A RABBI'S VISION

A CENTURY OF PROCLAIMING MESSIAH

A History of Chosen People Ministries, Inc.

by

Harold A. Sevener

CENTENNIAL EDITION
1894-1994

A RABBI'S VISION

A CENTURY OF PROCLAIMING MESSIAH

A History of Chosen People Ministries, Inc.

by

HAROLD A. SEVENER
President Emeritus
Chosen People Ministries, Inc.
Charlotte, North Carolina

DEDICATION

This history of Chosen People Ministries, Inc., formerly the American Board of Missions To The Jews, Inc., and originally the Williamsburg Mission To the Jews, Inc. is dedicated to the faithful staff of workers and to the members of the Board of Directors who have graciously given of themselves—of their time and of their God-given gifts and abilities—to lovingly bring the gospel to the Jewish people over the span of the past one hundred years.

This work is further dedicated to the countless hundreds and thousands of loving Christians who have shared in this ministry through faithful prayer support and sacrificial financial support of the Mission's world-wide ministry. Without the intercessory prayers of the people of God, and without their gracious financial gifts the outreach of the Mission could not have continued.

Finally, and foremost, this work is dedicated to the glory of God, in thanksgiving for His faithfulness in blessing His Word and in keeping His promises to the Jewish people.

To the glory of God, the story of Chosen People Ministries is a story of His faithfulness which has extended the vision of one Rabbi, saved by His grace and burdened with a desire to see his Jewish people accept their Messiah, to generation after generation of faithful men and women, producing a multi-faceted world-wide ministry proclaiming the gospel to all Jews everywhere.

A RABBI'S VISION
A CENTURY OF PROCLAIMING MESSIAH

CONTENTS

PREFACE

This extensive, encyclopedic history of Chosen People Ministries, Inc. chronicles the individuals and events which God has used to reach thousands of Jewish people with the gospel over the last one hundred years.

Chosen People Ministries, more than any other Jewish mission organization since the mid-1800's, was responsible for shaping and molding evangelism to the Jewish people around the world. It has been called the "grand-daddy" of Jewish missions in the United States. Most of the major Jewish mission organizations of the twentieth century had their roots in Chosen People Ministries, or the American Board of Missions to the Jews, as the Mission was known for over sixty-two years of its history.

While this work chronicles the history of Chosen People Ministries, its personnel, and its branches world-wide, it does a great deal more than that. It presents to the reader some of the behind-the-scenes events which were used of God to change, to modify, to refine, and to develop methodology for presenting the gospel to Jewish people—as well as for discipling new believers and establishing Messianic congregations which function alongside evangelism programs and branch and center ministries.

From the official Minutes of the Board of Directors, personal interviews, extensive research into archival material, and through the author's personal knowledge of and involvement with Chosen People Ministries, this history presents both the triumphs and the tragedies in the field of Jewish missions and evangelism.

The triumphs are seen in the stories of the faithful missionaries and support staff whom God has used through the years. Although the stories reveal that there were times when the personal lives of staff members and the work of the Mission were fraught with difficulties and problems, God's grace was sufficient and ultimately much fruit was produced to His glory.

The tragedies are seen in personality conflicts, politics and the struggle for power that seem to affect Christian organizations and churches as well as secular institutions. Tragedy is further seen in the frequent opposition to Jewish missions and evangelism from many Christian churches, as well as from the Jewish community. Opposition from the outside, coupled with power struggles and politics from within, led to misunderstandings, to resignations of staff members, and at one point to a split in the Mission itself. The events are recorded and detailed to show the reader that God is faithful; He uses His children—in spite of their imperfections and weaknesses—to fulfill His purposes. It is hoped that in detailing such events, the present generation of leaders and workers serving within the many Jewish mission agencies around the world will learn from the past experiences of those who have labored with Chosen People Ministries, and not repeat their mistakes but, instead, learn from their triumphs and victories.

Jewish missions and evangelism is, and has always been, on the "cutting edge" of gospel ministry. Yet it has often been considered the "orphan" or "non-essential" mission by the Christian community, and especially by the Jewish community. The author hopes and prays that in reading this detailed history of Chosen People Ministries, many Christians will be awakened to the necessity of bringing the gospel to the Jewish people; I pray that in the years to come, Jewish missions and evangelism will take its proper and legitimate place in the minds and hearts of Christians and Jews around the world.

HAROLD A. SEVENER

I

The Birth of Chosen People Ministries

The latter half of the last century (1850 to 1900) could well be called the "Golden Age of Jewish Missions," and the beginnings of the organization now known as Chosen People Ministries can be traced to those provocative years when spiritual awakenings were erupting throughout England and Europe.

Setting the Stage

The translation of the Scriptures into the language of the people, and improvements of the printing press were major contributing factors in bringing about this "Golden Age." The Scriptures had become available to the masses. Individual Christians were able to study the Scriptures for themselves.

As Christians studied the Scriptures, some discovered a renewed interest in the nation of Israel, and in the return of the Jewish people to their homeland. This renewal of interest in God's promises to Israel was another major contributing event to the "Golden Age."

Until the middle of the eighteenth century, the church, and most Christian theologians, held the position that the church had superseded Israel. Most theologians and the clergy taught that the Old Testament promises concerning Israel and the Jewish people found their fulfillment in the church. They further taught that the Jews were responsible for the death of the Messiah and were therefore under the curse of God. Such teaching caused Christians to look upon the Jewish people as renegades to Christianity—outcasts. But as some Christians and ministers began to study the scriptures, they recognized that God's program for the Church was inseparably linked with the Jewish people. Their study of God's Word led them away from popular opinion, and to the conclusion that God was not finished with the Jewish people.

Many concluded, in fact, that the Messiah could only return when the Jewish people were allowed to return to the land of Israel. Others went further, saying that the Messiah would not return unless the Jewish people returned to their land as believers in Yeshua as the Messiah; only then would the biblical prophecies concerning Israel, as well as the promises given to the church, be fulfilled. The outgrowth of these convictions brought about a renewed zeal for the Jewish people to accept Yeshua (Jesus) as personal Messiah and Savior.

As this teaching spread, it gave rise to the movement known today as "Zionism." The first Zionists were Christians. In his book entitled "Faith and Fulfillment," Michael Pragai wrote:

> Long before the emergence of a Jewish movement for the Return—the Zionist movement at the end of the nineteenth century—Christian belief in and support of the idea of the Return was clearly evident. Very important early contributions were made, primarily in Britain. Other countries followed, in particular, America. And inspiration for this support and understanding of the Return came from the Christian faith itself. When the Jews' own modern idea of the Return became a world political and practical movement, culminating in the Jewish State of Israel, there were many Christians who supported it and rendered it vital service on its arduous road. It is perhaps an odd irony that the Jewish return home was achieved partly, but significantly, through the instrumentality of that very faith which they, the Jews, have given the Gentiles.[1]

In Europe

For the first time since New Testament days, Christians were once again motivated to bring the Gospel to the Jewish people. During the latter half of the nineteenth century, over twenty-nine Jewish missions, or organized evangelistic outreaches to the Jewish people, were established. This is astounding, considering that prior to this awakening of concern for Israel, no sustained organized effort to witness to the Jewish people had been made, although occasional testimony had been presented through the efforts of individual Christians who were concerned. One such individual was Emmanuel Tremellius, a Jewish believer in Yeshua who was a professor at Cambridge. As early as 1554 he wrote a booklet entitled, "A Catechism for Inquiring Jews." This was his attempt to reach his brethren with the Gospel.

Germany, too, had one individual whose heart was burdened for the salvation of Jewish people. There, a Jewish believer by the name of Esdras Edzard devoted his life to the work of evangelizing his Jewish brethren. When he died, at the age of eighty, it was reported that hundreds of Jewish people had accepted Yeshua as Messiah and Savior as a result of his witness.

The Netherlands must also have had individual Christians who were concerned for the salvation of Jewish people, for church history reveals that in 1676 some of the synods of the Netherlands met together to consider how they could witness to the Jewish people. Out of that meeting came suggested methodology and increased awareness within the church in the Netherlands to reach Jewish people with the Gospel.

IN ENGLAND

But the greatest missionary movement to the Jews sprang up in the British Isles, with England and Scotland leading the way. Perhaps this can be attributed, in part, to Oliver Cromwell. As head of the English government from 1654 to 1658, he not only allowed Jewish people to live in England, he opened the doors for them to enter political and social life along side of their Christian neighbors. During his reign, and the reign of succeeding kings, many Jewish people come to faith in Yeshua.

In 1803, Joseph Samuel C. F. Frey, a Jewish believer who believed God was calling him to serve in Africa, went to England for the express purpose of contacting the London Missionary Society. While in England, he saw the plight of the Jews in London and he recognized how desperately they needed the Gospel. He shared his burden and concern for his brethren with other believers, and in 1809 he founded the "London Society for Promoting Christian Knowledge Among the Jews." The name of the organization was shortened and commonly became known as the "London Jews Society."

Thirty-two years later, in 1842, the "Society for the Propagation of the Gospel Among the Jews" was founded. Once again, God used a Jewish believer, Ridley Haim Herschell, to promote much of its organization and development. Mr. Herschell was of Polish Jewish background, having received rabbinical training under the Hasidim (a very strict orthodox Jewish sect). His search for faith began when he was a student at the University of Berlin. The story of his testimony relates that he went to a local grocery store one day and the infidel grocer wrapped his purchase in a printed page of the New Testament. Herschell stated that after unwrapping his purchase he read the page of the New Testament and it so touched his heart that he began to further investigate the claims of Yeshua. He later went to London; it was there that he heard the Gospel preached. After accepting Yeshua, Herschell started a ministry of establishing homes where Jewish believers could live after accepting Yeshua.

In the 1840's the Church of Scotland also began organizing and establishing missions to the Jews. The "Glasgow Society on Behalf of the Jews" (later named "The Friends of Israel") was established in 1845. This non-denominational society, supported by Christians who were not connected with either the established church or the Free churches, established mission stations in Glasgow, Edinburgh, Germany, and Africa. A few years after it was founded, this organization came under the exclusive control of the United Presbyterian Church of Scotland.

In 1876, John Wilkinson, who had worked for twenty-five years with the "Society for the Propagation of the Gospel Among the Jews," was led of the Lord to establish the "Mildmay Mission to the Jews." Branches of this mission were soon established throughout England, as well as in other countries of the world. The Mildmay Mission was also responsible for the publication and distribution of the New Testament in Hebrew and Yiddish. Their report, "The Missionary Review of the World," dated 1893 states: "According to Dr. Dalman, of Leipzig, there are 55 Protestant missionary societies for work among the Jews, with 399 missionaries, and an income of $406,000. During this century about 120,000 Jews have received Christian baptism, and about one fourth at Protestant hands."[2]

In 1899, in his work entitled "Judentaufen im 19 Jahrhundert," published in Leipzig, Germany, a French Jewish believer, Pastor de la Roi claimed that the Protestants had baptized 72,740 Jews, the Roman Catholics 57,300 Jews, and the Eastern Orthodox 74,500 Jews. He claimed another 19,000 were added to the church through miscellaneous means, including intermarriage, for a grand total of 224,000 converted Jews worldwide.[3]

During 1901 this same "Missionary Review of the World" reported: "over 125 converted Jews are now filling Protestant pulpits; converted Jews are found in nearly all denominations, and 4,500 of them are in the United States alone."[4] Using de la Roi's figures as a base, the report further stated: "The average number of Jewish baptisms is 1,500 a year, exclusive of the Roman Catholic Church. These are distributed as follows: Lutherans and Episcopalians, 800; other Protestant churches, 200; and the Greek Catholic Church, 500."[5]

Thus, during the latter part of the nineteenth century, the zeal and awakening on the part of Christians to bring the Gospel to the Jewish people spread from country to country: to Europe, to Israel, to Russia, Asia, and even to the United States.

IN AMERICA

In the Fall of 1810, Joseph Samuel Frey left England and the "London Jews' Society." He sailed to America. There he met with a group of Protestant ministers who were also interested in reaching Jewish people with the Gospel. In 1820 they formed a corporation in the state of New York called "The American Society for Meliorating the Condition of the Jews, Inc." The primary purpose and objective of the corporation was to provide relief to European Jews who were still being persecuted because of their faith, or because of the lingering effects of national and religious anti-Semitism still prevalent in Europe. But a secondary purpose stemmed from the belief that the society would also further the fulfillment of prophecy by transporting believing Jews back to Israel, thus bringing the entire nation to faith. The society wrote of itself:

> Is he a converted Jew? he [sic] has lost his cast, and feels himself solitary. To the Jew he is a Christian, and to the Christian he is a Jew: he is in fact both Christian and Jew, but he is in reputation neither, for by both he is neglected. What! A Christian neglected in a Christian land?…This stranger is left alone, without a friend, without a home, and without employment, until he finds a colony of his own religion and his own race…. From such institutions (as this) may yet arise hundreds of missionaries to their own brethren, that will accompany them on their return to Zion, where they shall see instead of the Crescent displayed triumphantly, the Cross in which they will glory.[6]

Elizabeth Charlotte, a Protestant who was concerned for the salvation of the Jewish people, also linked this prophetic theme with the evangelization of the Jews. In 1844 she wrote a letter to the Bishop of Jerusalem in which she urged missionaries not to encourage Jewish people to give up all of their customs and traditions when they accepted Yeshua. She felt it was all right for Jewish believers to observe such customs as the Sabbath, Passover, and circumcision. She wrote: "I do not believe…we are warranted to demand of the Jew that he become Gentile, or set at nought all that distinguishes him from the nations among whom his race is so scattered."[7] Her letter was eventually printed as a tract and used by The American Society for Meliorating the Condition of the Jews to convince Christians to support their ministry and to help them reach Jews with the Gospel, and thereby to help usher in the Kingdom.

Ministers across America began preaching similar messages. The evangelistic outreach ministries to the Jewish people that had erupted in Europe began springing up in America. On June 17, 1836, speaking at the fourteenth anniversary of the Palestine Missionary Society, Philip Colby delivered a sermon at Randolph, Massachusetts on the theme of the key role Jewish believers would have in evangelizing the world.[8] Soon, mainline denominations, as well as independent works, began stressing Jewish missions and evangelism.

One independent work in America was begun by Jacob Freshman, a second-generation Jewish believer. Jacob was born in Hungary—the son of a rabbi. When he was still a young boy, Jacob's father moved the family to Quebec, Canada. There, Mr. Freshman found a position teaching in a synagogue, but he also came into contact with faithful missionaries. Through their witness, he came to faith in Yeshua. He then set about to bring his entire family to faith in the Messiah of Israel. Jacob was the first to believe.

As Jacob matured in his faith, God led him into full-time ministry. For fifteen years he labored within the church in Canada, but his real desire was to reach his own people. In 1882 he left Canada and went to New York to minister among the Jewish people living there. He began publishing a magazine during the 1880's which he called "The Hebrew Christian." This magazine was designed with a two-fold purpose: to bring in support for his ministry, and to reach Jewish people with the Gospel. He also established a mission center where he had a reading room for Jews, and where he held regular prayer services, preaching services, and a Sunday School. As his ministry grew, Jacob saw a number of Jewish people accept the Messiah, and he discipled many Jewish believers who had come to America from Europe.

Among those who had come to America from Europe was a young Jewish man by the name of Hermann Warszawiak. The story of Chosen People Ministries begins with this man.

THE WARSZAWIAK STORY

Hermann Warszawiak was born in Warsaw, Poland in 1865. His great grandfather was the famed Rabbi of Breslau. Hermann was raised in a strict Orthodox Jewish home, and was educated in the best Jewish schools. But as he grew, he began to question some of his Jewish beliefs. He questioned why Jews no longer sacrificed animals, for it seemed to him that this was the only way of atonement for sin. He also had difficulty understanding Isaiah 53; it seemed to speak of an individual, not of the Jewish nation as he had been taught.

One of the great benefits of this era of spiritual awakening, during which time so many mission societies were established, was the plethora of tracts, books, and literature produced and printed to reach Jewish people with the Gospel. Written at a time when Messianic speculation was running high, both within the Jewish community and within the Christian community, most of the literature was written on a high scholarly level and therefore appealed to the rabbis and to the scholars of the Jewish community. These materials dealt with the promises of the Bible concerning the restoration of the Jews to Israel, as well as with the coming of the Messiah.

When a Christian minister heard that Hermann was questioning his belief in Judaism, he sent him a Hebrew edition of the New Testament and other materials that had been especially prepared for the Jews. The more Warszawiak read, the more he questioned. His friends soon began to call him a "Meshumad," or an "apostate." In July 1889, faced with compulsory military service by Russia and concerned by the ambivalence in his faith, Warszawiak fled to Breslau, to the home of his great grandfather, the famous rabbi. He was looking for answers in Judaism and in his traditions, but God had another plan.

The Church of Scotland, too, was caught up in the spiritual awakening to bring the Gospel to the Jewish people—to thereby hasten the Messiah's return—and in the providence of God, they had sent a missionary to Breslau to proclaim the Gospel to Jewish people living there. The missionary's name was the Rev. Mr. Daniel Edward, a Gentile Christian who had an overpowering love for the Jewish people.

One Sunday in July 1889, young Warszawiak, restless in mind and disturbed in spirit, walked down the streets looking for something that would give him peace. As he walked past some buildings he heard the sound of singing. He followed the sounds of the voices and they led him to the building where Mr. Edward was holding a service. Warszawiak stood by the door listening. He had intended to stay for just a few minutes—just long enough to satisfy his curiosity—but when the service ended he remained, to argue with the missionary, Daniel Edward.

God always makes divine appointments for his children, and for weeks after his initial visit with Mr. Edward, Warszawiak struggled with his belief in Orthodox Judaism and with the teachings he'd heard from Daniel Edward, that Yeshua was the promised Messiah. For weeks his spiritual and intellectual struggle was so intense that he could not eat or sleep. He was so distraught he could not even get out of bed; he thought he was going to die. One night, as his spiritual struggle grew more and more intense, he cried out to Yeshua to save him and to show him the truth. God answered his prayer. In his agonizing struggle, Hermann Warszawiak confessed Yeshua to be his Messiah and Savior. He then discovered that in Yeshua he had found what he had been searching for—the wonderful peace of God flooding his soul.

When Warszawiak's father learned that his son had accepted Yeshua, he was furious. He was a very influential man, and he threatened retaliation against his son and against Daniel Edward. In an effort to protect young Warszawiak, and to get him out of Poland where he was subject to persecution from his father and from other members of the Jewish community, Daniel Edward suggested that Hermann go to Edinburgh, Scotland where he could be baptized in the Barclay Free Church of Scotland. But Hermann Warszawiak would not hear of it. He insisted that he be baptized right there in Breslau, saying, "I am a great grandson of that famous rabbi who is known and honored in all the countryside. I want you to send out circulars to the thousands of Jews in this district, and I want you to tell them that on Sunday morning of October 6th [1889] Hermann Warszawiak, the great grandson of such and such rabbi, will be baptized into the Christian faith."[9]

The circulars were sent out. The entire Jewish community of Breslau was notified. On the morning of Hermann Warszawiak's baptismal service thousands of Jews, from the city of Breslau and from the surrounding villages and mountain regions, filled the streets. Most came out of curiosity; they wanted to see what their minds and hearts refused to accept, that the great grandson of the rabbi of Berezna would accept the Christian faith and be baptized.

True to his confession of faith, and despite the Jewish voices of protest, Hermann Warszawiak was publicly baptized on Sunday morning, October 6, 1889. But his belief in Yeshua as Israel's Messiah, and his personal Savior, created deep animosity toward him within the Jewish community. He was branded a "Meshumad" (a traitor) by his father and by other members of the Jewish community. His family declared him dead, while others threatened his life. Warszawiak's uncompromising stand for Yeshua stirred up such hatred and wrath toward him that it became clear he would no longer be able to remain in Poland. Daniel Edward convinced him to go to Edinburgh, Scotland. He knew his friends and associates within in the Church of Scotland would disciple this new Jewish believer, and prepare him for future ministry.

From the moment of his decision to accept Yeshua, Warszawiak sensed the call of God upon his life. He knew he wanted to bring the Gospel to his own people. They had to hear the message that had brought so much peace into his heart. God's timing is always perfect. There are no coincidences in His program. He always prepares in advance for the needs of His children, and Hermann Warszawiak was about to experience something of this wonderful provision from God. Some years later, a rabbi by the name of Leopold Cohn experienced a similar blessing from the hand of God through the very same individuals who so generously provided for Hermann Warszawiak.

God had a servant in Edinburgh, Scotland—a woman by the name of Miss Catherine G. Douglas. Lady Catherine, as she was affectionately known, was the daughter of Lord Douglas, who had been knighted for his bravery and military skills in defense of Scotland. The Douglas family was well-known and honored throughout Scotland. As the last member of the historic Douglas family, Lady Catherine lived in the ancestral castle on the hills high above the city of Edinburgh. She was a devout child of God, and served Him faithfully. Because of her love for God, and her willingness to be used as His servant, God used Lady Catherine Douglas to begin a series of events that ultimately led to the establishment of Chosen People Ministries.

Lady Douglas was an invalid for most of her adult life. She suffered from a form of paralysis for which the doctors had no cure. She was bed-ridden and suffered great pain. Daily she prayed to God to heal her and to give her deliverance from her paralysis. God heard those prayers. Joseph Hoffman Cohn, the son of Rabbi Leopold Cohn who knew Lady Douglas personally, wrote of her healing experience in this way:

> One day by some strange juncture a piercing and dazzling light seemed to shine into her inner consciousness, and the question was posed before her in the form of an imperative challenge, 'What have you done for the Jews?' This was a startling experience for Lady Douglas, and she turned over in her bed of agony, closed her eyes, and said to God, 'I hereby make this vow to Thee. If Thou wilt restore me so that I can get up out of this bed and walk again, I will spend the rest of my life and my money in helping to win Thy people, the Jews, to the Christ [Messiah]!'
>
> Within three weeks from that date, Lady Douglas arose from her bed, and under her own power walked across the room! She could hardly believe this miracle herself, and the doctors also found it hard to believe. But there it was in front of them, the patient walking and without pain!
>
> It was at this precise psychological hour that [Hermann] Warszawiak appeared on the scene. Timidly he pulled the bell knob on the iron gates of the Douglas castle. He was ushered into the marble halls of one of the proudest palaces of Scotland. Hermann produced the letter he had from that humble Scottish missionary in Breslau, Daniel Edward. Lady Douglas could hardly believe her eyes; for here she had now seen not only her body restored to health, but also a young Jew in her drawing room, presenting himself as a prospective missionary to his people! What more could she want by way of confirmation of the Lord's will for her? She bade him welcome to her home, and from that moment she became his devoted friend until the day of her homegoing. He lived in that home while she put him through the Free Church College in Edinburgh. He startled everyone with his brilliance of mind, his thirst for knowledge and his easy grasp of the most difficult theological problems.[10]

Shortly after completing his training, Warszawiak approached Lady Douglas with the great burden of his heart. He had come to love Lady Douglas as if she were his own mother, and he knew she and other members of the Free Church of Scotland wanted him to stay in Glasgow to minister among the Jews there. Joseph Cohn captured this moment when he wrote, "Came the time when young Warszawiak said to his benefactress, 'Mother, there are 300,000 Jews in New York City. There are only 1,000 in Glasgow and hardly 500 in Edinburgh. Let me go to America and preach to the 300,000 Jews of that great city!'"[11]

Cohn goes on to describe Warszawiak's departure from Edinburgh. He wrote, "With heartaches and tears, and many protests from the friends he had made in Scotland, including his own beloved pastor, Dr. J. Hood Wilson, at the Barclay Free Church, Hermann took up his bags one day, went to Glasgow and on to the steamer, and set sail for the glamorous city of New York. A great crowd was at the dock to see him off, and Lady Douglas pledged him her support and friendship for life, and told him she would become his honorary Treasurer for the British Isles, while he could carry on the work he was to undertake in New York."[12]

Warszawiak arrived in New York in April, 1890. He carried with him letters of introduction to Dr. John Hall, pastor of the historic Fifth Avenue Presbyterian Church. Dr. Hall was an Irish Presbyterian who had been called from Dublin to pastor this great church. Warszawiak also had letters of introduction to Dr. George Alexander, pastor of the University Place Presbyterian Church of New York. He also went to visit Jacob Freshman, director of the Hebrew Christian Mission of New York. Each of these men helped establish Warszawiak in Jewish ministry in New York. Jacob Freshman invited Hermann to speak at his mission services, and his ministry was well received. Hermann also joined the Fifth Avenue Presbyterian Church and became an active member, seeking to share his burden of Jewish evangelism with others there.

Yearning to accomplish more, Warszawiak secured the use of a building that was used by the old DeWitt Memorial Presbyterian Church. The building was in the very heart of the East Side of New York, on Rivington Street. It was there that he got his start in Jewish Missions. He did not stay there long however. Within a few months after beginning the work in that building, Jacob Freshman resigned as director of the Hebrew Christian Mission; Warszawiak was asked to become its new director. The name of the mission was changed to "The American Hebrew-Christian Mission." Within just a few years under his leadership, the American Hebrew-Christian Mission became one of the greatest missionary outreach ministries to the Jewish people that the city of New York had ever known. Nearly every Jewish mission established in the United States came about as an outgrowth of that mission.

The reputation of Warszawiak grew. He was invited to speak in churches across America. Wherever he spoke, the crowds overflowed to the doors. "When he finished his message, there was hardly a dry eye in the audience. When the ushers came up the aisles with the baskets, hardheaded merchants and bankers threw in their watches, emptied their pockets of what cash they had; women took off their diamond rings, and put them into the baskets. Such was the amazing power of the young man from Warsaw. It is not an exaggeration, also, to say that practically every Jewish Mission started in America, owed its existence to this young pioneer and genius."[13]

In New York, leading pastors, business men, and philanthropists supported Warszawiak, pouring their wealth into his ministry to help make it a dynamic and a phenomenal testimony to the Jewish people. During those years the streets and blocks on the East Side of New York surrounding Warszawiak's mission were teeming with multitudes of immigrants who had just gotten off the boats from Russia, Poland, Bohemia, Moravia, Galicia, Hungary, Romania—Jews from all walks of life came. Some were the bearded Hassids, with their peyotl (side curls) and heavy black coats. Others were silken bedecked Jews with rabbinical "Caftans," (Yarmulkes or turban type head-gear). Still others wore only rags, having just barely escaped from the country of their birth with their lives. These were the Jews that roamed the streets of New York, their new-found paradise. They were free from the nightmares of European massacres, free from the drownings and burnings at the stake, but they were strangers to the Truth that could truly set them free.

Hermann Warszawiak's ministry became well-known, and Christian workers visiting New York from various parts of America often scheduled time to visit his unique mission. Noted theologians, pastors, and missionaries like Dr. Andrew A. Bonar, of Glasgow, Scotland, Dr. J. Hood Wilson, Dr. A. F. Schauffler and Dr. William Cooper urged the Christian public to rally around this fearless pioneer and apostle whom they called "The Little Paul" or "The Little Messianic Prophet."

Just as God had carefully prepared the soil and the spiritual climate for the searching heart of Hermann Warszawiak, He also prepared the way for another searching Jewish immigrant who, in his longing to find the Messiah, had made his way to the shores of America. Though he did not know it, Leopold Cohn, a rabbi in search of the Messiah of Israel, was destined to begin where Hermann Warszawiak would leave off.

ENDNOTES

Chapter 1. The Birth of Chosen People Ministries

1   Michael J. Pragai, *Faith and Fulfillment*, (London, England: Valentine, Mitchell and Company Ltd., 1985), p 4.
2   *General Missionary Intelligence*, (The Missionary Review of the World, May, 1893), p 391.
3   See note above, November, 1899.
4   See note 2 above, August 1901, p 639.
5   See note above.
6   Alexander McLeod, *Address to the Christian Public by a Committee of the Board* (in Documents, New York: ASMCJ 1822), pp 11-12.
7   Elizabeth Charlotte, *Israel's Ordinances: A Few Thoughts on Their Perpetuity* (New York: I.P. Labagh, 1844) pp 16, 18-23.
8   Philip Colby, *The Conversion and Restoration of the Jews*, (Boston: Perkins and Marvin, 1836) p 20.
9   Joseph H. Cohn, *I Have Fought a Good Fight*, (New York: American Board of Missions to the Jews [now Chosen People Ministries, Inc.], 1953), p 155.
10 See note 8 above, pp 156, 157.
11 See note 8 above, p 157.
12 See note 8 above, pp 157, 158.
13 See note 8 above, p 163.

2

Leopold Cohn — The Rabbi Who Found Yeshua

In 1862, in the ghetto of the little town of Berezna in East Hungary a family of orthodox Jews joyfully welcomed a new son, Leopold Cohn. Jews who lived within the ghettos of Eastern Europe had little to do with Christianity or with Christians. Children were taught to evade the "goyim" (Gentiles), for their ways and customs were strange and forbidden. As he grew up, Leopold Cohn, like other children of the ghetto, equated Christianity with Roman Catholicism. In his autobiography, "A Modern Missionary to an Ancient People," Rabbi Cohn wrote:

> The Jews there [Berezna, Hungary] look upon Christianity as a phase of heathenism, for the Catholics openly exhibit their idolatrous habits, prostrating themselves on the public highways before crosses and images, practices greatly abhorred by the Jews because they were forbidden to Israel by Moses. Their priests are generally addicted to drink and are bitter enemies of the Jews, inciting the peasants to injure them in every possible way. Because of these things, I was taught to avoid Gentiles, not even to take a drink of water from their vessels.[1]

The Early Life of Leopold Cohn

Tragedy struck early in the life of Leopold. At the age of seven he lost both of his parents, and he, along with his brothers and sister, was left to shift for himself as best he could. The tragic loss of his parents, combined with the loneliness and isolation of ghetto life, caused Leopold to seek after God. He often found himself praying to God, asking God to teach him, and to show him what He wanted Leopold to do with his life. Leopold's older brother, Joseph, had become one of the best students in school and he tutored Leopold so he could enter Yeshiva.

At the age of twelve Leopold decided God was leading him to become a rabbi, a profession which, in those days, was seen as scholar and teacher, judge and spiritual leader. His livelihood as a rabbi would come either from a fixed salary, from payments for functions performed, or from a combination of both.

To become a rabbi, a student not only had a required course of studies, he was required to become a disciple or student of some recognized rabbi in the community. Young Leopold Cohn chose to study under the chief rabbi of Sziget, a miracle-working rabbi by the name of Zalmon Leib Teitelbaum. He was also affectionately called Zalmon Leib by his students and congregants. Leopold studied with Rabbi Zalmon Leib Teitelbaum for approximately three years. He then went to the larger Yeshiva in Presberg, Hungary where he studied for another year.

Years later Leopold wrote, "[By age eighteen] I was proficient in Hebrew literature and Talmudic law. I then received from several rabbis, in whose colleges I had studied, a diploma [semikah—or a Hattarat Hora'ah][2] containing a certificate of my good character and acquirements and also authority to become a rabbi. This was confirmed by my first and chief rabbi, a miracle-performer, Z. L. Teitelbaum in Sziget."[3]

Though orphaned and seemingly alone, Leopold's physical as well as spiritual and intellectual needs were faithfully provided for by God. And God's supply did not stop there! He also made provisions for Leopold to have a wife. In a town near Sziget, there lived a wealthy Jewish family by the name of Hoffman. Mr. Hoffman was a close friend of Rabbi Teitelbaum and he was very much interested in the progress of the rabbi's young protege, Leopold Cohn. This wealthy man wanted his daughter, Rose, to marry a promising rabbi, and Leopold seemed a likely candidate. Following the custom of Orthodox Jews of that day, the marriage was arranged and a "Ketubah" (marriage contract) was drawn up between Rose and Leopold. Leopold tells it this way: "When consent was given, I was called, and according to the custom there, arrangement was made as to how large a sum of money the father-in-law was to give me before I married his pretty and highly accomplished young daughter. Our marriage was consummated in 1880."[4]

Leopold was nineteen years of age when he was married. He gave the dowry he had received from his father-in-law to his brother-in-law, with the request that the brother-in-law invest it. It was his hope that the investment would provide for their future. Also, following the custom of that time, Leopold and his bride moved into his father-in-law's home. There, he was able to devote himself to the study of Talmud and Scripture. Of those early days Leopold wrote: "In the house of my father-in-law I was very happy, and always thanked God for giving me at last, after much hard labor in studying, so delightful a home. Many marks of honor were shown me, and I received tokens of love and of kindness on all sides and the days I spent under my father-in-law's roof were the brightest in my life."[5] But once again, tragedy struck. A year after Leopold and Rose were married, her father died. The young rabbi, Leopold, once again began to search the Scriptures, seeking after God and trying to find answers to the mysteries of life.

Knowing he was a rabbi, people from the town often came to Leopold, asking him for advice and help. He enjoyed counseling and advising these individuals, but the Jewish law of his day forbid him from using his skills as a rabbi because he lived in such close proximity to his teacher and mentor, Rabbi Teitelbaum, in Sziget. He was, however, allowed to gather a small group of students, and thus form his own little college of rabbinic studies. This he had established before his father-in-law's death and Mr. Hoffman, being a generous man, not only provided for Leopold and Rose, he also provided food and assistance for Leopold's students.

Five years later Rabbi Zalmon Leib Teitelbaum died, and Leopold Cohn was permitted to fully practice the office of Rabbi. For the next five years he served the Jewish congregations in the cities of Apsitza, Oyberapsa and Middleapsa. These were small towns in which the Jewish people made up less than 10% of the population. In Oyberapsa there were only about two hundred Jewish families; in Middleapsa, under three hundred Jewish families; and in Apsitza there were only about one hundred Jewish families. Since the Jewish community in each town was so small, none could afford to support a full-time rabbi. Rabbi Cohn therefore became a circuit rabbi, serving the needs of these small villages. As such, he became well-known among the Jewish communities in East Hungary. Regretfully, after he became a believer in the Messiah, Yeshua, his notoriety was used against him. Hearing the rumors of Rabbi Cohn's faith in the Gentile god, Yeshua, the Jewish leaders in Hungary became fearful that his belief in Yeshua would cause other Jewish people to accept Him as well. Accounts of that period of history record how they plotted to discredit him.

SEARCHING FOR THE MESSIAH

Serving as an itinerant rabbi kept Leopold busy, but never too busy to pursue the answers to his burning quest to know the mystery of the Messiah.

> 'During my leisure,' Cohn wrote, 'I had frequent recourse to my Talmud, in which I at one time read the following: "The world is to stand six thousand years, viz., two thousand confusion and void, two thousand with the law, and two thousand the time of Messiah." Rashi, the very first and most authoritative commentator gives as an explanation on the last clause: "Because after the second two thousand years, the Messiah must have come and the wicked kingdom should have been destroyed." This greatly excited my attention. I was accustomed to sit on the ground almost every Thursday night at twelve o'clock, weeping, crying, and mourning for about an hour, over the destruction of Jerusalem (called by Jews "Tickin Chazoss") and repeating the 137th Psalm. I was very anxiously awaiting the coming of our Messiah, and now I saw that his time was over two thousand years ago, according to the Jewish reckoning. I was surprised, and asked myself, "Is it possible that the time which God had fixed for the appearance of our Messiah had passed away without the promise of our true and living God being fulfilled?" I never had had any doubt of the truthfulness of Talmud; I believed every part of it to be holy, but now I looked upon this passage as a simple legend. It was then that I decided to search the Prophets concerning the time of the Messiah.'[6]

Leopold went on to state that his first thought was to study Daniel, but then he remembered that the Talmud curses anyone who studies concerning the end of the age, especially those sections of Daniel that refer to the coming of the Messiah, and to the end of the times. "'The bones of him who studies and calculates the ends (meaning the time of the Messiah) shall be blown up' says the Talmud."[7] The strength of this passage from Talmud sent terror into Leopold's heart and he stated:

> I thought that the minute I began to read that part of Daniel, a thunderbolt would come down from Heaven and strike me dead. But another thought came, suggesting that those Talmudists who made such statements must themselves have studied Daniel and the other Scriptures, concerning the coming of the Messiah, and if they did it, so would I. With fear and trembling, I opened the book, glanced over it, dwelling particularly on the ninth chapter. My research led me to blame myself for suspecting the holy words of the wise men. While I could see only as through a glass, for I was totally ignorant of Jesus (Yeshua) the Messiah, who was cut off not for Himself, and therefore could not understand thoroughly that the Messiah must have died for our sins, yet I realized dimly that the Messiah must have come about four hundred years after Daniel was told by the angel about the seventy weeks. There was gladness in my heart, to find it true that the Messiah should have come about that time, according to Daniel 9:24. But it was a joy mingled with sorrow.[8]

Leopold could not stop thinking and wondering about the Messiah. If Daniel was correct, the rabbis of Talmud were wrong. It was a contradiction of thought and study he could not dismiss. He believed his whole calling as a rabbi depended on its outcome, and his thirst for the truth drove him into a deeper study of the Prophets. Cohn wrote, "Whilst doing so, the pure spirit of God's Word took hold of my mind and heart. I then discovered that much of the Talmudic law is contrary to the Word of God. Then what a great struggle within, between light and darkness! I used to go into my large garden, and under an apple tree, cry like a little child, entreating, 'Open thou mine eyes, that I may behold wondrous things out of my law.'"[9]

He could find no rest, or peace, for his troubled heart and soul. Unlike Hermann Warszawiak, who had had the privilege of meeting and hearing the Gospel from the missionary, Daniel Edward, no missionaries had yet made their way to Sziget, and Leopold Cohn was isolated in the Ghetto; he was alone with his thoughts and fears, with no one to tell him of the Crucified One. No one had come to his village to share the Good News that the Messiah had come.

Years later, after Rabbi Leopold Cohn had come to faith in Yeshua, his recollection of his lonely struggle, of wanting to know the truth, and of not being able to find it, was one of the major factors that led him to establish the Williamsburg Mission to the Jews (now called Chosen People Ministries, Inc). Leopold did not want his Jewish brethren to go through the desperate search for truth about the Messiah which he had gone through. His desire was to let all Jews everywhere know that the Messiah had come, that His name is Yeshua, and that He had died to make an atonement for sin.

Cohn continued to study Talmudic references to the Messiah. The more he studied the more restless in mind and spirit he became. He wondered how all the Talmudic references to the Messiah could be reconciled with present day Judaism, and he began to ask other rabbis how they were able to reconcile Messianic statements in the Talmud with the Scriptures. How were they able to reconcile such Messianic statements with Judaism as it was being practiced and taught? Not one person was able to give him a satisfactory answer.

Leopold continued his search for answers to these ponderous questions, but he did so discreetly because of fear of persecution. He had no intention of mentioning the struggle going on deep within his heart to his little congregation. But to his amazement, he did tell them. Years after the incident, he stated that while he was preaching to his congregation during the celebration of Hanukkah, the Feast of Dedication, God literally intervened as he preached. Leopold wrote: "...God, who causes the dumb to speak, opened my mouth, and I revealed unto them all my discoveries. Probably they would have believed the discovery about the Messiah, since we were all ignorant of the fact that such a disclosure related to the Crucified One (Yeshua), but when they heard me finding so much fault with the holy Talmud, that was quite enough to make them hiss and wag their heads at me, and finally to leave me quite alone, preaching to the empty benches. Bitter persecution followed."[10]

It was not unusual for Jewish congregations of that day to persecute or to shun their rabbis when they digressed from the usual interpretation of Scripture, attacked Talmud, or differed from rabbinic tradition. Many rabbis had lost their congregations for such "free thinking." Some were even forced to leave their homes and communities. Many Jewish communities and synagogues had been torn apart because of teachings about the Messiah.

During this period in history, many people within the Jewish communities of Europe were just recovering from dashed hopes that a Messianic era would be established by Shabbetai Zevi, or by David Frank. Both men had been proclaimed to be the Messiah by the Jewish communities of Europe, but when their claims proved false, resulting in new persecution of the Jews, many Jews decided they wanted nothing more to do with teachings about the Messiah! This was especially true in Rabbi Cohn's congregation. Hence, their violent reaction when he attacked Talmud and the traditions of the rabbis.

Having no one at all with whom he could discuss the questions that continued to nag at his mind, Leopold found himself going to a rabbi in a distant town, far away from his own congregation, as he looked for someone who could help him find answers that would bring rest to his troubled mind and restless spirit. He told the rabbi about his studies, and about the questions these studies had raised. He also told the rabbi about the reaction of his congregation when he had revealed his discoveries to them. Although the rabbi acted surprised, he seemed to understand what Leopold was saying and feeling. Yet, his response to Rabbi Cohn was that he did not want to discuss the subject with him any further, and he warned Leopold that if he continued to preach and teach about the Messiah he would be discharged from his position. The rabbi told Leopold to go to America, where he would probably meet plenty of people who could tell him more about the Messiah. Those were the words Leopold Cohn was waiting to hear. He knew if he could get to America he would find the truth about the Messiah.

Years later, when reflecting on that conversation, Leopold stated that he believed this rabbi also knew something of the teachings of Yeshua and was, perhaps, a secret believer in his own heart. God does have His "ministering angels" whom He brings into our lives at just the right moments, and this particular rabbi was just such a "ministering angel" to Rabbi Cohn.

Arrival in America

So intent was Rabbi Cohn to relieve the burden from his heart and mind, that he made immediate preparations to leave for America. Afraid that his wife and her family would try to dissuade him from making such a journey, Leopold did not even return home to inform them that he was leaving!* Instead, he made immediate transportation arrangements from the village of Apsitza, Hungary to Budapest, Hungary; from Budapest, Hungary to Hamburg, Germany; and from Hamburg, Germany to Liverpool, England. From England he made arrangements to travel to New York by steamer. As if placed in a capsule in which time was accelerated, Leopold Cohn, a rabbi from Hungary, found himself passing through the immigration gates at New York's Ellis Island only some fifteen days after being advised to seek for the Messiah in America. The date was March 2, 1892.

Although his plans to leave Hungary and to journey to America had been made hurriedly, Leopold had managed to get word of his pending arrival in America to some friends and countrymen who were already there. One fellow-countryman who met him on his arrival, was Meyer Adler. Adler had also been born in Berezna, Hungary. He and Leopold had been playmates and had grown up together; he knew the Cohn family well. Meyer had moved to America in 1890 and had opened a tailoring shop in New York City. During his two years in America, he had established many friendships and knew his way around town. Meyer arranged to have a room ready for Leopold in the boarding house in which he lived—a boarding house on Columbia Street in New York City, owned by a Jewish baker by the name of Greenwald.

Rabbi Cohn's first order of business was to pay a visit to the Chief Orthodox Rabbi of his Orthodox sect, Rabbi Klein, who had a congregation on Rivington Street. This he did the day after his arrival in New York. As was customary, Rabbi Cohn gave Rabbi Klein his Haturah (his ordination paper and rabbinic references). Rabbi Klein proposed that Leopold open a school to teach the children of his congregation, but Rabbi Cohn wanted a congregation, so he turned the position down.

For several weeks after his arrival in America a strange procession could be seen each day as Rabbi Cohn, bearded and dressed in his Orthodox attire, walked with Meyer Adler, the well-dressed tailor, and Greenwald, the baker, as they made their way to the various Jewish synagogues of New York, seeking to find just the right congregation for Rabbi Leopold Cohn.

Days turned into weeks, and the focus of the Jewish community turned to the upcoming celebration of the Feast of Unleavened Bread and Passover which were about to begin. Rabbi Cohn still did not have a congregation, although he had accepted a temporary position. Like most Orthodox Jews, Leopold, too, was making preparation for the celebration of Passover, but thoughts of the Messiah continued to run through his mind, and the longing within his soul to find the Messiah could not be quieted.

The third Saturday after his arrival in New York dawned. It had been a little over a month since Leopold had left Hungary, and his wife and family. He was still no closer, so he thought, to finding the Messiah. Of that day Cohn wrote:

> …I went out for a walk, musing and thinking again about the Messiah, and passed by a church where there was a sign with Hebrew letters saying, 'Meetings for Jews.' I stopped, became curious and desired to enter. At my first step toward the door, however, I saw a cross at the top of the building. I was puzzled, and began to reason thus, 'If this is a Christian Church, what does that Hebrew writing mean? And what connection have they with the Jews? How can a Jew enter a building on which there is a "cross," that object which the so-called Christians in my country worship? And how are the Jew and Christian, between whom there is such great hatred in my country, here united?' As I stood musing and absorbed in these thoughts one of my friends passed by and said, in an awe-inspiring tone: 'Mr. Cohn, you had better come away from there.' 'Why?' asked I. 'Just come, please,' said he, and was so persistent that I had to follow. We went a few steps when he said, 'There are some apostates in that church who mislead our Jewish brethren.' 'How, how, I pray?' for he made me only more anxious to know. He told me at last. 'They say that the Messiah has already come.' When I heard that, I was nearly bewildered with joy and surprise, for this confirmed my discovery. I longed to enter that church to hear their ideas, but how could I get rid of my companion? I had already taken a lesson in my country not to speak about such things, so I freed myself from him by saying, 'Good-bye, friend, I have to go somewhere.' Glancing back until convinced of his disappearance, I ran hastily into the church, notwithstanding the cross at the top. [11]

To his utter amazement, there were some eight hundred Jewish men and women inside that building. Every square foot was occupied. There was hardly a place to stand. He looked toward the platform and once again, to his shock and amazement, on the platform were twenty-four Jewish girls, all dressed in blue frocks with white sleeves, and they were singing in Yiddish with great enthusiasm and great sincerity, "At the Cross, at the Cross, where I first saw the light!" Rabbi Cohn could hardly believe his eyes or his ears! "How could this be?" he wondered. "These are Jews!" he said to himself. Why are they are singing about the "goyim" (Gentile) god they call Jesus (Yeshua)?

While he was pondering the enigma of Jewish girls singing about Jesus, the room suddenly grew quiet. The girls quickly left the platform and the audience waited, as if they were expecting something exciting to happen. They didn't have to wait long. Suddenly, as if out of nowhere, a young man sprang onto the platform and, without introduction, he began preaching about the Messiah. "He ran back and forth on the platform, shouting with the force of a political orator, making his points with an assurance that brooked of no controversy. Suddenly, he leaped to one side into the wings of the platform, disappeared for a few seconds, and out he came again; and believe it or not, in his arms he brought a little live lamb! The audience gasped. Then he went on with his sermon about the Lamb of God and the Lamb in Isaiah 53."[12]

There are no coincidences in God's program! God's timing is always perfect. Rabbi Cohn knew well the story of the Exodus from Egypt, and the stories and traditions of Passover. In fact, he had just been reviewing those stories and traditions in his preparations for the Passover celebration. The story of God's redemption of His people, through the shed blood of a lamb, was well-versed and completely familiar, but as he listened to the message being preached Leopold Cohn heard, for the first time, how God's salvation was available to all who believed in the Lamb of God, the Messiah, Yeshua.

Along with the other Jewish people in the audience, Rabbi Cohn was caught up in the theatrics of the moment as he watched the young preacher, who seemed to be a born showman and a profound orator. Again, the speaker ran to the wings of the platform, handed the lamb over to another person, and came running out shouting at the top of his voice, "The Messiah has come, the Messiah has come!"[13] The audience erupted with shouts and halloos, some shouting "Messiah Yeshua," as others shouted curses and threats.

Leopold listened to the preaching for a while longer. He was fascinated by what he was hearing, but at the same time he was disgusted. He had been raised in the Orthodox tradition where men and women were separated during worship. Here, Jewish men and women were sitting together, and Jewish girls were singing songs about Jesus. What was even more appalling was that the young man who was preaching, who was a Jew himself, continually used the name of God, but he was not wearing a yarmulkah (skull-cap). To an Orthodox Jew like Rabbi Cohn, this was a great offense against God. He wanted to leave, to run from this place of blasphemy, but somehow his feet would not move because his heart wanted to hear more about the Messiah. This was why he had come to America. This was why he had left his wife and family.

Leopold struggled with his conscience; finally his background, tradition, and training allowed him to stay no longer. He pushed his way through the shouting, singing, praying congregation until he reached the door, but he found it was closed tight and guarded from the inside by the "Shamas," the caretaker of the building. Anxious though he was to leave, Leopold asked the Shamas for the name and the address of the young man on the platform who was preaching about the Messiah. The Shamas carefully wrote down the information and gave it Rabbi Cohn. He then helped Cohn escape through the doors into the mob on the streets outside.

Standing amidst the crowd on the sidewalk, Leopold was surprised to see a cordon of policemen who were guarding the building from the outside. He discovered that the door had been shut at 3:00 P.M., when all the seats inside had been filled and the service was ready to begin. The closed door held at bay Jewish people unable to attend the service because the room had been filled to capacity, as well as to keep out individuals who wanted to disrupt the service. The police were there to keep the mob from breaking down the doors.

That night Leopold could not sleep. He tossed and turned in his bed, while thoughts of the Messiah kept running through his mind. He could still hear the Jewish girls singing "At the Cross, At the Cross." He thought of his family, of his homeland, of the coming Passover celebration—and he thought of the words he'd heard about the Lamb of God.

At daybreak Leopold had his morning prayer service and, as soon as he could, he made his way to the address the Shamas had scribbled on the piece of paper. It was a home located on St. Mark's Place; it was the home of Hermann Warszawiak. In the providence of God, Rabbi Cohn had been led to the home of the young Jewish man mentioned in Chapter One of this book. He was standing at the doorsill of the home of the young Jewish believer who had been led to the Lord through the witness of Daniel Edward in Warsaw, Poland—Warszawiak, the young man Lady Catherine Douglas had helped and whom God had led to New York.

With some timidity, a troubled and still very upset Rabbi Cohn rang the bell of Warszawiak's home. When the door opened, the contrast between young Warszawiak who was still bare-headed, and the slim and bearded rabbi from Hungary who was dressed in his long silk caftan, wearing his rabbinical cap on his head, was striking. Rabbi Cohn looked every bit the part of the rabbi he was, and even before any greetings were exchanged his rabbinical and talmudic training and tradition got the better of him. He shouted, "How dare you get up on a platform and preach about God without your hat on your head! You are an 'am-ha-aretz' (ignoramus)."[14] Leopold seemed more upset with the fact that Warszawiak wasn't wearing a yarmulkah (skull cap) than with the fact that he was teaching about Jesus. Warszawiak's response was quiet. He had a most winning and interesting way about him, and when Leopold found out that he'd had some talmudic training, and that his grandfather was the famous rabbi in Poland, he calmed down and began to have a measure of confidence in what the young man was saying. When the subject turned to the Messiah, and Warszawiak saw Rabbi Cohn's interest in the matter and heard some of his questions, he knew he must not allow the conversation to erupt into an argument. Hermann was clever, and had no desire to get caught in an argument with this Orthodox rabbi who was so unquestionably his superior in Jewish tradition and Talmud. He simply said to Rabbi Cohn, "'I am going to give you a little book, and I want you to read it. After you have read it I want you to come back to me and we will talk. I will not say a word to you, I will not argue with you, I will do nothing, until you have read this Book'."[15] Warszawiak then went into a back room and returned with a book that was brand new to the world of that day; he handed Leopold Cohn a copy of the New Testament in Hebrew, translated by the famous Dr. Franz Delitzsch.

Once again, we are reminded that in God's program there are no coincidences. His timing is always perfect. Delitzsch's Hebrew New Testament had just been printed and was being proclaimed as the best translation of the New Testament into Hebrew. Warszawiak had just received a shipment of these Hebrew New Testaments from England. Had Rabbi Cohn appeared at his door even one week earlier, or a few days earlier, Hermann would not have been able to share a copy of this New Testament, for none would have been available in all of New York. Truly our great God, in His grace and mercy, leads us when we are searching to know the Truth!

The Rabbi Reads the New Testament

Clutching the little book, afraid to read it, and yet afraid not to read it, Rabbi Cohn hurriedly made his way back to his apartment. He hoped that none of his friends would see him, or ask about the little book he had tucked away under his caftan. Although no one could have noticed it, to Rabbi Cohn it seemed that everyone was staring at him and his little Hebrew book.

Upon his arrival home, Rabbi Cohn wasted no time in opening up the little book. For the very first time in his life he read the words, "This is the book of the generation of Yeshua, the Messiah, the son of David, the son of Abraham" (Matthew 1:1). Imagine his feelings, not only in reading these words for the first time, but also in reading them for the first time in his own sacred language, Hebrew. Recalling that awesome experience, Rabbi Cohn later wrote:

> My feelings could not be described! For many years my thoughts had been occupied almost continually with the coming of the Messiah. For that reason I had suffered and left my wife and children for a strange country, which I never expected to visit. I had inquired of several rabbis, searched the Scriptures, prayed and thought; my whole being was wrapped up in this one subject. And now at last here was a book that would tell me about the Messiah. 'Surely,' I thought, 'this book has come to me directly from above. God has sent it to me, and it will give all the desired information and lead me to the Messiah.' The words, 'Yeshua, the Messiah, the Son of David, the Son of Abraham' were sweeter to me than angelic music. I forgot all about my troubles and became very happy, and running as fast as I could to my private room, the doors of which I locked behind me, sat down to study that book. I began reading at eleven o'clock in the morning, and continued until one o'clock after midnight. I could not understand the contents of the whole book, but I could at least realize that the Messiah's name was Yeshua, and that He was born in Bethlehem, that He had lived in Jerusalem and talked to my people, and that He came at just about the time indicated by the angel's message to Daniel. My joy was unbounded."[16]

So excited was Rabbi Cohn with his discovery that he was unable to sleep. As soon as the sun arose and he had finished his morning prayers, he hurriedly made his way to share his discovery with Rabbi Klein, the head rabbi of the Orthodox sect of which Rabbi Cohn was also a member. Rabbi Klein was the rabbi to whom Leopold had submitted his rabbinical papers upon his arrival in New York.

Even though Leopold had said of his first experience reading the New Testament, "I could at least realize that the Messiah's name was Yeshua," there was much that he did not understand on first reading. For one thing, he had not identified the name, "Yeshua" (the Hebrew name for Jesus) with the "Jesus" whom the Gentiles spoke about as being the Son of God. His first reading of the New Testament led Rabbi Cohn to believe that the Messiah, whose name was Yeshua, lived somewhere in this country (America), and that He would be found ruling as King over a group of Jewish people, perhaps even the ten lost tribes. His joy could hardly be contained as he thought about how wonderful it would be to find this Yeshua, and to join the happy group of Jewish people who were living under the rule of King Messiah.

To our ears today, such fanciful thinking sounds like a "bubameis," a fairy tale. But we must understand the tradition, thinking, and background of Rabbi Cohn. At that time in history it was not uncommon for Jewish people to believe that the Messiah was alive, living in a different part of the world. We must also remember that Orthodox sects within Judaism during that era had very little contact with the Gentile world or, for that matter, with one other. The proclivity of the time was to solely follow the teachings and traditions of one's own particular chief rabbi. Further, Leopold spoke little English, and was unfamiliar with Christian terminology.

Jewish history is replete with stories of Messianic kingdoms and with the appearance and disappearance of false Messiahs who proclaimed they would bring the Jewish people back to Jerusalem. One of the earliest Jewish leaders who thought a Messianic kingdom existed was Abu-Yussf Chasdai ben Isaac Ibn-Shaprut (915-970), a member of the noble family of Ibn-Ezra, who made his home in Cordova, Spain. Because of his great learning and abilities he became the Caliph's personal physician, and was made an ambassador of the king's court. In his travels he'd heard of the kingdom of the "Chazars," a kingdom in Russia where the king and all of his people had converted to Judaism. Chasdai began corresponding with Joseph, the king of the Chazars. This correspondence is still in existence today. He mused that the citizens of the kingdom of the Chazars might be descendants of the ten lost tribes and that the Messiah (ben Joseph) ruled over them. In response to Chasdai's letter, Joseph, King of Chazars, wrote:

> ...'The Chazars were rather of heathen origin,'...[and] had been converted to Judaism. He went on to enumerate the successors of Bulan, [the first Chazar king to convert of Judaism], all of whom had Jewish names. He then describes the extent of his dominions, and various peoples that were subject to him. As regards the hopes of Messianic redemption which he also cherished, he remarks that neither he nor his people knew anything definite. 'We set our eyes upon Jerusalem,' he says, 'and also upon the Babylonian schools. May God speedily bring about the redemption.' 'You write,' he says, 'that you long to see me. I have the same longing to make the acquaintance of yourself and your wisdom. If this wish could be fulfilled, and I might speak to you face to face, you should be my father and I would be your son, and I would entrust the government of my state to your hands.'[17]

The most recent and most famous of the Messianic contenders was Shabbetai Zevi. He was born in Smyrna, Turkey in 1626, and died in Dulcigno, in 1676. Shabbetai was a mystic rabbi who was proclaimed to be the "Messiah" in his native city of Smyrna in AD 1666. Historical records indicate that the whole Jewish community throughout the world worshipped him as Messiah, and people of the city of Smyrna could be heard shouting when they saw him, or when his name was mentioned, "Long live our King Messiah!" Many Gentile Kings and Christians also believed he was the Messiah. Even his imprisonment did not squelch the confidence that his followers had in him, and they continued to seek his advice. After he converted to Islam many of his followers lost hope, but there were those who, even after his death, continued to believe, hoping that by some miracle he would return.

Rabbi Cohn knew all of these stories well. He, too, had spent years looking for the Messiah. Following the traditions of many Orthodox Jews and rabbis before him, he truly thought it was possible that somewhere in America the Messiah could be found alive and leading His people. After all, wasn't that what Messiah was to do? Wasn't that what this little Hebrew book was saying?

Arriving at Rabbi Klein's office, Rabbi Cohn could hardly wait to share his good news. Looking back on that visit Leopold later said, "I came to him with that book with great joy in my heart. I showed him, 'Why here I find something new.' He [Rabbi Klein] took that book, looked at it and threw it down to the floor. He showed a terrible temper and began to curse me for reading such a book."[18]

LEOPOLD COHN ACCEPTS THE MESSIAH

Confused and troubled, Leopold Cohn fled from the office of Rabbi Klein. The great joy he had experienced earlier was gone, and in its place depression and desperation filled his heart. He began to struggle with Rabbi Klein's words and with what he had read in his little Hebrew book, the New Testament. How was it possible that Yeshua, the Messiah, the son of David, could be the very same person whom the Christians worshipped? How could he have anything to do with this Yeshua if that was true? Why, that would be idolatry! Leopold wrote:

> For several days my heart ached with sorrow and depression. Then I renewed my studies and began to see the truth more plainly, as the sufferings of the Messiah were revealed to me. The fifty-third chapter of Isaiah was a most wonderful revelation, but what of it? How could I love that hated One? How could I take His name upon my lips since He is the Crucified One and since His followers in every generation and in every country have hated my people, robbed my brothers of all that was good and fair, killed, tortured and degraded them? How could I, a true Jew, join myself to such a band of the enemies of my own flesh and blood? But a small voice seemed to whisper in my heart, 'If He is the One of whom the Scriptures write, then you must love Him. No matter what others do in His name, you must do as He teaches.'
>
> Halting between the two opinions, I decided to fast a day and pray God to show me what to do. At noon time,

when instead of eating I began to pray, I held in my hands the Hebrew Old Testament and as I cried to God my body shook and the book dropped to the floor and opened for itself. Opening my eyes, I looked down and to my great consternation, read from the open page in the Hebrew, Malachi 3:1, which says literally: 'I am sending my messenger and he shall prepare the way before me and the Lord whom you seek shall suddenly come to His temple, even the angel of the covenant' (that word is identical with word 'testament') 'whom ye delight in: behold, He has already come, says the Lord of Hosts!' I fairly began to shiver; like an electric shock the words went through my whole system, and I felt as if the Crucified One stood beside me, pointing to that verse and particularly to the expression, 'Behold He has come already.' I was awe-stricken and fell upon my face exclaiming with all my heart, 'My Lord, my Messiah, Yeshua, thou art the One in whom Israel is to be glorified. Thou art surely the One who has reconciled Thy people unto God. From this day, I will serve Thee.' At that moment, a flood of light came into my mind and a stream of love to the Lord Jesus into my heart, and straightway I went and took a meal, breaking my fast and feeling altogether a new creature.[19]

God's Word is quick and powerful. It is a living Word. It is able to pierce the blindness of unbelief, of tradition, of hatred, and of fear. Rabbi Cohn's experience in coming to faith in Yeshua is a testimony of the faithfulness of God's Word and of His promises. It further demonstrates that His Word will not return unto Him empty but will, as He has promised, accomplish the purpose for which it was sent (cf. Isaiah 55:11).

While the Jewish community was celebrating Passover, Israel's exodus from Egypt, Rabbi Cohn was celebrating his own Passover. He now knew that Yeshua (Jesus) was the Messiah, his Passover Lamb, his Lord and Savior. He understood that his Yeshua was the very same "Jesus" whom the Gentiles worshipped, but it no longer mattered. He had found his Messiah and, for the first time in his life, he had peace within his heart and mind. He knew his sins had been paid for. He knew the God of Abraham, Isaac, and Jacob had not forsaken him, but had chosen him to share the life-giving message of forgiveness of sins and eternal life through the Messiah with all of his Jewish brethren.

As he thought about Yeshua, his Messiah, and about Passover, his thoughts began to turn to his wife and family whom he'd left in Hungary. How would they react? What would they say? Would he ever see them again? He closed his eyes and began to weep. His tears were tears of sadness for those who knew not the Messiah, mingled with tears of joy for God's miracle of grace in his own life. He purposed within his heart that he would trust God to reveal Himself to his family members and to others in the Jewish community as he shared the message of the Messiah.

He also thought about how quickly his life had changed. He had come to America on a search for his Messiah and in the short period of less than five weeks God had revealed Yeshua, the Messiah, to him and had clearly impressed upon his heart that he was to proclaim the message of Messiah to his Jewish people. Rabbi Cohn knew what that meant. He was well aware of the price he would have to pay, for he had already experienced a taste of that hatred and wrath from Rabbi Klein. However, he also knew he could not keep silent.

Keeping his promise to Hermann Warszawiak, Leopold went to him and told him that he had read the New Testament and that he now believed Yeshua was the promised Messiah. Warszawiak had not been looking forward to engaging in a debate or an argument with this talmudic rabbi, and he rejoiced with Leopold in his new-found faith and, at the same time, he rejoiced in the timing of the marvelous grace of God.

PERSECUTED FOR HIS FAITH

After leaving Warszawiak's home Rabbi Cohn was filled with "holy boldness" and he began telling any Jew who would listen that Yeshua was the Messiah. He told his friends, the shop-keepers, and other rabbis that he had found the Messiah of whom the prophets spoke. He told them if the Jewish people would accept God's Son, Yeshua, they would once again find favor in the sight of God. Leopold wrote:

...At first they thought that I was joking; then they said that I felt lonesome for having left my wife and children whom I loved so dearly, in the old country; my mind was affected and I was not responsible for my words. But as I persevered, they began to be more attentive to my condition and realizing that I was just as sane as ever, they persecuted me bitterly. They said: 'He is a traitor; he has forsaken our religion, our people and our God, and it would be a service to God if some one would lay hands upon him and kill him' (The Jews are no murderers, but their ignorant zeal for God knows no bounds).[20]

Rumors and accusations continued to be spread about Leopold Cohn, the rabbi from Hungary who believed in Yeshua. His picture appeared in both the English and the Yiddish editions of the Jewish newspapers. He was denounced as a "meshumad" (an apostate), a traitor, and every other name that was publishable. As the publicity grew, and as Rabbi Cohn became more and more unpopular in the Jewish community, he was forced to flee the room he had occupied in the rooming house with his other Jewish friends. He had become *persona non grata*.

Rejected by the Jewish community, Warszawiak arranged for Leopold to live with a Gentile Christian couple, Mr. and Mrs. Cruikshank, who lived on Avenue D in New York. The Cruikshanks were attending Dr. A.B. Simpson's Bible School and doing missionary work among the Jews, working with the Christian & Missionary Alliance. Mr. Cruikshank was assisted by Rev. A. E. Funk and others.[21] During his brief stay with the Cruikshank's, the persecution of Rabbi Cohn increased. Cables and letters were sent to Leopold's older brother in Hungary, telling him that his brother, Leopold Cohn, had become an apostate; he had announced his faith in the Gentile god, Jesus! A letter from Hungary came back stating, "I will give you 500 gulden if you shoot him."[22] Needless to say, Rabbi Cohn was heartsick. It seemed that his new-found faith in Yeshua was not only cutting him off from his own Jewish people, but would be the catalyst that would forever cut him off from his wife and family as well; he might never see them again.

The persecution of Leopold heightened, so that the Cruikshank's suggested to him that he change his name. He had, until that time, been using the name by which he had been known in Hungary, Isaac Leopold Kahan. Kahan was his family name, the name used in all of the newspapers and telegrams of that day, as well as the name that had been given to the immigration officials. At the insistence of the Cruikshank's, Isaac Leopold Kahan changed his name to Kohn, but Mrs. Cruikshank suggested to him, "We English do not use the K, you had better spell your name with a C."[23]

Rabbi Isaac Leopold Kahan became Rabbi Leopold Cohn. It was his new name, Rabbi Leopold Cohn, that was given and which appeared on his naturalization papers when he became a citizen of America on December 23, 1898.

The reader may ask why this name change becomes so important. The answer is that years after making the decision to change his name, after Rabbi Cohn had established his ministry of sharing the Gospel with his Jewish neighbors in New York, some members of the Jewish community in New York, along with Jewish and Gentile officials in Hungary, diligently sought to discredit him and to besmirch his character, his integrity, and his honesty. In their efforts to discredit Rabbi Leopold Cohn, they claimed that he had never been a rabbi but, instead, had been a saloon-keeper, an embezzler, and a murderer. They further claimed that his real name had never been Isaac Leopold Kahan, but had been Izsak Leib Joszovics, and they claimed he had used the name Steinmetz when he first came to America, to hide his true identity and his crimes in Hungary.

A full and detailed account of these accusations will be presented later in this history, and with it evidence will be given showing that Rabbi Cohn was, indeed, who he claimed to be. Mention is made here only to emphasize the scope of the persecution Rabbi Cohn suffered because of his belief in Yeshua. Yet, the more he was persecuted, the more determined he was to preach the Gospel to the Jewish people. His faithfulness to his calling, and his faithfulness to the Word of God resulted in many Jewish people coming to faith in Yeshua as their Messiah and Savior. This was the evident blessing of God upon Rabbi Leopold Cohn. However, the success of his ministry, as well as his strong determination to serve his Messiah, brought public and private persecution against Rabbi Cohn and, later, upon his family.

Because of the persecution and threats, all communication stopped between Leopold Cohn and his wife and other family members who were still living in Hungary. The Jewish communities in New York and in Hungary did everything they could to bring about total separation between Leopold and his wife and children. The thinking of the Jewish community was that it was bad enough that a rabbi had accepted Yeshua as the Messiah, but an even worse disaster, one that would be harder to explain, would be the acceptance of this "Yeshua" by his wife and family.

As the persecution of Leopold increased, the Cruikshank's felt they could no longer protect their guest. Rabbi Cohn, too, realized that it would be suicide for him to remain in America, so he went once again to his friend, Hermann Warszawiak. Hearing of what was happening to Rabbi Cohn, Warszawiak immediately called for a meeting with Dr. Schauffler and Mr. Leonard, men who had been helping him in his own ministry, and who loved the Jewish people. After some discussion it was decided that Scotland would be the safest place for Rabbi Cohn. A steamship ticket was purchased, and expense monies provided so that Rabbi Cohn could leave New York and go to Edinburgh, Scotland. Warszawiak also made arrangements for Leopold to stay with Lady Catherine Douglas, his honorary treasurer and his own benefactress. Also, because Leopold only spoke Hungarian, Yiddish, Hebrew, and a few other languages, but had not yet mastered English, Warszawiak arranged for Rev. Leonhardt, pastor of DeWitt Memorial Presbyterian Church in New York city, to accompany Leopold to Scotland and to stay with him until he learned enough English to manage on his own.

LIFE IN EDINBURGH

Driven by his search for his Messiah, and maligned because of his joy in finding his Messiah, a lonely Rabbi Leopold Cohn once again found himself aboard a steamship. So much had taken place since his arrival in New York approximately two months earlier, and now he was heading to Scotland. On his journey he was accompanied by his Messiah, and by Rev. Leonhardt. But he was also accompanied by, and haunted by, his recollection of the persecution he'd suffered from friends and family. He could not shake the thought that he might never again see his wife or children. What a strange paradox that one who so desperately wanted to tell his people about the Messiah was being forced to leave one of the largest Jewish communities to go to one of the smallest. On a small scale, Rabbi Leopold Cohn experienced what Rabbi Shaul (Paul) must have experienced after his Damascus road experience. He, too, was sent to a distant place to escape persecution and to be taught.

Upon his arrival in Edinburgh, Rabbi Cohn was introduced to the Rev. Dr. Wilson, pastor of the Barclay Free Church in Edinburgh. For the next few weeks, Leopold and Rev. Leonhardt attended every service held at the Barclay Church. Not only was Leopold hungry for the Word, he also wanted to learn English so he could communicate with the Christian community he was now living among. Lady Catherine Douglas was delighted to once again have a Jewish believer staying with her, and she made Rabbi Cohn feel most welcome in her home. For her, this was a glorious answer to prayer. Not only was she helping a Jewish believer, but a rabbi. She knew God had given her a special blessing.

But God's special blessings were not reserved for Lady Catherine Douglas alone. Following a Wednesday evening prayer service, shortly after Leopold's arrival in Scotland, Pastor Wilson and the board of elders questioned him about his belief in Yeshua. Satisfied with his answers, the elders unanimously agreed that Rabbi Leopold Cohn should be baptized the following Sunday morning, June 26, 1892. This momentous experience is best expressed in Leopold Cohn's own words. He wrote:

> ...That memorable morning impressed itself upon my heart with an indelible power. It was to me like Wellington's Waterloo. I had many enemies in New York, from whose persecution I had to flee, but that day, I met only one foe who would have been almost unconquerable, had it not been for the prayers of God's children. Early that morning, about daybreak, I awakened with a shiver, and it seemed as if someone spoke saying, 'What are you going to do today?' I sprang out of bed and walked up and down the room like one suffering from high fever, almost not knowing what I was doing. I had previously been anxiously waiting to be baptized as I was looking forward with joy to the time when I could publicly confess the Lord Jesus Christ before men, but now a sudden change came over me. The voice that seemed to be talking to me was that of the great enemy of mankind, though, of course, he was so sly that I could not perceive at that time that it was Satan. Very many questions were proposed to me rapidly one after another, and perplexed me so that I felt ill, mentally and physically. He questioned thus: 'You are going to be baptized, aren't you? Do you know that as soon as you take this step, you are cut off from your wife whom you love so dearly? She can never live with you again. Do you realize that your four children, of whom you are so fond, will never call you 'papa' or look into your face again? Your brothers, your sisters, all your relatives will consider you dead and their hearts will be broken forever. How can you be so cruel to your own flesh and blood? Your own people will despise and hate you more than ever before. You are a stranger here; you are cutting yourself off from your people; you have no friends in this world. You will be left alone to drift like a piece of timber on the ocean. What will become of you? You will lose your name, your reputation, your official position.'
>
> These thoughts put to me in the form of almost audible questions by Satan, whom I for the first time met as a personal enemy, distressed and almost unbalanced my mind. I could not sleep, neither could I eat. My friend [Pastor Leonhardt]...noticing this, tried to strengthen and encourage me in every way possible, but nothing availed. I knelt down in prayer to God, but that Satanic delusion was as strong as before.
>
> The time came to go to church. My pastor friend from America [Leonhardt] went with me and endeavored to cheer me, but awful sorrow and heaviness were in my heart. I merely went to church for the sake of my friend, for I was almost determined to refuse to be baptized that morning, and put it off for another time. The service began and the call came for me to go up to the platform. No one can imagine the terrible state of my mind, neither could I describe it. Walking up the aisle, I determined to say that I felt too ill for the baptismal rite and ask that it be postponed until next Sunday, but as I reached the platform, a sudden change swept over me, making me realize that my fears were all a fabrication of lies from the greatest enemy of my soul. My heart was strengthened, all the clouds disappeared, and I felt it the greatest privilege of my life to confess the Lord Jesus by baptism before so large a congregation, no matter what the cost might be.[24]

Rabbi Leopold Cohn never forgot that beautiful experience of baptism and the wonderful way in which the Spirit of God had moved upon his mind and heart. What made it even more memorable and miraculous to the Rabbi was a note he received from Dr. Andrew A. Bonar, a famous evangelist and Bible teacher. At the time he wrote to Leopold, Dr. Bonar was serving as pastor of a church in Glasgow, Scotland. Leopold had not met him, but Dr. Bonar knew of Rabbi Cohn, as did many Christians and Jews in Scotland. The "conversion" of a rabbi to Christianity is not something that can be kept a secret for long. Dr. Bonar wrote, "My people and I were praying for you this morning at our service."[25] At the close of his letter he wrote a verse in Hebrew, as he was also a well-known Hebrew scholar. It said, "How beautiful on the mountains are the feet of those who bring good news, who proclaim peace, who bring good tidings, who proclaim salvation, who say to Zion, 'Your God reigns!'" (Isaiah 52:7).

Rabbi Cohn kept that letter from his dear Christian brother as a constant reminder of the way in which God answers prayer. After reading Dr. Bonar's note he knew why his attitude had changed, and why he had been able to walk down the aisle to be baptized. Satan's power had been broken through the prayers of God's people. Leopold wrote, "Then I knew and understood that it was in answer to the prayers offered, perhaps at the very moment I began to walk up the aisle, that Satan was defeated by the power of Jesus, who is the mighty God."[26]

As a rabbi, Leopold Cohn had been accustomed to praying three times a day, but those had been ritual prayers. He now knew the living God in a personal way. He knew Him as his Heavenly Father. He knew that through Yeshua, his Messiah, his Heavenly Father could be approached any hour of the day or night. This was exciting. It was powerful. It was faith! In faith, Leopold believed that through prayer God would restore his family; through prayer God would grant him protection; through prayer God would fulfill the vision He had given him to reach his own Jewish people with the Gospel. However, his faith in answered prayer was tested almost immediately. His baptism had been announced in the local papers and as soon as the Jewish community heard that a rabbi was going to be baptized into the Christian faith they became irate. Some of the leaders of the community went to their rabbi and asked him to send a letter to the rabbi in Apsitza, Leopold's hometown, notifying him that Rabbi Cohn was an apostate (which to the Jews meant he was a bad Gentile, whose business it is to hate, rob, and kill the Jews) and was to be baptized. In the letter they also inquired about his character and questioned what kind of rabbi he had been. They could not believe that a real rabbi, a talmudic scholar, a reputable rabbi, would do something so unthinkable as to accept Yeshua as the Messiah. In their fury, they hoped for a bad report so they would be able to publish it in the newspapers of Scotland and England. This, they thought, would put an end to any other Jews believing in Yeshua. But to their dismay and utter shock, the rabbi from Hungary sent back a reply in which he warned them against maligning such a true and righteous Jew, and told them they should not believe the evil reports they had heard about Rabbi Cohn. He further reprimanded them, saying that Rabbi Cohn was a leader in Israel whom they should respect.

The reply first stunned and shocked them, but later rage boiled within these Jewish leaders. With the letter from the rabbi from Hungary in hand, the leader of the synagogue, along with a few other Jewish men, went to Rabbi Cohn. Some of the men were actually shedding tears of anger and frustration, but some shed tears of respect. Recounting this confrontation with the Jewish leaders, Leopold wrote:

> ...They said, 'The rabbis in your country do not want to believe what you have done here, that you publicly denounced Judaism and accepted the hated religion of our enemies.' They began to plead with me, begging me to return to the Jewish faith. I then showed them from the Scriptures that to believe in Jesus was Jewish faith, real Jewish faith, and that they had no Jewish religion whatever if they did not believe in the Son of God. They were struck with some Scriptures I quoted, and said: 'We will arrange for a meeting for you and our rabbi who knows the Scriptures better than we do, and let him decide whether you are right or not.[27]

Leopold was both excited and alarmed about a possible debate with a well-known rabbi selected by the Jewish community in Edinburgh. He was excited about the possibility of witnessing for his Lord, knowing the impact this would have upon the Jewish people. He was convinced of the power of prayer and he knew the power of God's Word. But he was alarmed because Dr. Wilson, the pastor who had baptized him, thought such a debate in a synagogue might be dangerous to Rabbi Cohn. Dr. Wilson believed such a debate could stir up more hatred and animosity against Leopold, forcing him once again to seek asylum in another country. If he were forced to leave Scotland where would he go?

As they prayed about the debate God gave them the solution. Perhaps the Jewish community would agree to holding the debate in a large private hall. In this way, anyone interested in such a debate would be welcome to come and listen. Dr. Wilson felt this would also provide more protection to Leopold Cohn, should any hostility break out.

Early on the morning of the scheduled debate, Rabbi Cohn met with Dr. Wilson and a group of leading clergymen and lay-Christians. Together, they prayed for this special meeting and the debate. The occasion marked Rabbi Cohn's first public debate on the subject of the Messiah since becoming a believer in Yeshua. It was his first public testimony of his faith before a large Jewish audience. He knew the power of God and he knew the power of prayer; he had experienced both, and after the prayer meeting he felt he was well prepared.

When Rabbi Cohn and his friends arrived at the hall they found it was already packed with Jewish people who had come from all over Scotland and England to hear the debate. In the middle of the room they spotted a small table, where the two rabbis would debate with one other. Leopold noticed that his opponent was already seated at the small table. In front of him he'd stacked all of his books and papers. He was ready and well-prepared for his debate with this so-called apostate rabbi. He was convinced that Talmud, along with rabbinic interpretation and Jewish tradition, would prevail and thus utterly defeat this heretic rabbi and his belief in the Gentile god, Yeshua. He glared at Leopold, challenging him by his very presence at the table. His mien and glower seemed to shout out that Rabbi Cohn would lose the debate and be crushed by the evidence of Talmud, and by his skilled argumentation. As Leopold approached the table a hush fell over the crowd. Some felt that Rabbi Cohn would, or should, be struck down by lightening before he reached his chair, but to their dismay nothing happened. Instead, he quietly took his place at the table. In his hand he held his only reference tools, his copy of the Hebrew Bible and the copy of Franz Delitzsch's Hebrew New Testament which Warszawiak had given him in New York. He held only two small books, but Leopold Cohn knew that he was also wearing the "full armor" of God. He claimed God's promise to Israel that "no weapon forged against you will prevail" (Isaiah 54:17). As the debate began Leopold's opponent immediately attacked him with rabbinic argumentation. Leopold said:

> ...He began by hurling at me his fiery darts in the shape of hard, puzzling questions and with great triumph ended the first question, turning to the people all around and showing his ability in argument, and that it was a foregone conclusion that this apostate could never answer him. But trusting the Lord, I calmly and gently replied, so that disappointment was soon noticed upon his face. The answer was so direct that nearly everyone in the room could understand plainly. The meeting lasted for two hours, the pride of the rabbi subsiding gradually with every answer to his questions until at last he had no more to ask. Then all went away, disappointed and discouraged, not being willing at the time to admit that this apostate was right in his belief in Jesus, the Messiah. Later on, some of them did acknowledge the truth as it is in Jesus.[28]

By September of 1892, Rabbi Leopold Cohn had learned enough English to begin studies in theology, and Lady Catherine Douglas arranged for his enrollment at New College in Edinburgh, Scotland. There he began preparing himself for the task which God had called him to do—to preach the message of salvation to his people, the Jews.

The events that had transpired over the nearly five months since he'd left his wife and family, and had hurriedly made his way to America in search of the Messiah, seemed almost unbelievable. His quest had taken him across the borders of many countries, traveling by rail, steamer, and by foot. He had encountered danger, hostility, and friendship. And the most unbelievable of all was that he had found the Messiah—not in the way he had expected, but in the way God intended. He was at peace for the first time in his life, but he also longed to see his wife and family once again.

Almost daily he faithfully wrote letters to his wife. He had written to her shortly after he had come to believe in Jesus, telling her about his faith in Yeshua, the Messiah. And when he heard that the leaders of the Jewish community were spreading rumors about him, and sending their lies and rumors to his family, he wrote even more letters. He wanted them to know the truth about what he was doing, and why! The response he received from his wife and family was silence. He waited in vain for a reply. His family's silence was a great source of emotional pain and anguish. Understandably, he suspected that his wife and his family believed the many rumors that were being circulated about him. In his heart he feared that his wife had declared him dead because of his faith and acceptance of Yeshua as the Messiah, but in spite of that nagging fear he could not forget the memory of his baptism and the promise he had made to God that he would follow Yeshua even if it meant losing his wife, his children, and everything that was dear to him in this world. In the flesh he wrestled with this promise. The spirit was willing, but the flesh was so weak! Leopold wrote of his pain and heartache:

> ...When I found myself alone, I would cry out, 'Rose darling, are you alive? Why don't you write to me how are you and how are our little ones getting on?' There would come on me a spasm of terrible pain in the heart so that I thought I could not stand it. But the Lord Jesus to whom I carried all my woes was my strength. After a little talk with Him, my troubled heart was calmed and soothed.[29]

What Leopold did not know, and would not find out until later, was that none of his letters ever reached his wife, Rose, for her family intercepted his letters. They knew she loved Leopold, and they knew she would be influenced by what he wrote. Instead of giving Rose his letters, they told her the lies and rumors that were being circulated among the small Jewish communities in Hungary. They also subtly intercepted all of Rose's letters to Leopold, so he could hear nothing from his wife or children. The motive behind their actions was their hope that this deprivation would bring Leopold Cohn to his senses.

In August of 1892, Lady Catherine Douglas, sensing Leopold Cohn's loneliness and deep concern for his wife and children, gathered together a group of believers. She told Leopold that she and the other believers would begin praying earnestly, night and day, for the reunion of his family. Leopold had experienced the power of prayer at his baptism and he was overjoyed. He knew God would hear and answer his plea, and as he waited he continued to write. It seemed a vain effort for he received no response, not even a negative one!

It was during one of the prayer sessions that God seemed to speak to each individual simultaneously, implanting the thought that perhaps the reason Rose had not responded to Leopold's letters was that she had not been receiving them. With this thought spurring them on, they decided that Leopold should send a cable. They reasoned that since Rose would have to sign for the cable, they could be assured that she would receive Leopold's message. After the message was sent they prayerfully waited for a response. They didn't have to wait long! Rose had been as anxious to hear from Leopold as he had been to hear from her. Cables were exchanged in rapid succession and when both Leopold and Rose realized what had been happening, they made arrangements for Rose to receive and to send letters under an assumed name in a different town. Leopold was overcome with joy! His Lord, whom he served, had once again wonderfully and miraculously answered prayer. Rabbi Cohn's faith and trust in the Messiah was growing by leaps and bounds. The prospect of hearing from his wife and family on a regular basis filled his heart with joy and he and Rose began writing long and frequent letters.

In her letters to Leopold, Rose told him about the news they had received from America, announcing his apostasy. She wrote that some people believed he was a Meshumad (apostate), but others did not. Some of his countrymen, she said, refused to believe the rumors being spread about him because none of them had ever known of any Jews who had accepted Yeshua as the Messiah, especially not a prominent Jewish rabbi like Leopold Cohn. Moreover, she indicated, it just wasn't possible for a well-educated Jewish rabbi to convert to Christianity. After all, she wrote, "the Jews are superior to the so-called Christians…in civilization, in morality, in commerce and in politics, thus making it impossible to believe that a prominent Jew would stoop so low as to associate with such a degraded class of people."[30] She went on to say that she believed some of Rabbi Cohn's countrymen had believed the rumors and stories about Leopold because the stories had come from such well-known Jews in America and Scotland. What made those Jews in America and Scotland write such malicious letters about Leopold, she asked? Why were so many Jewish people saying such bad things? What had he done to provoke such anger and wrath?

As Leopold read and reread Rose's letters, he wondered how he could answer her questions. He knew if he said too much Rose, herself, would begin to believe some of the stories being rumored about him. On the other hand, he did not want to deny his faith or his Messiah and Lord. He prayed that God would give him wisdom. Leopold knew if he told Rose he had become a Christian he would lose her forever. Her only knowledge of those who called themselves "Christians" was what she had seen and heard in the villages of Hungary and, like most Jews, she wanted nothing to do with "those Christians." He knew that she was well aware of his interest in the Messiah, so in response to her questions he simply told her that the reason the Jewish leaders were so angry with him was that he talked too much about the Messiah. He promised to explain things in greater detail when she and the children joined him.

REUNITED WITH HIS FAMILY

Leopold's response seemed to satisfied Rose, and she began to consider the possibility of making a journey to Scotland. She could then find out for herself if any of the stories she'd heard were true. The more she thought about it, the more she liked the idea. She was also angry with her family and friends who had kept Leopold's letters from reaching her, thereby forcing them into this secret correspondence. She was tired of the charade, tired of making excuses to visit other villages so she could receive her husband's letters. Rose wanted her husband back. She wanted the father of her children home. She wanted the family to be together again.

Rose had no idea that her actions and reactions were being influenced by the fervent prayers of Leopold and the small prayer group which Lady Catherine Douglas had organized. God was beginning a work in her life. For Rose it was a most perplexing time! Events had taken place which she had never dreamed would transpire. It had been bad enough during the long months after her husband left and no word was received from him. At least then she'd had her family and friends to talk to, and from whom she received some consolation. But learning of their plot to keep Leopold's letters from reaching her, she could no longer confide in them. Rose knew she needed someone who could help her sort through her feelings, questions, and confusion. She therefore sought the advice of one of the great miracle working rabbis, a rabbi like Rabbi Teitelbaum, her husband's teacher and mentor. After pouring out her story, Rose heard the great miracle working rabbi advising her not to believe the reports and stories being circulated about Leopold Cohn. His words calmed her troubled mind and heart. She believed he spoke by the power of the Holy Spirit. As he spoke, a quiet confidence began to build within Rose and she determined that she would gather up her children and her belongings and go to Scotland to be with her husband. She felt compelled to learn the truth, even if the cost meant giving up her country, her relatives, and her friends.

Rose wrote to Leopold, telling him of her decision to come to Scotland. She was still greatly perplexed by the hatred that had been generated toward him because of his longing to know the Messiah, and she told him she hoped the Messiah would come soon and confer great honor upon Leopold for all the persecution he and his family had endured. How could Rose have known then that they would be faced with even greater persecution in the days and years to come!

Leopold could hardly believe his eyes when he received Rose's letter saying she and the children would be coming to Scotland. He shared the good news with the family of believers who had been praying with him and, together, they rejoiced in the goodness and mercy of God. But joy turned to sadness when a second letter from Rose was received, in which she said that as she was making preparations to leave some of her relatives had discovered her plans and were taking steps to prevent her from leaving Hungary. She told Leopold that one man in particular, a very rich uncle, believed the stories about him and told Rose that, if necessary, he would spend half of his entire fortune to keep her and her children from going to Leopold. The uncle firmly believed that if Rose and the children left they too would become apostates. Rose's letter went on to say that her uncle had hired a "watchman," a security guard, to accompany her wherever she went; this guard was to prevent her from leaving Hungary.

Disappointed, but still trusting God and knowing the power of prayer, Leopold and his friends called a special prayer meeting. They fervently sought the intervention of God so Rose and the children would be permitted leave Hungary. They did not have to wait long for God's answer!

God, who knows the beginning from the end, chose to use a letter Rabbi Cohn had written to some of his family members shortly after he had become a believer in Yeshua. In that letter Leopold spoke about Yeshua, the Messiah. Through that letter one of his nephews, Joseph Kahan (Cohn), became very interested in Yeshua and he wrote to Leopold telling him that he, too, had come to believe that Yeshua was the Messiah. Joseph and Leopold continued their correspondence, sharing their growing faith in Yeshua. As boys, Joseph and Leopold had studied together in the Yeshiva in Marmoros, Sziget, and by God's grace, He had brought each to a knowledge of His Son, Yeshua. When Leopold received Rose's letter telling of her uncle's plan to prevent her and the children from leaving Hungary, he immediately thought of his nephew, Joseph Kahan. Here was someone he could trust. Leopold cabled Joseph and told him of their situation, asking him if he would help by making arrangements to take his wife and children by night to Berlin. He assured Joseph that arrangements would be made for someone else to bring them to Scotland.

Joseph agreed to help, and he immediately contacted Rose. Together they formulated a plan for the escape of Rose and her children. Of that fateful night Joseph Hoffman Cohn wrote that his mother "managed to escape from the alert relatives who were watching her day and night. It was one black midnight that I can still remember, as a boy of seven, that a lumber-box wagon drove up to our home in Berezna. The wagon was drawn by one rather bulky horse, and the driver was my father's nephew from the town of Sziget, some twelve miles away. Into the lumber-box body, all of us four children piled, and over all was spread a sort of tarpaulin canvas such as is used for tents. My mother climbed up on the seat with the driver, and off we went. All night we rumbled and rumbled along and early in the morning the poor bedraggled horse came to a stop in front of the little house in which lived my father's nephew and his family."[31]

No one, not even Rose, suspected that Joseph was a secret Messianic believer. He had told no one of his faith, fearing what would happen to him. The cable from Leopold had caused Joseph to realize anew how precarious his own position was, and he was more than happy to assist Leopold's family by helping them get to Scotland. Early in the morning he took Rose and her four children to the train station in Sziget to board a train to Berlin. That same morning in Sziget, the security guard's telephone message that Rose and the children were missing caused quite a stir in the homes of the relatives. They immediately began telephoning all of the train stations on the main routes out of Hungary, informing train officials that Rose and her children had been kidnapped; they were fugitives and should be apprehended. Leopold was fully aware of the family's determination to keep Rose and the children from joining him and, by the grace of God and in answer to prayers for wisdom, Leopold had prearranged with Joseph that Rose and the children should board the train, travel to the next town, and then take a different route to Berlin. Thus, they were able to elude all who were looking for them.

They were to arrive in Edinburgh at three o'clock in the morning and were to be taken immediately to the Lady Douglas castle where Leopold was staying. Needless to say, sleep came to no one that night. Instead, they maintained an all night prayer vigil. Even Lady Douglas agreed to stay up to welcome Rose and the children—the family they had so fervently prayed for. It had been well over six months since Leopold had seen his wife and children. His heart ached for them. He longed to hold them again in his arms and to hear their laughter around the table. He could hardly believe they were actually coming to Scotland; he could hardly contain his excitement over the prospect of seeing them again.

It was only after God intervened and had brought Rabbi Cohn and Rose together again that Leopold learned from Rose that she had been grieving as much as he had. She believed he had abandoned her and the children. She further believed he had lost his mind, and had gone mad. Because she did not know Yeshua, or the peace that He alone can bring, Rose's grief, loneliness, and heartache during those terrible months was greatly intensified. She revealed to Leopold that she'd felt completely alone and deserted; she'd felt she was a disgrace and a dishonor within in her own family and within the Jewish community.

At last the great knocker on the door sounded and the door was opened. Leopold saw Rose and the children standing there and he felt his heart leap for joy. He ran toward her with outstretched arms, longing to gather her and all the children in his arms and smother them with all the love he had suppressed during the long lonely months. But he was stopped short. Rose put out her arms, but not toward him. Instead, she placed them around her children as a barricade. She stared at Leopold Cohn and, with eyes that seemed to penetrate his very soul, she demanded that he first tell her about the rumor of apostasy.

Leopold hadn't expected such a response or such a greeting. He had been rehearsing what he would say to Rose when she asked him about his beliefs, but her query was too abrupt, too unexpected! He quickly prayed, asking God for guidance, and then began to tell her as briefly, but as fully as he could, about the Messiah. Of that confrontation he remembered telling her, "the Crucified One is our Messiah and that all the time I was searching for the Messiah I did not know that it was He, but now I found it out and would show it to her from the Bible as soon as we had opportunity."[32]

Rose burst into tears. What she had not wanted to believe was true. Her husband was an apostate. Her family had been right. She should not have come! Her whole world seemed to collapse. She felt repulsed by this one who had turned away from his people and she turned away from Leopold, gathering the children even closer to her. She then spun around to face Leopold and, glaring through her tears, she told him she and the children would return to Hungary in a day or two because she could not, and would not, stay with a man who believed in the Crucified One, Yeshua. After all, throughout her life she had been taught to abhor and hate "that man" whom the Gentiles worship.

Never had two days and nights seemed so long. They were like a hell on earth for Leopold Cohn. After the long months of separation his wife was now so close, yet so far. Each time he looked at her she would turn away. He tried to talk with her, but she would walk away, not wanting to be in the same room with him. As far as Rose Cohn was concerned, her rabbi husband, Leopold, the Jew, was dead. Such disappointment and hurt after their long-awaited reunion crushed Leopold's heart, but he knew all he could do was pray. He knew only God could resolve such a conflict, and he believed He would.

Rose was determined to leave Scotland in two days, but the two days turned into three and then four, and so on. Each day she made plans to leave, but as the time came to leave they were somehow prevented. During those days Rose remained firm in her determination not to speak to Leopold, but she did not forbid the children from talking with their father. The two older boys, Benjamin, age nine, and Joseph, age seven, were well educated for their ages. Being the sons of a rabbi, they knew the Torah well, and also the Psalms. In addition, they had been learning the Scriptures in Hebrew. They also knew of their father's ritual of prayer and Bible study. One morning the boys arose early, wanting to spend time with their father while their mother was making preparations for them to return that evening to Hungary. Their father sat reading from his Hebrew Bible and as he did so, they quietly slipped into the room and sat down in front of him. Leopold had been praying for an opportunity to speak to his boys about his faith in the Messiah, and now God had opened the door. Little did he realize how big a door God had opened! Of that special moment Rabbi Cohn wrote:

> ...I read the second Psalm with them, [and] showed that God spoke there of His Son and that He was the Messiah referred to in the second verse. I told them that this was the One in whom I believed and that through His death all our sins were forgiven and that He was sitting at the right hand of God, receiving our prayers and pleading for us. They, with childlike faith, accepted my teaching and joined me in prayer. This we did morning, noon, and evening, and sometimes between these set hours. They too offered their short prayers that the Lord would be merciful and lead their mother to accept this same Savior who could give her peace. She, from another room, was listening to our words, although we did not know it. Two days later as I and the boys knelt in prayer, I suddenly felt her arm around me, and opening my eyes in surprise, I saw her smiling, though with tears in her eyes, while she said, 'Do not worry, I will stay with you, for I see that you are the same child of God that you were. But I want you to promise to let me observe our religion as before. Then I will know that you are right'.[33]

Leopold agreed with her conditions, rejoicing in answered prayer and rejoicing that they could be a family once again. He also knew in his heart that one day Rose would come to faith in Yeshua.

Leopold continued in his study of God's Word with his children, and often Rose would listen to the exposition. Because of her upbringing in a strict Orthodox home, she believed women were not to study the Torah or the prophets; such study was for men only. Although Rose had been well educated and knew several languages, including Hebrew, and had been thoroughly taught in Jewish customs and traditions, she was reluctant to study the Scriptures or Messianic prophecies with Leopold because of her upbringing. She thought such studies were too deep and too mysterious for women. However, she did volunteer to help him in his mission work among the Jewish people in Edinburgh and Glasgow and she also took an interest in his studies at New College.

Word of Rabbi Cohn's missionary activities in Scotland began to filter back to the villages in Hungary and Rose's relatives became more and more bitter toward her. In one letter from her sister, who was very fond of her, Rose found a piece of black ribbon and her sister's words saying that she mourned for Rose as if she were dead. Rose's relatives even went so far as to try and have the family extradited from Scotland and brought back to Hungary so Leopold could face charges of kidnapping and theft. Letters were sent to the prominent members of the Jewish community in Edinburgh and Glasgow, and women from some of those Jewish families visited Rose. With tears and weeping they would try to convince Rose to take her children and leave her apostate, rabbi husband. They even tried to bribe her, and sent her letters stating that if she would leave Leopold she would never lack for friends or financial support. Even though Rose was not yet a believer in Yeshua, she told the Jewish women that she knew her husband better than they did, and that she had more confidence in him than in all the Jews in Edinburgh. She even told some they ought to accept Yeshua as the Messiah! Rose could see the change in her husband. She could see his peace and joy, despite the bitter persecution he'd received from his own Jewish brethren. Emotionally and spiritually, however, she was being torn apart, and the turmoil began to take it's effect upon her health. But she was determined to stay by her husband—even with her doubts.

With Leopold's love for his own people, and deep longing for them to know the Messiah, it wasn't long before he had established regular Messianic Bible studies as well as regular Friday evening and Saturday afternoon worship services. Rose attended the services but she did not want to study the Scriptures. Faithfully Leopold and his friends continued to pray for Rose's salvation. As the weeks turned into months, and then into years, the Holy Spirit softened her heart so that the Word of God could penetrate. Over those months and years, Leopold never lost faith that somehow God would reach Rose.

Return to America

In the latter part of September, 1893, Leopold approached Lady Catherine Douglas with the same burden Warszawiak had shared with her years earlier. He wanted to return to New York. His heart burned to minister to the hundreds of thousands of immigrant Jews who had fled, and were still fleeing, Europe. So, with Lady Douglas' blessings, and the blessing of the brethren in Scotland, Leopold Cohn, along with his ailing wife and four children, Benjamin, age 9; Joseph, age 7; Joshua, age 5; and Esther, age 3, boarded a ship for America.

Leopold Cohn had seen many miracles since boarding a similar vessel steaming its way between England and New York only a year previously. Aboard that first steamer he had been a man driven by a desire to find the Messiah, but also a man alone, restless, lonely for his wife and children, and totally uncertain about what the future held. This journey to America was in great contrast to the first, for he had found his Messiah, and now his beloved family was making their way to America with him. With his faith firmly fixed in his Messiah, and his family by his side, the future looked bright. He knew God had called him to bring the message of Messiah to the Jews of New York, and although he knew there would be persecution, he also knew God would see him through. It was by God's grace upon Leopold Cohn that he could not foresee how great that persecution and suffering would be.

The Warszawiak Scandal

The Cohn family arrived in New York in October, 1893. Leopold immediately contacted his good friend Hermann Warszawiak and when Leopold showed him the letters and credentials from the brethren in Scotland, Warszawiak promptly hired Leopold to work for him in the New York City Mission which was sponsored by the Church of Scotland. But, unknown to Leopold Cohn, a great controversy had begun to build around Warszawiak. His ministry had become too successful, too well-known, and many of the leaders in the Jewish community wanted his mission to the Jews closed. There were also Christian leaders who were not in agreement with Warszawiak's methods of reaching Jewish people with the Gospel. These Christians openly criticized him. They, too, were looking for ways to close his mission.

Amidst the rumors and speculations being spread, Hermann Warszawiak resigned his position as missionary for the New York City Mission in 1894. He stated that he felt God was leading him to establish his own independent mission.[34] However, his new endeavor was short-lived. The Synod of the Presbyterian Church began an investigation of Hermann Warszawiak and subsequently even more rumors began to be spread about him. It was rumored that he was a womanizer, a thief, and a gambler. Evidently, the first investigation brought back a guilty verdict upon the person and the ministry of Warszawiak. This verdict was appealed by Warszawiak and a later investigation did give him a new trial, but irreparable damage had already done to his ministry. The newspapers had a field day. It was a scandal equal to that of the PTL Jim Bakker scandal which rocked our nation in 1988.

News of the scandal reached Edinburgh, Scotland. Knowing that much of Warszawiak's support came from Lady

Catherine Douglas, a cable was sent to her, telling her that her "beloved son," Hermann, was a fraud, an impostor, and a swindler. Hermann left immediately for Edinburgh, for he wanted to tell Lady Catherine Douglas what had happened in his own words, to put the record straight. However, before he ever reached the castle of Lady Catherine Douglas, she had gone home to be with her Lord. As a woman in her eighties, the first cable she had received about Hermann brought on a stroke from which she never recovered.

The newspapers picked up on this choice sensational material and carried headlines such as "Warszawiak Exposed as a Fraud," "Mrs. Warszawiak Dragged Out of Church," and others.[35] On the matter of the headline concerning Mrs. Warszawiak being dragged out of church, Joseph Hoffman Cohn wrote:

> ...his wife,...went as usual on that Sunday morning to the service at the Fifth Avenue Presbyterian Church. She entered her pew and sat down. It was perhaps three or four minutes before the service was to begin. An usher came down the aisle to her pew, and bending over whispered in her ear, 'Will you please leave the church.' When she heard this she turned on him, and told him in not too polite language, 'I will do nothing of the kind; this is my pew and I have paid rent for it!' The usher went to the rear of the church, and came down once more, bringing another usher with him. The two men then seized her, one by each arm, and practically dragged her out of the church. Dr. Hall (the pastor) was already in the pulpit and witnessed the entire proceeding with the utmost embarrassment; some of the audience claimed to have seen sweat on his forehead as he agonized to see this terrible performance in his church.
>
> When Warszawiak came back from Edinburgh, a broken and vanquished man, he found his wife in the hospital, overcoming the effects of a miscarriage.[36]

The effects of this scandal were far-reaching. First, it had a profound effect upon Warszawiak's children. They were sneered at and insulted. In school the other children told them their father was a crook, a cheat, and a liar. Because of this terrible persecution, Warszawiak and his children were obliged to change their name. Secondly, it ended the ministry of Warszawiak. He left the ministry, moved to Colorado, and went to work for a Jewish businessman. Thirdly, it had a profound effect upon Jewish Christians and upon independent missions to the Jews.

As one so closely connected to Warszawiak and his ministry, Leopold Cohn bore the full brunt of the scandal and embarrassment that the Warszawiak incident caused. Not only had Warszawiak been instrumental in leading Leopold to the Lord, he had discipled him and helped him in his training. Then, too, Leopold had worked for Warszawiak and had also come to his defense. All of this was later used as fuel to feed the fires of antagonism against the mission work that Leopold established.

With Warszawiak embroiled in controversy and his mission work undermined, Leopold Cohn ultimately severed his ties with Warszawiak. Not long afterward, Leopold received a call from the Rev. John Wilkinson founder of the Mildmay Mission to the Jews in London, England. Rev. Wilkinson asked if Rabbi Cohn would prayerfully consider going to Toronto, Canada. Wilkinson had been visiting the United States and Canada, and was about to dedicate their new work in Toronto. He wanted someone of Leopold's stature to take over the ministry. But Leopold's heart was in New York. He knew God had called him to reach the Jewish people of New York, so he declined Rev. Wilkinson's generous offer.

Shortly after declining Wilkinson's offer, Leopold and a Jewish friend were taking the ferry from New York City to Brooklyn, crossing the East River. Leopold wrote:

> ...I was surprised to see the large crowds of Jews accompanying us. I started a conversation with some of them and asked if they knew of any mission work being done in Brooklyn. They did not even seem to know what kind of a creature a missionary was. Then a forcible thought came into my mind and heart that it was the place where the Lord wanted me to work. It came so suddenly that it made a tremendous impression upon me and I went home and told my dear wife the new thought that the Lord had given me and that I believed that it came to me directly from above. I had no rest day or night, for at meals and other times, that thought was always talking to me: 'There is your place.'[37]

BEGINNING A JEWISH MISSION

Having resigned from the New York City Mission, Rabbi Cohn and his family had no means of support. The friends from Scotland had discontinued sending support after the death of Lady Catherine Douglas and the Warszawiak scandal, and each day began a new challenge to see how the Lord would supply their needs. One day Leopold left his home, wondering how God would provide not only food for his family, but a place where he could begin his ministry. As he searched and prayed, he found himself in the suburbs of Brooklyn where a number of new Jewish immigrant families had settled. The neighborhood was called "Brownsville." It was a settlement of "Hassidic Jews," similar in background to that of Leopold Cohn. The neighborhood had a few houses with a number of vacant lots in between them; sidewalks had not yet been laid. The roads were muddy, but there were no cars running there. Leopold felt at home. Here was the place he would establish his mission. He wrote:

> Just then I met a Jew with a pack of garments on his back hurrying across a vacant lot. I stopped and asked if he knew of a store for rent. As the Jew is always inquisitive, he queried why I wanted a store. I told him, 'For a mission.' He did not know what that was so I explained and told him about the Lord Jesus who can save him as well as all the Jews in Brownsville from their sins. There were some geese, chickens and a few goats on the vacant lots around us and I thought that I was fulfilling the command 'preach the Gospel to every creature' to the very letter. Then this man showed me a store not far away and I rented it. The following Saturday I held a meeting there and my acquaintance of a few days before was present. Seven other Jews came in and wanted to fight when they heard me mention the name of Jesus, but soon they became quiet and listened to the preaching of the Gospel with interest. Next Saturday, sixteen Jews attended the meeting, and next, many more. So the attendance kept on increasing until all the chairs were filled.[38]

With a large measure of faith and very little money, Rabbi Cohn moved his family from New York City to a small house in Brooklyn—340 Jefferson Avenue—and thus, the Brownsville Mission to the Jews was founded in October of 1894. From this humble beginning, and through the vision and faith of Rabbi Leopold Cohn, God established the work that continues to this day under the name, Chosen People Ministries, Inc.

The first few months of his ministry at the Brownsville Mission brought bitter persecution to the entire Cohn family. Rose was not yet a believer. The hatred and persecution she had experienced from her family when she fled her home, and ultimately had decided to stay with Leopold, had greatly affected and weakened her physically. Once again, she found that she and her loved ones were becoming victims of persecution for the Gospel sake; this time the threats and hatred were being hurled from both the Jewish and the Christian communities. It was especially difficult for her to see her husband and children coming home bruised and bloody from beatings they had received from their fellow Jews. Of those first few weeks of ministry Rabbi Cohn wrote:

> The leading Jews of Brownsville, seeing the continuous and steady attendance at the mission, became bitter and started to persecute me as well as the Jews who came in. Several times, attempts were made to do me bodily harm, but they only once succeeded in decoying and giving me a good beating. It was done as follows: One afternoon as I was leaving the reading room in charge of another, word was sent asking me to bring a Hebrew New Testament to a certain house. Being glad at the request, I hurried to the given address. No sooner had I finished my errand, than the Jew, the head of the house, a powerful man, fell upon me, knocked me down and battered me severely with his fists, jumped upon me with his feet and took me by the ears, raising my head and dropping me to the floor many times. When he took hold of my ears, he repeated in Hebrew: 'These ears which heard from Mount Sinai, "Thou shalt not have other Gods beside me" and which now listen to the Christian god, must be pulled out of his head,' emphasizing his words, 'pulled out,' by a terrible jerk at my ears. But when it was about unbearable, the Lord sent another Jew who came in unexpectedly and my tormentor was startled and stopped persecuting me. So I gathered myself together and ran out as fast as I could. When I dragged myself home, my dear wife noticed the blood trickling down my face and was greatly shocked, but soon recovered and attended to my wounds, comforted and strengthened me in the Lord and in the blessed hope He gave us. She did not upbraid or triumph over me saying: 'Did I not tell you not to go to Brooklyn?' A number of times, however, I heard her murmur with a deep sigh, 'Oh, why was I so foolish as to leave Bonnie Scotland?' As a rule, she never complained under straitened circumstances, although she was brought up in wealth in her father's house where she never knew any need or want. Whenever I came home tired, she had a word of cheer, and with a heavenly smile on her face, always lightened my burdens.[39]

It was not just Leopold who was persecuted. The children also suffered, but they suffered more from the so-called "Christian" children. He wrote:

> On one occasion a number of boys took one of my boys, who was only six or seven years at that time; they stretched him on the floor, some holding him down while another stepped on his legs below his knees and fractured them. In spite of the agonizing screams of the boy, they laughed and said, 'That is the way the sheenies cry.' Then the boy was brought home helpless and one can imagine what great grief and vexation that caused us, and I thought, 'Now her (Rose's) faith will be weakened,' for Jewish people used to come in and when they learned of it, say, 'You see with whom you have to associate and who Christians are.'…On a later occasion, however, some other so-called Christian children took one of our boys, and while several held him by force, another came with a knife and cut his lower lip

through and through, and said: 'This is the way we have to do with sheenies.' Many other trials came in different ways from the hands of so-called Christians, and I always felt worried lest they should repel either my dear wife or some of my children from the Lord Jesus Christ, but thanks be to God it was not so.[40]

ROSE COHN ACCEPTS THE MESSIAH

Money was always scarce but Rabbi Cohn hung on to his conviction that God had called him to this neighborhood, and that God would not fail him in the hour of crisis. One month Leopold had no money with which to pay the rent on the mission building. From the moment she had joined her husband in Scotland, Rose had been observing his behavior as testings, and later deprivation, confronted them, but she had remained unwilling to consider the claims of Yeshua on her own life. When Leopold told Rose they had no money with which to pay the rent, she brought out the last pieces of jewelry which had been given to her as a remembrance of her mother, who had died when she was a young girl. The pieces of jewelry were dearly valued by Rose, but she told Leopold to pawn them and to pay the rent on the Mission building. Leopold said he told her they might never be able to redeem the jewelry, and he cautioned her that she might be sorry the rest of her life. To this Rose replied, "If it is lost here, your Jesus will return it to me in heaven."[41] This reply gave much joy to Leopold, for although Rose had not yet opened her heart to Yeshua, she was close. Her heart was becoming more and more open to God's truth, in spite of the persecution they had received and the opposition from the enemy of our souls.

It was the godly and devout life of her husband that finally led Rose to accept Yeshua. She had been observing him with suspicious caution, and as the months and years went by, she became convinced that his acceptance of Yeshua as the Messiah had not made Leopold a Gentile. He had not become a Jew-hater. Instead, she had observed that he loved his people more. In one of the first letters Leopold wrote to Rose after he had found his Messiah, Yeshua, he talked about a dream he'd had a few weeks before he sailed for America. He had mentioned the dream to Rose before he left Hungary, but at that time he'd had no understanding of the meaning of the dream. But now, he said in his letter, he understood what the dream meant. In his dream, Leopold said, he "…saw the sun rising in all its glory and brightness and not far from the sun were two moons, one very dark and the other full of light…. [He looked at them] with astonishment,…[and then] the dark moon fell from the skies and disappeared, while the bright moon stayed there with the sun."[42]

The dream had troubled Leopold and he longed to know its meaning. Because he had studied with a miracle-working rabbi and with mystics, he firmly believed that dreams held meanings. He believed they were symbolic of events in life. After Leopold had accepted Yeshua, he recognized the symbolism of his dream and in his letter to Rose he explained what he felt it's interpretation was. She never forgot it. He told her he believed the moon was symbolic of the Hebrew race and their religion, for as the moon has the renewal of her light after darkness, so the Jews will be renewed in their national glory after their fall. The sun was symbolic of the Messiah who is called the Son of righteousness. Thus, he said, "…in that dream the Lord showed me that the dark side of my Jewish religion would disappear, while the real Jewish faith which is full of light would stay and abide with me through the Sun of righteousness, the Lord Jesus who is the light of the world."[43] Rose could see that what Leopold had told her about his faith was true. His faith, the faith he had in the Messiah, Yeshua, was what was making him more Jewish than ever. She discovered she was not only falling in love once again with the Jewish rabbi she had married, she was also falling in love with his Messiah, Yeshua.

What settled the matter for Rose was the memory of the Passover they had celebrated together while they were in Scotland. Rabbi Cohn had been going through the traditional Seder service. On the Passover table were placed the three pieces of matzo (unleavened bread) which are always a part of the Passover Seder. These are wrapped together, but separated by a napkin between each piece. Together, they form a unity. Traditionally, as the father (or head of the family) performs the ceremony, he takes out the middle matzo and breaks it in half. One half of the broken matzo is hidden under a pillow of the lounge on which the father reclines during the meal. This ritual was not new to Rabbi Cohn, for he had been performing it year after year, but he had not realized its significance until after he had accepted Yeshua as his Messiah. As he read the New Testament account of the Passover meal which Yeshua kept with his disciples just before he died, Rabbi Cohn realized that Yeshua had used the "afikomen" (the broken piece of matzo which had been hidden away) and the cup which comes after the meal, the cup of redemption, to point to Himself. Yeshua had told His disciples, "This is my body given for you" and "This is the New Covenant" (Luke 22: 19,20).

Recalling his reaction to this new understanding Cohn later wrote, "…it suddenly dawned on me what it all meant. The three cakes represent Father, Son and Holy Spirit; the middle one, the Son, broken in halves, indicates the body of the Son of God, broken for our sins. Concealing it under the pillow signifies the burial of the broken body, and bringing it forth again at the third cup of wine indicates strikingly the resurrection of the Lord Jesus on the third day."[44]

As Rabbi Cohn shared his new understanding of the Passover Seder symbols with Rose and his children, they were all deeply moved, especially Rose. The symbolism of that broken matzo was sealed to her mind and heart. Leopold told them that it must have been the early Jewish believers in the Messiah, Yeshua, who had instituted this matzo-breaking ceremony so believers would not forget the price God had paid to redeem us from our sins. He went on, explaining to them that now Jews all over the world unwittingly show forth Messiah's death, burial, and resurrection, as well as the uniqueness of the triune God, when they celebrate Passover.

In her little home in Brooklyn, although confronted daily by evidence of the suffering and persecution to which her husband and children were being subjected because of their faith in Yeshua, Rose realized she could no longer straddle the fence; she needed to make a decision about this Messiah, Yeshua. In the quietness of her bedroom, she knelt in prayer and accepted Yeshua as her Messiah and Savior. The Cohn family was now united in faith. They were now united in their efforts and devotion to the task God had given them. Little did they know that God was preparing men who would help them in that task.

* Perhaps the reader will think it strange that Rabbi Cohn would leave his family and his country so abruptly, without so much as saying "good bye" to those he loved.

To understand, one must remember the time and circumstances in which Leopold Cohn lived. As an itinerant rabbi, Leopold was used to being away from home. In their quest for greater truth, it was not at all uncommon for rabbis and rabbinic students of that time to pursue answers to the enigmas of life, or of scripture, in far-away lands if it was felt the answers could be found there.

A second consideration was the matter of family pressures and control. As indicated in the early pages of this chapter, Leopold, like many rabbinic students, chose to move into the Hoffman family's home once he and Rose were married— an arrangement that enabled him to concentrate on his studies, but an arrangement in which he became financially dependent upon Rose's family and, therefore, somewhat under their control. Leopold's decision to simply "grasp the opportunity" removed any possibility that the family would object to such a trip and thereby end all hope of his finding the Messiah whom he so desperately longed to know.

ENDNOTES

Chapter 2. Leopold Cohn—the Rabbi Who Found Yeshua

[1] Leopold Cohn, *A Modern Missionary to an Ancient People*, (Brooklyn, New York: American Board of Missions to the Jews, now Chosen People Ministries Inc., 1908), p 13.

[2] *The Jewish Encyclopedia*, projector & managing ed. Isidore Singer, Vol. VI, (New York: Ktav Publishing House, Inc., n.d.), p 261. "Hattarat Hora'ah (lit. 'permission to teach and decide'): A rabbinical diploma; a written certificate given to one who, after a thorough examination, proves himself competent and worthy to be a rabbi. It is a substitute for the 'semikah,' which could be conferred only in Palestine, by a member of the Sanhedrin.... unlike the Christian ordination, [it] confers no sacred power, and is not a license; it is simply a testimonial of the ability of the holder to act as rabbi if elected.

[3] L. Cohn, *Ancient People*, p 15.

[4] See note above, p 15.

[5] See note above, p 15.

[6] See note above, pp 16, 17.

[7] See note above, p 17.

[8] See note above, pp 17, 18.

[9] See note above, p 18.

[10] See note above, pp 18-19.

[11] See note above, pp 20-21.

[12] Joseph H. Cohn, *I Have Fought A Good Fight*, (New York: American Board of Missions to the Jews, now Chosen People Ministries, Inc., 1953), p 160.

[13] See note above, p 160.

[14] See note above, p 161.

[15] See note above, p 161.

[16] L. Cohn, *Ancient People*, pp 21-22.

[17] Heinrich Graetz, *History of the Jews*, Vol. III, Ch. VII, (Philadelphia: The Jewish Publication Society of America, 1967), pp 221-222.

[18] Official Minutes: *In the Matter of the Investigation of Charges Preferred Against Leopold Cohn*, 1916, p 130.

[19] L. Cohn, *Ancient People*, pp 23-24.
[20] See note above, p 25.
[21] A.E. Thompson, *A Century of Jewish Missions*, (Chicago: Fleming H. Revell Co., 1902), p 243.
[22] J.H. Cohn, *Fought a Good Fight*, p 162.
[23] See *Investigation of Charges*, p 116.
[24] L. Cohn, *Ancient People*, pp 26-28.
[25] See note above, p 28.
[26] See note above, p 28.
[27] See note above, p 29.
[28] See note above, pp 29-30.
[29] See note above, pp 30-31.
[30] See note above, p 31.
[31] J.H. Cohn, *Fought a Good Fight*, p 108.
[32] L. Cohn, *Ancient People*, p 34.
[33] See note above, pp 34, 35.
[34] *Announcement*, The Hebrew Christian, December, 1894, p 1.
[35] J.H. Cohn, *Fought a Good Fight*, p 176.
[36] See note above, p 175, 176.
[37] L. Cohn, *Ancient People*, p 40.
[38] See note above, pp 41-42.
[39] See note above, pp 42-43.
[40] See note above, pp 48-49.
[41] J.H. Cohn, *Fought a Good Fight*, p 71.
[42] L. Cohn, *Ancient People*, p 36.
[43] See note above, p 37.
[44] See note above, p 38.

3

THE BROWNSVILLE MISSION TO THE JEWS

Rabbi Leopold Cohn faced an uphill battle in his struggle to establish an independent Jewish mission work in the New York area. Having resigned from the staff of the Hebrew-Christian Mission, he had no visible means of support. As a matter of fact, he had very few friends. The Warszawiak scandal had left pastors, Christian leaders, and denominational leaders very wary of any Jewish believer, especially of one who had assisted Hermann Warszawiak, or of one who was attempting to start an independent work.

THE BERNHARD ANGEL STORY

After Warszawiak's resignation as Director of the Hebrew-Christian Mission, the Church of Scotland and the Presbyterian synod appointed Bernhard Angel as the next Director.

Bernhard was born in Bucharest, Romania in 1860. He was trained in Judaism as a child, and later studied at the Jewish Seminary in Hanover, Germany. Aboard ship on his way to America, Bernhard met a Catholic woman whom he was very much attracted to. Despite his Jewish background and her Catholic upbringing, a romance blossomed. Their courtship continued after their arrival in New York and they subsequently married. Mrs. Angel opened her heart to the Lord following a visit by a Protestant missionary who came to her bedside when she was very ill. For six months following her conversion, Bernhard struggled with the issue of whether Yeshua was the promised Messiah. Finally he, too, came to believe in Yeshua, and not long afterward he felt the call of God upon his life to share the Gospel with his people. He enrolled in seminary in Chicago, and began to do mission work among the Jews there. After a time of ministry in Chicago, Bernhard was called to take over the directorship of the Hebrew-Christian Mission in New York.[1]

Because the Warszawiak scandal was still fresh in the minds of many Christians, Bernhard Angel began to write articles that he thought would help the Hebrew-Christian Mission recover some of the financial base it had lost as a result of the scandal. In the articles he addressed problems and issues that had plagued Jewish missions. The articles may have been of help to Angel's ailing mission, but they certainly weren't of any help to Rabbi Leopold Cohn, who was just starting his work and was attempting to gain financial support from pastors and Christian leaders. In one of his articles, Bernhard noted several mistakes he felt leaders of Jewish missions had made. He stated:

First Mistake- *It is a mistake to help a Jew financially too readily. There are a number of Jews surrounding every Christian mission who grasped the argument that because a Jew is persecuted, therefore he ought to be financially helped. Many Jews thus succeed in plundering the Gentile's pockets by pleading persecution, while by actual fact the persecution exists only in their imaginations.*

Second Mistake- *Equally unwise is it to furnish means for the emigration of professed converts to other lands…. No mission should this way shovel off its converts, either across land or ocean.*

Third Mistake- *It is a great mistake to baptize the inquirer too soon…. The uninstructed Jew has a vague impression that as soon as he is baptized the Christian church becomes his financial sponsor.*

Fourth Mistake- *It is a great mistake to make too much show at the baptism of a Jew.*

Fifth Mistake- *It is a mistake to think that nearly every Jewish convert should become a paid missionary.*

Sixth Mistake- *It is a mistake to think that because a Jew is willing to talk about religion therefore he is an inquirer.*

Seventh Mistake- *It is a mistake to trust any converted Jew as leader of others without very carefully examining his past history. There are many Jews who journey from mission to mission, staying in one until they have exhausted the patience of the missionary, and then going on to the other and being re-baptized for the same purpose. Jewish missionaries the world over, ought to have a clearing-house of information, and let each know when A, B or C of their converts have proved untrustworthy.*

Eighth Mistake. *It is a mistake to put in any Jewish convert as a leader without adequate training. If any one needs to be watched carefully, instructed systematically, and disabused of many of his former ideas, it is that Jew who leaves the religion of his ancestors and comes within the bounds of Christianity. Much evil has been done to the cause at large by entrusting its leadership to the hands of glib-tongued, smart, aggressive converts.[2]*

PROBLEMS OF JEWISH MISSIONS

Bernhard Angel's articles and ideas only served to promote increased hostility toward the Jewish people; they caused Gentile Christians to become suspicious of Jewish believers and of independent missions to the Jews. The Christian community no longer welcomed Jewish believers "with open arms," offering ready support with no questions asked. Instead, Gentile believers began to doubt the validity of the testimonies of new Jewish converts and of Jewish missions. They began to question whether the so-called "needs" presented by Jewish believers were, instead, simply despicable scams by those "immigrant Jews." The issues were complex and complicated.

Jewish believers and Jewish missions could no longer look to Christian groups for ready support. Nor could they turn to the Jewish community for endorsement of credentials. As immigrant Jews poured into New York, the leaders of the Jewish community diligently sought to keep the newcomers within the Jewish community. The rabbis and other leaders of the community were keenly aware that apart from what the new immigrants had experienced of church-state controlled religion in Europe, most had no knowledge of the Christian world. The concepts of the Messiah, of individual belief, the New Testament, missions, and the "Church," were unheard of to them. Many of the immigrants arrived in this new land without the language skills or the trade skills needed for their new lives in America. In their desperate attempt to keep the new immigrants from "straying," the rabbis and other leaders of the Jewish community did everything within their power to disparage the message proclaimed by Jewish missions, and to discredit the testimonies of Jewish believers.

America was a melting pot of people and ideas. Prior to 1820, fewer than 3,000 Jewish people resided in America. But when Napoleon was defeated, and the hopes of European Jews were defeated with him, many Jews began to leave Europe for America. Between the years of 1820 and 1850, the Jewish population in America grew to 50,000, and as revolutions and anti-Jewish feelings shook Europe more Jews left. By 1860 the Jewish population in America had swelled to over 150,000. The pogroms in Russia, and the anti-Jewish legislation adopted in Eastern Europe, led to more violence and hatred toward the Jews, until the only place of refuge for the Jew was America. America offered freedom and opportunity. America offered a respite from persecution. "Jewish immigration from Eastern Europe (Russia, Poland, Romania, Galacia, Hungary) due to physical, economic and political persecution, brought 2.5 million Jews to the United States between 1880 and 1930."[3] For most of the immigrants, the journey to this new land was an emotionally and physically draining experience. Once they reached the shores of America the majority of the new immigrants chose to remain in New York, close to their point of entry at Ellis Island. New York soon became the largest concentration of Jewish people in the world.

The impact of so many Jewish people pouring into one area in so a short time, bringing with them their unique culture, language, customs, and traditions, provoked an outbreak of anti-Semitism from the society around them. As new Jewish immigrants poured into the country, both young and old Jews flooded the school system as they attempted to learn language and work skills. Anti-Semitic feelings and attitudes flared in the work place as Jewish immigrants competed for jobs. Even within the churches anti-Semitic attitudes began to develop as Jewish immigrants turned to Christian churches and to missions for help and assistance. Many immigrants were willing to tolerate the message of Christianity in exchange for material assistance. Others were genuinely touched by the message of God's plan of redemption through the sacrifice of His Son, and accepted Yeshua as Messiah and Lord. During these turbulent days Rev. F. F. Ellinwood of New York City defended churches against charges of anti-Semitism in a published work entitled, "The Duty of Christendom to the Jews." He charged:

...Jews 'create prejudice' against them by their actions. First among these...is 'their phenomenal thrift.' He also pointed to their behavior at summer resorts where they are 'deemed undesirable guests on account of their rough and disagreeable manners.' But said he, they may be no more 'clownish or swinish than other races,' notably the Irish or certain classes of Americans.... Further, he charged Jews with 'money-getting passion which, in the course of centuries, has become a nature.' He was fearful of the power of Jewish bankers in Europe and that 'the main business thoroughfare of our great metropolis is exchanging the names of old American firms for the names of German Jews.' He was afraid that Jews will some day hold a 'magician wand' over our government just as Disraeli had over England. 'They are sure to become not only a great financial power but a strong social and political element in this country,'...'The logic of their twofold increase—by natural generation and by immigration—renders certain a great development.[4]

The solution Ellinwood proposed was similar to solutions proposed by other church leaders during that time in American church history when, for the first time, church leaders in America were confronted with the uniqueness of the

Jewish community. They recommended that Christians seek to convert the Jew and to assimilate him into the main-stream of Christian society. They believed that the Jews would ultimately be converted to Christianity, and they further believed that this would happen through gradual assimilation. Ellinwood went so far as to say, "Social absorption, inter-marriage, the assimilating influence of the common school, the fading out of the Jewish pride and prejudice of race are to be factors in God's plan of recovery."[5]

Anti-Semitism was gaining strength both within and outside of the Church. Gentile Christians expected Jewish missions to preach the Gospel to Jews and to assist in assimilating Jewish believers into the main-stream of Christianity, yet Jews who professed faith in Yeshua were suspect by both the Christian community and the Jewish community.

THE BROWNSVILLE MISSION BEGINS

It was into this turbulent society that Rabbi Leopold Cohn was led of God to begin his mission. His vision was not to reach Jews with the Gospel so they could become just like Gentile Christians. Leopold Cohn's vision was that Jews would come to believe in Yeshua, yet still maintain their Jewishness. Like others before him, Leopold patterned his mission program after the Jewish missions programs of Britain. But his mission was unique in that he determined to establish and maintain a Jewish-Christian congregation which, as a synagogue did for the Jewish community, would attempt to meet the needs of families within New York's burgeoning Jewish-Christian community.

Leopold's vision began to take on tangible properties when he rented his first building in Brownsville (Brooklyn), New York. God had supplied the means, as well as the Christian friends, to bring to fruition this first stepping stone of his vision. In the February 1896 issue of *The Chosen People* magazine, Rabbi Cohn wrote to friends of his ministry, saying: "The Lord put me here a year and four months ago to preach His glorious Gospel to His chosen people. This place made me sow in tears, and now He makes me reap in joy."[6] He then went on to rejoice over a number of Jews who had embraced Yeshua and, to keep friends of his ministry informed and involved, he included a description of the first "mission hall" from which his ministry was being carried on. The article stated:

> The place in which the work of the 'Brownsville Jewish Mission' is carried on is a low, small, unpretentious building, formerly occupied by an Italian shoemaker and his family.
>
> The location is admirably adapted to the work, as the hall is situated on Rockaway Ave., the principal thoroughfare of Brownsville; and while the hall is not in the centre of the Jewish quarters, it is accessible to all the Hebrew residents....
>
> The appointments of our hall are of the most primitive character,...
>
> We were unable to purchase shades for the large windows in front, so the painter's brush was called into requisition in order to provide a screen to protect us from the curious glance of the passers by, for the building is on a level with the street.
>
> As to carpets or matting, there is none, save a small piece provided for the teacher's use by a kind friend, a much needed provision, as there is no cellar, and consequently, the floor is very cold.
>
> A movable partition of the plainest kind is used to divide the hall into two rooms, when necessary. There are two windows in the rear. These are shaded with light calico curtains, scant in width, short in length. The papering on the walls of this room is an artistic wonder. Several different patterns are displayed, all arranged somewhat after the order of the 'crazy patch-work,' so fashionable a few years ago.
>
> Now as to the furniture, we have one hundred and sixty chairs, quite an increase over the forty-eight, with which the work was started. But even with this number we are greatly crowded on Thursday afternoons and evenings. We need at least fifty more chairs—for lack of these we seat the children in the window-seats, or on one of our school-tables, of which we have two.
>
> There is a clock, the gift of a lady interested in the work, and a piano. The latter is very old-fashioned, quite small, and can hardly be heard at the end of the room. We are very grateful to the owner, who kindly loaned it to us, but we need a more powerful instrument. We are indebted to the thoughtful kindness of a Christian lady who is greatly interested in the religious welfare of God's ancient people, for a good stove and a supply of fuel, which have greatly added to our comfort this winter.
>
> Gifts of mottoes and pictures for the walls have given a cheerful look to the rooms. We greatly need a book-case. We have had books given us by two Sunday Schools sufficient to form the nucleus of a lending library. As we have only one closet, so small it can hardly contain our Bibles, Testaments, school books, hymn books, and the work of the Sewing School, we have no place for our books.
>
> A library would be a great service to us. As soon as the men who attend the evening school can read English with any degree of pleasure, they ask for books to read at home. Such books could be also loaned to the larger girls at the sewing school.

> *Now in spite of our lack of the proper surroundings to make our hall cheery and comfortable, with all its disadvantages, it has become very dear to our hearts, and when on Thursday afternoons it is literally packed with bright-eyed, happy-faced girls, or in the evening with girls, boys, men and women, young and old, all singing together of a Saviour's love, it seems to us the most beautiful place in the world.*
>
> *Our great need is a suitable building in which to carry on our work. When we look back on the past year and recount all the blessings we have received, we are confident that in His own time this need will also be supplied.[7]*

Rabbi Cohn was providing six services a week in his effort to reach his Jewish people with the Gospel. On Saturday at 2:30 P.M., he held a preaching service in Yiddish. This was mainly attended by men, as women were not used to attending such services in the synagogues. On Saturday at 7:00 P.M., he held a Bible reading class. This was open to all. Mondays through Wednesdays at 7:00 P.M., he held an evening school, the purpose of which was not only to hear the Word of God, but also to learn English. On Thursdays at 3:00 P.M., he held a girls' sewing school. The sewing school was at first conducted by Leopold's wife, Rose. Later it was conducted by his daughter, Esther, with the help of other Christian women who volunteered their time. On Thursday evenings, he held a Praise Service. This was his evangelistic service, with singing, testimonies, and the preaching of the Word of God.

In addition to this heavy schedule, Rabbi Cohn advertised to the churches in the area that he was available to speak on Sundays and Fridays on subjects such as Jewish mission work, the Passover, the Tabernacle, the Second Coming of Christ, the Christian's duty to the Jews, and Jewish manners and customs. He advertised that no offerings would be taken. He also offered to be available to speak at mid-week services if arrangements were made in advance.

Rabbi Cohn spent every waking hour trying to reach the 15,000 Jews of Brownsville with the Gospel. He involved his wife and children in the ministry, as well as anyone else he could recruit. His vision for the ministry was to meet the needs of the Jewish community in as many ways as possible, while incorporating the Gospel message into each type of outreach. It seemed, however, that there were always more needs than money, and his greatest struggle was in trying to make both ends meet—both within his mission and within his personal life.

Recounting the difficulties of those early days of ministry, and praising God for His faithfulness, Rabbi Cohn said:

> *...One day when our children came home from school, there was only a cup of tea for their lunch. Upon explaining to them that there was no money to buy bread just now, one of the boys offered to go to the baker, who, he was sure, would give us a loaf of bread on credit. He went and returned without bread but with tears in his eyes; the baker refused to open an account with him and so hurt his feelings. Sadly disappointed, the children had to return to school without having a piece of bread with their tea. When I realized the situation that I as a father was not able to give bread to my dear children, my heart nearly broke, and I wept bitterly. Suddenly, the bell rang and the whistle of the letter-carrier shrieked loud, and behold, there was a registered letter with money in it. It was the rent for my dear wife's property, left her from her father, which she entrusted to her brother in Hungary before she left for Scotland. Her brother refused to send her the money for the previous two years on account of her staying with me. Now he sent it of his own accord. This was followed by a letter from Mr. E. Raphael, a Hebrew Christian in Edinburgh, promising of his own free will, to send us ten pounds monthly for a year.[8]*

The financial struggle was difficult for the entire Cohn family during that first year, but God was preparing the hearts of some Christian leaders who would share in Rabbi Cohn's vision of reaching the Jews of Brooklyn with the Gospel.

One Sunday in the fall of 1895, Leopold Cohn visited the Bushwick Avenue Baptist Church in Brooklyn. The church was located just a few blocks away from the mission hall on Rockaway Avenue in Brownsville. The pastor, Rev. Thomas J. Whitaker, spotted Rabbi Cohn immediately as he walked through the door. Whitaker had not met Cohn before, and at the close of the service he went to Cohn and asked him what he was doing there, and what he wanted. It was quite unusual to see a Jewish man, bearded and dressed in hasidic clothing, attending a Christian church service unescorted. Generally, if Jewish people attended services at all, they were brought by Christian friends or by a missionary. When Leopold told Rev. Whitaker that he was a Rabbi who believed in Yeshua, Whitaker was overjoyed. Cohn then shared something about his burden to see Jewish people come to faith in Yeshua, and about the work of the mission he had established. Whitaker became very excited. God had already been speaking to his heart, and he told Rabbi Cohn that he, too, had been desirous of seeing a mission for Jews established in Brooklyn. He further indicated that he would be willing to sponsor such a mission. Here was the beginning of the answer to Rabbi Cohn's prayer for needed funding!

Rabbi Cohn joined Bushwick Avenue Baptist Church, and in February 1896 he and his older son, Benjamin, were baptized by Pastor Whitaker. (Rabbi Cohn had been baptized in Scotland but the method of baptism by "sprinkling" was unacceptable at Bushwick Avenue Baptist Church; they required that Rabbi Cohn be immersed.)

THE CHOSEN PEOPLE MAGAZINE INITIATED

Pastor Whitaker encouraged Mr. H. O. Avery, a member of his deacon board, to get involved in Cohn's ministry, and a committee was formed to help in the mission as well. Rev. Whitaker became the Chairman of the committee, Mr. Avery was Treasurer, and Rabbi Leopold Cohn, the Director. The purpose of the committee was to oversee the finances of the mission, and to help give direction to Rabbi Cohn. One of the first things they encouraged Rabbi Cohn to do was to print a monthly newsletter which was to be sent to Christians, telling them of the need to evangelize the Jews of Brooklyn. It was believed that the newsletter would also help raise monies necessary for carrying on Rabbi Cohn's ministry. Leopold was delighted with the idea. So, among his other duties and responsibilities, he became the editor and writer of "The Chosen People magazine." The first issue of the magazine was sent out in October 1895. The early editions of The Chosen People Magazine stated:

> Our paper appears monthly, and is devoted to Jewish Mission Work, first in our own special field, located in that portion of the twenty-sixth ward formerly known as 'Brownsville,' where some fifteen thousand Jews reside.
>
> Our poor in Brownsville are suffering greatly at this time on account of the strike and slack work. We feel for them very much.
>
> When we visit their homes we see their great distress. We are sure that if any true Christian were to see four, five, and six children in one house, all ragged and barefoot, the mother sick, the father without employment, the rent overdue, a dispossess warrant expected,...he could not rest until he had tried to help such a family.
>
> There are four special quarters for Jews in Brooklyn. Each quarter is thickly populated with God's chosen people. Not one of the four has a smaller population than ten thousand souls: some number as high as fifty thousand Jews. Dear reader,...Did you ever think what you can do for them? Did it ever occur unto your mind that God had sent them to your very threshold for some special purpose?[9]

To help raise the needed funds to operate the mission, Pastor Whitaker offered to write a special article for The Chosen People magazine. Rev. Whitaker, Rabbi Cohn, and the other members of the committee hoped that such articles would help other ministers and other church congregations become more interested in reaching Jews with the Gospel. They were also hoping to allay some of the fears about supporting Jewish missions which earlier scandals and rumors had created. Rev. Whitaker wrote:

> The present outlook for evangelizing the Hebrew people surprises many Christians. The Lord's disciples have been idly waiting rather than anxiously watching for the fulfillment of prophecy respecting the Jews. The sun was above the horizon before we saw its coming. But now some are rubbing their eyes and wondering what the conversion of so many Jews portends. Can it be that God really meant what he said? Are the Orient People to be gathered on the old camping ground? Is the Lord about to appear unto them to lead them?
>
> It is high time that we awake out of our sleep, for the day is here. Israel has grown weary of her traditions and cries unto God for light. This cry, like the Macedonia cry of old, is waking up the Church of Jesus Christ, and she is shaking herself from her lethargy and is buckling on the armor for conquest.
>
> The planting of missions in the Hebrew districts of our cities is the order of to-day.
>
> To the ordinary Christian teacher a service at the mission is novel. The asking and answering of questions reminds one of our Lord's boyhood visit at the temple. Said a visiting pastor after a service, 'I have learned something to-day. This is the way to teach and reach the people.'
>
> Such questions as the following are often asked: 'If Christians love us, why do they treat us as they did in Russia?' 'How may we know that Jesus Christ is the Messiah?' 'Are all men Christians that are not Jews?' Answers to such questions are eagerly listened to, and the word of God settles all arguments with the Jew.
>
> There are some difficult and discouraging features about Hebrew mission work that we do not find among other peoples. One is the matter of support for the converts. When a Jew accepts Christ he is, in the majority of cases, immediately without work. For a Jew will not employ, nor work with, if he can dictate, any Christian Jew. The moment one of them seems interested in a Christian service, he is suspicioned and often persecuted, and not a few are driven from the missions by the fear of hunger coming to their homes. If some philanthropic and enterprising man or company could be induced to start an industrial plant and give employment to all who are thrown out of work by reason of their change of faith, it would be a mightier factor in solving the question of Hebrew mission work. The work at Brownsville is worthy of all help.[10]

The committee understood that Jewish mission work was, in reality, foreign missions at home and therefore required a broader scope of ministry and support than other types of home mission works. When a Jewish person accepted Yeshua, they were often ostracized by their family members and friends; they were left with no place to go but to the mission. Hence, the mission became responsible not only for their spiritual needs, but for their physical needs as well. Without the assistance of the mission, these individuals had no one to turn to for help. Financial pressure, family pressure, and social pressure were brought to bear on almost every Jewish believer in the Messiah. A good example of this kind of family pressure is found a in letter that Rabbi Cohn received from his brother in Hungary after Leopold had become a believer in Yeshua. He wrote:

> ...My dearly beloved brother—Remember how dearly we have loved one another, how delighted we were to talk together...how we expected one from another nothing but love and kindness.
>
> Now you have broken my heart, as well as the hearts of our other brother and sisters. You have made our lives not worth living. We cannot endure the shame, the grief, the vexation you have brought upon us. No respectable family here is willing to have any affinity with me or any of our family since there is an apostate in our number. I cannot come among people because of great confusion of face. When I walk in the street I cannot discern anybody, it is as if there was a thick darkness before my eyes. My strength is failing me day by day on account of your behavior. I used always to be in good health, but since I heard of your step I have often been sick. Oh, give up that Crucified One! Oh, pity me and your other brother and sisters, for God's sake, for our parent's sake, for our nation's sake, for your own sake, do, I beseech you, stop preaching that! Oh have mercy on me! Oh, spare my life! I am a father of children and I fear and say, as did David, 'I shall one day perish by the sorrow you have caused me.' Again, I ask you, my dear brother, 'intendest thou to kill me?'[11]

Cohn received many such letters from his sisters, his brother, and from his former friends and associates. He knew, first hand, how his Jewish brethren suffered because of their faith. Because of this suffering, his vision of reaching his Jewish people with the Gospel included meeting their physical needs as well as their spiritual needs. Within the issues of *The Chosen People* magazine Rabbi Cohn often appealed to the readership for support, and when he spoke in the churches he would challenge believers in the audience with the great need of reaching the Jews of Brooklyn with the Gospel, as well as the great need to provide for their physical welfare. If his ministry to the Jewish people was going to survive, Leopold Cohn had to offset the damage done to the support of Jewish missions through the circulation of Bernhard Angel's paper on "mistakes in Jewish missions."

As Rabbi Leopold Cohn faithfully served His Messiah, God honored his faith and supplied for his needs. Oftentimes his financial needs were met in the most unexpected of ways—ways that were nothing short of miraculous!

THE BAPTISTS DECIDE TO HELP

Rev. Whitaker became so impressed with the work Rabbi Cohn was doing that, unknown to Rabbi Cohn, he met with a group of ministers from the Baptist Church Extension Society of Brooklyn and the American Baptist Home Mission Society. With an eloquent and enthusiastic presentation, he persuaded them to join him at one of the mission's meetings, to see for themselves what a wonderful work Rabbi Cohn was doing among the Jews in Brooklyn. Rev. Whitaker believed if the men could actually see the work, they would be persuaded to support the work, and he was right.

It was on a cold, blustery Saturday afternoon in late February 1896 when ten of the leading Baptist pastors of Brooklyn made their way to the little Jewish mission in Brownsville, to see for themselves this remarkable work of God. They quietly slipped into the rear of the room and took their seats. Looking around, they discovered that they were surrounded by Jewish men, most of whom were shabbily dressed—Jewish immigrants searching for peace and prosperity in this new "promised land." Somehow, through the influence of Rabbi Cohn, they had been convinced to come, and hundreds of them crowded into the room.

As the Baptist pastors looked toward the platform they saw Rabbi Cohn, a thin man, not large, dressed like an Orthodox rabbi. His beard was very black; it seemed to make him look older than he actually was, but it also made him look scholarly and wise. On his head he wore the customary yarmulkah (skull-cap).

When Rabbi Cohn stood and began speaking, the pastors became spellbound. Because he spoke in Yiddish they could not understand the words he spoke, but they watched in amazement as the audience of Jewish men around them reacted to his words. Some of the men around them jumped up in their seats, and with violent gesticulation raised their fists and shouted angrily at the speaker. Nothing like this ever happened in their churches! They watched, fascinated by the argumentation and debate that was taking place between the speaker and his audience. They noticed the masterful way that Rabbi Cohn was able to control the seemingly violent crowd.

Soon the audience quieted down and Rabbi Cohn began preaching to them in earnest from the Word of God. Once again, the visiting Baptist pastors were amazed at the ability of the speaker to persuade his audience to listen to the Scriptures. And again, although they could not understand what Rabbi Cohn was saying, they could see and feel the reaction of the audience. They knew that the Spirit of God was at work. When an invitation was given to accept Yeshua as the Messiah, several Jewish people pressed forward to talk further with Rabbi Cohn.

When the service was dismissed, the ten pastors, along with Rev. Whitaker, remained to speak with Rabbi Cohn. They had been impressed with what they had seen. They recognized that God had called Rabbi Cohn to minister to his own people. They had felt and seen the Spirit of God at work as Leopold preached, and they asked him if he would take a few moments to share how he had come to faith in Yeshua, and how he had come to begin his mission work.

Rabbi Cohn began to share some of his testimony, of his call to the ministry, and of the burden on his heart to see his Jewish people come to faith in Yeshua. He told the men about the financial difficulties he'd been faced with, and of the marvelous ways in which God had thus-far met his needs. Their hearts were touched by the things Leopold shared with them and before they left they were in agreement that "...Mr. Leopold Cohn was to be the missionary under the American Baptist Home Mission Board, and that the Brooklyn Long Island Church Extension Society would undertake the costs of the mission hall itself,...they appointed among themselves a committee of three...to see the then secretary of the American Baptist Home Mission Society, a General Morgan."[12] The committee "...told General Morgan of their strange experience [at the mission], and concluded, 'Now we want you to appoint Mr. Cohn as missionary to the Jews under the American Baptist Home Mission Society; we want you to give him $1,000 a year salary; we are going to pay $600 a year from the Brooklyn Extension Society, and that will cover the rent and the maintenance of the Mission Hall."[13]

You can imagine Rabbi Cohn's amazement, shock, and delight! He knew this was a direct answer to his prayers. Once again, God had supplied far in abundance of what he had asked for, and quite apart from anything he had done, for he had not solicited support from the Baptist society. They were offering it of their own free will. Of that meeting Rabbi Cohn wrote:

> ...I told them that I would thankfully accept their support as I believed that the Lord sent them to my help, but I stipulated that I should not be interfered with in my methods of work in the spiritual dealings with my Jewish brethren whom I had studied from my earliest youth, knowing their characteristics, thoughts and daily life so well, and I also knew that Christian people had never studied Jewish life and consequently did not understand, humanly speaking, how to reach my brethren. I certainly believe, however, that God can use anybody, if He chooses, to work in a supernatural way. They agreed not to interfere with me and said they believed I was led by the Holy Spirit and they would not come in between Him and the work, but would share in it by supporting it.[14]

The committee comprised of Rev. Whitaker, Mr. Avery, and Leopold Cohn that was originally formed to oversee the finances of the mission and to help give direction to Rabbi Cohn, was expanded to include a new member—Dr. W.C.P. Rhoades, pastor of the Marcy Avenue Baptist Church in Brooklyn.

With the financial needs of the Brownsville Mission now backed by the Brooklyn Long Island Church Extension Society, Rabbi Cohn was relieved of the immediate financial pressures he had been laboring under and his heart began to be stirred by the Holy Spirit to consider the spiritual and physical needs of the broader Jewish community.

THE WILLIAMSBURG MISSION TO THE JEWS BEGINS

The year was 1896. The Williamsburg section of Brooklyn embraced a wealthier and better educated class of Jewish people than the Brownsville section. Yet, reasoned Rabbi Cohn, they are just as lost and just as in need of salvation as the Jews in Brownsville. Additionally, the Williamsburg section of Brooklyn had approximately 50,000 Jews, while the Brownsville section had only around 20,000. Without question, more Jews could be reached with the Gospel if a witness could go forth in the Williamsburg section of Brooklyn. Leopold knew God honored faith. He had trusted God for the financial backing needed to reach the Jews in Brownsville. Now he determined to trust God for the financial backing needed to establish a mission in Williamsburg.

Armed with faith, which was backed by much prayer, Leopold Cohn went to Williamsburg. He went directly to the Jewish section, and on his first visit he saw a very nice store which he felt was suitable for a mission. He wrote:

> ...I asked for the rent; it was thirty dollars a month; but I did not have the money, and I also needed to buy chairs and to put up a platform, and arrange for gas. I counted that about fifty dollars was absolutely required to commence. I had a talk with the Lord in my private closet and then gave five dollars as a deposit on the rent, asking the landlord to wait

two or three days, and if I did not bring him the rest, then the five dollars would be forfeited and he could rent the store to someone else. Two days later, a friend told me that a lady who had dined with her recently gave her a check for fifty-one dollars for the Jewish mission work. My friend had said that she knew of a rabbi who was doing mission work among the Jews, and the lady having never heard before contributed for Jewish mission work, wrote a check saying, 'Give this to your Jewish friend.' What joy it gave me that I could now rent that store and that the Lord had sent in the needed amount.[15]

While Leopold Cohn once again rejoiced in God's supply of his needs, some of the members of the Baptist Home Mission Society were not quite as happy. It seems that when Rabbi Cohn approached General Morgan, director of the Home Mission Society, telling him of the wonderful new opportunity for witness and of the miraculous provision God had given so that they could now have two missions to the Jews in Brooklyn instead of just one, General Morgan became furious and wanted to know by what authority Leopold Cohn had gone out and committed the society to pay the rent on another building. He informed Rabbi Cohn that the society wasn't going to do it. He further informed Cohn that he had never been in favor of Leopold being put on as a missionary with the Home Mission Society. He said the only reason he had given approval to include Rabbi Cohn as a missionary was to appease the ministers of Brooklyn who had threatened to withdraw their support if Morgan did not appoint Rabbi Leopold Cohn to be their missionary in Brooklyn.

It was obvious to Rabbi Cohn that General Morgan did not share his vision or burden for reaching Jewish people with the Gospel. In fact, he even seemed hostile to the idea. The news came as a blow to Cohn and he felt heart-sick. Had he run ahead of God? Yet the way God had supplied for the deposit on the building in Williamsburg had truly been a miracle. Leopold had committed himself to rent on the building. What should he do? After learning of the true feelings of General Morgan, it seemed like a miracle that his salary and the expenses for the Brownsville Mission were being paid by the Home Mission Society. He decided to prayerfully wait on the Lord. He didn't have to wait long!

Several months earlier, Leopold Cohn had been introduced to Mr. and Mrs. Ralph L. Cutter. Mr. Cutter was an elder in the Presbyterian church. When he'd first heard of Rabbi Cohn's ministry and learned that Leopold had been discipled by Church of Scotland missionaries, and had even attended their school in Edinburgh, he was fascinated. Mr. Cutter had a great interest in learning the Scriptures from a Jewish perspective, and he invited Leopold to come to his home on Monday nights to teach a Bible class. He even wanted Rabbi Cohn to teach him and his wife Hebrew so they could study the Bible in it's original language.

One of the evening meetings at the Cutter's home was held only hours after Rabbi Cohn's meeting with General Morgan, and when Leopold arrived at the Cutter's home, Ralph Cutter noticed that he was not his usual self. In his own blustery way, Mr. Cutter asked Leopold what was wrong. Leopold couldn't hold back his hurt and disappointment. He shared his vision of seeing the Jews of Brooklyn have an opportunity to hear the Gospel, and he shared the story of the commitment he had made on the rental of the building in Williamsburg, and of God's supply. Then he shared what he had been told by General Morgan. When Leopold finished speaking, without saying a word, Mr. Cutter took out his checkbook and wrote a check in the amount of $200.00. He handed it to Rabbi Cohn and said, "'Here is money for your first month's rent, and for buying the chairs and whatever else you will need to get the place furnished. Then I will be responsible each month for the rent. I will send you $35 each month from now on.'"[16]

Once again God had proven His faithfulness, and had confirmed to Rabbi Cohn that he was in the Father's will. Leopold knew God was with him, and that in spite of every obstacle, the Jews of Brooklyn would have an opportunity to hear the Gospel!

When Leopold left the Cutter's home that evening, with the rent money in hand, he could hardly wait for the next day to dawn. Sleep came, but he was awake early and he wasted no time in making his way back to Williamsburg. He gave the rent money to the landlord, signed all the necessary papers, and immediately began cleaning the building and buying the necessary chairs and equipment so his new mission could open.

The Williamsburg Mission building was located at 17 Ewen Street. Services were held on Wednesday evenings at 7:30 P.M. These were "Inquirer's Meetings." Preaching services in Yiddish were held on Friday and Saturday evenings at 7:30 P.M. It wasn't long before both mission buildings were filled with Jewish people, many of the Jews openly professing their faith in the Messiah. But, as the mission work grew, the problems also grew. It seemed each day brought more and more needs to be met. One of Leopold's greatest needs was for good Gospel materials in Yiddish—materials that could be distributed to Jewish people on the streets, or in outdoor preaching services. He needed tracts and discipleship materials that would readily communicate to Jewish people. So, on top of all his other duties and responsibilities, Leopold used the early morning hours to write tracts. He laboriously wrote each one out in Yiddish script. When he finally had them all finished, he gathered the pages together and once again made his way to the headquarters office of the American Baptist Home Mission Society.

The memory of his last confrontation with General Morgan in the headquarters office of the American Baptist Home Mission Society surfaced to harass Leopold as he made his way back to that building. But he knew General Morgan had since left his position at the society, and Leopold was hopeful that the new man, Dr. Morehouse, would be more sympathetic to reaching Jews with the Gospel. Sadly, once again, Rabbi Cohn was bitterly disappointed. Dr. Morehouse had no vision at all for reaching Jewish people. The more Leopold tried to persuade him of the need for printing his tracts, the louder the refutation became. Soon their voices could be heard echoing down the corridors of the Home Mission Society offices, as Leopold desperately tried to convince this Christian leader of the need to reach Jews with the Gospel. Dr. Morehouse argued that God was through with the Jews and that His message of salvation was to the Gentiles.

Realizing that his pleading and arguing with Dr. Morehouse was accomplishing nothing more than exacerbating an already volatile situation, Rabbi Cohn picked up his Yiddish tracts. With great heaviness of heart, feeling quite alone in his struggle to reach his people with the Gospel, he turned to leave the corporate office of this Christian leader. As he closed the door behind him, he couldn't help but notice members of the office staff staring at him as he made his way toward the elevator. He knew they had heard Dr. Morehouse shouting at him. He felt embarrassed and rejected.

It was difficult for Rabbi Cohn to understand the reasoning of this Christian mission leader, and the many others like him, with whom he had come into contact since beginning his ministry. When it came to evangelizing the Jews, Dr. Morehouse, like so many Christians, had a blind spot. He could only think in terms of evangelizing the great masses. He did not understand that Jewish people had to be reached in a special way. He did not seem to understand that Jews would not listen to the message of the "Gentile church." They had suffered too much persecution under so-called "Christians." Why couldn't Dr. Morehouse see this?

The more Leopold thought about his meeting with Dr. Morehouse, the more he realized that his ministry needed to educate two groups of people. He wanted to reach his Jewish people with the Gospel, but he would also need to spend time educating the "Christian church" of the necessity of witnessing to the Jew, and of the necessity of doing so in a Jewish context. Referring to his father's disappointing encounter with Dr. Morehouse, Joseph Cohn later wrote:

> As he [Rabbi Leopold Cohn] was deliberating in his mind about these things, standing there in the hallway, he found it hard to keep back the tears. Suddenly an arm swung around his shoulder; he looked up, and there stood Dr. Samuel McBride, a tall, lank Scotchman [sic], who was also employed as one of the Field Secretaries for the Home Mission Board under the direction of Dr. Morehouse. Dr. McBride had been in the office all during the time that my father was begging for these tracts, and now he had run out from the office to see if he could catch my father before he went down in the elevator. 'Brother Cohn, I want you to know that I am not party to all of this scolding and indifference. I think Dr. Morehouse is all wrong, and if I had my way, I would open wide the treasury of our Society for you. But this I cannot do. I am only a servant here. I can, and I now do, give you the solemn assurance of my friendship, and the promise that I will do all I can to help you.' With this assurance and comfort my father left the building and went home. All that afternoon he sat in his little study in our flat on Jefferson Avenue. He was indeed in the slough of despondency, and found himself bewildered to know how to understand this strange treatment he was receiving from men who should have been his strongest supporters.[17]

Joseph goes on to explain that about eight o'clock that same night there was a knock on the door of their flat, and when Rabbi Cohn opened the door, to his amazement, there stood Dr. Samuel McBride. Joseph, who as a young boy watched this drama unfold, wrote:

> ...He [Dr. Samuel McBride] walked into the room quite jauntily. His face was lit up with joy, and he said, still standing in the room, not having yet taken a seat, 'Brother Cohn, I have good news for you!' Then he sat down, and began to talk. He said: 'After we parted this morning in the hallway, I felt so under conviction and so ashamed, that I went out and hunted up an old friend of mine, a Scotchman [sic] by the name of John T. Pirie. He is not a Baptist, he is what they call a Plymouth Brother, but he and I are very good friends, and he has much confidence in me. I got an appointment with him for late this afternoon, and then I told him all about your story. And I told him of the tracts you had written, and that our Board could not see its way clear to pay for the printing. There were tears in his eyes as he reached for his checkbook. He made out a check, gave it to me, saying, "Give this to Mr. Cohn and tell him to go ahead and print his tracts, and there will be more for him when this money is gone!" So here I am tonight and here is the check [he then presented Leopold with a check in the amount of $400.00]. I cannot recall when I have had greater joy than I have tonight in giving you this money. May God bless you and give you many victories for the days to come.'[18]

Once again Rabbi Leopold Cohn had experienced God's faithfulness. From that day on, Mr. Pirie became a faithful and loyal supporter of Rabbi Cohn's ministry, as well as a personal friend.

Rabbi Cohn's struggle for recognition and help was not being waged solely with the Home Mission Society. He was also struggling to convince Christians, and Christian leaders to recognize his mission as a legitimate place of worship for the Jewish people in Brooklyn. Leopold was convinced that Jews should believe in Yeshua. He believed it therefore followed that Messianic worship was proper. The Jewish rabbis of Brooklyn, on the other hand, were furious with Rabbi Cohn. They claimed he was a fraud and said he was deceiving the people. These rabbis did everything they could to discourage the Jewish community of Brooklyn from attending any of the mission's meetings.

Late one Saturday night, shortly after the mission was opened in Williamsburg, a great fire broke out in the Jewish quarter of Brooklyn, just a few blocks away from the Williamsburg mission. The flames spread so quickly that before the fire could be put out, over forty Jewish families were left homeless. Everything they possessed was swept away in the flames, and they were left penniless and homeless. Some members of the Jewish community were quick to react. *The Chosen People* Magazine of May 1896 reported:

> On the Saturday after that great fire, which destroyed so many Jewish houses in the neighborhood of the Mission, a Rabbi preached from Isaiah 66:15, 16, showing that this fire, which put two hundred Jews to misery, came down from heaven as a rebuke from God because they allowed a Mission to exist in their midst, where hundreds of Jews gather to listen to the doctrines of the Crucified One.
>
> Some Jews, especially those poor sufferers who were made homeless, believed this, and of course, expressed their bitter feelings against the Mission. On that Saturday evening, when our meeting was held, the audience was a little smaller than hitherto. Many angry faces were seen outside the room. They peeped through the windows to see if there were any Jews present, and when they saw the people inside, they left with murmurings. We were not discouraged at the anger of these, since there were many others who laughed at their own Rabbi's ideas and continued to come and listen to the Gospel of Jesus, our blessed Lord.[19]

The incident wasn't to end there however. George C. Salter, one of the men Rabbi Cohn had trained to assist him in his ministry, wrote about his first week in the Williamsburg Mission. He said:

> My first week's experience at the Ewen street Mission in Williamsburg is something that I shall likely remember for some time to come.
>
> It was on a Friday evening. Mr. Cohn had been preaching from the text 'Awake, thou that sleepest, and arise from the dead, and Christ shall give thee light' Ephesians 5:14.
>
> During the service an old Jewish man rose to his feet several times and tried to interrupt the speaker. I went over to him and in a kind manner told him he must keep his seat, as Wednesday evenings was the only time when questions could be asked during the service. I noticed as I spoke to him that a number of men who were seated near him gave me some very unpleasant looks. I was at once convinced that they were friends of the old man and had come to this meeting with the intention of breaking it up.
>
> Hardly had I taken my place at the door, when they, with the old man, rose in a body and commenced upsetting the chairs. At this moment the old man called out in Hebrew, 'Fire.' Of course, that recalled to their minds the fire which had occurred in the neighborhood the week previous, and of which the Jewish Rabbi had told them that it was a judgment sent down upon them from God for attending the Christian services at the Mission.
>
> In an instant there was a mad rush for the front door by the old man and his followers, and I found myself lifted off my feet and pitched headlong on to the sidewalk.
>
> I felt just at that moment as if I could exclaim, in the words of the Psalmist, 'O, had I the wings of a dove, then would I fly away and be at rest,' for I was jostled and pushed in every direction by this crowd.
>
> Unmindful of the text 'Awake thou that sleepest,' the officer at the door was so taken aback by this unlooked for event that he seemed powerless to act, so that many of those who caused the trouble managed to escape arrest.
>
> In a few moments the old man came back again and remained quietly in his seat during the remainder of the service.
>
> Although quite a disturbance took place, strange to say, very few outside of those who caused the trouble, left the room, nor did they in any way approve of what had been done. As a rule, we have a most attentive and respectful audience.[20]

The reference by George Salter to a policeman (officer) being at the door was that, due to the large crowds of people attending the meetings, Rabbi Cohn had to have policemen come and stand guard at the entrance of the mission before and after services to maintain order, as well as to stop any persecution of himself, other Jewish believers, or Jewish inquirers who attended the meetings.[21]

In spite of the opposition, Rabbi Cohn persisted in his efforts to bring the Gospel to the Jews of Brooklyn. In October 1896 he began the first Boys' Club for the Jewish boys in Brownsville. It was called the Young Friend's Hebrew Club of Brownsville. Their meetings were held every Tuesday at 3:30 P.M. When they elected officers for the club they also included discussion of matters involving their physical protection as well as matters concerning spiritual growth, and elected what they called the "Inner and Outer Guard." As the boys entered, the Inner or Outer Guard took a password from them. This usually consisted of a verse of Scripture. In this way Rabbi Cohn had the boys memorizing the Word of God, while at the same time keeping troublemakers at bay.

One of the dilemmas in Jewish missions during those early days was that of finding ways to reach the women and girls with the Word of God, for within Judaism only the men studied the Scriptures. As he pondered this dilemma and prayed for a solution, Rabbi Cohn hit on two ideas that he felt certain would not only afford opportunity to share the Word of God, but would offer assistance to the women and girls of the community as well. He established a sewing class for girls, and an English language class for Jewish women. One problem remained. He did not have any helpers who were qualified to teach women. In *The Chosen People* magazine Leopold wrote:

> We frequently hear Christians visiting our missions, remark, with some surprise, 'Why, you have no women in the meetings.' They find a crowd of men listening to the Gospel and very often not one Jewess. The poor Jewish women are robbed of their right, and placed in a subordinate rank imposed upon them by traditions…. It was a Jewess who gave birth to the Lord Jesus Christ, also Jewesses who gave birth to Peter, Paul, James, John, etc. It was the Jewesses who erected the strong pillar of the Church of Jesus Christ, and now when they are blind as regards Christ their Messiah ought we not to do everything possible to give them the Gospel which would enlighten them and bring them to the Savior of mankind.
>
> …what we have said above, ought to be sufficient to show that a worker among the Jewish women is very much needed, a man cannot do it very well, but a devoted Christian lady could be used by the Lord to a larger extent than we can imagine, by visiting and holding meetings for them.
>
> We eagerly desire to do something in order to reach these women, and often earnestly pray to God. We decided to preach to our people both in Brownsville and in Williamsburg and by the help of God to show them plainly from Deuteronomy 31:12, 'Gather the people together, men, women and children, that they may hear, and that they may learn to fear the Lord your God and to observe all the words of this law,' that God commands women, as well as men, to know His Word. Then we referred to the New Testament which exactly agrees with the Old in considering women as rational beings and candidates for everlasting life, we also told them about the Christian women who study and know the Bible and worship God through the Lord Jesus. At the close of the service a man came forward and said: 'I have been several times to the Christian church you told me, and I have always found that there were more women in the audience present than men.' This is entirely opposite to our Synagogue services where there are men only, the reason for this I think is because, I read in the New Testament that the Christian women showed their great love for Jesus by visiting the sepulcher on the first day when it was yet dark, while the men were too slothful to rise so early. Then Jesus must have blessed the Christian women more than He did the men, and so they are blessed even unto this day, and come and worship God in much larger numbers than do the Christian men.[22]

To further emphasize his need, Rabbi Cohn placed prayer requests in *The Chosen People* magazine for a Christian woman to work among the Jews in Brooklyn. The only women working among the Jewish girls and mothers were his daughter, Esther, and Ella T. Marston, a volunteer, and daughter of Frank H. Marston who became one of the first Board members of Rabbi Cohn's mission. But in spite of Rabbi Cohn's pleas and prayer requests, it was several years before a qualified women's worker was found.

The opposition seemed never to cease, nor did the financial and staffing needs for Rabbi Leopold Cohn's growing mission ever seem to diminish. But in the midst of the opposition and other pressing needs, Rabbi Cohn was led of God to take another step of faith as he endeavored to meet the needs of his Jewish brethren in Brooklyn, and to share the Gospel with them. He opened a dispensary. Of this he wrote:

> …Three years ago when the Lord sent us to tell the Good Tidings to the Jews in Brownsville, we were engaged in visiting the Jewish houses indiscriminately for several months. This we did that we might become acquainted with the conditions and daily life of the Jews. Having seen much sickness and poverty in many houses, we prayed God for help,

and a dispensary was opened in the Mission room at 530 Rockaway Avenue. This being the only organization of the kind in Brownsville, among 6000 Jewish families, the room used to be crowded every day by sick people. On those occasions when the kind physicians in one corner of the room did their part in healing the patient's body, we, in another corner, administered to them the necessary remedy for their souls. In fact, we did not let one man or woman leave the room before we would tell him or her of eternal life through the Great Physician, even our Lord Jesus Christ. At this, the rulers and leaders of the different synagogues were alarmed: they published articles in the daily newspapers, stating they feared their poor co-religionists were being apostatized, and they made strong appeals to be assisted in building a dispensary of their own. Although they soon opened a place for dispensing medicines and urged the patients to leave our room and patronize their new establishment, yet the poor Jews who had seen the difference between other doctors and these Christian physicians with their kind and loving service for Christs' sake, felt reluctant about making the change.[23]

Eventually Rabbi Cohn was forced to close the dispensary on Rockaway Avenue. He was told his room was not adequate to serve as a dispensary. But Leopold Cohn was not easily discouraged; he simply took this as a sign from God that he should open the dispensary in some other location. A few years later, when the Mission was given property on Throop Avenue in Brooklyn, a new dispensary was opened.

The Girls' Sewing School continued to attract large numbers of Jewish girls and in an effort to stop what the rabbis of the Jewish community called "Cohn's proselytizing activities," the Jewish community raised money to establish a school of their own. Of this Leopold wrote:

...The opposing Jews, who have done all they could to keep away their people from the mission, have found themselves surrounded by so many young missionaries of the cross, and this to their great chagrin. Therefore they have lately organized a society, which collected enough means to conduct a sewing school for the Jewish girls, and also a kindergarten for the Jewish children in Brownsville.

A couple of months ago [October 1897] they opened a large hall for their schools. A large number of children, among them those whom we had turned away from our doors for lack of room, filled their place of instruction, but their leaders and founders were not satisfied.

All this would avail them nothing, so long as they saw the same large number of girls going in and out of the mission room at 530 Rockaway Ave. They printed hand-bills which were circulated not only in the streets, but also in the private houses. In it a strong appeal was made to the parents to forbid their children to enter the mission room, for the reason, that the missionary does 'entice' the little ones. Saying, 'Let us serve other gods.' Deut. XIII:7. and [sic] 'as it is written, "Train up a child in his way; and when he is old, he will not depart from it." Prov. XXII:6, these children will remain perverted apostates forever.' The circular went on to intimate that if the parents only wish was that their girls should learn sewing, their new founded sewing school was free to all and would, no doubt give them satisfaction in that respect, but if they desired (God forbid) that their children should forsake their fathers' religion, and the God of Israel, let them send their children to the missionary. Many of the parents who attend our meetings on Saturdays did not pay any attention to their appeals, but there were some who pleaded with their children and urged them to give up the mission's sewing school. One girl, when told by her mother to change schools replied, 'Mama, there is no use talking; all the girls say that Jesus' Sewing School is better.'[24]

As God blessed, the work grew, and as the work grew, God supplied additional staff to help Rabbi Cohn. In May 1898, Mr. B.M. Gordon was appointed as Assistant Missionary to Rabbi Cohn. Mr. Gordon was born in Kowna, Russia in 1875. He had been trained in Orthodox Jewish tradition, and he read and spoke Hebrew fluently. He also spoke a number of European languages, and was therefore well equipped to work among the Jewish refugees who were flooding into New York and Brooklyn during that period of time. Mr. Gordon had accepted Yeshua through the ministry of Rabbi Cohn and was baptized at the Marcy Avenue Baptist Church in Brooklyn.[25] Each addition to the work, whether a new method of outreach or a new staff member, was a step of faith for Rabbi Cohn. In hiring Mr. Gordon as a paid staff worker, Leopold took that step once again, trusting that God would supply the financial need for his growing ministry. And God did, in a most unexpected way.

A few years earlier, Rabbi Cohn had begun printing *The Chosen People* magazine. Within its pages he told the exciting stories of God's blessings upon his ministry. As the ministry grew, the circulation of the magazine grew as well. From just a few copies printed in 1895, Rabbi Cohn was printing five hundred copies each month by the time Mr. Gordon came on staff. Of the five hundred printed, one hundred forty-seven copies were mailed out to individuals on his mailing list. The remaining three hundred fifty-three copies he gave to his son, Joseph, who distributed them to Christians in Brooklyn. Each Sunday morning Joseph Cohn could be found standing outside the larger churches in Brooklyn, with a stack of the magazines. When the services were over he would distribute copies of *The Chosen People* magazine to the people as they were leaving church. On more than one occasion he was chased away by a church official who mistook him for being a Jewish beggar or peddler, but most of the Christians were delighted to receive the little publication. They would read it and often would then visit the mission or attend services. Some became avid and faithful supporters of the ministry.

Rabbi Cohn was acutely aware of the attitudes that some of the ministers and churches had toward independent mission works to the Jews. He therefore kept accurate and detailed records of all income and expenses of his two mission branches, Brownsville and Williamsburg. He listed the names of all contributors in *The Chosen People* magazine, along with the amount of their contribution. He also printed an audited financial statement in the magazine. The first such statement appeared in the March 1898 issue of the magazine. It showed income of $792.89 with expenses of $861.70, and a deficit of $68.81.[26] That deficit did not last long. God once again supplied for the need. By January 1899, the income had grown to $1,648.51, with expenses totaling $1,623.51. The balance on hand was listed at $25.00, and was earmarked for the Assistant Missionary's salary for the month of March.[27]

For the readers of *The Chosen People* magazine, the obvious blessings of God upon the work, the uniqueness of the ministry, and Rabbi's Cohn's zeal to bring the Gospel to his Jewish people came through the pages like arrows aimed at the heart. In the December 1898 issue Rabbi Cohn wrote an article, "Facts: and Worth Considering," in which he said:

> Fact One: *That when I began this testimony, four years ago, I could not get ten Jews together to whom to offer it; while today, on some occasions, I cannot get room enough to receive those who press to hear. This proves that God will bless the preaching of the Gospel to the Jews as richly as to any other race.*
>
> Fact Two: *That, because of their own eager importunity, I have had to commend to the churches for baptism a number of Jews, and that under much persecution these have, every one, continued steadfast to Christ. This proves that the Jew can be converted as radically as men of any other race.*
>
> Fact Three: *That after two years' labor in Brownsville, the door in Williamsburg was set open before me, and a year later an equally promising field in Manhattan—three mission stations in my hands to-day. This proves that it is God who is working, not man; and, that it is His purpose to give the Gospel to the Jews, and to enlarge the testimony.*
>
> Fact Four: *That ordinarily missions, to whatsoever class of people, costs $2,000 a year or more for their maintenance, or $6,000 for three. These three Jewish missions, conducted without any intervening official boards or expenses, are costing but little more than the usual cost of one. This proves an economic management, and guarantees to patrons the most effective use of money.*
>
> Fact Five: *That the history, habits of thought and present peculiar attitude of the Jewish race, demand the most accurate scriptural statement, and at the same time, because of their close and critical attention, admits of no repetitions. The testimony must always be new and striking and strictly Scriptural; That with six meetings every week no one man, dependent upon human powers alone, could possible meet this demand; yet, that this is being done, proves that the power is not of man but of God,—proves that the Lord Jesus Himself in a subtle and mysterious but glorious way is moving amidst the hosts of His ancient people.*
>
> Fact Six: *That a number of Jewish converts of these missions have been marvelously used of God in penetrating the darkness and bigotry of Roman Catholics, so difficult for Protestants to meet, and in delivering them both, women and men, from the bondage of their hierarchy 'into the liberty wherewith Christ hath made us free.' This proves that it is true, as the Bible declares, that the Jew is appointed to be God's ultimate and convincing missionary to the world, as it is written: 'Salvation is of the Jew.'*
>
> *Wherefore, dear Christian friends, consider these facts, briefly stated but most significant. Are they not signs of the times? Is not the Lord Himself at hand? 'Prepare to meet thy God!'*[28]

In every way, God was blessing—even in the production and printing of tracts. Early in his ministry Cohn had found the printed page to be a powerful tool in reaching Jewish people. This realization drove him to spend many evening hours searching the Scriptures and writing tracts in Yiddish for his Jewish people. One such tract was one he called the "Jargon Tract." It was published in December 1898, and in the January 1899 issue of *The Chosen People* magazine Cohn wrote:

> Readers of *The Chosen People* have been informed of the Jargon tract, issued last month, based upon Daniel 9:24, wherein Gabriel announces to Daniel the exact period to the Messiah, and to his being 'cut off.' The truths in this prophecy have hitherto been utterly hidden from the Jews through the irrelevant and intensely mystical interpretations of the Talmudists.

But the manifestation of God's blessing upon this tract has been quicker than our faith—coming before the tract was issued; for 'before they call I will answer; and while they are yet speaking I will hear.'(Is. 65:24.) When the Jewish printer who set the Jargon type brought to me the first edition of 1,000 copies, he burst forth at once with this testimony: 'This little booklet has surprised me and won my heart. While I have been setting it up, I have given my evenings to searching out the whole subject in the Bible, and I am glad to confess that the reckoning of the angel is not at all the mysterious thing which the Talmudists would have us believe, and which it is a sin for us even to think about, but is a clear and simple declaration of the coming of Messiah at the very time when Jesus of Nazareth appeared, and I am fully satisfied that He was, and is to be, our glorious Lord.'

Here let your missionary again make grateful acknowledgment to God for his goodness in securing the publishing of this tract, and for its blessed and multiplying results. The entire edition of 1,000 has already been called out, and is today in the hands of perhaps 5,000 readers; but, thanks to the provision for electroplating, it can now be reproduced at relatively small cost—namely, eleven dollars per thousand.[29]

As the ministry grew, Rabbi Cohn felt led of the Lord to establish a "Messianic congregation." Several attempts to build congregations of Messianic Jews had been tried by other missions and missionaries, but most had failed. Some had failed because they did not have the support of the Christian community; many Christians thought such congregations were rebuilding the "middle wall of partition" between Jews and Gentiles. Others failed because the congregations were not made up of true believers who were willing to break completely with rabbinic Judaism. But Rabbi Cohn believed it was within the realm of possibility to establish a congregation of Messianic Jews, and he further believed that such a congregation would serve as a wonderful testimony to the Jewish community.

No stranger to "stepping out in faith," Rabbi Leopold Cohn took another unique step of faith when he asked a nearby printer to print a number of small cards. Each card was, in effect, a ticket admitting one individual to a gathering of Messianic Jewish believers. To attend, the name and address of the individual presenting the ticket had to be printed on the ticket. The tickets were then collected as individuals entered the service.[30]

The February 1899 edition of *The Chosen People* magazine includes Rabbi Cohn's account of what happened when he gave out his tickets. He wrote:

To many of the Jews this [filling out a ticket] was a most startling proposition. Prejudiced and ignorant concerning Christianity, there are many superstitions still current among them, growing out from centuries of barbaric persecutions, so that some trembled with a mortal terror at the idea of committing themselves by signature to a Christian missionary. Thus it was said: 'If you give your signature to a Missionary on a slip of paper, or write it in his book, he thereby secures power over you (mesmeric, hypnotic, by black art, or something of that sort, is their idea), to change you (by metamorphose) into a dreaded diabolical Christian.' Another story was that these names were to be sent to the Pope at Rome, for to the Jew, the Christian is simply a persecutor, Catholic and Protestant alike, and then, certainly, the Jew's name is lost from the Book of God as soon as it reaches the hands of the Pope. It was whispered about, also, that this occasion was to be improved for a general branding with hot irons of the cross upon the arm after the manner of our recent antagonists of Spain. And with many such phantasms they frightened, threatened, and held back one another from signing the tickets; and on the night of the gathering delegates loitered about, peeping through cracks in the curtains to see what might befall their companions.

From these statements it will be readily seen, in view of the explicit announcement, that it was distinctively for believers in the Lord Jesus that the signing of the names became a most definite Profession of Christ—a crucial, determining Act of Faith.

For these reasons it was with the deepest interest that I watched the outcome. On the above conditions one hundred and twenty tickets were taken and nearly eighty were returned signed and as many persons were present; and of these persons there was not one but had signed the coupon, for the signatures were entered upon an alphabetical list and the men admitted not merely upon presentation of a ticket, but also as found and checked off from the list of signatures. Thus it happened that a good many with tickets were refused admission who may have been believers, indeed, but had lacked fortitude and faith to sign and confess openly....

About a week before this important gathering, I was stricken down with a very severe attack of the prevailing influenza or grippe, and on Tuesday, the 3rd instant, I was suffering the most intense pain in every member of my body. Yet, more intense than the pain, was my burning desire to see the faces of the men who would dare, by signing my coupons, to practically break forever with all their Judaic tradition and come forth courageously into the light of the Gospel of Christ. Wherefore, I cried unto the Lord,...'O Lord God, remember me, I pray thee, and strengthen me, I pray thee, only this once, O God.' And again, as a hundred times in the past, He showed the immutability of His

Word that 'I can do all things through Christ, which strengtheneth me.' And so it came about,...that I was borne, it seemed to me, by the Spirit's power, and had the great joy of seeing so many of my people, peculiarly entrusted of God to my ministry, gathered together in pronounced acclaim to the glory of Jesus Christ, my Lord.

The exercises were necessarily changed somewhat because of my sickness; but the Lord sent friendly substitutes and ordered the evening, I do not doubt, in His own best way. Mr. Frank H. Marston conducted the services.... My own remarks were necessarily brief,...but I was able, in their own tongue, to set forth the significance of the occasion, and to meet with a hearty and unanimous concurrence from all the Jews, assuring me that they were confirmed in their stand for Jesus.

After this, some simple refreshments were served—ice cream and cake. It had never been done before, and was a complete surprise, for it had not been announced, lest it might become, instead of the Lord himself alone, an incentive to some to seek to be present; but it stood in striking contrast to the predicted hot iron branding....

The moral in all this story to you dear reader, is simply this: That to the measure we obey God's command to preach the Gospel, men will be drawn to Christ, and it makes no difference whether it be to Gentile or to Jew.[31]

One additional, but necessary and continuing aspect of the ministry for Rabbi Cohn, was that of ministering to the needs of the poor Jewish immigrant. He had established a dispensary to meet their medical needs, a Sewing School for Jewish girls, and a language and training institute to help the immigrant Jews become a productive part of society. In the April 1899 issue of *The Chosen People* magazine Leopold expressed his feelings about the poor. It was a call to establish a "Poor Fund," and he wrote:

The poor Jews, who are driven to this free country by bitter persecutions, at the hands of so-called Christians in Europe, are in a pitiable condition. They come into a strange land they do not know, the language, the habits, the people, their methods of labor or commerce, and are utterly helpless. In their misery they are often compelled to work sixteen hours for fifty or sixty cents. They suffer hunger and nakedness, until they become sick and crippled for a lifetime. Yet they are not like other people who would go and beg; they never do so, and, therefore, people think the Jews have money. I believe that when the Lord Jesus said, 'For I was an hungered, and ye gave me meat; I was a stranger, and ye took me in; naked, and ye clothed me,' He plainly referred to these poor Jews, His brethren, who are strangers all over among the Christians. Don't you believe this, dear Christian friends? It is very plain! Those in comfortable circumstances do not know much about the misery and sufferings that exist in the Jewish quarters. But when the missionary goes out among these poor, unfortunate ones, and sees many suffering indescribable miseries, the Christian worker's heart is touched, and can only be cheered by seeing happiness coming into their lives through Christian ministrations in the Lord Jesus' name. No perfunctory visitations to the poor and suffering would do any good. To enlighten the poor and ignorant one, it is necessary to lighten him of the heavy load of misery and wretchedness, as well as of the burden of sin. It was much easier to talk about the soul to a person to whom sympathy was shown, than to a person who was suffering from cold, hunger, neglect and sickness. I write these words to people who love the Lord Jesus Christ. You certainly give your share to the fund for poor and needy of your different churches. I do not doubt that you freely contribute to the different charitable institutions. But remember that from these the Jews are excluded. Remember that the Lord Jesus would do good, first and chiefly to the Jews, His people. I do not think that He would approve of helping all other poor people, and leave out His brethren in the flesh; do you? Any donation sent to me especially for this purpose, will be kept by itself, thankfully acknowledged in this paper, reported to the committee, and judiciously dispensed.[32]

Many were God's blessings upon Rabbi Leopold Cohn as he stepped out in faith and followed God's bidding, but as the year 1899 drew to a close, a great disappointment befell him. He received word from the landlord of the Brownsville Mission Hall at number 530 Rockaway Avenue that he would have to move. Five years had passed since Rabbi Cohn had begun his ministry in the building at 530 Rockaway Avenue, and all of the Jews of Brooklyn, as well as the Christians, had come to associate that building with his mission. The reason given to Leopold was that the Principal of the public school had offered the landlord nearly three times the rent Leopold was paying. But Rabbi Cohn was a man who saw obstacles as God's opportunities to show His faithfulness, and as avenues for bringing glory to God through even greater ministry. To the readers of *The Chosen People* magazine he wrote: "Now, my dear friends, believing all things work together for good, and therefore that the Father will order all things well, and will use us as His workers or instruments, do you not think that now is our opportunity, and the time has come for us to put up a building suitable for the work?"[33]

His words were sincere as he challenged God's people to see the need and to come forward to meet the need. But even Rabbi Cohn could not have known that God would use this little announcement, an act of faith on his part, to change the direction and scope of his ministry. This announcement was the catalyst God used in a chain of events that not only brought increased pain and suffering to Rabbi Cohn personally, but caused his small ministry in Brooklyn to become Chosen People Ministries, Inc.—a world-wide outreach bringing the Gospel to all Jews everywhere.

ENDNOTES
Chapter 3. The Brownsville Mission to the Jews

[1] Bernhard Angel, *The Story of the Conversion of Rev. Bernhard Angel B.D.*, (The Hebrew-Christian, March 1894), pp 2-3.

[2] Bernhard Angel, *Mistakes*, (The Hebrew-Christian, July 1896), p 4.

[3] Abraham J. Karp, *Golden Door to America: the Jewish Immigration Experience*, (New York: Viking Press, 1976), pp 4-7.

[4] Daniel Joseph Evearitt, *Jewish-Christian Missions to Jews, 1820-1935*, Dissertation of D.J. Evearitt at Drew University, 1988, quoting from: F.F. Ellinwood: The Duty of Christendom to the Jews, The Missionary Review of the World, November 1890, pp 803-804, (Ann Arbor, Michigan: University Microfilms International Dissertation Information Service, 1989), pp 102-103.

[5] See note above, p 104.

[6] *The Chosen People*, Vol. 1, No. 5, (February, 1896), p 1.

[7] See note above, p 5.

[8] Leopold Cohn, *A Modern Missionary to an Ancient People*, (Brooklyn, New York: American Board of Missions to the Jews, now Chosen People Ministries, Inc., 1908), pp 44-45.

[9] *The Chosen People*, (February, 1896), p 6.

[10] See note above, p 8.

[11] *The Chosen People*, Vol. 2, No. 1, (October, 1896), p 4.

[12] Joseph H. Cohn, *I Have Fought A Good Fight*, (New York: American Board of Missions to the Jews, now Chosen People Ministries, Inc., 1953), p 73.

[13] See note above.

[14] L. Cohn, *Ancient People*, pp 49-50.

[15] See note above, p 51.

[16] J. Cohn, *Fought a Good Fight*, p 77.

[17] See note above, p 81.

[18] See note above, p 82.

[19] *The Chosen People*, Vol. 2, No. 1, (October, 1896), p 5.

[20] *The Chosen People*, Vol. 2, No. 2, (November, 1896), pp 4-5.

[21] See *The Chosen People*, Vol. 2, No. 3, (December, 1896), p 1.

[22] *The Chosen People*, Vol. 2, No. 6, (April, 1897), p 4.

[23] *The Chosen People*, Vol. 3, No. 4, (January, 1898), pp 3-4.

[24] See note above, pp 4-5.

[25] *The Chosen People*, Vol. 4, No. 1, (November, 1898), p 3.

[26] *The Chosen People*, Vol. 3, No. 6, (March, 1898), p 6.

[27] *The Chosen People*, Vol. 4, No. 5, (February, 1899), p 7.

[28] *The Chosen People*, Vol. 4, No. 2, (December, 1898), p 8.

[29] *The Chosen People*, Vol. 4, No. 4, (January, 1899), pp 6-7.

[30] *The Chosen People*, Vol. 4, No. 5, (February, 1899) p 4.

[31] *The Chosen People*, Vol. 4, No. 5, (February, 1899), pp 4-5.

[32] *The Chosen People*, Vol. 4, No. 7, (April, 1899), p 8.

[33] *The Chosen People*, Vol. 5, No. 8, (December, 1899), p 2.

4

THE FIRES OF AFFLICTION

When bad things happen to good people it is baffling, and seemingly unjust. Answers to our questions seem to elude us as we ponder why some of the really good people we have known have been faced with great suffering and loss. Rabbi Harold Kushner attempted to supply answers to such questions, as well as a measure of solace, through his book, "When Bad Things Happen To Good People."[1]

But individuals who are familiar with the Word of God—individuals who have faced life's hardest trials by first taking shelter in the Rock of their salvation—know that God often puts His servants through His refining fires, "fires of affliction," before He enlarges their ministries. No one but the Almighty One knows what is needed within the lives of His servants in order to refine them and to produce His perfect will in their lives.

Some might say Rabbi Cohn had endured enough persecution and affliction. Why would God require that he endure more? Yet as word spread of his troubles and persecution, and of his determination to persevere, both Christian and Jewish communities around the world became increasingly aware of his ministry. He was a man often misunderstood by both communities. He, in turn, had difficulty understanding his Christian brethren, and he and his family suffered greatly because of the alienation from his Jewish brethren. Rabbi Leopold Cohn was a man who lived, and moved, and ministered between two conflicting worlds.

Leopold Cohn's burning desire to find the Messiah had driven him to the point that he had willingly left his family and his native land of Hungary in order to pursue his search in America. But from the outset of his quest personal problems began to dog him. Leopold's wife, Rose, became ill shortly after he left Hungary, and her condition worsened when she and her family heard the whispered rumors that her beloved husband, the once respected Rabbi Cohn, had become a "Christian." Such rumors were being circulating among the villages, and they brought shame and reproach upon Rose and her family. Many of Rose's friends began to shun her—they would have nothing to do with her. Her own family forbid her to correspond with her husband and they kept her at home under constant vigil lest she, too, become a Christian.

THE DEATH OF ROSE COHN

As the months passed humiliation, emotional stress, and loneliness took its toll upon Rose and brought her to the point of nervous and emotional exhaustion. Yet, when a letter from Leopold slipped through the guarded family and reached her, she determined that she would take the children and join him in Scotland, despite her deteriorating physical and mental health. The trip to Scotland was nerve-racking and strenuous. The emotional stress of being reunited with her husband and of hearing "first hand" of his new and strange ideas was almost more than Rose could cope with. Her first and strongest instinct was to return to her home in Hungary and to forget Leopold, but as she watched her children's joy at being reunited with their father, and as she listened to the gentle way he spoke to them and prayed with them, her anger subsided and she agreed to stay.

During the months they lived in Scotland, Rose had ample opportunity to hear more about her husband's new beliefs, and to observe him. As she listened and observed, a spiritual battle began to wage within Rose. Then came the family's subsequent journey back to America—another culture to adjust to, struggles within the ministry, financial problems, rejection by her own people and, finally, the birth of their fifth child, and fourth son, David, in 1899. The combination of these circumstances left Rose in a state of mental and physical exhaustion (Rose and Leopold actually had seven children altogether, but two of them died shortly after birth). She did what she could to help Leopold in the ministry, but her physical problems multiplied. Of her illnesses, Rabbi Cohn wrote:

During last August Mrs. Cohn was taken ill, since which time she has been confined to her bed. She is now in a grave condition and I ask that you will please offer special prayer for speedy recovery of her health as she is much needed, first among her children and then in the work. Fifteen years ago when the news reached her in Europe that I had become a

Christian in America, instead of accepting a Synagogue as a Rabbi, it was a great shock to her nervous system. While two years later she was reconciled and accepted the Lord Jesus and became happy, yet the giving up of her sisters and brothers, whom she dearly loved, aggravated the condition caused by the former stroke, and about nine years ago she became utterly helpless. But her strong faith helped her to rally again in about a year's time, and she has been fairly well until last summer. I ask your earnest prayers in her behalf.[2]

On April 4, 1908, Rose Cohn went home to be with the Lord. Leopold wrote:

After the request for prayers on my dear wife's behalf, which was made in the March Chosen People, her critical condition changed so that there was hope for her recovery, several serious symptoms disappearing one after another, almost in a supernatural way. She herself, however, realized all this time, that she was going to leave us and hinted as much, tho' avoiding plainer talk for fear that it might distress me. Once during the time she said: 'I have been pulling with you hard uphill for so many years, waiting for the Mission building and now when almost to the top, the Lord wants me to go away. I have asked God to let me live to see the building and a Jewish-Christian congregation worshipping the Lord in it, but He says no, just as to Moses when he wanted to enter the Promised Land.' Mrs. Cohn, was so weak in the last few days that she could not move without assistance, yet a few hours before her death she expressed the desire to get up and 'go down on my knees and die praying, so that my soul may go up there with a special petition for the speedy conversion of my people.'

Thus at the end of two weeks she suddenly began to fail, and in two days slipped away. Saturday morning, April 4th, at 9:30, she began to lose consciousness and at 11:30 she breathed her last. [Born in 1866, Rose Cohn was only 42 years when she died.]

When the news spread abroad, it saddened the hearts of many who knew and loved her. She was of most cheerful disposition, always happy in the Lord, trying to make herself useful to every body. A number of friends, even from out of town, were so kind and came to comfort us. A large number of Jews who are not converted but who had heard Mrs. Cohn's short talks in the Mission, expressed in writing and personally their great sorrow and deep sympathy. On Monday evening the funeral service was held in our home. The Rev. W.C.P. Rhoades, D.D., her pastor, who baptized her twelve years ago, delivered an impressive address, and the following morning we accompanied her body to the cemetery. Upon our return David the youngest who is nine years old, cried bitterly as he began to realize what had happened. 'Where is mamma?' was his pitiful cry.[3]

A JEWISH "MATCHMAKER"

At the time of their Mother's death, all the Cohn children were still living at home, and the four eldest were actively helping their father in the ministry by writing for the magazine and traveling on behalf of the mission, seeking to raise funds for the desperately needed building in Brooklyn. Benjamin was 24, Joseph was 22, Joshua was 20, and Esther was 18. But the presence and help of his children did not keep Leopold, a widower at age 46, from feeling lonely. He wanted another wife, a helpmate in the ministry. It was inconceivable to Rabbi Cohn to marry a woman who was not Jewish. Therefore, following Orthodox tradition, he consulted a "Shadcahn," a Jewish match-maker.

Readers who come from different socio-cultural backgrounds may wonder why Rabbi Cohn would have visited a Jewish matchmaker when seeking a new wife. Others may go so far as to say he made a mistake by visiting such a person, and that he brought problems upon himself by doing so. But as a Jew, Rabbi Cohn was simply following the Jewish custom of that day—ignorant of the problems this would create for him in his new world, the Christian community. The lack of understanding of each community for the other made Rabbi Cohn and his ways an enigma to both communities, and years after his contact with the Shadcahn, individuals seeking to discredit Leopold and his ministry used this incident, as well as other grievances, in an attempt to defame his character and destroy his mission. (Rabbi Cohn's enemies were so vindictive in their attacks against him that it was eventually necessary for a trial to be held in order for Leopold to clear his name.)

Re-marry he did, but it is unclear whether his new wife was found through the efforts of the match-maker. Evidently the match-maker did introduce him to a number of young women whom Leopold interviewed as he sought to find the right helpmate. Some of the women who were interviewed, but not chosen, later vented their hurt and anger by spreading gossip and lies about Cohn. One Jewish girl, Miss Lena Dime, claimed Leopold had promised to marry her but had later broken his promise.

Lena Dime's "story" and other such statements were proven false years later when, in an effort to clear charges against him, a committee was set up to investigate the charges and rumors being circulated against Leopold Cohn. When summoned to testify before the Committee, Miss Ella Marston, a worker in the mission, stated that the matchmaker arranged for Leopold to meet and interview certain young women. The meetings took place at his office, with Ella present. Miss Marston stated that each young woman would enter the office, whereupon Rabbi Cohn would seat her at a table and give her a Bible to read. He would then return to his desk, to the work he was doing. After the young woman had ample opportunity to read several chapters, Leopold would ask her if she understood what she had read. He would then talk with her about the passage, and about his ministry. He wanted to find a wife who had spiritual insight and who was teachable.[4]

EVENTS LEADING TO INCORPORATION

Rose's death and the ensuing loneliness, along with the controversy over his method of finding another companion, was distressful for Leopold, to say the least. To make matters worse, his personal problems at that time were exacerbated by articles he had written for *The Chosen People* magazine concerning funds he stated were needed for the building in Brooklyn. These articles created a disagreement between Rabbi Cohn and the American Baptist Home Mission Society which seemingly could not be resolved. Rabbi Cohn was receiving some of his support from the Baptist Church Extension Society of Brooklyn. Additional support was being received from the American Baptist Home Mission Society which had begun supporting him in 1896. The dispute that ensued between Leopold and the American Baptist Home Mission Society was over money Leopold Cohn received for his "Building Fund" that the Home Mission Society contended he should turn over to them so they could disperse the funds as they saw fit. But Rabbi Cohn felt strongly that he would never see a dime of it for his new building, since some individuals within the Baptist Home Mission Society had made it abundantly clear that they were not interested in Jewish evangelism.

The issue came to a head when Rabbi Cohn received a gift of $10,000 toward his Building Fund from a Miss Frances J. Huntley. Miss Huntley, a generous supporter of the Baptist Society, had been greatly interested in the work of Rabbi Cohn for a number of years, and began supporting his ministry in 1896. Over the years she and Leopold had carried on extensive correspondence. She had met his family, had seen the work, and had been impressed by the Lord to invest her money in Jewish missions. Furthermore, she helped finance the education of Joseph Hoffman Cohn at Moody Bible Institute, and at Adelphi Institute and Adelphi College. Her home was always open to the Cohns.

Leopold's first mention of the need for a building appeared in the May 1903 issue of *The Chosen People* magazine. It was a small article and did not specifically ask for funds, but it reveals the problems he faced in trying to find rental space for his ministry. He wrote:

> There used to be in a fashionable summer resort a hotel with the above legend displayed at the entrance ["Jews Not Wanted: Dogs Not Allowed"]. *The Jews were very desirous of obtaining admittance to this hotel and they thought for a long time how to gain their end, but without any result, until they decided to buy the building from the owner. This they did and drove the hotel keeper away. The house is now a famous Jewish summer retreat.*
>
> *There is at Williamsburg, an unwritten sign before all the stores that are to let by Jewish owners, 'Jewish Christians not wanted: apostates not allowed.' Thus, you see, it is a very hard matter to get a suitable hall for mission purposes, as nearly all are owned by Jews and they would not rent it to a mission, either for fear of other Jews, or from their own scruples. The hall we have, though well filled at every meeting, is both inadequate to our needs, and too far out of the Jewish quarter. If we could have a hall on Graham avenue, the main Jewish thoroughfare, there is no doubt that a grand work could be done. But how is this hall to be obtained? Read the first part again. Now do you see? Buy it! It could not only be used for preaching purposes, but we could have more room for the Dispensary, the Industrial Plant, and a Home for destitute Jewish children, if some of His stewards would donate enough to purchase and fit out a building.*[5]

Cohn placed articles about the need for a building in each subsequent issue of *The Chosen People* magazine, and in the November 1904 issue of the magazine he said:

> To purchase and equip a building of this description would require at least fifty thousand dollars, and we have been led to lay this matter before the friends for especial prayer and consideration. We will adopt for our motto, 'Fifty thousand dollars before January 1st 1906.' We will devote this column for the report of the progress of this fund, from month to month. We trust that each friend of this mission will endeavor to help this cause by giving and collecting money from friends whom they can interest. Copies of The Chosen People will be sent free to any one who wishes to interest others. The time has come for an aggressive forward movement and we are ready and prepared to enlarge our sphere of activity and usefulness to the extent that our friends will enable us to do.[6]

Leopold then gave a listing of monies already collected toward the Building Fund. He listed $527.05 in the Building

Fund proper as of February 1904; $79.97 toward the Home for Children as of February 1904; and $15.00 received since February. The total monies on hand toward the needed fifty thousand was listed at $622.02.

When Miss Huntley received her November 1904 issue of *The Chosen People* Magazine and read Rabbi Cohn's request for fifty thousand dollars, she caught the vision and responded immediately by sending him a letter with an enclosed check in the amount of ten thousand dollars. In the letter she stated, "Go quickly and buy the land on which you have an option. Make this the first down payment, get possession, and then trust the Lord for all balances needed."[7]

The leaders, and especially Dr. Morehouse, of the Home Mission Society had a completely different reaction when they saw the November 1904 issue of *The Chosen People* magazine with its request for fifty thousand dollars for a building. They were furious with Rabbi Cohn! They told him they had not authorized him to make any such requests, and went on to say that any monies raised by his appeal were to be immediately turned over to the Baptist Home Mission Association for their determination regarding how those monies should be used.

Rabbi Cohn told Dr. Morehouse he had already received a gift of ten thousand dollars toward the building from Miss Huntley, whereupon Dr. Morehouse insisted that all monies in the building fund be turned over immediately to the Baptist Home Mission Association. To this Rabbi Cohn responded that he would be happy to turn the money over to Dr. Morehouse if that was what Miss Huntley wanted; he said he would be willing to abide by her decision in the matter. Dr. Morehouse immediately appointed a committee to meet with Miss Huntley. Included among the committee members was Dr. W. C. P. Rhoades, Rabbi Cohn's pastor and friend, who was also a Board member for the Baptist Society. He was caught in the middle. In recounting Dr. Rhoades' visit to Miss Huntley, Joseph Cohn wrote:

> And now he was in the home of Miss Huntley [Rochester, New York], and he told her of all that had been happening that winter. He told her that the Baptist brethren were men who could be thoroughly trusted, they were men of God, they were loyal to their trust, and were doing the best they could to advance the cause of Christ. He said that he had urged Mr. Cohn frequently to put himself in the care of these men, that they would always do the right thing by him. On the other hand, Mr. Cohn had repeatedly claimed that he could not trust these brethren, and that it would be betraying the trust of many Christian people who had put their confidence in him and were encouraging him to carry on independently. He explained that he had been sent up there to tell her these things and to urge her to instruct Mr. Cohn to turn the money over to them. Miss Huntley was not at all a well women, she had suffered much by her physical pain, and as she sat there in her large leather invalid chair, she looked at Dr. Rhoades in a most kindly way and asked him, 'Dr. Rhoades, have you done any praying about this matter before you came here?' Dr. Rhoades was quite embarrassed with the question; he told her finally that he was ashamed to say that he had not made this a matter of prayer. Then she asked him if he would not right then and there at his chair kneel down and ask God for wisdom in this perplexing problem. Dr. Rhoades knelt down and began to pray, but he did not get very far before he broke down with weeping. He arose, and went over to Miss Huntley and told her, 'Sister Huntley, you do whatever the Lord tells you, and we shall be satisfied.' After that he bade her goodbye and came back to New York.
>
> A few days later there came to New York two letters from Miss Huntley; one was addressed to Dr. Morehouse at the New York headquarters of the Home Mission Board; the other was sent to my father. In the letter to my father Miss Huntley explained that she was enclosing to him a copy of the letter she had just sent to Dr. Morehouse, and she wanted him to be guided by that letter. That letter, the words of which are still burned into my memory as though they had been branded there by fire, read as follows:
>
> 'While I have every confidence that you and the Baptist Brethren associated with you at the Headquarters of the American Baptist Home Mission Society, are earnest, sincere men, seeking only to do the Will of God, yet I have no confidence in your interest in the Jews, nor in your understanding of the Jewish problem. Therefore, while I gave the $10,000 to Mr. Leopold Cohn to do with exactly as he likes, I must now instruct him, under any condition, not to give it to you'[8]

When Dr. Morehouse received the letter, he immediately called Rabbi Cohn and asked him to come to a meeting at the home of Dr. Rhoades. According to Leopold Cohn, the following conversations took place:

> Dr. Morehouse said, 'Now, Mr. Cohn, you know that Miss Huntley trusts me, she gives money to our Society, and now that she said that you should keep the money, not give it to me, it must come from you [that] you persuaded her to say so, why did you do that? She would not have anything against you if you hand over the money to us now.' Then I said to him that I would not hand over the money out of my own account because I know that there is little interest in Christian people in the Jewish mission, that I am afraid that in time that money would not be used in the erection of a building for special Jewish work, but would be transferred to some other mission work, as there was a case of that kind

in New York some years ago, and this angered Dr. Morehouse very much, and he shook his fist in my face, 'You dare to tell me that I am not interested in the Jewish mission and I have been salarying you for eleven years;' and this made me feel very bad. I left the house and I came to my room and wrote down a resignation and sent it over to Dr. Morehouse, and a letter to Dr. Rhoades, and I said, 'You have seen the spirit of Dr. Morehouse, and I cannot work any more under him,' and I sent in my resignation.[9]

Thus, in 1907, after eleven years of ministry with them, Leopold Cohn severed his relationship with the American Baptist Home Mission Society and the society's support of Rabbi Cohn's work came to an abrupt end.[10] It is not clear if Miss Huntley continued her generous support of the Baptist Home Mission Society after Rabbi Cohn's resignation, but she did continue her support of Rabbi Cohn's mission. Not only did she supply further funding for the purchase of the land and a building for the mission, she also supplied funding for Rabbi Cohn to purchase a farm in Connecticut. The farm was to serve as a place where Jewish children could enjoy fresh air and life away from the city streets. The vision was that the farm would become an integral part of the ministry's program. However, the controversy that had developed over Rabbi Cohn in both the Christian community and the Jewish community, and the criticism of some of his "Christian" neighbors in Connecticut, hindered the development of the plans for the farm.

As advantageous and helpful as the generous gifts of Miss Huntley were, they also intensified the criticism surrounding Rabbi Cohn and his mission. From the time of his resignation from the Baptist Society, until September 30, 1911 Leopold operated the mission without an official Board of Trustees, and the mission was not legally incorporated. For nearly five years Rabbi Cohn continued to raise money, purchase property, and erect buildings in which to carry on his ministry, including hiring and paying salaries to mission personnel, without having an actual Board of Trustees. He was the Superintendent and the Treasurer. He, alone, maintained the financial records and published the audited statements that appeared in *The Chosen People* magazine. He published the names of donors and the amounts of their contributions in *The Chosen People* magazine, and he issued personal receipts of monies received. Rabbi Cohn's lapse in seeing that his mission was legally incorporated and functioning with an official Board of Trustees caused major problems as the years went by and as his ministry continued to expand.

Leopold's primary reason for not incorporating the work was based on his bad experience with the Board of the Baptist Association, and the attitudes and opinions that some Christians and Christian denominations clearly had toward Jewish mission works. He felt he could not entrust his ministry to an outside Board of Directors.

The matter came to a head when Dr. Rhoades learned that Miss Huntley was about to make another generous gift to Rabbi Cohn's ministry. In his testimony in the hearing that was held to consider the charges against Rabbi Cohn, Dr. Rhoades stated:

I had a letter from Miss Huntley's old pastor; he was a preacher in a Rochester Seminary—Dr. Mason. He did not mention Miss Huntley's name. He wanted to know my candid opinion of Mr. Cohn and his work, stating that he knew a person who was thinking of putting a considerable sum of money into that work if things were right, so I wrote a letter to Dr. Mason, of three or four pages, telling him my confidence in Mr. Cohn. I think I said in that letter that if I had to advise any one to give any considerable amount of money, I would advise giving it to the American Home Baptist Mission Society, because there was no Board of Trustees connected with Mr. Cohn's work. Sometime after that Miss Huntley gave $5,000.00 to Mr. Cohn's mission—toward the fund. I was a little disappointed. Then I heard that she was about to give more....so when I was at Rochester at one of the Trustee meetings of the Theological Seminary, I sought out Miss Huntley, and spent two hours with her one afternoon, telling her, 'Now, Miss Huntley, I have not come to influence you in any way with regard to money, but to relieve myself of any chance of trouble hereafter,...and I want you to understand me thoroughly in regard to my relations with Mr. Cohn's mission concerning money. If I were in your place I would give the money, as I said before, to the American Home Baptist Mission Society, in trust for that Mission, then none of it could be taken out unless authorized so to do. If Mr. Cohn should die, that would be held.'...She had been impressed with Mr. Cohn's sincerity, devotion and honesty, and she asked me questions. I said that I did not have anything to say against Mr. Cohn.[11]

Dr. Rhoades continued his testimony saying that he had received a letter from Miss Huntley, and he read from the letter:

Dear Dr. Rhoades, In reply to your letter of recent date I would say that if Mr. Cohn wishes to place the money which I have sent him for the building fund in the hands of the Home Miss. and Church Extension Soc's he can do so. I have for some years been sending him money for his work, long before I knew he was in any way connected with any Society, and have felt that he was worthy of confidence and capable of managing his Mission. I believe that a Jew understands the Jewish question and the best manner to deal with the Jews. It had not been in my mind when I sent him the money, that it would be necessary to pass out of his hands, except into the hands of a Board of Trustees of his own, and I charged him to keep it until then, and I suppose that he has a right to do so.[12]

Dr. Rhoades then went on to say that no Board had been appointed (c.1907). When asked if Miss Huntley continued to give more gifts to Cohn, he responded:

Yes. My object in seeing her was to make myself perfectly understood in the matter. I was about to go to the East for six months, and I was exceedingly anxious to get Mr. Cohn's business of the mission on a business basis. There was no chance to get a Board of Trustees then, but he did agree to have one; he said that if we would appoint a committee, any committee that would suit me, that he would agree to have a treasurer to have any monies that come in to the mission go into that treasurer's hands, and he would be advised by the committee. I laid my hands on Dr. Whitaker as the chairman of that committee, and he finally said he would attend to it, and I went off feeling a good deal less concerned than I did before. When I came back, I am not sure whether Miss Huntley had given any money in the meantime, I think she had given the money for that farm [the farm in Connecticut]; but the committee and Mr. Cohn had done nothing. I then told Mr. Cohn that I would not raise any money. He thought it was unkind of me; he could not understand it, and then Mr. Cohn incorporated the Mission and had a Board of Trustees appointed, and wanted to know if he could use my name as an advisor to refer to in his publication, and I said 'Yes', and he has done so, as far as I know.[13]

It must be recognized that Rabbi Leopold Cohn was a rabbi, not a businessman. God had called him to minister to his Jewish people. He was a missionary and evangelist. His heart's desire and vision was to have a congregation of Messianic Jews, a congregation that would reach out to, and care for the immigrant Jews of New York. His experiences and interrelations with the Christian community, and with Christian mission societies, was not the best. He did not understand them or their ways, and they did not share his burden to reach the Jews, nor did they understand his methodology. To establish a Board of Trustees that would exercise authority, direction, supervision, and control over the assets of his mission was not an easy step for Rabbi Cohn. He had witnessed what a Board had done to his friend, Hermann Warszawiak, and he had observed what had happened in other Jewish mission works once they had become organizations. However, he knew in his heart he had to incorporate or he would lose the credibility he had worked so hard to build for his ministry.

On September 30, 1911 the first meeting of the incorporators of the "Williamsburg Mission To The Jews" met in the offices of Messrs. Shaffer, Horrell and Hinds, at 207 Broadway, in the Borough of Manhattan. The first item of business was the election of officers, and a motion was made to elect Leopold Cohn as Chairman of the Corporation and his son, Joseph Hoffman Cohn (then age 25), as Secretary and Treasurer. Beside Leopold and Joseph Cohn, the incorporators of the Williamsburg Mission to the Jews were Curtis H. Muncie, John Donaldson, and Benjamin F. Knowles.[14] The next item of business was the reading and adoption of the By-laws for the newly formed corporation. The final item of business was the transfer of property, which had been held in the name of Joseph Hoffman Cohn, to the newly formed corporation. This transfer of property included a parcel of land at the corner of Throop Avenue and Walton Street in Brooklyn, New York. The Williamsburg Mission To The Jews was now a reality, holding it's own assets.

A Major Donor to the Rescue

In the five years during which Leopold Cohn ran the mission without a Board of Trustees, Miss Frances J. Huntley had donated gifts in excess of $60,000. These gifts were given for the purchase of property for the mission, and to build and finish the mission building in Brooklyn. She had also given Leopold Cohn the money to purchase the farm in Connecticut. With the exception of the farm, all properties and monies given were to go to the mission. Since there was no corporation, much of the property was held in the names of Joseph Hoffman Cohn and Leopold Cohn. However, once the corporation was formed the properties were transferred to the mission and the Cohns did take steps to see that the properties would be used for Jewish missions, should anything happen to them.

In his testimony before the Committee investigating charges against Leopold Cohn, Joseph Cohn stated: "I have given this property to my executor, the Peoples Trust Company, in trust, to pay over the income therefrom to my father during his life, and at his death the whole property to go to the Williamsburg Mission to the Jews."[15] When asked if he had made provision in his will for the disposition of the property if his father should predecease him, Joseph Cohn replied: "My wife agreed and she signed a release clause that she has no claim in that corner property at any time. I explained to her that I have a moral obligation on that property, and when I die it was to remain with the Mission."[16]

The question was then asked as to why the property had been placed in Joseph's name, rather than to remain in his father's name. Joseph gave two reasons. He said the property had originally been in his father's name, but that his father had put the farm in Joseph's name after Leopold's remarriage. He indicated that his father had done so because the farm was to remain in the Cohn family, according to the wishes of Miss Huntley. He went on to state that from the time he had been a small child, he had helped his father in the work of the mission and had felt the call of God upon his life but, he said, he had also been very much aware of the poverty and suffering his family had gone through for the sake of the mission. So, although he had been active in the ministry, he had also worked at a secular job after high school—a job which had trained him for the business world. He said he had reasoned that, if he could not be physically involved in his father's ministry, he would at least be able to financially support it, and thereby to make things easier. But, he went on to say, he'd never had any peace about remaining in a secular position and one day, while at Trinity Church in New York, he had asked God to show him a way out of his unhappiness. Of this time Joseph wrote:

> ...My business future looked bright, but true happiness seemed always to elude me. So came the day when I made the vow, right there in one of the pews of Trinity Church, 'Lord, if you want me to give up all this business and go into the work of the Mission with my father, you will have to open the way, and I will follow.'
>
> That night after supper my father said to me, 'Joe, I have received today a letter from a lady by the name of Miss Huntley, which I want you to read.' He gave me the letter and I read it. The letter said that she was sending a check for several hundred dollars to help my father in his up-stream battle. Her closing paragraph, however, was what my father wanted me to see. It read as follows, as nearly as I can remember, 'If you should happen to have any children who might feel called of God to consecrate their lives for His service among the Jews, I will be glad to help pay their expenses by way of education and training.'
>
> Thus my challenge had been met, to my utter astonishment. There was no way for me now but to accept this magnanimous offer, which had come out of a clear sky, and with nothing of my own doing to bring it about. My father wrote Miss Huntley and told her about me; and she wrote back promptly, enclosing a generous check, saying, 'This is to get Joseph started in some Bible School.'[17]

Thus, Joseph Cohn found himself in Chicago, enrolled in Moody Bible Institute and studying for the ministry. During his semesters of study there, he kept in constant touch with Miss Huntley. She was close to eighty years of age, and she wanted Joseph to consider her a foster mother. Whenever he would pass through Rochester, Joseph would stop and visit with Miss Huntley. She had prepared a special room for him in her home. During those visits Joseph would tell her about his involvement in the mission, and she would share letters she had received from his father. In a very real sense, Miss Frances J. Huntley had totally adopted the Cohns, especially Joseph and Leopold, as her own family.

After his mother's death and his father's resignation from the American Baptist Home Mission Society, Joseph felt it incumbent upon himself to leave Moody and to return home to help his father in the ministry. When he told Miss Huntley of his decision, she said it was essential that he have a good education and, once again, she became his benefactress. Joseph wrote:

> Miss Huntley had felt that I ought to undertake to make up for my lost education and go back to school and get at least a college degree [that Fall Joseph entered Adelphi Academy in Brooklyn, and later on went to Adelphi College]. She was a woman not only consecrated to the Lord's work, but with a keen understanding of the ways of the world. She was the owner of a large factory, and managed that factory with some 3,000 employees, from her huge leather invalid chair. So she felt that the world puts value on education, and she knew the importance of using the coin of the realm in making one's way through this mundane sphere. She thought that I would be better equipped and would receive better recognition if I should have a reasonably good education. She also knew that the Jewish mission work was perhaps the most difficult undertaking in all the world, and she wanted me to appear before the public adequately qualified to create confidence in the work we were doing and in our preparation and conduct of it. So she undertook the expense of my going to the little college in Brooklyn. And here it was that I entered. Thus by staying home instead of going away to college, I was able to help my father in the work, especially to carry on correspondence, and to keep the books, and help with the getting out of The Chosen People [magazine] each month.[18]

Thus, within his testimony before the Committee, Joseph gave further insight into the promises that had been made to him if he would agree to join his father in the ministry, which was a second reason the property had been placed in his name after Leopold Cohn's remarriage. Joseph testified:

...at that time [when the property had been put in Joseph's name] several things developed. One, that I was giving up my business connections entirely and would go into the work for good, and I said to my father, 'I am undertaking a risky thing, it is a hard thing to build up a Jewish work; it has never been successfully done as yet, if I did I ought have some kind of guarantee.' Miss Huntley agreed to the same thing that if I would promise her that I would spend my whole life in Jewish work that I would not do anything else, but do my best, and she would put her money in to protect me, if I would put my life in it, and that I would always administer that money; she gave me that stock...at the same time, and she intended to cover all cases.[19]

Thus, through the generous gifts of Miss Frances J. Huntley, the financial security of both Leopold and Joseph Hoffman Cohn, as well as the financial security of the Williamsburg Mission To The Jews, was secured. Miss Huntley's gifts gave the Cohn's and the Williamsburg Mission an appearance of wealth and success, and because of this Rabbi Cohn and his son, Joseph, once again found themselves between two worlds, neither of which liked or understood them.

During the years of 1905 to 1915, great struggles were taking place within ethnic groups that were pouring into America. As new immigrants grappled to find their places within the American society, believers within the churches became aware of the needs of the newcomers around them and in many cases efforts were made to reach out to meet those needs. But the Christians of America were struggling too. For the most part, the large denominational churches were involved in relief programs that supplied assistance to needy "Gentile" immigrants, but they were not interested in helping the Jews, or in reaching Jews with the Gospel. The accepted philosophy was to attempt to blend all social and ethnic groups into the main-stream of American life. The obvious success of Leopold Cohn's ministry among the poor immigrant Jews disturbed Christians who held to such a philosophy; his mission contradicted their view of Christianity. The Jewish community was even more outraged over Rabbi Cohn's ministry. A successful Jewish mission was anathema! The success of the Cohns in Brooklyn meant that other Jewish people might consider the claims of Yeshua and "convert" to Christianity.

While the Christian and Jewish communities grappled with questions and discussion of what should be done about the Cohns and their mission in Brooklyn, the Cohns forged ahead. Rabbi Cohn was determined to build a Messianic Jewish community. Joseph Cohn's vision was to reach all Jews everywhere with the Gospel, beginning in Williamsburg and spreading throughout the world. Both Cohns saw the financial base that had been given to them as evidence of God's blessing upon their ministry, so they forged ahead. In hindsight, it is clear that they should have followed the advice of Dr. Rhoades and incorporated the mission immediately, but they did not. Sadly, this failure came back to haunt them years later.

The Fresh Air Farm and Problems

In August 1906, a Dedication Service was held at the farm in Connecticut. Rabbi Cohn invited staff, pastors, and Christian friends to attend. At this service the farm was consecrated to the Lord for the work of the mission.[20] However, Rabbi Leopold Cohn and his son, Joseph, seemed never to be satisfied with the status-quo. God's supply of one need seemed to be the beginning of another need. Each answer to prayer, and each provision from the Lord, was an indication to reach out farther, to expand and enlarge the vision.

In November 1907, only a little over a year after the dedication of the farm, an article appeared in *The Chosen People* magazine stating:

Many changes have been made on our farm during the summer. Three thousand dollars were donated by a friend, as reported in this number, for necessary improvements and the work accomplished was as follows. A house of eight rooms was built for the farmer, a new barn was put up, the old barn was remodelled, stables for horses and cows were arranged, a tower, 30 feet high, with a tank holding 4,500 gallons of water was erected, a pumping engine was set up and through a system of piping, water is supplied to the two houses and stables.

People who know something about building now-a-days will understand how our money was exhausted before the work was completed, and so realizing the extravagance of leaving the buildings unfinished, I wrote to a few friends who readily permitted me to apply their donations for the building, and finish this work.

Now everything is completed and all we need is a dormitory to accommodate our school children for the summer. Few people can realize the great benefit this farm will be to the Gospel work among the Jews when once fully equipped. To talk to children or to men about Christ, for a few minutes, is one thing, and to be with them for fourteen consecutive days and away from the turmoil of city life is quite another. We also hope to establish there a home for destitute children. The only sad thing is that there is no other way of doing these things than through money. Will some who believe in philanthropy help us make this farm a place of happiness to Jewish children who never had such treatment from the

Church of Christ before. Is it not worth while to give this mission, upon which God has put His seal of approval, full scope, in the direction its pendulum is trying to swing?[21]

For Leopold Cohn—the missionary, the rabbi, the visionary—everything he had belonged to the Lord. Although the farm technically belonged to him, for his name was on the deed, and this was what Miss Huntley wanted, Leopold wanted the farm to be used for the Lord. He saw nothing wrong in asking for funds to expand and enlarge the farm, as long as it was being used for the Lord's work. He was always very careful to make it clear to his donors that gifts for the ministry were not used to develop or expand the farm. These were separate gifts apart from monies raised for evangelism and mission work.

Leopold's zeal for the Lord but lack of business discernment in failing to have a legal corporation for the mission set up came back to haunt him. As the farm was developed, and as new buildings and stables were erected, the neighbors, especially those critical of Leopold Cohn and of his Mission, only saw him as gaining in personal wealth. More than a few local Christians and pastors expressed concern, and even criticism, over the fact that Rabbi Cohn filled his car with Jewish children and went "sight seeing" on the "Christian Sabbath" (Sunday). They were also piqued that he often ignored the "Day of Rest" by sometimes working on his farm on that day. Leopold, on the other hand, could not understand why his neighbors were making such a fuss. From sundown Friday to sundown Saturday, he, as a Jewish believer, worshipped the Lord. He spoke in the services at the mission, prayed, and honored the Sabbath Day (the Jewish Sabbath). He did not ask his Gentile-Christian neighbors to reduce or stop their labors on Saturday, and he could not understand why they were not as amiable. Again, Leopold Cohn was caught in the middle—between two clashing worlds. Fear and jealously began to rise up within the hearts of those who did not know or understand Rabbi Cohn, and rumors began to be spread about this man and his farm.

Similar problems were developing in Brooklyn as Leopold and Joseph Cohn, using the funds provided by Miss Huntley, began buying up mortgages and entire blocks of houses surrounding the mission building. The income from those rentals was used to further expand their ministry. For the first time, rather than being the lessees, wondering if they would have a roof over their heads, they were the lessors. Without a legal corporation, the deeds to these properties were registered in the names of Leopold or Joseph Cohn.

As far as the Jewish and Christian public could see, the Cohn's were becoming wealthy land-owners. Their increased wealth and increased ownership of property in the Jewish sections of Brooklyn was cause for great alarm in the Jewish community, and rumors began to circulate. But Leopold and Joseph saw God's hand of blessing and direction in this enlargement of their financial base and ministry, so they forged ahead. They wanted to be true to the vision and calling God had given to them. From their perspective, it made sense that one provision from the Lord only meant that another, greater, provision should be expected.

A Building in Brooklyn

In the March 1908 Salutation of *The Chosen People* magazine, Leopold Cohn spoke of purchasing the property in Brooklyn, mentioning what would be needed to build. He wrote:

It is now over a year since the first large gift was received for the building fund of this Mission. It was then that I called your attention to 'the sound of a gong in the tops of the mulberry trees.' The amount received though large in itself did not warrant the purchase of the property we had in mind, the price then being $42,500. At that time it was also related to you how remarkably God had pointed out this property as most desirable for the Mission.

Then you prayed to God about these matters, as earnestly as if they were your personal affairs; and truly they were yours, for this work is yours and the workers are yours, by reason of your support. I know that you prayed for us, for the vast majority wrote me so. Let the following quotation from one of the many letters, suffice. 'We solemnly kept the fast for the day you fixed last Autumn, with fasting and prayers and tears. And we had the solemn assurance of friends that they prayed earnestly also for the Jewish Mission and the building that day and now we daily tell our dear Lord that we know He will finish what He has begun and that we are assured that we have already that building for which we have prayed so many, many times.'

So in answer to your prayers, that same desirably located property has been preserved for us. As reported last month another large gift has come from a dear soul stirred by the Holy Spirit and now at last the property has been bought for $40,000, $2,500 less than last year's price. The titles have passed and we, the children of the King...have seen His goings, the goings and motions of our God and our king in the Sanctuary or (literally) the things that are holy.

[The buildings]...cannot be used for the work but will bring in money to cover taxes, interest, and insurance. The property faces on three streets,...the Broadway front of 55 feet...contains two houses, one frame and the other,

brick. The side on Walton Street is 90 feet to Throop Avenue where it has a width of 60 feet. These lots are the most valuable that can be had in the vicinity and are a real bargain. Repairs must be made to the houses to remove a number of violations of the tenement laws which were neglected by the owner. These will require between two and three thousand dollars.

We had on hand $22,000. About $16,000 has been paid in cash to the owner and for a second mortgage of $6,000, this leaving a first mortgage of $24,000 and about $6,000 cash on hand.

The thing now needed on these lots is a suitable building which would cost between $30,000 and $40,000.[22]

During this time the income of the Mission grew from $1,861.27, as reported in the Financial Statement of March 1902 Chosen People magazine to $36,058.04 in the financial statement ending January 31, 1908.[23] Clearly, God was blessing the mission, both financially and spiritually, providing the means to meet the vision He had given to Rabbi Cohn.

Rabbi Cohn continued to keep friends of the ministry informed of God's provisions for the building in Brooklyn. In keeping with his faith, and his practice of trusting God for just a little bit more by urging God's people to catch the vision and dig down deep into their pockets, he mentions the cost of the building rising from $40,000 to $60,000. In the November 1908 Salutation of *The Chosen People* magazine, Leopold wrote:

As announced in the last issue, a new pledge of $10,000 was made, and since then has been realized. There is now on hand $14,000 in the Building Fund. We have been hoping for the Building for so many years, that on receipt of the new pledge, it was thought best not to wait until the whole sum of $60,000 needed for the entire plan, was collected, but to erect a portion of the Building, to occupy only as much ground as is vacant in the rear of the recently purchased property. This plot is 25 ft. x 58 ft., and an architect has drawn up plans for a whole building and then for this portion, so constructed that the remainder of the building can be properly added.

It was hoped that within a short time work could be begun, as we estimated that $14,000 would be sufficient, but when the architect had made up his figures, it was a disappointment to learn that it would cost $20,000.

I know that all our dear friends will join us workers in thanks and praise to God for His provisions so far in such a remarkable way. First, that the purchase of the property was made possible and second, that in less than a year since that purchase so much more money has come in.

A more unmistakable evidence of God's answer to your prayers cannot possibly be imagined. When four years ago, we announced a forward movement, having as its goal the raising of $50,000 for a Jewish Missionary Building in this great city, people were amazed; it was absurd that an unknown and unpopular mission (for Jewish missions have not been popular) should even dream of such vast possibilities. That was four years ago. To-day, the purchased property on Broadway alone is worth $50,000, and in addition, we have $14,000 as a nucleus of the building and a thoroughly equipped farm, which will prove a most wonderful co-operative agency in connection with the building plant in the city. In the face of these facts, we must simply stand aside and say, 'truly it is wonderful.'[24]

Leopold then went on to make a plea for the additional $6,000 needed to build the first phase of the building, and in the December 1908 issue of the magazine he printed the architect's sketch of the first section of the proposed building. In January 1909, contracts were issued for the erection of the building and Leopold wrote to his constituents:

I am glad to be able to report to you that contracts to erect that portion of the new building in Williamsburg, of which a sketch was given in the last issue of The Chosen People, have been signed. The contractor has already started to make necessary preparations and by the time you read these words the builders will be at work.

This building will give us, in the basement, ample room for carrying on the dispensary work. The next floor will make a good-sized church, accommodating comfortably 250 people and also having plenty of closet room for tracts, Bibles, and other literature. The floor above this will be for the children's work, for meetings of older girls and women, and for the educational department. The top floor will be used for the administration department. What a great relief from the present crowded condition this will be! I am already beginning to feel like one from whose shoulders a heavy load has been lifted. Words cannot describe my joyful feelings over this direct act of God in providing the Mission with a building after many years of patient prayer and waiting upon the Lord who has always done marvelously.[25]

The readers of *The Chosen People* magazine, and supporters of the mission, continued to receive updates on the progress of the building through Leopold's articles. Finally, the building was completed and the first service in it was held on Friday evening, July 2, 1909. Of this memorable occasion Rabbi Cohn wrote:

For two weeks previous we had announced this service, stating that all those who wished to be present must secure tickets of admission from the workers. About five hundred were eagerly taken by our Jewish friends so that when the time of the meeting arrived, streams of people began to flow toward the new building in such crowds that two policemen were required to keep them in order. We had crowded as many chairs as could be put into the hall so that about two hundred and twenty Jews were accommodated and it was estimated that perhaps four hundred more had to be turned away for lack of room. The windows on each side of the building held excited groups, craning their necks and straining their ears to catch the words spoken inside.

...How little did I imagine fifteen years ago, when the Lord thrust me into this field, that my eyes should witness such a scene; two hundred Jews worshipping the Lord Jesus Christ! My heart went up to God in joyful thanksgiving and in earnest prayer for still greater things.

A few Christian friends were with us on this occasion and some remarked that we would soon have to enlarge the building. Others expressed the regret that Mrs. Cohn had not lived to see the realization of her hopes, but I believe that her spirit saw it and was satisfied that her dying prayers were answered.[26]

With the building complete, the mission continued to grow and to attract new Jewish people to its services. Reports of Jewish people who had come to faith in Yeshua filled the pages of *The Chosen People* magazine. Through the mission, the Cohns were in contact with Jewish communities around the world, supplying support and literature, seeking to fulfill the vision God had given them of reaching all Jews everywhere with the Gospel.

But where there is victory, there is also opposition. God's Word has declared that the enemy of our souls "prowls about like a roaring lion, seeking someone to devour" (I Pet. 5:8). This applies to ministries of God, as well as to individuals of God. The more successful the Christian life, or ministry, the greater and more diabolical the attack of the Evil One.

A SMEAR CAMPAIGN

Hints at an attempt to discredit Rabbi Cohn were first mentioned by him in the December 1908 issue of *The Chosen People* magazine. He wrote:

Our friends are somewhat acquainted with the persecutions I have had to encounter ever since I took upon my self publicly to follow the Lord Jesus Christ. I had hoped that after seventeen years the bitterness of my Jewish friends would cease; but not so. A great fire has now been kindled among them whose flames are continually threatening me.

It originated in this manner. A false brother who professes Christianity wrote to the Jews in my native country that I am misleading many Jews, blaspheming against the Jewish religion, and publishing malicious articles causing the Gentiles to hate the Jews and thus bringing persecution upon them. Would not my countrymen therefore try to do something to stop me? This he wrote in the name of a rabbi of Brooklyn. The Jews in my country upon receiving this news last October when they were celebrating their holidays, were greatly stirred about it and thinking that the letter came from a rabbi whom they imagined to be over all the others, it carried great authority and a tremendous influence. They denounced me as well as my relatives in the all the synagogues where the news reached. I had sharp letters of warning from my own relatives saying that there is no telling what they will try to do to hurt me. Please pray for me.[27]

Rabbi Cohn was no stranger to persecution. He knew the malicious letter that was sent to the Jewish leaders in Hungry had once again stirred up animosity against him, but he was completely unaware of the fact that this was just the tip of the of the iceberg. He did not know that an organized plan was being developed to totally discredit him and his ministry.

Open opposition to his ministry intensified, and in the October 1911 issue of *The Chosen People* magazine an article stated:

Never before in the seventeen years of this mission did we have to encounter such serious opposition from a certain class of Jews as on the twenty-seventh of August of this summer. At half-past seven in the evening, the doors were thrown open as usual, and our doorkeeper was surprised to see a large crowd of Jews in front of the building. They did not want to enter, but stood there and watched. Presently, some of the usual attendants made their way through the people to go into the service, and the crowd then began to be troublesome. They divided into several groups; one company evidently was to stop the Jews that wished to go into the meeting, another band was to pick out the converts and give them a good beating, and sill another body of lads were appointed to be armed with bricks ready to throw them at a signal. All worked in perfect harmony, and although it was estimated that there were over a thousand Jews in that crowd, there was no confusion among them, with the result that the men who wanted to go in were forcibly turned away, some of the converts that spoke up for the mission and tried to remonstrate with the leaders were beaten severely, and the armed young Jews discharged their ammunition, making the doors and windows their target. Our janitor tried hard to save some of the converts from a beating, but he was hit with several stones, one striking the back of his head, while our co-worker, Mr. Englander, who came out of the building and pleaded with the crowd, had a brick thrown at his leg. The crowd grew more and more tumultuous, the uproar was great, the noise of the rowdyism could be heard for several blocks, and it looked as if the whole building was going to be demolished. One call after the other was made over the telephone to the Police Department, but it took fully half an hour before the police reserves from a near-by station came to the scene and dispersed the crowd. About half-past eight the auditorium was filled with a respectable audience and the meeting was held without any further disturbance.

This sudden attack of so many Jews upon the mission is the result of their fruitless attempts time and again to destroy this work. Once the rabbis of the neighborhood held a meeting to which they invited some Christian ministers, asking them to close up this mission, for they thought that the ministers could do it. They gave as reasons for their request that the mission makes converts and causes separations between children and parents, man and wife, etc., on account of the change in religion. Then they tried to establish sewing-schools in opposition to our school and then, thinking that we win the confidence of the poor Jews, helping them in their need and by giving them medical aid, an attempt was made by prominent Jews to have the Board of Charities close our medical department. But they could not accomplish that, so they have been collecting money for over a year and have now opened a large dispensary near the mission. They boasted that they would put an end to our medical department, and the day before their dispensary opened, they made a great demonstration by parading in the main streets of the Jewish quarter. They sent messengers from house to house, warning the Jews against the mission and urging their attendance at the new dispensary. They have also endeavored to establish new charitable organizations to help the poor. All these things did not avail them. Their last resort, therefore, was this foolish act of violence, a step for which they themselves perhaps are now sorry.[28]

The acts of violence against the Mission continued, but did not escalate. The leaders of these acts of violence soon found that such persecution resulted in Rabbi Cohn's ministry receiving more publicity, thus provoking more Christians to pray and support his ministry. This was evidenced by an article that appeared in the December 1912 issue of *The Chosen People* magazine which stated:

We have not, for a long time, had such a condition of excitement among the Jews of this large city as during the last month. Every Jewish paper has had something to say about the Missionary Cohn. Inciting articles were published, insinuating and suggesting violence against the missionary. Lengthy editorials and letters from individuals with blazing headlines were seen in the Jewish papers for days and weeks, causing all the Jews, who are ignorant of the activities of this mission for the good of the people, to feel very bitter against it. The beginning of this trouble was as follows:—

When we reopened the Sewing School in Brownsville, special invitations were given to the girls of the neighborhood to join us and thus the news of the School spread to new people. Some women living opposite the church where the School is held, met the girls and rebuked them for going into a church. The next Tuesday, when the sewing school was in session, a rabbi from Brownsville, accompanied by a president of his synagogue, came to visit the school. They asked the ladies a great many questions which were answered in a friendly way. Following that, on several occasions the girls were met by Jewish women and men, who rebuked them for attending the place where they are taught about Jesus. Some of the girls told them to mind their business. When the Jews pressed them to tell whether they really loved Jesus, the girls said, 'yes,' and that they had no right to interfere. This caused the rabbi to worry about the spiritual condition of the girls who attended our school.

He and some other Jews wrote letters to the English papers of the city, asking them to stop that Missionary Cohn from proselytizing the Jews. When a reporter asked me whether this was true, I assured him that as the Lord Jesus Christ came to proselyting [sic] the Jews so we His disciples, must do the same work. Then the Brooklyn Daily Eagle had a long article about the complaint of the Jews and what I had to say. This article, as well as the rabbi's letters to every Jewish paper, gave the Jewish editors material enough to write inflaming words about the missionary.

In the Brooklyn Daily Eagle there was a statement to the effect that there were about 10,000 Jews in this great city who believe in the Lord Jesus Christ, but who are afraid to confess Him publicly on account of their dependence on their own people for a livelihood. This statement sent terror into the hearts of the Jewish editors and rabbis. The Brownsville rabbi, who originated the agitation immediately organized a Sunday School for Jewish children with the main object to educate them to keep away from Christian missions. One of the editors said they owed thanks to Mr. Cohn, for if it had not been for his activities, the rabbi would not have organized this Sunday School.

> We have not had harmful results from this whole movement except that the Jewish girls in Brownsville are afraid to go to the sewing school because of the persecutors who meet them on the way and who send boys to taunt them when they leave the school. Still, we have quite a number who are bold enough to attend. The other Sewing School in Williamsburg has not been affected.
>
> One good result was that on the first Friday evening after these publications in the Jewish papers, the crowd which came to the meeting was immense and perhaps never before have there been so many Jews turned away from the hall for lack of space. It is amusing to read an article written by the rabbi of Brownsville, who describes his sorrow at the sight which he had to witness when he himself visited the building Beth Sar Shalom. Once, he says, he came on a Friday evening and saw the house literally packed with Jews. Then he came several times on Saturday afternoon and witnessed a large crowd of Jewish women going to our dispensary, and oh, how he bemoans that they go into a Christian dispensary and more than that, they take their little children with them. 'Perhaps,' he comments sarcastically, 'these pious Jewesses are afraid that their children will not know where this godly mission house, with its benevolent Christians is,' and then he goes on to call these Jews all sorts of names for doing that. Those Jews who come regularly to the mission have not been affected by this, but the ignorant have been made more ignorant and more bitter toward Christianity than ever before. We believe, however, that all things work together for good to them that love God, and that He is able to overrule all their zeal for the good and benefit of the Gospel of the Lord Jesus Christ.[29]

God's Word speaks of the tares growing up among the wheat. Satan always has his counterfeits. Jewish Christians are no less subject to Satan's attacks than Gentile Christians, and sometimes more so. No one likes to be duped—to be fooled. During this time, the Church and individual Christians were not prepared to recognize, or to deal with, organized attacks from members of the Jewish community or from a "professing" Jewish believer against another Jewish believer. Had they been able to recognize such treachery, perhaps Hermann Warszawiak, and other missionaries like him, would have received more backing from the Christian church and would thus have been able to continue in ministry. Nevertheless, the Christian community, and churches, remained unaware and unsuspecting.

Not only was Rabbi Cohn confronted with the daily badgering of hostile Jews within the Jewish community, he also had within his own ministry some "tares" in the form of disgruntled "professing" Jewish Christians. These wrathful individuals began working with the hostile Jews outside the ministry, devising a new plan of attack against Rabbi Cohn. They also enlisted the assistance of leaders from another Jewish mission who apparently harbored jealously over the success of the Cohns' mission. The plan was to totally discredit Rabbi Cohn personally. The assault used two well-tested tactics, the first of which was to discredit the character and morals of Cohn; the second involved creating doubts about his financial affairs. These tactics were carried out by creating and spreading vicious rumors and lies. Interestingly, similar tactics had been used by the leaders of the Jewish community in their efforts to discredit Hermann Warszawiak and his ministry.

The time and setting for carrying out their diabolical tactics were perfect. Both Hermann Warszawiak and Rabbi Cohn worked among immigrant Jews, most of whom were not educated and were very poor. It was a time when many Jews "converted" to Christianity for monetary gain. Such Jews would go from church to church, giving testimony of their faith just to receive an offering. In short, it was a way of making a living from the Christians. It was his awareness of this practice by some of the poor immigrant Jews that prompted Bernhard Angel to print his tract, warning churches and Christians about the "so-called" Jewish converts.[30]

NEUOWICH AND THE PLOT AGAINST COHN

The leader, and perhaps the instigator, of a group of three Jewish men who hatched the plot to try and discredit Leopold Cohn was a Mr. Alexander H. Neuowich, a fellow country-man of Rabbi Cohn. Neuowich claimed to be a Jewish believer, and prior to his peeve with Cohn his testimony appeared in the February 1904 issue of *The Chosen People* magazine (The spelling of his name is given as Alexander "Newitz." In later editions of the magazine his name is spelled "Neuowich." However, his picture always remains the same, and the facts remain the same).[31] In his testimony, Mr. Neuowich states that he had attended a meeting of Rev. Bernhard Angel and, while listening to the message, thought of Leopold Cohn. He stated:

> During the service I had been reminded of Mr. Leopold Cohn, whom they say in our country such men as this missionary misled, so that he became an apostate. But as he is highly esteemed by all the Jews who knew him, this counteracted the prejudice toward an apostate, and I resolved to go and see him. I asked Mr. Angel for Mr. Cohn's address and then went over to Brooklyn to his house.
>
> When I reached his home I delivered to him a message from his sister, and after having done so he gave me a

message from the Lord Jesus Christ. I was greatly astonished that a man like him who had been a rabbi in our country and who is still regarded very highly, should believe in that Crucified One.[32]

Neuowich's testimony goes on to relate how Rabbi Cohn gave him a New Testament and how he (Neuowich) accepted Yeshua. He tells of the persecution he endured because of his faith in Yeshua and how the Hungarian Jews in New York and his family wanted to send him back to Hungary; he speaks about a plot to have him killed, which he found out about through a relative of Rabbi Cohn. He said:

One Saturday afternoon last Spring, I invited a young man who is a relative of Mr. Cohn's, to accompany me to the Brownsville Mission. I talked to him about the Messiah and this perhaps caused him to reveal the secret to me and to Mr. Cohn. We had reason to believe the report, because the day before, two Jews, whose characters I suspected, accosted me in the street. I refused to pay attention to them, but they followed me closely for a distance until I appealed to some passers-by. Mr. Cohn would not let me go back to New York, and began to plan how I could leave the city altogether. He found a lady living in Easton, Connecticut, a Mrs. Silliman, who is a minister's widow, who was willing to take me into her house. After I had been baptized in the Marcy Avenue Baptist Church by the Rev. Dr. Rhoades, I went to Mrs. Silliman, where I stayed until January First. I would not miss this opportunity for mentioning that I could never find words enough to express my gratitude to this noble Christian lady, who has been more than a mother to me. She taught me English, explained the Bible to me, sheltered me and with great patience educated me in many ways.[33]

Why Mr. Neuowich later turned against Leopold Cohn, and would make up vicious lies about him, is unclear. Perhaps it was out of spite and anger over Leopold's refusal to endorse him, or perhaps it was out of his own desire to gain wealth and prestige through the development of his own ministry, for it is clear that he did develop his own work.

Under sworn testimony, when called to testify before the Committee investigating charges against Leopold Cohn, Mr. Neuowich stated that Mrs. Silliman had provided money for the mortgage so Leopold Cohn could purchase the farm in Easton, Connecticut and that Mrs. Silliman had become concerned about the character and actions of Leopold Cohn and wanted her money back.[34] Whatever his reasons, Mr. Neuowich either lied to the committee, or he lied in his testimony which was printed in *The Chosen People* magazine.

Regarding this same issue, Mr. Buckalew, a member of the investigation committee, submitted a letter regarding an interview he'd had with Mrs. Samuel Silliman. His letter stated:

Mrs. Samuel Silliman stated to the undersigned at her home on the afternoon of the above date (June 3, 1916) that Alexander Neuowich had been brought to her by Leopold Cohn several years ago and that she had taken an interest in Neuowich, helping him to study English and later sending him to the Mt. Hermon School. She said he wrote his name differently at various times such as "Norwich" and "Newitz" and then back again to Neuowich.

Mrs. Silliman became displeased with the many deceptions of Neuowich and his untruthfulness...She said that she has known Leopold Cohn for a number of years; that she knows he paid $2,750 for his farm and that she, Mrs. Silliman, had loaned him $3,000.00, taking a mortgage on the farm.

She said that Neuowich was very fond of Mr. Cohn and frequently spoke of him to Mrs. Silliman as having been a Rabbi in the old country, but that later Neuowich became unfriendly to Cohn and since then has told her that Cohn was a fugitive from justice.

Mrs. Silliman stated that she knows nothing against Mr. Cohn, that he had always acted as a gentleman so far as she knows. (signed) E.B. Buckalew.[35]

SCHAPIRO AND SPIEVACQUE JOIN PLOT

The other two malcontents who participated in Neuowich's plot to discredit Leopold Cohn were a notable Jewish believer by the name of Benjamin Aaron Moses Schapiro and a Mr. Philip Spievacque. Schapiro established a Jewish mission work in Brooklyn, called the Brooklyn City Mission, about the same time as Leopold Cohn started his mission. It would appear that both missions were established in close proximity to one another in Brooklyn, New York, and that they had similar programs.

Benjamin Schapiro was introduced to the Messiah through the testimony of Rev. Jacob Freshman, founder of the Hebrew Christian Mission, located at 17, St. Mark's Place, New York. The year was 1890. Benjamin, a native of Poland who had just arrived in America from Germany, was nineteen years old when he entered the Reading Room and first met Jacob Freshmen. Interestingly, Benjamin Schapiro's first encounter with Jacob Freshman occurred shortly after Hermann Warszawiak established his mission work as an outreach of the De Witt Memorial Church.

Jacob Freshman worked with Schapiro, teaching him English. It wasn't long before Benjamin Schapiro adopted the life-style and dress of the typical American of that day, and left Jacob Freshman's tutelage. In his book, "Some Jewish Witnesses for Christ," Rev. A. Bernstein states the following of Schapiro's second encounter with Jacob Freshman:

> Two years had elapsed since our first meeting. One evening, at the close of the service in a Hebrew Christian Church, we were cordially greeted by a young man. The native dress had been changed for American, the hair arranged in a different style, etc. So great was the transformation that at the first glance we failed to recognize our quondam pupil and friend. He then told us what had befallen him since we last met. He had, soon after leaving the mission, found employment with Mr. Benjamin Clayton, a butcher at Jamaica, L.I. Imagine, if you can, what a trial it must have been to one brought up to a strict observance of the tenets of Orthodox Judaism to have to handle "Gentile" meat, especially the abhorred pork.[36]

Some time after this second encounter with Freshman, Benjamin Schapiro publicly confessed his faith in Yeshua and joined a church in Brooklyn.[37] Not yet twenty-one years of age, Schapiro nevertheless felt the call of God to start his own mission to the Jews in Brooklyn. He used the limited resources he was able to solicit from friends. One friend, Mr. Horatio S. Stewart, helped pay Schapiro's tuition at Pennington Seminary. Like Leopold Cohn, Schapiro opened up his first mission branch in the "Brownsville" section of Brooklyn, New York.

> ...Saturday services were continued for more than two years. An evening school, where Jewish people, employed during the day, could receive gratuitous instruction in English, was carried on with a great degree of success....Mr. Schapiro, at his own expense, opened a soup-kitchen in his rooms, himself serving the tables, and for more than two weeks scores were fed....The missionary also opened a similar mission in the Sixteenth Ward, Eastern District, where there is a Jewish population of 50,000, and for nearly a year carried on the two stations, holding a service at Brownsville on Saturday morning, and a second one in the new mission in the afternoon. Finally his committee deemed it best to confine his labours entirely to the Eastern District station, . . .
>
> After seven years of mission work [c. 1899], owing to the combined labour of carrying on the service and collecting funds for the maintenance of the mission, his health [Schapiro] broke down and he gave up the work.[38]

In his book, "A Century of Jewish Missions," A. E. Thompson reported:

> ...In 1899 he [Schapiro] surrendered the supervision of it [the Brooklyn Christian Mission to the Jews] to Philip Spievacque and devoted himself to the publication of a quarterly magazine, The People, the Land and the Book, which set a new literary standard for Jewish missionary journals.[39]

Interestingly, the third man involved in the conspiracy against Leopold Cohn was none other than Philip Spievacque. Why these three men would conspire against Leopold Cohn is open to conjecture and can only be speculated upon. However, recognizing the competition that exists even today among Christian organizations as they seek to carve out their specialized fields of endeavor, one can imagine what it must have been like during the formative days of independent Jewish missions.

How many of the other eight or so existing Jewish missions of that day were approached by Alexander Neuowich, with his plot to discredit the Cohns, is not known. However, it is to the credit of the missions established by Jacob Freshman, Rev. A.C. Gaebelein, et al., and to leaders of the denominational missions to the Jews that they did not believe the rumors that were circulated about Leopold Cohn and his mission.

As the scope of Leopold Cohn's work enlarged, as the readership of his magazine grew, and as he and Joseph purchased more and more property for the Mission, many of the smaller Jewish ministries felt threatened. Perhaps this was the case with Neuowich, Schapiro, and Spievacque.

Evidently, Schapiro and Spievacque felt so strongly about the Cohns that when Neuowich came to them with his plan to discredit Leopold Cohn, they went along with the scheme. Once entangled, they could not extricate themselves and sadly, because of their actions, the ministry begun by Benjamin Schapiro, and later directed by Philip Spievacque, soon fell into disrepute and eventually closed.

Satan is the great deceiver, and oftentimes those caught in his web of deception are unable to see the harm they are doing to themselves, to others, and to the program of God. So it was with these three men. Having determined among themselves to destroy the ministry of Leopold and Joseph Cohn, Neuowich, Spievacque, and Schapiro set their plans in motion and began to circulate their vicious rumors. As one tactic failed, they would devise and consummate a new plot.

Their ultimate scheme was to make Rabbi Leopold Cohn appear to be a "womanizer," an imposter, a swindler, and a murderer.

At first, they tried to discredit Leopold as a "womanizer" by accusing him of taking young girls to the farm in Connecticut for immoral purposes. In perpetrating this rumor, they sought to get women whom Leopold Cohn had met through the Jewish match-maker to come forward and give testimony of sexual advances which Rabbi Cohn had supposedly made toward them in his office. Leopold was incensed at this defamation of his character, and he promptly had his accusers arrested. As was his practice, Rabbi Cohn wanted friends of his ministry to be informed about such situations when they arose so he asked his lawyer, F.M. Sheffield, to write a statement for *The Chosen People* magazine. It said:

> On January 13, 1913, Mr. Leopold Cohn obtained from the Magistrate then sitting in the Essex Market Police Court, Manhattan, a warrant for the arrest of David Rose, Alexander H. Neuowich, Philip Spievacque, and Mr. Levin. This warrant was issued on the testimony of three witnesses and the affidavit of Mr. Cohn, which affidavit set forth that the four defendants had violated Section 580, of the Penal Law, which section applies to conspiracy. Neuowich and Spievacque were arrested, the others were not found. After several adjournments, examination of Spievacque and Neuowich was started on February 10th, and completed on the following day, the 11th. Several witnesses were examined on behalf of the prosecution and Spievacque and Neuowitch [sic] took the stand themselves. Although both denied any conspiracy, the Magistrate held both Spievacque and Neuowich under bail of $500 each, for trial in Special Sessions. The charge was that the four defendants named had conspired falsely to institute and maintain an action or actions against Mr. Cohn; that they had conspired to prevent Mr. Cohn from following his lawful calling as a missionary, and that they had conspired to obtain money from Mr. Cohn by methods which, if consummated, would be criminal. The testimony was that one Rose Steinberg had been approached by two of the defendants, who urged her to bring an action for breach of promise against Mr. Cohn, although she had no claim of that kind against him, but was engaged to marry another at that time. Another girl, Lena Dime, testified that she had been urged by all four of the defendants to bring an action for breach of promise against Mr. Cohn and that all four of the defendants had been at her house at one time to induce her to bring such an action; that the defendant Spiveaque [sic] had taken her to an attorney before whom she had signed papers. It was shown that the defendant Spiveaque [sic] was a stranger to the girl until he approached her with that proposition. It was shown that Neuowich called on Mr. Cohn, and offered to stifle all of several actions and charges which were to be brought and made against Mr. Cohn, if he, Mr. Cohn, would pay him, Neuowich, $200.00.
>
> Upon the defendants being held for Special Sessions, the District Attorney's Office drew up a new information, or complaint, upon which to sustain the charge in that court. The affidavit upon which the proceeding was based in the Magistrate's Court was superseded by his new information. When the case was called for trial on April 17th, one of the attorneys for the defendants made a motion to dismiss the information or complaint upon the ground that it did not state a crime under Section 580, of the Penal Law. After deliberation, the Court granted the motion because the information of complaint did not state that the defendants had conspired falsely to institute an action....the Court decided that it could not proceed where the information or complaint was inadequate;...No explanation was given as to why the variation between the original affidavit and the information drawn by the District's Attorney's Office existed. The judges in Special Sessions heard none of the facts in the case. They did not pass upon the truth or falsity of the charges as the Magistrate had done, but on the contrary, they were prevented from doing so by the failure of the information or complaint to set forth the proper charges.[40]

THE STRANGE STORY OF IZSAK JOSZOVICS

With their plot thwarted, Cohn's enemies then began spreading the rumor that Rabbi Leopold Cohn was not a rabbi at all, but was in reality a man named Izsak Joszovics, who had been a Saloon-keeper in Berezna, Hungary. The rumor went on to declare that this Izsak Joszovics had swindled an old couple out of their property, then committed murder, and fled from Hungary. According to the rumor, the Hungarian authorities were still looking for him. Their story purported that Rabbi Cohn was Izsak Joszovics, and that he had changed his name to Rabbi Leopold Cohn after coming to America. In an effort to make their new charges "stick," Leopold's enemies went so far as to write to officials in Hungary, obtaining forged documentation to support their claims, and they began to harass him at his farm.

Once again, Leopold took legal action against the men involved. He obtained a restraining order and, taking it one step further, sued them for trespassing and for defamation of character. This was just the reaction some of the hostile leaders in the Jewish community had been looking for. At last they had him! They would tie Leopold Cohn up in court, besmirch his reputation, deplete his funds, and put a final end to his ministry by causing the Christian Community to label him an imposter and a charlatan. Such tactics had worked in the past with other Jewish missionaries, and they were confident that they could now put an end to Cohn and to his mission. But Leopold Cohn's enemies had failed to reckon with the God who had called him to do a work among the Jews of New York. God had provided Rabbi Cohn with Christian friends, as well as with a financial power base; these provided support for Leopold during these attempts to discredit his person and his ministry.

As court cases went back and forth, and as rumors and innuendos spread, Mr. Pierson, then the editor of a paper called "The Missionary Review of the World," picked up some of the stories and rumors that were being circulated by the Jewish Community. Mr. Pierson's letters and editorials were brought to the attention of Dr. James M. Gray, then the President of the Moody Bible Institute of Chicago. Dr. Gray contacted Rabbi Cohn and told him that with such rumors and allegations being spread about himself and his mission, Dr. Gray would no longer be able to accept advertizing from the mission in Moody's publications.

A COMMITTEE SEARCHES FOR THE TRUTH

To this, Rabbi Cohn proposed that a committee be appointed to make a thorough investigation of the charges against himself and his mission work. He proposed further that Dr. Gray appoint a representative of his choice to the committee, and that Mr. Pierson (his accuser) should appoint a second member to the committee. These two committee members were to meet in New York and to then select a third committee member. Dr. Gray agreed. He appointed Mr. Edmund B. Buckalew, Secretary of the Extension Department of the Moody Bible Institute, to be his representative on the committee. Referring to this incident, Joseph Cohn later wrote:

> Mr. Buckalew started at once to see about having a committee formed. Mr. Pierson named Mr. Hugh R. Monro, formerly President of the Montclair National Bank, and a highly-respected leader in many commercial enterprises, as well as a much-sought-after counsellor in the upper echelons of the Presbyterian Boards....Mr. Buckalew and Dr. Monro met duly and they discussed whom they might select as third member of the committee. They thought that Dr. John F. Carson, at that time the Moderator of the General Assembly of the Presbyterian Church of America, and also pastor of the Central Presbyterian Church of Brooklyn, would be an excellent choice for a third member of the committee. Mr. Buckalew called on Dr. Carson to ask him if he would become the third member. Dr. Carson flatly refused, and said, 'I don't want to have a thing to do with those crooks!' [meaning the Cohns]. Mr. Buckalew came over to my father that night and told him what had happened. The next morning my father went to see Dr. Rhoades, his own pastor, of the Marcy Avenue Baptist Church, to tell him of the impasse. It so happened that Dr. Rhoades was a member of the same clergy club to which Dr. Carson belonged. He went to his telephone and called up Dr. Carson: 'John, I want you to go on that committee; I cannot go on because I am Mr. Cohn's Pastor, and they would claim that I was prejudiced. But I want you to go on.' Dr. Carson indignantly replied: 'I will do nothing of the kind. I want nothing to do with those crooks.' Dr. Rhoades came back with the appeal, 'John, if those men are crooks, I want you to expose them, and as soon as you find out that they actually are crooks, I will help you to expose them.' So Dr. Carson consented, a rather unwilling investigator, and fatefully prejudiced. He had been convinced beyond all contradiction that Leopold Cohn and his son were frauds.[41]

Prior to the first meeting of the Investigation Committee another member was added, a Mr. Roy M. Hart. He served as counsel to the committee. The committee began taking depositions in May 1916, and continued their work for nearly two months. A written transcript of all testimony given by the witnesses was kept, and the original transcript is still kept in the archival library of Chosen People Ministries, Inc. It is a typewritten manuscript of approximately 269 pages, consisting of questions asked and answers given, plus letters and evidential documents.

One of the primary tasks of this committee was to determine if, indeed, Leopold Cohn was who he claimed to be, or if he was, in reality, an imposter—the Mr. Izsak Joszovics. The witnesses against Leopold Cohn, primarily Mr. Spievacque and Mr. Schapiro, went to great lengths to produce supposedly "official" documents from Hungary to prove their claim. Leopold Cohn and Joseph Cohn, on behalf of the ministry, began their response to the charges by stating:

> The only points which concern us directly in these alleged documents, are...of a person called Izsak Joszovics, whom our enemies are attempting to identify as Mr. Leopold Cohn. We reply in general, however, as follows:
> 1st. What assurance is given to the Committee or to us that this document (the Hungarian Document which gave the description of Izsak Joszovics identified as Leopold Cohn by his accusers) is genuine? So far as we know the original document of which this claims to be a copy, has never been seen by anyone,...are we expected to take the simple statement of a man of the known unreliability of Mr. Spievacque that this is a real copy of a genuine document? We have a right to demand the original document which we do now demand.
> 2nd. Assuming...this copy is a genuine copy of an original document from the Hungarian Government:- What

proof is there as to the truth of the statements in the document? We are very intimately aware of gross corruption in Hungarian political and judicial circles, as are all persons who possess general knowledge of conditions in Austria-Hungary; the corruption there is so notorious that for a given sum of money it is possible to secure a genuine, official document that most any designated person has been a criminal in Austria-Hungary.

3rd. The description [of Izsak Joszovics] reads as follows:-

'Izsak Joszovics, thirty years old, Hebrew, has wife and children, Farmer, birth place Berezna, last residence Apsicza (County of Maramoros) speaks Hungarian, Russian, German and Hebrew, 169 centimeters tall, of wiry build, long face, brown complexion, hair, mustache, eyebrows, black, high forehead, eyes black, mouth regular, teeth defective, chin round, special mark of recognition a red spot under his left eye.'

...our enemies are claiming that this description exactly fits Mr. Leopold Cohn. The truth of the matter is as follows:- about 7 or 8 years ago Mr. Spievacque together with Mr. B.A.M. Schapiro took it into their heads to go up to the farm of Mr. Leopold Cohn near Bridgeport, Conn. for the purpose of annoying him, etc. Of course they were not allowed on the farm grounds themselves, but they sat around outside on the road making grimaces and shouting all kinds of offensive names so that Mr. Cohn's family was greatly annoyed and disturbed. No resistance being offered by Mr. Cohn's family, these two men grew bolder and made their way into the barn, whereupon one of Mr. Cohn's sons, Joshua Cohn, was compelled to draw a revolver on them and as Mr. Schapiro saw the gun he turned about and ran as fast as he could, crying in the meantime at the top of his lungs, 'Philip! Philip! he wants to shoot me!' This action on the part of Joshua Cohn resulted in the two leaving the place. However, while they were there during that entire day they had with them a little pad and whenever they would catch a glimpse of Mr. Leopold Cohn they would write down something on the pad of paper. Mr. Cohn was at a loss to understand what they were writing continuously, and it was about a year later that he discovered what they had been writing. It seems that they had hatched out the scheme of securing from Hungary some kind of a document proving Mr. Cohn a criminal and in order to do this they had to have a description of him which would be fairly accurate. Hence this sudden visit to the farm. But unfortunately for them, they made a ridiculous botchery in their description; in their eagerness to incriminate Mr. Cohn, they overreached themselves and proved too much. We call attention to several such blunders:

1st: ...great stress is laid in this alleged document, as to...'A red spot under his left eye';...the joke is this, when Spievacque and Schapiro saw Mr. Leopold Cohn at the farm,...they saw the red spot and naturally assumed it must have been a birth mark. Now that actual fact is that when Mr. Cohn came to America in 1892, he had absolutely no red spot under his eye.

The red spot under the eye came after Mr. Cohn had come to America the second time, in the year 1893, and had already begun missionary work among the Jews in Brownsville in the year 1894; on his way home from his mission one day a band of Jews, angered by his missionary activities attacked him and threw stones at him; one of the stones struck him under the eye and opened up the flesh. Mr. Cohn was confined to his bed for a number of days afterwards; he was visited at that time by his treasurer, H.O Avery, Esq., still living at 820 Quincy Street, Brooklyn, who will testify whenever the Committee says, to the fact that the red spot was not there in any way, manner, form, or suggestion, until this accident just mentioned, and after the wound had healed this red mark was left. Rev. T.J. Whitaker, Pastor of the Bushwick Avenue Baptist Church of Brooklyn will also testify to the same fact; he having known Mr. Cohn for the last 22 years, or almost since Mr. Cohn's return to America in 1893.[42]

Regarding the red mark under Leopold's eye, the Minutes of the Williamsburg Mission to the Jews, as well as Joseph Cohn's book, "I Have Fought A Good Fight," record the following incident which took place when Joseph Cohn was preaching at Calvary Baptist Church in Whittier, California:

...I was delivering a message one night in the Calvary Baptist Church in Whittier, California. At the close of the meeting, just before the collection was to be taken, a middle-aged brother got up and asked the pastor if he might say a few words. It appeared that he was a deacon in the church, and the pastor knew him. So he replied, 'Go right ahead, Brother Gordon.' This brother thereupon turned to the audience and began his story. As nearly as I can recall it, he said something like this:

'I enjoyed tremendously the story that Dr. Cohn told us tonight. He may not know that I have in my possession the autobiography of his father in a book entitled, "A Modern Missionary to an Ancient People." In that book one paragraph has always fascinated me. He tells there that one day he was on his way home from the Mission Hall in Brownsville, in Brooklyn. It was a snowy afternoon in late November, and he was walking briskly down Rockaway Avenue toward Fulton Street. A group of Jewish boys had begun to follow him, calling him names and throwing stones at him. One stone hit him on the cheekbone, and caused blood to flow quite freely. He tells that he went home and went

to bed and they called a doctor to take care of the wound. What fascinated me was that he ends that story with these words: "I am still praying for those boys that they may be brought to Christ."'

Then this deacon of the church turned once more around so that he could be seen by the whole audience, and called out, 'The boy whose stone cut the face of Leopold Cohn is standing before you tonight!'

…He then continued to tell how he went a few months longer to the Mission on Rockaway Avenue, and then his parents moved to California. But what he had learned at the Mission stayed with him, and finally he came out openly in a confession of faith in the Lord Jesus Christ, and now was a deacon in this church. I never forgot that incident.[43]

It should be noted, as well, that included in the testimony presented before the Committee was a signed statement by the doctor who treated Leopold Cohn, stating that the scar was the result of a wound which he (the doctor) had treated, and was not a birthmark.

In their rebuttal against the charges that Rabbi Leopold Cohn was, in reality, one Izsak Joszovics, Leopold and Joseph's prepared statement to the Committee continued:

We now come to another glaring discrepancy; the description says 'teeth defective,' 'chin round.' Both of these descriptions are untrue as regards Mr. Leopold Cohn; it is generally known among Mr. Cohn's friends that he has a very remarkable sound set of teeth, and the most casual glance will show that his teeth, by the greatest stretch of imagination, cannot be called defective; then as regards the chin being round, the joke here is that Mr. Cohn had never shaved in his whole life until within the past year; it is a very strict law among the orthodox Jews never to shave, and this law Mr. Cohn followed to the letter. Therefore when Mr. Spievacque and Mr. Schapiro made up their description, they just assumed that the chin must be round, because the beard looked as though the chin might be round. Now the Committee having seen Mr. Cohn themselves many times, with his beard shaved off can judge for themselves as to whether his chin is round; we think that the best description of Mr. Cohn's chin would be 'long and square.'

Finally, we have one more blunder to expose, and that is in the description "eyes black"; again our friends Mr. Schapiro and Mr. Spievacque have betrayed their sinister purpose;…they just assumed that because Rabbi Cohn's hair was black and his complexion dark, his eyes must be black; if the committee will look for themselves they will find that Mr. Cohn's eyes are what are known as Hazel color and not black, nor could anyone by the wildest stretch of imagination pass them as being black.[44]

The rebuttal to the Committee went on to say that the description given in the "Hungarian Document" would apply quite aptly to possibly 50,000 Jews in New York City, and went on to suggest that the committee should note that the description never referred to a beard, "although Mr. Cohn had a beard when he came to America as we will show by a picture submitted to your committee, published in the year 1895."[45]

As to why and how the document from Hungary was obtained, Leopold and Joseph Cohn's rebuttal statement to the Committee offered the following theory:

Mr. Spievacque and Mr. Schapiro, being both desirous of forcing Mr. Cohn to a position of subjection to them so that they could both keep on securing funds under their false pretence of their being Christian workers, tried on many occasions to compromise Mr. Cohn but each time without success. Finally it appears that a new plot occurred to them, which if carried out would completely accomplish their purpose; this plot was very simple; it consisted of simply sending to some lawyer in Austria-Hungary and offering him as much money as would accomplish the purpose, to secure for them a document bearing the official Hungarian seal to the effect that Mr. Cohn had been a criminal. This would be a very easy thing to do, and all that would be required was a fairly accurate description of Mr. Cohn. The only way to get this was to see Mr. Cohn personally. This was done by the trip which Mr. Schapiro and Mr. Spievacque made to the farm of Mr. Leopold Cohn…within 3 or 4 months of this visit to the farm by these two men, they had secured a document from Austria Hungary and began exploiting it wherever possible. We have never yet seen the original document, and about a year ago during the trial in the court of the Neuowich suit, Mr. Spievacque was in the witness chair and talked a good deal about the document; the curious fact is that while he claimed to have that document in his inside pocket, yet he refused to show it to the judge or to the jury.[46]

In verification of his claim to be Leopold Cohn and not Izsak Joszovics, and that he was, indeed a rabbi, Leopold submitted the following evidence to the committee:

1st. An original Municipal Certificate in the Hungarian language, from the Judge (mayor) and the Town Clerk of Berezna, Leopold's birth place. This was translated by Prof. Didovics, of Bloomfield Seminary. The certificate read: "The undersigned judge (mayor) of the township of Berezna hereby testifies that Leopold Kahan, who has left this town 25 years ago, and who at present lives in America, 47 years old, so long as he lived a Berezna, has shown a good moral and political conduct. Berezna, April 27, 1909."[47] The document was signed by the magistrates and witnessed and contained the official seal of the Hungarian government.

2nd. He submitted sworn affidavits by Max and David Kahan, of Detroit, Michigan, who stated that they were nephews of Mr. Cohn.[48]

3rd. He submitted a copy of the February 1904 Chosen People magazine that contained the testimony of Mr. Alexander Newitz, in which Newitz stated that he knew Mr. Cohn as a Rabbi, and that he was highly regarded in Hungary.[49]

4th. Rabbi Cohn entered a translation of an article from the Jewish Express Supplement, London, May 29, 1899 bearing the heading "Yet a Jew."[50]

5th. He submitted a copy of a "Scattered Nation," that contained a report of a visit to Mr. Cohn's mission by Mr. Landsman, associate of David Baron, who described an address given by Mr. Cohn indicating that he was a rabbi and that he had a thorough knowledge of the Hebrew, and great familiarity with Rabbinic literature.[51]

6th. He submitted a copy of the February 1916 issue of "A Friend of Israel" that contained an extract from an article in The Chosen People, by Leopold Cohn, with a footnote stating that he was formerly a Rabbi.[52]

7th. He submitted a March 1894 copy of Mission News, from Mr. Warszawiak, published by Miss Douglas, and containing the following note. "The February number of Hebrew Christians contains an excellent portrait of Mr. Cohn with a narrative of his conversion, written by himself, and any one who is not a subscriber to that periodical and wishes to have the February number, it may be obtained by application to Miss Douglas."[53]

8th. He submitted a copy of the October 1895 issue of The Chosen People magazine, "containing a reprint of the article of Mr. Warszawiak's paper, above referred to, together with Mr. Cohn's portrait."[54]

Some readers may ask, "Why didn't Rabbi Cohn simply submit his credentials, showing that he was a rabbi?" Unfortunately, he did not have them. Upon his arrival to America, according to protocol, Leopold had given his credentials to the Chief Rabbi, who was to then endeavor to find a synagogue for him. When Leopold became a believer, he did not think he would need the credentials any longer. When he finally did try to recover them, he found that the Chief Rabbi would not return the documents to him.

Evidently the Committee tried to obtain duplicate copies of the credentials, only to learn that no records had been kept on the names of rabbis who had been appointed to the small villages and towns in Hungary during the time when Rabbi Cohn claimed to have served. The Committee therefore did the next best thing; they sought out an expert on rabbinic and Talmudic studies—someone who was familiar with the historical setting of that day.

After extensive questioning of Leopold Cohn concerning his background, training, and the villages in which he had served as rabbi, the Committee sought out the assistance and the expertise of Dr. Edward A. Steiner, a Talmudic scholar, historian, and authority on the immigrants and conditions of Southern Europe. Mr. Buckalew of the Committee arranged for an interview between Dr. Steiner and Leopold Cohn, for the express purpose of determining if Leopold Cohn's background and knowledge of Talmud would qualify him to serve as a rabbi.

The following letter was entered into evidence for the Committee's consideration:

My dear Mr. Buckalew,
    At your request I had a conversation with Mr. Cohn. In the brief time I had at my disposal I found that Mr. Cohn possesses such knowledge of Rabbinical literature and law as to enable him to hold such a position as he claims he held. I do not find that he claims to have done the work of an appointed Rabbi; the semi-official position he held is in harmony with his attainments. Sincerely yours,
    (sd.) E.A. Steiner.[55]

Dr. Buckalew also asked Dr. E.A. Steiner whether it would have been possible for an individual to serve in the capacity of rabbi in Hungary, as Leopold Cohn claimed to have done, without having been officially appointed by the government. In his response to the Committee Dr. Steiner replied:

My dear Friend Buckalew,
    In answer to your question, whether a man could have been a Rabbi in Hungary twenty-five years ago without being recognized by the Government, I would say my impression is that in the smaller towns Rabbis held semi-official positions and were not recognized by the Government. In latter years the Government has grown very strict because the Rabbis make records of births and deaths, and I doubt that such a position can be held now. I think the change

occurred about twenty-five years ago.
Very sincerely yours,
E.A. Steiner[56]

The Committee accepted into evidence a number of letters verifying the character of Rabbi Cohn; among them was a letter from Dr. George H. Sandison, of the Christian Herald. He offered regrets that he was unable to attend the Committee's sessions and went on to state:

This movement against Leopold Cohn, the Hebrew Christian missionary worker of the Eastern district, is simply a continuation of similar crusades against successful Hebrew Christian missionaries, which have gone on at intervals during the last twenty or twenty-five years....The purpose is always the same; to drag down, discredit, and destroy the work of such missionaries when they attain any notable degree of success. It seems to be a settled policy that his should be done and I regret to say that I have seen it successfully done in a number of cases.

My own acquaintance with Leopold Cohn and his son has extended over a period of twelve or probably fifteen years. I have never visited the mission personally. My impressions of the Cohns have been favorable from the outset, and I resolved, as a matter of principle, to give them credit for honesty of purpose, sincerity of religious profession, and truthfulness of statement as to their work. I have at the present time found no reason to doubt them in regard to any matters that related to their work, nor to withdraw my confidence. At a time when they were peculiarly harassed by enemies, I made various suggestions which resulted in the mission becoming a corporate body with regular officers, and in other ways conducting its business in a satisfactory manner according to the laws governing religious corporations. My associates and I have made various suggestions which the mission managers accepted, and which were calculated to strengthen their position against attacks and to give assurance of public confidence in the methods of management.

With regard to the past of Mr. Cohn, I have no personal knowledge nor have I ever made it a matter of investigation, God in His wisdom has seen fit to use many kinds of instruments for His work, and to me it matters little what the past of a man has been, if he be truly regenerated and sincere now and living a correct Christian life. Some of the best mission managers in New York and elsewhere have had a clouded past, which God's grace had covered, while He made them notable workers in His Harvest fields.

I believe you told me that one of the chief witnesses against Mr. Cohn was a certain man now engaged in home missionary work in another city. I came in contact with the person referred to some twelve or fifteen years ago, possibly longer, (I have not the exact date at hand) under peculiar circumstances. He represented, to one of my associates of The Christian Herald, that he was the founder and head of a mission in New Jersey, and offered a photograph of the mission building, as he called it. An article on this subject appeared in the Christian Herald, and a few days after its publication, I was visited by Mr. Adolph Benjamin, an Orthodox Hebrew and an agent of the Hebrew Society for preventing proselyting work among Hebrew children. Mr. Benjamin offered to submit proof that the article was fraud and that there was no such mission. I accepted his offer of submitting proof, which he brought me within a week, in the shape of a letter signed by practically every business man in the place, stating that the photograph was not a mission but a public school, and that the entire story was absolute fiction. I took occasion to meet the original informant and, in the presence of witnesses told him in pretty strong terms what an outrageous thing he had done. From that day to this, I have not met him. It may be that he has become a better and more trustworthy man than he then was. In any event, I should want assurance of a change of heart before believing any evidence he had to offer on a matter of importance now.

I trust that your committee may be wisely guided in making this investigation, in order that full justice may be done to Mr. Cohn, who has suffered much, fought bravely, and borne himself, as far as my observation goes, always like a true Christian and good citizen. He has hidden nothing from me which I have ever asked, and has tried, I am sure, in every way to live up to the privileges and responsibilities of his position. Yours very sincerely, (sd.) Geo. H. Sandison.[57]

After listening to all of the witnesses, and after reviewing all of the testimony and evidence submitted, the Committee issued a unanimous decision exonerating Rabbi Cohn of all charges brought against him.

At a special meeting of the Board of Trustees held on June 27, 1916, at 2:30 P.M., Joseph Cohn was asked to bring a report of the Committee's investigation to date. The official Board Minutes record the following:

...The sessions of the Committee lasted nearly two months and their work was most through and exhaustive. A large amount and variety of evidence was examined and charges made by anyone were looked into. A lawyer consulted real estate records and a special accountant examined the books of the Mission. Testimonies of witnesses were taken stenographically so that full records may be preserved.

The Committee is now preparing a statement for publication, fully exonerating Mr. Cohn but until that is in permanent form, a preliminary notice is to be given out and published in the Brooklyn Daily Eagle.

Many pleasant letters had been received, approving the work of the Committee and rejoicing that the work and character of the Mission would be so fully established.[58]

The full report of the Committee was published in the November 1916 issue of *The Chosen People* Magazine entitled, "A REPORT OF SPECIAL IMPORTANCE TO EVERY READER." It read as follows:

Upwards of twenty years ago the Williamsburg Mission to the Jews was founded by Leopold Cohn, a Hebrew, who a short time previous had been converted to Christianity. The Mission has become widely known, has acquired a considerable property and enlists the interest and support of Christians in all parts of the country. For several years rumors reflecting on the conduct of the Mission and its superintendent, Mr. Cohn, have been in circulation and more recently circular letters and printed statements containing specific allegations as to irregularities and misconduct have been sent through the mails to friends of Jewish work.

At the suggestion of several Christian organizations and Christian workers, and on the initiative of Dr. James M. Gray, editor of the 'Christian Workers Magazine,' and Mr. Delavan L. Pierson, editor of the 'Missionary Review of the World,' steps were taken early in the present year to form an independent committee of investigation which would thoroughly examine the charges made against Mr. Cohn and inquire into every phase of the conduct of the missionary enterprise of which he is the recognized head. The committee as constituted consisted of Rev. John F. Carson, D.D., of Brooklyn; Mr. Hugh R. Monro, Vice-President of the Niagara Lithograph Co., of New York, and Mr. E.B. Buckalew, Secretary of the Extension Department of The Moody Bible Institute, Chicago. Mr. Roy M. Hart, attorney-at-law, served as counsel to the Committee.

Sessions of the committee extended over a period of nearly two months, during which a large number of witnesses were examined and much documentary and other evidence. The mission premises were visited, the equipment inspected, and careful inquiry made into all branches of the work through the employed workers, converts and others. Financial and accounting methods were examined by a leading firm of public accountants on behalf of the committee and investigation was made of real estate records, bank accounts, minutes and other evidence bearing on the conduct of the Mission and the relation of Leopold Cohn and his son, Joseph Cohn, thereto.

CLEARED OF ALL CHARGES

The charges laid before the committee may be grouped under three general heads: (1) Financial irregularities; (2) Inefficiency in the conduct of the work; (3) Charges affecting the personal character of Mr. Cohn. It was the original intention of the committee to limit its investigation to specific evidence on these points, but the inquiry was broadened to include a wide range of matters developed or suggested during the examination of witnesses....As the result of this extended inquiry, the committee presents the following conclusions:

(1) Mission finances: We find the charge that money subscribed for the work of the mission was devoted to other purposes, and that the financial methods are generally lax, is wholly without support....the committee is convinced that the expressed wishes of the donors are being carried out to the fullest extent. The expert accountant employed by the committee, rendered a favorable report on the accounting system of the Mission, and this opinion is sustained by a personal examination of the system by the members of the Committee.

(2) General Efficiency of the Work: The Committee finds that the charge of inefficiency is not sustained. The Headquarters of the Mission at 27 Throop Avenue is a large, well equipped building...The workers are an intelligent and earnest body, and we believe the measures employed are well calculated to lead those who attend the Mission into an intelligent faith and to build them up in the Christian life. A Hebrew Christian Church has been formed, made up largely of converts, who worship in the Mission Building with Mr. Cohn as pastor. The testimony of a number of these converts, together with that of several pastors and Christian workers of high standing, and who have had long and intimate knowledge of the work, tends to show that the labors of Mr. Cohn and his co-workers have been fruitful in a large measure.

(3) Character of Leopold Cohn: Charges reflecting on the personal character of Rev. Leopold Cohn the committee finds to be wholly unsustained. These charges, which are of the gravest nature and specific in character, called for the most searching inquiry. In addition to the direct examination of witnesses the Committee was able, through the assistance of a number of disinterested Christian workers, to follow up practically every clue which seemed to afford the slightest evidence as to these matters, and the result has been to prove conclusively that Mr. Cohn has been the victim of

persecution of the most outrageous and conscienceless sort. Many of the accusations in this respect have proved to be without a shred of foundation, while others were built up with shrewd cunning in an effort to attach a sinister significance to the most innocent circumstances. The Committee cannot express in too strong terms its condemnation of several men who joined in this shameless attempt to defame Mr. Cohn and destroy the influence of the Mission, the upbuilding of which has been his life's work. Other good men have doubtless been led unwittingly to give support to these baseless charges,…practically all of the evidence presented to this Committee tending to call in question the sincerity, integrity, and ability of Mr. Cohn, was evidently the influence of this small group of accusers, who for various reasons, had conceived a violent prejudice and become bitterly hostile to him and his work.

As a result of these weeks of painstaking inquiry the Committee has found no evidence which could be substantiated which affords a reasonable basis for any of the charges made by his accusers. On the other hand there has been abundant testimony by pastors, missionaries, and other Christian workers of the highest character, who have been in close association with Mr. Cohn and his work for periods of from five to twenty years, affirming in strongest terms his integrity and self-sacrificing devotion to the cause of Jewish evangelization. This testimony has been confirmed by correspondence, sworn statements and documentary evidence of such unimpeachable character as to produce in the minds of the Committee the conviction that Rev. Leopold Cohn is entitled to the confidence of the Christian public and that the Williamsburg Mission to the Jews is an effective Agency. Signed Hugh R. Monro, John F. Carson, E.B. Buckalew.[59]

"Behold, I have refined you, but not as silver; I have tested you in the furnace of affliction" (Isa. 48:10). Leopold Cohn and his ministry had been put through the refining fires, the fires of affliction. To the glory of God, both came out unscathed. God had called him to reach his people with the Gospel, and to the best of his ability Rabbi Cohn had tried to do that. A jury of his peers had combed through the most intimate details of his life and ministry. What they found was a humble rabbi, a Messianic believer, a true child of God, seeking to do the will of God.

ENDNOTES

Chapter 4. The Fires of Affliction

[1] Harold Kushner, *When Bad Things Happen to Good People*, (New York: Schocken Books, 1981).

[2] *The Chosen People*, Vol. 13, No. 6, (March, 1908), p 2.

[3] *The Chosen People*, Vol. 13, No. 8, (May, 1908), p 3.

[4] Testimony of Miss Ella T. Marston, *In the Matter of the Investigation of Charges Preferred Against Leopold Cohn* (Unpublished, 1916), p 175.

[5] *The Chosen People*, Vol. 8, No. 8, (May, 1903), p 2.

[6] *The Chosen People*, Vol. 10, No. 2, (November, 1904), p 8.

[7] Joseph Hoffman Cohn, *I Have Fought a Good Fight*, (New York, New York: American Board of Missions to the Jews, now Chosen People Ministries, Inc., 1953), p 100.

[8] See note above, pp 104-105.

[9] Testimony of Rabbi Leopold Cohn, *Investigation*, p 140.

[10] See Appendix A. Journal entries for the reports of the Brooklyn Baptist Church Extension Society and the Long Island Baptist Association from 1896 - 1912.

[11] Testimony of Dr. Rhoades, *Investigation*, pp 64-65.

[12] See note above, p 65.

[13] See note above, p 66.

[14] *Minutes of the Williamsburg Mission to the Jews*, September 30, 1911, pp 1-5.

[15] Testimony of Joseph H. Cohn, *Investigation*, p 149.

[16] See note above, pp 149-150.

[17] J. Cohn, *Fought A Good Fight*, pp 45-46.

[18] See note above, pp 66-67.

[19] Testimony of Joseph Cohn, *Investigation*, p 150.

[20] *The Chosen People*, Vol. 12, No. 2,(November, 1906), p 6.

[21] *The Chosen People*, Vol. 13, No. 2, (November, 1907), p 7.

[22] *The Chosen People*, Vol. 13, No. 6, (March, 1908), pp 1-2.

[23] See note above, p 7 [The equivalent of the 1902 dollar amounts of $1,861.27 in today's currency would be almost

$29,000.00. The reported income of $36,058.04 in 1908 would be almost $540,000 in 1992 U.S. dollars].

24 *The Chosen People*, Vol. 14, No. 2, (November, 1908), p 1.

25 *The Chosen People*, Vol. 14, No. 4, (January, 1909), p 1.

26 *The Chosen People*, Vol. 15, No. 1, (October, 1909), pp 3-4.

27 *The Chosen People*, Vol. 14, No. 3, (December, 1908), p 2.

28 *The Chosen People*, Vol. 17, No. 1, (October, 1911), p 3.

29 *The Chosen People*, Vol. 18, No. 3, (December, 1912), p 3.

30 Bernhard Angel, *Mistakes*, (The Hebrew Christian, July 1896), p 4.

31 *The Chosen People*, Vol. 10, No. 4, (January, 1905), p 5; compare with *The Chosen People*, Vol. 12, No. 5, (October, 1907), p 6.

32 *The Chosen People*, Vol. 9, No. 5, (February, 1904), p 3.

33 See note above, p 4.

34 Testimony of Mr. Neuowich, *Investigation*, p 92.

35 See note above, (insert) pp 121-123.

36 Rev. A. Bernstein, *Some Jewish Witnesses For Christ*, (London: Operative Jewish Converts' Institution, Palestine House, 1909), p 451.

37 See note above.

38 See note above, pp 455-456.

39 A. E. Thompson, *A Century of Jewish Missions*, (Chicago, IL: Fleming H. Revell Co., 1902), p 244.

40 *The Chosen People*, Vol. 18, No. 8, (May, 1913), pp 9-10.

41 J. Cohn, *Fought a Good Fight*, pp 212-213.

42 Testimony of Joseph Cohn, *Investigation*, pp 1-4.

43 J. Cohn, *Fought a Good Fight*, pp 220-221.

44 Testimony of Joseph Cohn, *Investigation*, pp 4-5.

45 See note above, p 5.

46 See note above, pp 6-7.

47 See note above, p 110.

48 See note above, pp 111-112. [See Appendix B, Sworn affidavits of Max Kahan and David Kahan].

49 See note above, p 124.

50 See note above.

51 See note above.

52 See note above.

53 See note above, pp 124-125.

54 See note above, p 125.

55 See note above, p 180.

56 See note above, p 179.

57 See note above, pp 181-182.

58 *Minutes of Williamsburg Mission*, June 27, 1916, p 31.

59 *The Chosen People*, Vol. 22, No. 2, (November, 1916), pp 5-6.

5

THE WINDS OF CHANGE

"Adversity is the diamond dust Heaven polishes its jewels with,"[1] said Robert Leighton. Throughout the years of being "polished" by opposition, adversity, and then by the hardship of the investigation into his personal life and the work of the mission by the Committee, Leopold Cohn remained firm in his faith, and steadfast to the course God had set before him. As the heat of the furnace hardens clay, the fires of affliction produced in Rabbi Cohn strong, tensile faith. God faithfully kept His servant, and when the fires of affliction subsided He blessed the ministry with steady growth and outreach as well as increased staff. But increased growth also brought the inevitable—change.

The winds of change swept across the mission in the way the great prairie winds swept across the land. Some changes were welcomed, like a refreshing breeze. Other changes came unexpectedly, sweeping in with the force of a hurricane or tornado. But whether they blew in as a whirlwind, or as a gentle breeze, God was in both, shaping the ministry and guiding the leaders as they held fast to the course of reaching all Jews everywhere with the Gospel.

Change is often difficult, but for Rabbi Cohn it was especially trying as he saw his vision of a Messianic church and a Messianic community changing into an organization. He had experienced some of the problems which accompany rapid growth during the "infancy years" of his mission, and he had learned from his mistake of not incorporating the Williamsburg Mission sooner, but now he began to struggle with the tug-of-war of doing "ministry" and heading an "organization." Leopold Cohn was a rabbi, a teacher. He wanted to help his suffering Jewish brethren. Most of all, he wanted to minister to them the life-changing Good News, the Gospel of the Lord Yeshua. Without question, he had come to realize that he could not do this without proper organization, but forming an organization ultimately meant setting up a Board of Directors, hiring staff, and staying abreast of all the laws governing not-for-profit corporations—including existing laws and the multitude of ever-changing and developing laws. Being the head of an "organization" meant becoming an administrator, a task far removed from preaching, teaching, and helping which Rabbi Cohn yearned to do.

SOME EARLY WORKERS

The birth of the mission had come to pass because of Leopold's deep burden for his own people. His co-workers in those early days were his own family members who, in spite of persecution and trials, remained faithful in the ministry through the years. Esther, Leopold's daughter, continued to work in the ministry until her marriage. She worked with the girls and women. Benjamin and Joshua helped in the boys' classes (Benjamin later became the secretary to Judge Dykes). Joseph eventually succeeded his father as head of the mission; it was Joseph who built the mission into a world-wide outreach.

Leopold enjoyed the early days of the mission when he had a free hand. He went wherever God led him; he went wherever there was an open door. As the ministry grew, and as he needed additional help, he hired workers who shared his vision—Jewish believers or Gentile believers. Some were volunteers, some were paid. He hired Mr. B.M. Gordon, his first Assistant Missionary, Mr. George C. Salter, and Miss Ella Marston, who worked with Esther Cohn teaching the girls and women. Ella later served as Secretary to the Board of Directors of the Williamsburg Mission to the Jews.

MISS SUSSDORFF AND MISS BIGELOW

In the early days of the ministry, Rabbi Cohn was invited by Pastor Dr. Ditmas, to speak to the young people's group at Hope Baptist Church in New York. During that service Leopold challenged the young people to come and sing at his Mission. He challenged them to consider working in Jewish missions. At that time the Mission was located on Manhattan Avenue and Varst Street in Brooklyn. Two young girls, Miss Augusta Sussdorff and Miss Bigelow, accepted Rabbi Cohn's challenge and they came to sing. Both young women were impressed with what they saw, and they continued to come on Friday and Saturday evenings to sing. Although they were not Jewish, they also began to participate in the social meetings that were held at the mission and their presence began to attract other girls and women. This was a major turning point because, as indicated earlier, the audience in the early days of ministry was composed mainly of men. Jewish girls and women did not study the Torah.

Rabbi Cohn had a great desire to see women coming to the mission so that they, too, could study and know the Scriptures. His advertisements for women workers had not produced one woman who was qualified and willing to help in this area, but as the months went by, Augusta Sussdorff and Miss Bigelow began to express interest in serving in the ministry in some way. Leopold and his daughter, Esther, knew the desire of the young women was genuine so they began to groom Miss Sussdorff, as well as Miss Bigelow, for missionary work. Records of the work during those days indicate that these two young women began attending mission services and serving as volunteers around 1904, and joined the mission as paid workers sometime in 1912-1913.

In her testimony before the Committee,[2] Miss Sussdorff stated that part of their requirement as staff workers was that they hold four meetings a week for Jewish girls and women; they were permitted to hold more, depending upon the need. Miss Sussdorff conducted Mothers' Meetings, a Sewing School, a Saturday morning Bible class, and a Sunday afternoon class. She also attended a Thursday class conducted by Miss Marston. Altogether, she attended about eight classes a week. Attendance at these classes ran between twenty-five and thirty women. In addition to the classes she held or attended, Miss Sussdorff also visited in homes, distributed clothing to those in need, and assisted in finding jobs for Jewish immigrants who could speak English. Additionally, she assisted individuals with financial need in obtaining aid through the Poor Fund of the Mission.[3]

Her duties did not end here, however. Miss Sussdorff further elaborated on her work at the Mission by stating that on Tuesdays, Thursdays, and Saturdays she assisted in the Dispensary which was open from one o'clock until four o'clock in the afternoon. During that time she would assist between fifteen and fifty patients. Her main responsibility at the Dispensary was to get the patient information for the doctors, but she had opportunity to witness to the patients as well.[4]

Miss Sussdorff was typical of the early missionary workers that Rabbi Cohn recruited and trained for his mission. He did not require that they be Jewish, but he did require that if they were not Jewish, they be acculturated. Gentile believers working on the Mission staff had to learn Yiddish, as well as the customs and traditions of Orthodox Jews.

PHILIP ENGLANDER

Another faithful worker of the early days of the Mission was Mr. Philip Englander, a Jewish believer who began his service with the Mission as a part-time worker around 1907-1908. Rabbi Cohn put Mr. Englander in charge of the weekly Bible meetings at the Brooklyn mission. He also helped in the Dispensary. In addition, he was responsible for "...pastoral visitation, looking after the spiritual and physical needs of our scattered congregation, counselling those in fear of persecution or in need of employment, and assisting in publishing and distributing *The Shepherd of Israel*"[5] (a Yiddish Gospel newsletter).

Philip Englander had another talent that made him a valuable worker. He was a musician and a writer of Jewish hymns. Leopold Cohn wrote of him:

> One interesting feature of his service here is his ability to sing Jewish hymns, the words of which he writes himself. We have printed a little booklet containing over a dozen of his songs and these are distributed through our audience, many gladly joining in as Mr. Englander sings. His little daughter plays the Jewish music for him and in some hymns sings the chorus. In one such piece which our assistant wrote, on the Second Coming of the Lord Jesus, the chorus sung by the little girl asks the question, 'Oh, who will that be?' and the answer comes from Mr. Englander, 'The Lord Jesus the Messiah'; then she asks again, 'Oh when will that be?' and the answer comes, 'Very soon in our days.' The little daughter again questions, 'And what will happen when He comes?' and the reply enumerates a lot of good things which will take place at Christ's Coming. Then the girl utters a closing cry which both the words and suitable tune fittingly express, as if from a panting and thirsty soul, 'Oh, let Him come right away.' Mr. Englander has also written a hymn on the Trinity which our audience enjoys singing very much and in this, too, his daughter participates for she sings the chorus which is John 3:16, in Jewish words in rhyme.
>
> During these past years we have been able, because of lack of means, to engage Mr. Englander for only a part of his time. But we now very much need his entire time that we may open up new avenues of work and that he may be able to more thoroughly aid me in carrying the Gospel to our brethren. So I want to place this matter, under God before you, for your consideration. Six hundred dollars more yearly, will be needed to increase his salary to an amount sufficient to

pay for his entire time and if six friends would contribute $100 each, or twelve, $50 each, the end would be accomplished. Who will be one of six, or one of twelve or one to assume this helpful responsibility?[6]

The funds came in, and Mr. Englander was hired as a full-time missionary. Although he was not the first full-time missionary Rabbi Cohn had hired, he had the distinction of being the first Messianic song-writer on staff, producing hymns for the Messianic congregation established by Rabbi Cohn.

In an article that appeared in *The Chosen People* magazine, Mr. Englander spoke about how God had blessed him and used him, even though he was exhausted from a very heavy schedule. He said:

Every Wednesday evening, a meeting is held at 626 Broadway, and until recently this has been especially used for asking and answering questions. At such time the Mission-Hall is filled with young, intelligent Jewish people who come to ask questions concerning Prophecy and Christianity, and to listen to the answers given under the guidance of the Holy Spirit.

But for the last few weeks these meetings have been turned into Bible conversations, taking a chapter and explaining it verse by verse, while at the close of each verse, questions may be asked upon it. The result has been that the evening is not spent on questions only but also in reading the Word of God and the questions themselves have been much more profitable as they must be related to the subject of the chapter.

The interest is so great that we can never close at the appointed time, for all want to stay, no matter how late, to learn the precious truth of our Lord Jesus.

One day recently on coming home from my daily business, I was astonished to find in my home, a regular meeting of six new Jewish faces, four men and two ladies. Being afraid to call at the Mission, on account of their parents, they were advised to call on me at home. Oh, what a glorious conversation! No matter how tired I come home I gladly pointed them to the Lord Jesus as the true Messiah.

It is only a short time since the Lord most wonderfully answered one of my prayers. One of my uncles (President of a great Orthodox synagogue) who has always been very bitter and my greatest enemy, since the confession of my faith in Christ, was taken seriously ill and sent for me. When I entered his room, I found him at his morning prayer, saying, 'O lord, let a new Light shine from Zion, that we all may enjoy His light.' O what a precious prayer.

I...had often told him of the Great Light which had shone for 1900 years and yet is always new. Now, at last, I had the joy of seeing my uncle rejoicing in that Light and praising God for His goodness. If he recovers what a blessing he will be to my great and Orthodox family. Yes indeed, the Lord answers prayer.[7]

HARRY BURGEN

At one special meeting of the Board, Leopold reported that he had hired a new part-time student missionary. He said, "Harry Burgan [sic], a young Hebrew Christian whom we have been educating in the Practical Bible School for a couple of years, is to work for the Mission this summer and was engaged at a salary of $50.00 a month."[8] Harry Burgen eventually became a full-time worker and served with the Mission for over fifty years.

There were many others who assisted Leopold Cohn in those early days of ministry, some whose names and deeds, will be listed upon the journals of Heaven along with other "heroes of the faith." Only eternity will be able to measure the selfless dedication of the early workers who labored side-by-side with Rabbi Cohn, enduring great persecution and the scorn and hatred of family and friends in order to bring the Gospel to the Jews.

JOSEPH HOFFMAN COHN

From the ranks of dedicated workers during those early days of ministry, one individual became a leader of great influence and prominence. That worker was Leopold Cohn's son, Joseph Hoffman Cohn. Joseph shared his father's vision but, being a very strong personality himself, he was not content to simply share the vision. He took his father's vision and, to use a colloquialism, "ran with it." He enlarged upon the vision of his father and, in a very real sense, changed the course of the Mission by doing so. Understandably, this resulted in friction between father and son. No organization can have two heads. No organization can have two leaders setting the vision.

Joseph was involved in the ministry from the very beginning. He was only eight years old when his father began the work in Brooklyn. Even at that early age he felt the call of God upon his life and he would follow his father to the mission, attend the Bible classes, distribute copies of *The Chosen People* magazine, tracts, and *The Shepherd of Israel*. At the age of twelve he began writing for the magazine, and by the time he was sixteen he was conducting a Boys' Club for the mission. In one issue of *The Chosen People* magazine Joseph wrote:

I had not been attending the meetings in the Manhattan Avenue Mission this fall very long before I noticed that a meeting for boys specially, would not be out of place; for there were a number of boys who regularly attended the meetings for adults; and, as the Jews do not like young people to be mingled with older ones, and, also, as the boys would not very well appreciate the sermons intended for the men, it was decided to have meetings for boys. I felt that the Lord wished me to have a part in His work, and that this was the part he wished me to take. I told my friends, the Doctors Muncie of my plan, and they and their family became much interested in this work. Many thanks are due to these dear friends for the deep interest manifested by them. Curtis, their son, of nearly my own age, immediately wanted to help and so we planned about the meetings. We decided to hold two meetings a week, one on Sunday afternoon at 3 o'clock, which was to be carried on like a Sunday School, and another on Monday night when the boys could enjoy themselves by playing games and reading books. We secured some magazines from several friends; and Mrs. Barnes gave us a few games. I did not like to ask my father for money to buy these things, for I knew that the other departments of the work needed the money more than this, so we contented ourselves with what we had.

At the first meeting (which was on a Sunday), there were present some fourteen boys. The number surprised me for I did not expect nor did I wish more than six or seven boys at the first few meetings, because I was afraid that we could not manage them; but these fourteen behaved very well, and listened attentively to Mr. Sibli, a friend of Dr. Muncie's, whom I asked to speak.

So we went on,…The attendance varies and numbers anywhere from six to fifteen boys.

On Monday, December 23, through the kindness of Miss Hilton, Miss Hudson, Miss Raye, and Dr. Wiggins, we were enabled to give the boys an excellent entertainment. These friends recited and sang for us. We had about fifty boys present, for we allowed each regular attendant to bring his friends with him that night. Through this entertainment, we secured a number of new regular attendants.

Now, dear friends of Israel, we wish to ask your help in several matters. First we want you to pray that these meetings may be factors of great good to the boys and that they may, in time, accept Christ as their Savior (They are all Jewish boys). Second we would be glad to receive from any one interested, books, reading matter suited for the boys who are from fourteen to eighteen years of age, and interesting games. We should like to start a circulating library, if we had the means. And last, but not least, we would ask the readers to pray the Lord to put it into the heart of some Christian lady or gentleman to come down on Sunday afternoons and sing for us, for at present, we have no music,…We have an organ for anyone to play if he or she should feel it in her heart to come. It is a glorious work and may be productive of much good, for the boys' addresses are taken and their parents are then visited.[9]

In another article Joseph related how he helped his father distribute Bibles, tracts, and literature to the Jewish people of Brooklyn. He wrote:

…In those days the New Testament in Yiddish was unknown, but one day came a sensation in the form of the first translation in history of the New Testament in Yiddish. Someone in London, where the translation had been made, sent to my father a box containing 500 of these New Testaments, the first ones off the press.

In those days our Mission hall was a corner store on what is now known as Manhattan Avenue. This hall was jammed every meeting night, literally packed to the doors.

…at the close of such meeting[s]…I as a youngster of perhaps fourteen, would stand up on a chair in the middle of the room, and for a matter of fifteen minutes would peddle out these New Testaments in Yiddish at one cent a copy. The theory was that if a Jew should be obliged to pay one cent for the book, that would be some assurance that he would not throw it away when he got out into the street….And so each night I had a hundred New Testaments given to me, and it did not take long to dispose of the entire hundred, so eager were the Jews for those copies. As I stood up on the chair, I would shout, 'A penny a book! A penny a book!' And they all swarmed around me, and snatched the books out of my hand.[10]

On Friday afternoons Joseph was assigned the job of going through the streets of Williamsburg in Brooklyn, distributing circulars in Yiddish. These circulars announced the services that were being held at the Mission. Although Friday was a school day, Joseph would only attend classes in the mornings. He would then go home for lunch, and rather than go back to school, he would proceed to the Mission to pick up the circulars which were ready for distribution. The school soon noticed his absences and reported this to his father, Leopold Cohn. According to Joseph, the Principal of the school was willing to make some concessions, but Joseph felt he'd had enough of high-school, so he dropped out. He would have remained a high school drop-out had it not been for the concern and intervention of Miss Frances J. Huntley who insisted that he should finish his education, and paid his way to return to school.

With Miss Huntley's financial assistance and encouragement, Joseph went on to study at Moody Bible Institute. It was while he was at Moody that his father resigned from the American Baptist Home Mission Society (see Chapter Four). Joseph understood the impact this would have upon the mission. He remembered the financial struggles of those early years of ministry, and he felt it incumbent that he return home to assist his father. But he did not abandon his studies altogether; he attended Adelphi Academy and college while assisting his father in the ministry. It was during this period that Joseph also began to develop his innate business, investment, and communication skills.

Rabbi Leopold Cohn was a visionary, a scholar, and a missionary. While Joseph shared his father's vision, he also had a keen sense of organization, of promotion, and of business. In this way he was the exact opposite of his father. He wrote of these contrasting characteristics, stating:

> ...I have to smile further when they accuse my father of having been a shrewd scheming exploiter. The truth is that he never had one executive hair in his head. He knew nothing about business management; he knew nothing about the schemings they accuse him of. His was a very simple mind, and a simple soul, whose one driving force was that he must reach the Jews with the Gospel. I remember that as work was developing I began to beg him to buy a typewriter. The very idea seemed to appall him, and I remember he replied, 'A typewriter, are you crazy?' I told him that I was not crazy, but that the time would come when we would need six typewriters! He then thought that I was a dreamer of impossible dreams.[11]

Joseph Cohn added further:

> It was the hardest job to get him out from the bondage of his devotion and attachment to the Mission, just for a few days, to come with me and to speak in certain conferences which I had previously arranged. He just would not give up his meetings at the Mission. The Jews had a profound respect for him. They recognized his powers as an expounder of the Word of God. He spoke with authority and they knew that as a rabbi in the old country, he had even in his early youth made his mark among the Jewish leaders of his community. Many of the older rabbis had predicted for him a brilliant future and were deeply shocked when the news came that he had become a follower of the Lord Jesus Christ.
>
> When I finally would get him to come with me to speak at some meetings, the first thing we would do, once he was settled in his room at the hotel, would be to have me lay out on his bureau the time-table showing what train he would get, and on what day, that would take him back to New York! It was this devotion and faithfulness to his Jewish audience in New York that made him so beloved to the people of Israel to whom he was ministering.[12]

The founder of the Mission was Rabbi Leopold Cohn, the persecuted rabbi from Hungary who had found his Messiah—the visionary whose sole desire was to see Jewish people reached with the Gospel, and whose heart longed to see a congregation of Messianic Jews established in New York. But it was Leopold's son, Joseph Hoffman Cohn, who envisioned the world-wide ministry, and who saw how this could be accomplished. It was Joseph Hoffman Cohn's expanded vision for the ministry, his drive, that was responsible for building the support base of the growing ministry.

Joseph's endeavors to expand the mission into a world-wide ministry and to build the support base of the mission created tension between father and son. His drive, and the resulting changes within the Mission, generated increased problems for the Mission as well as additional personal problems for Leopold. Many Christians could not understand why the Cohns needed to build such large reserve funds, or why they felt it necessary to secure their Mission work by owning property, stocks, bonds, etc. Other faith missions of that day did not seek to build reserve funds or to own property. Funds raised for other faith missions went in their entirety toward the support of their missionaries and to their branch ministries. More than a few Christians questioned why the Cohns did not handle their income in like manner.

Such questions may even be asked by believers in our day, and the author urges readers to endeavor to understand by developing an awareness of the world in that day from a Jewish perspective.

Leopold and Joseph Cohn ministered among the poor immigrant Jews of New York. As members of the Jewish immigrant population of that day themselves, and as a part of a hated minority group, they had either heard about, or had witnessed first hand, what was being done to the Jewish people in the name of Christianity. Daily, they experienced the expressions and attitudes of anti-Semitism. Additionally, they knew that because of their faith in the Messiah, Yeshua, they could never ask for help, or expect to receive help, from the Jewish community without renouncing their faith—something they would never do. As believers, they understood the New Testament. They understood the prophecies regarding the future persecution of Israel and the Jewish people. They understood the teaching of God's Word that there would come a day when the entire world would turn against the Jews, something they'd had a small taste of from the churches of Europe. They firmly believed that without a reserve fund the Mission would never be able to carry on it's witness to the Jewish people, should the hard times come. Leopold and Joseph Cohn were also very much aware of the fact that the majority of Christians, and Christian churches, were not interested in reaching Jewish people with the Gospel. They therefore believed it was incumbent upon them as leaders of the Mission, in order to fulfill the vision God had given to them, to build up reserve funds sufficient to carry on the ministry until the Lord returned, or until all Jews everywhere had been reached with the Gospel.

Thus, the baton for raising funds to support his expanded vision for the ministry fell to Joseph Hoffman Cohn, and he was both willing and able to pick up the baton and to run with it. God had given him the innate abilities and had prepared him well for the task.

While still a student at Moody Bible Institute, Joseph exhibited his ability to raise funds for the ministry when he took speaking engagements in nearby churches. His approach was very simple: teach the Word of God, impress upon the audience the need to reach Jewish people with the Gospel, share how this was already being done through the Mission, and give people an opportunity to financially support the ministry through a free-will offering or through a pledge for future financial support. Finally, and perhaps most importantly, get the names and addresses of people in attendance so issues of *The Chosen People* magazine could be sent to them. Both Leopold and Joseph Cohn firmly believed that by receiving *The Chosen People* magazine, Christians would be: (1) educated to the need for reaching Jewish people with the Gospel, (2) kept informed of what the Mission was doing, and (3) challenged to become a part of the on-going work. Joseph also believed that such supporters would form a world-wide prayer link that would continue to sustain the ministry before the Lord in prayer.

After Leopold's resignation from the American Baptist Home Mission Society and Joseph's return to New York from Moody Bible Institute, Joseph began to assume the role of director and leader of the Mission. By January 1910, *The Chosen People* magazine mast-head carried the words: "*The Williamsburg Mission to the Jews*, under the direction of Leopold Cohn, and his son, Joseph Cohn." Prior to this, only the name of Leopold Cohn had appeared as "Director." Inasmuch as the Mission had not yet been officially incorporated, there are no minutes to verify exactly when, and why, this change was made. Perhaps it was partly due to the legal struggles ensnaring Leopold Cohn at that time, as well as to their co-ownership of the property Miss Huntley had given to Leopold and Joseph Cohn. Whatever the reasons, Joseph soon assumed the leadership role, while his father remained a figure-head leader.

THE BROOKLYN BUILDING ENLARGED

The Scriptures say, "Where there is no vision, the people perish" (Proverbs 29:18). Like his father, Joseph understood that people support "vision." They do not give to a finished work, but to an on-going work, a growing work, an expanding vision. Only two years after the new building in Brooklyn was completed, the November 1911 issue of *The Chosen People* magazine carried an article entitled, "The Opportunity of a Century." While Joseph's name is not listed as the writer of this article, the style and content are in keeping with Joseph's style of writing more than with Leopold's. The article stated:

> To somebody, somewhere, a wonderful opportunity presents itself. We think it so great that we have called it, the opportunity of the century; to that individual, or that group of individuals who may eventually respond to the cry, it will be the opportunity of a lifetime. It is this: to erect, equip and endow, the first really complete Jewish missionary plant on this continent. Such a task must bring the unmistakable blessing of the Lord Jesus Himself, as well as eternal gratitude in the hearts and lives of those whom such a foundation will reach and continue to reach, throughout the years to come, and until He himself shall return to earth.
>
> We have a building; it is the only building of its kind in America, it is even the largest of its kind in America; but if the truth must be told, it is far too small for our needs, and far too inadequate to cope with the strategic situation in which New York finds itself at present. When we first talked about putting up this building, the plans were for a plant three or four times the size of what we now have, but the proposal seemed so tremendous that even we ourselves were somewhat timid, and it was decided to buy ground sufficient for the large building, but only erect upon it a small part of the original plans. Even then our friends said we were building too largely, and the mission would not be filled, and it would simply be a burden on our hands. From the first day that the building was opened, God showed His approval by sending to us, and continuing to send until this day, crowds of Jews, men, women, and children, so that from that day the building has proved far too small for what the Lord would have us accomplish. We dare not carry on an active propaganda among the Jews because our hall is too small to accommodate those that come even now, without active efforts. We believe that we could very readily secure weekly audiences of at least 1,000 Jews if we had the auditorium in which to put them. Our medical work is woefully handicapped, and although the total number of patients treated last year was approximately 15,000, yet this could be increased to at least 50,000. The school for the children could be

enlarged, to double and treble what it is now, if we had the space, and the workers that would be required to handle a situation of this kind. Then, there ought to be new work undertaken, such as night school, trade classes for Jews, and industrial work for the Jewish men who are thrown out of work by reason of their belief in Christ; lack of this industrial work is at present the greatest hindrance to the acceptance of Christ by vast multitudes of Jews. If a Jew accepts Christ, his own Jewish friends and neighbors have no more to do with him, and a welcome among the Gentiles is practically unknown; so where shall the poor man turn? We believe that he has a right to ask of Christianity, at least an opportunity to earn his own living. The field here in Greater New York is tremendous. Just think for a moment; a million and a quarter of Jews almost within a stone's throw of the Mission building, and we are practically powerless to reach them as they should be reached. Is this not a reflection on the church of Christ, and are there not some true Christians who will see the wonderful vision, and make this the really one achievement of their whole lifetime?

To accomplish our purpose, we need at least $250,000; of this sum, we want $50,000 for the erection of the building itself, and $200,000 for a permanent endowment. The need is great and we are convinced from the nature of God's working in our midst that it is His will that this need shall be supplied. We have not the least idea where this money is to come from; we do know, however, that this is the Lord's work; He has, by many unmistakable signs set upon it the seal of His ownership; and being His work, He will provide for it through His stewards to whom He will whisper that His is the silver and the gold. In 1904 we were led in this same way to lay before our friends the need of a building. We did not know at that time how, or in what way, the Lord was going to supply that building, but we stated in The Chosen People that the building was needed, and kept on praying to God until it came. It took five years of prayer and patient waiting, for it was not until 1909 that this building was finished and dedicated. We ask all to join us in earnest prayers to God for this crying need.

We shall be glad to hear from our friends concerning this matter, and to record any pledges that you may be led to make. To any Christian steward, we again say that this is an opportunity to do the will of God, the like of which has not been presented to you in your lifetime. You will equip and endow a perpetual testimony to the Jews that shall combine a mission, a church, a school, and industry, and a university for training workers among Jews.

One thing more; please do not let this conflict with the regular needs of the work. We are maintaining the mission at a constant and increasingly heavy expense, and this must of course be supported as usual. Gifts for the enlarged Building must be in the nature of extra contributions.[13]

Although $250,000 does not seem such a large request in today's world, calculating the equivalent in today's dollars brings the realization that Joseph was asking for a little more than 3.7 million dollars, and he was asking for the bulk of it, $200,000 (three million in today's dollars) to be set aside as an endowment fund. It is little wonder that the Cohns encountered problems with their Christian brothers and sisters!

Once the Williamsburg Mission was officially incorporated, and regular Board Meetings were being held, the work began to advance at a rapid pace. Joseph carried three titles: he was Treasurer of the Corporation; Field Secretary; and Office Manager, instituting the day-to-day operations and policies for the staff, as well as overseeing the handling of the mail and the finances.

As Field Secretary, Joseph traveled extensively on behalf of the Mission, raising funds and enlisting new donors and subscribers to *The Chosen People* magazine. In this capacity he would often travel 15,000 to 20,000 miles a year. As he traveled, he not only raised funds and developed new donors, but he was always on the look out for new areas in which the ministry could develop. In one of Joseph's reports to the Board, the secretary recorded the following:

Mr. Joseph Cohn then gave a report of his work as Field Secretary during the winter months when he visited the Pacific Coast and spoke in the principal cities. He reported the results to be encouraging, about $5,000 exclusive of expenses to have been raised. A number of invitations were extended to him for next winter and many individual friends for the work were made. At a number of points, Jewish missions could be established if we would oversee them. He hoped to continue this work.[14]

At the Second Annual Meeting of the Corporation in January 1913, Joseph Cohn gave the audited financial report that showed the annual income at $18,036.11, and expenses at $15,095.71. He then told of his field work and travels. The Minutes continue, stating:

The President [Leopold Cohn] reported crowded meetings on Friday and Sunday nights at Beth Sar Shalom. Persons are being turned away for lack of room and there is continued need for an enlarged building. There have been many encouraging testimonies at the Convert's meetings on Monday evenings. The opposition by the Jews have for the last two months been very severe in all directions but the possibilities on all sides are great.

The medical work continues unabated and the Dispensary is so crowded that the State Board of Charities recommends that we have larger quarters.[15]

It was at this meeting, as well, that the members voted to expand their Board to include the following new members: Mr. R.H. Richards, Mrs. A.L. Ogden, and Miss C.E. Masters. At an earlier meeting (June 4, 1912) they'd voted to make the following individuals Honorary Board Members: Mr. R. L. Cutter, Miss Frances J. Huntley, Mr. J. T. Pirie, Dr. H. A. Kelly, Mr. F. H. Marston, and Mr. A. A. Hyde.

At the Second Annual meeting of the Corporation the Board was also informed of the new format of *The Chosen People* magazine, effective with the February 1913 issue. The reason given for the change was to allow more space for information concerning the work and the workers.

A special meeting of the Board was called for June 11, 1913, for the purpose of discussing needed changes in the By-laws and Constitution of the newly formed Corporation. The members were duly notified of the proposed change, and voted to change the By-laws to read, "a quorum shall consist of five members of the corporation" instead of "two-thirds of the entire number"[16] as formerly stated. Reports were given from all departments of the Mission, indicating that the work was progressing well. Joseph Cohn's field report was most interesting. The secretary recorded:

> The Field Secretary told of his winter and spring trips in the Middle West. In Denver, [a] local Jewish work had been started as a result of the interest in the subject. A committee of one hundred had been formed, a hall rented and $700 raised for the purpose. It has been arranged that Morris Zutrau, the young man converted during the fall, shall go next fall to Park College, Missouri. A special plan has been developed this Spring to send an advance agent to a city preceding Mr. Cohn's coming who arouses interest in the work and brings the subject to the attention of the people. One large meeting is held soon after Mr. Cohn's arrival and thus much is accomplished in a short time. The Field Secretary reported about $4500 in cash and pledges raised in the first five months of the year. In the fall he is planning to visit Eastern Cities.[17]

Of particular interest is the mention of the tactics which Joseph developed to enlarge the crowds at his meetings, and to open new doors of opportunity for ministry. They are the same tactics being used by larger evangelistic organizations today. In many ways, Joseph Hoffman Cohn was far ahead of his time in his development and methodology of enlarging the financial base and ministry of the Mission. Joseph and his ideas shook the status quo; he was willing to try different methods to reach the goals he felt God had given him. But of course, this added to the controversy and problems surrounding the ministry as it grew.

At the Fourth Annual meeting of the Williamsburg Mission, it was reported that the annual income of the Mission had risen to $22,584.67, and that all expenses had been met. It was also noted that there was continual opposition to the ministry by the Anti-Missionary Society, and that several times the police had to be called because of near riots. Leopold Cohn, the President, then reported the following:

> ...last spring it was thought wise to make a change of doctors in the Dispensary. The Jewish doctors whom we had previously employed were objecting to the Gospel signs around the dispensary and so two Christian physicians, Drs. Richardson and Cooley were engaged in their places. The head Jewish doctor soon after this, opened another dispensary just below our building and for a time succeeded in drawing away many of our patients but our numbers are again increasing and all conditions are more satisfactory than they were previously.[18]

A Gospel Mail Ministry Established

Leopold went on to report that a new phase of work had been started during the Fall. He stated that a Miss Merriam, who was greatly interested in the distribution of the Scriptures, had made it possible for the mission to mail ten thousand Scripture portions, accompanied by a special letter inviting the receiver to visit the Mission and receive a copy of the Gospel of Matthew. He reported that only a few responses had been received, but that it was noticeable at the meetings that a larger number of well-to-do Jews were attending—"the class which we are hoping to reach by the letters."[19]

The mail ministry and the travels of Joseph Cohn broadened the horizons of the Mission. No longer was the main thrust of the ministry primarily to the poor immigrant Jews of Brooklyn, New York. Certainly, immigrant Jews in New York continued to be reached and ministered to, but strategy now began to be developed and planned to reach Jews world-wide with the Gospel.

In her lifetime, Miss Merriam may never have realized the full impact of her gift to the ministry. In effect, she was responsible for beginning the Gospel Mail Department of the Mission. At the 1916 Annual Meeting of the Williamsburg Mission, Leopold Cohn reported:

> Miss Merriam who last year had made it possible for us to mail ten thousand letters and Scripture portions to Jews in Brooklyn and New York continued this work for another year and 10,000 copies of Mr. Cohn's tract, 'To Both The Houses of Israel,' had been sent out with a letter in Jewish and English on the first page. Fewer replies to the tract had been received than to the letter, but three definite conversions had resulted.
>
> The Gospel by Mail Department, instituted last Spring, is planned to reach Jews in any part of the country with the Gospel. Anyone interested in a Jew may send us his name and fifty-cents and we will mail him an appropriate letter with tracts and a New Testament if it is desired. Since the opening of this department, less than a year, 300 names had been corresponded with and two people had been converted.[20]

By 1917 the Gospel Mail Department had proven to be a great success in reaching Jewish people. It was reported: "The Gospel By Mail Department is proving to be a great work. During the summer six consecutive letters were sent out to 5,000 Jewish names of Brooklyn. A large correspondence had resulted and two or three conversions. We were thus able to reach a class not otherwise touched by the Mission. Tracts and these six letters are now being sent to Jews all over the Country."[21]

A Cemetery For Jewish Believers

Reaching Jews with the Gospel was always a primary goal for Rabbi Cohn, but he also recognized early in his ministry the need for a cemetery for Jewish believers. He addressed this matter in the November 1912 issue of *The Chosen People* magazine stating:

> It is impossible for our friends who do not know the Jews to have an adequate idea of the various problems which a missionary to that nation has to encounter. Ever since Jacob, Joseph, and others of the Jewish fathers expressed a desire to be buried with their ancestors, there has been a strong feeling in the heart of every Jew along that direction. It has grown up into some sort of a religious principle that one must be buried among Jews, and the Jewish cemetery must consist merely of Jewish corpses and those only of moral persons. No bad Jew can be buried there. Every Jew, while he lives, provides in some way or another for his burial place. To be buried among Gentiles is the greatest shame for the family still living, as well as for the dead.
>
> No sooner did we organize our little church, consisting of a number of the converts, than they began to discuss the matter of burial. Where shall the bodies of the believers be buried? One of the members, a widow of about forty, who is one of the staunchest converts, became sick from working in unhealthy shops. A skillful physician told her she might fall dead at any minute, as her lungs were in such a condition that she might have a hemorrhage at any time. She gathered up all her strength one day, and came to us, and said, 'I may die any day, and I am ready to meet the Lord Jesus; I am not afraid of death, but am glad to meet my Savior. I want to give you written authority to conduct my funeral services and bury my body among Christian people' (thinking that Christians, too, have a separate cemetery like the Jews). Presupposing the usual trouble at such a funeral, as Jewish relatives bitterly opposing such a course, she wanted to give me the right in writing so as to make such opposition of no avail. The poor widow has children, and would like to bring them up in the faith of the Lord Jesus Christ. Please pray for her. We knelt down with her in prayer to God and when we rose from our knees she looked happy, not a trace of worry was seen in her face. What a comfort it would be to have a special cemetery for these Hebrew Christians, as that would settle all these difficulties. If some of our friends should be led to buy a cemetery for these brethren, it would be greatly appreciated.[22]

The pleas of Leopold Cohn for the need of a cemetery for Jewish believers seemingly went unheard. But Leopold did not forget the matter. The Minutes of the November 8, 1916 Board Meeting record his proposal: "Mr. Cohn then presented the need of a Cemetery plot for the burial of Hebrew-Christians, and suggested that a special plot be purchased by the Mission and Hebrew-Christians allowed the privilege of burial there after the payment of a weekly rate. After discussion it was decided that legal advice should be taken on this matter before the Board approves of such a plan. Mr. Knowles and Mr. Joseph Cohn were appointed to look into the matter."[23]

On this same issue later minutes record: "In regard to the matter of a cemetery for Jews, Mr. Hart, the lawyer, wrote that under the present charters neither the Williamsburg Mission to the Jews, nor the Sar Shalom Association could own such property and receive weekly payments from Jews towards the graves, guaranteeing them burial expenses and free burial in the plot. Mr. Cohn strongly urged the necessity for owning such a burial place, hoping some arrangement could be made to purchase one. Mr. Knowles was appointed to look into this subject as he knew of a lady who was desirous of disposing of some lots in Cypress Hills Cemetery."[24]

SAR SHALOM ASSOCIATION AND CONGREGATION

It should be noted that the Sar Shalom Association mentioned here was an organization that had been formed as an outgrowth of the Messianic congregation Leopold Cohn had established. It's original name was the "Mevasser Tov Association." An article about this association appeared in the February 1910 issue of *The Chosen People* Magazine, stating:

> We have on several occasions mentioned to our friends that the gathering of Jewish Christians, consisting of the converts of this Mission, is continuing to flourish. This Society began about two years ago and was then called the Mevasser Tov Association (Society for publishing the Good Tidings), but since being in the new building, it was voted to change the name to Sar Shalom Association.
>
> This movement is unique and very interesting and we are making progress in membership and in spiritual growth. There are between forty and fifty that belong to the congregation and we have about thirty paying members who contribute ten cents a week to our Treasurer. This money is kept for cases of emergency, to help a needy member. Most of our number are married and represent large families....
>
> It is a joy to the workers to see so many of the converts attending these special meetings for converts every Monday evening. We have very encouraging testimonies from these brethren. For instance the oldest member, who is eighty-four,...testified that during the last four or five years since he had begun to believe in the Lord Jesus Christ, he is feeling younger every year the Lord answers his prayers in the name of Jesus,...The manner and the spirit with which this oldest brother testifies causes a shout of hallelujahs and cheers up the brethren. Another member told of an incident during his wife's sickness when at a critical moment he offered a prayer to God in the name of the Lord Jesus. Help came immediately and a woman friend who was present, seeing the remarkable answer of God to the brother's prayer, accepted the same Savior. She came with him to the meeting and testified, confirming the statement.
>
> We take courage at every meeting and thank God for this outcome to the working power of the Lord Jesus Christ in our midst. We do pray and hope that the Lord will keep this congregation steadfast and increase it so that it shall grow mightily and stand out as an example which very likely other Jews will follow, that when converted they may establish other Jewish Christian congregations.[25]

Clearly, the vision and hope of Leopold Cohn was for the establishment of a Messianic community that would provide for the needs of individuals from the cradle to the grave, including the establishment of Messianic congregations. Joseph Cohn, on the other hand, recognized the need for the congregations, but saw his role as one of developing support to fund the missionaries and the programs, thus enabling the ministry to reach all Jews with the Gospel. He had no problem leaving the development and problems of the congregations to his father.

A report on the type of service Leopold had adopted for his congregation appeared in the December 1910 issue of the magazine. It stated:

> The following article was written by the well-known Hebrew Christian poet, Mark Levy, who is now helping in this mission. When he addressed our meeting for the first time, he was greatly surprised and said that he had never seen such a large and respectable Jewish audience in his life. He has traveled a great deal and has seen Jewish missions all over the world.
>
> 'Personally, there were several causes for thanksgiving and rejoicing. We met on the eve of the ancient Sabbath,...we were under the leadership of a son of Israel's priestly tribe, in the direct Aaronic line (Cohn). The singing was led by a brother of Judah who had set to old Hebrew congregational melodies several original hymns written to glorify the Messiahship of Jesus our Lord (Englander). The hall was filled with Hebrew men and women, youths and maidens, who throughout the service displayed a degree of interest and sympathy I have never seen equalled in a Jewish mission. And above all, I rejoiced in the opportunity of telling our unconverted brethren that the mercy of God is most compassionately manifested in the forgiveness of sin through the precious blood of Jesus the Messiah, who came as the Lamb of God to take away the sin of the world.'
>
> 'Throughout my Christian career, I have deplored the Gentilizing methods that prevail in presenting the Gospel to our Jewish brethren. The effort on Hebrew Christians and on our unconverted kinsmen has been deplorable; and therefore the opinion is wide-spread in Jewry that loyalty to Christ involves disloyalty to Moses. The note here struck of presenting the truth, as it is in Israel's Messiah, to a Jewish congregation in a Jewish form was never more happily

demonstrated to the writer.'

'Reverence and order, joy and thanksgiving prevailed throughout the service. That Mr. Cohn and his fellow-workers are exercising love and wisdom in this respect, none should doubt and that the time may speedily come when in this great city of New York, with its million Jewish population, there shall be many halls and churches filled with Hebrew congregations, singing the praises of our Blessed Messiah, should be the fervent prayer of all His loyal followers.'[26]

The matter of the cemetery for Jewish believers was still not settled, and was addressed again at the November 20, 1917 meeting of the Board. The Minutes state:

The subject of the value and need of a cemetery plot owned by the Mission or some corporation of Hebrew Christians, as a burial place for Hebrew Christians, was again discussed. Mr. Knowles reported that is seemed impossible to locate the lots in Cypress Hills Cemetery, previously referred to, and the Cemetery was unwilling that an outside surveyor be brought in, so it was thought best to drop the subject of those lots. Mr. Donaldson then spoke of Mt. Olivet and Maple Grove Cemeterys [sic] and suggested that we try there for suitable lots. On motion, Mr. Knowles was asked to inquire about Mt. Olivet and Maple Grove Cemeterys and report and if necessary the Secretary should call a special meeting to take action in the matter.[27]

Leopold's dream of obtaining a burial place for Jewish believers was finally resolved at a special meeting of the Board. The Minutes of January 16, 1918 reflect the following: "Mr. Leopold Cohn then presented a report of the general work of the Mission for 1917. He said that a cemetery plot in the Mt. Olivet Cemetery containing 48 graves had been purchased for the sum of $1267, approval of the purchase having been obtained from the members of the Board by the Secretary, as directed at the last meeting."[28]

The Minutes go on to report that the deed was being recorded. The use of this plot, it was decided, should be for the members of the Sar Shalom Association and any others whom they might decide to include, but the title was to remain in the name of the Mission. "Burial expenses are to be met by the Sar Shalom Association from the dues which shall be paid by those desiring burial in the plot. Thus a Hebrew-Christian Cemetery has been established which we hope may be a testimony to the power of Christ and a comfort to His people if they need it."[29]

Four years later, in the year 1922, the cemetery was finally completed and the Minutes of the Executive Committee of the Williamsburg Mission recorded: "The cemetery lot which the Mission owns has at last been put in order and fenced in and an appropriate tablet placed upon the gate. The latter reads as follows:

MACHPELAH
A BURIAL PLACE FOR JEWISH CHRISTIANS.
ESTABLISHED BY THE WILLIAMSBURG MISSION TO THE JEWS.
BROOKLYN, N.Y. IN 1916.[30]

Because of Leopold Cohn's deep love for his people and his earnest desire to provide for their needs (cradle to grave), and because of his tenacity and persistence to provide a place where Jewish believers could be buried with honor, Machpelah became a blessing and a place of testimony to Jews and Christians alike. Many Jewish believers buried there had forsaken all—family, friends, and fortune—in order to serve the Messiah, and reading the register of names at Machpelah is like reading a listing of the "heroes of the faith."

The work continued to grow. At a January 1917 Annual Board Meeting the report was given, "eleven more persons were baptized during the year (1916) and a number of others professed conversion, but were fearful of making an open confession."[31]

At this same meeting, Rabbi Cohn announced a plan which the Board adopted regarding Jews who wished to study the Scriptures to prepare themselves for missionary work. Instead of sending them away to Bible training schools at a distance, "it has been decided to teach them at the Mission. Mr. Cohn [Leopold] giving them regular lessons, and letting them gain practical experience by helping in the work of the Mission. This method has been commenced with Mr. Maisels and there is another promising young man whom we hope may also join him."[32]

A third item on the Agenda was the resignation of Mr. R.H. Richards, who stepped down from the Trustees Board because he moved to the Pacific Coast. Mr. Paul H. Graef was appointed to replace him.[33]

Interestingly, around the time of Leopold's break with the American Baptist Home Mission Society, articles began to appear in issues of *The Chosen People* magazine, announcing the Mission's acceptance of "wills and annuities."[34] These announcements continued, and such bequests and annuities became a growing part of the Mission's finances.

At their April 17, 1917 meeting the Board decided to allow the Treasurer, Joseph Cohn, to continue to hold annuities for the Mission in his name, providing he was bonded. This decision ultimately had serious repercussions that could have been avoided had the decision been made to set up all annuities and investments under a separate committee of the Board, or in a separate foundation. Unfortunately, the decision approved by the Board made Joseph Cohn vulnerable to attacks similar to those levied against his father. However, the decision approved by the Board was legal for that day.

In his report to the Board at their meeting held April 1917, Leopold Cohn spoke of the "unusual opportunity to reach Jews in connection with the Billy Sunday Campaign in New York. Many Jews are attending the meetings and linger around the outside of the building and seem especially approachable. Two workers from our staff have therefore been assigned to that particular field and have been distributing literature and having interesting conversations with Jews."[35] The need of a temporary headquarters in that vicinity was discussed and on motion, the Board of Directors was authorized to put forth efforts to obtain a store opposite the Sunday Tabernacle for preaching and distribution of literature on condition that special funds for this purpose be secured, and that no extra expense be incurred from the General Funds.[36]

Both Leopold and Joseph made appeals for the funding of such a building. There was concern over the finances and over the increasing overhead of operating the Mission. The Treasurer reported: "It is proving increasingly difficult to obtain large sums of money for our work...but our list of small contributors is increasing. This is of course a very safe condition but it means additional office work as the mail is heavy. We are now employing six stenographers. We have a list of 1,000 paid subscribers to *The Chosen People* magazine and 2000 pledge names."[37]

By November 4, 1918 things had improved. It was reported that the contributions had come in steadily all summer so that on October 1, 1918 there was a balance of at least $4,000 in the General Fund, as well as monies designated for the building.

The Board Minutes of the meeting held November 4, 1918 note a general discussion on various buildings and suitable locations for the new branch. "If possible, it was thought desirable to rent a store first but the difficulty in this direction was realized. Two buildings in the neighborhood of the Williamsburg Plaza were suggested."[38] Permission was granted to the Cohns to look for a building at a rental which was not to exceed $100 per month. If they found such a building they were "empowered to enter into a lease for a term of not exceeding a year."[39]

At the June 1918 meeting of the Executive Committee, mention was made of the necessity to ordain Rabbi Leopold Cohn. Mr. Cohn told the Board that the Baptist Ministers of Brooklyn had previously agreed to accept his studies as a rabbi in place of theological studies; they had therefore considered him to be an ordained minister and had so recorded him on their lists. However, Leopold said, since his enemies were making such a point of this, the Marcy Avenue Baptist Church had applied for his regular ordination. He stated that he planned to meet the Committee on Ordination which would decide on the subject.[40]

Mention of this is made to remind the reader that throughout the ministry's early years of growth and expansion, throughout the realization of his dreams for the Mission, Leopold Cohn was involved in law-suits with individuals who were untiring in their efforts to destroy his character and the work of the Mission. The legal struggles for Rabbi Cohn did not end until 1918-1919.

The Plaza Branch

On December 5, 1918 a special meeting of the Board of Trustees was called to discuss the progress made by the committee appointed to locate property for the previously discussed new branch. It was reported:

> ...it had been impossible to rent a store in the neighborhood of the Williamsburg Bridge Plaza as Jewish owners would not consider the Mission as a tenant and one Gentile owner declined to do so fearing the other Jewish tenants would be disaffected.
>
> The Committee therefore reported that a very desirable piece of property at 235 So. 4th St. was for sale and that Mr. Knowles had obtained the low price of $17,000 on it. The lot is 20x95 ft. in size. There is a four story brick building on it, in good repair. The store floor is suitable for a Mission hall for us and the location is unusually fine. There is a mortgage of $10,000 on this property so $7,000 cash would be needed.
>
> The Treasurer reported that on October first there was a surplus of $7,000 in our General Fund and recently pledges for $1600 toward buying a Branch Mission had been received.[41]

The Board voted to buy the property and allowed for an additional $500.00 to be spent on "painting, furnishing, lighting, heating, etc., the meeting rooms in this new building."[42]

The story of the "Opening of the Plaza Branch" appears in the February 1919 issue of *The Chosen People* magazine.

The branch was dedicated and opened on January 19, 1919. Once again, success was measured by opposition: "Since first writing this article a number of very well attended meetings have been held in the Plaza Branch, and great interest shown. Inquirers have come in to the Reading Room each day. Opposition is also developing, the rabbis in the neighborhood warning their congregations against the place and urging them to stay away from it."[43]

A 1919 REPORT OF THE MINISTRY

A full report of the scope of the Cohns' ministry also appeared in the February, 1919 magazine. Highlights of that report stated:

THE GENERAL MISSION DEPARTMENT: *Workers employed, full time or part-time: Leopold Cohn, Philip Englander, Harry Burgen, Miss Augusta E. Sussdorff, Mrs. M. Randolph, Rev. Harry Rubenstein.*

Gospel meetings maintained Friday and Sunday nights with an average attendance throughout the year of about seventy-five. A meeting has been held Monday nights for the Jewish converts of the Mission who gather and are organized as a small church body. The Missionary department also was engaged constantly in house to house visitation among the Jews of our district; these visits, in accordance with our established custom, are never tabulated, but it is safe to estimate that their total number would run into many thousands. The visitation work consists of calling at a home, presenting a tract or a New Testament, and talking with the persons concerning their soul's salvation. Sometimes such a visit ends with a prayer and an expression on the part of the person visited of deep concern for his or her salvation.

Owing to the peculiar conditions surrounding Jewish work, it is impossible to present a figure of conversions throughout the year, but the workers all bear testimony that literally hundreds of Jews, men and women, have made confessions to them of their secret faith in the Lord Jesus Christ. A strong evidence of that statement can be secured by a visit to any of the gospel meetings on Friday or Sunday nights, because the visitor will notice by looking into the faces of the audience that from seventy-five to ninety per cent of the people are in the fullest sympathy with the Mission and its teachings concerning the Lord Jesus Christ.

WORK AMONG WOMEN, CHILDREN AND GIRLS: *This department is under the supervision of Miss Ella T. Marston, with a number of volunteer workers and Miss A.E. Sussdorff as the salaried worker. The work among the children consists of sewing classes on Thursday afternoon and a kindergarten on Wednesday afternoon. In both meetings the principal object sought and accomplished, is to teach the children the love of the Lord Jesus Christ and to feel their need of Him as a Savior. The Wednesday afternoon class is of unusual interest because it consists almost entirely of the children of the mothers for whom Miss Sussdorff conducts a meeting on the same afternoon. These mothers cannot leave their children at home because there is no one to care for them, so they bring them here to the Mission and while Miss Sussdorff gives them a Bible lesson in a separate room, other workers take the children in charge and provide occupation and Bible study of a type suited to their minds....*

A class is also held on Thursday nights for working girls. This was established in response to the need of keeping in touch with the girls who are growing up in our sewing classes and going out to make their own living. The girls come from shops and offices directly to the Mission building; a simple but substantial supper is served to them at seven o'clock, after which there is a regular Gospel meeting, with a definite Bible lesson, followed by sewing, knitting or sometimes games. The work done through these meetings has justified many times their existence; a number of girls have married and some bring their husbands to the services, sometimes they bring them to the general Gospel meetings on Friday and Sunday nights. While many are not free to live in their homes the Christian life, yet we trust that they are in their hearts, believers in the Lord Jesus Christ. The average attendance during the past year was twenty.

BIBLE AND TRACT DISTRIBUTION: *This is an important and increasingly large department of our work. The word tract is so, so misleading that we feel the word book would better apply to the bulky literature which we send out under the name of tracts. Our tracts are of large sizes, five inches by eight inches, and they vary from twelve pages to sixty pages in thickness. We printed during 1918 over 30,000 tracts; our stock on hand always amounts to a minimum of some 20,000 tracts. These tracts have had wide distribution; not only in Brooklyn and in New York, but they have found their way throughout the entire country....we distributed over one thousand of these bulky tracts at the Billy Sunday Tabernacle meetings a year ago....We also sent at least five thousand in small amounts to Christian people over the entire country who are using them for distribution among their Jewish tradesmen, peddlers, etc.*

GOSPEL BY MAIL: *As a division in our Bible and Tract Department, there is a very important work being carried on which we have called the Gospel by Mail work. This consists of sending specially prepared letters to Jewish names throughout the country, accompanied by our entire set of eight tracts in a separate package....The total number of letters sent in this department went to 560 individual names, to whom we sent six letters each, making a total of 3,360 separate letters, and a total of 4,480 tracts.*

In addition to this direct method of Gospel by Mail work, we also sent out through the kindness and co-operation of a friend, 40,000 circular letters under one cent postage to Jews whose names were selected from telephone books, and directories, taken from the large cities of this country.

RELIEF TO THE POOR: This is another effective part of our work and consists of the helping of the poor among whom we are situated, with gifts of clothing, groceries, and actual cash. Also we are many times called upon to act in an advisory capacity to our Jewish people in cases involving many serious problems; such problems consist of placing children in various homes in this city and elsewhere, putting sick men and women in hospitals, securing employment for those that are out of work, and many other peculiar cases, requiring a great deal of time and wisdom to handle.

THE EDUCATION FUND: This fund has not been as large as in other years, but we are always on the lookout for promising young men, to send to some institution for training for Christian work; during 1917 we helped two such young men to go to the Moody Bible School. One of our workers here in the Mission was entirely educated by us in this way, and we bore the full expense of his training for a period of nearly three years.

FIELD SECRETARY - EXTENSION DEPARTMENT: This department of work is far-reaching in its influence; while on the surface it would appear that the one object is to do promotion work and raise funds, yet that is only a beginning of the work actually accomplished. We employed during 1918 for full time, Mr. Joseph Cohn as Field Secretary; Rev. E.S. Davidson and Rev. E. Zimmerman as Assistant Field Secretaries, for part time; all of these are Jewish Christians. In addition we also employed other helpers for part time work. Each one of these field workers is always on the lookout to reach Jews in the various towns which they visit, and there have been a substantial number of Jewish conversions through their work, although we do not tabulate such conversions, owing to the fact that such Jews join the Church in which the field worker has been preaching. Mr. Joseph Cohn reports frequently that Jews come to him at his hotel privately to discuss the question of their believing in the Lord Jesus Christ, and he has had a great many very interesting conversations with a large percentage of private confessions of faith in the Lord Jesus Christ. There is no way by which we can show the value of this phase of the work, and yet it is not an exaggeration to say that if we did not have these field workers great loss would be incurred; not from a financial standpoint, but because many Jews...being given the gospel message would not hear in any other way. So these Field Secretaries are really a missionary force traveling over the country.

BY-PRODUCTS: A result of this extension work has been accomplished which is beyond measure and without which, it is conservative to say, as letters constantly affirm, there would be little Jewish mission work done in America excepting in a few established centers. This result is the reflex stimulus which has come to Christian people in almost every city where our secretaries have gone, to engage in some form of Jewish missionary work. Our secretaries have found that Christian people were totally ignorant concerning the needs of Jewish evangelization and a part of their task has been to arouse these Christian people so as to make them eager to go out at once and reach the Jews in their own towns and vicinities. As a result we have definite Mission work carried on in at least 5 cities in this country, in some cases by our own converts.

Individual efforts are also being made by Christians in many of the other large cities.

...It is a well known and accepted fact among Jewish Christians throughout this entire country that the remarkable rise of the Jewish mission movement in America largely owes its development to what has been done by the Williamsburg Mission to the Jews through its publicity department.

For all this we give God the thanks and honor and are striving continuously to make the Mission more effective, more faithful to Him, and more aggressive in the wide spreading of the Gospel of the Lord Jesus Christ among the Jews of this country, so that the Mission shall not be purely a local restricted activity, but as wide as America itself.[44]

As the winds of change continued to sweep through the ministry, there were a number of pressure points being applied from the outside. One was the growing acceptance of Zionism by both Jews and Christians. Another was the signing of the Balfour Declaration; this opened the door for the possibility of a homeland for the Jews in what was then called "Palestine." Political changes were taking place in Europe—changes that ultimately led to World War I. Christians wondered how all of the political changes and Jewish issues could be understood in the light of Bible prophecy. Liberalism was making in-roads into Christianity, undermining the Word of God, evangelism, and missions. Each of these events, world-views, and Christian-views had an impact, internally and externally, upon the direction and thrust of the Mission's programs.

As early as December 1916 an editorial appeared in *The Chosen People* magazine that was critical of a new resolution passed by the Episcopal Church. It stated:

Quite a stir was created over the country when a few weeks ago the Episcopalians at their annual convention at St. Louis, passed a resolution giving liberty to any Jews joining their church to observe Jewish rites and ceremonial customs. The Jews generally have taken this as a direct overture to them and as a proselyting attempt and a great many sermons have been preached by rabbis attacking this resolution. They also have spoken sarcastically of those who would now give them the privilege of obeying the law which they have been following for 3,500 years.

We wish however that the Episcopal Church was officially doing some active work to reach the masses of Jews in this city, or any other in the United States, for then this action at St. Louis would come with greater force....If all the evangelical denominations in the United States were vigorously conducting missions to Jews it would not be long before all would have an opportunity to hear the truth. We are glad that the Lord has a few of His people who not only allow the Jews to come in, but actually are willing to help us go out into the highways and bring them in.[45]

This editorial reflected the growing trend within the denominations not to proselytize (evangelize), but to accept all groups into fellowship, regardless of what they believed.

The November 1916 issue of *The Chosen People* magazine included an editorial entitled, "Until," that generated a host of letters from readers of the magazine. In response to the many letters the following response was given:

Our editorial of last month, which makes the second coming of our Lord contingent upon the conversion of the Jews, has caused many comments and inquires. A number of friends have written us giving the usual program and order of events in this age according to prophecy, namely: the completion of the Remnant according to the election of grace; the calling out of the Church; the Coming of Christ in the air for his Bride; the Tribulation, and then the conversion of the Jews as a nation.

...Likewise the Church leaving the future in God's hands, should keep the order given her by her Lord and Master and preach the Gospel to the Jew first, that in the Great Tribulation those who did not accept Him may remember what they heard and finding the truth proved by the events of the time may cry out for their King to come.[46]

From its inception until this point in time, Rabbi Cohn's mission had not formally adopted a Doctrinal Statement; it had not seemed necessary. But events transpiring in the world of that day—the upheavals taking place in Europe, and impending war, coupled with cries for relief and charity—were bringing about a renewed interest in teachings concerning the Lord's Return. Eschatology was becoming an issue, and the Cohns took a stand through the Editorial in the February 1917 issue of *The Chosen People*:

Now dear reader, may we ask you in the words of II Cor. 6:15, 'What concord hath Christ with Belial? Or what part hath he that believeth with an infidel?' How can you as a Christian, unite with unbelievers and blasphemers in giving money for purely philanthropic work? Are you really honoring Christ in this way? Have you a right to use the Lord's money for this purpose? We are amazed to see War Relief organizations composed of infidels, unitarians, and agnostics having the effrontery to appeal to the churches of Christ. What claim have they upon the church of Christ? The only Scriptural way in which the church can act under these conditions is to send money to some genuine Christian society which will see to it that it shall be given to the suffering people in the name of our Lord Jesus Christ. A gift from the church in any other way than this is a distinct dishonor to our Lord Jesus Christ; and if we continue to have fellowship with the workers of iniquity, God tells us we become partakers in their iniquity.

We would not be misunderstood as lacking sympathy for the peoples in Europe suffering such frightful butcheries; on the contrary, our hearts are torn in sorrow. But, what use is there of relieving the physical suffering, if at the same time the souls of those peoples are allowed to go down into hell?...

If we are Christians, we ought to realize that there is too little Christian money in the world to justify our spending it for that which properly belongs to humanitarian philanthropists. Let the dead bury the dead, is a statement as true today as when our Lord made it, and if the unbelievers of America give their money for relief work, we shall be thankful; but it is not our business, as Christians, to join with them in a task which omits honor and credit to the name of our Lord Jesus Christ.

The time has come to call upon true Christians to withdraw their support from everything that is not distinctly honoring to Christ. You have a right to ask of any organization which appeals to you for help, 'Are you going to use my money for the Lord's glory?' If the answer is doubtful, hold back your gift! Is this narrow? Then let us be narrow! So was Christ narrow! So was Paul narrow! God give us more narrow men! God needs them badly in this wide age. Let us refuse to support any institution which is ready to compromise the faith once for all delivered to the saints. Our business is to win precious souls for Him, and to make ready for His appearing....

Are you willing, dear friend, to grasp this great vision? Are you willing to consecrate yourself anew to the task of spreading the Gospel of Christ among His own brethren and in this way bring about the speedy return of the King? These are solemn words; our earnest prayer is that they may not fall on barren ground. We need a tremendous awakening to a new sense of our neglect, and to God's compelling urgency upon us to evangelize the Jew now, on a scale hitherto undreamed of. With the moral and material support of a united body of Christians in America, we can strike a mighty blow for the Gospel of our Lord, among the Jews. We are ready. Are You?[47]

Having taken the Christians to task, the Cohns then directed their editorials toward the Jews and toward the Christians' attitudes to the Jews. The most out-spoken of Leopold Cohn's editorials appeared in the March 1917. He based this editorial on riots that had recently taken place in New York:

It is not generally known throughout the country that the leaders of these riots were for the main part Jews. This is surprising, because Jews have always preferred to suffer rather than to take up violent measures. We quote further, but now from 'The Jewish Daily News' of New York City, one of the prominent papers in circulation among the Jews of this country:

'The Jewish Anarchists, Socialists, Birth Control agitators, and other irresponsible persons who seek to make capital of the great poverty and the fight against high prices in the Jewish quarters, yesterday over-stepped all limits of respectability, when they made a riot in the great synagogue on Norfolk Street. They threatened the rabbi of the synagogue, the great rabbi Salom Alchanon Yafa and the offices. They polluted the holy place with the most ugly words and broke pulpits and chairs. The police came just in time to restore order and to save the rabbi from danger. The readers will recollect that a few years ago when there was a fight against lack of work, Jewish "comrades" began to make raids upon churches.'

This admission made by a Jewish paper is nothing short of a revelation, and must come as a shock to every right-minded Christian. The poor Christian people of America have been deluded and blinded into a peculiar belief that 'the Jew is all right as he is,' and for the past four hundred years, ever since there began to be settlements of people in America, we have criminally left the Jew unevangelized. What a strange people we are! We have seen by the light of history that the Jew, without God, is desperately wicked; and we know that the Jew who rejects Christ is rejecting God, (John 15:23; 14:1)....

The Jew is an extremist; either he is a mystic, or he is an anarchist; either he is all bad or he is all good; either like Saul, he goes about killing the Jews who believe in Christ, or like the same Paul, touched by the power of the Holy Spirit, he turns about and becomes the greatest missionary of the Cross this earth has ever known....In this country the Jew began to breathe the ozone of this so-called liberty, which he soon began to interpret into infidelity, atheism, and anarchy. We became so extravagant with our ideas of liberty, that we barred from our public schools every shred of Bible teaching, and began to educate these Jewish children, to sharpen their wits, to develop their shrewdness, but failed to give them the one thing which alone would make for a stable future for our government—the moral stamina, without which education is wicked. What is the result? We are facing the most serious hour of Jewish history in America. Judaism has become bankrupt; . . .

It is inevitable that a nation which has lost its grip on God must eventually sink to a low plane of morality, and this is just what is happening today within the confines of Judaism. Last summer, when rigid investigations were made in New York into the White Slave Traffic, there appeared before the District Attorneys, one Yushe Botwin, said to be the head of the White Slave Trust. Botwin admitted that he had been a white slaver for 25 years. He implicated other Jews in this unspeakable business. It is well-known that the East Side in New York is honey-combed with the abominable cadet system, gangsters, etc. When the Rosenthal murder was in the spotlight, there were four accomplices sentenced to the electric chair at Sing Sing, besides Lieutenant Becker; three of these were Jews. (It is noteworthy that American born and educated Jews manifest these alarming tendencies!) So we could go on, naming one by one the frightful conditions of spiritual and moral bankruptcy which pervade modern Judaism. The Jew is rapidly becoming the intellectual leader in this country; we tremble, when we realize what that means for the future of Christianity in America. Everywhere throughout the land, these so-called Reformed rabbis are charming away good Christian people into a mawkish sentimentality and into a denial of that for which the martyrs shed their blood. Over and over again, misled Christians allow in their pulpits these Reformed rabbis and listen to their superficial sophistry. One prominent Rabbi loves to parade himself over the land and repeat that which he knows is a wicked falsehood — "There never was a converted Jew in all history who was worth anything!" and we foolish Christians sit quietly and let him say this without a word of protest, while we know down in our heart that if it were not for Jewish Christian supermen like Paul, Peter, James, John, Edersheim, Herschell, Neander, etc., ad infinitum, Christianity, humanly speaking, would not be in existence today.

Why do you let yourself be so misled? Why doesn't the church of Christ in America awake and turn to the Jew with a tremendous missionary campaign such as has never been known before in our history? Are we asleep? Oh for a Luther who will thunder up and down our land until the church of Christ shall upon bended knee come to God for forgiveness and a new vision of duty to this people![48]

Needless to say, such editorials were not looked on kindly by liberal Christians and by Jewish leaders. They only added fuel to the fires of persecution that were already raging around Leopold and Joseph Cohn. They were, however, a rallying cry to fundamentalists, independents, and to those in far-right extreme camps within Christianity. Many denominations began to phase out their Jewish mission works in their entirety, in favor of dialogue. Fundamentalists groups and the evangelicals, however, picked up the cause—but these groups tended to link evangelism to the Jews with dispensational teaching and with prophetic end-time events. In his travels as Field Secretary, seeking to gain supporters for the Mission, Joseph Cohn recognized this new trend among the fundamentalists and evangelicals.

WINONA LAKE PROPHECY CONFERENCE

In August 1917, at the Winona Lake Conference Grounds in Winona Lake, Indiana, the Mission held the first of many annual conferences on "The Jew in Prophecy." A report on this conference was included in the October issue of *The Chosen People* magazine. It stated:

One of the memorable events in the history of this Mission was the Conference on the Jews which we were permitted to conduct a Winona Lake, Ind., this past summer. The very thought of such a Conference was in itself radical for us, and we confess that we undertook the arrangement with fear and trembling. It was most encouraging to hear from many of you that you were praying earnestly that God would bless richly those three days set apart for the study of God's Word concerning the Jews....

On Sunday night, the third session of the Conference, the address was given again by Mr. Joseph Cohn. The more solid work of the program began on Monday morning, for we had planned a heavy schedule, every hour of the day being taken with some address dealing with the Jewish problem. A fair idea of the scope of the conference can be obtained when I mention some of the subjects treated, like 'The Jewish Sword,' by Dr. Buswell; 'They that did the King's Business Helped the Jews,' by Rev. C.H. Irving; 'The Responsibility of the Church in Relation to Israel,' by Rev. B.B. Sutcliffe; 'Christ the Keystone in Israel's History,' by Dr. Van Osdel; 'The Hidden Remnant,' by Mr. Flacks; 'The Day of Jacob's Trouble,' by Dr. Van Osdel; 'For Such A Time as This,' by Dr. Buswell. We were amazed to see the remarkable attention given to the different speakers as they opened up the Word of God concerning His future plans for Israel....When the sessions were opened for questions, they came thick and fast and before we knew it, we had used up, not only the hour allotted to the questions, but also the next hour. The people expressed themselves in terms of utmost astonishment because of the new revelations of truth that had come to them through this Conference. We have been receiving letters ever since from those who were in attendance, telling us how much blessing they received and of how deeply they were touched with the various presentations of the Jewish need.[49]

These conferences, which were developed by Joseph Cohn, served to place the Mission at the forefront of prophetic teaching and as Joseph rallied around him Bible scholars, teachers, and pastors who held like doctrine, it was not long before the Mission needed a formal Doctrinal Statement.

The Revision Committee for the By-laws brought a draft of the Revised Constitution to a special meeting of the Board held on Wednesday afternoon January 7, 1920. The draft was read and discussed, article by article, with "free expression being given by all the members as each article was carefully considered. Several minor changes were made and at the conclusion Mr. P.H. Graef moved as follows: 'That we adopt the revised Constitution as a whole with the changes agreed upon.' This was duly seconded and carried. Miss Masters moved that we adopt the revised By-laws as a whole, covering the changes agreed upon. Seconded and carried.[50]

One of the important changes contained in these new By-laws was the inclusion of a Doctrinal Statement. It reads as follows:

ARTICLE IV. DOCTRINAL BASIS
SECTION 1

The members of the Corporation hereby declare and affirm their belief in the Divine inspiration, infallibility and authority of the Old and New Testaments; in the Triune God, the Father, the Son and the Holy Spirit; in the Deity of the Lord Jesus Christ as the only begotten Son of God; in the sacrificial blood atonement of the Lord Jesus Christ at Calvary and His bodily resurrection from the dead; finally, in the lost condition of every human being, whether Jew or Gentile, who does not accept salvation by faith in the Lord Jesus Christ, and, therefore, in the necessity of presenting the Gospel to the Jews.

SECTION 2

Only such persons who give assent to the doctrinal basis as contained in Section One of this article, either verbally or in writing, as may be required by the Board of Trustees, and who are known to be interested in the evangelization of the Jews, shall be eligible to membership in this Corporation.[51]

The Mission not only took a stand, doctrinally aligning itself with the fundamentalists of the day, but the very wording of the statement in it's By-Laws and Constitution, along with the additional safeguard of requiring verbal or written assent, were steps that were deliberately taken to protect the Mission from the in-roads of liberalism that were sweeping through denominations and denominational missions of that day. Theological statements included in the Doctrinal Statement reflect some of the issues of the day—the deity of Christ, the inspiration and infallibility of Scripture, the sacrificial blood atonement, the bodily resurrection, the lost condition of all mankind, and the need for including the Jew when preaching the Gospel.

It is interesting to note that the statement did not include a reference to the pre-tribulation or pre-millennial return of Christ. However, a pre-millennial statement was added later. The doctrines of the imminent return of Christ, pre-Tribulation, mid-Tribulation, and post-Tribulation were still in their infancy. Dispensationalism had been put forth by William Darby in the late 1800's and was, at this period in time, being popularized by Dr. C. I. Scofield. World events (i.e., the Balfour Declaration, Zionism, the return of the Jews to Palestine) had set the stage for such teaching, and dispensationalism was rapidly gaining a foot-hold among the fundamentalists.

As the Mission continued to hold Prophetic Conferences, the conferences continued to grow in popularity and in size. Literature, tracts, and other materials produced by the ministry began to be more closely aligned to the Dispensational position and with pre-Tribulation and pre-Millennial teachings regarding the return of Yeshua. This is not to say, however, that Joseph Cohn was in complete agreement with all of the prophetic teachings of that day. There were areas which he steadfastly proclaimed needed to be looked at from the perspective of the Jew and of the Jewish Christian. Some dispensational teaching of that time did not include the need to evangelize the Jew; Jews were viewed as a people with whom God had dealt in the past and would deal again in the future. In an editorial in the May 1919 *Chosen People* magazine, Joseph addressed this erroneous interpretation of God's Word. He wrote:

A friend wrote us a few days ago as follows: "I wish you could write an article on the futility of praying for Christ's return and preaching on this subject, and never once praying for the conversion of the Jews. Does not the last mentioned come first, and isn't that the work to be busy about just now? Don't you think there is a veil over Christian eyes as well as Jewish?"

To all of which we respond with a hearty Amen. Because God has begun to work mightily in the closing days of this age, by causing the fig tree to 'put forth leaves,' as evidenced in the renaissance of the Jewish nation, it has become suddenly popular to talk about the Jews, about Prophecy, about the return of our Lord, and on kindred subjects. Conferences are being held in many parts of the land, great gatherings of people are being brought together to attend such conferences, speakers of national and world reputation are secured, great addresses are given dealing with almost every conceivable phase of the pre-millennial doctrine, excepting one. The past history of the Jews is carefully and analytically gone into, their achievements properly eulogized; the Abrahamic covenant is fully explained, expounded and expanded; then comes a sudden hiatus, and leap in the dark as it were, for speakers suddenly jump several thousand years into space and land at a point called the Millennium, which they describe as a period when the Jew shall have a wonderful and glorious time; but we wait and wait, and wait, with long drawn out patience, for just a word about the Jews right here and now, but never a word do we hear!...

May we now ask, of what use is it to a dying Jew to be told that 'tomorrow,' in the millennium, the Jews will have a wonderful day in their beloved land? If the Word of God be true that a soul that dies out of Christ is lost forever, what kind of a tomorrow can you possibly hold out to the dying Jews, who will never live to reach Palestine? Do you not see the inconsistency of it all? We protest most vehemently, this cannot be true pre-millennialism, nor indeed is it, when measured by the square rule of God's Word.[52]

During this period, as the Mission grew and *The Chosen People* magazine gained more and more subscribers, the editorials, salutations, and articles appearing in the magazine began to reflect a growing world-view of ministry and of teaching from a Jewish-Christian perspective. Joseph Cohn seemed to view himself as a "watch-dog" for issues affecting Jewish Christians around the world, and he used *The Chosen People* magazine as a forum from which to present his viewpoint.

It is difficult to measure the impact that Joseph Cohn and the Mission had upon the theological issues of the day. One thing is certain however—without Joseph Cohn's writings and hard-line editorials, without his articles in which he expressed his personal concern for the salvation of Jewish people and challenged Christians to share his concern, there would not be the interest in Jewish missions that exists to our day. Every issue—theological, social, political, etc.—was analyzed and scrutinized as to its affect on the Jews and as to whether it would have any effect upon their opportunities to hear the Gospel. Joseph's editorial entitled, "The Red Terror," is a good example of this. He wrote:

The Red Terror. It is now here; it stalks brazenly and blatantly up and down our streets. It calls itself "Bolshevism," "Soviet rule," "Socialism," "I.W.W.," and other "uplift" epithets. It hails from that land of brute savagery whose chief delight for many centuries has been the butchering of helpless and innocent Jews,—Russia; where murder, rapine, and other crimes too hideous to describe or mention, are perpetrated upon Jewish men, women and children daily,...

Its cause is the fundamental cause of all the evils now in the world. It is Christlessness. Russia has rejected the Lord Jesus Christ as far back as history recalls. In the light of this fact, what else could be expected from such a people, but murder of Jews? For that is the surest sign of one without Christ—he hates the Jews. And no one can genuinely love Christ without also loving His nation....

And so the Red Terror stalks in our land. And for many decades we, who call ourselves Christians, have been helping to pave the way for it. We have given of our money and of our time to help establish institutions which under the mask of Christianity, were undermining the vitals of our faith, and of the faith of our children. We have endowed colleges with Christian money, given by Godly men and Godly women, only to discover years afterwards with a feeling of faintness, that these very schools were turning out educated and cultured infidels and Christ-haters....

And in these latter days a new movement has taken unto itself wings and is spreading over the land, and is deluding thousands of innocent Christians. It calls itself "Christian Americanization." And it includes in its ambitious program, the 'Americanization of the Jews.' And many poor, earnest Christians now imagine that this is Christian Mission work! It is a delusion on the face of it. Every one knows that the Jew is "at home" anywhere. He is the first to become a citizen in whatever country he settles. He needs no Americanization. But if he does need it, our government is well able to do it, and is doing it admirably. The church's duty is to preach her Lord, not to usurp the powers of our government. "But," it is argued, "we can in this way convert the Jew!" To which we reply, that the moment you try to approach the Jew through a camouflage, you become to him an object of contempt. And if you really mean to convert him, why not be a man, and say so openly, and call yourself a Mission to the Jews, and not a "Community Center" or an "Americanization movement?"...

And the Red Terror goes mercilessly on and leaves desolation it its wake. And we remember the words of our Lord. 'But as the days of Noah were, so shall also the coming of the Son of man be' Matt. 24:37.[53]

Over the span of a few short years (1894 to 1907) the winds of change that blew from within, and from without the mission, carried the work along from being a small, obscure mission to the Jews in Brooklyn, to being a recognized, well-funded ministry to the Jews with a voice (*The Chosen People* magazine) that was reaching into the homes of thousands of Christians by the years 1907 to 1920. Its speakers, Joseph Hoffman Cohn and others, regularly preached in some of the most prominent and significant pulpits in the land, challenging Christians regarding their duty to reach the Jews with the Gospel.

In just thirteen short years (1907-1920)—the length of time it takes a Jewish boy to be Bar Mitzvah and declared an adult—Rabbi Leopold Cohn's Mission to the Jews reached adulthood. Taking its place alongside of other independent mission organizations, the Williamsburg Mission to the Jews became a recognized voice, a force within fundamental Christianity, and the "spokesman" for Jewish Christians and Jewish Christian ministries in America.

THE CHANGING OF THE GUARD

Behind the scenes, however, the winds of change had left disarray in their wake. For reasons which may never be known to this author, or to the general public, at the Annual meeting of the Board of the Williamsburg Mission, on January 28, 1920, it was moved that Leopold Cohn be given the title of Superintendent Emeritus and that he be given the current fiscal year as a time of rest and vacation, at his pleasure. The reasons for this decision are not reflected in the official Minutes of the Board Meeting, or in any of the official papers of the Mission.

It was then moved and seconded to "appoint Mr. Joseph Cohn Field Secretary and Manager at his present salary, his duties to be determined by the Executive Committee. Recorded and unanimously approved."[54]

At the next Board of Directors Meeting in June 1920 Joseph asked that his salary by increased. The Board agreed that the request for an increase was warranted and moved that "the salary of Mr. Joseph Cohn be increased to $400.00 per month from June 1st for the balance of the fiscal year."[55]

We can only surmise as to the reasons for the change of title and "vacation" given to Rabbi Cohn. Perhaps the Board felt Rabbi Cohn had been under too much pressure due to the many lawsuits and charges that had been brought against him, or perhaps there were family problems, or personality conflicts due to the changes that were taking place within the organization. What we do know is that the Board's action evidently did not please Rabbi Cohn, for at the very first Executive Board Meeting of the Williamsburg Mission the subject was brought up for discussion and action. The minutes reflect the following:

> Mr. Donaldson asked Mr. Knowles to open the meeting with prayer after which Mr. Joseph Cohn reported that Mr. Leopold Cohn would be pleased if the title Emeritus, given to him by the Board at its last meeting, should be changed, also if he should not have to take his vacation just at present and if in the meantime he be allowed to take up some of his duties at the mission, as he feels able.
>
> After discussion the Committee decided that they would be very glad to have Mr. Leopold Cohn's assistance in the matters of writing for The Chosen People, opening the mail and speaking at the meetings, as he had mentioned, and in any other matters they would be glad if he would consult the Executive Committee. As Mr. Cohn's vacation was given him by the Board, "at his pleasure" the Committee saw no reason why he could not defer it until later. The subject of the title "Emeritus" would be considered, other titles being suggested and the subject be referred to the Board at its next meeting.[56]

The next Executive Committee meeting was held on March 24, 1920 and "the subject of the title to be used by Mr. Leopold Cohn was re-opened and further discussed and at length on motion it was decided that Mr. Leopold Cohn retain the title of Superintendent."[57]

While nothing was mentioned directly, it would appear that tension had developed between Leopold and his son Joseph, over who was actually in charge of the Mission and it's affairs. When the Williamsburg Mission was incorporated there were only three voting directors, two of whom were Leopold and Joseph. But when the new By-Laws were adopted it became necessary to immediately amend them to allow for nine directors rather than three. The minutes reflect the following action:

> Resolved that the number of Directors of this Corporation be increased from three (3) the present number, to nine (9) and that said Directors be hereafter called Trustees and they are hereby authorized and directed to sign, acknowledge and file proper amended certificates, pursuant to section 14 of the Membership Corporations Law, and to take any other steps that may be necessary to carry out and effectuate such increase in the number of Directors.
>
> This resolution was made necessary because of the changes in the By Laws affecting the Charter of the Mission and at the suggestion of Mr. R. M. Hart, counsel for the Mission, who was present and explained the matter, the amended certificate was to be filed at Albany.
>
> This resolution was there put and being duly seconded was unanimously passed.[58]

Rabbi Leopold Cohn had resisted incorporating his Mission out of fear that he would lose control, and within nine short years after its incorporation his fears became a reality—control of the Mission was turned over to his son, Joseph. From that time until his death, although Leopold continued to play an active role in the on-going work of the Mission, and although he continued to serve on the Board, he no longer set the direction for the ministry. The vision for the ministry and the control of its leadership—the power—belonged to Joseph.

Perhaps there were other considerations that entered into the Board's decision to change Leopold Cohn's title to "Superintendent," and thus to essentially remove him from his position as head of the Mission. One such consideration could have been the farm in Connecticut. The farm had been given to Leopold and he had advertized it as a "Fresh air farm for the children of the Mission." As indicated earlier, he had received monies to make needed repairs and improvements on the property and had turned it into a rather elaborate affair. Although it was used for children of the Mission for a short period of time, after the Investigation of the Charges against Leopold Cohn all references to the Farm were dropped from the pages of The Chosen People magazine, as well as from the Minutes of the Corporation. Perhaps the Board, as it increased in size and began to take a more active role in the financial affairs and policies of the Mission, felt this farm and the controversy over how it was acquired, as well as the innuendo over monies spent on its expansion, would forever be a subject that would provoke questions and incite insinuations of impropriety on Rabbi Cohn's part. To date, the farm has not been included as a part of the Mission's assets. It has remained in the Cohn family.

The Board may also have been wrestling with Leopold's obsession with trying to clear his name of the numerous charges that had been brought against him. In his determination to clear his name, Leopold was continuously engaged in lawsuits. As has been mentioned, the last lawsuit was finally settled in 1918. The Minutes of the Board reflect that members of the Board were never in favor of these lawsuits, yet they felt an obligation to assist Leopold because they believed he would not have been engaged in such problems had he not been a missionary serving in Jewish missions. They therefore gave him some financial assistance, but they also warned him not to continue pursuing the lawsuits. To their dismay, Leopold persistently continued until all legal means were exhausted. The continuous negative publicity that resulted from the lawsuits was emotionally draining, time consuming, and a source of considerable expense to the Mission.

The transition in leadership was smooth and uncomplicated. Joseph had already been doing most of the work; he had already been developing all of the programs for the broadened outreach of the ministry. Under his leadership the Mission continued to grow at a steady pace. Income grew, the conference ministry continued to bring in new names, and the Branch Ministries continued to reach Jewish people with the Gospel.

A Yiddish and English Newspaper is Born

Joseph, as has been mentioned, was always on the lookout for new methods of reaching Jews. As he mingled with the Jewish masses in New York he was quick to observe how effective the Yiddish and English newspapers were in gaining the attention of the Jewish people. He observed that they almost "devoured" such papers and he felt if he could develop such a paper, with a Gospel emphasis, he would be able to reach many more Jews with the Gospel. He was so convinced that this method of communication would be successful that he established The Publishing Salvation Department of the Mission which printed a Yiddish and English newspaper called *The Shepherd of Israel*. Joseph was right, and the impact of *The Shepherd of Israel* went beyond even his expectations! Even he never dreamed that God would use this little paper to open up a foreign branch of the Mission. He wrote of this in *The Chosen People* magazine stating:

> ...we began to feel more and more keenly the power of the Jewish press,...
>
> Out of all of the above as the background, was born the thought of...a newspaper to be published once a month, and to be given wide circulation among the Jews, and to deal with news items and problems of the moment, and to give them proper Christian interpretation, so that we should have a Jewish audience numbering into the thousands, to whom our message would go month after month in the printed page and who would in this way be reached with a true interpretation of Christ and His Gospel....
>
> We have called the paper, The Shepherd of Israel. The object of the paper is primarily educative; that is, we want to destroy in the Jewish mind the mainly false teachings they have had through their newspapers and through their rabbis as to what Christianity is, and as to who Christ was; after we have done this, we want at the same time to build up in the Jewish mind a true knowledge as to who Christ was and as to what Christianity is. Our present undertaking is to send out 10,000 of these papers through the mails under one cent postage, to 10,000 Jewish names that we have already selected from the Brooklyn Directory; we will send 10,000 papers again in October to the same 10,000 names, and we will continue doing so for twelve consecutive issues. Then we will discard the list of 10,000 names, and take up the next 10,000 and send them the publication every month for a year. To give you an idea of the enormity of the task, if we limit ourselves to 10,000 names each year, it will take us at least forty years to send a copy of the paper for one year each to every Jewish family in New York City; this estimate is based on an accepted population of two million Jews in New York, divided into approximately 400,000 families.[59]

This was a very ambitious program which was to continue as long as funds were available. As Joseph had predicted, within just a few years after the Jewish community was introduced to *The Shepherd of Israel* publication, the Mission began seeing results. At the Executive Committee on April 25, 1922, Joseph Cohn reported:

> The value of The Shepherd of Israel continues to be realized more fully as various incidents are brought to our attention. One Jew wrote asking us to change the address on his copy as he was moving and evidently did not want to miss receiving any numbers. Another Jew from Cleveland came to the Mission recently and reported that he had been converted some month's previously through reading The Shepherd of Israel.[60]

At the Annual meeting of the Board on January 25, 1922 Rabbi Leopold Cohn reported on work accomplished in 1921. The Minutes of his report state:

> *The Superintendent, Mr. L. Cohn, then made his report for the year 1921, stating there had been good meetings at the Mission all winter, in spite of opposition in many forms, many strangers being present, largely because of our new paper [The Shepherd of Israel]. There were 3 baptisms and 60 confessions of faith (estimated). At the Plaza Branch little was done, and on November first Mr. Cohn [Leopold] personally undertook the weekly meetings, the attendance gradually increasing from 2 to 25. He further spoke of the great success of our paper, The Shepherd of Israel, 20,000 copies being sent out monthly, of its question column, and of the prize contest with its few objections, and his belief that the paper reaches 100,000 people. He also told of the splendid effect which the weddings of two Jewish couples, converts of the Mission, and held at the Mission, had on the work. He also called attention to the fact that 9 converts of the Mission are missionaries.[61]*

The twenty-seventh Audited Statement of the Williamsburg Mission for the months of January-December 1921, showed receipts of $75,409.52 against $57,167.63 in disbursements. The total net reserves of the Mission stood at $90,891.89.[62] In today's dollars the income would have been reported as approximately $568,000. with net reserves at approximately $684,000. Financially, the Mission was in good shape. The programs that Joseph had developed were creating a sound financial base for The Williamsburg Mission to the Jews.

The Mission's Name is Changed

But the winds of change continued to blow. At the March 1923 Executive Board Meeting the subject of changing the name of The Williamsburg Mission to the Jews was brought up for discussion. "As our work and interests are extending in so many directions it is felt that a less restricted title, which suggests so local a work, would be a more appropriate one. Various new names were suggested such as American Jewish Missionary Society and The American Board of Missions to the Jews but no conclusion was reached in the matter. It was asked that each one consider the subject and submit to the next meeting various appropriate new titles."[63]

The Executive Committee met again in May and the advisability of a name change was once again discussed. All members of the committee agreed that they liked the name, The American Mission to the Jews. The only individual who objected to the name change was Leopold Cohn, but he was persuaded to go along with it. Mr. Hart, the attorney for the Board, was to be consulted as to the "methods of making such a change and whether the words, 'Successor to' or 'Continuing' be used."[64]

At their June 27, 1923 meeting the Executive Committee once again addressed the matter of the name change. A report was made that the full Board had discussed the matter and had given their approval for such a change. Mr. Hart was therefore instructed to prepare the necessary documents to effect the change of name from The Williamsburg Mission to the Jews to The American Mission to the Jews. However, as Mr. Hart worked on the documents he discovered that the name selected could not be used because it was already being used by another mission corporation. The other mission was no longer actively involved in doing missionary work but their corporation had never been dissolved. The matter was "tabled" until the November 7, 1923 meeting of the Executive Committee when, after some discussion, the committee members voted to change the name to The American Board of Missions to the Jews.[65]

After further investigation into the matter of changing the name of the ministry, the Board's attorney, Mr. Hart, advised that it would be in the best interest of the ministry to establish The American Board of Missions to the Jews, Inc." as a new corporation rather than to simply change the name of the Mission. Therefore, on May 1, 1924, after duly notifying all Board Members, a special meeting was called. The Executive Committee Minutes state the following:

> *Mrs. Marston also reported that on May 1st, 1924 nine persons interested in Jewish work met to incorporate a new society called The American Board of Missions to the Jews. The names of the Incorporators were as follows: Frank H. Marston, Paul H. Graef, John C. Medd, Ella T. Marston, Benjamin F. Knowles, Philip A. Benson, H.E.D. Deubke, Leopold Cohn, Joseph Hoffman Cohn.[66]*

Subsequently, on September 15, 1924 a special meeting of the Board of Trustees of The Williamsburg Mission to the Jews was held. The purpose of the meeting was to pass a resolution in which the Williamsburg Mission to the Jews would request that the newly organized American Board of Missions to the Jews assist them (the Williamsburg Mission) in the conduct of their missionary activities. The following resolution was then unanimously adopted:

WHEREAS the American Board of Missions to the Jews, Inc., has been incorporated under the laws of the State of New York, and has for its object the preaching of the Gospel of the Lord Jesus Christ to the Jews, and

WHEREAS the trustees of the Williamsburg Mission to the Jews are of the opinion that it would be desirable to have the American Board of Missions to the Jews, Inc., assist it in carrying on its mission work, and

WHEREAS the American Board of Missions to the Jews, Inc., will incur certain expenses in such cooperation, and

WHEREAS the Williamsburg Mission to the Jews has on hand certain funds contributed to its work and may, as the Lord provides, receive other contributions, and the trustees are of the opinion that if the American Board of Missions to the Jews Inc., so assists in such mission work, it lays upon the Williamsburg Mission to the Jews, the duty of helping the American Board of Missions to the Jews, Inc., financially,

NOW, THEREFORE, be it resolved that the Williamsburg Mission to the Jews shall request the American Board of Missions to the Jews, Inc., to assist it in its work and activities as such Mission on and after January 1st, 1925, and this Board does hereby direct that if such request be granted, such cooperation shall begin on January 1st, 1925; and this Board does further consent and approve of paying to the American Board of Missions to the Jews, Inc., such sums monthly as the American Board of Missions to the Jews, Inc., may need in carrying out this request.

It is further resolved that this request and offer be communicated in writing to The American Board of Missions to the Jews, Inc., and a copy of the resolution be sent to it, and that a copy of the communication and any reply received therefrom be placed on file.[67]

The Chosen People magazine, the voice of the Mission, heralded the name change in the October 1924 issue under the caption: "Important Announcement." The article went on to say:

Growing pains are often accompanied by other symptoms. Sometimes these symptoms prove an embarrassment to the suffering but happy patient. This has been the experience of The Williamsburg Mission to the Jews for the past few years. Our friends are well acquainted with the growth of the work and the rich blessings which God has given to every effort put forth here for its enlargement, until it has become an institution with a scope wider than America. The constant travels of our Field representatives, from coast to coast, their daily contact with Jews and Christians in all parts of the this great country; the nation-wide, and, indeed, world-wide distribution of our Gospel tracts among the Jews of every clime and nation; and finally, the more recent achievement of the Mission, the publishing of a monthly Yiddish paper which now counts its Jewish readers by the thousands; all these far-visioned activities have made the name of the Williamsburg Mission to the Jews known throughout the world. On this far-flung battle line are to be found, England, Russia, Germany, Palestine, China, India. For The Shepherd of Israel is actually read by the Jews of London, of Odessa, of Hamburg, and of Jerusalem, of Canton and of Bombay.

But the name, Williamsburg Mission to the Jews, meant nothing to all these world-citizens. Williamsburg is only a small section of Brooklyn, and Brooklyn is only a Borough of New York, ... To many Christians in America likewise, the name meant very little, and failed to reflect the large work actually being done.

For several years our Board grappled with the problem; and finally, after prayer and lengthy considerations, a plan was agreed upon that would fully meet all the needs of the situation.

A new corporation was formed, known as the American Board of Missions to the Jews, Inc. The old Williamsburg Mission to the Jews does not lose its existence. It will still live and continue to hold all property now vested in its corporate name. But the new American Board of Missions to the Jews, Inc. will hereafter conduct the activities of the Williamsburg Mission to the Jews, in accordance with a legal request from the latter that the American Board do so. A majority of the members of the Williamsburg Mission to the Jews are members of the American Board of Missions to the Jews, Inc., so that there is virtually no change in the personnel of the management.

What this really means to our friends is that hereafter the new name, American Board of Missions to the Jews, Inc., will truly reflect the complete scope of our work; and it should stimulate a larger and more intense cooperation from God's children everywhere to realize that here is a Society desirous of coping with the Jewish problem in America, consistent with means and workers made available to us.[68]

Why Mr. Hart, legal counsel for the Mission, advised the Board to form a separate Corporation rather than to simply change the name of the "Williamsburg Mission to the Jews" to "the American Board of Missions to the Jews, Inc." is not clear. Quite possibly he was attempting to shelter the new corporation from the vast amount of bad publicity that the Williamsburg Mission had received by virtue of the attacks on Leopold Cohn. Whatever the reason, by incorporating under this method, the Mission, in effect, became two organizations. The Williamsburg Mission and its Board (all of whom served on the American Board) held all of the Assets of the corporation (i.e. the buildings, properties, investment funds, estates, wills, annuities, etc.). The American Board of Missions to the Jews, Inc. (some of whose board members served on the The Williamsburg Mission Board) maintained the ministry, and received and receipted all gifts and donations. When additional funds were needed for its operations, The American Board of Mission to the Jews, Inc. would request such funds from the investment account of the The Williamsburg Mission to the Jews. This somewhat awkward system worked for a number of years but year by year it led to increased problems. The assets of the The Williamsburg Mission to the Jews continued to grow. Separate Minutes and audited financial statements were kept, as required by law. But because all board members of The American Board did not serve on the board of The Williamsburg Mission, suspicions arose and with the suspicions, rumors and gossip began to erupt. It was rumored that Joseph Cohn was building up vast reserves of monies, and that he was free to spend as he saw fit rather than to use all of the monies for missionary work. Such persistent rumors followed Joseph throughout his years as General Secretary of the Mission and caused a division within the board which ultimately led to a split in the Mission itself.

The author would like to remind readers once again of the uniqueness of Jewish missions, especially during the late 1800's and early 1900's. Jewish missions has never been a popular missionary activity; it has always been subject to attacks from both the Jewish community and the Christian community. Jewish missions stand between two worlds, and those who work within Jewish missions are often caught in the cross fire as those worlds clash. Rabbi Leopold Cohn's mission had always been dependent upon the gifts of God's people as its only source of income. The future of the Jews was always uncertain and the Cohns, as well as members of the Boards, believed the Mission had a responsibility to assist and help the Jewish people (both physically and spiritually) in every country where they were scattered. To do this an investment fund was necessary, even though other missions and evangelistic organizations of the day did not follow such a practice. In many ways, Joseph's skills in business organization put the Mission far ahead of his time. This was not always understood by his Christian brothers, however. The problems that arose within the American Board came as a result of questions that arose over the ethical and moral issues of raising funds through one corporation, while holding fairly large assets and investments in the other. Nothing illegal was done either by the Board of the Mission or in the activities of Joseph himself. The corporations had been duly established under New York law, and were governed by duly appointed and elected board of directors.

HEWES HOUSE

One of the major achievements of the Williamsburg Mission to the Jews, just before the formation of The American Board of Missions to the Jews, Inc., was the purchase of a building to be used as "A Home For Jewish Christians." For Rabbi Cohn the establishment of such a home was a fulfillment of his long-held dream of developing a "Messianic community." He shared his excitement with the readers of *The Chosen People* magazine, writing:

> *The Williamsburg Mission to the Jews marks another milestone in its history. For years an outstanding need of Jewish Mission work in America has been a Home—a home where aged Jewish Christians left penniless and without a friend in the world might find a haven of rest; a home where new converts might have at least a temporary shelter while readjusting themselves to the new life they must face, and a home where children left alone in the world might find a place where they may have the privilege of a true Christian bringing up. Frequently have we in our work witnessed the orphans of some of our converts taken and put into Jewish asylums and thus lost to the cause of Christ.*
>
> *In England where Jewish Mission work has been carried on for over one hundred years, the value of such a home was long ago realized and there are a number of such institutions both in England and continental Europe.*
>
> *For years it had been our earnest desire to establish such a home in America, but thus far we have been unable to realize this great hope. And now as the natural growth of the Mission has brought on new needs and enlarged opportunities, there has come the next logical step, a home for Jewish Christians. The appeal for this Home was first made last spring through the columns of The Chosen People, and found such a wide response on the part of our friends and such a deep interest that we felt truly it was the Lord's will to undertake this new enterprise. Accordingly our Treasurer, B.F. Knowles, Esq., set about to find a suitable location; after a long search such a property was found at 141 Hewes Street, at a price considerably below the current market for similar houses even in the same block....*
>
> *The Home will be in the charge of Mr. and Mrs. Duff who have been laboring so faithfully at the Plaza Branch. It will not be a Home in the sense of an orphan asylum. It will be the kind of a home that we have described in the beginning of this article, our idea being to make it more a temporary shelter rather than a permanent home for any one.[69]*

Mr. and Mrs. Marvin Duff had been hired by the Mission in the summer of 1922 to work in the Plaza Branch, as well as to conduct the Open Air Meetings for the Mission. Previously, Mr. Duff had worked with the National Bible Institute who recommended him to work with the Mission because of his love for Jewish Gospel work.[70]

Because of its street address, the home for Jewish Christians became known as the "Hewes Home." Sadly, after such a glowing report of its establishment, it soon became known within the Mission that things were not working out for the Duff's. They resigned their position at the Plaza Branch, but they asked to remain as caretakers at the Hewes Home until a new family could be found.

Within the providence of God, such a family was found—a family that ultimately played an important role in the growth and development of the Mission. The surname of the family was Fuchs. Mrs. Fuchs was a Jewish believer who had come to faith through the outreach of the Mission. Executive Minutes of the Mission state: "Mrs. Fuchs, a widow with three grown children, a convert of the Mission has been engaged to live in Hewes St. and take charge of the house. We know that she is clean and neat and a good housekeeper as she has previously done work for us. We will give her fifty dollars a month and her rent and she will give us most of her time. When she concludes outside engagements and can give us all of her time, we will increase her salary to $65.00 a month."[71]

Mrs. Fuchs did increase her hours, and was not only the housekeeper for the Hewes property, but she also took charge of cleaning the Doctor's offices and the Drug Room in the Dispensary.[72] The names of Mrs. Fuchs' three grown children were John, Judith, and Daniel. As Mrs. Fuchs labored for her Messiah at the Hewes Home, and as she and her children lived at that residence, God used their experience there to shape and mold two of her children for missionary work. Both Judith and Daniel felt led to become missionaries with the American Board of Missions to the Jews. Judith worked among the women and girls until her engagement, and Daniel served in a number of capacities, ultimately becoming President of the American Board of Missions to the Jews, Inc., and then Chairman of the Board of Directors. John chose secular work.

The influence of the many visitors played a vital role in shaping the lives of Daniel and Judith. Leopold Cohn shared comments about one such visit with the Executive Committee, saying:

> The Mission has had the pleasure of entertaining at the Home in Hewes St., Mr. and Mrs. Auerbuch [sic] of Kichineff, Bessarabia, missionaries of the Mildmay Mission to the Jews of London. Mr. and Mrs. Auerbuch had been visiting in this country and while in New York made their headquarters in Hewes St. They visited several of the meetings and Mr. Auerbuch preached and sang and played his violin. With the approval of the Executive Committee one hundred dollars was given to Mr. Auerbuch at the Communion Service on Sunday Morning, to purchase a cemetery plot for the burial of Hebrew Christians in Kishineff. Conditions in Bessarabia are very serious and the people in great poverty.[73]

Thus, the house on Hewes St. not only provided a place for Jewish believers to stay, it was also the training ground for two more workers for the ministry.

Somewhere along his travels, Joseph Cohn saw an electronic model of the old stereopticon (for showing pictures). The new electronic model was called a Cutler Automatic Stereopticon. Joseph immediately realized its potential for reaching Jews with the Gospel. He therefore purchased one, and soon thereafter the Mission began using this new invention. Unlike the old stereopticon machines, the new machine was capable of exhibiting a series of stereopticon slides automatically, throwing a picture approximately two feet square on a specially prepared silk screen. The whole machine was so compact that it fit in the window at the Plaza Branch where Mr. Daniel Finestone was working. Mr. Finestone had come to the mission to do volunteer work, but in 1924 Joseph Cohn hired him to work with the boys during Vacation Bible School, to do visitation, and to do open-air preaching. While at the Plaza Branch he was also responsible for the operation of the Stereopticon. He wrote of the impact this new machine had upon his ministry:

> The average Jew knows very little regarding the life of Jesus Christ. Only a few have read the New Testament. The rabbis, however, have not failed to acquaint them with their fanciful legends concerning Him.
>
> One of these, perhaps the most familiar to the Jew, is the legend in which Jesus is pictured as flying through the air. It was this, they claim, which gained Him the notoriety, leading many of the people to believe in His Messiahship….
>
> To acquaint them with some of the facts is our task, but how to accomplish it, is our difficulty. Prejudice and carelessness must be overcome, and an interest aroused.
>
> This we have endeavored to do in a novel, and we believe, an effective way, by means of pictures of the life of Christ in our Mission window at the Plaza Branch. The passing throng of Jews, both old and young, evince great interest in this story. A capacity audience quickly gathers around the window, and as the simple facts are unfolded before their eyes, an earnest, serious expression comes over their faces.
>
> The facts relating to His birth, His care for the sad and suffering, present a new impression to many, who only thought of Jesus Christ as the Founder of a religion of hate.

The account of His rejection, crucifixion and death reveals to them that He is their brother, loving them even unto death.

But God's vindication of His Son by raising Him from the dead and setting Him at His own right hand, found expression in the exclamation of a little boy who rejoicingly said, 'He didn't stay dead.'

A young man came into the Mission, after seeing the pictures one evening, and accepted a gospel, which would give the further information he desired. A short time later he came again, rejoicing in his new-found love for Him whom he once hated.

Some, however, have bitterly opposed the thought that Jesus is the Jewish Messiah. A band of Jewish young men for several evenings took it upon themselves to disturb the on-lookers, but only succeeded in creating greater interest among the passers-by. Some even stayed to see the pictures all over again, and they take over half an hour to show.

One evening, a little Jewish girl stopped me on the street, and pointing to the Mission window said, 'I believe it's all true. Do you know, I believe?' The sunshine in her little face told me there was sunshine in her heart too.

Thus the old story has lost none of its power.[74]

QUEST FOR NEW WORKERS

Under the new name, "The American Board of Missions to the Jews, Inc." the ministry continued to grow and expand. There was a constant need for new workers, competent workers, trained workers. Some of the workers who had been with Rabbi Cohn from the beginning of the Mission were getting up in years. Some were leaving to get married and have families—such was the case with Esther Cohn, the daughter of Leopold. In the summer of 1922 she married Mr. John Lolis and resigned from the ministry. Esther had faithfully worked among the Jewish girls and women since being a teenager herself.

Miss Grace Bigelow, who had first come to the Mission around 1904 as a result of Rabbi Cohn's challenge to the young people's group at Hope Baptist Church, remained a faithful helper with the music at the evening meetings in the Mission for over twenty years. She became ill with tuberculosis, however, and had to go into a sanitarium. The Mission helped with her expenses, but sorely missed this faithful worker.[75]

After Esther's marriage, Leopold and Joseph were the only members of the Cohn family still involved in the work of the Mission. Leopold's sons, Benjamin and Joshua, had never become part of the Mission staff as adults, nor had David, Leopold's youngest son, who died on November 10, 1931 at the age of 31. While attending Colgate University, David had enlisted in the U.S. Army, and during his time of service in the Army he became ill with tuberculosis. He was treated in the government hospitals in Asheville, North Carolina; Fort Snelling, Minnesota; and finally, at the Government hospital in Hines, Illinois. Rabbi Cohn shared the tragedy of his son's illness with readers of *The Chosen People* magazine saying, "Lying on his bed his suffering and pain did not hinder his testimony for the Lord Jesus. The Chaplain of the institution wrote that he enjoyed visiting David and was much helped by the talks on prophecy that the boy gave him. He preached the Gospel to his Jewish physician and gave him some of our literature."[76]

Thus, Leopold and Joseph had to rely more and more on the workers they had hired and trained. They were especially anxious to have converts of the Mission developed for missionary work. They wanted their workers to be Jewish believers. If, however, they found Gentile believers who shared their concern for the salvation of Jewish people, these were welcomed as well, but were required to be acculturated and to work along side of Jewish believers. Joseph Cohn expressed this thinking in his editorial entitled, "Our Testimony." He wrote:

Many of our readers are a bit confused as to the relative value or effectiveness as between Gentile Christian missionaries and Jewish Christian missionaries in doing Jewish Mission work.

It has been pointed out that a Gentile Christian worker addressing a Jewish audience always gets a less boisterous hearing than a Jewish Christian gets, particularly in open air work. And this has been used as an argument for the superior advantage a Gentile Christian has in approaching the Jew. We, ourselves, have heard earnest Gentile Christians tell of the crowds of Jews they had addressed in the open air, and how quiet the Jews were, and tolerant, and even cordial. But when we asked such a brother, 'Did you have any definite, permanent conversions?' the silence became almost cavernous.

In other words, the brother was only superficial. He thought that getting an audience was the only objective of his work, and that having gotten his audience, that was its own reward. And he thought that because the Jews made no protest, and no riot, that this was a sure sign he is a successful Jewish missionary.

Now as a matter of fact, just the opposite is true....

...And yet in these days how many there are among Gentile Christians and even among preachers, who when called upon to address a Jewish audience, tremble at every word for fear they may offend the Jew by even mentioning

the name of Christ!

And we ourselves often stop to hear some of these speakers, and what we hear only confirms what they themselves tell us when we ask them, 'Well, what did you say to them?' For the main burden of these talks seems to be to tell the Jews what a great nation they are, and what a wonderful future they have, and how they are going back to Jerusalem, etc., etc. And not a word of the fact that the Jew is a lost man, in need of a Savior right here and now....

It is argued that when a Jewish Christian talks to Jews, it makes trouble. Of course it does, and most certainly it should. Just read the record in the Book of Acts, and see how much trouble Paul caused—and Peter!...

Not that we would minimize Gentile Christian testimony to Jews. God forbid. On the contrary, we welcome with open arms every true child of God, be he Jew or Gentile, so long as he has been called of Him to labor among the Jews, and is willing to give the Jews a clear message of salvation through the blood of the Lord Jesus Christ.

But the Gentile worker alone, is under a serious handicap, and on that account we have been convinced that his best labors will only be of value if he is associated with Jewish Christian guidance and cooperation. The Jewish psychology is of this type: 'Yes, you were born a Gentile, or a Christian (the names are, erroneously and unfortunately synonymous to the Jew) and what you say is all very nice for you. But I was born a Jew, and we Jews were taught of God to be the world's religious leaders; so how can you teach me anything?' So he listens with sophisticated tolerance.

But if, on the other hand, he hears one of his own blood, a Jew, speak to him about the love of Jesus, that is a different matter. And at once he is aroused; 'A Traitor! An Apostate!' And when you have him aroused, you have done a good day's work. Saul had become so aroused that he went about killing Jewish Christians! But see what kind of a Paul you got afterwards!

And so we want our friends to know that ours is a testimony of Jews to Jews. The same sort of testimony as was that of Peter to the crowds on Pentecost; and of Stephen, whom they stoned to death; and of Paul, who suffered many tortures from them. The old saying is 'diamond cuts diamond'; and a Jew is the best one to reach a Jew. That is why we should encourage all young Jewish converts to enter training for Jewish work.[77]

HARRY BURGEN—THE PHILADELPHIA BRANCH

Harry Burgen was a good example of the type of Jewish worker Joseph Cohn was looking for. Harry was first hired by the Mission while he was a student at the Practical Bible Institute. He was a Jewish believer who had been saved at one of the Mission services when he was a young man. The Mission subsequently provided him with funds for his education. Throughout his years of training, Harry continued to do colportage work for the Mission, faithfully distributing tracts and Gospel books to the Jewish people. His testimony was included in *The Chosen People* magazine:

I was born in Malat, a small town in Lithuania in the year 1893. My parents were very strict orthodox Jews, who earnestly sought to observe all the precepts, according to the Law of Moses and the innumerable precepts handed down by the Jewish Rabbis. At the age of six I was sent to 'Chader' (Hebrew School) where we were taught the Hebrew alphabet to begin with, the daily prayer book, then the early Books of the Old Testament, also man-made books and commentaries. I attended until I reached my thirteenth year, when I became 'barmitzvah' (the age of responsibility). I was no longer allowed to pray without the phylacteries. Thus, in my early years a reverence and Godly fear were instilled in my heart for the Word of God and I very earnestly tried to obey what I was taught.

As I became older a longing grew in my heart for something I did not find in the synagogue or in all my religious observances. Often I was so unhappy and used to find some satisfaction in stealing away and repeating portions of the psalms and meditating. But still I was troubled, for I saw myself a sinner before God and wanted assurance of forgiveness for my sin. After my thirteenth year I was sent out to learn a trade and later left my native town for a larger city where I secured a position and though among strangers I carried out the religious training of our home.

Some years later my older brother who had already immigrated to America sent me a steamship ticket and in the year 1910 I landed at Ellis Island, making my home with relatives in Brooklyn who lived in the Williamsburg section. Like other immigrants I soon obtained work in one of the factories and began to earn my own living. I thought I would be happy then, for I had everything I needed and still kept attending the synagogue; on the other hand seeking all the worldly pleasures of which our native town was bereft. Yet in the midst of it all, I knew it was barren, giving no lasting joy, peace or hope.

One day in the early part of 1913, a young man in the factory told me of some meetings he attended regularly at a Jewish Mission. Though he was an unbeliever he insisted on my accompanying him saying they had lots of fun there annoying and mimicking the missionaries. This was altogether new to me for I had not heard of missionaries in my native town. I consented to go with the young man, attending a Friday evening Gospel meeting. I listened attentively to the story of the Son of God and it touched my very heart strings. The words I heard were as a 'balm of Gilead' to my *soul.*

I began to attend the meetings regularly but mingled with the throng who mocked and sneered, thinking they were 'doing God service' to persecute the one who dared to acknowledge Christ as Israel's true Messiah. Rebellion arose, with doubts and questioning, 'If this were so would not our learned men tell us these things?' etc. In this frame of mind I endeavored to break up the meetings, destroying Christian literature until I was ordered out of the Mission for misbehavior. Once outside the door regret and sorrow filled my heart for having rejected the Word of Life which I knew then was the Truth. I was miserable at my work and was impelled to go once more to the meetings.

I decided to take a back seat; in case I was recognized I would not have far to go. On entering I took a seat away from those who mocked and laughed. To my joy no one asked any questions and after the service I took with me one of the tracts written by Mr. Cohn and read it carefully from cover to cover. Thus I began to attend the meetings again, gradually moving up front and drinking in every word. Each time I took a different tract and finally read the New Testament for the first time in my life and my eyes were opened to the Truth as it is in Christ.

Reports were brought to my uncle, in whose house I lived, that I was attending the Mission. He was greatly displeased and he told me to choose between his home and the Mission. That same day I found a room with utter strangers and left my uncle's house.

On the 20th day of October, 1913, it was my blessed privilege to acknowledge the Lord Jesus Christ as my personal Savior by being baptized at the Mission, and was later sent by these dear friends to the Practical Bible Training School at Binghamton, New York in preparation for the blessed service of making Christ known to our people, that He is indeed the Christ, the Son of the living God, according to Moses and the Prophets. From the depths of my heart I bless God for His 'unspeakable gift' and for opening my eyes to know Him, the One who satisfieth the longing soul. 'Taste and see that the Lord is good, blessed is the man that trusteth in Him.'[78]

After finishing his schooling, Harry returned to work at the Plaza Branch of the Mission. In 1921 he married Miss Rebecca Young, a Jewish believer, and God blessed their marriage with one son and three daughters. Sadly, one of their little daughters died at the age of six—a tragedy that seemed to have had a lasting affect on Rebecca.

At their December 21, 1926 meeting, the Executive Committee appointed Harry Burgen to open a new branch of the American Board of Missions to the Jews in Philadelphia, Pennsylvania. This was the first official branch of the Mission to be opened outside of New York, with a full-time paid worker. The Jewish population of Philadelphia was around 240,000; this represented over 70% of the Jewish population of the entire state.

On January 1, 1927 Harry Burgen and his wife moved to Philadelphia, where Harry faithfully labored for over forty-seven years. At the beginning, he rented a store front building at 535 Spruce St., in downtown Philadelphia. This was used as a reading room and as a meeting room until the mission purchased property at 717 Walnut Street in Philadelphia in 1945. While serving at the store front building Harry affectionately became known as the Mission's "Trap Door" Missionary. He was given this name because of the way he worked in his store front building. Using all of his creative talents, he would cleverly decorate the store front window with Scripture verses, objects of art, or other items that he felt would attract the attention of a Jewish passer-by. He would then wait behind the curtain at the window. As soon as a curious person would stop to look, like a trap-door spider springing out of its nest after its prey, Harry would quickly spring out the door to engage the person in conversation. He was a master at this, and as a result of his patience and his loving witness, many Jews and Gentiles came to faith in the Messiah.

Harry was an ardent soul winner and excellent missionary, and he also had a great burden for the Jewish population in Atlantic City. In October 1928, after getting the Board's approval, Harry opened a branch of the Mission in Atlantic City. The Board also authorized that a young Jewish man, Fred W. Haberer, who had recently graduated from the Jewish Studies Department at Moody, serve as Harry's assistant. Fred had been recruited in August 1928 by Joseph Cohn to work in the Brooklyn and Plaza branches of the Mission.[79]

The work in Atlantic City proved to be a difficult field. The local authorities flatly refused to give Fred and Harry permission to preach on the Boardwalk, where thousands of Jews visited annually. God blessed as meetings were held and a handful of Jewish people did come to know Yeshua through the work being done. However, the February 1932 issue of *The Chosen People* magazine included this announcement: "While many may be disappointed to learn that our Atlantic City Branch will be discontinued after December 31st, yet we believe…it is a wise move. This is the most costly of all our Branches and since so very few Jews come in to the services, it was deemed unwise to continue the expense."[80]

Harry was not only responsible for opening the work in Philadelphia, he was also indirectly responsible for opening the door for the Mission's ministry in Lithuania. The story is a remarkable testimony to the power of the written Word of God.

The story began while Harry was still doing the work of a missionary colporteur in Atlantic City, New Jersey. One day, as he was distributing copies of *The Shepherd of Israel*, a Jewish man accepted one. After taking the paper in hand, the man read the title of the paper aloud in Yiddish. Harry immediately recognized his Lithuanian accent and questioned the man about his homeland. To his amazement, Harry discovered that the man came from the same village in Lithuania that he'd come from. Through this common bond, a friendship between the two "landsmen" (countrymen) formed and Harry began visiting the man in his home. He met other members of his family as well, and it wasn't long before the entire family had come to faith in Yeshua—all but one brother who still lived in Lithuania that is. Harry obtained the brother's name and address and sent him a personal letter. In the letter Harry told the man how, after coming to America, he had found the Lord Jesus Christ, the true Redeemer of Israel. He expressed how anxious he was for this man to find the same Redeemer, just as the other members of his family had. Not long afterward Harry received a reply from a fellow-country man named Simon Aszur. It said:

> Dear Friend Harry: I have read the letter which you wrote to Benjamin, and he, himself, does not want to answer you because he does not know what to answer and does not understand you, in that you are a reasonable man and should accept the thought that Jesus of Nazareth is truly the Savior of all mankind. There was no evil thought in Him against anyone and is the Friend of all. I understand the faith and am well pleased with it.
>
> Now dear companion and friend, I will allow myself to write who I am. I remember you very well. We went to 'Chader' (Hebrew School) together. I am Simon, (if you remember a red-headed boy), the son of Moses the Rabbi. Certainly you must remember me.
>
> Now to the main point again. I can hardly tell you my friend, how happy I am that I have found such a close companion as you to talk over about the same thought which I have long hidden in me. But now I do not withhold or hesitate to speak openly, and as much as possible to prove to others that the enmity is only a 'hatred without a cause.'
>
> When it is possible for you, send me the necessary literature that I may have more material to make the faith known to more people. Your Companion and Friend, Simon Aszur.[81]

We can only imagine the joy that filled Harry's heart when he received Simon's letter. He immediately replied and sent Simon more of Leopold Cohn's tracts in Yiddish. In fact, he was so anxious to see that his old friend had enough material about the Lord that he sent him a rather large parcel. Harry then received the following letter from his friend, Simon:

> My dear brother Harry: I have received the package of literature which you sent me but I have had considerable aggravation concerning it, in that I was informed I would have to pay a certain amount of duty and I did not possess a cent. I did not have where to borrow because I am so hated by my surrounding Jewish brethren because I have acknowledged Christ as my personal Savior. I could not allow myself to let the package go back, so I obtained a customer for a good overcoat of mine, which I did with joy. For a part of the money I redeemed the package and two dollars in American money is my remaining portion. Up till the present I was working as an electrician but my employer being an orthodox Jew, dismissed me because of my faith. But I trust to God, with the help of our Lord Jesus, that you will consider my need and come to my aid.[82]

Harry continued his correspondence with Simon, doing what he could to assist him and to disciple him through the mail. After a time of sickness and persecution because of his faith, Simon wrote to Harry again, expressing his desire to continue his witness to his Jewish brethren despite persecution. He wrote:

> ...Dear Harry, one cannot hold the blessed Tidings for himself alone, no! but he desires that the hearts of others may rejoice also, even though he makes numerous enemies as soon as a word is spoken concerning the Truth. I am altogether open before my brethren who go astray. My desire is for them to be saved. Perhaps some among them will acknowledge the glory of the Christ of God, that His words in Luke 15:7 might be fulfilled. Simon Aszur.[83]

Ministry to Europe

Simon's letters to Harry always blessed his heart, but they also stirred him and created within him a great desire to witness to his brethren in Lithuania. With this burden on his heart, Harry prayerfully took some of Simon's letters to Joseph Cohn and asked if there was any way of using Simon in the ministry. Joseph, too, was impressed with Simon's sincerity as he expressed himself in his letters. Joseph therefore decided to have Mr. Joseph Flacks, whom he knew was a devoted Christian, interview Simon. Mr. Flacks reported that he had been very favorably impressed, and on that recommendation Joseph asked the Executive Committee of the Mission to hire Mr. Simon Aszur as the Mission's missionary in Lithuania. He requested that Simon move to Kovno, the capital of Lithuania, and begin a ministry of personal work and of distributing *The Shepherd of Israel*.[84]

Simon Aszur became the first foreign missionary supported by the American Board of Missions to the Jews. Interestingly, it was the distribution of the Shepherd of Israel that God used to open the door for this new phase of ministry. As early as 1923, Joseph Cohn began reporting stories in *The Chosen People* magazine of Jewish people in other European countries who had come to faith in Yeshua as a result of reading the Shepherd of Israel.

One such man was Mr. Yekel Katz, who lived in Poland. Yekel was a twenty-four year old man who had spent eighteen years studying in Hebrew Schools. A neighbor who had immigrated to America started sending copies of the Shepherd of Israel to Yekel's sister, Rose Katz, who also lived in Poland. Yekel visited his sister and saw a copy of the publication and, being intrigued by the title, asked to read it. He soon learned that his sister received other materials from the Mission as well, and he wanted to read it all. After reading the Gospel literature he became convinced that Yeshua was the Messiah. Sadly, when he told his parents about his faith they threw him out of their home.[85]

When Yekel wrote to the Mission, Joseph immediately wrote to Mr. Moses Gitlin. Moses was a Polish Jew who had accepted Yeshua while he was in America; he had been baptized by Leopold Cohn. He had since returned to Poland and was living and working near the town in which Yekel lived.

As copies of *The Shepherd of Israel* had greater distribution world-wide, more and more contacts with individuals abroad were made, and word of more and more conversions reached Joseph's ears. Clearly, the Jewish communities outside of America were ready for a publication like The Shepherd of Israel. Armed with this confidence, Joseph entered into arrangements for the circulation of *The Shepherd of Israel* into Great Britain, Germany, Russia, Palestine and other parts of Europe.

He arranged with Pastor Arnold Frank, a Jewish believer in Hamburg, Germany, to distribute 300 copies of the paper each month on the steamship docks in Hamburg—to Jews who were immigrating to America. Pastor Frank, in turn, arranged for Dr. Lev, in Danzig, to distribute an additional 200 copies per month another seaport and debarkation port. Thus, immigrant Jews leaving Germany not only received a copy of *The Shepherd of Israel*, they also received the address of the Mission in New York which was given on the back of the paper.[86]

Members of the Jewish community became irate as they realized what was happening. Yiddish newspapers in New York began running articles about the Williamsburg Mission and the deceitful practices of their "soul-snatching" missionaries. An excerpt from such an article appeared in the December 1923 *Chosen People* magazine:

> 'Until now America has provided the poor Jews of Europe with its dollar, to save the body. But we discovered during the last weeks that there is in America a certain group who wants to provide for the souls of the European Jews. Do you want to know their address? Here it is: It is New York's central Mission, called Beth Sar Shalom, corner Throop Avenue and Walton Street, Brooklyn, N.Y. There is the group of those crazy people who think that they can catch Jewish souls and apostatize them just like little lambs who have gone astray and are now coming back to their Shepherd! They are the 'messengers of the Messiah' as they call themselves in their paper The Shepherd of Israel. It is too little for them to catch in their net ignorant Jews in the United States, but they also spread themselves out over the miserable suffering Jews of Europe. There used to be here and there a missionary in Europe who would occasionally make a speech; but they did not make much progress until now, when they have renewed their activities through the help of the American missionaries. Those American missionaries, who say that it is their task to declare unto the Jews the true Messiah, have opened one of their departments in Danzig. There is a certain apostate by the name of Dr. Lev, who is agitating the Jews, asking them to accept Jesus the Messiah. Especially is he active among the emigrants who go through the Danzig port to countries over the ocean.'[87]

The Shepherd of Israel continued to open doors for missionary activity throughout Europe, parts of Asia, and the Middle East, and Jewish readers responded by sending letters to the Headquarters office expressing their questions, interest, etc. Joseph Cohn was always quick to respond to the letters because he realized that they represented God's answers to his prayers to reach all Jews everywhere with the Gospel.

AN ATLANTIC CITY BRANCH ESTABLISHED

Growth continued to take place in America as well, and on November 30, 1928 the Mission purchased property at 2603 Pacific Avenue in Atlantic City, where a second branch outside of New York was opened. Although the resident Jewish population of Atlantic City at that time was only about 15,000, it was a resort city that attracted thousands of Jewish people throughout the year. In sharing the news of how the Mission was led to establish a branch in Atlantic City, Joseph Cohn wrote:

It really didn't happen. Nothing happens in the affairs of this Mission—every step is ordered of God; it is He that keeps us, and it is He that is planning for us every advance that is made. But the circumstances that brought about this new undertaking have their human elements, and only serve to reveal His ways of working. In the first place, there is a small group of praying people in Atlantic City; these faithful children of God banded themselves together some fourteen years ago into a Friends of Israel Circle, and for fourteen years the burden of their prayer has been 'Oh Lord, open up a Mission to the Jews of Atlantic City!' Never once has their faith faltered.

In the second place, almost three years ago when we were so definitely led to engage one of our own converts, Brother Harry Burgen, and establish him as Missionary to the Jews in Philadelphia, he felt an unavoidable conviction of God that he must include Atlantic City as a part of his field. In this we agreed, and so over all this period, at least one day a week was always spent by Brother Burgen in Atlantic City....

Thirdly, no sooner had we undertaken this one-day-a-week ministry in Atlantic City than the Lord began to work. Hostility, of course, was in abundance; we expect that...But with hostility came also tokens of His grace, for there were hungry souls...Our Field Secretary (Joseph Cohn) went down to Atlantic City and held some meetings. Some of the Jews who had shown kindness to Mr. Burgen, came to the meeting, and lo, one family made open confession of faith in the Lord, and was baptized in a local church. Since then others have come, and still others are friendly but need the encouragement and the help which a Center of our own can give them. So, slowly, but surely we were being driven to face the need of a Branch Station....

So we went down to Atlantic City to rent a store for a Mission. With Brother Burgen we trudged the streets of the Jewish quarter. 'There's just the store we want!' we both exclaimed. And to the agent we hurried. 'What! a Jewish Mission? Are you crazy? Never!' A Jew was the owner! Again and again we went through this same experience; and we came home baffled. Did the Lord not want us to open a Branch? Surely He did. But it took us nearly another month before we saw the light—we must buy.

So again we went, and to make the ending short, we bought. And even this buying was beset with baffling blockades. The wisdom of a serpent, the harmlessness of a dove—these were needed and used at every turn. And now we can announce we have the property![88]

The building cost $21,000. The Mission took a mortgage of $12,000 and a second mortgage of $6,000. The property, like most properties of the Mission, was purchased in the name of Joseph Cohn, and the title was later transferred to the Mission. Purchases were handled in this way because most owners were reluctant to rent property to a Jewish mission, but they were even less inclined to sell property to a Jewish mission. As laws against discrimination were enacted purchases made in this way were no longer necessary.

Over and over again, the enemies of the Mission, and of Joseph Cohn in particular, sought to discredit both the Mission and Joseph by continually making accusations implying wrong doing regarding the purchase and holding of real estate. However, the Minutes of the Mission show that every piece of real estate purchased for the Mission in the name of Joseph Cohn was later transferred to the Mission and became a part of its corporate assets, and a part of its audited financial statement.

JOHN SOLOMON—THE PITTSBURGH BRANCH

The Mission continued to expand its outreach to the Jewish community throughout America, and in 1929 a third Branch outside New York was opened in Pittsburgh, Pennsylvania. It was established by Mr. John Solomon.

Joseph Cohn had first approached Mr. Solomon in March 1920, to inquire if he would consider accepting a position with the Mission at the Plaza branch in New York. John Solomon had been serving as a missionary to the Jews in Cleveland. Although he accepted Joseph's invitation to work with the Mission, he later declined because of family problems. During the intervening years John had moved to Pittsburgh, serving as a missionary with the New Covenant Mission. But much of his time was spent traveling, raising funds for New Covenant Mission, and he was ready for a change. He was an experienced missionary with a wonderful testimony and reputation, as well as over twenty-five years of experience in reaching his own people with the Gospel, and he had a desire to establish a mission station.

At the Executive Committee meeting held June 4, 1929, an employment contract was issued to Mr. John Solomon to begin working for the American Board of Missions to the Jews, Inc. His primary responsibility was to establish a Branch of the Mission in Pittsburgh.[89]

The employment agreement with Mr. John Solomon was typical of the way in which Joseph Cohn hired new workers for the Mission although, depending upon the circumstances of the individual, there was some variation. Such "contracts and details" as devised and used by Joseph had never been used by Leopold. This was one of the many changes made by Joseph Cohn which created division between himself and his father. Leopold had always looked for workers who shared his vision and his dedication to witnessing to Jewish people. He wanted the freedom to hire any Jewish believer, or Gentile believer, who had a desire to share the Gospel with Jewish people. If they needed money, he would help them. If they didn't need money they would work as volunteers. If they wanted to stay with the Mission, they stayed. If they wanted to leave, they left. Leopold had a difficult time combining business practices with ministry.

John Solomon was a choice servant of the Lord, a faithful missionary to the Jews. The opening of the Pittsburgh branch with John Solomon as the missionary in charge proved to be one of the wisest decisions Joseph Cohn ever made. John's testimony is remarkable. He wrote:

> I was born of Orthodox parents in the city of Yassy, Roumania. My parents claimed to be of the tribe of Levi: direct descendants of Abraham according to the flesh. I was circumcised on the eighth day to become a child of his covenant....My father, being a prominent leader and Hebrew teacher, considered it his duty to fulfill Deut. 33:10, 'They shall teach Jacob thy judgments and Israel thy law.'
>
> As I look back now to those years of my youth, I recall that they were spent more in the fear of man, than the fear of God. I was trying to observe the precepts of the rabbis, but the more I tried, the more disappointed and miserable I felt, because they became a burden to me.
>
> In the year 1898 Roumania went through a great crisis. During this time of pressure the Jews were the scapegoats and suffered the most. This created in my heart a longing for freedom, and a desire to live in a country where Jews had liberty to develop their intellectual, commercial and spiritual capabilities.
>
> As I was now a young married man, Mrs. Solomon and I agreed to leave Roumania and seek our fortune in a land of opportunities. After thirty-six hours of railroad traveling we reached Budapest, the capital of Hungary. A friend from Roumania had given me a letter of introduction to a gentleman of very fine character in Budapest. Immediately upon acquaintance he offered us both help and advice, which we refused to accept, for we learned in the course of our conversation that he was a Christian minister. Mrs. Solomon most emphatically refused, saying, we have suffered enough from these 'Goyim' (Gentiles). Rev. Dr. A.M. seeing that we were unwilling to stay in Budapest, gave us a note to Rev. David Baron, London, England. He assured us that he was Hebrew having the highest and finest principles.
>
> Arriving in London, I found employment within the first week. On Sunday afternoon, my wife and I took a walk on Whitechapel Road. The singing at an open air meeting attracted our attention. This was the first time in our lives that we heard a group of Jews in the Yiddish vernacular singing, praising, exalting 'Jehsuah' Jesus, as the Messiah of Israel, and the Savior of the World. We listened eagerly, while the crowd around was restless. At the close of the meeting, one of the speakers, recognizing that we were newcomers, gave us an invitation to come to the Saturday afternoon meeting, he told us that Rev. David Baron would speak. 'Rev. David Baron?', I asked, 'Why, we have a note to Rev. Baron: I wonder if this is the man?' Curiosity brought me in contact with that dear messenger of God.
>
> When I met him, his countenance radiated sunshine, love, understanding and welcome, lending to his whole appearance a dignity and bearing not easily portrayed. Instinctively, I knew I was in the presence of a friend.
>
> 'Faith cometh by hearing and hearing by the word of God.' Three years passed; then a stirring sermon was preached on Numbers 21:8 compared with John 3:14 and Psalm 22. The whole message seemed to be directed to me only, as though the speaker knew all about my hatred for the Cross. They sang the words of the hymn: 'See from His head, His hands, His feet. Sorrow and love flow mingled down. Did e'er such love and sorrow meet, or Thorns compose so rich a crown?'
>
> A sudden picture of the Cross came before my vision, and grief and sorrow pierced through my heart.
>
> The Holy Spirit brought conviction to my soul, so that I could not refrain from crying. At the close of the meeting I was asked to come to the prayer room. Special prayers were offered in my behalf. Upon request, I earnestly repeated, 'Lord, be merciful unto me a sinner!' The blessed Holy Spirit worked out the new creation within my soul, and gave me the assurance that my sins are all washed away by the blood of Christ on Calvary's Cross.
>
> Having therefore obtained the help of God, I continue unto this day, witnessing both to small and great, saying none other things than those which the prophets and Moses did say should come; that Christ should suffer, that He should be the first that should rise from the dead, and show light unto the Jewish people, and to the Gentiles.[90]

During his missionary tenure with the Mission, John Solomon was used of God to lead a young rabbinical student to the Lord. That student's name was Charles Lee Feinberg. Charles was attending the Yeshiva (rabbinical school) in Pittsburgh. The impact which the life and testimony of this young rabbinical student had upon the Mission, and upon evangelical Christianity, can never be measured. (Further consideration of his contribution to the Mission will be enlarged upon in later chapters.) John Solomon's life and selfless ministry touched Charles Feinberg and many other Jewish people in the Pittsburgh area. He was a faithful and beloved worker for our Lord.

LEOPOLD COHN HONORED

Nine years of growth and change had passed since that fateful day when the Board of the Williamsburg Mission had "moved to appoint Mr. Joseph Cohn Field Secretary and Manager" of the Mission.[91] During those years Rabbi Leopold Cohn continued to faithfully carry on his ministry as Superintendent of the Williamsburg Mission and as pastor of his Messianic congregation in Brooklyn. He retained the title of Editor of *The Chosen People* magazine until January 1933, but in reality Joseph had created an Editorial Department, of which he was the head. More than a few of the conflicts that erupted between Joseph and his father came as a result of their differing ideas over how the vision of the ministry should be presented to the readers of *The Chosen People* magazine. To Leopold, the ministry would always be the Williamsburg Mission to the Jews, a Messianic community. Joseph, however, saw the broader scope of the work in "The American Board of Missions to the Jews, Inc.," a world-wide ministry which was reaching out to all Jews everywhere with the Gospel.

Wheaton College, at their Commencement Exercises on June 18, 1930, conferred upon Leopold Cohn (then age 68) the degree of Doctor of Divinity. Thus, after thirty-six years of dedicated ministry to his Jewish people—after enduring personal, physical, and emotional struggles that would have crushed a lesser man—Rabbi Leopold Cohn, the humble rabbi from Hungary who had diligently and faithfully served his Messiah, received national recognition for his ministry and his accomplishments. By conferring this degree upon Rabbi Leopold Cohn, Wheaton College not only publicly repudiated the rumors and false charges of Leopold Cohn's enemies, they also gave endorsement to the cause of Jewish missions and evangelism. Wheaton College took a stand that day, proclaiming that they recognized Jewish missions as an honorable field of service for servants of the Lord Jesus Christ.

The winds of change had been relentless, and for Rabbi Leopold Cohn they had caused drastic and often undesired changes within his ministry. Rabbi Cohn, God's servant, continued to faithfully share the message of the Gospel, but Leopold, the man, must have often felt that he was being pushed aside. This must have been especially true as the Board of Directors grew in number, resulting in new members who had no knowledge of the affliction, the suffering, and the devotion of Rabbi Leopold Cohn to his people and to his Mission.

It is heartening to know that Rabbi Cohn's fellow workers followed Wheaton College's lead in recognizing the achievements and the blessings of God upon Leopold and his ministry. The Minutes of the January 1934 Board Meeting record the following:

> Nominations for officers for the ensuing year being in order, Mr. Graef expressed his conviction that because of the changes in Mission management within the past year or two, and the diminished participation of Mr. Leopold Cohn in the work, it would be a very appropriate conclusion to elect Mr. Cohn as Honorary President for the remainder of his life, in recognition of his being the Founder of the Mission, and of his many years of untiring and faithful labor and service, under God, in its building up.
>
> He thereupon moved the election of Mr. Leopold Cohn as Honorary President for the remainder of Mr. Cohn's life. The motion was seconded, and after several of the members present had expressed their warm approval, it was carried, and Mr. Cohn was declared elected as Honorary President.[92]

For the next few years Leopold attended the Board meetings as he was able, and he made every effort to attend the Mission meetings that he so dearly loved. But the years of struggle and bitter persecution had taken their toll upon his physical strength, and as the years progressed he became weaker and more frail in health.

THE DEATH OF LEOPOLD COHN

On December 19, 1937 Rabbi Leopold Cohn went home to be with his blessed Lord whom he had served so faithfully. The February 1938 Chosen People magazine included several pages of an article entitled, "In Memoriam." Excerpts from that article are as follows:

> Dr. Cohn became suddenly ill on Saturday afternoon of December 11th, 1937, with hemorrhages. On Sunday the 12th he was removed to the Brooklyn Hospital where the hemorrhages were diagnosed as coming from a stomach ulcer which had apparently broken through the blood vessels. By Tuesday evening the treatments began to show definite results, for the bleeding had stopped and Dr. Cohn was taking nourishment. On Wednesday morning, however, pneumonia had developed, and the oxygen tent was at once resorted to. His condition however from that time on became gradually weaker and weaker, although several blood transfusions were given. On Saturday, December 18th, Dr. Cohn went into a coma from which he did not recover; the end came peacefully on Sunday morning, December 19th, at 4:29 o'clock.

...we will print hereunder an account which appeared in the Brooklyn Daily Eagle. [The Brooklyn Daily Eagle was the paper that had so often carried the stories of Leopold's persecutions and battles with those who had sought to destroy his ministry.]

'The Rev. Dr. Leopold Cohn, founder and president emeritus of the American Board of Missions to the Jews, Inc., of Brooklyn, N.Y., the largest Jewish missionary agency in America, and the second largest in the world, died early yesterday morning in the Brooklyn Hospital after an illness of one week. He was in his 76th year.'

'Educated in the Yeshivas of Central Europe, Dr. Cohn was a rabbi of an orthodox synagogue in Austria Hungary, and shortly after his arrival became a convert to Christianity. So devoted was he to his new found faith that after further studies at the Free Church College of Edinburgh, Scotland, he returned to America and undertook immediately to preach the Gospel to the Jews in the Brownsville section of Brooklyn. His efforts at first encountered the most bitter hostility, and for years Dr. Cohn waged a militant battle for the Gospel.'

'A total stranger when he first arrived in America, his struggles soon won for him friends from the various Christian denominations, and these began to rally to his support. Slowly, and under many handicaps, there developed a society known as the Williamsburg Mission to the Jews, because the principal work then had come to be established in the Williamsburg section of Brooklyn. Again the work grew and enlarged until it began to reach out over the United States by means of branch stations and missionaries.'

'Branches were later established in Poland, Germany, France, Latvia and Palestine. The name was changed to The American Board of Missions to the Jews. At the headquarters building in Brooklyn many hundreds of Jews have been baptized, and a large congregation of Christian Jews remains as a testimony to the 43 years of labor of Dr. Cohn. From these headquarters buildings have gone out missionaries to all parts of the earth.'

'Dr. Cohn was honored with the degree of Doctor of Divinity by Wheaton College of Wheaton, Illinois in 1930. He was for nearly 40 years a member of the Long Island Baptist Ministers' Association, also a member of the Marcy Avenue Baptist Church of Brooklyn. Surviving are a wife and four children, Benjamin Cohn, the Rev. J. Hoffman Cohn, Mrs. John Lolis and Dr. Joshua Cohn.'

'Funeral services will be held at the Marcy Avenue Baptist Church, Marcy and Putnam Avenues, tomorrow night at 8 p.m. [The Brooklyn Daily Eagle, Monday, December 20, 1937].'[93]

The service was held on Tuesday, December 21, at the Marcy Avenue Baptist Church. The building was filled to capacity; many who attended were Jewish people who had come to faith in Yeshua through Leopold's dedicated ministry and faithfulness to God's Word. Before he died, Leopold had left strict instructions that he wanted a Hebrew Bible opened to Isaiah Chapter 53 placed in the casket with him. He told his Jewish congregation that when he entered into the presence of the Lord Jesus Christ he would simply point to that chapter as his admission ticket. In accordance with his wishes, the Hebrew Bible, opened to Isaiah 53, was placed on Leopold's casket for all to see and read.

Rev. Dr. W. H. Rogers, pastor of the First Baptist Church of New York, and many of the other ministers who took part in the service, were from the Long Island Baptist Minister's Association. Some had known Leopold from the time he began his ministry. Among the laymen present was Dr. Hugh R. Monro. His tribute to Rabbi Cohn was as follows:

I am glad this evening to bear a simple word of tribute to this valiant soldier of Christ who was my friend for many years. As far as I have been able to draw from the remarks that have been given tonight, I think that my acquaintance extended over a period almost as long as that of any of the speakers this evening, nearly forty years. I treasure this fellowship as one of the inspiring things which has come into my life, one of the real influences. I owe a great debt to this true soldier of the Cross. He was indeed a soldier, for, as several have indicated, he knew what strife was, what warfare was, on behalf of the Lord. There are probably not many in this audience who know how acute the suffering of this servant of Christ was in his early ministry. The anguish that he went through over a period of years. It is one of the phenomena of the spiritual history of this city and it is hard to account for it. I can hardly think of a parallel in the religious history of this country. To find an exact parallel I should have to go abroad to a celebrated case in France in which one of his own people was concerned a generation ago. The simple fact is that his life was in constant peril for years in his early ministry. He was the victim of assault more than once. How strange this is when we think of the gentleness of his spirit, and his humility, and his one passion, and that to serve others. Yet for some reason this violent opposition, not only on the part of his own people, but on the part of some Gentiles, developed and for many years he was hounded and haunted night and day by opposition, by obstacles, by vilest slander and misrepresentation. It sounds like a chapter out of the dark ages. Perhaps some day that history will be written. I think there would be a value in the record. We live in days of such indulgence and softness we know little of what our forefathers had to pass through. The things that put fight into them and iron in their blood. But Leopold Cohn knew all about it. Another impression I have, and that was his singular poise and stamina. Leopold Cohn knew his Bible as few men know their Bible. He was steeped in its teaching. He had a full-orbed message. In the first Epistle to the Corinthians there is a list of the endowments that are given to the Saints of God, fruits of the Spirit. In the Epistle to the Ephesians there is a catalogue of God's gifts to His Church. And when our Lord ascended on high he gave gifts unto men, and these gifts were prophets, apostles, pastors, evangelists, and teachers. Now I can think of our beloved Brother right in the midst of that catalogue. He was in truth a gift of our Lord to the Church. He had the true spirit of the under shepherd. He had a passion for souls. He had a keen responsiveness to the voice of the Spirit. How unslightingly did he labor during all these years in this very community. Starting amidst discouraging circumstances and with only a few kindred spirits behind him to share his afflictions and persecutions, the work which he founded is reaching out, as has been observed, to almost all quarters of the globe. Our Lord is the great Vindicator. He has a way of seeing his children through, and he has a way of settling accounts and squaring things. What a satisfaction and joy it is to realize as we meet here tonight, that even while still in the flesh he knew his Lord's vindication. He had led him out into this large and wealthy place. So I salute this true soldier of the Cross. I would like to lay some worthy tribute upon his casket. He has fought a good fight. He has finished his course. He has kept the faith. Henceforth there is laid up that crown of righteousness, which the Lord, the righteous judge, will give him: not to him only but to all those that love His appearing.[94]

Among the thousands of significant testimonials that were received about Leopold Cohn, was one written by the Rev. Jacob Peltz, B.D., Secretary, The International Hebrew Christian Alliance, of London, England. Both Leopold and Joseph had been involved in the beginnings of the American Chapter of the Hebrew-Christian Alliance. Jacob Peltz, wrote:

Please accept my profound sympathy in the great loss you and your family have sustained personally and in the loss the Jewish Mission field has suffered by the passing of one of its greatest missionary pioneers and leaders.

It was my privilege and pleasure to meet and have conversation with your father on three or four different occasions and each time I felt that I had been in the presence of a great Hebrew Christian scholar and one of the most gifted Jewish missionaries in the world. How proud and happy I am to have known your distinguished father.

How happy your father must have been after spending forty-three years of labor as a Jewish missionary (and I know that some of those years were full of pain, suffering, persecution, when all the satanic powers were at work to undermine him and the great work he was establishing) to be able to see such a harvest as a result of his indefatigable and faithful labors: Jewish converts everywhere, a network of Jewish mission stations in the United States and other countries of the world, a Jewish missionary periodical which is having untold influence over the minds of thousands of Jews the world over. I know of no Jewish Christian since the time of the Apostles who has left so much evident, visible and tangible fruits of his labors as your dear father.

I am quite aware that it is due to your great organizing ability, your genius in administration, that the American Board of Missions to the Jews has had such a phenomenal growth and expansion during the last decade but none of us will forget that it was your father who built the foundation and weathered the storm when it was raging during the most violent tempests of controversy.[95]

What makes this testimonial stand out is that it comes from one of Leopold's peers, someone who was also directly involved in Jewish missions and evangelism. Both Leopold and Joseph Cohn often had differences of opinion with individuals within the International Hebrew Christian Alliance regarding direction, focus, and methodology, yet they had respect for one another's respective ministries and callings. This testimonial is also of interest because it expresses Jacob Peltz's recognition of Joseph Cohn's genius in organizing and administrating the Mission during it's time of expansion and growth (a genius others recognized as well).

On Wednesday morning December 22, 1937 Leopold Cohn's body was laid to rest in the burial plot in the Cypress Hills Cemetery in Brooklyn, New York. The humble rabbi from Hungary was with his Lord, but his memory and his ministry lived on. The violent winds of change and the growth he created within the Mission may have side-tracked Rabbi Cohn's vision of establishing a great Messianic community (one that included Messianic congregations), but his vision for those needs was not extinguished. As the winds of change continued to buffet the Mission, Rabbi Leopold Cohn's vision for Messianic congregations remained, to be rekindled many years later in the hearts of future Mission leaders.

ENDNOTES
Chapter 5. The Winds of Change

1. *The Encyclopedia of Religious Quotations*, edited & compiled by Frank S. Mead, (Westwood, New Jersey: Fleming H. Revell Co., 1965), p 1.
2. The Committee investigating charges against Leopold Cohn, *In the Matter of the Investigation of Charges Preferred Against Leopold Cohn*, Official Minutes (Unpublished, 1916).
3. Testimony of Augusta Sussdorf, *Investigation*, p 164.
4. See note above.
5. *Down On Throop Avenue*, (Brooklyn, New York: American Board of Missions to the Jews, Inc., now Chosen People Ministries, Inc., n.d.), p 11.
6. *The Chosen People*, Vol. 15, No. 5, (February, 1910), p 5.
7. *The Chosen People*, Vol. 13, No. 8, (May, 1908), p 6.
8. *Minutes of Williamsburg Mission to the Jews*, June 27, 1916, p 32.
9. *The Chosen People*, Vol. 7, No. 4, (January, 1902), pp 5-6.
10. Joseph Cohn, *I Have Fought A Good Fight*, (New York, New York: The American Board of Missions to the Jews, Inc., now Chosen People Ministries, Inc., 1953), pp 40-41.
11. See note above, p 123.
12. See note above, pp 124-125.
13. *The Chosen People*, Vol. 17, No. 2, (November, 1911), p 5.
14. *Minutes of Williamsburg Mission*, June 4, 1912, p 9.
15. See note above, January 15, 1913, p 11.
16. See note above, June 11, 1913, p 13.
17. See note above.
18. See note above, January 21, 1915, p 20.
19. See note above.
20. See note above, January 19, 1916, pp 27-28.
21. See note above, January 17, 1917, p 37.
22. *The Chosen People*, Vol. 18, No. 2, (November, 1912), pp 5-6.
23. *Minutes of Williamsburg Mission*, November 8, 1916, p 31.
24. See note above, January 17, 1917, p 40.
25. *The Chosen People*, Vol. 15, No. 5 (February, 1910), pp 3-4.
26. *The Chosen People*, Vol. 16, No. 3, (January, 1911), p 5.
27. *Minutes of Williamsburg Mission*, November 20, 1917, p 44.
28. See note above, January 16, 1918, p 46.
29. See note above.
30. *Minutes of the Executive Committee*, Williamsburg Mission to the Jews, October 16, 1922, p 29.
31. *Minutes of Williamsburg Mission*, January 17, 1917, p 36.
32. See note above, p 37.
33. See note above, p 39.
34. *The Chosen People*, Vol 13, No. 3, (December, 1907) p 2; *The Chosen People*, Vol. 18, No. 4, (January, 1913), p 2.
35. *Minutes of Williamsburg Mission*, April 17, 1917, p 43.
36. See note above.
37. *Minutes of Williamsburg Mission*, November 20, 1917, p 45.
38. See note above, November 4, 1918, p 53.
39. See note above.
40. *Minutes of Williamsburg Mission*, June 13, 1918, p 52.
41. See note above, December 5, 1918, p 54.
42. See note above.
43. *The Chosen People*, Vol. 22, No. 5, (February, 1919), p 6.
44. See note above, pp 7-10.
45. *The Chosen People*, Vol. 22, No. 3, (December, 1916), p 5.
46. See note above, p 12.
47. *The Chosen People*, Vol. 22, No. 5 (February, 1917) p 5.
48. *The Chosen People*, Vol. 22, No. 6, (March, 1917) pp 3-5.

[49] *The Chosen People*, Vol.23, No. 1, (October, 1917), pp 3-4.

[50] *Minutes of Williamsburg Mission*, January 7, 1920, p 61.

[51] See note above, pp 63-64.

[52] *The Chosen People*, Vol 24, No. 8, (May, 1919) p 5.

[53] *The Chosen People*, Vol. 25, No. 3, (December, 1919), pp 5-6.

[54] *Minutes of Williamsburg Mission*, January 28, 1920, p 74.

[55] See note above, June 2, 1920, pp 76-77.

[56] *Minutes of the Executive Committee*, March 10, 1920, p 2.

[57] See note above, March 24, 1920, p 4.

[58] *Minutes of Williamsburg Mission*, March 3, 1920, p 69.

[59] *The Chosen People*, Vol. 26, No. 1, (October, 1920), pp 10-11.

[60] *Minutes of the Executive Committee*, April 25, 1922, p 25.

[61] *Minutes of Williamsburg Mission*, January 25, 1922, pp 85-86.

[62] See note above.

[63] *Minutes of the Executive Committee*, March 13, 1923, pp 34-35.

[64] See note above, May 14, 1923, p 37.

[65] See note above, November 7, 1923, p 42.

[66] See note above, July 16, 1924, p 48.

[67] *Minutes of Williamsburg Mission*, September 15, 1924, p 103.

[68] *The Chosen People*, Vol. 30, No. 1, (October, 1924), p 8.

[69] *The Chosen People*, Vol. 29, No. 1, (October, 1923), p 11.

[70] *Minutes of the Executive Committee*, November 21, 1922, p 31.

[71] See note above, June 21, 1927, pp 69-70.

[72] See note above, October 3, 1927, p 74.

[73] See note above, March 19, 1928, p 79.

[74] *The Chosen People*, Vol. 31, No. 2, (November, 1925), p 8.

[75] *Minutes of the Executive Committee*, December 20, 1921, p 22.

[76] *The Chosen People*, Vol. 37, No. 3, (December, 1931), p 11.

[77] *The Chosen People*, Vol. 32, No. 7, (April, 1927), pp 4-5.

[78] *The Chosen People*, Vol. 32, No. 4, (January, 1927), pp 7-8.

[79] *The Chosen People*, Vol 34, No. 3, (December, 1928), p 10.

[80] *The Chosen People*, Vol. 37, No. 5, (February, 1932), p 8.

[81] *The Chosen People*, Vol. 32, No. 4, (January, 1927), p 9.

[82] See note above, pp 9-10.

[83] See note above.

[84] *Minutes of the Executive Committee*, December 21, 1926, p 63.

[85] *The Chosen People*, Vol. 28, No. 8, (May, 1923), p 5.

[86] *The Chosen People*, Vol. 29, No. 3, (December, 1923), p 7.

[87] See note above.

[88] *The Chosen People*, Vol. 34, No. 3, (December, 1928), pp 6-7.

[89] See Appendix C. Stipulations of Mr. John Solomon's employment contract with The American Board of Missions to the Jews, Inc.

[90] *The Chosen People*, Vol. 35, No. 1, (October, 1929), pp 4-5.

[91] *Minutes of Williamsburg Mission*, January 28, 1920, p 75.

[92] See note above, January 24, 1934, p 141.

[93] *The Chosen People*, Vol. 43, No. 5, (February, 1938), pp 5-6.

[94] See note above, pp 7-8.

[95] See note above, p 13.

6

The Vision Expands In America

Joseph Hoffman Cohn, next to the eldest son of Rabbi Leopold Cohn, had worked by his father's side in the ministry for many years before Leopold's death. Leopold had gently and lovingly shared the Scriptures with Joseph and his siblings when they were reunited as a family in Scotland. God used those quiet moments of Bible study and prayer to speak to young Joseph's heart, and on one of those occasions Leopold led Joseph in receiving Yeshua as his Messiah. Joseph was about eight years of age. At the time, neither Leopold nor Joseph realized that their lives, their ambitions, and their ministries would be intertwined throughout the remainder of Leopold's life.

Early Life and Training of Joseph Cohn

Joseph was familiar with the discipline of including scheduled times for daily Bible study and prayer prior to his family's move to Scotland. He wrote:

> ...At the age of three and a half, in the old country of Austria-Hungary, I had been started in the Hebrew School. The first lesson I learned was in the Hebrew language, 'In the beginning God made the heavens and the earth.'
>
> ...By the time I was seven years old I had gone through the five books of Moses three times. As a sort of incidental supplement I was compelled to memorize the Psalms, and I think that before I reached the age of eight I could recite the first 75 Psalms in the Hebrew.[1]

The daily discipline of study and prayer was continued under his father's tutelage. As an adult Joseph recalled:

> Coming to America my father kept up the same ritual with us. Every morning we had to read one chapter either of the Torah or of the Psalm book, in the Hebrew, and then translate it before him, into the Yiddish, so that he knew we understood the chapter. Only after we had done this could we have our breakfast. Coming home from school in the afternoon we were not allowed to play with the boys in the street, but we had to stay in and study in the Book of Isaiah. Also in Hebrew. This, of course, was a terrific depriving of our play hours, and we boys resented it. But, as the time went on, I began to be thankful for it because I realized that if I had been playing with the boys in the street, I might have gotten into a good deal of mischief. As it was, I learned nothing about gang rule, nothing about what now seems to be so prevalent, juvenile crime. All that passed me by, but only because of what at the time seemed to me a ruthless control of our every hour.[2]

The study discipline learned, and the knowledge and understanding gleaned from the years of training in the Word of God, prepared Joseph well for the leadership role he eventually assumed in the Mission. But the years of discipline and training also seemed to create a "work-alcoholic" mind set from which Joseph was never able to extricate himself (and which caused him personal and family problems).

From childhood Joseph evidently possessed a proclivity for understanding the Scriptures in the Hebrew and Yiddish languages. He was an accomplished communicator, with excellent written and verbal skills. He also exhibited an ability for writing and for organizing. He possessed a keen business sense and an innate ability to make money.

In his book, "I Have Fought A Good Fight," Joseph shared an incident that happened while he was a student at Moody Bible Institute. This story gives the reader insight into the thinking, the character, and the abilities of Joseph Hoffman Cohn. He wrote:

The school allowed fifteen cents an hour to boys who wanted to earn a little money to help pay for room and board. For fifteen cents an hour the students would have to scrub floors, make beds, wait on tables, and do the thousand and one manual labors necessary in carrying on the operation of a well-organized building. Miss Huntley [mentioned in earlier chapters] was paying my board, but I wanted to earn my own money for clothes and personal needs. I was not quite satisfied with fifteen cents an hour; so I hired my roommate and gave him fifteen cents an hour to scrub the floor of our double room. Then I went downtown and got a job putting up white enamel and gold letters on store windows, work which netted me a good profit, oftentimes as much as one and two dollars an hour. This sort of made me a plutocrat among the students, and I am afraid that I may have stirred up a bit of jealousy. But after all, I felt that if I were capable of earning one or two dollars instead of fifteen cents, that was the proper thing for me to do. The parable of the talents, ten talents, five talents and one talent, would come before me many times as I would ponder over the problem posed by this activity. And I could not see where I was doing wrong.[3]

Another example of Joseph's penchant for making money occurred while he was a student at Moody Bible Institute. It seems the school was using a "Stereopticon" that showed pictures illustrating their lectures in the churches. On one occasion the stereopticon operator did not show up, so Joseph operated the system. The Mission had been using a stereopticon in their programs, therefore Joseph was familiar with the machine. Once the school officials learned that Joseph could operate the machine, they asked him if he would like the job on a regular basis. Of this incident Joseph wrote:

...I told him I would be glad to do this, and I asked him how much they expected to pay me. He replied, 'The usual rate.' I asked, 'What do you mean by the usual rate?' He answered, 'Why, fifteen cents an hour, of course.' I looked at him in surprise, and said, 'I am afraid you've got the wrong man. Let me ask you how much do you have to pay the man that comes up from downtown, who failed to show up last night?' He replied, 'That is none of your business, and has nothing to do with this case.' I answered, 'Mr. H., I am sorry to disagree with you, because it is certainly my business to ask how much you pay a professional man, and it is my business also to expect from you remuneration somewhere within decent distance of what you pay for the downtown professional. Not only that, but the downtown man comes only for the one hour, to run the machine, and then he goes back home. But my job, as I understand it from you, will be that I shall haul all this machinery to whatever place you are going to have the lecture, that I am to see to it that the oxygen and the hydrogen tanks are delivered to that church, that I am to get there an hour or two before the meeting, and I am to set up the machine. I am also to set up the screen, I am to show the pictures, and after the whole thing is over, I am to pack up everything, come down to the depot, wait for a train and come back here anywhere from eleven o'clock at night to one in the morning. I happen to know what you have to pay the man; it is seven dollars, and this just for one hour. I am going to ask you to pay me exactly one half that amount, that is $3.50 for each performance, and I will see to it that the machinery is brought to the place of exhibit, and brought back again at night.' The manager looked at me with contempt. When he got control of himself, he finally said to me, 'You ought to be ashamed of yourself, trying to make money out of the Lord's work. I do not get $3.50 for an hour's work, why should you ask that from us?' I answered him rather brusquely, 'Perhaps you had better excuse me from taking the job.' And so I left him in a state of puzzlement, and went to my room. An hour or two later I received a message from him saying that they would agree to my terms, and I was to report at a certain town the next night, with the equipment, and to operate the machine.[4]

These insights and others into the character of Joseph Hoffman Cohn indicate that he was, without a doubt, a different man from his father, Leopold. He had a firm grasp of the Scriptures and a deep love for the Lord, but he was also a very practical man. He firmly believed that sound business principles could and should be applied to the work of the Mission. Unlike his father, Joseph evaluated every part of the ministry by its effectiveness. During his years of leadership he made it known that his philosophy for the staff was that every barrel had to stand on it's own bottom. In other words, he wanted to know the bottom line. He wanted to know the bottom line costs to the ministry for every project undertaken—from the cost of operating a branch ministry, to the cost of hiring a missionary. Programs that were ineffective were terminated; workers who were not producing were let go. People who knew Joseph Cohn either loved him or hated him.

From his childhood, Joseph had a zeal for the work of the Mission and as he grew to adulthood he had a vision for the Mission, and a direction he wanted to go with that vision. His decision to devote his life to the work and advancement of the Mission was made early; he began working full-time for the Williamsburg Mission in 1907; he was twenty-one years of age.

Joseph welcomed assistance from those who accepted his vision and direction, and he rewarded them accordingly. But those who opposed him, those who sought to thwart his vision for ministry, quickly became his enemies. Thus, controversy constantly surrounded Joseph Cohn—like bees swarming around honey. Criticism was sparked over the way he lived and traveled. He stayed in only the finest hotels and ate at the best restaurants. When he traveled abroad, he would avail himself of a luxurious state-room. Some members of the Christian community were outraged over his seeming lack of propriety, but Joseph believed if the heads of corporations in the secular world could travel this way, the head of a corporation whose purpose it was to bring the Gospel to Jews and Gentiles should travel in like manner. He believed God's servants should travel first class, not steerage. But many Christians, including some of the Mission's board members and supporters, failed to share Joseph's belief in this regard.

MARRIAGE AND FAMILY OF JOSEPH COHN

At the age of 30, in the year 1916, Joseph married Miss Josephine Stone. Josephine was related to the Kellogg family. Her father was a very successful businessman who, according to Joseph, approached him prior to the wedding and encouraged him to leave the work of the Mission. Joseph stated that Mr. Stone, his future father-in-law, offered him five or six times the salary he was receiving if he would work for him instead of the Mission. But Joseph had made a commitment to serve the Lord. He had also made a commitment to his father and to Miss Frances Huntley that he would never voluntarily leave the Mission. Whether a rift was caused over Joseph's refusal to accept Mr. Stone's offer, or whether a rift developed as a result of some other incident that took place, Josephine's father, and later Josephine herself, seemed to have second thoughts about the marriage.

The union of Joseph and Josephine produced three children: Cordelia, Joseph Hoffman Jr., and Huntley (named in loving memory of Frances Huntley, the benefactress to Joseph, Leopold, and the Mission). Evidently, it was not a happy marriage. As has been mentioned, Joseph was a workaholic; the Mission and his service for the Lord always came first in his life. Joseph's travels for the Mission kept him away from home for weeks at a time. It was not unusual for him to travel over 50,000 miles a year on Mission business. Adverse publicity about the Mission, and about Joseph himself, also affected his family and created problems and embarrassment for them. As the Mission grew in size and influence it was a constant source of irritation to the rabbis and to the Jewish community, as well as to some churches, ministers, and Christians. Additionally, the threat of anti-Semitism was growing. With the rise of Nazism, being Jewish, or having a Jewish name, was a definite liability for those who wanted to travel to Europe, and this was evidently something Josephine wanted very much to do. Her married name created an obstacle for both herself and for her children. She solved the problem by changing her surname and the surname of her children back to her maiden name, Stone, when she applied for their passports.

We can only surmise the feelings and atmosphere within the family. What we do know is that the name change and the trip to Europe was the "beginning of the end" for Joseph and Josephine's marriage: They separated. They never did obtain a legal divorce; neither one ever remarried. Joseph's children retained their mother's maiden name; none of his children ever became active in the work of the Mission. However, after Joseph's death, his son, Huntley Stone, served as a member of the Mission's Board of Directors until 1965.

Joseph poured all of his energies into the Mission; it was his life. After his separation from his wife, the Mission took the place of his family. In order to be closer to the Headquarters Office, he took up permanent residence at the Beacon Hotel in New York City. His God-given talents and leadership ability, combined with his love of a challenge, drove him as he tirelessly worked to develop and to enlarge the unique ministry that by that time bore the name, "The American Board of Missions to the Jews, Inc."

The Mission was not unique because it was a ministry reaching out to Jews with the Gospel. There were many other Jewish missions working in America during those years. Most other Jewish missions were local works, established with the goal of reaching the Jews of a particular city; others were denominational works. Many of the missions were established years before Leopold Cohn began his outreach to his neighbors in the Williamsburg section of Brooklyn. The American Board of Missions to the Jews was unique because never before had there existed in America such a large, independent, financially successful mission to the Jews.

Leopold Cohn had been the founder of the Mission, but Joseph became its aggressive leader, whose vision for the scope of the ministry's outreach went far beyond the Jews of New York—it went beyond the Jews of America. Joseph Cohn's vision for the ministry's outreach included sharing the Gospel with Jews, and meeting the needs of Jews, wherever they lived. How could this be done? Joseph's mind was constantly at work, searching for answers to that question. He had no role model for developing such a ministry. The methodology used by missions to Gentiles could rarely be adapted to reaching Jews.

Hurdles to be crossed came from the Christian community and from the Jewish community. A major hurdle to cross in the Christian community was to somehow convince Christians that Jewish people need to hear the Gospel. Almost all Christians readily agreed that the heathen needed to hear the Gospel—but the Jews? Many Christians, pastors and laymen alike, felt it was not necessary. Then there was the hurdle of educating the Christian community to understand that in order to attract Jewish people to a mission outreach, the ministry needed to appear successful, and the missionaries needed to be a part of the Jewish community in which they ministered. This often means that missionaries to the Jews live in more expensive areas of the community than their Gentile counter-parts; the salaries needed are consequently higher than other missionary workers, etc. This is a problem which continues to affect Jewish missions to our day.

The hurdles to cross in the Jewish community seemed endless. The American Jewish community during the mid-1920's to the late 1950's was steadily making inroads into mainstream society; it was beginning to win the battle against discrimination. Jewish immigrants discovered that within American society being Jewish, for the most part, created no problems—as long as one did not call attention to the fact of his "Jewishness." The Jews wanted to "play down" their Jewishness; they wanted to assimilate as quickly as possible and become a part of the sum total of American society. But Joseph Cohn and his editorials in *The Chosen People* magazine constantly drew attention to the distinctiveness of the Jews. He constantly pointed out that the Jews needed the Gospel; he pointed out that without the Gospel they were lost. At a time when the Jewish community was seeking acceptance by American society, the writings of Joseph Cohn and the work of the Mission grated upon the feelings of the Jewish community like fingernails on a blackboard. The Mission was a continual source of irritation and embarrassment to the Jewish community.

METHODOLOGY LOOKS BEYOND THE IMMIGRANTS

To be a successful outreach to the Jews, the Mission had to evolve with the Jewish community. Joseph Cohn understood this. Most of the Jewish people who immigrated to America were industrious; they worked diligently to gain financial wealth and security in their new country, making every effort to shed their immigrant status as quickly as possible. Reaching the immigrant Jews with the Gospel remained an integral part of the early ministry of Williamsburg Mission to the Jews and The American Board of Missions to the Jews, but Joseph was looking beyond the immigrants, to the Jews who were becoming more affluent. He wanted the programs of the Mission changed to include their needs.

To effect such changes, Joseph Cohn and the Mission had to cross the hurdle of the "culture problem"—a matter that continually created misunderstandings between the Jewish community, the Jewish believers, and the Christian church. Gentile Christians and pastors within the church pressured Jewish believers to forsake their Jewish culture and be like other "Christians." Jewish believers were encouraged to eat non-kosher foods (ham, shrimp, lobster, etc.). If they succumbed to the pressure and ate the non-kosher foods, they were hailed as being "true Christians," but if they did not eat the non-kosher foods, they were accused of hanging onto their Jewishness and of "keeping the law." Those who would not bow to the pressure of the Christian community, or who tried to retain something of their Jewish culture, failed the "test" and were criticized for being Judaizers, or of perhaps not being true Christians at all. Many found they were no longer welcomed into the activities of the church.

Members of the Jewish community, on the other hand, would accuse the Jewish believers of being deceptive, or of being rabble rousers by drawing attention to their Jewishness. If Jewish believers totally assimilated into the Christian community, never being identified as Jewish, the Jewish community used them as examples saying, "The Christians are making Gentiles out of the Jews they convert," or "The Christians and missionaries to the Jews are soul snatchers, robbing Jews of their identity and heritage."

Joseph Cohn understood the difficulties that the "cultural games" created for Jewish believers within the Church. Many true Christians had a stereo-typical idea (based on reading Scripture) of what they thought the Jews should be like. Some thought all Jews should be gentle, kind, and loving like the greatest Jew who ever lived—the Lord Yeshua. They found it difficult to accept their new Jewish neighbors when they did not measure up to their preconceived ideas. Other Christians believed that all Jews were stiff-necked and rebellious against God. Still others thought the Jews were responsible for the crucifixion of Yeshua and were therefore under a curse from God. Being well aware of such attitudes on the part of some Christians in America, Joseph Cohn did not mince words when he addressed these issues in his editorials in *The Chosen People* magazine. One such article appeared in the May 1929 issue of the magazine. He wrote:

> *'I hate the Jews.'* So said a gentleman to us a few weeks ago. We were consulting him about renting one of his stores for a Jewish Mission, *'They are tricky,'* he continued, *'and you can't trust them behind your back, and they are always trying to beat you.'*
>
> We found the gentleman was a Quaker, although not working very hard at it. But we told him a number of things which many similarly-minded and otherwise cultured people either do not know, or do not consider, when they attempt an appraisal of the Jews enmasse. And we want to pass on to our readers, and through our readers to many other

Christians, some of the things we told this Quaker.

If you had been brought up in Russia, a land of terror and indescribable brutality, and your fathers before you had been brought up in the same land, and you went back 800 and 900 and 1,000 years, and...if for 800 years back you had been kicked about as a yellow cur, with no home to call your own, and no promise of the same bed to sleep in for two nights in succession, perhaps you too, like the yellow dog, might snarl back if any one made advances to you.

A Jew in Russia was not allowed to own property; his children were not allowed to go to the public schools; like cattle the Jews were roped off in their respective quarters and were compelled to remain within the ropes; if a Jew was caught outside of the ropes he was instantly put to death....

Whenever a Russian Czar wanted a little extra money, all he did was to make a raid on the Jews, take what they had, squeezing them dry like a sponge, and letting them start life all over again. These frequent and well organized raids finally drove the Jew to the necessity of dealing only in such businesses as would enable him to make a quick escape and to take with him his belongings. That is why so many Jews engaged in the jewelry business, likewise the money lending business. These possessions could usually be placed in the pockets and quick escape be made.

Now it must be remembered that something like 90% of all the Jews in America have come here originally from Russia. It can easily be understood therefore that these Jews would bring with them all of the old, bitter memories of Russian trickery and cruelty. You cannot expect therefore that the first generation of these European Jews is going to grasp immediately the fact of fundamental justice and fairness that prevails in America. In the Jewish mind is that thousand year old fear and distrust of anything which savors of the so-called Christian....If we could take these Jews who come here with all the bitterness of old Europe in their hearts, and quickly inculcate into their minds the true spirit of Christ and Christianity, they would respond to that just as quickly and beautifully as the flower bud responds to the warmth of the June sunshine that pours upon it.

And the Quaker friend said to us, 'You have taught me a great deal this morning, and I want to thank you. I shall know better from now on how to handle the Jews whom I meet.'

And may we hope that many of our readers will also have a little better understanding of the Jewish background, and on that account a little more sympathy and just a little more desire to give the Jew the Gospel message.[5]

Throughout the days of his ministry, Rabbi Leopold Cohn buffeted the problems caused by the collision of two worlds and their cultures—Jewish and Christian. Joseph Cohn now stood in the gap. Thus, much of the criticism that was heaped upon Joseph Cohn, and on the Mission as it grew and expanded into a world-wide ministry, came about as a result of cultural misunderstandings of the role of Jewish believers in the Church, and in a pluralistic society. This is not to say that Joseph Cohn did not make mistakes; he did. But oftentimes his mistakes, like the mistakes made by his father, were brought about by misunderstandings, and magnified out of proportion because of those misunderstandings.

Under Joseph's leadership the Mission saw steady growth, but the most rapid growth took place during the years of 1926 through 1953. Joseph was constantly watching the world around him—looking for the trends, searching for effective ways to reach the Jewish community with the Gospel. He saw the Jewish people beginning to assimilate into mainstream society and he saw their eagerness to stay abreast of the world around them by reading the daily newspapers, so he established The Publishing Salvation Department of the Mission which produced the paper, The Shepherd of Israel. This publication was first published in Yiddish and English and, as was mentioned in the previous chapter, God used it to open the doors for the Mission's first foreign branches—branches that ultimately assisted many Jewish families in their escape from the Holocaust as it swept across Europe and Russia. The story of the development of the foreign branches and the brave men and women who served Yeshua in those branches will be told in a subsequent chapter of this history. Of the Mission and of Joseph Cohn's vision for the ministry it could be said, as Mordecai said to Esther, "and who knows whether thou art come to the kingdom for such a time as this?"[6]

During the early 1900's vast numbers of Jews, fleeing the rising tide of anti-Semitism in Europe and the growing threat of Nazism, poured into New York and Joseph Cohn was anxious to have the Mission at the forefront of evangelism. It was clear to him that the Mission, if it was going to be effective in its outreach to the influx of sad and disillusioned immigrants, would have to develop new methodology and produce new literature. He recognized as well, that the Mission would have to hire and train additional missionary workers and support staff to carry out the programs of the ministry. The Mission was to leave no method untried in the effort to reach Jews with a message of hope—the Gospel.

Recognizing the need, and believing that the Mission was the means God wanted to use to meet that need, Joseph Cohn began to develop his strategy along two fronts. First, to increase the Mission's support base and the Mission's profile among Christians in North America. Second, to establish new branch ministries. To accomplish the second goal, Joseph knew it would not only be necessary to hire and train new missionaries, a "net-work" system of volunteers would be needed as well. His ultimate goal in the establishment of branch ministries and the development of volunteer workers was to elevate the profile of the Mission, and to educate Christians to recognize the need for reaching out to their Jewish neighbors with the Gospel.

The Brooklyn branch of the Mission became the model. It also served as the National and International Headquarters for the Mission. Despite his hectic schedule of travel, speaking, writing, etc., Joseph Cohn faithfully attended the meetings that were held at the Brooklyn headquarters. He often preached at the services, and when his father, Leopold Cohn, could no longer baptize new believers, Joseph gladly assumed the task.

By 1934, the Mission's headquarters building in Brooklyn was overcrowded. More often than not, the Monday night Converts' Testimony Meeting had standing room only. The unique Mothers' Class that had been started by Miss Augusta Sussdorff and Miss Dorothy Rose was attracting forty to sixty Jewish mothers each week. Through that class the Mission not only reached Jewish mothers with the Gospel, but the truths taught went home with the women, to be shared with their children and their husbands. Ultimately, many of the children and husbands began to attend meetings at the Mission as well. Nearly every occasion for meetings—Daily Vacation Bible School, Friday night Gospel services, the annual Thanksgiving celebrations, the annual Christmas programs, and Jewish holiday services—drew large crowds to the Brooklyn building, resulting in a very overcrowded facility.

Word of mouth about the services held at the Brooklyn headquarters was not the only factor that drew the crowds. The increased printing and mailing of literature brought many inquisitive Jewish immigrants. The Shepherd Of Israel was being printed and sent to France, England, China, Austria, Palestine, Czechoslovakia, Australia, Latvia, Denmark, Romania, Canada, Poland, Sweden, Scotland, Bulgaria, and Turkey. Joseph wrote concerning the ministry of The Shepherd of Israel: "This is truly a far flung battle line, and we can only look upon it with thanksgiving and with praise. Forty different Mission stations are included in these statistical summaries, and the number of papers sent to these various Missions total anywhere from 25 to 2000 copies a month."[7]

In addition to The Shepherd of Israel, the Mission continued to publish and mail issues of The Chosen People magazine, plus a number of tracts and other publications. Sharing some of these figures with his readers, Joseph wrote:

> A ministry which has received little mention from us throughout the years, is the shipping from our headquarters building of thousands of tracts and leaflets, of all kinds; many of these are tracts which are sent for by our Christian friends to be used by them in their personal dealing with their Jewish friends. Other tracts are those which serve as a ministry to the Lord's people, tracts dealing with the place of the Jew in God's order for the present day, tracts dealing with the nearness of our Lord's return, tracts dealing with direct Gospel presentation,…Just one month alone will give you a fair idea of the vast amount of work involved, showing shipments not only in all parts of America, but to all parts of the world,…The figures for the month of December, as an example, show 3961 pieces of literature sent to 75 individual addresses. In this connection, may I mention also that all of this work is done in the office in addition to the regular daily mail, the acknowledgment of all contributions, and the regular bookkeeping entries. (To give you an idea of the vast amount of work involved, we received 10,034 individual contributions during the year 1933, almost an average of 900 a month.)[8]

The Mission's headquarters building was also home to its Dispensary—a medical clinic that was operated until the early 1950's. This unique clinic provided much needed medical care for newcomers to the country who could not afford other medical care. In 1933 the Dispensary treated over 6,000 patients. But beyond dispensing medical care and advice, the Dispensary was also used of God to reach many Jewish families with the Good News of the Gospel.

To Joseph Cohn, the crowded conditions at the Brooklyn facility confirmed that God was blessing the work of the Mission. However, Joseph also saw the overcrowded conditions as a hedge around what God could do if the limitations of space were not holding Him back. Expansion was needed at the Brooklyn headquarters facility! In the February 1934 issue of The Chosen People magazine, Joseph asked readers to pray with him about this special need. He stated that such an expansion of the facility would cost in the neighborhood of $20,000.[9]

MARSTON MEMORIAL HALL

One year later, in February 1935, Joseph announced to his readers that the Mission was moving ahead with its plan to enlarge the Headquarters building in Brooklyn. He informed readers of answered prayer—some $15,000 over and above the usual gifts for the ministry had been received, and Joseph wanted his readers to know that the Mission planned to break ground for the expansion in March.[10]

The March 1935 issue of The Chosen People magazine included a picture of the architect's drawing of the new building. Readers were informed that work on the new building had already been started, and that the Mission expected to occupy the new space by June 15, 1935. The new building was to be named the Marston Memorial Hall, in honor of

Mr. Frank H. Marston.

Mr. Marston first met Rabbi Leopold Cohn in 1896, just two years after Leopold started his ministry. He served as a faithful member of the Board of Directors from the time the Mission was incorporated, and was appointed to serve as the Chairman of the Board—a position he filled until his death. Frank H. Marston was a close and dear friend of the Cohns and of the Mission. Joseph Cohn wrote of Frank Marston:

> ...Of his time, his money, his consecrated wisdom, he gave freely and sacrificially. When the work was buffeted in the crucible of persecution, and its enemies seemed about to overwhelm us on all sides, it was this man of God who stood on the firing line with us, with a self-abandon that said, 'If the ship is to sink, I'll be the last one to leave.' And it was he who used to say at our Board meetings, where, as our honored head until the day of his home-going, he presided with such grace and courtesy, 'I want that whatever we do at this meeting, we shall not be ashamed to have appear on the front page of The New York Times tomorrow.'[11]

Joseph was pleased to announce to his readers that the building had not only been completed on time, but that God had supplied every penny required for the expansion; they would be able to dedicated the building debt free. The Dedication Service was held exactly as planned, on June 17, 1935.[12] It was a service that lasted six hours—from four o'clock to ten o'clock P.M. Several pastors from the area brought messages; Joseph Cohn and some of the missionaries shared reports of God's blessings; there was singing, prayer, and thanksgiving. To top the praise celebration off, a special meal was prepared and served to the guests in the new Marston Memorial Hall.

Mr. Irwin H. Linton, the President (Chairman) of the Board attended the Dedication Service, although to be there meant he had to travel all the way from Washington D.C. Mr. Linton was elected to the Board at the annual meeting held January 25, 1933. He was a lawyer—a member of the Bar of the District of Columbia and of the Supreme Court of the United States. He served as President of the Board until January, 1960. During that time, Mr. Linton stood shoulder-to-shoulder with Joseph Cohn as they sought to expand the Mission's vision and to protect the Mission's reputation when it was being attacked by individuals who opposed its expanding ministry and influence.

AUGUSTA SUSSDORFF—HER STORY

One of the testimonies shared at the Dedication Service was that of Miss Augusta Sussdorff who, by that time, had been on staff for over thirty years. She spoke of the early days of the Mission—of the days when persecution of the Mission and of the missionaries had caused great suffering. As Miss Sussdorff spoke, Miss M. Helen Biber, who had joined the staff of the Mission in 1931, listened intently. Miss Biber had previously served in Chicago at the Marcy Center, a Jewish work conducted by the Methodists. Remembering Miss Sussdorff's testimony, Miss Biber later wrote:

> ...In closing, Miss Sussdorff paid tribute to Mr. Marston and his devoted daughter [Ella] who is carrying on in the spirit of her sainted father. It occurred to me as I listened to her story that we missionaries of the last decade have found work among the Jews so different from the standpoint of persecution, and that we have missed some of the fellowship of His sufferings which the pioneer missionaries experienced.[13]

For Joseph Cohn, the expansion of the Mission's headquarters building in Brooklyn was cause for rejoicing; it meant the work could continue to grow. But that was not his greatest cause for rejoicing. Joseph Cohn was a business man "through and through," but every business transaction, every program put into place, every piece of literature developed—all was done to reach Jewish people with the Gospel. The reports from the dedicated staff of missionaries and volunteers telling of Jews who had accepted Yeshua brought Joseph the greatest joy.

Joseph, too, was moved as Augusta Sussdorff gave her testimony at the Dedication Service. And as Joseph gave his report about the workers who had so faithfully served the Mission and the Lord, his mind reflected back on one fact that others at the service did not know. Joseph Cohn knew that three years earlier, Augusta Sussdorff had submitted her resignation to the Board, stating:

> Brethren:- Owing to my physical condition, I can no longer do my work as it should be done. I therefore resign my position. I would like the privilege of doing as I have done for the past six or seven months, days I felt able I served all day, other days I was here part time. On Wednesday the Lord always supplied the needed strength. Praise His Name. I do know a younger worker is needed. The dear mission is part of myself and I would love to serve a while longer in this small way, if the Brethren so decide.[14]

The Minutes reflect Joseph's great reluctance at losing such a dedicated worker. He told the Board:

> *Miss Sussdorff has been with us for thirty-three years. For the past year or more she has not been at all well, and is not getting any better. Last year she wanted to resign and have her salary stopped. I told her that we could not do that in view of the fact that for many years she had worked without getting any money for her services. Finally it was agreed that she was to receive her full salary and if she wished, she could give back a donation to the Mission. This was a relief to her and so she has been returning $50 each month.* [15]

The Board agreed to pay Miss Sussdorff $60 a month, saying she could give as much or as little of her time as she desired. This dear saint of God, Miss Augusta Sussdorff—a Gentile Christian woman, not a Jewish Christian—gave over fifty years of her life in active missionary service with the Mission. Because of her witness, her loving way of teaching, and her godly life, many Jewish people came to trust in Yeshua as Messiah and Lord. Some of her spiritual children became missionaries with the Mission; others became pastors or Christian workers in other fields of the Lord's vineyard.

Augusta Sussdorff was born on October 8, 1867 to German immigrant parents who were living just off the Bowery on New York's lower East Side. Soon after Augusta was born, her parents moved to the Williamsburg section of Brooklyn. They lived on the edge of a neighborhood called Dutchtown—thus called because of the large number of Dutch families that had settled there. The Sussdorff family joined the Central Avenue Baptist Church on Marcy Avenue, and it was during one of the meetings at that church that she accepted the Lord at the age of thirteen. She became intensely interested in Sunday School work and in foreign missions.

From time to time, the young people of Central Avenue Baptist Church visited other churches in the area, and it was on one of those occasions—when the young people were visiting Hope Baptist Church on the occasion that Rabbi Cohn had been invited as a guest speaker (as mentioned in Chapter Five)—that Augusta had first learned of the mission to the Jews in Williamsburg. Out of conviction, but also out of curiosity, Augusta decided to join her friend, Grace Bigelow, and visit the strange Mission. Miss Sussdorff wrote about that first experience, saying:

> *…The Jews who came to hear Mr. Cohn were rough-looking and unfriendly. They seemed more interested in embarrassing the speaker and breaking up the meeting. One of them sat down in front, almost at Mr. Cohn's feet. He had a habit of springing to his feet during the discourse, shaking his fist under the speaker's nose, and exclaiming in Yiddish, "Say that name again and I'll blast you!" Other Jews shouted and gesticulated. Through it all, the speaker maintained his tranquility and dignity and held his audience by the sheer force of his sincerity and faith in his Lord.* [16]

Because German was the language spoken in their homes, Augusta and Grace had little difficulty understanding Yiddish. Soon they were speaking Yiddish as if they, themselves, were immigrant Jews. They began attending almost all of the services, volunteered their time to visit and to assist as they could, and even gave of their meager resources to financially assist the struggling ministry. Augusta Sussdorff and Grace Bigelow became Leopold Cohn's first volunteer assistants, and even after the Mission had become well established they continued on a volunteer basis, not wanting to receive money for the time spent in sharing the Gospel with Jewish people.

Of her years of ministry with the Mission, Augusta Sussdorff said: "I prayed to love the Jews! In spite of their indifference and unfriendliness, in spite of their rejections and their ridicule, in spite even of their persecutions, I prayed to love the Jews! And my prayer was answered. Right from the beginning of my ministry I have been able to say, 'I love the Jews!'" [17]

On the occasion of Miss Sussdorff's 89th birthday, a great celebration in her honor was held at the Coney Island branch of the Mission. Over one hundred guests showed up for her birthday party, many of whom she had not seen in years. The guest list was comprised of her spiritual children, her spiritual grandchildren, and, yes, her spiritual great-grandchildren—people who had attended her classes as children, who were now adults with children of their own! This wonderful saint of God, who never married, but who gave her life to reaching Jews with the Gospel, wrote of the great blessing it was for her to be honored in such a way. She said:

> *In our world old parents are in the way, but not so with the born-again children of God's family. There were beautiful cards reading 'To my other Mother,' and cards that would not have been sent if the poems did not mean what they said. Some of the gifts had no names on their cards, just 'because we love you.' Oh, how many lonesome mothers and fathers would live again to get such love and devotion! But these were our children spiritually. Some had come from great distances to be present and let me know their love for me.*
>
> *Then there was singing of the hymns I love; and speeches with testimonies of God's power to save. I just drank in*

more and more, until the cup of joy in the Lord was full to overflowing. When my turn came, my mouth was too full to talk. I wanted to say, 'Lord, take me now.' To see that those I had labored with for so many years had held on and were faithful to Him in whom we trust, even our Lord and Savior, Jesus Christ!

A word of thanks for Miss Hilda Koser, who was one of my little girls in the old Throop Avenue Mission in Brooklyn, who always wanted to be 'like Miss Sussdorff.' As a child she used to 'play mission' in her yard with her sisters and other children. Her dear mother used to tell me, 'You should see Hilda stand on a box and play she is Miss Sussdorff and get the children to sing.' Today her dream has come true, and she is our missionary in Coney Island. [The Coney Island branch was under Miss Koser's leadership by this time.]

Then a number of adults who were children stood around me, all believers in the Lord Jesus. One man, taller than all, had come to the Brooklyn Mission as a little boy living across the road. Then he brought his mother. She joined the Mothers' Class, and accepted the Lord and was baptized. Then this boy Albert, as he grew up, accepted the Lord and was led to go to Bible School. He had no suitcase for his things, but God sent him three suitcases and money to get to school. Today he is known as the Rev. Albert Runge, Resident Pastor at our Mission Headquarters, 236 West 72nd Street, New York City.

Another of the adults who stood around my chair was a man named Daniel. His mother was one of the first young girls in my Sunday school class at the Mission in the early days. She was able to lead her mother and sisters to the Mission where they found Christ. Today her son, Rev. Daniel Fuchs, is Director of Missionary Activities, a member of our Board of Directors and also edits The Chosen People. Oh, how wonderfully the Lord is using him!

As I think back I praise God for the privilege that was mine of studying under Leopold Cohn, the founder of the American Board of Missions to the Jews, who gave such wonderful talks in Hebrew and Yiddish. And best of all, as I gazed around my spiritual family in the Lord I realized anew, 'one sows, another waters, but God gives the increase.' I rejoice always that the Lord used me in even a small part to win these many Jewish souls for Him.[18]

BERNHARD SCHATKIN—THE PLAZA BRANCH

Another faithful worker mentioned by Joseph Cohn in his report at the Dedication Service was Mr. Bernhard Schatkin, who had served on the Mission's staff for twenty-eight years. During those years, Bernhard had led many Jewish people to the Lord.

Bernhard was born in Minsk, Russia on September 15, 1877. His family immigrated to the United States in 1892 and, like many of the Jewish immigrants, they settled in New York. Bernard was fifteen years old—an impressionable age. New York was so different from the little town of Minsk! Opportunities for fame and fortune seemed to present themselves everywhere. Perhaps it was naivete, or simply the thrill of doing things he had never known about before, but Bernhard seemed drawn to all of the wrong elements within society, and began to align himself with the forces of liberalism. He soon joined the numerous soap-box orators who lined the streets and parks of New York—from Union Square to Columbus circle. He developed a talent for rabble-rousing, and convinced himself that he was an atheist and a communist. But deep within his heart, Bernhard knew his life was empty.

Bernhard was twenty-four years old, and still espousing his atheistic and communistic philosophy from the soap-box, when God sent a young Gentile girl his way. The two fell in love and were married in 1901. As a married man, Bernhard knew he had to provide for his wife; he could no longer spend his days on a soap-box in the park, so he took a job selling pianos. The energy and enthusiasm which he had channeled into preaching his atheistic philosophy was now channeled into selling pianos. Soon he was the top salesman in the firm.

There was no question in his mind—Bernhard knew he loved his wife. He also knew he enjoyed his work, and that he was good at it! But something was still missing. He knew there had to be more to life than what he was experiencing. What was it? Where could he find it? He continued to maintain his belief that God did not exist, in spite of the feelings of emptiness that his atheistic philosophy produced. To fill the void, he sought love and comfort from his wife and family. Then one day he heard that there was a Mission to the Jews in New York. Recalling that moment, Bernhard later said:

...Curiosity led me to attend one of the meetings. A missionary handed me a copy of the New Testament. I took it home and began to read it. The wonderful life therein depicted of Jesus the Messiah made a profound impression upon me. I had never heard of the New Testament before. I read for the first time of the wonderful Prophet of Galilee and of how he gave sight to the blind, cleansed the lepers, and even raised the dead. I began to attend Christian services, in an effort to learn more of this wonderful Person. I found many friends among those who attended these meetings and I soon began to realize that true believers in Christ love the Jews. It was not long before I felt that I too, must believe in Him as Lord and Messiah and to put my trust in Him for time and eternity.[19]

Bernhard accepted Yeshua as his Messiah in 1909. He was thirty-two years old. He grew quickly in the faith, and soon his wife and family were also believers in Yeshua.

On September 21, 1927 Joseph Cohn hired Bernhard Schatkin to replace Mr. Kern as the Missionary in Charge at the Plaza branch of the Mission. Mr. Kern had resigned because of illness.[20] Within the first few months after Bernhard was put in charge of the Reading Room at the Plaza branch, 112 Jewish people visited the Reading Room, and one man openly professed his faith in the Messiah and wanted to be baptized.[21]

Bernhard Schatkin was ordained in 1935 by the Free Methodist Church in New York. He remained a faithful and loyal worker for the Mission in Brooklyn and in Manhattan until the Lord called him home on June 22, 1956.

Joseph Cohn also mentioned Miss Dorothy Rose in his report—one of the Jewish students whom the Mission had sent to Moody Bible Institute for training in Moody's Jewish Missions Department. Dorothy graduated from Moody in the Spring of 1929. She then joined the Mission's staff as an assistant to Miss Augusta Sussdorff. Dorothy proved to be an excellent worker, although she suffered from poor health. In February 1945, Joseph reported to the readers of *The Chosen People* magazine that Miss Rose would be taking an indefinite leave of absence due to her failing health.[22] During her sixteen years of ministry, Dorothy not only endeared herself to her co-workers, but to the many hundreds of Jewish mothers and young people whom she had served with genuine sympathy and Christian love.

The Brooklyn ministry was running smoothly, and the newly expanded Headquarters building was a facility teeming with activity. Additionally, the Philadelphia branch that had been established earlier under the direction of Rev. Harry Burgen, and the Pittsburgh branch, established under the direction of Rev. John Solomon, were thriving.

Satisfied with what had been accomplished, and eager to expand the scope of the Mission further, Joseph began to turn his attention to the needs of Jews in other cities in North America, and his energy to the task of raising support to finance the Mission's growing work.

CHICAGO BRANCHES AND STUDENT TRAINING

Joseph Hoffman Cohn recognized the value of collaboration and interchange long before the word "networking" became a catch word. He knew if he invested time and resources into the lives of young, gifted Jewish believers (or Gentile believers), it would not only pay big dividends for the Mission, but for the Kingdom of God as well—and he was right! Joseph used this method of "networking" to attract missionaries, to raise support, to open new mission branches—all of which expanded the ministry of The American Board of Missions to the Jews as the Mission sought to reach Jews around the world.

In meshing programs that would bring about expansion of the ministry, with needed personnel to carry out those programs, Joseph was a master tactician. One example of this was the way he brought Mr. Solomon Birnbaum, Director of the Jewish Studies Department at Moody Bible Institute, together with his desire to establish a work on the South side of Chicago. Perhaps some would say Joseph Cohn was a master at "playing one side off against another." In this case, he asked the Board to financially help Solomon Birnbaum in his "mass evangelistic" campaigns, since brother Birnbaum was distributing the Mission's literature. He then asked Solomon Birnbaum if he would take over the leadership of the South side branch if the Mission would support it.[23] Solomon agreed, and thus a new branch of the Mission was opened in Chicago—one that was also tied to Moody Bible Institute. The Branch became the training ground for Moody students who were interested in Jewish evangelism.

Mr. A. E. (Eric) Priestly, was a young man who had been led to the Lord during one of the Mission's Bible conferences, and discipled by Mr. Harry Burgen. Not long after he became a believer, Eric indicated that he felt the call of God upon his life to witness to the Jewish people. Although he was a Gentile believer, Joseph Cohn was so impressed with this young man's dedication to bring the Gospel to the Jewish people that he placed Eric on a scholarship so he could attend the Jewish Studies Department at Moody Bible Institute. Joseph reported to the Executive Committee:

> …we have agreed to pay him [Eric Priestly] $50.00 a month while he is in Chicago, at a salary as missionary colporteur among the Jews in Chicago. Mr. Birnbaum, the head of the Jewish Mission Department, has undertaken to supervise this young man's work and to direct him as to his visits in the Jewish homes. It is expected that he will distribute about 2,000 copies of The Shepherd of Israel each month in certain Jewish districts of Chicago which are not now cared for by any Jewish Mission. In this way he will develop a personal contact with the Jewish families in their homes and it gives us a new outlet for The Shepherd of Israel in Chicago.[24]

The Jewish Studies Department at Moody Bible Institute, under Mr. Birnbaum, became the training and educational base for many of the future missionaries of The American Board of Missions to the Jews. Young Jewish believers who expressed a desire to reach their own people with the Gospel by serving as missionaries with the Mission, were sent to Moody through a small scholarship fund of the Mission; it was called the "Student Aid" program. But Gentile Christians who had a burden to reach Jewish people with the Gospel, and who wanted to serve on staff with the Mission, were directed to Moody as well—as was the case with Mr. Priestly. The financial need of the individual dictated whether he or she would receive a full scholarships or a partial scholarship.

Adjustment to life at a Christian school wasn't always easy for the Jewish students. The Minutes reflect an experience of Mr. Harry Orenstein who had been sent to Moody: "Harry Orenstein, one of the two boys who went to Moody recently, has returned to Atlantic City. It seems that he is of a very sensitive disposition and could not stand the jokes of his fellow students. His lack of English also hindered him."[25]

It is important to remember the difficulties put upon Jewish believers during the years under discussion. Most Jewish believers came from very poor, immigrant families. Some spoke very little English. Those who spoke English often had heavy accents. It was not uncommon for Jews who professed Yeshua as Messiah to be cut off by their family members and friends; the families of Jewish believers often had them committed to mental institutions, or considered them dead and thus held funeral services for them. Jewish believers were also subjected to the prejudices and bigotry that was directed toward all Jewish people during that time. People within American society, including some Christians, had difficulty adjusting to the hundreds and thousands of immigrant Jews who were pouring into their neighborhoods. Some of the immigrant Jews were assuming places of leadership, buying properties, establishing corporations and department stores. They became a source of irritation to their Gentile neighbors when their hard work and close-knit families allowed them to become prosperous. It became apparent that the old-line prejudices and hatred of the Jews, passed down from generation to generation in the communities of Europe and other countries of the world, thrived in America as well.

A year or so after the Mission's branch had been established on the South side of Chicago, Joseph recognized a need for a branch on the North side of the city. He approached Solomon Birnbaum with the proposal of establishing another branch and, once again, Solomon was persuaded to accept the additional responsibility. Thus, a new North side Chicago branch was opened under the supervision of Solomon Birnbaum in the Fall of 1936.[26] As before, Moody students who were interested in entering the field of Jewish Missions were involved in the work of the branch. As a result of his work with the Mission, and in view of the support he was receiving, Solomon Birnbaum was made the honorary missionary for the Mission in Chicago.[27]

BEN KOLTON—HIS STORY

Another Jewish student whom the Mission assisted as he trained in the Jewish Studies Department at Moody, was Mr. Ben Kolton. Ben accepted the Lord only two short weeks after first hearing the Gospel. He was led to the Lord by Mrs. Olive Chattaway, a worker who normally assisted in the Mission's branches in New York and Philadelphia. But on one occasion Mrs. Chattaway was sent to Atlantic City to fill in for Mr. Haberer who had gone to Indiana for a visit. In less than one month after he accepted Yeshua, Ben was attending Bible School, but before leaving for school he wrote out his testimony and gave a copy to Joseph Cohn. His testimony is typical of the many Jewish young people who came to faith in Yeshua through the Mission's branch ministries. Excerpts from Ben's testimony are as follows:

> On December 29th [1930], I arrived in Atlantic City from New York, looking for work, with funds very low. Walking to Texas Avenue to inquire for the Secretary of the Working Men's Circle...[I] saw the sign, 'Messiah of Israel.' I thought I would go in and inquire where I could get a more reasonable room than the one I had. Going in and finding a lady there, I asked this information about the room. I found her to be very friendly,...We started to talk, I explained my atheistic views of religion, and attacking everything which she pointed out to me in the Old and New Testaments, and trying to show her how much of a fake everything she told me was. But seeing the pained look in her face, I was interested, yet amused, to find anyone so truthful in the world;...Therefore, I decided to find out if she were truly sincere; so I asked if I might come again the next day, to study further and see whether she and the things she believed were true or a fake.
>
> So on January 1st, I came in the Mission between 2 and 4 P.M., and was greeted in a very friendly way. We started in to battle about my religion. The lady pointed to the prophecies of Moses and Isaiah regarding the Messiah, which I did not believe in at all,...But I admitted to her that I once read some passages in the New Testament while stopping in a hotel, and that in my eyes I saw her Lord Jesus Christ (Who is also mine now - Praise the Lord) was the greatest Socialist in the world, and greater than any Old Testament prophet....At this, the lady asked me to do her a favor. I consented and she had me promise that I would...pray honestly from my heart to God that He should reveal to me whether Jesus Christ is the Messiah, the Son of God. It amused me much, but for her sake I felt I must promise, so I did. Before I went she invited me to the Saturday evening meeting, as Mr. Burgen of Philadelphia, would be there. I gladly promised. That evening I prayed the prayer I promised to pray, but I had no direct answer.

Saturday evening, January 3rd, I attended the meeting and met Mr. Burgen and talked with him, telling him my ideas. During the meeting my interest grew in the plain people who attended. By studying them and their faces, I saw in each and every one how they listened and enjoyed the message and were really very happy. When the songs were sung, the question that came to me was, 'Why are they so happy?' That night I prayed again, thanking God for the desire I had to read the New Testament, for I really enjoyed it. The next day,...I spent my time reading. I was so sorry I had no one to explain to me some things which I wished to know,...At 7 P.M., I came to the Mission and told Mrs. Chattaway that I had read that day Matthew, Mark, Luke, and had begun in John. After prayer...she pleaded with me that I should study more earnestly and she was sure I would see the truth.

...The next Saturday, Mrs. Chattaway invited me again to the evening meeting. Mr. Burgen of Philadelphia, was again the speaker....It seemed to me that things were clearer, and for the first time it came to me that the Lord was revealing things to me. When Mr. Burgen asked for hands to be raised for all those who believed in Jesus as the Messiah, something in my heart told me to raise my hand, but my Jewish blood in me (or Satan) hindered me....

In the evening we attended the service in Mr. Burgen's Mission, but had to leave early for Atlantic City. In the bus,...When Mrs. Chattaway asked me how I enjoyed the day and the sermon, I could hold out no longer and had to say, 'Very much; it was wonderful and the sermon impressed my very much.' She said, 'Do you now accept Jesus as your Messiah?' I said, 'Yes.' She said, 'Right Now?' I said, 'Yes, with all my heart and all my soul.' She said, 'You take Him, believing through His blood that you are redeemed?' I said, 'Yes, and I am giving my body and soul to serve Him for the rest of my life.' Oh, how greatly Mrs. Chattaway rejoiced....Thus, the Lord answered my prayer and revealed to me the Truth, for which I thanked Him.

...my joy is continuing from day to day. I realize that if the Lord would have given me all that joy the first day that I prayed to Him, that I never would have been able to bear it. Therefore, I am hoping and praying that whoever reads this testimony, especially an unbeliever, shall see the wonderful change wrought in me, and if he really searches for happiness, let him come to the Lord with a true heart and ask that it will be given unto him, ...

On Sunday, January 18th, 1931, I and another son of Israel, were baptized in Chelsea Baptist Church, by Mr. Fuller, the pastor. Afterwards, I asked Mr. Fuller to give me a certificate of baptism, so that I could show it to any unbelieving friends who might say that I had been paid to say I was baptized.[28]

Shortly after her experience of leading Ben Kolton to the Lord, Joseph Cohn asked Mrs. Chattaway if she would be willing to embark upon a new adventure. He said he had received a number of requests to open up a new branch among the more than 100,000 Jews who were living in the Detroit area. Joseph asked Mrs. Chattaway to open that branch. Mrs. Chattaway was willing to accept the challenge, and the Detroit branch opened in January 1931. The following report was included in *The Chosen People* magazine:

Mrs. Chattaway, our Missionary, arrived January 24, all enthusiasm for the opportunities of this new field, and before night of this first day had seen and approved the Rooms at 7709 Oakland Avenue, which we have finally succeeded in securing for the work; she located also her home quarters. She has just completed her third week with us and has made ninety-five calls in Jewish homes where she had encouraging access and gave a clear Gospel testimony leaving always literature in English and Yiddish. She made also ninety-seven calls at doors which she was not invited to enter. In these cases she left literature. Nearly two hundred visits in all— ...

In one Jewish home, Mrs. Chattaway found a woman whose Jewish brother-in-law in Chicago is a Christian believer who had taken her to a Mission in Chicago, who maintained family worship in his home, and because of whose faithful testimony, the mind and heart of his sister-in-law was, and is, open to the Gospel. We trust she may be one of the first sheaves to be gathered. One elderly Jewish man listened with tears in his eyes to Mrs. Chattaway's story of Mr. Kolton's conversion in Atlantic City.[29]

CHARLES LEE FEINBERG—HIS STORY

The evidence of God's blessings upon the work of the Mission was seen in its growth and expansion into new cities throughout America, in its hiring of new workers, in the many decisions for the Lord in the branch ministries, and in the number of Jewish believers the Mission was sending to Bible School. God's Spirit was at work, producing fruit from the efforts of the faithful missionary staff.

This was especially true in Pittsburgh, where Rev. John Solomon had opened that branch in 1929. His work had outgrown its first building and he had rented a second, larger building located in the middle of the Jewish community of Pittsburgh. Understanding the importance of prayer to undergird his work, John had established a prayer circle comprised of some of the women who attended the Mission's meetings. These women met daily in a home, or at the Mission.

They had a great burden for the young "yeshiva bochers" (rabbinical students). They not only prayed for these young men, but sometimes they would even venture forth with Mr. Solomon to give them tracts, or copies of The Shepherd of Israel. When this could not be accomplished, they would place the literature in the young men's letter boxes. The December 1930 issue of The Chosen People magazine gave testimony of God's blessings on the prayers and labors of these women and Mr. Solomon. John Solomon wrote:

> One Monday afternoon, the telephone rang. Mrs. Solomon, in my absence answered the call. 'This is Rabbi F. speaking, at what time will Rev. Solomon be in?' 'He is out on his visitation tour and will be home after 9:00 P.M.' Arrangements were made to meet the inquirer at the close of my class that evening.
>
> Carnegie Library was the place where we first met. We introduced ourselves. He was a young man, just graduated from the University, he also holds two diplomas from Hebrew Schools, and was ready to enter the Hebrew Rabbinical Seminary this Fall. He wished to discuss some important religious subjects and because the Library was too public, we decided that my office would be the right place for that purpose.
>
> On the following day in my office Mr. F. told me 'that for some months Christian tracts, and The Shepherd of Israel, had been placed in my letter box. They were from the Williamsburg Mission to the Jews.' He did not know that I was the one who that had put these tracts there. He read these tracts very carefully and in secret so that his parents, who are orthodox Jews, should not know anything about it. After he had read them he destroyed them.
>
> 'God works in a mysterious way, His wonders to perform.' These tracts had stirred up his mind and made him restless. He sought to discuss these religious problems with a university student, Mr. M. This young man happened to have been one of my pupils in a Hebrew class, and he advised Mr. F. to see me. This is why he came, anxious to hear how I would explain these problems.
>
> For several hours we talked on sin and repentance, 'How can a sinner approach God direct without a mediator, or High Priest?' With the Bible open, I tried to persuade the young man to accept the Messiah, the Lord Jesus Christ as his personal Savior. But he said, 'I cannot say anything just now; please give me time to consider the matter very carefully. Goodbye.'
>
> After he left, we prayed earnestly asking the Holy Spirit to touch his heart and bring conviction to his soul.
>
> About ten days later he came again to the Mission and said, 'I am ready to be in the will of God, and to do whatever He wants me to do.' From that day, he attended the services regularly, also told us that he is fully convinced that Jesus is the Messiah and Savior of Israel. 'I want to be a shining light to my Jewish brethren.'
>
> The burden of this newly born brother began to press upon us more than ever before. Here was a fine young man, a university graduate with a B.A. degree, and a Hebrew teacher. What were we to do with him? Where could we send him to establish a sound Christian foundation, and prepare him for the ministry? Where was his support to come from? In answer to prayer, I came in contact with Dr. Bob Jones, who was conducting evangelistic services in Pittsburgh at the time. I mentioned the problem to him. That same evening the young man and I attended the service. Dr. Jones was so impressed with this young man that he offered to give him free tuition, also board and room at the Bob Jones' College in Florida....The only remaining problem was money for the transportation. Our Field Secretary Mr. J. H. Cohn, passed through Pittsburgh the very next day, and stayed over for a few hours, talked to Brother F. and discussed matters with Dr. Jones, and immediately advanced the money for the transportation to college.
>
> Since then, letters have come from Bob Jones College, telling us how God is already using this brother's testimony for the saving of other precious souls.[30]

The Lord had given Joseph Cohn the unique gift of being able to quickly evaluate potential workers, and he immediately recognized the potential of the young rabbinic student from Pittsburgh. He knew the young man would be a great worker for the Lord and a great blessing and help for the Mission if he could receive the proper theological training. The young rabbinic student's name was Charles Lee Feinberg.

While Charles was in Florida, attending Bob Jones College, Joseph Cohn was laying ground work for the continuing education of this promising new worker. Joseph was in contact with Dr. Lewis Sperry Chafer who had just founded the Evangelical Theological College of Dallas, Texas (later known as Dallas Theological Seminary).

Charles was a brilliant student and an avid student-worker for the Mission. Not only did he carry a full schedule of classes at the Evangelical Theological College of Dallas, but every week-end he engaged himself in speaking for the Mission. In May 1932, Charles sent Joseph Cohn a progress report of his work and studies. He indicated that he had received all A's and A+'s in his class work, and wrote:

> ...In connection with my thesis for graduation I have already received permission to write on 'The Mystery of

Israel's Blindness.'

Aside from my regular school work I am still teaching at Fire Stations in the city on Sundays. I am teaching four times now instead of twice. I was substituting in one place but they made me promise to come permanently. I have had the opportunity of preaching at the Scofield Memorial Church last Sunday. My subject was 'The Messiah in the Talmud.' The Lord was gracious in blessing the meeting. I have been asked to preach again the middle of April.[31]

Joseph Cohn's instincts were correct about the abilities of this young rabbinical student, and about the impact he would have upon the Mission and the doors of opportunity he would open for the Mission, as well as for other Jewish believers. Charles not only completed his degree from the Evangelical Theological College of Dallas, he went on to become a member of its faculty. A bulletin published and circulated by the college stated:

Dr. Charles L. Feinberg had been elected by the Board to take the History department. When the Department of Semitics became vacant it was deemed wise to avail ourselves of his long training in Hebrew and Old Testament, and request his transfer to that department.

Dr. Feinberg was reared in an extremely orthodox Jewish home and synagogue life. He studied Hebrew fourteen years at the Hebrew Institute of Pittsburgh, an institution of high rating, the latter part of which time he had in view rabbinical training. He also taught Hebrew three years. He completed the four year course at the University of Pittsburgh for the A.B. degree in three years, winning membership in Eumatheia, Nat. Hon. Scholastic Fraternity, Phi Alpha Theta, Nat. Hon. History Fraternity, and the Association of Honor Graduates. After his conversion to Christ he came to Dallas and laid out his work to win all three of the degrees offered by our Seminary. These he won with the following predicates; Bachelor of Theology and Master of Theology, each Magna cum laude; Doctor of Theology, Summa cum laude, the latter honor being the first ever won in this Seminary. Due to his training and proficiency in Hebrew he was able to cover all the work for these three degrees in four years with some summer work, majoring in Systematic Theology in his graduate work. He was Fellow in Church History during his last year. His Doctor's dissertation, entitled The Premillennial and Amillennial Systems of Bible Interpretation Analyzed and Compared, will be published early in the fall by a prominent religious publishing house.[32]

Recognizing the important role that a Jewish believer could have in the educational world—both religious and secular—Charles went on in his education to complete a Master's degree at Southern Methodist University in Old Testament, and then to complete a Ph.d degree in Archaeology and Semitic Languages at John Hopkins University.

After teaching at the Evangelical Theological College of Dallas (now Dallas Theological Seminary), Dr. Feinberg left the faculty to join the staff of Talbot Theological Seminary, a new school that was established in Southern California. At Talbot, Dr. Feinberg held the position of Dean and Professor of Old Testament and Semitic Languages.

When queried, years later, what it was that had caused him to investigate the claims of Yeshua, Dr. Feinberg said:

More than a quarter of a century ago when as a university student and prospective candidate for the rabbinate, [I] was studying at home, there was one day deposited in the doorway…a small paper which, upon examination, was found to be a copy of The Shepherd of Israel. With curiosity the little paper was skimmed to ascertain its main message. Some of the material was in English, while another portion was in Yiddish. What held [my] attention…was a striking picture of a bearded, venerable aged Jew. He was reading the Scriptures at Isaiah 53, and the Hebrew text was reprinted in the paper in full. At the top of the Spiritual portion was the question, "Of whom is the prophet speaking?" But more arresting than this was the fact that the aged Jew, clothed in the traditional prayer shawl, was reading with his back to the light. The caption under the picture read, "Standing in his own light." The impression made upon me at the time has never left me, and it proved to be seed sown upon good ground, which the Spirit of God caused to bring forth fruit to eternal life in the days that followed. The words proved to be a shaft from the Lord which went directly to the heart, and ultimately wrought conviction.[33]

Throughout the years, until his recent retirement, Dr. Charles Lee Feinberg wrote, traveled, and spoke on behalf of the Mission. He influenced countless young men and women who were considering going into Christian ministry, always impressing upon them the need of sharing the Gospel with the Jews.

OSCAR WAGO—THE COLUMBUS, OHIO BRANCH

In June 1932, God once again honored the prayers of John Solomon and his prayer circle by directing Oscar Wago to attend a meeting being held at the Pittsburgh branch. Unlike the young rabbinic student, Charles Feinberg, Oscar was neither young, nor a student; he was an automobile engineer.

Oscar Wago was born into a very strict orthodox Jewish family in Hungary in 1869. His father was a rabbi—one of the great talmudic teachers of the day.

Oscar's religious training began when he was three years old. When he was seven, he was brought before a congregation of rabbis to display that though he was young, he already knew all the precepts and traditions that govern the life of an orthodox Jew.

At age thirteen Oscar was made Bar Mitzvah. His father, who was eager for him to receive as a good an education as possible, enrolled him in the nearest high school (gymnasium)—a Roman Catholic school. Being Jewish, Oscar was often taunted and teased about being Jewish, but he persevered.

Oscar pursued graduate studies, with the help of scholarships, at universities in Vienna, Berlin, Paris and Zurich. He graduated with a diploma as an automotive and aeroplane designing engineer. Throughout the years in the Catholic high school and in the various universities that he attended, no one ever spoke to him about Jesus, or about his need to accept Jesus as his Messiah and Savior.

When World War I broke out, Oscar became an officer in the German Army. He was wounded twelve times; at the end of the war he received sixteen medals, one of which was placed on him by Kaiser Wilhelm, himself.

Although Oscar had been a loyal citizen of his country—one who had been honored for his service in the military— he was politely, but firmly, told to leave the country after the Nazis came into power. The reason—he was a Jew.

With great sadness of heart, Oscar packed his meager belongings and said goodbye to his friends and to the country he had come to love. He had booked passage to America.

Once on American soil, Oscar made his may to Pittsburgh. Although he had arrived in America during the "depression years," he felt certain he would be able to find employment and use his engineering skills there.

One Friday night as he walked through the Hill District—the Jewish section of Pittsburgh—he heard singing. It seemed a very strange thing to him that people would be singing when they likely had little food and clothing for themselves and their children. He paused to listen, and then turned in the direction of the joyful sounds. But when he reached the building, the singing suddenly stopped.

The building appeared to be a small storeroom, although there was a large window at the front. In the window he noticed a lovely display of Jewish and English literature and Bibles. He thought the storeroom was probably a small Jewish synagogue.

Just as he turned to leave, the singing suddenly started up again. This time he could hear some of the words. He listened attentively. Yes, he distinctly heard the name of Jesus Christ!

Oscar felt as if he had been struck by lightening! How could it be? A Jewish synagogue where people were singing of Jesus Christ! Impossible!

The singing went on, and again, he distinctly heard the name of Jesus Christ. He couldn't believe his ears. Who were these people? Seeking to satisfy his curiosity, Oscar opened the door and went in. There, to his amazement, sat a group of Jews and Gentiles worshipping together—all singing of Jesus Christ their Savior!

When the singing stopped, a little Jewish man got up and read from the Scriptures. He read the words in Hebrew, and then explained them in Yiddish and English. He was aghast when he heard the little man say that Jesus Christ was spoken of in the Old Testament! Oscar later recalled:

...I felt like shouting, 'It's a lie!' But he went on and on and I had to sit there quietly, listening to him telling the people that Jesus Christ was spoken of in the Old Testament and that He was the promised Messiah of Israel! This truly burned me up. I kept my eyes on the door, resolved to get out of the place as soon as the meeting was over.

The Jewish man finished, a benediction was pronounced, and I jumped to my feet and made for the door. Before I could reach it, the little man was there before me. He reached out his hand, saying, 'Pardon me! What is your name?' I felt compelled to answer, 'My name is Oscar Wago.' He replied, 'My name is John Solomon.' I then said, 'I'm pleased to meet you, Mr. Solomon—good bye!'

I didn't escape so easily, however. Mr. Solomon said he wanted to know me better and asked me to wait a few minutes so that he could talk to me. Still upset and angry, I said, 'There is no use talking to me. When I came in here I didn't know what kind of place it was, but now that I know, the best thing for me to do is to get out as quickly as possible. I was born a Jew and I'm going to die as a Jew, and no one in the world is going to convert me!'

Mr. Solomon smiled and said, 'My friend, I don't want to convert you. I couldn't if I wanted to. I just want to talk to you.' I answered angrily, 'You may tell these people that Jesus Christ is in the Old Testament, but you can't tell it to me. I know my Bible.'

I thought I had settled the matter, but I was mistaken. Mr. Solomon answered kindly, 'I would just like to talk to you for a few minutes as one gentleman to another.' His mention of the word 'gentlemen' did the trick. I relented and said,

'Very well. I will give you just a few minutes.'

After all the people had gone, Mr. Solomon took his Bible and we sat down to examine the Word of God together—a bit stiffly, to be sure, because each of us was trying to find out how much the other knew of his Bible.

Time passed and I was tired. I wanted to go home and I told Mr. Solomon so. Before leaving Mr. Solomon asked me to do him a favor. He handed me a slip of paper upon which he wrote the references to a few Bible passages and asked me to look them up when I got home and read them, and not only to read them but also to meditate upon them. He said, 'If you find that I am right, then like one gentleman to another, come back and tell me so; but if you find that I am wrong, also come back and tell me so, and we'll compare our differences.'

I took the piece of paper and saw at once that I was familiar with most of the passages. But since Mr. Solomon appealed to me as a gentleman, I thought there might possibly be something I had forgotten in these passages, and decided to give him the benefit of the doubt. So home I went, took out my Hebrew Bible and looked up the passages he had written down. I found each and every one of them to be as I thought they would be. But while I meditated on them, something happened to me. It was not that I felt I was being converted. Conversion is not so quickly accomplished. But I was disturbed. That cock-sure feeling I always had that I couldn't be wrong, instilled in me by my teachers, the best Rabbis, and my father, the greatest of them all, was somehow shaken.

The following day I went back to Mr. Solomon and said to him, 'I don't believe a single word you said, but I confess I am not so sure of myself either.' Again we sat down and read certain portions of the Bible together. It was then that Mr. Solomon gave me a New Testament. It was the first time in my life I had ever seen one. I had heard that the New Testament was a wonderful book, but it doesn't prove anything to a Jew.

I decided to accept it and take it home and read it with an unbiased mind. The references given to me in the Old Testament enabled me to find the fulfillment of certain prophecies in the New Testament, and as I read and compared the two I had plenty of time to meditate on their relation and significance. While doing this, little by little God opened up new meanings to me. This did not take place suddenly or easily. For weeks and weeks I was so nervous I wanted to see nobody, and talk to nobody. Night after night I never closed my eyes. Exhausted and wary, I fell asleep one night and when I woke up in the morning I noticed my pillow was wet. I must have cried in my sleep, although I never cried even at the horrible things I saw during the war. This upset me to such an extent that I got out of bed and fell on my knees, wondering if I was out of my mind. I cried out, 'Oh God, I can't stand this any longer. Help me and show me the truth. What am I to believe, what my father taught me, or the things I am being taught by Mr. Solomon?'

As I prayed thus, I was given a sign by God's grace. Suddenly there flashed before my mind's eye the vision of my old high school back in Hungary and the inscription over the entrance to the building, 'I am the way, the truth, and the life' standing out in glaring letters.

I honestly and devoutly believed this to be an answer to prayer, the evidence of the working of the Holy Spirit of God in my heart pointing out to my troubled spirit the answer to all my doubts and inner conflict, the Lord Jesus Christ, my own personal Saviour, Redeemer and the true Messiah of Israel. It was He who said, 'I am the way, the truth, and life,' and at last I had the courage to accept it.

I could hardly wait to get to the meeting place of the Jewish Mission that night. When Mr. Solomon invited any of those present to testify as to their acceptance of Jesus Christ as Lord and Saviour, I fairly jumped to my feet and in the hearing of all present, said, 'I know and I believe that Jesus Christ is my Saviour; that Jesus Christ is my Messiah and coming King, for Whom we Jews are praying three times a day and for three hundred and sixty-five days a year! I know it!'

From this time on the reality and assurance of my salvation has been ever precious and the same, and when occasionally I ask a Christian brother if he is saved and he answers, 'I think so, I *hope* so!' I am able to tell him with full assurance, 'I don't *think* so, I don't *hope* so, I *know* so!'[34]

After Oscar opened his heart to receive Yeshua as Messiah and Lord he became John Solomon's "right hand man." He helped in the ministry and with the publication of "Christ's Life," a magazine funded by the Howard Banks Estate. In sharing his testimony, Oscar loved to tell of the night when he found his Messiah:

It was there, in that humble mission room that I for the first time in my life heard...in Jewish terms of the great Jewish Messiah, the Lord Jesus Christ. I heard new words of love, and hope for the sinner and the downtrodden, and soon became an interested listener. From the first day on, I couldn't help but be inspired by the beauty of the teaching of the Gospel. Yet there was the inherited Jewish...mistrust of the ancient Jewish race towards Christianity,...I fought a hard battle for many weeks against the acceptance of the new doctrine. But, I thank the Lord that His Holy Spirit, working in me, gained victory. Searching...the Holy Scriptures, and looking at my life in the light of the new teachings, I saw myself as a hopeless condemned sinner without atonement. I prayed to Jehovah, and cried for His help to lead me out of the hopeless darkness. One day suddenly the light dawned on my soul that there is but one way to salvation and that is through Christ, the Messiah; and that redemption of my sins cannot come any other way but by the blood of the Savior, who died for us,...

Since I first confessed Christ as my Savior I have lost many dear Jewish friends. But I know that I found in Him a true friend who never will forsake me.[35]

In 1933, only one year after he was saved, Oscar was on the platform at the Erieside Ohio Bible Conference, sharing his testimony and preaching the Word. In his introductory remarks he said:

While I represent the Pittsburgh Branch of the American Board of Missions to the Jews, in the absence of Rev. John Solomon, I do not speak in any official capacity, but as a recent convert, led to Christ my Messiah and Savior, by our beloved Brother Solomon. I feel it my duty to speak about the wonderful work done by this Mission among God's Ancient People, and raise my voice that the Command given by the Captain of our Salvation, to bring to all nations, and to the Jew first, shall be carried out.[36]

After hearing this address, Joseph Cohn recognized that Oscar Wago was one of God's choice "jewels." It made no difference to him at all that Oscar was sixty-two years of age when he accepted Yeshua as his Messiah and Savior. It mattered not that Oscar was an automotive engineer who had received no formal theological training. What *did* matter was that Oscar Wago was bright and articulate; he was a quick student who drank in the Word of God like a thirsty sponge soaks up water.

As Joseph worked to enlarge the horizons of the Mission, he was a man who utilized men with a diversity of backgrounds. Instinctively, he knew that having Oscar Wago on staff would pay big dividends for the Mission, and he acted quickly in hiring him. The Minutes reflect: "Oscar Wago, a convert of the Pittsburgh Branch, is now working with "Christ Life" but this keeps him busy three days a week. It was suggested that we might use him for the other three days and let him do field work and help Mr. Solomon. Carried."[37]

In March 1935, in response to the pleas of a number of Christians in Columbus, Ohio who wanted a mission outreach in their area, Joseph Cohn sent Oscar Wago and his wife, Hannah, to Columbus to serve as itinerant missionaries. A report of this change, and of the Wago's new duties and responsibilities, appeared in *The Chosen People* Magazine:

The labors of Mr. Wago have been, and will continue to be, two-fold: one phase has been to enlist the sympathy and cooperation of the Christian forces of the city, so as to insure a cordiality and a Christ-like attitude to the Jews, if any should attend some of the church services. The other work has been with the Jews themselves. In this phase of the work, Mr. Wago had been calling on the Jews in their homes, in the market, and on the streets. A Bible Class has also been maintained in the small apartment where Mr. and Mrs. Wago live; and to that class come both Jews and Christians.

In both undertakings there has been experienced an abundant outpouring of the Lord's blessings. The churches and pastors have opened their doors and their hearts to Mr. Wago. And from the Jews, there has been a cordial response. They receive gladly the testimony, both by mouth and by the printed page of The Shepherd of Israel. A number are attending the Bible classes. We have just spent a few days in Columbus and saw first hand what the Lord has done. In our meetings were many Jews, and those with whom we spoke, had only praise and love for Mr. and Mrs. Wago.[38]

The ministry in Columbus grew rapidly, and whenever Oscar preached in the churches, pastors would report that people had received Yeshua. Then tragedy struck. Oscar had been ill for a number of months, and his doctors had advised him to go to Florida for the winter months. This they did, but just before dawn on the day after their arrival in Lakeland, Florida, Oscar suffered a swift and massive heart attack. He was seventy-one years of age. Within a few hours, he was with his Lord. Funeral services were held at the Central Presbyterian Church in Columbus, Ohio. Oscar Wago died on January 2, 1940, but his ministry and testimony did not end. Hannah Wago, Oscar's wife, took up the ministry where he left off. The story of God's hand upon her life and testimony will be told at a later point in the narration of the history of The American Board of Missions to the Jews.

Sanford Mills—Washington D.C./Columbus

Several months before Oscar Wago's illness, he had led a Jewish family to the Lord—husband, wife and two children. He had also baptized all members of the family except the baby, who was only two and a half years old. Joseph Cohn mentioned the family in his February 1940 editorial in *The Chosen People* Magazine, saying: "...the father has felt with a powerful conviction the call of God that he shall labor in the Lord's vineyard. We hope our friends will remember this brother in earnest prayer, that the way shall be opened for him to undertake special training, and that later on he will prove to be a mighty instrument in God's hands for preaching the Gospel to His own brethren."[39] The family Oscar had led to the Lord was Mr. and Mrs. Sanford Mills, and their son Gerald. Evidently God's people did heed the call to pray, and Sanford Mills was led to join the staff of The American Board of Mission to the Jews. The Minutes of the Board state:

> Mr. Cohn told of the telegram which had come from Chas. Sanford Mills, mention of whom was made in previous Minutes, in which telegram he tells of having lost his position because of his faith in Christ. We have instructed him to move his family and his furniture to Brooklyn. We will pay him $100.00 a month, $25.00 of which he will return as rent for one of the now vacant apartments at 235 South 4th Street. It is planned that he will study with Mr. Birnbaum in the morning and do further study at the National Bible Institute. We hope that he will some day become an effective missionary worker.[40]

By October of 1940 Sanford Mills and his family had settled down in the Brooklyn apartment provided for them by the Mission, and Joseph reported to the Board:

> ...He [Sanford Mills] has been spending his mornings in study under Mr. Birnbaum and has attended classes at National Bible Institute. It is now time to decide what his future field of labor shall be, and for what work he is particularly fitted. There is a possible place for him in Dallas, Texas, where there is a group of Christian people anxious to start and support a Jewish work. We have not reached any conclusions regarding Mr. Mills.[41]

But the Mills family was not sent to Dallas, Texas. Instead, they were sent to Washington D.C. In his report to readers of *The Chosen People* magazine, Joseph said:

> ...By remarkable direction of the Holy Spirit, some friends in Washington wrote us begging that we send a worker there to engage in visitation work among the Jews and offering to carry the larger share of the budget. We were convinced that this was the Lord's opening and arrangements were made for Mr. Mills to go. Our friends are earnestly reminded to keep this young brother before the Throne of Grace. He is a sort of Timothy to that stalwart giant Oscar Wago, and needs much prayer that the Lord will enable him to grow in grace.[42]

Sanford Mills planned his "witnessing strategy" for the Washington D.C. area like a General would lay plans for battle. Unlike New York, Washington D.C. had no Jewish ghetto—Jews were scattered all over the city. It was obvious that door-to-door visitation was impossible. Street meetings were also ineffective. It was clear to Sanford that the field to which he had been assigned called for "mobile ministry." His plan of action included doing visitation, holding home meetings, and taking church meetings. With his strategy planned, he was ready to go into action, and the first thing he did was to request a small car from the Mission. The board was taken aback by his request! It seemed to be such an excessive request, and one made by such a new worker! But when the members of the board understood the unique field in which Sanford was laboring, they agreed to supply him with a car. Sanford's program worked. Within the first few months of his arrival in Washington D. C. he had led several Jewish people to the Lord. Joseph reported to the readers of the magazine: "...Already the Lord has given some remarkable conversions, and he is in constant demand to call upon these different homes where he receives a respectful hearing and a grateful response. Mr. Mills has won the friendship of some of the leading pastors of Washington, and they have learned to trust him with their confidence."[43]

Oscar Wago's sudden death was a great blow to those who knew and loved him in the Columbus, Ohio area. They had all expected the Wago's to return to Columbus after spending the winter in Florida. Realizing the importance of maintaining the ministry and relations with pastors and churches in the Columbus area, Joseph Cohn began to talk to the Board about the possibility of moving Sanford Mills and his family to Ohio. Hannah Wago could then be moved to Denver, Colorado to work in that city.[44]

In February 1943 Joseph announced the closing of the Washington D.C. branch of the Mission. Readers were told that the Mills' family was being transferred to Columbus, Ohio. Joseph said:

> ...the Washington field has in it some difficult peculiarities with regard to the Jewish work; there is practically no Jewish ghetto, no center assembly of Jews, but they are scattered in all parts of the District. Many of them are employed by the government, and their hours of employment are irregular. To visit in these homes became more and more prohibitive as gasoline shortages became pronounced.[45]

Knowing that some of the readers would be wondering about the continuing work of Mrs. Wago, Joseph went on to say that Hannah was being transferred to Denver, Colorado. He wrote:

...In Denver there have been local Jewish mission undertakings for some years past, and Mrs. Wago has identified herself with some of these friends, and has explained her desire to be of help to them rather than to undertake anything new or separate. These friends have welcomed her help, and she is slowly finding a niche and a place of service for the Lord.[46]

Hannah faithfully sought out Jewish people with whom she could share the Gospel message. One day God directed Hannah to the door of a young Jewish woman whose heart He had been preparing for a number of years, although the young woman was not aware of it! She had never attended church, but God used the words of Christmas carols to burrow deep into her heart. Almost fourteen years to the day after Oscar Wago's death, Hannah knocked on this young woman's door. Introductions were exchanged, and the young woman told Hannah that her name was Ceil—Ceil Rosen.

Hannah shared her husband's testimony and some verses from the Word of God, and Ceil's heart was receptive. The ripples of Hannah's many meetings with Ceil Rosen went out and touched her husband, Martin Meyer Rosen (now Moishe Rosen). Through Hannah Wago's faithful witness and persistent challenge, both Ceil and Martin opened their hearts to receive Yeshua. Hannah was instrumental in encouraging them in obedience to God's call upon their lives to serve as missionaries with the Mission. Martin Meyer Rosen was a worker who *greatly* impacted the Mission—a story that will be told in greater depth in a subsequent chapter of this history.

Although Joseph Cohn was still a young man (in his forties), his business prowess and drive made him appear older. The challenge of finding and interacting with topnotch people, and of ultimately meshing their unique talents or contacts with the Mission's expanding program, was exhilarating to Joseph. He saw his net-working ability as being a good steward of the Lord's resources.

ELIAS ZIMMERMAN — THE LOS ANGELES MINISTRY

One well-known Christian leader with whom Joseph had come into contact was Dr. Arnold Frank, pastor of the Evangelical Church in Hamburg, Germany, and editor of a Hebrew-Christian journal called "Zion's Friend." Dr. Frank was sympathetic with Joseph Cohn and with the work being done by the Mission, and he agreed to let Joseph know of Jewish believers who were planning to immigrate to America. One such individual was Elias Zimmerman.

Elias Zimmerman was born in Russia on April 14, 1892. His father was a rabbi, and at the age of thirteen Elias was sent away from home to receive his rabbinical training. Between the ages of thirteen and nineteen, Elias studied in some of the most famous rabbinical schools in Europe and Russia, including the famous Vilna Academy. While he was a student at the Vilna Academy, some missionaries slipped Elias a tract about the Messiah, Yeshua. After reading it, Elias felt sure he could defeat the arguments presented about Yeshua in the little tract. He went to the missionaries to argue, but instead he was given a New Testament to read. He later stated that the more he read of the New Testament, and the more he compared it with the Old Testament, the more convinced he became that Yeshua was the Messiah. He stated that one night as he was reading the Scriptures, the Holy Spirit convicted him of the truth. He fell upon his knees and accepted Yeshua as his own personal Messiah and Savior, but like so many before him, he was persecuted for his new found faith and he was ultimately forced to leave Russia because of his belief in Yeshua.

Elias fled to Germany where he was introduced to Dr. Arnold Frank. Over the weeks and months, Dr. Frank discipled Elias, and later baptized him. During that time Elias' father, the well-known rabbi, had tracked him down and made it clear that he wanted his son to return to Russia. He was insistent that his son give up his absurd new ideas, and return to Judaism. His father contacted other rabbis in Germany, and tried to work through them to force Elias to leave Germany. When this did not work, his father decided to send him to America to live with his brother Morris, an orthodox Jew. He hoped that in America Elias would come to his senses, but even if he did not, he would no longer be an embarrassment to the family in Russia.

Elias agreed to move to America, but before he left Germany Dr. Frank wrote to Joseph Cohn, telling him about this young rabbinical student who was studying for the ministry. Joseph immediately offered the Mission's help. A very weary Elias Zimmerman arrived at Ellis Island in 1910. He had exactly one dollar in his pocket and was unable to speak a word of English. The Mission helped him learn English and assisted him financially so that he could enter Dubuque University, in Iowa.

In 1914 Elias moved to Texas, where he enrolled at Austin Seminary. While he was studying there, Elias received a letter from Joseph. Joseph reminded Elias of the urgent need to reach Jewish people with the Gospel, and he asked Elias if he would be willing to represent the Mission in the Presbyterian churches in the South. Elias responded by telling

Joseph he would pray about the matter. But Joseph was not satisfied. He continued to write to Elias, pressing him to join the Mission's staff.

Elias transferred to, and graduated from, Columbia Theological Seminary. After graduation he was ordained, and took a position as the pastor of the Smyrna Presbyterian Church in Smyrna, Georgia—a suburb of Atlanta. With his usual tenacity, Joseph continued writing to Elias until, after two and a half years, Elias knew what Joseph Cohn had been certain of all along—that God wanted Elias Zimmerman to serve with the Mission.

Elias was soon accompanying Joseph on his many trips; the two men traveled together from coast to coast, speaking, teaching, and witnessing as they raised financial support for the Mission. In 1921, on one of his trips to Los Angeles, California, Elias met Miss Helen Brinkmeyer, a pastor's daughter. They fell in love and were married four years later.

Once married, Elias and Helen made Los Angeles their home base, but Elias kept the Pacific coast highway "hot" as he held meetings for the Mission. He also traveled to the mid-western states and to Canada as he worked to build the support base for the Mission, to enlist volunteers to help with the work, and to recruit missionaries for the staff.

In 1935 a group of Christians in the Los Angeles area contacted Joseph Cohn. In their letter they explained that their group was small and their resources were limited, but they stated that they were anxious to start a work among the Jewish people; they asked if the Mission would be interested in cooperating with them. The Board voted to help the group by sending $20.00 a month toward the rent of a "Gospel Center" from which they could begin to reach the Jews of Los Angeles.[47] Not long after this decision, further action was taken. The December 1935 Executive Minutes state: "Upon motion it was agreed that we hire Mr. Elias Zimmerman to take charge of the Reading Room in the newly launched Mission work in Los Angeles, at a salary of $50.00 a month. It was also voted that we increase our rent allowance for the rent of this store to $22.50."[48]

Joseph wrote a glowing article in *The Chosen People* magazine about the opening of the new branch ministry in Los Angeles. His opening statements reflect his philosophy of "networking" with interested Christian groups whenever and wherever possible. He wrote:

> Once more the Lord enlarges our borders. And once more our friends will rejoice and give thanks with us that He enables us to buy up Gospel testimony opportunities just as rapidly as he opens them to us, and directs our paths.
>
> This time in Los Angeles, California, and with great joy we are able to announce that a branch of the American Board of Missions to the Jews has been opened at No. 2005 Brooklyn Avenue, Los Angeles, with Rev. Elias Zimmerman as missionary, and with Mr. Joseph W. Johnston, together with a group of friends associated with him, as local sponsor.[49]

Once established, the Los Angeles work proved to be an exciting and fruitful outreach. By early Spring 1936, Mr. Johnston was reporting to Joseph that in January they ministered to 150 Jews, and by February their attendance had jumped to nearly 400. He told Joseph that the interest in the ministry was so great that they had to keep the Mission open every night, besides having meetings twice on Sunday.[50]

Elias, too, sent reports of growth and of answered prayer. The Minutes state:

> The work in Los Angeles has developed in a much greater way than was even hoped for. Mr. Zimmerman reports that already two young Jewish men, converts of the Los Angeles Branch, were baptized in one of the churches of that city....
>
> When the work was started it was thought that Mr. Zimmerman would spend perhaps three or four afternoons in the Reading Room, but now he is having meetings every night and seems to be carrying on a full program of work. Therefore Mr. Cohn suggests that his salary of $75 a month be increased to $100.[51]

For eight years, Elias and Helen operated the only Jewish Rescue Mission in the country. During those eight years, thousands of young Jewish men who went to Los Angeles seeking work found "Zimmie's Mission" instead.

"Zimmie" (as Elias was affectionately called) and Helen ministered tirelessly to the homeless, friendless, and penniless people who came to their rescue mission. In addition to filling hungry stomachs, Elias held preaching services six nights a week in a hall crowded with men who were spiritually hungry. Large numbers of Jewish men and boys openly confessed their faith in Yeshua and were baptized.[52]

Pearl Harbor, and the end of World War II brought the Jewish Rescue Mission work of Zimmie and Helen to a sudden halt. Elias wrote:

> ...It caused havoc with our Mission, and it tore our work in shreds. Many of our boys did not wait to be called to the colors. They enlisted and volunteered. Others were drafted later on. Only a few, the unfit, were left behind.

We soon saw the handwriting on the wall as far as our work among the boys was concerned. We realized that we must change the nature of our activities. This we did all along ever since we plunged into the war. We have been seeking to reach the local Jews, giving out many thousands of The Shepherd of Israel, literature, tracts, New Testaments; we also conducted street meetings, in addition to our regular Gospel services indoors on Wednesdays and Sundays....

In spite of all the difficulties and hardships, the Lord has been good and gracious unto us. Now and then the Mission is pretty well filled, and the hall again rings with the singing of gospel hymns. Now and then we receive a letter from our soldier boys; or some of them stop off to see us, as they pass through the city to the different training camps or on their way to the South Pacific....The Lord has also given us some souls for our hire. A number made public confession of their faith during the year, and three, two Jews and one Gentile, were baptized recently in the Second Brethren Church of Los Angeles.[53]

Elias went on to mention the need for the ministry to find a new location. It was difficult to get people to attend meetings because the Mission's building had become so closely identified as a Rescue Mission. Elias reported:

Since we have changed the nature of our activities, we have realized more than ever the need of a different location and a better equipped building. Many of our difficulties and discouragements have been due to the fact that we are poorly located and poorly equipped for the kind of work we are doing. For one thing, some of the local Jews have come to look upon our Mission as a rescue mission for down and outers, for those in distress and in need; and so they are ashamed to come in. Then the entrance to the Mission is too conspicuous for other Jews who would like to come to the services. The Mission is on the main street, and so some are afraid that they are being watched and reported and talked about when they visit the Mission. On several occasions we were asked by some Jewish women if we had some side or back door so that they could slip in without being seen. One day I persuaded a cultured and intelligent Jewish mother and her daughter to come to the service at the Mission. I drove up in front, and when they stepped out of the car they stood there on the sidewalk not knowing whether they would walk in or go back home. I could see in their behavior that they were embarrassed and confused. They were anxious for me to drive them back home. And it took a good deal of persuading on my part to get them to come in, but only after they looked around on every side and made sure that nobody saw them enter.[54]

A new location was found—the Calvary Baptist Church, an independent Baptist church on St. Louis Avenue in the Boyle Heights neighborhood of Los Angeles. Elias had hoped that the church would sell the building to the Mission, but they were only willing to allow him to rent space for his meetings. From this new location, Zimmie's ministry continued—this time reaching out to a different class of Jews in Los Angeles.

In 1946 Daniel Fuchs gave a report on the work of Elias Zimmerman, saying:

...I was privileged to minister with our Brother Elias Zimmerman.... The first... was the regular Friday night street meeting on Brooklyn Avenue. For one and a half hours the Gospel message was faithfully proclaimed and I was given the opportunity of adding a word of testimony and of distributing our Gospel newspaper, The Shepherd of Israel. In all of my experience I never met with such intense opposition to the Gospel message as we faced that night. Bitter, vituperative remarks were hurled at me until I wondered when they would cease. I glanced over to Brother Zimmerman to see how he was faring.... what a contrast! With a radiant countenance he calmly faced the people and lovingly but firmly presented the message of salvation to them.

The following Wednesday evening we attended the regular mid-week meeting at the Mission. What a contrast to our experience on the street corner! It was joy to meet other Jews of like faith in the Lord Jesus, our Messiah. Instead of opposition, we had fellowship in the Lord.... It was a heart-warming experience to join in singing the old hymns of the faith, and to join in prayer for the requests both spoken and unspoken which were made by the brethren. Especially did we remember "Zimmie's boys," so many of whom were serving in the armed forces. We were again privileged to minister the Word of Life to the people. But in place of the bitter antagonism of the previous Friday evening, we were conscious of the intense interest of the people in the message....

But it was a contrast made possible only by the faithful ministry of Brother and Sister Zimmerman. Only a servant who was called by the Lord could faithfully preach on the street corners against such opposition. Only one who loves his Lord and his people could patiently and lovingly win these people one by one as Brother Zimmerman has done.[55]

HELEN GRABER—LOS ANGELES

Like Joseph Cohn, Elias quickly learned to "network" with individuals interested in Jewish evangelism. One such individual was Miss Helen Graber, a Gentile Christian with genuine love for the Jewish people. As a professional nurse, Helen came across many Jewish patients. Meeting Elias and Helen Zimmerman was an answer to her prayers! With their friendship and counsel, Helen was able to lead numerous Jewish women and children to the Lord. For eleven years (c. 1943) Helen worked as a volunteer for the Mission. During those eleven years she organized children's and women's classes, visited in homes, and distributed tracts and copies of the Shepherd of Israel. She joined the staff of the Mission on a full-time basis in the Fall of 1953. The many Jewish people Miss Graber led to the Lord helped to form the nucleus for an ongoing ministry in Los Angeles. Shortly after coming on staff Helen wrote:

> ...A goodly number of Jewish children have thanked Jesus, their Messiah, that He suffered and died for all their sins; they have taken Him into their hearts. Several adults also have made a profession of their faith in Christ, their Messiah....
>
> Marilyn, now ten years old, heard the plan of salvation at a street corner. She went home, knelt down, and took Jesus into her heart. A few weeks later she again came to that street corner and received more children's tracts, and she then asked me to her home to teach her God's Word. Her parents consented to my coming, but not too willingly. For several months it has been my privilege to go to her home and teach her and her younger sister. This sister also took Jesus into her heart. Sometimes their mother listens in on the Bible story....
>
> Another day a middle-aged Jewess, in whose apartment we have read the Bible for several years, surprised me by saying, 'I believe in Jesus.' Thank God for that. She is a widow, without children, without health, and without this world's goods.[56]

Helen gave a brief report of the extensive street work carried on in Los Angeles in 1955. She wrote:

> For our street work we go to different Jewish sections of the city and one large beach resort with an extensive Jewish population. There we meet our Jewish friends twice a week and distribute The Shepherd Of Israel and tracts. In the course of the year we distributed about half a million tracts, more than 20,000 of The Shepherd of Israel, 285 New Testaments, and 40 Bibles. To as many as will listen we make plain the way of salvation. We dealt with a goodly number of children, and to our great joy many received Christ as their Savior from sin.[57]

During her visitation in homes, Helen Graber met a Jewish woman who was extremely bitter and hostile to Helen's witness. She explained to Helen that her daughter had turned to the Gentile's god, Jesus. Through Miss Graber's persistent visitation, and faithful and loving witness, the day came when the once-bitter Mrs. Faye Cohen prayed to receive Yeshua as her Messiah and Lord. "Mama Cohen" became a much-loved worker at the Los Angeles branch ministry!

God gave Elias and Helen Zimmerman one additional worker—Rev. Ashton Holden, a Gentile believer. Ashton only worked in Los Angeles for a couple of years, before Joseph transferred him to work in the Montreal branch of the Mission in 1953.

JOINT MINISTRY WITH KEITH L. BROOKS

As Joseph directed the affairs of the Mission, and sought to promote an awareness of the Mission, he looked for every possible opportunity to develop cooperative ministry ventures with other organizations. In 1933 he approached the Board with a recommendation for a unique partnership between the Mission and Keith L. Brooks, a well known radio speaker and editor of a paper called Prophecy. The Minutes reflect this uncommon partnership. They state:

> In California Mr. Cohn made a tentative arrangement with Mr. Keith Brooks. He agreed that from now on through his paper Prophecy which has a circulation of 5000, he will become our exclusive 'promoter' on the Pacific Coast. He will come on our Advisory Council and he is to be honorary treasurer on the Pacific Coast. Every month he will devote two pages of Prophecy to telling something about our work. For this we are to pay him $10.00 a month and he will do everything he can to cooperate with us to help our work on the Coast.[58]

Joseph encouraged readers of The Chosen People magazine to subscribe to Mr. Brooks' Prophecy Newsletter.[59] Not only did this arrangement work well for both organizations, but later, when Joseph came under attack by individuals seeking to discredit him and the Mission, Mr. Brooks used his influence to help Joseph and the Mission. Keith L. Brooks' friendship and association with the Mission continued on, well beyond the time of Joseph's death.

Joseph also recognized the importance of advertizing. He knew if new revenue and support was going to be generated, the "product" had to be kept before the Christian public—and Joseph Cohn made sure that it was! The Minutes reflect his action taken: "...A special full page advertisement in the Moody Monthly and The Sunday School Times brought in over $4,000 of new money, in a two months period. A friend in the West paid for this special advertising."[60]

Herman Juroe—Field Evangelist

Joseph Cohn's penchant for meshing his ideas with individuals who could support or carry out those ideas was also used to expand his team of field evangelists—men who worked diligently to raise additional funds for the growing ministry. During 1936, Joseph recruited a worker to serve as a field evangelist and itinerant missionary for the state of Iowa. He told the Board:

> Mr. Herman Juroe, a Jewish Christian, came to New York at our invitation recently and spent about two weeks with us. Mr. Juroe was converted in New York some twelve years ago. He went to Moody, also to the Seminary in Dallas. He has been a pastor in Des Moines but has not been very happy in this connection. There is a group of Christians in Des Moines anxious for him to do itinerant missionary work among the Jews in the State of Iowa. Mr. Juroe wrote us in this connection and we asked him to come to New York so that we might become acquainted with him and that he might become thoroughly familiar with our methods. From here he went to Pittsburgh to spend a week with Mr. Solomon, and then on to Columbus, where Mr. Wago took him with him on his speaking engagements. Mr. Cohn suggested that we engage Mr. Juroe as itinerant missionary for Iowa, and surrounding territory, which has a Jewish population of 75,000. $105 will be needed to take care of his family needs and the rent of an apartment which is to be used for missionary work (Mrs. Juroe is to conduct classes for mothers and children). We also should pay his expenses on the road [This was approved on a month to month basis].[61]

Herbert Amster—Field Evangelist

Another Field Evangelist was added to the staff of the Mission in the Spring of 1937, when Joseph met Rev. Herbert H. Amster. Herbert, a graduate of the Denver Bible Institute, was already an ordained minister and an independent itinerant evangelist when the two men met. Seeing Herbert's potential, and needing additional Field Evangelists for the Mission, Joseph encouraged Herbert to join the Mission's staff.

Herbert was Jewish; he was born in Vienna, Austria. To escape persecution, his family had converted to Roman Catholicism before his birth. Herbert was therefore christened into the Roman Catholic church, but in daily life the family did not practice or teach any type of religion in their home.

Herbert's introduction to religion came when he entered Catholic High School at the age of eleven. There, he learned the rituals and traditions of the Catholic church, but he heard nothing about the Messiah, Himself.

When he was twenty years old, Herbert immigrated to America, thinking he would find more answers to life in the new world. He became a part of the Jewish immigrant community, and began to identify with fellow Jews in his work and social life. As far as religion was concerned, Herbert decided he was an agnostic. He threw himself into a whirlwind of activities and concentrated on becoming a *good* Jew by practicing some Jewish traditions. Strangely, however, he discovered that in spite of his outward motions at being a *good* Jew, there was a growing emptiness inside—an emptiness that nothing seemed to dispel. He had tried to forget about God, but God had not forgotten about Herbert!

One night, while staying in a hotel in St. Louis, Herbert picked up a Gideon Bible and began to read it. As he read, God spoke to his heart. He understood that he was reading a Jewish book, and he understood that it was speaking to him—a Jewish person. The message was clearly telling him what he needed to do to become a good Jew. He went to the telephone directory to look for help. Remembering that night, he later wrote:

> ...I had determined I would become a 'good Jew.' I knew what Gentile Missions were for—to 'rescue the perishing' Gentiles. I had read the familiar slogan 'A man may be down, but he's never out.' I had never heard of a Hebrew Mission. That, I reasoned, would turn a wayward Jew into a good orthodox Jew.[62]

As Herbert's eyes had scanned the pages of the telephone directory, they had fallen on a listing for the St. Louis Hebrew Mission. He made note of the address and quickly made his way to the building.

When he arrived at the proper address, to Herbert's surprise, he was met by a Scottish gentlemen—a man with a heavy Scottish brogue—not an orthodox Jew as he had expected to find at a *Hebrew* mission. When he was coaxed into the lobby of the building, Herbert's worst fears were realized. There on a table, laid a blotter with the words of Romans 1:16 written on it. Herbert did not have time to read the whole verse, but he did see the words: "...To the Greek...The Gospel of Christ." Fear filled his heart, and he wondered what he had gotten himself into. He later said, "I was willing to become an orthodox Jew, but not a Greek Orthodox—Never!"[63]

Before Herbert could turn tail and run, a white-haired gentlemen approached him—a Jewish believer in the Messiah. As the gentleman spoke, Herbert found that he was fascinated by the testimony the older man was sharing. Soon his doubts and fears were replaced with a desire to know God personally, and to have the peace and joy that the men at the mission demonstrated.

As he was returning to his hotel, Herbert rehearsed the testimonies and conversations he'd had with the men at the mission. Once in his room, he read the little tracts he had been given and he read more of the Bible. Then he quietly knelt down beside the bed and asked Yeshua to be his personal Savior and Messiah. He wrote:

> ...I believed then that the Lord Jesus had died for my sins and that I needed the salvation he thus offered. A heavy burden was rolling off my shoulders, and a new day was dawning. Three days later I made an open confession of my faith, no longer able to repress the joy which demanded utterance.[64]

Herbert served as one of the Mission's Field Evangelists for only a short time before Joseph sent him to Seattle, Washington to open a new branch. The first public service of that branch was held on October 10, 1939, with 100 people in attendance.[65]

During the summer of 1940, Herbert was transferred to serve as a Field Evangelist in Denver, Colorado.[66] He later left the staff of the Mission, but returned to work as a volunteer in the Los Angeles and San Diego branches of the Mission until his death.

WALTER ATKINSON—HIS STORY

Joseph's network disclosed that a Jewish believer by the name of Rev. Walter Atkinson was carrying on an independent work among the Jews in the Bensonhurst section of Brooklyn. Walter had worked for a time with the Lutheran Board. At first Joseph just asked the Board to send $25.00 a month toward Mr. Atkinson's support,[67] but it wasn't long before he recruited Walter as a full-time missionary for the Seattle branch. Joseph reported to the Board:

> ...Mrs. Robert Fleming, who is sponsor for our work in Seattle, was visiting in New York several weeks ago and at that time she heard Mr. Atkinson speak in the Mission. She also heard Mrs. Atkinson sing a solo, and was impressed that this was the couple for Seattle.[68]

By March 1941, Walter and Elizabeth Atkinson were the new missionaries in the Seattle, Washington branch.

Walter Atkinson was born into a conservative Jewish family in the imperial Berlin of the Kaiser in 1899. He was educated in Berlin and also received his Jewish education for Bar Mitzvah. At seventeen he was drafted into the army, and upon his return home he decided to study medicine; he therefore enrolled in the University of Berlin. Unfortunately, Walter's family could not afford the expense of his medical training, and after three years of medical school he had to drop out. His job search led him to a brokerage house in Berlin. They agreed to accept Walter as an apprentice. Buying and selling on the Berlin Stock Market during the volatile days of the breakdown of the German armies at the Western front, Walter found himself in the "eye of the storm" during the economic collapse of the old Reich. Like many others who worked for banks and brokerage houses, Walter lost his job. Unable to secure any type of employment, he decided to move to Holland, but he found that there, too, jobs were scarce. The job he finally secured was a far cry from the "white collar" jobs he had previously held. Working on a "coaling" gang, Walter's job was to help fill empty bunkers with coal. It has hard, dusty, dirty work—but it was work, and it did supply money for a room and for food.

Unsatisfied with his life as it was, Walter decided that perhaps travel would fill the void he felt. He applied for a job as Steward aboard a small freighter, and was hired. Serving on one ship after another, he visited Belgium, England, Scotland, Gibraltar, Egypt, Malta, Palestine, Syria, Constantinople, Rumania, Bulgaria. He even served on a ship that went around the Scandinavian peninsula to the North, to the Russian port of Archangelsk, north of the Polar Circle. But the sights of the world did not diminish the dissatisfaction Walter felt deep within his own soul.

One day his ship's route took him to New Orleans; it was Walter's first time on American soil. Walter fell in love with America, and with New Orleans—so much so that on his return to Europe he made immediate application for an American immigration visa. This was granted, and in July 1928, Walter Atkinson, the searching refugee Jew from Berlin, Germany, was admitted as an immigrant to the United States.

Because he had fallen in love with New Orleans, Walter looked for a job that would allow him to live there. A position as a night orderly was available in the Southern Baptist Hospital of New Orleans. There are no coincidences in God's divine program, and of that job and the ultimate consequences it brought into his life, Walter later wrote:

> ...and it was here that I first came under the influence of the Lord Jesus Christ. The superintendent of this hospital gave me a complete Bible containing both the Old and the New Testaments, and the Gospel in song began to influence my life. Every morning as I waited for my relief to come on duty, the student nurses had their chapel service and their

singing filled the halls. A great favorite of their's was: 'There is power, power, wonder working power, in the blood of the Lamb.' I must have heard this hymn four or five days out of seven. It has stayed with me ever since.

At that time a friend of mine introduced me to a Hebrew-Christian missionary who was working in New Orleans under interdenominational auspices. His patience helped to break down my prejudice and after a while I was willing to listen to his reasoning that the Lord Jesus came as the Messiah promised in the Old Testament. Then he was transferred to a distant city, and I felt quite lonely. In time a feeling of homesickness for my friend, the missionary, began to develop. One day I could stand it no longer. I quit my job, took my savings and bought a ticket to the city where he was now located, and followed him. He received me graciously, and we read again the New Testament together. But now it took only a few days until the veil was drawn away and the scales fell from my eyes, and I realized that I had become home-sick not so much for my earthly friend but for my heavenly Friend and Savior, my Messiah, the Lord Jesus Christ. My struggle had lasted more than twelve months, and it was on December 22, 1929, that I confessed my Savior in Baptism. He saved me and has kept me ever since.

I spent the first nine months of the year 1930 in the Moody Bible Institute of Chicago, where He had led me, so that I might be grounded securely in the Faith and in the Bible. Then I was guided to Princeton Theological Seminary and was graduated by that school in 1933 having taken the full course. As there seemed to be no opening for me following my graduation, I was advised to continue my studies and did so in Philadelphia at the feet of Dr. Machlen of sainted memory and at the Lutheran Seminary where I did graduate work.

During this period I was called to the pastorate of a church and served this church until the spring of 1936. Here the Lord also gave me my helpmate, my beloved wife Elizabeth, whose melodious soprano voice is dedicated to the service of God. Early in the year 1936 we left for Brooklyn, N.Y., to take up work among the many Jews of that metropolis. God by His grace enabled us to establish two mission stations in Jewish neighborhoods. I felt particularly called to minister to the poorest of the poor among Jesus' own brethren according to the flesh, the refugees, whose language I speak. This work the Lord blessed with several conversions, praise His name.

We were privileged to continue our work, also including that among the refugees, under the auspices of the American Board of Missions to the Jews, Inc., [Chosen People Ministries] and are happy now to be God's servants in Seattle, Washington, where we arrived a short time ago. The Christian friends in Seattle have received us with open arms and have made us feel at home. We covet your prayers for our work among God's chosen people.[69]

Joseph Cohn was delighted to see the way the work was growing, and to see the financial needs of the Mission being met as God's people rallied to each new challenge. But, as he considered the overall scope of the ministry from his office in New York, Joseph's heart was once again drawn to an awareness of the huge Jewish community living in that city and its boroughs. With renewed concern for the Jewish people living in the area where the Mission had first been established, Joseph told the Board: "…Things are going on nicely generally but there is a need for more missionaries right here in Brooklyn. We should have them in the various sections of Brooklyn."[70]

DANIEL FUCHS—HIS STORY

Joseph already had additional workers in mind for the Brooklyn ministry. He told the Board: "…we have now taken on Daniel Fuchs hoping that eventually he can take complete charge of the young people's work. We will pay him $100 a month. Part of his time will be given to study at Columbia so that he may secure his degree, and the rest will be spent in the Mission work here."[71]

Daniel Fuchs and his sister, Judith Fuchs, were both hired by Joseph Cohn to work for the Mission. Judith worked with the children, while Daniel worked with the Jewish boys. As was mentioned in the previous chapter, the involvement of the Fuchs family came as a result of the faithful witness of Miss Augusta Sussdorff in her Mothers' Meetings. Daniel told the story in this way:

One day Miss Sussdorff visited 220 Stockton Street, Brooklyn, and knocked on the door of the Salinsky's apartment. The girl who opened the door later became my mother. My grandmother was not at home. Miss Sussdorff explained the purpose of her visit to my mother and invited her to come to classes in Bible study at the Mission. When my grandmother returned, my mother asked for permission to go to the Mission. This was refused. She was told that we [sic] should receive a whipping if she ever went.

Jewish children are different from Gentile children—or are they? Tell a Jewish child not to go to the Mission, and that's where he'll go! My mother went to the Mission, and for the first time in her life heard that the Lord Jesus Christ was Israel's Messiah. When she went home she began asking some questions and let 'the cat out of the bag!' The visit to the Mission meeting was discovered and my mother received the promised thrashing. She was told that the following week she would have to come directly home from school and be locked in what was called the front room. But my grandmother made a serious error in strategy. There was a fire escape outside the room, and because of the cold weather my mother threw her coat out the window to her sister (my Aunt Mary) and both went to the meeting. Upon her return my mother climbed back up the fire escape, and found my grandmother waiting for her.

But no amount of opposition or punishment hindered my mother from attending the Mission classes and one Thursday afternoon following the teaching of the Bible lesson by Miss Sussdorff, my mother accepted the Lord Jesus Christ as her Messiah and as her Lord and Savior….my mother continued going to the Mission. Subsequently she met a young Jewish believer in the Lord, they fell in love, and were married and covenanted together that, by God's grace, they would have a Christian home.[72]

Daniel was born on November 3, 1912, the second of three children. His older brother's name was John. His younger sister's name was Judith. In 1919 Daniel's father died. Daniel was just seven years old. The Mission had arranged to have Daniel's father buried in Machpelah, the Mission's cemetery. Speaking of that dreadful day, Daniel wrote: "…We wept together with my mother as they lowered the body of my father into the grave. I re-lived that frightful experience over and over again in the nightmares of my early childhood. Deep down in my heart there were two emotions: a dreadful fear of death, and a deep-seated rebellion against God who would take my father away from us."[73]

Daniel's mother was only twenty-seven years old at the time of her husband's death. Because of her faith in Yeshua, she had been forced to leave school before she even graduated from elementary school. With little education and no skills, her only means of providing for her little family was to take employment scrubbing floors. She was convinced that her decision to take such employment, where she was free to pray for her children, was preferable to leaving her children with her sympathetic, but still unbelieving, Jewish family. Daniel remembered: "Each morning before she left home for the drudgery of another day's work the three of us were gathered together for family worship. This had been the habit of my father before he was called Home. Thus right from the start our rebellious hearts were nurtured on the Word of God."[74]

Daniel's heart remained rebellious for a number of years. Speaking of the day after his father's burial, Daniel wrote: "…my mother began teaching us the fourteenth chapter of John. I rebelled, laughed, and parodied the Scriptures, but with a steadfastness that was anchored in the sure promises of God my mother kept on. One by one we dropped out of the family worship, but we were never separated from the influence of her prayers."[75]

As she was able to, Mrs. Fuchs continued to attend meetings at the Mission. After some months she was hired by the Mission to be a housekeeper for some of the Mission's buildings. As was mentioned in the previous chapter, when the property on Hewes Avenue in Brooklyn was purchased, Mrs. Fuchs was eventually hired to live in the home—to keep it clean, and to provide for Mission guests who were invited to stay there.

It was while the Fuchs family was living in the Mission's "Hewes House" (as it was known), that the earnest prayers of Mrs. Fuchs for her family members were answered. On March 10, 1930 Daniel accepted Yeshua as his personal Lord and Savior. Through the faithful prayers and witness of Mrs. Fuchs and her friends at the Mission, other members of the family opened their hearts to receive Yeshua, too. Daniel wrote: "My aunts and uncles and even my grandmother came to the Lord. My grandmother had persecuted my mother not because she hated her, but actually because she loved her and thought she was doing God a favor. As an old lady, almost blind, she accepted the Lord and was one of the thousand baptized by Leopold Cohn."[76]

In April 1931, the Fuchs family moved out of the Mission's house on Hewes Avenue. God had accomplished His purpose. The family was united in faith. Daniel and Judith became involved in Mission activities; their older brother, John, left to seek secular employment.

Judith Fuchs continued to work for the Mission until April 1941. While she was serving on the staff of the Mission, Joseph Cohn heard about a young Jewish man in Europe who had come to know Yeshua through the ministry of Mr. Moses Gitlin. Joseph knew Moses Gitlin—he had become a believer in Yeshua under the ministry of his father, Rabbi Leopold Cohn. Moses had also been baptized by Leopold.[77] The Mission had helped Moses attend Moody Bible Institute. More about Moses Gitlin and his ministry in Europe will be discussed in a later chapter of this history.

Just as the Mission had provided help for many other Jewish believers in Europe, funds were provided to bring the young Jewish believer, Raphael Hoffman, to the United States, and to assist him while he attended the National Bible Institute. Judith Fuchs and Raphael Hoffman fell in love, and planned to be married. But there was one problem. A difference of opinion had come between Raphael and Joseph that had severed the relationship between the two men. The Mission was no longer supporting Raphael, and Joseph strongly opposed Judith's engagement to him. Seeing no future for Raphael within the Mission, Judith also resigned. Through the years she was an excellent worker for the Mission, and her loss in working with the Jewish young people was deeply felt.

Daniel Fuchs remained a faithful and devoted worker. Over the years, he was involved in almost every aspect of the ministry. He began by directing the Boys' classes in Brooklyn; he assisted in the Buffalo branch and the Coney Island branch; he served as a Field Evangelist; he served as a writer and then as editor of *The Chosen People* magazine; he served as Missionary Secretary of the Mission; he then became the Mission's President. During his last years of service with the Mission, until his death, Daniel served as Chairman of the Board. Further details of the life and ministry of Daniel Fuchs will be given as the story of the Mission's history unfolds.

Expanding the Branch Ministries

That God was adding His blessings to Joseph Cohn's vision for the ministry, and to the dedicated service of the Mission's staff, was evident. But that did not mean there were no crosses to bear. Heartbreak and disappointments were a very real part of the daily life of many of the Mission's workers. One worker who continued to faithfully serve his Lord in spite of great heartache and financial burden, was brother Harry Burgen of the Philadelphia branch. During the early months of 1937 Harry's wife, Rebecca, was severely disabled by mental illness. Doctors were consulted and friends and family prayed, but by the Fall of 1937 she had to be institutionalized. Rebecca was never able to return home. It was a severe blow to Harry and to the children, yet God sustained them, and He brought to the Burgen family a Christian woman who felt called of the Lord to cook for the family and to love the children.[78] It was hard to imagine why one so faithful in God's service would be called on to bear such a burden, but Harry carried on without complaint.

When Harry opened the Philadelphia branch in 1927, the ministry was carried on from a store front building on Spruce Street in downtown Philadelphia. But as God blessed, and as the ministry grew, a larger facility was needed. Harry mentioned the need to Joseph Cohn in 1937 and, after a diligent search, a suitable building was located at 717 Walnut Street. The Dedication Service for the new facility was held in the Fall of 1938. One year later Harry wrote a report of his activities for *The Chosen People* magazine in which he stated:

> We have completed our first year at 717 Walnut St., Philadelphia. We came to this new location at the end of October, 1938.
>
> Since coming to this new location we are meeting with increased opportunities of reaching Jews, Gentiles and Christians. The Lord is giving us a ministry among them all....
>
> Recently we have had contact with many refugee Jews, who have fled for their lives from lands of oppression. They pause at our window, hesitate and are fearful of coming in but finally take courage and step in. They are amazed and overwhelmed at the kindness shown them. Most do not know why we are here. They ask for employment or seek to sell merchandise. Some ask for literature which is displayed in the window. In every case it is our chief joy to magnify the Name of the Lord Jesus Christ and endeavor to win each one for Him.[79]

Harry did magnify the name of the Lord—not in a spectacular, flashy way; Harry Burgen lifted up his Lord through his faithful and consistent witness to God's Truth and Grace.

The Board of the Mission had moved to essentially "turn over the reigns" of leadership of the Mission to Joseph Hoffman Cohn in 1920. Seventeen years later, Joseph's accomplishments in the field of Jewish evangelism were being recognized and lauded by the Christian community. In the Spring of 1937 Joseph told members of his Executive Committee that he had received a telegram informing him that the Los Angeles Baptist Seminary of Los Angeles, California had honored him with the degree of Doctor of Divinity.[80] Joseph remarked to members of the committee that the honor had come as a complete surprised to him!

The early months of 1937 held another surprise for Joseph Cohn and the Mission. Joseph received a letter from a committee of Independent Baptists who asked if the Mission would be interested in merging with a Jewish mission in Buffalo, New York—the Buffalo Hebrew Christian Mission, a work that had been established by Mr. Abraham B. Machlin in 1920. A number of months earlier the Mission had been contacted by the same committee, asking if the Mission would be willing to financially assist the mission in Buffalo. The Minutes state:

> After discussion, it was voted that we send $50.00 monthly to the friends in Buffalo, for a period of six months, with the distinct understanding however that the Board is in no way responsible for the work done there, the responsibility and supervision to be undertaken by the brethren in Buffalo. Carried.[81]

After receiving the committee's second communique, in which it was suggested that the Mission take over the work in Buffalo, the Board became excited about the prospect of having a branch in Buffalo, and an agreement for a merger of the two ministries was worked out. Joseph transferred some of the staff from the Brooklyn branch, as well as from other branches. The dedication service for the Buffalo branch was held in the Fall of 1937. The opening of the new outreach was a joyous occasion, but the joy soon turned to frustration, and then to heartache, as difficulties and misunderstandings mounted. The details of the Buffalo branch will be told in greater detail in a separate chapter of this history.

As Christian people across North America heard more and more about the Mission, they began to understand the responsibility and opportunity they had for being used as God's channels to reach Jewish people with the Gospel, and branch ministries began to open across the country.

In Erie, Pennsylvania a branch of the Mission was opened under the direction of Mrs. Thelma Blair, a full-time volunteer worker who had a deep love for the Jewish people and for Israel. Thelma invited Jewish women from her community to her home each week. She opened her heart to the women and shared her testimony and, together, they would look into the pages of Scripture. Joseph saw to it that Thelma received a monthly supply of The Shepherd of Israel, New Testaments, Gospel tracts, and any other materials she requested for her outreach in Erie.[82]

As a result of Joseph Cohn's extensive contact with pastors and churches, a branch of the Mission was also opened in Indianapolis, Indiana in 1943. The workers were somewhat on "loan," but Joseph was nonetheless very pleased, and wrote:

> ...The dislocations of the world war brought us at least this much of blessing, that as a result of the disbanding of the American missionaries of the Belgian Gospel Mission in Brussels, and their return to the United States for the duration, the Misses Esther Hoyt and Lulu Sommers have sort of loaned themselves to us until in God's good providence they can go back once more to their first love in Brussels. These two consecrated and industrious missionaries have been salaried by the Wealthy Street Baptist Church of Grand Rapids, Michigan, and it was this church which said to us, "Here are these two girls, you are welcome to use them in the Jewish Mission work, and we will continue paying our previous salaries to them."
>
> And so both were assigned, in God's leading, to Indianapolis. There they found shelter and an open door welcome with our beloved friends, Rev. Robert S. McCarthy and Mrs. McCarthy, and the members of the 31st Street Fundamentalist Baptist Church. Miss Hoyt is a virtual dynamo, while Miss Sommers is gifted as a Bible teacher. Both set to work immediately and already the reports are coming of the most remarkable blessings attending their faithful class of Jewish refugees who come to their home regularly for Bible study, and they have endeared themselves to Jews and Christians alike.[83]

Florida, too, with its mushrooming Jewish population, was a state where a branch of the Mission was established. This branch, like other branches of the Mission, was largely staffed by people who volunteered their time. In February 1943 Joseph wrote about the Florida branch, saying:

> ...Here dear Mrs. Lindsey is carrying on in a rented hall on 502 N. Miami Avenue, and we are helping her with the rent, besides providing the literature she needs month after month. As our contribution further, we have the privilege of paying the salary of a Jewish Christian young woman, Geraldine Larsen; this girl has suffered much because of her faith in the Lord Jesus Christ, but she is a welcome visitor in the Jewish homes of which there are many thousands in the Miami and Miami Beach area. To give the work a proper organizational standing, we arranged for some of our ministerial brethren of Miami Beach to be responsible for the day-to-day activities. And so Brother John Maxwell Cook, Rev. Jas. H. Christie, Rev. Wm. C. Cumming, are a Committee to whom Mrs. Larsen is responsible and through whom she reports to us her monthly activities. These pastors are happy in this new undertaking, and we likewise are thankful that it is our privilege to have this fellowship with them.[84]

In the Spring of 1944, Rev. Mr. Leslie J. Batchelder paid a visit to the Mission's headquarters office in New York and while he was there, he shared his testimony with Joseph Cohn. Joseph, who had been thinking about expanding the Mission's work in Florida, listened to the testimony with interest.

Rev. Batchelder shared with Joseph that he was a Gentile Christian. He had come to faith in Yeshua in 1926. Feeling God's call upon his life, Leslie trained for the ministry and had become a pastor. When the depression years came along, money was scarce and became a matter of concern. The Mission had placed an article in a Christian periodical with the caption "To the Jew First." Rev. Batchelder told Joseph that as he read the article his heart came under conviction, and he realized that he had done nothing for the Jewish people. Then and there, he made a commitment to give a portion of his tithe to the Mission, and God's promise, "I will bless those who bless thee [Abraham and his seed through Isaac]..."[85] became a reality for him. God brought about a complete reversal of his financial situation, and his ministry began to grow. Over the next thirteen years he had remained in the pastorate, faithfully sending a portion of his tithe to the Mission.

Toward the end of 1943, Rev. Batchelder said he'd felt constrained to witness to the Jewish people—so much so that he'd resigned his pastorate and begun a small independent work among the Jewish people. Of the small independent work he started, Rev. Batchelder later wrote:

> ...This was purely a venture on faith, and it was blessed of God. I visited the stores and homes of Jewish people and testified to them of the true Messiah Jesus. Some resented it, but on the whole the Jews were very receptive to the Gospel message. They accepted tracts, Scripture portions and New Testaments. Christians and churches became aroused and interested, and rallied to my support....The American Board of Missions to the Jews first made me conscious of my obligation to the Jews; through them I have been able to bless the Jew and have been blessed myself, therefore I am happy to be a member of this great family seeking to win to the Lord Jesus, the lost sheep of Israel.[86]

The sincerity of Rev. Batchelder's testimony, and his obvious love for the Jewish people resulted in Joseph offering him a position as a missionary worker in Florida.

Month by month, and year by year, the "network" of key individuals enlisted by Joseph for personal involvement in the ministry, or for support of the ministry, continued to grow. Joseph viewed each person hired, each volunteer, each friend of the Mission as God's link in the expansion of the Mission's outreach to both Jews and Christians.

Joseph told members of the Executive Committee about one such "link"—a Rev. David T. Cant, who had been doing independent work among the Jews in Seattle, Washington. Joseph first met Rev. Cant when he and Mr. Abraham Machlin (additional information about Mr. A.B. Machlin will be given in a subsequent chapter of this history) were in Seattle, seeking to raise support for the Buffalo branch. Joseph said: "...He [Cant] has a very fine effective way of approaching the Jews through personal contacts, and the Lord has blessed him in this, so that he has quite a number of splendid converts."[87] He then proposed that Mr. Cant be hired to represent the Mission in the Northwest territory including the states of Oregon and Washington, and going as far as Vancouver in British Columbia. He further stated that he had already worked out a financial arrangement with David Cant:

> ...This arrangement that I have outlined with him is that if he raises any funds for the Mission, we will return to him all monies up to a gross total of $100, so that he may have that to use in the local work, in the Northwest. Above this $100, we are to retain all income. Our net obligation, therefore, is only $50 a month. We ought to undertake this for the sake of not losing the opportunity of a good approach to the Jews in this northwestern territory, where practically nothing has been done for the Jews by way of gospel work.[88]

RADIO—A NEW VENTURE

The closing of the Atlantic City branch had been a great disappointment to the entire Mission staff, but Joseph Cohn was not one to give up. He continuously looked for new avenues of witness, and in 1937 his ears "perked up" when he heard about the excellent outreach to Jews of the Atlantic City area that was being accomplished through the radio broadcast of Rev. Coulson Shepherd, pastor of the First Baptist Church in Atlantic City. Joseph therefore suggested to the Board that the Mission help support Rev. Shepherd's radio ministry. The Board was in agreement with his suggestion.[89]

During the mid to late 1930's, radio was being recognized as an effective tool for evangelism. Not being one to miss an opportunity, Joseph had mentioned the possibility that the Mission have its own radio program even before he'd requested that the Mission support Rev. Shepherd's broadcast. In a letter to the Executive Committee, in lieu of their regular meeting, Joseph wrote:

> This is not a request for an appropriation, it is only a foreshadowing of something I would like to bring up when our full board meets. I have requested Mr. H. (Herman) Centz of Philadelphia to prepare 40 radio programs of 15 minutes duration. My desire is that we go on to a radio hook-up this winter on some reasonably good sized station, and conduct over 40 weeks a Jewish Christian hour. When Mr. Centz will submit to me the 40 programs, which I hope will be soon, I will go over them with several other people, and then if I think they are worth adopting, I will ask our board to approve a radio program for the winter. I will also secure figures of cost, etc., so we will have all the data for us which will enable us to act intelligently. In the meantime, this is something we may be all praying about very definitely.[90]

Unfortunately, the broadcast programs produced by Herman Centz were a great disappointment to Joseph. He told the Board that Mr. Centz had worked all summer and had only been able to produce two programs, neither of which was satisfactory. Mr. Paul Graef, the Treasurer of the Board, had been reading through old copies of The Shepherd of Israel and he suggested that topics from that publication would be very suitable for radio broadcasts. He believed that thirty or forty programs could quite easily be prepared from them. The Board was delighted with Graef's idea, and suggested that Joseph be allowed to spend up to $10,000 for such a broadcast.[91] Joseph further suggested that the Mission's broadcast be aired every Friday evening, just prior to the broadcast aired by Temple Emanuel of New York City. He reasoned, "…if we could take the time immediately preceding this broadcast there might be some Jews who would turn the dial to WHN ahead of time, waiting for the service, and so they would hear at least a portion of our broadcast."[92]

In getting a radio program off the ground, and keeping weekly broadcasts going, Joseph was faced with a number of problems. With his hectic schedule, the first problem he faced was in trying to find the time to make the tapes—a task that took precious time away from other pressing matters. Yet Joseph knew if he asked another worker to make the tapes they, in effect, would became the "radio voice" of the Mission—a detraction from the leadership image of Joseph Cohn.

By 1943 Joseph told the Board he was again thinking of trying to have Herman Centz produce some radio tapes. This time Joseph wanted Herman to go to Buffalo to make the tapes because a radio station in Buffalo had promised to give the Mission an available time slot. Joseph remarked to the Board that Mr. Centz was not happy about this plan.[93]

Joseph then told the Board he had discussed a media idea with Mr. Iver Iverson, a member of Calvary Church in New York. The idea was to use radio "spot announcements" in the cities where Joseph had speaking engagements arranged. He had already experimented with such announcements, and had found that the attendance at his meetings was greatly increased. He told the Board: "…With these 'spot' programs, we are able to hook into any station. The cost is somewhere in the neighborhood of $60.00 for 50 words, on the large chains, and we could use these words to tell the radio audience about the Mission, suggesting that they send for information about the work, or for tracts for Jews, etc.[94]

The Board voted to use monies that had been set aside for a radio broadcast, to make the "spot announcements." The amount appropriated was $10,000.[95]

At a Board meeting less than two years later, in January 1945, Joseph once again broached the subject of the need for the Mission to have its own radio broadcast. Joseph set his proposal before the members of the Board, and once again they approved his proposal, giving him a budget of $15,000 to work with.

In his proposal to the Board, Joseph told the men that Rev. R. Paul Miller, General Secretary and Treasurer of the Brethren Churches of America, had volunteered to help him with the broadcasts. Joseph had known Rev. Miller for over thirty years. The two men had first met when Paul Miller was pastoring a small Brethren church in Spokane, Washington. Paul told Joseph he had become interested in Jewish evangelism and in The American Board of Missions to the Jews through the Mission's field evangelist, Rev. Elias Zimmerman.

After their initial meeting, Rev. Miller became a staunch supporter of Joseph Cohn and of the Mission, and when he resigned from his position with the Brethren Home Mission Society, he went back to his first love of being an independent traveling evangelist. But, like Joseph Cohn, the more he thought about radio and about the valuable tool it could be in teaching the Word, and in exhorting the cause of Jewish Missions and evangelism, the more he was drawn to that medium. He wrote to Joseph and said:

> …I believe this is going to be the biggest thing we have yet done for Jewish Missions…Joe, this thing is getting into my blood. I'm even beginning to dream about it. Maybe I need to see a doctor or take a trip to Florida! One thing is sure, I am willing for His will to be done. If it be His will for me to leave the evangelistic field temporarily or permanently, even though it has been my life work, I am not averse to it if I know my own heart. I love Israel and I am willing to go down the line for them any time He says so.[96]

Joseph proposed to the Board that they take Rev. Miller up on his offer; allow him to continue all of his church engagements, but engage him for the time he was not speaking in churches to experiment with radio work for the Mission. Joseph estimated the radio expenses and Rev. Miller's time at about $15,000 a year. He told the Board:

> …I feel we will get more than this amount back in a year's time. But even if we do not get one dollar return, it will be a marvelous testimony. I propose to call it The Chosen People broadcast, with a three point program. We propose to reach the Jews with the Gospel message, also we will do our part to combat anti-semitism, and we will have a message for the Gentile Christian.[97]

The Board was delighted with the plan and immediately approved it. It proved to be a wise decision! The radio ministry was a real answer to prayer. The broadcasts gave Joseph (the Mission) an audio voice that he needed to teach and to preach about the need for sharing the Gospel with the Jews. The sincerity of Joseph's voice, his manner, his expository skills, and his ability to communicate, soon made *The Chosen People* broadcast one of the most-listened-to Christian radio programs in the country. The broadcasts helped to establish confidence in the Mission as Christians listened to Joseph Cohn, the Jewish evangelist, expound the Word of God, and as they received and read through the monthly issues of *The Chosen People* magazine.

In spite of previous attempts at establishing and maintaining a radio broadcast, Joseph told members of his Board he hadn't realized how difficult radio communication could be. In his usual style, he tackled the problem and reported to the Board:

> ...I went out to Detroit a few weeks ago and Rev. Paul Miller and myself made a number of records....There I cut my eye teeth. We found that we made three or four mistakes. We had shipped five records to be broadcast in Waterloo. Three of them were rejected. I sat with the head man of the station and he showed me exactly what the trouble was. He said 'I am with you 100% but I am sitting here listening with the ears of the public and I know just what their reaction will be. In defending the Jew, as you are endeavoring to do, you must be very careful not to antagonize the Gentiles.' So we must reset some of the records. From nine in the morning till five p.m. each day for a whole week, I sat in Detroit and dictated the material for 40 manuscripts.
>
> We have been told that we must not expect any results from this broadcasting for the first six months. After that time we will get responses from both Jew and Gentiles.
>
> We will make 50 master records. From these we will have copies made and forwarded to our field men. They in turn will 'peddle' them to the small stations in the various towns and cities as they go about. We are satisfied if we can use the facilities of only the small stations. We do not make any appeal for funds in our broadcasts. We are defending the Jews against Anti-Semitism. There is no such message on the air at the present moment. In the Detroit studios the two men with whom I dealt were Jews. They looked at me as if I were a curiosity, but after they listened to some of the messages, one said, 'You have something on the ball. I never heard anything like this before in my life.*[98]

Paul Miller was a God-send for Joseph Cohn and for the Mission. One year after this initial agreement, with the radio work growing and producing good results, Joseph told the Board that Paul was needed on a full-time basis. The Board agreed, and Rev. Paul Miller was hired as a full-time worker with the Mission.[99]

Paul Miller gave this excellent report of the radio ministry:

> Our first program started on Station WOAI, San Antonio, Texas. This soon followed with a program over KARK, Little Rock, Arkansas. WOAI began broadcasting The Chosen People program the first week of April [1945]. KARK started in June [1945]. On August 12th, God opened the way for us to broadcast over WTOL in Toledo, Ohio. Hardly had this opening come, than an opportunity came to get on the strong station, WRNL, Richmond, Va. These stations are now carrying The Chosen People program every Sunday morning....
>
> Other stations are being added right along, and they will be announced each month on this radio page. If you are living near enough to any of these stations, be sure to listen in—and tell your friends to listen in also. If you receive a blessing through listening, write and tell us so. If you have Jewish friends, or business acquaintances, be sure to tell them to listen in. There never was a time in history when Jewish hearts were so disturbed over world conditions, and so fearful for their own future with the tide of Anti-Semitism rising steadily. Many of you may have been wondering what you can do to help Israel to know Christ. This is one thing you can do! You can tell your Jewish friends or storekeepers about this program, and then pray that God will use it to lead them to Christ. With the world in the state that it is, no one can foresee how soon all radio privileges may be removed from religious programs. So, do not delay, but do all you can at once.[100]

And listen they did—both Jews and Christians! As indicated earlier, *The Chosen People* radio broadcast soon became a main vehicle of evangelism and of support for the ministry. New stations were added almost daily.

In relating to the readers of *The Chosen People* magazine some of the problems they had faced in airing the radio broadcasts, Joseph wrote:

> ...The results have been thrilling, as you have read in the reports of our brother, R. Paul Miller. This dear brother has given of himself sacrificially and God has used him effectively in getting these programs under way. The problem was rather intricate because we could not approach the broadcasting stations here in America with a straight-out Gospel-preaching campaign. No radio company would permit us to go on the air with a program of what they call "proselyting the Jews." So we had to ask of God, and from Him we received divine wisdom. The result is that Jews have begun to

listen to the programs and are making complimentary comments on the way we have been handling the Gospel question. We explained to the broadcasting people that our purpose is to help eliminate anti-Semitism, and our message would be that only through the Lord Jesus Christ can there come an end to Jew hate or to any other kind of hate. We think often of that beautiful passage in Ephesians 2 where it is shown so clearly that through Christ and through Him alone, is there the breaking down of the middle wall of partition, and the securing of peace both for Jew and for Gentile. The Lord blessed our explanation and our radio program was accepted.[101]

The work that Rev. Paul Miller established in putting together a radio broadcast for the Mission, in securing radio time, and in overseeing that part of the Mission's outreach lasted long after both he and Joseph had gone home to be with the Lord. Paul Miller may never have fully realized how much his love for the Jewish people, and his commitment to bringing the Gospel to the Jewish people was influencing his own son. But the writer is certain that Rev. Paul Miller would have been very pleased to know that because of his faithful and dedicated service to the Mission, his son, Robert E.A. Miller, and Robert's wife, Althea, gave up a successful pastorate in Glendale, California to serve on the Mission's staff as missionaries in the Washington D.C. and Los Angeles, California areas.

When Joseph Hoffman Cohn passed away, the Mission continued to air his taped messages. It is true that through the wonder of the air waves even the dead can continue to speak, but such a ministry cannot promote growth. By the time God called Rev. Paul Miller into his presence on February 20, 1964, the radio ministry had nearly expired as well.

THE CONEY ISLAND BRANCH ESTABLISHED

During the same period of time that Joseph and Rev. Miller began working to establish a radio ministry for the Mission, a new branch of the Mission was established in Coney Island, and grew rapidly under the direction of Miss Rose and Miss Sussdorff. The ministry in Coney Island began as a challenge from Joseph Cohn to Miss Dorothy Rose and Miss Augusta Sussdorff in the early months of 1938. The story was told in *The Chosen People* magazine, by Dorothy Rose:

'Go ahead and do it' was the sentence that started us off to work among the many thousands of Jews in Coney Island. For a long while Miss Sussdorff and I had had a burden for the mothers in Israel living in that district. A number of women who had at one time attended the mission in Williamsburg had moved to Coney Island and could not come to the mission any more. Some had been away fifteen or twenty years, others but a short while; but Miss Sussdorff had kept in touch with them through visitation.

In conversation one day with Mr. Cohn I expressed a wish that we could start a mother's class in Coney Island. His answer was, 'Go ahead and do it.'[102]

So the dynamo team—Augusta Sussdorff and Dorothy Rose—rose to the challenge and "went out and did it!" They spoke to the Jewish women with whom Miss Sussdorff had remained in contact; they met with area pastors; they did door-to-door visitation. The meetings started in a home with just a few women attending, but by early Fall sixteen mothers were regularly attending. Soon Miss Sussdorff and Miss Rose thought it was time to open a children's class. Once again, God opened doors and by late Fall they had twenty-seven girls enrolled in the class. Miss Rose wrote:

God has shown Himself mighty in our behalf in giving us a group of women and class of girls,—the beginning we trust of a permanent mission work among the multitudes of Jews in a section that is practically untouched by the gospel of the Lord Jesus Christ. Pray for victory in Coney Island.[103]

Just as the Mission's programs had drawn in the Jews of Brooklyn, the meetings held in Coney Island appealed to the Jews of that community. It was not long before the cry came for more space and for more staff. Joseph reported to the Board:

The Coney Island work under the leadership of Miss Rose is growing rapidly and so it seemed imperative that we rent a store. We found a store admirably suited for our purposes, but when it came to leasing we found that there were so many requirements of the city to be met, that it was useless to consider it further. So we are continuing the Coney Island classes in the home of one of our converts, though we are much crowded for space. Last week we had 34 children, and Miss Rose told the girls not to bring any more friends.[104]

For two years they diligently sought suitable property for the Coney Island branch. Miss Dorothy Rose wrote:

Up one street and down another. Expectantly and persistently we searched. 'For Rent' and 'For Sale' signs held a certain fascination for Miss Sussdorff and me as we looked for a suitable house to use as a mission station in Coney Island, but it seemed of no avail. One after another, each place was eliminated with such notations as,— next door to a synagogue; too far away from our former location; rooms not suitable for our purpose; in bad condition....

September came and as we went through the streets the children and mothers eagerly questioned, 'When will classes begin?' 'Where will we meet this year?' It was then that we heard of a house for sale by the Home Owners Loan Corporation. When we saw it, newly decorated and modernized, our hearts leaped with joy. It was ideal. God had planned it just for us. It was in a choice location, half way between two public schools, near a public playground, and right in the midst of the neighborhood where the families lived that we already knew. But obstacles innumerable seemed to pop up from everywhere. The price needed adjusting, others were interested in the place, red tape with government and real estate agents consumed so much time; but finally the day came when the American Board of Missions [Chosen People Ministries] took title to the house of our prayers—the Coney Island Branch....

The first meeting was the last week of November and our hearts were filled with thanksgiving to God for the fulfillment of our dreams and prayers....

The old members responded to our invitations and together with the new ones we have nineteen mothers and thirty-nine girls in regular attendance. Others are interested in coming and will soon be in the classes.[105]

HILDA KOSER—HER STORY

As the Coney Island ministry grew, additional staff was greatly needed. Joseph felt the work needed another woman—someone who could work well with the women and children, someone young enough to continue developing the work beyond the years that Miss Sussdorff and Miss Rose would be able to devote to it. He knew the Mission already had, within its own ranks, just such a young person—a Jewish girl whose family had been saved through the Mission. She was a girl who had come to faith in Yeshua because Joseph had made it possible for her to attend a Christian summer camp—Camp Pinnacle—in the Catskills of New York. The young girl's name was Hilda Koser.

Hilda's mother was from Vilna, Lithuania; her father was from Lodz, Poland. Both parents were from orthodox Jewish homes. Her mother's family had immigrated to America along with thousands of other Jews who were seeking a better life. Her father, seeking to escape the pogroms and persecution of Jews in Poland, had taken a job as a ship's carpenter. Thus, a young ship's carpenter and a fifteen year old girl whose family was seeking asylum in America, met on board a ship steaming its way to America. By the time the ship docked in Philadelphia the two young people knew they were in love, and shortly after arriving in America they were married.

Seeking a better life for himself and his expanding family (three daughters), Hilda's family moved to the Williamsburg section of Brooklyn. Her father was one of the carpenters who helped to build Luna Park in Coney Island.

The pogroms of Poland had given Mr. Koser an aversion to anyone who called himself a Christian. But one day, while working on some scaffolding at Coney Island, he slipped and severely injured himself. Like many immigrants of that time, Mr. Koser did not have sufficient funds to go to the hospital so he went home, but his condition continued to worsen. He knew he needed medical care. He had heard that there was a free clinic in Williamsburg; what he did not know was that the clinic was run by the Mission. Had he known that the clinic was a place where the staff also preached the Gospel, and where Jews believed in Yeshua, he would have died before entering its doors! Many years later, Hilda wrote of that fateful day:

Twenty-two years ago, [c.1916] a man walked into the Mission dispensary. After he was examined, the doctor walked over to the missionary in charge, and said, 'Miss Sussdorff, that man will never live to get home. If I were you, I'd follow him and see if he has a family.' That man was my father.

Miss Sussdorff followed him and found my mother and three little children. I was the baby. She spoke to my mother, and invited her to the Mother's Club.[106]

Miss Sussdorff and Leopold Cohn continued to visit with the family in spite of the strong protests of Mr. Koser. He did not die from the injuries sustained in the accident, but it was soon discovered that he had tuberculosis, and he was sent to a sanitorium in Denver, Colorado. This afforded the Mission's workers greater opportunity to visit with Mrs. Koser and her little girls, and little by little the family began attending the services of the Mission. As they attended, Mrs. Koser accepted Yeshua and was baptized. Her little daughters' faith in the God of Abraham, and in His Son, Yeshua, began to grow as well. But that was not all that was growing—the size of the family was also growing! Hilda wrote:

...my father who was in the sanitorium in Denver, Colorado, managed to sneak out of the hospital at least once a year.

He would make his way to Brooklyn (absent without leave) and almost every year there would be another child, until the family consisted of eight children.

My mother continued attending the mission and brought all of us with her. In time God answered our prayers concerning my father, and he was declared cured, and was able to come home to live. He was very nervous and with eight children who could blame him! We made him feel uncomfortable for he couldn't remember all of our names. We were all about one year or so apart. Some people called us "the steps" and wondered when they would see my mother without a baby in her arms. We were seven girls and one boy.[107]

Like the other Koser children, Hilda was virtually raised in the Mission, but it was not until she was fifteen years of age that she actually accepted Yeshua as her personal Messiah and Savior. Later in the year, she had another life-changing experience. She wrote:

...That summer, Mr. Cohn sent me to a Christian Camp—Camp Pinnacle—and there for two whole weeks, I was among Christian people and lived a pure and wholesome Christian life; for you see, though my mother was a Christian, my father was not, and all our moves and actions had to be closely watched for fear of what he would do. At Camp Pinnacle, I was offered the chance of attending a Bible School with all my expenses paid, but I felt I owed my family a debt and so refused.[108]

The seed had been planted in Hilda's heart and mind, and after she went home from camp she continued to think and pray about Bible School, and about God's claim and call upon her life. She wanted to serve the Lord, but she was also afraid of what her family would think—especially her father. He was adamant in his hatred of anything "Christian." Hilda wrote of turmoil and anguish:

I'll never forget my first night home. I went to my room which had no door. I opened my Bible, got down on my knees and began to read and pray and my father saw me. Now my father loved me, but when he saw me, his daughter, on her knees with an open Bible, he reached for the first thing his hands could grab, a wooden hanger. He beat me with it and cried, 'How could you, my child, believe in a Jesus who killed your grandmother, your grandfather, your aunts and uncles.' The memory of the pogroms (massacres) in Poland was still very real and my father believed Jesus had done this.

After the beating my father gave me, I cried to the Lord, 'It costs too much to follow Thee. I'll graduate from high school and go to work. I'll support any missionary you care to send. But, please, Lord, don't send me.'[109]

Hilda finished High School and went to work. Whenever she felt the call to go to Bible school, she smothered the thought. But the Lord gave her no rest. She wrote:

...Never, if I live to be a hundred, will I forget the last summer. My life was so miserable. I prayed for death. Trouble and misery just seemed to be crushing me. Trouble seemed to dog my path no matter where I went. My home life, my social life, my business life, my spiritual life, they were all in a turmoil. I just didn't know what to do. I prayed, but couldn't get close to the Lord.[110]

One night some friends invited her to go with them to a concert. As they traveled by subway, one of Hilda's friends told her that she believed the Lord was calling her to go to Bible College. Hilda had never told her mother, her Mission teachers, or any of her friends of her own inner turmoil because of God's clear call for her to serve Him. She was badly shaken when she heard her friend declare that she had heard God's call and that she was *willing* to obey His call and attend Bible school. Hilda wrote:

...I left the train at the next station and ran all the way home. This time I went into my sister's room which had a door, and told the Lord every reason why I would fail as a missionary. As I presented each reason to Him, He gave me the answer, 'What is that to thee? Follow thou Me.' (John 21:22c). Finally I yielded my all, and cried, 'Lord, wherever you lead me, I will follow.'[111]

Still testing the Lord, Hilda went to each of the family members and told them of her decision to go to Bible school. She was certain they would all be upset with her decision, but to her great surprise she found that God had prepared the way before her, and each family member she approached only encouraged her in her decision.

Hilda's teachers at the Mission were thrilled to hear of her decision, as was Joseph Cohn and, just as he had done so many times before, he agreed to pay the first year's expenses at the Bible Institute of Pennsylvania (now called Philadelphia College of the Bible) for both Hilda and her friend, Esther Shernow.

In June 1939 Hilda and her friend, Esther, graduated from the two-year program of the Bible Institute of Pennsylvania. Esther went for further study at Columbia Bible College in South Carolina, but Hilda, knowing God wanted her to be a missionary, accepted a position with the Mission. She was sent to the Pittsburgh branch to work with Dr. and Mrs. Solomon. The Minutes of the Board reflect the dedication and ability of Hilda. They state:

> *Miss Hilda Koser is now in Pittsburgh working with Mr. Solomon. Mr. Solomon speaks very highly of this young Jewish girl, which means a great deal because Mr. Solomon is not easily pleased and requires much from those who labor with him.[112]*

Hilda did not remain in Pittsburgh for long however. Her abilities and innate gift in working with women and children brought her once again to the attention of Joseph Cohn. As one who possessed a gift of assessing individuals and their talents, and in matching those individuals with particular needs within the Mission, Joseph knew Hilda Koser was the worker they were looking for to replace Miss Sussdorff and Miss Rose in Coney Island. The October 30, 1940 Minutes of the Board record these comments of Joseph Cohn: "Miss Hilda Koser is doing a splendid work in Coney Island. She has five different classes and last week over 125 different children attended the various classes. Mr. Birnbaum is now planning to start an evening class for the fathers of the Coney Island attendants. The first meeting will be Wednesday night, November 6th."[113] (note: Solomon Birnbaum was the founder and former Director of the Jewish Studies Department at Moody Bible Institute.)

As a "child of the mission" herself, and as one who deeply believed in the importance of reaching children with the Gospel, Hilda Koser emphasized the need of continuing something like the "Fresh Air Summer Camp" that Rabbi Leopold Cohn had established. Joseph took her concern seriously, and the May 1940 Minutes record that Joseph told members of the Board he wanted to establish a "Summer Camp for the children who come to our various classes, and also some of the refugee children."[114]

The Chosen People magazine carried a report of the new Summer Camp venture. Dorothy Rose, who wrote the report for the magazine, stated that the children were transported by bus from Brooklyn to Camp Fernwood in Roseland, New Jersey. That summer (1940), the girls camp began on July 14; sixty-one girls attended. The boys camp began on July 22; fifty-five boys attended. Each group stayed at the camp for eight days. The counsellors who served were: Dorothy Rose, Hilda Koser, Helen Machlin, Mrs. Daniel Fuchs, Lottie Furth and Martha Singer. In addition, Mr. Daniel Fuchs and two other Hebrew Christian young men helped in both the boys' and girls' camps.[115] Two volunteers not mentioned in Dorothy's report, but who gave their time and their love to the children at Camp Fernwood, were Clara and Joe Rubin. Although she was five months pregnant, Clara helped with the girls' camp. Joe helped at the boys' camp.[116] (Additional information about the ministry of Clara and Joseph Rubin will be covered in a later chapter of this history.)

Through the years, the summer camping program became an integral part of the Mission's evangelistic outreach. Camp locations have changed, and new programs have continued to be developed as the Mission's staff has endeavored to stay "in tune" with the times, but the Gospel emphasis of the camps has never changed. *The Chosen People* magazine continues to include stories and testimonies of Jewish and Gentile children who have come to faith in Yeshua while attending "Camp Hananeel" or "Camp Yeladim" (Hebrew, for Children's Camp). The camping program is still a viable means of reaching Jewish children and their parents with the Gospel.

The work at Coney Island continued to grow, and was a source of great encouragement to Joseph Cohn. Writing about that branch of the work in February 1941, he said:

> *Here the Lord has given the most stimulating tokens of approval and blessing. Under the faithful labors of Miss Dorothy Rose, Miss Sussdorff and Miss Hilda Koser, the meetings have had to be split and then split again much as the bees do when they swarm, and each time the new group has been adding to itself still larger numbers. Miss Koser reports a total well above 150 mothers and children who attend the meetings. And when it is considered that all this work was begun and is carried on in a district 100% Jewish and much of it of the orthodox and racially conscious type, the miracle takes on still further significance.[117]*

Hilda, too, was greatly encouraged by the work God was doing among His people in Coney Island. But the work at Coney Island was not all "sunshine and mirth." In one of her reports Hilda wrote:

I call the work in Coney Island my bitter-sweet. For, in the work, there is much bitterness caused by the opposition of Satan. But, there is also much sweetness caused by the joy and happiness of seeing the little ones being won to the Lord.

The past year the Lord has blessed abundantly. For, in spite of all opposition and trouble, I found in re-checking my roll book that He had sent in over 250 Jewish children in my own classes. Many have had to drop out, but praise God many have remained. And, at the end of June, I had 150 children attending my classes. Those who dropped out, I know have heard God's plan of salvation. We can plant, others may water, but the Lord giveth the increase.[118]

During her ministry in Coney Island, Hilda experienced and endured a constant barrage of persecution and hatred directed both toward herself and toward the Mission. Joseph understood the unique community in which Miss Koser ministered, and he shared some of the problems she faced with readers of the magazine. He said:

...Here an all-year-round population of about 100 thousand Jews gives us a challenging field, with sometimes as many as 300 to 500 thousand during the heated summer season. The heartaches, the joys, the difficulties, the persecutions, of this unique field will never be known by any of us, we suppose, until the records are revealed on the eternal shores where sorrow and sighing will be no more. But to this almost titanic challenge, our dear and faithful Hilda Koser has consecrated every fiber of her being. Rabbis, Jewish school teachers, officials of various Jewish clubs, Parent and Teacher Associations, all these apparently motivated by Satan's most desperate machinations, seem to have combined in a furious assault to make the life of Miss Koser at times a nightmare. The block where our building is located has been picketed day after day, and children have been seized and threatened with all sorts of dire consequences if they dared to attend the Gospel meetings. Be it said that some of these children have their hearts so deeply planted in the love of the Lord Jesus Christ, that they defy these threats, and come anyhow! And God has moved in wonderful ways to put to nought these unconscionable persecutions.[119]

In 1942, Joseph hired a young Baptist minister and his wife, Rev. and Mrs. Harry Fargo. They were to train for the ministry under the guidance and direction of Hilda Koser. The Fargo's were to live at the Mission's property in Coney Island. Harry was to care for the buildings, and to assist in the ministry as needed.[120]

Harry Fargo had a genuine love for Israel and the Jewish people but, being a Gentile Christian, he had little knowledge of Jewish culture and tradition. He wrote about the approach used during his training experience at Coney Island, and of the patience it took to become a worker in that field. He said:

Upon our arrival here, to begin the glorious task of spreading the glad tidings to Israel, our beloved Dr. Joseph Cohn,...called me into his office and told me that nothing much would be expected of me in the way of actual service for at least six months. He advised me to attend the meetings, go with the workers in their visitation work and the passing out of literature on the street. In this way, he said, I would become familiar with the ways and means of reaching the Jewish heart with the Gospel. Later when opportunities and privileges of ministering to them would come, it would be natural to so speak and deal with them that they would not be offended by our approach. Thus I would gain their confidence to the point where the presentation of our Savior to them as their Messiah would be an attraction to them.

After eight years of preaching the Gospel as a pastor, before coming to New York, it was hard to sit by week after week and watch others do the witnessing. But God had taught us the value of patience during those years of pastoral labors. The first opportunities of witnessing came by way of music and song at the meetings, and in personal testimony at the street meetings; also, during the course of our daily contacts with the people on the street as we distributed circulars and literature in the various sections of Brooklyn.

My first opportunity for real responsibility came the next summer when I was privileged to have the oldest group of boys at camp, to live with them, and to teach them the love of our Lord Jesus.

Here was the first test of the value of the long winter of observing and waiting and learning.

These boys, about ten of them, with the exception of two refugee boys, were American born and educated. English was as familiar to them as it was to me, a Gentile, but the language of the Scriptures, apart from the familiar stories of the early history of the human family and the kingdom of Israel, was almost as strange to them as their Yiddish and Hebrew were to me.

But boys being boys, no matter what their race or religion, we had a good time together and through the years that have followed, many of them have developed into true believers in the Lord Jesus as their Messiah and Savior.

Most of this development, of course, is the result of the work and prayers of their own club teachers in Coney Island and Williamsburg, but it has been a great encouragement to me to know that we have won their confidence and now that they are nearly grown men they come to us often for advice on their personal and spiritual problems.

Among the older people, too, the days of tarrying were not without blessings. In the meetings in Williamsburg the joy that spread over their faces the first time we sang a hymn in Yiddish was a sight worth many hours of labor to behold. And then as they would seek to point out features or characteristics in our faces and gestures that they thought bore a Jewish resemblance, we realized that we were accepted among them as part of the family and no longer considered as an alien to their people....

...I have come to realize that to witness effectually to Israel takes patience which must be endured to the breaking point. From there it must be carried on by a dogged love, until that love shall reach through us in penetrating power, piercing the prejudice and fear,...

In spite of all this justified prejudice and fear, it is amazing how in the street meetings, in the reading room and public services, and also in their homes, that they are eager to hear and discuss, yes, even believe, the truth as it is presented to them from the Word of God. Many are accepting Him as their Savior and Lord of their life.[121]

Harry Fargo continued in ministry at Coney Island and in various New York branches of the Mission for more than forty years.

Over a span of thirty-seven years, Hilda Koser faithfully served her Lord in Coney Island. Through her children's programs, mothers' classes, Sunday school program, Holiday services, Dorcas society, etc., thousands of Jewish people heard the Gospel. She served as counselor, match-maker, and mother and father to her "Coney Island kids." Because of her love for people (children in particular) the Mission at Coney Island became known around the world. Many of the "Coney Island kids" went on to Bible college and are now serving as pastors, teachers, and missionaries; some are even serving as missionaries with the Mission (now called Chosen People Ministries).

Time changed Coney Island, and over the years it became like an orphan child among the boroughs of New York. The amusement park, board-walk, and beaches were no longer attracting the crowds they once did; the buildings and properties in the area began to deteriorate—Coney Island was becoming a slum area. By the mid 1970's the Government stepped in and condemned all of the buildings in the area surrounding the Mission's buildings. The city's Urban Renewal Program set forth the proposal that low-cost affordable housing for minorities and refugees seeking asylum in America be built on the land. On the city's early plans, the Mission's buildings were exempt from demolition, but later they, too, were included. Hilda and the Mission fought to retain the buildings, but in the end the Mission's buildings were condemned, and were taken over by the Government.

Building after building was vacated, then demolished. Many stood empty for weeks, and sometimes for months, as demolition crews worked their way through the neighborhoods. The families that had occupied the houses and apartments in the buildings were forced to move. Standing amidst the debris and rubble, the Mission's buildings were among the last to be demolished. By that time the area looked like a war zone.

As the weeks turned into months, and the months turned into years, Hilda Koser faithfully maintained the Mission's work in Coney Island, and God blessed her ministry. Hundreds of Jewish people heard about and accepted Yeshua through the meetings that were held, and Hilda continued to train new workers for the Mission. But during those last few years, as the neighborhood buildings came down around them, and as she watched the ministry slowly erode away, her heart was breaking.

Hilda had only taken a few vacations from her "beloved" Coney Island throughout thirty-seven years of ministry. She needed a rest—a vacation from the years of ministry and from the heartbreak of the inevitable destruction of the buildings and property that had been her life for so many years. She therefore requested that the Mission allow her an extended leave of absence so she could go to Florida.

Hilda had already recruited and trained a capable staff of young people. In her absence, and until the building felt the blow of the demolition ball, the Mission's work continued under the supervision of Mr. Larry Feldman. Helping him were Cynthia Rydelnik, and Linda Schwartz, as well as a staff of volunteer workers and student workers whom Hilda had trained.

LARRY FELDMAN—HIS STORY

Knowing that the day would come when she would eventually retire, Hilda had been corresponding with Dr. Louis Goldberg (who, by that time, was the Director of the Jewish Studies department at Moody Bible Institute). In response to her inquiry about a possible candidate for the Coney Island work, Dr. Goldberg had suggested to Hilda that she contact Larry Feldman. Hilda followed through on Dr. Goldberg's suggestion and eventually met with Larry. She later wrote: "...praise God, as soon as I saw him and talked with him, I felt this was God's answer to my prayer."[122]

Larry Feldman was born in Philadelphia, Pennsylvania in 1948. He was raised in a conservative Jewish home, and was Bar Mitzvah (a ceremony held at age thirteen, in which a young Jewish boy becomes a 'son of the law'). Like many Jewish people, Larry had been taught that "Jesus" was a name associated with the Gentiles and with their God, but that Jewish people had nothing to do with that name, or with individuals who claimed to be followers of Jesus.

Larry's confrontation with the Messiah came in suburban Philadelphia when Joe and Debbie Finklestein moved into the neighborhood where Larry's family lived. The Finklesteins turned their home into a Messianic witnessing center that became known as "Fink's Zoo." In relating the story, Larry wrote:

At first, all I said I wanted was proof.

'Prove to me that Yeshua is the Messiah,' I told my friend Mark when he explained he had become a believer in the Messiah. 'Prove that God really wants me to believe it.'

Since I knew he'd never be able to prove it, I figured that would end the discussion. Frankly, even before Mark told me he believed in the Messiah, I was sick of the subject.

The whole controversy of Jews believing in Yeshua as the Messiah had hit our middle-class Philadelphia neighborhood about two years earlier [c. 1970], when Joe and Debbie Finklestein moved in.

The Finklesteins were an outgoing Jewish couple with a very outspoken belief: They said that the Messiah had come, that His name was Yeshua and that the only way to have a personal relationship with God was through Yeshua.

Their belief in Yeshua, the Hebrew name for Jesus, had slowly changed our entire neighborhood.

The Finklesteins had opened their house and their lives. Almost everyone in the area knew them, and most of the people had at least stopped by to hear what they had to say. Their place was so popular that we started calling it 'Fink's Zoo.'

Soon you couldn't go anywhere without hearing people talk about Joe and Debbie, and the people from the 'Zoo' were everywhere in the neighborhood, talking about Yeshua.

Naturally my friend Mark and I were above all that. It was one thing for a bunch of losers to discover religion, but not us.

We were real Jews. We'd graduated college. I was planning on going to medical school. We didn't need that kind of thing.

The problem was that we liked Joe and Debbie and couldn't really call them losers. They were warm, intelligent people. Joe had his master's degree in chemistry and was a research chemist for a respected firm. They were interesting to talk to and enjoyable to be with.

Still, Mark and I knew better.

Then one day Mark told me it was all true. I wasn't sure what he meant.

'You know—Yeshua, the Bible, the whole thing. The Bible really does point to Him coming, and He really does fulfill the prophecies.'

I went a little crazy. We'd been friends since we were five years old; we'd made fun of the weird people in Fink's Zoo. He had told me, 'I'd rather be in hell with you than in heaven with them.'

When I got over being mad at him, I said, 'Fine, as long as it doesn't change your life.'

But his life did change, and the biggest change of all was that he was always reading the Bible to me.

Rather than get mad and argue, I told him, 'Just prove it, then I'll believe.'

There was no telling what kind of proof it would take. I was an agnostic, convinced that there was no way anyone could know for certain that God exists. I thought maybe I'd see a miracle, but since I refused to believe in an emotional experience, I knew that wouldn't be enough.

But Mark kept coming over, telling me what the Bible said. We'd be talking about baseball, and pretty soon he'd be talking about the Bible. We'd discuss women, and suddenly I'd be hearing about the Bible. He was getting irritating to listen to. Most of all, he was making a lot of sense.

More and more I silently started asking God to show me the truth. He answered that prayer through Mark...and the Bible. The more Mark showed me in the Bible, the more I realized God had something specific to say to me.

For instance, on a moral scale, I figured I'd hit just about the middle—better than some, worse than others. The Bible categorized all this as sin, and said it separated me from God. The Bible also said God didn't want this separation.

The question seemed to be, 'How do I find peace with God?'

The Bible even had an answer for this, Mark explained. He asked if he could read me something.

'Okay,' I agreed, with one qualification, 'if it's from the Old Testament. That's my book.'

'It's from Isaiah.'

'Is that from the Old Testament?'

'Yes.'

'Even if it is, I'm not going to understand it because no one can understand the Bible.'

'Just let me read it, and you tell me what you think.'

I nodded assent and kept quiet while Mark read. Then he read this,

'Surely he hath borne griefs inflicted by us, and suffered sorrows we have caused: Yet we did esteem him stricken smitten of God, and afflicted.' 'But he was wounded through our transgression, bruised through our iniquities: the chastisement of our peace was upon him, and with his wounds we were healed.' Isaiah 53:4,5

'Stop right there.' I was insulted! 'Anyone knows your [sic] reading about Yeshua.'

'Yes, I am, but did you know that Isaiah was written about 750 years before Yeshua was born?'

He also read to me from another part of Isaiah, chapter 7, where it said the Messiah would be born of a virgin. Then he showed me in Daniel 9 that Messiah would come before the destruction of the Temple, which occurred in A.D. 70 and that, according to the prophet Micah, Messiah would be born in Bethlehem.

He also showed me that Psalm 22 indicated that the Messiah would die from crucifixion. In Zechariah 12:10, I recognized that the pierced Messiah could be none other than Yeshua.

From reading all these prophecies, I now knew God had made it clear how Messiah would come.

After a while, there didn't seem any way to avoid it. The Bible very convincingly proved that Yeshua was the Messiah. The Bible also made it very clear that God, the Jewish God, wanted me to know Him.

Something deep inside me held me back. It was clear that my hesitation was an emotional one. The Bible made it clear that I needed to do more than say it was true: I needed to make a decision to accept it for myself. It was a heart, as well as a head, decision.

'I can't do it,' I told Mark. 'I'd feel like a Gentile or a traitor or something awful.'

I said this, even though I saw in Mark's life, in Joe and Debbie Finklestein's lives, and even in the others who hung around Fink's Zoo, that they were still Jewish. Still, it was too foreign to me.

The days and months passed. Mark kept talking about Yeshua. I began praying regularly, asking God to show me the truth.

In a sense, I was trying it on for size. I'd talk the talk and even tell other people what the Bible said. I almost forgot that I didn't really believe it with my heart.

One day I said to Mark, 'You know, when we get to heaven...'

'What do you mean?' he interrupted. 'You're not going to heaven. The only way you can do that is to accept what Messiah did for you. Personally.'

Thinking about his words made me realize that I wanted to experience a relationship with God for myself, but that I only wanted to try it out: I only wanted God there for a few minutes.

So, late at night, laying in bed, I tried. Almost like a dare, I prayed, 'If you are real, come into my life.'

Nothing happened.

'Okay,' I thought. 'At least I tried. Subject closed.'

But not for God.

A few weeks later Mark invited me to a film. The title was Dry Bones, and it was about the prophecies relating to the rebirth of the state of Israel.

The movie was interesting and all, but honestly, I don't remember much about it. I only remember that a man stood up at the end and said, 'If there is anyone here who would like to accept Yeshua for the first time, raise your hand.'

Strange as it seems, I knew I had to raise my hand. God had somehow answered my prayer: There was no doubt in my mind what He wanted me to believe.

'Yeshua, I believe You died for me,' I began. 'I believe You died for my sins. I want to receive You into my life.'

Nothing looked different as I raised my eyes. Yet inside I felt changed. I was changed, not into a Gentile, but into a Jew who had found his Messiah.[123]

Larry received the Lord Jesus as his Messiah and Savior on January 15, 1972. In the days that followed, he stated:

I attended conferences, Bible studies and became involved in testifying for my Lord. I soon realized that I needed Bible school training. When I learned that Moody Bible Institute had a course in Jewish studies, I applied and was accepted. At the end of the school year, I felt it was time for me to become active in full-time service and a teacher at Moody told me of the Coney Island Branch of ABMJ [Chosen People Ministries] and of their need for a young man to be in charge of the Sunday School and eventually take over the work.

I corresponded with Miss Koser, the missionary-in-charge, and after an interview with her and much prayer, decided that this was where God wanted me. On June 1, 1974 I officially started my work and had a six-month training program, during which the Lord, knowing it is not good for man to live alone, gave me a wonderful wife whom I had met several years before [Fran]. She also is a Hebrew Christian, and we were married in August.

I have been teaching the adult class on Thursday nights, the older teen-age group on Friday nights, the adult Bible class in Sunday School, and have acted as pastor of the Sunday School. The work has kept me very busy, but there is no greater joy than teaching the Word of God. The visitation programs and the personal experiences with these people have given me great joy. I know that God has something wonderful in store for me and I am willing to do whatever He would have me to do.[124]

With a young energetic staff trained and in place, Hilda felt free to go to Florida. At first all went well, and Hilda wrote for *The Chosen People* magazine:

'Take a Sabbatical!' 'Go for a rest!' 'Your Body is exhausted!' 'Hasn't the Lord sent you a staff?' ' Haven't you trained them?' 'Now is the time to go.' So said my doctor. Thirty-eight years of constant ministry in Coney Island, N.Y. had taken its toll. I was very tired and I had also developed high blood pressure.

After much prayer and counsel I was advised to take a sabbatical. So off I went to Daytona Beach, Florida.

Almost immediately, I found an apartment....Have you ever dreamed of an apartment and found it furnished the way you wanted it? Well I did.

I could hardly believe my eyes. It was right on the ocean where I could watch the waves from my patio. The beach was right there, too; and I could walk for miles and feel no pain in my arthritic toes, as I had in New York.[125]

The apartment was wonderful. Being away from the pressures of Coney Island, with the condemnation proceedings continuing against the Mission's buildings, was wonderful. But not being one to "sit around," Hilda did not just relax in the sun. She went out—wherever she knew she would find Jewish people to witness to. It wasn't long before she was speaking at "Winning Women" groups in the area's churches, or speaking at Bible study groups. She was almost as busy as she had been in Coney Island. She wrote:

...Praise God for the many opportunities He has given.

In the meantime the staff in Coney Island is doing a great job. My prayer is to be used of God wherever and whenever He leads. Pray for me as I speak, teach and write my book on the Coney Island ministry.[126]

In Coney Island, the city continued its condemnation proceedings. But the community and its structures were not the only changes taking place at that time. A transitional period in Jewish missions and evangelism had begun—almost unnoticed at first. The wave of Jewish young people who had come to faith in Yeshua during the late 1960's and early 1970's were seeking to find an expression of their Jewishness in their worship and faith. Following the 1967 Six-Day War in Israel, both religious and non-religious Jewish young people began to take pride in their Jewishness. Those who had grown up with close ties to their Jewish identification and culture did not want to forfeit their "Jewishness" or their identity with "Israel" because of their faith in Yeshua. And Jewish young people who had grown up in families whose members had completely assimilated within Gentile American society wanted to re-identify with their Jewish heritage once they opened their hearts to the greatest Jew of all times—Yeshua, the Messiah of Israel.

A new era had begun—a time when young Jewish believers wanted to develop ways in which to express their Jewishness and their faith in Yeshua at the same time. The concepts of Rabbi Leopold Cohn for a Messianic congregation and community were being rekindled in the hearts and minds of many young Jewish believers—a phenomenon that is continuing in its development up to the present time.

Larry Feldman, being one of the young Jewish believers who wanted to express his Jewishness within worship, began to introduce Messianic language, songs, traditions and customs into the programs at Coney Island. Incorporating new ideas into worship is not an easy task. Many of the people who had continued attending the meetings at Coney Island after Hilda Koser had left for Florida were people whose family members had attended through several generations. They felt "at home" with the status quo, and did not like the changes introduced by this new staff worker. Hilda began to receive a barrage of letters and phone calls from members of her "family" in Coney Island who were unhappy about the changes taking place. The Mission also received letters and telephone calls.

Not many months later, Larry Feldman, himself, notified the Mission that he felt called of the Lord to continue his education. He and his wife, Fran, left for Dallas, Texas, where Larry enrolled at Dallas Theological Seminary. While they were in Texas, Larry continued to work for the Mission's Dallas branch on a part-time basis. After graduation from seminary, Larry and Fran returned to full-time service with the Mission. They established, and have maintained for the

Mission, a Messianic congregation in Livingston, New Jersey, and have continued to be faithful, God-honoring workers up to the present time.

STEVE SCHLISSEL — HIS STORY

When Larry and Fran left Coney Island, Steve Schlissel, another Messianic Jewish believer, was placed in charge of the struggling work there. Steve first heard about the Mission when a local Christian radio station made an announcement about a Jewish Evangelism seminar the Mission was sponsoring at a church in Queens, New York. Steve was intrigued by the announcement. He told his wife, Jeanne, about the seminar, and they decided to attend. Steve wrote of that encounter:

> ...It was to be a seminar about sharing the Good News of Messiah Jesus with Jewish people. Although I am Jewish I was completely ignorant of the proper tact, knowledge and sensibilities which are required to effectively witness to my brethren according to the flesh. That seminar was the beginning of the end of that ignorance.[127]

After the seminar, Steve and Jeanne wasted no time in contacting the branch of the Mission that was nearest to their home. Steve wrote:

> If the seminar was great, the fellowship at the Coney Island Branch, then directed by Rev. Larry Feldman, was greater. From the first Bible study we attended Jeanne and I knew the Lord was calling us to be a part of this work. If you'll excuse the expression, we attended meetings religiously, missing very few of the thrice-weekly gatherings over the next two years.[128]

Being an astute business man, Steve received several good promotions, but the higher he advanced in the business world, the more clearly he heard the still small voice of God calling him into Jewish ministry. Finally, unable to resist God's call upon his life, Steve made application and was accepted into the Mission's training program. In fact, Steve and Jeanne attended the training program together. Just as it had been in the business world, Steve's leadership ability was evident. He was excited about using his experience, knowledge, and abilities for the Lord, and he shared some of his excitement and vision for the Brooklyn Ministry (as it was called by that time) with the readers of *The Chosen People* Magazine. He wrote:

> The training experience has been invaluable. We have formed strong bonds with Dr. Fuchs, Rev. Sevener, the headquarters staff and, of course, our fellow "trainees" who will bring the Good News to the Jews from Phoenix to Farmingdale, and Brooklyn to Buenos Aires. We have studied Biblical Theology, Mission Programming, Hebrew, Yiddish, Israeli Geo-Politics, Messianic Prophecy, Bible Survey, Jewish Theology—traditional and contemporary—and many other subjects to equip us to do His will. The entire training process has been an experience of growth in our Lord....
>
> The means of reaching our people [in Brooklyn] will be varied. Hopefully we plan to have new and innovative experiences—in His will.
>
> In addition to our Bible studies, the Brooklyn Beth Sar Shalom has the musical ministry of Ammi (Hebrew for 'My People'). Ammi ministers to residents of nursing homes, local college students and distant churches and others, declaring in song and testimony the reality of the risen Messiah.
>
> We will continue to seek well-known Christian speakers to give their testimonies within the framework of talks on timely topics of interest to the Jewish community. Attractive services focusing on the true significance of the Jewish holidays should continue to result in many unsaved people hearing the Gospel. Aggressive tract distribution and pavement pounding will result in many more learning about the real Jesus, the Jesus who loves Israel and the Jewish people, and Who gave His life as a ransom, that whoever hears His word and believes will have crossed over from death to life.
>
> There will be challenges, difficulties, and resistance, I know. And sometimes there might even be despair. But as God enables, Brooklyn will continue to be a fruitful field.[129]

Shortly after Steve Schlissel was appointed Director of the Brooklyn ministry, the government finally took over the Mission's buildings and forced the Mission to relocate its ministry. After a lengthy search, a building was purchased in a Jewish neighborhood in Brighton Beach—within the Borough of Brooklyn, but several miles from Coney Island. The first meeting in the new building was held on Rosh Hashanah (New Year) September 22, 1979. Reporting on the schedule of activities, Steve wrote:

Our current schedule offers a Young Adult Bible Study, prayer meetings, Hebrew lessons, a Friday night Bible centered meeting, Sunday School and Sunday service as well as local tract distribution, visitation and counseling. Our plans include a direct-mail ministry—bringing the Gospel to the mailboxes of the local residents—tract distribution at New York's two major airports, newspaper advertising, door-to-door contact, campus evangelism and much more.

As our profile gets higher and our spectrum of activities gets wider, our dependence upon the prayers of God's servants increases. Please remember the Brooklyn ministry in your prayers.[130]

ENDING AN ERA

The Coney Island branch of the Mission had been "home away from home" for many, and they were homesick. They missed Miss Koser, they missed the old building, they missed the way meetings had been handled, and the feeling of "family" they had known there. With the relocation of the ministry to a new building, and with an emphasis that now sought to reach the changing Jewish and ethnic community of Brooklyn, many of the people who had faithfully attended the Coney Island branch stopped attending services. They wrote to Hilda, pleading with her to return and re-establish the old Coney Island branch ministry. But she could not. The buildings were gone, and Hilda's health was failing. Her sabbatical turned into retirement. She wrote:

...my work there has come to an end. Not the way I thought it would, however; but then, nothing in Coney Island happened the way I thought it would. There were very few nights that I didn't fall asleep with my pillow wet with tears. Yet, if I had my life to live over again, I would not change it. I knew this was God's place for me from the first day I entered the new building that the Mission had purchased....

The houses on our streets and most of Coney Island were demolished but the Word of God can never be destroyed. The letters, phone calls, and visits from my spiritual family in Coney Island who 'Came and Got It' [as referred to in the title of Hilda's autobiographical book, "Come & Get It," on Coney Island] encouraged my heart and now I can say as John wrote of old:

'For I rejoiced greatly, when the brethren came and testified of the truth that is in thee, even as thou walkest in the truth. I have greater joy than to hear that my children walk in truth' (3 John 3,4).[131]

Miss Hilda Koser continues to live in Florida, and in spite of health problems she continues to carry on an active witness for our Lord.

The ministry in Brooklyn also continues on, but as the neighborhood and community needs have changed, the ministry has also changed. As of the writing of this history, the neighborhood has become a great "pocket" of Russian immigrants. The work of the Mission there is now comprised mainly of meeting both the physical and the spiritual needs of those newcomers to our country. The work is being carried on under the leadership and direction of Rev. Israel Cohen and his wife, Judy. Steve and Jeanne Schlissel were able to develop the Beth Sar Shalom congregation into an established local church that continues to minister to both Jew and Gentile alike.

The story of Coney Island is an application of the truth of Scripture, as Paul wrote:

What, after all, is Apollos? And what is Paul? Only servants, through whom thou came to believe—as the Lord has assigned to each his task. I planted the seed, Apollos watered it, but God made it grow. So neither he who plants nor he who waters is anything, but only God, who makes things grow (1 Corinthians 3:5-8 NIV).

EMIL GRUEN JOINS THE STAFF

At the same time Joseph Cohn challenged Miss Rose and Miss Sussdorff in 1938 to "go ahead" and develop a ministry in Coney Island, another opportunity for expansion had presented itself. At the April 20, 1938 Board meeting Joseph reported:

We have tentatively agreed to take over the work of Rev. Emil Gruen, a Jewish Christian, in Philadelphia. Mr. Gruen's father started this work many years ago, but the father and mother both have died, and the young son has found it almost impossible to continue, for it means that he must not only take care of the work but must also go out to raise the necessary funds to support it. He came to us and asked if we could be of help. He publishes a German paper, Israel's Hoffnung, which he sends out to some 800 or 900 German Christians. This subscription list he will hand over to us, and his paper will be merged with our German edition of The Chosen People. Mr. Singer, Mr. Gruen and Mr. Cohn will be associate Editors. The plan is to have him do field work and also to do actual Jewish Mission work in the enlarged work we are hoping to undertake in Philadelphia. A three months' trial was suggested to see if he would be able *to raise a sufficient amount in the German churches to care for his salary and expenses. We are not in any way bound to continue his connection with us. His salary will be $125 a month.*[132]

The Board unanimously approved the arrangement for a "three month trial" which, in fact, turned into over thirty-four years.

Before the turn of the century, the Gruen family lived in Romania. Emil's father was a businessman—a sales manager for magazine publishers in Europe—whose life was changed when he traveled from Romania to Constantinople to attend a sales conference.

During the dinner hour a missionary entered the hotel's dining room and approached a table at which several Jewish businessmen were sitting—a table adjacent to Mr. Gruen's own table. The missionary boldly spoke about the Messiah and the Scriptures until the outraged Jewish men drove him away from their table.

As he ate his meal, Mr. Gruen mused over some of the missionary's comments which he had overheard. His curiosity had been whetted. He wanted to hear more, and he was relieved to see that the missionary was still in the hotel's lobby.

Mr. Deutch, the missionary, recognized Mr. Gruen as he approached him. He felt his heart begin to pound, but his apprehension gave way to thanksgiving when Mr. Gruen simply introduced himself, and gave him his address, as well as an invitation to visit the Gruens home whenever he was in the area.

Mr. Deutch recognized that God had been preparing the heart of this Jewish businessman, and he followed through in visiting the Gruens' home. Soon after his first visit, Mr. Gruen professed his faith in Jesus as his Messiah and personal Savior.

The Jewish community where the family lived was small and close-knit, and Mr. Gruen's new beliefs were not well received by his Jewish friends and neighbors. Soon the family was forced to move to the city of Hamburg. There, Mr. Gruen began doing work as a colporteur for Pastor Dollman. He loved taking gospel books, tracts, and other literature to the homes of the many immigrant Jews who lived in the city.

As persecution of the Jews of Europe began to increase, Mr. Gruen felt led to immigrate to America where he believed he could carry on his ministry among the thousands of immigrant Jews in the city of New York. He left his family in Hamburg, and sailed to New York in 1914. Two years later, after establishing himself and his ministry, he sent for his family. Unfortunately, because of the war and enforced conscription, only boys who were too young to serve in the military were free to leave. Thus, Mrs. Gruen tearfully left behind two sons as she began her journey to America with her two remaining children—a daughter and a young son, Emil.

The Gruen family settled into the German immigrant community of New York, and joined the German Baptist Church in Harlem. Through the active witness of his father, and the teaching and preaching of the Word, Emil soon professed his faith in the Messiah and he was subsequently baptized.

By 1929 Emil began to sense God's call upon his life to share the Gospel. He enrolled in Eastern Baptist Seminary in Philadelphia, graduating in 1932.

Pennsylvania was home to a large German population, and Emil was in Philadelphia. Mr. Gruen concluded that his ministry could be carried on just as effectively in Philadelphia, and soon the family was together again.

Father and son began ministering in the German-speaking churches, telling Christians of the need to share the gospel with Jewish people. They also began publishing a German paper called "Israel's Hoffnung," which was mailed to 800 to 900 German Christians each month. Soon, father and son were ministering in German churches throughout the Mid-Atlantic and North-Eastern states.

In the Fall of 1933, God called Mr. Gruen home to glory and Emil was left to carry on the ministry alone. He struggled to keep the work going, knowing the importance of reaching his Jewish people with the gospel, but it seemed that at every turn in the road a new obstacle would arise. The final blow came when the building they were renting was abruptly sold, leaving the ministry without a place to meet.

Joseph Hoffman Cohn was familiar with the work of the Gruens' in Philadelphia; word about the problems the ministry was facing had also reached him. He believed the two ministries could be merged, and thereby strengthen both works, and he telephoned Emil to discuss the possibility. Emil readily agreed to the merger of the two ministries. Both he and his wife, Dorothy, whom he married in September, 1935, believed the merger to be an answer to prayer.

Emil Gruen joined the staff of the Mission in April, 1938. He was hired to work with Mr. Herbert Singer as an associate editor of the German edition of *The Chosen People* Magazine, to continue ministering in German-speaking churches, and to enlarge the Mission's missionary work in Philadelphia.

On October 2, 1938, shortly after Emil's appointment, Mr. Herman Juroe, the Mission's worker in Iowa, passed away suddenly. He left a wife and three children. His wife, Esther, asked if she might be allowed to stay on staff and carry on the ministry of visiting in Jewish homes, conducting some Bible classes, and trying to carry on the work of the ministry for at least six months. The Board agreed to her request, but they also felt Dr. Emil Gruen should be sent to Iowa, to carry on the field ministry there. The reasoning was that such a move would not only help Emil raise his support, but would also help the Mission maintain the contacts that Herman Juroe had made in the churches.[133]

By April 1939 Dr. Gruen was in Iowa, exploring the possibility of settling there permanently. Joseph Cohn wrote to *The Chosen People* family:

> ...Mrs. Juroe, who had had a good deal of experience in Jewish work in New York some years ago, has remained in Des Moines, and from her little home she goes out and carries on a faithful house-to-house visitation in the Jewish residences, and has been used wonderfully of God in breaking down prejudice and in opening Jewish hearts to receive the Gospel message. In the home itself she maintains a weekly Bible Class for Jewish women. To replace Mr. Juroe, whose work had been largely out on the field, Rev. and Mrs. Emil Gruen, after much prayer and after a special visit to Des Moines, felt definitely that it was in God's will for them to go out to the Iowa field and settle in Des Moines as a central point from which to carry on the work of itinerant evangelism. In that territory which includes Iowa and the adjoining boundary cities such as Kansas City, Missouri, etc., there are about 75,000 Jews; they are scattered in the smaller cities and villages in these rural communities, and in many cases they have no communal Jewish life, no rabbi, no synagogue. To these cities the Gruen's go; make their visitation in these scattered Jewish homes and stores, then try to connect them with some local church which has an understanding of the Jewish problems and a love for the Jews; in this way the ice is being broken slowly but surely, and the Jew is beginning to feel that there is a place for him in the Church of Christ after all. Mr. Gruen seeks openings in one of the churches, and then the Jews are invited to his services. In this way a contact is established and when the Gruen's leave the town, the Pastor and people of the church are left to follow up the work that has been begun. We are happy to report that both Mr. and Mrs. Gruen are overjoyed with their work, and see daily evidences of God's dealings with them.[134]

Dr. Emil Gruen faithfully served on staff with The American Board of Missions to the Jews, Inc. until his retirement in 1972.

VICTOR BUKSBAZEN — HIS STORY

Joseph Cohn continued to maintain contact with Dr. Arnold Frank, pastor of the Evangelical Church in Hamburg, Germany. As he had done over the years, Pastor Frank continued to let Joseph know about Jewish believers who wanted to immigrate to America. In 1940, Pastor Frank highly recommended to Joseph a Jewish believer by the name of Victor Buksbazen. Mr. Buksbazen was living in London, England, and the Board was not sure when he would be able to leave England to come to America, but the October 30, 1940 Minutes record that a call was extended to Mr. Buksbazen.[135] The January 22, 1941 Minutes further record:

> Mr. Cohn referring to unfinished business items in the Minutes announced the arrival of Mr. Buksbazen of London. Bookings on the Cunard Lines were so heavy that the Buksbazen family took passage on a little Polish cargo boat sailing from Glasgow to Sidney, Nova Scotia. They arrived in New York on Sunday, January 12th, with just one dollar left. He is now settled in the Home at Hewes Street. First impressions of the man are favorable. Mr. Buksbazen is a graduate of the University of Warsaw, and has degrees from the Anglican Seminary there. He was for three years in charge of the London Jews Society in Cracow.[136]

Victor Buksbazen began his ministry with the Mission preaching, teaching, and visiting in Jewish homes in New York.

Victor's story began in Warsaw, Poland. He was born into an "unusual" Orthodox Jewish family. His father was a believer in Jesus—but his mother was adamantly opposed to her husband's belief; she wanted nothing to do with Jesus!

When Mr. Buksbazen was invited to attend a Mission meeting in the year 1900, he had gone with the sole purpose of convincing the missionaries that they were preaching about a false Messiah. But to his amazement, he soon found himself drawn to the person of Jesus—to the beauty of His teaching and to His holiness. Soon he was openly professing his faith in the Messiah Jesus.

Victor's earliest recollection of his father's faith occurred when he was just three years old. Father and son had gone out for a walk along the streets of Warsaw one starlit evening. A brilliant moon was suspended low in the sky, and in his childish way Victor thought he could grasp it if only he could stretch his hands out far enough. Impressed by the moon's beauty, Victor asked his father, "Daddy, who made the moon?" His father quietly said: "God made the moon, and the stars, and the sun. In fact, God made the whole world and everything you can see." This was Victor's first lesson in theology; it was a lesson he never forgot.

As he grew older, Victor began attending meetings at the Mission with his father. As an adult, he recalled that the long sermons of the missionaries bored him almost to tears. They were far beyond the understanding and comprehension of a child. One day, however, Victor paid particular attention to the missionary's frequent references to someone he called "Yeshua."

Following the meeting Victor asked his father, "Who was Yeshua?" His father replied, "Yeshua was the Son of God, the Savior and Messiah of Israel, long hoped for by the Jewish people." He went on, "God sent Him to deliver men from their sins and to make them children of God. But when He came, they did not recognize Him, but rejected Him, because they hoped for a different kind of Savior who would make them a strong, independent ruling nation. Thus when Yeshua (Jesus) came and wanted to deliver them from the power of evil, they were disappointed and delivered Him to be crucified." His father spoke so lovingly concerning Yeshua that Victor too began to love Him.

In 1920, when Victor was just sixteen years old, his father died and he was left to take care of his mother and his two younger sisters. They were difficult days. The hardship of his situation was intensified by the fact that the Jews in Poland were beginning to feel the persecution and hatred of anti-Semitism. Yet, despite the outward circumstances, Victor continued to faithfully attend the Mission and to study his Bible. He often sat up until late in the night "burning the midnight oil," in a literal sense, since during that time linseed oil lamps were the only means of illumination in Poland. Often his mother and sisters would complain about his study of the Bible; they claimed he was using their precious oil on a worthless book!

Victor also had to contend with his family's attempts to dissuade him from openly professing his faith in Jesus. His mother begged him not to be baptized. She finally conceded that he could believe in Jesus if he would not mention Him publicly. But other members of the family were not so lenient. They insisted that Victor go with them to visit prominent Jewish scholars, and one day Victor found that angry family members had shredded his beautifully bound and illustrated Yiddish version of Bunyan's Pilgrim's Progress. When the family's hostility toward him reached the point that one of his uncles threatened to kill him, Victor was forced to leave home.

Victor had been rejected by his family, but he was not abandoned by God. God led him to a Christian couple who took him into their home. They provided for his needs as if he was their own son, and they encouraged him to complete his high school education.

Victor was baptized on May 2, 1922, and as he grew in faith he began to recognize God's call upon his life to become a missionary to his own Jewish people. To prepare himself for the Gospel ministry, he entered the Theological Seminary of the Warsaw University but when he graduated in 1931, he was immediately called into the service of his country.

When his tour of duty ended, Victor returned to Warsaw. As he prayed for God's leading in his life, he received a call to become a missionary with the British Society for the Propagation of the Gospel among the Jews. He established a mission station in Cracow following his ordination in the Reformed Church of Poland—a Presbyterian body. During his four years of ministry among the Jewish people of Cracow, the Lord richly blessed his efforts.

In 1937, the British mission society transferred Victor to assist in their work among the English Jews. But by the end of 1940 the imminent danger of invasion, the air raids, and the fact that Victor was not a British subject made his work nearly impossible in England.

Knowing of his plight, Dr. Arnold Frank of Hamburg, Germany, contacted Joseph Cohn. For many years Dr. Frank had kept Joseph informed of Jewish believers in Yeshua who wanted to immigrate to America. Cohn wasted no time in contacting Victor, and in arranging for his immigration to America. It was not an easy trip. The Buksbazen family had a rough sail over. Because of the War, it was impossible to book passage on the major steamship lines and the Buksbazens were forced to take passage on a small Polish cargo boat sailing by way of Glasgow, Scotland, and Sidney, Nova Scotia. By the time they reached New York, the family was nearly dead from exhaustion, exposure to the elements, and lack of food.

As God's people upheld the Buksbazen family in prayer, they began to regain their strength and soon Victor was strong enough to begin preaching, teaching, and visiting Jewish homes in New York.

Like Joseph Cohn, Victor Buksbazen had an entrepreneurial spirit. He was also blessed with gifts of administration. Victor, who had started his own work in Europe, and had directed other works in England, was used to being in charge. He found it difficult to fit into the program of the Mission (it was well known that Joseph Cohn was not the easiest person to work for), and after two years on the Mission's staff he began to fear that he might end up as a "desk jockey." That fear led him to resign from his position with the Mission.[137]

At the January 27, 1943 Board meeting, Joseph announced that Victor Buksbazen had resigned.[138] Victor had come on staff at a time when it was obvious that an internal struggle for leadership was taking place within the Mission; a polarization of staff was taking place which Victor may have felt he did not want to be a part of.

Soon after leaving the Mission, Victor and his wife, Lydia, established a ministry called the Friends of Israel Gospel and Relief Society, Inc. Victor also produced his own magazine called "Israel My Glory." Their ministry, now known as The Friends of Israel, will commemorate fifty years of testimony to the Jewish people in the year 1993.

The history of the ministry first known by the name "The Williamsburg Mission to the Jews," and better known under the name "The American Board of Missions to the Jews" (now Chosen People Ministries, Inc.), reveals that God used the ministry in multitudinous ways. He used the Mission over the years to proclaim His Truth to thousands of Jewish people. He used the Mission as a training ground for individuals who felt called of God to share the Gospel message with Jewish people. He further used the Mission as a vehicle and a catalyst to begin many other Gospel ministries to the Jewish people, and thereby to multiply the opportunities for Jewish people to hear the message of redemption through Yeshua's atonement.

Many of the people with whom Joseph "networked," and many whom he hired to work for the Mission, made life-long commitments to the ministry. Others came on staff, but later left to enter other areas of ministry, or to go back into secular work. Through the years a goodly number, like Victor Buksbazen, left to establish new ministries to the Jews—but even in this God led, as each new work formed was the outgrowth of that worker's vision and burden to increase the effectiveness of the Gospel witness to the Jewish people. Joseph Cohn, like many mission leaders and Christian leaders, learned to say:

> It is true that some preach Christ out of envy and rivalry, but others out of good will. The latter do so in love, knowing that I am put here for the defense of the gospel. The former preach Christ out of selfish ambition, not sincerely, supposing that they can stir up trouble for me while I am in chains. But what does it matter? The important thing is that in every way, whether from false motives or true, Christ is preached. And because of this I rejoice (Philippians 1:15-18 NIV).

ENDNOTES

Chapter 6. The Vision Expands in America

[1] Cohn, Joseph, *I Have Fought A Good Fight*, (New York: American Board of Missions to the Jews, Inc. [now Chosen People Ministries, Inc.], 1953), p 284.

[2] See note above, pp 284-285.

[3] See note above, p 49.

[4] See note above, pp 51-52.

[5] *The Chosen People*, Vol. XXXIV, No. 8, (May, 1929), pp 5-6.

[6] See Esther 4:14.

[7] *The Chosen People*, Vol. XXXIX, No. 5, (February, 1934), p 5.

[8] See note above.

[9] See note above, p 4.

[10] *The Chosen People*, Vol. XL, No. 6, (March, 1935), p 5.

[11] *The Chosen People*, Vol. XL, No. 6, (March, 1935), p 3.

[12] *The Chosen People*, Vol. XLI, No. 1, (October, 1935), p 3.

[13] See note above, p 11.

[14] *Minutes*, ABMJ, (January 17, 1932), p 85.

[15] See note above.

[16] *The Chosen People*, Vol. LIX, No. 5, (February, 1954), p 14.

[17] See note above, p 15.

[18] *The Chosen People*, Vol. LXII, No. 9, (May, 1957), pp 8, 9.

[19] *The Chosen People*, Vol. LIX, No. 6, (March, 1954), p 16.

[20] *Minutes*, ABMJ, (January 25, 1928), p 15.

[21] See note above.

[22] *The Chosen People*, Vol. L, No. 5, (February, 1945), p 15.

[23] *Minutes of the Executive Committee*, ABMJ, (December 10, 1935), p 2.

[24] See note above, October 8, 1929, pp 99-100.

[25] *Minutes*, ABMJ, April 15, 1931, p 74.

[26] *Minutes of the Executive Committee*, ABMJ, (June 18, 1936).

[27] See note above.

[28] *The Chosen People*, Vol. XXXVI, No. 6, (March, 1931), pp 5-7.

[29] See note above, p 11.

[30] *The Chosen People*, Vol. XXXVI, No. 3, (December, 1930), p 9.

[31] *The Chosen People*, Vol. XXXVII, No. 8, (May, 1932), p 8.

[32] *The Chosen People*, Vol. XLI, No. 2, (November, 1935), pp 10, 11.

[33] *The Chosen People*, Vol. LXIX, No. 5, (January, 1964) p 6.

[34] *The Shepherd of Israel*, Vol. 45, No. 2, (October, 1960), p 1,2.

[35] *The Chosen People*, Vol. XXXVIII, No. 2, (November, 1932), p 8.

[36] *The Chosen People*, Vol. XXXIX, No. 2, (November, 1933), p 8.

[37] *Minutes, ABMJ*, (October 25, 1933).

[38] *The Chosen People*, Vol. XLI, No. 2, (November, 1935), p 8.

[39] *Minutes, ABMJ*, (January 24, 1940).

[40] *Minutes, ABMJ*, (May 15, 1940).

[41] See note above.

[42] *The Chosen People*, Vol. XLVI, No. 1, (October, 1940), p 14.

[43] *The Chosen People*, Vol. XLVII, No. 5, (February, 1942), p 10.

[44] *Minutes, ABMJ*, (January 28, 1942), p 2.

[45] *The Chosen People*, Vol. XLVIII, No. 5, (February, 1943), p 8.

[46] See note above, p 9.

[47] *Minutes, ABMJ*, (October 16, 1935), p 5.

[48] *Minutes of the Executive Committee, ABMJ*, (December 10, 1935).

[49] *The Chosen People*, Vol. XLI, No. 4, (January, 1936), p 8.

[50] See *The Chosen People*, Vol. XLI, No. 7, (April, 1936), p 10.

[51] *Minutes, ABMJ*, (April 15, 1936).

[52] *The Chosen People*, Vol. LIX, No. 8, (May, 1954), pp 11, 12.

[53] *The Chosen People*, Vol. XLIX, No. 5, (February, 1944), pp 12, 13.

[54] See note above, p 13.

[55] *The Chosen People*, Vol. LI, No. 7, (April, 1946), p 13.

[56] *The Chosen People*, Vol. LIX, No. 4, (January, 1954), p 13.

[57] *The Chosen People*, Vol. LX, No. 7, (April, 1955), p 8.

[58] *Minutes, ABMJ*, (April 19, 1933).

[59] *The Chosen People*, Vol. XXXVIII, No. 8,(May, 1933), p 6, 7.

[60] *Minutes, ABMJ*, (January 17, 1932), p 85.

[61] *Minutes, ABMJ*, (October 28, 1936).

[62] *The Chosen People*, Vol. XLIII, No. 6, (March, 1938), p 14.

[63] See note above.

[64] See note above, p 15.

[65] *The Chosen People*, Vol. XLV, No. 2, (November, 1939), p 12.

[66] *The Chosen People*, Vol. XLVI, No. 1, (October, 1940), p 15.

[67] *Minutes, ABMJ*, (October 30, 1940), p 7.

[68] *Minutes, ABMJ*, (April 16, 1941).

[69] *The Chosen People*, Vol. XLVI, No. 8, (May, 1941), pp 11, 12.

[70] *Minutes, ABMJ*, (January 27, 1937), p 2.

[71] See note above, p 10.

[72] *The Chosen People*, Vol. LXX, No. 9, (May, 1965), pp 2, 3.

[73] *The Chosen People*, Vol. LXIII, No. 10, (June, 1958), p 1.

[74] See note above.

[75] See note above.

[76] *The Chosen People*, Vol. LXX, No. 9, (May, 1965), p 1.

[77] *The Chosen People*, Vol. XVIII, No. 8, (May, 1913), p 6.

[78] *Minutes, ABMJ*, (October 20, 1937), p 4.

[79] *The Chosen People*, Vol. XLV, No. 7, (April, 1940), p 10.

[80] *Minutes of Executive Committee, ABMJ*, (June 4, 1937), p 2.

[81] *Minutes*, ABMJ, (October 16, 1935).

[82] *The Chosen People*, Vol. XLVIII, No. 5, (February, 1943), p 8.

[83] See note above, p 8,9.

[84] See note above, p 9.

[85] Genesis 12:3.

[86] *The Chosen People*, Vol. L, No. 1, (October, 1944), p 9.

[87] *Minutes of Executive Committee*, ABMJ, (August 18, 1937), p 4.

[88] See note above.

[89] See *Minutes of Executive Committee*, ABMJ, (August 18, 1937), p 4; compare with *Minutes*, ABMJ, (October 20, 1937), p 1.

[90] *Memorandum to Executive Committee in Lieu of Meeting*, ABMJ, (August 18, 1937), p 5.

[91] *Minutes*, ABMJ, (October 20, 1937), p 5.

[92] See note above.

[93] *Minutes*, ABMJ, (October 27, 1943), p 1.

[94] See note above, p 2.

[95] See note above.

[96] *Minutes/Special Meeting of the Board*, ABMJ, (June 8, 1945), p 2.

[97] *Minutes*, ABMJ, (January 23, 1945), p 4.

[98] See note above.

[99] *Minutes of Executive Committee*, ABMJ, (February 18, 1946), p 2.

[100] *The Chosen People*, Vol. LI, No. 3, (December, 1945), p 11.

[101] *The Chosen People*, Vol. LI, No. 5, (February, 1946), pp 9, 10.

[102] *The Chosen People*, Vol. XLIII, No. 4, (January, 1938), p 13.

[103] See note above, p 14.

[104] *Minutes*, ABMJ, (October 19, 1938), p 8.

[105] *The Chosen People*, Vol. XLV, No. 5, (February, 1940), pp 15, 16.

[106] *The Chosen People*, Vol. XLIII, No. 7, (April, 1938), p 11.

[107] Hilda Koser, *Come & Get It*, (Orlando, Florida: Golden Rule Book Press, Inc., 1987), p 20.

[108] *The Chosen People*, Vol. XLIII, No. 7, (April, 1938), pp 11, 12.

[109] H. Koser, *Come & Get It*, pp 23, 24.

[110] *The Chosen People*, Vol. XLIII, No. 7, (April, 1938), p 12.

[111] H. Koser, *Come & Get It*, pp 24, 25.

[112] *Minutes*, ABMJ, (October 19, 1939), p 2.

[113] *Minutes*, ABMJ, (October 30, 1940), p 2.

[114] *Minutes*, ABMJ, (May 15, 1940), p 8.

[115] *The Chosen People*, Vol. XLVII, No. 1, (October, 1941), p 9.

[116] *The Chosen People*, Vol. LXXXII, No. 4, (December, 1976), p 13.

[117] *The Chosen People*, Vol. XLVI, No. 5, (February, 1941), p 4.

[118] *The Chosen People*, Vol. XLIX, No. 2, (November, 1943), p 8.

[119] *The Chosen People*, Vol. LI, No. 5, (February, 1946), pp 8, 9.

[120] *Minutes of Executive Committee*, (December 9, 1942), p 2.

[121] *The Chosen People*, Vol. LII, No. 3, (December, 1946), pp 11, 12.

[122] *The Chosen People*, Vol. LXXX, No. 10, (June, 1975), p 17.

[123] *The Chosen People*, Special Issue, (October, 1987), pp 4-6.

[124] See note above, pp 17, 18.

[125] *The Chosen People*, Vol. LXXXII, No. 11, (July, 1977), p 8.

[126] See note above, p 9.

[127] *The Chosen People*, Vol. LXXXV, No. 2, (October, 1979), p 7.

[128] See note above.

[129] See note above, pp 7, 8.

[130] *The Chosen People*, Vol. LXXXV, No. 6, (February, 1980), p 11.

[131] H. Koser, *Come & Get It*, p 71.

[132] *Minutes*, ABMJ, (April 20, 1938), p 5.

[133] *Minutes*, ABMJ, (October 19, 1938), p 7.

[134] *Minutes*, ABMJ, (January 24, 1940), p 3.

[135] *Minutes*, ABMJ, (October 30, 1940).

[136] *Minutes*, ABMJ, (January 22, 1941), p 2.

[137] See testimony of Victor Buksbazen in: *The Chosen People*, Vol. XLVI, No. 7, (April, 1941), pp 9-12.

[138] *Minutes*, ABMJ, (January 27, 1943), p 3.

7

THE VISION EXPANDS TO EUROPE AND BEYOND

It has been said that only eternity can measure the value and scope of a man's worth. Surely this adage applies to Joseph Hoffman Cohn. He was a man totally dedicated to the task of reaching all Jews everywhere with the Gospel, taking advantage of every opportunity, networking with every individual who was known to have an interest in the Jewish people and Israel. He sacrificed his family, his social life, and the personal wealth he could have attained had he continued toward his goal of a business career—all was put aside for the cause of Jewish evangelism—all was forfeited as he threw himself into the task of expanding the outreach of the American Board of Missions to the Jews (Chosen People Ministries, Inc.).

Many branches of the Mission had been established in strategic cities of the United States from coast to coast. An impressive network of missionaries, field evangelists, pastors, and Christian leaders had joined forces to support Joseph's efforts. Satisfied with what had been accomplished, he began to look across the Atlantic—to Europe and to the problems of reaching the increasing numbers of refugee Jews with the Gospel.

Joseph's roots were in Europe. He had been born in Hungary and still had relatives living there. Had God's hand not directed his father, Rabbi Leopold Cohn, to America in his search of the Messiah, Joseph might well have been one of the Jews trapped in Europe, facing the concentration camps or the gas ovens of the Nazis along with millions of other Jews. Joseph was cognizant of the privilege God had bestowed on him—to have had the opportunity to hear and respond to the Gospel, to be an American citizen where he was free to proclaim the message of Messiah to his Jewish brethren. He was also aware of the fact that with privilege comes responsibility, and he deeply believed that the Mission had a responsibility to reach the Jewish community beyond the shores of America.

Copies of the Mission's paper, The Shepherd of Israel, had already made their way into the hands of Jews living in Europe. The early response to that little Yiddish publication had been astonishing and exciting! As has been mentioned in the previous chapters, God used The Shepherd of Israel not only as a vehicle to proclaim the Gospel message, but as the vehicle to open the doors for the Mission's first foreign branches—works that ultimately helped thousands of Jews flee the rising tide of Nazism and find peace and safety in other parts of the world.

BRANCHES OPENED IN LITHUANIA AND RUSSIA

The first foreign branch of The American Board of Missions to the Jews, Inc. was established in Lithuania; Simon Aszur was the Missionary-in-charge of that branch (Simon's testimony and the story of the opening of the branch in Lithuania was given in Chapter Five of this history).

The second foreign branch was established in Russia. The distribution of The Shepherd of Israel played a vital role in the establishment of the Russian branch, just as it had in the establishment of the branch in Lithuania. Because of the paper's circulation, the Mission began to receive letters with requests for help from people in Russia and Poland. Joseph and the Mission staff began to pray, asking God to reveal ways that they could help the Jewish believers living in those countries and, at the same time, expand the Gospel witness to other Jews living there. The answer came in a most amazing way.

Rev. and Mrs. Peter Smoljar were missionaries serving under the Mildmay Mission to the Jews of London. Their mission field was Riga, Latvia, a seaport town located on the Baltic Sea. But prior to being sent to Riga, the Smoljar's had worked in Russia and had established a work in Ekaterinaslav, in the southern part of Soviet Russia. Under Mr. Smoljar's leadership, a Jewish-Christian church had been established—a church that was fully organized and which had some forty members. Mr. Smoljar had also established missionary contacts in a radius of over one hundred miles from his center in Ekaterinaslav. At a time when the work was reaching its highest spiritual peak, a time when more and more Soviet Jews were attending the meetings, the Soviet government laid plans to seize Mr. and Mrs Smoljar, to exile them to Siberia. But God intervened. When the Smoljar's heard of the government's plans, they escaped from Russia and went to Riga, Latvia. In 1932, Joseph reported to the Board:

...[we have] an opportunity...of engaging what appears as being a very competent young man as a missionary in Riga, Latvia....This young man, Mr. Joseph Schwartz, will work under Mr. Smoljar who will be responsible for him and will direct his activities....The young man is to go out traveling to the little villages and towns surrounding Riga and distribute 1000 copies of The Shepherd of Israel each month, and later we would hope to increase it to 2000 if he can distribute them without waste. Mr. Joseph Cohn recommended that we try this young man beginning November 1st.[1]

Joseph included a report of the opening of this new Branch in the November 1932 issue of *The Chosen People*.

Following the escape of Mr. and Mrs. Smoljar from Russia, their assistant, Mr. Gregory Guberman, continued to pastor the flock, with the work still under the support of the Mildmay Mission to the Jews. But the Soviet government passed such restrictive measures governing Jewish mission work being done by outside organizations that the Mildmay Mission to the Jews reluctantly had to withdraw all of their activities in the Soviet Union. For several years the American European Fellowship undertook the support of the Guberman's, but they, too, encountered financial difficulties and had to drop their support.

It was at this time that Joseph had been investigating the possibility of establishing a work in Russia. The Mission had been sending a small amount of aid in response to the letters from people who received the Shepherd of Israel. Joseph and the Mission staff had been prayerfully considering how the Mission could do more when Joseph received a visit from the Smoljar's of Riga, Latvia. Joseph told readers of *The Chosen People* magazine:

...these good people of God not only confirmed verbally all that we had learned through correspondence, but they begged us with tears in their eyes, that we should take up the support of Mr. Guberman and certain workers with him, and that we must not under any condition forsake those destitute brethren who are now left as sheep without a shepherd....

After prayer and consideration, we have been won over, and are ready to say to our friends, 'Come and help us undertake a work in Russia'! We have done everything possible to safeguard the investment of any money which we are going to ask you to put into Russia. It has been our determination that we will never undertake work in Europe unless we can be assured that we can administer it in such a way as to keep the confidence of our friends. And now we feel we have just that opportunity.[2]

With the approval of the Board, Joseph hired Mr. Gregory Guberman to be the Mission's worker in Russia.[3] Upon receiving the news that the Mission would support him, Mr. Guberman wrote the following letter to Joseph Cohn:

Thanks be to God, He at last has heard our prayers of His true servants, and is giving us again the possibility to spread the gospel of the Kingdom among our suffering brethren who are in the depths of sin and unbelief, without hope....

The first thing that is necessary is to rent a hall where to hold meetings....Yet do I venture to present to you several expenses which are necessary at the very beginning:—chairs, a platform, a small foot organ, and other similar expenses. Of course all these things must be begun on a small scale. Our ecclesia is called 'The House of Meetings for the Hebrew Christian Congregation.' We speak and sing hymns in Yiddish. The Jewish people who visit our meetings feel themselves at home, not like in the Russian Church where they feel strange. In this district there are about forty believing Jews, among whom there are some able preachers. They all help in the work, but alas, there are among them sick ones and many who suffer from lack of means. It will be necessary therefore at the beginning of the work to help them a little at this very hard time. This will refresh them, and their painful hearts will be strengthened.

If the Mission will permit, I would like also to make a missionary tour to Moscow, Kiev and Odessa, for the purpose of uniting the Christian Jewish brethren in those cities into one band and in this way to be able to report to the Mission concerning all the circumstances in which our brethren are to be found.[4]

The cost of supporting such a missionary in Russia in those days was between fifty and sixty dollars a month, plus an additional expense of fifty dollars to rent a hall for meetings. Joseph made an appeal for support of Mr. Guberman to the readers of *The Chosen People* magazine, saying:

Briefly, $50 or $60 a month will support a full time missionary in Soviet Russia or in Poland; $50 a month will pay the rent and incidental expenses for a preaching hall in Dnjepropetrowsk or Odessa or Kiev. If you feel led to support a missionary for full time, or if you feel able to pay half the salary of a missionary, we will appoint a missionary with your money, and give you his name so that you may know exactly who your missionary is, and may pray for him definitely.[5]

So it was, that at a time when the "Great Depression" was beginning to tighten its grip upon the economic situation in America, God chose to expand the Mission's outreach into Russia—to Jews who were suffering greatly from economic depression, persecution, and social and cultural deprivation. The commitment to the work in Russia was a big step of faith for the Mission. It meant becoming responsible for Russian Jews who came to faith in Yeshua. On the other hand, the Russian Jews were already being persecuted by the Communists. They knew that the price of openly professing Yeshua could be their very lives!

On June 6, 1929 the Mission building in the little town of Dnjepropetrowsk (formerly called Ekaterinaslav)[6] was opened and dedicated. Mr. Guberman wrote:

> It is with great pleasure that I can tell you, dear Brother, that after lots of patience and great expense I have at last received an official permit to open our Meeting Hall, where we gather every Saturday, Sunday, and Wednesday and preach the Gospel to Jews....
>
> We had our official opening on Sunday, June 6th, and we had great joy in seeing the victory over darkness. The meeting lasted the whole day, from 10 A.M. until 7 P.M. Many stopped in front of our Hall to read the sign, 'The Church of the Hebrew Christian Congregation' and were astonished. At this time when Churches and Synagogues are taken for other purposes, when people are trying to throw off all religious convictions, even at such a time here are found people who believe in God. Some say this with friendly amusement and others with hate and sneering.
>
> Praise God that in the midst of unbelief, yet we had at our meeting about thirty believing members and several others who are very near believing.
>
> The whole day was spent in praise and prayer, in preaching the Word and in sweet communion. This day will be remembered by a monthly feast, and the first day of March by a yearly Mission feast....
>
> I am sorry to say that a number of our Jewish Christians didn't take part in our great feast. Some were afraid to have their pictures taken, because in time it may hurt their business. We ended the feast with a cup of tea and with the doxology 'Praise God from Whom all blessings flow.'[7]

As always, especially in ministry to the Jewish people, Satan was ready to attack and to do everything possible to hinder the work. No sooner had Mr. Guberman opened his mission station in Ekaterinaslav than Soviet Russia closed it down. A report of Joseph Cohn to the Executive Committee expresses the dismay and concern felt by workers of the Mission:

> Word has come to us that the Government of Soviet Russia has seized our property in Ekaterinaslav, and evicted our missionaries. The excuse given was that the Government needs the building for residence purposes. The Soviet government is determined at all costs to destroy every Gospel effort. We however dare not forsake Mr. Guberman and some 40 Jewish families at Ekaterinaslav, but we ought to continue supporting him, waiting the time to come, as it surely will come, when the masses of the Russian people will arise and revolt; at that time there will of necessity be a wide open door for Gospel proclamation. Mr. Guberman is going to hunt for a new location and if he finds it we should be prepared to pay the rent and at the same time be prepared to lose it again. Of course it is possible, and we must face that also, that Mr. Guberman and other missionaries with him may be exiled to Siberia. In such an event we of course can do nothing further. But I suggest we continue helping him so long as we can maintain communication with him.[8]

Not only did Satan attack the work in Russia, he also attacked the work in Lithuania. Joseph Cohn had not heard from Mr. Simon Aszur for several months and began to worry that something may have happened to him. He asked Mr. Smoljar of Riga if he could possibly learn anything about Mr. Aszur. Joseph reported this sad word to the Board of Directors:

> A Jewish missionary in Kovno, [Lithuania]...visited the town where Simon Aszur lives and found the young man with his wife and baby and mother, in a nice little cottage. He is in the electrical business. His mother and neighbors and other relatives had so worked on him by pressure and threats, that they shut his mouth, and he could do no missionary work. When we sent him copies of The Shepherd of Israel he would go to a town ten or twelve miles away and put the papers in the letter boxes. In the meantime he was receiving our checks but never sent a report of what he was doing. He was too ashamed to write to us. We finally sent him a check for $50 and told him to go with his family to Riga and work under Mr. Smoljar, and that we would not send him any more money until we heard from him in Riga. He took the money but did not go and was too ashamed to write. The missionary reports that the young man believes in Christ and in his private life he reads the New Testament, but beyond that he cannot go.[9]

The problem of trying to supervise the foreign branches of the Mission was a constant concern. It was not unusual that workers who thought they were called to do missionary work among the Jews could not, or would not, continue when pressures and persecution became too great. Shortly after the incident involving Simon Aszur, the Board asked Joseph to begin scheduling regular visits to Europe for the purpose of interviewing missionary candidates and to visit the branch ministries. The Board also began to develop guidelines and policies related to the foreign workers and outreach ministries.

Unlike Simon Aszur, who broke under the pressures brought to bear upon him as a result of his missionary activities, Mr. Gregory Guberman thrived under the pressures and threats. He believed that the God he served was greater than any man-made government. When the Russian government shut him down, he simply moved to another city. He would hold his meetings in the homes of people who were brave enough to offer their homes for such use until he could find another building. Joseph reported:

> ...A recent letter from Mr. Guberman tells us that he is ready to meet the fate of many others who have labored for Christ in recent months in Russia—either exile to Siberia or immediate death. Such is the situation this consecrated worker is facing, and we, here at this end, are unable to do one least thing in a human way to help. Our dependence only is upon God and asking every reader of The Chosen People who sees these lines, to offer up a plea to God not only to protect our missionaries there, but to do something to intervene for the salvation of Russia.[10]

Joseph Cohn went on to encourage readers of *The Chosen People* magazine by including excerpts from some of the letters he had received from Mr. Guberman which said:

> Our work here is the only one in all Russia, and no matter how small the fire is burning, no one has any right to quench it. I am in full hope that some day this little fire will become a great one, and will light up many dark spots through the Lord Jesus Christ, who is the light of the world. Dear brother, the time is very serious....many of those who were with us have now become our worst enemies, and are persecuting the followers of the Lord. Others have become weak and are staying away. Please pray that the dear Lord may give us much strength and courage to withstand all difficulties and troubles.[11]

Persecution of the missionaries continued in Russia as the Communists sought to eliminate all vestiges of religion, especially missionaries of Christianity. At the annual meeting of the Board of Directors on January 22, 1930 Dr. Cohn reported:

> Mr. Guberman in Russia says it is impossible for him to send us any regular reports of his work as his letters are censored and conditions are very difficult. We are thankful that Mr. Guberman can continue his work but there is great danger of his being sent to Siberia. He is doing his work quietly. He visits certain Jews who come to his meetings and thru these visits he reaches a few others.[12]

No further correspondence was ever received from Mr. Guberman, and his fate was not known. However, shortly after the Board meeting in January 1930, word was received that the government had once again seized the Mission's properties. Joseph shared this news with readers of *The Chosen People* in an article entitled, "We Are Driven Out Of Russia":

> Word came last month just after The Chosen People had gone to press, that the Soviet Government had for the second time seized our Mission Station, and that our workers were in flight. For the protection of our workers there, we will from now on withhold all specific public mention of their names, the locations of our work in Soviet Russia, if any, and the future movements of our workers. The system of espionage is so thoroughly organized now that one single slip on our part might cost the lives of some faithful Jewish Christians on the other side....
>
> For the time being we are of course unable to forward money to Russia, but we will be ready to do so again just as soon as we receive definite word as to where our workers are located. Let us all join in earnest prayer that by the time we greet you again in these columns next October, we may have good news to bring from this sin-cursed and Christ-hating land of the North.[13]

Since no further word was ever heard from the Mission's workers in Russia, it was assumed that they were either killed or sent to Siberia because of their fearless testimony for our Lord. Opportunities to witness to Russian Jews became almost nonexistent. From time to time the Mission was able to smuggle a few copies of the Bible into Russia, or a few Gospel tracts, or copies of *The Shepherd of Israel*, and when Joseph Cohn made visits to Europe he was occasionally able to get some relief funds delivered to some of the believers who were being held in Communist countries. But the door for the Mission to once again have a viable witness in Russia did not open again until the late 1980's and early 1990's.

Ministry Begun in Palestine/Israel

With the door to Russia closed, Joseph stayed in close contact with Jewish believers working and living in other parts of Europe. He was constantly looking for new opportunities and new ways for the Mission to reach out to his suffering Jewish brethren in other parts of the world.

Frank Boothby

Jews were already beginning to pour into "Palestine" from Europe and from other countries of oppression. Aware of the trend, Joseph Cohn wanted to have a vibrant testimony for the Gospel in the Jewish homeland. For nearly twelve years, he had been supplying copies of The Shepherd of Israel to a man in Jerusalem. The Minutes of the April 19, 1933 Board of Director's meeting state:

> There is a missionary to the Jews in Jerusalem by the name of Mr. Frank Boothby. He has been distributing 200 copies of the Shepherd of Israel each year for the last twelve years. The Jews in Jerusalem like our paper and ask for it, if it happens to be late in reaching Mr. Boothby. It is the only Yiddish literature they will accept as they prefer reading Hebrew. Mr. Boothby has a little room in which he keeps gospel literature to hand to all those who pass by. He calls it the 'Gospel Gate Room' but he seems unable to continue the rent of it. Mr. Cohn asked if the Board was in favor of agreeing to pay the rent of the Gospel Gate Room for one year, which is 10 pounds sterling or about $50.00.[14]

Receiving the Board's unanimous agreement of his proposal, Joseph's dream was realized. The Mission had an outreach in Palestine. Whether or not the work began as a cooperative effort with the British Foreign Missionary Society is unclear. From the Minutes and from articles written at the time, it appears that Mr. Boothby was no longer receiving support from the British Foreign Missionary Society. If he was, it was not enough to pay for the expenses of the ministry in Palestine. It is also a possibility that the British Foreign Missionary Society retired Mr. Boothby, since he was retirement age and was not in the best of health. The Minutes reflect something of the problem:

> The idea of sending Moses Schiff to Palestine has had to be abandoned because his wife is not a Christian. Mr. Cohn has thought that Mr. Fred Haberer, our former worker might be suitable as he is a good Hebrew student. Mr. Boothby our present worker in Palestine is an old man and may soon be incapacitated. It is essential that we have someone there to keep us informed as to events. Our friends are intensely interested in the Holy Land and keep asking us for the latest events and how they fit in with prophecy.[15]

Finding a competent worker in Palestine was not an easy task. Joseph's first trip to that land brought him face-to-face with the monumental difficulties that existed in trying to evangelize the Jews there. He reported to the Board:

> As to doing missionary work in Palestine, there are no competent workers to be had. The Jews are in such a condition that you cannot reach them with the Gospel. All around they see Roman Catholic Churches, Greek Catholic Churches, the Coptic Church, etc. The place is filled with all kinds of paganism, and the Jews have a contempt for this. There is a man called Mr. Gabriel who carries on a little work under the Christian Alliance Church, but it seems very hopeless. You see perhaps 7 or 8 Arab children. No Jew in Jerusalem would dare to confess Christ for they would tear him limb from limb. Nationalism is very strong.
>
> However there are Jews that do ask for Hebrew New Testaments. They come to Mr. Boothby, in charge of the Gospel Gate, and ask for The Shepherd of Israel and the New Testament. We purchased 500 of thest [sic] Testaments from the British and Foreign Bible Society. Mr. Boothby thinks these will last for 3 or 4 months. It is impossible to hold a public meeting for it is against the law.[16]

Because of the great difficulties in finding workers and suitable buildings for missionary work in Palestine, Joseph was delighted with the arrangements he had been able to make with Frank Boothby; at least the Mission had a foot-hold in the land. Quoting partly from a letter he had received from Mr. Boothby, Joseph told the readers of *The Chosen People* about the new worker in Jerusalem:

The Gospel Gate Room…is on one side of the North gateway of the Russian Compound, Jerusalem.…

This Gate Room preaches the Gospel in print by wall text and window text, and is also used for the distribution of Gospel portions and New Testaments (chiefly in Hebrew or English or Yiddish) and any appropriate Gospel literature such as The Shepherd of Israel, *etc. Being a very little room, it is not large enough for mission services, and we have to avoid crowding in this situation. Many times have I seen individuals standing before the windows and reading the Gospel truths as though they had never read anything before to enlighten or feed their souls. Many of these souls attend synagogue where of course the Gospel or name of the Lord Jesus is not mentioned for salvation.…*

In conclusion we may say further that this Gospel Gate Room is now apparently at the heart of the present growing Jerusalem.[17]

The ministry in Jerusalem and other parts of Palestine always faltered between the continuation of their struggling existence or closing down, yet the work was vital because it was a contact with refugee Jews who were pouring into the country. It also served as an important catalyst for raising funds for refugee work that was being done in other parts of the world. But more importantly to Joseph, was that he believed that one day the Jewish people would return to the land of Israel and he wanted the Mission to be there, prepared and ready for a Gospel witness to the returning Jews, and to those living in the land—even through the Tribulation period!

Frank Boothby's reports to Joseph included details about the difficulties and perils of living in Palestine during the days when the Jews were returning to the land. He spoke about the Jews rebuilding the cities and waste places, as well as about the unrest and conflict their activities caused within the Arab community. He considered each incident a further fulfillment of prophecy—an indication of the imminent return of the Messiah. He wrote:

Water has been expected to flow up to Jerusalem since it was promised over two months ago. But on January 7th 1936, the supply of water from Ras-el-Ain, below the foot of the mountains, started to fill the Romema Reservoir in Western Jerusalem. Since that date between four and five hundred thousand gallons daily have been provided from that source. The reservoir has a total capacity of about two million gallons (2,000,000). The long standing anxiety for the inhabitants of Jerusalem has at least temporarily passed away.[18]

In his October 1936 report, Mr. Boothby included a news clipping from the *Palestine Post.* The article described an Arab strike and malicious damage to the water supply system, and it stated:

…Jerusalem is now faced with a serious water shortage. A part of the pipeline was again blown up yesterday and owing to recent damage no water from this source has reached Jerusalem during the last four days.[19]

Further word of the difficulties within the land were revealed in Boothby's December 1936 letter. He wrote:

The increase of armed forces for protection is very noticeable in Jerusalem. The terrorists are still active. To hear shooting and bombs exploding is not restful to the nerves. However, it drives one who has tasted of the Lord's saving power to look to Him for deliverance and peace. The little Gospel Gate Room still continues to serve as a Gospel lighthouse for passers-by who, in a state of dread, look to us for comfort. There would be desolation indeed if we were to close this room for Gospel purposes. Pray for its continuance.[20]

Two years later (c. 1938), as the struggle for a Jewish homeland continued, Frank Boothby's report to Joseph spoke about the Jewish immigrants who were leaving Palestine. Life was too difficult, and the war-weary immigrants were hoping to find an easier existence elsewhere. He then informed Joseph about the Jewish believers in the land. He wrote:

…As to Hebrew-Christians, it is even more difficult for them to find their way through. A recommendation from Christian quarters is generally impossible, for when it becomes known that Jews have turned toward Christ they are faced with bitter hatred and boycott from all Jewish sides, and the Missions have yet not found the means to sustain them or to provide jobs or work of a lasting kind. You will know about the Hebrew-Christian Alliance-Scheme for a H-C Colony in the Holy Land, but so far every effort to secure suitable land has failed, and it seems as if the Lord did not approve of this plan, as again and again negotiations had to meet with breakdown at the very eve of conclusion.[21]

Boothby went on to tell Joseph about the numbers of Jewish refugees, especially young men, he had been able to help through the relief funds sent by the Mission. He wrote:

> *...I have quite a number of young Zionist men, who used to call on me and who attend the meetings....many [are] without work; there is no Jewish Social Welfare Center that cares for the workless and needy in an adequate measure, and they expect from the Christians, who proclaim the message of goodwill among men, especially unto their Jewish brethren, that they should come to their rescue. All I can do is to provide a warm meal now and again....Thank you once more, that you have undertaken to assist me in these cares, that are truly sent by God to open up opportunities, where before because of prosperity there seemed to be no response to the Gospel message, 'Our difficulties become our opportunities by the blessing of our Lord.'* [22]

Boothby then gave a graphic description of the terrorist activity near the Mission's "Gate Room," saying:

> *I have hardly been able to keep account of terrible events that have happened within the past month or so. However I have endeavored to keep my business in the Lord going on. Terrorists have been trying to work near our Gate Room for at least a month. On the 14th of October [1937], two bombs thrown into a Restaurant Grocery just diagonally opposite our Gospel Gate Room, would doubtless have killed ten men sitting there, but for a quick move of some one to extinguish the burning fuse within half an inch of the explosive material. It was estimated, had it exploded, that the Gospel Gate Room would have been blown to pieces, and a block of buildings or so demolished, and some 200 people killed or injured seriously. It was a wonderful escape.* [23]

The war in Europe continued to escalate and by March 1940 Joseph received a communique from Herbert Singer, the Mission's worker in charge of Jewish Refugee ministry. Herbert wrote of the disillusionment of thousands of Jews who were trying to flee the horrors and savagery being brought down upon them in Central Europe. He spoke of the countless thousands of Jewish refugees who were being smuggled into Palestine through Syria and Lebanon, from Egypt, from Persia, and directly from the Mediterranean. He stated:

> *...It is reported that many ships are still drifting about the Mediterranean, each loaded to the rails with hundreds of these poor helpless creatures, scanning eagerly the coast lines of Mediterranean shores, for a possible unpatrolled gap, into which their little ship might slip unobserved, and thus land their heart-weary cargo of human derelicts. It is thought that there must be between 15,000 and 30,000 Jews now in Palestine, who have smuggled themselves in illegally....Your Mission is doing what we can to come to the help of these poor miserable and destitute human beings, but what we can do seems so small in the face of the appalling need, that we find ourselves bewildered and staggered. Out side of Jerusalem, we have no missionary work in Palestine of our own. But we have been privileged to cooperate with other missionaries, and to be used in God's hands as a help to them in their relief work.* [24]

Every letter from Frank Boothby and from Herbert Singer convinced Joseph of the need to expand the Mission's outreach in Palestine. Recognizing the need, he set about to do something about it. Through his networking system, he worked out an arrangement with the British Jews' Society to have their workers in Haifa, Mr. F.J. Plotke and Mrs. Rohold, handle the disbursement of funds which the Mission was sending to assist incoming refugees. [25]

In the May 1940 issue of *The Chosen People* magazine Joseph told readers about 1,300 Jewish refugees who had finally made it to Palestine, only to be arrested by the British Government officials. He said:

> *...Concerning these pitiful cases our friends in Haifa, through whom we are privileged to distribute relief funds, cabled for immediate relief moneys. Among such refugees there are always a certain number who are Christian Jews, true believers on the Lord Jesus Christ; and our brother begs us to help in a ministry to them. Although our own funds are greatly diminished, we had not the heart to say no, but we cabled immediately the sum of $500 at least as a beginning and as a bit of encouragement. More of course we must send and will send just as soon as the Lord replenishes our own treasury.* [26]

SIGOURD BIORNESS

Only a few months later, in September 1940, Joseph was informed that Mr. Frank Boothby had suddenly passed away. Not wanting to lose the contact in Jerusalem with the Gospel Gate Room, Joseph appointed Mr. Sigourd Biorness, a Norwegian missionary, to be the Mission's new worker in Jerusalem. [27]

Mr. Biorness's report to Joseph in the Spring of 1941 spoke about the dire situation in Palestine—the scarcity of jobs and the need for food and clothing. Then he stated: "The Shepherd of Israel is eagerly received. Everybody is hungry for fresh reading matter....The Gospel Gate Room is a lively place these days. Mrs. Biorness and I are changing off every forenoon and sometimes we are both there."[28] He also spoke about a number of secret Jewish believers. Most of them were from the Kibbutzim (communal farms). He wrote:

> ...A good many of these visitors are young people from the colonies and we have come in contact with them in the Bible shop. They come and want both Bibles in English and Hebrew; so we have had many interesting talks with these people....Last Saturday a Cheqoslovak Jew came to our shop and told he was a Jew, but believed in Christ as the Messiah. 'There are many in the colonies like me,' he said, 'they believe but have no chance to get out as they will lose their jobs.' This has been my conviction also that there are more believers in Palestine than we know about, only they cannot come out—yet.[29]

With each passing year the situation in Israel grew more desperate. In May 1942 Joseph received the following word from Mr. F.J. Plotke, the Mission's cooperative missionary in Haifa:

> ...The cost of living has increased by 140% since last year, and our people find it most difficult to make ends meet. They may earn enough for their daily bread, but they cannot manage to save up money for rent or for schooling of their children, and as soon as any small misfortune comes their way, they are finding themselves in narrow straits....You cannot imagine how hard it is over here to openly confess allegiance to our LORD.[30]

As the war in Europe was drawing to a close, more and more Jewish refugees were making their way from the concentration camps to Palestine. The numbers of illegal immigrants and refugees in the country swelled. By the Spring of 1943, Joseph received a letter from Mr. Biorness in which he suggested that the Mission purchase land for the establishment of its own colony in Palestine. Joseph was in favor of such a plan. In fact, he had discussed setting up a program for the re-settlement of refugee Jews with some members of the International Hebrew Christian Alliance some months earlier. Reporting on Mr. Biorness's suggestion, Joseph told the Mission's Directors:

> ...he tells of his desire to start a little colony of needy Jewish Christians. Many refugees have come from Poland, Romania, etc. They are in the country illegally. The cost of living in Palestine has increased 300% and these refugees are almost starving. The employment situation in the country is bad.
> Mr. Biorness has been negotiating with a party who has a piece of land for sale, located about 4 miles from Jerusalem...[it] will cost about seven hundred pounds, which Mr. Biorness considers reasonable.[31]

Joseph asked the Board to approve an allocation of $5,000.00 to purchase land for such a project—if other believers in Palestine concurred that it is a good effort to pursue. Permission was granted to investigate and to proceed with the purchase of property if Joseph's contacts in Israel agreed to the project.[32]

Subsequently, Mr. Biorness was unable to purchase the land he was negotiating on, and Joseph either changed his mind about the project or was convinced by his committee in Israel that it was not a good idea. Part of the problem may have been over the fact that Mr. Biorness had proposed that the colony be established for Jewish Christians who were in the country illegally. Joseph Cohn did not agree with the British in their governmental policy concerning Palestine, but he did not want to break the law by having the Mission harbor illegal refugees. It was a sensitive issue, especially to those living in the land.

As Jewish refugees poured into Palestine it was clear to believers within the country that the sad-eyed, broken-hearted newcomers needed to hear the message of healing, hope, and life through Yeshua, but the message was one that was extremely difficult to preach because of what the refugees had suffered. Additionally, the war had essentially closed most of the shipping lines and it was next to impossible to get Bibles, tracts, and Gospel literature to Palestine. By 1946 Mr. Biorness informed Joseph that there were many Jewish people asking for Bibles and New Testaments, but there were no Bibles to be had in Jerusalem.[33]

Three years elapsed and no property had been purchased for the establishment of a colony for Jewish Christians. Evidently Mr. Biorness was so upset about this that he submitted a letter of resignation. The Minutes of the April 1946 Board meeting include the following notation:

> A letter from Mr. Sigourd Biorness, our missionary in Jerusalem, was presented by Mr. Cohn, in which Mr. Biorness tendered his resignation effective as of March 31, 1946. Mr. Graef moved that the resignation of Mr. Biorness be accepted and that the Board is sorry for the attitude and hasty action that he has taken. The motion carried.[34]

With the resignation of Mr. Biorness, the Jerusalem Gate House ministry came to a close. It is not known what became of the building and materials, but it is likely that much of it was destroyed in the War of Liberation prior to the establishment of the State of Israel.

Although the Mission no longer had a worker in Jerusalem, Mr. Plotke, Joseph's missionary in cooperation with the British Jews' Society, continued to keep the Board abreast of the situation in Palestine. In May 1947 Mr. Plotke wrote:

> ...I am unable to enlarge today upon my news of March 5, concerning conditions over here. Sunday evening a schooner with 650 illegal immigrants was brought into Haifa. The unfortunate folks aboard were forcibly trans-shipped for Cyprus....
>
> The baptism of four adults under my instruction was celebrated at the evening service in the Church of Scotland by courtesy of the minister, who is most understanding, and I was escorted home after the service by military jeep and security convoy.[35]

In preparation for the end of the war, Joseph had thousands of copies of the Yiddish New Testament printed. He also made preparations to go to Palestine during the summer of 1947 for a first-hand look at the needs, as well as to ascertain the possibilities for expanding the Mission's outreach there. His trip preceded the establishment of the State of Israel— at the time when the United Nations was seeking to partition the land. A report of his visit to Palestine was included in the October 1947 Chosen People magazine. It stated:

> ...You remember we stated in May that we might have to open a hostel in Haifa to care for homeless Jews smuggled in by means of the blockade-running of the Zionist fanatics. But I soon discovered when I reached Haifa that if we engaged in this sort of business we would be harboring illegal immigrants in Palestine and, to that extent, we would be criminally guilty of violating the laws of Great Britain as the Mandate power for Palestine. So here again I suggested that we need not build any special house or buy any special property, but, if there were legitimate cases of need, we would pay for the room of every Jew who was in Palestine legitimately so that he might find a place to live, either in some private home or in a rooming house. We would have no part in illegitimate entry. And this, too, seemed to settle the problem to the satisfaction of everybody.[36]

While he was in Palestine, Joseph made contact with Mr. & Mrs. E. B. Shelley, an older couple who agreed to carry on some relief and correspondence work for him. The Shelley's were from Britain, but they had spent over fifty years in Palestine. Mr. Shelly was eighty-seven years of age; his wife was eighty-one.

In 1948, when the War of Liberation broke out, the Shelley's refused to leave Jerusalem. A portion of one of Mr. Shelly's letters to Joseph was included in the April 1948 issue of *The Chosen People* magazine. It stated:

> Our King's city is not only stirred, but soaked in Jewish blood. Its most important street in a total ruin, with the above record of 54 killed (so far) and 130 (so far) injured under the British flag.
>
> Isaiah 4:3, is our ordained orbit as being left in Zion. And to be called holy, sanctified for such service, indicates that our Lord has not put two aged ones,...alone here. For there are millions praying for Zion who don't know the aged ones. You can understand how close we are to the scenes of slaughter, when I report to you that the clerk of my chamber was rushed, with babies and in night apparel, off the roof of his house; it is now level with the street, demolished and everything lost. And he is only one of the outraged....
>
> We have been protected in the midst of a battle all around us; the attack was against a Jewish colony which old Montefiore established a hundred years ago. How long, oh Lord, how long?[37]

HAIM HAIMOFF

In June 1949, after the War of Liberation and the establishment of the State of Israel, Joseph made another trip to Israel. This trip brought him into contact with a Jewish believer whose name was Mr. Haim Haimoff. Joseph was impressed with Haimoff; the two men shared the same prophetic vision for the land of Israel. Joseph's enthusiastic report of Haimoff appears in the Minutes of the August 1949 Board meeting. It states:

> While Mr. Cohn was in Jerusalem in June he was brought into contact with a Jewish Christian brother from Sofia who is currently associated with the Christian Missionary Alliance in Jerusalem. This contact was made through Mr. Stanley Clark, a believing Christian, and Manager of Barcley's [sic] Bank. This man, Haim Haimoff, was converted some years ago in Sofia. He is in his early forties and is married and has three children. He is very anxious to work with

this Mission and conduct a Branch for us in Jerusalem. He has now about 25 Jewish Christian families with whom he is working, and he would like to establish a place where they can meet for fellowship and for worship. He has been recommended by Mr. Clark as being the best person in Jerusalem now for this work.[38]

The Board agreed to hire Mr. Haimoff as the Missionary-In-Charge of Jerusalem, Israel.

Haim J. Haimoff was born of Jewish parents on April 27, 1905 in Doupnitza—not far from Sofia, the Capital of Bulgaria. Although his father was a "free thinker" who didn't attend synagogue regularly, he did attend a few services each year during the holy days of Rosh Hashanah and Yom Kippur. When Haim was very young, his father took him to the "Selichot" (the early morning prayers offered in the synagogues during the month before Rosh Hashanah).

Many years later Haim recalled that the prayer services made such a great impression on him that thereafter, although he was only four or five years of age, he got up every morning at between four and five a.m., dressed himself and, alone, made his way through the dark, muddy, winding streets to the synagogue. He stated that, even though he was very young, he felt that through these prayers he was expressing his devotion to God. As the years went by, longing to be a devout Jew, he spent most of his time in the synagogue, attending the Friday and Saturday services and all of the prayer services.

Haim finished his pro-gymnasium (school) at the age of thirteen. His father then sent him to continue his studies at the American College conducted by the Congregational Church in the nearby town of Samokov. It was while he was attending this school that Haim came into contact with the New Testament of the Bible. His job as a librarian of the college afforded him unlimited access to other books as well.

Haim had a deep desire to know absolute Truth, and toward this end he read the great philosophical systems and classical literature; he read everything he thought might help him in his quest, but nothing quenched his thirst for the Truth. Only his brief exposure to the New Testament had bathed his heart with peace.

As he was approaching graduation, an inner voice urged him to read the New Testament Scriptures once again, but he never seemed to find the time. Of that period in his life Haim wrote:

> *...At times I thought myself a Christian, but the question of the Trinity was unclear to me. I trembled before the thought of accepting Jesus as the Son of God without understanding it and unless I would trespass the first of the Ten Commandments. Then I said: I have so great a love and faith in God that I am sure He will find ways to reveal to me in an unquestionable way the whole truth concerning Christ. So I reconciled.*[39]

Haim graduated from the American College in September 1923, and continued his studies at the University of Zurich, Switzerland. Lonely, and still searching for the truth, he often walked along the shores of Zurich lake when he was not in classes. The Salvation Army Corps members held open air meetings in the same area and as Haim walked he could hear the singing and preaching. The hymns brought back fond memories of his days at the American College. The Salvation Army people also passed out tracts written in German. Haim was just learning German, so after their meetings he would take a handful of tracts, which he then took back to his room to translate.

One day he accepted a tract that changed his life. It was a tract that spoke about the imminent return of the Messiah, the Lord, Yeshua. As Haim translated the words, they penetrated his heart and he realized that if the teaching was true he ought to read it for himself. He hurried to the Bible House and bought a New Testament in English. He decided that this time he would not just read it, he would study it in depth—for if this was Truth, he wanted to know it. He later recalled that he read the Sermon on the Mount again and again, as God's Spirit seared the words to his heart. He wrote:

> *...Oh, at last I found the thing I was looking for so many years. I found just what my whole nature believed to be the truth. And if Christ revealed it, then he could not be a liar. He must be what He claims to be. Then I knelt beside my desk on which my New Testament was, still open on that wonderful discourse and asked God Almighty to reveal me at last the truth. Then the power and glory of the Eternal covered me and the Holy Spirit whispered in my ears: In Christ is the Truth. He is Truth...and I believed it....*
>
> *When I returned home from Zurich and made known to my parents my new beliefs, they did not say anything about it. But later my father used to tell me: You may believe what you want, but don't tell others about it. And when he saw I did not keep silent,...he simply told me one day that I had to choose between home and the Gospel....My father's words did not, however, represent an alternative for me. For my choice was already made long ago. By faith I understood that the Lord was leading me to the land of Israel. And by the end of May 1928 I left Sofia by train. Not long after that I came to Jerusalem and at once entered the Bible School near Bethlehem.*[40]

Haim graduated from the Bible School near Bethlehem in 1932. He returned to Bulgaria for a visit with his family in 1939 but, because of the war, he was unable to return to Israel until 1944. By that time he had married. Of the Jews in Bulgaria during the war years, Haim wrote:

> About two months after we [Haim and his wife] left Bulgaria my father died in a small town…where my whole family had been deported….a miracle happened with the Jews in Bulgaria. Though the German Army stayed there for a few years, not a single Jew was killed or deported to Poland….It seems He [God] found ten righteous Jews for whose sake He preserved the lives of all.
>
> …God heard my prayers concerning my mother, who had never opposed me in my Christian views. She has come safely to Israel and is staying with us. She is fully persuaded in the Messiahship of our Lord, is praying in His Name, and is reading the New Testament in Ladino (Spanish jargon the Jews of Balcans speak) with great interest.[41]

The Directors of the Mission were delighted with the work Haimoff was doing in Israel and they agreed to raise the annual amount they were spending in Jerusalem to $10,000.00 a year. The money was placed on deposit with Barclay's Bank in New York and Haimoff was permitted to draw down $750.00 a month for expenses—and more if approved by Joseph Cohn.[42]

In the Spring of 1950 the Board gave Joseph permission to spend up to $40,000.00 for a suitable building for the Mission's work in Jerusalem. They were also examining the legal ramifications of a foreign corporation owning property in Israel.[43]

THE MCCLENAHANS

Additionally, Mr. W. L. McClenahan, a Gentile Christian who had been in the land for some thirty years, was hired to act as a treasurer for the work in Jerusalem and to function in a legal and advisory capacity for Mr. Haimoff. Mr. McClenahan was given Power of Attorney to register the Mission as a foreign corporation in Israel.[44] Mr. & Mrs. McClenahan were experienced missionaries who had a deep love for Israel and the Jewish people, and Joseph felt they would be good co-laborers for the Haimoffs.[45]

Friends of the Mission were kept abreast of the outreach in Israel through Joseph's articles in *The Chosen People* magazine. *The Shepherd of Israel* also heralded stories of God's blessings on the work in Israel. One such "miracle" story was that of Rabbi Daniel Zion, a seventy year old rabbi who had become a believer. The rabbi, who had been the Chief Rabbi of Bulgaria, had immigrated to Israel; he made his home in Jerusalem. The January 1951 *Shepherd of Israel* carried the full story of Rabbi Zion, as well as a sequel with the comments of outrage that took place because of his faith in Yeshua. The article stated:

> …So great were the outcries of abuse and condemnation, that at long last the high officials of Jewish religious institutions met together, held an examination of Daniel Zion, and then, believe it or not, they pronounced him 'Mad!' And they relieved him from the official office as Rabbi.[46]

Rabbi Zion himself shared his story with readers of *The Shepherd of Israel*. He stated:

> I was born in Salonica, Greece, and was brought up by my parents of Rabbinical origin, who were prejudiced concerning Jesus and the New Testament. When I first bought a Bible in French with the New Testament contained within, they tore out the New Testament part; for we were not allowed to have the New Testament in our home. Later, when I came to Sofia, the capital of Bulgaria, I had the chance to talk with some Bulgarians who quoted verses from the New Testament. I was surprised to find in it great contents and high morality. Consequently I started to read the New Testament more attentively. The more I wondered why it was that the Jewish people did not read that precious book, especially because of the fact that it contained so many quotations from the Old Testament. Still greater was my surprise, when I got convinced that Jesus was a divine person. Why did they condemn Him to death?
>
> For many years there contained [continued] to be a link between the New Testament and myself. In my preaching I quoted quite often from it. At the same time I used to tell my followers in Sofia to read that book.
>
> On one occasion, I was invited by Mr. and Mrs. Joseph Haimoff, a noted Jewish family of Sofia, to bless their son, Mr. Haim Joseph Haimoff, and their daughter-in-law, who had just been married by a Baptist pastor. I accepted the invitation, though I knew very well Mr. Haim J. Haimoff as an outspoken believer on the Lord Jesus Christ as the Messiah of Israel and the Son of God.
>
> But my faith in Jesus as the Messiah was weak in me, though He became my guide, since I saw Him in a vision—crucified.

Since I came to the State of Israel, my faith in Him kept growing from day to day stronger and stronger. Specially when my guide sent me to Jerusalem, and I was left entirely alone for a whole month. I had been living in Tel Aviv, but now for a month, I was to live all alone in Jerusalem. As I was fully separated from the outside world, I deepened myself in the New Testament writings and at the end of the month I received a revelation by the Holy Spirit, who told me: 'You must go to Tel Aviv and tell two persons of the chief Rabbinate, that you believe in Jesus as the Messiah and that He offered Himself for the Jewish nation, that their sins might be forgiven....'

Then I called together all members of my family, whom I told the same thing. Some of them tried to oppose me, using different considerations, but of course did not succeed. And so I continued to spread my faith for a few weeks and many of them understood me, but few fully believed.[47]

As Mr. Haimoff sought to share the Gospel with the Jews in Israel, he visited on the Kibbutzim, in hospitals, and in the homes of individuals. He also distributed tracts and literature. His greatest needs were for a Mission building in which to hold meetings, and a store front for use as a Reading Room.

Meanwhile, Mr. McClenahan's efforts toward registering the Mission as a foreign corporation in Israel came to fruition. The May 1951 issue of *The Chosen People* magazine included a picture of the Mission's official registration in Israel. A free translation of the certificate read:

State of Israel. Registration Certificate of a Foreign Society. [No. 010]. This is to certify that the American Board of Missions to the Jews, Inc., a Society established in the United States, has been registered in Israel according to the 1929 Regulations governing Corporations. Issued by signature in Jerusalem on the 30th day of the month of Shevat, in the year 5711 (February, 1951). The Chief Registrar, Registration of Societies, State of Israel.[48]

Alongside the picture of the registration was another notation which stated: "The American Board of Missions to the Jews is now registered under the laws of the State of Israel—the first and only independent missionary society in the world to enjoy that privilege."[49]

Following the establishment of the State of Israel a "Messianic frenzy" broke out among many Christians who saw the state as a fulfillment of prophecy—one that would hasten the return of Yeshua. In their zeal to win as many converts as possible before the Tribulation Period, and before the return of the Messiah, Christians clamored to move to the newly formed state. But the State of Israel was founded on Zionist principles and entry into the country was therefore very restrictive to Christians. Only those missionaries who had been in the land prior to the establishment of the State were allowed to return. Regarding the Mission's work in Israel Joseph wrote:

Suddenly everybody seems to be 'called of God' to go to Jerusalem as a missionary! It seems to be a sort of sensation of the hour, a spellbinder to earnest Christian people who have not the facts to enable them to understand the fallacies of these well meaning brethren.

...the Israeli regulations will not allow a missionary to come into Palestine. The only exceptions are in cases where the missionary was established in Palestine before the Jewish-Arab War began. It is necessary that such a missionary shall prove that he was so established, had only fled the country at the approach of the War, but now was returning to his old status. [Cohn did not mention that often such missionaries had already lost the respect of the Israeli for leaving the country.] But new missionaries, seeking to take advantage of present chaotic conditions, will not be allowed to enter....

The only alternative left to missionaries who are determined to enter legally or illegally, is to enter Palestine by making false statements in their visa applications....Is it to be wondered at that the Jewish leaders over there develop a strong aversion to 'this thing called Christianity?'

You may trust to the judgment of the administrators of your Jewish Mission that we will deal in such matters only on the highest plane of integrity and responsibility....it will be on such a basis as will comply with the legal restrictions of the new Israeli Government, and will command their respect and confidence.[50]

Christians who were unable to enter Israel as new missionaries joined with other believers who earnestly prayed for a harvest of Jewish converts. Together, such individuals began channeling money and material goods into Israel. Unfortunately, their gifts oftentimes ended in the hands of Christians who were in the land illegally, or who were winning Jewish converts through bribery or through other subtle means of deception. For the poor refugee Jews, and for many disillusioned Zionist Jews, the profession of faith required by the missionaries was a small price to pay for needed food and funding. Joseph wrote scathing castigation of such schemes, leaving the reader with little doubt about his (and the

Mission's) position on the issues. In one article he wrote:

> Other missionaries…should also be sent home, for they are doing irreparable harm to the cause of Christ. They know nothing about Jewish work. I have read reports from some of these zealots, containing the wildest fantasies, in some cases deliberate falsehoods, and in most cases unjustified exaggerations. One woman writes to her 'prayer warriors' that she has had her first convert and she is so happy! What she does not know is that the 'convert' is just a shrewd Israeli who goes around to these women, each in a different place. He fawns around them and tells each one privately that he has received more blessings from this particular missionary than from anybody else in all his life! He then gets a box of food and few piasters. Then goes on to the next missionary and tells her the same story. And so it goes on, round and round, and suddenly all the typewriters get busy and each missionary sends a report to her 'prayer-warriors' that she has a new 'convert!'…
>
> The basic difficulty is that these well-meaning 'missionaries' run off to distant places and undertake to do whatever they wish, when they wish, and how they wish, all without supervision from anybody. This is a sort of escapism from conscientious obligations.
>
> …One of these American 'Missions' which claims to be working in the 'Holy Land' although they are one of the most notable of the quack exploiters, had the audacity to write to us recently a proposition that they would give us 20% of their 'take,' if we would supply them with the mailing list of The Chosen People! May we assure our friends that their names are never given, or sold, or loaned, to anyone under any circumstances….[a policy that the Mission continues to keep to this very day.]
>
> One trouble is that everybody now wants to run to Jerusalem. It has become a sort of sentimental Hegira. Everybody runs there and rushes back to America to announce that he or they have now got either a 'representative' or a 'correspondent' in Jerusalem. In one case one exploiter picked upon that poor misguided rabbi, who really does not know what salvation is, and who publicly states that he does not believe that Christ was God. This poor groping rabbi the exploiter announced as his 'missionary' for Jerusalem! This same exploiter picked upon a woman whose reputation is something devastating to contemplate, and this woman also is his 'missionary!'
>
> The whole situation, as the American missionary leader said when she saw it, 'is a mess.'[51]

For Joseph, "the mess" would not go away. In the same article, he informed his readers that he'd had to sever connections with Haim Haimoff, the Mission's worker in Jerusalem. No explanation was given either in *The Chosen People* magazine nor in the official Minutes of the Board, but there is no reason to attach any wrong doing to Mr. Haimoff. As mentioned earlier, Haimoff wanted very much to develop a "colony" or a "kibbutz." It is likely, therefore, that differing opinions over how the ministry was to be developed was the catalyst that brought about the separation between the two men.

In sharing his vision for the Mission's work in Jerusalem, Joseph wrote:

> …We are not seeking to make capital of our undertakings in Israel, we are only trying to do an honest work there; and if we cannot do an honest work we will prefer to do no work. We do want you to pray earnestly that the Lord will enable us to solve effectively the perplexities of the Jerusalem situation; we need desperately the right kind of a missionary in whom we can have the fullest confidence. And we need also a building of our own in Jerusalem, properly located in the center of traffic, where we can maintain a Bible House, with window display; a Reading Room where we can have a missionary in charge…We still retain as our Adviser in Jerusalem our dear brother, William L. McClenahan; it has been remarkable how, in spite of his advancing years, Mr. McClenahan has continued with vigorous testimony both to Arab and to Jew.[52]

As Joseph indicated in his article, Mr. McClenahan was a man in the sunset of his life. Shortly after Joseph Cohn passed away in 1953, William L. McClenahan also went home to be with his Lord. The Minutes of the Board reflect that Mr. Harold Pretlove and Mr. William Jones, members of the Executive Committee, contacted Mrs. McClenahan, asking if she would be the Mission's representative in Israel.[53] Evidently the reply from Mrs. McClenahan was positive, as her name continued to be listed as the Mission's missionary in Jerusalem through May, 1956.

Israel Through the Eyes of Charles Kalisky

In the Spring of 1955, Mrs. McClenahan requested that the Board allow her to make a visit to the United States for a six to eight month period of time so she could arrange for schooling for her two children, Elizabeth and David. In arranging for a temporary replacement for her, the Mission contacted Mr. Charles Kalisky, a Christian from Britain. He agreed to a four-month stint of ministry in Israel, during which time he consented to do personal work among the Jews but he also wanted to do observation and investigation of the over-all missionary effort being done in the country.[54] Mr. Kalisky went to Israel during the summer of 1955. His observations of the missionary work being done in there were shared with readers of *The Chosen People* magazine. He wrote:

> *The number of missionaries stationed in the country, permanently and temporarily, is relatively far larger than in any other mission field in the world. As a result, the sum of money contributed for the work there is out of all proportion to the size of the country, which is somewhat smaller than the State of New Jersey....*
>
> *The fact remains that in the city of New York alone the number of Jews is three times the entire population of the State of Israel. Yet the number of missionaries working among the Jews in New York is no more, and possibly less, than the total number working in the city of Jerusalem alone, which has a population of about 135,000! This may seem remarkable, but I wrote down the names of all the different missions represented there, and found that there were no less than twenty mission stations, some having more than a single missionary. In addition there are many unattached freelance or 'faith' missionaries whose number I could not ascertain. In all I would estimate that the total number of Christian workers in Jerusalem alone is at least thirty. It is doubtful if New York has so many full-time missionaries to the Jews, with its Jewish population of between two and three million!*
>
> *...In Israel today I noticed that most of the missionaries are using the methods that won Jews to Christ in the past, but this does not signify that the same methods will be successful today. Many are ignorant of the fact that the Gospel is a form of Judaism, and that it is talmudic Judaism that has misled the people of Israel. The Gospel should be presented in its old Jewish form, not as an alien religion but as an integral part of Biblical Judaism. This is necessary because of the reborn nationalism of the Jews in Israel.*
>
> *I found many missionaries, even some of those who had been many years in the country, unable to present the Gospel in Hebrew and quite unfamiliar with the Jewish way of life or thinking. As a result they were confused, disappointed, discouraged and sometimes even chagrined and angry with the unresponsiveness of the Jews.[55]*

A further report of Mr. Kalisky's observations of missionary work in Israel was included in the May 1956 issue of the magazine. In this report he made it clear that there were many areas open for the Mission to have an "effective" witness to the Jews in Israel. He wrote:

> *...A very effective witness is being carried out by several small groups in the country who stoutly affirm their Jewishness yet believe in the Messiah Who came from Nazareth. I met and spoke with several of these groups. One in Jerusalem particularly impressed me. About 25 Jewish believers met for worship together in an upper room each Sabbath morning at the time other Jews were in the synagogues. The service was conducted in Hebrew, as were the services of the early Christians two thousand years ago in this self-same city. The Old Testament was read and expounded as was the New Testament in the language of the Bible, and finally a brief sermon was given in Hebrew. I had the joy and privilege of addressing this meeting several times. They belong to no mission, but they are just an assembly of Jewish believers in the Messiah. They have their own small funds for their different needs, and their leader visits them in their homes. They were short of Hebrew hymn books, so I undertook to revise and reprint such a book, and this is one way in which your Mission is helping this group....*
>
> *After many inquiries I came to the conclusion that another useful piece of work your Mission can do is to produce a special edition of The Shepherd of Israel in Hebrew and French. English is spoken less and less, and there are so many Jews from Morocco, Iraq, Romania and Turkey who speak French that the monthly issue of this paper can serve a good purpose provided it is carefully and prayerfully distributed....*
>
> *I also noticed that the intensive efforts of several years ago to place the Scriptures in the homes in Israel have had the result that in almost every home I entered, except among the more orthodox people, I found a Bible in Hebrew or some other language containing the New Testament. Not all of them are read of course, but there it is, and who would dare to limit the power of the Holy Spirit to use the Word of God at any time—even years later.[56]*

A further observation of Kalisky strikes at the heart of many pseudo-evangelistic efforts that were being carried on in Israel (Such works are still being carried on in Israel. They may one day open the door to future witness, but they cannot be considered to be Jewish evangelism). Kalisky stated:

> *Another phase of misinformed missionary activity that I encountered was that some non-Jewish workers were highly pleased if they succeeded in visiting some well-known Jew in his home, or if they were able to make friends with a Jewish*

family. One thing is certain, such invitation would not be repeated, nor would the friendship endure, if the name of Christ was mentioned often. To show love to Jews by non-Jewish Christians is always a good thing. Love draws when argument fails. But it is a mistake, in my view, to believe that the presence of a Christian anywhere, in such circumstances, can be a means of winning anybody to Christ. 'Faith cometh by hearing, and hearing by the Word of God.' 'How shall they believe unless they hear. . .?' Elsewhere such a witness can be effective only if there is a background of Christian teaching, but to a Jew whose tradition and culture have conditioned him against Christianity I doubt the effectiveness of such an approach.[57]

It is not known if Mrs. McClenahan returned to Israel after her leave of absence to the United States, but if she did, she did not return as the Mission's worker. After Mr. Kalisky's temporary assignment in Israel, the Board appointed Rev. Elias Zimmerman to be their "Appointed Foreign Inspector." Elias visited Israel and Jerusalem in 1957, but he gave no report of the Mission's activities there.[58] It would appear that the Mission had no salaried missionaries in Israel from 1952, when Haim Haimoff left the staff, until the Fall of 1963. During those years, a number of attempts were made to find workers in Israel, or to send workers to Israel, but no trained worker could be found to work exclusively for the Mission.

Paramount in the Mission's difficulty in finding qualified workers for Israel was the fact that while the land was under British Mandate rule, prior to the establishment of the State of Israel, its quota of missionary workers in the land was never registered. When official registration was sought, Joseph had the Mission registered as a "foreign corporation" in Israel. Because Israeli regulation restricted Christian missionaries to those individuals who had been serving as missionaries prior to the establishment of the State (or to their replacements), new missionaries had to be sought from among the believers who were already citizens of Israel—a factor that severely limited the choices.

PETER GUTKIND

During the early Fall of 1961, in his position as Missionary Secretary of the Mission, Daniel Fuchs made a trip to Israel. While he was there, he made contact with Peter Gutkind, a Jewish believer who lived in Haifa. The Minutes of the May 1962 Board meeting reflect Board action taken following Mr. Fuchs' report of his trip to Israel: "After discussion of the proposals of the missionary secretary, Mr. Stone moved that Mr. Fuchs be given authority to immediately hire Mr. Peter Gutkind as our missionary in Israel."[59]

Mr. Gutkind's work consisted mostly of distributing the Mission's care packages, doing personal visitation, distributing literature, and establishing Bible classes. Reports of his ministry began to appear in *The Chosen People* magazine by 1964, and the September 1965 issue of the magazine included his report which told of the special Seder (Passover) service held during the Spring of 1965, and of the baptismal service to two Jewish believers. He wrote:

The baptismal service for these two believers was a very blessed, joyful and happy one, rich in touching experiences not soon to be forgotten. The baptism took place at wonderful Bethsaida, in Galilee, near Capernaum. We improvised a meeting at the Sea of Tiberias, had our breakfast there, and at eleven o'clock went to the home of one of our faithful friends, where, with ten believers, we celebrated the Lord's Supper,...Later that day we returned to our apartment in Haifa for the Saturday evening meeting, where...Three of our brethren gave messages on the Gospel during the evening....

In general, during the month of April, we kept up a lively contact with numbers of our Jewish-Christian friends, as we did in March, totaling about 50 visits, and, in addition,...we distributed many copies of the Holy Scriptures,...[60]

Mr. Gutkind's missionary work soon brought him to the attention of some orthodox Jewish radicals. On August 9, 1965 the Mission received a cablegram stating: "Many fanatics attacked home August fifth broke in forcefully some damage family unharmed police chief promised protection came late following attack arrested six."[61]

Efforts to contact the Gutkind's were unsuccessful, and an around-the-clock prayer vigil for their safety was quickly established. When word was finally received, it came in the form of a news item from the Hebrew newspaper, *Maariv*, in Haifa. It stated:

More than one hundred Yeshiva Youth, including members of the 'Activist Group' laid siege last night to the home of Theodore (Peter) Gutkind, aged 62, of Jaffa Street in Haifa. They threatened to use force against him if he did not cease from disseminating the propaganda of the 'Jewish Christianity Movement.'

Several dozen of the demonstrators broke into his home and destroyed items in the apartment. It was only with great effort that the police succeeded in dispersing the crowd and arrested five young men.

In an interview with a 'Maariv' reporter this morning, Mr. Gutkind said that these religious young men threatened him for many days. They set guards around his house who continually annoyed him. Once they hurled stones at him, another time they blocked his lock with plaster, they destroyed his doorbell, and personally threatened him.

Last Thursday the Police advised him to seek safety for himself because they could not assure his safety.

Gutkind then hid himself with relatives at Kiriat Hayyim, but after two days the same young men discovered his hiding place. A large group gathered as one of them entered the apartment and wanted to talk to him.

According to Gutkind, this young man represented himself as the "representative of the religious ones" and said that if he would not stop preaching for the 'Jewish Christian' movement, his life would be in danger, but if he did stop they would assure him of life to the age of 120 and that they would find him a respectable occupation.

Theodore (Peter) Gutkind is a Jewish apostate who immigrated from Poland seven years ago. For five years he was secretary of a Government school in Haifa.[62]

Once it was known that the Gutkind's were safe, the Mission began taking steps to purchase an apartment for them in Haifa. They looked for a place that would afford safe living quarters, as well as providing office space for the ministry and a meeting room for believers. The search revealed that it would be necessary to purchase such a property in the name of an individual, rather than in the name of the Mission, because of the hostility toward such a mission. When a suitable property was located, it was decided that the property would be purchased in the name of Peter Gutkind; Daniel Fuchs made a trip to Israel to finalize the arrangements for the purchase. He later wrote:

...I conferred with several government officials, and am happy to report that, while they personally did not approve of missions or missionaries, they nevertheless deplore the persecution of Peter Gutkind by the aforementioned group [Torah Activists] of fanatics. We are confident that, if the attacks should be repeated, Mr. Gutkind will receive the protection he needs. However, because our enemies are still very active we will not make any of the details of this arrangement public until the purchase of the property if fully and legally registered.[63]

Registering the property was a web of complexity that was compounded by the fact that the Mission was registered as a foreign corporation doing business in Israel, rather than as a "not-for-profit" organization in the land. Foreign corporations operating in Israel were subject to Israeli corporate taxes on property and business. Mr. Fuchs attempted to avoid taxation by having the property registered under the Mission's corporate name "Beth Sar Shalom" (House of the Prince of Peace), but his efforts were unsuccessful because the new name had not been previously registered and therefore had no standing in Israel at all. Fraught with problems at every turn, it was finally decided that the title of the property in Haifa would be placed in Mr. Fuchs' name until such time as the name "Beth Sar Shalom" could be registered in Israel. Shortly thereafter, the Six Day War (June 1967) broke out in Israel.

EXPANDING THE MINISTRY THROUGH RADIO

Because of the difficulty of finding qualified workers for Israel, and because of the limitations put upon doing ministry within Israel, Mr. Fuchs began investigating the possibility of establishing a radio ministry into Israel.[64] Toward this end, he contacted HCJB in Quito, Ecuador—a station that was just beginning to beam short-wave radio broadcasts into Israel. He also sent Dr. Henry Heydt to Quito to work out the details of producing broadcasts in Hebrew, Yiddish, and English. Unfortunately, HCJB ran into difficulty trying to get their signals beamed into Israel. But Mr. Fuchs was not to be deterred. He approached Trans World Radio (TWR). They informed him that TWR had an exclusive arrangement to broadcast the programs of the American Messianic Fellowship (originally known as the Chicago Hebrew Mission) into Israel. Not willing to forego the idea, Mr. Fuchs requested that a meeting be set up between himself, a representative of TWR, and a representative of AMF (American Messianic Fellowship) for the purpose of working out an agreement whereby the two Missions could jointly support a broadcast into Israel. In his January 1969 report to the Board, Daniel stated:

...The broadcast now goes out seven days a week for fifteen minutes each broadcast. If we join them, it will be brdcast [sic] for a half an hour. No names of missions will be mentioned. This would be a ministry through the Christian church in Israel and would be produced in Israel, not an American broadcast translated into Hebrew. The cost would approximate $20,000 not including production costs.[65]

The Board approved the plan and authorized an expenditure of up to $25,000 for producing and broadcasting a fifteen minute program into Israel over TWR, with the provision that it was tied to the fifteen minute broadcast of AMF. But it wasn't long before Mr. Fuchs discovered that additional funds were required to produce the programs in Israel and he requested an additional $10,000 to purchase the necessary broadcasting equipment in Israel.[66]

With the broadcasts to Israel in place, the American Board of Missions to the Jews and the American Messianic Fellowship entered into an historic agreement to reach the Jewish people of Israel with the Gospel. The agreement was unanimously approved by the Board. It stated:

1. *The American Board of Missions to the Jews and the American Messianic Fellowship have entered into an agreement to give financial and spiritual support to Christians in Israel to enable them to reach the people of Israel by means of regular radio programs, recorded in Israel (in part) and aired on Trans World Radio.*

2. *The glory of God and the salvation of souls and the edification of the saints are the objective toward which we work, and not the promotion of either of the involved mission agencies.*

3. *Since the American Messianic Fellowship has already made a substantial investment in equipment, this shall be taken into account in the initial expense now being undertaken to purchase editing equipment.*

4. *The expense of remodelling the new building and the monthly expense of operation are to be limited to the budget submitted by Victor Smadja, and will be shared equally by the American Board of Missions to the Jews and the American Messianic Fellowship. Bills will be sent to the General Director of the American Messianic Fellowship, who will duplicate them and send copies to the American Board of Missions to the Jews.*
   Each mission will send its part of the total expense to the account established in Israel for the care of these radio expenses, with Victor Smadja as the custodian of that fund. Any deviation from the budget must be requested from the two participating missions in advance of the expenditure.

5. *Each mission will keep the other informed of any items of interest or of business that are likely to affect the relationships between us and our Christian friends in Israel with whom we are involved in this strategic ministry.*

6. *We covenant to pray, each for the other that the Lord will use this new relationship, and project in which we are engaged, to bless the lives of many in Israel, and to speed the day 'when all Israel shall be saved.'[67]*

The Gospel broadcasts went well and were gradually increased from thirty-minute programs to sixty-minute programs. The agreement between the two organizations also worked out well until 1973, when the American Messianic Fellowship had a change in leadership. Their new director felt their part of the funds spent on radio broadcasts into Israel could be better spent on ministry to the Russian people.

Knowing that the Mission could not carry the expense of the broadcast by itself, Mr. Fuchs reported to the Board that he was seeking other missions with whom the radio ministry could be shared, but no other mission with resources for a radio broadcast into Israel could be found.[68] By 1974 the broadcast was cut back to a thirty-minute program, and Mr. Fuchs reported to the Board that he had been unable to locate anyone in Israel who could make the broadcasts.[69] Various Jewish believers were selected to make the broadcasts, but by the mid-1980's it was determined that short-wave/medium-wave radio broadcasts were no longer an effective means of getting the Gospel into Israel, and the Mission closed its radio ministry there.

During the same time when Daniel Fuchs proposed that the Mission enter into a AMF/ABMJ sponsored Gospel radio broadcast into Israel (September 1969), he also put forth a policy statement concerning the Mission's work in Israel—a policy that affected the Mission's role in Israel for years to come. It stated:

Because of the difficulties which confront the testimony of the Lord Jesus Christ in Israel, we, the members of the Board of Directors of the American Board of Missions to the Jews, Inc., do hereby set the following policy.

A. *Under the present laws of Israel the American Board of Missions to the Jews is not permitted to send missionaries to Israel. It is, therefore, our policy to be a cooperating agency, not a sending agency.*

B. *The American Board of Missions to the Jews will actively cooperate and will actively seek the cooperation of every Christian agency witnessing in Israel, whose doctrinal beliefs and principles of practice agree with those set forth in the By-Laws of the American Board of Missions to the Jews.*

C. *Because of the tenuous situation of all missions in Israel we give highest priority in our program to strengthen and train the Hebrew Christians who now live in Israel. It is our hope and prayer, that if the Lord tarries, the indigenous church in Israel will soon be so strengthened and so well-trained in the Scriptures that it, empowered by the Holy Sprüt [sic], will maintain a strong, effective witness of the Gospel in the State of Israel.*

D. *The American Board of Missions to the Jews will encourage and train Hebrew Christians, especially those of unusual skills; such as, physicians, lawyers, teachers, etc.; to migrate to Israel under the laws of the state, to earn their own living in Israel in their chosen profession, and to join the testimony of the local church in its witness.*

E. *If, another eveangelical [sic] missionary agency decides to vacate its testimony in Israel, and the American Board* of Missions to the Jews, as the Lord provides, seeks to maintain the agency's witness, it is expressly understood

1. That the worker so aided will be a believer of the highest character whose testimony and doctrinal beliefs concur with the standards of the American Board of Missions to the Jews.
2. That the salary of the worker will be on a level of similar workers who are citizens and residents of Israel.
3. That the worker maintain the standards and discipline of the American Board of Missions to the Jews.
4. The maintaining of any particular witness does not necessarily entail the purchase of any property. Every property so offered shall be considered on its own merits and must be evaluated on the overall program of the American Board of Missions to the Jews.
5. The General Secretary of the American Board of Missions to the Jews shall regularly report to the Board of Directors concerning all such opportunities to contiue [sic] the work of any agency. All arrangements shall be made with the express understanding and concurrence with the agency vacating the field. The Board of Directors of the American Board of Missions to the Jews must approve the hiring of any workers recruited under the terms of this policy.[70]

The reason for this policy, which is self-explanatory, becomes immediately clear. Dr. A. Michelson, founder of the Los Angeles Hebrew-Christian Witness to Israel (Ed. of the Jewish Hope Magazine) had passed away. His daughters, who had taken over the work, had decided to close their branches of ministry in Israel, Greece, and France. The Minutes show the following action taken.

...Mr. Fuchs reported that two of the missionaries who had been working for Dr. Michelson are available for service with the American Board. Mr. Jacob Goren, who is well known to Mr. Fuchs, is in Jerusalem, and the missionary in Athens is recommended by Mr. Zodiates of the American Mission to the Greeks. After discussion, Mr. Fuchs moved and Mr. Ivins seconded the motion that we employ Mr. Jacob Goren in Israel and the missionary in Athens, Greece (to be supervised by the American Mission to the Greeks). Mr. Goren's salary is be adjusted in accordance with our Statement of Policy in Israel,...[71]

JACOB AND LEAH GOREN — THEIR STORY

The story of Jacob and Leah Goren begins in Poland. Jacob's family name was Gorfinkel—a name he shortened when he and his wife, Leah, immigrated to Israel. In sharing his testimony, Jacob wrote:

My first contact with Christianity goes back to my childhood days. I was born in a little Polish town near Warsaw in 1915. My parents were Jews by name, but they despised all religions. I was sent to public school and my parents did not oppose my attending classes in religion, directed by a Roman Catholic priest. Another Jewish boy also attended these classes and I recall that one day the Gentile boys protested our presence. They said, 'We are Christians, we don't want Jews to study our religion with us.' At that time I knew already a little bit about Christianity and I said: 'But why not? Doesn't Jesus belong to us also? Wasn't He a Jew?' Thus the matter ended.

When I reached the age of 14, my parents sent me to Warsaw to continue my studies. Here I came in touch with the Halutzim—the Pioneers of the Zionist Movement. I was convinced of the rightness of their purpose and joined their ranks. However I soon lost my enthusiasm, for God must have already planted a different longing in my restless soul.

The deep yearning of my heart was soon to be fulfilled. A friend of mine whom I visited who belonged to the same Pioneer movement, told me that he was occasionally attending the meetings of the Mission branch in Warsaw [a work directed by Mr. and Mrs. Moses Gitlin, whose ministry will be covered in greater detail at a later point in this history]. I was restless and curious so I joined him and others and went to the meeting.

The message of the Gospel answered the yearnings of my heart. I was gripped by a new joy of fulfilled longing. I therefore took the matter seriously and began to think deeper about the messages from the Word. The decisive day for me was December 31, 1936. On that evening the Jewish Christians of Warsaw had a united New Year's service. They sang the customary Yiddish and Polish gospel hymns. Then the Scriptures were read and many of the Jewish believers rose to their feet to tell of their salvation through the Lord Jesus the Messiah and Savior of their soul. No human being urged me to do so, but my heart was open to the Holy Spirit of God and it was surely He who moved my heart and feet to go forward, to stand before the people and declare that I too had come to know the Lord Jesus to be my Messiah and my personal Savior and that the new birth had begun in my life.[72]

Shortly after Jacob came to faith in Yeshua, Moses and Clara Gitlin led a young girl by the name of Leah to the Lord. The Gitlins faithfully taught the Word of God to Jacob and to Leah, and in many ways they became spiritual parents to the young believers. By 1939, when Moses and Clara Gitlin were forced to leave their ministry in Poland and move to the United States, they turned the oversight of their ministry over to Jacob and Leah. Clara Gitlin wrote:

> Closest of all, however, clings to us our dear spiritual child Leah. She came to us at the beginning of 1937, was converted and till this day worked in our house as a servant girl. Beside her is Bro. Jacob Gorfinkiel [sic] [Goren] who was converted in our home a few months before Leah. He was helped by our Mission Board through the Warsaw Bible School where Mr. Gitlin taught. This couple have just married and are undertaking to carry on the work in our place.[73]

When the war escalated to the point that it was no longer possible for Jacob and Leah to maintain the ministry in Poland, they fled to the East and lived in Russia until 1946. During their years in Russia, they did what they could to minister to the physical and spiritual needs of their Jewish brethren; their family was also enlarged by the births of two daughters. In 1948 the opportunity came for them to immigrate to Israel. Leah shared her memories of those days:

> …In spite of the fact that we had opportunities to go to other countries, we had survived the Holocaust and therefore felt that our place was in Israel.
>
> We felt that we had to build the country; the metropolitan city of Tel Aviv was then only a village. We also wanted to make our living 'by the sweat of our brow,' desiring that our testimony to our countrymen be most effective.
>
> Both desires were very difficult. For, though we worked very hard, there were days when we and our children were hungry, without enough bread to eat. In the minds of our brethren in the flesh, we were traitors to our people.
>
> Slowly, the Lord helped us to win the trust of some and they stopped thinking of us as traitors and started thinking of us simply as crazy people.
>
> Often I thank and praise the Lord for the strength He gave us to ignore the humiliation and continue to plant those seeds, with dreams that they would grow for His glory.…
>
> When we arrived in Israel, there were very few believers, and those that existed were spread out in different congregations led by foreign leaders.[74]

Jacob and Leah struggled to maintain their testimony and witness within the Jewish communities of Israel, but by 1952 Jacob realized that the call God had placed upon them to be missionaries in Israel necessitated their working under a Mission agency. In 1954 he resigned from his job so that he and Leah could conduct a home for Jewish children in connection with Dr. A. Michelson's work. They faithfully ministered the Gospel with that organization until its outreach in Israel was phased out in 1969. At that time, The American Board of Missions to the Jews (C.P.M.) picked up their support.

When the Directors of the Mission agreed to hire the Gorens, they were very much interested in purchasing the property of Dr. Michelson's work as well. Daniel Fuchs and this author, who held the position of Missionary Director of ABMJ at the time, met with the Michelson family to discuss the possibility of purchasing their property in Israel—at a reasonable cost, and in accordance with the Board's policy on property in Israel. However, Israeli government regulations, along with other difficulties, ended those negotiations and, once again, the Mission undertook the difficult task of locating housing in Israel for its workers there. Prayer was answered when a lovely apartment in Jerusalem became available for purchase. As in the case of the Haifa property, the apartment, purchased in the name of Daniel Fuchs, served as a place where the Gorens lived and from which they carried on their ministry.

Joseph Alkahe—His Story

At about the same time that the Gorens came on staff, Mr. Fuchs came into contact with another Jewish believer in Tel Aviv, Israel whom he felt would make an excellent worker—Dr. Joseph Alkahe. Dr. Alkahe was a lawyer who held a degree in theology from the University at Zurich, as well as a doctorate in law from the University in Rome. His struggle to come to faith in Yeshua began shortly after he graduated from law school. Relating his story, he said:

> Inferior.…I was an Italian, my own country now legally classified me as 'racially inferior.' Even though I was a recent graduate from law school, I was forbidden to practice my profession. Why? Because I had been 'yellow tagged' as a Jew—it was the yellow badge of shame pinned to my chest. I stared at it in disbelief.
>
> To understand the road that led me to Jesus, one must first remember that crazy world where Nazism was coming to the zenith of its power: My beloved homeland was bleeding under the heel of Hitler and Mussolini, and I began my quest for personal freedom in a world at the end of its tether.
>
> Amidst the numerous absurdities surrounding me, I was longing for freedom. Finally, I took the fateful, frightful

step to leave Italy and resettle in Palestine. Here, in my Jewish homeland, I found a brave, new world. One which I would help to build....In my brave new world, I could also seek the God who was mighty to save—for to me, He was evident in this ancient land. His existence seemed daily evidenced as I saw the swamps turned into productive land, and wasteland into groves and orchards.

My very life was devoted to fighting for that which was meaningful to me. I was living on a kibbutz (communal settlement) to help build a future with my fellow Zionists. I served in the British Army during World War II, defending my new homeland against repeated invasions. Yet, for all my fighting and struggling the goal of peace seemed no closer. A permanent state of war seemed to blunt human sensitivity to injustice and suffering. Even within Israel, though we struggled toward the same dream, I saw tensions which fostered internal discord.

I saw that our common religion was not enough to unify us. Various beliefs, nationalities, and cultures within the religion seemed to create storm centers for disharmony, rather than peace. But still, I longed for peace, for a deeper freedom, even though the world, my nation, and people all around me lacked these qualities.

For years I wrestled and meditated on the matter, all the while wondering...where was this peace? Where was this freedom?

I seriously studied the Bible—for the first time, both the Old and the New Testaments. Finally, I even started to meet with various Christian groups. This was no small step to a man who had clung to his religion through the era of Hitler, a move to Israel and the tumultuous days of the early State. I found in these small groups of people who loved Christ, no betrayal of that which I believed.

'Perhaps,' I thought, 'religion and culture are not what I should cling to. Perhaps, instead of the religion of Israel, I should seek the God of Israel.'

Yes, I found a message of love and of peace. A message of Jesus, the Jew, the Son of God, the Messiah....

Peace, security, and freedom flowed to me from the heartbeat of Jesus' love and His death for me, as I accepted Jesus as my Lord, amidst a world at the end of its tether.[75]

As Joseph Alkahe grew in his faith, he felt the call of God on his life to serve his Messiah in full-time ministry and, like many believers in Israel, he soon found himself thrust into leadership roles within the Messianic community. For a number of years (prior to 1970) he served as the pastor of a small church in the suburbs of Tel Aviv, but the denomination under which he served believed that the promises of God to Israel had been transferred to the church—a belief that put Alkahe in an awkward position, so he resigned and made application to the Mission. In his correspondence with Mr. Fuchs, Joseph Alkahe presented a report of his work. Some of the ideas mentioned reflect, in part, the formative stages of the Messianic congregation movement in Israel. He said:

1. *After my resignation from the congregation, weekly prayer meetings have been held in my home, with friends and neighbors participating in numbers varying from twenty-nine to forty-eight. Since last November I have moved to other living quarters, which are less centrally located and less suitable to such prayer meetings than my former home, these have been more recently held in different homes according to an agreed schedule.*

2. *I have been for some time engaged in an active visitation program covering a wider area. It is my firm conviction that the time is ripe for the formation and gathering of local congregations within a close range of their members' homes, so that each neighborhood has a central location for local assemblies. This method is substantially that adopted by Paul during his journeys, when he visited first the local synagogue and talked there to those open to his message. This is as sound a strategy today as it was then. Many people are alive to the meaning and the call of a newly-won freedom which extends to every sphere of life, and primarily to the religious principles of life itself.*

3. *Once treading this narrow, but well-chartered path, the need will arise, at a certain stage of development, to secure a suitable place to meet and pray together. Each local congregation should, in my view, be self-supporting from its inception. All the members should pledge themselves to defray the expenses involved in their religious activities. Provision should be made also for a central or associational fund to help toward meeting expenses connected with the first needs of any rising community (such as leasing a prayerhouse, buying chairs or other equipment, etc.), or with inter-group assistance to guide and promote local growth.*[76]

The Board was delighted with the Mission's new staff of workers and branches in Israel—Jacob and Leah Goren in Jerusalem; Mr. and Mrs. Joseph Alkahe in Tel Aviv; Mr. and Mrs. Peter Gutkind in Haifa. The Mission was also working closely with Mr. Victor Smadja, a Jewish believer who had established a publishing company in Israel called 'Ya'netz Press.'

Jewish believers in Israel were hard pressed to find employment. They were harassed and discriminated against on every hand when seeking employment through normal channels. On the other hand, if they were employed as missionaries by "foreign" mission organizations, other Israelis looked upon them with great disdain. Mr. Smadja's publishing company provided Jewish believers with legitimate employment, and demonstrated that believers in Israel were not dependent upon income earned from "missionary" groups to sustain their lives in Israel. (It is not within the purview of this history to tell the story of Victor Smadja and Ya'netz Press, and all that Mr. Smadja has done to assist, shape, and develop the Messianic movement in Israel. Perhaps, one day, a history on ministries and businesses such as Ya'netz Press will be written.)

Working with Mr. Smadja and Ya'netz Press was in keeping with the policy established by the Board for the Mission's work in Israel. Daniel Fuchs wrote:

> *...(Readers of The Chosen People will remember that two years ago [c.1969] we provided an offset camera for Mr. Smadja which our Rev. Burl Haynie [staff worker in charge of printing department for ABMJ/CPM in New York] installed.) This year the Hebrew edition of the Jewish Art Calendar is being printed in Jerusalem by Mr. Smadja; because last year it was printed in Indiana and not only was some of the information in English, but the times for the lighting of the candles, etc., was in American-city time. Now it is being printed entirely in Hebrew and in Israel time. An edition of 20,000 is being printed in four colors, the same as our other editions; and it will be offered over radio, and in newspaper ads and already a large mailing list has been prepared. So far as we know, this is the only Gospel literature that Israeli's actually ask for.*[77]

MARY ANN SLEICHTER—HER STORY

At the January 1970 Board of Directors meeting, Daniel presented one additional experimental missionary program for Israel—an apprentice program—unanimously adopted by the directors. He outlined the program as follows:

> *...under which a missionary between the ages of 21 and 30 who has been on our staff for two years and who agrees to remain with us for two more years, and who wishes to study in Israel for a year at his own expense, may be placed on half salary for the year in Israel.*[78]

The first candidate for the new apprentice program was a young girl who qualified for the program and who seemed to be the candidate around which the program was built. Her name was Mary Ann Sleichter.

Mary Ann was raised in a Christian home, although the family had its church membership in a liberal denomination. When Mary Ann was still in high school, her mother, who was an accomplished organist, asked Mary Ann if she would accompany her to a local Bible church where she had been asked to play for their services. Mary Ann agreed to go. As the pastor presented his message on the book of Revelation, Mary Ann, who had never heard anything like that before, found that she was fascinated. After that service she began attending the Bible church on a regular basis and it wasn't long before she accepted Jesus as her Savior.

As Mary Ann approached college age, she had not actually dedicated herself to full-time Christian service, but she did have a desire to go to a Christian college. The Lord led her to Cedarville College. There she became acquainted with Arnold Fruchtenbaum, a young Jewish student who had accepted Yeshua through the work of the Mission (more about Arnold Fruchtenbaum and how God used his life and ministry will be given in a later chapter of this history). Through her friendship with Arnold, Mary Ann first learned of the role of the Jewish people in God's redemptive program, and of the responsibility of believers to share the Gospel with Jewish people.

In her sophomore year at Cedarville, Mary Ann experienced the call of God upon her life, and she dedicated herself to serve Him as a missionary to the Jewish people. After her graduation from Cedarville in June 1968, she applied to the Mission for work in the camping programs and in the Daily Vacation Bible School at Coney Island.[79] She then entered the six-month training program conducted by the Mission in New York City, and soon became an experienced personal worker and soul-winner for the Lord.

Mary Ann's musical ability and friendly out-going spirit drew young people to her like bears are drawn to honey. It was an era of the "hippie movement" and of "coffee-houses." Young people were looking for answers to life; Jewish young people were rebelling against traditional family and religious life, and Mary Ann was an asset to the Mission's staff as it sought for "unorthodox" ways in which to present a Gospel witness to Jewish and Gentile young people who were caught up in the spirit of the times.

Mary Ann had a special burden for Israel and for the Jewish young people living there. She was delighted when she was told that the Board had approved an "Israel Apprentice Program"—a program in which she was the sole apprentice. Thus, in 1970, Mary Ann Sleichter found herself living and working for the Mission in Jerusalem, Israel. Daniel Fuchs shared information about the Board's new experiment in Israel with the readers of *The Chosen People* magazine, stating:

The Gorens were thrilled with a new experiment we started last year. One of our new workers, Mary Ann Sleichter, paid her own fare to Israel and registered at Hebrew University. We supported her at $200 a month (adequate for living expenses in Israel). Mary Ann has a vivacious personality, plays the guitar, and readily makes friends. Originally it was planned that she would work with the local assembly [Messianic congregation in Jerusalem] in its witness....

Jerusalem is a small city (250,000) and students do not have too many means of recreation. A coffeehouse ministry has been started: Mary Ann with her guitar, college-trained young people who know how to witness, the only place in Jerusalem where one can get a good 25-agorot (about 8 cents) cup of coffee. Saturday nights the place has been filled.

...Your Board has approved the recommendation that we immediately seek to recruit a team of ten concerned Christians who would like to spend a year studying and witnessing in Jerusalem. The cost of the year including travel would approximately be the same as one year of college in the U.S.A. These young people could raise support for this project from their churches. The function of the A.B.M.J. would be recruiting, selection, and training.[80]

While the program sounded exciting, it was not successful. Not only did the Mission have difficulty recruiting students to participate, there was growing hostility in Israel about Christian students coming into the country to evangelize. Jewish believers in Israel also complained that they were left to bear the brunt of such evangelism long after the students left.

Following her year in Israel, Mary Ann Sleichter returned to New York (1972).[81] As she continued her ministry, she decided to change her name from Mary Ann to Miriam, and she moved to California to assist in the Mission's outreach in San Francisco. There, she met (and eventually married) a young Jewish believer who had recently come to faith in Yeshua. He was a student at Simpson Bible College. His name was Sam Nadler. The story of how God continued to use Miriam and Sam Nadler will be expanded upon as the history of Chosen People Ministries unfolds.

CONTINUING THE WITNESS IN ISRAEL

In Israel, the Gospel message continued to go out to the Israelis through the radio ministry and through the faithful testimony and outreach of the Alkahes, the Gorens, and the Gutkinds. The Mission encouraged each couple to work through established Messianic congregations, or to establish new congregations. Jacob and Leah Goren became active in the Jerusalem Assembly. Jacob served as an elder, while Leah worked with the women and children. Leah wrote about those years of transition. She spoke of the changes that took place going from "colonial" methodology which imported western Christian culture, to "indigenous" methodology that utilized Jewish and Israeli culture to teach an indigenous Christianity to the Jewish people of Israel.

Through the "Israel policy" which the Board had adopted, true cross-cultural missionary work was finally taking place in Israel. Messianic congregations that were self-supporting, self-governing local churches, utilizing Jewish and Israeli culture could finally be established in Israel, without interference from an outside Mission board. Leah wrote:

...As the Lord multiplied the brethren, He caused me to dream further...to dream of making the testimony more effective and creating Hebrew congregations that would be led by Hebrew Christians. I believed it was very important that the Word of God be preached in Hebrew, so that our brethren coming into the congregation would see that he was among his own and hear the Word of God as he used to hear it in cheder (religious school). By His grace, this part of the dream has also been realized.[82]

The Lord called Jacob Goren into His presence on November 10, 1981; Leah continued to faithfully serve on the staff of the Mission until her retirement in 1988. She continues to live in the apartment that the Mission provided for them, and she is still active in the Messianic Assembly in Jerusalem and in personal witness and visitation to her many Jewish friends and neighbors.

As for Peter Gutkind, he continued his ministry in Haifa until his retirement in 1972.[83] Following his retirement, the Mission sold the apartment in which the Gutkinds had been living in order to purchase Mission property for Joseph Alkahe. A smaller, less expensive apartment was secured for the Gutkinds. Peter is now in his nineties; he lives in an old age home in Haifa. In his correspondence he tells of his continuing witness there.

Joseph Alkahe wanted to pursue the program which he had outlined to Daniel Fuchs and the Board, but his plans did not materialize. As local Messianic congregations developed in Israel, they remained independent of one another. Additionally, as the years passed, Mr. Alkahe's doctrinal position seems to have changed. His emphasis in ministry turned more toward the Zionist doctrine of developing the land as a means of ushering in the Messianic age, and less toward the need for individual belief in the deity of Yeshua and of His work of redemption at Calvary. In 1981 the Board voted not to continue support of Joseph Alkahe.[84]

The retirement of Peter Gutkind essentially closed the outreach in Haifa; the decision to no longer support the ministry of Joseph Alkahe closed the work in Tel Aviv; the sudden death of Jacob Goren was a blow to the outreach in Jerusalem. In a matter of months, the Mission's outreach in Israel was severely limited—but a witness did continued through the radio ministry, through Leah Goren's continued work, through the Mission's involvement in several institute programs in Israel, and, later, through a tour ministry that was developed.

The purpose of the "See Israel Through Jewish Eyes" tour ministry was two-fold. It gave Jewish and Gentile Christians an opportunity to tour Israel with a group that was doing more than just seeing the traditional Christian sights in the land and, as the tour members participated in love offerings that were taken and then donated to various relief projects in Israel, the tours opened new doors of witness and involvement for the Mission. The love gifts from the tour groups were given to hospitals, youth centers, etc., with the clear understanding that they were being given in the name of the Messiah, Yeshua.

The contributions made by the "See Israel Through Jewish Eyes" tour groups made the tours visible. That, in turn, opened the door for contact with rabbis and with Israeli government officials who were involved in tourism, education, immigration, etc. They, and other Israelis, saw the donations as "good deeds" (faith put into action). The tour ministry of the Mission has thereby functioned as a "good-will ambassador" in Israel even though there has been a clear understanding that the purpose and work of the Mission is to share the Gospel with the Jewish people.

The concept, "See Israel through Jewish Eyes," was initiated and developed by the author and Mr. Gary Selman, a Jewish believer from New Jersey whose thirst for an understanding of the Word of God seemed unquenchable, and whose zeal for sharing the Gospel with Jewish people made him fearless in his witness. The Mission's headquarters office was near his home, and in the months just after he came to faith in Yeshua he often stopped to spend the early morning hours studying the Scriptures with the author, or to research Jewish sources for references to the Messiah. But he did not just take the Word in, he frequently called later in the day to share the good news of someone he had led to the Lord.

Gary's "Jewishness," his high energy level, and his love of sharing the Gospel with Jewish people made him a great asset as plans for the Mission's unique tour ministry were developed and then initiated. For a number of years he served as the Tour Director. His involvement not only increased his growth in the Messiah, it also increased the Mission's outreach into the Jewish community, both within the United States and in Israel. On one tour Gary asked if the author would baptize him in the Jordan River; he wanted his baptism to serve as a testimony to Israeli friends.

As the years went by, and as Gary's faith grew, he became more and more involved in the establishment of a Messianic congregation in New Jersey, and in a radio broadcast in the New York/New Jersey area called "Two Jewish Boys." He continues in these ministries, and God has blessed him in each one.

Once the Board decided to discontinue support of Joseph Alkahe, the building the Mission had purchased for his ministry was sold. The funds from the sale of the building were invested in Israel. In 1988 the Board gave the author permission to use a portion of those funds to produce three documentary videos centering around different aspects and questions of the Messiah. The videos, "The Messiah," "Armageddon—The Return of the Messiah," and "The Temple at Jerusalem" are still being sold in book stores and retail outlets throughout Israel.

Avner Boskey—His Story

In May 1988, after seven years without a full-time worker in Israel, the Lord opened the door for the Mission to hire Mr. Avner Boskey, a graduate of Dallas Theological Seminary.[85] Avner had worked as a missionary with Ariel Ministries while he was a student at Dallas Theological Seminary (the story of Ariel Ministries and its founder, Arnold Fruchtenbaum will be given later in this history), and shortly after his graduation from seminary he and his wife, Rachel, immigrated to Israel. They purchased an apartment in the suburbs of Jerusalem, and continued their work with Ariel Ministries, as well as becoming actively involved in the Messianic Assembly in Jerusalem.

Avner also took the Israeli government's required courses which trained him to become a licensed tour guide, but he soon learned that guiding did not offer him the income or the opportunities for ministry that he thought it would. He longed to do more ministry; it was that longing which prompted him to contact the Mission, stating his desire to serve as a missionary and inquiring if the Mission would be willing to meet the financial support he needed to keep his family in Israel. The Board received Avner's request as a direct answer to prayer! New workers were needed in Israel, and the fact that the Boskey's were already Israeli citizens met the Board's policy regarding the hiring of workers for Israel.

Avner Boskey grew up in Montreal, Quebec, Canada—a city with a thriving Yiddish speaking Jewish community. As a child, he attended the Jewish Peretz School where his mother was a teacher. Like many people in Montreal, Avner became multi-lingual. He studied English, French, Yiddish and Hebrew. As he approached the age of thirteen, and began preparing for Bar Mitzvah, he had many questions which the rabbis and his teachers could not answer—questions about justice, oppression, and the ultimate purpose of life.

Avner's parents were both raised as orthodox Jews, but in their teens each had made a conscious decision to abandon the Jewish lifestyle and belief system. His father had served as a cantor at one time in his life, but he had decided that he could not sing about, or put his faith in, a God who allowed for so much social injustice to exist in society. He had concluded that God was dead! Destitute of faith in God, Avner's parents were persuaded that the answers to man's problems—to oppression and social injustice—lay in the political transformation of society. They believed that only through the redistribution of wealth, through the protection of the rights of the common man, and through fighting social hypocrisy, could the world be made a better place in which to live.

Enamored by the belief system and values of his parents, Avner determined to follow in their footsteps. He enrolled at McGill University with a major in political science. His goal was to learn how to transform society through politics. Of this university experience Avner wrote:

> It did not take me long to come to a shocking realization: though my professors and political heroes alike were convinced that their political theories, if applied, would create a brave new world and transform all human relationships, they themselves were still unchanged people, trapped by greed, suspicions and jealousies.
>
> Their own philosophies had proven powerless to change their own lives—how could they believe that others would be transformed? I did not believe that I could trust my teachers with my own life 'come the revolution,' nor would I continue to do it now. I had learned an important lesson: society and its institutions cannot be changed from the outside in, merely by manipulating social and economic forces. On the contrary, a changed society can only result from changed individuals![86]

During the late 1960's, when many young people were exploring Eastern mystical solutions as the answers to life, Avner was swept away in the tidal wave of such teachings. With the eager curiosity of a child set free in a toy store, he set out to explore and to examine every spiritual alternative that came his way. Eager to experience the 'spirit world' for himself, he dove into the worlds of Alan Watts, Lobsang Rampa, TM, Guru Maharaji, macrobiotics, Kundalini yoga, LSD. As a statement of his free thinking, he wore his hair in a long pony tail and he dropped in weight to 145 pounds. (Avner is 6'1"!) For six long months he forced himself to remain in a basement apartment as he sought peace and the answers to life, only allowing himself to come out of the apartment long enough for a midnight stroll. In his own words he stated:

> Yet, with sadness I noted that all of my gurus and 'masters' were still struggling with the same base motives that had troubled my political science professors. The more deeply I concentrated on the inner light or meditated on universal or cosmic energy, the more I saw that my spiritual innards were indeed in a terrible state.
>
> By the end of this four-year process, I had come to the same conclusions as had Jeremiah the Hebrew prophet…'The heart is more deceitful than all else and is desperately sick; who can understand it?' (Jeremiah 17:9). I had learned a second important lesson: man is not able to solve his internal problems by himself—though his essential nature needs changing, he is powerless to bring about that change.
>
> Toward the close of this period I met a former Texan who called himself 'Ebony.' He was involved in Satanism, and told me that he had encounters with powerful spiritual forces belonging to Lucifer.
>
> Through contact with him I, too began to discover a hidden world of great power and mystery. For the first time in my life I was having powerful encounters with supernatural forces, many of them quite frightening. I realized a third spiritual lesson: not everything in the spiritual realm is friendly or good: there are also spiritual forces of great power and wickedness…
>
> This realization caused me to ask…since Satan and his power were all too real, could it be that God Almighty, the God of the Bible, also exits?…
>
> At that time I was working as an assistant production manager of a plastics company. The office manager was a likeable Dutch fellow named Nick Swart.…
>
> He told me some astounding news—that he had a personal relationship with God. There was no pride in his voice when he communicated that, and I could see that Nick was not perfect. But that presence of something in his life kept drawing me back to listen. And I knew inside that I deeply wanted such a personal relationship with God. Could it really be possible?…
>
> Nick prayed privately for my salvation. I began to read the Gospel accounts of Yeshua and His ministry. The truth of Yeshua's words penetrated to the depths of my heart;…
>
> I was traveling on a bus on my way to work when I decided to pray. Hesitant, I spoke to God in silent prayer: 'If

it's true that You exist, and that You truly are Lord of the universe, then I must be Your enemy. For twenty-odd years I have ignored You, used Your name as a curse, laughed in Your face. And yet in spite of this You seem to love me, and want me to have a personal relationship with You. If this is all true, If Yeshua is indeed my atonement and my Messiah, if You're listening to me now, then please: forgive my sins, come into my life and make me Your child.'

Immediately, personally, and in a way simultaneously both powerful and tender, God poured His Spirit into my soul, opened my eyes spiritually and gave me new life....

My calling is to proclaim Messiah Yeshua to His chosen people, to let Israelis know that a personal relationship with God is free for the asking, thanks to Yeshua's atoning death and resurrection. [87]

After joining the staff of the Mission, Avner revealed that he felt led of the Lord to establish a new Messianic congregation in the town of K'far Saba, a suburb of Tel Aviv. The remaining invested funds from the sale of Dr. Joseph Alkahe's apartment, along with additional monies, were used to purchase an apartment for the Boskey family in K'far Saba, and Avner began the task of developing the ministry God had laid on his heart. He worked with other Jewish believers, realizing that a cooperative effort between the various ministries in Israel would accomplish far more for the Lord than the efforts of a single congregation, mission agency, or evangelistic team. He also served on a number of committees and councils in Israel. Reporting on his ministry and on the joint activities of the Messianic believers in Israel, Avner wrote:

For the past five years the National Evangelism Committee has planned and spearheaded evangelistic outreaches in Israel with national participation....

Its members are active in planning and carrying out evangelism to the people of Israel, and bring with them many years of evangelistic experience. This group has directed outreaches in Tel Aviv and Haifa, and is working on the development of educational materials which will equip believers around the country for more effective outreach.

These evangelistic campaigns draw on a wide variety of Jewish and Gentile believers from across the spectrum in Israel, Eilat, Tiberias and Nahariya, Jerusalem, Tel Aviv and the Galilee—all contribute time and prayers to these endeavors.

The fellowship and evangelistic joy which characterize these times of outreach are most striking. I have had the privilege of helping to lead some of these campaigns over the past few years and can personally express my own joy to be part of such a national cooperative effort.

What happens during a typical campaign? About 20 believers gather for training in evangelistic techniques, legal rights of the believer in Israel, how to deal with opposition, street discipline, the strategic importance of prayer, etc. Then they don T-shirts emblazoned with logos like 'There is a Messiah Now!,' 'Yeshua is the Messiah,' or 'Messianic Jews.' With tract bags full of Bible portions, Messianic literature, and tracts in Hebrew, Arabic, and Russian, they depart three to four times a day for pre-arranged sites on street corners and beaches.

As they hand out literature to passers-by they're always prepared to present a reason for the hope that lies within them, yet with gentleness and reverence (1 Peter 3:15).

An outreach like this usually lasts a number of days, during which time tens of thousands of tracts and hundreds of Scripture portions are distributed. Hundreds of in-depth Gospel presentations are given, addresses of interested people are collected for follow-up, and Jews and Arabs are even led to pray the sinner's prayer right on the streets of Israel's busy cities.

Our outreach in September (1990) saw up to 40 people out on the streets of Haifa, with good participation from represented congregations.

Jewish and Arab believers went out together to evangelize, some to Haifa's Arab areas, but most to its Jewish majority. Some teams went down toward the harbor, where drug addicts and prostitutes converge. Others went to the commercial and office areas; still others to entertainment spots or beaches.

Approximately 17,000 tracts were handed out, many of them on the theme of Rosh Hashanah (the Jewish New Year). This tract raises the question: 'How Does One Know That One's Sins Really Are Forgiven During The High Holiday?'

An additional 471 pieces of follow-up Messianic literature were distributed to those curious people who questioned us about our beliefs; 289 Scripture portions or Bibles were also handed out. In one touching scene, a Russian Jewish immigrant who had been in Israel for less than 24 hours could not believe that he was being given a free Bible by a Jewish believer in Jesus.

His eyes widened with amazement—to think that here in Israel Bibles can be distributed freely on the street! Truly Israel must be a country which values religious liberty, he thought.

Our ministry to newly-arrived Russian Jews was bolstered immeasurably by Albert Davis [Israeli]. Albert, a Jewish believer of Russian background who heads up Chosen People Ministries' Russian work in Toronto, Canada, translated one of our tracts into Russian. He was in his element here, sharing the Gospel with scores of Russian Jewish immigrants 'right off the boat,' both individuals and families.

Six people (including two Russian Jewish immigrants) prayed to receive Messiah Jesus' atonement for their sins. We thank God for this time of planting and harvesting.[88]

The fact that Albert Davis (he is now using his given surname, Israeli) was in Israel for the campaign was not only a blessing to Avner and to the ministry, it was also a precursor of things to come. Toward the end of 1990 Avner Boskey informed the Mission that he had embraced the teachings of John Wember (a charismatic signs and wonders movement that began in the United States several years earlier). His desire to teach the Wember beliefs within the congregations in Israel began to create problems with many of the other workers there. Additionally, the Boskey's had received word of the severe illness of members of Rachel's family in the United States, and they were dealing with the serious health problems of one of their own children. They therefore decided to return to America where they would have opportunity to be with their respective family members, as well as have time to study their positions further regarding the Wember Movement.

Reluctantly, the Board accepted the resignation of the Avner and Rachael Boskey, praying that one day God will again lead them to Israel and that once again they will be led to work for Chosen People Ministries.

As the Boskey's prepared to leave the ministry and their friends in Israel, God was preparing new workers to stand in the gap—workers who were already thoroughly prepared for ministry there, since both had lived in Israel as teenagers; they were not going to a foreign land, they were going "home."

ALBERT AND GRETTA ISRAELI—THEIR STORY

Albert and Gretta Davis (Israeli) were hired by the Mission in June 1987, in spite of the fact that the Mission had a moratorium on hiring new workers. The Board had passed a resolution that the budget *must* be balanced, but the doors to Russia were just beginning to open and when the staff and the Directors heard Albert's testimony they all agreed that, in his case, the moratorium should be lifted. The Mission wanted to be on the "cutting edge" of the new opportunity to reach Soviet Jews with the Gospel, and Albert was just the worker needed! The moratorium was therefore lifted, and Albert was hired to do missionary work and to hold Bible study classes among the Russian Jews in Toronto, Canada. He also agreed to produce a Russian radio broadcast for the Mission—a broadcast that was to be beamed into the Soviet Union, directed toward the Jewish people living there. (Additional information about Albert and Gretta's ministry in Canada will be shared in the chapter devoted to the expansion of the Mission in Canada.)

Albert Israeli (the surname was changed to Davis when Albert's father moved his family to Canada in 1977) was born into a family of very observant, traditional Jews who lived in Georgia, in the Soviet Union. Albert was thirteen years of age when his family, including his grandparents, immigrated to Israel. He tells his story in this way:

To some it seems a surprise that a Jewish family could live as Jews in the Soviet Union. I think this is because few people understand that the Soviet Union is actually fifteen separate countries, and even though communism is the only officially recognized 'religion' in any of the countries, the enforcement greatly differs from place to place.

I lived in Georgia, which has a very old and established Jewish community. The Jews of Georgia have been there since the Babylonian captivity, and most families can trace their ancestry back for hundreds of years. There was no interference when we wanted to celebrate Jewish holidays or attend synagogue.

Because I attended public school, I was not a product of the old traditions, but was very modern and 'enlightened.' I knew there was no God, that science had disproved Him, and that He was mostly a myth invented by old men and capitalists to control others.

Although I had great love for my Orthodox grandparents and would do nothing disrespectful in their home, I thought I was much too smart to accept their empty traditions. Even when I was very young, I could see that their belief was in a heritage and not in a God....

In 1973, the year we arrived in Israel, was the Yom Kippur War. I had never seen so many planes and so much fighting before. In my kibbutz we were often wakened at night by the sound of artillery.

It was very, very, frightening to see so much death and danger....

Yet, despite the harsh impact of the war, I loved Israel. From the moment I arrived I felt something I never knew before: a true home.

I suffered no culture shock—perhaps being only thirteen helped—and I soon loved my new country. It was this love that made the war all the harder to bear.

It gave me a great sadness when, in 1975, my father decided we must leave. He didn't want his children growing up with the hardships and sadness this land held.

We went to Frankfurt, Germany, where we applied for visas to the United States. We were refused. Next we tried Canada, then Australia, New Zealand, and South Africa. But with no family and no money, we were refused everywhere.

The months were long and the worries great as we waited for more than two years, always with the fear that our temporary German visas would not be renewed and we would be without hope. Finally, in 1977 we received permission to immigrate to Canada.

It was in Canada that I met my wife [Gretta]. Her family had left the Ukraine, another section of the Soviet Union, and moved to Israel the same year mine had. Like us, they had been saddened at the facts in the Promised Land and had immigrated to Canada.

After we married, we lived among the Jewish community and had a Jewish home but my view of God never changed.

One time out of curiosity, I picked up a Bible. After reading the beginning chapters of Genesis I thought, 'How can people read this all their lives and not be bored?'

By 1984, though, many things were changing. I had decided to go to college, which I knew was going to be very difficult. Not only did I have a family to support, but I would have to pass a written English exam which was said to be very difficult.

At this same time I met a neighbor of mine, Alex Bonderevsky, who was also Russian. He told me he was a Jew who believed in Jesus.

All of a sudden my very atheistic, indifferent view of religion changed. How dare he believe that! Didn't he know that Jesus was for Christians, for people who liked to kneel in front of statues?

I found myself going back to Alex to argue with him. He gave me a Bible.

It was only two days away from my big English exam, but when I started to read the Bible, I could not stop. By the time I got to the end of Matthew, I loved this Messiah Jesus. I was involved with Him. The things He taught were so beautiful; I knew if I could live like that nothing would ever be the same.

Then, in Matthew 15 when He said He was sent to the lost sheep of the house of Israel, I knew He was sent for me. Although I wasn't sure what to do, I knew I believed.

I had done nothing about this when I went in to take my exam. When I opened the English portion of the test and looked at it, I knew I had no chance.

I started to close the book, feeling complete despair and resignation, when Jesus' words came to me, 'Ask and you shall receive.'

So I prayed to God to help me with the exam and promised Him I would study all summer so that my English would be good enough by the time school started.

But I had no faith as I blindly answered the multiple-choice questions and even less hope when I tried to write an essay. I went home and told my wife, 'I have failed the test.'

I was very depressed over this and moped around the house. I had forgotten my love and desire for Jesus. Then two weeks later the school called to say congratulations, that I had been accepted.

I knew it was the hand of God. In the next week, even before I started to study English as I promised I would, I read the entire New Testament. I almost couldn't stop, not even to eat and sleep, so hungry was I for this message....

One night,...I heard a voice say, 'Get up and go to your bedroom.'

As I stood,...I knew I was in the presence of God....

I had never even prayed before, but there I was for almost forty minutes, talking to God....

Since that night, nothing has been the same. My wife and children also believe, and God has given us a burden to reach our Russian brethren with the Gospel.[89]

In the Spring of 1991, Albert and Gretta agreed to immigrate back to Israel so Albert could minister to the influx of Russian Jews who were pouring into the land. In Israel, Albert resumed using his original surname, "Israeli." Both Albert and Gretta were well prepared for the ministry in Israel since both were already Israeli citizens, and both spoke both Hebrew and Russian (as well as a few other languages, including English). The Mission's apartment in K'far Saba became their new home.

Albert's frequent trips to Russia and to East European countries prior to his family's move to Israel had brought him into contact with hundreds of Soviet Jews—Jews who are now immigrating to Israel. When asked why he wanted to move his family back to Israel, Albert replied:

> So many of the people I witnessed to in the Soviet Union are headed to Israel. They are, as are many others just like them, very open to the Lord, very curious, very eager to discover for themselves. Once they get to Israel, I want to be there and minister to them.[90]

Together with other believers in Israel, Albert and Greta have carried on a strong and vibrant work among the scores of Russian Jewish immigrants. Of this great opportunity, Albert wrote:

> ...I think there is a special movement of the Holy Spirit among the Jewish people right now. God has brought Soviet Jews out in massive numbers. He has prepared their hearts in unique ways. And there is something very important happening in Israel right now. I want to be a part of it.[91]

In the early 1920's, when the Jews were beginning to pour into Palestine to escape the scourge of hatred and persecution against them in Europe, Mr. Frank Boothby opened his little Gospel Gate Room because he believed God was preparing His people to hear His voice. Others, too, have shared his conviction that a Gospel witness must go forth to His people in their land. Indeed, Albert and Gretta Israeli and other workers of the Mission have been a part of this unique movement of God in Israel. To the glory of God, seventy five years after Frank Boothby opened his ministry, the Mission still continues to have an active witness to the Jewish people in Israel.

Networking in Europe

The closing of the doors for ministry in Russia in the early 1930's was a source of great disappointment to Joseph Cohn and to the Directors of the Mission. But Joseph was not a man who let the disappointments of one day undermine or squelch the opportunities of the next day! In May 1934, he reported to the Board that the International Hebrew Christian Alliance (an organization that was founded in Hamburg, Germany in 1925) would be holding their Triennial Convention in London during the latter part of July. He indicated that he felt it would be good for him to attend in order to re-establish a relationship with the various ministries and missionary workers in Europe. He also wished to visit some of the ministries that the Mission was already supporting. The Board approved Joseph's trip, with the reservation that he not visit Germany or Russia due to the danger and hostile feelings toward the Jews in those countries.[92]

Joseph's participation at the IHCA Triennial Convention not only enlarged his network of European pastors and Christian workers, it was a trip that sealed the plight of the refugee Jews to his heart and mind, and thereby initiated the Mission's expansion into Europe with a large relief ministry to refugee Jews who were fleeing war-torn Europe.

Sir Leon Levison served as the first President of the IHCA. As he led the organization, he made it clear that part of his concern was to see that the needs of Jewish Christian brethren were being met. The power and influence of the Nazis was increasing. Committees were being formed to protect the rights of Jewish people and the rights of Christian people, but Levison pointed out that none of the committees had representation from a Jewish-Christian. The result was that Jewish believers of Europe had no representation. The Jewish community claimed that Jewish believers were Christians, and therefore wanted nothing to do with them. The Christian community, on the other hand, claimed they were still Jews and likewise would not help. It was clear that except for organizations like the IHCA, or other concerned Jewish missions, Jewish-Christians of Europe stood alone.

Two other concerns under discussion at the IHCA meetings were matters that were close to Joseph Cohn's heart. One was the issue of Messianic churches. Joseph knew how much his father, Rabbi Leopold Cohn, had longed to see such congregations established and flourishing. The second, and perhaps more pressing topic under discussion, was the need for establishing a colony, either in Israel or elsewhere, for the thousands of Jewish believers who were fleeing the rising Nazi threat. These two pressing needs seemed to seal themselves to Joseph Cohn's heart.

At the convention Joseph was introduced to Pastor Arnold Frank, a founder-member of the IHCA. Pastor Frank was one of the leading evangelical Jewish believers in Germany. His church (a Jewish mission), established and funded by the Irish Presbyterian Church, was the place where many German Jews had come to know the Messiah. He was also the editor of a paper called *Zion's Freund* (Zion's Friend)—a paper he founded in 1899, and continued to edit until it was suppressed by the Nazis near the end of 1936. Zion's Freund reached into all parts of Europe, the U.K., and even into the United States; its circulation was nearly 40,000. The relationship between Arnold Frank and Joseph Cohn developed into a close friendship as the two men maintained correspondence and held meetings together over the years.

While he was in London, Joseph arranged to meet with Mr. Moses Gitlin—a Jewish believer who had come to know Yeshua under the ministry of Rabbi Leopold Cohn. Moses was baptized by Leopold Cohn,[93] and the Mission helped him attend Moody Bible Institute. After his training at Moody, Moses was sent to do missionary work in Poland. He then went to Russia as an evangelist under the auspices of *The Sunday School Times*. During his years of ministry in Europe, Mr. Gitlin also served with the American European Fellowship, and then with a Mr. Tetler. But the working relationship with Mr. Tetler was evidently an unsatisfactory one for Moses, due to the fact that Mr. Tetler wanted him to limit his ministry to the task of raising support rather than doing direct evangelism. But Gitlin, an evangelist known throughout Europe and Russia, who had led over thirty young Jewish men to Yeshua, wanted to continue sharing the Gospel with Jewish people.

Joseph Cohn and Moses Gitlin had maintained correspondence over the years, and from time to time the Mission had helped Moses financially. The Mission had also supplied him with copies of *The Shepherd of Israel* for use in his ministry. Occasionally news of Mr. Gitlin's work would appear in the pages of *The Chosen People* Magazine under headings such as the one in the October 1930 magazine, "From One of Our Boys in Poland."[94] When Joseph learned that Moses Gitlin wanted to leave the employ of Mr. Tetler, he saw it as an opportunity for the Mission to open a branch of ministry in Poland. He immediately offered him a position with the Mission, conditional upon ratification of the Board of Directors at their next meeting.[95] The Board approved the hiring of Moses Gitlin. They also approved the hiring of his assistant, Moses Schiff. The November 1934 issue of *The Chosen People* Magazine carried the full story of this new branch opening in Poland.[96] Moses Gitlin's reputation, and the reputation of his ministry, was impeccable. His long involvement with key evangelical ministries throughout Europe, and his articles that had been published in the prestigious *Sunday School Times*, opened many new contacts for the Mission.

HENRI VINCENT — THE PARIS MINISTRY

As the summer of 1935 approached, Joseph made plans to return to Europe. This trip included a stop in Paris, where he made arrangements to meet with a Mr. Henri Vincent. Once again, he returned home with a burning desire to expand the Mission's network in Europe and he asked the Board to consider establishing a new branch of the Mission in Paris. The Minutes show the following action taken:

> Mr. Cohn then asked the Board whether they are in favor of undertaking a small work in Paris. When Mr. Cohn was abroad last summer he contacted Pastor Henri Vincent who is the pastor of a Baptist Church in the Montparnasse section of Paris. Mr. Vincent is a very devoted Christian.
>
> One of the members of Pastor Vincent's church is a highly educated Jewish Christian woman who would be willing to translate suitably The Shepherd of Israel each month into French at no cost to us. We could therefore print a French edition of The Shepherd of Israel in Paris.
>
> Mr. Vincent has also met a fine Jewish Christian named Mr. Frankl, a French Jew, the story of whose conversion has been sent to us. He would be willing to distribute The Shepherd of Israel and begin a small work in Paris under our support.
>
> The expenses of such an undertaking would be about $115 a month; $75 as salary for Mr. Frankl, and $40 for the printing of the French edition of the Shepherd of Israel.
>
> [Motion carried to undertake an experimental work in Paris]...for a period of six months beginning February 15th.[97]

Joseph wasted no time in making the announcement of the new Paris branch within the pages of *The Chosen People* magazine. The story of the beginning of that branch is worth retelling, for its founder, Henri Vincent, remained a faithful and trusted partner in the Paris branch for over fifty-four years—until his death on November 4, 1990.

The beginning of the story goes back to the year 1911, when Joseph Cohn was first introduced to the name of a young Frenchman, Paul Vincent, who was studying at the Theological Seminary in Rochester, New York. The contact came through a Miss Bedley, a supporter of the Mission and also a student at the seminary. Miss Bedley told Joseph that if he was ever in Paris, he should look up Paul Vincent and his family because they had developed a large evangelical work in France and, perhaps, could be of help to the Mission. Joseph had completely forgotten about the matter until he was in Germany during the summer of 1935. That summer, he saw the thousands of Jewish refugees who were fleeing Germany, headed for France in an attempt to escape the hated Nazis. The refugees were hungry, haggard, and sad beyond description—forced to leave their homes and villages with only the clothes on their backs. Joseph's heart went out to them, and as he began to pray and to think about who he might know in France that could help the poor Jewish immigrants, the name "Vincent" came into his mind.

Although his itinerary did not officially include a visit to France, Joseph changed his plans immediately and headed for Paris. Once there, he began his search for anyone who knew a "Vincent" family. He learned that there was a Baptist church on Avenue du Maine, in the Montparnasse district of Paris. The pastor's name was Vincent. With that information in hand, he telephoned the church and asked to speak with Paul Vincent. But the individual who answered the telephone responded that Paul Vincent had been drafted into the army and had never returned. The individual informed Joseph that he was Paul Vincent's younger brother, Henri Vincent. Joseph persuaded Henri to meet him at his hotel, to discuss what could be done in the name of Yeshua to help the Jewish refugees who were pouring into the city of Paris. Henri was taken aback by Joseph's request, for he, himself, had been praying that God would raise up someone to meet this need. Now this brusk American Jew was asking if he would help.

At their meeting together the two men discussed the refugee situation for several hours. Henri explained to Joseph that, as President of the Baptist Union of France, and as a busy pastor, he didn't see how he could possibly devote himself to the task of helping the Jewish refugees. But the need of the Jewish immigrants had taken a hold on Joseph and he was determined to find a solution for the need. He asked Henri if he would at least try to find a man who was a Jew and a Christian who could help Henri publish *The Shepherd of Israel* in French, and who could help distribute relief funds to Jewish believers and to other needy Jews in the name of the Messiah, Yeshua. Henri's response was that he didn't know any Christian Jews, but that he would see what he could do.[98]

On the way back to his church Henri began thinking about, and praying about, the events of the day. He was burdened and eager to help. Who did he know who was Jewish and also a Christian? Suddenly, like a bolt of lightening from the sky, Henri remembered that his own secretary, Mademoiselle Marie Solomon, had told him she was a Jewish-Christian—a fact that had completely slipped his mind. Because of the persecution and anti-Semitism toward the Jewish people of Europe, most Parisian Jews who had accepted Yeshua as the Messiah had completely integrated into the life and structure of the church so that no one would suspect them of being Jewish (a sad fact that is true even in our present days).

When Henri told Mlle. Solomon of his conversation with Joseph Cohn, she reminded him of a Christian Jew who had come to see them the previous year. Unfortunately, neither one of them could remember the man's name, so they sought the Lord in prayer. The next morning there came a knock at the door of Pastor Vincent's study. When he opened the door, God's answer to prayer was standing before him. Henri recognized the man immediately—it was the Jewish-Christian man he and Mlle. Solomon had prayed about the previous day. As the man before him spoke, introducing himself as Andre Frankl, Henri Vincent was offering up a prayer of thanksgiving to God. Henri quickly invited Mr. Frankl into his study, and in the moments that followed, Henri shared the story of his meeting with Joseph Cohn, and of Joseph's vision to help the Jewish refugees by providing relief assistance and by sharing the Gospel with them. Pastor Vincent did not have to press hard. God had already prepared the heart of Andre Frankl—he was ready to help.

Within two days of Joseph Cohn's arrival in Paris, the Paris Branch of The American Board of Missions to the Jews was established. It was decided that Mr. Andre Frankl would be the missionary, while Pastor Vincent and Mlle. Marie Solomon would translate the issues of *The Shepherd of Israel* into French. The French edition of *The Shepherd of Israel* was to be called, le Berger d'Israel. Pastor Henri Vincent agreed to be responsible to oversee the ministry in Paris, and to oversee the disbursement of all relief funds.

Once home, Joseph Cohn shared his vision for the Paris ministry in a lengthy article in *The Chosen People* Magazine, saying in part:

> ...Mr. Frankl...shall do a work of visiting evangelism among the nearly 200,000 Jews of Paris. Many of them are of the better class, to whom Mr. Frankl's message should have a special appeal. Then, he is to deal more particularly with the 12,000 to 15,000 refugee Jews, and see that as many of these as possible, who are on their way to Palestine, shall go there with the Gospel message in their hearts, and The Shepherd of Israel in their pockets, and other suitable literature and Gospels, and New Testaments. This plan has in it wonderful possibilities of blessing and soul-saving opportunities.[99]

Sir Leon Levison, the first President of the International Hebrew-Christian Alliance died in 1936, and Joseph expressed his concerns to the Board at their meeting in December 1936. The Minutes state:

> Mr. Cohn first spoke of the death of Sir Leon Levison, President of the International Hebrew-Christian Alliance. Sir Leon was a man of influence and [lived] the Christian life of faith. The Alliance is therefore now without a leader. There are other Hebrew Christian groups in Germany (under Pastor Frank) and in other countries with whom we must work who must be held together and given leadership.
>
> Mr. Cohn pointed out that doubtless there would be special needs in 1937 for our overseas and Jewish refugee work. Also we have a large cash balance which ought not to be carried forward on our books. It was therefore moved and carried that $15,000 of our funds be allocated for oversees and Jewish refugee relief work in 1937.[100]

Emanuel Lichtenstein — His Story

Joseph also asked the Board, and they approved, that the Mission increase the amount of money they were sending to Pastor Arnold Frank and to Mr. Heinrich Poms, a co-laborer and missionary to the Jews. Pastor Frank was elected to succeed Sir Leon Levison as President of the IHCA in September 1937.

Through their on-going correspondence, and through the meetings they had together when Joseph was in Europe, Pastor Frank assisted Joseph in every way he could with the Mission's relief work in Europe; he also assisted the Mission by helping to provide missionary workers. But as hatred and persecution mushroomed in Germany, the Nazis threatened to close his church. The church was spared through the intervention of the British Foreign Secretary, Anthony Eden, because it belonged to the Presbyterian Church of Ireland, but Arnold Frank did not escape the war years totally unscathed. He, along with a number of other German pastors and Jewish believers, was arrested in 1937 and held prisoner by the Nazis. After nine days of imprisonment, once again through the intervention of the British Foreign Secretary, he was freed (though he was confined to his home). In spite of hardships endured, God blessed Pastor Frank with a long life. He died on March 19, 1965 in Belfast, Ireland, at the age of 106!

The summer of 1936, like the two preceding summers, found Joseph Cohn in Europe. While he was in Vienna, he met a Jewish believer by the name of Emanuel Lichtenstein. Emanuel was the grandson of one of the most prominent orthodox rabbis in all of Budapest—Rabbi Ignatz Lichtenstein of Tapio Szele, Hungary. A brilliant man who had become a rabbi at the age of twenty, Rabbi Lichtenstein taught in different Jewish communities throughout Hungary. He finally settled in Tapio Szele, where he became the district rabbi, and where he lived for over forty years.

On one occasion during his years as a rabbi, Ignatz Lichtenstein discovered one of his students reading a New Testament. He confiscated the book and hid it in his own library. Later, during an anti-Semitic outbreak in his city, he decided to read the New Testament to see what was in the book that caused such hatred of the Jewish people. As he read the little book, the Holy Spirit moved within his heart and convinced him of the truth that Yeshua was the Messiah. The more he read, the more he fell in love with Yeshua. He gradually began to bring passages of the New Testament into his sermons in the synagogues. He also began to write pamphlets and articles in which he put forth the idea that perhaps Yeshua was Israel's Messiah. Some members of his congregation became upset with his innuendos about Yeshua, and they asked the chief rabbi of Budapest to investigate. This the chief rabbi did, and when he questioned Rabbi Lichtenstein about his opinion about Yeshua, Lichtenstein replied that he believed in the crucified Messiah, Yeshua. The chief rabbi was aghast, and immediately asked for his resignation. Without hesitation, he complied and afterwards he openly preached the Gospel to the Jewish people until his death in 1909.

Emanuel Lichtenstein went to live with his grandfather after the death of his parents. Rabbi Lichtenstein arranged for Emanuel to attend a boarding school and gymnasium (high school equivalent). Living together provided a natural environment in which Rabbi Lichtenstein could shared the truth of the Gospel with his grandson, and in time Emanuel, too, came to faith in Yeshua and was baptized.

As an adult, Emanuel was employed as a journalist. But when the Nazis marched into town they killed Emanuel's employer, and Emanuel himself had to flee for his life. Starving, and in need of shelter and work, he was led by God to the Swedish Mission in Vienna. The staff there was helping him keep body and soul together when Joseph Cohn met him during the summer of 1936. Once Joseph learned who Emanuel was, and learned of Emanuel's desire to serve the Lord, he immediately offered him a job doing missionary colportage work, visitation, etc. Emanuel was forty-five years of age, and he had a small family. The salary of $50.00 a month which Joseph offered him seemed a real answer to prayer! Joseph arranged for all funds to be sent through the Swedish Mission. Emanuel was to work under their auspices, and under the direct supervision of Pastor Friedrich Forell, the director of the Swedish Mission in Vienna.[101] In his report to the friends and contributors of the Mission, Joseph wrote:

> …The brethren in Vienna cannot express enough gratitude to us, that we have in this way contributed a worker to help them in their efforts to reach the Jews of that city. Vienna at the present time has many thousands of poor desperate Jews that have escaped from Germany, and are in a state of starvation and suffering beyond the power of language to describe. I visited in some of their homes last summer, and was deeply touched with the unspeakable poverty and need. And yet in the midst of such terrible conditions, there was present a silence born of self-respect; so far as possible they were determined to keep their suffering and their hunger to themselves.[102]

From 1934 through 1948 the amount of relief sent by The American Board of Missions to the Jews to its foreign branches steadily increased. In 1936 the Mission sent just over $14,000 (the equivalent of approximately $147,000 in 1992). By 1948 the amount had increased to $127,000 (the equivalent of approximately $715,000 in 1992).

HERBERT SINGER—RELIEF MINISTRY IN EUROPE

The growth of the overseas refugee ministries resulted in the need for additional staff to oversee the various works. Thus, in March 1937 Joseph introduced members of the Executive Committee to Mr. Herbert Singer. Mr. Singer was from Hamburg, Germany. He had worked as Pastor Arnold Frank's assistant for twenty-nine years.

Herbert Singer was born in the city of Cottbus, Germany in 1884. Each morning, as a member of a very strict orthodox Jewish family, young Herbert had to recite the traditional Jewish prayers before having breakfast. He did not really understand why he had to do these things; he did them in obedience to his father.

Throughout his childhood, Herbert attended synagogue regularly. On Yom Kippur, he fasted all day, as did other members of the Singer family. He knew that when he was old enough, he would be required to put on phylacteries and recite the prescribed number of prayers in the Jewish prayer book.

Herbert wanted to love God. He longed for a real relationship with God. He was being taught to fear God, but even though he was just a boy, the rituals and traditions of his religion did not satisfy him.

He had a schoolmate whose home he often visited and he was impressed with the family's prayers at mealtimes; they would fold their hands and thank God for the food and for His other blessings in simple, plain language. The family members talked to God as if they knew Him personally, and he enjoyed the atmosphere of peace and harmony within the home.

Herbert wished that he could know God in the same way. He wished he could pray to God without a printed prayer book. In his friend's home, Herbert heard the Lord's Prayer recited for the first time in his life. The words of the prayer seemed to meet his own spiritual need. He memorized the words, and prayed it every evening in his bed.

When Herbert was twelve years old his family moved to Berlin. Until he was twenty-four years old, Herbert never again came into contact with any genuine Christians—although most of his high school friends called themselves "Christians."

One Sunday afternoon as Herbert was walking through the streets of Berlin, someone handed him an invitation to attend an evangelistic meeting at the Y.M.C.A. He decided to attend the meeting; it was the first time in his life that he had heard the gospel message. As he listened, Herbert knew without a doubt that Jesus was the only One who could still the longings of his heart. He had made certain to take a seat at the rear of the meeting hall so he could quickly escape if he did not like what he was hearing, but in spite of that, a Jewish missionary sought him out at the conclusion of the meeting. The missionary recognized that Herbert was also Jewish, and he invited Herbert to his home. As they walked, Herbert spoke about his longing for peace, and the missionary told him more about the Lord Jesus, who alone is able to give permanent joy and peace.

Their discussion continued at the missionary's home. As Herbert listened, he realized that he was hearing the Truth. It wasn't long before he was kneeling, asking the God of Abraham, Isaac, and Jacob to continue to reveal His Truth to him. Before he left the missionary's home, Herbert gratefully accepted a copy of the New Testament.

Not many months later, Herbert decided to leave Berlin. He planned to go to Hamburg to find a better-paying job. But before he left, his missionary friend gave him the address of Pastor Arnold Frank in Hamburg. Herbert promised he would contact Pastor Frank, but his promise was forgotten during his first weeks in Hamburg. He was too occupied with his frantic search for work and for a place to live.

On a cold, rainy day weeks after leaving Berlin, Herbert was wandering the streets of Hamburg. He was still out of work, and he had no place of shelter. Without thinking, he put his hand into his pocket. His fingers touched a tattered piece of paper, and he suddenly remembered his promise to the missionary.

Herbert located the address on the paper and rang the doorbell. He was not sure what to expect, but when the door opened, there stood a Jewish man with a broad smile. Pastor Frank quickly invited Herbert to come in out of the rain. He led Herbert into a hall where about twenty-four young Jewish men were sitting at a long table—each one with an open Bible before him. They had been listening attentively to a lecture being given by Pastor Frank.

Herbert entered the Mission of Pastor Frank in February of 1909. It was a life-changing day! As he took his place alongside the other young Jewish men that day, Herbert sat enthralled by Pastor Frank's teaching. The atmosphere was permeated with love and peace; Herbert wanted very much to be one of the young men who were privileged to live there. To his joy, Pastor Frank granted his request.

Some three months after the cold, rainy day when he first knocked on Pastor Frank's door, Herbert opened his heart to receive Jesus as his Messiah and Savior. The long search to know God in a personal way was over. Herbert experienced the joy of knowing his sins were forgiven. The peace of God ruled in his heart! On Easter Sunday, 1909, Herbert openly confessed his faith by being baptized.

Herbert's new-found joy was marred by only one factor—his family did not share his delight in having found the Messiah. His father wrote that he considered Herbert to be insane. He stated that Herbert should never write to him or to any member of the family again. He told Herbert that he regarded him as dead.

Two years passed without one word from his family. Then Herbert received a telegram from his father urging him to come to Berlin. His mother was seriously ill; she wanted to see her son before she died.

Herbert quickly made arrangements to go to Berlin. When he arrived at his parents home, he found his mother still alive, but very weak. With tears in her eyes, she told her son that she forgave him for his decision to accept Jesus. Herbert remained with his mother until the hour of her death, and although his father would not speak to him, his younger brother, Fritz, was open and receptive to the Word of God.

After his return to Hamburg, Herbert tried repeatedly to become reconciled to his father. When, to his surprise and delight, his father broke his wall of silence, Herbert asked his father to let Fritz come to Hamburg. To his great joy, permission was granted.

Fritz lived with Herbert at the Mission house, and it wasn't long after his arrival in Hamburg that Herbert had the privilege of leading young Fritz to the Lord. Fritz, too, became a sincere believer in the Lord.

Hundreds of young Jewish men came under the preaching of the Word of God as Herbert and Arnold Frank faithfully carried on a witness for the Lord; many of them accepted Jesus as Messiah and Lord of their lives, and some went on to proclaim salvation through Christ to Jews and Gentiles all over the world.

As the turmoil of Hitler's madness began to be felt throughout Europe, the work of Pastor Frank's mission was greatly affected. Finally, the Mission house in Hamburg was closed, and Pastor Frank, then 80 years old, was thrown into a concentration camp.

Fritz, and other members of Herbert's family, were taken by the Nazis to Hitler's death camps. Herbert never saw or heard from them again.

But in His Divine Plan, God spared Herbert. As the clouds of persecution and of impending war loomed on the horizon, Pastor Frank had contacted Joseph Hoffman Cohn and the Mission, to ask for assistance. Frank told Joseph about the wonderful work of Herbert Singer, and Joseph immediately began making arrangements to help him get out of Germany.

Joseph told the Board:

> ...We have now found a use for his [Herbert Singer's] services in the publishing of an eight page edition of The Chosen People in the German language. Pastor Frank had a 40,000 circulation for his paper in Germany....Mr. Singer will write over to get these names so that we can send The Chosen People to them....He is also gradually to work himself into the missionary activities of our work....He wants to do actual missionary work and then to go out into the churches to tell them about what he is doing....He is very much liked by all of the workers.[103]

Within a few short months Herbert became Joseph Cohn's right-hand man as he assisted with the refugee work. His knowledge of the German language made him invaluable as he translated letters and corresponded with Joseph's many European contacts. Herbert was also responsible for seeing that items of clothing, food supplies, Bibles, and Gospel literature reached the many refugee centers that had been established by the Mission. By 1940, Joseph Cohn referred to Mr. Singer as the individual "in charge" of the refugee work—a title and position Singer bore until his death on January 30, 1948.[104]

As has been mentioned, the idea of a colony for Jewish believers (as discussed at the 1934 meeting of the IHCA in London) appealed to Joseph Cohn. There were problems to be resolved, however. One issue was that the leadership of the IHCA wanted the colony to be established in Israel. When it became clear that establishing such a colony in Israel would be virtually impossible, the leadership conceded to settle for any country where Jewish people could live in safety.

The other issue was not as easily resolved. Members of the various branches of the IHCA were unwilling to use funds raised for evangelism to establish such a colony. During Sir Leon Levison's term as President of the IHCA, strong feelings over this issue nearly split the Alliance. Evidence of the depths of feelings on the matter can be seen in Frederick Levison's book, "Christian And Jew—Leon Levison—1881-1936," where he states:

> ...the Rev. Henry Carpenter, himself a Hebrew Christian and a missionary in Poland, was a stumbling block. He asserted that money given for evangelistic purposes could be used for that alone. 'I regret,' said Leon [Levison] 'having to differ from Mr. Carpenter. The bogey that money is only to be used for evangelizing is all wrong. We cannot get money to bring people to Christ...and let them die. This we must oppose. The phrase 'dedicated money' used in this manner is almost irreverent. We must remember that Christ told us to feed the poor.[105]

When a majority of the member mission organizations of the Alliance (IHCA) failed to show up for a meeting to discuss the establishment of a colony, not even sending representatives in their places or letters of apology for their absence, Sir Leon Levison was even more angry. Then, when the director of the Barbican Mission showed his disinterest, and the Mildmay Mission wrote a letter saying they could not support such a colony, Leon Levison, commenting on the spirit of Jewish mission leaders, said: "A spirit…that breaks one's heart….I would rather play third or tenth fiddle than show such a spirit."[106]

The leaders of some Jewish missions did show up for the meeting, and gave their approval of a colony but "…after returning to their committees they wrote regretting that for financial reasons they could not participate, and Leon [Levison] was moved to make an unusually caustic remark: 'If money can be spent travelling about in first-class carriages and staying at first-class hotels it could be put to helping our Hebrew Christian brethren.'"[107]

How involved Joseph Cohn was in these proceedings, or whether he supported Levison's position on using evangelistic funds for colonization purposes, is unclear. Correspondence does indicate that he did encourage his foreign branches to cooperate with the Alliance (IHCA) whenever the purposes of the two organizations did not conflict and wherever there was agreement between the workers.[108]

WORK AMONG REFUGEE JEWS

Joseph Cohn's own position on the matter, and the Mission's position as stated in *The Chosen People* magazine, was that no relief would be given without a corresponding witness for the Gospel.[109] Joseph had, in fact, refused to cooperate with a Quaker missionary in Paris because she did not believe in direct Jewish evangelism. The Minutes record: "When Mr. Cohn visited Paris he found a young Quakeress who is doing relief work among the Jewish refugees from Germany, but she would not agree to a Gospel program in connection with her work, so that it will be impossible for us to cooperate with her."[110] Along these lines, Joseph Cohn reminded supporters of the Mission that The American Board of Missions to the Jews was not just a relief organization. He wrote:

> It may be important to stress here once more, that we are not a relief agency, nor a Refugee Society. Ours is a God-commissioned work of presenting the message of salvation through the Lord Jesus Christ, and this we do in season and out. Refugee relief we use only as a means to a vital end—the salvation of men and women. Frankly, we are not interested in relief work for its own sake—there are many organizations doing that, and they, of course, as our Lord reminded us, have their reward. But our work abroad is saturated with the Gospel, and while we try to help in His Name all who come to us, our more substantial help naturally is extended especially to the Household of Faith, those Jews who have given up their all, even their racial connections, to identify themselves for all time with Him who bought them and gave Himself for them.[111]

Joseph Cohn was a man of action. He did not wait for the divisions within the Alliance (IHCA) to be solved. He made a decision to move ahead on his own to help resettle Jewish refugees, making it clear that he would be willing to cooperate with the IHCA, or with other missions whenever they wished to assist him in the effort.

Over 25,000 German Jewish immigrants were living in Paris illegally. It was against French law for them to be employed. As illegal aliens, they had no passports and they risked being deported at any time. They became victims of anti-Semitic riots and fell prey to the slurs of anti-Semitic politicians who, like the Nazis, wanted to find a solution for Paris' growing "Jewish problem." Reporting on the desperate situation, Joseph told readers of *The Chosen People* magazine that the only feasible solution to the Jewish refugee problem in France and Germany seemed to be "…to pick up the families bodily and transplant them into a new world with a new hope and a new rootage,…"[112] This was not possible, however, so Joseph Cohn, Henri Vincent, and Andre Frankl "brainstormed" until they came up with a way to provide relief for the Jewish refugees without violating French law. Joseph told readers of *The Chosen People* about the unique plan:

> I arranged…to open up a relief station where we shall be able, in the name of the Lord Jesus Christ, to bring immediate relief to substantial numbers of these destitute families. Our method is to give them tickets which entitle each one to one meal in a restaurant in the Jewish ghetto district of Paris, down below the Bastille. These tickets will then be returned to us by the restaurant keeper and we will redeem them at the price of 3.5 francs per meal, about 24 cents in our money, at the old rate of exchange. We will also provide, whenever we can, clothing, either by purchases or from gifts, which Pastor Vincent will receive from friends in France. Pastor Vincent will also form a central committee which will have charge of this relief work. Let us pray that his venture on our part will be used of God to bring the saving knowledge of our Lord Jesus Christ into the hearts of many of these who now seem to have lost all hope. We must remind them that Israel's God still lives, and that He will send help when all else fails.[113]

Joseph also told the Board he wanted to investigate the possibility of finding Christian families in the United States who would be willing to adopt the children of Jewish Christians from Germany and Poland. He stated that Pastor Frank had written, saying: "...there are many Jewish Christian parents in Germany who are anxious to send their children to the United States for adoption into Christian homes. Mr. Cohn has made inquiries from the Immigration Department and hopes that it will be possible for us to bring at least a few such children here and place them in the homes of some of our friends."[114]

The problems were monumental. People were desperate. Once again, Joseph Cohn went back to the thought that the only real hope was to establish a colony of refugee Jews. At the next Board meeting, he asked that the Board set up a "resettlement fund" to be used to resettle Jewish refugee families in South America—one of the few countries that was willing to accept Jewish people. The Board approved his proposal.

The first family to be resettled was a German Jewish family by the name of "Daltrop." The involvement for the Mission went far beyond just supplying the funding for them to be resettled in Montevideo, Uruguay.[115] The procedure was arduous. Visas had to be secured, an almost impossible task for German Jews; a security deposit had to be given to the Uruguay Government; steamship tickets had to be purchased; funding had to be provided for the family once they arrived in Uruguay. Joseph Cohn involved the readers of The Chosen People magazine, making them aware of this new project and its needs. Just as they always had, God's people responded and funding for the "resettling of refugee Jews" began to pour in.[116]

The persecution of the Jews in Europe intensified, and as it did Joseph Cohn intensified his efforts to establish colonies of Jewish refugees in countries where they would be safe. He received numerous letters from supporters of the Mission asking how they could help, and in response he wrote:

> ...Many are asking us what are we doing in the matter? And we want to answer now: -1st, We are sending relief funds into Europe as rapidly and as efficiently as we can. 2nd, The International Hebrew Christian Alliance, with headquarters in London, with whom we have been in friendly cooperation for several years past, has received word from the Government of Ecuador, that they are willing to set aside enough land to take care of 100 Jewish families, each family to be given 100 hectares of land. This is equivalent to about 247 acres. The land is represented as being suitable for growing cocoa, coffee, sugar cane, cotton, nuts, and fruits. Each family that enters Ecuador must have $1,000 cash, so that the government may be assured that they can live until the land begins to produce.
>
> Also, there is a possibility of some similar settling to be done in the island of Cyprus in the Mediterranean. And there is a little encouragement with regard to the Argentine and to Uruguay.
>
> Therefore we make bold to announce once more our Resettlement or Colonization fund. We have already committed ourselves to the International Alliance up to the sum of $15,000. If we could have the ears of all America in this heart-breaking need, one million dollars could be raised and used over the next six months just for this colonization plan alone.[117]

Joseph went on to tell readers about two other German Jewish families that the Mission had already re-settled in Uruguay. He told the readers: "They not only have been successful in breaking up the virgin soil, and establishing themselves economically, but they have been at the same time evangelizing the natives. So in this way we have done a twofold work; we have helped establish Jewish Christian families in distress and we have given the Gospel through them to hitherto unevangelized peoples."[118]

The Vienna Ministry—Emanuel Lichtenstein

The web of Nazi terror continued to engulf Europe and threatened to close the foreign branches of the Mission, including the work in Vienna where Emanuel Lichtenstein was working in cooperation with the Swedish Missionary Society. During the dark days of 1938 through 1942, Emanuel remained a faithful laborer for the Lord. He wrote about the first time he was interrogated at the Gestapo Headquarters in Vienna. Some months before the incident, Emanuel had received a copy of the December 1937 German edition of The Chosen People magazine called, "Das Auserwahlte Volk"—an issue which carried a front page article, "Rabbi Lichtenstein's Grandson Becomes our Missionary in Vienna." The report was illustrated with photos of Lichtenstein's grandfather, and of Emanuel himself. He was very proud of the article, and carried a copy of the magazine with him wherever he went. He happened to have it in his pocket when the Gestapo ordered him to appear at their headquarters. It seems that the military censor had opened some of his mail and he wanted Emanuel to explain why he was receiving foreign correspondence. Lichtenstein began to explain who he was and what he was doing, and as he did so, he reached into his pocket and pulled out The Chosen People magazine and showed it to the Gestapo officer who was interrogating him. Lichtenstein wrote:

...He looked distrustingly on both pictures, but he studied very, very keenly all I showed him. Quite suddenly he called out (using the true Gestapo voice): 'What?! What's that you say of yourself here? You are a follower of the Lord Jesus Christ?' He then held that page of The Chosen People (Auserwahlte Volk) under my eyes with those two photos and the explanation underneath in German as follows: Grossvater und Enkelsohn, beide Nachfolger des Herrn Jesu Christi (Grandfather and grandson, both followers of the Lord Jesus Christ.) I explained that the text was not written by myself and that, of course, it would never try to convey such a Nachfolge as the Pope pretends to be, but that 'to follow Christ Jesus' is a usual characterizing of believers in the Lord Jesus of any and all races, languages, and peoples, who see in and confess the Lord Jesus as their only and true Saviour Who died for their own personal sins and those inherited by all men.

When the other Gestapo-man, who had sat opposite 'my' man, left the office for some few minutes, 'my' man's rancour changed into quite a different tune. He said it was not his intention to argue with me on religious matters that he did not understand. But he warned me not to write any more letters into foreign countries, after which he bade me farewell as follows: 'And now try and get out quickly! Go away in Jesus' name!' And he handed me the written permit to leave the Gestapo building. I felt truly that he did not say 'in Jesus' name ironically. But I felt sure that this man— usually cruelty personified against all kinds of innocent people—had for just a single moment been made bland and soft just for this occasion. Perhaps he felt himself that he could never find any justification before God for himself to have proceedings against a follower of Jesus Christ unjustly, unfairly, and without any reason whatsoever. But after I came through the strongly-guarded barring of the gates of that terrible building into the open and free air, I breathed heartily again and thanked God that He had worked with me and for me, as it really was an exceptionally rare case that a Jew entered the Gestapo building and was free to leave it within a few hours as a free man and as healthy as he had entered.[119]

With God's help, and in spite of the Nazi threat of imprisonment, torture, or death hanging over their heads, Emanuel Lichtenstein was able to build up a staff of over twelve workers. Some of these brave believers helped him arrange for papers and visas; others served as doctors or pharmacists; still others ministered to the spiritual and physical needs of the refugees. Time after time the Nazis tried to shut the doors of the Mission, but miraculously the doors of the Mission not only remained opened, the work even grew. Through the relief funds sent to him by the Mission, Emanuel and his staff opened a "soup kitchen" to feed the hungry refugees. He wrote:

The tasks in our mission work increase from day to day, and the stream of Jewish people, applying for help, becomes larger every day. We know that we would not be able to solve these tasks without God's help and support.
We receive many letters from Jews and Hebrew Christians, who already have left Austria,...[120]

Joseph Cohn had always enjoyed a good challenge, and in the matter of dispensing relief funds his natural ingenuity proved very valuable. As the war in Europe continued to escalate, some of the Mission's supporters were concerned that the monies they were giving toward relief for needy Jews might fall, instead, into the hands of the Nazis. Whenever possible, Joseph handled the matter by giving out the relief funds personally. But when this was not possible, he had to rely on trusted friends and on his carefully thought through plans.

One example of Joseph's creativity in dispensing relief funds was the elaborate system which he and Emanuel Lichtenstein used in Vienna—a system that was used in other countries as well, when it was feasible to do so. All monies designated for Vienna were sent directly to the Swedish Mission Society in Stockholm, Sweden. Since Sweden was still on friendly terms with Germany, their workers had certain freedoms to carry on ministry, including the transfer of funds for Gospel and relief work. Reporting on this system to the Board, Joseph said:

...In Vienna, if a Jewish person is fortunate enough to secure permission to leave the country, whatever money he has must be confiscated to the German Government. So instead of losing his money to the Government he gives all he has to our missionary in Vienna. Then that Jew leaves and goes to Stockholm, where the money which we have been sending over awaits him, and with this money he goes to various parts of the world, the destinations having been prearranged by correspondence with the various governments by Mr. Lichtenstein or by the Swedish Missionary Society in Stockholm. One such family is with us now, Mr. and Mrs. Unger.[121]

Still, there were certain risks involved in trying to get funds to the workers, or relief funds to Jewish believers. Joseph expressed this in a letter to Mr. Jean Tanguy, a worker who had replaced Henri Vincent in Paris when Henri went into the army. He wrote:

It is impossible for us to send money to Mme. Slowik in Frankfort. There is no possible way of our getting money through to her—every avenue of approach is blocked. We are still fortunate in our dealing with Mr. Lichtenstein in Vienna, because that money we send to Stockholm, and the Swedish friends somehow are able to get the money to Vienna; but if they should be caught in any suspicious shifting of money in any other parts of Germany, it might mean much trouble to them, it might even mean that Lichtenstein could be arrested, and it might mean that the Mission itself in Vienna might be closed down by the Nazis. Therefore you see what a great risk we are running when we try to do a thing like that. We have heard nothing whatever from Pastor Lowy in Frankfort, ever since I came back from Europe, and this means that he must be in trouble also. My heart truly aches for Mme. Slowik, but I am helpless, as you can readily see.[122]

Thousands of refugees were touched with the Gospel through the loving and dedicated ministry of Emanuel Lichtenstein. Two such refugees were Josef Israel Herschkowitz and Lottie Furth; both were helped by the Mission in Vienna, and both later accepted Yeshua and become faithful workers of the Mission.

Lottie Furth

Emanuel Lichtenstein arranged for Lottie to escape to London, and from London she immigrated to New York. Once in New York, she and six other Jewish believers from Vienna were baptized by Joseph Cohn in the Brooklyn branch of the ministry. Joseph then arranged for Lottie to attend the Bible Institute in Philadelphia. After graduating, she enrolled for nurse training at William Booth Memorial Hospital in New York City and when she received her state license she was hired by the Mission to work with the Jewish refugees who daily poured into the Mission's Dispensary.

Josef Herschkowitz — His Story

Josef Israel Herschkowitz' story was different. He was born into an orthodox Jewish home in Vienna in 1898. When his brother was drafted into World War I, he decided that he could not believe in a God who would take children to be soldiers; he therefore became an atheist.

After he married, his wife, Hermina, became seriously ill. Josef believed that only God could save her, but he refused to pray. Miraculously she survived, but Josef still refused to acknowledge God. When the Nazis occupied Austria in 1938, they drove Josef out of his house. He had no relatives or family outside of Austria; he had no hope of escape. His wife was an Aryan and she had heard about the Mission, and about Emanuel Lichtenstein, so she suggested to Josef that they go to the Mission to see if someone there could help get him out of Austria. Because he was in such desperate straits, he agreed to go. At the Mission no promises or commitments were made, but brother Lichtenstein agreed to do whatever he could to get Josef safely out of Austria. While they waited for the necessary papers, Josef and Hermina began attending the Sunday and Wednesday services at the Mission. There, they heard the Gospel for the first time.

On November 10, 1939, as Josef was making his way to a Mission meeting, the Nazis arrested him. He was sent to Dachau Concentration Camp in Germany. It was the experience of being a helpless, persecuted prisoner—forced to watch the torture and slaughter of his own Jewish brethren—that finally brought Josef to the place where he cried out to God in prayer. Six months later, through the help of Hermina and the Mission, he was released from Dachau. The Mission arranged for him to go to a Protestant refugee camp in Holland. There, he joined with others in the study of the Bible. Again he acknowledged that perhaps God existed, but he could not accept the deity of Yeshua or the doctrine of the Trinity.

Hermina, who was still living in Vienna, had been given the name of a Hebrew Christian in Detroit. This contact, in turn, put her in touch with some friends of the Mission—Mr. and Mrs. Blair of Erie, Pennsylvania. It was Mr. Blair who signed an Affidavit so Josef Herschkowitz could get a visa to enter the United States.

It was people in desperate situations, like that of Josef Herschkowitz, that prompted Joseph Cohn to place an announcement in *The Chosen People* magazine which stated:

We are besieged from Europe with pitiful letters asking that we provide Affidavits of Support so as to enable destitute Jewish refugees to come to America.

An Affidavit of Support is a form which any one in America can sign and in which the signer agrees to be responsible for the support of the family for whom he is signing the Affidavit. The law requires now that every Jewish family seeking entrance to America from any European point must present to the American Consul in that district an Affidavit of Support signed by someone in America guaranteeing that the family will not be dependent upon the United States Government.

If you feel that you would like to help us by agreeing to sign some of these affidavits won't you please drop us a postal card and we will list your name, and then when a specially worthy family makes application to us for an Affidavit we will call upon you to execute the form. We will also give you our Mission guarantee that any such families that will come over because of your affidavit will be cared for by the Mission and that you will be protected by us against any possible claims.[123]

In the case of the Blair's, though their hearts were in the right place, they simply didn't have sufficient funds to guarantee Josef the necessary entrance Visa, or to sponsor him once he arrived in America. Deeply disappointed, Josef Herschkowitz began to pray. He put out a fleece to God; he asked God to give him a sign that Yeshua was His Son, and of the reality of the Trinity, by causing the American Consul to issue him a Visa. Within a few days, the American Consul contacted Josef, and when he went in for an interview they issued him a Visa. God confirmed the truth of His Word to Josef! Fourteen days later he was baptized, and three days after his baptism he left the refugee camp in Holland (and his wife who was still in Vienna), and was on his way to America.

Josef Israel Herschkowitz arrived in New York on May 16, 1940. After his disappointing experience with the Blair family, he did not want to live with them but that is exactly where The Committee For Christian Refugees sent him to live. They did so because Josef could not speak English and could not get a job.

The Blair's were wonderful Christian people and they immediately adopted Josef into their family. They took him everywhere, including to their church—a strong evangelical fellowship. The more he attended the church, the more Josef realized it wasn't enough just to know the doctrines about Yeshua, the Trinity, and other doctrines of the Scripture. He realized that he needed to accept Yeshua as his personal Messiah and Savior, so he made a public confession of his faith in Yeshua and was once again baptized. In his testimony he stated, "The Lord is wonderful. He is above all human understanding! He never takes away things from us without giving us much more for it....I had lost all the things I loved most but He gave me Himself, Jesus Christ and through Him joy and happiness."[124]

For a period of seven years, Josef Herschkowitz attempted to stay in touch with his wife and to seek her release from Nazi-held Austria, but all of his efforts seemed to be in vain. During those years, he learned English, went to Bible school, and became a missionary on the staff of the Mission. Hermina, on the other hand, lived through those years with determination to remain faithful to her husband even though the Nazis continually hounded her to divorce that "Jew." When Austria was liberated, by God's grace, Hermina found herself in the American Zone. Had she been living in the Russian or the French zones she would not have been permitted to immigrate to America. The Mission arranged for her transportation, and Josef made arrangements for her to enter into Canada. In January 1947 Hermina and Josef were reunited after eight long years of Nazi forced separation. The Hamilton (Ontario) Spectator printed the full story of their reunion, and the story was shared in *The Chosen People* magazine as well.[125]

Emanuel Lichtenstein's dedicated labors in Vienna continued, and Joseph Cohn kept readers of *The Chosen People* abreast of his tremendous accomplishments. He wrote:

Emanuel Lichtenstein was continuously in correspondence with more than eighty world governments, seeking outlets for desperately driven Jews who had come to the Mission doors in their last effort to find deliverance. And so through him, a steady stream of Jewish exiles kept crossing the seven seas to find harbor and new homes for themselves and their little broods. So greatly did the work in Vienna increase that Mr. Lichtenstein built up an organization of twelve fellow-workers, all of them volunteers; and through them he carried on almost a country-wide labor of relief and hope and comfort for the hapless victims of Nazi cruelties. He endeared himself to the refugees whom he served; we ourselves saw once in our Paris Mission, whither he had gone with us from London, strong men embrace and kiss him when he came into the hall and they recognized him; he had been their means of deliverance from the hell that was Vienna; we saw men and women weep like children when they had to bid farewell to him as he insisted on returning there against the pleadings of the many who had escaped and who knew that only agony awaited him if he should go back.[126]

LICHTENSTEIN FORCED TO FLEE EUROPE

But the day came when the situation in Vienna was so perilous that it was imperative that the Mission help the Lichtensteins flee the country. Joseph told readers of *The Chosen People*:

The startling news was that the Nazis in control of the city of Vienna had resorted to the shameful and diabolical crime of setting loose among the Jewish population of Vienna the germs of typhus so that the poor Jews of that city have become infected with typhoid en masse, and this has given the Nazis their excuse now for wholesale deportation of Jews. Many are packed in cattle cars, and others are driven across the fields of Austria to some place of quarantine in Poland

> 'for their protective safety!' Of course, the obvious objective is clear enough, and this is the utter destruction of these helpless victims of Satanic fury. Our friends are asked especially to pray for our Missionary in Vienna, Rev. Emanuel Lichtenstein, for the numerous other missionaries with whom he was associated there and for the many hundreds of Jewish Christians who flocked to the Mission of Seegasse as a shelter in the hour of terror. We are doing our utmost to get Mr. Lichtenstein out of Vienna and to transfer him to some South American port such as Buenos Aires where he can continue as our missionary. There are a good many thousand refugee Jews in Buenos Aires now. We are also trying in case it proves to be impossible to get Mr. Lichtenstein into the Argentine, to locate him in Shanghai, where at the present time there are about 20,000 refugee Jews many of them believers on the Lord Jesus Christ. Will you please pray earnestly for God's over-ruling hand in this terrible crisis hour.[127]

The prayers of God's people were answered, and in March 1941 the Lichtenstein family escaped by plane to Stockholm, Sweden. The escape was not without incident however. When Emanuel and his family arrived at the Berlin airport, a customs officer saw a cross in Emanuel's luggage. The cross, which bore the Latin inscription, *sitio* (I have thirst), had been on his desk throughout his ministry. Of this incident he related:

> …The customs man thrust his finger on my passport wherein not only the Nazi-placed name 'Israel,' but even a greater and larger 'J' (Jude—for Jew), called his attention to the fact that I belonged to the Jewish people. With his other hand he showed me the cross: 'What does a Jew need a cross for?' He hardly listened to my explaining answer, but he ordered a bodily search that almost let me lose my plane. But God helped me this other time. And the cross continued to adorn my home in thankful remembrance of God's wondrous ways to save me from the Nazi clutches, for which our Mission had put the necessary means at my disposal.…
>
> With regard to the question of that customs man, I am ever since repeating to myself this same question every morning that He kindly lets me see and every night as I lie down to rest, late as I may be: 'Just what does the Jew need the cross for?' Because I feel that in this short sentence there is what the work amongst Israel, there is what the entire work of our Mission stands for, and our whole task amongst The Chosen People of God. 'What does the Jew need the cross for?' In finding and conveying the correct answer to this question is all the success and all the failure of our Mission and its work.[128]

THE BUENOS AIRES BRANCH

The Mission and the Swedish Missionary Society, with whom the Lichtensteins were staying while they were in Stockholm, worked feverishly to obtain visas for their entry into South America. After six months of continuous work, the permits and tickets were secured; their journey was to take them from Stockholm, through the English Channel, to Buenos Aries, Argentina.

The complicated business of arranging for passage and negotiating visas for the Lichtenstein's immigration to South America gave Joseph Cohn another opportunity to exercise his "networking" ability. Emanuel was not just a minister of the Gospel—he was a missionary to the Jews, and the Argentine government had placed a ban on the entrance of all new missionaries and missionary endeavors in the country. There was a ruling, however, which stated that if a church or mission society had an established work, the organization could replace an existing staff member with a new pastor or missionary. This was just the loop-hole needed! Through staff members of The Swedish Missionary Society in Stockholm, Joseph learned that the Lutheran church had an established church in Buenos Aries, Argentina. He immediately contacted Dr. Henry Einspruch, a Lutheran pastor, to see if he could arrange a meeting between Joseph and the Board of the Lutheran Missionary Society.

Dr. Einspruch was also the director of the Lederer Foundation in Baltimore, Maryland—a foundation that had been established for the purpose of printing and distributing Gospel literature for the Jewish people. Through their common interest in reaching Jewish people with the Gospel, Henry Einspruch and Joseph Cohn had become good friends. In fact, the Lederer Foundation was working in cooperation with the Mission by translating and publishing a Yiddish New Testament. Joseph's hope was that the Lutheran church would be willing to issue a call to Emanuel Lichtenstein to serve on their staff in Argentina.

Dr. Einspruch made the necessary calls, and the meeting between Joseph and the Board of the Lutheran Missionary Society was held. Of that meeting Joseph wrote:

> …And these brethren not only gave us sympathetic ear, but went promptly into action, and cabled their leaders in Buenos Aires to issue a call by cable to Mr. Lichtenstein in Stockholm. And so it was done, and the technical obstacles were removed, and the Lord gave us the open door.

But the greater advantage is that all the equipment, and the ministry, and the visiting staff, all are at our disposal in Buenos Aires. And further, Mr. Lichtenstein will carry on his work, not only as an official and legal member of the Staff, but with their fullest cooperation and, more yet, under their supervision. And this means, he is not sent there by us as a lone, unsupervised worker, with only his judgment to fall back upon. He has a responsible directing body with him, and over him, right there on the field....Indeed, this sort of method has been the Mission's policy wherever we have established Stations either here, or abroad, and it has made for the most efficient administration of your funds.[129]

In Buenos Aires, Emanuel Lichtenstein entered a missionary field that was already prepared. The expectations of his ministry were outlined in a letter that Mr. Armbruster, pastor of the Lutheran Church that was sponsoring him, sent to Joseph. Armbruster stated:

First of all, may I say that Mr. Lichtenstein has been very busy renewing the contacts that he made in his work while in Europe and is establishing new contacts thru mutual acquaintances here. Last night at our service we had the joy of baptizing two adults, whom Mr. Lichtenstein met very shortly after his arrival in Buenos Aires and whom he has had under instruction for baptism for the past several weeks. Last Saturday Mr. Lichtenstein held his first meeting with a group of people he had invited, and before an audience of forty people (a number that we consider large, given the short time that he has been in the country) he related his recent experiences in Europe, told of the work of your Board and invited his hearers to manifest their opinions as to the possibility of establishing Bible study groups, etc....

The most feasible work to be undertaken by Mr. Lichtenstein is...house to house visits, learning to know from friends the names of other people who should be interested in his exposition of the word, and then hold group meetings from time to time, where he can talk to his people in an informal way, hold Bible study and then top off the afternoon with a tea....

Then there is a second object that he has in mind that is most certainly a happy one and a much needed one in our community, the establishing of an evangelical bureau somewhere in the center of town, where those refugees from Europe who are already of our faith, as well as others who profess no belief at all, may find a welcome material and spiritual help. Such committees, with their respective centers of work are maintained by the Jews and by the Roman Catholics, but the refugees of evangelical faith have had up to now no place to which they might go to receive advice and a helping hand. Mr. Lichtenstein, with his European experience behind him, I believe, would be the ideal person to head up such a committee and take charge of such a place for evangelical and other refugees.[130]

The December 1943 issue of *The Chosen People* magazine carried a glowing report of the Mission's new Branch in Buenos Aires. Approximately 200,000 Jews were living in Buenos Aires by 1942. Many of them were Jewish refugees who had either received help from Lichtenstein through his vast relief network in Europe, or individuals who had become believers in Yeshua through his ministry in Vienna. As word of Emanuel and Justina Lichtenstein's presence in Buenos Aires spread, people from many parts of Argentina began to find their way to the Mission. Emanuel's open witness for the Lord, his integrity and impeccable reputation, and his ability to get things done won him a reputation as someone to turn to when help was needed.

It was no secret that Emanuel and the members of the Swedish Lutheran Mission were anxious for the Mission to purchase a building for the ministry in Buenos Aires, but the Board was hesitant to invest in property there due to the unstable conditions in Argentina. Still, Lichtenstein persisted. He wrote:

Your statement explaining the position of your Board of Directors at the present time, was no surprise to us. Pastor Armbruster had in view only the best interests of our work and especially the stabilization of our expenditures for rent for the Mission and the dwelling of the missionary, when he counseled me to send the cablegram. Pastor Armbruster is of the decided opinion that real estate of the Evangelical churches and of Jewish societies here is in no more danger than in any other part of the world, which today is so restless and given to constant changes of policy. He also stressed the constant value and marketableness of the real estate in question, in order to give you a clear picture in a few words, and advised the inquiry by cable, even though he knew well enough how carefully the people in the U. S. still weigh everything in connection with Argentine affairs.[131]

While the matter of the purchase of a building remained unresolved, the ministry continued to move ahead. Emanuel was a familiar sight among the Jewish shopkeepers and merchants as, each week, he faithfully distributed tracts and invitations to the Mission's services. He also recruited the assistance of local Lutheran pastors. Rev. and Mrs Graefe agreed to give Spanish and English lessons. Axel Krebs, of the Danish church, participated in the Mission's Bible classes.

Emanuel's faithfulness reaped a harvest for the Lord as he worked at building a Jewish-Christian Lutheran congregation in Buenos Aires; he reported that the attendance remained steady at forty to sixty-five adherents. He also followed Joseph's advice to have New Testaments printed, so that those who attended the weekly Bible study on Saturdays could read the corresponding passages together, and he introduced a voluntary offering system at his evening Bible class. A portion of the collection was used for relief efforts among the refugee Jews who were flooding into Argentina; the remaining portion was used to help the Lutheran relief efforts. Lichtenstein wrote to Joseph, saying:

> ...The results of our collections from March 13 to the end of April were a total of $110.50. We have used of this amount $100 for the contribution to the cost of a bed of the Old Men's Home of the United Lutheran Church, in remembrance of the beloved Rev. Dr. Leopold Cohn, as also we had done some months ago for their Old Ladies Home....
>
> Already in some former report I have informed you, that Pastor Armbruster facilitated $120 for the M_____ family with six children, that enabled them to move from their unhealthy, damp quarters in a wood and corrugated iron shed into a better flat. The shifting into their new apartment was realized in the April month, and our Mission Station will refund the money to the United Lutheran Church in $10 monthly installments, because our weekly collection of offerings is now a regular institution which enables us to do so.[132]

In 1947, after ten years of service with the Mission, Emanuel wrote to Joseph, saying:

> Today it is exactly ten years since I entered the service of the American Board of Missions to the Jews. This important anniversary in my life has been made more important still by my being ordained as a pastor of the United Lutheran Church in my condition as the head of your Mission Station here in Buenos Aires. This solemn act took place last night [c. September, 1947].[133]

He continued his letter by thanking Joseph and the Board for assisting him over the ten year span. He also thanked them for assisting him as he continued his theological education.

In 1951, at the Lutheran Synodal Congress, pastor Lichtenstein was elected by the Argentine United Lutheran Church (ULC) to fill a vacancy in the Directing Council of the local United Lutheran Church. Later that year the Society of Women of the local ULC congregations held their annual conference at the Mission's Center in Buenos Aires, and Mrs. Justina Lichtenstein was elected President of the Congress of Evangelical Women. The leadership of the Lutheran church was in hopes that the election of the Lichtensteins (who were not only Jewish believers, but missionaries to the Jews as well) would help their ministry, as well as to dispel rumors that the Lutheran church was anti-Semitic.[134] Unfortunately, soon after Emanuel's election to the ULC Council, many churches in South America, like the churches of North America, began to struggle with the affects of Liberalism and Modernism. Theological disputes triggered splits within some of the Lutheran churches in Latin America, and some pastors, including Rev. Armbruster, left their churches. Emanuel wrote:

> ...In our Evangelical church...since the disappearance of the late Pastor Armbruster, we have had to go through many hard problems. On account of the differences between pastors and people, a woman sustained a wound in her soul so...she has left the church and just comes into the Mission Station saying that with us she feels that we not only preach the true Spirit of Christ but also try and practice it.
>
> Naturally, your Mission Station is...not only a meeting place for Jew and Gentile,...but mainly a place of preaching the good Tidings of Salvation in Christ to the Jews. And so it is great joy to us that...a Jewish-Christian family of four, who heard of our work in Argentina already in Europe, have found their way to us, and come to our meetings every week.
>
> Not only for spiritual needs but—as far as God fills our hands—also for material needs we are trying to help.[135]

In his zeal to reach Spanish speaking people—Jew and Gentile alike—Emanuel worked on Spanish translations of the Scriptures, as well as on Spanish and German Gospel literature. Some materials he wrote himself, other materials he simply translated, making sure that they were sensitive to the Jewish people. He wrote:

> ...this year we recalled Dr. Cohn's word: 'A Mission without a literature is like a bird without wings.' Therefore, this mission station edited two booklets in Spanish, 'A Christian Congregation Witnesses to its Jewish Neighbours,' and in German, 'One Holy Christian Church of Jews and Gentiles.' These booklets are now being distributed in all Spanish-

speaking countries including Morocco, and in the USA and Canada principally through the brotherly cooperation of Brother Atkinson.[136]

Over the years word of the Mission and of the Lichtenstein's ministry continued to spread throughout South America and Europe, and after a dozen years of ministry in Argentina Emanuel wrote: "...during the twelve years of mission work in Buenos Aires, this mission has grown to be something like an institution. Our presence is, however, a continual reminder: We preach to you Jewish men and women, your very own Messiah, crucified and risen from the dead, Jesus of Nazareth."[137]

The Chosen People magazine also heralded the story of the work in Buenos Aires as Emanuel's reports of decisions for the Lord, baptisms, or other avenues of testimony were presented in the magazine. Like Joseph Cohn, Emanuel was constantly looking for ways to put hands and feet to the message of the Gospel. In some of his reports, he spoke of the broad scope of their ministry. He reported:

Mrs. Lichtenstein and I often don't feel like brothers and sisters to our friends, but like parents; for, thanks to the great sacrifice of our Mission's Board of Directors, we are able to help all needy and dependent with doctor bills and medicine and the in-the-modern-medical-methods indispensable but very expensive radiographs and analyses, as well as with all kinds of other everyday difficulties and problems not so easily coped with by the exile as by the one at home. Still many Christian Jews have to flee from Hungary and come to us after having obtained our address in Austria, or are sent to us by immigrants here. The housing and language problems are the most difficult ones for the new-comers.[138]

Several months later he wrote:

Other features of our work are to intercede for the Jews who have illegally entered Argentine and help them to obtain their residing status; applying for home pensions for German and Austrian immigrants, arranging for the hospitalization of the ill; seeking medical care and medicines for the needy at Mission expenses; making regular calls on the ill and the infirm; helping families in the upkeep and education of their many children during this tremendous inflation; providing for clothes and shoes, books and whatnot; assisting women expecting children and lacking the means for adequate care; and intervening to the best of our possibilities in all that our proteges may need. A lawyer's office would have quite enough work with our tasks.[139]

A Congregation Established

As for his congregation, called "Congregation El Mesias (Messiah)," Emanuel reported:

...our 1959 Advent Reunion seemed to impress us as of more than usual significance because it was marked by a special fraternization of Jews and non-Jews,...This came about, we believe, because many Jewish and Jewish-Christian friends have been taking part in the monthly services of our "Congregation El Mesias (Messiah)" of which I am the pastor. The steady attendance of our Jewish and Jewish-Christian friends at these monthly services seems to have aroused the respect and admiration of the non-Jewish part of the congregation. The result of this fraternization led a delegation of our non-Jewish members to take part in our Reunion at the YWCA [The Mission had been moved from the church where it had been meeting, to the local YWCA. This afforded them more room as well as a more neutral place for the Jewish people to meet]. Our small quarters at this place were crowded to capacity, with almost a hundred persons present....

We are looking forward to the day—which may be, with God's help, before Easter of this year—when our Mission Station and our Congregation El Mesias will be under the same roof. I am sure this will promote a closer community feeling and unite us more completely, and at the same time establish us more firmly for the still greater spreading of our mission work for Israel.[140]

Emanuel's prayers were answered. On October 2, 1960 the Cangallo Chapel, the new home of Congregation El Mesias, was dedicated. Over one hundred sixty people attended the service. Lichtenstein opened the celebration with the lighting of the Menorah in honor of Rabbi Leopold Cohn, and Dr. Villaverde, President of the Iglesia Evangelica Luterana Unida, brought the message. In the message, Dr. Villaverde emphasized that the dedication of the Cangallo Chapel was the result of nearly twenty years of faithful proclamation of the Gospel by Emanuel and Justina, combined with the faithful testimony of the congregation to the needs of the community. On the Saturday following the dedication of the Cangallo Chapel, a special dedication service was held, in memory of Joseph Hoffman Cohn, to dedicate the official opening of the "Mission Room."[141]

With a new chapel for the congregation, and a new Mission room, the Lichtenstein's (by now in their late sixties) worked even harder as they sought to reach the German, Hungarian and Austrian Jewish immigrants in Buenos Aires with the Gospel.

Three years after the dedication of the Cangallo Chapel, during the summer of 1963, Daniel Fuchs (who was then serving as Missionary Secretary of the Mission) made his first trip to South America. Emanuel Lichtenstein was a spry seventy-one years of age. Daniel gave this description of him:

> ...Although I had never met Emanuel Lichtenstein before, I had learned to know him and to love him through our correspondence. Right from the start there was a bond of understanding and fellowship. If I ever write an article on 'My Most Unforgettable Character,' that character will be Emanuel Lichtenstein. Although he is already in his early seventies, he is a man of limitless energy. He walks with a limp, but at times I found myself hardly able to keep up with him. He is a big man, but he has to be one, for he has a great heart.[142]

Of the work being done in Buenos Aires, Daniel reported further:

> ...I heard testimonies that thrilled my heart. These children of Israel had found the Lord through the faithfulness of this unusual child of God. From one meeting to another, each day was filled with the warmth and joy of Christian fellowship. I went from home to home where I heard different words on the same theme. Thank God for His grace, for Emanuel Lichtenstein, for the American Board of Missions to the Jews!
>
> Jews are still flocking to the Argentine; it is an open door, but there are many adversaries. Not only many of the victims of the Nazis fled there but also many of the Nazis themselves. I saw red paint spilled as blood over the entrance of a synagogue at Buenos Aires. The walls of many buildings were covered with virulent anti-Semitic diatribe. We must tell these Jews about the real love of our Lord.[143]

The outreach and ministry that Emanuel Lichtenstein had accomplished in cooperation with the Lutheran church was impressive indeed, but Daniel Fuchs returned from his trip to Buenos Aires both elated and burdened. He was elated with what Lichtenstein had accomplished, but the congregation at the Cangallo Chapel was comprised mainly of East European Jews, and Daniel returned home burdened for the growing Sephardic Jewish communities of Latin America— Jewish people that the Mission was not reaching. As he pondered how the Mission could reach out to yet another Jewish community, Daniel did not know that God had already prepared a worker to meet the need.

VICTOR AND DEBORAH SEDACA

Even before his trip to Buenos Aires in 1963, Daniel had given thought to the eventuality of the Lichtensteins' retirement, and of the need for locating and training a worker who would be able to continue, and to expand, the work in Argentina. With this realization in mind, he had contacted Arthur Glass, a missionary who went to Buenos Aires in 1936 under the auspices of the International Hebrew Christian Alliance. Daniel wanted to know if Arthur knew of anyone who would be qualified to carry on the work among the immigrant Ashkenazi (East European) Jews, and to expand the outreach so it would include the indigenous Sephardic communities of Buenos Aires. In response, Arthur suggested that Daniel contact a Jewish believer by the name of Victor Sedaca; he was pastor of a church in Montevideo, Uruguay.

Victor Sedaca was born in Argentina in 1918. His parents were Spanish Jews. His father died when he was just a boy, and when his mother could no longer care for Victor and his older brother, she placed the boys in an orphanage in Buenos Aires.

When Victor was eighteen years of age he heard Arthur Glass preach the message of the Gospel. He could not believe that God loved him—a Jewish orphan. God moved upon his heart, and Victor became the first of many Jewish people who came to faith through the ministry of Arthur Glass. Later he enrolled in seminary, and after he had completed his studies, he married a young lady whose name was Deborah Ruth.

Victor and Deborah had not been married long before he felt led to answer an urgent call to pastor a church in Barcelona, Spain. In Barcelona they underwent great persecution for the Gospel's sake—their church was burned, Victor was imprisoned because of his witness for the Messiah, and Deborah's health was severely impaired. Yet they persisted, despite the suffering and persecution, knowing that God had called them to serve Him in Barcelona.

During their years in Spain, God used Victor in many areas of responsibility. He was Professor of Theology and Homiletics at the Baptist Theological Seminary, President of the Baptist Convention, and representative of the Spanish believers in the European Evangelical Conference and at the World Baptist Alliance. Yet, he was not at peace. The sight of the physical maladies of his Jewish brethren (ailments brought about as a result of suffering and oppression at the hands of the Nazis) created within him a desire to help relieve the physical needs of his people, as well as their spiritual needs. So great was this desire, that the Sedacas returned to Argentina so Victor could enroll in medical school. He remained active in missionary work during his five years of medical training and eventually he accepted a call to serve as pastor of a church in Montevideo, Uruguay.[144]

Daniel followed through on Arthur Glass's advice to meet with Victor Sedaca. He already knew of Victor through his association with the International Hebrew Christian Alliance; Victor was serving in an honorary capacity while pastoring the church in Uruguay. Daniel arranged his travel itinerary during the summer of 1963 to include a visit with Victor in Montevideo. This afforded him an opportunity to see a little of Victor's ministry there. He then invited Victor to Buenos Aires so Victor could observe the ministry there, as well as to meet with Emanuel Lichtenstein.

In the Spring of 1964 Victor entered the six-month training program of the Mission which was being conducted in Los Angeles, California under the direction of Mr. Martin Meyer Rosen (Moishe). Mr. Rosen was the Missionary-in-Charge of the Los Angeles branch of the Mission (his title was soon thereafter changed to Director of Recruiting and Training).[145] At the completion of the program, Victor was sent to serve as Missionary-in-Charge of the Pittsburgh branch, rather than being sent back to Buenos Aires as originally planned. This action was taken because Rev. Albert Runge, the Missionary-in-Charge of Pittsburgh had resigned to take a position with the Christian Jew Foundation in San Antonio, Texas, and the Mission desperately needed trained leadership for this old, established branch of the ministry. Knowing that God had called him to minister among his people in Buenos Aires, Victor agreed to the temporary reassignment in Pittsburgh—with the understanding that it was just until new leadership could be trained. But it was not until 1966, two years after entering the training program, that Victor was able to return to Argentina.

Victor's official title was Missionary-in-Charge of Buenos Aires. Emanuel and Justina Lichtenstein were named "Misionero Emeritus" (honorary missionaries) and they continued working among the German and Hungarian refugee Jews within the Lutheran church. The Sedacas worked with the Lichtensteins, but at the same time they worked to establish an indigenous work among the Sephardic Jews of Buenos Aires, and among the new generation of Jews who were immigrating to South America. On September 4, 1966 the Lord called Mrs. Justina Lichtenstein home. Emanuel Lichtenstein was then named Director Emeritus, a title he bore with honor until the Lord called him home at the age of 87, on August 22, 1979.

The methodology taught at the Missionary Training Program during the years when Victor Sedaca attended (c. 1964-65) was a "Center" approach to Jewish evangelism. Under this approach, the Mission would establish a branch from which all staff and programs of evangelism and ministry were generated. It was an approach that had been used by the Mission for many years, but it was a method of evangelism that required a building from which to work, and although Emanuel Lichtenstein and members of the Swedish Lutheran Mission had been anxious for the Mission to purchase a building in Buenos Aires, such a purchase had not been made.

It was not until 1965 that the Board began to consider following a centralized and unified program for all branches, including the foreign branch ministries. This was a matter which required that the Mission have registration in each country. Additionally, gaining tax exempt status required that the Mission be duly incorporated in each country. Action was taken to pursue the possibility of obtaining registration in Argentina.[146]

By September 1966, the Mission had obtained official registration in Argentina, but it did not follow through with incorporation. Shortly thereafter, problems developed between Victor Sedaca and Emanuel Lichtenstein. Each man had his own ideas regarding vision and direction for the ministry. With the hope that he could restore harmony between the two workers and their respective and joint ministries, Daniel Fuchs scheduled a visit to Buenos Aires in the Fall of 1967. But his negotiations did not accomplish the desired reconciliation; the Mission therefore severed its relationship with the Evangelical Lutheran Churches—churches that had sponsored the ministry in Buenos Aires from its inception.[147]

In many ways the severing of the Mission's joint ministry with the Lutheran Churches of South America resulted in the birth of a totally new work for the Mission. Under the leadership of Victor Sedaca, the ministry began to focus on the Jewish people of Buenos Aires, rather than on the European refugee Jews. The split also meant that the Mission had to locate another building, and the new work under Victor had to establish its own identity.

Victor Sedaca reported to readers of *The Chosen People* magazine that Emanuel Lichtenstein planned to continue his ministry among the German speaking Jews, with the help of Brother Juan Jorge Hecht, a German Lutheran pastor who established a bi-lingual ministry. The reason for the bi-lingual ministry was stated by Brother Hecht. He wrote:

> *During the last years our Argentine group was steadily increasing, and therefore it was advisable to translate German preachings into the national tongue. Whereas the older generation of Jewish immigrants continues in the German*

language, the younger ones prefer Spanish. For me it's a marvelous experience to talk in Spanish and in German about the same thing, as each tongue has beauties of its own. Sometimes a truth becomes clear to me in the Spanish text of the Bible, after having gone unnoticed in the German. It is a good thing to praise God in all languages and this is our experience.[148]

Victor went on to report that he and Deborah were "enlarging" the ministry to the Spanish-speaking by holding meetings for women at the Cangallo Street Church every Wednesday, by conducting Bible studies in their home every Tuesday evening, through visitation ministry among the 300,000 Jews of Buenos Aires, and deputation ministry among the many evangelical churches of the city.[149]

BUENOS AIRES BUILDING DEDICATED

In the Fall of 1969, the Board authorized the purchase of property in Buenos Aires, and in November 1970 the Mission's building was joyously dedicated.[150] Of that occasion Victor wrote:

'Dedicating living souls, not stones...' These were the culminating words which our General Secretary, Dr. Fuchs, used in his address on the occasion of the dedication of our new Mission Center in Buenos Aires in November, 1970.

At last it has became a joyful reality. Through God's grace we now have our own beautiful building in Calle Billinghurst 417 in this enormous capital city of Argentina. We will never forget that Sunday when a large crowd of members and friends of our Mission gathered outside the premises waiting for the moment when Dr. Fuchs would cut the ribbon, symbolically opening our Headquarters.

Our beloved guest also unveiled a commemorative plaque in the Mission hall, and said, 'This property is dedicated to the glory of God and to the salvation of Israel!'

Once in the auditorium, a varied program began...Pastor Lichtenstein gave a short outline of the history of the Mission in Argentina, which dates back to 1942. In its beginning the Mission was guest of several Christian institutions until quite a few years ago when it was welcomed to the premises of the Congregation El Mesias of the Lutheran Church.

The Buenos Aires churches and Christian institutions sent words of salutation and good wishes for God's blessing....

The pastors and missionaries came forward for the solemn moment of the dedication prayer of the Argentine Baptist Convention, Rev. Pedro Bachor.[151]

With a new building, a new focus, and a new identity, the ministry began to flourish and many Jewish people came to faith in Yeshua. Deborah Sedaca was also intensively involved, working with women's groups of the Mission and in the churches. She was often called upon to present the Jewish meaning of the feasts and the Jewish calendar to Christian women's group. From her many lectures, and under the auspices of the Baptist Women's Convention of Argentina, she wrote a book entitled "The Christian Woman and Her World." Of her book, she wrote:

...It has been a best seller in its field and also has been the means of gaining concern in the churches and women's groups for our Mission. Pastor Lichtenstein is mentioned in one of the chapters and because of this many have wanted to know about our outreach to the Jews. In the presentation of the book it is clearly stated that Mrs. Sedaca is working among the Jews in Argentina as a part of the ABMJ staff in Buenos Aires.

Everywhere I go for speaking engagements, I take our tracts to show the great need of making known the message of salvation to Israel.[152]

Following the Six-Day War and the Yom Kippur War, the eyes of the world were on Israel. People in South America, as well as in other countries of the world, wanted to know what the Scriptures had to say about the nation of Israel. Victor wrote:

The recent crisis provoked by the Middle East War [c. 1973] has enabled us to increase our literature ministry to the Jews. The booklet, 'The Indestructible Jew' (El indestructible pueblo de Israel) is being gladly accepted by almost everyone. With the help of brother Richard McMullin, thousands of these booklets have been distributed to the Jews, sponsored by the Million Testaments Campaign. As a result of such mass distribution, hundreds of Jewish people have written asking for the Prophecy Edition of the New Testament. Some people have even sent their requests 'registered mail' or 'special delivery!' A few weeks ago I received an eager request over the phone for a New Testament from a Jewish person who had just attended a Jewish mass meeting in a sports stadium. I told him that he would receive the

Testament the next day. Early the next day he called again and reminded me, 'Please remember that you promised to send me a New Testament.' He received it with much prayer to the Lord that he may know the Messiah as he reads the Word of God. The Spanish edition of the 'Shepherd of Israel' has had a warm acceptation. Please pray that we may continue translating and publishing this every month.[153]

As the work grew, volunteers and additional staff members were added. Rev. and Mrs. Peter Clark, missionaries to the Jews under the Churches Ministry to the Jews in England, assisted the ministry by teaching Hebrew and English to the Spanish Jews.[154]

Victor also began a weekly radio broadcast to the Jews in Buenos Aires and Montevideo. He said:

Every Sunday at 9:45 a.m. the entire coast of the River Plate and the Atlantic Ocean is being hit by the 'Messianic Voice,' a very high quality radio program featuring Hebrew songs, Hebrew Christian testimonies, an offer of literature and New Testaments, and a central prophetic message of 8 minutes, closing the program with a cordial, sincere, 'Shalom, amigos.'[155]

The Jewish children of Buenos Aires were not overlooked by the Sedacas as they proclaimed the Gospel message. Through a cooperative program with the Baptist Association of Entre Rios, Victor was able to participate in teaching the three hundred or so young people who were in the program, sharing truths about the Messiah and about God's plan for Israel.[156]

David Sedaca

In 1974 the author (who was then serving as Executive Vice President of the Mission) received a letter from Victor Sedaca in which he asked if the Board would consider hiring his son, David Sedaca, as a possible worker for the expanding ministry in Buenos Aires. David was already doing volunteer work for the Mission, while working at a secular job and pastoring a church. In one of his letters to the author, Victor wrote:

As you can imagine, brother Sevener, I feel very happy that the Lord has called David to devote his life to His service in the field of Jewish missions. Even happier to know that he has chosen our Mission as channel for his ministry.

According to your suggestion given to David in your letter of November 13th, I am glad to report that David is already working as part-time volunteer in the Buenos Aires branch with visitation, preaching, Bible studies, and many other minor activities of the mission, such as, taking people home in the Mission car, mailing, and taking care of some building repair.

As soon as he will be appointed as full-time missionary, his main job in the mission will be Minister of Visitation, along with other regular activities of the branch.[157]

The Board shared Victor's joy over David's desire to devote his life to Jewish mission work, and they recognized David's potential. They realized, as well, that there was a need for additional workers in Buenos Aires, but the consensus of opinion was that it would be unwise to hire David for the Buenos Aires branch and thereby place him directly under the supervision of his father. The author therefore wrote to David Sedaca, telling him of two possible openings for Mission service in branches other than Buenos Aires—one in the Los Angeles branch, the other in the Toronto, Canada branch.[158] David and his wife, Julie, prayed for God's leading and then contacted the Board saying they felt God was leading them to the Toronto branch of the Mission. While waiting for acceptance, visas, and travel arrangements to be made for their move to Canada, David continued to assist his father with the work in Buenos Aires.

David Sedaca was born on June 9, 1947 in Uruguay. At the time of his birth, his father, Victor, was pastoring the church in Montevideo, Uruguay. In 1956, through the influence and teaching of his parents, David accepted Yeshua as his Messiah. When he was old enough, David was sent to the United States for his schooling. He became involved in the Mission's summer camping program as a teenager, and it was during his teen years that he surrendered his life to the Lord and felt God's call upon his life for full-time service. As a student at Biola college, he became involved in the Los Angeles branch of the Mission, attending the Sunday afternoon services and participating with staff members as they went to MacArthur Park and to other areas to preach the Gospel.

After leaving Biola, David returned to Argentina. There, he continued his training at the Baptist Theological Seminary. He also took a position as assistant pastor of a church; it was at that church that he met the lovely young church organist and Sunday School teacher, Julia, who eventually became his wife.

Serving the Lord in a part-time capacity pleased David because it gave him opportunity to be involved in the business world as well. He took a job with General Motors of Argentina. Later, he took an even better position with the Goodyear Tire and Rubber Corporation. Eventually Goodyear asked him to take over Goodyear's branch operations in Mendoza, Argentina—a very important promotion. At last David had achieved the financial and social status he had been looking for. Not long after their move to Mendoza David accepted an invitation to become the Assistant Pastor of the West Mendoza Baptist Church. Things were going well for David and Julia Sedaca—they were building a new home and they had purchased a new car. But quite suddenly the Pastor of the church left, and the deacons asked David if he would be willing to be ordained and become their pastor. Their proposal interjected turmoil into David's previously well-ordered lifestyle. He knew acceptance of the position as pastor would require that he give up his job at Goodyear—something he did not want to do. As he prayed about it, he felt God leading him to ask the company if they would allow him to accept the pastorate, *and* maintain his position at the company. David knew God had intervened when the President of Goodyear made an exception in company rules, allowing him to become the pastor of the West Mendoza Baptist Church and retain his position as an executive with Goodyear at the same time.

After pastoring the West Mendoza Baptist Church for four years, David told Julia of his desire to resign the church and to quit his job with Goodyear. In the months that followed, they sold their new home and gave up the new car; they put themselves and their two little children totally into the hands of the Lord. David served as the vice president of the Baptist Churches Association of Mendoza. He was a member of the radio and television committee of the Argentine Baptist Convention. He produced Christian radio and T.V. programs, and was in charge of the broadcast of the evangelistic programs of Billy Graham for that area of Argentina, and for the Luis Palau radio programs in the Republic of Chile. He was even able to use his hobby of photography for the Lord by producing motion pictures. But an emptiness within remained. In his heart, he longed to see his Jewish people come to faith in Messiah. As he and Julia prayed, God continued to burden their hearts for the salvation of Jewish people. It was then that David made application to join the staff of the Mission.

With assurance in his heart that the right decisions had been made, David arrived in New York in the middle of March, 1979. He was there to take part in a six-month training program, after which he was to move with his family to Toronto Canada. But within weeks after his arrival in the States (June 1979), he and the Mission received word that Victor Sedaca had died of a sudden massive heart attack. Ironically, on the day before his death, Victor had preached a message entitled, "I have fought a good fight." Only two months later, on August 22, 1979, Pastor Emanuel Lichtenstein, the faithful and beloved founder of the Mission in Buenos Aires, died. Within a period of only a few short months, the Mission in Argentina was stripped of leadership.

SOUTH AMERICAN BOARD ESTABLISHED

Following the sudden deaths of Emanuel Lichtenstein and Victor Sedaca, an agreement was reached between the Mission's Board of Directors and David Sedaca that he would return to Argentina to serve as the Missionary-in-charge of Buenos Aires for a period of two years. During that time, he was to stabilize the work by working toward establishing an Argentine Board of Directors and by locating and training replacement staff. At the conclusion of the two year period, with the aforementioned goals accomplished, the Board agreed that it would then transfer David and his family to serve in the Toronto, Canada branch.

The American Directors recognized as never before the formidable task of administering a foreign branch of the Mission from the United States, and realized the need for a local Board of Directors to oversee the personnel and to control the finances of the work in South America. The proposal that such a board be established was agreed upon by the American Board, with the understanding that two members from the American Board would also serve on the Board in South America.[159]

On December 14, 1979 a Board of Directors for the Argentine branch of the Mission was established. The Board's membership was comprised of outstanding Christian businessmen and Christian leaders in Argentina. Mr. Jose Abadi, a Sephardic Jewish believer, was elected to serve as the Chairman of the Board—a position he continues to hold at the writing of this history. Jose was born in Egypt. As an adult, he founded a paper manufacturing, book binding, and printing business called "Fabril Encuadernadora Inc." He has served as President of his company, and has also served on the Stewardship Committee of the Baptist Convention of Argentina. Other members of the Argentine Board included: Mr. Samuel Martinez, President of "Martinez, Sarmenti & Co.," manufacturer of office equipment and supplies. Samuel also served on the Executive Committee of the Baptist Convention of Argentina. Dr. Luis Arroyo, a lawyer and professor of history and economy at Moron University in Buenos Aires. Mr. Sebastian Impelluso, former sales director of General Motors Co., then a member of the Board of Directors of Toyota Sales Co. He also served as President of the Argentine Chamber of Auto Dealers, and as a member of the Board of a Bank Pool of Tokyo in South America. Mr. David Somoza, Executive Secretary of the Argentine Bible Society, and an economist. Dr. Daniel Tinao, President of the Baptist Theological Seminary of Buenos Aires. Dr. Tinao is also a psychiatrist and a well-known author and professor. He served as the pastor of Once Church.

With the help of these Board members, the ministry increased in its outreach and influence among the Jews and the Christians of Argentina. David Sedaca wrote of the new Argentine Board:

> ...By this important step, our ministry will depend more than ever before on the efforts of Christian churches. It will actually become part of the mission work of the local churches. With their support we will be able to hire full-time missionaries to help us. We already have the workers, and we are sure that God will supply the means.
>
> Argentina will become the center for Jewish outreach throughout South America. Brazil, Uruguay, Venezuela and Chile have large Jewish communities that need to hear of their Messiah. In fact, Sao Paulo, Brazil, has the fastest growing population in the world...and they need to know about Jesus.
>
> ...we have started street meetings in a square two blocks away from our mission building. While these young people teach Bible lessons to the children, I and a group of believers preach the Gospel to the Jews. Every Sunday at 5 p.m. a street meeting is held, and many Jews hear for the first time that Jesus is the promised Messiah.[160]

As an astute businessman, David also located and trained a young woman who literally became the "man Friday" for the ministry in Buenos Aires. When she joined the staff of the Mission her name was Miss Giselle Sparks. She later became Mrs. Giselle Grancharoff. Nothing was too small a task or too great a task for Giselle to accomplish. She was an invaluable and astute worker who handled the details of the expanding work with diligence and love. When David was transferred to Canada, she stayed as the "bridge" to stabilize the work and to assist the new director in his activities.

David's two-year commitment in Argentina was drawing to a close and the Canadian Board of the Mission was requesting a full-time missionary for Toronto. David was the obvious candidate, but there was considerable concern over who would replace him in the Buenos Aires branch. Before any decisions had been made, civil war broke out in Argentina. Inflation rose several hundred percent and support for the ministry from local churches in South America dropped drastically, while expenses skyrocketed! The Board agreed that under the circumstances, David and his family should be immediately transferred out of Buenos Aires to Toronto. The ministry in Buenos Aires was to be put "on hold" until things settled down, but David was to maintain contact with the Board in South America and the search for a Missionary-in-Charge for the Argentine branch was to continue.[161]

In the midst of the Sedacas' move to Canada, and in the midst of turmoil regarding the long-range future of the Argentine ministry, God raised up a choice servant for the work there. Roberto Passo, a well-known pastor, evangelist, and soul-winner was willing to become Missionary-in-Charge of the Buenos Aires branch.

ROBERTO PASSO—HIS STORY

Roberto Passo was born in Buenos Aires, Argentina on May 1, 1936. He was a child of a mixed marriage—his mother was of Sephardic Jewish background; his father was a Gentile. As an adult, Roberto recalled that in his parents' home love and peace were almost nonexistent. It was a home in which the children often watched helplessly as their father physically and verbally abused their mother, and Roberto recalls moments when he felt so bad that he wanted to kill his father. As a result of the turmoil in the home, Roberto's childhood and teenage days were problematic. When he was nine years old the situation became so bad that he considered suicide.

Roberto looked for love and peace outside his family's home but, unfortunately, he looked in all the wrong places. He began to follow the ways of the world, and soon his life was full of sin. He recognized that many of the things he was doing were wrong, but he felt helpless to stop his own actions.

When he was sixteen years old, Roberto began working in his father's repair company. Frequently he was called to make repairs at a Baptist Church near his home. The members of the church were very friendly and they often invited Roberto to attend the services, but he wanted nothing to do with religion or with God. One day was different however. Years later, in broken English, Roberto shared his testimony, saying:

> I was there in the temple of the Baptist Church, where I was making several repairs, and feeling that something special was in the atmosphere. I had always thought that the members of that church must be mad, because I had never known about God. But in that moment, I felt his Presence there, and for the first time I prayed to Him, in that way: 'God, If this is the real religion, Please make me come here.'[162]

It did not take God long to answer Roberto's prayer. One of the members of the church came to his home and personally invited him to come to the church with her. Since she had come personally, to invite him, Roberto felt he could not refuse her warm invitation. Of that visit Roberto wrote: "The worship did not mean nothing to me, but what really stroke [sic] my life, was the atittude [sic] of the members. Some of them were neighbors. They received me so warmly, with such a concern, that the following Sunday I went for myself."[163]

Roberto continued attending the services and the warmth of the church fellowship, combined with the teaching of the Word of God, began to melt his hardened heart. It wasn't long until the Holy Spirit of God brought conviction upon his heart, and Roberto openly professed Jesus as his Messiah and Lord.

Roberto continued working at his father's repair company, but he also began taking classes toward a Masters of Technical Engineering. After graduation he formed his own repair company, and he made a commitment to God to support missionaries with the money he made. He believed in this way he could fulfill God's calling upon his life.

He was an active church member and a successful businessman who regularly supported a number of missionaries when he met Azucena Laura Richetti, a student in her last year at the Baptist Theological Seminary. For Roberto, it was love at first sight, but he didn't have the courage to tell Azucena of his love for her because of his past life. After much prayer, he summoned up all of his courage and declared his love for Azucena. Her response was that she would pray about his intentions. As she prayed, God showed Azucena that she truly loved Roberto and they announced their engagement.

With his fiancee working in a missionary program in another city in Argentina, Roberto bowed his head before eating his lunch one day, and God used that moment to speak to his heart in a way that changed the course of his life. Remembering that experience, Roberto wrote:

> ...before having lunch, I began to pray. I felt His presence very strongly. I knew that God wanted all my life, but I did not want to hear His voice. I was working a lot in the ministry of my church, I was attending a Biblical Course, but that was not God's will. In that moment, I opened my Bible and God spoke very clear through the passage, where I read, '...And they immediately left the boat and followed Him' (Matthew 4:22). I felt upset, and shut the Bible. But I had there a magazine which cover said: 'Lord, I sold you today, because I prefered [sic] my plans to yours.' I threw it also. In that moment, crying I said to my Lord, 'Take my life, and do whatever you want with it.' Since then, I felt peace and joy in my heart. I left the Repair Company and began my theological study at the Baptist Theological Seminary. And now, I have serving as ordained pastor for seventeen years. And what is really important in my life, is not how and how long I live, but yes for whom. I live for the Glory of God, and my favorite passage is: 'Commit thy way unto the Lord; trust also in him, and he shall bring it to pass.'[164]

Indeed, God brought to pass His will in the lives of Roberto and Azucena Passo. Not only did Roberto serve the Lord as a pastor for seventeen years, he was also used of the Lord as an evangelist. His ministry has resulted in countless thousands of Gentiles and Jews coming to faith in Jesus.

Through the late Rev. Victor Sedaca, God impressed Roberto with the need of sharing the Gospel with his own people—the Jews. Victor faithfully encouraged Roberto to minister among the Jews, and although Victor did not live to see the day when Roberto joined the staff of the Mission, Victor's son, David Sedaca, actually recruited Roberto for the Mission's staff.

Roberto joined the staff of the Mission in 1982. He has served as Missionary-in-charge of the South American ministry since that time. Under his capable and godly leadership the work has blossomed. His vision for the work, his boundless energy, and his commitment to the Lord and to the task of preaching the Gospel message have been the impetus that has enabled the work to develop beyond the borders of Argentina; he became a "Johnny Appleseed" for the Mission throughout South America. Wherever he went, Jews and Gentiles responded to his message by coming to faith in Yeshua; others responded by volunteering their services as missionaries and as support workers.

As more and more volunteers came forward to express their desire to begin a Gospel outreach to the Jews in their communities, Roberto recognized the need to equip the volunteer staff with the knowledge and with materials to make them effective soul winners. He therefore established an annual Jewish Evangelism Training Seminar which is held in Buenos Aires in conjunction with an annual Prophetic Conference. Under this program Rev. Passo has trained workers and assisted in establishing branches of the Mission in many other Latin American countries including Chile, Uruguay, and Peru. The author (who was serving as President of the Mission at the time the seminars were first established) was often invited to join Rev. Passo, and the Jose Abadi (Chairman of the Board for South America) as a speaker at the annual conferences. It was a great joy to see the nearly two hundred volunteers, most of whom traveled to Buenos Aires at their own expense, gather each morning for training and instruction on how to witness to the Jewish people. In the evenings, the auditorium was filled to capacity as the volunteers gathered to hear the messages on Israel, prophecy, and Jewish evangelism. Oftentimes, curious passers-by stopped to listen through open windows as the message of the Gospel was presented, and when the invitation was given, dozens of Jewish people came forward to accept Yeshua as Messiah.

One year, over seventy-five Jewish people made their way down the aisle to proclaim their faith in Yeshua.

Under the leadership of Roberto Passo and Jose Abadi the ministry in South America today reaches into nearly every Jewish community on that continent. As the work spread, the demand for a Spanish edition of *The Chosen People* magazine grew. Giselle Grancharoff faithfully worked on translating the magazine and today "El Pueblo Elegido" is being circulated throughout South America, as well as into other Spanish-speaking areas of the world.

ELIAS HABIF

The growing South American ministry was also much in need of another full-time missionary. In the Spring of 1990, God answered prayers for a qualified worker for the work in Argentina in the person of Mr. Elias Habif. Elias is a product of the ministry in Buenos Aires. He has the distinction of being the first missionary appointed by the South American Board, with the approval of the American Board. With his appointment, the South American Board agreed to help raise part of his support in South America.

Elias Habif was born in Buenos Aires, Argentina on December 6, 1949. In sharing his testimony with readers of *The Chosen People* magazine, Elias wrote:

> ...*My family was a poor Sephardic Jewish family, where I was brought up with love and care amidst a Jewish culture, celebrating festivities and trying to keep God's commandments.*
>
> *I studied some years at the Talmud Torah Shalom, a Hebrew Yeshiva of the Sephardic community, in front of my house. When I was 13 years old, I was Bar Mitzvah and knew then that I was responsible for my own acts. According to Jewish tradition, I was now able to participate in the minyan, the required number of men to hold religious ceremonies, and several times I did.*
>
> *I knew and understood Judaism's beautiful traditions but I did not personally know the God I should love and to whom I should render all my acts. Many years would pass before I would know a real relationship with God and the true meaning of those festivities. I needed time to know the Way, the Truth and the Life, the Messiah of Israel.*
>
> *I lived a different life in those years. Only now am I able to understand that God was directing everything. One of those circumstances was that when I turned fifteen years old, I started thinking that I would die at the age of 33.*
>
> *This thought stayed with me for a long time. I had a common life, as any young man; in high school I studied guitar. But, as I grew, I grew further from my Judaism.*
>
> *As Judaism grew less vital for me, I had another dream. This time I was 20 years old. In that dream my person appeared double; one of them was listening to the other who was preaching in a big room with a Bible in his hand. Both of them were me, and the audience included both Jews and Gentiles! It was a quiet and harmonious dream, but it was crazy. I was an atheist, I could not participate in meeting like this. Yet I had dreamed this dream several times!*
>
> *I entered college for an accounting degree. Then I turned to music, working and playing in different pubs and bars. When I got my degree as a guitar teacher, I started teaching and doing some recitals. Everything should have been fine, but my life lacked something. There was a terrible spiritual need in me: I lacked hope and faith.*
>
> *On the street someone gave me a New Testament tract which I read. But on the other hand, I was also attending some courses on spiritual education; going to the spiritualistic school and other Eastern religions. But I felt badly. None of these could fill my heart.*
>
> *When I was 26 years old, I met a man who studied the Bible. After telling him 'no' many times, I finally accepted and started attending his Bible study. They were really interested in showing me the prophecies about the Messiah of Israel in the Old Testament. Only through His death and Resurrection, could I find peace and eternal life, they told me. God was working on me, but I didn't realize it.*
>
> *At the age of 29, I started working at a Catholic school, teaching guitar. Every day for the next five years, I passed in front of an organization of believers in Jesus (Campus Crusade for Christ) two blocks from my job. But I did not want to enter there. I thought only a miracle could make me enter. But God was preparing that miracle.*
>
> *In March 1983, while crossing a park near the school, I met a young man from that organization. He approached me and after some questions, talked to me about God. Here was my miracle! My surprise grew when he invited me to Chosen People Ministries, a place where Messianic Jewish believers met.*
>
> *I went for the first time, and was introduced to Pastor Passo and his family. After several meetings, the moment came for me—I accepted Jesus as my Savior and Messiah! He filled my heart and took possession of my life. My old life died, and I began a new life—exactly when I turned 33 years old. After two or three months of being a believer, Pastor Passo asked me to conduct the music for worshipping God in our meetings. When he asked me to teach a Bible Study, I understood that my dream had been a message from God. Finding the Messiah at Chosen People Ministries was the end of a long journey, but what is more important, it was the fulfillment of God's prophecies to me. There is still*

a long way to go, and God is still working in my life, making progress every day. Along with Pastor Passo, other brothers and sisters, and my fiancee Rosa (whom I met at Chosen People Ministries [Rosa is now Mrs. Rosa Habif c.1989]), we visit many churches sharing the work of the ministry.[165]

After their marriage, Elias and Rosa began a second outreach ministry in a suburb of Buenos Aires. They continue to work along side of Roberto Passo and the Board in South America, seeking to reach many more Jewish people with the Gospel.

Fifty years have passed since the Lichtenstein's fled Vienna and re-established their lives and ministry in Buenos Aires. Their Gospel testimony to the Jews of Argentina is continuing today, and has spread beyond the borders of the Argentine, through the ministry of Rev. Roberto Passo and his dedicated staff.

OTTO SAMUEL—MINISTRY IN GERMANY

Only months after Joseph Cohn met and hired Emanuel Lichtenstein to be the Mission's worker in Vienna, he hired Rev. Otto Samuel to continue the Mission's outreach in Germany. The year was 1937. Herbert Singer and his family had immigrated to America, thus creating a great need for someone to pick up the baton of testimony and assistance of the war-ravaged German Jews. Like Herbert Singer, Otto Samuel's name was give to Joseph Cohn at the recommendation of Pastor Arnold Frank.

Persecution of the Jews of Germany was increasing at an alarming rate, and Nazi activity was making the outreach at Pastor Frank's mission difficult, but at the time Otto Samuel was hired neither Joseph Cohn nor Pastor Frank realized that Frank's mission in Hamburg would soon be forced to close. With his usual optimism, Joseph Cohn hired Otto to work under the direct supervision of Pastor Frank; he was to be responsible for distributing the relief money which the Mission sent to Germany. As always, the announcement of the new work was heralded in *The Chosen People* magazine:

We have also engaged at full-time salary the services of Rev. Otto Samuel who will represent us in doing itinerant work throughout Germany as our missionary and relief disbursing agent...He is going to carry on his activities in connection with the Paulus-Bund, which is a union of some 80,000 non-Aryan Christians who have sought by joining forces to help each other with a work of cheer and with mutual fellowship in the hour of suffering.[166]

Otto Samuel was born on March 10, 1887. His father was a merchant. His mother died while he was a young child.

During his childhood, Otto worked hard to get good grades in school so that he would be able to attend college. He had an interest in philosophy. His grades would have allowed him to pursue his interest in college, but his father denied him this dream. It seemed Otto was destined for the same profession as his father; it made him very unhappy.

After two years as an apprentice merchant, despite his unhappiness, Otto advanced to the position of foreign forwarding clerk—a position which gave him an opportunity to travel as well as to pursue his studies in philosophy, away from his father's watchful eye.

It was through his study of philosophy that Otto first came in contact with the dogmas and teaching of Christianity. Intrigued, he began reading the New Testament as well as other books on Christian doctrine and theology, but the mystery of the gospel had not yet been revealed to him.

In 1914 war broke out in Europe. Otto was twenty-eight years old. His father had recently died, and he was inducted into the military. He was sent to Merzig on the Saar for military training. While he was there he became seriously ill and had to be taken to the military hospital.

In a hospital bed next to Otto lay a soldier who was a believer in the Lord Jesus. He told Otto he had prayed for years that the Lord would grant him the opportunity to share the gospel with a Jewish person. Otto later recalled:

...A conversation arose between us which lasted until late at night,...during the course of which my friend, Leo Hoffman, gave his testimony. Finally he asked me to pray that if Jesus of Nazareth should really be the Messiah, He might reveal Himself to me. When I was alone, I followed this advice in true simplicity. The Lord Jesus Christ revealed Himself to me in His whole Majesty and Glory. Above all He also revealed Himself to me as the Savior of sinners. I fell on my knees before Him and confessed my sins, and He awarded me forgiveness. I who had been an arrogant philosopher and who even then was speculating on the unity of God, became very humble. A new life began for me....I had a burning desire for the Word of God. My friend loaned me his Bible, until I could get one for myself. I read over and over again the entire New Testament. Worlds opened before my mind.[167]

Throughout the war, Otto continued his study of the Bible and theology. He started a Bible study among the others soldiers who were stationed with him in Namur, and soon many of them also came to faith in Jesus.

After the war, Otto went to see Dr. Everhard Arnold, the co-editor of the "Furro" (Furche). Dr. Arnold, who pastored a church in Halle-Saale, had published a number of Otto's philosophical essays in the Furro. As the two men spent time together, Dr. Arnold asked Otto to become his assistant at the church.

Otto eventually succeeded Dr. Arnold as the pastor of the church in Halle-Saale—a position he held for five years. He was then asked to become the pastor of the Free Evangelical Church of Gelsenkirchen-Horst, where he remained for ten years—until Hitler's troops began rounding up the Jews of Europe for torture and for certain death in the concentration camps.

Resigning his pastorate to help his own Jewish people, Otto wrote:

> *The peculiar conditions of today have for a long time made it appear very desirable for me to resign my ministry here in my community and to try to help my Hebrew Christian brethren according to the flesh. Whether the Lord will grant me a short or long life, I pray God to make me fit to give my all to this huge task, which has sprung up from this new situation.*[168]

After resigning from his pastorate, Otto contacted Pastor Arnold Frank, asking if he could assist him in helping refugee Jews. Pastor Frank, in turn, contacted Joseph Hoffman Cohn, asking if the Mission would pick up Otto's support. Cohn immediately agreed, and thus the Mission had a new staff worker in Europe.

But neither Otto Samuel nor the Mission realized the full extent of suffering and persecution Otto would have to endure because of his decision to help his Jewish brethren. As he sought to bring help and relief, as well as the gospel message, to the suffering Jews of war-ravished Europe, Otto Samuel became a hunted enemy of the Nazis!

Like Herbert Singer, Otto Samuel, was forced to flee Germany. But although he was forced to forsake his country, he did not forsake the Gospel, or his ministry. Instead, he re-established his work in Brussels, where The Belgium Gospel Mission graciously allowed him office space in which to carry on his work among refugee Jews who were fleeing Germany and other parts of Europe.[169]

Otto wasted no time in establishing a relief ministry for the refugees in Belgium and Antwerp. Rev. John C. Winston, the Head Secretary of the Belgian Gospel Mission, wrote to Joseph Cohn concerning the missionary efforts of Otto Samuel, saying:

> *I should like to assure you that it is a real satisfaction to me to have a small share in the splendid efforts which Mr. Samuel is exerting to bring spiritual and material assistance to a large number of the Jewish refugees who are helplessly stranded here in Brussels. Ever since he reached here last April, he has been holding meetings, making visits and having private interviews with numbers of German and former Austrian expatriates who have sought asylum in Belgium. I have been particularly pleased to notice that his interest in the spiritual welfare of these poor unfortunates is even greater than his care for their physical needs. I feel sure that many of them will realize in later years that the awful trial of this hour has come to them as a blessing in disguise, for God will have used it for the salvation of their souls through the ministry of His servant. And all who come in contact with him here will have cause to be thankful for his labor of love on their behalf.*
>
> *When he came to me a few weeks ago to tell me of the means that you were placing at his disposal for the opening of a soup kitchen for Jewish refugees in Brussels during the hard months of winter, I rejoiced and I continue to rejoice in the present realization of that plan. It is heart-rending to see the plight of many who, as foreigners in a strange land, without resources, without friends, forbidden to work by the law of the land and with a very dark outlook for the future are in most cases entirely dependent on charity. To about one hundred of these Mr. Samuel is now giving one warm substantial meal a day. Moreover, those who have no fire in their own cramped little rooms, here find a place to sit and be warm. They also have a chance to hear the Eternal Gospel of our Lord Jesus Christ.*[170]

Shortly after Joseph received that letter, the Nazis ravaged Belgium, sweeping up Otto Samuel in their web of hate and destruction. For the second time Otto was taken prisoner. This time his captors took him to an internment camp in Perpignan, located in the Spanish Pyrenees. Joseph was able to get some money to him, and he received a letter from Otto as well. Otto told Joseph that he had been taken to the Internment Camp along with about forty other refugees from his work in Brussels, and about fifty non-Aryan Christians. He told Cohn:

> *My situation here is very hard. We are lying in very bad barracks on straw. The walls are broken and when the mistral east wind Storms (this is a sand storm) we are getting always covered with sand. During the day time it is very hot, and*

> *at night we have terrible cold. This coldness which comes from the ground has made me sick. I have terrible pains in my kidneys and in the chest. From day to day I am getting weaker, very often I cannot get up in the morning, and my physical condition is getting weaker every day. It is the highest time that I get help. With all my troubles I do my duty just like in Brussels. I have my meetings and I give the little I have to my comrades.*
>
> *From my poor wife, I know nothing! Alas! Please pray for us, that the Lord will deliver us and guide us together. The Word of the Lord is every day my great consolation. Excuse my faults, I may not be in possession of all my forces [faculties]. I must write this letter on my knees, we have no tables.[171]*

By January 1941, Joseph reported that he had received word that Otto Samuel had been moved from Camp Perpignan to Camp de Gurs, in the unoccupied area of France. Furthermore, he'd heard that Otto had been made chief chaplain of all the Protestants and the non-Aryan Christians in the new camp. Joseph had also learned that Mrs. Samuel was alive, and was living in Brussels, anxiously waiting her husband's release.[172]

The May 1941 issue of *The Chosen People* magazine announced that Otto Samuel had finally been released from Camp de Gurs, and had made his way to Marseille, France, where he was awaiting a ship to America. The report went on to say that his wife was still in Brussels, which was under Nazi control, and could not get out. Joseph wrote:

> *...He is physically in the most deplorable condition, indeed it is a wonder that he is alive after all that he went through in the concentration camps. We praise God that his life has been preserved and now we are doing everything in our power to get him to America; once here, we want to give him every benefit of medical treatment, and then as the Lord restores him to his former strength, we want to send him out again in some other refugee center where he can carry on the work that God has given him to do.[173]*

At the June 24, 1941 meeting of the Executive Committee, Joseph Cohn told members of the Board that he had received a wire informing him that Mr. Otto Samuel had at last been able to sail from France, on a ship leaving for Trinidad; he was scheduled to arrive in New York on June 27th. The message in the wire also mentioned Otto's failing health and the possibility that he might need hospitalization. It also mentioned that Otto had a brother who lived in Brooklyn, and that he had prepared a room for Otto.[174]

Some 8,000 Jewish refugees had settled in the Philadelphia area, and Otto was sent to work under Harry Burgen in the Philadelphia branch of the Mission. At the October 1941 Board meeting, Joseph told the Directors that the Mission had been given the use of a church in North Philadelphia. Otto Samuel's responsibility would be to conduct one gospel meeting a week for the Jewish refugees, and give them lessons in English. Several Christian women in the Philadelphia area had volunteered to help Otto with the English lessons.[175]

The official Minutes of a meeting held May 13, 1942 includes the last, sad, entry regarding Otto Samuel. They state:

> *...we have been having some difficulty with Otto Samuel but we have been hoping that it might finally blow over. Perhaps the terrible experiences through which he has passed in the camps in Europe have unbalanced his mind so that he is super-sensitive. The other workers in Philadelphia have found it impossible to work with him and he refused to cooperate, and finally resigned.[176]*

There is no further word on what happened to Otto Samuel after he left the Mission. We can only hope and pray that our Great Physician healed any and all problems so that he could continue in the ministry God had called him to.

In Europe, just as the deadly web of Nazism had entangled the Jews of Vienna, Belgium, and Germany, it was beginning to encompass the Jews of Poland (The stories of Nazi torture and persecution of the Jews of Poland is infamous).

MOSES GITLIN—MINISTRY IN POLAND

Prior to the Nazis invasion of Poland, Moses Gitlin traveled throughout that country sharing the Gospel with Jewish people who lived there. In the city of Warsaw, where he lived, a number of young Jewish believers who had come to know Yeshua through his ministry had requested that he establish a Bible Training School—a kind of Messianic Yeshiva. In April 1936, Joseph Cohn reported to the readers of *The Chosen People* magazine that the Mission had granted permission to Moses Gitlin to move to a larger apartment—one that would better accommodate his growing ministry and provide space for the Bible School.[177]

Moses Schiff, Mr. Gitlin's assistant wrote glowing reports of Mr. Gitlin's travels throughout Poland. In one statistical report to Cohn, Schiff reported: "...To those who are interested in statistics, here are a few:—Days on journey 49; places visited, 30; distance covered in kilometers, 1190; sermons preached, 63; attendance at meetings, 4,550; tracts distributed, 1,335; individuals dealt with, 216; homes visited, 115."[178] This was a very busy schedule considering the fact that most travel was done by foot, by horseback, or by mule-drawn carriages.

Schiff also reported: "...It is hard to stop the flow of the masses of Jews that come to our doors. And to stop we must; for our meeting room has room for about forty, and with the adjoining room we could accommodate let us say some sixty or seventy people. They come, they fill the places, they take up all the standing room, and still they keep dropping in, till we simply have to lock the doors, and say that there is no more room."[179]

Clearly, Mr. Gitlin and Mr. Schiff were reaching out to the Jewish community with the Gospel—but they were also meeting a need within the Jewish community. Of an "Oneg Shabbat" (a Sabbath Gathering) that they held in Warsaw, Mr. Schiff reported:

> Representatives of missions in Warsaw, Lodz, Pinsk, and other cities, admire our beautiful and blessed 'oineg shabosim.'...The selected audience which number from 20 to 40 have each time more pleasure and profit from it. The audience is seated in a circle. We feel ourselves extraordinarily in the cozy atmosphere of our Beth Sar Shalom. Every time we have a different theme for the evening, and to this theme are adapted all the remarks, recitations, singing, prayers or sermonettes, and instrumental music. We have a break during the two and a half hours of our oineg shabos, during which Mrs. Gitlin serves tea and some nicely prepared and tasty Kosher sandwiches.[180]

Joseph Cohn visited the work in Poland during the summer of 1936, and saw firsthand the remarkable way in which God was blessing the ministries of Moses Gitlin and Moses Schiff.[181] Despite increasing anti-Semitism, the ministry remained undisturbed until the Fall of 1937. It was then that Joseph received a letter from Moses Gitlin in which he mentioned a great dilemma: the church they attended, and which they had encouraged Jewish believers to attend, was no longer going to allow Jewish people to attend. The letter stated:

> On Saturday, October 9, while I was still abroad, there came to Mrs. Gitlin the associate pastor of our church, and told her that the pastor wished her to announce at our Gospel meetings in the church that no Jew should come to the church services on Sunday, seeing that the 'Nationalists' have threatened to demolish the Gospel hall if any Jews will be found there.
>
> According to the wisdom which the Lord gave bountifully to my dear wife, she did not tell any long story to the audience, but simply announced that henceforth the services on Sunday will be held in our mission hall and the Jews need not go to the church meeting place.
>
> And so it was. On Sunday morning and evening services were held in our own mission place.
>
> Upon my arrival from abroad,...Alas, we became also convinced that it was not only the outside pressure from the nationalists which had forced him [the pastor] to put a taboo on Jews coming to the church; but that, alas, also some of the church members have become infected with the anti-Semitic epidemic and have availed themselves of the demand of the nationalists and suggested the taboo.
>
> The only solution to the problem that Pastor S. could propose is that we form ourselves into a Hebrew Christian church and that as a church unit we enter into the Union of Evangelical Christian Churches of which he is the President....
>
> Up to the very last minute I was asked to preach twice a week regularly and sometimes thrice a week at our church. Mrs. Gitlin and I, as well as many of our Jewish brethren paid in their membership dues, and liberally contributed to every church need....
>
> Judging by what we go through now you can imagine what the regular unbelieving Jew has to go through now in this land. On the other hand the unconverted Jews are a big and powerful body, and can appeal directly and indirectly, while we are such a tiny handful, and we dare not voice any protests and dare not make any open appeals. Pray for us, Please.
>
> What a pity, that now, when the Lord works again so mightily in the hearts of Jews, we should have such a setback. May the Lord be pleased to make the wrath of men to praise Him, and make all things work together for good to them that love Him.[182]

But conditions got worse, not better. The long night of Jewish suffering continued. The persecution of the Jews in Poland was far more hideous than in Germany; it just did not receive the publicity. Quoting the Manchester Guardian, *The Chosen People* magazine reported: "...more than 1,000 Jews were injured in riots and persecutions in Poland in the year 1936. In some towns there has been a wholesale destruction of property designed to make it impossible for the Jews to live. For the first time in the history of Poland, Jews have been branded officially as being racially inferior.[183]

As the satanic attack of anti-Semitism fell upon the Jews of Poland, the personnel of the Mission also fell under satanic attack. In his April 1937 report to the Board, Joseph Cohn stated:

Mr. Schiff, our worker in Warsaw has had a moral break-down, and it has been necessary to discharge him from the work. He is without question the most able Talmudical scholar in all Poland and is a gifted man. He has had a most unhappy home life....Under such conditions perhaps we should not have engaged him, but Mr. Gitlin felt that this situation could be overcome. The matter got into the newspapers and has caused disgrace and disturbance among the believers.[184]

The work in Poland was different from the other foreign branches. It was different because Moses Gitlin shared Joseph Cohn's vision to see a Hebrew Christian church established, and he worked diligently toward that end. This vision was realized when, just prior to January 1, 1938, such a congregation was established.[185] In an article in which Joseph described the sufferings of the Gitlin's and the uncertainties of maintaining the work in Poland, he said:

...The policies and methods pursued in Warsaw are sui generis, a piece of work uniquely patterned by Mr. Gitlin and his good wife, along lines which the Lord has allowed them to develop, lines peculiar to the needs and environment of the situation in Poland. Mr. Gitlin has reached out in every direction, and has given unstintedly of his time, and talent, and experience,...On a number of occasions the rising tide of Jew hate has seemed to threaten to close down the work in Warsaw entirely;...Last year he was assaulted in an open street in Warsaw, by some of the Anti-semitic hoodlums, and was seriously disabled for a number of weeks. In his modesty he never said a word to us about it in his reports; but last summer when I was in London, I heard about it from another missionary worker, and then I spoke to Mr. Gitlin, and he rather reluctantly admitted the assault, but seemed to make light of it. However I learned that he was still suffering from the effects of those blows and beatings....There were a good many conversions throughout the year and a number of baptisms.[186]

The next issue of *The Chosen People* magazine included a report in which Moses Gitlin gave the testimonies of some of the believers who had been baptized,[187] but that issue of the magazine also included Joseph's announcement that the Gitlins would be leaving their beloved Poland. Joseph shared further with the Board, saying: "The agitation against the Jews in Poland is becoming very severe. Mr. Gitlin, as an American citizen can no longer remain in that country and do missionary work."[188]

In July 1939 Moses Gitlin and his wife, Clara, left Poland. They traveled to England, and in August 1939 they came to America. Clara Gitlin shared her impressions of their last days in Poland with readers of *The Chosen People* magazine. She wrote: "All during the last week folks came and wept over our going. To all of them our house was a Bethel, and to many of them it contained the gates of heaven. It was their house of refuge, and a haven of rest, and they wept as children whose parental nest was broken up."[189] She told of the many Jewish believers who had come to faith in Yeshua through their ministry—men and women who had been taught, discipled, and baptized by her husband. She spoke of their meetings with pastors and Christian leaders, and of meetings with government officials. Clara related how when Moses had met with some of the more important government officials, under whose jurisdiction they had lived and worked, they, too, had expressed sorrow that the Gitlins were leaving Warsaw. To show their confidence in us, she wrote, "...they not only granted us return visas but also kindly gave us formal permission to make arrangements to continue our work by leaving a successor whose ministry will be independent of any denominational protection. For this we are very thankful to God, for it is a high privilege, especially when remembering that several foreign representatives of other missionary organizations were obliged to leave the country."[190]

The successors of the Gitlins, as mentioned earlier were Jacob and Leah Goren (Gorfinkel). They continued the Mission work throughout the long, perilous days of the war—faced with the threat of imminent death, as were all Jewish people. God blessed their faithfulness and their witness for Him but, sadly, the war destroyed the Mission's outreach in Poland and like other Jewish ministries in Poland, it was never re-established.

In planning for the Gitlin's return to the United States, Joseph suggested to the Board that they take over the work in Buffalo, New York. A report of their return to the States, and of their transfer from the Warsaw branch to the Buffalo branch was included in the October, 1939 issue of *The Chosen People* magazine.[191] This arrangement did not last long however. The Minutes state: "Mr. Moses Gitlin resigned as of October 7th. After several weeks in the United States he feels himself unfit for work among the American Jews, and will devote his time and energy to reaching the Russians and Poles."[192]

Although *The Chosen People* magazine did not carry any further reports about this choice servant of the Lord, Moses Gitlin faithfully continued his ministry of reaching both Jew and Gentile with the Gospel. On April 24, 1944 Joseph Cohn received a letter from Moses Gitlin in which he apologized for his abrupt severance with the Mission, and stated that, in many ways, he wished that he had remained on staff. But God was blessing in his ministry with The Hebrew Christian Mission in Detroit, Michigan. Gitlin wrote:

> *Esteemed Dr. Cohn:*
>
> *Kindly allow me to unburden myself of a load that has been of late pressing upon my conscience.*
>
> *I feel that I owe you and your Board an apology for my leaving Buffalo and not giving you the commonly accepted time and opportunity to act on my resignation.*
>
> *Leaving out secondary considerations I must say in justice to myself that my main difficulty was that after a busy and blessed ministry in Poland, I found myself circumscribed and ineffective in my ministry in Buffalo. I thought it unethical not to earn sufficiently my bread and butter, and then too, my pride was hurt.*
>
> *When I came to Detroit I found conditions here quite similar. My natural inclination was to give up, but I was constrained to wait upon the Lord. Some two years later we were led and enabled to open up a reading room. Then we commenced a radio ministry. Thus by the grace and help of God I found my place of usefulness and effectiveness also in the States.*
>
> *Were I to have had the patience and humility while in Buffalo to wait on the Lord and confer with you, the Lord could have similarly led me there, and under your mission my ministry would have been facilitated by better conditions and crowned by greater results.*
>
> *Hence, I most sincerely regret my lack of patience and humility before God and my lack of persistent propriety before you, and I apologize for my hasty and unjust action.*
>
> *You have been kind to me and my family all along. I am sorry that I did not sufficiently show my recognition of it and reciprocity for it by being more considerate and consistent. I want to assure you of my esteem and love in which my family joins me.*
>
> *I shall appreciate it if you would deem it proper to convey this my apology also to your Board.*
>
> *Respectfully yours, [signed] Moses H. Gitlin.*[193]

This letter of apology and friendship from Moses Gitlin to Joseph Cohn helped to ease some of the pain and difficulty that Joseph was going through as a result of the divisions and strife taking place in the Buffalo branch of the Mission—a matter that will be discussed in greater depth in the following chapter of this history.

THE PARIS MINISTRY AND THE NAZIS

In Europe, Nazi hatred was rampant. As its stronghold increased, the Mission's Paris Branch was threatened with closure. But Pastor Henri Vincent and his assistants, Andre Frankl and Mlle. Marie Solomon, labored on—faithfully translating and printing a French edition of *The Shepherd of Israel (le Berger d'Israel)*. These they distributed to the Jews of Paris and to the hordes of Jewish refugees who were flooding into Paris. They also held Bible classes, conducted door-to-door visitation, and provided clothing, shelter, and food. Henri Vincent wrote:

> *...Every Tuesday afternoon, Mr. Frankl receives the people that come and listens as they explain their sad situations. If he finds it absolutely necessary, he is allowed to give something immediately. As a rule, however, it is understood that he makes an inquiry to make sure of the truthfulness of the stories that are told. Every caller is told that help is given by us in the name of Christ, invited to come to the meetings, and receives a Gospel or a paper, or some Christian literature. Several people who have come to receive money, have become attendants at the Bible meetings, although no obligation has been placed upon them to do so.*[194]

He further told how they would administer relief aid once it was determined that such aid should be given. He said:

> *...It is almost impossible to help find work, but in several instances we have helped a man to secure some goods and earn his living selling them. As far as possible we have not given money, but meal tickets, tickets for lodgings at the Salvation Army houses, tickets to buy shoes. When help is necessary for the rent, we have paid it directly to the landlord. And so for the papers from the police, and for the doctors when we send them to some home, and the medicines. In order to give these tickets we have made an agreement with two restaurant owners, from whom we buy tickets for meals at a low price,...with a shoe factory, which at a low price, with a ticket gives away shoes, which we reimburse each month. We also give clothes; we collected some for that purpose and have some at our disposal in the Church.*
>
> *When people need the visit of a doctor, either they come to the dispensary of the Church, or we send them a doctor. The doctor we send is a German Jewish refugee, who having no legal right to practice in France, works under the*

responsibility of a French doctor, but is very poor. Helping the sick people, we help at the same time the doctor. Help in money has seldom exceeded frs.15 at a time. However, in some instances we have given a larger help, when we thought such a help would enable a man either to earn his living or bring him out of a very bad position.[195]

In spite of the hardships and the suffering all around them, and in spite of his busy schedule of ministry, Andre Frankl found time for romance. He and another relief worker, Mlle. Germaine Melon-Hollard, fell in love. They were married during the summer of 1939. Joseph Cohn was in Paris that summer, and he attended the ceremony. He wrote: "The Church was crowded, and people were standing all about. I should say that one-third of the audience was made up of our own Jewish refugees, the larger part of them Jewish Christians; another one-third might have been the members of the church itself, and the final third I judge was made up of the Quaker friends of Mlle. Germaine Melon-Hollard."[196]

MINISTRY AMONG THE REFUGEES

Once married, Mme. Germaine Frankl worked side-by-side with her husband. Because she was able to write in English, she soon took charge of handling correspondence—letters to Joseph Cohn, and letters on behalf of refugee Jews who were seeking help and asylum. In one of her first reports to Cohn, Mrs. Frankl revealed a behind-the-scenes look at the enormous task which the Mission in Paris faced in helping refugee Jews. She wrote:

...we see nearly every week: First, new refugees who come from Germany and Austria (most of them by illegal way, as the frontiers are nearly always closed for them). When they arrive in France, most of them do not receive permission to stay. Second, refugees, or foreigners, people (from Hungary, Poland, etc., with or without nationality) who are in France for a long time, but have no more permission to stay because of the more and more severe law in France (expulsions in great deal). Third, the refugees who did not leave France when they received expulsion (because, where to go?...), and had punition with 6 months in prison. They have after that, 8 days or so to leave France. If they do not leave, they have then 2 years in prison. And then? Fourth, the refugees who have, or will have papers in order, and permission to stay in France, but live in great misery....Some of them can find work if we give them money to begin something, and pay their "Carte d'Identite" [Identification Card]. The others could never earn regularly, because of chronic illness, or too many children, or do not find work. Fifth, the refugees who have papers and can earn more or less their living, and do not ask for financial help, but come regularly to my husband's [Andre Frankl] Evangelization Meeting.

For the First, we have both to keep them alive, and do the necessary steps in the Police & Ministers to try (how difficult it is) to obtain for them permission to stay in France. Their misery is beyond description.

For the Second, we urge them to leave France, if they are not political refugees, and if they can return to their country without persecution. For Hungary, Poland, etc., it is so. But sometimes those people are 'apatrides' and then, no country accepts them. In one case or another, we keep some of them on hand for some weeks.

For the Third, it is our despair. It is simply no solution for most of them, because the permission to stay in France, after all, and after enormous efforts, is so rare!

For the Fourth, (A) we try not only to keep them alive, but help them in building a new life, and find private work. It would be very necessary to give them 'initial sum'—fonds de roulement, from time to time for that purpose, but the trouble is that we have now so many new refugees for whom to give first relief, food tickets, etc., constructive work can't be arranged as it would be necessary to do so. For the Fourth (B) regular money is urgently needed to pay their rent, and give food, at least from time to time.[197]

Henri Vincent wrote further of the problems of the refugees as the war escalated in France. He said:

As for the work of the help to the refugees themselves, the situation is growing worse than it was....Now, on account of the decision of the French Government, it is practically impossible that we receive in France new refugees, except those who cross the borders unnoticed, and these are not many....For many years the police has shut their eyes on them [refugees], but now on account of the imminence of war, at the end of September, and the foolishness of some foreigners in France at that time, the Police have become more severe.

The refugees who have regular papers (identity cards) are not troubled, but those who have not are sometimes threatened with expulsion and sometimes thrown into jail.[198]

Yet in the midst of these desperate circumstances, God was blessing. In the same letter, Pastor Vincent reported that he had baptized eight new Jewish believers, and he said several others had asked to be baptized.[199]

Joseph Cohn's trip to Paris during the summer of 1939 gave him a "first hand" look at the plight of the Jewish refugees. He wrote:

All day long, without let-up, there has passed before me a procession of men and women with hungry, gaunt faces and eyes in their hollow sockets, beseeching eyes, pleading more eloquently than oratorical outbursts for a deliverance that seems hopeless. And still, hoping against hope, those eyes keep asking, 'Can you not do something to get me and my beloved ones out of this hell?' It is the dumb plea of the dying, and while in my heart of hearts I realize that humanly speaking there is not hope, yet I try to keep a cheerful face, and a brave smile, and I keep repeating over and over again, 'Only in God is our hope—He still lives; He who crushed a Pharaoh, who hanged a Haman, who humbled a Nebuchadnezzar; He is still in His heaven, and He has promised a day of Vengeance!'

All morning we hold consultation in our headquarters in the Eglise Evangelique at 123 Avenue du Maine. Some hundred refugees are in the waiting hall, by appointment. In they come, one at a time, or two, if they be man and wife; more, if they are family groups. To each we give attentive ears as the tale of anguish is unrolled, and then we struggle to find some way to help, even if with only a hundred Francs.

Strong men stand before us, able-bodied men; some have been men of brain as well as brawn, back in their beloved Austria or Germany. Among them are lawyers, physicians, university professors, chemists, manufacturers, bankers, salesmen. All, all find themselves suddenly thrust out of the country they and their ancestors helped for centuries back to build, and here they are, derelicts washed up on the shores of a world suddenly gone mad with demoniacal Jew-hate.

A formerly prominent jurist of Berlin is telling us of his plight. Gentle, kindly and cultured, this brother (he is also a brother in Christ, as well as one in the flesh) timidly produces his dismissal papers from a French jail. He had been arrested for being in Paris without legal permission, kept two months in jail, and now released with the ultimatum that within 30 days he must leave France or he will be re-arrested, and this time for a six months' imprisonment! Back in Berlin are his wife and precious brood of little ones, to whom he has sent no support for several months. Shamefaced, he dare not write them of his desolation, this family on whom he had so joyously bestowed every care and provision in those better days when he was a celebrity in Germany. He takes from his pocket a small photograph and with trembling hands passes it over to us. A beautiful picture of his loved ones as they used to be. And as he himself gazes upon it, he suddenly breaks down in uncontrollable hysteria. Our missionary, Andre Frankl, embraces him...and whispers words of comfort and hope. A word of prayer, and the dear brother quiets down. We ask him how much he needs for immediate help and he tells of two months arrears in rent, of all possessions pawned, of nothing eaten since yesterday. We give him several hundred Francs, and tell him it comes in the Name of the Lord Jesus, in Whom he must trust, as he has trusted hitherto. At the sight of the money he breaks down again, sobs fairly convulse him, while we ourselves, Pastor Vincent, Mr. Frankl, Mme. Frankl, and I find it impossible to refrain from tears. 'Never before in my life,' he sobs, 'have I asked or taken money like this. Who would have thought I should ever come to such an hour?...'

A morning like that, then the afternoon, after a trip downtown for lunch, spent in visitation in unspeakably pitiful tenement rooms. We walk up five, six, and seven floors, to find a family in one room, in squalor and wretchedness of which the less said the better. Sickness, misery, death, stalk in these hiding places of the hunted and haunted Jewish refugees.[200]

The Mission in Paris assisted refugee Jews from all over Europe, locating places of haven for them while at the same time sharing the Gospel. Throughout the war years the staff in Paris remained faithful in spite of the fact that some of them suffered great persecution because of their faith and because of the assistance they were giving to the Jewish refugees. Nearly every issue of *The Chosen People* magazine during the years 1939-1946 carried news of the ministry in Paris.

In February 1939 Henri Vincent wrote to inform Joseph that a Paris branch of the International Hebrew Christian Alliance had been organized on January 24, 1939. Mr. Forell was elected President, and Mr. Frankl was elected Vice-President. Pastor Vincent went on to say that the workers in Paris would cooperate with the Alliance, but with the understanding that their first emphasis would be upon bringing the Gospel to the refugees. Vincent wrote:

...Mr. Forell is not of the same Christian temperament as we, being a German Lutheran Minister; he is more of a social director than of an evangelist. We feel that our first duty is preaching the Gospel, and bringing people to a sense of repentance and faith in Christ as Saviour from sin, and for us the help given to the refugees is only a complement to the spiritual work. However, as far as the work of helping the refugees is concerned, we may well cooperate with Mr. Forell and the Hebrew Christian Alliance, in the measure of their own willingness.[201]

In the same letter, Pastor Vincent told of a letter he had received from a pastor Rev. Verne J. Swann from Petersburg, Alaska, in which Pastor Swann stated that he would be willing to sponsor one or two Jewish families if the Mission could get them to Alaska. Both Cohn and Vincent agreed that they would try to send some families to Rev. Swann just as soon as visas could be arranged.

In June 1939, Joseph received another letter from Henri Vincent. In it, Vincent informed Joseph that Rabbi Ignaz Hauser, whom the Mission had been helping, would be coming to the United States via Vienna and Prague. Rabbi Hauser had obtained a three year teaching contract in a Jewish school in Cleveland, Ohio, and would be traveling to the U.S. on a regular visa. The letter stated that Rabbi Hauser would contact the Mission in Brooklyn upon his arrival in the United States.[202]

Two prominent outreach ministries of the Mission in Paris are deserving of being expanded upon further—the "Children's Home" for refugee children, and the "Soup Kitchen."

A CHILDREN'S HOME

Although Henri Vincent had discussed the need for a Children's Home in his correspondence with Joseph during the early months of 1939, it was not until April of that year that the home became a reality. Vincent's letter to Joseph informed him that an international committee had been established to oversee the home. This allowed them to solicit funding for the home in France, Switzerland, the United States, etc., without objections from the French authorities. This international committee for the Children's Home was called the Patronage Committee. The home was located in Nurieux, France. Pastor Vincent told Joseph:

> We have made an arrangement with a Baptist woman, Mlle. Revoy, member of my church, who has a home for children in a section of France near Switzerland, to take several Jewish boys and girls at a low price (250 fr per children under 5 years, and 300 fr above 5 years, per month: $7 and $8). At the same time, we have made arrangements with our Baptist Union to transform the private home of Mlle Revoy into a Baptist orphanage, so that the children we send get the Christian education we want for them. We feel that in that way, the Jewish boys and girls, mixed with French boys and girls, will adapt themselves more easily to the French life and also to the Christian life. I am to visit with Mr. Frankl next month and we have already several children to send. It will involve no cost except the payment of the board at the above rate.[203]

By the time Joseph Cohn received Pastor Vincent's April 1939 communique, the home already had five Jewish boys and girls. The Patronage Committee worked in conjunction with other groups, using some of their funds to place Jewish children in safe homes because the home in Nurieux could only house fifteen to sixteen children. Vincent's letter suggested the possibility of enlarging the home at a modest cost. It also mentioned that the cost of feeding and housing the children in the Nurieux home would be approximately 4500 francs a month—about $120.00 a month.[204]

The December 1939 issue of *The Chosen People* magazine included a picture of the "Children's Home" in Nurieux, France and a glowing report of this new missionary project. Joseph told his readers:

> We now have twelve children in the Home, and they are a happy lot, far removed from the heartaches and burning memories of the cruelties and sufferings heaped upon their helpless bodies and souls because of Nazi evictions. The parents are in Paris, being looked after by our workers; some of the men have been drafted into the war area. One of our Jewish Christian girls, Katy, volunteered her service and went down to Nurieux, and there is acting as general helper and nurse to the children. Her mother and father are with us in Paris, and they have gone through heart-breaking sufferings and losses.
>
> The cost? We agreed to pay $100 a month for the first year, which means that just a little more than $8.00 per month per child takes care of that child, food, clothing, and nursing! And so we have a whole orphan asylum, although these children are not orphans, for nearly $100 a month. We leave it to our readers to judge as to whether this is not an unusually wise and thrifty investment of the Lord's money. This is always our earnest desire, that we shall make your missionary dollar in the Jewish work go the farthest distance possible, in buying one hundred cents' worth of value. So, we pass on this report to you, that you may give thanks with us, and then make this also another addition to your list of the things dear to your heart, and worth praying for day by day.[205]

SOUP KITCHENS ESTABLISHED

In responding to reports of the great need for food for the refugees, the Board authorized the establishment of "Soup Kitchens" or "Food Depots" in Paris, Brussels, and Vienna. The date was November 15, 1939. The "Soup Kitchens" were to provide a simple, but substantial, noonday meal—such as a bowl of beef stew, some bread, and a beverage. After the meal there was a Gospel service with testimonies, etc.[206]

Pastor Vincent and his staff began gathering supplies to open a Soup Kitchen in Paris, but before it was opened France entered the war. Henri wrote to Joseph: "I did not believe war was possible, but I am obliged to acknowledge I was mistaken. I could not believe Hitler was quite as mad as he really is. For there is no hope for Germany they will finally lose."[207] The words of Henri Vincent were prophetic, and proved to be true. He knew the promises of God—that no nation that brings harm to the "apple of God's eye" can stand. Henri Vincent and his staff had personal knowledge of what Hitler was doing to the Jewish people.

Henri's letter to Joseph went on to assure him that Paris had not yet been bombed and that everyone was safe. However, he said, he had been inducted into the Army and was scheduled to leave for active duty the following week. In his humble way, he assured Joseph: "Due to the fact that I did not leave immediately, on account of my age and family, I had time to arrange everything so that our work and the Church and the Union of Churches will not suffer. I have charged one of my church members [Mr. Jean Tanguy], who will not be drafted, and who is very able, I trust in him as in my own self to take my place for all the many enterprises which I directed."[208]

In the spirit of the pastor and the evangelist that he was, Henri Vincent had taken steps to ensure that the work of the Lord would continue. He let Joseph know that he had engaged a part-time secretary who would carry on the correspondence and would give Joseph a forwarding address for himself once it was known where he was to be stationed. He stated:

> We have suspended all meetings for the present. But when the situation of the Refugees is settled we shall be able to start again a meeting in the afternoon. Many of the Refugees, between 18 and 50, have enlisted as soldiers or worjers [sic] for the government. But the women and the older men will remain. Many of them will be taken care of in camps, for a time at least.
>
> We do not know yet what form the work will take, but we are thinking in addition to the meeting when it is possible to resume it, to do more visiting and writing. We shall go on editing the Berger d'Israel, but probably in French only, and giving some news of the work and the people. We will do our best to keep together our people, and to evangelize in spite of everything. It is more necessary than ever.
>
> I am sure the team of Mr. Tanguy, Mrs. and Mr. Frankl will go on beautifully with the work. And we must trust in God for the rest.
>
> Mrs. Frankl will write you soon and give you more details. I will also write you when I am settled in my new life. I do not feel very prepared for my new work, but God will help me, and I will keep up my witness for Christ wherever I am. I am going with faith and confidence and hope. Perhaps this war will not be as long as the last one.[209]

Rev. Vincent was an excellent administrator, and the staff he appointed served God with complete dedication throughout the war. Once the Nazis invaded Paris it was impossible for the Mission to get funds directly to them, yet those dear servants of Yeshua bravely and sacrificially carried on. Henri had arranged for the staff to borrow funds from the Baptist Federation if necessary, but they also often used their own limited funds, trusting that the Mission would reimburse them once communication was be re-established.

VINCENT TAKEN PRISONER

Henri Vincent, himself, was taken captive in June 1940 when the Germans invaded France. Within the French Army, he served in the capacity as Chaplain. When the Germans took over they sent him to serve as a Chaplain at a Prisoner of War camp near Dunkirk. Many years later Pastor Vincent told this writer:

> Since the Germans wanted to invade England and they didn't have enough troops to care for the hospital, they began to release the prisoners. But I was not put on the list. So, when I saw the cars that were leaving for France somewhere, or Germany, I asked the officer. He said, 'Well, your name is not on my list.' I said, 'What shall I do?' I was supposed to stay there, but I said there are no English soldiers left. So I went in the car and I stopped in a hospital in the north of France.[210]

At the hospital, Vincent was very persuasive, (he said the Germans were not too well organized at that time). He convinced the officers that under the Geneva Accords he, as a Chaplain, should be sent back to Paris. In effect, Vincent arranged his own escape. On July 14, 1940 a Nazi officer who didn't realize Henri was an escaped prisoner of war, drove him to Paris.

During the months that Henri Vincent was in the Army and was held prisoner, Mr. Jean Tanguy and Mme. Germaine Frankl corresponded with Joseph Cohn, keeping him abreast of the work in Paris and of the overall situation in France. But when the Nazis invaded Paris, all communication stopped; it was as if a heavy curtain had fallen over Paris, blanking out the city and the Mission. No further word was heard from the workers in Paris until one bright and happy day many months later when the mailman delivered a postcard to Joseph Cohn. It was dated October 19, 1944. Henri Vincent had written to let Joseph know he was still alive and well.

On November 18, 1944 Henri Vincent penned more than a postcard to Joseph. He sent him a letter in which he gave Joseph first-hand information about what had happened in Paris during the war, giving insight into his problems with the Gestapo. He also mentioned the current status of the relief work. He wrote:

> I myself was several times suspected by the gestapo. My house was searched, my wife questioned. I was arrested and handcuffed, but soon freed. I was accused of having given refuge in my home to two Jews, and I did not deny it, as it was true. The hand of God was over me all that time, in a very wonderful way. My activity to help not only our people, but the Jewish community in Paris was never entirely suspected, although I had to answer quite often questions of the German police as well as the French.
>
> Since the liberation of Paris, the work has been entirely resumed, except for the publication of The Shepherd of Israel (for lack of paper). Many of the refugees from Central Europe are still in a great misery. We do what we can, with what resources we have. We are keeping 8 children of deportees or whose parents are gone from France. We are also helping several poor Jews.
>
> With the liberation, some of the refugees from Germany have gone in trouble, because they were Germans, there is a strong anti-German feeling in France, as we have suffered so much from them.[211]

It is not certain if Joseph ever received that letter, or sent a reply. Indications are that he did receive the letter but, because of the slow mail service to France after the war, Joseph's reply (if one was sent) did not reach Henri before he wrote a second letter to Joseph. Henri's second letter bore the date March 10, 1945; it gave the following details:

> We have had some very hard times during the war, but with God's help, we have been able to endure all hardships and go through all dangers unhurt.
>
> The work has been going on all the time. Most of the Jews whom we ministered to were dispersed in 1940, some went South, in the part of France that was not occupied by the Germans.
>
> I was taken a prisoner in Dunkirk in June 1940, but was sent home, according to the Geneva agreement, as a chaplain, in July of the same year. Mr. and Mrs. Frankl came back from Southern France some time later, and Mr. Frankl resumed his work with the few Jewish people that were still in Paris.
>
> Then came the Jewish laws, obligation to wear the yellow star, beginning of the arrest of the Jews of foreign origin. Mr. Frankl, being Hungarian, was obliged to wear the yellow star, but was not arrested, but many of our people were arrested or obliged to take refuge in the country under false identities.
>
> We did our best to procure false papers and hide the people, especially the children.
>
> In 1943, things became worse, and we not only helped our own people, but many Jews, and we cooperated with some Jewish organizations to secure hidings and false identities to many Jews.
>
> In the Church itself, we gave refuge to several people.
>
> Then, in 1944, things became very bad. Hungarians Jews were arrested and deported. Mr. Frankl then had to secure false papers, and hide himself. But he remained in Paris and as he could, continued to minister to the few that were still in Paris and free. Mlle. Solomon took refuge in the country, with some fine people.
>
> All the time, I was under suspicion of the Gestapo, that came very often to see me for inquiries. I will tell you some time how God helped me in a wonderful and I may say miraculous way, in one occasion when my home was searched, I was handcuffed, and my wife terrorized by the Gestapo men, because I had given refuge to two [French] Jews for two weeks, and they wanted to know where they had gone from my home.
>
> It is impossible in a short letter to tell you of all the troubles we have had, especially since January 1944, trying to save some people, have them out of prison, and prevent their deportation. Unhappily, if we succeeded in securing hidings and [helping] people to escape arrest, we could not prevent those that were arrested from being deported. We of course never had news from those who were deported.
>
> Now, the work has started again. It never stopped entirely, Mr. Frankl always held a private prayer meeting, and visited the people. Of course, now we are free to work openly. There is a meeting on Friday and Sunday afternoon.[212]

LIBERATION OF PARIS—MINISTRY RESUMED

Henri told Joseph that a few of the Jewish Christian families were beginning to return to Paris. He mentioned the Piotrkowski family and said, "...M. Piotrkowski is always a faithful Christian. During his stay in the Army and in the South of France, he gave a very good testimony to the Gospel. He is now working in a factory in Paris."[213]

Pastor Vincent also gave an ominous word concerning the Jews who were deported from Paris by the French authorities and by the Nazis. He stated: "None of our deportees has come back yet, and we have little hope that any of them shall come back. We have had the visit of Mr. Chonotni, a Jewish Evangelist in Warsaw, liberated by the allied Armies. He came to Paris, but does not intend to go back to Poland."[214]

Joseph Cohn wrote to Pastor Vincent, asking for a full accounting of their funding during the War; he wanted to fulfill the agreement he'd made with Henri to reimburse him for monies spent in helping the Jewish refugees. Henri replied that their accounts showed that Mr. Tanguy had received a check from the Mission in 1940, while Henri was still in the army. That was the last check the Paris branch had received from the Mission. Henri then shared some of the inventive ways in which the workers in Paris had continued to finance the ministry during the War. He said:

> As we had no more money left by that time, I made an arrangement with an American citizen who was returning to America, who left money with me, and to whom I gave in return several receipts, which were to paid by the Board in Brooklyn, if you accepted the arrangement made. I kept copy of the sum borrowed in that way for a time, but after a first search of the Gestapo at my home, I had to destroy the receipts, and as the Gestapo has seized our books in 1942, I do not know how much money we borrowed in that way. If you paid the money in N.Y. it is not due any more. I should like to know how the thing has come through.
>
> When the advance was exhausted, we asked the Federation of Baptist Churches in France to take up the salary of Mr. Frankl, which it did. And up to June 30th 1945, the amount advanced by the Federation (as we paid Mr. Frankl on the basis of the French Pastors) was frs 138.996.
>
> The two remittances of $500 received since the liberation have been used to diminish the debt, so that the amount due is really on the 30th of June: frs 89.590.
>
> All the other salaries have been suspended.
>
> As we had several children to keep in several places, and some temporary help to give to some Jewish friends, for which purpose we spent during the time: frs 169.505,70, we were obliged in order not to increase our debts and fulfil what we thought was our duty, to call for some money from some friends, and we received during the same period: frs 152.845,20.
>
> This left a difference of 15.959 which I advanced personally so that it is due to me.
>
> Together: frs 105.540, which were all advanced in Francs, and should be reimbursed at the actual rate of exchange of frs 49 for 1$, i.e.: $2.150.[215]

But this was not all—more money was due as they had been paying the rent and taxes on Frankl's home. Also due was Mr. Frankl's current salary and the part-time salary of Mlle. Solomon. Henri did not ask for any salary reimbursement for himself, but he did ask for minimal office and travel expenses so the work could continue. He also asked for money to carry on the relief. He told Joseph:

> To this may be added whatever grant may be made for relief and help. Although the number of our people has largely diminished through deportation and death, the situation of some of our people is just as bad as it was, if not worse for some of them, before the war, and the cost of living is 5 times that of 1940. We have still some children for which we are to care, and the help we have received throug [sic] various organizations during the occupation will be soon cut off.[216]

Henri told Joseph: "...Everything is extremely expensive. Very little can be had, no shoes, no clothing to be bought, transportation is not easy due to the destruction of bridges, locomotives, and railroad cars and trucks and the lack of gasoline and automobiles."[217] But in spite of conditions around him, Henri Vincent's spirit was undaunted. Always the pastor and evangelist, he shared his plans for the ministry's future, saying:

> Among the things which we plan for is the publication of some tracts and treatises, as soon as the paper can be had. There is a great need of litterature [sic] at the present, and now is the time to evangelize, not only the foreign Jews, but the French Jews. Could you send us if possible and as soon as possible, as many of the tracts which you may have in English (2 or 3 copies of each) so that we can immediately work on the translation and adaptation of those that we may think useful in France.

We plan also to resume the publication of the 'Berger d'Israel' (The Shepherd of Israel) as soon as paper is available. We think however that, for the present, we should put it in French only.

Along the same lines, we wonder also if it would be a good thing to publish a quarterly review intended in France for the Christians interested in the Evangelization of the Jews. Surely such a publication would be most timely as more and more the French Christians are interested in the question....

I may simply say that I feel that the work must be carried more and more in French and for the French Jews, without neglecting the others.

I may add that a very good piece of service could be rendered immediately. Since I hear that parcels are now allowed to be sent from America to the Continent. Could it be possible to send some food packages to about 30 of our Jewish Christians people, directly to the addresses we could give? If it is possible, we would gladly furnish the names.[218]

Joseph's response to Henri's letter was immediate. He was anxious for Henri to proceed with his plans! He was especially concerned for the Jewish children, and was pleased that Pastor Vincent was planning to help them. Some correspondence between Joseph and Henri, in which financial matters were discussed, was sent through Mr. J.R. Miller. This was done to prevent any possible misunderstandings through the translation between French and English. Joseph put Pastor Vincent on a regular expense budget just as he had before the war. In his letter to Mr. Miller, Joseph explained:

...We are doing this so as to give Brother Vincent a little fuller scope and leeway in carrying on the work at the present time, hoping that in this way he will not be too much hampered for lack of immediately necessary funds. This should cover at least a modest honorarium to Pastor Vincent,...Then there should be money left over for helping to care for those little children; in fact I would feel for myself personally that we should encourage him to gather together even additional Jewish children whose mothers and fathers are gone and who have no one to care for them. Tell him I think we would have little difficulty here in America to raise the funds for caring for such children. The hearts of the American people are deeply touched with the tragic condition of those children, and I am sure they will respond if once we put the pictures before them.[219]

Joseph promised to send tracts and materials for publication in French, and also promised to send food packages for needy Jewish believers in France.

Henri Vincent was jubilant! He was delighted that Joseph Cohn was willing to help the Jewish children, to send the food packages, and to supply funding to help in the ministry to the Jews of Paris. His letter to Cohn reflects not only his own concern for the Jewish children, but also the concern of the Baptist Federation. He also shared what was happening with many of the refugee children. He wrote:

I am very glad of what you say about the interest Americans should take in children's work. We are taking care at present of only two children, one of which will in due time be sent to England where her parents have taken refuge, and who have asked the girl to be sent to them as soon as we may do so. At the same time we are helping in a small way some women left alone with their children, but who want to keep them with them.

But we are solicited to take care entirelly [sic] of three children more, and our intention is to have them in our Baptist home for children, due to open next October, in Tremel, Britany. This home is a gift that has been made during the war to our Union. At present we are using it for a summer camp, and a summer or fresh air home for children. We have sent already several young Jewish boys and girls there for the summer. We have found the money for that partly in the Churches.

The three children are: 2 boys, 5 and 7, whose father has been deported and died in Germany. The mother, Mme Podmener is obliged to work and will not be able to take care of the children properly. She is willing to give us the 2 boys.

One boy 4, whose mother Mme Tandler is not married, the father having refused to marry her, in 1941, when he found she was a Jew. We have known her recently.

Concerning the children of deportees and displaced persons. There are many Jewish children in Germany, and whose parents were deported from Roumania, Poland and Tchecoslovaquia. The parents have disappeared, dead or lost, and the children have been freed by the allies. I do not know what happens of them in American or British held territories, but in the territories held by the French, those children Jewish or not, are all sent to France, with the intention of making French citizens of those boys and girls, of whatever nationality they may be.

This has given some concern to the Jewish organizations in Paris, which in some cases have hastened to send some Jewish children to Palestine, without taking sufficient time for the parents to show up. In some cases at least we suppose that it is possible that the parents come back. I was told last Sunday of 40 Roumanian children, Jewish children, sent to

Palestine in that way, by one of the leading officers of a Roumanian relief organization in Paris, which was not very pleased with such haste.

There is no doubt that among all the children coming to France in that way, there are some for whom we could and perhaps should care. We shall make further inquiries into the matter. We must not go too fast. Up to the present time relief organizations for deportees and Jews, official help given by state administration to all displaced persons take care of the need of many. But there is a time when official help will naturally be suspended, and relief will fall mostly on the private relief organizations. I will let you know about the development of that situation.

Life is getting a little better and easier now in Paris. However I send you the names and addresses on a separate sheet of the people for whom a food package would be most welcome.[220]

ANDRE FRANKL EXPANDS THE PARIS MINISTRY

Word of the revived mission in Paris began to spread throughout Europe. Andre Frankl began a hectic schedule of meetings and travel to promote the ministry. They started a French paper for French Christians who were interested in Jewish evangelism and Zionism; the paper was called "Tous-Unis." Mr. Frankl maintained a heavy schedule of visits to the sick, held Bible Studies classes, worked making arrangements for the placement of "orphan Jewish children" in good homes, as well as arranging for the children to participate in the Baptist Federation's summer camps. In one report he stated:

I have many children—half-orphan—in my work. These are made up of mixed marriages, the fathers Jewish-Christians, and the mothers Aryans. The Jewish fathers were 'liquidated' and these poor 'Aryan' mothers are left by themselves with the enormous task of raising these children.[221]

By the end of 1946 Mr. Andre Frankl was recognized as the leader of the Mission in Paris. He was traveling on behalf of the Mission and speaking with the heads of other evangelical groups in Europe as he endeavored to help them recognize their obligation to help the Jews of Europe—to assist the orphaned Jewish children and immigrant Jews in their efforts to immigrate to Israel.

Jewish refugees continued to pour into Paris. As they did, Henri Vincent and Andre Frankl (along with their staff of dedicated workers) assisted them in every way they could. The reputation of the work of the Mission was beyond re-proach, and the level of interest which Andre Frankl had been able to raise among evangelical Christians in Europe was remarkable—yet these factors had worked together to create a most unexpected problem. Frankl wrote:

Paris, being the strongest Jewish center in Occidental Europe, we see an actual rush of missions towards the City. There was a time when I was alone in Paris, and now we have here representatives of the Swedish Mission, Rev. R's Mission, a Dutch Sister, a missionary of the Big Brothers (Mr. Samuel), the missionary family of Rev. Wilinson. And others are still coming over to establish themselves here. The working methods of all these new co-workers is not always at its best. Thus to eliminate clashes, confusion and jealousies, which cannot be anything but inevitable, I, as their elder, have the intention of inviting these brothers to monthly meetings.[222]

Untiring in his efforts to enlarge his Gospel testimony to the Jews, Andre Frankl pressed on. During the summer of 1947, he made a whirl-wind trip through Europe. In Lausanne, Switzerland he met with Jean Jacques Bovet, a reformed pastor who had once carried on a work in Paris, but who was being transferred to Stockholm. In Zurich Frankl had hoped to attend the Zionist Congress, but when he was not permitted to attend he passed out tracts and witnessed to Jews who were attending. In Denmark he met with the President of the Baptist Convention, as well as with the President of the Swiss Baptist Congregation, Rev. Pfister. Continuing on, he went to Oslo, Norway where he met with the leaders of the Jewish mission of the Norwegian State-Church (Lutheran)—at that time they had stations in Romania, where Wurmbrand and Solheim were pastors. From Oslo, Frankl went to Brussels, and from Brussels he returned to Paris. A report of his trip, including his thoughts about how the future of the ministry in Europe should be established, was included in the December 1947 issue of *The Chosen People* magazine. He wrote:

We have in Europe a very favorable and far-stretched working field. The interests for the Jewish question are aroused everywhere. The Gentiles want to repay what the Jews had to suffer from the Neo-heathens, and will repay with evangelization. In all states there are various efforts at Jewish missions, but the different denominations all want their own Missions. It does not seem absolutely necessary to start our own Stations; very often it is sufficient to show them our good will and help them with tracts and personal visits. We should encourage and deepen our connection with

Brother Wainer [He met Dr. Wainer in Oslo, Norway]. These brothers are very well known and with their help we will be able to penetrate into the Scandinavian countries (Norway, Sweden and Finland).

Such trips should be made more frequently in the future, because: (1) The connections formed must be maintained through personal visits. (2) They make known our Mission. (3) The proclamation of the Word of God to the Jews is the biggest task of Christianity. (4) We have to work as long as it is still day; the time of Jacob's Trouble will arrive soon.[223]

Cohn gave Frankl the green light to continue his travels, and to network with the Christian leaders of Europe. As a result, the funding of the Paris work increased, as did the number of food packages being sent to needy Jewish believers and to the Jewish refugee children. God blessed the ministry of Andre Frankl because his priorities were always God-honoring: He first presented the Gospel, then he offered relief in the name of Yeshua, the Messiah.

Under the leadership of Mr. Frankl, and with the supervision and organizational skills of Henri Vincent, the Paris ministry continued to thrive in post-war Europe. In 1950 Frankl wrote to Cohn, reporting that he had been able to baptize six more Jewish believers. He also expressed his thanks to Dr. Cohn for allowing him to have an assistant, Miss Ursula Flatow—a Jewish believer who had studied in Berne, Switzerland during the war. Miss Flatow had a diploma in kindergarten teaching, and after the war she also took training in a Bible School near Paris.

By the end of 1950 the Paris branch was printing 3,500 monthly issues of *le Berger d'Israel* (*The Shepherd of Israel*) and dispensing, either through the mail or through personal contact, over 38,000 copies of the publication each year. Andre Frankl had a volunteer staff of seventy-eight Christians assisting him in the work. Mr. Frankl also translated into French fourteen tracts that were originally published by the Mission in English; he and his staff of workers distributed these tracts to Jews throughout France and Europe.

In 1951 Andre Frankl wrote of a strange phenomenon that was taking place. Instead of ministering to Jewish refugees who wanted to immigrate to Israel—the Jewish homeland—he was beginning to minister to more and more Jews who were leaving Israel. He wrote these alarming words:

Characteristic of this year has been the return of Jews and Jewish-Christians from Palestine. Hardly a week goes by that new emigres do not come to our Mission. Ofttimes whole families come with children born in Palestine. Disillusionment and bitterness is very evident when they speak of their experiences in Palestine, especially of the social boycotting of the Jewish believers. Surely the Lord is leading our people through a difficult schooling; possibly to toughen and equip them for their participation in the tribulation and agony still to come.[224]

Two years later, Andre Frankl expressed his anguish over the Jewish emigres, saying:

The problem of the Jews streaming back from Eretz (the land of Israel) has caused us much concern in this year too. There are some precious pearls amongst these twice homeless ones. The French State gives no permit to stay to these persons; the Jewish organizations give them no assistance. I can bring them the Word, and this is of course the main thing. But I have no possibility to help them to permanent living quarters or to an earthly existence.[225]

In 1952, Andre Frankl told Joseph Cohn that approximately 550,000 Jews still remained in French territory—"that is, in France, Northern Africa, Belgium and in French Switzerland."[226] Frankl wanted to reach them *all* with the Gospel!

In the Spring of 1964, God called his faithful and dedicated servant, Andre Frankl, into His presence. The loss to the Paris mission and to the entire European work was cataclysmic! Frankl had been the spark-plug for the European ministries; he had kept the European network operating for the Mission.

After Frankl's death, Henri Vincent did his best to hold the European network together. He continued the Bible studies, the publication of le Berger d'Israel (The Shepherd of Israel), and the publication of the French tracts. He also maintained contact with the refugees, the emigres, and the orphaned Jewish children. He did all this for the Mission while still maintaining his position as a pastor, and while maintaining his position of leadership within the Baptist Federation.

In June 1965 Rev. Henri Vincent was invited to attend the Board of Directors meeting of the Mission. At that meeting, he gave the Directors a brief history of the Paris branch. In appreciation of his sacrificial work on behalf of the Mission in Paris, the Board passed a resolution honoring Henri Vincent.[227]

ANDRE-RENE BOULAGNON

At the same June meeting, the Board approved the hiring of Mr. Andre-Rene Boulagnon, who had formerly worked for Mr. Michelson (The Jewish Hope magazine and broadcast). Mr. Boulagnon was hired with the stipulation that he would enter the Mission's six-month training program which was being held in Los Angeles, California. After he completed the required training program, he returned to Paris. The April 1968 issue of *The Chosen People* magazine carried the story of the revitalized work in Paris. A building was being renovated for the ministry, and Mr. Boulagnon wrote:

> ...These premises are close to Rothschild's Home for Aged people where hundreds of Jews are living.
> We shall have regular meetings here. However, we do not intend to set up a Hebrew or a Hebrew-Christian Church, but rather an evangelization center of neutral appearance.[228]

Mr. Boulagnon continued to print *le Berger d'Israel* (*The Shepherd of Israel*) and continued to hold Bible study meetings in Lyons, France. He also began a ministry to reach Jewish children with the Gospel. Another avenue of witness that opened for the Mission was the opportunity to have a French radio broadcast, called *Shalom Israel*. The broadcast was a thirty minute weekly Gospel program in French. Boulagnon was responsible for preparing the messages and for speaking on the programs. In his report of the first few weeks of broadcasts, he wrote: "We have now received 40 letters, among these listeners 10 have requested the courses on Isaiah. This is a very good starting as the French are long to make up their minds."[229] The course on Isaiah was a correspondence course which the Mission had developed; this had been translated into French.

Andre Boulagnon's leadership of the Paris branch of the Mission continued for a few years, but the day came when he announced that he felt the Lord was calling him to a pastorate in Paris. The Paris branch was once again in need of leadership.

Jacque Guggenheim

Times had changed and the entire scope of the work in Paris, as well as the entire European work, had also changed. Joseph Hoffman Cohn and Andre Frankl, men who possessed networking skills matched by few, could no longer be called on for their assistance or expertise; they were enjoying the presence of the Lord. The Lord met the need of a new missionary worker in Paris by leading Mr. Jacque Guggenheim and his wife, Renée, to accept the position. But it was decided that a committee was needed to oversee the Paris ministry. Committee members were to include: Pastor Henri Vincent as Honorary Director; Mr. Ernest Gutknecht, a member of the Baptist Federation and a member of the Mission; and Mr. Jacque Guggenheim, who was to continue the radio ministry, the Bible studies, and the visitation programs, as well as continuing the publication of le Berger d'Israel which, by the late 1960's, had a distribution of over 6,000 copies to Jewish people each month.

The Mission staff in Paris was increased as Sylvain Romerowsky was hired to translate the Shepherd of Israel into French. Mrs. Denton and her daughter, Ellen Denton, also joined the staff. A number of volunteer workers and part-time workers also gave of their time and talents. Jacque Guggenheim and his wife, Renée, continued on staff with the Mission until 1991 when the Board felt the time had come to "cut the umbilical cord." The decision was made to let the Paris ministry continue as an independent European work.

As of the writing of this history, the Paris ministry continues to exist under the leadership of Mr. Jacque Guggenheim. He continues to publish and distribute "le Berger d'Israel" for Jews and Christians in Europe and throughout the world.

The Russian Ministry and the War

As mentioned earlier, the response of the Jews of Europe to the distribution of The Shepherd of Israel had opened Joseph Cohn's eyes to the need for sharing the Gospel message with the Jews of Europe. Clearly, there was a spiritual hunger within some Jews of the European Jewish communities, and Joseph seized the opportunity to satisfy that spiritual hunger when he hired Simon Aszur to be the Mission's first European missionary in the early 1920's.

The distribution of The Shepherd of Israel then opened the opportunity for ministry in Russia and, as was mentioned at the outset of this chapter, the Mission undertook the support of Mr. Gregory Guberman in Dnjepropetrowsk (formerly called Ekaterinaslav), Russia after Mr. & Mrs. Peter Smoljar escaped and went to Riga, Latvia. To the dismay of Joseph and the many prayer partners of the Mission, the ministry of Mr. Guberman was cut off in the early months of 1930 and, as has been mentioned, his fate was never learned.

But the ministry of Mr. Gregory Guberman in Dnjepropetrowsk was not the Mission's only involvement in Russia. Throughout the 1930's Joseph enlarged his network of European contacts, and the Mission steadily increased its involvement in Europe. It was through these contacts that Joseph became aware of a colony of Jewish believers in Kischineff, Bessarabia—a territory between the rivers Prut and Dniester, and bordered by the Black Sea. Bessarabia was a part of Moldavia until the Russians annexed it in 1812 as a part of the "Pale of Settlement." Strategically located to Rumania, it was a territory in almost constant dispute. For the Jews who lived there, life was extremely difficult and persecution was an everyday occurrence.

JOSEPH RABINOWITZ

The colony of believers was established in the late 1800's by world famed Jewish lawyer, Joseph Rabinowitz—a Jewish believer whose published sermons and other writings were scattered widely throughout Russia. His bold testimony and influence led many Jewish people of Russia and the surrounding countries to faith in Yeshua; the outgrowth of his ministry was essentially the beginning of the Hebrew Christian movement in Russia.

Joseph Rabinowitz was born at Resina on the Dniester, September 23, 1837. He died at Kischineff, Bessarabia (Russia) in 1899. He was the son of David ben Ephraim—a rabbinic family.

When his mother died, Joseph was taken to her father's home to live. Nathan Neta, Rabinowitz's grandfather, educated his grandson in Torah and in the Scriptures, and by the age of six he could recite the entire book of the Song of Songs by heart.

In 1848 Rabinowitz left his grandfather's home to live with other members of the family. He was betrothed to be married by the age of thirteen. The Jews of that time were under Imperial orders to learn the Russian language—a skill that opened a new world to him—the world of literature.

In 1855 Jehiel Hershensohn (Lichtenstein), Joseph's future brother-in-law, gave him a copy of the New Testament in Hebrew and told him to read the book. Lichtenstein further told Joseph that he believed that Jesus of Nazareth may be the Messiah—an announcement that surprised Joseph and impelled him to read the book, but he was not immediately persuaded that Jesus was the Messiah. He continued reading various books and literature however, including the New Testament, and the knowledge gleaned from his reading eventually caused him to leave the "Hassidism" (strict orthodox).[230]

Rabinowitz was married in 1856, at the age of nineteen. He continued his study of the Bible and his secular studies in the law and, as an activist for Jewish causes—especially the cause of education for Jewish children—he became an influential citizen in his small community. He was a frequent lecturer and contributor to the local Jewish newspapers.

In 1878 he wrote an article in the Hebrew paper, "Haboker Or," in which he requested that the rabbis work to improve the condition of Russian Jews by teaching them to become an agricultural people. He set the example himself by creating a garden. This seemed to be a precursor to the establishment of "kibbutzim" (communal farms) in Israel. When persecution broke out in that part of Russia, the Jewish community sent him to Palestine to check into the possibility of establishing a Jewish colony there.

As he packed his baggage for the journey to Palestine, Joseph placed the little New Testament (which had been given to him years earlier) at the bottom of the bag. Once in the land, he was drawn to pull the little book out of the bag and compare its words with the places he visited.

> …when he arrived in Jerusalem and saw the sad temporal and spiritual condition of the Jews there, his heart sank within him, and he was about to leave the Holy City in despair. Before doing so, he went to the Mount of Olives, once more with that marvelous Book in hand. There he sat down in deep meditation, and reviewing the sad history of his unfortunate people, the thought came to him as an inspiration: 'The key to the Holy Land is in the hands of our brother Jesus!' Returning to Kischineff, he startled the Jewish community with the announcement, 'Brethren, I have found the place of rest for our people! It is in the hollow of the side of our crucified Messiah!' He drew up thirteen theses, the substance of which was that Jesus is the only Saviour of Israel as well as of the whole world. With great courage and enthusiasm he then undertook by word and pen to propagate his discovery, and in a short time gained many adherents at Kischineff and in other towns of Bessarabia.[231]

Rabinowitz was baptized in Berlin by Professor Mead of Andover, Massachusetts (USA) on March 22, 1885.[232] Soon after his baptism, his wife and seven children, his brother and his family, and a number of other Jews who had heard him preach confessed Christ as their Messiah and Lord. That year he also published the "Symbols of the Israelites of the New Covenant"—a series of seven articles that put forth the principles for his new movement. The articles were based upon the thirteen principles of Moses Maimonides, but each article was tied to the fact that Jesus was the Messiah and the Savior of the world.[233]

By 1887, encouraged by Professor F. Delitzsch and by Rev. John Wilkinson, founder of the Mildmay Mission to the Jews in Glasgow, Scotland, Rabinowitz formed an association to help support his work and his followers who called themselves "Israelites of the New Covenant."

Leon Awerbuch

In 1938, Joseph received a letter from Mr. Leon Awerbuch asking if there was anything the Mission could do to financially assist the colony which was at the brink of disaster due to increased persecution and the threat of war. Awerbuch had served as the Director of the colony for twenty years or so (c. 1918).[234] Joseph Cohn knew Leon Awerbuch, and the Mission had given assistance to the colony of Jewish believers in Bessarabia prior to 1938. Joseph mentioned the colony in one of his articles in *The Chosen People* magazine, stating:

> It was our privilege to fellowship with the Kishineff brethren...We purchased for them a plot which was dedicated for a number of uses. Among them was a portion set aside as a cemetery for Jewish Christians, another portion for a children's playground and picnic area, and on still another piece of ground is the tomb stone covering the place where rests the body of their beloved Rabinowitz. We also were able from time to time to send generous gifts to help in the carrying on of the work, until the war made further support impossible.[235]

Shortly before the war machine moved into Bessarabia, the Awerbuchs escaped to England where they began working with the Barbican Mission to the Jews among the Jews of London. From London Mr. Awerbuch wrote to Joseph, stating that he would continue the Mission's relief efforts to the colony of Jewish believers in Kishineff for as long as he was able. In his letter Leon Awerbuch said:

> We thank you for your letter, and also for the check. I will forward the money to Kishineff as soon as possible, after the crisis of war is settled, and the brethren also will write to you. We have learned from their latest letters that there are great persecutions for the believers. The authorities ask for such formalities and conditions to have religious meetings, that it is hard to fulfill. Several preachers have been put into prisons for having prayer meetings, which now are illegal. We do not know what may happen with our community at Kishineff. It is impossible to stand all the new regulations. In spite of all the difficulties the brethren are very brave, and grow spiritually, thank God.[236]

Additional insight into the plight of the colony of Jewish believers in Bessarabia is revealed in the March 1946 issue of The Shepherd of Israel which states:

> ...A colony of believing Jews was formed, which existed all through the passing years, until only a few years ago the Nazis swept down upon the helpless town, and with savagery unprecedented tortured these very Jewish believers, until all were done to horrible death.[237]

Ministry in England

When the Awerbuch's could no longer get relief funds into Russia and into Europe, they continued working with the Mission by carrying on a relief ministry among the growing Jewish refugee community within London—a work they faithfully carried on until August 16, 1941, when the Lord called Leon Awerbuch home. Mrs. Marie Awerbuch shared her thoughts of that sad hour in a letter to Joseph Cohn. She said:

> ...My dear, dear friend, my all I had on this earth is now with the Lord. He will suffer no more, and no calumny or calamity will hurt him anymore....He was only fifty six years old, but the doctor said that he is worn out. Certainly not by years....He was conscious to the end....he asked me for a piece of paper as he wanted to write something. It was very difficult for me to decipher his writing, but I managed it. It was in Hebrew: 'The Lord Jesus Christ is Victory.' When I read it to him he said, 'Yes, that is for you and for me.' That small piece of paper is such a treasure to me....
> He was ill six months and oh, how patient he was—always thinking of others....My joy, my pleasure, was to help my husband, and when I saw he was content and pleased with it, that was my best reward.[238]

In 1942, just a few months after the death of Leon Awerbuch, Joseph Cohn appointed Marie Awerbuch to carry on the Mission's outreach among the refugee Jews in London. Reports of her many experiences appeared within many of the issues of *The Chosen People* magazine. Her love was demonstrated in her selfless acts of charity, and through her witness many Jewish people came to faith in Yeshua.

By 1945 Joseph Cohn was planning "post war strategy" for the Mission's European outreach. His plans included using London as the base for a European Headquarters of the Mission. He began laying the ground work in London by hiring additional staff. Rev. Peter Smoljar, who had served as a missionary in Russia under the Mildmay Mission to the Jews of London, had also returned to London as the war engulfed Russia. Joseph had hired a young Jewish believer,

Abraham Gradowsky, to work for the Mission in Birmingham, England.[239] When Joseph learned that Peter Smoljar was in London, he asked him if he would be willing to train Abraham Gradowsky to be one of the Mission's post-war missionaries for Europe.

ANNE RAYNER—HER STORY

In the spring of 1945, Joseph hired another worker for his post-war missionary team. Marie Awerbuch's health was beginning to fail (on February 3, 1946 the Lord called Marie Awerbuch into his presence), so Joseph hired Miss Anne Rayner, a Jewish believer from Bessarabia. Anne's testimony appeared in both the Shepherd of Israel and *The Chosen People* magazine. She wrote:

> I was born in Bessarabia, Rumania, of orthodox parents; but rumours of war and persecution of the Jews caused my parents to bring my elder brother and me to England whilst my age was still counted in months.
>
> My parents, being very religious, naturally brought up their children…to observe all the ritual of the Jewish faith.…the name of Jesus Christ was never mentioned by my parents, the only occasions on which I ever heard it was when street urchins used it in blasphemy.…
>
> At eighteen I was engaged to be married; my fiancé was an orthodox Jew, religious and upright, and I counted myself one of the happiest of girls. Then, suddenly, my mother died and it was necessary for me to take her place, so far as I could, in the home. Everything was changed. I felt unequal to the task; there seemed no one to whom I could turn for advice and comfort.…and God seemed to be so far away.
>
> One day, going about my household tasks, I could hear singing in the street.…and, being curious, went out on the street to see what was happening. An open-air meeting was in progress and,…I listened with interest to the missionary who was speaking of the Messiah, whose coming was prophesied in the Old Testament. I had a pencil and a scrap of paper in my pocket and noted the references the speaker quoted from: Isaiah 9:6, 4:14 and chapter 53.…
>
> I was a member of a religious Zionist movement, the Young Mizrachi, and I went to their reading room, borrowed an Old Testament in English, for the Bibles we had at home were in Hebrew; and, to my amazement, I found the references were exactly as they were quoted by the missionary I had heard. I began to wonder why our rabbis apparently did not believe what was written in our own Bible. I decided to visit the mission to the Jews to hear more.…
>
> The meeting had already commenced and I sat in a corner in the back row, hoping I would not be noticed. The missionary who first captured my attention was speaking again, and somehow he seemed to be addressing me alone. He said I was a sinner…and to myself I said, 'These missionaries are artful; they saw me come in and they are specially trying to win me over; but they won't get me!' Before the meeting was over I slipped away, resolved never again to go there. But the following Sunday evening found me in the same place at the back of the hall.…Again it seemed as if all the speakers were addressing only me; and again I was filled with anger and resentment that they should dare speak as they did. Yet I could not prove them wrong. This time before I could get away unobtrusively, one of the missionaries stopped me, inviting me to a discussion the following evening. I went and afterwards began reading my Bible, the Old Testament, with a new interest, comparing it with the New Testament which had been given to me.
>
> …One night I was too restless and thoughtful to sleep, and in my heart I cried out to God for help, asking Him to show me the truth and what to do about it, and, like a flash, the light dawned on me and I accepted the Lord Jesus Christ as my Saviour.…
>
> …as my new faith became known at home, so persecution began. My father tried to commit suicide; for, he said, he could no longer face the Jewish people…since his daughter had brought such disgrace upon him; my elder brother threatened to kill me; wherever I went I was followed; when I brought a Bible home it was burned; no matter where I hid them, they were found and destroyed. I told my fiancé of my conversion; at first he thought I was not serious and replied that 'such jokes are in bad taste'; when he realized I was in earnest he stormed for a time and then pleaded with me to give up 'such madness,' and it was only by the Grace of God that I stood firm. My fiancé promised to wait a year and, if I had given up my new faith and had 'returned to sanity,' he would still marry me.
>
> Eventually I became ill, but somehow my family did not cast me out. God in His mercy strengthened me and, when I recovered, I found I still could not read my Bible at home; so I would visit the reference library for hours at a time and pore over chapter after chapter of the Scriptures, committing long passages to memory; no one could rob me of them then.…
>
> When war broke out in 1939 I was called up for Civil Defense Service. At first I was nursing and assisted with First Aid Training.…The hospital I was in was badly bombed during the Battle of Britain in 1940. I was transferred to the Ambulance Service and learned to drive an ambulance.…
>
> Mark Kagan, the missionary whose words…changed the course of my life and led me to Christ, has been a

spiritual help to me ever since, and I thank God for him. Because I have found Jesus to be so wonderful a Saviour to me I long that all my Jewish brethren may also find salvation through Him and be led with joy into everlasting life.[240]

God blessed the faithful missionary efforts of Mr. Mark Kagan, Miss Anne Rayner and others, and the work prospered. In 1950 Joseph Cohn announced to the readers of *The Chosen People:*

So wonderfully has the Lord been blessing the sacrificial service of our Miss Anne Rayner in London, that now the stakes need to be strengthened, and the lines lengthened.

Accordingly, we are happy to report the following organizational changes: Mr. S. V. Scott-Mitchell, a devout and highly respected Christian layman of London, has in his generosity of heart responded to our need by agreeing to be our Honorary Treasurer for all funds sent to us from the British Commonwealth of Nations....

Also, Mr. Mark Kagan, a Jewish Christian brother much beloved as a Bible teacher in Christian circles all over the British Isles, will devote more time to the work there as our Honorary Director, giving an abundance of his ability in assisting our Miss Anne Rayner.[241]

Another report of the work in London appeared in the October, 1950 issue of *The Chosen People* magazine. It was written by Alexander Marks, who had returned to post-war England to visit the scenes of his childhood, and the sacred spot where he had found the Lord Jesus. In his report Mr. Marks said:

...The bombings of London scattered Jewish people and made Jewish missionary work more difficult. For instance, in the East End before the war, there lived more than one hundred thousand Jews. Today there are only twenty-five thousand. The Jewish Mission buildings were all bombed with the exception of two; and numbers of Jews and Christian Jews were killed in the air raids.

Many Jews moved from the East End to the north of London. Here, our Missionary, Miss Anne Rayner, is doing a noble work for the Lord. She has Gospel meetings for Jews in her home and she visits hospitals, Jewish stores and Jewish homes. In this way she has been able to reach many Jews with the Gospel and all in a section which has not before been touched by any Jewish Mission or Missionary.

It was my privilege to give three messages at Miss Rayner's home. I was delighted to meet Jewish people of all walks of life who were interested in the Gospel. The meetings in our Mission are being conducted strictly on spiritual lines, and it is a joy to hear the Gospel story sung by Jewish believers....

Miss Anne Rayner is doing the work of two people. She needs larger quarters to accommodate the Jewish people who come to her meetings.[242]

FINAL DAYS OF MINISTRY IN ENGLAND

The ministry in England was growing, and in an effort to ensure the continuation of the Mission's outreach there, and to bring about the realization of Joseph Cohn's dream for a European Headquarters in London, the Board passed a motion at their August 30, 1950 meeting to immediately seek to have the Mission registered as a foreign corporation in England. They also authorized Mark Kagan to locate and move toward the purchase of a building for the ministry in London.[243]

Properties suitable for the ministry were sought, and Mr. and Mrs. Gaylord A. Barcley (Mr. Barcley became a member of the Board of Directors in 1943) offered to donate one fourth of the purchase price on a property,[244] but such a building was never purchased. Instead, Joseph Cohn secured some rented rooms in a building that belonged to the Mildmay Mission to the Jews.[245]

The Mission did, however, obtain registration in England. It was registered as The American Board of Missions to the Jews Limited.[246]

The Mission's hesitancy to purchase property in London evidently generated some difficultly with the staff there. Although nothing is mentioned in the Minutes or in *The Chosen People* magazine regarding the workers in London being disgruntled, the February 1952 issue of *The Chosen People* magazine, in a section entitled Transition, states:

In London, our newly appointed missionary is Joshua Wilkowsky, a brother who has known the Lord for over 35 years, and who has the respect of the Jewish population of London wherever he goes....Miss Rayner is no longer with us.[247]

Joshua Wilkowsky was born c. 1891, having come to faith in the Messiah at the age of seventeen. At the time he was hired as the Mission's worker in London, he was a man of sixty-one years of age. There is no mention of his background in either the official Board Minutes, in correspondence, or in *The Chosen People* magazine. Nor is there any mention as to why he was hired. It would appear, however, that he was to be a "transition" worker until such time as Joseph could put a staff and a work back together again—action that was never taken due to Joseph's untimely death in October, 1953.

Although Joshua Wilkowsky remained on staff until 1963, Joseph Cohn's death essentially effected an end to the Mission's outreach in London. Wilkowsky's main duties and responsibilities were to visit Jewish shop-keepers, to do hospital visitation, to distribute copies of The Shepherd of Israel, tracts, etc. He also maintained a monthly prayer meeting for the ministry. His wife assisted him in the work, and they faithfully reported on their activities to the readers of *The Chosen People* magazine. In 1956 the Wilkowsky's reported:

> ...*The prayer fellowship which takes place the first Saturday in each month has been growing steadily.*
> *To sum up the year's activities: Over 2000 calls have been made at Jewish homes; 4000 copies of The Shepherd of Israel have been distributed, and about 2000 tracts handed out. For all of this we thank the Lord.*[248]

Subsequent to Mr. Daniel Fuchs' appointment as Missionary Secretary of the Mission in 1957, he made several trips to London to assess the work and the prospect for continued outreach there. Following one of his trips, the Board approved the following action regarding the Mission's work in England:

> *Mr. Fuchs told of his feeling that some changes should be made in the organization of our English work and that an aggressive effort should be made to interest the churches and people in the work. Rev. Alexander Marks is going to England and Ireland for his vacation this summer. Mr. Fuchs met a very fine Christian man who was anxious to do deputation work for the Mission on weekends while he was in England....the Board appropriate[d] a sum not to exceed $500 for deputation work in England this summer, and Mr. Fuchs should try to arrange for Mr. Fields to accompany Mr. Marks on visits to churches while he is in England.*[249]

At their October 1963 meeting, after lengthy discussion on the matter, the Directors voted to retire Mr. Joshua Wilkowsky, placing him on a pension from the Mission's Canadian funds.[250] Further action was taken at the annual meeting of the Board held on January 29, 1964. At that meeting a motion was made and unanimously passed to, "...terminate our English work as of February 29, 1964 and that a letter be sent to our mailing list in Great Britain informing them of this change....It was also moved that a gift of 100 pounds be given to Mr. Kagan in appreciation of his services as our honorary director.[251]

With this action, the Board brought the Mission's Gospel outreach in England to a close. In subsequent years, several attempts were made to revive the ministry there, but the consensus of Board opinion has been that since the British Societies to the Jews are still actively involved in reaching the Jewish community of England, the Mission's resources are better utilized in evangelizing other areas of the world.

Joseph Cohn's dream of a post-war ministry throughout Europe, with its Headquarters in London, was never realized. But his dream for a vibrant testimony to the Jews in Israel and in South America became a reality, bearing fruit until this day!

Endnotes

Chapter 7. The Vision Expands to Europe and Beyond

1   *Minutes*, ABMJ, (October 19, 1932), p 104.
2   *The Chosen People*, Vol. XXXIV, No. 7, (April, 1929), p 8.
3   *Minutes of the Executive Committee*, ABMJ, (March 5, 1929), p 90.
4   *The Chosen People*, Vol. XXXIV, No. 7, (April, 1929), pp 8-9.
5   See note above, p 9.
6   See note above, p 7.
7   *The Chosen People*, Vol. XXXV, No. 1, (October, 1929), p 7.
8   *Minutes of the Executive Committee*, ABMJ, (October 8, 1929), p 100.
9   *Minutes*, ABMJ, (October 17, 1929), p 41.
10 *The Chosen People*, Vol. XXXV, No. 6, (March, 1930), p 7.
11 See note above, pp 7, 8.

12   *Minutes*, ABMJ, (January 22, 1930), p 44.

13   *The Chosen People*, Vol. XXXV, No. 8, (May, 1930), p 9.

14   *Minutes*, ABMJ, (April 19, 1933), p 3.

15   *Minutes of Executive Committee*, ABMJ, (June 18, 1936), pp 2, 3.

16   *Minutes*, ABMJ, (October 16, 1935), p 2.

17   *The Chosen People*, Vol. XXXVIII, No. 8, (May, 1933), pp 8, 9.

18   *The Chosen People*, Vol. XLI, No. 6, (March, 1936), p 10.

19   *The Chosen People*, Vol. XLII, No. 1, (October, 1936), p 8.

20   *The Chosen People*, Vol. XLII, No. 3, (December, 1936), p 10.

21   *The Chosen People*, Vol. XLIII, No. 6, (March, 1938), pp 11, 12.

22   See note above.

23   See note above, p 13.

24   *The Chosen People*, Vol. XLV, No. 6, (March, 1940), p 9.

25   *The Chosen People*, Vol. XLIX, No. 7, (April, 1944), p 6.

26   *The Chosen People*, Vol. XLV, No. 8, (May, 1940), p 6.

27   *The Chosen People*, Vol. XLVI, No. 5, (February, 1941), p 14.

28   *The Chosen People*, Vol. XLVI, No. 8, (May, 1941), p 15.

29   *The Chosen People*, Vol. XLVII, No. 3, (December, 1941), pp 9, 21.

30   *The Chosen People*, Vol. XLVII, No. 8, (May, 1942), p 8.

31   *Minutes*, ABMJ, (April 27, 1943), p 2.

32   See note above.

33   *The Chosen People*, Vol. LI, No. 5, (February, 1946), p 7.

34   *Minutes*, ABMJ, (April 23, 1946), p 1.

35   *The Chosen People*, Vol. LII, No. 8, (May, 1947), p 11.

36   *The Chosen People*, Vol. LIII, No. 1, (October, 1947), p 9.

37   *The Chosen People*, Vol. LIII, No. 7, (April, 1948), pp 16, 17.

38   *Minutes*, ABMJ, (August 30, 1949), p 49,50.

39   *The Chosen People*, Vol. LVI, No. 3, (December, 1950), p 10.

40   See note above, pp 10-12.

41   See note above.

42   *Minutes*, ABMJ, (October 26, 1949), p 52.

43   *Minutes*, ABMJ, (April 26, 1950), p 68.

44   *Minutes*, ABMJ, (October 25, 1950), pp 77, 78.

45   *The Chosen People*, Vol. LV, No. 7, (April, 1950), p 9.

46   *Shepherd of Israel*, Vol. 34, No. 5, (January, 1951), p 2.

47   See note above.

48   *The Chosen People*, Vol. LVI, No. 8, (May, 1951), p 11.

49   See note above.

50   *The Chosen People*, Vol. LV, No. 2, (November, 1949), pp 16, 17.

51   *The Chosen People*, Vol. LVIII, No. 1, (October, 1952), pp 16, 17.

52   See note above.

53   *Minutes*, ABMJ, (April 28, 1954), p 116.

54   *Minutes*, ABMJ, (April 27, 1955), p 135.

55   *The Chosen People*, Vol. LXI, No. 8, (April, 1956), pp 8, 9.

56   *The Chosen People*, Vol. LXI, No. 9, (May, 1956), p 11.

57   See note above.

58   *The Chosen People*, Vol. LXIII, No. 7, (March, 1958), pp 3-5.

59   *Minutes*, ABMJ, (May 23, 1962), p 210.

60   *The Chosen People*, Vol. LXXI, No. 1, (September, 1965), p 7.

61   See note above, p 10.

62   See note above.

63   *The Chosen People*, Vol. LXXII, No. 4, (December, 1966), p 1.

64   *Minutes*, ABMJ, (December, 1968), p 22.

65   *Minutes*, ABMJ, (January 22, 1969), p 24.

[66] *Minutes*, ABMJ, (July 16, 1969), p 30.

[67] *Minutes*, ABMJ, (September 17, 1969), p 33.

[68] *Minutes*, ABMJ, (June 27, 1973), p 92.

[69] *Minutes*, ABMJ, (January 23, 1974), p 101.

[70] *Minutes*, ABMJ, (September 17, 1969), pp 34,p35.

[71] *Minutes*, ABMJ, (November 19, 1969), p 37.

[72] *The Chosen People*, Vol. LXXVI, No. 5, (January, 1971), p 12.

[73] *The Chosen People*, Vol. XLV, No. 1, (October, 1939), p 10.

[74] *The Chosen People*, Vol. XCIII, No. 9, (May, 1987), p 9.

[75] *The Chosen People*, Vol. LXXXVII, No. 5, (May, 1981), p 14.

[76] *The Chosen People*, Vol. LXXVII, No. 1, (September, 1971), p 4.

[77] See note above, pp 3, 4.

[78] *Minutes*, ABMJ, (January 28, 1970), p 41.

[79] *The Chosen People*, Vol. LXXIV, No. 4, (December, 1968), p 10.

[80] *The Chosen People*, Vol. LXXVII, No. 1, (September, 1971), p 3.

[81] *The Chosen People*, Vol. LXXVII, No. 4, (December, 1971), p 6.

[82] *The Chosen People*, Vol. XCIII, No. 9, (May, 1987), p 9.

[83] *Minutes*, ABMJ, (January 21, 1973), p 86.

[84] *Minutes*, ABMJ, (January 28, 1981), p 2.

[85] *Minutes*, ABMJ, (May 6, 1988), p 1.

[86] *The Chosen People*, Vol. XCX, No. 9, (May, 1989), p 9.

[87] See note above, p 10,11.

[88] *The Chosen People*, Vol. XCVII, No. 3, (November, 1990), pp 10, 11.

[89] *The Chosen People*, Vol. XCII, No. 8, (April, 1986), pp 13, 14.

[90] *The Chosen People*, Vol. XCVII, No. 10, (June, 1991), p 9.

[91] See note above.

[92] *Minutes of Executive Committee*, ABMJ, (May 24, 1934), p 1.

[93] *The Chosen People*, Vol. XVIII, No. 8, (May, 1913), p 6.

[94] *The Chosen People*, Vol. XXXVI, No. 1, (October, 1930), p 12.

[95] *Minutes of Executive Committee*, ABMJ, (October 2, 1934), p 3; *Minutes of the Board*, ABMJ, (October 17, 1934), p 11.

[96] *The Chosen People*, Vol. XL, No. 2, (November, 1934), pp 5-7.

[97] *Minutes*, ABMJ, (December 10, 1935), pp 6, 7.

[98] Harold A. Sevener, *Personal Interview With Henri Vincent*, April 19, 1990.

[99] *The Chosen People*, Vol. XLI, No. 7, (April, 1936), p 10.

[100] *Minutes of Executive Committee*, ABMJ, (December 8, 1936), p 1.

[101] *Minutes of Executive Committee*, ABMJ, (August 18, 1937), p 3.

[102] *The Chosen People*, Vol. XLIII, No. 3, (December, 1937), p 14.

[103] *Minutes*, ABMJ, (April 21, 1937), pp 5, 6.

[104] Testimony appears in: *The Shepherd of Israel*, Vol. XXVIII, No. 11,12, (July-August, 1946), pp 1, 2.

[105] Frederick Levison, *Christian and Jew—Leon Levison—1881-1936*, (East Lothian, Scotland: The Pentland Press, 1989), p 212.

[106] See note above.

[107] See note above, p 13.

[108] *Personal correspondence*, J. Cohn and H. Vincent, November 29, 1938, December 13, 1938.

[109] See *The Chosen People*, 1936-1947.

[110] *Minutes*, ABMJ, (October 28, 1936), p 4.

[111] *The Chosen People*, Vol. XLV, No. 1, (October, 1939), p 5.

[112] *The Chosen People*, Vol. XLII, No. 2, (November, 1936), p 5.

[113] See note above, p 6.

[114] *Minutes*, ABMJ, (January 27, 1937), p 10.

[115] See note above.

[116] *The Chosen People*, Vol. XLII, No. 5, (February, 1937), p 4.

[117] *The Chosen People*, Vol. XLV, No. 3, (December, 1939), p 9.

[118] See note above, pp 9, 10.

[119] *The Chosen People*, Vol. LXIII, No. 6, (February, 1958), pp 6, 7.

[120] *The Chosen People*, Vol. XLIV, No. 3, (December, 1938), p 12.

[121] *Minutes, ABMJ*, (October 30, 1940), p 2.

[122] *Personal correspondence: J. Cohn to Mr. Jean Tanguy*, November 11, 1939.

[123] *The Chosen People*, Vol. XLVI, No. 2, (November, 1940), p 12.

[124] *The Chosen People*, Vol. XLVIII, No. 2, (November, 1942), pp 7, 8.

[125] *The Chosen People*, Vol. LII, No. 7, (April, 1947), pp 9, 10.

[126] *The Chosen People*, Vol. XLVII, No. 7, (April, 1942), p 12.

[127] *The Chosen People*, Vol. XLVI, No. 6, (March, 1941), p 10.

[128] *The Chosen People*, Vol. LXIII, No. 6, (February, 1958), pp 7, 8.

[129] *The Chosen People*, Vol. XLVII, No. 7, (April, 1942), p 7.

[130] *Minutes, ABMJ*, (May 13, 1942), p 2.

[131] *The Chosen People*, Vol. LII, No. 1, (October, 1946), p 11.

[132] *The Chosen People*, Vol. LII, No. 2, (November, 1946), p 19.

[133] *The Chosen People*, Vol. LIII, No. 3, (December, 1947), p 12.

[134] See *The Chosen People*, Vol. LVII, No. 5, (February, 1952), p 10.

[135] *The Chosen People*, Vol. LVIII, No. 4, (January, 1953), p 11.

[136] *The Chosen People*, Vol. LX, No. 6, (March, 1955), p 9.

[137] *The Chosen People*, Vol. LIX, No. 3, (December, 1953), p 14.

[138] *The Chosen People*, Vol. LXIII, No. 10, (June, 1958), p 6.

[139] *The Chosen People*, Vol. LXIV, No. 6, (February, 1959), p 7.

[140] *The Chosen People*, Vol. LXV, No. 8, (April, 1960), pp 4, 5.

[141] *The Chosen People*, Vol. LXVI, No. 7, (March, 1961), p 3,4.

[142] *The Chosen People*, Vol. LXIX, No. 4, (December, 1963), p 3.

[143] See note above.

[144] *The Chosen People*, Vol. LXXXV, No. 1, (September, 1979), p 4.

[145] *The Chosen People*, Vol. LXXII, No. 1, (September, 1966), pp 10, 11.

[146] *Minutes, ABMJ*, (June 23, 1965), p 248; *Minutes, ABMJ*, (November 17, 1965), p 252.

[147] *Minutes, ABMJ*, (April 19, 1967), p 285.

[148] *The Chosen People*, Vol. LXXIX, No. 6, (February, 1974), p 7.

[149] *The Chosen People*, Vol. LXXII, No. 6, (February, 1967), p 12.

[150] *Minutes, ABMJ*, (April 22, 1970), p 43.

[151] *The Chosen People*, Vol. LXXVI, No. 6, (February, 1971), p 8.

[152] *The Chosen People*, Vol. LXXIX, No. 6, (February, 1974), p 8.

[153] See note above.

[154] *The Chosen People*, Vol. LXXX, No. 6, (February, 1975), p 7.

[155] See note above, p 8.

[156] See note above.

[157] *Personal correspondence: V. Sedaca to H. Sevener*, January 30, 1976.

[158] *Personal correspondence: H. Sevener to D. Sedaca*, May 25, 1977.

[159] *Minutes, ABMJ*, (January 23, 1980), p 2.

[160] *The Chosen People*, Vol. LXXXV, No. 7, (March, 1980), p 10.

[161] *Minutes, ABMJ*, (October 21, 1981), p 4.

[162] Roberto Passo, *Personal Testimony/Application*, (May, 1982), p 1.

[163] See note above.

[164] See note above.

[165] *The Chosen People*, Vol. XCX, No. 7, (March, 1989), pp 10, 11.

[166] *The Chosen People*, Vol. XLII, No. 5, (February, 1937), p 5.

[167] *The Shepherd of Israel*, Vol. XIX, No. 6, (February, 1937), p 1.

[168] See note above.

[169] *Minutes, Executive Committee, ABMJ*, (June 12, 1939), p 1.

[170] *The Chosen People*, Vol. XLV, No. 8, (May, 1940), p 11.

[171] See note above, p 4.

[172] *The Chosen People*, Vol. XLVI, No. 4, (January, 1941), p 12.

[173] *The Chosen People*, Vol. XLVI, No. 8, (May, 1941), p 16.

[174] *Minutes of Executive Committee, ABMJ*, (June 24, 1941).

[175] *Minutes, ABMJ*, (October 16, 1941).

[176] *Minutes, ABMJ*, (May 13, 1942), p 2.

[177] *The Chosen People*, Vol. XLI, No. 7, (April, 1936), p 10.

[178] *The Chosen People*, Vol. XLI, No. 3, (December, 1935), p 9.

[179] *The Chosen People*, Vol. XLI, No. 8, (May, 1936), p 11.

[180] See note above, p 11,12.

[181] *The Chosen People*, Vol. XLII, No. 4, (January, 1937), pp 7-9.

[182] *The Chosen People*, Vol. XLIII, No. 2, (November, 1937), pp 7, 8.

[183] *The Chosen People*, Vol. XLIII, No. 3, (December, 1937), p 8.

[184] *Minutes, ABMJ*, (April 21, 1937).

[185] *The Chosen People*, Vol. XLIII, No. 5, (February, 1938), p 12.

[186] *The Chosen People*, Vol. XLIV, No. 5, (February, 1939), pp 5, 6.

[187] *The Chosen People*, Vol. XLIV, No. 6, (March, 1939), p 10.

[188] *Minutes, ABMJ*, (April 19, 1939), p 4.

[189] *The Chosen People*, Vol. XLV, No. 1, (October, 1939), p 9.

[190] See note above, pp 9, 10.

[191] See note above, p 13.

[192] *Minutes, ABMJ*, (October 19, 1939), p 3.

[193] *Personal correspondence: M. Gitlin to J. Cohn*, April 24, 1944.

[194] *The Chosen People*, Vol. XLII, No. 5, (February, 1937), pp 10, 11.

[195] See note above.

[196] *The Chosen People*, Vol. XLIV, No. 2, (November, 1938), p 7.

[197] *The Chosen People*, Vol. XLIV, No. 4, (January, 1939), pp 10, 11.

[198] See note above, p 13.

[199] See note above.

[200] *The Chosen People*, Vol. XLV, No. 1, (October, 1939), pp 4, 5.

[201] *Personal correspondence: H. Vincent to J. Cohn*, February 14, 1939, p 1.

[202] *Personal correspondence: H. Vincent to J. Cohn*, June 20, 1939.

[203] *Personal correspondence: H. Vincent to J. Cohn*, February 14, 1939, p 2.

[204] *Personal correspondence: H. Vincent to J. Cohn*, April 18, 1939.

[205] *The Chosen People*, Vol. XLV, No. 3, (December, 1939), p 7.

[206] *The Chosen People*, Vol. XLV, No. 4, (January, 1940), p 10.

[207] *Personal correspondence: H. Vincent to J. Cohn*, September 10, 1939.

[208] See note above.

[209] See note above, p 2.

[210] *Personal interview: H. Sevener with H. Vincent*, April 19, 1990, p 4.

[211] *Personal correspondence: H. Vincent to J. Cohn*, November 18, 1944.

[212] *Personal correspondence: H. Vincent to J. Cohn*, March 10, 1945.

[213] *Personal correspondence: H. Vincent to J. Cohn*, June 12, 1945.

[214] See note above.

[215] *Personal correspondence: H. Vincent to J. Cohn*, July 7, 1945.

[216] See note above, p 2.

[217] See note above.

[218] See note above, pp 2, 3.

[219] *Personal correspondence: J. Cohn to J. R. Miller*, July 13, 1945.

[220] *Personal correspondence: H. Vincent to J. Cohn*, August 8, 1945.

[221] *The Chosen People*, Vol. LII, No. 3, (December, 1946), p 13.

[222] See note above, p 14.

[223] *The Chosen People*, Vol. LIII, No. 3, (December, 1947), p 12.

[224] *The Chosen People*, Vol. LVI, No. 6, (March, 1951), p 12.

[225] *The Chosen People*, Vol. LVIII, No. 7, (April, 1953), p 10.

[226] *The Chosen People*, Vol. LVII, No. 7, (April, 1952), p 13.

[227] *Minutes*, ABMJ, (September 15, 1965).

[228] *The Chosen People*, Vol. LXXIII, No. 8, (April, 1968), p 10.

[229] See note above, p 13.

[230] A. Bernstein, *Some Jewish Witnesses for Christ*, (London: Operative Jewish Converts' Institution, 1909), p 420.

[231] *The Shepherd of Israel*, Vol. XXVIII, No. 7, (March, 1946), p 1.

[232] A. Bernstein, *Some Jewish Witnesses*, p 421.

[233] See note above.

[234] *Minutes of Executive Committee*, ABMJ, (June 12, 1939), p 3.

[235] *The Chosen People*, Vol. XLVII, No. 4, (January, 1942), p 8.

[236] *The Chosen People*, Vol. XLIV, No. 4, (January, 1939), p 8.

[237] *The Shepherd of Israel*, Vol. XXVIII, No. 7, (March, 1946), p 2.

[238] *The Chosen People*, Vol. XLVII, No. 4, (January, 1942), p 9.

[239] *The Chosen People*, Vol. L, No. 3, (December, 1944), p 12.

[240] *The Chosen People*, Vol. LIV, No. 2, (November, 1948), pp 7, 8.

[241] *The Chosen People*, Vol. LVI, No. 1, (October, 1950), p 15.

[242] See note above, p 16.

[243] *Minutes*, ABMJ, (August 30, 1950), p 75.

[244] *Minutes*, ABMJ, (April 27, 1943), p 3.

[245] *Minutes*, ABMJ, (April 23, 1952), p 92.

[246] See note above.

[247] *The Chosen People*, Vol. LVII, No. 5, (February, 1952), p 17.

[248] *The Chosen People*, Vol. LXI, No. 7, (March, 1956), p 7.

[249] *Minutes*, ABMJ, (May 23, 1962), p 211.

[250] *Minutes*, ABMJ, (October 23, 1963), p 224.

[251] *Minutes*, ABMJ, (January 29, 1964), p 229.

8

THE VISION IN THE MIDST OF DISSENSION

As the Mission grew in strength and influence, Joseph Hoffman Cohn's reputation also grew. He was in constant demand as a speaker. His networking system brought him into contact with Christian leaders on the highest echelon of the Christian world. Never before had an independent Jewish mission had such acceptance within Christian circles; never before had the leader of any Jewish mission been so in demand on the platforms and programs of major churches, conference grounds, Bible colleges, and seminaries. Joseph's abilities as a leader and as a visionary were unparalleled in the field of Jewish evangelism during his day.

The Mission was becoming recognized overseas as well, as Joseph "networked" with key individuals and established branches of the Mission in Europe, Russia, the United Kingdom, and Israel. Joseph's vision was to reach Jews in every country with the Gospel. But the enemy of our souls was not in agreement with Joseph's vision. The task of the Great Commission—of sharing the Gospel, "the power of God for the salvation of everyone who believes: first for the Jew, then for the Gentile" (Romans 1:16 NIV)—is a task of engaging in spiritual warfare.

At the same time Satan was using his influence to produce the blind hatred motivating Nazism and anti-Semitism in his effort to destroy the Jewish people physically, he used his knowledge of mankind's sin nature to produce "spiritual warfare" within the Mission. The Scriptures state that it is the little foxes that spoil the vine (Song of Solomon 2:15), and Satan knows which "little foxes" he can use to spoil or to destroy an effective witness of the Gospel. In this world no Christian, or Christian organization, doing an effective work of evangelism is immune from Satan's attacks. Joseph Cohn had had much opportunity to observe and to experience such warfare—especially as he had watched his father go through the fires of affliction—but time and the successes of ministry had dimmed his memory of those difficult days.

At a time when the Mission was at its zenith—at a time when it was necessary—*vital*—to get the Gospel to Jewish people who were experiencing the horrors of the holocaust, Joseph Cohn and the Mission became entangled in a spiritual battle that left all combatants battle-scarred and weary. It was a battle that was waged from 1943 through 1950—a seven year period of personal tribulation for Cohn, and a dark period in the history of the Mission.

Yet, despite the problems that this spiritual conflict brought to Joseph Cohn and to the Mission, the Gospel witness to the Jewish people was never interrupted. Through the faithfulness of God, and the perseverance of Joseph Cohn and the staff, the Gospel witness continued to be proclaimed through the American Board of Missions to the Jews, and Jewish people continued to respond to its message!

To grasp an understanding of the little foxes Satan used in his effort to destroy the testimony of the Mission, and to destroy the man, Joseph Cohn, who was the driving force behind the Mission, the reader must recall that Joseph Cohn was a man of great self confidence, firm convictions, clear vision for the Mission, and a man of great determination. As was mentioned earlier, he was a man people either loved or hated.

To the Christian public, the work of The American Board of Missions to the Jews (CPM) was a thriving enterprise—a work that was obviously enjoying God's blessings. But those who were on the "inner core" knew that year by year an undercurrent of discontent was swelling. Joseph Cohn set the vision for the organization, he had complete oversight of all staff and branch ministries of the organization, he was in charge of all of the Mission's publications. He served on the Finance Committee, making investments for the Mission as he saw fit. He also called the meetings of the Board of Directors, and any special meetings of the Board he deemed necessary to escalate action on his plans and projects for the expansion of the work. Joseph seemed to perceive the Mission as his extended family, of which he was the father. He trusted and followed his instincts, but his self confidence often caused him to move ahead of the Board.

Unable to harness the vision and drive of their leader, members of the Board of Directors found that in time they were approving policies and making decisions affecting the Mission's finances which they had neither had time to think about or pray about. For a few years the Board, in effect, became a "rubber stamp" for the plans and programs of Joseph Cohn.

As the son of the founder of the Mission, and as one of the original incorporators of the Williamsburg Mission to the

Jews, Joseph had known and served on the Board with several of the men for many years. The nucleus of the Board had known Rabbi Leopold Cohn almost from the Mission's inception; others elected were close friends of the Cohns. The Minutes of the Board reflect that some Board members did question many of Joseph's ideas and proposals, but in the end, more often than not, the Board went along with him because of the sheer force of his personality and convictions. The Minutes also reflect that it was only as the years went by, and as new Board members were added, that the Board began to exercise some control over Joseph.

As it was alluded to in an earlier chapter, the undercurrent of discontent within the Board began with the merging of the Mission with the Buffalo Hebrew Christian Mission in Buffalo, New York.

Abraham Machlin—His Story

Abraham Machlin, founder of the Buffalo Hebrew Christian Mission, was born of Jewish parents in Mogileff, Russia (c. 1886). Theirs was a typical Jewish family, and Abraham attended Hebrew school (Cheder) until the age of thirteen. When Abraham was in his early teens his family moved to Kiev. It was there, as a young man attempting to find work, that Abraham began to experience the cruel hatred and persecution that was so often directed toward Jews in Russia during those days. Hatred swelled within Abraham's heart as day by day he faced the vengeful actions of the Gentile citizens of Kiev. The Greek-Catholic Church (Russian Orthodox) was the religion of the State, and Abraham began to hate both the Russian government and anything "Christian."

Like many Jews, Abraham believed that all Gentiles were "Christians," and in his experience Christians had become the hated enemy. The Social Revolutionary Party was formed in Russia in 1901. It called for the end to autocracy; it called for a classless society, for the distribution of land to peasants, and for the self-determination of minorities. Abraham Machlin believed in the organization's statement of purpose, and he joined the Party (c.1905). He became very involved in all of its activities and was soon arrested and sent to prison. After serving his sentence he threw himself back into the Party's activities, breaking his parole. Again, he was arrested. This time he was sentenced to five years hard labor in Siberia, but in less than a week Abraham managed to escape the labor camp. He returned home and doggedly pursued his activities with the Party. In less than one month the authorities caught up with him. Once again, he was sent to Siberia, but this time he was sent to a labor camp over 2,000 miles into the interior of Siberia.

Abraham Machlin was evidently a man of great inner strength and determination, for he managed to escape a second time from the labor camp. When he reached his home, he learned that his mother had died. Knowing that the authorities would sentence him to death if they caught him again, his family and friends advised him to flee the country. They suggested that he go to America.

Abraham followed the advice given to him, and made arrangements to sail to America. Upon his arrival, he immediately joined the American Socialist Party, but soon became disenchanted with their principles and methods of operations so he resigned. Of that period in his life, he later wrote:

> All those years I had sought for excitement and for expression of self, but all I found was trouble and misery and sin and dissatisfaction and discontent. In my heart there was a longing for something which I could not explain. My soul was made for God and the rubbish of this world with which I was filling it could not satisfy me. While in this state of mind, I came across a Jewish mission in Philadelphia and went to one of their services. I was deeply impressed with the meeting and was further drawn to that mission by the kindness of a Christian lady who graciously talked with me after the services. She spoke so kindly of a Jewish Messiah who satisfied her longing soul. Though at that time I did not yet understand what she meant, still I could sense from her testimony that she had a wonderful peace and satisfaction in her faith, a satisfaction which I sorely lacked.
>
> Later I became anxious to learn more about this Messiah, and when I was about to leave for New York that same lady advised me to get in touch with the Williamsburg Mission to the Jews in Brooklyn, New York, now the American Board of Missions to the Jews. This I did, and one of the first things I saw on entering the mission hall was the fifty-third chapter of Isaiah inscribed on the wall. Rev. Leopold Cohn, the superintendent of the mission, happened to take his message that evening from the same chapter, in which he painted for the audience a vivid picture of Christ our Messiah as the One who gave His life for us that we might live. My heart was touched. I went forward and told Mr. Cohn that if he could prove to me from the Old Testament Scriptures that Jesus Christ was the Messiah, I would believe. Mr. Cohn patiently presented to me such passages as Genesis 49:10, Daniel 9:25-26 and Zechariah 12:10. All these were new to me, as my rabbis had never taught me these Scriptures. I was so thoroughly convinced of the truth of these passages of Scripture that I was led to receive Christ right there and then, and soon after I made public confession of my faith [c.1914].
>
> After having attended several services at this mission, I told my relatives that I had found Him of whom the

prophets did write. I had peace and joy in my soul because of my faith in the Messiah, and I expected my people to accept this same Jesus also, but, alas, they refused to have anything to with Him or with me....

Soon after this I went to Boston. All my letters to my people were returned unopened.... At the end of two years, however, I received a letter inviting me to come home. It was Passover season, and when I arrived I found that four of my relatives came together to celebrate the feast (seder)....

My uncle took the three unleavened cakes (matzos), and broke the middle-one in half, hiding one half under the pillow upon which he reclined, and distributing the remaining half among us. After the supper he took out the other half (afikomen), and broke that also and divided it among us. I could not resist saying to him, 'Uncle, would you like me to explain what these three unleavened cakes represent?' He gave me permission and I said, 'They represent the Trinity: God, the Father, the Son and the Holy Spirit. The middle cake which you broke represents Jesus our Messiah who was broken for our sins.' I also told him in the course of our conversation that because of my having found the Messiah I loved him more than ever before and was constrained to pray for them all, as the Lord did while on the cross, 'Father, forgive them, for they know not what they do.' At this he wept, and took my hand, saying, 'I believe you are sincere and may God bless you.'[1]

Abraham Machlin continued to study the Scriptures, and soon felt God's call upon his life to become a missionary to his own people. He decided to open a Gospel outreach to Jewish people in Buffalo, New York. In developing his mission, Abraham attempted to duplicate in every way the example he'd seen in Rabbi Leopold Cohn's mission, the Williamsburg Mission to the Jews in Brooklyn, New York.

He enlisted the support of a few interested Christians in the area, as well as some sympathetic pastors. These individuals formed a committee of support and concern for the new mission. By the winter of 1920 A.B. Machlin was ready to move his small ministry into a facility in which meetings could be held. The Buffalo Evening News carried a report of the opening of the new Hebrew mission, along with a picture of the building and a picture of the Machlins. The article stated:

Buffalo's new Hebrew mission which opened this week is known as The House of the Prince of Peace [Incidently, this was the same name used by Leopold and Joseph Cohn for all of the branches opened and operated by the Mission].

Rev. A. B. Machlin is to be in charge of it.

Mrs. Machlin is also helping him in the work.

The building, which was formerly an apartment house, has been made into a community center.

Beside the rooms for services and classes, there will also be a public reading room on the first floor. In the basement, it is planned to open a manual training school. On the third floor, a gymnasium is being fitted up.

Another feature of the mission will be a free clinic. Dr. Edwin R. Gould will head it.

'Our plan is to preach Jesus Christ among the Hebrews of Buffalo,' said Mr. Machlin, in explaining the purpose of the mission.[2]

During its first year, Abraham Machlin's mission was the target of great opposition. Time and time again the Jewish community organized, to try to close the ministry. There was open violence against the mission's workers and vandalism of the mission's property. A less tenacious man would have given up in discouragement and despair, yet Abraham persevered and after a number of years suspicion largely gave way to trust and confidence on the part of the community—Jew and Gentile alike. Abraham enlarged the circle of volunteers helping him in the work, and the ministry continued to grow.

A Buffalo, New York Branch Established

A group of faithful constituents of the Buffalo Hebrew Christian Mission attending an annual banquet and business meeting in 1927, heard A.B. Machlin give the following report:

A year has passed and God has been with us teaching us how to be workers together with Him, then crowning our efforts with success.

1. *Daily Vacation Bible School. When we began planning our Vacation Bible School, we felt uncertain as to whether or not our school would be all it has been in past years. This year the Jewish Community House discontinued the Vacation School they have held the past three years, mainly as a protest to our school, and announced their camp would open to girls the second week in July. We have had little fear for their school because the children come to us in preference to their own, but when it comes to a summer vacation, every mother longs to have her children in the*

country near a cool beach and we cannot blame them. When our school closed, we felt like children who have listened to a sad story with a happy ending. But we are praying for a summer camp!

2. *Open Air. As usual, we had a blessed time in the open air. Twice a week the Jewish throng heard the story of Redeeming Love and gladly accepted Gospels and Tracts.*

3. *Broadcasting. A new field of activity was opened to us this year, perhaps the greatest afforded us to reach the adults. We have been broadcasting a regular program every Friday evening at 8:00 P.M. over Station WKBW in Yiddish and English. Tune in!*

4. *Mailing Literature. Another new feature of the work this year has been mailing a letter and several tracts at regular intervals to those we cannot reach in any other way. We have a mailing list of 5,000 and keep a complete record of letters and tracts sent. Also personal replies received.*

5. *Visitation. We have continued house to house visitation throughout the year and many opportunities of usefulness have opened to us. Certain days are devoted to distribution of literature and others to visits and discussions in friendly homes of those who attend regularly.*

6. *'Knell Memorial Hall'. Since our very beginning we have worked under great difficulties. We did not have a room large enough for the children to play, or place where we could invite children and parents for a night together and when it came to equipment of the boys, we had nothing to offer. But—October 22 our new addition, 'Knell Memorial Hall,' was completed and Sunday, October 23, dedicated for service.*[3]

Clearly, the Buffalo Hebrew Christian Mission was enjoying God's blessings, but A.B. Machlin discovered, just as Joseph Cohn had, that continued growth and expansion requires not only the prayers and faithful support of God's people—it requires an ever increasing base of support as well. As he sought to expand his mission, A.B. Machlin found himself traveling from city to city—seeking pastors, churches, and Christians who would be willing to help support his mission. He found that when he was away from Buffalo he could raise some support, but not enough. And when he was away, the support from the Buffalo churches diminished because of his absence from the area. Time became a commodity—there simply wasn't enough time to do both missionary work *and* fund raising!

By 1936 the Hebrew Christian Mission in Buffalo was in dire straits. Abraham Machlin was spending most of his time trying to raise funds, while the committee of pastors and Christians did more and more overseeing of the missionary work. Funds were running low; the mission was having difficulty paying the rent on its property. It was then, after much prayer, that members of the committee sent a second communique to Joseph, to ask if the American Board of Missions to the Jews would be interested in merging with the Buffalo Hebrew Christian Mission. One of the prominent committee members was Dr. John Palmer Muntz, an influential Christian, and the pastor of the Cazenovia Park Baptist Church in Buffalo, New York. The committee proposed that Mr. A.B. Machlin be placed on the Mission's staff as an Itinerant Evangelist and Field Representative. They further suggested and recommended that the Mission send a worker, of the Mission's choice, to do the actual missionary work in Buffalo. It was stated that Dr. Palmer Muntz was willing to locally direct the work.[4]

Dr. Muntz was a well-known personality in the Christian world. He was born and raised in Buffalo. After completing his studies at Northern Baptist Seminary in 1924, he accepted a call to serve as pastor of the Cazenovia Park Baptist Church in Buffalo, New York—a position he held from 1924 through 1963.

His interest in the separatist, fundamentalist Baptist movement began in the 1920's, and over the years he was involved with the Fundamentalist Fellowship of the Northern Baptist Convention and the Baptist Bible Union, as well as with the Conservative Baptists from the initial days of their founding. He also had a great love for the Jewish people. It was this love and concern that led him to devote time, energy, and support to the Buffalo Hebrew Christian Mission from its inception.

In 1932 the Los Angeles Baptist Theological Seminary awarded him with an honorary doctorate; it was the first of eight honorary doctorates he received.

In 1935 Dr. William Biederwolf invited Dr. Muntz to speak at a conference at the Winona Lake Bible Conference grounds in Winona Lake, Indiana. That opportunity was not only the beginning of a close friendship that developed between Dr. Biederwolf and Dr. Muntz, it was also the beginning of Muntz's involvement with the conference ministry at the Winona Lake Bible Conference grounds. Dr. Muntz eventually became an assistant to Biederwolf, and went on to succeed him as Director of Winona Lake Bible Conferences from 1939 until 1958. During his tenure as Director, the conference program grew from a one week conference to a six week conference, followed by the Conference on Prophecy and the Jews.

When Joseph Cohn saw that Dr. J. Palmer Muntz was going to be personally involved in the oversight of the ministry in Buffalo, he wasted no time in getting his Board to act. He knew Dr. Muntz's influence would open the doors of many churches and the cooperation of many Christian leaders. Muntz's involvement would also assure the continuation of the Mission's "Conference on Prophecy and the Jewish People" at the Winona Lake Bible Conference Grounds. For Joseph, the letter from the committee in Buffalo was an answer to prayer. It opened another opportunity to expand the work of the Mission!

The committee's letter informed Joseph that a new facility would need to be obtained. They suggested the purchase of a building they knew was available, and which they felt would be suitable for the needs of the ministry in Buffalo. The purchase price of the building had been looked into and was quoted to be $1,600. The suggestion was put forth that the Baptist group in Buffalo would contribute $800.00 toward the purchase of the building, and the Mission (ABMJ) could contribute the remaining $800.00. It was further indicated that Mr. Machlin would agree to raise money for the Mission, in return for which the Mission would fund the Buffalo branch with a budget of $3600 a year.[5]

The Board approved the plan, but just before it went into effect the seller of the property in Buffalo raised his price. The decision was made to proceed with the plan to hire Mr. Machlin, and to rent the home in which the Machlin's had been living for the Mission's activities[6] (In hindsight, this small set-back was just the "tip of the iceberg" of greater problems to be faced as a result of the merging of the two ministries).

At the time, it seemed that God's will was being accomplished—especially so when, by early Fall, the owner of the property again changed his mind and agreed to sell at the original price quoted, $1600.00.

Joseph Cohn announced the opening of the new Buffalo branch of the Mission in the November 1937 issue of *The Chosen People* magazine. The Dedication was a week long event, with services that began on Monday, October 10, 1937 and concluded on October 17, 1937. A number of notable Christians were asked to participate as speakers that week, including: Dr. John (Palmer) Muntz; Dr. Harry A. Ironside, pastor of the Moody Memorial Church of Chicago; Rev. Joseph Flacks of Minneapolis, Minnesota, well-known evangelist and Bible teacher; Rev. Dean S. Bedford, from Rochester, New York; Dr. William Edward Biederwolf, President of Winona Lake Bible Conference.

Dr. Muntz handled the arrangements for the Dedication services and he presided at all of the meetings. It was announced, "The Machlins will be assisted by many Christian volunteers in the city, and will have as staff workers, Mr. Daniel Fuchs, a former student of the National Bible Institute of New York; and Miss Elfrieda Mann, a graduate of the Moody Bible Institute of Chicago."[7] Daniel was transferred from the Brooklyn branch of the Mission to help in Buffalo. Miss Mann was transferred from the Chicago branch, where she had been assisting while finishing the Jewish Studies course at Moody.

It was also announced, "…that Mr. Machlin was in receipt of a telegram from Dr. Albert G. Johnson, pastor of the Hinson Memorial Baptist Church of Portland, Oregon, announcing their contribution of $1,000 to make the Chapel [the building purchased for $1600.00] a memorial to the late Dr. Walter B. Hinson, 'friend of God and lover of Israel' and best wishes to the Machlins' new work in Buffalo."[8]

Because of the years A.B. Machlin had devoted to fund raising for the Buffalo Hebrew Christian Mission, he had already built up a large number of pastors and Christian leaders who had confidence in him, but Joseph apparently felt that the support of Mr. Machlin's network of pastors and Christian leaders was more of a camaraderie—one that lacked financial backing. This was unacceptable to Joseph's business nature. In a report to the Executive Committee of the Board, Joseph stated:

> To help the Buffalo work to get started on good foundation, I had to go with Mr. Machlin clear out to the Pacific Northwest, Portland, Tacoma, Seattle, etc., where an important group of Mr. Machlin's friends have pastorates. This involved much traveling and a hard campaign. But it resulted most happily, and we were able to secure guarantees from the various churches which will provide at least for one-third of the entire year's budget in Buffalo. I have gotten Mr. Machlin started now on other similar work for the next two or three months while I am away, which holds promise of equally good results.[9]

Mr. Herman Centz, who had been sent to Buffalo to make tapes for the radio broadcasts, did not become the radio voice for the Mission. Instead, Joseph decided to use him as a missionary in the Buffalo outreach.

HERMAN CENTZ—THE BUFFALO BRANCH

Herman had known Joseph for many years, having been baptized by Rabbi Leopold Cohn. In his testimony, Herman recounted that he was born in Russia, the son of a highly placed orthodox Jewish family. In 1912, while still in Odessa, Russia, Herman first came into contact with some Christians who introduced him to the New Testament. He said: "Earnest study of the Scriptures soon brought me to the conclusion that God had indeed visited His people with salvation at the time appointed, but that in blindness we had missed the day of His visitation."[10] On Easter morning in 1913,

Herman prayed to accept Yeshua as his Messiah and Lord. He arrived in the United States in the Fall of 1913. He stated, "Here I was providentially brought in contact with the American Board of Missions to the Jews. In the warm atmosphere of the Mission fellowship my faith grew to maturity, ...and on October 20, 1913, I received baptism from the late Dr. Leopold Cohn."[11]

Herman trained for full-time Christian ministry, and in 1920 he returned to Europe to do evangelistic work. Upon returning to the United States he served as a pastor and evangelist, and in 1927 he became associated with the National Missions work of the Presbyterian Church, U.S.A. He worked with them until he accepted a position on the staff of the Mission in the early months of 1937—just a few months before the death of Rabbi Leopold Cohn. He served the Mission as an itinerant evangelist until Joseph asked him to move to Buffalo. In Buffalo, he served as the Missionary-in-Charge whenever Abraham Machlin was away doing deputation work for the Mission.

Joseph knew Herman was not happy about going to Buffalo; he (Joseph) had mentioned Herman's displeasure to the Board shortly after he had asked Herman to go to Buffalo to make the radio tapes.[12] It is not known, at least by the writer, if this unhappiness was the impetus that caused seeds of dissension to take root in the heart of Herman Centz. What is known is that seeds of discontent and dissension did take root in Herman's heart, and as they grew everything good that could have been produced through a harmonious God-honoring ministry in Buffalo, was choked out. Perhaps disappointment had turned to anger when Joseph rejected the radio programs Herman had labored on during the summer of 1937 (See Chapter Six of this history). Or perhaps jealousy sprang up in Herman's heart when Joseph failed to use him for the radio ministry—even after sending him all the way to Buffalo to make radio tapes. The dissatisfaction that took root in Herman's heart soon spread to the entire staff in Buffalo, as well as to some members of the committee who had been a part of the independent work in Buffalo. Buffalo became a "hotbed" of unrest.

PROBLEMS OF JOSEPH COHN

The problems in Buffalo were not the only problems Joseph was dealing with at that time. His wife, as was mentioned in an earlier chapter, had left him. They were not divorced, but they were legally separated. After years of separation, Mrs. Cohn had begun to publicly express her dissatisfaction with Joseph Cohn and with his leadership of the Mission. The feelings and opinions she aired with a number of influential leaders within the Christian community added fuel to a fire of discontent which was already smoldering in the hearts of some staff members and Board members in the Buffalo ministry.

Rumors of the unrest in Buffalo, and of Joseph Cohn's personal problems, reached Mr. A.B. Machlin who was out on the field raising funds for the Mission. Mr. Machlin had a personal interest in the Buffalo branch—it was *his* mission— and the rumors that reached him created bitterness in Machlin's own heart.

To get to the bottom of the matter, and to determine the competence or incompetence of Joseph's leadership of the Mission, a meeting of an ad hoc committee of the Board of Directors was held on September 27, 1938. Mrs. Cohn and her attorney were invited to attend. Mrs. Cohn turned down the invitation, but the committee proceeded with its interrogation of Joseph Cohn. The Minutes of that meeting state:

> *After thorough questioning of Mr. Cohn and consideration of statements made by him, some of which were supported by record evidence, and after consideration of a report by one of the officers of our Board, who had for several weeks past been making special investigation as to certain rumors and accusations, it was the unanimous and thoroughly convinced decision of the Committee and directors of the American Board of Missions that the charges made against Mr. Joseph Cohn were utterly false and without a basis in fact.*[13]

While most members of the Board of Directors accepted the report of the committee, the seeds of doubt and dissension had been planted, and some Board members who were not a part of the ad hoc committee never regained their confidence in Joseph Cohn, or in his ability to properly run the affairs of the Mission. As a result, full-blown accusations against Joseph later developed within the Board of Directors. Further, the rumors of impropriety and the accusations of Joseph's wife regarding his leadership of the Mission added verification to the mistrust and dislike which A.B. Machlin and Herman Centz both felt toward Joseph Cohn. In spite of the findings of the ad hoc committee neither of these men ever regained their confidence in Joseph's leadership of the affairs of the Mission.

In October 1940, in an effort to ease some of the tension between himself, the staff, and some committee members in Buffalo, and in an attempt to further consolidate the work in Buffalo, Joseph invited Dr. Muntz to sit in on the Board meeting.[14] Three months later, at the annual meeting of the Board in January 1941, Joseph presented the name of Dr. J. Palmer Muntz as a member and Director of the Board, and moved that "...he be elected to fill an unexpired term of two years."[15] The motion was duly seconded and approved. Dr. J. Palmer Muntz became a member of the Board of Directors of the Mission in 1941. But even this action did not bring about the reconciliation Joseph had hoped for.

By 1943, the volcanic situation that had been created by mistrust and innuendo began to shake the foundation of the Mission. Accusations of impropriety, mismanagement of Mission funds, and a character assassination of Joseph Cohn spread from within the Board and Mission staff to Christian leaders and churches. The final eruption created a split within the Board of Directors, and resulted in some of the Mission's workers and Board members leaving, to form a new mission organization. The aftermath of the blow up nearly brought an end to Joseph's ministry and an end to the Mission itself.

How clever the enemy of our souls is! Although problems and misunderstandings had surfaced almost immediately after the merge of the American Board of Missions to the Jews with the Buffalo Hebrew Christian Mission, the difficulties were being dealt with and Joseph believed solutions would be found. But the ingredient that caused the whole situation to "boil over" began with one brief telephone conversation—a conversation during which one board member, Mr. Robert O. Fleming, mentioned information from a recent Board meeting to two staff workers—Mr. A.B. Machlin and Mr. Herman Centz. Mr. Fleming revealed to the staff workers that at their April 1943 meeting, the Board had agreed "...that Mr. Cohn be given discretionary powers to increase the salaries of our workers on a *bonus basis* up to 25%."[16] Mr. Fleming went on to reveal that two workers, Mr. Machlin and Mr. Centz, were to receive even more.

It is possible that Mr. Fleming revealed this information because he was a close friend of both men; he was also a close friend of Joseph Cohn. Cohn, Centz, and Machlin had been arguing over some expense account items, as well as about the roles Centz and Machlin would have in the future leadership of the Mission. Knowing this, it may be that Mr. Fleming was seeking to reconcile the men before further damage was done to their friendships and to the ministry. It also appears that Mr. Fleming felt A. B. Machlin and Herman Centz had some legitimate grievances. Mr. Fleming wrote to Joseph and stated:

> ...we discussed the affairs of the mission and naturally my wife and I were very sorry to learn that there was no immediate prospect of a new missionary for the Seattle area. This brings up a matter which I mentioned at the time of our last visit and which is giving us increasing concern. It seems to us that the Mission is entirely out of balance; that too much emphasis is being put upon the raising of funds and too little upon the actual missionary effort. What is the use of being the world's largest Jewish mission without being able to produce converts, and we haven't heard of one in the last twelve months? [This was not an altogether true statement. Reports for this period show that their were decisions for the Lord, but in Cohn's reports to the Board, he did not stress them. Instead he was talking about further expansion of the ministry; buying a building in Manhattan; Bible Conferences, etc.; also, Centz and Machlin were not missionaries, but Field Evangelists] Don't you think this ought to cause grave concern and drive us to our knees to ascertain wherein lies the trouble?
>
> I think you should know that the boys [Centz & Machlin] divulged to me, not only as a friend but as a member of the Board, something of the difficulty which has recently disturbed their relationship with you. What causes them the most uneasiness is the threat of a ruptured friendship. I read both the personal and circular communications, and it appears there is more behind them than the ostensible laudable desire to curb what you consider to be extravagant travel expense. I am not attempting to judge any matter in dispute but as your friend I feel that a breach between you and the brethren would cause irreparable damage to the cause we both love.[17]

After the telephone and personal conversation with Mr. Fleming, Abraham Machlin sent Joseph a five-page letter, exhorting him to reconsider his treatment and attitude toward himself and Herman Centz. In his letter, Mr. Machlin rehearsed all the things that he, personally, had done to help Joseph and the Mission achieve world-wide recognition. Just as Mr. Fleming had done in his letter to Joseph, A.B. Machlin stated that he felt the Mission was out of balance; in his opinion, the Mission needed more missionaries on staff. He then turned to the matter of the expense accounts, writing: "And now you have started a campaign of vilification against us and all of your staff, trying to make it out that we are petty thieves who cannot be trusted with a few pennies of field expense money.... With respect to us, that is Centz and me, if no other condemnation were possible, your letters alone would brand you as unjust and ungrateful to men who tied their lives to yours, sink or swim."[18]

Joseph was incensed! His dispute with Machlin and Centz over their expense accounts had already angered him. Abraham Machlin's letter added fuel to the fire by providing proof that a Board member and long standing friend, Mr. Fleming, was divulging Board information to staff members—something no Board member should *ever* do!

As the month of December 1943 approached, Herman Centz and Abraham Machlin were interested in knowing how much their "extra bonus" was going to be. Thinking it might be given as a Christmas bonus, the two men kept "nudging" (pressing) Joseph. He finally told them they would be getting a 20% increase and a $500 bonus.[19]

When Centz and Machlin returned to Buffalo, they apparently contacted Dr. J. Palmer Muntz. They revealed to him that Robert Fleming had given them information about the Board's decision to grant 25% increases to the Mission's staff. They further revealed that they had gone to see Joseph Cohn, and that he had stated they would be receiving only a 20% increase. Since Dr. Muntz was a Board member (and since the three men had shared other grievances regarding Joseph Cohn and his leadership of the Mission), Centz and Machlin wanted the discrepancy known and dealt with. They felt Joseph was trying to renege on the amount to be given, or to undercut them on the promised bonus.

Not long afterwards, Joseph and Dr. Muntz had a meeting. During their conversation the subject of raises and bonuses came up, and Dr. Muntz told Joseph that he had been informed of Mr. Fleming's conversations with Herman Centz and A.B. Machlin regarding the Board's approval of a 25% increase. Muntz revealed that the two men had come to him after their meeting with Joseph, because of Joseph's statement to them that the increase was to be merely 20%. Joseph was genuinely embarrassed over the fact that he had not correctly remembered the percentage of salary increase voted on. He pressed Dr. Muntz to see if he remembered if the Board had voted 20% or 25%, and Dr. Muntz assured him that the amount voted on had been 25%. Joseph assured Muntz that the mistake had been an honest one and that nothing was intended to the contrary—but the conversation revealed to Joseph that *two* of his Board members had been talking with Centz and Machlin about Board information and policy.

The next day Joseph went to his secretary, Miss Pithman, to verify the exact amount the Board had agreed to. She read the Board Minutes which stated that the Board had approved an increase on a bonus basis up to 25%.[20] (There is nothing in the Minutes indicating that Joseph ever apologized to Centz or Machlin, or attempted to set the record straight.)

Another issue came up before the end of 1943 which triggered additional anger and resentment on the part of Herman Centz and A.B. Machlin—Mr. Paul Graef, treasurer of the Board, alleged that he found irregularities in the expense reporting of the two men. Mr. Graef alleged that he had found that Centz and Machlin used some of their offerings of meet their daily expenses. He further alleged that he had discovered that they had charged the mission for first class Pullman seats, while riding coach—keeping the difference for themselves.

Joseph asked Paul Graef to design a new expense voucher form—one that would correct accounting problems and improve the reporting system of the field evangelists and missionaries, but when it was introduced to the workers, Herman Centz and Abraham Machlin refused to use it. Joseph reported to the Board that as of April 1944, neither man had submitted any expenses. He further told the Board that in November 1943 he had written to all of the field men, stating; "in the future we want an analyzed expense ccount [sic]. Mr. Centz …said that no one can question his account…. Mr. Machlin flet [sic] the same way."[21]

Joseph told the Board that instead of dismissing the two men, he had decided to relieve them of all deputation and field work; he planned to transfer them into direct missionary work. Abraham Machlin was to be sent back to the Buffalo branch, and Herman Centz was to be transferred to Seattle. Joseph asked for a motion to support his action. A majority of the Board supported the motion, but he did not have his usual unanimous decision. The board members in attendance at the meeting were: Messrs. Linton, Graef, Dembke, Cohn, Barcley, Fleming, and Muntz.[22]

In discussing possible action against Mr. Centz and Mr. Machlin for their insubordination, members of the Board agreed that "…nothing more serious than a charge of irregularity shall be entered into our books against Mr. Machlin and Mr. Centz."[23]

Although it may have gone unrecognized at the time, it was an historic moment in the history of the American Board of Missions to the Jews—a crucial turning point in the contest of power between Joseph Cohn and some members of his staff and Board. The fiery resentment against Joseph Cohn had not been quenched in Herman Centz and A.B. Machlin. They enjoyed camaraderie with several of the Board members, including Dr. Muntz, and they continued to go to them with stories of Joseph's mistreatment of his staff, his alleged dishonesty, his alleged marital problems, etc., as they sought to get Joseph fired, or to force his resignation. Nor did they limit their audience to Board members. They laid hold of every opportunity to undermine Joseph Cohn and his leadership of the Mission as they shared with pastors and with other Christians.

Joseph began to receive letters and telegrams from pastors, and from friends and acquaintances of Centz, Machlin, and Muntz. What had begun as a quarrel among the "Mission family," was spreading to the Christian community and to supporting churches. Christian leaders were being pressed to take sides. The Mission's staff was lining up on one side or the other. The groundwork had been laid for a power play within the Board of Directors—initiated by Board members Dr. J. Palmer Muntz and Mr. Robert Fleming, and carried to the Mission's staff and to others by A.B. Machlin and Herman Centz. The respect and admiration Joseph's staff had once felt toward him turned to disrespect and disapproval, as seen in a letter dated May 3, 1944 that Elizabeth Goodrow sent to her friend Grace Bredehoft in Danville, Illinois. Elizabeth had worked for Joseph as a bookkeeper for a few months. She wrote:

As you might know, we lost out. We were closeted with him [Cohn] practically all day, but he is too slick for old country hicks like us. And we knew what to expect. The men feel he is not worth fighting for, and are withdrawing as a body, me being with them. That may throw some weight around, 6 withdrawing at one and the same time. But he has too much at stake and he doesn't care.

He will probably keep you as he is so short of help, but you may as well know that it wouldn't be for any longer than he could help,...Mr. Machlin is going to try to get you something else, in case.... He [Cohn] never raised his voice to me once, but he tried hard to becloud the issue, and to twist things around, and each time I yelled at him, 'Mr. Cohn, that is not true,'...He still believed in me even when I showed the books to the directors. I felt bad about being a Judas, but he is such a one.[24]

The Minutes of the May 8, 1944 Executive Committee meeting state:

Mr. Cohn reported that due to certain circumstances that had developed within the last few weeks among certain members of our Board of Directors, he had become disturbed concerning his future administration of the work. He had consulted with Mr. Linton, our President, and with Miss Marston, the Secretary of the Board, also with Mr. Graef and with Mr. Dembke and all had emphatically come to the conclusion that certain steps must be taken to safeguard Mr. Cohn's future position with the work, and his financial security.

Mr. Dembke moved that in recognition of the forty years of service rendered by Mr. Joseph H. Cohn, and to provide for his future financial security in the event of unforeseen changes in the management of the American Board of Missions to the Jews, or to any other emergencies, the Treasurer be instructed to purchase an annuity contract which will provide for Mr. Cohn an income of not less than $450 a month as long as he shall live. This contract shall be an Installment Refund Annuity Contract, and shall provide that any balance remaining in the fund that shall be paid over by us to the insurance company, in the event of Mr. Cohn's death, will be repaid to the Mission either in one lump sum or in continuation of the installments. Carried.

It is moved that from the date that Mr. Cohn will begin to receive the installments on the Annuity Plan, his salary from the Mission shall be reduced by the amount of the payments.... Carried.[25]

RESIGNATIONS PROVOKE CONFRONTATION

At this same meeting Cohn told the Executive Committee he had received a letter of resignation from Herman Centz. It was to take effect immediately.

Herman Centz sent his letter of resignation directly to Joseph Cohn, but Abraham Machlin sent his resignation to Mr. Irwin Linton, President of the Board. In his letter, dated May 10, 1944, Machlin expressed his grievances against Joseph, and asked Mr. Linton not to accept his resignation until May 31, 1944—after a special Board meeting that had been scheduled for May 24, 1944.[26] (Herman Centz and A.B. Machlin were both valuable and popular workers. Evidently they were hoping they would have enough support on the Board so that neither man's resignation would be acted on. From the way their resignations were submitted, it would appear that Centz and Machlin wanted to force the Board to a no confidence vote in the leadership of Cohn—thus forcing him to step down.)

Mr. Linton, however, shared Machlin's letter of May 10th (which also contained Machlin's resignation) with Joseph. Joseph, in turn, sent Machlin a letter dated May 12, 1944, officially informing him that he (Cohn) had accepted Machlin's resignation effective May 10, 1944. Cohn had accepted both men's resignations, but he needed Board action to ratify his action.

Prior to the special Board meeting scheduled for May 24, 1944, Joseph received a telegram from Dr. David Otis Fuller, pastor of Wealthy Street Baptist Church in Grand Rapids, Michigan, and from Rev. R. L. Powell, pastor of Temple Baptist Church in Tacoma, Washington. Both men were well-known leaders in the Christian world; their advice and opinions were heeded by the Christian community. At some time between the dates of May 12 and 15, 1944, they sent a telegram to Joseph, giving him the following message:

We are deeply distressed over reports reaching us of serious irregularities in Mission administration. We cannot urge too strongly that representative Christian leaders who have the confidence of the nation's Christian constituency be elected at an early date to your Board. Would suggest such men as Johnson, Howard, Brownville, Taylor, Strathean [sic], Ironside, Bauman. We are waiting to know what you plan to do. Our people will demand action.[27]

The telegram from Dr. Fuller and Dr. Powell was more than a "suggestion" from the movers and shakers of the evangelical world of that day. Joseph had been urged (instructed, if he wanted the continued support of the Christian community) to expand his Board. The message read like an ultimatum. But Joseph Cohn knew the course of action being recommended would result in the dilution of his own power within the Board of Directors. Joseph knew of his father's hesitancy in putting together a Board of Directors; he remembered his father's fear of losing the control of the Mission. He saw it happen to his father. In some ways, as he took control of the Mission, he helped it happen to his father—but he did not want the same thing to happen to him!

Miss Ella Marston, Secretary of the Board, sent out a letter to Board members notifying them of the special meeting of the Board to be held at 27 Throop Avenue on Wednesday, May 24, 1944. Only four Board members responded by showing up—Mr. Irwin H. Linton, President; Mr. H.E.O. Dembke, Vice President; Mr. Paul Graef, Treasurer; and Joseph Hoffman Cohn, General Secretary. The number was insufficient to make a quorum of five (as required by the constitution). Miss Marston had been ill for nearly one year, and had not been well enough to travel to Brooklyn for the special meeting. It was decided that the meeting would be adjourned to Miss Marston's home. This would allow them to have an "official" Board meeting—Miss Marston being the additional member needed to make up the quorum.[28] (While this was legal according to parliamentary rules, the maneuver gave further cause for criticism that Joseph was attempting to control the Board.)

At the meeting, Mr. Frank E. Davis was elected to serve as a member of the Board, to fill the vacancy in the class of 1947.[29] The Directors also passed a resolution stating: "RESOLVED, that the number of Directors of this Corporation shall be not less than seven nor more than fifteen, and that the Directors be and are hereby authorized and directed to sign, acknowledge and file amended Certificates pursuant to Section 30 of the Membership Corporations Law and to take any other steps that may be necessary to carry out and effectuate such changes in the number of Directors of this Corporation."[30]

They further passed two amendments to the Mission's constitution. Article V was amended to include the statement, "The Board shall have full power to fill vacancies occurring between the annual meetings, such Directors so elected to hold office for the balance of the unexpired terms which they are elected to fill."[31] Article VI, paragraph three, was amended to read: "The members shall vote by ballot on the admission for election to Directorship of this proposed new member. Only those whose names have been submitted in accordance with this article shall be voted upon. A majority vote of those present shall be required to elect to membership."[32]

After approving these amendments to the Mission's constitution, the quorum then voted that Mr. James W. Ames of Montclair, New Jersey, and Mr. William Jones of Hamilton, Ontario, Canada, be elected Directors, and that "...such election being subject to, and effective, immediately upon the due filing of the aforesaid amendment to the Certificate of Incorporation."[33] Three Board vacancies were now filled. Only one vacancy remained.

Evidently these actions seemed necessary to Joseph, to ensure his control within the Board. Copies of Joseph's personal correspondence, telegrams, and the Minutes from that period of time all clearly indicate that staff members, Centz and Machlin, along with the board members, Fleming and Muntz, were planning a "power play" within the Board, to force Joseph's resignation. Joseph saw it too, and to offset the inevitable, he wanted to be sure that he had a sufficient number of Board members who were loyal to him.

Mr. Fleming, Mr. Muntz, and Mr. Barcley had chosen not to attend the special meeting of the Board held May 24, 1944, but when Fleming and Muntz received news of the action taken by the Directors at that meeting, they were furious! They immediately contacted Dr. Otis Fuller, knowing that Joseph Cohn and Dr. Fuller were good friends. But Dr. Fuller was also a close friend to Muntz, Fleming, Machlin and Centz. Dr. Muntz was hoping that Dr. Fuller would be an arbitrator, and that somehow a reconciliation could be worked out.

In the meantime, however, Joseph evidently sent out a mailing to the Mission's constituents in Buffalo, informing them of changes that would be taking place in the Buffalo branch. Following that mailing, Dr. Muntz began receiving telephone calls from his congregants, asking what the changes were all about. In response to the telephone inquiries, Dr. Muntz sent out his own letter, indicating that the real problem was with Joseph Cohn and the Board. He stated:

> A serious situation has indeed developed but not here in Buffalo as Mr. Cohn very well knows, but rather in the board meetings of the Mission. I became one of the directors in 1941 and have consistently stood back of Mr. Cohn and the work of the Mission. Not only here but throughout the country many hundreds of friends and Christian leaders have given him their support because of my attitude in spite of the cloud he has been under.
>
> Recently, however, undeniable facts have come to the attention of some of us who are directors which have caused us utterly to lose confidence in him and to make charges against him of an unethical and unChristian attitude toward his co-workers, over-emphasis on money-raising, failure to develop the spiritual work and in general properly manage the Mission.... Mr. Machlin and Mr. Centz have resigned, as has also the head bookkeeper and accountant because she could no longer 'conscientiously support his administration of Mission affairs.'

The simplest way out for us would have been also to resign, but we have for the time being retained our positions at the urgent request of representative and nationally-known Christian leaders who are aware of the issues involved and recognize with us that the testimony of the Mission and the proper use of the large funds entrusted to us are at stake. We have been hoping that the situation would be adjusted within the Mission so that it would not again come into disrepute and hence have purposely refrained from making any public statement. I have not before even hinted to you of our church of any disaffection nor made this explanation as to why I have had to spend so many extra days out of the city.

Though Mr. Cohn has belligerently refused the advice of interested friends and the recommendations of some of his advisory council, stating that these things are 'my board's business,' now he 'feels it necessary' to inject the situation into our church life and that of our Buffalo constituency by the wide circularization of a letter, obviously designed to cause embarrassment even if only by its inferences. As far as Mr. Machlin is concerned, he is a deacon of this church and we, as pastor and people, have the highest regard for him....

I regret that on the other hand, we feel Mr. Cohn's purposes in the past months have been malicious and selfish and we have been forced to question his trust-worthiness and his truthfulness.

Let me say in closing that you must not let these things affect your purpose to send the message of salvation to the Jew. We will advise you later about developments and it may yet be possible to avoid a wider public statement, though of course copies of Mr. Cohn's letter and of this one will have to go to key leaders throughout the country who with us have been disillusioned and distressed beyond measure at the turn things have taken.[34]

The letters—of both men—only served to broaden the involvement of the Christian world in the Mission's internal conflict, further polarizing both groups.

ATTEMPTS AT RECONCILIATION

On Tuesday, June 13, 1944, Dr. Otis Fuller and a committee from the board of Wealthy Street Baptist Church met with both sides in the controversy. They met with Muntz, Machlin, Centz, and Goodrow at 1:30 P.M., and with Cohn, Jones (a new Board-member), and Sanford Mills (staff worker from Columbus) at 6:00 P.M. Dr. Fuller then wrote to Dr. Powell, giving Dr. Powell his impression of the meeting. He wrote:

...In listening to both sides we were convinced of one thing, both sides had done and said things which were absolutely wrong. At the close, around 9 P.M. we had both sides present and asked them frankly if they thought a reconciliation was possible. Neither side seemed to think that it was possible. I asked Machlin and Centz if they would admit that during this whole flare up that they had done or said things which they believed were wrong. Both admitted that they could have said and done things which were wrong under such pressure and circumstances, and probably did, tho they didn't specify. I asked Br. [sic] Cohn the same question twice, but he would not admit that he had done or said anything wrong. I then said that I didn't believe any man on earth could go through such an unpleasant set of circumstances without doing or saying something that wasn't wrong. I have my faults, you have yours, and Dr. Cohn has his, and obviously one of them is, he won't admit he is in the wrong.

After we saw that there seemed no possibility of a reconciliation, we asked all to leave except the two board members, Mr. Jones and Palmer Muntz. We then asked them if they would be willing to have an impartial committee of known Christian leaders investigate this whole matter and render a decision. We suggested the names of Dr. Ironside (Chairman), Dr. Powell of Tacoma, Dr. Culbertson, dean of the Moody Bible Institute, Dr. Oswald Smith of Canada, Dr. W.H. Rogers of the South, and Dr. Louis Talbot of California. More could be added if it was felt necessary. Both Jones and Muntz seemed to be agreeable to such a proposal.

We then talked with Dr. Cohn alone. We strongly recommended that an independent audit be taken of the books of the Mission immediately. He said he had already contacted a number of known auditing companies, but all were swamped with work. We saw the letters of refusal. One company, Ernst and Ernst said they could do it in a few months. Dr. Cohn said that he already contracted with this company to make this audit as soon as possible. [As it turned out, Cohn needed the audit sooner, and he was able to get the firm of Haskins & Sells CPA to do the audit—completed by July 12, 1944.]

We also urged that a more representative group be appointed on the Board of the Mission from across the country, having recommendations come from churches such as ours which have been vitally interested in the work for years. He seemed agreeable to such a proposal.

Now, Dr. Powell, God knows my heart, and He knows there is no person in America that would like to see this matter cleared up more than I would, but I'm not going to be swept off my feet. I want the facts. Our committee agreed after Dr. Cohn left, that we felt about 60-40 in the matter, sixty for Cohn, forty for the other side, and we will reserve decision until the audit is made and this committee has investigated. Just because I have not made any decision in this matter as yet does not mean that I am afraid to and am stalling for time. These are my honest convictions, and also those of the committee.[35]

One week after his meeting with Dr. Fuller and his committee, Joseph attended a special meeting of the Board that had been called for June 21, 1944. The purpose of the June 21st meeting was two-fold: To promptly elect a new Secretary to the Board (Miss Ella T. Marston, who had been ill for many months, had passed away), and to present a Resolution for adoption to amend the Certificate of Incorporation per the amendments passed at the May 24th meeting—a meeting that Dr. Muntz had deliberately boycotted. If the meetings with Dr. Fuller and his committee had opened even the slightest chance for reconciliation, it was squelched as the June 21st meeting progressed.

Completely ignoring the admonition of the telegram sent to him by Dr. Fuller and Dr. Powell (as well as Dr. Fuller's personal comments on the matter when Joseph met with him and the committee), that new Board members of the American Board of Missions to the Jews be representative Christian leaders who had the confidence of America's Christian constituency, Joseph put forth the name of Miss Elsie Olsen to succeed Miss Marston, as a Director. Miss Olsen and her family had been long-time friends of the Mission and of the Cohn's. Her name and nomination were proposed for the Board's consideration in a letter dated June 10, 1944—a letter advising Board members of the Special Directors' Meeting called for June 21st. The June 10th letter to the Directors makes mention of the fact that the "prompt election" of a new Secretary was in accordance with the by-laws amendments made at the May 24th Board meeting.[36] (Putting forth Miss Olsen's name in the letter of June 10th allowed enough time before the June 21st meeting for the 10-day notification required by the constitution.)

At the June 10th meeting, Dr. Muntz vigorously opposed the actions taken by the Board at the May 24th meeting. He especially opposed the election of Frank Davis to the Board, declaring that it was illegal according to the constitution. However, Irwin Linton, President of the Board, and also a practicing attorney, assured Dr. Muntz that the meeting itself had been a legal meeting according to the constitution, and that the actions taken at the meeting were legal as well. To appease Dr. Muntz, and to assuage any fears that Frank Davis' appointment might not be on the "up and up," the Board was asked to vote on Mr. Davis again, to confirm his appointment to the Board.

Dr. Muntz objected, as well, to Miss Olsen's nomination, and complained that nominations by other Directors had not even been considered. He suggested the name of Dr. Otis Fuller, and asked the Board to waive the necessity for giving the Directors a 10-day notice of nominees' names, so he could nominate Dr. Fuller. Mr. Graef objected, stating "...the absent members of our Board could not legally waive their rights to the ten day requirement, ...Dr. Muntz should show sufficient respect for the provisions of our Constitution, to follow such provisions."[37]

Joseph, too, objected, reminding Dr. Muntz of the long standing policy of the Board which was to elect laymen as Directors. Dr. Muntz, himself, had been the only exception to the rule. (It would appear at this point that Joseph Cohn had no intention of following Dr. Fuller's advice to elect a representative Board of a cross-section of pastors, Christian leaders, etc.)

A piqued Dr. Muntz asked to be allowed to "withdraw my presence from the earlier part of the meeting, before any motions were made."[38] The Board refused consent.

Joseph again moved the nomination of Miss Elsie Olsen to succeed Miss Marston, and after the vote Mr. Linton announced that Miss Olsen was duly elected a Director of the Board. With this election completed, all vacancies of the Board were filled.

Joseph Cohn then asked the Board for permission to sell the Mission property in Buffalo. He stated that he felt the property was no longer in a Jewish area and was unsuited to the Mission's use.

The reader will recall that Joseph had "inherited" A.B. Machlin as a worker because of the merge of the Mission with the Buffalo Hebrew Christian Mission. Herman Centz, too, had been sent by Joseph to serve as a worker in the Buffalo branch. Further, it was because of the purchase of the property in Buffalo, and the need for supervision of that branch while Mr. Machlin was doing field evangelism, that Dr. J. Palmer Muntz had become so closely involved— ultimately becoming a Board member. Dr. Muntz was still pastoring his church in Buffalo, and that area was still the base of operation for Machlin and Centz. Realizing the possibility that a split in the Mission might be inevitable, Joseph may have decided to sell the Buffalo building just to ensure that the others would not inherit it. He suggested that the Mission rent a store front in a Jewish area, from which they would conduct the ministry.

If Joseph was trying to push Dr. Muntz's "hot button," he knew which button to press! Muntz objected vigorously to this proposal, telling the Board:

...the people in Buffalo are not in favor of the property being sold. They feel that the house...is a suitable location

241

for the Buffalo work, and they voted, in a recent meeting held in Buffalo, expressing disapproval of the property being sold, and further voted that the property be retained. They feel that the property shall be controlled by a group in Buffalo.[39]

Mr. Jones reminded Dr. Muntz that the members of the committee in Buffalo were under his influence, since most of them were members of his own church!

Joseph agreed to withdraw his motion on the condition that a corporation, or group, suitable to the Directors of the American Board of Missions to the Jews, be found to take over the ministry. He stated that if the Board was satisfied that the group was doing a real Jewish work in the city of Buffalo, he would consider renting the property to them for $1.00 a year. This proposal was made in the form of a motion and approved with the following exception presented by Paul Graef: "I do not want Dr. Muntz to go back to Buffalo and say that we will agree to anything, for the consideration of $1.00 a year."[40]

Joseph Cohn may have pressed Dr. Muntz's "hot button" at the meeting, but his was not the only hot button pressed! Mr. Jones brought up the issue of finances. He reminded the Board that "...when he was at the meeting in Grand Rapids the people asked that several Christian leaders be appointed to make an investigation into the affairs of the Mission."[41] Joseph Cohn hit the roof, stating:

I believe we are sufficiently competent to do our own investigating. How far would we get if we tried to investigate the Moody Bible Institute, or the Cazenovia Church [where Dr. Muntz was pastor], or the Sudan Interior Mission?

We have submitted to a new audit of our books and we will submit a new account. I think we should resist stubbornly any such scheme as they propose; we should say we are sufficiently competent to do any investigation. They should submit any charges in writing and the Board will investigate. We will not abdicate our trust to any outside group, no matter by whom suggested or under what circumstances they may be suggested. We welcome any sincere inquirer who wishes to come to our Mission and in good faith to seek any legitimate information to which he may be entitled.[42]

In his letter of June 14, 1944 to Dr. Powell, Dr. Fuller gave the impression that Joseph was agreeable to such an investigation. Evidently Joseph's attitude toward an investigation of the affairs of the Mission had changed. Perhaps during the week between June 13th and June 21st Joseph had reflected back in time to the investigation of the affairs of the Mission when his father was alive, deciding that another such ordeal was just more than he was willing to face.

The reader will recall that the outside investigation of the Mission made during the time of Rabbi Leopold Cohn had cleared the Mission of any wrong doing—no improprieties were found with the financial accounting systems of the Mission. However, the very fact that an outside group had been called in to investigate the affairs of the Mission had caused irreparable harm to the ministry by planting doubt about the Mission's integrity in the minds of many pastors, Christian leaders, and constituents. The investigation had been a blight on the Mission's testimony to the Jewish community as well—as if confirming that such an organization should be shut down. It is understandable that Joseph would not want to repeat such an experience! All of the Board members, with the exception of one, agreed with Joseph's sentiments.

The firm of Haskins & Sells CPA was contacted to do a complete audit of the Mission's books. Their full examination of the Mission's accounting system disclosed that there was nothing out of order. Satisfied that the findings of the audit would help assuage any lingering doubts about his mishandling of the Mission's funds, Joseph sent a copy of the audit to Dr. Fuller and suggested that he share its findings with the committee. However, the audit only added fuel to the fire.

On July 19, 1944 a notice was sent to the Directors informing them of a special Directors' meeting called for August 1, 1944. The notice stated that the purpose of the meeting was three-fold: to discuss the audit that had just been completed by Haskins and Sells CPA firm, to further discuss the matter of the property in Buffalo, and to act upon two proposed amendments to the Constitution.

The first amendment proposed to be added to the Constitution seemed to be aimed directly at the two Board members who were giving Joseph the most trouble—Fleming and Muntz. It stated:

The Board of Directors and/or the Members shall have the power to expel any Director or Directors from membership on the Board, and/or from membership in the Corporation, if in the judgment of the majority of those present such expulsion should be deemed to be for the best interests of the Corporation. Such action to expel may be taken at any regular or special meeting of the Board.[43]

The second amendment proposed was directed at the designated use of funds given to the Mission. For a number of years, Joseph had been raising money for the Foreign ministry. However, in the Articles of Incorporation, the stated purpose of the Corporation was to spread the "...Gospel of the Lord Jesus Christ among the Jews in the United States of America,...." The proposed change was to amend the statement to read: "...The object for which it is to be formed is the spread of the Gospel of the Lord Jesus Christ among the Jews in the United States of America and in all parts of the world."[44]

Evidently, when the auditors went through the books they noticed that money was being raised, and was being held, for Foreign ministries. They questioned this, in view of the Mission's Statement of Purpose. Joseph and the Board had done nothing wrong, but this amendment of the Mission's Statement of Purpose clarified that the Mission was an international ministry and that funds could be raised and disbursed accordingly.

The Minutes of the August 1, 1944 meeting of the Board reveal that the resolution to amend the Mission's Articles of Incorporation to indicate that the ministry was intended to be an international work, was passed. There is no reference to the proposed amendment regarding the expulsion of Board members.

Dr. Muntz was absent from the meeting, but he had sent a letter to Joseph in which he stated that a committee was being formed in Buffalo "...with the idea of taking over the work ...and they wanted to rent the [Mission] property for $1.00 a year for a period of five years, and they [the committee] would make the necessary repairs on the property."[45]

The Minutes of the previous meeting were consulted. The Board agreed that they had not made any commitment to Dr. Muntz, to either rent the property for $1.00 a year, or to sell it for that amount. What their motion did state was that the property would be rented or sold to a committee or to an institution approved by the Board. (By that time, Joseph Cohn would never have approved a committee sponsored by Dr. Muntz!) The Board then voted by resolution to sell the Buffalo property and to re-locate the ministry to a more suitable location in the Buffalo area.

At the meeting Mr. Linton shared a letter they had received from a critic of the Mission and of Joseph Cohn. Charges made within the letter were discussed point by point, after which the following motion was unanimously approved:

> In view of the communication that our President has read to us as having been received from a critic of the work, and in view of our having analysed [sic] every accusation that has been made, and gone into every detail with minute thoroughness, we as a Board wish to have recorded a vote of confidence in our General Secretary, as to his personal character, integrity, fidelity to his Master, and to his conduct in presiding over the work and affairs of the American Board of Missions to the Jews [now Chosen People Ministries].[46]

Directors who attended the August 1, 1944 meeting were given copies of the audit done by Haskins & Sells CPA so they could examine the findings. Dr. Muntz, who was not at the meeting, never received a copy of the audit. The fact that a copy of the audit was not sent to Dr. Muntz was certainly a tactical error on Joseph's part! This, plus the action taken by the Board regarding the Mission's property in Buffalo, was like a slap in the face to him! He was a very influential pastor—one who had been responsible for opening many doors for Joseph Cohn and other workers of the Mission. Dr. Muntz had been a close friend to Joseph Cohn, but his friendship was reaching the breaking point!

The attacks on Joseph Cohn's personal character and on his leadership of the Mission which began in 1943 with disgruntled workers and a misunderstanding over expense accounts and bonuses, continued on through 1944—but they did not seem to dampen Joseph's determination to continue his program of expansion of the Mission. One of his goals for the ministry was that it would one day have a building in Manhattan—a branch in the very *heart* of New York! Like a pit bull locking his jaws around an object, Joseph was single-minded in his determination to find such a building for the Mission! The details of this matter will be discussed in the following chapter of this history. Suffice it to say here that in his haste and resolution to purchase a building in Manhattan, Joseph made a costly mistake—one that was used to further inflame the rumors of his incompetence to lead the Mission.

At the April 25, 1944 Directors meeting, Joseph reported: "...we [Joseph] have put a deposit on a building on East 54th Street, ...the purchase price of which is $70,000. It is planned to make this building a center for Hebrew Christian Fellowship, also we are to have a Reading Room, and a number of other activities."[47] The Minutes go on to state that Joseph told the Directors he had gone ahead on the matter after speaking with Mr. Linton by telephone. Mr. Linton, in turn, spoke to Miss Marston, Mr. Graef and Mr. Barcley. Joseph and the other Directors were delighted with the purchase, but their joy was short-lived. They soon discovered that building housed a restaurant that had a license to sell liquor. To break the restaurant's long-term lease would be a costly matter! Joseph wanted to evict the tenants, pay the charges for breaking the lease, and take possession of the building, but some of the Board members felt breaking the lease was not an option due to the expense of such an action, and due to the OPA laws of New York City. They felt the Mission should wait out the lease and treat the building as investment property. The compromise decided upon was that they would try to sell the building as soon as they could, and find some other suitable building in Manhattan.

The fact that this purchase was made only months after the run-in with Herman Centz and A.B. Machlin over the bonuses and their expense accounts, and at a time when Joseph was "under fire" from the continuing discontent of Centz and Machlin, as well as from at least two of his Board members and other Christians who were beginning to take sides, gave one more opportunity for Joseph's enemies to find fault. It was scandalous that the Mission should own a piece of property where liquor was being sold, and Joseph Cohn was responsible for the purchase of the property! The property was sold as quickly as possible, but not soon enough to stop the rumors and gossip.

The Scriptures state, "The tongue also is a fire, a world of evil among the parts of the body.... no man can tame the tongue" (James 3:6a,8b NIV). Rumor begets rumor. Gossip begets gossip. Isolation breeds suspicion; suspicion breeds doubt; doubt breeds uncertainty; uncertainty breeds loss of confidence; loss of confidence breeds hatred. Christians are not immune. Satan was using the little foxes to spoil the vine.

Joseph Cohn and Dr. J. Palmer Muntz had once enjoyed great respect and love for one another. They had worked together, prayed together, and taught and preached together. Dr. Muntz had a great love for Israel and the Jewish people. He was desirous that every opportunity be given to reach Jewish people with the Gospel. Mr. Fleming, too, shared the same burden. But egos, pride, and suspicion had destroyed the love and respect the men once enjoyed toward one another.

At some time during the months of 1944, Keith L. Brooks published an article which appeared in his paper, "Prophecy." The article, which bore no author's name, indicated that Herman Centz and A.B. Machlin had been released from service with the Mission because of dishonesty.[48] Since the publication, "Prophecy," was advertized in *The Chosen People* magazine, many of the Mission's readers likely saw this article defaming Centz and Machlin. While no one on the Mission's Board or staff would admit to writing the article, or to giving information for the article, it added fuel to the fires of hostility!

A SPLIT IN THE BOARD OF DIRECTORS

By the Fall of 1944, the battle lines had been drawn. There was no thought of retreat. The Board meeting held on October 24, 1944 was the site of a raging battle. Minutes were kept of this historic meeting, as well as the notes from which the minutes were recorded. The heart of God must have been deeply grieved. But the enemy of our souls must have been rejoicing. Looking back, one wonders why reconciliation could not have been made before the matter got so out of hand. It was a battle that had no victors!

Present at the meeting were "Messrs. Linton, Graef, Dembke, Jones, Davis, Cohn, Barclay [sic], Fleming, Muntz, and Miss Olsen.... present as a guest...was Dr. David Otis Fuller, pastor of the Wealthy Street Baptist Church of Grand Rapids, Mich."[49] Dr. Fuller had contacted Cohn and Linton, asking if it would be alright for him to attend the meeting. He felt if he attended, Muntz and Fleming would also attend, and perhaps a reconciliation could be affected. Cohn and Linton agreed and extended an invitation for him to attend.

Dr. Muntz and Mr. Fleming began comments by reflecting back to the May 24th special meeting of the Board, declaring that it had been illegally called and that none of its actions, including the election of Frank Davis, were therefore valid. The other Board members, and the attorneys on the Board argued that the meeting had been valid, as were all actions taken at the meeting. They further stated that the issue was dead, since subsequent Board meetings had ratified all of the actions taken—to appease Dr. Muntz and Mr. Fleming.

The issues of the suspected dishonesty of Centz and Machlin with regard to their expense accounts, and the accusations that they had taken funds from the Mission for their own personal use were then addressed. In response, the Board reminded Muntz and Fleming that the only charge they had entered against Centz and Machlin in the official record was one of "irregularity," not dishonesty. But Muntz and Fleming wanted the Board to state categorically that the two men were not dishonest. The other Board members remained firm on the action previously taken. This was a crucial issue for Muntz and Fleming; losing this issue meant they did not have enough votes within the Board to call for a no confidence vote in Joseph Cohn.

Nevertheless, they persisted. They attacked the Minutes and record keeping of the Mission, indicating that the Minutes did not reflect accurate information of Board proceedings. The other Board members took exception. Muntz and Fleming then attacked the audit that had been done by the Haskins & Sells CPA firm. At this point, Joseph asked Dr. Fuller to address the Board.

Dr. Fuller thanked Joseph and Mr. Linton for allowing him to attend the meeting, indicating that the only reason he had come was in the spirit of fairness and reconciliation. He told the Board that since his church and responsibilities kept him a thousand miles away, it was difficult to see both sides of the misunderstanding. He did indicate that there seemed to be a great deal of confusion over the way things had been handled with regard to Herman Centz and Abraham Machlin. He said, "…For a number of years we have held in practically as high regard as Dr. Cohn, both Brother Machlin and Brother Centz."[50]

Dr. Fuller went on, saying,

> …we have been connected with this Mission for 30 years or more, I as long as I have been pastor, …and Dr. Cohn has come as long as I have been there and Dr. Leopold Cohn came before his son. I believe that you will agree with me that I am interested in this. If I had not been I would not be here tonight. We are interested to the extent that we spend [t] some $200 in Grand Rapids to have both sides come to Grand Rapids and have stenographic notes made of all the proceedings. I want to be, I have tried to be thus far, absolutely fair in all this and have earnestly sought to harmonize the two sides.[51]

Dr. Fuller then addressed the issue of a statement that Joseph had made of Keith L. Brooks, which may have led to the "dishonesty" article that appeared in his paper. He assured Cohn that he believed Joseph had not done anything intentionally, but that perhaps there had been a misstatement. Joseph (surprisingly) agreed that this was a real possibility and that he may have made certain assumptions, based upon what he believed to be true. He promised that he would immediately send a letter of apology to Brooks recanting anything that he may have said.[52]

Dr. Fuller then addressed the matter of the Mission's finances, he told the Board:

> …We were satisfied with the complete audit that was sent and we appreciate it and we want you to know it, it was sent to Brother Beers and upon Dr. Cohn's consent Brother Beers allowed the committee and the complete Board to have it. Brother Beers said it was splendid.[53]

While Dr. Fuller stated that he and the committee had been satisfied with the audit, he mentioned another concern that the audit had highlighted—the matter of the surplus in the Reserve Fund of the Mission. He stated that he believed all monies coming into the Mission should be used immediately, but that the audited report showed $724,000 in the Reserve Fund, of which $80,000 was reserved for buildings, $133,000 in annuities, $109,000 in the Post War Fund, and $2,000 in the Paris Branch Fund—leaving $320,000 not designated. Dr. Fuller stated that he felt that was too much money to set idle; he believed it should be spent on evangelism. He told Cohn and the Board: "My point is this, now I want to be honest, I feel *strongly* with all my heart that when the money comes it should be given out as fast as possible for the work."[54]

Cohn and Linton then pointed out that over $100,000 of the Reserve Fund was being held for annuities, and that they had not defaulted on one annuity, as some other Christian organizations which did not set the money aside had. They further remarked that monies being held for overseas work were for the branches of the ministry that had been opened before the war broke out. They stated that the funds were being held for post-war development of the ministry; they felt that this was wise stewardship on their part.

Dr. Fuller commented that he still felt the sum was too large, and should be spent on staff. Cohn responded that he would be happy to spend the money hiring additional staff, but he said: "…I am not going to hire any incompetent men…. this mission has the finest staff of Jewish mission workers in the world."[55] He went on, saying that the Mission was always looking for workers, but that there just weren't enough competent people. This, of course, was a sore point with Dr. Fuller, Dr. Muntz, and Mr. Fleming. After all, the Mission had, in their opinions, just let two very competent workers go—and it was because of issues over how and why they had been let go (salaries, expenses, treatment of staff) that the whole unpleasant business at hand was under discussion.

Joseph pointed out that no one questions the great reserves of the American Bible Society, or of the tract societies, or of other evangelistic or denominational groups. He pointed out that for some reason, such funds seemed to be questionable only when held by independent Jewish mission agencies. He stressed that it was vital to the future of Jewish evangelism that missions such as The American Board of Missions (CPM) have reserve funds. (As has already been stated, Joseph Cohn believed in the imminent return of Yeshua. He believed in the Tribulation. He further believed that during the Tribulation, Jewish people would be saved, and that a Jewish believer would be raised up to carry on the work of the Mission during the Tribulation. He wanted to be certain that Jews always had an opportunity to hear the Gospel. His vision, like that of his father, Rabbi Leopold Cohn, was that finances would always be available for sharing the Gospel with the Jewish people. He believed strongly that there would come a day when Jewish missions would not be able to count on churches for support. Therefore, unless the Mission had sufficient reserves on hand, Jewish people would be forgotten.)

Dr. Fuller accepted Cohn's explanation, but he was never fully convinced of the need for such a large Reserve Fund. He didn't have one in his church, and he couldn't see the need for the Mission to have such a fund.

Dr. Fuller then put forth his last question. He asked if the Board was planning to become a representative Board—that is, to draw its members from across the country, rather than to limit selection of members to those individuals who personally knew Joseph Cohn and who lived in the Northeast. This was a sore point with Joseph—something he had not yet discussed with the Board, but something he had addressed with subtlety in his proposed amendments to the Constitution at the May 24, 1944 Board meeting.

The notes to the Minutes indicate that Joseph's response to Dr. Fuller's question was interrupted because Mr. Fleming and Mr. Muntz once again brought up matters concerning the audit, the financial statements, Minutes, etc. Mr. Fleming stated, "After the April meeting I went down to Washington to see Mr. Linton. I asked for a special meeting. I stayed around ten days. Directly [after] I left ...they called a special meeting. I can't have anything to do with a Mission who has a man of that character.... I am sorry gentlemen but in the past I have enjoyed fellowship with you but I can see nothing at all in it, as long as Dr. Cohn is running the Board, and I am sorry to reiterate that statement, I just can't stay on."[56] The notes to the Minutes then state: "He added something to the effect that the Board was just a rubber stamp for whatever the Gen. Sect. does."[57] Only moments earlier Mr. Fleming had stated:

> ...Mr. Cohn was the insubordinate one. In any event gentlemen, if you listen to the General Secretary talk, I certainly get the impression that he does everything, personally. It is I, I, I. I resign because he looks upon the Mission as his own personal property.[58]

Dr. Muntz also stated his belief that the Board's decisions, and the audit that had been done, were nothing but "rubber stamp" actions, and he asked to have his resignation included with that of Mr. Fleming. In defending his actions as a Board member, Mr. Dembke said he had been in Christian work for over fifty-six years, and had served on the Mission's Board for over twenty years. He stated: "...that he had been faithful to his trust. He believed absolutely in Mr. Cohn. As a member of the Finance Committee he had to give approval to actions taken and that nothing was done by the Board without the approval of the Finance Committee."[59]

Joseph immediately made a motion to accept the resignations of both Mr. Fleming and Dr. Muntz. After some discussion both resignations were accepted, with thanks for the years of service both men had given to the Mission. Mr. Linton remarked, "Brethren, you seem to have severed your connection with us."[60] Fleming replied: "We regret very deeply our utter loss of confidence in the Board and in the General Secretary."[61] The meeting adjourned. Dr. Fuller had come to the meeting pleading for unity, but it did not happen.

The battle within the Board of Directors was over, but the war was just beginning! As stated earlier, when Christian leaders do battle there are no winners. The scars remain long after the battle. "War stories" continue to do harm within the Christian community and, ultimately, the testimony of the Messiah also suffers. Gossip, rumors, and speculation about what took place at the October 24th Directors' Meeting spread like wildfire.

THE A.A.J.E. FORMED

The public explosion came shortly after the Board meeting, when J. Palmer Muntz published a pamphlet entitled "To Whom It May Concern." It was an eight page booklet in which he presented his views, as well as the views of Machlin, Centz, and Goodrow as to why they had left the American Board of Missions to the Jews, Inc. This booklet was widely circulated among Christian leaders and among the Christian public. The name of the pamphlet was later changed to "Why We Resign from the American Board of Missions to the Jews, Inc." The reasons given were basically a rehash of the issues that had been raised by Herman Centz and A.B. Machlin, and those raised at the Board meetings by Fleming and Muntz. But there were two new things mentioned under the headings of Item 12 and Item 13, on the last two pages of the pamphlet. They stated:

> Item 12: A new agency has been formed under the name of the American Association for Jewish Evangelism, Inc., for the channeling of the gifts of God's people interested in reaching the Jews for Christ and desirous of proper administration of such funds. The directors of this new corporation will not be a self-perpetuating body, amenable to no one, as is the case with Mr. Cohn's Mission, but will be elected by a nation-wide council of representative Christian leaders named annually by the contributors.
>
> Item 13: Further information will be available in the near future. Meanwhile communications and contributions may be addressed to the American Association for Jewish Evangelism at Winona Lake, Indiana. We shall be glad to hear from any who love the Lord and desire the consolation of Israel, and will do our best to answer any questions which may arise.[62]

The "Why We Resign" statement included a listing of the Board and the Advisory Council of the newly formed American Association for Jewish Evangelism, Inc. Some of the names included on the Board are: Joseph W. Hakes, General Secretary; Hyman J. Appelman, President of the Board of Directors; J. Palmer Muntz, Vice-President; B.E. Allen, Elmer B. Funk, R.L. Powell, Harry E. Jessop, Robert O. Fleming, Albert G. Johnson, Peter MacFarlane. The Advisory Council listing included the names of forty-two pastors, Christian leaders, educators, etc. Among them were: Harry A. Ironside, Chairman; Louis Bauman, Herbert W. Bieber, John W. Bradbury, Herman B. Centz, Lewis S. Chafer, Frank E. Gaebelein, Earle G. Griffith, Will H. Houghton, J.A. Huffman, A.B. Machlin, John G. Mitchell, Harry Rimmer, Paul W. Rood, Harold Strathearn, and Louis T. Talbot.

The advisory council included most of the men with whom Joseph Cohn had participated in the Mission's Congress on Prophecy and with whom he had ministered at the annual prophetic Bible conferences at Winona Lake, Indiana—conferences that had been held since the early 1900's.

The "Why We Resign" pamphlet was circulated among all of the churches and associations represented by the Board and Advisory Council of The American Association for Jewish Evangelism, Inc., as well as to individuals and churches on the mailing list of The American Board of Missions to the Jews, Inc., that became available through Board and staff members who had resigned from the Mission. The fact that the pamphlet was circulated over the signature of Dr. Harry A. Ironside made it creditable to most Christians who read it. Almost over night, doors that had previously been open to the Mission were tightly closed. Former friends, pastors, and Christian leaders shunned Joseph and the workers who remained on staff with The American Board of Missions to the Jews (CPM).

In mid-December (1945), Dr. Muntz sent out another circular to the mailing lists he had obtained. This communique was sent on the letterhead of The American Association for Jewish Evangelism, Inc. The letter was intended to answer inquiries relative to the Buffalo work. Dr. Muntz stated:

> You may recall that originally we expected to use the name of 'American Jewish Missionary Society' and then, during our conference on Prophecy and the Jew at Winona Lake, Dr. Ironside suggested that we call it 'American Jewish Evangelistic Society.' However, Dr. Cohn's men advised him of our announcement and he immediately tried to prevent our using either of these names by himself applying for incorporation papers under both of them. Nevertheless, God used even this to our advantage, leading us to change to the above corporate name, which is still more descriptive of our purposes.
>
> You will be heartily pleased to note that Dr. Hyman J. Appelman, noted Jewish-Christian evangelist, is our President; Dr. Harry A. Ironside, the chairman of our national Advisory Council and Dr. Joseph W. Hakes, our General Secretary. The personnel of the Board and Council is in itself an emphatic protest against the conditions which called into existence and made necessary this new movement. Nevertheless, we want it distinctly understood that while information as to those causes and conditions must be available to the Christian public, this organization is not going to engage in a controversy, but rather go ahead with a constructive work of its own as God leads and supplies the means.
>
> The testimony to the Jews at Buffalo has been reestablished, with Mr. Machlin as Superintendent, under the direction of a strong local committee and a new building has been secured for the work. You will be kept advised as to progress made.[63]

In November 1944 word came that the Church of the Open Door and BIOLA would no longer support or carry the advertisements of the Mission. In a letter to Keith L. Brooks, Louis Talbot wrote:

> While I was in the Middle West, I came in contact with those involved in the Cohn controversy. I am very much afraid that the work of the Lord is going to come into disrepute as a result of this trouble. I am not taking sides in it. I feel that the course we are taking here is the wise one until the matters in the mission are cleared up. I have come to this conclusion after learning from Dr. Muntz that certain Christian leaders such as Dr. Harry Ironside and Dr. Otis Fuller urged Mr. Cohn to meet these brethren half-way which it is reported he has refused to do. We at BIOLA are under serious fire because we have carried his ads for such a long time. However, there must be something seriously wrong for such brethren as I have named to reach the conclusion they have. I do trust for the Lord's sake a solution may be reached with a view to furthering the Gospel of Christ as preached among the Jewish people. Mr. Daniel Rose has been insisting upon space in the King's Business for a long time; however, it has not been given him because we did not want to break faith with Mr. Cohn, in spite of the derogatory rumors regarding divorce, his use of tobacco, etc. However, we feel that in the light of present events, we must save ourselves from further criticism.[64]

Thankfully, not everyone jumped on the band-wagon to discredit Joseph Cohn and the Mission. There were some

Christian leaders who gave Joseph the benefit of the doubt. One such individual was Dr. W. H. Rogers. In responding to a personal letter, Rogers wrote:

> Concerning the matter of the Brooklyn Mission. There has been considerable trouble with which I am quite familiar. I have read considerable literature from both sides and many letters that were written to others and I am convinced that it is another wile of the Devil to stir up trouble and hinder the good work the mission is doing. I have friends on both sides and I do not want to take issue with any one of them. I have reached the conclusion that perhaps the division will ultimately mean more work done for The Chosen People of God. Those that have pulled out from the mission did so suddenly after they were called upon to give an itemized account of their travel and expenses. There had also been some evidence of their desire to take the mission into their own hands and get out the present personnel. That was the beginning of the trouble. The things of which they accuse Dr. Cohn are the very things for which they are responsible before the break came. The fact that the board has clearly and publicly exonerated Mr. Cohn of all the charges that were made, is sufficient to convince me that I should stand by and support the work. While I do that I shall pray that the other work might be blest of God to the end that jews [sic] will be saved. I am carefully sifting through my own mind everything I hear and intend to be positively fair in the conclusions I reach since I hold no brief for anyone.[65]

Loss of Support

In the wake of all of the controversy, the pastors of some churches began to withdraw support, or to transfer support to other ministries. This was the case of Paul Jackson, pastor of the First Baptist Church in Ceres, CA. He wrote to Emil Gruen:

> We appreciate all that is being done for the Lord by the American Board of Missions to the Jews, although we are not in sympathy with some of the policies of the Mission. I am thinking particularly of large funds which are being held inactive for future use. I also feel that the Mission is using in an unscriptural way the slogan 'To the Jew first.' So while I have no idea at all of starting any discussion or controversy upon these things with you, I am frankly saying that we are throwing our support behind our own independent Baptist Mission with which we are thoroughly in sympathy.[66]

William Houghton, President of Moody Bible Institute, wrote a letter to a Mr. Dodge, and sent a copy of the letter to Keith L. Brooks. Houghton said to Mr. Dodge:

> I am sorry to see you have gone to the bat for a certain Brooklyn gentleman, answering in advance charges which you have not as yet heard. This means nothing in my young life, but brother I hate to see you climb out on a limb. It is going to be embarrassing for some folks if and when it is proven that most of his final defenders were subsidized, some for as little as twenty-five dollars a month.[67]

Back and forth the battle went, as Christian leaders and laymen chose sides. Some supported Cohn, but the majority did not. A few chose to remain neutral. As the drama continued to unfold, several additional workers of the Mission resigned. Some took positions with the new organization commonly known as the AAJE; others took pastorates or took positions with other Jewish missions.

It was ironic that forty years after the Mission had very nearly been destroyed by two Jewish Christians, history was repeating itself. The difference this time was that there would be no investigation of the charges. Joseph's refusal to accept Dr. Otis Fuller's suggestion to allow for an outside committee investigation, meant that unfounded charges, gossip, and rumors were destined to be tried in the Christian tabloids of the day.

Feeling betrayed, deeply hurt, and frustrated, Joseph sent a personal letter to Dr. Harry Ironside on March 7, 1945. He stated:

> Dr. Muntz is sending out broadcast printed copies of certain letters that he claims you wrote to Dr. Keith L. Brooks, in which are statements defaming the work of the American Board of Missions to the Jews, and myself personally, although there is an assertion that you have no intention of doing so!
>
> Do you not believe that you should stick to the truth? For instance it is not true that I refused an investigation [Minutes show that he refused the committee investigation suggested by Fuller & Muntz; Joseph never refused investigation by individual Christian leaders—in fact, he welcomed it]. The records show that we have repeatedly urged you to come to New York, even at our expense and to make any investigation of our Mission that you wish. We have made the same offer to a good many other brethren, and some have accepted, have come here and have gone away

more devoted to the Mission that ever before.

Your behavior in adhering to the Muntz-Winona-LeTourneau-Stratheam line-up has staggered me, and completely shattered my faith in you as a man of God, and a man who really wishes truth and justice. By and by if the explosion comes, the truth will be revealed, and I am afraid your judgment will prove to have been sadly at fault....

Speaking of truth, I may say that it is not true that you had looked only to Messrs. Muntz and Machlin for information and endorsement of this Mission. You forget that over thirty years ago it was that I used to sit with you by the hour in the back of your store on Telegraph Avenue in Oakland, and that we used to discuss at that time many phases of the Jewish problem in which we had a common interest....

Perhaps you will remember that a good many years ago you were very glad to speak with me on the same platform, such as Eaglesmere, Camden, N.J. and here in New York, even in our own Mission building; and all of these occasions took place before I ever heard of Muntz or even Machlin.

Speaking further of truth, can you in all honesty consider it fair or even truthful, to say that you have lost confidence in me, when the only time you ever saw me on this question was last July, 1944, and that for a matter of about two hours, with Mr. W. Jones being present? You seemed already so to have mistrusted me that you insisted on bringing in one Arthur McKee from Winona Lake. At that two hour conference your behavior and your trifling with important matters that I brought before you, were such that Mr. Jones and I went away fully satisfied that you were so biased in advance that there was no possible chance of expecting either justice or fair play from you. And in this fear, your actions of the last eight months, how many times have you met with our accusers, and in how many places and for how long periods? Just put one against the other, and ask yourself whether you have dealt fairly, honestly and in truth with us.

Will you kindly ask yourself what degree of fairness you displayed when, without hearing the witnesses we could present, you permitted your name to be affixed to a paper containing accusations against the ABMJ and at the same time gave your consent to the formation of a new Jewish organization using a very important part of our name i.e., of an already existing organization. As to this last point it looks as if some one intended to deceive the friends of Jewish people by leading them to believe that they were giving to the Jewish organization with which they have been so long familiar.

It is more of a grief for me to write you these lines than I can express to you and I can only hope and pray that the Lord somehow will touch your conscience and cause you to see that you have been woefully misled and misinformed, and all of this by men who have been lashed into fury by the fact that they have been balked in their schemes to gain control of this Mission and its work, with a honorable history for 51 years of service.[68]

Joseph waited five long years before he received a reply from Dr. Ironside on these matters. During those years, he did his utmost to clear his name and reputation, and to forge ahead with his Mission's program. But it wasn't easy. As the stories and gossip spread from person to person, church to church, and denomination to denomination, it became clear that the old stories about Rabbi Leopold Cohn being a fake, a thief, a swindler, and murderer, had not died. Two individuals, whose hearts were filled with hatred toward the Cohn's and the Mission, had kept the stories alive through their writings.

Although the November 1916 issue of *The Chosen People* magazine included a full report of the Committee to Investigate Charges Against Leopold Cohn, a man named Colonel Alexander Bacon did his best to continue spreading the vicious lie that Rabbi Cohn was, in reality, a fake. Col. Bacon perpetuated his belief through a booklet he wrote and published in 1918, entitled, "The Strange Story of Dr. Cohn and Mr. Joszovics."

A few years later, a man by the name of Colonel E.N. Sanctuary busied himself extrapolating the lies and innuendos that he found printed about the Cohn's in Col. Bacon's booklet and in newspapers, etc. These he compiled and published in booklet form in 1939. The booklet was titled, "Making Ananias a Piker." Col. Sanctuary published a rehash of the same information in 1943 under the title, "A Foundation of Sand." He said the book was a sequel to Col. Bacon's book, "The Strange Story of Dr. Cohn and Mr. Joszovics."

It is difficult to understand the reasons behind Colonel Sanctuary's attacks against the Mission, but a possible explanation may be revealed in the Minutes of a Board meeting held in October 1935. They state:

...Mr. Joseph Cohn showed a copy of the New York Times of October 9th [1935] in which Col. Sanctuary is announced as one of the chief speakers at a Nazi Rally in New York City. This may explain the Colonel's hatred of our Jewish mission.[69]

These Minutes also reveal that Joseph met with Dr. Arno Gaebelein and requested that he try to stop the malicious gossip being spread by Col. Sanctuary. They state:

> *Mr. Cohn told of his recent visit with Dr. Gaebelein. Dr. Gaebelein is a member of the American European Fellowship and Mr. Cohn wondered whether the Fellowship was aware of Col. Sanctuary's activities against the Mission and whether they sanctioned such activities. This meeting resulted in Dr. Gaebelein's calling a meeting of the Fellowship at which a resolution was passed instructing Col. Sanctuary that he must cease his attacks upon us.[70] [A letter of appreciation was sent to Dr. Gaebelein.]*

Dr. Gaebelein's efforts may have helped some, but they did not completely abate Col. Sanctuary's attacks on the Mission, as shown in the Minutes of June 1936 Directors' meeting:

> *...As a result of Col. Sanctuary's malicious activities against us, we were suddenly notified on May 5th that our advertising in The Sunday School Times was to be suspended, pending investigation on the part of Dr. Trumbull and Mr. Philip Howard. Mr. Cohn wrote protesting ...a reply came that on reconsideration they felt that we were right and that they would continue the advertising temporarily and promised to insert a pending advertisement in the next issue. Four or five days latter ...he reversed himself completely and announced they would not print the advertising.... Finally on June 9th a conference was held in Philadelphia with Dr. Trumbull, Mr. Howard, and Mr. Cohn. Mr. Linton [was] also...present,...At this conference Mr. Linton was overjoyed to see how completely we had demolished the false accusations of Col. Sanctuary, but Dr. Trumbull and Mr. Howard refused to give a decision. Dr. Trumbull admitted that the evidences Mr. Cohn presented were thoroughly convincing but in his own words, he refused to 'adjudicate the matter.' Mr. Cohn protested and tried to show him how unfair he was, but to no avail. It was left however that we will hear later and we believe the decision will be in our favor. In the meantime we must suffer from the injustice of this temporary unfairness.[71]*

A number of Christian leaders contacted Joseph directly to inquire about the validity of Col. Sanctuary's accusations. Joseph welcomed the opportunity to have genuinely concerned Christians visit the Mission and discuss the charges put forth in Col. Sanctuary's materials. One Christian who contacted Joseph, asking if he might visit the Mission and discuss the charges of Col. Sanctuary, was Mr. Harold Strathearn. Mr. Strathearn was the Secretary of the Interstate Evangelistic Association (a Baptist organization comprised of 2,000 ministers). He had been influenced by Sanctuary's publications and by meetings where Sanctuary had spoken, but after a personal visit to the Mission's Headquarters office, he left convinced that the writings of the Colonel were not true. The Minutes reflect the results of Mr. Strathearn's visit to the Mission. They state:

> *The Rev. Mr. Strathearn,...spent the day visiting the Mission and inquiring into its history and methods. The members of the Executive Committee met him. Recently Col. Sanctuary had spoken in Pennsylvania and Western New York and after his regular meetings had severely attacked our mission, speaking against it in every way and making many incorrect statements. Mr. Strathearn was much concerned about these stories as he had known Mr. Joseph Cohn, so he came over to investigate for himself.*
>
> *He was greatly pleased with all that he saw and heard and much distressed that he had listened to these malicious tales and wished to do all he could to stop them and their influence from proceeding further.*
>
> *He decided to send a letter to the 2000 members of the Association telling of his visit in Brooklyn.[72]*

Unfortunately, after the split on the Board, Mr. Strathearn sided with the Centz-Machlin-Muntz camp. He joined the newly formed AAJE as a member of that organization's Advisory Council, and used his influence to further discredit Joseph and the Mission.

W. B. Riley, President of the Northwestern Theological Seminary and Bible Training School, had also been influenced by the writings of Col. Sanctuary. The circumstances and rumors that prompted the formation of the AAJE gave Riley further cause to perpetuate the lies of Col. Sanctuary by peddling his books to students and to the subscribers to his ministry. Dr. Riley was totally convinced that Joseph Cohn should be stopped, and the Mission shut down. When word came to him on April 14, 1945 of the imminent split within the Mission, he wrote to Irwin H. Linton, attempting to persuade him to resign from the Board, and offering him copies of the scurrilous booklets.[73]

When Mr. Linton shared Riley's letters with Joseph, he was so infuriated by what was being said about him that he wanted to take legal action against Riley. Not only were some of Riley's statements libelous, some were blatantly anti-Semitic. But Joseph's lawyers told him Riley's statements were only libelous by "...innuendo, rather than direct libel, since the statements are cleverly phrased."[74] On his attorney's advice that he would not be able to win such a suit, Joseph took no further action.

Although it took Dr. Ironside five years before he responded to Joseph's letter, his response to a letter from Keith L. Brooks was prompt. Brooks had remained a loyal and faithful friend of Joseph and of the Mission. In a reply to Brooks, Dr. Ironside wrote:

I have no desire to attack the Cohn work. I do not understand that this was Dr. Muntz' motive. The point with him and Mr. Fleming was this: Their presence on the board helped to give prestige to that movement and literally thousands of people, myself among them, had their fears quelled as to the untrustworthiness of that work because of the very fact that men of integrity like Muntz and Fleming were on the board, and also because of the fact that faithful men like Machlin and Centz expressed their confidence in it. Now, when these men lost confidence and a thorough investigation was refused, they felt they owed it to those whom they had interested, to tell them the facts. Unfortunately, a great deal more publicity has been given to it all than they originally intended should be the case.[75]

As a young man, Joseph Cohn had agreed to join his father in ministry. Further, he had promised to spend his whole life in Jewish work, and to do his best at it.[76] He had kept his promise. The reader will recall that he was separated from his wife (a legal separation, not a divorce), he was separated from his family, he lived alone in the Beacon Hotel in New York City. His every thought and every action focused on the Mission. He had sacrificed all for the ministry, but as God had blessed his efforts, his self confidence was bolstered and his pride had swelled. God was now demanding his pride as well. God knows what must be done to make a servant and, when necessary, what must be done to break a servant—when the servant has forgotten his status as clay in the Master's hand.

Alone in his room at the Morton Hotel in Grand Rapids, Michigan, Joseph took some stationary out of the desk drawer. In his unique European style of writing, scratching out phrases as new thoughts came to him, he expressed his innermost feelings and thoughts:

Envy is a deadly cancer, and too common a sin among certain Christian brethren in highly placed positions. Like the Pharisees of old, they sit in Moses' seat, and 'say, but do not.' They preach platitudes to the rest of us, that we must guard the unruly tongue, must not speak evil of one another. But Shakespeare's exhortation of 'man's inhumanity to man' is but an incident when we come to examine the back-biting, the knifing, the character assassinations, the cruelties of condemnations, of which some of them are guilty, when once they have determined that certain so and so must be 'rubbed out,' or once their pride has been hurt, or their power challenged. Is this also a sign of the last days?

And is it terrifying to think that a handful of such leaders, holding the confidence of some of the Lord's people, should conspire together, under the reckless sway of two or three evil minded men bent on relentless revenge, to destroy, if possible, a work which God has so signally honored and blessed for 50 years, so that it is now the largest Gospel testimony to Israel in the whole world, and must be destined for a strategic place in His purposes for these end-days. Is it not clear, that this can only be the work of Satan? Still more appalling is it that these same men will do crimes, in the name of their Christian profession, which the unbelievers in the street would despise, and which the courts of our land have punished over and over again under indictments of criminal libel. Indeed many friends have urged us to initiate such libel suits, as the only means of bringing these men to an abrupt accounting of their deeds. One of these conspirators is none other than the President of a Bible Institute; and it is the boast of the undercover instigator of all this evil that this 'master in Israel' delivered a 300,000 mailing list of his institutions, so that the libels might be sent broadcast from coast to coast! If this be true, then that Institution has some investigating to do! And it takes money to carry on their evil propaganda—where does it come from?

But we see Jesus. And we see our friends on bended knees, holding us up before the Throne of Grace, that the Lord Himself shall lay bare His arm of deliverance; that He Himself shall keep us steadfast and unmoved, for it is a lonely struggle at best. May He give us the continuing grace to abide in the exhortation of 1 Peter 2:23, 'Who, when He was reviled, reviled not again; when He suffered, He threatened not; but committed Himself to Him that judgeth righteously.'

Now forgive us this digression. We have kept still now nearly a year, and we had hoped never to bring these matters to you. But now we are forced to do this, only that you may have at least some of the facts. Then you will know what to do. If we told everything it would require a book, and might rock America.[77]

Dr. Ironside Apologizes

The monthly issues of *The Chosen People* magazine during the years 1943 to 1950 carried no mention of the raging controversy; Joseph did not dignify the controversy by writing about it. However, once he was exonerated by Dr. Ironside, he published Dr. Ironside's apology in a small booklet entitled "Dr. Ironside Corrects An Injustice."

Dr. Harry A. Ironside's exoneration of Joseph came by way of a letter dated October 6, 1950. It said:

For some time I have felt constrained to write you that I feel it was a great mistake to allow myself to be drawn into the controversy between you and Dr. Muntz, Centz, Machlin, and others. I believe I would have honored the Lord more if I had kept clear of the entire matter, as it was 'strife belonging not to me.' As you know I resigned from the chairmanship of the Advisory Board of the A.A.J.E. some months ago, and am no longer connected in any way with that Association.[78]

Further correspondence between Ironside and Joseph Cohn indicated that, before his death, Dr. Ironside wrote to a number of Christian leaders, publishers, pastors, and friends in an attempt to undo the harm he felt he may have brought upon Joseph Cohn and the Mission. On November 24, 1950 he wrote this word to Joseph:

This is to acknowledge your gracious letter of October 25 which I received upon arrival here last Tuesday. I feel greatly relieved in my own mind since clearing my conscience of complicity with the attack upon you and your work into which I had allowed myself to be drawn. I do sincerely hope that whatever harm was thus done may at least to some extent be reversed.[79]

Keith L. Brooks, also suffered because he stood with Joseph and the Mission throughout the bitter attacks. In the January 1951 edition of Prophecy magazine he wrote the following statement:

Any who, during the past few years, have been disturbed about attacks upon the work of the American Board of Missions to the Jews and its General Secretary, Dr. Joseph Hoffman Cohn, may receive some enlightenment through a statement just issued by Dr. H. A. Ironside. It is relative to his deep regret that, without proper investigation, he allowed his name to be used as 'Chairman' of an organized group that has been principally engaged in trying to destroy Dr. Cohn's work. Dr. Ironside renews his complete endorsement of the American Board of Missions to the Jews and authorized the use of his statement with any who may have been influenced by the fact that his name has been used to dignify these smear attacks. His resignation from this group has been met with statements that it was because of 'failing eyesight' that he gave up his connection. Dr. Ironside wishes it made clear that he does not endorse the affairs of this association in any way.[80]

Dr. Ironside's letters of endorsement of Joseph and the Mission accomplished what he hoped they would. The pastors of key churches, and Christian friends throughout the world who received his letters, began to recant and to once again invited Joseph and the Mission's representatives into their fellowship. Joseph Cohn and the Board had learned some very hard lessons—lessons that served to shape and mold the selection of future Board members and future leaders of the Mission.

As for the American Association For Jewish Evangelism, Inc., it became an effective ministry of outreach to the Jewish people. It also continued the Prophetic Bible Conferences at Winona Lake—conferences Joseph Cohn initiated in the Summer of 1917,[81] but the organization never grew to the size and position of prominence that its founders envisioned.

Final Attempt at Reconciliation

In 1981, Dr. J. Palmer Muntz approached Dr. Daniel Fuchs, who was then the Chairman of the Board of The American Board of Missions to the Jews, Inc. (CPM). He asked if the Mission would be interested in affecting a reconciliation and merger of the two organizations once again. Dr. Fuchs and the author, who was at that time serving as President of the Mission, met with Dr. Muntz and members of the Board of the AAJE on several occasions, to discuss how such a merger could be realized. On May 1, 1982 the Executive Committees of both missions met together and enjoyed renewed fellowship, yet it was unfortunate that the discussions made it apparent that a merger of the two ministries was outside the realm of possibility. Over the years each organization had developed its own vision, direction, and methodology. Each organization was making a contribution to the goal of reaching Jewish people with the Gospel—in different ways. Ultimately, each group felt it best, unless God clearly directed otherwise, to keep the organizations separate. Each ministry continues the task of reaching Jews with the Gospel. God alone knows if He will work to bring the two organizations together at some time in the days ahead.

ENDNOTES

Chapter 8. The Vision in the Midst of Dissension

1 *The Shepherd of Israel*, Vol. XX, No. 11-12, (July-August, 1938), n.p.

2 Reprint, *Buffalo Evening News*, (January 20, 1921).

3 Reprint, *Annual Banquet and Business Meeting*, Buffalo Hebrew Christian Mission, (December, 2, 1927).

4 *Minutes of Executive Committee*, ABMJ, (March 30, 1937), p 2.

5 See note above.

6 *Minutes*, ABMJ, (April 12, 1936), p 5.

7 *The Chosen People*, Vol. XLIII, No. 2, (November, 1937), p 7.

8 See note above.

9 *Minutes of Executive Committee*, ABMJ, (June 4, 1937), p 1.

10 *The Chosen People*, Vol. XLIII, No. 7, (April, 1938), p 9.

11 See note above.

12 *Minutes*, ABMJ, (October 27, 1943), p 1.

13 *Minutes: Special Meeting of the Executive Committee*, ABMJ, (Granada Hotel, Brooklyn, New York: September 27, 1938), p 2.

14 *Minutes*, ABMJ, (October 30, 1940), p 1.

15 *Minutes*, ABMJ, (January 22, 1941), p 1.

16 *Minutes*, ABMJ, (April 27, 1943), p 3.

17 *Personal letter: R. Fleming to J. Cohn*, March 27, 1944.

18 *Personal letter: A. Machlin to J. Cohn*, April 15, 1944, p 4.

19 See *J. Cohn's work sheets*, (April 25, 1944, edited for April 25, 1944 Special Board Meeting).

20 *Minutes*, ABMJ, (April 27, 1943), p 3.

21 *Notes for Minutes*, ABMJ, (April 25, 1944), p 2.

22 *Minutes*, ABMJ, (April 25, 1944), p 1.

23 See note above.

24 *Personal letter: Elizabeth Goodrow to Grace Bredehoft*, May 3, 1944.

25 *Minutes of Executive Committee*, ABMJ, (May 8, 1944), p 1.

26 *Personal letter: A.B. Machlin to Irwin H. Linton*, May 29, 1944.

27 *Telegram: O. Fuller and R. Powell to J. Cohn*, received between May 12-15, 1944.

28 *Minutes*, ABMJ, (May 24, 1944), p 1.

29 See note above.

30 See note above, p 1,2.

31 See note above, p 2.

32 See note above.

33 See note above.

34 *Mass mailing letter: J.P. Muntz to his constituency and others*, June 1, 1944.

35 *Personal letter: D.O. Fuller to R.L. Powell*, June 14, 1944, p 2.

36 *Minutes*, ABMJ, Notice of Special Directors' Meeting, June 10, 1944.

37 *Minutes: Special meeting of the Board*, ABMJ, (June 21, 1944), p 2.

38 See note above, p 3.

39 See note above, p 5.

40 See note above, p 6.

41 See note above, p 8.

42 See note above.

43 *Minutes*, ABMJ, Notice of special Directors' meeting, (July 19, 1944).

44 See note above.

45 *Minutes*, ABMJ, (August 1, 1944), p 1.

46 See note above, p 2.

47 *Minutes*, ABMJ, (April 25, 1944), p 1.

48 See *Notes for Minutes*, ABMJ, (October 24, 1944), pp 14, 15.

49 See note above, p 1.

50 See note above, p 8.

51 See note above.

52 See note above.

53 See note above, p 9.

54 See note above.

55 See note above, p 12.

56 See note above, p 16.

57 See note above.

58 See note above, p 15.

59 See note above.

60 See note above, p 17.

61 See note above.

62 *Why We Resign from The American Board of Missions to the Jews, Inc.*, N.A., n.d.

63 *Circular letter: J.P. Muntz to supporting mailing lists*, 1944/45.

64 *Personal letter: L. Talbot to K. Brooks*, November 21, 1944.

65 *Personal letter: W.H. Rogers to A.L. Griswold*, February 20, 1945.

66 *Personal letter: P.R. Jackson to E.D. Gruen*, October 31, 1944.

67 *Personal letter: W.H. Houghton to K.L. Brooks*, September 6, 1944.

68 *Personal letter: J. Cohn to H. Ironside*, March 7, 1945.

69 *Minutes, ABMJ*, (October 16, 1935), p 1.

70 See note above, p 5.

71 *Minutes of Executive Committee, ABMJ*, (June 18, 1936), p 1.

72 *Minutes of Executive Committee, ABMJ*, (June 5, 1935), pp 1, 2.

73 See *Personal letter: W.B. Riley to I.H. Linton*, April 14, 1945.

74 *Personal letter: Douglas Hall, Law offices Helstein and Hall, to Joseph Cohn*, June 23, 1945.

75 *Personal letter: H.A. Ironside to K.L. Brooks*, February 14, 1945.

76 See testimony of Joseph Cohn, *Investigation of Charges Against Leopold Cohn*, p 150.

77 J. Cohn, *Personal notes*, (Morton Hotel, Grand Rapids, MI), n.d.

78 *Personal letter: H.A. Ironside to J.H. Cohn*, October 6, 1950.

79 *Personal letter: H.A. Ironside to J.H. Cohn*, November 24, 1950.

80 Keith L. Brooks, *Prophecy magazine*, (January, 1951).

81 See *The Chosen People*, Vol. XXIII, No. 1, (October, 1917), pp 3, 4).

9

TILL DEATH DO US PART

The scope and variety of ministry activities that Joseph Cohn was involved in, and the depth of his commitment to those activities, is "mind boggling" to consider. At the same time he was opening branches across America, he was also opening branches in Europe, South America, and Palestine. The establishment of each new branch required the hiring of new workers, recruiting and training of new volunteers to assist, and increased responsibility for Joseph in supervising his growing "world-wide" staff. Additionally, he was writing and editing *The Chosen People* magazine, writing books and tracts, developing films, and carrying on a radio ministry for the Mission.

Joseph's entire life and all of his energies were given to the task of expanding the Mission's outreach. He was a man blessed with boundless energy—a man driven to advance the cause. Failure to advance meant "retreat," a word that was not in his vocabulary where the work of Jewish evangelism was concerned. The Mission—overseeing the work of the Mission, expanding the work of the Mission, networking on behalf of the Mission—occupied his every waking thought (and probably most of his dreams). He had made a commitment to the Lord, as well as to his father, Rabbi Leopold Cohn, and to Frances Huntley, that he would carry on the work of the Mission and thus fulfill his father's dream of a time when many thousands of Jews would proclaim Yeshua as Messiah.

YIDDISH NEW TESTAMENT PUBLISHED

One of Rabbi Leopold Cohn's deep desires was that the Mission would produce and print a new Yiddish translation of the New Testament. He had mentioned this to the Board on more than one occasion. The Board Minutes of October 17, 1938 (less than one year after Leopold's death) reveal the Board's approval to produce and sell a book titled, "When Jews Face Christ." A handwritten notation in the margin of the Minutes book stating, "Money to be used in printing a new Yiddish New Testament,"[1] indicates that revenue from the sale of the book was to be set aside to realize Rabbi Cohn's dream of a new Yiddish New Testament.

In 1940 Joseph Cohn once again reminded the Board of the need to produce a Yiddish New Testament. His reminder prompted the appointment of a committee to investigate the need for such a New Testament, and the feasibility of producing one. Their findings were reported to the Executive Committee. The Minutes state:

> There is a shortage of Yiddish New Testaments in this country as they have previously always come from Europe. Also the present translation is considered very faulty. Dr. H. Einspruch, of the Lutheran Jewish Mission Society of Baltimore has been working for years on a new translation which is just about completed. Mr. Cohn suggested that we appropriate $5,000. for printing 10,000 New Testaments of this new translation. The translation and the type setting would be the gift to us of the Lewis and Harriet Lederer Foundation which has been sponsoring Dr. Einspruch's work for years. We would pay for the actual printing, binding, paper, etc., and our Mission's imprint together with that of the Lederer Foundation will appear on the title page. The Testaments are to be given away freely, no charge is to be made for them.[2]

The Executive Committee unanimously approved the report and the subsequent motion.

Dr. Einspruch's Yiddish New Testament was completed as scheduled, and in the Fall of 1941 Joseph told Board members that he had already received many enthusiastic letters commending the Mission for publishing this new translation.

World conditions had people longing for peace. Many who had never before sought God were willing to consider the truths of His Word, but the escalating war in Europe was wreaking havoc on efforts to conduct ministry in that part of the world. The air-raids in England had destroyed most of the literature used by the Mission's workers and by other ministries there. Joseph therefore proposed to the Board, and they unanimously agreed, that the Mission would send 10,000 copies of its special tracts and large quantities of the new Yiddish New Testament to the Barbican Mission in England. They, in turn, had agreed to distribute the materials to other Jewish ministries in England and in other countries of Europe.[3] This plan never came to fruition however. The steamship company refused the Mission's request to ship the literature due to the fact that the war, and war materials, had first priority. The following report was given to the Board:

> ...they were forced to decline this request until after the war is over. The shipping facilities are so crowded, that they have sort of Gentlemen's agreement with the Government not to use such facilities unless absolutely necessary. As soon as the war is over they will be very happy to act as our agents for the distribution of these books, and at no cost to us.[4]

In his report Joseph went on to say that he had been able to send 1,000 copies of the New Testament to Mr. C. H. Gill of the London Jews Society. He informed the Board that the shipment had been divided and sent in two boats—an effort to protect the literature in case of attack. The Minutes reflect that the shipment did arrive safely.[5]

With the new Yiddish translation of the New Testament so well received, Joseph again contacted Dr. Einspruch and asked him to produce a special Yiddish edition of the Gospel of Matthew that could be circulated among Jewish servicemen. Soon it, too, was being requested by other ministries around the world.

1st Congress on Prophecy

Members of the Board knew Joseph well. They knew he was continuously looking for new ways to promote the Mission—to increase its base of operations—while at the same time promoting the Gospel message. In May 1942, while World War II was raging, Joseph proposed a program that completely caught the Board off-guard. He proposed bringing together forty or fifty of the leading ministers and Bible teachers in the country for a Mission-sponsored "National Prophetic Convention." He stated:

> ...There has arisen a movement in this country which attempts to break away from the traditional teaching of Scofield, Moorhead, and such men of a generation ago, particularly on Ezekiel 38 and Revelation 20, disclaiming that there will be a revival of the Roman Empire. I see it more and more as I go about. We used to have in this country men like Dr. James M. Gray who was what we might call, in the finest terms, a little theological pope. People had respect for him and his views and they rallied to his pronouncements. But Dr. Gray is gone and there is no one to take his place. My scheme is to call a National Prophetic Convention. I have picked out abut fifty men all over the country. We would plan to bring these men to Chicago, with Dr. Ironsides of the Moody Memorial Church as host for the Convention. We would put on a three day program, with an opening address by Dr. Albert Johnson of Portland. Another address by Dr. Louis Bauman, and then a closing address by Dr. Harry Ironsides. We would have all day meetings for the many people who would attend such a convention. I would suggest seven creedos. My theory is to write to each of these men 'Here is an affirmation and manifesto. If you are with us on the basis outlined, you are invited to come to Chicago at our expense, and then we will have time to work out each paragraph on these credos.'
>
> We will get these 50 men to sign the final document, and then copies will be sent to 500 ministers and laymen for secondary signatures all over the country so that the entire proceedings will be broadcast throughout the land.[6]

The Board was so taken aback by the scope and immensity of the plan that they were unable to come to a decision on the matter, but after much discussion Joseph proposed a motion which was unanimously approved. It stated:

> ...that the Mission [would] encourage and sponsor the calling of a national gathering of leading premillennial brethren to some central place for the purpose of getting a united expression of affirmation as to dispensational truth, the place of the Jew in the program of the Church, the imminence of our Lord's return and the probable development of events as we believe they are outlined in prophetic Scripture. It is further voted that the sum of $5000 be appropriated to meet the expense of such a Convention.[7]

Across America the Mission's name was already linked with good prophetic teaching and scholarship—an association that had been steadily building since August 1917 when the first of many annual conferences on "The Jew in Prophecy" was held at the Winona Lake Conference Grounds in Winona, Indiana.

With the Board's approval of a Mission-sponsored "National Prophetic Convention," Joseph Cohn wasted no time in making the arrangements. The only major change the Board had made in Joseph's original proposal was to change the proposed location from Chicago to New York. It was reasoned that this change would afford those attending the convention an opportunity to visit the Mission's work as well.

The October 1942 issue of *The Chosen People* magazine heralded the news of this epoch-making Conference on Prophecy. Joseph wrote:

> So everything else has been set aside and the tracks have been cleared for this one great momentous event. We have called a National Congress on Prophecy, to be held in Calvary Baptist Church, New York, from Lord's Day to Lord's Day, November 1st to 8th, to consider one thing only, namely the application of prophetic truth to the present crashing hour of world history.[8]

The listing of thirty-five dispensational/evangelical speakers reads like a virtual Who's Who list of well-known pastors and Christian leaders of the day.[9] Many more Christian leaders signed the "manifesto" but were unable to attend the conference because of conflicts in their own busy schedules.

Joseph encouraged readers of the magazine to pray for the special conference and to support it financially. He also assured readers that the Mission would produce a book containing the messages given at the Congress so that individuals who were unable to attend the sessions would be able to share in the wealth of Bible knowledge and inspiration generated at the conference.

It was no surprise to Joseph that the first National Congress on Prophecy, held in November 1942, was a tremendous success. The book containing the messages given at the Congress was published as promised, and was ready for distribution by January 1943. The success of the congress confirmed to Joseph that there was a great desire on the part of Christians to have such an arena of sound Bible teaching, and for many years thereafter (until the time of Joseph Cohn's death) the Mission sponsored a Congress on Prophecy. Following each congress, messages given were published in book form. After Joseph's death smaller versions of the Congress on Prophecy continued to be conducted by the Mission. The last such Congress on Prophecy was held in Philadelphia in 1976, in honor of America's Bi-centennial celebration (See Chapter Twelve of this history).

Although Joseph maintained an office at the headquarters building in New York, he certainly did not spend a great deal of time there. He was always out on the field; he was always "checking the barometer" for changes within the Jewish community or the Christian community, or checking on opportunities for the growth of the Mission, or on needs of the staff. In 1941, after returning from one of his field trips, Joseph called a special meeting of the Board to suggest that the time had come to establish a pension fund for the Mission workers. He said:

> …It has seemed to me that the time has come when the Mission should take definite steps to provide some retirement income for our workers. With conditions as they are today, uncertainty as to our currency system, all the big denominations are making provisions along these lines. Take for instance the case of Mr. Zimmerman, who is working in Los Angeles. He has been with us fully 25 years. He is not at all well. He is still a young man, probably under 50. He is wondering what will become of him if he becomes disabled. Several of our workers have spoken to me for they are concerned for their future when they are no longer able to work.[10]

Joseph suggested that the Board consider putting into place some type of retirement plan that would allow a worker to retire at age sixty-five and, based on length of service with the Mission and on the worker's average earnings during the entire time of service, receive from the Mission a monthly sum for the rest of his or her life. The Board approved his suggestion, telling him to act on it immediately. They stated:

> …as of tomorrow in order to secure the rates which are now in force, so that when they [the insurance company] make the examinations of those men who will be nominated later on by the Committee, we will have the benefit of the present rates for them. It shall also be understood that we adopt as a general plan of retirement income for those not protected in our insurance and retirement income policies, that of making a suitable arrangement with each individual case based on a thirty year service basis.[11]

Another field trip took Joseph to churches in the South—a trip that disclosed the fact that many Christians in the South knew little about the teachings of the second coming of the Messiah or about the role of the Jew in God's prophetic program. These same Christians showed great interest in learning about such things however, and Joseph realized he needed to find workers to open the South for the work of the Mission.

DR. HARRY MARKO—HIS STORY

In answer to prayer, during the Fall of 1942, he heard about a remarkable Jewish doctor who was preaching the

Gospel throughout the state of Texas. Joseph was eager to find a vibrant Jewish believer who could help him open the South-west for Jewish evangelism and for the Mission's support, so he arranged a trip to Texas where he met Dr. Harry Marko.

Harry Marko was born in Romania, the child of an orthodox Jewish couple who conscientiously taught him the Hebrew Scriptures from the age of four. Harry was only eleven years old when his father died.

As he grew to adulthood, Harry became involved in synagogue life. He was a gifted singer, and was asked to be the cantor of a synagogue—a position that frequently involved taking singing trips across Russia. But medicine, not music, was Harry's first love, so he enrolled in college in Vienna and embarked upon the study of medicine at the age of sixteen. In his spare time he continued voice lessons under the tutelage of a noted singer at the Vienna Opera. He completed his medical training and received his credentials as a Doctor of medicine by the age of twenty. During the same year he received a certificate from the Vienna Opera as a singer.

With his studies completed, twenty-one year old Dr. Harry Marko became restless and, like many men before him, he embarked upon a journey to America thinking perhaps he would find fame and fortune there. His travels in America eventually took him to the state of Texas—a state he liked so much he decided to open a medical practice in one of its small towns. His practice did well; he was known as the "Singing Jewish Doctor."

On one occasion, Dr. Marko was called to a neighboring town for consultation. On his trip home, he noticed a hitch-hiker standing on the side of the highway. Harry had never before stopped for a hitch-hiker, but he later stated that he'd felt compelled to stop for the man. To break the uneasiness of riding with a stranger, he began making small talk. The stranger listened politely for awhile, but then he interrupted Harry and began asking him probing questions regarding his beliefs about death, heaven, and hell.

In his testimony, Dr. Marko said he began to feel very uncomfortable and had tried to change the subject. The hitch-hiker went right on talking, telling Harry the story of his own life. To his amazement, Harry found himself intrigued by the man's story. Gently and carefully, the stranger wove portions of Scripture into his testimony. Harry was fascinated; he had never heard such things before. The Scripture verses made an impact upon him, cutting away at his proud, rebellious, hardened heart like his own surgical knife cut through the diseased flesh of his patients.

Dr. Marko's heart came under conviction; he realized that he was lost. He pulled his car over to the side of the road and, like the Ethiopian Eunuch (see Acts 8:26-39), he asked his passenger what he had to do to be saved. The man explained the plan of salvation to Harry and then both men got out of the car and knelt together in the gravel beside the car. For the first time in his life Harry prayed, saying, "Lord, be merciful to me a sinner." Harry had kept his appointment with God, and in that moment he accepted Yeshua, God's Son, to be his Messiah and Savior.

When Harry got up from his knees, his passenger told him he would not be going any further. The two men said good-bye to one another, and Dr. Marko started down the highway toward his home. He had driven only a short distance before he realized that he'd forgotten to get the name and address of his passenger. He turned his car around and went back to the spot where they had exchanged their good-byes, but the man was not there. He drove up and down the highway but the man was not to be found again. He never met the hitch-hiker again. He later wrote a pamphlet entitled "How a Hitch-Hiker Led a Jewish Doctor to Christ." Harry knew he'd meet the hitch-hiker again in heaven.

After accepting Yeshua, Harry continued to practice medicine, but on Sundays he traveled the length and breadth of Texas, sharing his testimony and preaching the Gospel in churches throughout the state. His testimony and his presentation of the Gospel message moved the hearts of many people, and soon Dr. Harry Marko was in great demand as a speaker and evangelist. His medical practice began to dwindle as he found greater and greater satisfaction in preaching God's Word, seeing people healed spiritually from the disease of sin.

By the time Joseph Cohn and Dr. Harry Marko met, Harry was ready to serve his Lord on a full-time basis. There was no hesitation when Joseph asked him to join the staff of the Mission; he agreed immediately. He became a member of the Mission's staff in the Fall of 1942, and faithfully served his Lord on the Mission's staff until his death on October 24, 1960. Like the hitch-hiker who had introduced him to Yeshua, Dr. Marko became an itinerant evangelist, traveling the highways and byways of the state of Texas, sharing the Gospel with everyone he met. Joseph wrote:

In Texas, our Brother Marko,...continues an aggressive program of testimony and exhortation throughout that State. It is his custom, when he visits a town, to call on the Jewish merchants, and to invite each one to the preaching services at the church. Often the pastor of the church goes with him, and a liaison friendship develops between pastor and Jew, which continues long after Dr. Marko has left the city. Thus we are doing in Texas a unique piece of work which we call 'Itinerant Evangelism.' In this way Jews are being reached who would never in the ordinary course of Gospel effort hear the Message of Salvation.[12]

The October 1947 issue of *The Chosen People* magazine includes a picture of Dr. Harry Marko with a group of Jewish believers and a portion of the letter he sent with the picture. He wrote:

> Enclosed find a group picture in which there are twenty-one Christian Jews, all baptized believers, each and every one of them belonging to a New Testament Gospel Church, representing six families of Austin and San Antonio. These are the visible results of the years that I have been connected with our Mission. Again I want to say that they are the results of much prayer, patient witnessing, and much travel to and fro.[13]

Because of the remarkable ministry of Dr. Harry Marko, the Mission eventually opened branch ministries in the cities of Dallas, Austin, San Antonio, and Houston. Among the many faithful servants of the Lord who continued the Mission's witness to both Jews and Gentiles in Texas was Dr. Harry Marko's grand-daughter, Celia Law.

Jack Schwartz—His Story

During 1943, less than a year after meeting Harry Marko, Joseph met another Jewish believer in the South—Mr. Jack Schwartz, a Southern Baptist. Through his conversations with Jack, Joseph realized that Southern Baptist people are "missionary minded," and will support what they believe in. It became clear to him that the Mission needed to expand its base of operations to include the Southern Baptist Convention. He recognized the strategic importance of having a trained Southern Baptist missionary on staff to accomplish this, and he told the Board:

> ...I made the acquaintance of a Jewish Christian by the name of Jack Schwartz. His wife is a Gentile, and they are a fine couple. He was in the insurance business at the time of his conversion. He gave up that business and entered the Baptist Seminary in Fort Worth. He had enough money to get started but when his money gave out he turned to Jacob Gartenhaus for help. Mr. Gartenhaus is a Jewish missionary for the Southern Baptists, but he was not in favor that money should be spent for the educating of converts to become missionaries. At the time I met him he was attending school in the day time and working in a defense plant at night, but this is a severe strain on his strength. It would require $125.00 a month to take care of this couple at the Seminary, where it is required that both man and wife shall study. This means that his wife is unable to work. I am anxious that they shall graduate from a Southern School because this will give them a standing with the Southern Baptists. During the summer months I want to bring this couple up north so that they may attend Moody School, where they will get dispensational teaching. Also, they will be able to attend the Conference at Winona Lake. Then in the fall they may return to the south and will eventually be first class workers, and because of their diplomas from a southern Baptist Seminary they will be recognized.[14]

Alexander Marks—His Story

In the Fall of 1943, another Jewish believer with unique abilities was brought to the attention of Joseph Cohn. Mr. Herbert Singer was directing the Mission's refugee work in Brooklyn. He needed help in the "Street Ministry,"—the forte of Mr. Alexander Marks.

Alexander was born into an orthodox Jewish home in the Jewish section of London. His mother's father had been a rabbi at Lodz, Poland. As the daughter of a rabbi, his mother was a strict religious Jew who attended synagogue faithfully and who was able to recite perfectly all of the Hebrew prayers she had committed to memory. She was also adamant in her instruction to her children that they should not mix with the Christians. Having witnessed much of the suffering of the Jewish people in Poland, she believed that anyone who was not Jewish was a Christian—therefore, the persecutors of the Jewish people were all Christians.

Like his Jewish friends, Alex went to the Talmud Torah school where he studied for his Bar Mitzvah. He was very interested in the Old Testament, although he found it hard to understand.

One day he met a Christian woman who had been a missionary to the Jews in Romania. She told him that his Jewish Bible was full of teachings about the Jewish Messiah, the Lord Yeshua, and she pointed out specific verses. As she spoke, Alex was surprised that a Gentile woman knew so much about his Scriptures. Before they parted ways, the woman gave him the copy of the New Testament that she had been reading from.[15]

Alex was intrigued by the things the woman had shared with him; he was eager to read more, but he knew his Orthodox parents would never approve of him reading the little New Testament so he smuggled it into the house and quickly hid it away. His only opportunity to read the wonderful words of the Messiah was in the bathroom; he would sneak the book under his shirt. He soon became convinced that Yeshua was the Messiah, and he quietly prayed to receive Him as Savior and Lord.

Each day the desire to tell someone about his new belief grew more intense, but Alex knew he could not tell his parents. His dilemma had not resolved itself when he made a trip to Poland to visit his grandfather—the rabbi. After his arrival in Poland, Alex could hold his secret no longer and he confessed to his aged grandfather that he believed that Yeshua was the Messiah of Israel. He expected his grandfather to give him a stern lecture on why Yeshua was not the Messiah, or to berate him for being a traitor to his people. Instead, his grandfather shared that he had come to believe in Yeshua over forty years earlier. With a note of sadness in his voice, the old rabbi shared the fact that he had not told anyone of his belief for fear of being thrown out the synagogue, and he encouraged Alex to share the truth of the Gospel boldly with the Jewish people.

Alex took his grandfather's admonition to heart and he began to openly testify for his Lord. He often proclaimed the Gospel of Yeshua from the soap-boxes in Hyde Park, London—a message that prompted zealous young Jews who had no use for him, or for his message, to pull him off the soap-box and beat him. But the next day, beaten and bruised, Alex would return to preach about Yeshua.

The Jew who was preaching from the soap-boxes soon came to the attention of the Church of Scotland, and under their auspices Alex was discipled, baptized, and given the opportunity to attend London Bible College. Following his graduation from London Bible College, Alex was ordained as a minister of the Church of Scotland and he began a ministry among the Jewish people in London's East End.

When World II broke out, Alex immigrated to Canada. There, he continued doing missionary work among the Jewish people—mainly immigrant Jews who, like himself, had fled the terrors and persecution of war-torn Europe.

Alex's love for the Lord, his zeal for witnessing to the Jewish people, and his experience in confrontational evangelism made him the perfect candidate for the Street Ministry in New York, and Joseph Cohn did not waste time in offering him a position on the Mission's staff—nor did Alex deliberate long before accepting Joseph's proposal.

By November 1944 the first of many reports about Alex's ministry appeared on the pages of *The Chosen People* magazine. The first report told of a street meeting he had organized on the corner of Nostrand Avenue and Eastern Parkway—right in the heart of the Jewish center in Brooklyn. With him was Dr. Solomon Birnbaum, who had joined the staff of the Mission in the Fall of 1939 after serving for nearly fifteen years as the director of the Jewish Mission Department of the Moody Bible Institute in Chicago. In the report Alex stated:

The attendance at these street meetings grew increasingly. Sometimes more than 300 Jews stood and listened to the Gospel. One week a number of Jewish young men came with the purpose of asking questions. When the older Jews saw how interested the young people were in the meeting, they got angry, and one of them tried to break up the meeting; but another Jew stepped forward and said, 'I am not a missionary; you all know me. I am the president of the Jewish synagogue. More than twenty years ago a Jewish missionary came to Brownsville to speak in the street. Our Jews threw things at him; that missionary was the late Dr. Leopold Cohn. We are more civilized now and we should allow every man to say what he wishes.'[16]

In December of 1945, Joseph Cohn wrote an article about Alexander Marks entitled "A Wandering Witness." It was the story of Alex's nine-month journey through Virginia and North Carolina, witnessing and distributing literature to every Jewish person he could find—including the rabbis.[17] But not long after his trip South, Alex wrote to Joseph and told him of problems he was experiencing with his eyes. The doctors informed Alex that an infection which had started in one eye due to a detached retina, had spread to both eyes. Three serious operations were performed on his eyes in the hope that his eyesight could be restored, but to no avail. Alexander Marks—the Street-Preacher, the Wandering Jewish Evangelist, the out-going personal worker—was totally blind!

The loss of his eyesight was not the path he would have chosen for himself, but by God's grace, the indomitable Alexander Marks determined to turn his personal tragedy into a triumph for the Lord he served.

Joseph Cohn gave this report to the Board after learning of Alex's blindness:

...He has taken this with a great deal of grace, and has begun with much courage his readjustment to a completely new life. He is studying touch typing and Braille. He plans to return to New York October 29, [1946] and will take over the work of the Sunday afternoon meetings, etc., for a while, and later may do some evangelistic work in the field. Mr. Linton expressed the opinion of the Board by saying that he felt that everything possible should be done to help this brother in his adjustment to a new way of living.[18]

Neither Alexander nor Joseph saw Alex's blindness as a handicap; it was a readjustment of lifestyle. Joseph recognized Alex's determination to continue his ministry and he supported him by assigning areas of ministry that showed his confidence in Alex—such as asking him to preach and teach at the many services that were held at the Headquarters building (then located at 236 West 72nd Street, New York), and placing him in charge of the Mission's Reading Room and window display at the Headquarters building. The latter was a strange assignment for a blind man, but Cohn knew that with the Lord's help, Alex would be able to exercise the special "spiritual sight" that God had given him.

Joseph's confidence in Alex and his abilities were evident at the April 1947 Executive Committee meeting when he announced that, in making plans for his first trip to Europe after World War II, he had taken steps to place Alexander Marks in charge of the missionary staff; all missionaries were to report to him during Joseph's absence. He also reported on a three-month deputation and evangelistic trip through Canada on which Alex was planning to embark after Joseph's return from Europe; Daniel Fuchs was scheduled to travel with Alex as companion and fellow worker.[19]

The joy of serving his Lord as an itinerant evangelist filled Alex's heart as he and Daniel spoke in churches throughout Canada, and Alex became convinced that he *must* take steps to ensure that his ministry would not be limited to one location because of his blindness. He therefore took the training necessary to receive a guide dog. With his faithful dog by his side (through the years he had several dogs), he was once again free to travel. And travel he did! The pages of *The Chosen People* magazine are replete with stories of Dr. Marks adventures (he was awarded a Doctor of Divinity degree— a degree some members on staff teased him about, saying it meant "Divine Dynamite" degree). And, with tongue in cheek, he loved to state: "I have the only Christian guide dogs in the world. They fall asleep when I begin to preach, and they wake up the moment I say 'Amen'."

In overcoming his blindness, Alex developed a keen memory for voices, names, and for portions of Scripture. When he would return to churches where he had previously spoken, he constantly amazed people by his ability to recognize voices. He would then address individuals by name, rehearsing where he'd met them, and remembering something about their family. He spent hours listening to God's Word on tape, or being read to him by a companion, as he worked on new messages.

In 1988, Alexander Marks was stricken with cancer. But even painful chemotherapy treatment, and later thrice weekly dialysis, did not prevent him from taking every opportunity to witness and speak out for his Lord. Alex faithfully proclaimed the Gospel message until he entered the presence of his Messiah on November 14, 1990.

The Mission in Manhattan

During the early 1940's, while Joseph was busily expanding his team of Field Evangelists and the missionary staff, he was also concerned about the Mission's image in New York. The building in Brooklyn served a dual purpose; it served as a branch of the ministry, and it served as the Mission's Headquarters. There was also a branch in Coney Island. But Joseph suggested to the Board that the time had come for the Mission to have a building in Manhattan. He said:

> ...If we do not go forward we will go backward. We have a grip on both Jew and Christian all over the country. We have gone far beyond what we ever dreamed or thought possible a few years ago. People look to us for leadership. It seems fitting that we shall do something at this time when we are celebrating the JUBILEE year of the Mission's existence, as a sort of memorial to my father. The book 'Under Cover' exposes what is going on in this country by way of Nazi propaganda and a spirit of anti-Semitism is spreading over the land. In order for us to be in a position to cope successfully with the threatened deluge of anti-Jew propaganda in the post-war year period, it seems to me of the utmost importance that we shall buy a building on 5th Avenue, somewhere near Rockefeller Center; we have reasonable expectations that property in this section will not decrease. When the war is over we will be located at the world's cross roads. In such a location we would be able to reach the better class Jews. The ground floor windows could be used for display purposes, and we would have a high class Reading Room on that floor. On the second floor we could have one large room to serve as a Directors Room. the rest of the floor might be the Chapel, with some appropriate Hebrew name. This building will also be a center for a fellowship of all the Hebrew-Christians in the United States.[20]

Joseph went on to tell the Board that he had already been looking at a piece of property located at 588 Fifth Avenue. The property was assessed at $470,000, but Joseph thought the owners would accept an offer of $200,000 cash. He suggested:

> ...We can easily pay out of our current checking accounts $100,000 cash. Then we could borrow $100,000 from a bank, at 3%, and we would pay off the loan in four years. It must be remembered that once the building is used for Mission purposes we will not need to pay taxes. The money invested in such a building would not be lost, for it is expected that we could always sell the building at somewhere near the purchase price.[21]

The Board unanimously passed a motion empowering Joseph to set up a committee "...to guide him in the purchase of a suitable building on Manhattan Island, with the understanding that the approval of the Board shall be obtained before the purchase is consummated."[22]

Joseph and his committee made a closer inspection of the building at 588 Fifth Avenue, but to their disappointment they discovered it was not at all suitable for the Mission's purposes. Another property was located, but once again their plans for it were dashed when they discovered it was tied up as a part of an estate. In the meantime, the building at 588 Fifth Avenue sold for $555,000—nearly triple what Joseph had planned to offer.[23]

When a property located at 12 East 54th Street in Manhattan came on the market, Joseph made an immediate inquiry. Upon learning that he would be able to purchase it for a mere $70,000, he quickly made telephone calls to some of the members of the Board. In this way he obtained Board approval to put a deposit on the building. The sale was thus consummated, but in his haste to purchase the building Joseph (and the Board) had neglected to check the terms of an existing lease agreement. To their dismay they discovered that the building had a long-term lease agreement with a tenant who operated a restaurant—one that served liquor as well as food.

Joseph and the Board were faced with a dilemma, for in his usual zeal, Joseph had already made an announcement about the building to *The Chosen People* family in the October 1944 magazine.[24] If he tried to break the lease the tenets would most certainly take the Mission to court and the Directors did not want the Mission's constituents to know that the tenants of the new building were restaurant owners who served liquor.

In an effort to quell embarrassment to the Mission, and to avoid displeasing the supporters of the Mission, Joseph and the Board agreed that they should sell the property as quickly as possible. However, when no offers came forward, the Board voted to "...continue with the lease and deal with the tenants with the finest of Christian courtesy."[25] Joseph put an announcement in the December 1944 issue of *The Chosen People* magazine stating:

> *Further news about our Manhattan Building, ...Our Directors decided that we must act the part of Christian gentlemen when we deal with those out in the world, so that our actions and deeds shall not be evil spoken of. They felt that when we bought the building, we bought it subject to the lease then existing on the property. It would be manifestly unfair to the tenants who had entered into that lease in good faith with the previous owners for us to dispossess them summarily. So it was voted unanimously that we allow the lease to run through to its expiration date.[26]*

Supporters of the Mission had sent in over $80,000 to the Jubilee Fund—a fund which Joseph had begun in 1943 for the purchase of a building in Manhattan on the Mission's Jubilee year (the anniversary of its founding).[27] Joseph believed the gifts indicated that God's people shared his vision for the Mission to have a building in Manhattan. He also believed God can over-rule man's mistakes, so he continued to pray and to look for a suitable building. The Minutes of the January 27, 1945 meeting of the Board record how God answered his prayers:

> *Mr. Cohn told of a new building at 236 W. 72nd Street, Manhattan, which has been offered to us for sale. Both Mr. Birnbaum and Mr. Singer are 'utterly' enthusiastic with the possibilities for doing Jewish work from such a center. The building is located in a section of the city where a good many Jews live, many of them being refugees. It is easily accessible to those living at a distance, since the IRT subway is just a short distance away.[28]*

Potential buyers for the building were limited by the fact that the owner needed money and would only sell for cash. Through God's blessings the Mission's financial base was good. The Year End financial statement for the twelve months ending December 1944 showed the total receipts (income) for the Mission at $384,183.61, with total disbursements at $221,830.32. The Mission also held $885,357.14 in assets, stocks, bonds, real estate, reserve funds, etc.[29]

The Board mandated that the property at 12 E. 54th Street, Manhattan should not be sold at less than $110,000.00, and that the purchase of the building at 236 W. 72nd Street, Manhattan should not exceed "...a price of $65,000, or within $2,000 of this price."[30] The result of the sale of one property and the purchase of the other would therefore provide the Mission with a profit of $45,000—money to be used for missionary work.

By the Spring of 1945 the building on 72nd Street had been purchased for the cash price of $65,000.00; the building at 54th Street was sold for $105,000.00.[31] The purchase of the building on 72nd Street, Manhattan, New York was more than just the purchase of a *building* to Joseph Cohn. He believed the move of the Mission's Headquarters office to Manhattan was vital to the overall scope of Jewish evangelism and Jewish missions. The Mission had become a world-wide organization. No longer was its sole focus to reach out to the immigrant Jews of Brooklyn; the ministry was reaching beyond the boroughs of Brooklyn to Jews who had shed their immigrant status and were moving "up" in society. Joseph was convinced that being in Manhattan would give the Mission the opportunity to have its finger on the pulse of America—on the pulse of the Jewish community. Not only that, having a building in Manhattan seemed a fitting memorial to his father, Rabbi Leopold Cohn, whose vision was to reach out to all Jews with the Gospel—the down-trodden as well as those who were socially and financially well-off. The building in Manhattan would honor Rabbi Cohn's vision; it would be called the Leopold Cohn Memorial Building.

THE MANHATTAN BUILDING DEDICATED

On Sunday, October 28, 1945 the Mission's building at 72nd Street in Manhattan was dedicated. The dedication celebration continued throughout the week. Joseph captured the excitement of the occasion in his Salutation in the December 1945 issue of *The Chosen People* magazine. He wrote:

> *The crowds just poured in all day, and the glory of God filled the house. By one of those unforeseen fortuitous providences of God, it so happened that New York City was celebrating Navy Day both on Saturday, October 27, and Sunday, October 28. The awe-inspiring array of battleships was anchored off our own 72d Street, just a few steps from our building, on the Hudson River, or North River, as the New York section of the Hudson is called. And so 72d Street became the funnel through which uncounted thousands and hundreds of thousands of people streamed down to the river front to Riverside Drive, to the West Side Highway, and to the Yacht Basin out on the docks. Right under our windows came the procession escorting President Truman on Saturday on his way to the Battleship Missouri. You may well imagine what a gala business all of this was and what a God-send it was to the Mission, because thousands have stopped at our windows and gazed with wonder and curiosity at our display. Thus we became known to large numbers of the Jews of New York City in a matter of a few days more intensely and extensively than might ordinarily be possible through a five-year normal operation of the Mission. Your Mission leaped, as it were, to the front, in just the twinkling of an eye. Who shall say that the honor and the thanksgiving for this miracle shall not be given to the Lord, the One who has guided our footsteps through these over fifty years of toil?*
>
> *Promptly at three o'clock the capacity audience arose in the Leopold Cohn Memorial Building, and the majestic cadences of that matchless Coronation Hymn sent their waves of joy and praise to the heavens above, and the hall itself echoed and re-echoed the feeling of triumph and jubilee that seemed to be in the hearts of everyone present. Dedication Week was on. A substantial part of the audience was made up of the very Jews who had been passing by the building these many days of preparation and now had made their way into the opening meeting to discover what it was all about. While the session was going on, in the back of the room at the entrance doors, there was a constant moving of traffic in and out, many standing up, many Jewish inquirers coming in, asking for Gospel literature, receiving it, standing up awhile, and then going out again. This kept on all afternoon, as well as into the evening....*
>
> *Outside of the building there was even more interest, if that were possible, than on the inside. Crowds were gathered, reading eagerly the varied contents of the attractively dressed show window, talking excitedly, gesticulating, and arguing, one with the other. Our Brother Harry Burgen, having come in from Philadelphia, was out there, delighted beyond words and eager for the battle. We suppose more Jews heard the Gospel yesterday here, both inside and outside, than we could have reached in a normal schedule of meetings for a whole year in any other of our world branches. Some of the conversations and remarks, revealing an abysmal ignorance on the part of the misinformed Jewish men and women, would make you laugh if we had the space to put them down in these pages.*
>
> *...we looked about the crowded hall and there saw the children and supporters of the Mission who came to us from many parts of the country.... Brother John Solomon came in from Pittsburgh; Mr. and Mrs. Mills from Ohio; our Brother Paul Miller from Indiana; Dr. Charles Feinberg from Texas; Brother Karl Goldberg from Canada; and so on. We could take a whole column just to list the beloved ones who are with us. To all it is the crowning day of our history. It is the assurance that we are on the threshold of the greatest era of Gospel preaching we have ever known. What a future God has in store for us if only we shall remain humble before and faithful to Him, and our beloved friends shall continue in prayer and in fellowship with us for the days ahead![32]*

True to his vision for Manhattan, Joseph Cohn turned the new Headquarters building—the Leopold Memorial Building—into a bee-hive of activity. During the Fall of 1945, he transferred Dr. Emil Gruen and his family from Des Moines, Iowa to New York. Emil was given the title of National Field Evangelist, and he was given an office in the Leopold Memorial Building.[33] In addition to the regular meetings held, Joseph also established a Jewish Missionary Institute at the Manhattan building. His vision was to see the institute grow into a recognized institution of specialized training. He wrote:

> *...we will begin humbly with a few classes each week, until these courses shall have gathered enough momentum to make an impress not only here in our own city of New York, but upon the whole country. Then gradually we shall*

develop an established curriculum, graded classes, semester work and regular academic accomplishments. We are beginning with such courses as 'The Messianic Stream of Revelation' from the Garden of Eden to Calvary; 'World Religions' in contrast with Christianity,... 'The personal life of the Jewish Missionary,' courses in 'Hebrew Christian Biographies,' courses in the Yiddish language, courses on doctrines...[34]

He also established meetings during the month of August which he called a Summer's End Conference. These were held at the Leopold Memorial Building in Manhattan, as well as in various key churches throughout the New York area. Emil Gruen was responsible for planning and setting up these Bible conferences. The highlight and finale to the Summer's End Conference were the meetings held at the Leopold Memorial Building. They gave the Mission's constituents from around the world an opportunity to meet the missionaries, to see the physical plant in Manhattan, and to become more closely attuned to the vast and progressive ministry of The American Board of Missions to the Jews (CPM). The Summer's End Conferences were very successful and the Mission's friends and supporters looked forward to the annual event.

ELEANOR BULLOCK—HER STORY

Joseph also hired several new workers during this period of time; among them was Miss Eleanor Bullock.

Eleanor was a Gentile Christian who had been raised by godly parents. The Lord placed a love for the Jewish people in her heart during her childhood. As a high school student, she took a summer job at a concession stand in a bus station that provided bus service to the Catskill mountains in New York. Hundreds of Jewish people passed though the station on their way to the Jewish resorts in Liberty and in Monticello, New York, and as Eleanor would wait on them, and talk with them, her love for the Jewish people increased and her desire to see them accept Yeshua as Messiah also increased.

After graduating from high school Eleanor enrolled in a commercial school, but after finishing the one year course she was unable to find work. God then led her to the Practical Bible Training School in New York. Her study of God's Word, combined with the events transpiring in the world during the early 1940's, increased her burden for the Jewish people—a burden she shared with her Messianic Theology professor. In the providence of God, as Eleanor neared graduation from Bible school, her Messianic Theology professor received a letter from Joseph Cohn asking if any of the women students at the school would be interested in working with the Mission's outreach to Jewish women. Miss Dorothy Rose was seriously ill, and it was imperative that another worker be found to replace her. Knowing of Eleanor's burden for the Jews, the professor told her of the letter from Joseph and, after praying about it, she contacted Joseph to let him know of her willingness to work for the Mission.

Eleanor joined the Mission's staff on June 15, 1945. Several months later, a report of her initial impressions of the work, about her part in the work of the Mission during the time the building in Manhattan was being readied for outreach, and of her joy in being a part of the Mission's staff appeared in *The Chosen People* magazine. She wrote:

June 15, 1945, was one of the happiest days in my life. It was on that red letter date that I came to join the band of workers at 27 Throop Avenue, Brooklyn. That first evening I attended the regular Gospel Service in Jewish, and although I did not understand the message, the presence of God was felt in a very remarkable way. I received a great blessing through the bond of fellowship with those of like precious faith. During the service, the words of John came to my mind, 'He came unto His own, and His own received him not. But as many as received Him, to them gave He power to become the sons of God, even to them that believe on His Name.' Yet there in my presence was a group of people, members of the race from which God chose to bring to us our Messiah, brothers in the flesh to our Lord, praising God and giving due honor to the Lord Jesus Christ. This great fact overwhelmed me and deepened my desire to take the Gospel to the many yet outside of Christ....

Under the prayerful guidance of my fellow-workers, I was privileged to work with the Mother's Groups in Brooklyn. This phase of the great work has, time and again, inspired me and brought to my heart joy in His service. As I learned to know each member of the class personally, I could see the sincerity in their desire to learn of the Messiah. The opportunities here are manifold and my heart is thrilled as I find myself anxiously looking forward to those meetings.

Many times I have marveled at the faithfulness of these people in regularly coming to the class in the very face of bitter persecution. The price which is required of them to pay for their faith in Jesus the Messiah is startling.

During August when our building at 72nd Street was being redecorated, it was my privilege to welcome some of the many inquirers as they stopped to ask questions concerning our work. We gave out many tracts and found wonderful opportunities to witness to the saving power of our Lord Jesus Christ. Some who came in only wanted to argue, while others were earnest in their desire to hear about the Messiah....

We are looking to the Lord for wisdom and guidance in this new field, knowing that God's Word will not return unto Him void, but that it will accomplish that which He shall please.[35]

Throughout her years of service with the Mission, God abundantly blessed Eleanor and used her in reaching many Jewish women and mothers for the Lord. For a number of years she was in charge of the various outreach classes that were established on Long Island. When the Headquarters was moved from Brooklyn to Manhattan in 1946, she began a Tuesday afternoon Women's Bible Class in the 72nd Street building—an outreach she faithfully continued until 1972. Like Miss Augusta Sussdorff and Miss Dorothy Rose, Eleanor Bullock was known and loved by the Jewish and Gentile women with whom she ministered.

As one of the Mission's most faithful, effective, and loyal missionaries, Eleanor Bullock served on staff for forty years—a Biblical generation—until her retirement on July 1, 1985. Over the years she saw changes in personnel, programs, and in methodology, as the Mission sought to adapt itself to the changing needs of the Jewish community. But she remained steadfast in her testimony to the Jewish people and she adapted to the new methods and to the new programs. In her retirement, like other workers of the Mission, Eleanor has continued an active witness for the Lord.

Paul Wilson—in Cuba and Buffalo

The new Headquarters building in Manhattan was not the only new branch of the Mission to open during 1945. In the Spring of 1945 a new branch was also opened in Havana, Cuba, where over 10,000 Jews had settled. This branch came about as a direct result of the radio broadcasts developed by Rev. Paul Miller and Joseph Cohn. Mr. Paul H. Wilson, who had spent nearly four years working at the Buffalo branch, was asked to serve as the Missionary in charge of the Cuba branch.

Paul Wilson was a graduate of the Lancaster School of the Bible in Lancaster, Pennsylvania. He was a member of Calvary Independent Church of Lancaster, where Frank G. Torry was pastor. With his home church supporting him, Paul was hired by the Mission in the summer of 1941, and was sent to assist in the Buffalo branch in October 1941. At that time, Joseph reported to the readers of *The Chosen People* magazine:

> ...His [Paul's] *labors in Buffalo will consist in house to house visitation work, following a careful survey of the Jewish population of that city, so that as far as possible every Jewish home will be visited in due course, and copies of The Shepherd of Israel left in each home, together with our Gospel tracts, and other Gospel literature. A part of this work will include the careful distribution of our newly accomplished American translation of the New Testament in the Yiddish language.*[36]

During his tenure in Cuba, Paul was responsible for arranging for a radio broadcast that was aired over a Havana station. In the United States the broadcast was known as "*The Chosen People* Broadcast." The programs were produced in Yiddish, Spanish, and in English, and were aired over "The Voice of Cuba" under the name, "The Message Of The Christian Jew." In a letter reporting the first visible results of his ministry in Cuba, Paul wrote:

> ...*I think I wrote to you some time ago about a young German Jewish refugee [Rolf] whose parents were killed by Hitler's madmen, and who suffered much through the London bombings. He escaped to England, and his sister got to Uruguay. We were enabled to show him some kindness when we met him here and after some instruction in the Scriptures he has confessed Christ as his Savior and Messiah.*[37]

A continuation of the story of Rolf was included in the April 1946 issue of *The Chosen People*. Paul wrote:

> ...*He is witnessing among his own people and distributing our literature among them, and he is getting his first taste of persecution. The gracious manner in which he replies to his critics has astonished me. A young Jewish medical student said to him: 'I believe that we must keep the Law to the best of our ability and keep ourselves clean to be saved.' Instantly Rolf replied: 'You are a medical student and know the aseptic requirements of an operating room. Now suppose I had on a white suit and looked very clean, would you permit me to come in off the street into the operating room? Of course not. I might look clean but I would carry into the operating room all kinds of disease-producing organisms. And so with God, a man might look clean to men, and feel clean to himself, but God sees the hidden sin in the heart, and will let nothing unclean into Heaven....'*
> *Because of his sufferings, and the loss of his parents, and the separation from his sister, and the unspeakable atrocities of the Nazi fiends, Rolf for four years constantly thought of taking his own life. But for some unexplained reason, he was unable to commit the terrible deed. Now he understands why. Today he came to the house for more New Testaments and copies of* The Shepherd of Israel *to distribute; he plans to go to the homes of some very religious Polish Jews who are longing to go to Palestine, but who say: 'We will not go before the Messiah comes.' He is taking*

with him the Yiddish New Testament *and* The Shepherd of Israel. *There will either be a rejoicing or a riot, for these Polish Jews here are very religious.*[38]

By October of 1950, Paul had completed five years of missionary work in Cuba. The radio ministry was reaching into many homes, and he was sending out Gospel literature in Spanish, English, and Yiddish to many Jewish and Gentile listeners. He was also sending out copies of the New Testament to anyone who requested one, and he had begun a Bible class in conjunction with the radio broadcast. Paul told Cohn that he was distributing, on average, about 1,500 tracts a month. He wrote:

…This tract distribution does not mean that tracts are carelessly or promiscuously thrown away. Each tract or piece of literature is given personally and individually. Many are distributed in buses and street cars and are almost invariably read immediately. The work of visiting homes and business places has been most encouraging, not only in Havana, but in the cities and towns of the interior.[39]

Paul also gave this encouraging report of his work in Cuba:

About two years ago we made our first visit among the Jewish people of Cardenas in the province of Matanzas. We gave a Yiddish New Testament to each family. We followed up this visit by personal correspondence and the sending of The Shepherd of Israel each month together with other suitable literature in Spanish. We again visited the city in September with the promise to return in December for a meeting in the home of the Baptist pastor of Cardenas, who is much interested and cooperates fully in trying to win the Jews of his city. On December 4th we returned, and that night in the pastor's home a fine Jewish gentlemen about sixty years of age confessed faith in Jesus as Lord and Messiah. He had been reading his Yiddish New Testament, and when we showed him that night from the Yiddish and Hebrew Old testament Scriptures what Moses and prophets had said concerning the Messiah, he believed….
We also had a most happy meeting with seven Jewish men in the old Colonial city of Trinidad, on the Caribbean coast.[40]

Paul Wilson remained in Cuba until February 1952 when, because of tensions within that country, as well as the Mission's need for workers elsewhere, he was asked to replace the Mission's worker in Montreal, Canada.[41] (See Chapter Fourteen.)

As was discussed in the preceding chapter of this history, the Buffalo branch was beset with problems and personality conflicts from the earliest days of the Mission's involvement there. Staff changes were one of the ways in which Joseph sought to bring about harmony among the workers, and to maintain control of that branch of the Mission. After transferring Paul Wilson to Cuba, two workers were sent to the Buffalo branch—Mrs. M. Helen Johnson, and Mr. Joseph Serafin.

Helen Johnson—In Buffalo

Joseph hired Helen Johnson for the Buffalo ministry because of her ability to work with women and children. (Mrs. Johnson was the former Miss Helen Biber, spoken of earlier in reference to the Dedication Service of the Mission's enlarged Headquarters facility in Brooklyn, New York. Miss Biber, who joined the Mission's staff in 1931, worked with women and children at the Brooklyn branch until she married the Rev. Mr. George Johnson.) After her marriage, Helen resigned from the Mission and she and her husband moved to Baltimore where they labored for the Lord among the Catholics, but when Mr. Johnson died Helen wrote to Joseph.

In a praise report in *The Chosen People* magazine, Joseph shared how God had answered prayer with regard to the need for a worker in the Buffalo branch. He stated:

We found ourselves under the burden of a lady worker being needed in Buffalo to undertake a work for women and children. While these anxieties were burdening our souls, came a letter from Mrs. M. Helen Johnson, …Mrs. Johnson wrote to us that she was yearning to come back to her first love, and if we have any place in our Mission staff where she could serve God, in behalf of Israel. A place we certainly did have. Was this not the Lord's own answer to our need? No sooner was she settled in Buffalo than we received grateful letters both from herself and from several friends, telling how clear was the evidence that God had sent her there. Mrs. Johnson keeps writing us how happy she is in the work and how the Lord is giving her entrance into the homes of Jews who had never before been brought into contact with the Gospel.[42]

Joseph Serafin—in Manhattan and Buffalo

Mr. Joseph Serafin was transferred from the Manhattan branch to the Buffalo branch, to serve as the Missionary in charge. Of Serafin's labors in Buffalo, Joseph wrote:

> The work in Buffalo is enjoying an era of God's blessing such as we have not had since we first started our work there. Our good brother, Joseph Serafin, is doing heroic service, and has earned the love of the pastors in that city. In season and out of season, this brother stands upon the highways and the byways of Buffalo, and with a glow of love and kindness, approaches Jew after Jew with a Gospel tract, a copy of The Shepherd Of Israel, and a cheerful 'God Bless you.' So cordial is Mr. Serafin in his approach to these Jews that they are overwhelmed by his very appearance before them. The secret behind this, we have discovered, is that hours are spent by Brother Serafin upon his knees, pleading with God that He shall plant in his heart a glowing love for the children of Abraham.[43]

Joseph Serafin was born in Rumania in 1884. Like many other Jews of that time, his family immigrated to America. Evidently Joseph did not enjoy school and did not continue his education. Instead, he left school to take a job as a bartender.

Because of his background and treatment by Christians, Joseph had a hatred of Christianity, and of anyone who had anything to do with the name of Jesus. But, miraculously, God touched his life and he came to know Jesus as Messiah and Lord. Not long after receiving Jesus, Joseph lost his job. As he walked the streets, wondering what he should do, the Lord directed him to the Mission where he met Joseph Cohn. Although one man was highly educated and the other only minimally educated, the two men became immediate friends. Joseph Cohn recognized that God had placed within Joseph Serafin a servant's heart.

After being hired to work for the Mission, Joseph Serafin served in any capacity he was asked to handle—from sweeping the floors, to running the elevator, to preaching on street corners, or to visiting the sick. Those who had known him as the rowdy barkeeper now heard him preaching on the streets and they mocked him, calling him "Holy Joe"—a name he wore with pride!

Any and every task he was asked to do, Serafin did with love and humility. Perhaps it was for this reason that Joseph Cohn sent him to serve as Mission in charge of the Buffalo branch. But he only remained in that capacity for a couple of years before he was transferred back to New York to continue his work in the Manhattan and the Brooklyn branches. He continued to faithfully serve his Lord with the Mission's branches in New York until his death on November 16, 1954.[44]

Ruth Wardell—Her Story

In 1946, a young Gentile Christian girl in Ontario, Canada was asking God to provide money so she could attend a Child Evangelism Fellowship training school in Dallas, Texas; her name was Ruth Wardell. Ruth's father was a pastor and through his influence, at the age of nine, she had opened her heart to receive Yeshua. When she was twelve, she surrendered her life to the Lord for full-time missionary service.

Ruth had a love for children, and after her graduation from London Bible College in Ontario, she wanted very much to work with Child Evangelism Fellowship, but she needed $500.00 to attend their training school in Dallas, Texas. She sought the Lord in prayer, asking that He would provided the needed money if it was His will for her to go to Texas.

Several months earlier Isabel Smith, one of the Mission's workers in the Hamilton, Ontario branch had started praying that God would send her five students who would become missionaries to the Jews. Isabel was also an alumna of London Bible College. When she heard of Ruth's desire to attend the training school for Child Evangelism Fellowship, and of her need for funds, Isabel wrote to Ruth. She told Ruth she would supply the needed funds, and she invited Ruth to the Hamilton office so they could meet one another. During their visit, Isabel shared her burden for the Jewish people. She told Ruth how she had been praying that God would send her students who felt called to the Jewish people; she shared, too, how she had been saving from her meager salary to help sponsor those students in their preparation to enter the field of Jewish missions. As Ruth listened to Isabel talk, she was very impressed with this godly woman and with her sacrificial spirit and deep desire to bring the Gospel to the Jews. At the conclusion of their visit Ruth thanked Isabel for her willingness to help her, even though she did not feel called to work in the field of Jewish evangelism. Ruth went on to Texas, but her visit with Isabel left an indelible impression—one that ultimately changed the direction of her missionary calling. She later wrote:

> One night as I read in Matthew 10:5, 'Go not into the way of the Gentiles…but go rather to the lost sheep of the house of Israel,' God showed me my future work was to be among His own chosen people, the Jews. The thought was new

and strange at the time, but since then I have realized the privilege God has given me and my heart rejoices that He has called me into this service.[45]

When Ruth called Isabel to tell her how God had spoken to her heart, Isabel was delighted! She confided that she had known all along that Ruth was to be one of the five missionaries she was asking God to supply.

Soon thereafter Ruth was on a bus bound for New York. The agreement was that she would serve on the staff of the Mission for a three-month trial period. Ruth wrote:

> ...*it has been my joy for the three months of October, November, and December [c. 1946] to observe the work of the Mission in the three branches of Manhattan, Brooklyn, and Coney Island. As I have studied all phases and methods of the work my heart greatly rejoiced to see the many classes of Jewish children, young people, and adults who meet from week to week to hear of the Lord Jesus Christ, their promised Messiah. It has also been a great blessing to me to hear their testimonies, and my heart has burned within me as I have listened to the stories of the sufferings of these dear people for their faith in the Lord Jesus Christ. I now look forward eagerly to the future work, and my prayer to God for Israel is that they, too, might be saved.*[46]

Ruth's three-month trial period with the Mission turned into nearly forty-two years of faithful missionary work with the Jewish people.

Joseph Cohn recognized Ruth's abilities with children almost immediately. In 1947, just one year after joining the Mission's staff, he placed her in charge of the Mission's summer camp at Stony Brook, New York.[47] From that time Ruth remained involved in the Mission's summer camp program in one way or another. Her outgoing spirit and her enthusiasm for life, and for the Lord, was something neither children, young people, nor adults could resist. They all loved being with Ruth!

It was obvious that Ruth loved the work God had called her to. Having grown up in the environment of love and security, her heart went out to the young people who attended the Mission's meetings. Jewish young people who came to faith in Yeshua faced tremendous pressures from their family members and from their friends. They greatly needed individuals who could counsel them as they faced subtle persecution, or open hostility, and Ruth always made herself available to them. One such teenager was a boy whose name was Arnold Fruchtenbaum. His story will be shared in greater depth at a later point in the narration of the history of the Mission.

Over the span of her career with the Mission, Ruth Wardell helped in the establishment of most of the Mission's branches on Long Island, and she worked with the children's and youth outreach programs at most of the branches in New York. The last years of her service with the Mission were devoted to the Mission's outreach in Southern California—the North Hollywood and San Fernando branches. She retired from active full-time service with the Mission on September 1, 1987, but like other workers who have retired from the Mission, she continues to actively witness for the Lord and she continues to serve as confidante, counselor, and consultant to younger workers on staff.

RECRUITING NEW BOARD MEMBERS

Throughout his tenure as General Secretary of the Mission, Joseph Cohn continually wrestled with the problem of appointing new Board members. Over the years, some of his Board members had resigned, others died. Finding replacement members was always a problem for him. He wanted men he could trust to carry out his vision for the work. However, some of his new Board members did not always share his vision.

When Mr. Robert Fleming and Dr. J. Palmer Muntz resigned from the Board in 1944, Joseph was left with two vacancies. Dr. Otis Fuller (pastor, Wealthy St. Baptist Church, Grand Rapids, MI) advised Joseph to fill the vacancies with Christian leaders, but Joseph did not heed his advice. Joseph, like his father, felt that the interests of the Mission could better be served by Christian laymen; he believed Christian businessmen were more innovative and creative in their thinking. His experience with, and relationship to, the one pastor he had placed on the Board (Muntz) had, in his mind, created nothing but problems. It had certainly not increased his desire to add Christian leaders to the Board. In fact, the pastor served on the Board less than two years, while many of the businessmen had served with him for many years.

One of the Board vacancies was filled in 1945, when Mr. Linton, the President of the Board (Chairman), nominated Mr. Lewis Fisher to serve on the Board. His nomination was approved.[48]

Two years later, in 1947, Mr. Frank Davis presented the name of Harold B. Pretlove for membership to the Board of Directors. The nomination was unanimously approved, with a note in the Minutes which states, "...[Mr. Pretlove] avowed that he ascribed to the doctrinal statement and to the premillennial belief 100%."[49]

For the next few years the Board of Directors consisted of the following members: Gaylord A. Barcley, Joseph Hoffman Cohn, Frank E. Davis, H.E.O. Dembke, Lewis H.Fisher, Paul H. Graef, William Jones, Irwin H. Linton, Miss Elsie L. Olsen, Harold B. Pretlove. Members who died were not replaced and, in keeping with Joseph's unwritten Board selection policy, nominees for the Board were businessmen. Joseph Cohn wanted a Board of Managers, not a Board of influential religious people. He wanted sole control over setting the policy and the vision for the Mission. This is clear from two projects he submitted to the Board. The Board made it clear that they were not in favor of either project, but Joseph persisted in moving ahead in spite of their objections.

THE TRIBULATION FUND

One of the projects was the establishment of a "Tribulation Fund." Joseph believed strongly in the imminent return of the Lord. He further believed in a Pre-Tribulation Rapture (that the Church will be removed [taken out of the world] before the seven year Tribulation begins). He was convinced that many Jews would be saved during the Tribulation Period, and that one of those Jews would step forward to take control of the assets of the Mission and use those assets for Jewish evangelism. Believing this, he wanted the necessary funds set aside. The Minutes of the Board's April, 1945 meeting include their discussion regarding Joseph's "Tribulation Fund":

> Mr. Cohn told of an idea which has come to him, 'It is like this, you may remember some years ago we made a sensation in The Chosen People. We proposed that our Mission shall now appoint nine able Jews in New York City who would carry on the Mission after the Tribulation [Rapture]. We got an avalanche of letters, but since a few of them were unfavorable we did nothing further about it. Over and over come inquiries from our friends as to what happened to the plan. The other day a lady in Oregon sent us $1,000 which she has specified to start a fund called 'Tribulation Days Missionary Fund.'...I tried to persuade her not to specify the money this way but to allow us to use it partly for the new building and partly for the radio work, but she felt that the Lord has definitely laid it on her heart to do this. I proposed to Mr. Davis that he prepare a contract with the National City Bank or with another bank, in which they will agree to take over the Mission in the event of the Rapture. We will try to get the bank to agree that in case we are taken up they will step in and take over our assets and they will appoint any nine men who at that time will agree to a creedal statement that we will prepare now, and these nine men will carry on the Mission in the Tribulation days.[50]

The Board was far from unanimous as they wrestled with Joseph's idea. The Minutes state:

> Mr Graef felt that perhaps this is a much more important matter than we can think of at the present time.
> Mr. Fisher said, 'What Mr. Cohn is asking is if there is any objection to his putting a statement in The Chosen People asking our friends what is their reaction to the establishing of such a Tribulation Days Missionary Fund.'
> Mr. Dembke expressed his opposition to the whole plan as he felt that we should leave the future of the Mission in the Lord's hand.
> Mr. Graef said, 'We have received $1,000 from this dear child of God who sent it in all good faith, and we must in all integrity act on that. I do not think that Brother Jo [Cohn] should act on that alone, as regards committing the Mission to any course of action'.[51]

The Minutes show that no conclusion was reached on the matter. But Joseph Cohn had reached a decision. He went ahead with his plan! The Financial Statement for 1945 shows a new item under income received: "Tribulation Day Missionary Fund —— $3,532.45."[52]

Joseph was very eager to have the Board approve his idea of a Tribulation Fund because he had written an article about the "Tribulation Days Missionary Fund" for the April 1945 issue of The Chosen People. The May issue of magazine carried this response from one of the Mission's supporters:

> I have just read your article with reference to 'Our corporate persistence and existence beyond the actual event of the Rapture.' I have never heard of or read anything so startling, so awakening and so timely as that article. It has aroused my own heart and mind to think that you have planned or rather are bringing forth such a proposition for nine men to carry on if you are caught up with the Rapture. What is our Christian church doing and what plans have we formulated with reference to the Rapture? You are certainly giving us a good example and I hope and pray that your objective will cause a stir among us and be crystallized to such an extent that the Christian Church, meaning all Christendom that believes in the Rapture, will prepare for what follows. Naturally, according to the Word, the Jews will be the Evangelists during the tribulation; but could we not make some definite plans that also may be realized during the tribulation?[53]

Always moving ahead, Joseph then put an announcement of the new "Tribulation Days Missionary Fund" in the October 1945 issue of *The Chosen People* magazine. He evidently received a great deal of mail following that announcement, for in the November issue of the magazine he wrote:

> The response to our October announcement that we are establishing a new fund to be called the Tribulation Days Missionary Fund, was electric. We felt unquestionably sure, as He had given us a conviction in these matters, that we were touching something which was peculiarly and desperately needed by way of a ministry to thousands of those who keep closest in step with the Lord's revealed will for these latter days. The evidence accumulates that we really are in God's will. One of the largest banks in America is now considering the contract we referred to in October, and will give us a decision within a few weeks. If the decision is favorable, we will print forms of the contract so that friends may have copies for their study and use. Naturally there are many unsolved difficulties inevitably existent in so unusual a problem as this—the arranging for the testimony to Israel to continue through the Tribulation days, after the Church has been taken out. Such a problem, so far as we know, has never before been grappled with by any human agency on this earth.
>
> Therefore, as we boldly take up the questions involved, we know our friends will be patient with us and make allowances for initial mistakes.... We must ask our friends not to divert their regular giving into the Tribulation Days Missionary Fund, because that would present a serious handicap to us in carrying on our ever-increasing, world-wide testimony.[54]

It may well be that Joseph lived to see the day he wished he'd not gone ahead of his Board's consultation and advice. His "Tribulation Days Missionary Fund" became a great source of controversy for many years; his critics saw the fund as one of his "gimmicks" to build up reserve funds for the Mission.

The American Fellowship of Christian Jews

Joseph also felt there was a great need for an organization that would bring Jewish evangelism missions and agencies together for fellowship and interaction; his Board did not agree that such a need existed. Once again, Joseph ignored his Board and acted on his own instincts, obligating the Board to finance the organization. The January 1945 Minutes state:

> Mr. Cohn reported the organizing of a new Society to be called American Fellowship of Christian Jews, in which he and a number of the other Mission workers have had a dominant part. The newly formed Fellowship is to be sponsored and supported by the American Board [Chosen People Ministries], its aims being to develop and encourage the Jewish Christians in all parts of the country into a closer fellowship with each other, and to encourage the younger generation to consider seriously the call of God for service as Missionaries to the Jews. Mr. Barcley raised the question as to why the necessity for a separate corporation to do that which we already were undertaking to do and doing quite successfully. After some discussion it was concluded that we do not recognize the Fellowship as a separate organization, that we not supply funds to it through a separate Treasury, but that we consider it as one of the Branches of our work, and that we advance at our discretion any funds needed for the carrying out of its objectives directly from the Mission Treasury, and to the individuals to be benefitted by the paying out of such funds.[55]

Rebuilding the Ministry in Europe

With the war in Europe over, and the rebuilding of cities and of lives begun, Joseph Cohn was anxious to return to the countries in which the Mission had established branch ministries. He was eager to assess the damage, and to begin the work of re-establishing the Mission's extensive foreign ministry. When he told the Board of his desire to return to Europe, they were enthusiastic. Funds had been kept in reserve so the ministry could be resumed when the war was over. There was one stipulation, however, before they would grant Joseph permission to go. That stipulation was that he was to delegate authority to qualified workers, and to outline a plan of strategy for the Mission organization in his absence.

If Joseph Cohn had a glaring weakness, it was his inability and unwillingness to train people to run the ministry in his absence. His was a "one man show" style of leadership. It had been his unwillingness to delegate authority to competent people that had led to problems with workers like Machlin, Centz, and other Jewish believers who had joined the Mission's staff, but who later left. Joseph Cohn's style of leadership left little room for advancement or for growth within the organization.

In compliance with the Board's stipulation, Joseph set about to delegate authority to certain members of the Mission's staff so that the many facets of the ministry would continue to function while he was in Europe. He reported to the Executive Committee:

...steps were taken and completed which responsible head to whom all the workers shall give account both at the staff meetings and throughout the week. All workers were very happy in this arrangement, and showed every eagerness to cooperate with Mr. Marks and look to him for leadership.

In the office our key workers are Miss Pithman [Mrs. Christian], Miss Chesley [Dorothy], Mrs. Cele Pauli, Miss Morgan. With these we have made arrangements so that the mail will be handled in order, one provision being that there shall always be two girls to open the mail and to pass it on to the bookkeepers upstairs. Miss Chesley is to have charge on the second floor of routine matters, but is to refer to Miss Pithman either in person or by telephone any unusual circumstances. Miss Pithman in turn is to make decisions as she feels she is able to from past experience in similar cases, and if she is not able to make the decision, she will consult with Mr. Graef [Treasurer of Board]. In the last analysis if there are still any items that cannot be handled, the office will have at all times a daily schedule of where they can reach us by cable either in Europe or in Palestine or aboard the ship.

We have arranged for the summer camp at Stony Brook, Miss Ruth Wardell being in charge with Miss Bonnie Hayes as assistant. They will operate from June 30 to July 25, there are to be three sets of children to go out, both boys and girls. Also excursions have been arranged up the river for early June for our Refugee group, and our adult clubs in Brooklyn, the arrangements having been made early so that Mr. Marks can participate just prior to his leaving for a three months deputation and evangelistic trip through Canada. Mr. Marks is having with him Daniel Fuchs as companion and fellow worker.

Vacations are all set for the office and missionary staff.

Mr. Gruen will make a deputation trip throughout the middle west, Mr. Zimmerman up the west coast, Mr. Davidson in New England and the other workers will be in their respective territories.

The programs are already in the hands of the printer for the various summer conferences, Asbury Park, Avon, Atlantic City, Ocean City, Indianapolis and the Summer's End Conference in New York.[56]

Joseph's concerns for rebuilding the ministry in Europe, the burden of the oversight of his growing staff, and many years of total devotion to the ministry were beginning to take their toll. He expressed his weariness in his February 1946 editorial, saying:

The burdens are heavy; sometimes when the day is finished we feel an ache and a sense of weariness, and look up to Him for the needed strength and wisdom to carry on even for another day. I think we need someone such as Moses had in his father-in-law, Jethro, who not only gave good advice, but actually helped Moses organize and delegate the work to stronger shoulders....

So you see it is our next task to try to delegate some of our duties, to find other shoulders able to carry them; and we do want you to be praying definitely that somehow relief may come and your servant shall have a little respite from the burden and heat of the day.[57]

But as weary as he was, Joseph found it difficult to delegate more than just minor responsibilities. He did reorganize the office and, at the Board's insistence, he set up a system for accountability in his absence, but he remained firmly in control. He continued his writing, his radio ministry, and his Board activity—including his role on the Finance Committee. He was also preparing to resume his role of networking in Europe so that the Mission's branches in Europe could be restored. To *The Chosen People* family he wrote:

Your Mission is on the brink of the greatest era of all its fifty-two years of history. We want 1947 to break all records in every department of the work. I can say now definitely that I have booked passage for the first of April to go across the water. I hope to take with me several hundred thousand dollars, that I might in your behalf bring a bit of cheer to the desolate, food to the hungry, clothing to the naked, and above all, the Gospel message to the millions that now walk the fields and thoroughfares of Europe in a daze of desperation, turning here, turning there, asking each other, 'Was there ever sorrow like my sorrow?' All of this help is to be brought to these derelicts of a diabolic civilization, in the name and to the honor of the Lord Jesus Christ. I am already having estimates prepared over in Europe for printing the New Testament in Yiddish and in Hebrew, and that will be the first task attended to. I think the least number of these New Testaments for the first printing should be 200,000 copies. I mention all this so that you may know about these plans as far ahead as possible, that might be praying about the trip and praying for God's journeying blessings and care, praying for success on the undertakings in all the lands where I shall visit.... You will also need to pray that God will watch over this Headquarters Building and all of our work in America while your General Secretary is on the other side.[58]

In April 1947, just before leaving for his extended trip to Europe, Joseph reported to the Board that he had been able to purchase a building in Manhattan located at 241 W. 71st Street—property that directly abutted the rear of the Leopold Memorial Building at 236 W. 72nd Street. The property was purchased for $18,500.[59] Less than a year later, at the January 27, 1948 meeting of the Board, Joseph told the directors he had purchased a building located at 247-249 West 72nd Street for the sum of $80,000.[60] Always the businessman (as well as missionary/evangelist), Joseph wanted to buy all of the property surrounding the Leopold Memorial Building in Manhattan.

On April 19, 1947, Mr. Herman E.O. Dembke went home to be with the Lord. Mr. Dembke had been a member of the Board since October 1924—twenty-three years of faithful service. Miss Elsie Olsen also submitted her resignation due to a lengthy illness, but Joseph persuaded her to remain on the Board until he returned from his trip to Europe.

Supplying Yiddish New Testaments

Joseph's trip to Europe was scheduled for late Spring, 1947. The itinerary included visits in London, Holland, Belgium, Switzerland, Paris, Cairo, and Palestine. He was to be away for more than two months. As has been mentioned, part of his agenda included distribution of copies of the Yiddish New Testament—to individuals, as well as to workers and ministries that had long been without them. To accomplish this, he had to obtain the permission of the British and Foreign Bible Society of London. They had printed the original Leopold Cohn Yiddish New Testament Memorial Edition in 1901, and they held the copyright. But Joseph Cohn retained the original plates.

In order to avoid shipping fees, Joseph scoured Europe to find a printer who could "off-set" print 50,000 Yiddish New Testaments, but to his dismay he could not find such a printer. He was told it would be a year or two before printers in Europe would be able to handle such a job because most had experienced extensive damage to their equipment during the war and replacement parts were virtually nonexistent.

Joseph Cohn was a man of determination. He therefore dug out the old plates and began contacting printers in the New York area to see if any would print the New Testament in Yiddish. There were sixteen printers with the capability of printing materials in Yiddish, but not one was willing to print a Yiddish New Testament. Joseph was at his wits end when the Lord brought to his mind the printer who had been printing issues of *The Shepherd of Israel*. Because his printing operation was so small, Joseph had not thought to contact him. To his great delight, the printer told Joseph he was not only willing to do the job, he assured Joseph of his ability to print the quantity needed and guaranteed that he would have the materials shipped to Paris where they would await Joseph's arrival and subsequent distribution.

Joseph's agreement with the London Bible Society was that, in return for their permission to reprint the Yiddish New Testaments in the United States, he would supply them with 1,000 copies of the New Testaments for their distribution. In addition, he agreed to give them the "Yiddish plates" since theirs had been destroyed in the war. They would then reprint editions for the Mission's use after the repair of their equipment.[61]

Joseph worked out an agreement with the Mennonite brethren in Virginia to underwrite the expense for the printing of 20,000 Yiddish New Testaments. In return for their generosity, he promised to dedicate the frontispiece to them. In sharing this information with readers of *The Chosen People* magazine, he wrote:

> …Thus the Jews who will receive these books in Europe, in Palestine, will also know that certain true believers in the Lord Jesus Christ from among the Gentiles so loved the Jews that they gave of their money that these exiled Jews now may read about their own Messiah, the Lord Jesus Christ.[62]

The World Fellowship of Christian Jews

Detailed accounts of the conditions Joseph found in Europe and in the Middle East were given in the Mid-summer letter of 1947, and in the October 1947 issue of *The Chosen People* magazine. In those publications Joseph informed his readers of his activities during the two months he was overseas. He stated that he had been able to arrange for the distribution of the Scriptures to Jewish refugees who were waiting to immigrate to Palestine; he had worked on negotiations to get the Scriptures into the internment camps on Cyprus; he made arrangements for the Paris branch to become the Mission's headquarters in Central Europe for assisting the Jewish refugees; he explored the possibility of purchasing property in areas where it would benefit the ministry of the Mission; he'd set up programs to provide food and shelter for Jewish people in need. He mentioned how he was especially concerned about meeting the needs of the many orphaned children. Last, but not least, he had been able to organize a new society called The World Fellowship of Christian Jews. About that society he wrote:

> …Here in this country we have its original counterpart in The American Fellowship of Christian Jews, with headquarters here in our own building. We were able to organize this American Fellowship five or six years ago and it has had a

flourishing life ever since. But now we are organizing the same thing in Europe; Paris will be our headquarters for the European section of the Fellowship with our own Pastor Andre Frankl as President. This undertaking has in it far-reaching potentialities for blessing and help to all Jewish Christians who may need its protecting wings.[63]

Joseph's trip was so successful that the Board authorized him to take a second trip to further implement the plans and programs he had put into action. The second trip was scheduled for the Fall of 1947, and the Board authorized him to take any staff members he felt need of from the US staff or from the staff in Canada.[64]

ELIAS AND MARGARET DEN AREND—THEIR STORY

As has been stated, Joseph maintained an office in the Headquarters building in Manhattan but it was often empty as he carried on his heavy schedule of speaking and ministry oversight. In the providence of God, however, he had just returned from his second tour to Europe and was occupying his office on the day in December 1947 when a Jewish believer from Holland, Mr. Elias (Eddy) den Arend, entered the building.

Elias den Arend was born August 25, 1907 in a small village in Holland. His parents were orthodox Jews of Sephardic background. Elias was an avid student and an accomplished cellist, who received a doctorate in music in Leipzig, Germany and a teacher's certificate that qualified him to be an instructor of music.

In 1940, when the War broke out in Europe, Elias and his wife, Greta, and small son, Benjamin, were living in Antwerp, Belgium. Holland was mobilizing for the war, and as a native of Holland, Elias was called into immediate military duty. His destination was the town of Leiden. Because of his background in music and education, he was assigned as a leader of a branch of the army called "Recreation and Education." His task was to keep the soldiers busy in spiritual and cultural activity, and thus keep them off the streets at night and out of the taverns.

During his tour of duty in the Recreation and Education division, Elias came into contact with many chaplains and ministers from the Christian Soldiers' homes, etc. Their testimonies rolled off him like water rolls off a duck's back, but Greta listened with interest as the men discussed the Bible and talked about the need to receive Yeshua as personal Savior. One evening after listening to the men talk, Greta prayed and asked Yeshua to be her Messiah and Savior. She was afraid to tell her husband what she had done, but she told their young son, Benjamin, and one day he, too, prayed to receive Yeshua as his personal Savior.

As the horrors of the war progressed, Elias' heart became more and more calloused toward God. Like many, he was unable to reconcile the terrible suffering of his people with the existence of a loving God. Surely if God existed, He would put an end the war's atrocities!

On May 10, 1940 the war reached Holland. In the early morning hours as the soldiers prepared themselves for battle, one of the chaplains came into the barracks to offer prayer before the men left. Elias observed the reaction of the men, and saw how the chaplain's prayer and words brought encouragement, comfort, and strength to the men. The chaplain prayed for the Queen, for the government, for the Church; he even prayed for their enemies. Elias was very impressed by that prayer. He couldn't believe anyone would pray for his enemies.

The war in Holland didn't last long; Holland capitulated to the enemy within five days. But for Elias den Arend, the real battle had just begun. He could not bear to see his Jewish people suffer, so he decided to join the Dutch underground. Elias den Arend, the mild mannered teacher, the quiet musician, was about to become a "freedom fighter"—a member of the Dutch Underground—a part of the Resistance Movement. He did not know this would bring about a change in his heart as well. Of those awesome days, he later wrote:

On May 24, 1940, I received a secret order to contact a person in den Haag, and assist him in establishing Saboteurs in every Province of the Netherlands. My first duty was to gather persons who were reliable, and whom we could trust in those terrible days. Soon I gathered 24 persons, among whom were two girls who were willing to help the Underground. At that time, women saboteurs were not so readily suspected by the Germans; ...Our first acts of sabotage were to cut the wires of communications, so that the Germans could not get in touch with other. They retaliated by placing men on watch at night in those places where the sabotage had occurred; and they threatened to shoot their own men on watch if sabotage were repeated. We had to look for other means of sabotage, so we reversed the signs on the roads. This brought about hopeless confusion amongst the German troops, since they were constantly sent in the opposite direction by the signs which had been reversed. We also cut the tires of their cars, emptied the gasoline tanks, etc. Every day we met in different places, often in the parsonage or church. Before we went out upon our work of resistance, prayer was offered, and upon return, thanksgiving was offered for our safe return. This made a deep impression upon me, and out of formality, I also folded my hands and prayed. The Lord was working with His spirit in my heart.

Then came June 1942 with its persecution of the Jews, and we had the added task of finding hiding places for these unfortunates. Soon the Lord provided hundreds of addresses where we could place Jews in hiding.

The transportation of Jews was very difficult, since the enemy suspected all those who had a Jewish appearance. When caught, both the Jews and their protectors were sent to the gas chambers or the Concentration Camp. We had to provide these people in hiding with all sorts of documents, such as identification papers, breadcards, etc., as well as money. All these items had to be obtained by raiding the offices of distribution, city halls, etc. These places were all under the control of men who collaborated with the Germans; so we would put on German Uniforms and only those who spoke perfect German were assigned to this task of stealing what we needed. Most often our men had already disappeared with their loot before the enemy had any idea of what was going on. Many times, some of our bravest men lost their lives in this line of duty.

On one of my assignments in the city of Amsterdam, I saw Jewish infants torn from their mothers' breasts by the German police, and thrown from second and third story windows and crushed to death.... At another time, I was teaching a class of Jewish children who were no longer allowed to attend the public schools because they were Jews, when my father came and warned me that four men from the Gestapo were waiting for me at home to arrest me. My dear wife managed to escape through the garden and met me and our little son who was with me at school. One of our men from the Underground in Den Haag had been arrested, and after much torture was forced to give names of his friends who helped in the resistance. My name had been mentioned, and hence we were sought. We left my parents' home to begin our wanderings, which lasted for more than three years.

While on the way to Eindhoven, my wife prayed often that we might reach our friends in Eindhoven safely. The trip was not without danger since my wife and son had a very Jewish appearance, but my wife assured me that she trusted in the Lord Jesus Christ who would protect us from all our enemies. Her son was her companion in the faith [Elias knew of his wife and son's belief in Yeshua before this time, and with his own involvement with some of the 'true' believers who were helping the Jewish people, his heart had softened somewhat]. It was difficult to find refuge for my family since all the available places were given to those in hiding; and to the homes of our comrades we dared not go, since their names may have been given to the Gestapo, who would then be waiting in their homes for us.

After being in Eindhoven for 2 days, my wife told me that she awoke at night and had a feeling that danger was near; so we left for Rotterdam, and although the trains were filled with Germans, we were not molested. We learned later that an hour after we left the house in Eindhoven, the Gestapo made a raid on the house!

In Rotterdam, we went to a church, and the minister placed us with a Christian family where I studied and fought against my unbelief. My wife noticed my spiritual struggles and would come to me and understandingly say to me, 'The Devil tries to keep you from believing. He tried to tempt our Lord also, but He drove him away. Just pray to our Lord for strength.' And so, during the day I studied, and at night I would battle the Germans in order to get the necessities of life for our unfortunate people, and to prevent them from being slaughtered or sent to work in German factories to make weapons for our destruction.

Finally, after having been steeped in the age-old superstition of being a Jew and yet not knowing why, I came to the conviction that Jesus was my savior to whom I could tell all my troubles. I had been re-born by the Holy Spirit. I was a new man in Christ Jesus. I knew that He could forgive my unbelief and that He would protect me and be my highest good.

In the meantime, I was informed that my parents and relatives as well as those of my wife, had been sent to Poland to be gassed and burned to death. Again my faith was severely tried, and we were much in prayer; and the Lord strengthened us.

That the faith of my wife was stronger than mine is clear from this experience. While I was away on duty, the Germans raided the homes of the neighborhood, and also our house, and there was no time for my wife and son to escape. Yet, while they clearly appeared Jewish and while they even spoke with her, they did not molest her. It seemed the Germans were made blind for the moment. When I got home she told me the experience and when I asked her if she were not afraid, she said, 'Trust in the Lord.' [Greta and Elias told the author that during this time she and Benjamin were given a place of hiding in a tiny secret attic of a Christian's home; they spent three years in that attic. Occasionally, at night, the Christian couple would signal to them that it was safe to come downstairs, but throughout the long days they had to remain locked in the secret attic, completely silent, lest any guests in the home, the neighbors, or a passing stranger hear them and report it to the Germans. Many days they had nothing to eat because it was too dangerous for the couple to approach the entrance to the secret attic. One can imagine the difficulty of keeping a young, active boy quiet through such terrifying days—when life and death hung on a mis-spoken word, a cry, or even a whisper.]

By this and many similar experiences, I was forced to put my trust in Jesus Christ. Pastor Rijpert, a Christian Reformed Pastor, and soldier for freedom and for Christ, was arrested with his wife, two sons and two daughters. They were thrown in a Concentration Camp and were placed in a bunker which was made of cement and was too small for *anyone to lie down, stand up or get rest. Finally came the trial, which was worse than brutal; but the Pastor refused to tell where the weapons were hidden or who belonged to the Underground Movement. Pastor Rijpert and family refused to obey anyone but God and the legitimate government of Holland. The Germans threatened to shoot them, yet they would not yield. Mrs. Rijpert declared that if they killed her husband and children, then some day the Germans would have to answer for this deed before God Who would judge them. A few days later, she heard footsteps early in the morning and the voices of her husband and two sons singing 'A Mighty Fortress is Our God.' Then she heard a salvo of shots and she knew that her dear ones had been faithful unto death. After the Liberation, Mrs. Rijpert and her two daughters were released.[65]*

When the war ended and liberation came, the den Arends had no reason to remain in Holland. All of their family members had been killed by the Germans. Confused and uncertain of the future, they felt God was directing them to immigrate to America. They arrived at Ellis Island, New York at 6:00 P.M. on June 30, 1947.

Elias was in need of employment on that December day when he found himself in the Mission's building on 72nd Street in Manhattan. His friends had suggested that he look for work in the Jewish section of Brooklyn. He thought he was headed for Brooklyn when he boarded the subway at Seventh Avenue, but when he got off the train he discovered he was on 72nd Street. As he walked along, he passed the Mission's large window display. As his eyes scanned the Scriptures displayed in Hebrew, Yiddish, and English his heart warmed, and he wondered to himself if the display meant that there were other Jews who believed in Yeshua. He couldn't resist the temptation to enter the building. The receptionist was friendly, and as they made conversation Elias acknowledged that he was a believer in the Messiah Yeshua. The receptionist eagerly introduced him to Joseph Cohn; once Joseph heard Elias' story he told him to return on Monday and Cohn would have a job for him. When Elias returned, he began working as the elevator operator at Headquarters.

In addition to operating the elevator at the Mission, Elias den Arend worked on learning the English language and once his language skills enabled him to enroll in Bible classes, Joseph saw to it that Elias received the training he needed to equip him to serve on staff as a missionary.

Joseph put his new missionary worker, Elias den Arend, under the supervision of Sanford Mills. Almost immediately, the two men became inseparable. They worked as a team as they represented the Mission in the churches. Elias, the accomplished cellist, began the service with music and then gave his testimony; Sanford would then present the message. But it wasn't long before Sanford requested that the Board supply him with a saxophone. The Minutes record his unique request:

> *...since Mr. Mills and Dr. den Arend have been working together, Mr. Mills had wished to learn to play a musical instrument so that they could play together when they go out to the various churches. Mr. Mills has been studying the saxophone under the instruction of Dr. den Arend, and has been using a borrowed instrument, loaned to him by Dr. den Arend's son. Now that Mr. Mills has learned to play the saxophone he would like to have an instrument for his own use, and he has found that he can secure one through a friend at a cost of $200.00, the retail cost of same is $280.00. He asks that the Board consider the purchase of a saxophone for his use.[66]*

The Board approved the request, and Mills and den Arend began playing duets in the churches where they ministered.

For a number of years, the den Arends made their home in Muskegon, Michigan. When Elias was not traveling for the Mission, he was conducting home Bible studies and doing personal visitation in Jewish homes in his area,[67] or he was preparing for his Ordination. His official service of Ordination was held at the Washington Avenue Baptist Church in Ludington, Michigan on January 26, 1951.

By 1955 Elias and Greta had moved to San Jose, California. They had decided to use "English" names, and they became known as Eddy and Margaret den Arend. Eddy's English had improved so much by that time that he was made a full-time Field Evangelist for the Mission. He had put away his cello (he told the author he greatly missed playing his cello but, he went on to say, he wanted to be remembered in the churches for his ability to teach the Word of God rather than for his ability to play the cello).

During their thirty-two years of ministry with the Mission, Eddy and Margaret traveled the length and breadth of the Pacific Northwest and the Pacific Southwest, faithfully witnessing to Jewish people and ministering in the churches. On February 22, 1979 God called his servant Elias den Arend into His presence.

HERMAN NEWMARK, A POSSIBLE SUCCESSOR

Mention has already been made of Joseph's reluctance to delegate authority. For years he ignored the Board's pleas, and then their demands, that he train someone to help him. He therefore took the Directors by surprise at their January 1948 meeting. The minutes state:

> *Mr. Cohn reported that while he was in London in December he met several times with an English Jewish Christian who was born and brought up in England, and who for some time has been associated with Rev. E. Bendor Samuel in the Hebrew Christian Testimony to Israel. [The Hebrew Christian Testimony to Israel was founded by David Baron in 1894, the same year Rabbi Leopold Cohn founded his mission in Brooklyn, New York.] This man's name is Rev. Herman Newmark. He is about 53 years old.... Mr. Cohn said that he felt this man was the first one he had ever met who seemed to have the qualities necessary to perhaps one day be his successor in the work of the American Board of Missions to the Jews, and that he would like the permission of the Board to invite Mr. Newmark to come to America this spring for a vacation trip and during that time to have a chance to see the work here, and to meet the Board of Directors without incurring any obligation on the part of anyone.*[68]

Herman Newmark was born and raised in England. His Jewish family taught him to be proud of the fact that he was a Jew, but they did not practice their religion. In fact, as Herman grew to manhood, he concluded that God did not exist. He believed that the Old Testament was "...a man-made book of morals which could be safely ignored as out of date."[69]

At the end of 1912, at the age of twenty-one, Herman left London and set sail for Yokohama, Japan. His younger brother had preceded him in making a move to Japan; both men believed that Japan offered better business opportunities than their homeland.

The beginning of World War in 1914 caused the sudden return of Herman's brother to London, and Herman was left alone in a heathen land. The outbreak of the war brought disillusionment to the young businessman who had long dreamed of a coming world brotherhood. He concluded that men were not in themselves capable of uniting as true brothers. For the first time in his life he wondered if, perhaps, there was an intelligent Creator of the universe who made men, and who could put men right.

Far from family and friends, surrounded by Shintoism, Herman felt compelled to learn whether or not God existed. He went to the Welsh landlady in whose boarding house he lived, and asked her if he might borrow her Bible. He wanted to see if it really was God's message to mankind. Herman later recalled:

> *...I quietly read through the Old Testament and it impressed me at once as being what it claims to be—'The Word of God.' There I learned the history of Israel and saw that their dispersions and sufferings were all foretold by Moses before they even entered the promised land under Joshua.... In addition to this I learned for the first time in my life that God Himself had promised to send a Messiah to restore Israel to Himself and to their land, and so make them a blessing to all the world.*[70]

God's Word penetrated Herman's heart, and soon he prayed to receive Jesus as his Messiah and Savior. In 1918, when his term of service with the Asiatic Petroleum Company ended, Herman felt constrained to relinquish his business career and return to England to share the Gospel with his Jewish brethren. Once in London, he immediately went to work for the Hebrew Christian Testimony to Israel—the ministry he was faithfully serving with when he was first introduced to Joseph Hoffman Cohn.

Joseph Cohn and Herman Newmark first became acquainted in December, 1947. Cohn was in England to assess ways in which the American Board of Missions to the Jews (C.P.M.) could increase its ministry to the throngs of European Jews who were displaced following World War II. Herman's concern for the salvation of Jewish people, and zeal for ministry, greatly impressed Cohn. The two men were "kindred spirits."

Following that trip, Joseph made the first mention to the mission's Board of Directors that he may have found a successor to himself. Herman Newmark was the first person Cohn ever named as a possible successor to himself.

Cohn went further than just to mention Herman Newmark's name to members of the Board. He asked the Directors for their permission to invite Herman to visit America later that year (c. 1948). Permission was granted.

Herman Newmark and his wife arrived in the United States on August 13, 1948. They attended the Summer's End Conference, and Herman was invited to a special meeting of the Board that was planned at that time.[71]

At the Fall 1948 meeting of the Board, Joseph presented a letter from Mr. Newmark. The Newmarks had returned to England, but Herman's letter stated that he had discussed the matter of his coming to New York with the Board of The Hebrew Christian Testimony to Israel. They had given approval for Herman and his wife to return to New York for the months of January through April (1949). The London Society agreed to pay Mr. Newmark's full salary during those months; the Mission was to cover all of his travel expense.[72]

During his four-month trial period, Herman Newmark ministered on behalf of the Mission and taught classes at the Missionary Training Institute—the training program Joseph had set up in the Leopold Memorial Building in Manhattan. He told the Board he was delighted to be in America, and stated that he would like to move to America permanently. He said he thought it would be possible for him to return to New York on permanent status around June 1950.[73]

The Board was very pleased with Mr. Newmark as a possible successor to Joseph Cohn—like Cohn, he saw the larger picture, and he had a vision for reaching all Jews everywhere with the Gospel. A formal call was extended at the Board of Directors meeting on April 27, 1949. The Minutes state:

> Mr. Jones moved that this Board extend a call to Mr. Herman Newmark of London, England to join the staff of the American Board of Missions to the Jews, Inc., in the capacity of superintendent of the New York stations of the Mission, Coney Island, Brooklyn and 72nd Street, under direction of the General Secretary, ...and to make himself of such help in other activities of the Mission as may be found appropriate from time to time.[74]

The motion was passed and the Board seemed delighted to have a man who could assist Joseph, but God evidently over-ruled. At a special meeting of the Board in August 1949 Joseph reported:

> ...Mr. Newmark is not resigning from the Hebrew-Christian Testimony to Israel but will remain in England, and not come to the United States to work with the American Board of Missions to the Jews, Inc.[75]

The Minutes of the Directors meeting do not enlarge on the reasons for Mr. Newmark's abrupt change of mind, nor is there any correspondence that sheds light on the matter. One can only speculate as to the reasons behind Newmark's change of mind and as to the direction the Mission might have taken if Mr. Newmark, a man with impressive abilities, had joined forces with Joseph Cohn. Without question, the Mission's involvement and influence in Europe would have realized continued expansion.

With Herman Newmark out of the picture, Joseph Cohn again had no successor in the wings. He continued to work alone. But one worker was of great help to Joseph because he kept the weekly services going at the Headquarters building in Manhattan. That worker was Rev. Sydney Parker.

SYDNEY PARKER—IN MANHATTAN

Sydney Parker accepted Yeshua as Messiah and Lord while he was a college student. In writing about the amazing way in which God touched and changed his life, he said:

> I was at college and enjoying the new world of learning I had entered, and the whole wealth of interesting subjects that were spread before me. Anything scientific, particularly if it had a medical aspect, had always attracted me. Consequently, at the City College of New York I set out on a course of study which was designed to prepare me for a medical career.
>
> Whilst crossing the college campus one day, I saw a group of students engaged in an animated discussion, and out of curiosity I joined them. In the center of the group I found a man speaking about God and distributing some little books. Some of the students, fresh from listening to lectures on philosophy, psychology, evolution, and other thought-provoking subjects, were entering into heated arguments with this lone stranger who seemed pleased at the opportunity to speak with these youngsters and debate with them. I did not join in the discussion, but just listened for a while, and as I left I took one of his little books which I found to be the New Testament—a book about which I knew almost nothing.
>
> Travelling home that night to Brooklyn on the subway, I began to read it the same way I would read any other book. I began at the beginning, and read the words, 'The book of the generation of Jesus Christ, the son of David, the son of Abraham....' and found to my surprise that I was reading a Jewish book about a Jew.
>
> From that very first contact with it, the New Testament completely captivated me, and I read it again and again. Here I found subject matter more fascinating and more practical for the problems of daily life than all my college courses. This Book became my constant companion, and my favorite reading.
>
> Gradually the great central figure of the New Testament, Jesus Christ, impressed Himself on my heart and mind. He was a Jew who knew the Law and the prophets, and did the works of God. I discovered, one day with a start, that He WAS God. Indeed, reading and learning His beautiful sayings and teachings, and following Him around as He traveled and taught and healed in the hills and valleys of the Holy Land, became food and drink to me. His promise of forgiveness and eternal life to those who believe in Him beckoned and drew me, until one day I put my trust in Him, and accepted Him as Savior and Lord. Only God can forgive sins.
>
> I, as a Jew, found much of beauty and grandeur in the New Testament, but beyond the pages of the Book I have found more of spiritual satisfaction than I ever dreamed of, for I have found the Messiah, the only begotten Son of God!
>
> He fulfills His promise day by day to be with me always, and at all times, and in my heart I have the peace of God.

Life, to a follower of Jesus Christ, the Redeemer of Israel, is richer and fuller, and will continue more and more so until the dawning of the perfect day in eternity.[76]

As a new Jewish believer, Sydney found his way to the Brooklyn branch of the Mission. There, he was "smitten by Cupid's arrow" when he met the nurse at the Dispensary—Miss Lottie Furth (a worker whose story was told in Chapter Seven of this history). Lottie had served as a nurse at the Dispensary for over ten years before she and Sydney met, fell in love, and were married.

When Sydney revealed to Joseph that he believed God was calling him into full-time ministry, Joseph brought the matter before the Board and they agreed to extend student aid to him so he could embark upon and complete a course in Bible training.[77] At their Spring 1950 meeting, the Directors voted to hire Sydney for a period of two years.[78] Part of his ministry included working in the Reading Room at the Mission's Headquarters building. Of that experience, Sydney wrote:

The Reading Room is a wonderful place of opportunity and education. It is an opportunity to give out the good news of God to Jews. It is an education by means of which one may observe people and see 'what makes them tick.'[79]

Following Sydney's ordination service at the Parkchester Baptist Church on January 31, 1951,[80] he became the resident pastor for the Mission's outreach at the Headquarters office in Manhattan. He loved the work. Like other workers who had served as "pastor" at the Headquarters building, Sydney had a pastor's heart. He found that the more he counseled people, and discipled new believers, the more he felt drawn to pastor a congregation on a full-time basis.

Rabbi Leopold Cohn's vision of developing a Messianic congregation had gotten lost in the explosive expansion of the Mission under Joseph Cohn's leadership. The "congregations" that had developed within the branch ministries were under the direction and the control of the Mission's programs. Joseph's method of developing "branch outreaches" met the need for Jewish evangelism, but did not meet the need of the congregations for growth as indigenous, self-supporting, and self governing bodies—independent of the Mission's support and involvement. The Mission did not have, and did not encourage, congregations where Jews and Gentiles could worship together under the leadership of a pastor.

Eventually Sydney's desire to pastor a congregation, along with some changes in his own doctrinal position, led him to submit his resignation to the Mission. He became the pastor of the Dover Plains Methodist Church of Dover Plains, New York, but he and Lottie loved the Mission and never lost touch with its ongoing ministry. On November 11, 1962 their daughter, Susan, was baptized at the Mission, along with seven other Jewish young people. Daniel Fuchs did the baptizing and Sydney brought the message.[81]

Replacing Aging Board Members

Mr. Paul Graef, who had given over thirty-one years of faithful service as a Board member, was in attendance at the January 1948 Directors meeting when Joseph reported his desire to invite Mr. Herman Newmark to meet the Board and to be a candidate as his successor. But Graef passed away during the Spring of 1948, and did not have the opportunity to meet Newmark when he arrived in New York that August. Several of the members were getting quite elderly; over a period of three years the Board mourned the loss of a number of their dear friends.

At the January 26, 1949 meeting of the Board, Dr. Frank Morris was elected to replace Paul Graef.[82] At the October 1950 Directors meeting, Joseph reported that he had met a man by the name of John Melhorn, whom he thought would be interested in serving on the Board.[83] Mr. Lewis H. Fisher passed away on November 21, 1950, and at their January 1951 meeting the Board elected Mr. John Melhorn to serve as one of their members.[84] Another new member was added to the Board's ranks in April 1951—Mr. Francis E. Simmons of Washington DC.[85] The Board then stabilized.

Replacing Aging Staff Members

Many of the workers were aging as well. Joseph was concerned about Mr. John Solomon, whose faithful wife and help mate had already gone home to be with the lord. A special service was held at the Pittsburgh branch in her honor on February 2, 1945 and a report of that service was given in *The Chosen People* magazine, stating:

...What a wonderful memory we all have of Sister Solomon. Though suffering a number of years, her dear face was always radiant, greeting all of us with her sweet ready smile of welcome. Friday she stood up and gave forth a clear testimony of her love for Jesus and what He meant to her through the years since Jesus came into her heart and she loves to tell the Blessed Story of Salvation to all—especially to His brethren, the Jews.
Saturday she seemed as well as her condition permitted, but suddenly, Sunday evening, she became very ill. A physician was called, but in a short time after kissing her dear old companion good night here, she passed on into the

arms of Jesus where she will never feel pain any more, neither sorrow, nor crying. Amen![86]

After his wife's death, John Solomon aged rapidly. In 1946 Cohn told the Executive Committee that the situation in Pittsburgh was not going well; he thought that it would be advisable to send Miss Eva Zipper to Pittsburgh to assist Solomon in case he should decide to retire.[87] But John continued to serve his Lord for nearly three additional years. It was not until January 1949 that Joseph announced to readers of *The Chosen People* magazine that, at eighty-four years of age, John Solomon had retired. He had served with the Mission for over fifty years—most of the years had been in Pittsburgh. After his "official retirement," John continued his devoted missionary work until the Lord called him home on February 10, 1951.

ARNOLD AND MARGARET SEIDLER—IN PITTSBURGH

Although Eva Zipper was sent to Pittsburgh to assist John Solomon, she was not put in charge of the branch. Instead, Joseph asked Rev. Mr. Arnold Seidler to take over the Pittsburgh branch. Seidler had been a missionary for over ten years with the Hebrew Christian Testimony to Israel in London, England—the same work Herman Newmark was associated with. His wife, Margaret Seidler, was the sister of Mr. Ashton Holden, a worker who served with the Mission's staff in Los Angeles, California and later in Montreal, Quebec, Canada.

Seidler was born to orthodox Jewish parents of Polish descent. His parents had fled to Germany from Russo-Poland to escape the Czarist pogroms. From early childhood, Arnold had learned to hate and to shun anything that had to do with Christians. His family had experienced the horrors of anti-Semitic hatred from many Catholic and Greek-orthodox people who called themselves "Christians." In Germany, the Seidler family added "Protestants" to the list of those who hated and persecuted the Jews. Remembering some of his experiences as a child in school, Arnold Seidler said:

> *...On one occasion I was beaten until nearly unconscious, which confirmed me in my dislike, to put it mildly, of anything that was in any way connected with Christianity. I was proud of the fact that I was a Jew and was sustained in the most cruel persecution which I had to undergo, by the thought, implanted in my mind by my mother when a youngster, that one day we Jews would be reinstated into the favor of God and the Gentiles would then receive their just reward. As I look back on my school days I remember even the day when I was barred from religious instruction by the teacher, who said that they were now starting to read the New Testament and that was not for Jews. At that time I considered Christianity to be a religion of idol worship, having been told of the way the Russian and Polish peasants worshipped their ikons.[88]*

After he finished high school, Arnold received orders from the Polish Consul to enlist in the Polish army, but he refused to go. Instead, he remained in Germany until his passport expired—a decision he lived to regret. The Polish Consulate refused to renew his passport until he reported to the military authorities at Lublin, Poland, but the German authorities would not give him an exit visa because he did not have a valid passport. Arnold was caught in a "Catch-22" situation. In desperation, he slipped across the border into Poland on his own. To his amazement, the Polish military rejected him from military service because of his poor eyesight. He then tried to return to Germany, but he found he was not able to get back into the country. The frustration of his predicament was almost more than he could cope with!

While waiting for the proper authorities to decide if he would be allowed to re-enter Germany, Arnold met a young Jewish man who had become a Christian. He listened as the young man told him about the Messiah, Yeshua. One evening the young man invited Arnold to go with him to a Bible class. It was there that Arnold learned, for the first time in his life, that "true" Christians do not hate the Jews, nor do they worship idols; he learned that they, too, worship the God of Abraham, Isaac and Jacob. Arnold was greatly impressed with the things he heard and saw, and he continued attending the Bible class. Through his contact with these new friends, his attitude toward Christians and toward Christianity began to change. He later stated that God used two Bible messages in particular to pierce his heart and convict him of his sin and of his need to accept Yeshua. He said:

> *On the second occasion the subject was, 'When I see the blood I will pass over you.' He painted this ancient scene vividly before our mind's eye and showed us that Christ Jesus fulfilled the passover type in every detail.... Again it seemed as if he spoke to me personally and, sitting there, I realized that I was in truth the sinner for which Christ had died. I lifted my heart in prayer to God and said, 'Lord, be merciful to me, a sinner.' There and then I found in Christ the forgiveness of sin and peace of heart I so desired.[89]*

When Arnold wrote to his parents, telling them of his belief in Yeshua, they were livid! They wanted nothing more to do with him. For six years they would neither write to him nor visit him. But God gave Arnold a wonderful new family of "spiritual" mothers, fathers, sisters, and brothers.

God also opened the way for Arnold to go to England so he could prepare to study for the ministry. At the completion of his studies, God led him to work for the Hebrew Christian Testimony to Israel—an organization he served with for fourteen years. But of his last two years with that organization he wrote:

> ...my heart was burdened with the greater need of His people and at the same time that He was dealing with me, He spoke to my wife, making her willing to leave her native country if He so desired. Through a mutual friend of ours and the American Board of Missions to the Jews, the need for a witness among the Jews in the U.S.A. was brought before us and an interview with the General Secretary of the Mission, who was on a visit to Europe, was arranged. The outcome was an invitation to visit the headquarters in New York, which has subsequently extended to a call to serve under the Board's supervision.
>
> With the resignation and retirement of Rev. John Solomon, I was detailed to take charge of the Pittsburgh work. By the time these few lines appear in print I shall have spent some months of work in the Pittsburgh area where my wife and daughter, recently arrived from England, have joined me.[90]

The year 1949 was a "red letter year" for the Pittsburgh branch. Not only did God provide a new missionary family, He provided a new building for the ministry there. At the April 27, 1949 meeting of the Board, Joseph announced that he would finally be able to close on the Mission's new building in Pittsburgh—property located at 5808 Beacon Avenue.[91]

Arnold Seidler, like his predecessor John Solomon, found a fruitful field among the Jews in Pittsburgh. He found acceptance among the Gentiles and Christians as well, and his ministry steadily grew in scope and influence. He wrote:

> We have nothing spectacular to report. We have done what was in our power to give out the Word of God, and during the last year over 3,000 copies of The Shepherd of Israel have been handed to the Jews in Pittsburgh. Large numbers of our other tracts, hundreds of Gospels and many New Testaments, as well as Bibles, have been accepted, and Jews have been dealt with both here in Pittsburgh as well as in other cities of Pennsylvania. Some of those approached by us never before heard that Christ Jesus came into the world to save sinners. The need of our people is great indeed. Not so long ago some elders of one of the synagogues in our street called on me and we had a long and, I believe, profitable talk about the prophetic and messianic Scriptures. In our journeying we have visited Jews in their homes and stores and they in turn—at least some of them—have attended our meetings. From their attitude we realized that the Lord had spoken to them and we covet your prayers that the Lord may finish His work in their hearts.
>
> Finally we are grateful that we can report that the Lord has used us to the salvation of several Jews and Gentiles.[92]

Over the years, God used Arnold Seidler to lead many Jewish people to Himself. Arnold faithfully and lovingly discipled new believers in his home, or in the classes at the Pittsburgh branch. On Monday, December 7, 1959, while returning from a missionary conference in Denver, Colorado, Arnold suffered a massive heart attack. The Lord quickly called this choice servant home. Mrs. Margaret Seidler remained at the Pittsburgh branch. The continuation of the story of Mrs. Seidler and the Pittsburgh branch will be given in a subsequent chapter of this history.

It has been established that Joseph Hoffman Cohn was a man who was driven to see his vision and goals for the Mission accomplished. He was a man who was blessed with a high energy level, but cursed by his need to be in control. He spread himself thin, but one man cannot be in every place at the same time. His solution to his desire to be representing the Mission in *every* church, in *every* state and in *every* country was to use Field Evangelists. The Mission's team of Field Evangelists was essential to the on-going support base of the ministry.

ELMER S. DAVIDSON—FIELD EVANGELIST

One of the first Field Evangelists hired by Joseph was Mr. Elmer S. Davidson, who came on staff just after graduating from Houghton College in 1914. Elmer left the Mission when he was called to military service in World War I. After the war nothing more was heard from him until 1938, when he showed up at a meeting at Park Street Church in Boston where Joseph was speaking. After the service, Elmer asked Joseph if he would re-hire him, and Joseph said "Yes."

Joseph's expectations from the Field Evangelists during those early days was that they represent the Mission in the churches, and "sell" Christians on the need for sharing the Gospel with the Jews and on the need for them (the Christians) to support the Mission in its task of preaching the Gospel to the Jews. Joseph looked for men who had a burden for the Jews and Israel, but, for the Field Evangelists, Bible knowledge and training was not an "essential." Oftentimes the

Field Evangelists only had a select few messages. These would be preached over and over as the men traveled to different churches in different parts of the country. Many of the men made no effort to keep up with their own in-depth study of God's Word, nor did they stay current with developing trends in theology and Biblical studies. Evidently Elmer Davidson was one such individual.

By the late 1940's, with the resurgence of interest in prophecy which developed during World War II, and with a greater number of Bible conferences developing across the country, many pastors, and the Christian body in general, were becoming more "sophisticated." Having men like Elmer Davidson on staff was becoming detrimental to the Mission's reputation. This is clear from the Board Minutes of 1949 which state, " ...Over a period of time complaints have come from various parts of the country concerning his [Davidson's] doctrinal views, and statements that he has made while speaking, but although investigation has been made nothing has ever been able to be actually proven. He has also written a number of letters to Mr. Cohn that did not exhibit the finest of Christian spirit."[93]

The Board instructed Joseph to personally interview Elmer, but they further instructed that when he did, he was to have another Board member present. Joseph asked Harold Pretlove and Mr. Davis to handle the task with him, and the three men reported back to the Board:

> ...He [Davidson] didn't give a satisfactory answer to any question that was asked, and at times was very arrogant. He was excused for 15 minutes to write a statement of his faith which might be presented to the Board as evidence on his own behalf for the consideration of the board and this speaks for itself. Mr. Davis said that his personal reaction as far as Mr. Davidson was concerned was that he was not a satisfactory person to represent the Board.[94]

This incident may seem to be obscure, but it is included in this history to show that, as new members were added to the Board, it (the Board as a body) was beginning to take a firmer grip on the ministry. Joseph had ignored their pleas to hire and train an Assistant who could share his work load. He was the Editor of *The Chosen People* magazine; he was the Director for the foreign work; he was in charge of the radio ministry, the Dispensary, etc. The entire Mission and ministry rotated around Joseph Cohn. But by the late 1940's the Board was becoming increasingly involved with staff problems as they came up. They passed new By-Laws for the Corporation which gave them broader powers. They also amended the Certificate of Incorporation to include the Doctrinal Statement in Section I and in Section II—a statement of assent which stated: "Only persons who give assent to the doctrinal basis as contained in Section 1 of this article, either verbally or in writing as may be required by the Board of Directors and who are known to be interested in the evangelization of the Jews, shall be eligible to membership in this Corporation."[95]

Establishing Foreign Corporations

During 1950 Joseph continued to shuttle back and forth between the United States, England, Europe, and the newly formed state of Israel. He was intent upon seeing the work in Paris expand. He was equally determined that the Mission's witness in Israel would flourish. He also spent a great deal of time in London, seeking for ways to either merge the Mission with an established Mission to the Jews in England, or for a way to establish a branch of the ministry there.

In August 1950 the Board approved a motion for the Mission to take the necessary steps to become a foreign corporation in France, England, Israel, and Canada.[96] Acting on this motion, the Mission became a legal corporation in England in September 1951. The work was called The American Board of Missions to the Jews Limited.[97] But in France and in Israel, the Mission continued to function as a foreign corporation doing business in those countries. This was not a problem in France, but it was not workable in Israel. It is unfortunate that Joseph and the Board did not press for the Mission's recognition under British Mandate law governing religious organizations operating within the country prior to the establishment of the State of Israel. Had they done so, the Mission would have been entitled to send into Israel the same number of missionaries the organization had there during the Mandate and Turkish rule. Their failure to exercise this provision in the law has hampered the Mission's efforts to bring qualified missionaries into Israel to the present time.

Ruth Backus—the Portland, Oregon Branch

At the January 1953 meeting of the Board, Joseph introduced members of the Board to Miss Ruth Backus. Ruth was from Portland, Oregon. She had received a year's training at the Mission's Training School in New York, as well as practical Jewish missionary experience in the New York branches. In keeping with their new "hands on" policy of management, the Board interviewed Ruth. During the interview, she stated that she was interested in starting a work for the Mission among the Jews in Portland. The Board then authorized Joseph to proceed with the establishment of a work in Portland,[98] but he never had the opportunity to open that branch.

PERSONAL MEMOIRS PENNED

The February 1950 issue of *The Chosen People* magazine held the first of an ongoing series in which Joseph penned his personal memoirs. He wanted to tell the wonderful story of the American Board of Missions to the Jews (CPM) in his own words. The series was concluded in the October 1953 magazine. At the same time as he was writing his memoirs in serial form for *The Chosen People* magazine, it was being prepared for publication in book form. The title Joseph selected for the manuscript was, "I Have Fought A Good Fight." Four days after he had penned the word "finis" in his large bold hand on the last page of the manuscript, the Lord quietly and quickly called him home. Joseph Hoffman Cohn entered the presence of the Lord on October 5, 1953.

His last editorial in *The Chosen People* magazine seems almost prophetic. In it he recounted and gave tribute to many who had faithfully and sacrificially labored to bring the Gospel to the Jewish people. He wrote:

> ...My father's own record was 43 years of continuous self-sacrificing devotion to the cause to which God had called him. Mr. Philip Englander rolled up 46 years of faithful labor in the Mission, at the time when the Lord took him home, some five or six years after my father had gone. Miss Augusta Sussdorff, whom we consider now our veteran missionary, served 50 solid years as missionary under our Board, and is now retired on pension. At this writing, she is 85 years old, and even at this advanced age she still insists on coming to the Mission, working with us just as though she had never been retired. Such is her devotion to the Mission that I believe she would crawl on her hands and knees if she could get here no other way.
>
> Our first Office Secretary [Miss Helen Pithman {Mrs. Helen Christian}] spent some 36 years caring for the office, and then was also retired on pension.
>
> Mr. Bernhard Schatkin, still with us, has a record of some 30 years of consecrated labor. And so on it goes down the line....
>
> Our brother Harry Burgen who found the Lord in the Brooklyn Mission, now has passed thirty years of service with us....
>
> Out in Los Angeles our faithful Brother Elias Zimmerman labors, in charge of the branch in that city. He has passed his 32nd year with us.... Of course it is true, and we have to admit the charge frankly, that for the most part, our workers are Christian Jews, brethren who either through the ministry of our own Mission, or through some other channel, found in the Lord Jesus Christ their hope, their Messiah, their salvation. But our door is always open to Gentile Christian workers, and among them we have, I believe, the finest in America by way of workers among the women and among the children, consecrated young women like Miss Eleanor Bullock, Miss Ruth Wardell, Miss Bonnie Hayes....
>
> To mention just two or three more, there is Miss Hilda Koser, who grew up in the Mission from childhood. Now in charge of the Coney Island Branch, she has an enrollment of over 300 Jewish children, and has stirred Coney Island from end to end. Then there is Daniel Fuchs, also brought up from childhood in the Mission halls, now Dean of the Jewish Missionary Training Institute, and a worthy worker with us, well approved, that needeth not to be ashamed. He is now rounding out some 20 years of service. There is also Emil D. Gruen, with a service record which already has passed the 16th milestone. And what more shall I say? For time and space would fail us to tell of the galaxy of brightly shining stars that have studded the testimony of the Mission.[99]

Joseph reminisced further about the Paris ministry, the European work, and the refugee work. He concluded by writing:

> Here the story must stop again, but will continue, the Lord willing, next month. It is simply another buttressing pillar to show again how the Lord guided the course of your beloved American Board of Missions to the Jews. Who shall dare say in the face of all these overwhelming evidences, that it was not God who watched over the early planting of the work, the watering of it, and the fruitage of it? We have grown now into a large company, we who have combined together by prayer and by gift to make possible this world wide sweep of labor and testimony for the Lord Jesus Christ. And together 'we are journeying into the place of which the Lord said, I will give it to you; come thou with us and we will do thee good; for the Lord hath spoken good concerning Israel.' And indeed we are travelling on to the New Jerusalem. Some day we shall hear from Him His 'Well done thou good and faithful servant, enter into the joy of thy Lord.'[100]

THE DEATH OF JOSEPH HOFFMAN COHN

Joseph did not know when he penned those words that he, himself, would be called suddenly into the presence of his Lord. He was a difficult man, a hard task master, but his life was devoted to the work of sharing the Gospel with his kindred—the Jews—and devoted to the growth and continuation of the Mission which his father, Rabbi Leopold Cohn, had founded. When he entered glory he must have heard his Lord say, "Well done thou good and faithful servant, enter into the joy of your Lord,"[101] for he had "fought the good fight"—he had "finished the course."

It was well known to the Mission's staff that when he was in town, Joseph Cohn was almost always the first one to arrive at the Headquarters building in the morning, and the last one to leave at night.

On the day of his death, Miss Dorothy Chesley, his personal secretary and administrative assistant, arrived at the front door of the Leopold Memorial Building and was surprised to find it locked. Since she had a key, she opened the door, turned on the lights, and went to her desk. Soon after Miss Chesley's arrival, Miss Helen Pithman (Mrs. Helen Christian) arrived. Miss Pithman had been Joseph's secretary for over thirty-eight years. By the time of his death she was retired, but she still enjoyed coming to the office one day a week to take dictation from Joseph and to help Miss Chesley by freeing her to handle the mail and to do other things in the office.

Dorothy Chesley was hired by the Mission in 1941. She had served as Joseph's personal secretary for twelve years, and she knew his habits very well. She was disturbed by the fact that she had arrived before he had. When Joseph had *still* not arrived by the time Miss Pithman arrived, both women knew something was wrong. Joseph Cohn was exacting; he left a precise schedule of where he would be every moment of each day.

For a number of years Joseph had made his home at the Beacon Hotel—a hotel not far from the Mission's Headquarters building. The two women remembered that Henry Heydt lived close to that hotel, so they called him and asked him to see if Joseph was alright. When Henry arrived at the Beacon Hotel he found the hotel manager and, together, they went to Joseph's door and began knocking. Getting no response, the manager opened the door and the two men found Joseph's body. He had been in the presence of the Lord for sometime—there was nothing more that could be done.

To say that Joseph's death was a shock to the Mission's staff, Board, and constituents is a profound understatement. It was utterly traumatic, a catastrophe. His sudden death threw the Board, the staff, and the entire program of the Mission into utter chaos and confusion. News of his death went from floor to floor in the Leopold Memorial Building, and hit the workers like shock waves. Time seemed to stand still. The workers were devastated.

Dorothy Chesley had the presence of mind to call Daniel Fuchs who, in turn, helped them call Huntley Stone, Joseph's son. From that point things began to move more swiftly. The Executive Committee of the Board was called; they stepped in and took over the daily affairs of the Mission, as well as the funeral, burial, and memorial service arrangements. They also worked with the staff so that the January 1954 issue of *The Chosen People* magazine was produced as a Memorial Edition in honor of Joseph Hoffman Cohn.

The funeral service was held on Thursday night, October 8, 1953 at the Leopold Memorial Building in Manhattan. Every seat in the main hall of the building was taken, and additional seats were set up on the third and fourth floors of the building.

Although he had long been separated from his wife, Josephine did attend Joseph's funeral service, as did his son, Huntley Stone. His brothers and sister also came—some with their family members. His funeral may quite possibly have been the last time the family members came together. Except for Huntley Stone, who joined the Board of Directors after his father's death, none of the other members of the family ever became involved in the ministry. The extent and involvement of other members of Rabbi Leopold Cohn's family in the work of the Lord is not known, although it is known that Joseph's brother, Joshua, maintained a wonderful Christian testimony in Minnesota. It is also known that Joshua's daughter, Esther, has been an active member in Church work throughout her life. The vibrant testimony of Joshua Cohn also touched Esther's son and his family, and at the time this history is being written, they are praying about being missionaries in the Far East.

Although some members of the Cohn family may not have esteemed Joseph for the work he accomplished in the Mission, other people did. Tributes in his memory came to the Mission from all over the world. Highlights from the message of Dr. Charles Lee Feinberg, a child of the Mission and a protege of Joseph Cohn, describe the commitment of Joseph to the Lord and to the Mission. Dr. Feinberg said:

> *…First and foremost he was man of deep convictions. Small men hold or entertain opinions and views; big men are held as in a vise by convictions. All who knew Dr. Cohn realized immediately that he was a man of clear-cut and well-defined convictions. There was never any doubt where he stood on the full inspiration of the Word of God. All who saw and heard him minister the Word, knew by his handling of it, that he believed it implicitly. Throughout his life he tried to penetrate always more deeply into its infinite truths. There was never any doubt about his loyalty to the Lord Jesus Christ…. In a ministry of over 50 years this Mission saw some of our largest denominations literally rent asunder over the doctrinal divisions and liberal inroads. During all this time there never was a breath of doubt about where this*

Mission stood on the fundamentals of our faith…. In the matter of Jewish Missions, Dr. Cohn was a life-long exponent of the truth of Romans 1:16: 'I am not ashamed of the gospel of Christ: for it is the power of God unto salvation to every one that believeth; to the Jew first, and also to the Greek.' 'To the Jews First' was not a shibboleth with him, nor a fetish, nor a clever means for gaining support, as some may have fondly surmised, but it was life of his life and flesh of his flesh. He believed this with all his heart. He was willing to nail this truth to the mast of the ship and go down fighting for it. Yes, dear friends, this man of God was characterized by deep convictions on these basic matters, and he was unswervingly faithful to them.

In the second place, Dr. Cohn was characterized by mighty deeds. Under God he was used to transform a small mission in Williamsburg into a world-wide testimony where truly 'their line has gone out into all the world.' This he did, by the help of God, by dint of ceaseless work. As a young man he found himself by an inner compulsion knocking at the doors of ministers throughout the land, when the going was always hard, in order to get his message to people. He knew it was an almost endless task to indoctrinate generation after generation in the churches in the Biblical basis of Jewish Missions, but he went about the task decade after decade. He brought countless blessings to the churches where he ministered, as many of us know from experience. He carried on an almost unbelievable ministry in correspondence with friends of the Mission. Throughout the land friends still speak of filing away these letters. Then he gave himself to setting forth in print, in The Shepherd of Israel, The Chosen People Magazine, and in tracts, pamphlets, and books the need for evangelizing the Jew here and now. In addition to all this, he looked personally after the financial welfare of the work, as well as the many phases of the foreign work of the Mission, and the individual problems of all the missionaries. He had a brilliant mind, and ceaselessly sought to promote the work of the mission to which God had called him. He was an untiring worker, and easily did the work of three men or more. He was empowered of God, and like Stephen of old, was full of good works.

Finally, Dr. Cohn was characterized by tender sympathies. Only his friends who were nearest him, knew the depth and tenderness of his feelings. His love for his people Israel burned as a fire in his bones. No one can realize the agonies he underwent as he learned again and again throughout Europe of the Nazi persecution of the Jews, as bereaved one after bereaved one poured his or her tale of woe into his ears and heart. He tenderly loved his family. There is not one of them but what he was proud of every accomplishment, whether daughter, daughter-in-law, sons, or grandchildren. The memories of the early home life of his children were spoken of so tenderly. He had a heart for every child of this Mission. He bore with faults and defended shortcomings because of his great love. He was blessed by God with a love for all people, and gained unnumbered friends by his warm and constant sense of humor. His relations with the Lord were very sacred, and in recent years he spoke to me of them. His heart was tender toward God, and he was grateful for the way God had led him. He was ready to go when God called him up higher.[102]

Dr. Charles H. Stevens, Pastor of the Salem Baptist Church, Winston-Salem, NC, said:

A number of things have impressed themselves upon my mind in my association with Dr. J. Hoffman Cohn. I have known him as a loyal friend. He was a lovely character. Our people loved him, for somehow he symbolized to us one of the most precious movements on earth—the evangelization of Israel. He had a deep love for Israel. Dr. Cohn came into our midst and typified what we believed a Christian Jew should typify, and we had a contact that enriched our hearts and lives. I think of his testimony, his love for Jesus Christ. It wasn't simply a system of beliefs; he knew Christ personally. I do not believe there is a man in this generation who has done more to consistently perpetuate the Blessed Hope than Dr. Cohn. He believed it; he lived it; he proclaimed it. The life, the teachings, the writings of this man epitomize the great truth of the living, personal Christ.[103]

Further tributes were given by Dr. W. H. Rogers, former Pastor of the First Baptist Church, New York, New York; from Keith L. Brooks, President American Prophetic League, Los Angeles; John S. Ironside, Manhattan, Kansas; Dr. and Mrs. L. Sale-Harrison, author and Bible teacher; Alexander A. Murry, Pastor, North East Bible Presbyterian Church, Philadelphia, Pennsylvania; Dr. W.E. Pietsch, Director, Evangelize America Program.

The Rev. Gote Hedenquist, Director, Committee on the Christian Approach to the Jews, International Missionary Council, recalled:

…I also am very indebted to him [Cohn] for the great help he rendered me before the last World War in my work in Vienna, Austria. By his support I was enabled to start and maintain for a rather long time a daily meal for about 125 Christians of Jewish origin in the Swedish Mission to the Jews there. At my last visit to his office in New York in 1951 his optimistic views on Jewish Missionary Work in USA were most encouraging and inspiring to my own present duties.[104]

Tributes also came from members of the staff, members of the Board of Directors, and from faithful friends and supporters of the Mission.

Joseph Hoffman Cohn's body was laid to rest on Friday morning October 9, 1953 next to his mother and father in the burial plot in Cypress Hills Cemetery, Brooklyn.

It was the end of an era for the Mission. The end of the Cohn family leadership of the Mission. Many people saw the death of Joseph Cohn as the demise of the Mission, and it almost was—but for God!

ENDNOTES
Chapter 9. Till Death Do Us Part
1 *Minutes*, ABMJ, (October 17, 1938), p 8.
2 *Minutes of Executive Committee*, ABMJ, (September 11, 1940), p 3.
3 *Minutes*, ABMJ, (October 15, 1941), p 1.
4 *Minutes*, ABMJ, (January 28, 1942), p 2.
5 See note above.
6 *Minutes*, ABMJ, (May 13, 1942), p 4.
7 See note above.
8 *The Chosen People*, Vol. XLVIII, No. 1, (October, 1942), p 4.
9 See Appendix D. Listing of speakers at the first National Prophetic Convention held at Calvary Baptist Church, November, 1942.
10 *Minutes*, ABMJ, (December 30, 1941), p 1.
11 See note above.
12 *The Chosen People*, Vol. LI, No. 5, (February, 1946), p 5.
13 *The Chosen People*, Vol. LV, No. 1, (October, 1949), p 10.
14 *Minutes*, ABMJ, (April 27, 1943), p 2.
15 *The Shepherd of Israel*, Vol. 30, No. 6, (February, 1948), p 2.
16 *The Chosen People*, Vol. L, No. 2, (November, 1944), p 14.
17 *The Chosen People*, Vol. LI, No. 3, (December, 1945), p 12.
18 *Minutes*, ABMJ, (October 22, 1946), p 3.
19 *Minutes of Executive Committee*, ABMJ, (April 9, 1947), p 4.
20 *Minutes*, ABMJ, (April 27, 1943), p 4.
21 See note above.
22 See note above.
23 *Minutes*, ABMJ, (January 27, 1944), p 8.
24 *The Chosen People*, Vol. L, No. 3, (December, 1944), p 8.
25 *Minutes*, ABMJ, (October 24, 1944), p 2.
26 *The Chosen People*, Vol. L, No. 3, (December, 1944), p 8.
27 *The Chosen People*, Vol. XLIX, No. 5, (February, 1944), p 11.
28 *Minutes*, ABMJ, (January 27, 1945), p 2.
29 See note above.
30 See note above.
31 Joseph Cohn, *I Have Fought a Good Fight*, (New York: American Board of Missions to the Jews, Inc. [now Chosen People Ministries, Inc.] 1953), p 310.
32 *The Chosen People*, Vol. LI, No. 3, (December, 1945), pp 3, 4.
33 *The Chosen People*, Vol. LII, No. 5, (February, 1947), p 5.
34 *The Chosen People*, Vol. LII, No. 1, (October, 1946), p 4.
35 *The Chosen People*, Vol. LI, No. 6, (March, 1946), p 11.
36 *The Chosen People*, Vol. XLVII, No. 1, (October, 1941), pp 14, 15.
37 *The Chosen People*, Vol. LI, No. 2, (November, 1945), p 10.
38 *The Chosen People*, Vol. LI, No. 7, (April, 1946), p 14.
39 *The Chosen People*, Vol. LVI, No. 6, (March, 1951), p 12.
40 See note above.
41 *The Chosen People*, Vol. LVII, No. 5, (February, 1952), p 17.

42 *The Chosen People*, Vol. L, No. 5, (February, 1945), p 15.
43 See note above, p 14.
44 *The Chosen People*, Vol. LX, No. 3, (December, 1954), p 10.
45 *The Chosen People*, Vol. LII, No. 5, (February, 1947), p 6.
46 See note above.
47 *Minutes of Executive Committee*, ABMJ, (Obtober 8, 1947), p 2.
48 *Minutes*, ABMJ, (January 23, 1945), p 1.
49 *Minutes*, ABMJ, (January 28, 1947), p 1.
50 *Minutes*, ABMJ, (April 24, 1945), p 2.
51 See note above.
52 *The Chosen People*, Vol. LI, No. 5, (February, 1946), p 12.
53 *The Chosen People*, Vol. L, No. 8, (May, 1945), p 20.
54 *The Chosen People*, Vol. LI, No. 2, (November, 1945), pp 3, 4.
55 *Minutes*, ABMJ, (January 23, 1945), p 9.
56 *Minutes of Executive Committee*, ABMJ, (April 9, 1947), pp 3, 4.
57 *The Chosen People*, Vol. LI, No. 5, (February, 1946), p 9.
58 *The Chosen People*, Vol. LII, No. 4, (January, 1947), p 10.
59 *Minutes*, ABMJ, (April 22, 1947), p 21.
60 *Minutes*, ABMJ, (January 27, 1948), p 30.
61 *Minutes*, ABMJ, (April 22, 1947), p 22.
62 *The Chosen People*, Vol. LIII, No. 1, (October, 1947), p 8.
63 See note above, p 9.
64 *Minutes*, ABMJ, (October 28, 1947), p 27.
65 *The Chosen People*, Vol. LIII, No. 4, (January, 1948), pp 8-11.
66 *Minutes*, ABMJ, (January 26, 1949), pp 44, 45.
67 *The Chosen People*, Vol. LVI, No. 7, (April, 1951), p 12.
68 *Minutes*, ABMJ, (January 27, 1948), p 30.
69 *The Shepherd of Israel*, Vol. XXVIII, No. 6, (February, 1946) p 1.
70 See note above.
71 *Minutes*, ABMJ, (August 31, 1948), p 36.
72 *Minutes*, ABMJ, (October 26, 1948), p 38.
73 *Minutes*, ABMJ, (January 26, 1949), p 43.
74 *Minutes*, ABMJ, (April 27, 1949), p 47.
75 *Minutes*, ABMJ, (August 30, 1949), p 50.
76 *Shepherd of Israel*, Vol. 36, No. 11, (July-August, 1953), p 2.
77 *Minutes*, ABMJ, (January 25, 1950), p 65.
78 *Minutes*, ABMJ, (April 26, 1950), p 68.
79 *The Chosen People*, Vol. LVI, No. 7, (April, 1951), p 11.
80 *The Chosen People*, Vol. LVI, No. 6, (March, 1951), p 18.
81 *The Chosen People*, Vol. LXVIII, No. 7, (March, 1963), p 6.
82 *Minutes*, ABMJ, (January 26, 1949), p 40.
83 *Minutes*, ABMJ, (October 25, 1950), p 76.
84 *Minutes*, ABMJ, (January 24, 1951), p 79.
85 *Minutes*, ABMJ, (April 25, 1951), p 84.
86 *The Chosen People*, Vol. L, No. 8, (May, 1945), p 11.
87 *Minutes of Executive Committee*, ABMJ, (March 14, 1946), p 4.
88 *The Chosen People*, Vol. LIV, No. 7, (April, 1949), p 9.
89 See note above, p 10.
90 See note above, p 11.
91 *Minutes*, ABMJ, (April 27, 1949), p 47.
92 *The Chosen People*, Vol. LVIII, No. 3, (December, 1952), p 13.
93 *Minutes*, ABMJ, (August 30, 1949), p 49.
94 *Minutes*, ABMJ, (October 26, 1949), p 53.
95 See note above, p 60.

[96]   *Minutes*, ABMJ, (August 30, 1950), p 75.

[97]   See *Memorandum and Articles of Association of The American Board of Missions to the Jews Limited*, 499351, September 12, 1951.

[98]   *Minutes*, ABMJ, (January 28, 1953), p 96.

[99]   *The Chosen People*, Vol. LIX, No. 1, (October, 1953), pp 2, 3.

[100] See note above, pp 7, 8.

[101] Matthew 25:21.

[102] *The Chosen People*, Joseph Hoffman Cohn Memorial Edition, (January, 1954), pp 5-7.

[103] See note above, p 7.

[104] See note above, pp 11, 12.

10

THE VISION RE-KINDLED

"He has gone. His chair is empty. A vacancy has taken place in the hearts of multitudes. Thousands upon thousands throughout the land and across the seas, bow in sorrow in the loss of a great friend,..."[1]

Joseph Cohn—the Mission's "powerhouse," visionary, great fund raiser, networking genius—was dead. His death brought to a sudden halt an era of missionary endeavor that was unparalleled in the annals of Jewish Missions, and very nearly brought about the demise of the Mission he had poured his life into. Joseph's strengths and drive had built a small neighborhood outreach into an international ministry. Throughout the world, "the American Board of Missions to the Jews" was so closely identified with the Cohns, and particularly with Joseph Cohn, that pastors and Christian leaders often referred to it as "Cohns' Mission." But for all of his strengths, Joseph's need for control—his insistence on placing his stamp of approval on every worker, every project, and every program of the Mission—had left the Mission with no one groomed to be his successor. No one was prepared to "pick up the baton" for aggressive leadership and development of the vision of Leopold and Joseph Cohn.

SEARCHING FOR A NEW LEADER

The Board had recognized the need for a trained successor and they had pointed out that need to Joseph. To his credit, Joseph did make one attempt to groom a successor when he suggested that the Board issue a call to Mr. Herman Newmark. When that did not work out as he had hoped, he may have been looking for leadership qualities in some of the men who were later hired, although he made no mention of grooming any one of them as his successor.

Dr. Henry Heydt, was hired to replace Daniel Fuchs as Director of the Jewish Missionary Training Institute. Mr. Charles Kalisky, a Hebrew Christian originally from Britain, was hired to assist in the Training Institute, to assist in writing *The Shepherd of Israel*, and to help in the missionary work. Kalisky was an avid scholar, writer and teacher. After Joseph's death he took over the "Notes From Israel" column in *The Chosen People* magazine, and he served as an interim missionary in Israel for four months during the summer of 1955 (as mentioned in Chapter Seven of this history). After returning from Israel, Kalisky continued writing for the magazine, and he also became the Mission's Field Evangelist for the New England area. Mr. Chester Webber was hired to serve as a member of the Field Evangelism team. Rabbi Asher Levi, a well known Jewish believer, was hired to work at the headquarters building in Manhattan. Mr. Cordis Hopper, a graduate of Moody Bible Institute, was hired to assist with mailings and publications and to assist with the boys' work at Brooklyn and Coney Island.[2]

Joseph's death struck at the very heart of the Mission's staff and its programs. But more devastating was the fact that his death struck at the very heart of the Mission's Board of Directors. For the greater part of his adult life, Joseph Cohn had been the power behind the Board. He set the agenda and the vision; he presented the policies and the programs for the Mission, and made sure others went along with them. It was only during the last few years of his life that the Board began to exercise a measure of control over Joseph's programs and policies, and began to assume more responsibility for the financial control of the Mission. By the late 1940's, with no heir apparent and with Joseph spending more and more time in Europe, the Board began to function as a "hands on" committee, involving themselves in the day-to-day operations of the Mission—interviewing potential workers, approving student scholarships, etc.

The funeral service for Dr. Joseph Hoffman Cohn was held on Thursday, October 8, 1953. Following the service, a special meeting of the Board of Directors was called. The mood of the meeting was somber indeed. The purpose: to determine a course of action to hold things together until a successor for Joseph Cohn could be found.

It was moved and seconded that the Executive Committee would have the authority to run the day-to-day operations of the Mission.[3] The Executive Committee, as elected at the annual meeting held on January 28, 1953,[4] was comprised of three members—Mr. Joseph Cohn, Mr. Frank Davis, and Mr. Harold B. Pretlove. Mr. Pretlove also served as the Secretary of the Board, and as the Executor of Joseph Cohn's estate.[5] Mr. Davis was Vice-President and Treasurer, having replaced Paul Graef following his death. With Joseph Cohn gone, the task of running the Mission fell into the laps of Mr. Pretlove and Mr. Davis, but the Board was also intent on remaining involved in the day-to-day operations of the Mission. Toward this end, they amended their By-Laws, Article IV, Section 2 to state:

> The Executive Committee shall consist of not less than three and not more than five members, three of whom shall hold the office of President, Treasurer, and Executive Secretary, the others to be named by the Board of Member-Directors. The Committee shall meet regularly once a month, during the absence of the regular Board Meetings, and 3 shall constitute a quorum.[6]

Thus, the monthly meetings of the Executive Committee, held with the Executive Secretary (a Board member), was to enforce all existing policy of the Board and see that the Mission was proceeding as the Board intended.

In hindsight one wonders why there was no discussion of establishing a Search Committee to locate a successor either from within the organization or from outside its staff of workers. But no such discussion is recorded in the Minutes, nor is there even a passing reference to such a proposal. At the time of Joseph's death the staff of the Mission included a number of Jewish believers who were veteran missionaries to the Jews—Walter Atkinson, Harry Burgen, Daniel Fuchs, Emil Gruen, Henry Heydt, Charles Kalisky, Asher Levi, Harry Marko, Sanford Mills, Arnold Seidler, and Elias Zimmerman. Any one of these men might have been appointed as Interim Director, thus giving the Board time to ultimately choose a successor. From outside the Mission's own staff, the Board could have considered a successor by contacting men who were saved through the ministry of the Mission, such as Dr. Charles Lee Feinberg, et al. Or they could have once again contacted Mr. Herman Newmark, Joseph's original choice as a successor. But, once again, there is no mention within the Minutes of the special Board meeting to indicate any such considerations. It was not until three years after Joseph's death that Mr. Pretlove proposed to the Board that they contact Herman Newmark; only then was the suggestion put forth that the Board attempt to work out a merger between the two organizations. The incentive to the Hebrew Christian Testimony to Israel for such a merge was that they would be allowed to have the oversight of the foreign branches of the Mission.[7] But such a merger was never consummated.

HAROLD B. PRETLOVE—EXECUTIVE SECRETARY

The regular Fall Board meeting was held on October 28, 1953, just twenty-three days after Joseph Cohn's death. At that meeting, Mr. Harold B. Pretlove was elected the Executive Secretary of the Mission.[8] *Nothing*, other than the sudden death of Joseph Cohn, could have shocked the missionaries and staff more. None of the men on the Board were qualified to be Executive Secretary, but the least qualified was Harold Pretlove, who had only served on the Board for six years. He was elected to the Board in January 1948, at the recommendation of Frank Davis. He had never been a missionary to the Jews. He was not an ordained minister. He'd had no formal training in the Scriptures. And, he was a Gentile Christian. The missionary staff at the time of Joseph Cohn's death was over 70% Jewish believers, most of whom came from orthodox Jewish backgrounds. The majority of the missionary staff spoke Yiddish. Those who did not, quickly learned a few words and expressions. With the exception of the Board of Directors, the Mission was a ministry established by Jews, run by Jews, for the purpose of reaching Jews with the Gospel. The Board's appointment of a Gentile Christian as Executive Secretary was an invitation to problems. Even the choice of the title given to Mr. Pretlove raised a red flag to the staff. "General Secretary" was a common title for mission directors of that day. But, to the missionaries and the staff, the title "Executive Secretary" meant that Mr. Pretlove was totally in charge.

The reasoning behind the Board's decision to appoint Harold Pretlove as Executive Secretary is unclear. But Mr. Pretlove told this author, and others, that he was Joseph's choice for the position and that Joseph had shared that fact with Board members on several occasions.

Mr. Linton, President of the Board, made the announcement of Harold Pretlove's appointment in the Salutation of the March 1954 *Chosen People* magazine. He wrote:

> ...Naturally all of our friends have been wondering and asking who will be the one who will assume the many, many duties and tasks that were formerly so ably handled by our beloved departed brother, Dr. J. Hoffman Cohn. Humanly speaking, such a vacancy seems almost impossible to fill, but nothing is impossible with the Lord, and we know that He has been preparing Mr. Harold Pretlove through the past years for the task which the Directors of the Board have asked him to undertake, namely, the management of this world-wide testimony to the Jews.... When various persons would ask Dr. Cohn who he thought might take over the leadership of the work in the event that he no longer would be able to do it, without any hesitation the answer came, 'Harold Pretlove.'[9]

But Mr. Linton, and individuals who knew Joseph Cohn personally, knew that such remarks were often made casually and were not to be taken seriously. Nothing within the Minutes, or within Joseph Cohn's personal correspondence, indicates that he ever selected a successor apart from Herman Newmark.

At the Directors special meeting of October 8, 1953, following Joseph's funeral, a resolution in his memory was passed. Copies were later given to members of his family. In part it read:

A Tribute to Dr. Joseph Hoffman Cohn

He slipped away so quietly, at the peak of his activities—his book of the history of the Mission just finished—the material for The Chosen People *for November and December, just finished—the birthday gifts delivered to his grandchild, whose birthday was yet in the month to come—just as though the Lord had said to him (maybe He did, who knows) 'son get ready, you're coming home to Father's house.'*

Those who were in close association with him during the past two or more decades, best realize what it meant to have fellowship with this great man of God. The days ahead are going to be hard for them. They will have to lean hard on Him Whose everlasting arms were always round their leader.

Dr. Cohn was chosen of God for a great work, and God signally equipped him for his monumental task. As the Apostle Paul was signally prepared of God for the ministry to which God called him so Dr. Cohn was prepared for his great assignment; and one cannot think of his genius apart from God's endowments.

God gave him rare executive and administrative ability; gave him great gifts of writing, so that one could hardly finish one paragraph, in anticipation of what the next would reveal; gave him great gifts as an expositor, so that he was totally unable to meet the demands for his ministry, that came to him, from all over the country; gave him great gifts in appraising men and women, enabling him to penetrate through the exterior and determine what was in the heart, that the personnel of the Mission would be above reproach; gave him great reserves of faith and strength to withstand the Satan inspired attacks that were levelled at him through the years; gave him great courage in his writings, in which he unsparingly attacked those whom he regarded as the enemies of his Lord; gave him great powers of discernment in the study of the Scriptures, enabling him to answer multitudes of those seeking light; gave him a phenomenal memory, a quick mind, ability to reach immediate decisions with exceptional inerrancy; and so we could go on and on before reaching the bottom of the well of God's reserves.

And he has left a great work, firmly established, with world wide recognition. In his meticulous care of details, he has seen that every phase of the work of the Mission, is in running order, with a consecrated personnel, so that the great ministry of the Mission may go forward, not only without abatement, but to scale greater heights in its witness for the Master.

We shall best revere his memory, by giving ourselves unstintedly to the wonderful stewardship with which God has entrusted us.[10]

This resolution spelled out in detail how the Board felt about Joseph Cohn. It further spelled out the characteristics in Joseph that God had used to build the work of the Mission into a world-wide ministry. They were characteristics that the Board should have been seeking in Joseph's successor—but they did not.

In choosing Harold Pretlove, the Board chose a man who was the exact opposite of Joseph Cohn. Harold Pretlove was a fine Christian gentleman and a loving husband and father, and God used him to carry the Mission through some very difficult years. But the qualities of leadership in Joseph Cohn that God used to expand the work of the Mission, and which were so evident to the Board, were not present in Harold Pretlove.

Members of Cohn's family, as well as staff members who served under Joseph Cohn, have stated to the author on a number of occasions that Joseph did not believe the Mission would survive ten years beyond his death. It could very well be that members of the Board felt this way too. Perhaps they were acting out this belief when they appointed Harold Pretlove as Joseph's successor. This would explain, in part, many of the Board's later decisions regarding staff, as well as their decision to spend off the Mission's assets.

Such thoughts are merely speculation, but one thing is certain—God never intended for the Mission founded by Rabbi Leopold Cohn to cease in its tireless efforts to bring the Gospel to the Jewish people. The work begun by the fearless rabbi, and expanded by his determined son, has continued to be blessed of God so that now, one hundred years after its founding, it is still a vibrant testimony reaching Jews everywhere with the Gospel.

Historic Staff Conference

In the months immediately following the death of Joseph Cohn, the morale of the missionary staff and other workers of the Mission was at its lowest possible state. Recognizing the workers feelings of abandonment and frustration, the Board called the first general staff meeting, or "Workers' Conference," in the history of the Mission. The entire North American staff was to meet together from December 14-16, 1953. The purpose of the conference was to boost the morale of the staff and to try to rekindle the flame of hope for the future of the Mission, as well as to engender staff confidence in their decision in selecting Harold Pretlove as the successor to Joseph Cohn.

All fifty-four staff members attended the conference, which was held at the Leopold Memorial Building—the Headquarters building in Manhattan. For some, the conference was a time of reunion. For others, it was their first opportunity to meet their fellow workers. For most, it was their first opportunity to meet members of the Board of Directors.

The conference began with prayer and devotions. Then the members of the Board of Directors and the members of the Executive Committee were introduced. They told of their plans for expanding the overall work of the Mission, as well as strengthening of the Mission's existing branches. Such assurances were a necessary part of the conference because many of the workers believed that the Mission would soon be closing it's doors; they did not see how it could survive without Cohn's leadership. Yet they clung to any ray of hope that it would survive.

The Board then introduced a film which Joseph Cohn had completed only weeks before his death. The title of the film was, "I Found My Messiah." The story line of the film was about a young Jewish soldier who returned to his home and business after World War II; he was given Dr. Cohn's tract, "What is a Christian?" and subsequently accepted Yeshua as his Messiah. The film was unique for its time because it portrayed typical questions within the mind of a seeking Jew; it showed the reasons for the prejudices of the Jews toward Jesus and toward Christians; it tenderly and tastefully, but with tremendous emotional impact, showed the struggle which the young Jewish soldier went through as he literally "sweated out" the choice he had to make between his family and the Lord. The film closed on a note of climactic victory as the young man chose Yeshua, and God gave him back his family.

This film proved to be a true legacy from Joseph. Because some members of the cast were Jewish believers who had found the Lord through the Mission, the film was very real to the workers and it became a rallying point for them.

A report of the Workers' Conference, and of their experience in viewing Joseph's film, was given in *The Chosen People* magazine. It states:

>...*When the lights were turned on there was not a dry eye in the audience. In viewing the picture many of the workers had re-lived their own experience.*
>
>*After dinner we met again to discuss the picture and the best means of presenting it. All agreed that it is a wonderful presentation of our message; it preaches the gospel; it creates interest in bringing the gospel to the Jew; it shows the difficulties involved and the reasons for them; it shows how to reach the Jew effectively with the gospel.... We believe that this is one of the finest Christian films yet produced.*[11]

The discussion did not end there however. The report goes on to state:

>*With all of this your workers agreed heartily,...Your Mission is built on Bible teaching and not upon entertainment. If this picture is to be effective, it must be made a part of our Bible-teaching ministry. Friendship made through the means of audio-visual education may not be very long lasting, but a friendship based upon the solid rock of God's Word will weather the storm. With this in mind, it was decided that the picture would never be shown on a rental basis. At each showing a field-worker of the Mission must be present, and there must be an appeal for Jewish Missions that is based upon a message from the Word of God.*[12]

Given vision and hope, and an exciting new means of financing and supporting that vision, the missionaries and other workers were ready to fight the up-hill battle of keeping the Mission going without the strong leadership of Joseph Hoffman Cohn.

Continuing to build upon the momentum already created, the next two days of the conference were like icing on the cake. The entire staff was taken to Brooklyn, to the old headquarters building at 27 Throop Avenue, where it had all begun. The sight and smells of the old building brought back vivid memories for many members of the staff; it was the place where many had been baptized. It had been said by Cohn, and by others, that fully half of the Christian Jewish missionaries in America found the Lord in the Mission's building at 27 Throop Avenue. It was also claimed that over one thousand Jews were baptized by Leopold and Joseph Cohn in that building. Ruth Wardell was a new missionary on staff, and she had the privilege of being present, when the 1,000th Jewish believer was baptized!

When the Headquarters operation was moved from Brooklyn to Manhattan in 1946, the Brooklyn building became the home for the large youth and teenage ministry of the Mission. As visitors, the staff of missionaries watched as the young people read and recited Scripture, and sang praises to the Messiah in Yiddish and English. The old hall was crowded as the visiting missionaries and the young people mingled, but it was a joyful occasion—Jewish children, young people, whole families and missionaries all joining together in praise to the Lord.

A report in *The Chosen People* magazine included an anecdote that expresses the response of the staff to their visit to the old Brooklyn headquarters. It states:

> At the close of the meeting a little heart-warming and enlightening incident occurred. Our veteran missionary, Elias Zimmerman, had been standing at the door waiting for transportation to his hotel room. One of the young people, Joe Rubin, spied him standing there and excitedly exclaimed, 'Zimmie, why, I haven't seen you for years!? Fifteen years ago (c.1937) homeless and heart-sick, Joe came to our Mission in Los Angeles needing a place to sleep. He received shelter and heard the gospel before he went on his way. His path finally led to Brooklyn where he met one of our girls, Clara Krop, who led him to the Lord and thence to the matrimonial altar. And now, several years later, they brought their daughter to our Christmas celebration where she played Christmas carols on the accordion. Los Angeles and Brooklyn, three thousand miles apart, yet your Mission preached the gospel to two widely separated souls who later became one in the Lord. And so another Christian-Jewish family was begun.[13]

Having seen the old Brooklyn headquarters, the staff was also taken to Coney Island. Like Brooklyn, the building was jammed packed—there was not one empty seat—and, again, the staff thrilled at being a part of a ministry that was clearly doing an impressive job of reaching the Jewish community with the gospel.

The workers were also invited to attend sessions of the Jewish Missionary Training Institute, a program that was under the leadership of Dr. Henry Heydt, the founder and former President of the Lancaster School of the Bible, in Lancaster, Pennsylvania. Dr. Heydt was a gentle man of God, with an excellent knowledge of the Scriptures, and as the staff observed the faculty and the quality of teaching at the Institute, they became convinced of their desire to see their Mission carry on this vital phase of the ministry.

As the workers returned to their individual stations, the vision of reaching all Jews everywhere with the Gospel had been rekindled in their hearts. The conference had accomplished what the Board had hoped that it would: The workers returned to their places of service determined to fulfill the call of God that had led them to serve with the Mission.

For Harold Pretlove, the task of holding the work together in the aftermath of Joseph's death was an extremely difficult one, but God used him and blessed him. Eventually, however, the work took its toll upon his physical health.

Harold Pretlove joined the Board while he was employed by Dugan Brothers Baking Company—a well-known bakery firm in the Northeast, whose owners were Christian businessmen. Harold began his employment at Dugan Brothers as one of their accountants, but as the years went by he moved up the ladder until he held an executive position within the company. Mr. Pretlove often shared with the author that Mr. Dugan had a burden for sharing the Gospel with the Jews, and that he often stopped at the Mission to pick up a bundle of tracts. He would then stuff his pockets full of tracts and go out to distribute them on the streets of New York. Pretlove said Dugan's devotion to witnessing to Jews impressed him and was the motivating factor that instilled in him an interest in witnessing to the Jews.

Harold Pretlove had been a faithful employee of Dugan Brothers for twenty-eight years when he resigned to accept the position as Executive Secretary of the Mission. Throughout his secular business career, he had maintained active roles in various ministries. Not only did he serve on the Board of the Mission, he served as President of the New York Bible Society for four years, he served on the Board of the Christian Business Men's Committee, and he was active in other evangelical Christian groups as well. He was not without experience and ability in serving on the boards of Christian organizations!

In his position as Executive Secretary, Mr. Pretlove was immediately faced with a number of challenges. One matter of prime concern was the need to fill Joseph Cohn's place on the Board. Mr. Pretlove therefore nominated Mr. Huntley Stone, one of Joseph's sons, who was a successful lawyer and businessman in Bridgeport, Connecticut. Even though Joseph and his wife had been separated for many years, and Huntley had retained his Mother's maiden name, he had remained in contact with his father and he had a genuine interest in the Mission which his father and grandfather had built. The author had opportunity to visit with Mr. Stone, and as the conversation developed he indicated that the Board was in no way considering him as a successor to his father. Rather, the invitation was extended to him because of the Board's desire to maintain ties with the Cohn family. Huntley was unanimously elected to the Board, and faithfully served until 1965.

The challenge of preparing the monthly issues of *The Chosen People* magazine was another major hurdle for Mr. Pretlove. At their October 1953 meeting, the Board had decided that the Executive Committee would be responsible for preparing the January 1954 issue of the magazine[14] (the special Joseph Hoffman Cohn Memorial Issue). But it was not the preparation of the magazine that posed the problem; it was deciding who would write the Salutation that Joseph wrote each month which presented a dilemma. Because the magazine was prepared three months in advance, Joseph had already prepared materials for that period of time. But nothing had been written for subsequent issues of the magazine. Mr. Pretlove knew he was not prepared to write the articles. He also knew the Mission could not run Joseph's previous Salutations over and over again (although he did run a few). He finally decided to approach Daniel Fuchs about writing the Salutations for him, since Daniel had helped Joseph put the magazine together from time to time, and since he also had experience using the old metal plated "addressographer" which was used to label the magazines for mailing.

Daniel gladly accepted Pretlove's proposal. From April 1954 through February 1955, the Salutations in *The Chosen People* magazine carried no signature. Readers assumed they were being written by Harold Pretlove when, in fact, they were being written by Daniel Fuchs. The March 1955 magazine is the first instance where the Salutation carries Daniel Fuchs' signature. From that time, until his death on May 24, 1988 (a span of 34 years!), Daniel Fuchs wrote for the monthly issues of *The Chosen People* magazine. He wrote the Salutation and an editorial, and when he became Chairman of the Board he wrote a post-script, message, or an article that was carried in serial form.

An Editorial Staff Appointed

In the weeks and months following Joseph's death, the magazine—the writing of the Salutation, the matter of credit being given to the individual who wrote the Salutation, the editorial position of the magazine, the content of the magazine—became the "baby" over which the entire Mission family was fighting. The matter of the signature for the Salutation became an issue between Daniel Fuchs and Harold Pretlove; the missionary staff did not feel the Executive Committee of the Board had the "know how" or the experience to produce a magazine. By the latter months of 1954, the situation was intolerable. It was resolved at the January 26, 1955 Board meeting with the following action recorded:

> Mr. Jones moved and Mr. Stone seconded the motion that an editorial staff consisting of Harold B. Pretlove, Executive Secretary, Daniel Fuchs, Henry J. Heydt, Charles Kalisky and Hilda Koser be appointed for the publication of The Chosen People, The Shepherd of Israel, and our other publications. The Salutation Letter in The Chosen People is to be written by Mr. Fuchs and is to be signed by him. The names of the editorial staff are to appear in the front of The Chosen People. Mr. Pretlove's name is to appear as Executive Secretary. It was so voted.[15]

At the same meeting, the Board voted to begin publishing ten issues of the magazine (September through June) rather than eight issues (October through May), as previously published. They further voted to send out a "Mid-Summer Letter" in either July or August.[16] The addition of two issues of the magazine, plus a Mid-Summer Letter, constituted a major change and generated a considerable amount of additional work. But more than that, the Board's decisions initiated the evolution of power from Harold Pretlove to Daniel Fuchs. By the April 1955 Board meeting, Daniel Fuchs was named Chairman of the Editorial Committee. From that time on, he reported directly to the Board of Directors.[17]

Tension Among the Mission's Staff

The tension and conflict created over the preparation of *The Chosen People* magazine would have been enough, but the Conference ministry and the Missionary Department (national and international) were also drastically affected by Joseph Cohn's death. The Executive Committee was running the Mission, under the direction of the Board, but no one was setting vision. Ideas for the Missionary Department were presented, but were not well thought through. One example of this was a plan for the expansion of missionary work which Mr. Pretlove presented to the Board on behalf of the Executive Committee. The Minutes state:

> Mr. Pretlove explained …the desire of the Executive Committee to expand our missionary activities throughout this country, Canada and the world, this program to start with an enlarged missionary program in our Los Angeles Branch— the first step to be taken would be to find a suitable building (either to rent or buy, preferably rent) to hold classes such as we have in New York, Coney Island and Brooklyn. Then it would be necessary to find suitable missionary workers to staff these stations.[18]

The Board approved the plan—action that reveals the lack of missionary experience by Harold Pretlove and members of the Board. This was not the way Cohn had built the ministry. It is not the way to build mission stations. The Directors had the cart before the horse. Buildings come last, not first. Committed workers and missionaries come first. Buildings are the result of ministry, they do not create ministry.

The veteran missionaries on staff began to balk. Some of the staff had been enraged over the appointment of Harold Pretlove, and as they became aware of decisions made by the Board many of them began to write letters of complaint.

Arnold Seidler, the missionary in Pittsburgh, was the most vociferous with his complaints. He apparently went so far as to suggest to the Board that they remove Harold Pretlove from the position of Executive Secretary and name Rev. Elias Zimmerman as his replacement. The Minutes show the following action taken:

> As each member of the Board had received a mimeographed letter from Rev. Arnold Seidler making certain suggestions as to the appointment of members of the staff, and as this letter apparently has been sent to other than the Board members, Mr. Davis moved. . .that the Executive Secretary be authorized to write to Mr. Seidler thanking him for his letter which has been considered by the Board of Directors. For various reasons important among which is the fact that Mr. Zimmerman's health has caused him to consider retirement, the Board was obliged to dismiss the suggestion. The Board is always open to suggestions from the workers but as in this case the letter was mailed rather widely to other than the Board of Directors, the Board is obliged to remind Mr. Seidler that this is an unwise practice and does not promote the best interests of the American Board of Missions to the Jews. Accordingly the Board requests that he refrain from any such action in the future and that he advise us the exact mailing of the letter outside of the Board of Directors so that they can consider an appropriate reply.[19]

The action taken by Arnold Seidler in voicing his dissatisfaction and his suggested replacement for the position of Executive Secretary was unethical, and the Board was correct in reprimanding him. But in receiving Seidler's letter, the Board was confronted with two glaring facts: the unrest and dissatisfaction among the Mission's staff over their appointment of Harold Pretlove as Executive Secretary had not abated; Harold Pretlove would never be able to win the confidence of the missionary staff—he would never be able to supervise them or set the vision for their activities.

Problems also arose because of Pretlove's lack of experience in handling the conference ministry. Joseph Cohn had brought Emil Gruen to the Headquarters building, and had placed him in charge of setting up the conferences (although Cohn always helped in the selection of speakers and, of course, had the final veto). Pretlove's position as General Secretary directly impacted Gruen's ministry, and conflicts erupted over how far Gruen's authority extended in planning the conferences. Was he now over the Field Evangelists? What was their relationship to him going to be?

A NEW ADMINISTRATIVE STRUCTURE

In an effort to quell the contention between the workers, and find viable solutions for the problems at hand, a special meeting of the Board was called for March 1, 1955. At the meeting the members approved a motion stating: "...that Rev. Emil D. Gruen be appointed as director of Conference planning for those conferences which do not come directly under the supervision of our field representatives."[20]

A further effort to ease the tension between Mr. Pretlove and Mr. Fuchs was undertaken by the Board at their October 1955 meeting. The Directors approved "...the motion that a new position be created with the purpose of expanding the missionary activity of the Board, and that Daniel Fuchs be a appointed to be the Director of Missionary Activity."[21]

In their efforts to resolve the tensions that existed within the missionary staff and programs, the Board ultimately assigned more and more authority to Daniel Fuchs. His assignment to the position of Director of Missionary Activity, further reduced the authority of the Executive Secretary, Harold Pretlove. Daniel now reported directly to the Board as Chairman of the Editorial Committee, and as Director of Missionary Activity.[22]

At the January 16, 1957 meeting of the Board, Fuchs presented an organizational function chart which he, Gruen and Pretlove had prepared. The chart outlined the functions of the various departments of the Mission. The Board of Directors was listed as the foremost body. Under the Board of Directors was the Executive Committee, whose function was listed as policy interpretation and investment planning. Under the Executive Committee was the Joint Planning Committee, whose function was coordination, advertising, radio, publications, and student training. Under the Joint Planning Committee, with access to the Executive Committee, were three departments: Executive Secretary, Conference Secretary, Missionary Secretary.

The duties of the Executive Secretary's department were shown to be: business management, administrative, income, expenses, equipment, investment management, study and recommendations, real estate, equipment, acquisitions, sales, maintenance.

The duties of the Conference Secretary's department were shown to be: Bible conferences—New York and area wide.

The duties of the Missionary Secretary's department were shown to be: missionary and evangelistic activities, branch and field personnel, programs, Jewish Missionary Training Institute, headquarters, Bible schools, churches; editorial—Chosen People, Shepherd of Israel, etc.

This chart, which was adopted by the Board and remained the functional and operational chart for the Mission until September 1968, essentially made the leadership of the Mission a "troika"—a leadership team of three. The essential power and authority for all decisions rested in the Joint Planning Committee (a committee which formed a team of the three men: Harold Pretlove, Daniel Fuchs, and Emil Gruen), but the Executive Committee of the Board had the final authority.

DANIEL FUCHS APPOINTED TO THE BOARD

The Board's unanimous approval of the functional chart indicates that the Directors recognized that if peace within the ranks was ever going to be realized, the mantle of leadership of the Mission would ultimately have to fall on Daniel Fuchs, a Jewish believer. This was confirmed by further action taken at the meeting. The Minutes state: "The name of Rev. Daniel Fuchs was presented for membership on the Board of Directors in the Class of 1958. Mr. Fuchs has subscribed to the doctrinal statement of the Board…. It was so voted."[23]

Daniel Fuchs' appointment to the Board gave him equal authority with Harold Pretlove. The Directors saw the appointment as a necessary step in making the Joint Planning Committee function without creating more friction. Previous to this appointment, both Fuchs and Gruen had been invited to Board meetings to give their reports but once their reports were given, discussed, and appropriate action taken, the men were dismissed. With the appointment, Daniel would have access to all Board information. The fact that the Board did not present the name of Emil Gruen for membership indicates that they had decided that Daniel Fuchs would eventually become Joseph Cohn's successor.

The appointment of Daniel Fuchs to the Board defused much of the tension within the missionary ranks. When Joseph Cohn was alive, all of their dealings had been with him; communication between the workers and the Board members was virtually nonexistent. But when Cohn died, many of the missionaries felt they no longer had a voice in the Mission, or a sympathetic ear within the Mission. Daniel Fuchs was a Jewish believer, a child of the Mission, a missionary himself. His appointment to the Board and his position as Missionary Secretary allayed many of their fears and rekindled their hopes for their futures with the Mission.

RABBI ASHER TZADIK LEVI—HIS STORY

One of the workers who was on fire for the Lord was Rabbi Asher Tzadik Levi—a man whom Joseph Cohn led to the Lord in 1952, and who joined the staff of the Mission shortly before Cohn's death. Rabbi Levi's story is a wonderful account of God's faithfulness in blessing His Word and in using willing hearts to share the Gospel.

Rabbi Levi was a practicing Jewish rabbi according to the traditions of the Spanish and Portuguese Jews for over thirty-five years, serving in Sephardic (Spanish) synagogues in Turkey, Belgium, and England before he came to America. In America, he served in a synagogue in Miami, Florida.

In 1950 the days and weeks seemed to offer nothing but turmoil and unrest for Levi. He could not seem to find answers or solutions to the problems that beset him, and in desperation he turned to a well-known Jewish businessman for advice. What he did not know was that the businessman, a Jew from Baghdad, was a believer in Yeshua.

The Jew from Baghdad had come to America some years earlier, and had made a fortune in real estate. He owned several hotels in Miami Beach. One morning, as he was leaving one of his hotels, a Christian handed him a Yiddish copy of "The Shepherd of Israel." He was intrigued by the Hebrew and Yiddish, and began to read it. The words touched his heart and he wrote to the Mission requesting more information. Joseph Cohn responded. Soon Joseph received another letter from the Jew from Baghdad. This time he enclosed a check for $500.00 and asked for copies of all of the materials the Mission had in stock. The materials were sent immediately, and Joseph then left for Europe. When he returned it was time for the Summer's End Conference in New York. To his amazement, the Jew from Baghdad attended the conference and gave his testimony of how he had found his Messiah through the literature of the Mission. He concluded his testimony with a prayer request for a Jewish rabbi who was living in one of his hotels in Miami. He asked for prayer for the rabbi, and for a door of opportunity to witness to him.

God answered prayer in a most amazing way. As the Jewish businessman sat in his office one day, Rabbi Asher Levi walked right into the office and began pouring out his story of woe. He spoke of his marital problems and of his separation from his wife. He also revealed that during the time he was serving as a rabbi in Miami Beach, someone had given him literature from the American Board of Missions to the Jews (Chosen People Ministries). He read the literature. In fact, he had pored over it. But the more he read it, the more questions it raised in his mind. He began to question his calling and profession, and in wrestling with his confusion and doubts about Judaism, he revealed that he had resigned his position at the synagogue and was in need of work. He wanted to know if the Jewish businessman could help him.

The Jewish businessman listened, and then picked up an old envelope from his desk. He turned it over, carefully wrote three words, and handed it to Rabbi Levi. The three words said: Isaiah fifty-three. Seeing the puzzled look on the rabbi's face, the businessman told him, "If you are a Rabbi, read the 53rd chapter of Isaiah and then come again to see me."[24] Astonished, curious, and confused, Rabbi Levi returned to his room. There he picked up his Bible and read Isaiah 53. He wasn't sure what to look for, so he read it again and again. At last the Spirit of God touched his heart and he began to think, "of whom does this prophet speak?" He could only think of one name, "Yeshua!"

After his discovery, Rabbi Levi returned to the office of the businessman, who then suggested that Levi write to Joseph Cohn and ask for a visit with him. When Levi arrived in New York he had one question for Cohn—how could the Messiah be the "Korban" (atonement) for our sins. Cohn shared additional Scriptures with him and in a few minutes Rabbi Levi prayed to receive Yeshua as his Messiah and Savior. On Resurrection Sunday, 1952, Joseph had the privilege of baptizing Rabbi Asher Tzadik Levi.[25] Watching the baptism through the lens of his camera was Daniel Fuchs.[26]

Not long after Rabbi Levi's baptismal service, Joseph Cohn made a trip to California. Levi had mentioned that his wife lived in California, so Cohn looked her up. He shared the news that Asher now believed that Yeshua was the promised Messiah, and to his surprise Mrs. Levi shared that she had been a believer in Yeshua for many years. Cohn was able to reunite the family; they were now one in the Messiah.

Joseph arranged for Levi to attend some Bible classes and to take the courses at the Jewish Missionary Institute in New York. In 1953 Cohn hired Levi to work at the Mission's Headquarters building. After Cohn's death, Levi was transferred to Miami Beach, Florida, where the Lord used him to lead many Jewish people to the Lord. Later he was transferred to California, where he opened a branch of the Mission in Beverly Hills. But Levi did not confine his ministry to the Jewish community of Beverly Hills; he witnessed to the Jews of the greater Los Angeles area, and as far north as Santa Barbara. Of his ministry in California Levi wrote:

> My leaflets, 'How a Rabbi Found Salvation' and 'The Chosen People—Am Segula,' recently published, are being circulated here in Los Angeles and have attracted favorable attention. I continue to receive letters asking for copies. One letter from a well-known radio broadcaster in New York asks permission to broadcast my testimony over a large 5-station network that would reach many of the Jews in the New York Metropolitan area of which there are more than two million.
>
> There are large numbers of Spanish-speaking Jews in Los Angeles, and I was recently invited to speak to some of them in Spanish. At a meeting which my wife and I attended in our Beth Sar Shalom Mission we met a Spanish Jewess who told us she heard me offer a prayer in Hebrew and was so thrilled she told her husband and they promised to bring ten people to the next meeting.[27]

MARTIN AND CEIL ROSEN—THEIR STORY

As the Mission continued in this transition phase of its history, more staff was added. In the Fall of 1954, one year after the death of Joseph Cohn, a young Jewish believer entered Northeastern Bible Institute of Essex Fells, New Jersey, and thus began his career with the Mission. Martin (Moishe) Rosen's life, ministry, and commitment to Jewish missions and evangelism rivals that of Leopold and Joseph Hoffman Cohn. In many ways he thought of himself as the successor to the Cohns' and sought to pattern his life and ministry after theirs.

Martin Meyer Rosen was born to Reform Jewish parents in Kansas City, Missouri in 1932. In 1934 his family moved to Denver, Colorado. There, Mr. Rosen opened a scrap metal business. He was hoping his son would help him in the business but, like many teenagers, Martin had other plans for his life. He did not want to make his career in scrap metal so he tried to find another job, but he soon discovered that jobs for Jewish boys were few and far between. He therefore lied about his age and enlisted in the National Guard artillery unit. But even there, anti-Semitism raised its ugly head in the form of continual harassment from his sergeant. It reached the point where Martin could take it no longer, and he attacked his sergeant physically—an act that resulted in Martin having to guard the motor pool for thirty-six straight hours, after which he ended up in the hospital from sheer exhaustion.

Each new anti-Semitic experience reinforced Martin's pride in his Jewish heritage; the episodes also reinforced his belief that there was no God. He fancied himself an agnostic. Culturally, he was proud to be a Jew but religiously, he was an agnostic.

Martin met and fell in love with a beautiful Jewish girl named Ceil. After they were married, he became a salesman for a sporting goods store; he also enrolled at the local college, taking business courses. Everything seemed to be going his way—until the day he met Orville Freestone, a local pastor.

Orville and Martin met at bus stop on Yom Kippur, October 3, 1949. Their first visit wasn't a lengthy one, but it was long enough for Orville to witness to Martin and to hand him a New Testament. Because his witness was done with such love and tact, Martin accepted the New Testament. He put it in his dresser drawer when he got home. As he closed the drawer he tried to forget about the incident, but Orville's words kept coming back to him. He had never heard anyone explain Christianity the way Orville had. Orville had urged him to read the New Testament, but Martin feared that if he read it, and if he believed what it said, he would be a Christian. He would then be an outcast to his family and to his own people, so he decided to leave the whole matter alone. But Orville Freestone had a burden for Martin Rosen, and in the weeks following their initial visit he continued to witness to him and to pray for him.

One day Ceil found the little New Testament in Martin's dresser drawer. She took it out and began to read; the more she read the more convinced she became that it was true. She remembered that Martin had introduced her to Orville Freestone, telling her that he (Orville) was a true believer in the Messiah. But when she tried to contact Orville she learned that he and his wife had moved.

God's faithful servant, Hannah Wago, was also living in Denver, Colorado at the time. Before her move to Denver, Hannah had served the Lord as the faithful help mate of Oscar Wago, the Mission's worker in Columbus, Ohio. Mention was made of the their vibrant ministry, and of Oscar's sudden death, in Chapter Six of this history.

Although she deeply missed Oscar, Hannah continued her zealous witness to the Jewish people after her husband's death. In Denver, Hannah soon became known as the person to contact when help was needed in presenting a testimony to the Jews of that community. That is why, in January 1953, she received a letter from Rev. Orville Freestone asking if she would visit a young Jewish couple—Martin and Ceil Rosen. Although the Freestone's had moved to a new community, Orville was still praying for Martin's salvation—in spite of the fact that Martin had told him, "Look, I appreciate your concern and all, but you're not going to convert me. I really don't want to talk about Jesus anymore."[28]

Hannah preceded all of her visits with prayer, so she began to ask God to open an opportunity for her to visit Rev. Freestone's young friends. The answer to her prayers came several weeks later when one of the Jewish women she visited regularly called to say she was sick. As Hannah hung up the receiver, the Lord reminded her of the Rosens.

It was a cold, blustery day. As Hannah made her way to the Rosen's home the cold wind stung her face. She hadn't called to make an appointment, but she felt certain someone would be home on such a bitter day. As she raised her hand to knock on the door, Hannah offered a prayer for God's guidance and blessing. Then the door opened, and she was face to face with a young Jewish woman—Ceil Rosen. Hannah later wrote:

> ...When I mentioned our mutual friends and their request that I stop in and bring their regards, she was very friendly. In fact, she seemed delighted and asked me to please take my coat off and stay a while....
>
> We first talked a little about our mutual friends. Then I inquired a few things about the little family and learned that they had come from the East several years ago. She then asked some questions of me, and I told her a few things about myself. I then took the opportunity to tell her about Mr. Wago, and before I realized it, I told her the story of his conversion.
>
> My young friend was preparing supper for the little family and had to go past me several times to the pantry. Each time she was very polite and apologized for interrupting. The second time she went to the pantry, I stopped a moment until she came back, and she said, 'Please go on now; I am really interested; I want to hear the rest of the story." I finished the story, and she seemed so impressed she had tears in her eyes. After she put things in the oven, she came and sat beside me and said, 'Mrs. Wago, you were sent here today. I have been seriously thinking about those very things for about a year, and I have been wanting to know more about the Bible, I half believe it, but I would like to know more about it.'[29]

Ceil Rosen indicated to Hannah that she'd been thinking about spiritual things for over a year, but in her testimony Ceil revealed that she had begun wondering about Israel's Messiah and about Christianity since the time when, as a teenager, she and other members of the high school choral group had participated in a Christmas pageant. As a part of the program they sang a Christmas carol that included the words, "Oh come, Oh come, Emmanuel, And ransom captive Israel." Ceil stated:

> ...I wondered if Jesus could really be the One Israel was waiting for. But then I didn't think about it again until a few years later, after we had been married for a year. It was Christmas of 1951, and I was sitting at home listening to Christmas carols. Again, the words of a song, this time 'O Little Town of Bethlehem,' raised the same question in my mind. I prayed and said, 'God, would you show me what is the right way? Is there anything to what they're saying about Jesus? Is Christianity true? If it is, I'd like to know about it. Otherwise, I'll go back to Judaism, if You show me that I should. Please show me what's true!'[30]

Ceil recognized that God had sent the answer to her prayers in the person of Hannah Wago. She told Hannah her husband was aware of her search for the Truth. She had revealed to him that she'd found the little New Testament in his drawer, and that she'd been reading it. He was so busy with work and school that he didn't make a fuss; he advised her to talk to someone who might be able to answer her questions. Hannah told Ceil she would be happy to visit her once a week to study the Bible with her. In telling about her first visit with Ceil, Hannah stated:

I wanted to pray with her before I left, but her father dropped in to see the only grandchild [Linda], and a little later her husband [Martin] came home early. I promised to be back the following week, but the very stormy weather made it impossible. So I telephoned her, and for a couple of hours we had a Bible lesson over the phone—I hope to the displeasure of the 'prince of the power of the air.' I suggested that when somebody wanted the phone we'd give it to him a while, and then we could pick up where we left off. We were interrupted four times, but each time we waited a few minutes, then continued.

The next week we again had some precious hours of Bible study together. Her mother stopped in a few times, but we hid our books, and when she was gone we dug them out again…. I left some literature and…I suggested she let her husband read these things and keep him informed on the things we were studying so that he might not feel left out or become indifferent.

On the Thursday before Easter, we had at least two and a half hours of study concerning the importance of Christ's death…. Before I left, I mentioned how nice it would be if she (or she and her husband) could enjoy an Easter service and have the inspiration that comes from worshipping with other believers. The young woman said her husband had attended church one time; she never had, but she was thinking about it. She said she would talk to her husband about it, and I promised to make arrangements if she could go….

Later in the afternoon she called me once more, and …she said she decided to go to church, and I could make arrangements…. I called Mrs. E. and informed her that our young friend decided to go, and I asked her to stop for her in the morning. I continued to pray and trust.

I didn't get to contact Mrs. E. again until about four o'clock Sunday afternoon. You can imagine my joy when she told me that our young friend [Ceil] not only enjoyed Sunday school and the inspiring service, but when the invitation was given she went courageously forward to publicly accept the Lord Jesus Christ as her Messiah and Saviour….

My new little sister in Christ called me the next day to supply a little more of the detail I was wondering about. She informed me they had gotten themselves a TV set, and Saturday evening before Easter there was a beautiful portrayal of the life, death and resurrection of Christ. She and her husband were up until midnight watching it. She said her husband seemed especially impressed, and he was visibly touched when he heard Jesus say to His followers, 'He that loveth father or mother more than me is not worthy of me.' His parents are very sweet to them, and he doesn't want to hurt them.

After the picture on TV they went to bed, but they talked until three o'clock in the morning. The young husband was puzzled that their rabbis did not speak of these things, and the little wife remembered that, because Israel rejected the Messiah, blindness in part has happened to them, that seeing they will not perceive, and hearing they will not understand, etc. She said she showed her husband Daniel 9:26 to show that Messiah must have come, and then, as best she could, explained 'The Times of the Gentiles' and 'The Seventy Weeks' of Daniel to him, for I had made her a chart of this. She said she thought her husband would laugh at her, but he didn't. Instead, he took it all in.[31]

The whole affair had come full circle. Through Orville Freestone's persistent testimony, Martin had heard the Gospel and had received a copy of the New Testament, and because of Orville's continued concern, and his letter to Hannah Wago, Ceil had responded to the Gospel and was now a believer in Yeshua.

Less than six weeks had passed since Hannah had paid her first visit in the Rosen's home, and in that time Martin felt that his whole life had been turned upside down. Even though he had been impressed with the program he and Ceil had watched on TV, and even though he had displayed interest as they had discussed the program together, he didn't want anymore of this "Christian" thing in his home and he told Ceil he did not want her to talk with Hannah Wago anymore. Enough was enough!

But Hannah was persistent—and so was Ceil. Their telephone conversations continued. This so angered Martin that one day he tore the telephone out of the wall. Recalling that incident, Martin later wrote:

Ceil was embarrassed, but she remained surprisingly sweet. She said, 'I love you, but please don't make me choose between Jesus and you.' I was in agony. I didn't know what to do with her. As a last resort, I downed a couple of double shots of whiskey and went over to see my father. Ordinarily I kept liquor in the house only for guests, but I needed to do something to give me the courage to discuss such an unpleasant topic.

'Dad, I have a real problem,' I began. 'Ceil says she believes in Jesus. She reads the New Testament, she prays. I don't think she's flipped, but how I can live with her when she's going on like this? Do you think we should get a divorce?'

'Shame on you,' my father said, ignoring the question. 'You've been drinking.'

'You know I usually don't drink. It's just that I'm worried.'

'You can't be serious about divorcing her. She's a nice Jewish girl, from a nice family. You shouldn't drink if you make such silly jokes.'

We didn't really get anywhere in our conservation because I didn't know exactly how to explain my predicament. I didn't tell my father Ceil was a Christian, because to me that meant being a church member and she had never joined any church. In fact, she had honored my demand that she not attend church.[32]

Martin continued to struggle with his beliefs and with Ceil's confession of faith in Yeshua. Hannah's suggestion to Ceil was that she put some of the Mission's tracts and pamphlets around the house. Ceil followed Hannah's advice and it became almost a game to Martin who loved to read them and then remark to Ceil and to himself, "this is a bunch of *goyish* (Gentile) nonsense." But one evening Ceil carefully laid a tract about heaven where it would catch Martin's eye. He picked it up, expecting to make his usual snide remarks, but as he read the words he thought to himself, "What if this is true? What if there is a heaven?"[33] In recalling this moment of crisis and decision Martin (Moishe) later wrote:

A few days later, on a Saturday evening, I was sitting in my favorite chair, and I found myself asking, 'What do I really believe?' I suddenly realized that it might all be true. That was an awesome moment. Many Jews reach that point. They believe it just might be true. Faith grows slowly; it creeps up on you. When I looked inside myself, I realized I actually believed what my wife had been saying, and I didn't know what to do next. It was scary. I told Ceil, and she started throwing Bible verses at me. We began to pray. Kneeling had always been out of the question for me, because it had seemed such a gentile custom. But we actually knelt at our bed that evening. By then I was so devastated inside that I would have done anything. If she had said, 'Stand on your head and pray,' I would have stood on my head and prayed. I was completely pliable and had lost all my bearings at that point. Five minutes before, I had possessed a coherent, secular-Jewish philosophy of life. Now, that was all in the past. I had known who I was, what I wanted, where I was going, but now I was like a baby that needed to be taught everything from the beginning.

We went to church the next morning—it was Pentecost Sunday of 1953—and I went forward and professed my faith publicly, as Ceil had done on Easter Sunday. My whole outlook on life changed drastically after that. If Jesus was really the Promised One, the Messiah—and I believed deeply now that He was—then it seemed important for me to learn all about Him as quickly as possible and model my life after His.[34]

And learn he did—partly because of the intense prodding of Hannah Wago, whom Martin felt was a very imposing presence in their lives. Her bedside manner in discipleship may have left something to be desired, but for her it worked. Evidently she knew how to handle Martin Rosen which, under the best of circumstances, was no easy task. He told the author:

…She always imposed herself on me. I wasn't afraid of her, but to me she was a voice of righteousness. I felt that she was right, and she had me memorizing six Bible verses a day—every day. And she would call me up on the telephone and badger me. It was about two months before I found out that not all Christians were required to memorize so many Bible verses. But by then, I'd memorized quite a few. When I entered Northeastern, in 1954, I'd been a Christian for about eighteen months. We all had to take a Bible entrance exam and I got the top score. That was not broken until 1978.[35]

But Hannah Wago attributed their growth as new believers to their pastor and church family. She wrote:

…As soon as Celia and Martin were brought in contact with Trinity Church, Pastor MacDonald and his fine people of the church took them into their hearts and helped them to grow in grace and in the knowledge of their Lord and Savior.[36]

Martin and Ceil were soon baptized, and they began to sense God's call upon their lives to serve Him in reaching Jewish people with the Gospel. Through Hannah Wago and the literature she had given to them, they knew of the Mission—of Joseph Cohn, of his recent death, and of the various branches of the Mission—but Hannah was the only missionary from the Mission they had met, and Martin told the author:

…I was impressed with her as a person. I had never encountered anyone who had the stubborn drive that she had, and there was a certain amount of admiration. But at the same time, she lived in an apartment that was very sparsely furnished, although she had a lot of books, and I knew that she was poor. That created a negative impression on me—

her poverty. But when Emil Gruen [the Mission's Director of Conferences and Field Evangelist] came into town I was much more favorably impressed. He seemed to be a sophisticated man of the world, and kindly. He encouraged me. I was doing all right financially. I had a part of my father's business and I was working at the sporting goods store.[37]

Feeling certain of God's call upon their lives, and encouraged by Emil Gruen, Martin and Ceil decided to pack up their belongings and move to New York, to attend Bible school and to work with the Mission. The trip was a long one with a toddler (by that time their daughter Linda [Lyn] was in her second year), and when they arrived some of the promises that had been made by Joseph Cohn when he was alive were not kept, but they remained convinced that God had called them to serve with the Mission. In recalling those days, Martin told the author:

We arrived in New York at the end of August, during the Summer's End Conference—1954. You know, coming from Denver, I had not met many Jewish believers. A lot of the people who attended the Summer's End Conference were Christians who had come to town for that purpose, but there were still a goodly number of Jewish believers too. I'll tell you, that really made a profound impression on me. They had a Passover Banquet in 1955 (a Passover Seder) and they had so many people that they had to use five floors (of the Headquarters Building on 72nd Street) and the people still kept coming. That building, in general, was a dingy place—poorly lit, chairs that belonged to the mid-30's—but still they had about 150 people coming in 1954 and 1955.

Over in Brooklyn they had forty at a Yiddish service, and I had to re-learn Yiddish because I had to go over once a month. Then I started going once a week. Those services were taken over by Jonas Cohen. But just the large numbers of Jewish believers impressed me.[38]

During his years of Bible training at Northeastern College, Martin worked part-time for the Mission. He took classes at the Jewish Missionary Training Institute held at the Headquarters building, and was exposed to every aspect of the Mission's work as he was asked to teach Bible classes, conduct street meetings, and carry on personal witnessing and visitation work.

In the Spring of 1957, after his graduation from Northeastern, Martin was hired by Daniel Fuchs to be the Missionary in charge of the Los Angeles branch. Elias Zimmerman, the founder of that branch, had requested that the Board allow him to retire, effective January 1, 1956.[39] However, he later asked that his retirement be delayed until July 1, 1957 so he could do some field work in the southern part of the country—mainly Florida. The Board approved the delay in "Zimmie's" retirement at their Fall 1956 meeting.[40] Then at the Spring 1957 meeting of the Board, Daniel Fuchs suggested that, in the absence of Joseph Cohn's tours to Europe, Elias Zimmerman be asked to make an "inspection tour" of the Mission's European and Israel works. The Board was delighted with the suggestion, and they approved a maximum three-month tour for Zimmerman to make the visits.[41]

Daniel Fuchs' strategy was well planned. The delay in Zimmerman's retirement ensured that the Mission would have a worker in the Los Angeles area until Martin Rosen was ready to take over that branch after his graduation from Northeastern. And, asking "Zimmie" to make a foreign "inspection tour" helped ease the transition that exists when the founder of a ministry retires, and a new worker is appointed.

Once again, Martin Rosen and his family (the addition of another daughter, Ruth, enlarged their family to four) made the long drive from one coast to the other. The trip included one significant stop in Denver, Colorado. On August 9, 1957 Martin appeared before an Ordination Committee that had been called by their home church—Trinity Baptist Church; Martin's service of ordination was held at the church on August 28, 1957. In some ways, the service was also a commissioning service—the passing of the baton of leadership from one worker of the Mission to another, as Elias Zimmerman delivered the charge to the candidate. When the service concluded, the church body covenanted to pray for the new missionary workers,[42] and soon the Rosen family was back on the road—headed for California and the many opportunities for witness and ministry God would open for them there.

INVESTING RESERVES IN MISSIONARY OUTREACH

During the years of 1954 through 1957 the Board authorized the addition of many new staff members, and the purchase of a number of buildings and properties—expansion that created considerable financial strain on the General Fund of the Mission. To lessen the strain, the Directors approved two major changes; neither would have met with Joseph Hoffman Cohn's approval. First, they voted to dissolve the "Tribulation Days Missionary Fund" which Joseph had fought so hard to establish. This step was taken after some Board members had visited a number of banks and had discovered that none could provide the legal assurances necessary to administer such a fund. In a resolution approved by the Board, the following action was taken:

...it is hereby RESOLVED that we authorize the transfer of the Tribulation Days Missionary Fund to the General Missionary Funds to be used exclusively in Israel for missionary purposes, relief, and the distribution of food parcels.[43]

Secondly, the Board authorized transfers of money from the Mission's investment accounts to the General Fund for the purpose of subsidizing the missionary program. This action was diametrically opposed to Joseph Cohn's belief that the Mission should maintain a large investment fund to ensure that the testimony to the Jewish people would continue through the Tribulation Period, and to his belief that every worker and every department of the Mission had to raise the funds needed for their ministry.

Members of the Board were in agreement with Joseph's belief in the imminent return of the Lord, but they did not all share his belief that the Mission needed to hold large amounts of capital. A number of the Directors felt it was dishonoring to the Lord to hold a large reserve fund when there were so many Jewish people who needed to hear the Gospel in their own days. Thus, the Board approved expansion of the personnel and programs of the Mission, drawing from the financial reserves of the Mission, without taking steps to develop programs that would increase its financial base.

For twenty-five years the missionary program of the Mission was funded by its reserve funds and by funds raised through the work of the Field Evangelists and Bible conference ministry. From time to time suggestions for other methods of fund-raising were presented, but these were squelched because the Field Evangelists or workers in the Bible conference ministry saw such suggestions as a criticism of their effectiveness. Other suggestions for fund-raising were disregarded because some leaders of the Mission believed that the Mission had an "unwritten" policy never to ask for money (Leopold and Joseph Cohn never maintained such a policy!).

Because the missionary program was being subsidized by the reserve fund in order to reduce the reserve, there was never any pressure for workers or departments to raise support to cover the cost of programs or projects undertaken. This was a total change from the financial policy of Cohn who insisted that every barrel must stand on its own bottom, and that every department had to raise any monies it spent.

The Board deviated from Joseph's methodology regarding staff in other areas as well. For the most part, Joseph located and recruited his staff through his world-wide network of contacts. Many of the people he hired were already doing the work of Jewish evangelism; he simply provided them with funding so they could carry on the work they were already doing. Workers were hired at the lowest possible wage, and benefits supplied to the workers were not meted out with equality. He made arrangements for a pension program for some of his workers, but not for all; he supplied cars to some of his workers, but not to all. Assistance with medical bills was given on an individual basis.

After Joseph's death, the Board sought to rectify some of the inequities that had existed for so long. They increased the salaries of all workers. They adopted a formal pension plan for all workers—a fair program at no cost to the employees, although it was expensive for the Mission to carry.[44] They adopted a formal medical health care plan for all full-time employees. And, they adopted a formal plan to supply automobiles, and to cover the cost of maintaining the automobiles, for all full-time missionary staff.

The Minutes of the Directors' meeting in January 1955 reveals that serious consideration was given to the type of automobiles that were to be supplied to the workers. Of primary concern was the image that the cars would project, and how that might impact the overall work of the Mission. The Minutes state:

The new cars this year in the low price field are much heavier than in the past and indeed are comparable with more expensive cars of the years past. The new cars are also very garish in style and trim and it would be disadvantageous to the Mission for our men to drive many of these cars. Mr. Pretlove suggested after making a study of the new models and makes that the staff be limited in the purchase of the new cars to the following:

That all cars be either solid black or solid gray with as little chrome trim as possible. That they be either Chevrolet, 4 door; Plymouth, 4 door, Savoy; Ford, Custom Line, Ford, V8.

That the equipment on the car be limited to automatic transmission, heater, directional signals and undercoating.[45]

As humorous as this action may appear in today's world, the provision of an automobile to a worker during those days was equivalent to a sizable increase in salary; it was a non-taxable benefit, paid out of the Mission's current income and reserve funds, with no mention made to the workers of the need to increase personal support to offset the benefit.

The increased benefit package, plus the practice of hiring workers without requiring that they raise their own support, attracted many new workers to the Mission. But the attitudes of many who applied were vastly different from the attitudes of workers who joined the Mission's staff to assist Leopold and Joseph Cohn. During the 1700's and 1800's, Christians who entered the field of Jewish evangelism were highly motivated. Jewish Christians who embarked upon a ministry of Jewish evangelism were not only highly motivated, they were highly educated—many had been schooled in rabbinics, the Scriptures, theology, etc., and they were respected for their educational backgrounds as well as for their commitment to the Lord.

Joseph Cohn continued to look for workers who were highly motivated to reach the Jews with the Gospel, and he did want his missionary workers to have at least basic Bible training, but higher education was not a requirement, nor was it stressed, and oftentimes the workers did not have the educational background or the theological background to gain the respect of either the Christian or the Jewish communities.

HENRY HEYDT—HIS STORY

Cohn recognized that this posed a problem. His attempt to solve the problem was the establishment of the Jewish Missionary Training Institute. As mentioned in the opening paragraphs of this chapter, Dr. Henry Heydt was hired to serve as the Director of the Institute; under his leadership, Cohn was hoping the Institute would develop into an accredited training school for missionaries and scholars in the field of Jewish Missions.

In 1929, Henry Heydt was a young pastor of the Moravian Church in Lancaster, Pennsylvania. He was seated behind his desk at the church one day when a small dark-haired man came into his study and introduced himself as Mr. Myrl Hanenkrat, a Field Evangelist for the American Board of Missions to the Jews. Mr. Hanenkrat didn't have an appointment, and Henry was puzzled over what had brought him to his church.

Several months earlier, through his vast networking system, Joseph Cohn had become aware that the pastor of the First Baptist Church of Findley, Ohio had a unique love for Israel and the Jewish people. That pastor was Rev. Myrl M. Hanenkrat. As he had done so many times before, Joseph made a point of arranging his schedule so he could meet this unusual pastor, and in the Fall of 1929 he invited the Hanenkrat's (Gentile Christians) to join the staff of the Mission as Field Evangelists.[46] Hanenkrat's major task was to represent the Mission in church meetings, and to emphasize within his messages the place Israel holds in God's dispensational program. In representing the Mission, he was to serve as an "advance" man to open the doors of churches for the ministry of Joseph Cohn. Thus, he had made his way to Lancaster, Pennsylvania and had entered, unannounced, into the office of Henry Heydt.

After introducing himself to Henry, Hanenkrat went on to explain that he had visited every church in the town of Lancaster with the hope of getting a meeting, but the pastors of the other churches had made it clear that they did not want any speakers who were associated with a Jewish mission. Hanenkrat was surprised when Henry expressed interest in the Mission and asked him to tell him more about it. Henry had asked, so Hanenkrat told him that Joseph Cohn was planning a trip to the Lancaster area and that he would like to have meetings in Henry's church if he could. "And Henry said, 'He certainly can. I'll be happy to have him.' But when he told his Board about it they said, 'Pastor, you're supposed to clear that with us.' To that Henry just said, 'I've already done it!'"[47]

On the Sunday that Joseph was scheduled to speak at the Moravian Church, Henry Heydt went over to the church early to make sure everything was in order. To his surprise, he found that the church was already half filled. In remembering the event, Mrs. Margaret Heydt said that her husband came home and said,

> *The church is half full already. The people are coming in, expecting to sit in their 'pet pews,' and they're already taken. He was so tickled. Dr. Cohn didn't realize that people from all around the area, even up to Philadelphia, …came to the church to hear him. And from that moment that church was blessed…. So Henry learned that the blessing of God was on the church that opened its doors to Jewish missions and from that time on the church grew.[48]*

Over the next four years, Joseph Cohn returned as a guest speaker at Henry Heydt's church many times, and he and the Heydts became close friends.

Henry was a fine scholar, theologian, and teacher of the Scriptures. His dream was to start a school that would teach seminary subjects with a Biblical basis. He made that dream a reality when, in the early thirties, armed only with his old text books from college, with the encouragement of his wife, and with the blessing of the Lord, Henry began the Lancaster School of the Bible. With Joseph Cohn's help and frequent visits, courses on Israel, the Jewish people, and Jewish evangelism were also introduced into the curriculum at the school. Henry's notes for those classes formed the basis for his first book, "Studies in Jewish Evangelism," which was published by the Mission in 1951. Although this book is now out of print, it remains a classic text in the field of Jewish evangelism.

Heydt served as the school's President from its commencement until March, 1953, when he joined the staff of the Mission. Joseph had pleaded with him for years to move to New York so he could take over the Jewish Missionary Training Institute, but Henry had refused the offer. Finally he agreed to teach at the Institute two days a week. But it was a long trip each week and after much prayer and the continual cajoling of Joseph, Henry accepted the position of Director of the Jewish Missionary Training Institute.

Margaret and Henry Heydt moved to New York, and under Dr. Heydt's direction both the student body and the curriculum of the Institute grew. The Institute offered classes in Biblical and Conversational Hebrew, Methods of Jewish Evangelism, History and Customs of the Jewish People, Messianic Prophecy, and intensive Bible study courses. Before Dr. Heydt's acceptance of the position of Director of the Institute, the enrollment had only been thirty full-time students. But under his direction it jumped to over sixty students attending various classes.[49]

Joseph Cohn's dream that the Institute would become an accredited training school did not become a reality. Dr. Heydt attempted to develop a school that would fulfill Cohn's vision, but the Board did not follow through with the accreditation. The Minutes record the following action taken:

> *The matter of having our Jewish Missionary Training Institute become accredited under the State Board of Regents was discussed, and it was felt that this was not necessary at this time.[50]*

No mention of further discussion on the matter can be found in the Minutes, but it is known that the Institute never received accreditation and that the attendance and quality of teaching waned as Dr. Heydt became more and more involved in teaching at the Coney Island branch of the Mission and in speaking on behalf of the Mission within the churches.

In March 1955 Dr. Heydt took over the task of researching and answering theological questions asked in the many letters that poured into the Mission from its constituency—a task he willingly did long after he had retired. His wife faithfully assisted him by typing his diligently researched responses. As space allowed, the answers were printed in a "Question and Answer" column in *The Chosen People* magazine. This column became one of the favorite sections of the magazine. The researched answers became the basis for a book that was published by the Mission in 1976 entitled, "Question and Answer Box II." It was a sequel to "*The Chosen People* Question Box," written by Joseph Cohn and published by the Mission in 1945. Both books were prized by the Mission's constituency.

As the years following Joseph Cohn's death went by, it became apparent that the combination of the Mission's relaxed attitude toward formal training, plus the easier hiring practices, had created a "revolving door" staff. A number of workers who were hired left because they felt inadequate for the task; others left because they recognized their need for further education—but oftentimes the educational institutions they attended did not stress the need for Jewish evangelism and their ministry goals were diverted to other areas of Christian service. The new attitudes and procedures also created problems for the veteran missionary workers. Those who had received training and graduate degrees felt that the Mission was diluting the quality of its staff by hiring so many untrained workers. On the other hand, workers who did not have graduate degrees, but who had years of "field experience," were wary of new workers who had the educational training but no experience. Then, too, the influx of new untrained staff occasionally created difficulties between Jewish and Gentile workers. This was especially true when Gentile workers made it clear that they felt no need to acculturate to Jewish customs, traditions, and needs.

A Minneapolis Branch Established

One of the Mission's "veteran workers" who re-applied for a staff position shortly after Joseph Cohn's death was Rev. Josef Herschkowitz. Josef had left the Mission's staff when he immigrated to Canada in order to join his wife there (the story of their long separation during the war years was told in Chapter Seven of this history). In re-applying, Josef indicated that he was interested in returning to the United States to establish a branch of the Mission in Minneapolis, Minnesota. He also indicated that he would do Field Evangelism work in the states of Minnesota, Wisconsin, North and South Dakota. His application was accepted by the Board in April, 1954.[51]

Josef and his wife, Hermina, started the Minneapolis branch in their home. Josef wrote: "I do try to gather Gentiles, Jews, and Christians in my home whenever there is an opportunity for it. One time I had thirty-six people in my home; some of them were unconverted Jews, some converted, and it really proved to be a blessing to all of us."[52] Later he wrote:

> *Redeeming the time seems one of the hardest things to do. We are so busy doing the Lord's work that there is often little time left to do the Lord's work. Sounds like a contradiction, but nevertheless it is a fact.*
>
> *As I have been traveling through the Northwest during this past year I often thought about the work which should be done in Minneapolis. Day after day I prayed the Lord to send me someone to help me right here in the Twin Cities—Minneapolis and St. Paul. There are perhaps 20,000 Jews in Minneapolis and about 10,000 Jews in St. Paul. I knew I had to do something about reaching these groups, but because I was away from home so much of the time, the Lord led me to attempt a new approach.*
>
> *I started a series of monthly meetings right in the heart of Minneapolis, in the Curtis Hotel. It is only a small*

beginning, it is true, but I feel that the Lord is blessing our efforts and that we are making progress. Jews in small numbers are beginning to come and are hearing God's Word...we covet the prayers of the entire Chosen People family, that we may soon develop these monthly meetings into weekly meetings to the end that precious Jewish souls may find their Messiah, the Lord Jesus Christ.[53]

Although Josef labored diligently to keep the meetings in the Curtis Hotel going, and although a few Jewish people opened their hearts to receive Yeshua at those meetings, Josef's heavy travel schedule kept him from fully developing the work in Minnesota.

In the summer of 1961, after the death of Dr. Harry Marko (the singing Jewish doctor whose story was given in Chapter Nine of this history), the Board transferred Josef and Hermina Herschkowitz to Austin, Texas. Herschkowitz was to take the place of Dr. Marko as the Field Evangelist in that state.

Like Harry Marko, Josef Herschkowitz was well received by the churches and by the Mission's friends in Texas. He carried on a vibrant ministry in that state for a period of ten years—until the Lord called him into His presence in the Spring of 1971.[54]

ALBERT RUNGE—HIS STORY

At about the same time that Josef Herschkowitz re-applied for a staff position with the Mission, David Albert Runge, a "child of the Mission," was applying for a staff position too (Miss Sussdorff mentioned Albert Runge in her testimony on the occasion of her 89th Birthday party [see Chapter Six]).

Albert's first contact with the Mission came when he was just a child, and his family was in great need. Being Jewish, his parents had suffered through many of the pogroms in Russia. Like many of their fellow Russians, they immigrated to America and, like other immigrant Jewish families, they settled in the Jewish quarter of Brooklyn—not far from the Mission's Dispensary.

Mr. and Mrs. Runge set about to find sufficient work to keep a roof over their heads and food on the table. It wasn't easy, as the hard days of The Great Depression cast its ominous shadow over them. They were desperately poor.

Albert's parents fled Russia because of the persecution they had experienced as Jews, but Albert had been too young to be aware of the persecution. He did not experience such a thing until he was about seven years old—in America—when one of his playmates who attended a parochial school asked him if he was Jewish. Albert answered proudly that he was. It was Easter time, and his young friend told Albert that he could no longer play with him. When Albert asked why, his young Christian play-mate told him bluntly that it was because he crucified Jesus.

Albert didn't know what the word "crucify" meant. He didn't even know who this person, Jesus, was. Totally confused, he thought perhaps he had hurt someone without knowing about it, and he was ready to make amends so he told his friend he would apologize to Jesus. But his young friend just ran away.

Troubled over what had happened, Albert ran home to ask his mother who Jesus was, and why his playmate had accused him of hurting Him. Mrs. Runge told her young son that Jesus was the God of the Gentiles, and that the followers of Jesus hate the Jews because they believe the Jews killed their God. Then she told Albert about the suffering and persecution she and her family had gone through at the hands of the so-called "Christians" in Russia. After hearing his mother's story, Albert wanted nothing more to do with Gentiles, or with their God.

One day, Louis, Albert's little brother who was five years old, wanted to follow his father and grandfather when they went for a walk. His father told him he could not join them, and to placate him, Albert's mother gave him a few pennies to buy an ice-cream cone in the drugstore located immediately below the flat where they lived. Happy once again, little Louis bought his favorite ice-cream cone and sat down on the curbing to eat it as he watched some other children playing stick ball in the street. Louis was so engrossed in watching the children, and in the enjoyment of his ice cream cone, that he didn't notice he'd sat down behind a delivery truck. He didn't notice the driver of the delivery truck get into his vehicle—nor did he hear the engine start up. In hurrying to make his rounds, the delivery man had not noticed the small boy sitting on the curb directly behind his truck either. He just jumped into his truck and quickly threw it into reverse. The noises made by the meshing of gears, and the noise of the engine as he accelerated backward, drowned the screams of Louis and of the other children, until it was too late. Louis was killed instantly as the rear wheels of the truck crushed the life out of his small body.

Minutes after the tragic accident Albert's father and grandfather, who were just returning from their walk, saw the crushed and lifeless body of little Louis laying on the sidewalk. Albert's father went into shock; he could not speak for three days. Little Louis' sudden and tragic death instilled a feeling of uncertainty of life, and a fear of death in Albert—feelings that lasted until he became a believer in the Messiah.

Albert's mother also went into shock, but in spite of her grief she made the funeral arrangements. She went to the local rabbi for comfort, but he was not able to give comfort or hope when she asked him where Louis was now. Grieving over the loss of her son, and finding no hope or comfort, Mrs. Runge soon became seriously ill. After a time she could no longer care for Albert and his two sisters, and the three children were placed in a Jewish home for children—waiting for the day when their mother would recover and take care of them again.

That day did come, and Albert and his sisters returned to their apartment in Brooklyn. A few days later, as Mrs. Runge was walking down the street, she saw a sign on a building that she had never paid attention to before. It said, "Free medical treatment for Jewish people." She qualified—she was Jewish, and they were poor and therefore needed free medical help. She decided she should investigate. What she did not know was that the free clinic was run by the Mission. Nor did she know that the people inside—the young Hebrew doctor and Miss Augusta Sussdorff—were missionaries. Had she known, she probably would not have entered!

Upon entering the Mission's Dispensary, Mrs. Runge was immediately impressed with the sincerity and love of the staff—especially with Miss Sussdorff because she was the first Gentile Mrs. Runge had ever met who showed genuine love and concern for the Jewish people as a whole, and for herself and her family in particular. When Miss Sussdorff made a visit to their home a few days later, Albert's mother was even more impressed. Before she left their apartment, Miss Sussdorff invited the family to attend the Mission's activities. Afterwards, Albert's mother told her three children that they could visit the Mission, and go on some of the outings to Coney Island and other places, but they were not to believe anything the missionaries said about Jesus or about their religion.

It wasn't long before Albert was a regular participant in all of the Mission's activities. He joined the Boys' Club and the Camera Club, both of which were taught by Daniel Fuchs. And as he attended the club meetings and the other functions at the Mission, Albert was impressed with the faith and with the love demonstrated in the lives of Miss Sussdorff and Daniel Fuchs. He had heard some of the Bible stories from the rabbis, but somehow at the Mission they seemed different—more alive, real. He learned about faith and hope, and about a personal God who loved each individual. And he heard about personal salvation through the Messiah, Yeshua (Jesus). He liked what he heard at the Mission, but Albert was afraid to believe it so he went to the rabbi. The rabbi told Albert that Jews don't believe those things. Then he quoted Isaiah 55:9, "As the heavens are higher than the earth, so are my ways higher than your ways and my thoughts than your thoughts." The rabbi told Albert that his conclusion, based on that verse, was that there was no hope to ever know God.

The rabbi's answer seemed logical to Albert, but it didn't satisfy the hunger to know God which was growing in his heart. The seed of faith had been planted and was being nourished by the Mission's teachers, and as each week passed Albert became more convinced that the teachers at the Mission knew God personally—even if his rabbi didn't.

Albert's parents began to notice how much of his time was being spent at the Mission and they began to worry, so they forbid him to attend the services. He was obedient to his parents, but God did not forsake Albert. Even when his family moved away from Brooklyn a few years later, God kept His eye on Albert. It wasn't just coincidence that led them to move into a home located directly across the street from an evangelical church!

Albert asked the pastor of the church if Jews could attend the services. The pastor assured him that he would be more than welcome, so Albert decided to attend. Remembering the eventful night when he attended his first church service Albert later recalled:

> As I listened to the pastor's message that night, I knew what he was saying was true. I knew I was a sinner and that I was lost. I knew I didn't have a personal relationship with God and if I died that night without accepting Christ, I would go to hell. Ever since my brother's fatal accident I had a fear of death. So when I fell under conviction for my sins, I wanted to be forgiven and have eternal life. I was convinced of the fact that Jesus was God's Son, my Messiah. I was certain that He had died for my sins and that He was physically raised from the dead.
>
> Yet, when the pastor asked those who felt the moving of God in their heart to accept Christ, to raise their hands— I couldn't. In synagogue, you raised your hand to make a financial commitment, and I wasn't going to do that. I wasn't ready to get that committed!
>
> Still, I knew I wanted Christ in my life. So, when I got home that night, I got down on my knees and confessed to God that all these convictions I had felt in the meeting were true. At that moment, something wonderful happened in my heart. I had the assurance that my sins had been forgiven and now I was a child of God.
>
> Surely, this wasn't something to keep secret from your parents. I wanted to tell them the good news that I had found a personal relationship with God. But I didn't know how to tell them because I didn't know anything about Christians. Then I remembered years before at the mission someone had said, 'Amen.' Then someone else said, 'Praise the Lord.' So, I thought, this must be the way Christians talk.
>
> Now that I knew what to say, I boldly walked into the room where my mother and father were sitting and joyfully

declared, 'Amen! Praise the Lord! I've been saved!'

At first, my mother thought I was just making fun of Christians. When she saw, however, that I was serious she immediately went out to the store to call her cousin who was a psychiatrist. Fortunately, his fees discouraged her from putting me into psycho-therapy. Instead, she came back to our apartment, patted me on the head and said, 'Don't worry, Albert, you're going to outgrow this.'

I was only 14 then, but I knew what I had would last a lifetime. God was real. He loved me. And I had been born again into His eternal Kingdom.[55]

When God saved Albert He placed within his heart a desire to preach the Gospel—but for Albert this was a seemingly insurmountable problem. From the time of his birth he had been severely allergic; tests showed that he had allergic reactions to 103 substances. He also suffered from sever asthma, and his eyesight was so poor he was nearly blind. He had used his inability to see as an excuse not to study. As a result, he had to repeat the fifth grade three times. By the time he reached ninth grade he was hopelessly behind and he flunked out. After that, he dropped out of school and took odd jobs to support himself. But he was frustrated because he still felt called to serve the Lord. Then he heard the story of Dwight L. Moody, and how he overcame all of his liabilities because he wanted to be a man wholly yielded to God, and Albert prayed Moody's prayer, "Lord, let me be that man!"

After that, Albert began to look for a school that would accept him in spite of his poor transcript. A Christian school in Toccoa Falls, Georgia agreed to accept him, and the church he was attending took up an offering for him. It was enough to pay for his bus ticket and one month's tuition. So, with little money in his pockets, but a great deal of faith, Albert Runge headed for Georgia.

Albert spent the next three years studying to complete his high school education. During that time God opened the doors for him to work at a number of jobs. He was surprised to find that subjects he had once failed, he now passed. In fact, his grades placed him at the top of his class. God was answering his prayers, and as Albert saw God's hand upon his life he became more convinced of his call to ministry.

After graduating from high school, Albert continued his studies. The Mission provided him with financial assistance through the Student Aid Scholarship Fund while he attended Nyack Missionary Training School and Houghton College. After graduating from college he attended, and graduated from Eastern Baptist Seminary.

After his graduation from seminary Albert became the pastor of a small church in New Jersey, but he had not forgotten the Mission or the need to bring the Gospel to his Jewish people, so he decided to ask if there was a place of service for him on the Mission's staff. The Directors discussed his request at their March 1955 meeting. The Minutes state: "…He feels that this coming summer [1955] the church will be in a condition where he can resign without harm to the church and go into Jewish work, and he would like to be employed by the Mission."[56]

Circumstances did not work out as planned however. Albert did not begin employment with the Mission until after January 1, 1956. His first assignment was to do missionary work in New York at the Headquarters branch. His ministry was so effective that Daniel Fuchs recommended he be appointed the Resident Pastor of the New York ministry—a position Daniel Fuchs had been filling on a temporary basis. The Board agreed with Daniel's suggestion, and followed through by making the appointment.[57]

As time permitted, Albert was also involved with the other branches of the Mission in New York. He wrote:

In Coney Island we continued our Thursday night class for adults and children. Several new Jewish people attended, but they have shown fear of the Jewish community….

Our Daily Vacation Bible School in Coney Island had 60 Jewish mothers and children in attendance. There was one new Jewish boy that showed a real interest in the things of God….

We kept our Yiddish and English class going on Friday night at our Brooklyn Mission.

Besides these classes there were street meetings, personal work, visitation and our Book Room ministry; not, of course, forgetting our literature work and tract distribution.

As you can see, your Mission's doors are never closed.[58]

In 1957 Albert requested of the Board that they assist him in financing a home he wanted to purchase in Lakewood, New Jersey. Since he planned to use his home for missionary meetings once or twice a week, the Board agreed to make the loan.[59] He was not the first worker to receive a low interest loan from the Mission. After Joseph Cohn's death, such loans became one of the benefits that the Board extended to the workers of the Mission because the funds enabled staff members to purchase homes in areas where they were ministering. The Board was anxious for the ministry to go forward; they were also very concerned about the well-being of the staff. They knew the workers' salaries were low, and they tried to offset that by extending very generous benefits. But the loans to staff members, while being generous and beneficial, also further reduced the investment fund of the Mission.

By 1959 Albert was serving as a Field Evangelist for the New York area,[60] but that phase of his ministry came to an end when Arnold Seidler, the Missionary in Charge of the Pittsburgh branch of the Mission, passed away on December 7, 1959. Pittsburgh was the second oldest branch outside of New York/New Jersey (Philadelphia was the first) and the Board did not want that branch of the work to close. John Solomon and Arnold Seidler had poured their lives into reaching the Jews of Pittsburgh with the Gospel. Another Jewish worker was needed for that vital branch of the Mission and the Board asked Albert Runge to be that person. By March 1960 the Runges had made the move to a new house and a new ministry. At the close of his first year of ministry in Pittsburgh Albert wrote:

> Early in our first year here in Pittsburgh, Mrs. Runge and I became aware that God's hand was at work. We started a class of Jewish women and in five short weeks it had grown from two or three to eight....
>
> Our monthly family night meeting has grown rapidly in attendance. We had sixty-three people at a recent meeting.... We have had a number of experiences that indicate that God is working among our Jewish people here. Just this week we had a young Jewish man come all the way from Cleveland, Ohio, to talk to us about his spiritual problems. He spent several hours with us discussing matters pertaining to the Messiah. Just before he left for his home in Cleveland he definitely gave his heart to the Lord Jesus Christ as his Saviour.[61]

In March 1962, after completing two years of missionary work in Pittsburgh, Albert wrote a glowing report of God's blessing upon the ministry—but he also mentioned their disappointment over the fact that some of the Jewish children had been forbidden to attend the Children's Bible Club, and he mentioned a disappointment of a personal nature. He wrote:

> ...Our little girl, Robin, age 6, has developed an ulcer, our doctor informs us. In an effort to discover the cause, I found out that Robin, as a faithful missionary, has been witnessing to her small Jewish friends, whose parents told her that if she talked of Jesus to their children she would not be allowed to play with them. Robin's anxiety and worry over this incident is what probably resulted in the ulcer. Please pray for Robin that she may be restored in body and spirit.[62]

Albert patterned his ministry in Pittsburgh after the Brooklyn branch of the Mission—the branch he'd known in his childhood. He had an extensive literature ministry. He also started a ministry among Jewish prisoners, and had the joy of seeing some of the men place their faith in Yeshua. After his release from prison, one of the men even attended Bible College in preparation to become a missionary to the Jews. Speaking of his aspirations for penetrating Pittsburgh's Jewish community with the Gospel, Albert wrote:

> We also have some future hopes. One of these is a radio ministry in the Pittsburgh area to reach the Jews. A second is a plan to add volunteer workers. We need teachers for our classes, personal workers and office helpers. We hope to start a gospel witness to Jewish high school and university students. We are now in the process of training a group of volunteer workers at our Friday evening course in Jewish evangelism for house-to-house visitation.[63]

Under Albert's leadership, and with God's blessings, the ministry in Pittsburgh was growing substantially—so much so that in September 1962 the Board agreed to send Miss Marilyn Hicks to the Pittsburgh branch to assist Albert in the work there.

Marilyn was a Gentile Christian who had grown up with many Jewish friends. After graduating from Wooster and Western Reserve colleges in Ohio, she began her career as a school teacher. But as she studied the Word of God, she remembered the Jewish friends she'd grown up with, and she became increasingly concerned about their need to hear the Gospel. Finally, she left the teaching profession and she enrolled in the Mission's Jewish Studies course at Northeastern Collegiate Bible Institute (Northeastern Bible College), in Essex Fells, New Jersey. While she was a student at Northeastern, she wrote a term paper on Daniel's Seventieth Week. The Mission published her paper in two issues of *The Chosen People* magazine.[64] As a former school teacher, Marilyn's abilities in working with the women and children made her a perfect candidate to assist the Runge's in their expanding ministry in Pittsburgh.

In addition to Marilyn's help, Albert was also assisted in the ministry by Mr. and Mrs. Howard Anderson who volunteered their time to the ministry. Their unique God-given gifts were put to use in working with young people.

Albert also developed an active training program for the training of new missionary workers, and in the Fall of 1964 the Board agreed to send Mr. Jack Levin to the Pittsburgh branch. He was among the first candidates trained in Albert's program, and following his training his primary responsibilities were to develop the visitation program and the popular potluck dinner "Family Night" program.[65]

Albert's dream of establishing a radio outreach as an expansion of the Pittsburgh ministry was never realized. But an opportunity for radio ministry was offered to him when he was asked to be one of the radio teachers on the "Christian Jew Hour," sponsored by Dr. Charles Halff in San Antonio, Texas. It was an opportunity Albert felt he did not want to pass up, so after nearly ten years of service with the Mission, he resigned. In subsequent years, the Lord not only used him in radio ministry, but He has used him in the pastorate as well. Albert served as the pastor of one of the largest Missionary Alliance churches in North America. Over the years, he has reached many thousands of people with the Gospel.

In the late 1970's, while participating as a guest speaker at a Prophetic Bible Conference at Sacandaga Bible Conference Grounds, the author discovered that Albert Runge and his wife, Lee, were guests on the conference grounds; they had come for rest and relaxation. Albert had not forgotten the Mission or the important role it had played in his life, and as he and the author shared in a time of fellowship together, Albert laughed and reminisced about the "good ol' days" with the Mission.

Following the conference, the author mentioned his time of fellowship with the Runges to Dr. Daniel Fuchs. God used that conversation to convince both Daniel Fuchs and the author that it would be good to have another "son of the Mission" serving on the Board of Directors. The author therefore nominated Albert Runge to become a member of the Board at the Directors meeting in October 1984.[66] Albert served as a Board member until 1993, when he regretfully resigned from the Board due to the heavy demands of his pastoral schedule.

CLARA AND JOE RUBIN—THEIR STORY

In July 1956, just six months after Albert Runge joined the Mission's staff, Clara Rubin (Krop) opened her home in Huntington Station, Long Island, New York to be used as another branch of the ministry. For six months Clara served as a "volunteer missionary," but in December 1956 both she and her husband, Joe, joined the staff of the Mission. Together they directed the missionary activities of the Huntington Station branch until their retirement on December 31, 1983.

Like Albert Runge, Clara Krop was a "child of the mission." Her parents, Harry and Zena Krop, had immigrated from Russia. They arrived in America in 1911, and settled in the Williamsburg section of Brooklyn—just three blocks away from the Mission's headquarters at 27 Throop Avenue. Five years later, on December 16, 1916, Clara was born.

A year or so before Clara's birth, Mrs. Krop noticed the large sign on the building advertising free medical treatment for Jews at the Mission's Dispensary. Like Mrs. Runge, she was curious so she went to see what it was all about. Once inside the building, she saw another sign that said in large bold type:

This Dispensary is maintained by the Williamsburg Mission To The Jews. There are Christian People who Love the LORD JESUS CHRIST Our Messiah, and they give the money to carry on this work so that you also may learn about the Messiah. EVERY TRUE CHRISTIAN LOVES THE JEWS.[67]

The sign had been placed on the wall deliberately so the immigrant Jews who entered the Dispensary would realize that there was a difference between "true Christians" and the so called "Christians" they had known in Europe. The love and patience of the staff as they gave medical assistance demonstrated that they *did* love the Jews, and Clara's mother, like many other Jewish immigrants, was impressed with the clinic—so much so that she continued to visit the Dispensary when she became pregnant with Clara.

After Clara was born, Miss Sussdorff continued to maintain contact with Mrs. Krop by making visits to her apartment. During her visits, she invited Mrs. Krop to attend the Mission's meetings; on one occasion she also gave Mrs. Krop a copy of the Yiddish New Testament. Mrs. Krop responded to Miss Sussdorff's friendship and loving invitations by attending some of the meetings, but it took over fifty years of friendship and prayer before she accepted Yeshua as her personal Savior and Messiah.[68]

When Clara was old enough to attend the children's activities at the Mission, her mother allowed her to participate. But, as mentioned in the early chapters of this history, the orthodox Jews who lived in the Williamsburg section of Brooklyn did everything they could to disrupt the ministry of the Mission and they ridiculed, and often violently attacked, Jews who attended the services. Even the children were subjected to their taunts and threats as a means of discouraging them from attending the Mission's meetings.

Clara endured the ridicule and taunting from outside the Mission's building because she enjoyed the love, attention, and kindness showered upon her and the other children once they were inside the building. Love and attention was something many of the children did not receive at home during those days of hardship and poverty. But the teasing and ridicule affected her. To protect herself from the insults, she built up a wall of defiance. Soon she became a disruptive problem child. To her amazement, in spite of her uncourteous, rude attitude and behavior, Miss Dorothy Rose and Miss Sussdorff continued to show her love. She was amazed at their patience and love despite her terrible conduct. These "true Christians" were demonstrating their love in action—just like the sign in the Dispensary said. Years later, Clara wrote:

> The week of Thanksgiving, true Christians from nearby churches would come and prepare an entire Thanksgiving dinner for all the mission families. An Episcopalian minister who loved the Jews would attend wearing the priestly collar, and many Jews seeing him would be afraid to come in, saying, 'See—a golloch, a golloch,' mistaking him for a Catholic priest, and saying, 'This proves the mission is trying to make goyim of us.'[69]
>
> Christmas time at the mission lives forever in my heart. After the program which we children took part in, shopping bags were distributed, filled with candy, fruit, and gifts for each member of the family.
>
> Miss Sussdorff called out families according to size, to expedite emptying the room. In the bags were Sunkist oranges, which, to us poor people, were something for the millionaires to eat.[70]
>
> For special outings at end of season and end of month-long Daily Vacation Bible School, we rode large, open-air, jitney buses to park or beach, singing all the way there and home. This, too, was a millionaire's treat.
>
> I remember my kindergarten teacher at the mission, Miss Amy Blomquist, tall, very beautiful, and very loving. Her hair was in beautiful braids around her head or over her ears. Her smile was from ear to ear, and after our lesson with her, we would be served cocoa and broken cookies on our little kindergarten chairs. Our mothers would be in the large room doing embroidery work and then, after their Bible lesson, would also enjoy cocoa and cookies.[71]

At the age of ten, Clara began to attend Hebrew school at one of the local synagogues. In the few months that she attended, she was amazed to find that the Old Testament Bible stories which she was learning at the Mission were the same stories she was being taught in the synagogue. She realized then that the Mission's teachers were teaching her things that were really Jewish and not just "narishkeit" (foolishness).

Two years later Clara saw a film on the life of Christ. The picture portrayed in detail the good that He did while He lived on earth, and when the scene of Jesus' crucifixion was shown, she began to cry. In telling the story of that moment in her life, Clara said:

> …What a pity and shame, I thought, to do that to someone who did nothing but good.
>
> I realized then that what I heard in the Mission, about Jesus, how he died for my sins so that I could have eternal life, was true. So I accepted Christ, but it was merely a head belief. I did as I well pleased. My behavior was atrocious and I continued to be mischievous to Miss Dorothy Rose, my teacher.
>
> As for Jesus, my attitude was—yes, it is true—but so what? Thanks again to Miss Rose for her patience with me for two more years, when I became 14.
>
> She taught me not to use Christ as a license for sin, but to allow Christ to live within me, and to walk in His path, trusting Him all the way. I yielded then with all my heart, and I was eager to study all about my Lord.[72]

So, in 1930, at the age of fourteen, through the loving and patient guidance of Miss Dorothy Rose, Clara accepted the Messiah Yeshua as her personal Savior—and as the Lord of her life.

Just as Clara had given herself wholeheartedly to being a mischief-maker, she now gave herself wholeheartedly to sharing the good news of the Gospel with her fellow Jews. She ignored the threats and the insults of the orthodox Jews when, at the age of sixteen, she would accompany Daniel Fuchs to a nearby street corner where they would pass out literature and proclaim the Gospel message. Of this time in her life, Clara wrote:

> I started the teenage classes, the young adult classes, and later on the classes for working adults. At our Throop Avenue Mission with Miss Dorothy Rose doing the teaching, I witnessed wherever I stood and wherever I went.[73]

Because of her bold and persistent witness, God used Clara to lead her fifteen year old friend, Beatrice Kaufman, to the Lord. Years afterward, Beatrice joined the staff of the Mission and she began the Flushing branch of the Mission (This branch was later known as the Hollis branch; it was a part of the Long Island ministry of the Mission).

Mrs. Krop, Clara's mother, was not yet a believer, and she was not happy about all of the time Clara was spending at the Mission; worse still was Clara's decision to accept Yeshua as her Messiah, and her missionary activities—something she was very outspoken about. But the coup de grace came the day Clara, at age sixteen, announced to her mother that she was going to be baptized. Her mother hit the roof. Mrs. Krop told her daughter she *refused* to have a "goy" (Gentile) for a daughter, and she threatened to jump off the roof. She further told Clara that no Jewish boy would every marry her if she went through with the baptism; not to be married was the worst fate a Jewish girl could endure!

Clara's response to her mother was that she would get married first—then she would be free to do as she pleased. After that conversation with her mother, Clara began to pray that God would not only send her a good Jewish man to marry—she prayed for a Jewish man who also believed in Yeshua. She told the Lord that such a match would be a real witness and testimony to her family. God heard Clara's prayers, and He began preparing the heart of young man named Joseph Rubin.

Joseph Rubin was an orphan. He was raised at the Daughters of Miriam Orphans' Home in Clifton, New Jersey. As soon as he reached the age of majority, he left the orphanage in search of answers to life—a search that ultimately took him to the West Coast, where he ended up at the Rescue Mission run by the Mission's worker in Los Angeles, Rev. Elias Zimmerman.

Joseph was so intrigued by the message about Yeshua, and by the love extended by "Zimmie" and his wife, that he sought out the Mission's Headquarters building when he returned to the East Coast. It was there that he met Clara Krop, and "Cupid's arrows" pierced both their hearts. After Joseph became a believe in Yeshua, he and Clara were married. The date was October 10, 1937. Clara's prayers had been answered. She had married a nice Jewish boy—one who also believed in the Messiah. Now she could be baptized. At the age of twenty-five, eleven years after accepting Yeshua as her Messiah and Savior, and after waiting patiently for the Lord to answer her prayers so that she would not be disobedient to her parents, or a disappointment to them, she followed the command of her Lord, and was baptized.

Throughout the years, Mrs. Krop had continued to attend the Mission's meetings, although she had remained unwilling to accept Yeshua as her Messiah. She went primarily because of the sewing classes. She was an excellent seamstress and the Mission provided a place for her to use her sewing ability.

After their marriage, Clara and Joe found a home in Brooklyn so they would be close to the Mission. They gave every spare moment volunteering their time to the work of the Mission, and soon they found themselves in charge of many of the meetings. During the summer of 1940, although Clara was five months pregnant, Joseph gave up two weeks of pay from his job so they could help in the Mission's Summer Camping program. Their daughter, Ilayna, was born on February 2, 1941. From the time of her birth, Clara and Joe dedicated their daughter to the Lord, and they involved her in their missionary activity and in the meetings at the Mission. As she grew, Ilayna learned to play the accordion and she often accompanied her parents to street corners and to the parks. As Ilayna played her accordion, the crowd would gather, and then Clara and Joe would boldly witness for the Lord.

History has a strange way of repeating itself. An event that took place one afternoon as Clara, Ilayna, and Clara's mother, Zena, were walking to the Brooklyn Mission is evidence of this fact. As they walked toward the Mission's building, several angry Jewish women began to shout at them. They not only shouted abuses, they shouted out warnings to Zena that her grand-daughter would never be able to marry a Jew if she continued to let her attend the Mission. Their words were more than Zena Krop could stand. It had been bad enough when she'd endured the brunt of her neighbors comments about her daughter, Clara. She was not going to take it again because of her grand-daughter. She therefore told Clara she was not going to attend meetings at the Mission any more. Later, both Mr. and Mrs. Krop told Clara that if she continued to allow Ilayna to go to the Mission and get baptized, they would kill themselves. The rest of the story, written by Clara many years after the incident, is best told in Clara's own words:

> My heartfelt prayer to God, from the moment of her birth, when we dedicated our daughter [Ilayna] to Him, was that God would give her, when the time came, a Hebrew Christian husband. This we felt would make it evident to all our Jewish friends that believing in Yeshua Hamashiach, the Lord Jesus Christ, didn't make us Gentiles, and that it would be a testimony to our faith in Him.
>
> When Ilayna was in hospital taking nurses' training, she met a Jewish young man who professed to love her. His family liked us, too. However, when I gave him Christian tracts to take home, his parents were angered and sent him to their rabbi for advice. The rabbi told him that Hitler killed the Jews because of people like us, that we were the worst kind of people—traitors. So the young man told Ilayna she had to make a choice between him and her religion, whereupon she took her stand for the Lord Jesus Christ. This upset him very much and as a result he wrote her a very rude letter and left it for her at the nurses' residence.
>
> This incident was the beginning of friction in our family, reminding my mother of all the old taunts of the unsaved Jews, and it left me with no opportunity for further witnessing so far as our family was concerned.
>
> I believe it when God's Word says, 'Be ye not unequally yoked together with unbelievers,' so I added to my prayer that God would provide a Hebrew Christian husband for Ilayna—'O Lord, let my daughter's husband have saved parents, and that they might also be soul winners.'
>
> However, other Jewish young men proposed to Ilayna, and she refused them because they weren't even interested

in God. My mother took this to heart and became critically ill. My family said I was killing my mother, and that my religion was a handicap to Ilayna? Why, they wanted to know, did we so desire that Ilayna marry a Hebrew Christian? I told them that we had dedicated her life to the Lord and that God, in His own time, would provide a worthy husband for her. She was 21 years old and her love for the Lord came first in her life, even before her love for her parents and her grandmother.

I asked my mother, who was sick in the hospital, 'How long do you want God to plead with you before you accept the Lord Jesus Christ as Messiah? You heard the Word of God 50 years ago at our Jewish Mission.' She said she wanted a sign from God. I took her home and nursed her back to health. I prayed that the Lord would not let her die before she was saved. Shortly thereafter, God perfected that which pertained to me, as He had promised.

On October 5, 1963, Ilayna was married to a Hebrew Christian young man whose parents are saved and are in Christian work. She is now Mrs. David Klayman. The marriage was performed by brother Daniel Fuchs, our Missionary Secretary, at a beautiful ceremony attended by many Hebrew Christians and others and a whole host of unsaved relatives from as far away as Spain, who sat and listened to the message of the Gospel of the Lord Jesus Christ who was given preeminence on that occasion. David's father was brought to the Lord at a tent meeting in Brooklyn, 29 years ago, by one of the Mission's beloved workers, the late Joe Serafin. [As will be seen later in this chapter, David Klayman's father and mother, Martin and Pauline Klayman also became workers for the Mission.]

We found that it was also the 27th wedding anniversary of the Klayman's, and our own 26th. So the wedding party became also a time of testimony to the sustaining grace of our precious Lord.

My mother has now confessed that this was the sign that she had asked God for when she lay ill in the hospital. She believes that Yeshua brought all this to pass because of our faith in Him. Once again we have the joy of freely witnessing for our Lord to all of our family and we pray that God will use us to His glory. How grateful we are to God for honoring our prayer that He would provide a Hebrew Christian husband for Ilayna, and to use this family affair as a sign and a witness.[74]

THE HUNTINGTON STATION BRANCH ESTABLISHED

Over the years, Clara and Joe began to notice that the Jewish community they had known and loved was changing; as success had come to many of their Jewish friends and neighbors, they were gradually moving out of Brooklyn into the suburbs. One by one, the families moved away but the prayers of Clara and Joe followed them. After awhile, God put it upon the hearts of Clara and Joe that they, too, should move; they should follow the migration of Jewish people into the suburbs and continue a witness among them. In May 1955, Clara and Joe put a deposit on a home in a new subdivision in Huntington Station, Long Island. God's confirmation upon their move was evident to Clara when she learned that their new address was going to be 27 Liberty St. All she could think of was 27 Throop Avenue—the address of her beloved Mission in Brooklyn. She immediately telephoned Eleanor Bullock (under whose supervision Clara had been volunteering her time), to say that she and Joe wanted their home to become the Huntington Station branch of the Mission.

It was fifteen months before their new home was ready for occupancy. As soon as they moved in, Clara and Joe dedicated their beautiful new home to the Lord. They wanted everyone who entered to learn about Yeshua the Messiah, and about salvation through His shed blood. They had made plans to hold their first meeting two weeks after moving in, and they were both anxiously awaiting that day. They already had three Jewish people who had indicated that they wanted very much to come. But instead of the joyful event they were looking forward to, tragedy struck. It would appear that Satan did not want the strong testimony of the Rubins on Long Island.

Early one morning, as Joe was on his way to work, a car sped along the highway and neared the rear of his car. It came so close that its bright lights temporarily blinded him. Then it swerved out from behind Joe and quickly cut in front of him—so close that it struck his car, cutting him off, and causing him to lose control. Joe's car careened off the road and crashed into a telephone pole. The other car sped off into the darkness. Joe was so badly injured that by the time help arrived, and the medics were able to get him to the hospital, the doctors gave little hope for his survival.

Clara did not know Joe was hovering between life and death as she helped make arrangements for her parents' move into a new apartment that day. When the telephone rang, she thought it might be her sister to inform her of further arrangements for her parents' move. Instead, it was a call about Joe. Relying on the inner strength that only God can give, Clara hurriedly made her way to the hospital where Joe lay with two broken legs (the right leg broken in three places), a broken jaw, extensive internal injuries and the possibility that he would never walk again.

As if that wasn't enough, when Clara left the hospital and returned to help her parents, she found her father seriously ill and in need of hospitalization. She spent the remainder of the day trying to locate a hospital that would admit him. As they drove from hospital to hospital, Clara offered up a continuous silent prayer, and she fervently witnessed to her father—as she had so often done in the past. At last she found a hospital that was willing to admit him.

Once he was settled into a bed, Clara asked her father again if he believed in Yeshua. Hesitatingly, he said "Yes," and Clara prayed with him. But as she left his bedside to go back to the hospital where Joe lay so seriously injured, her heart was still heavy because she was not sure if her father really meant what he said. Five days later Clara's father died, and to this day she prays and hopes that her father really accepted the Messiah. She had been faithful and bold in her witness to him, but only eternity will reveal if he believed her witness.

The tests of Clara's faith kept coming. She had buried her father and was still feeling his loss, and her husband still lay in critical condition in his hospital bed, when another unexpected event struck. As Joe laid in his bed with his jaws wired closed and his lower body encased in a plaster cast, he suffered a major heart attack. He then developed further complications and almost died of blood clots in the lungs. Clara did the only thing she could do, she turned to God in prayer. Her many friends gathered around her and joined her in uplifting Joe and his needs before the Lord. And as they prayed, God provided. They prayed for nurses, and God sent nurses from the Mission, from churches, and from among their friends. They prayed for healing, and God proved Himself to be the Great Physician, the Great Provider, and the Friend who sticks closer than a brother. Clara later wrote:

> I faced the hardest tests when I had to see Joe in such dreadful pain. But, as I prayed, I realized how God could see His own Son, the Messiah of Israel, suffer the pain of death, and, because of this pain, the world received salvation. I would tell Joe, 'God has plans for you, and good must come from your suffering. Perhaps God has work for you to do for Him, and this is the only way for Him to mold you to His Will,' and with that, I would be comforted.[75]

God answered the prayers of His children and He healed Joe. Four months later, Clara and Joe held their first Bible study in their new home—although it was held at Joe's bedside. Subsequent meetings were held in the large "rumpus room" they had carefully prepared for that purpose when their home was still in the planning stages. Thus, Clara and Joe Rubin's ministry from 27 Liberty Avenue had its beginning—and as the days, months, and years went by their address became known around the world as the place where Christians could bring their Jewish friends to hear and learn about the Messiah Yeshua.[76]

In giving readers of *The Chosen People* a little insight into their ministry on Long Island, Clara wrote:

> This section of Long Island in and around Huntington Station has many Jewish people who have never heard the Gospel of love before and are not too receptive to it. Our neighborhood has Jews and Gentiles living together. There are many new churches being built here, and when they open their doors to us, we acquaint them with Jewish missionary work and ask them to help us tell their Jewish neighbors about their own Messiah, the Lord Jesus Christ. We leave tracts and literature for them to hand out to their Jewish friends.
>
> Every second Wednesday we hold Bible classes for Jews here in our home, the adults meeting downstairs and the children upstairs. We send out about 500 letters with The Shepherd of Israel every month and invite people to attend our Bible class.
>
> Two teen-age Jewish girls, sisters accepted the Lord Jesus last August....
>
> We do much witnessing by telephone and letters. Many times we get threatening calls by telephone.[77]

As God poured out His blessings upon Clara and Joe's ministry at 27 Liberty Avenue, that branch of the Mission was rapidly becoming another 27 Throop Avenue—just as Clara had prayed that it would. She wrote:

> On the second Saturday of every month we hold our regular Gospel Meeting for Jews at 8:00 p.m. at our Huntington Station Mission. In preparation for this we have a busy day, putting the meeting rooms in shape, borrowing extra chairs, providing refreshments, sending out notices and invitations, and bringing some of the folks in by car. The price of admission to Gentiles is, 'Free if you bring a Jew.' At a recent meeting we had 23 Jews, many of them coming for the first time, a total attendance including Gentiles of 45. Two carloads of our people came from Connecticut, several unsaved Jews among them. A Jewish lad from nearby Hollis, on his first visit, stayed till nearly 3 a.m., listening hungrily to God's Word.[78]

But the Huntington Station branch was not the only new extension of the Mission's outreach. The reader will recall that after Joseph Cohn's death, the Board adopted a policy of "Mission Expansion," and appointed Daniel Fuchs as the Missionary Secretary to develop and oversee that program of growth. By mid-1967, five new branches of the ministry had been established in the boroughs and suburbs of New York. The Huntington Station branch was just one among the five.[79]

In establishing the other branches of outreach to the Jewish community of New York, Daniel enlisted the help of Ruth Wardell, Sydney Parker, Albert Runge, Kenneth Anderson and Eleanor Bullock. Albert and Sydney were to do the preaching, Eleanor was to work with the women, and Ruth was to work with the children and young people. It was a good team—each worker's gifts complemented the gifts of the others. Using this "team effort," branches of the Mission were established in Jamaica, New York; Flushing, New York; East New York; Rockaway, Long Island; and Levittown, Long Island.

The Jamaica, New York outreach was begun in January 1955, in the home of Mr. and Mrs. Gilbert Maggi (Mrs. Maggi was the young Jewish friend [Beatrice Kaufman] whom Clara Rubin led to the Lord when they were both teenagers). After Beatrice married, she and her husband moved to an apartment in Jamaica, Queens, New York—but she had stayed in touch with the Mission.

THE QUEENS BRANCH—BEATRICE (KAUFMAN) MAGGI

Ruth Wardell and Sydney Parker visited Beatrice, telling her of the Mission's desire to open a branch in Queens, and asking if she and her husband would be willing to open their apartment for a new missionary venture. Beatrice responded:

> ...We were thrilled at the prospect of helping in the Lord's work. I had for some time felt that the Lord would use me in some way and had prayed earnestly for this privilege which now, it seemed, was to become a reality.
>
> Fortunately our apartment was large enough to accommodate separate classes for children and adults, and so the work was begun. The Lord blessed our labors: and we had many wonderful meetings, as many as fifteen to twenty gathering weekly. There were some folk who had formerly attended our other mission branches but now lived in Queens, and they were happy to have a place to meet in the neighborhood. We also had several new people, among them a teen-age girl, who later came to know the Lord.[80]

As the work continued to grow it became difficult for the Maggi's to hold the meetings in their apartment, so the search began for a suitable property in the area. Such a property was located at 164th Street and Jewell Avenue in Flushing; the building was purchased and Mr. & Mrs. Maggi moved in. A dedication service was held in the early Spring of 1958.[81]

THE FLUSHING BRANCH

In describing the ministry in the new Flushing location, and revealing some of the problems encountered when a missionary to the Jews moves into a new neighborhood, Beatrice Maggi wrote:

> ...It is now almost a year since we started our work here and we have had some interesting experiences which we would like to relate.
>
> Ours is the last in a row of five new homes on the block in Flushing. We were the first family to move in and we wondered how our immediate neighbors would react when they learned of our purposes here....
>
> It wasn't long, however, before Mrs. G. learned that we were here to witness to Jewish people concerning their Messiah. She lost no time in going around to neighbors across from us and voicing her displeasure. At this time we were especially concerned about the family who would come to live next door, as their living room adjoined our meeting room and they would be sure to hear the hymn singing.
>
> We prayed earnestly about this, and soon learned that the new Jewish family was very orthodox, Mr. and Mrs L., a young refugee couple and their two little girls. They were so orthodox, in fact, that they had two sinks installed in their kitchen in order to wash meat and dairy dishes separately.
>
> After our first meeting we became the recipients of some far-from-pleasant looks, but as good-will ambassadors for the Lord we continued to be friendly, pretending not to notice. I tried especially to show that I had not become a goy (Gentile) by using yiddish expressions when I had opportunity,...
>
> ...Then one day Mr. L. confided to Gilbert [Mr. Maggi] that he listened every morning to a Jewish Christian man on the radio and found it most interesting.[82]

Beatrice Maggi's love and testimony made the Flushing ministry a true "light house" in the community, and it came as a tragic blow when it was discovered that she had cancer. Her illness made it impossible for her to continue the ministry, and in a matter of months she went to be with the Lord.

After Beatrice Maggi's death, her husband, Gilbert, moved out of the Mission's building. The Flushing branch then became a "training branch"—something of a revolving door for new missionaries on staff.

In 1961 Mr. and Mrs. James Marrow occupied the home and served as missionaries in Flushing. Jim Marrow wrote:

> *My wife and I have been greatly blessed in our work here in Flushing. The Lord has brought us into contact with a number of Hebrew Christians in this area so that we have been able to start a monthly Bible class and several unsaved Jews have come to it. Also, two Jewish children have been coming once a week to hear Bible stories and work at handicraft.*
>
> *Recently we have added a new activity—classes in elementary Hebrew; and our people are supporting it enthusiastically. God is indeed blessing our work and day by day He is giving us new opportunities for service.*[83]

One day the Lord directed two yeshiva students to the door at the Flushing branch. They had seen the sign advertising the Beth Sar Shalom meetings, and they were curious as to what it all meant. Jim was thrilled to explain to them that the Mission taught about the Messiah who had already come—Yeshua of Nazareth. He had a taped message which Sam Stern had given him at one of the Mission's recent services—Sam had been a rabbi, but was now a believer and a co-worker with Jim in the ministry. Jim invited the two young yeshiva students into the house to listen to the tape. As they listened, they questioned Jim about his beliefs and about the things Sam spoke about in the taped message. When the young men left, they promised to return—a promise they kept. Later that evening they brought other boys from the Yeshiva with them, giving Jim opportunity to witness further. Before the boys left, he gave each one a copy of the Gospel of Matthew and told them never to criticize a book without first reading it.[84]

Soon after that encounter, the Morrow's resigned from their position with the Mission in order to further their education and training for the Lord's service. They did not return to full-time service with the Mission, but they remained committed to the cause of bringing the Gospel to the Jewish people.

BILL AND JO ENNIS—THEIR STORY

Shortly after the Marrow's left the Flushing ministry, Daniel Fuchs transferred Bill and Jo Ennis from the Dallas branch of the Mission to the Flushing branch.

From his background, Bill Ennis seemed an unlikely candidate as a Jewish missionary—but when God calls an individual to a particular ministry He supplies the gifts needed to accomplish the tasks He has called that servant to do. Such was the case with Bill Ennis!

Bill is a Gentile, raised as a Catholic in Ardmore, Oklahoma. As a boy he knew very little, if anything at all, about the Jewish people. His knowledge of Jewish people had not increased much when, in January 1942, he enlisted in the Army Air Force. During his three-and-one-half year stint in the Army Air Corps, he served as a 1st Lieutenant, 1st Pilot, and as a Combat Pilot. He and members of his unit made thirty-five raids on occupied Europe, with two hundred fifty hours of combat flying time. Bill was awarded the Distinguished Flying Cross, the Air Medal with three Oak Leaf Clusters, and two Combat Stars in ETO. He was also a flight instructor.

As the war continued, Bill saw many of his students and friends leave for over-seas duty, never to return. It was disconcerting to him because it brought up issues he didn't want to think about—death, and the possibility of life after death. For quite some time his wife, Jo, had been witnessing to him but somehow, with his Catholic background and training, he just couldn't accept the things she told him. They sounded good, but in his heart he knew he just didn't believe it.

In 1943, while on a routine training mission, the plane Bill was in suddenly ignited into a ball of fire. Five of the eight men on board were killed, but Bill miraculously survived—without so much as a broken bone. He did not recognize God's hand upon his life, but the plane crash did leave an indelible impression upon him. After the crash he feared that if he went over-seas, he would be shot down and be killed. That thought was frightening enough, but even more frightening to him was the thought of what would happen after death.

Late in 1943 Bill's orders came. He was being sent overseas. He knew he had to settle the matter between himself and the Lord, but somehow nothing worked. One day he met with Jo's Sunday school teacher. Unlike others who had argued with him when he spoke of his unbelief, she wept over him as he spoke of it. When she left, Bill felt even more unworthy of God's love. He could not understand why he was unable to grasp hold of God, and of His peace, like others had. He dreaded each day and night, knowing each one brought him closer to the fateful day when he would have to go overseas—to meet certain death. But before that day arrived, Bill agreed to go to church with his wife, Jo.

Bill remembers slinking into the church, hoping no one would recognize him—a "sinful Catholic"—sitting in a Protestant church. When he saw Jo smiling at him from the choir loft, her peaceful smile made him more uncomfortable and angry. He had tried and tried, but he just couldn't believe. He knew how real God was to Jo, and to other members of her family, but He just wasn't real to Bill. That morning he didn't hear a word the preacher said because he was so focused on his own misery. Then he heard the choir singing "Come Home, Come Home, Ye who are weary, Come Home." As the words reverberated in his ears, his heart told him that was what he wanted to do—to come home. As he looked toward the front of the church, he did not see the pastor or the choir; he only saw a cross, and hanging on the cross was the figure of Jesus. As he watched, transfixed by the wonderful scene, he saw the hand of Jesus reaching out to him in a welcoming, loving, kindly gesture—inviting him to come home! In that moment he knew that God loved *him*; he knew that Jesus had died for *him*. He stepped away from his seat and made his way down the aisle to receive Jesus as his Savior and Lord. On that Sunday morning in February 1944, Bill Ennis "came home!"

Bill was discharged from military service in May 1945, but while he was finishing his tour of duty he faithfully read his Bible, and when he wrote letters to Jo, he told her about various Scriptures that had become especially meaningful to him. God also used that time and experience to open Bill's eyes to the plight of the Jewish people. As his understanding of the Word increased, his love and concern for the Jewish people increased as well. By the time his tour of duty was over he had a burning desire within his heart to share the Gospel with the Jewish people.

Within a year after returning from military service, Bill was certain that God wanted him to preach the Gospel, so he enrolled at the First Orthodox Bible Institute in Ardmore, Oklahoma. While he was attending Bible school his burden for the salvation of the Jewish people weighed so heavily upon his heart that he often attended the orthodox synagogue services. He wasn't sure how to witness to them, but he would put a yarmulke on his head and he would try to share the Messiah with them from the large Bible he carried with him. Some of the Jews got very upset, but most loved his earnest sincerity and the love he showed. They referred to the big Bible he carried as the "Wild Bill" translation.

After graduating from Bible school in 1949, Bill pastored Baptist churches in Perth, Kansas and in Fitzhugh, Texas until 1953. It was during their years in Fitzhugh, Texas that Bill and Jo discovered that one of their son's was deaf. They learned that the nearest School for the Deaf, where their son could receive help and training, was in Austin, Texas, so they made the move to Austin. There, Bill conducted a radio program for Maranatha Bible Broadcast for two years. He also continued to seek out Jewish people to witness to.

One day Bill's Mother-in-law gave him a copy of *The Chosen People* magazine. As he read it, he saw the name of Dr. Harry Marko. He was thrilled to learn of a Jewish believer who lived and ministered right there in the state of Texas. As soon as he could, Bill contacted Dr. Marko. The two became immediate friends. Not long afterwards, Harry told Bill that as he had been praying for Bill, and for his family, he'd felt impressed by the Lord that Bill should be in Jewish mission work. Bill had been praying about the very same thing; Harry Marko's conversation was simply the Lord's confirmation to him.

When Dr. Marko contacted Daniel Fuchs to tell him about this prospective missionary candidate, Daniel arranged his schedule to include a trip to Texas. During their meeting Daniel was impressed with Bill's sincerity, with his love for the Lord, and with the fact that he was already witnessing to Jewish people. He was convinced that Bill would make a good missionary to the Jews, so he invited Bill to participate in the Mission's two-month training program.

New York was a new experience for someone who had grown up in Oklahoma and who liked wide open spaces. But Bill took the Missionary Training Program seriously and, along with other missionary candidates, he did the classroom work and the practical work with diligence. God had already prepared Bill well, but the training program further refined his God-given gifts.

AT THE DALLAS BRANCH

At the completion of the Training Program, Bill and Jo joined the staff of the Mission. They were assigned to work at the Dallas, Texas Branch—a branch that opened as a direct result of the Field Evangelistic work of Dr. Harry Marko. Because of his ministry, a number of Christian people and pastors had become interested in having a branch of the Mission established in Dallas. Their desire became a reality on January 11, 1959, when the Dallas branch was opened. Dr. Marko reported:

> *Our prayers for a Mission Station in Dallas, Texas, have been answered. The Lord has opened a way for us to have a place of worship there, and has given us a wonderful missionary family, the Rev. and Mrs. William T. Ennis, who are very faithful in witnessing to the Jews. Brother Ennis is completely consecrated to this work as he spent much of his time before becoming a member of the staff of the American Board of Missions to the Jews in bringing the Gospel to God's chosen people wherever he could.*[85]

When the Dallas Branch was dedicated nearly one hundred people were present. The service was held in Embrey Hall of the First Baptist Church of Dallas. Those participating in the service were Dr. Harry Marko, Dr. Daniel Fuchs, Dr.

Harlan Roper, pastor of Scofield Memorial Church of Dallas, Dr. Jase Jones, Southern Baptist state leader for Texas in Jewish Missions. Several other Jewish Ministries were also represented by Mr. Tom Roth, Mrs. Mary Kaley, and Mrs. Jewel Daniel.

Dr. W. A. Criswell, who throughout his ministry has had a great love for the Jewish people and for Jewish evangelism, also went out of his way to help with the establishment of the Mission's work in Dallas. He and his children gave gifts of furnishings to help equip the new branch.[86]

For the first few years the branch in Dallas operated as a storefront ministry. Bill and Jo Ennis labored long and hard to developed the work; they proved to be one of the most effective couples the Mission had on its staff. Their love for the Jewish people was obvious, and their sensitivity to the needs of the Jewish people attending their meetings endeared them to all who came. Through their loving and faithful ministry, a number of Jewish people came to faith in Yeshua. Bill wrote:

> ...What a privilege it has been for us to present to these friends, and have them accept, the Lord Jesus Christ as their true Messiah, and to experience the joy of seeing them bear witness to their faith, in baptism, and to testify to Jew and Gentile alike of their salvation in the Lord Jesus as their Messiah.
>
> Among these friends is M.D., a Jewess, who recently followed our Lord in baptism, now a member of our church, who enjoys hearing Dr. Criswell preach the Word. Another Jewish friend, Jordan M., was baptized within two weeks of M.D., and expressed a desire to accompany us when we go out to testify to his people because he speaks impeccable Yiddish and is able to present the Gospel to them in their own familiar language.[87]

At the Flushing Branch

In the Fall of 1962, Bill and Jo Ennis were transferred to the Flushing, New York branch. Daniel Fuchs needed an experienced missionary to take over the leadership of the Mission's Long Island ministry, as well as the Mission's camping program, and Bill and Jo were the perfect candidates!

After making the move to the Northeast, Bill shared his vision for the ministry in New York with readers of *The Chosen People* magazine. He wrote:

> Our plans for 1963 include the following activities: First, participation in the work of our New York Headquarters; second, developing our work at the Flushing Branch; third, Sunday evening assemblies in homes in Levittown, Long Island; and fourth, a plan for adding a feature to our next summer's Camp Sar Shalom for training our Jewish young people in conducting outdoor meetings.[88]

Establishing a Deaf Ministry

As a part of their participation in the ministry at the Headquarters building in Manhattan, Jo Ennis pioneered a ministry to deaf and hearing-impaired Jewish people—a group previously unreached. Of this new and exciting part of the ministry, Bill wrote:

> ...An important new feature of our work at the New York Mission, and perhaps the most rewarding, is a Sunday afternoon meeting for our deaf Jewish people. This ministry is pioneering in a new field for our Mission, and is especially dear to the hearts of Mrs. Ennis and myself since our youngest and oldest sons are deaf. God has blessed us richly in this ministry, and also has sent us an extremely capable and devoted interpreter in the person of Miss Kay Mancill, who has volunteered for this work as a service for the Lord.[89]

The ministry to the deaf continued to be an important part of the Ennis' ministry. Even in retirement, Jo continues to use her knowledge of "signing" to witness to Jewish people, to disciple new believers, and to teach deaf Christians about the need to reach Jewish people with the Gospel.

Directing the Summer Camp Program

As they worked to expand the Mission's summer Camp Sar Shalom program, Bill wrote:

> ...Already plans have been made by a God-blessed dedicated staff of Mission workers to provide an additional outdoor spiritual experience for our Jewish teenagers. They will conduct open-air meetings in a number of the Pennsylvania communities adjacent to our Camp Sar Shalom at Honey Brook, Pennsylvania, during the coming summer camp. By this means we believe our Jewish young people will gain strength and confidence in proclaiming the Gospel of Salvation through the Lord Jesus Christ.[90]

As the staff laid plans for the camping program, it was decided to divide the program into separate programs for the young married couples, the older teenagers, the younger teenagers, and the juniors—down to six year old's. A record attendance was reported, and the camping program was a great success. Bill wrote:

> The month of July was divided into two equal periods, as in previous years, the first two weeks for the junior boys and girls, and the last two weeks for the teenagers. This year there were 79 juniors from New York, Brooklyn, Coney Island, Long Island, Washington (D.C.), Pittsburgh, Englewood (N.J.) and New City (N.Y.). These 79 juniors returned to their homes as the young married couples and older and younger teenagers arrived for the last two weeks of camp. The total attendance of all groups this year was 150 campers, a new attendance record. From the juniors 18, and from the teenagers five confessed their faith in the Lord Jesus Christ, and a large number from all age groups dedicated their lives anew to the Lord.[91]

Ruth Wardell gave further insight into the results of the new, invigorated youth program. She wrote:

> Groups of our boys and girls accompanied by their counselors would take to the road as an evangelistic party, and spend the week-end at some not-too-far-distant point from New York Headquarters. On the way they would organize open-air meetings, particularly on a Saturday afternoon, and on Sunday morning conduct a worship service in a church. Thus they would experience the joy of presenting the good news of salvation on their own responsibility to the 'mixed multitude,' on the one hand, and give their testimony to Christians, on the other.
>
> It will cheer the hearts of all who read these lines to know that the Mission's work with our teenage boys and girls has taken on a new impetus this year. In addition to the week-end pilgrimages, which are being continued, our group has established its newsletter, 'Teens for the Messiah,' on a monthly basis, with a member of the group acting as 'Editor.' Although 'Teens for the Messiah' has been published by our young people for a number of years—in fact, since about 1950—this is the first time our teenagers have taken such an active interest in the paper as to undertake the work of writing the contents themselves.[92]

Under the leadership of Bill and Jo Ennis, the camping program continued to grow. It was an area of ministry that greatly impacted many Jewish and Gentile young people, and which influenced more than a few young people to devote themselves to full-time missionary service with the Mission, or with other ministries.

OPENING THE HOLLIS BRANCH

When the Ennis's were not laboring at the Headquarters branch, or at Camp Sar Shalom, they devoted themselves to the development of the ministry in Flushing, New York. That branch, too, experienced growth under their leadership, and in 1967 it became necessary to move the ministry to a larger facility. A suitable building was located in Hollis, Long Island. It was a large home, in close proximity to the Jewish community and to the bus and rail commuter lines. Daniel Fuchs shared the good news of this expansion with the readers of The Chosen People magazine, stating that the new building in Hollis would be open in the Fall of 1967.[93] But unforeseen problems delayed the opening. The delays, which were disappointing at first, turned out to be God's blessings in disguise. Jo Ennis wrote:

> ...building codes and fire laws must be observed, and so repairs and installations began. To our keen disappointment, it was obvious that we couldn't begin our regularly scheduled Fall classes in that building. What to do? Pray and look for an open door, of course. The Lord is always faithful. We were able to rent a store building on a busy street. There was also a shopping area nearby. We had an attractive window display and arranged a reading room and desk for inquirers. Also we have two class rooms. Rev. Burl Haynie, Mrs. Pauline Klayman and Mrs. Sarah Urbach, as well as ourselves, have kept the reading room open 10 a.m. to 6 p.m. Misses Eleanor Bullock and Ruth Wardell, Bob Gross, and Rev. and Mrs. Bill Ennis are providing classes for all age groups, with both day and evening meetings. It has proved to be a blessing which the Lord wanted us to have.
>
> Many, many Jewish people have come in for literature and witnessing. Some have attended meetings and been visited in their homes. At least one woman has accepted Jesus as her Messiah. The fact that we have become known in this area will be a tremendous help when we open the new Mission Home in the near future.[94]

The dedication and open house of the new Hollis branch was held on May 30, 1968—months after the projected opening date and two years to the day subsequent to the date in that summer of 1966 when members of the Brooklyn staff and the Long Island staff decided that the time had come for a branch of the Mission in Queens, Long Island. Over two hundred seventy-five people attended the dedication service.

By the time the Hollis building was purchased, Bill was serving as Missionary in Charge of the Long Island ministries; the building itself was remodeled to function as a multi-purpose facility. It served as a branch for ministry, as a headquarters for the Long Island ministry, and as the Ennis' living quarters.

As a branch of the ministry, the Hollis building became a bee-hive of activity. One of the very successful weekly meetings held there was the Ladies' Bible Class, taught by Eleanor Bullock. The class had been started by Eleanor twenty years earlier, in Brooklyn, but when the Hollis building was opened the class was relocated to that facility. Under her excellent teaching the class continued to grow and to draw women from miles around. Readers of The Chosen People magazine were told:

> These dear ones, some past 70 years of age, come faithfully regardless of weather conditions. One day last winter we had a heavy snowfall and our meeting was scheduled for the next day. We did not expect any one, but were pleasantly surprised to see many come. When we were settled, they laughingly said that it would take more than a little snow storm to keep them from the Word of God.[95]

A host of other meetings were held as well, and as Bill and Jo worked with the Long Island staff, their love and patience enabled them to draw out the best in each worker, and to thereby enhance the overall work being done.

The Flushing property continued to be used as a branch of the Mission, as well as a home for many of the new missionary workers. But when it was no longer possible to carry on a viable ministry from that building because of the changes in the neighborhood, the property was sold.

The East New York Branch

After the opening of the Flushing branch of the Mission in January 1955, the next new branch opened was in the old Brownsville section of Brooklyn—the very section of Brooklyn where Leopold Cohn had started the ministry before moving it to Williamsburg, Brooklyn. This branch was called the East New York branch.

The Brownsville section of Brooklyn was still one of the most densely populated Jewish areas in New York—an area that housed over 150,000 Jewish people and more than thirteen synagogues. With such a concentrated Jewish population, there was a definite need for a Gospel witness in Brownsville. But there was an additional consideration that led to the establishment of a branch in that area. It seems that quite a few Jewish people who had attended the Mission's meetings in other areas of Brooklyn had moved to the Brownsville area; they had requested that the Mission establish a branch there.

As the Mission surveyed the area and sought a building in which to hold meetings, pastor Don Marsh of the East End Baptist Church offered his facilities for the Mission's use. He was deeply concerned for the salvation of the Jewish people who lived near the church, and he and his congregants had been praying that a mission to the Jews would come into the area. They therefore gladly opened the church and the church house for the Mission's use.[96]

Even before the Mission knew of pastor Marsh's generous offer of a facility for meetings, the Lord had supplied a worker. In the Spring of 1956 the Mission hired Rev. Kenneth C. Anderson to begin a work in East New York.[97]

Because it was located in an extremely difficult area, the East New York branch never really developed. But Rev. Anderson reported a few successes as the Lord blessed his witness. He wrote:

> ...We provide crafts for the children, sewing for the ladies, hold regular classes for the teaching of God's Word, and enjoy fellowship with those of 'like precious faith.' We cannot boast of large numbers, but in the weeks that have passed there have been additions—those who are unsaved and others who have grown in grace. Who are these people and how do we find them? Only God can direct us as we distribute the invitations among the pushcarts of Blake Avenue, or mount the countless stairways of Brooklyn's labyrinthine streets....
>
> There are the sick to visit, programs to be planned, lessons to be taught. The subways of New York and Brooklyn have become familiar routine as we pursue the various tasks and methods to reach the Jew for Christ.[98]

Arnold Fruchtenbaum—His Story

Ruth Wardell taught the children's classes and youth classes at the East New York branch. One day, Daniel Fuchs gave Ruth the name of the Fruchtenbaum family, and asked her to pay them a visit. This Ruth did the following day. When she arrived at their apartment, she saw thirteen-year old Arnold, and his brother and sister, standing outside. She was involved in teaching the youth, so without hesitation she introduced herself and proceeded to invite the young people to attend one of her Bible classes. To her surprise, they agreed to come and they all piled into her car. She did not know, nor did Arnold or his brother and sister know, that Mrs. Fruchtenbaum had given their family's name to Daniel Fuchs a few years earlier. At the time, the Mission did not have any missionaries working in that area so Daniel had put the name in his file—awaiting the day when the Mission would have a worker in the area who could visit them.

The East New York branch only existed for about six years—but that was time enough for the witness to reach the Fruchtenbaum family. God's grace is marvelous? To understand the scope of His grace and mercy with regard to Arnold Fruchtenbaum and his family, the reader must journey back to the end of World War II.

Arnold was born of Jewish parents in Siberia, Russia on September 26, 1943—in the midst of the raging war with the Nazis. At the time of his birth, Arnold's father was being held in a Communist concentration camp. After the War was over, the Fruchtenbaum family made their way back to their home in Poland, but they found they were trapped behind the Iron Curtain of Communism. It was during their attempt to flee from Communist-controlled Poland, that the Fruchtenbaums first heard about a mission to the Jews. The story is best told in Arnold's own words:

> My first contact with the American Board of Missions to the Jews occurred in 1947 in West Germany. Through the work of the Israeli Underground, my parents and I escaped from behind the Iron Curtain and were soon moved into the British Displaced Persons Camps, which were to be our homes for five years. Working among these Jewish D.P.'s, was a representative of the American Board [of Missions to the Jews] whose main job was to hand out food and clothes to Jewish people escaping from behind the Iron Curtain. The first clothes we had to wear were those purchased by the American Board, although this was something we did not know until many years later. The minister, suspecting that someday we might come to the United States, tore off the cover from the October 1948 issue of The Chosen People magazine, on which Joseph Hoffman Cohn's name and the American Board headquarters' address were printed. My mother was told that if and when we went to the United States, we should contact these people and they would be able to help us.
>
> My mother accepted the magazine cover, put it into her purse and kept it there for three years. In 1951, when we received permission to immigrate to the United States, we left Germany and moved to Brooklyn, New York. Soon after this my mother, having the information from the magazine cover, found her way to the New York Headquarters and asked to speak with Dr. Cohn. Since he was out of town, one of their missionaries, Daniel Fuchs, who is now the General Secretary, spoke to her and took our name and address promising us that we would be contacted as soon as it would be feasible.[99]

Daniel was normally very prompt in following through with such requests. When he put the Fruchtenbaum name in his file, he expected to send a worker to visit the family in a few weeks or so. Never in his wildest dreams would he have put off visiting a Jewish family for nearly six long years. But that's what happened. God has His plans, and man has his. But God's plans are sovereign. He knew that a thirteen year old boy, named Arnold, needed to hear the message of salvation. He knew that the thirteen year old boy who had already studied the Scriptures with the rabbis, and who was already deeply religious and searching for the truth about the Messiah, would be far more receptive to the Gospel than the seven year old boy who had just arrived in America. God also knew that the early rabbinic training and lessons in the Hebrew Scriptures would serve as a strong foundation upon which a strong testimony of Gospel witness to the Jewish people would one day be built.

When Ruth invited Arnold and his brother and sister to attend her class, she did not know how ill-prepared she was for the searching, in-depth questions young Arnold would be asking. Arnold could read Hebrew and he had a good grasp of the Hebrew Scriptures. He knew some of what the rabbis taught about the Messiah. According to Jewish tradition, he was very religious. Even though he was only thirteen, he had already spent years studying the Hebrew Scriptures, Jewish traditions, history, and theology with the rabbis. He was on his way to becoming a "yeshiva bocher" (a rabbinical student), and perhaps a rabbi.

Arnold's probing questions threw Ruth off-guard. After their first classroom experience together she went home and immediately pulled out her Isaac Leeser translation of the Hebrew Bible (at the time, this was the most accepted English translation of the Bible for Jewish people). Painstakingly, she went through every Messianic prophecy, comparing the translations of various Bibles with the Isaac Leeser translation. She wanted to be fully prepared for her next encounter with this knowledgeable Jewish teenager! While she studied, she prayed that God would speak to Arnold's heart and she prayed for the ability to communicate the Truth so that he would one day come to faith in Yeshua.

When Arnold returned home after his first classroom experience at the Mission he was bombarded with warnings from the other Jewish kids who'd heard that he had gone to the "missionaries" place. They told Arnold that the Mission would tatoo crosses and wicked emblems on his back, and make a "hated" Christian out of him. Arnold took the warnings seriously, and when Ruth dropped by to invite him back to the Mission, he politely declined. But Ruth was not one to give up easily, so she continued to press and to encourage him to attend her class. Arnold didn't want to tell Ruth about the warnings he'd received from the other Jewish children in the neighborhood, and he didn't have a good excuse for not going, so he finally relented and jumped into the car for his second visit to the Mission.

Through her study of the Word, God had prepared Ruth's heart. In the intervening time, He had also prepared Arnold's heart. Arnold, too, had been studying the Messianic claims within Scripture and as he and Ruth talked, and compared the Scriptures, his heart began to soften toward the person of Yeshua. Before he left the Mission that day, he prayed to receive Yeshua as his Messiah and Savior.

After his second visit to the Mission, Arnold faithfully attended Ruth's Bible studies and the other activities of the Mission. God had blessed him with a quick mind and, although he had an impressive knowledge of Scripture when he began attending Ruth's classes, his knowledge of the Scriptures increased as he eagerly drank in the Word of God.

When summer arrived, Arnold joined the other young people who were attending the Mission's summer camping program. There, at the age of fourteen, Arnold preached his first sermon—a study of the book of Job. Ruth still remembers how impressed she and the other missionaries, counselors, and staff workers were when the small Jewish boy, with the little yarmulka on his head, stood and expounded the book of Job as if he were a seminary graduate. After that, Ruth and the other missionaries knew they had another potential missionary to the Jews—one who would make a profound impact upon the Jewish community.

The Fruchtenbaum family moved to Los Angeles in 1958—just a year or so after Arnold's acceptance of Yeshua. Arnold's new belief and his involvement with the Mission had been the cause of considerable conflict and dissension within the family. In fact, Mr. Fruchtenbaum had not spoken to him since learning of his faith in Yeshua, and when the family gathered around the table for a meal, he would act as if Arnold was not even there.[100] When Arnold persisted in proclaiming his belief in Yeshua, and in attending meetings at the Mission even after the family's move West, Mr. Fruchtenbaum decided he'd had enough of his son's heresy. But Mrs. Fruchtenbaum was the person who delivered the news to Arnold of his father's decision. One night, while he was reading in bed, Mrs. Fruchtenbaum slipped into Arnold's room and told him that his father had issued an ultimatum—he was to get out of the house as soon as he graduated from high school!

As Arnold prayed about what to do, he felt that the Lord was directing him to return to New York—where he had first met his Messiah. Remembering that traumatic time in his life, Arnold wrote:

> ...Fully convinced of this, I prepared to leave Los Angeles knowing I would have only $160 with me. But the Lord opened the way for me to be provided with transportation by car and for most of my expenses to be taken care of by people who did not realize that they were being used as His instruments. I finally reached New York, two weeks later, with most of my small capital still intact.[101]

The next several years were filled with many tests of Arnold's faith, and demonstrations of God's faithfulness to him as he exercised his faith. One such test involved the matter of his college tuition fees. He wrote:

> Only a few weeks passed by before I had to exercise my faith again. This time the problem was whether to start college with the $140 left or go to work for a year and make some additional money. I asked Him for a sign so that I would be sure of His will for me. In a most remarkable and totally unexpected manner a sign was given that removed all shadow of doubt from my mind, and I knew I had to go to college.
>
> So I went to Shelton College. My bill for the first semester was $713.25. I exercised my faith and trusted God to keep His promise. By the end of the semester not only was the whole bill paid but the college owed me money.[102]

God continued to faithfully supply for Arnold. He went on to Cedarville College, graduating with a B.A. in Hebrew and Greek. Then he went to Israel, where he took graduate work at the Institute of Holyland Studies and at the Hebrew University in Jerusalem. He later attended Dallas Theological Seminary, graduating with a Th.M. in Old Testament and Semitics.

Throughout his years of study, Arnold continued to be involved with the Mission. He especially enjoyed working with young people in the camping program—an activity of the Mission that had been close to his heart since his first experience with the program when he was fourteen. It was through the camping program that he also met, and fell in love with a young girl named Maryanne, who later became his wife.

In 1977 God led Arnold to establish his own mission to the Jews. He called it Ariel Ministries. While he was developing Ariel Ministries, Arnold also took graduate studies at the Jewish Theological Seminary in New York and then went on to complete a Ph.d. in Jewish studies at New York University.

Although Arnold no longer serves on the staff of the Mission, he continues to be involved in many of the Mission's activities, and he is a popular speaker at Mission conferences. A close cooperation exists between Ariel Ministries and Chosen People Ministries.

Thus, although the East New York branch of the Mission only remained open for a relatively short time, the investment of time, resources, and personnel was blessed by God. It was an investment that continues to touch lives even today through young people and adults who found the Messiah there.

MAX DORIANI—THE ROCKAWAYS BRANCH

In March 1956, a third new branch of the Mission was opened in New York—in the Rockaway section. The branch was called the Rockaways-and-Five-Towns branch.[103] The Rockaways are comprised of a narrow strip of land, ten to twelve miles long, stretching along the coast of Long Island toward Brooklyn and Coney Island, and jutting out into the Atlantic Ocean. It was mainly a Jewish resort area, but there were also year-round residents—many of whom were Jewish. Many prominent rabbis lived there, and there were a number of prominent synagogues in the area, as well as the Long Island Hebrew Institute. It was an excellent location for a Gospel witness to the Jews!

Like the East New York branch, the Rockaway branch enjoyed the use of a church facility—the parish house of a church. The building was located near the large Jewish section of Far Rockaway. The few Jewish Christians who already lived in the area attended the first meeting in March 1956, and made up the nucleus of the congregation thereafter. The missionary worker was a Jewish believer from Russia—Mr. Max Doriani.[104] Max had accepted the Lord some ten years earlier (c. 1946). His native tongue was Russian, but he spoke English and a smattering of other languages as well. He loved the Lord, and wanted only to serve Him as a missionary to His own people.

Meetings at the Rockaways branch were held twice a month at first, but by the Fall of 1956 they were being held on a weekly basis. Max reported:

> …Because of its location it is important to have a Branch here as a base of operations for our evangelistic work and also as a place of worship and spiritual growth for those who are already believers in the Lord Jesus Christ, the Messiah. The children's work, under the able direction of Miss Ruth Wardell, is an important part of our program. We also have special programs which we present to churches, showing the importance of giving the Gospel to the Jews and making for a better understanding of the Mission's program of missionary work among the Jews.[105]

In addition to his responsibilities at the Rockaways branch, Max Doriani also assisted Jonas Cohen at the Williamsburg branch, where Friday evening services were conducted in three languages. Reporting to readers of *The Chosen People* magazine, Max said:

> …Mr. Jonas Cohen (no relation to Joseph Hoffman Cohn) and I work together. He conducts the service and gives a message in Yiddish. I give a message in English and follow it with a message in Russian. Inasmuch as most Jews in this area come from either German or Russian dominated countries, there is hardly a Jew who would fail to understand the gospel message because of a language barrier. We hear many stirring, heart-warming testimonies on what Jesus the Messiah of Israel means in the lives of these people.[106] [The reader will learn more about Jonas Cohen in Chapter Eleven of this history.]

While the work at the Rockaways never grew into a large branch, it was an effective branch. In November 1958 Max reported:

> We are now in our second year at the Rockaways branch of our Mission….
> During the past year five of our members were baptized. Another member professed her faith in the Lord Jesus Christ, our Messiah, at a meeting of the Billy Graham Crusade. The husband of another of our believers came to a saving knowledge of the Lord last fall. Another who was a professional singer now sings at our meetings. Through this latter feature a Jewish family is taking an interest in our work.[107]

The longer Max worked in the Rockaways, the deeper was his burden for the Jews of Long Island, and the greater was his desire to share the Gospel message with every Jew who lived on the island. Everywhere he went, he saw new opportunities for expanding the outreach. He knew that a branch of the Mission was being established in Levittown, but he longed to see other branches opened too. As he ministered in the churches, such as Carle Place Baptist Church in Carle Place, Long Island, where the congregation was twenty-five percent Jewish, he shared his vision that more branches of the mission would be opened on Long Island. God answered his prayers and made his vision a reality when some friends of the Mission arranged for meetings to be held in a wonderful conference building in Westbury, Nassau County, Long Island. Max wrote:

> ...Our first meeting was held December 11, 1957. It was an impressive sight to see the large number of Christian Jews who attended this meeting. A goodly number of inquiring Jews also came. This meeting place at Westbury will, God willing, serve as another beacon on Long Island where still more of God's scattered and bewildered people may hear the Gospel of salvation through faith in the Lord Jesus Christ, their true Messiah. [108]

The ministry that Max started at Westbury was ultimately developed by other workers of the Mission. Max continued his efforts to establish additional Mission stations on the island. He wrote:

> The Rev. and Mrs. Fred Keil joined us in prayer as we met to seek God's guidance in the matter of opening a new Mission station at Port Washington (Long Island) in the Keil home. The need for starting a work among the Jews in this location is urgent because of the large Jewish population in the section and in nearby Great Neck. Weekly meetings were started and have continued without interruption. Two Jewish women have already accepted the Lord. We are studying the Bible and seeking the salvation and upbuilding of all who come, and God is blessing our efforts. [109]

Like Joseph Cohn, Max Doriani kept his eyes and ears open for opportunities for witness. One unusual avenue of witness that he used was to join forces with other evangelical ministries on Long Island to set up a booth at the county fair. He wrote:

> Because of the large Jewish population in Nassau County on Long Island, our Mission, for the first time, joined with other evangelical Christian agencies in setting up a booth for the distribution of our literature at the Nassau County Fair during October, 1960. Thousands of copies of our tract, 'What is a Christian?' from our series of 'What Every Jew Should Know,' were handed out to visitors, and proved to be most effective in directing the attention of all who read it to the importance of reaching the Jew for Christ at this present time. [110]

Later other workers of the Mission also utilized county fairs, and even the World Fairs, as platforms from which to present a Gospel witness to Jewish people.

God used Max Doriani mightily in reaching Jewish people with the Gospel—both on Long Island and in Brooklyn. But the long days, the heavy travel and speaking schedule, and the inter-personal staff problems began to take their toll, and one day Max told Daniel Fuchs that he felt the Lord was directing him to take a church. He felt that as a pastor, he could encourage more Christians to witness to their Jewish friends and neighbors. Max Doriani resigned from the Mission in the Fall of 1962, to pastor the First Christian Church at Ebensburg, Pennsylvania. In December 1963 he was pastor of Big Run Baptist Church in Pennsylvania.

During his years in the pastorate, Max did just what he said he wanted to do—he encouraged his congregants to become involved in sharing the Gospel with the Jewish people. He also wrote a number of articles about how pastors and Christians could be effective witnesses to the Jewish people. One of the articles is as relevant today as it was the day it was written. It states:

> There are thousands and thousands of small towns in the United States in each of which are Jewish families, few or several. The sum total of these rural and small-town Jews is undoubtedly very large.
>
> What is the religious life of these country Jews? How are they regarded by their Gentile and Christian neighbors? Aren't they often looked upon as a people apart? Even earnest Christians, who hear so often in church and Sunday school that the Jew is part of the great Hebrew-Christian tradition, do not know exactly how to meet and exchange ideas on religion with their Jewish friends and neighbors.
>
> A field representative from a Jewish mission may come to speak in one of these small-town churches and remind its members that Jews need Christ and that the congregation should not only pray for the salvation of the Jews but also make some evangelistic effort to reach them for our Lord, by doing it themselves locally or by contributing to a dedicated missionary program.
>
> Are there special conditions which prevail in small towns and country areas which differ from those that prevail in the larger cities? I think there are. In small towns everybody knows everybody else. Jews know pretty well what is going on in the local churches and what kind of people church members are. A Jew will judge the claims of Christianity by the

people who belong to the local church. The average church has among its membership some very good clean-living people. So has the local synagogue. Church membership also includes some who are not too good and not too bad. So does the membership of the synagogue. There are church members who are trouble-makers and squabblers. The synagogue also has some. The church will occasionally have a member or two who is downright evil. And so may the synagogue.

Yet it is a Christian imperative to witness to the Jew. Jews are intellectually inquisitive. Some, if only to satisfy their curiosity, would like to know more about the Christian faith. Many Jews are waiting for someone to take the first step to bring them into a larger fellowship with their Christian neighbors. They, like some of us, don't know how to make the first move.

Can we talk to a Jew about Christ and the need of a personal relationship with Him? Of course. But not about subjects which he would consider abstractions, or philosophical theories, such as justification, the visible and invisible church. The Bible is the Word of God and has to do with God's dealing with people, and this is the important thing to discuss with the Jew.

How many Jews in small towns and rural communities can be reached with the Gospel? If there is a church in the town that is really close to Christ, with a real Christian spirit, this is the church which has the golden opportunity to reach the local Jews. A closer walk with Christ on the part of the congregation and each individual Christian is the answer. Members of such a church should think out an intelligent approach to the Jew and familiarize themselves with it. They should make a simple and sincere effort to welcome Jews to their meetings.

A minister's attitude toward the Jew is a gauge by which his Christian spirituality can be measured. A modernistic minister has no interest in the Jew, a neo-orthodox minister may have some, but a minister who goes by the Word of God is intensely concerned about the Jew. This is true of a congregation in still another way. A lukewarm though doctrinally sound congregation has no real interest in Jewish evangelism. A congregation spiritually close to the Lord Jesus Christ is intensely interested in the Jew. When we have the right spiritual equipment, we may look for great rewards and blessings.[111]

The Levittown Branch

While Clara and Joe Rubin carried on the ministry at the Huntington Station branch, and while Max Doriani worked to oversee the Flushing branch, the East New York branch and the Rockaway branch (as well as participating in other areas of evangelistic outreach), a branch of the Mission was also established in Levittown, New York.

Levittown was a giant experiment in sociology. When World War II ended, many of the G.I.'s who returned home were immediately discharged from military service. Scores of the men were married, and their return to the States created an urgent need for homes for them and their families. The government therefore enacted the G.I. Bill which provided low interest mortgages so the men could buy homes with little or no money down. Mr. Levitt, a Jewish business-man and land developer, saw a wonderful opportunity to capitalize on the returning G.I.'s, and on government financing, so he developed Levittown—a sprawling community of nearly-identical small single-family homes built on postage-stamp sized lots. The residents of Levittown were mainly G.I.'s, although the community was comprised of people of mixed ethnic and religious backgrounds—including Jews. Levittown provided Jewish G.I.'s, as well as young Jewish families who wanted to move from the changing areas of Brooklyn, a community in which they could find affordable housing.

If Levittown was an experiment for sociologists, it was also an experiment for the Mission. Reaching the Jews of Levittown, like the Jews of the other suburban cities on Long Island, required new methods of ministry. The Jews of suburbia were quite different from the Jews of the close-knit Jewish families of Brooklyn.

The branch at Levittown was started by Ruth Wardell and other workers of the Mission who, for more than one year, had made regular visits to a Jewish believer in Levittown whose name was Sally Frankel. Sally was introduced to the Mission through *The Chosen People* radio broadcast. Although it had been more than two years since Joseph Cohn's death, tapes of his messages were still being aired and at the conclusion of the taped message the address of the Mission was given. Sally, who had problems and personal needs, contacted the Mission and subsequently some of the Mission's workers began meeting with her for Bible study, prayer, and counseling. Ruth Wardell and Beatrice Maggi were two of the workers who met with Sally. Their loving counsel, along with the Bible study, created within Sally a great burden for her Jewish friends. She said:

About a year ago [c. 1955/56] Ruth Wardell, Mrs. Maggi and I were sitting together in my home. We had just closed our Bibles after a meeting at which the Word of God had been presented to us. As we sat together I told them of certain Jewish friends of mine in Levittown and wondered if there wasn't some way of bringing the peace of the Lord to them. My own home was hardly suitable as a place for holding meetings; so Miss Wardell asked me to keep an eye out for some house that would be suitable.

After making the rounds of several real estate offices and watching the real estate section of the local newspaper, I found a home with a semi-finished attic about two blocks from the main shopping center. I'll never forget the rainy day when Miss Wardell and Mrs. Maggi called to tell me the Mission liked the house and would lease it.

Our first gathering in the name of the Lord was shortly before Christmas. It was a wonderful experience to celebrate the Lord's birth together. The Rev. Daniel Fuchs attended and prayed that though we were small in number we might be great in the Holy Spirit.

This, then, is the story of 'Our House.' Here Miss Wardell gives us patient and loving instruction for our Christian life, while Ruth Koffler supervises the children in our well-stocked playroom. Here, too, we have the sure knowledge that Christ dwells in the midst of us. We sing together, we learn together, and what's more important, we pray together in His name.[112]

The meetings continued to be held in 'Our House' until Ruth Wardell moved to Levittown in 1958. After that, they were held in Ruth's home; her home became her primary base of operations from which she traveled all over Long Island, or to the Williamsburg branch, until 1973 when the Mission transferred her to Los Angeles.

The staff in New York was doing a commendable job making inroads with the Gospel to the many Jewish people who had moved from Brooklyn into the boroughs of New York, while on the West Coast, Martin (Moishe) Meyer Rosen was mapping out his strategy for developing the ministry in Los Angeles, California. His program and approach to suburban Jewish missionary work ultimately affected the overall course of the Mission and its growth.

The Los Angeles Ministry Expanded

Following his ordination in Denver, Colorado on August 9, 1957, Martin and his family made the last leg of their trip to Los Angeles. As has been mentioned, they were to replace Rev. Elias Zimmerman, the founder of the Mission's work there. During the last few years of his ministry in Los Angeles, Elias' health had not allowed him to maintain a full schedule of activities, and by the time Rosen arrived on the scene the Los Angeles work had declined substantially. Daniel Fuchs' purpose in sending Martin to Los Angeles was to infuse new life into the West Coast ministry—something he certainly did!

Realizing that the Los Angeles ministry was in decline, the Mission had made an effort to revitalize the work in 1956 by purchasing a building on West Pico Boulevard in West Los Angeles. Mr. Burl Haynie was hired to assist Elias Zimmerman (Burl was a former worker for Dr. David L. Cooper's ministry—the Christian Research Society). Two years earlier (c. 1954) Mr. Kenneth Reeves had also been hired to assist in the ministry, but in spite of these efforts the work continued to decline.

Elias Zimmerman first met Kenneth Reeves at a Passover dinner that was being held at the Biblical Research Society. Ken and Elias sat at the same table, and as Elias told Ken about the Mission, Ken felt that he would like to serve the Lord in such an organization. Both Ken and his wife, Marguerite, were Gentile Christians, but each had developed a deep love for Jewish people while attending BIOLA college. As students at BIOLA, they had taken every Jewish studies course offered and taught by Dr. Oren Smith.

After making application with the Mission, Kenneth and Marguerite Reeves assisted Elias Zimmerman in the Los Angeles ministry for four years. They were transferred to San Diego, California in 1958, to open a new branch of the Mission.[113]

By the time the Rosen's arrived in Los Angeles in 1957, attendance at the meetings in Los Angeles was so small that Martin felt like he was pioneering a new work rather than assuming leadership of an existing ministry. In an interview with the author, Moishe (Martin) mused over the fact that his Bible training in New York had not included any practical training on how to begin a new outreach ministry—so he "muddled along" as best he could. He began by contacting local believers, pastors, and anyone he knew of who had expressed an interest in Jewish evangelism. His wife, Ceil, helped by beginning a work with children. God added His blessings to their efforts, and soon they had a core of faithful volunteers assisting them in the work. In reminiscing about those days Moishe said:

...Anyway, I was muddling along and Daniel Fuchs came out.... Daniel stayed in our house. He stayed with us for two weeks. He went with me and did everything with me. What surprised me was that he didn't know any more than I did. But in a sense, that two weeks turned me around because it was just having somebody there, doing the work with me.... Daniel was willing to listen to me and then he'd offer suggestions, and his suggestions were good. But I was surprised to find out that he, personally, had not had any experience in doing what I was doing.... But the thing that I admired about him was ...that there was no job he wasn't willing to do. I was also impressed with the fact that he could admit when he didn't know something.[114]

The Los Angeles ministry began to blossom again. It enjoyed an era of unparalleled growth from 1960 to 1974. By 1961-1962 Martin's staff included himself, Ceil, Miss Helen Graber, and Mr. Kenneth Reeves (plus the help of some part-time students).

A New Training Program Developed

Part of Martin's strategy for ministry growth included personal growth. To achieve this goal he enrolled in classes at Fuller Theological Seminary. As he gleaned information from the classroom, from colleagues, and from first-hand experience in ministry, he began to systematize and develop guideline materials for use in training other missionaries to establish branches of the Mission and for evangelizing the Jewish community. He shared his ideas and the materials he'd prepared with Daniel Fuchs, and Daniel was so impressed that he transferred the entire recruiting and training program of the Mission to Martin, and the Los Angeles branch of the Mission—action which set up a chain of events and a power struggle within the Mission that ultimately led to Martin's resignation from the Mission and the formation of the Jewish mission called "Jews for Jesus."

As mentioned in earlier discussion of this chapter, the Directors of the Mission had assigned Daniel Fuchs responsibility over the publications of the Mission and over the missionary work of the Mission. But the responsibility for the executive, financial, and administrative work of the Mission was under the jurisdiction of other individuals—namely Harold Pretlove (administrative) and Emil Gruen (Conference Ministry). With the success and growth of the West Coast ministry, Martin Rosen's sphere of influence and authority grew as well, and his programs began to impact other departments within the Mission. It appeared to some of the workers, as well as to some of the Board members, that there were two separate ministries within the one organization—one ministry run by Daniel Fuchs with Martin Rosen; the other ministry run by Harold Pretlove and Emil Gruen, with the Field Evangelists somewhere in between.

In many ways, Martin (Moishe) Rosen was a true successor to Joseph Cohn, and, like Cohn, he generated controversy. Although the two men had never met, they had similar traits, and they were similarly single-minded where reaching Jewish people with the Gospel was concerned. Like Joseph Cohn, Martin Rosen was a born strategist and tactician. But unlike Cohn, Rosen was able to delegate responsibility so that individuals trained could grow within the organization. Martin was far more organized and structured in his administration than Cohn, but like Cohn, he demanded accountability from each worker under his authority. Over a span of ten years (1960-1970) Martin Rosen developed a recruiting and training program, a deputation program, policy and procedures for the hiring and placing of missionaries in the field, and a strategic plan for opening new branches.

It has been mentioned that following the death of Joseph Cohn in October 1953, there was no strategic plan outlining direction for the Mission. The Mission's vision was being set by the "Executive Planning Committee." Further, the Board had voted to use the Mission's reserve funds to hire staff, to purchase buildings, and to expand the ministry. Hence, branches were opened and missionaries were hired based on the interest in a given area, or based on the interest generated through the work of the Field Evangelists, rather than based on a long-range strategic plan for the ministry. Additionally, the branches and workers gave little or no thought to the need of raising support.

In setting up his training program, Martin instructed prospective missionaries to utilize strategic planning in their ministries; he encouraged them to develop long-range goals for the branches they would be establishing and, as a part of the long-range plans, Martin (like Cohn) insisted on the importance of each branch raising support for their programs.

The training program was excellent, but it created differences of opinion regarding methodology between newly trained workers and long-standing members of the staff. The new staff had a certain allegiance to Martin because, for the most part, he was the person who had recruited them, trained them, and ultimately assigned them to their respective areas of ministry within the Mission (in accordance with his overall long range plan for the Mission).

As the new workers began raising support from the churches in the areas of their respective branches, the Mission's Field Evangelists, who looked at such churches as being "their churches" were angered over the infringement on their territories. The matter of workers raising support for their branch ministries also caused problems for the Conference Ministry of the Mission, because once a missionary had spoken in a church, and had taken an offering for the support of his branch, it was difficult (and often impossible) to book a Prophetic Bible Conference in the church during the same year.

Not only was Martin Rosen a good mission strategist and tactician, he was (and is) one of the best missionaries to the Jews that this century produced—in the same league as Leopold and Joseph Cohn. Early in his ministry in Los Angeles, he gave the following report to the readers of *The Chosen People* magazine:

> 'It's a different Los Angeles today,' Martin Rosen said. 'Thousands of newcomers throng the city and its suburbs. Among our Jewish people today there is a new spirit of inquiry, a willingness to consider the claims of the Gospel. The Jew who will listen to the Gospel is there if we will go out and find him.'

'How do we go about finding him? We still rely on our tried and true methods of evangelizing the unsaved,—tract distribution and open-air meetings. Also, many Jewish people are referred to us by friendly churches, that is, the pastor or a member of an evangelical congregation may know of a Jewish person who shows an interest in the Gospel, and this person will be referred to us, and some one from the Mission will follow the matter up. Our missionary workers are always on the alert in seeking opportunities for witnessing to the Jews at open-air meetings, door-to-door visitation, and talking with callers at the Mission....'

'How do we deal with Jewish folk who show interest in the Gospel? Do we have a program for dealing with such a one? Yes, we do. Here is where our Home Fellowship meetings come in. These are most effective when they are sponsored by the local church. The meeting is held, when possible, in the home of a well-known lay member of the congregation, not on church property. Church members personally invite their Jewish acquaintances, or invitations are sometimes mailed. The meetings follow a simple form, opening with a brief prayer, singing, a talk on a spiritual Bible topic, and a time of visitation, with refreshments. The visiting period offers opportunities for personal work. The tone of the meeting is one of friendly informality, avoiding both the social party idea and the religious service. These Home Fellowship meetings are directed at unconverted Jews. At the present time we are holding six meetings a month at various locations in the Los Angeles area. We hope soon to increase this number to twenty a month.'

'Then at our local mission center on Pico Boulevard we hold a regular weekly Bible Study. This is very much like our Home Fellowship meetings except that we do not have guest speakers as a rule and the spoken message is planned for the benefit of Jewish believers. At the present time we are studying the book of the prophet Isaiah. We don't send out invitations to these regular weekly meetings, and, in spite of this, our attendance has been packed.'[115]

NETWORK OF VOLUNTEER WORKERS DEVELOPED

Martin Rosen, like Joseph Cohn, developed a great "net-work" of volunteers—individuals, pastors, churches and other Christian organizations from within the Los Angeles environs. Included in the group of faithful volunteers he used were Albert and Muriel Stoltey, Elizabeth Leitch (Freston), Lois Hurwitz and Mrs. Waldo Spear. These individuals, and many other committed Christians, gave liberally of their time and talents to further the testimony to the Jewish community of Los Angeles.

Another individual who helped Martin Rosen as he developed the ministry in Los Angeles was Bill Counts, the campus leader for Campus Crusade For Christ. Through Bill, Martin was able to arrange for meetings on the Southern California campus of the University of California. Bill also helped Martin arrange for an annual Jewish Evangelism Seminar for Christian students on campus who wanted instruction on how to witness to the many Jewish students who attended the university.

The Jewish Evangelism seminars were not limited to students at the university. Martin planned to include such seminars in his expansion of the overall ministry of the Los Angeles branch. He told readers of *The Chosen People* magazine:

About our plans for the future? We hope to have at least ten meetings a month instructing Gentiles on how to witness effectively to the Jews. We will call these meetings Jewish Evangelism Seminars and will conduct them in co-operation with the evangelical churches in this area. We also hope to have a children's work under way soon and to intensify the work of every department of the Branch as soon as we acquire the facilities and staff.[116]

As the lectures from the Jewish Evangelism Seminars were refined, the notes became the basis for Martin's booklet entitled, "How To Witness Simply and Effectively to the Jews," which the Mission published in 1969.

THOMAS MCCALL—HIS STORY

In addition to volunteer workers, Martin also made use of several students. One such individual was the Rev. Thomas S. McCall.

Tom was born in Dallas, Texas in 1936. His parents were Christians. As a member of the First Baptist Church of Dallas, Tom was greatly influenced by his godly pastor, Dr. W.A. Criswell, who loved the Jewish people and the nation of Israel. The example of his pastor, combined with Tom's personal study of the Old Testament, were used by God to direct him into Jewish missions.

In his pursuit of an education that would prepare him to enter the field of Jewish evangelism, Tom moved to Southern California. There he enrolled at Talbot Seminary where he studied under Dr. Charles Lee Feinberg, who was Dean of Talbot and the chair for the department of Old Testament Semitic languages.

As a part of his "practical training," Tom became one of the first missionary candidates to go through Martin Rosen's Missionary Training Program. He joined the staff of the Mission as a part-time "associate missionary" in 1958.

As part-time workers, Tom and his wife, Carolyn, moved into the Mission's building on Pico Boulevard. From there, they carried on an extensive visitation program, they counseled Jewish people who made inquiry about the Mission and about the Messiah, they arranged for meetings, and Tom spoke in churches on behalf of the Mission.

DEVELOPING THE DALLAS BRANCH

After Tom completed his graduate studies at Talbot in 1962, Daniel Fuchs transferred the McCall's back to Dallas, where they replaced Bill and Jo Ennis when they were transferred to New York. In Dallas, Tom applied the systematized programs he had learned in Martin's training program in Los Angeles. To readers of *The Chosen People* magazine, he reported:

> There are three phases to our ministry among the Jews of Dallas:
> The first phase is visitation. We are striving to visit the homes of all our unsaved Jewish acquaintances to present the message of Christ and invite them to our meetings, which are held as noted.
> The second phase is our Jewish Fellowship meeting. This meeting is held on the second Thursday night of each month in the home of our good Christian friends, Mr. and Mrs. Rutledge. It is an evangelistic meeting designed for the unsaved Jewish people that they might hear the Gospel in an atmosphere conducive to their understanding.
> The third phase is our weekly Tuesday night Bible study. This meeting is held in our home and is designed to build up the faith of the Jewish Christians and prepare them for active church membership. These Bible studies constitute a very important phase of our ministry. Most new Jewish Christians have so small a knowledge of Christian doctrines and fundamentals that they come to the classes eager to learn all we can give them. Interested Christians are also welcome to attend and many have received a blessing through these studies.[117]

By the Spring of 1964, Tom was reporting that the monthly fellowship meetings in Dallas had grown steadily, with a "…regular attendance of fifty people, about half of whom are Jewish Christians and unsaved Jewish people. The rest are interested Gentile Christian friends."[118] The Thursday night Bible class increased to an average attendance of about 18 or 20.[119] Tom also began an annual Jewish Fellowship Dinner at the First Baptist Church of Dallas. In his report telling about the dinner that was held in the Spring of 1963, Tom reported:

> …There were at least seventy unsaved Jewish people who came, and a total attendance of over 300 people. The theme was the Passover Feast, and the Rev. Mr. Kurtz (a Jewish-Christian pastor) and Dr. Criswell of the First Baptist Church spoke on 'The Meaning of Passover to Christians and Jews.' I was master of ceremonies. This banquet followed a week of a 'Study Course on Jewish Evangelism' in the church, which I was privileged to teach. There were over 40 members and we made a detailed study of the subject.[120]

By the fourth annual Jewish Christian Passover Banquet at the First Baptist church of Dallas, there were over seven hundred people in attendance—two hundred of them were unsaved Jewish people![121]

In addition to hosting the annual Jewish Christian Passover Banquets, the First Baptist Church of Dallas also agreed to host an annual "Conference on Prophecy and the Jew." These conferences continued as annual events at the church until the mid-1980's; they were phased out when the leadership of the Mission's Dallas branch underwent further changes.

During his years of leadership at the Dallas branch of the Mission, Tom McCall used a number of students from Dallas Theological Seminary as part-time missionary staff. Among the student workers were Arnold Fruchtenbaum, Bill Beck, Louis Lapides, Larry Feldman, and Gary Derechinsky, to name a few. Arnold worked with Tom the longest, helping him develop the "Southern States Region" for the Mission. Through Arnold's ministry, many new churches and opportunities for evangelism were opened for the Mission.

DEDICATING A NEW BUILDING

The work in Dallas continued to enjoy growth, and as it did, the need for a larger facility arose. God's answer for that need came in a most unexpected way. Mr. and Mrs. Troy C. Bateson offered to donate their beautiful home and half of the value of the entire property to the Mission. Their generous offer made it possible for the Mission to purchase the house and property for the Dallas branch (and Texas headquarters office). With minimal remodeling the Bateson home was transformed into a beautiful meeting hall and offices for Tom McCall and his staff. The new facility was joyfully dedicated on September 11, 1966.[122] As word of the Mission's beautiful new facility spread among the Christians and Jews of the Dallas area, both the attendance and the number of activities at the branch increased.

ASSISTED BY STUDENT WORKERS

The close proximity of the Dallas branch to Dallas Theological Seminary, Dallas Bible College, and to other Christian schools in the area made it a "natural" as a training ground for students who were interested in entering the field of Jewish evangelism. Many students worked as part-time staff, or used the Mission's outreach to fulfill their Christian service assignments. Tom mentioned this phenomenon to readers of *The Chosen People* magazine, saying:

> *Three Hebrew Christians in the Dallas area who are studying for the Lord's work, have been on the Mission's scholarship program during the past year. Two of them are students at Dallas Theological Seminary. Jack Meadows and his wife are graduates of Portland Bible College, and he is now in this third year at Dallas Seminary. Marvin Rosenthal is yet another Hebrew-Christian student at the seminary. He is in his second year toward the Master of Theology Degree, having already been graduated from the Philadelphia College of the Bible. Marvin and his wife Marbeth have been working with our Tuesday night Bible class at the mission station.* [Marvin Rosenthal later became the Executive Director of the Friends of Israel Gospel Ministry. He has now established his own organization called Zion's Hope.]
>
> *The third scholarship student is David Solomon who is attending Baylor University. He came to the Lord about two years ago and has dedicated his operatic singing ability to God and is preparing for His service.*[123]

MARTIN WALDMAN—HIS STORY

One other youth worker hired by Tom McCall to work at the Dallas branch was Martin Waldman, a young Jewish believer who, with the assistance of the Mission's Student Aid program, was attending Dallas Bible College.

Martin Waldman was born to Jewish parents on September 6, 1949 in Queens, New York. He was raised in a traditional Jewish home and, like many other Jewish boys, he became more interested in social issues, the environment, and ecology than he was in God or in Jewish traditions and religion. His concerns regarding ecology and the changes in the environment were reinforced during his years as a student at Los Angeles Valley Junior College. Sharing his views and concerns was another young student—Marleen O'Brien—who eventually became Mrs. Marleen Waldman. Marleen had grown up in a Christian home; she had opened her heart to the Lord as a child, but as a teenager she wandered from the Lord and from her family.

After they were married, "Marty" and Marleen set about to live a simple life-style—one that was in harmony with nature and would not harm the environment. But as honorable as their goals were, they both sensed an emptiness in their lives; something was missing—something "nature" could not fill.

As the Spirit of God witnessed to her heart, Marleen recognized her need to come back into fellowship with God, and shortly after the birth of their daughter, Sabra, she rededicated her life to the Lord. She was fully aware that her decision might cause problems with Marty, but she knew she would never know true peace and contentment until she was back in fellowship with the Lord.

Marleen began to read the Bible, to pray, and to actively witness to Marty, and a few days later he picked up the Bible on his own. As he glanced through the New Testament, he was astounded to find the book of Revelation. As he read through it, he was even more astonished to see that it spoke about things that will happen to this earth in the future. This was exactly what he had been looking for.

The more Marty read the Scriptures, the more the Spirit of God began to bring about conviction within his heart. He was surprised to learn that many of their friends had read the Bible and were familiar with Bible prophecy. With their encouragement, Marty agreed that he and Marleen would attend church services with them. On January 5, 1975 (only two weeks after Marleen rededicated her life to the Lord), Marty accepted Jesus as his Messiah and Savior.

The Bible became Marty's favorite book after he came to faith in Jesus. He read and studied God's Word daily, and as he did, God began to impress upon him the need to share the Gospel with his own Jewish people. He wrote:

> *…the Lord began working on my heart. I felt a calling to be a witness to my own people, the Jews. My zeal was such that I wanted to be on the streets handing out tracts and telling people what had happened to me, but I didn't know much about the Bible and what it really said. The Lord soon led me to apply at Dallas Bible College [c. August 1975] and provided a part-time job with the Mission here in Dallas.*[124]

Marty served as the youth worker for the Dallas branch, the Minister of Visitation, and finally as the Missionary-in-Charge. As a result of his ministry, a number of Jewish people received Jesus as their Messiah and Savior. He told readers of *The Chosen People* magazine about two Jewish people he led to the Lord. He said:

> *Martha had heard about Jesus from Christian friends in college. She was interested in knowing more, and yet, always*

held back. 'After all,' she thought, 'I'm Jewish.' Now, two years later, a gentile co-worker was telling her about the Lord. She was willing to come to our Bible study with him, but she didn't really believe she would change her mind.

After the study, we began talking. She told me that for her, the main obstacle was fear of friends and family. She wondered what they would think, and she admitted, 'I'm afraid I'd be ostracized and alone.'

'Yes, you might be cut off from your family,' I agreed, 'However, I can only tell you about what God wants and what He offers you.' We went through the Scriptures together. Still, she couldn't take the step of faith. After almost an hour of talking together, I felt a strong and heavy need to pray for this young woman. So I earnestly prayed for Martha as her friend began talking with her.

When her friend walked away, I said, 'Martha, would you like to pray to receive the Messiah?'

'Yes,' she admitted. 'But I can't, I'm afraid.'

'Do know why you are afraid?'

'No,' she said very quietly.

I gently responded, 'There is one who doesn't want you to believe, and will try to keep you from accepting the Lord. If you'd like, I'll help you and I'll show you how to pray. But only if you'd like.'

'Yes, I would,' was her reply.

The Holy Spirit had given her victory in answer to my prayer. She had overcome her fear, and now she bowed her head and quietly invited Jesus into her life.[125]

Marty also told about Sam. He wrote:

Sam was not a believer in Messiah when he first came to our Bible study, but he had heard about the Lord from Zola Levitt, a Jewish believer in Jesus. While Sam was curious enough to want to know more, he was not convinced enough to believe. He was Jewish, in his mid-40's, a distinguished looking man who worked as a sales representative for a local corporation. He attended the Bible studies regularly, but always refrained from investigating Christ's claims too seriously.

One Saturday, after lunch at my house, Sam and I began talking about a number of things, including spiritual matters. 'Sam,' I asked, 'have you gone through the Bible yet, to see what God says about salvation?'

'No,' he replied, shaking his head.

Somehow I sensed the timing was right, and asked if he would like to begin such a study.

'Yes,' he agreed.

The next time we got together, we began looking at a number of Scriptures. When we came to Isaiah 53, I asked, 'What do you think this means?'

Sam replied, 'I understand that it's talking about Jesus, but I don't know how to believe. I don't feel anything.'

I explained that people don't always feel things, but if they trust, such trust comes from the heart. I encouraged him to simply trust and accept what the Bible says about Jesus. 'As for not knowing how,' I volunteered, 'I'll pray with you.'

'All right,' Sam said. 'I'd like that.'

I began to pray, and then Sam followed in his own words. As he continued, he confessed his inadequacy before the Lord. Then, the man who didn't know how, very simply asked Jesus to come into his life.

Sam is now studying and walking with the Lord.[126]

Marty served as the Missionary-in-Charge of the Dallas branch through the transition and sale of the Dallas property and the re-organization of the staff to a more de-centralized approach to Jewish evangelism. In December 1983 he resigned from the Mission's staff to assume the position as pastor of a Messianic congregation that grew out of the Bible studies and monthly meetings of the Mission in the Dallas area.

Tom's responsibilities within the Mission increased as the Dallas branch expanded. In addition to running the branch operation, he was appointed Regional Director for the Mission's Southwest territory. Later, he was appointed Mission Conference Director—a position which gave him oversight of the Mission's family conferences and multi-church conferences. To ensure that the branch ministry would not be neglected as Tom assumed more and more regional and national responsibilities, new staff workers were assigned to help with the Dallas ministry. Rev. Paul B. Cawthon was hired as Coordinator of Visitation; Mr. Irwin Chalek was hired as Minister of Church Relations; Mr. Clifford Marquardt was hired as Youth Director; and Mr. Louis Lapides was hired to work with High School youth.

One new Jewish believer in the Dallas area became a particularly close friend of Tom's during the busy days when he was serving as Missionary-in-Charge of the Dallas Branch. The young man's name was Zola Levitt, mentioned above. When Tom and Zola met they became instant friends. Zola was hungry to know the Word of God, and Tom was anxious to teach him. As they studied together, they also began to work together. Soon Zola was Tom's "right hand man." Tom appointed Zola to be one of his regular speakers and evangelists for the Southwest region. The two men also began writing books together. Their first book, entitled "Satan In The Sanctuary," became an immediate best-seller. It was followed by a book entitled, *The Coming Russian Invasion of Israel*. A third book was titled, *Raptured*. Tom also edited the Mission's Congress on Prophecy book entitled, *America in History and Prophecy*. It contained the messages from the Mission's prophecy conference held in honor of our nation's bi-centennial celebration.

While Tom McCall was working to develop the Dallas ministry, Martin Rosen continued his agenda of expansion of the Los Angeles ministry and his program of recruiting and training new workers for the Mission.

A New Building in Los Angeles

The building on West Pico Boulevard that had served as a home for the Rosen's and for the McCall's, as well as a facility for meetings and offices, was clearly too small. It's limited space prohibited further growth of the branch, and did not provide adequate space for the training program. God's supply was more than adequate—it was beyond the hopes and dreams of those who had been praying. Daniel Fuchs gave a glowing report in *The Chosen People* magazine, saying:

> ...When you receive this issue of The Chosen People we will have dedicated the largest, best-equipped Jewish missionary building on the West coast. The new address for our Los Angeles work from now on will be 6136 Lexington Avenue, Hollywood 38, California. How we thank God for our entire Los Angeles staff. Originally it was our veteran missionary, Elias Zimmerman, who was our Nehemiah there. He faithfully built the walls. But the last two times I spoke at our old building on West Pico Boulevard, we needed wall stretchers—there were people actually standing outside looking in. What has happened in Los Angeles during the last five years is a modern missionary miracle. Building on the foundation laid by 'Zimmie,' Martin Rosen has been enabled to train a competent group of workers, many of whom are volunteers, into a staff whose ministry has been signally blessed by our Lord. Two years ago when together with Mr. Rosen we drove all over the city of Los Angeles 'inspecting the walls,' I turned to him and said, 'Martin, what you need here will cost a quarter of million dollars, and we just don't have it. The land alone will cost $100,000.' But our Lord provided— and it didn't cost a quarter of a million dollars. When Zimmie started his testimony, the first converts were baptized at the Calvary Bible Church in Hollywood. This church met at Mary Pickford's old home. During the years the church grew and renovations were made, until now they had a well-equipped building complete with parking lot in the heart of Hollywood, near transportation. After World War II the neighborhood changed—the Jews moved in and, instead of moving out, the Calvary Bible Church invited us in. They sold us the land for $5,000 less than its assessed value and gave us the building![127]

The Minutes reflect that the total price paid for the Calvary Church property was $60,000.00.[128] The property on West Pico was then sold for $20,000.00, leaving a net expense of $40,000.00 for the well-equipped and strategically located Mission building.[129]

Participating in the World's Fair

Nearly ten years had elapsed since the death of Joseph Cohn, and the Mission was carrying on an aggressive missionary program to the Jews on three major fronts in the United States—New York, Los Angeles, and Texas—although ministry was being done in other areas of the U.S. and outside the U.S. as well. In January 1963, Daniel Fuchs suggested to the Board that they consider underwriting the expense for a national missionary project. He wanted the Mission to participate in the World's Fair which was to be held in New York in 1964 and 1965. He told the Board:

> ...We have been offered 15x10 space in the Education Building in a very good location where a booth can be set up to show our literature and a trained worker be on duty. The rental cost would be $15,000 and the cost of setting up the booth would probably be about $5,000. A large supply of literature would have to be printed.[130]

The Board unanimously approved a motion giving Daniel permission to enter into a two year lease for space in the Education Building. The Directors further requested that "...Mr. Fuchs work on plans for the staffing of this project and other arrangements and bring back a detailed report at the next Board meeting for approval."[131]

No detailed plan for the booth at the World's Fair was reported in the Minutes, but they do reflect that the Mission was able to rent space. However, the cost of the lease was increased by $5,000.00.[132]

Fuchs reported to the Board that he had contacted Dr. David Cooper of the Biblical Research Society in Los Angeles and arranged to display and distribute their books and materials through the Mission's booth at the World's Fair.

The Directors' discussion on this matter states: "...a very nice sign would be prepared for use with these books saying they have been placed in the exhibit through the cooperation of the Biblical Research Society of Los Angeles."[133] (For those not acquainted with this material, Dr. David Cooper was an outstanding Hebrew and Talmudic scholar. He was a Christian with a great love for the Jewish people. His books were written to reach rabbis, the Orthodox, and scholarly Jews with the Gospel.)

Fuchs also entered into negotiations with Dr. Henry Einspruch, President of the Lederer Foundation to distribute some of their material in the Mission's booth. The Minutes state:

> ...an invitation to the Lederer Foundation ...to cooperate with us and that we use their Good News According to Matthew as a prominent display in our booth, with a clear understanding that the management of the exhibit is definitely with the American Board of Missions to the Jews. It was further suggested that we pay to the Lederer Foundation the actual cost of the books and material which will be used in our exhibit. It was so voted.[134]

When Fuchs reported to the Directors that additional workers would be needed to help man the booth at the World's Fair, they approved that he could "...hire temporary part-time workers to help in manning our booth at the World's Fair."[135] The discussion then turned to the need to rent apartments for workers who planned to help at the booth. The Minutes record the decision reached:

> After discussion of the need for apartments or living quarters for those who will be coming to the World's Fair, Mr. Pretlove moved and Mr. Fuchs seconded the motion that Mr. Pretlove be authorized to arrange for the renting of two apartments in a nearby hotel suitable for our use during the time the World's Fair is open, beginning about April 1 and continuing through November. It was so voted.[136]

Other than the mention of the initial leasing expense for the booth at the Fair, nothing further is mentioned regarding the actual costs incurred for this outreach. It is known, however, that during that period of time of the Mission's operations, funding for the national missionary projects, and for all of the Mission's missionary programs, came from the General Fund and from the Mission's Investment Funds. The financial health of the Mission was good, but the ratio of expenses over income was creating a problem. The General Fund was inadequate to meet the operating expenses, and the Investment Fund was being borrowed on heavily to make up the deficit. The Investment Funds were further depleted through the purchase of properties and through the Board-approved national missionary projects.

The opportunity for evangelistic work at the World's Fair was the first of several national missionary projects. Each one of the programs was worthy of support, and each was blessed of God in reaching Jewish people with the Gospel. But the projects not only drained the reserve funds of the Mission, they created tension within the Mission over whether available funds would be designated to missionary programs or to the Board-sponsored national missionary projects. The Board was still working on the principle that the Mission needed to spend its Investment Fund on direct missionary evangelism (a worthy goal), but it had not instituted a policy determining how large an Investment Fund was needed to adequately fund the salary and benefits of Mission personnel, branch expenses, costs for special programs, or projected staff and ministry needs. Further, no long-range plans had been made to maximize the benefit created by the national missionary projects, and the Mission did not have the resources in place for the ministry to grow in different directions at the same time.

The announcement concerning the Mission's booth at the World's Fair created quite a sensation. Daniel gave a glowing report in his Salutation letter in the April 1964 Chosen People magazine. He said:

> We believe that, by God's grace, our Mission will reach more Jews with the Gospel at the New York World's Fair than we have been able to reach with all of our stations since the Lord founded this ministry through Leopold Cohn in 1894. World's Fair authorities expect a minimum of ninety million people to visit the Fair. We expect that one quarter of all the Jews in the world will attend it. Is it any wonder that we thank God that 'a great door and effectual is opened' unto us?
>
> We also believe that the location of our Mission exhibit is strategic. Only our Lord could have opened such a door. The greatest attraction at the Fair will be the Pool of Industry. All day long there will be fountain displays of untold beauty. They will be synchronized with the music of the nations. The Pool will be a symphony of sight and sound.... These fountain displays are free for all to enjoy, but they should be enjoyed from the best vantage point.
>
> Now allow me to let you in on a little secret. The Pool of Industry will be the focal point of the Fair. Just to the west of the Pool, and bordering on it, you find the Hall of Education. You will easily recognize this building. It is the only one

that has a balcony. This balcony is the vantage point from which to view the display.... But in order to get to the balcony you will have to take an escalator.... After you're on, just look up and you will see the exhibit of your Mission. As you leave the escalator, follow the crowd to the right and come in and see us.

The feature of our exhibit that will naturally attract your eye will be the world's most unusual clock. It was designed and produced by our Rev. Burl Haynie, assisted by our brother Mogens Mogensen, both of our Headquarters staff. It is a revolving timepiece. On one side is a regular clock that will display the correct time—correct to a split second. Surrounding the clock with the correct time will be the Scripture:

...Behold, now is the accepted time; behold, now is the day of salvation (2 Corinthians 6:2).

Check your watch quickly for the clock revolves rapidly. On the other side there is another clock. The hands of this clock swiftly move over a map of the world, and around it are the words? 'It is even the time of Jacob's trouble,' quoted from Jeremiah 30:7.

Brother Haynie has arranged a beautiful booth where the Word of God will be displayed and distributed in a way that will honor our Lord's Name. From ten o'clock in the morning until ten o'clock at night the Gospel will be proclaimed by means of a sight-sound synchronized display of the pictures I took in Israel last year. Two of our workers and several specially-trained volunteer attendants will staff our display at all times. Many of these volunteers will be our own young people. We praise God for them. Special editions of our tracts are being printed by the hundreds of thousands. By God's enabling grace and power the door has been opened; by His strength we will enter and occupy the land. We need and earnestly solicit your prayers.

The World's Fair opens, the Lord willing, on April 22nd. For seven months in 1964 and seven months in 1965, if our Lord tarry, we will have this wonderful opportunity—seven months, seven days a week, twelve hours a day. Only our Lord can give us the necessary strength. Several of our workers have covenanted with the Lord to be used by Him in any way possible during this special ministry. How I thank God for the missionaries of our staff; to me they are the finest group of missionaries in all the world. You will understand what I mean when you realize that they are whole-heartedly giving their time in addition to their regular work. Summer time is busy enough with camp, street-meetings, extension work, etc., but in addition to this they are willing and eager to contribute their all to further this unusual opportunity.[137]

But the Mission's booth at the World's Fair also generated controversy. Daniel wrote:

...opposition was evident every step of the way. For instance, when the cornerstone of the Hall of Education was laid, the name of our Mission appeared prominently near the head of the alphabetical list on the program: 'American Board of Missions to the Jews, Inc.' Later, when the capping ceremonies were conducted, somebody edited our name so that it appeared merely, as American Board of Missions. When we protested we learned that some officials of the Fair had vigorously objected to our presence in the Hall of Education. We had been very frank and open in our negotiations; our lease was made in our full name and the approved plans for our exhibit had our name prominently displayed on the original drawings. The fact that we, a missionary organization, were permitted to erect a display at the Fair was in itself a miracle, and we had a signed lease which the enemy could oppose but could not cancel.

At this point I made a decision realizing that some people would object to the prominent display of our name. Since our purpose was to preach the Gospel, not to advertise the Mission, I agreed to subordinate our name, instead of displaying it as originally planned. At the suggestion of the lawyer who represented the Hall of Education, we built an attractive cabinet presenting a beautiful and readable display of the history and the purpose of the Mission. However, one had to enter the exhibit to read it; it was not visible from the outside. Outside, in front of the exhibit, was the moving clock...'Israel—God's Timepiece.' We had no intention of deceiving anyone with the name 'Israel.' We did not dream that anybody would come to our display thinking that we were an Israeli organization. But that was exactly what happened. We received many queries about Israel and hundreds of our Mission tracts were distributed to people who would never have entered our exhibit if our name had been displayed in front. I want to emphasize that we did not plan this. Our Lord was once more using the opposition to confound our Adversary![138]

There was another incident, too, which the Adversary attempted to use to close down the Mission's booth at the fair. It took place on Sunday, May 31, 1964, when a twelve year old Jewish boy approached Rev. Burl Haynie who was one of the workers manning the booth that day. The boy was alone, and appeared to be very interested in the materials displayed. He asked Burl a question about the Messiah, and Burl wanted to answer, but with the crowds around it was impossible. Sensing the boys interest, Burl suggested that the boy go with him to the Billy Graham Pavilion where the film, "Man in the Fifth Dimension," was about to be shown. Burl felt the film would answer the boy's questions. Burl's suggestion appealed to the boy, who said nothing about being with friends or relatives, so they walked the short distance to the Billy Graham Pavilion.

When Burl and the boy returned to the Mission's exhibit, Burl was surprised to find the boy's mother and their rabbi frantically looking for him. Burl apologized to them both and explained what had happened. There was no backlash to Burl's explanation, and when they left the incident appeared to be excused and over. But the head rabbi of the Jewish Center where the boy attended classes was not going to let the incident pass. He wrote a letter to the Fair's officials, and then released copies of his letter to the newspapers. On June 12, 1964 (about two weeks after the incident) the following story appeared in the *New York Times*:

"MINISTER AT FAIR ACCUSED BY RABBI"
Attempt to Convert Jewish Boy Laid to Missionary

A rabbi has accused a staff member of a religious exhibit at the World's Fair of spiriting a 12-year old Jewish boy from his classmates and his mother in an attempt to influence the boy's beliefs.

The rabbi, Alvin M. Poplack, of the Bellerose Jewish Center in Floral Park, has protested the incident and the presence of the exhibit at the Fair.

The exhibit, which has the word 'Israel' across the top, is that of the American Board of Missions to the Jews, Inc., established in 1894 to 'promulgate the Gospel of the Lord Jesus Christ among the Jews.'

The man accused of taking the boy away for 'some 30 or 40 minutes' on May 31 is the Rev. Burl Haynie, a Baptist minister in charge of the mission exhibit in the Hall of Education.

Mr. Haynie said yesterday that he had taken the boy to see part of the Billy Graham film, 'Man In The Fifth Dimension,' but that he did not know the boy's mother or classmates were present at the fair. He said the boy was away from his group 20 to 25 minutes.

'I admit I made a mistake,' Mr. Haynie said, 'but the lad was so eager, so full of questions. I was overeager to help him out....'

He explained that since that time 'we have changed our entire policy in dealing with children.'

'We won't even talk with them,' he said. 'We just let them take the literature.' A rack of small pamphlets is available at the exhibit.

Rabbi Poplack, in his letter of protest to Robert Moses, president of the fair corporation disputed Mr. Haynie's contention that he thought the child was alone. He charged 'complicity' by the personnel of the exhibit in 'this criminal act,' in not telling the boy's mother where Mr. Haynie had taken him.

The boy was Fred Hoishman. According to Rabbi Poplack, he was with a class of 80 students of the center's religious school, visiting the Hall of Education when the incident took place. Rabbi Poplack was not present himself. The school's principal, Rabbi Benjamin Stephansky, was in charge of the class.[139]

The entire incident was carefully investigated by the officials at the Fair, and the Mission's exhibit was allowed to remain. What was meant to harm, God used for good and the publicity generated by the incident created a desire within people to visit the "controversial" booth at the fair.

When the New York World's Fair was over, the Mission's workers spent many months following up on the new contacts that had been made at the booth. This follow-up work resulted in many decisions made for the Lord. The workers also evaluated lessons that had been learned during the Mission's first national evangelistic project, so strategy could be developed for future media attempts at bringing the Gospel to the Jewish people.

The Mission's exhibit at the World's Fair had been the focus of the ministry on the East Coast, but on the West Coast the emphasis had continued to be on the training and recruiting program, and on the expansion of the Los Angeles ministry. Martin (Moishe) Rosen had been given a "green light" from Daniel and the Board to proceed with the recruitment and hiring of new workers.

DEVELOPMENT OF DISTRICT METHODOLOGY

As a part of his training program, Martin had developed a "Church Survey" questionnaire which he mailed out to pastors of churches across the United States. The questionnaire was a vehicle to acquire information about the pastor and about his knowledge of Jewish missions and evangelism, but it was primarily designed to serve as means of opening church doors to the deputation program of the Mission, and it was very effective. Soon there was a need to add additional staff to meet all of the requests for Mission meetings. This need was discussed at the December 1964 meeting of the Directors. The Minutes state:

Mr. Fuchs spoke of the necessity of adding to our field representatives, as at the present time there are only six and they cannot fill all the requests which come in for the presentation of the Jewish work in churches all over the country. Through a mailing program to interest the Christian churches in this work, we have many requests. In the past few summers we have been able to use students from Bible schools and seminaries and they have opened many new doors.[140]

One such student worker was Terryl Delaney, a student at BIOLA college in La Mirada, California. Terryl became interested in the Mission when he joined one of the evangelistic teams organized by Martin Rosen. The teams served a dual purpose: They enabled Bible college students and seminary students to fulfill their Christian service assignments, and they helped the Mission bring the Gospel to Jews who gathered in MacArthur Park in Los Angeles each Sunday. The teams also served as a means of introducing students to the Mission, and some students, like Terryl, were then recruited as Mission workers.

Terryl joined the team as a volunteer in 1961. He was a popular speaker and writer, and soon he was leading the outdoor meetings. Terryl was a Gentile Christian from a small railroad town in the state of Washington. With a name like "Delaney," it was obvious that he was not Jewish, yet God had given him unique qualities for communicating the Gospel.

Throughout his years of training at BIOLA, Terryl faithfully gave of his time to do volunteer ministry with the Mission. He served as a full-time field worker for the Los Angeles branch during the summer months, and during the summer of 1964 he was asked to embark on a 16,000-mile deputation tour across the United States to raise support for the Mission and to witness to Jewish people in the cities where he had meetings scheduled. His tour took him through seven western states, including the city of Denver (the city where Martin Rosen came to faith in Yeshua).

Martin knew that Hannah Wago, who had been instrumental in opening the truths of God's Word to himself and to Ceil, was reaching retirement age and his long-range strategy for the West Coast ministry was to have Denver serve as the key city for the development of "the Rocky Mountain District." The district was to be developed along the guidelines outlined in his training program which included a broad deputation schedule that was different in concept and in practice from the existing deputation program of the Mission. Terryl Delaney was being groomed to develop the Rocky Mountain district. In fact, his 16,000 mile deputation tour initiated Martin's new program of district development.

The established deputation program of the Mission had called for the Field Evangelists to spend several days, or even weeks, at a given church. Rosen's program differed in that it called for a worker to hold only one meeting per church, or at most, a morning and evening service. His theory, which was later proven correct, was that the financial benefit to the Mission was greater holding one meeting per church than by holding multiple meetings at the same church. He also demonstrated that the ratio of income to expense was better when workers held one meeting rather than multiple meetings at the same church. Martin further called into question "pledge giving"—a type of giving that was strongly emphasized by the Mission's Field Evangelists. Rosen questioned whether the pledges were ever given and, if so, in what percentage. The answers to his questions were not forthcoming since the Mission did not have its mailing lists and other records computerized at that time.

Rosen's training program and new theory of "one meeting per church" created a great deal of tension between the established Field Evangelists and their programs and Martin's new recruits who were doing deputation according to his new guidelines. This controversy, as well as the controversy over Rosen's division of the ministry into "districts" (with the Missionary in Charge having oversight of said district) was discussed and was partially resolved in what was referred to as "the Salt Lake City Convention" that was held November 14-15, 1966.

The workers who attended the Salt Lake City Convention were: Dr. Daniel Fuchs, Dr. Sanford Mills, Rev. Martin Rosen, Dr. Elias den Arend, Dr. Thomas McCall, Dr. Walter Atkinson, Mr. Harry Bucalstein, and Rev. Terryl Delaney. Invited, but absent, was Rev. Joseph Herschkowitz.[141] Several members of the staff were not invited and were conspicuous by their absence—e.g. Dr. Emil Gruen, the Conference Director; veteran missionaries from the Mid-West and from the East, including New York. No explanation is given within the Minutes for the omission of these workers. It would appear, however, that the purpose of the convention was to provide the Field Evangelists (who were being directly impacted by the new programs Rosen already had in operation in the Western states) with a better understanding of his theories and programs and thus to promote unity and healing of the rift.

Sadly, the convention did not accomplish its goal of bringing about unity. In effect, there were now two separate missions operating within the one organization. Under Martin Rosen's supervision and leadership, the Mission in the West and in some of the mid-western states was operating under a "district" program. Under the supervision and leadership of Daniel Fuchs, the mission in the eastern states and the foreign work was operating under a "branch" and "Field Evangelist" program. Why Fuchs allowed this to happen is uncertain. He made it clear at the Salt Lake City Convention that he wanted the work to develop under Rosen's district program, but he also stressed that every Missionary in Charge, as well as each Field Evangelist, was to continue reporting directly to the Missionary Secretary—himself. In the paper he presented at the convention, Fuchs wrote:

> ...if you look at a map you will observe that there are still large areas of the U.S.A. where we have neither field representatives nor missionary witness. Our task is to bring the gospel to all Jews everywhere—we are not yet doing the job.
>
> It was to meet this situation that the district method of operations was initiated. Under the branch method each missionary labored in a specific community and reported to the Missionary Secretary. The field evangelist considered a single area as his territory or assignment—he also reported to the Missionary Secretary. We frequently tread on each other's heels while vast areas remained untouched.
>
> Under the district method of operation each area will be the responsibility of our [one] person in the Mission. He is in charge of all activities—both missionary and deputational.
>
> Each district will be viewed as a unit in itself. A supervisor (Missionary-in-Charge) will be appointed to each district, and will exercise oversight with regard to the staff. It will be his task to develop the testimony to reach as many Jewish people as possible. Likewise he will seek to enlarge the influence of the Mission within his sphere of operations. The Missionary-in-Charge will strive for proportionate growth,...In his relation to the churches he will strive to gain sufficient support so as to permit this growth without making other districts suffer. The converse will also be true. When donor income increases, plans for expansion can be initiated.
>
> The Missionary-in-Charge reports to the Missionary Secretary. The field evangelist will work closely with the Missionary-in-Charge but will still report to the Missionary Secretary. It should be clearly understood that we are timing this transition so that the old and new methods will be used to carry out a well-organized witness in every area. Such words as 'phase out' do not apply. The status quo of the older workers is not being changed by this growth.
>
> Our program is being initiated in the western states where we serve the largest area and which, believe it or not, presents the fewest problems. A pilot program is also being initiated in the D.C.-Virginia district where no problem of old versus new overlay exists. As we learn our lessons, and as changes in area personnel become necessary, we expect to expand this method to the whole country. This method has been presented to the Board of Directors where it was completely examined and discussed and unanimously approved.[142]

Several items should be noted about this new policy statement in Mr. Fuchs' report:

1. He stated, "Such words as 'phase out' do not apply. The status quo of the older workers is not being changed by this growth." In effect, he was stating that the older workers of the Mission would continue working under the old "established" policies and procedures—only the new workers would be affected by Rosen's new policy. Rather than to bring about the desired unity, this statement only served to create further tension between new workers trained in Rosen's program, and the older workers on staff.
2. The program was to be "...initiated in the western states..." By initiating the new policy only in the West, Fuchs was once again dividing the Mission rather than unifying it. The purpose of the District Program, as outlined by Rosen, was to unify the overall work of the Mission. It affected all workers and programs; none could be exempt if the program was to work. By excluding some while the program was being phased in, tension was added to an already explosive situation.
3. Fuchs stated that each Missionary-in-Charge and all Field Evangelists were to report directly to him. Most of the staff was already reporting directly to Fuchs, but by making this statement he added to his load of supervision. This procedure also created tension among the new workers who had been recruited and trained by Rosen, and had been taught by implication that they were to report to him. Once they were made Missionary-in-Charge of a district, they felt torn between two bosses—Fuchs and Rosen.
4. Daniel stated that Rosen's new "district" method of operation had been "completely examined and discussed and unanimously approved" by the Board of Directors of the Mission. Fuchs may have perceived this to be the case, but it was not altogether the case. The only reference in the official Minutes of the Board to the training program, appear in the Minutes of the November 17, 1965 meeting. They state:
   > Mr. Fuchs read his report as missionary secretary and presented each director with a copy of a proposed plan for the extension of our work and also a copy of a training program Martin Rosen is using in Los Angeles for study.
   >
   > Mr. Leonard moved and Mr. Melhorn seconded the motion that his report be accepted with great thanksgiving and placed on file. It was so voted.[143]

If the Directors' acceptance of Daniel's report (including Martin Rosen's proposal for extending the work [no mention is made whether this proposal included a plan for District Expansion] and his training program) was understood as a motion to approve its adoption, then Daniel was correct. (This was often the way the Board approved certain projects and programs, so Daniel could have been led to believe that the Board had approved the training program, and with it the District Program.) However, the Minutes of the Board are devoid of specific motions, or adoptions of policy and procedures regarding Rosen's training program and the district method of operation. Later, when personalities became an issue and when tension reached the breaking point, some workers on staff accused Martin of initiating policies and procedures that were never approved by the Board—accusations that could not be disproved by the Minutes.

The whole issue of the recruitment of workers was further muddled by the fact that although Rosen had been given a "green light" for recruiting and training, Fuchs, as Missionary Secretary, continued to recruit workers as well. Further, because the policy stipulating the qualifications for missionary service had not been established, there were instances when a prospective new worker had the approval of the Missionary Secretary (Fuchs), but not the approval of the "unofficial" Director of Recruiting and Training (Rosen). The Mission's "troika" leadership (Pretlove, Fuchs, Gruen) was moving toward a further split in the leadership—this time within the Missionary department.

NEW WORKERS RECRUITED

Despite the tensions that existed within the Mission's leadership during the years 1964 to 1973, new workers were hired and the overall growth of the ministry continued. Two workers, Mr. Emil Olsen and Mr. Mogens Mogensen, came on staff as a direct result of their involvement in manning the Mission's exhibit at New York World's Fair.

EMIL OLSEN

Emil Olsen first became acquainted with the Mission when his mother, Elsie Olsen, served as one of the Mission's Board members and as Secretary to the Board—a position she held for a number of years. Emil's knowledge of the Mission was increased when he became interested in the Hebrew language, and enrolled in classes at the Mission's Jewish Missionary Training Institute in New York. After completing the courses at the Institute he moved to Israel, where he studied at the Hebrew University in Jerusalem.

Emil was hired to work at the Mission's booth at the World's Fair because of his concern for the salvation of Jewish people, but also because of his language aptitude. He spoke fluent Hebrew and Scandinavian, as well as related languages—skills which were very helpful in communicating with the many ethnic groups visiting the Mission's display. He did such a fine job at the World's Fair that he was asked to remain on staff. Martin Rosen then recruited him to oversee the Deputation Program he was developing for the Mission's District method of operation, and in 1966 Emil was transferred to Los Angeles where he helped Rosen with the Training Program, as well as helping to further develop the District Deputation Program.

MOGENS MOGENSEN

Mogens R. Mogensen not only helped to man the Mission's booth at the World's Fair, he did most of the work building the booth. Mogens was a native of Denmark who, before entering full-time ministry for the Lord, had served as a ship's officer. He was also a trained engineer, and was an extremely creative individual. His wife, Marjorie, worked by his side at the booth. She, too, was dedicated to the task of sharing the Gospel with the Jews.

When the fair closed, Mogens and Marge served the Mission in Pittsburgh, Pennsylvania for a time. They then moved to New York City, where Mogens completed the Mission's training program in 1968. Marge not only helped Mogens in his ministry, she also became an assistant secretary to Muriel Fuchs (Daniel's wife), and she helped edit the monthly issues of *The Chosen People* magazine, as well as tracts, books, and pamphlets published by the Mission.

On August 4, 1973 a boating accident claimed the life of Mogens R. Mogensen. He was swiftly called into his Master's presence. Marge continued serving as a part of the Headquarters Office staff until 1980, when the Mission opened a new branch in Boston, Massachusetts. Marge's sister lived on Cape Cod and she felt she would be able to accomplish two of her deepest desires by moving to Boston—she could get back into direct missionary work after fourteen years working at Headquarters, and she could be near her sister. Marge therefore requested that she be allowed to work at the new Boston branch. Her request was granted, and she faithfully continued sharing the Gospel with the Jews of Boston until her retirement in February, 1986.

THE AUTHOR—HIS STORY

A new worker was also hired for the Los Angeles staff. That worker was the author, Harold A. Sevener. During the Spring of 1964, the Mission mailed out letters to a number of Bible colleges and seminaries across the country. The

CHOSEN PEOPLE MINISTRIES: PHOTO ALBUM

RABBI LEOPOLD COHN

PROFESSOR BIRNBAUM'S
TUESDAY NIGHT
YIDDISH CLASS

LADIES' SEWING CLASS

FRIDAY EVENING GOSPEL MEETING

STREET MEETING,
CITY HALL PARK,
NEW YORK

CELEBRATING THANKSGIVING AT THE MISSION

WINDOW MINISTRY,
MARSTON MEMORIAL
BUILDING

SUNDAY
AFTERNOON
MEETING,
LEOPOLD COHN
MEMORIAL BUILDING

WAITING
TO ENTER
THE MISSION'S
DISPENSARY

DISPENSARY
STAFF

SOUP KITCHEN,
PARIS

REFUGEE DINNER,
SINGER'S
REFUGEE
DEPARTMENT

REFUGEE LUNCHEON,
PARIS

CHILDREN'S CLUB

purpose of the letter was to inquire of faculty members whether they knew of students or other qualified individuals who might be interested in joining the Mission's staff. There was an opening for someone to serve as "Resident Missionary" for the Los Angeles branch, located in Hollywood, California. One such letter was sent to Dr. John Schimmel, Academic Dean of Western Baptist College, then located in El Cerrito, California.

After graduating from high school, I enrolled at Western Baptist Bible College (W.B.B.C.). Dr. Schimmel was one of my professors. Following graduation from Western, I spent several months studying in Israel and then returned to California to complete graduate work at the San Francisco Conservative Baptist Seminary. While attending seminary, in addition to serving as Interim pastor at Miramar Community Church and working full-time for the Alameda County Library, I accepted a part-time teaching position at W.B.B.C.

John Schimmel became a close personal friend who knew of my interest in Israel, the Jewish people, and in Jewish missions. He therefore gave the Mission's letter to me, saying, "With your background, interests, and abilities, I think that you should prayerfully consider this opportunity."

During my months of study in Israel (c.1960-1961), I had witnessed the sad condition of Jewish missions in that country. With the exception of the work being done by Mr. & Mrs. Kauffman, who conducted the Messianic Assembly at the YMCA in Jerusalem, the ministries which were purportedly evangelistic outreach ministries to the Jews in Israel were organized to function like American churches. Services were held promptly at 11:00 a.m. each Sunday—a factor that eliminated Jewish attendance, since Sunday is a work day in Israel. Further, they were an insult to the Jewish community because very little or no effort was made to use Hebrew, even though it had been the national language since the establishment of the State of Israel in 1948. Services were conducted in English, using the hymns and liturgy of America or England. It is little wonder that the small congregations were made up of a few Gentile Christians, a few Arab believers, and a very few older Jewish believers who were looking for fellowship. From time to time, the services were also attended by "spies" from the Department of Religious Affairs who would then report on any new Israelis who attended the meetings, and report on new activities being planned by the missionaries.

Many of the missionaries with whom the author spoke were genuinely discouraged over their futile efforts to evangelize the Jews in Israel. They were discouraged, as well, by the fact that congregants had been lost when, just prior to the establishment of the State of Israel, Arab members and friends had heeded the warnings of Arab leaders and had fled to the east. Many of those Arabs became "displaced persons" when the United Nations partitioned the land; they did not return to occupy their homes and therefore no longer attended the services being held in Israel. Warehoused in the storage areas of many of the Mission buildings were stockpiles of Bibles, tracts, and literature in Arabic and Hebrew—gathering dust. In spite of the surge of interest in Israel on the part of Christians, much of the genuine missionary activity among the Jews actually came to a halt when the nation of Israel was established.

In visiting with the various missionaries in Israel during those days, my wife, Grace, and I heard the ministry of Mr. & Mrs. Kauffman criticized and castigated as being "Judaizing." The Kauffman's group met on Saturday, the Sabbath. They conducted their services in Hebrew and English, incorporating the use of Jewish customs and traditions as they sought to reach the Jewish community with the Gospel. As a result, their services were well attended by Jewish people; their ministry served as the beginning of the Messianic movement in Israel.

It was through our attendance of Kauffman's services that the realization dawned that it was not the Gospel message that most Jewish people were opposed to, it was the "Christian/Gentile" culture in which the Gospel message was encased that they objected to. Thus, while we did not want to be like most of the missionaries working among the Jews in Israel during that era, we had prayed about returning to Israel to demonstrate our faith in a Messianic Jewish way in every day life.

As I drove home from the Bible college with the Mission's letter in my pocket, I wondered what my wife's reaction would be. Both Grace and I had a desire to return to Israel, but we had not even considered working among the Jews in America.

Grace had been raised in a Christian home. Her father, the late Dr. James Franklin Prewitt, had been one of the founders of Western Baptist College, now located in Salem, Oregon. During the fifty years he served with the school, he taught classes in the areas of Jewish history, geography, the Life of Christ, the Life of Paul, and Biblical Backgrounds. He had also served as the Director of the Institute of Holy Land Studies in Jerusalem from 1960-1962.

Dr. Prewitt's great love for Israel and the Jewish people was communicated early to his daughter, Grace. She accepted Yeshua as Savior at the age of seven, and as she observed the dedication of both her mother and her father to the Lord's service, she learned valuable lessons of God's faithfulness to those who commit themselves to Him—lessons that have served her well as she has labored by the author's side in ministry.

Like Grace, I, too, was raised in a Christian home. My father came to faith through the preaching of the Word over the radio and my mother, who had trusted the Lord as a child, rededicated her life to the Lord at about the same time. As we children were born (three girls and myself), my parents dedicated each one of us to the Lord.

My parents not only taught us to love the Lord, they taught us to love the Jewish people, and they made it known to us that they supported a number of Jewish mission works. My father's ancestors were from Alsace Lorraine, where there was a large Jewish community at one time. It was known within the family that our surname had been changed, and my father's heart was always so drawn to the Jews that we often questioned whether he had descended from Jewish heritage. He never tried to prove or to disprove the idea. Instead, he stressed the need to understand the Scriptures from a Jewish perspective, and from an understanding of God's dealings with the nation of Israel, both historically and prophetically. My own interest in the Jewish people and in the nation of Israel came through the influence of my parents.

I was born on July 24, 1936 in Los Angeles, California. A few years later my father accepted a position as an accountant for the Navy, and the family moved to Chula Vista, California. When World War II broke out, precautionary steps were taken against the possibility of a Japanese invasion of the Pacific coast; the Navy transferred all civilian personnel working on sensitive accounts for the Seventh Fleet to the state of Utah. Those were traumatic days for our nation, but they were traumatic days for our small family as well. My father was sent immediately to Utah; the family remained in Chula Vista. There were air-raids and black-outs; even the children were aware of the pervading fear that at any moment the Japanese would attack the base in San Diego, as they had done at Pearl Harbor. Adults talked about the war in Europe and about the horrifying persecution and deaths of the Jewish people. Every night my mother would remind us to pray for Jewish people who were suffering at the hands of the Nazis and others.

At Christmas (c.1941), my father surprised us with a visit. He told us he had found a house in Utah; we would be moving shortly. Within a few weeks we were on the train, winding our way to a new home in Ogden, Utah.

Utah was an interesting state. I soon learned that there were people living there who called themselves "Mormons." I also learned that the Mormons believe they are the actual descendants of the tribe of Naphtali—as revealed to the prophet Joseph Smith, and recorded in the book of Mormons. As far as they are concerned, they are Jews and everyone else is a Gentile. This teaching created a great dilemma for me because although I was young, I reasoned, "If the Mormons were the real Jews, then who are the Nazis killing in Europe?" "Why do some people think that we are Jewish?" And, "Why don't they like us when they think we were Jewish?" It was a puzzle to me that if people believed we were Jewish, they didn't like us, but if they thought we were Mormon (and thus Jews by the Mormon definition) they liked us!

During this time as well, I began to wrestle with my own faith in Yeshua. I knew what my parents believed. My father had become a "lay chaplin" for the Armed Services and every Sunday morning he would get up early in the morning and make the rounds of the various Air Force bases in the environs of Salt Lake City, Ogden, and Logan, Utah. Oftentimes I would accompany him, and as he explained the Scriptures and the plan of salvation to the wounded servicemen I would listen carefully. I was impressed with my father's faith, and with the comforting words that he shared with the men. My father and mother also started a Bible study group in our home; from that Bible study a local church was soon established.

By the time I reached the age of twelve, I was firmly convinced of the truth of God's Word, and of Yeshua's death on my behalf. I understood that I could not be saved by my parents' faith, or by their example, so I openly professed my faith in Yeshua. I also knew at that time that God was calling me to serve Him, although I had no idea what He was calling me to do.

Not long after I professed my faith in Yeshua, one of my father's friends learned that he was being transferred to California. He wanted to drive his car, but gasoline was being rationed and he did not have enough "ration stamps" to get him to California. He therefore offered to trade his extensive library for my father's extra ration stamps. My father agreed to the trade and we soon found ourselves with enough books to fill every room in the house. The books were a God-send to me, for among them were volumes on Judaica, philosophy, and religion.

Year by year my interest in the study of God's Word increased. I was eager to learn Hebrew, Aramaic, Greek, Latin, German, and French—languages which I knew would help me in my understanding of Scripture, history, religion and philosophy. These language studies were not available to me in school, so I began to study some of them on my own and as I did, I became increasingly interested in Gematria (the study of numbers in the Bible and Talmud). My eighth grade thesis consisted of the Jewish and Christian understanding of the number seven in the ancient Scriptures from the Hebrew, Aramaic and Ugaritic usage. It was an attempt to demonstrate the inspiration of Scripture by the multiple usage of the number seven. In careful handwritten calligraphy, I printed in Hebrew, Aramaic, and Ugaritic the various characters and verses. I loved the project, and found that my faith was enriched because of it.

The more I studied the Scriptures, the more I felt the hand of God upon my life to teach the Scriptures and theology *from a Jewish perspective—distinctively showing that God has a plan for the Jewish people (Israel), for the Church, and for the Gentile world.*

When the War ended my father asked to be transferred to California. Our family moved to the San Francisco Bay Area in 1949. Once again, my father used his unique gifts to establish a number of Bible classes and to assist a new church in a nearby neighborhood. From time to time I was called upon to substitute teach for his classes. I also served as the church pianist, organist, and then as choir director.

When I was fifteen, a civil service position opened at the local library. I was very anxious to have the position, but to do so I had to pass a civil service examination. I also knew I would have to be able to work full-time and still finish high school. As I prayed about the whole matter, the Lord seemed to indicate that I should pursue it, so my mother and I went to the school principal to ask if I could attend school part-time and work full-time. The principal knew I was preparing to go to college so he tried to discourage me, but when he realized I was determined to try to do both, he worked out a class schedule that allowed me to take all required courses during the morning hours. I then took the civil service examination, passed, and was hired for the position at the library. Once again, this was a God-send—a direct answer to prayer. My library position gave me unlimited access to books on all subjects!

Upon graduation from high school I enrolled at Western Baptist Bible College (then located in Oakland, California), arranging my class schedule so I could continue my employment with the library. I was also actively involved in the youth ministry and the music ministry at Mt. Eden Presbyterian Church in Hayward, California. At the age of nineteen, through a special dispensation from the San Francisco Presbytery, I was ordained an elder and became clerk of the Session.

It was unusual for a young elder of the Presbyterian Church to be studying for the ministry at a Baptist school, but I had chosen Western because I agreed with the school's position on the Scriptures and the theological distinctions they taught between Israel, the Church, and the Nations—distinctions which most other denominational Christian schools were no longer teaching.

While registering for my last semester at Western, I met Grace Prewitt. She was also registering for classes. Her father, Dr. J. Frank Prewitt, had been one of my teachers and as we spoke casually, she mentioned that her father had been asked to direct the Institute of Holy Land Studies in Jerusalem for the years 1960-1962, while the school's founder, Dr. G. Douglas Young, returned to the States to develop the support base for the school. I had not heard of the school, but I was intrigued? I later questioned Dr. Prewitt about the program at the Institute, and he suggested that I contact Dr. Young directly. That evening I telephoned Dr. Young at his home in Evanston, Illinois. He told me about the school's purpose and program, and invited me to attend the program in the Fall of 1960.

For several months before leaving for Israel, I joined the Prewitt's in a conversational Hebrew class. Some months later, as Grace and I studied together, and as we toured the land of Israel as students, our love for the people and for the land grew daily—and so did our love for one another. We were married in Jerusalem on February 14, 1961.

We returned to the States in time for me to enroll in the Fall 1961 semester at the Conservative Baptist Seminary in San Francisco. It was while I was finishing my last year at the seminary that Dr. Schimmel gave me the letter and application form from the Mission.

Although we had not considered doing missionary work among Jewish people in the States, both Grace and I felt we should at least give the Lord opportunity to direct in our lives by completing the application, and by speaking with someone about the Mission's methods of reaching Jewish people with the Gospel. This opportunity came shortly after the completed application was mailed. Martin (Moishe) Rosen—the Missionary-in-Charge of the Los Angeles branch, who was also the "unofficial" Director of Recruiting and Training for the Mission, came to our home in Castro Valley, California to interview us. As he told us of the background of the Mission, we were encouraged to learn that the Mission was open to using Jewish customs and traditions in its witness. We were told that a number of programs had already been developed incorporating the Gospel with Jewish culture.

Shortly after the interview with Rosen, we were notified that Daniel Fuchs was planning to be on the West Coast for meetings; I was asked to fly to Los Angeles for an interview with him. During our conversation together, I asked Dr. Fuchs, "If we come with the Mission can we reach Jewish people for the Lord within their own culture?" With a broad smile, and a twinkle in his eye, he replied, "as long as you preach the Gospel, you can use any means possible to reach Jewish people with the Gospel." It was just what I wanted to hear!

By end of the interview I felt convinced that God was directing us to work with the Mission, and I agreed to accept the position in Los Angeles—making a two year commitment to the Mission. We moved to Los Angeles in October, 1965 and I joined the training program being conducted by Martin Rosen. Our "two year" commitment has now covered a span of almost thirty years.

Henry Johnson

Several other missionary candidates were also involved in the training program during the Fall of 1965. Andre Boulagnon was being trained to take over the Paris branch of the Mission. Another trainee was Rev. Henry Elmer Johnson, who was being trained to work in the Pittsburgh branch of the Mission. Henry was a Gentile believer—a graduate of the Reformed Episcopal Seminary in Philadelphia. His decision to come with the Mission had been prompted by his love for the Jewish people, and by his desire to openly preach the Gospel among them. He had served as a pastor of Reform congregations for ten years.

Henry had served as pastor of a church in Pennsylvania for eight years when members of his congregation began to feud. The strife ultimately ended in a split within in the church, and on October 28, 1962 a decision which was made within the congregation forced him to resign. But a contingent of the congregation who were leaving the church asked Henry if he would consider being their pastor at a new location. One of the couples donated a parcel of land for the new church building, and on March 6, 1963 ninety-two charter members organized as "Christ Church." Building plans were drawn up and a building fund was established. By February 2, 1964 the congregation joyfully celebrated their first worship service in their new auditorium. Fresh from starting this new work, and excited about evangelism and reaching new people with the Gospel, Henry applied to the Mission. He wanted to put his experience in evangelism to work among the Jews.

Irvin Rifkin

While Henry was involved in the training program, God used him to lead a Jewish young man named Irvin Rifkin to the Lord.

Irv was born in Philadelphia, Pennsylvania of Jewish parents on November 23, 1939. He was raised in a kosher home and attended Chedar (Jewish school) in preparation for his Bar Mitzvah. After his Bar Mitzvah, Irv's religious training ended and his religious interest waned. He kept the Jewish holidays, but only attended synagogue occasionally at other times of the year. On the occasions when he did attend synagogue, he found that the services were devoid of any spiritual fulfillment; he would leave feeling as empty as when he'd come.

In 1960, Irv's mother died very suddenly. The shock of her death caused him to begin a search for the meaning of life. His search brought him to California. He took a job making mannequins for Hollywood studios and department stores and there his boss, a Jewish believer, would witness to him. Eventually Irv's boss brought him to the Mission's meetings in Hollywood. It was there that he met Henry Johnson.

A bond of friendship formed between the two men immediately. Over the weeks and months, Henry patiently answered Irv's many questions and helped him through difficult times. Irv began reading the Scriptures, as Henry had suggested he do. One evening in 1966, after a Bible study in Pasadena, Irv accepted Yeshua as his Messiah and Savior. In a matter of months, Irv felt God's call to Jewish evangelism. He enrolled as a student at BIOLA college; the Mission helped him by providing scholarship funds and by supplying part-time employment.

In January 1968 Irv married a young woman whose native home was Central America. Cordelia had enrolled at BIOLA because she wanted to be a missionary to her own people in Central America. But as she spent time with Irv, and as their love for one another grew, Cordelia's love for the Jewish people and burden for their salvation grew. It wasn't long before she shared Irv's burden to reach Jewish people with the Gospel.

After his graduation from BIOLA, Irv entered the Mission's training program in Los Angeles. He graduated from the training program in 1972, and remained as a worker in the Los Angeles area for a few years. The Rifkins were then transferred to San Diego, where they have faithfully labored through the years. Because of Cordelia's fluency in Spanish (Irv also learned Spanish) they have been able to reach many Spanish-speaking Jews and Gentiles with the Gospel in the San Diego/Los Angeles areas, as well as in Mexico and Central America.

After his graduation from the Mission's training program, Henry Johnson was sent to serve as Missionary-in-Charge of the Pittsburgh branch (the reader may recall that the Pittsburgh branch was one of the earliest branches of the Mission established outside of New York). Pittsburgh was an influential branch, not only because of the workers who had labored there, but also because of the numbers of Jewish people who had come to faith because of the ministry there.

Harry Bucalstein—His Story

Another missionary candidate in the Fall 1965 class was a former pastor by the name of Harry Bucalstein—a man who was short in stature, but big of heart!

Harry Bucalstein was born of Jewish parents in Bereza Kartutska, Poland on March 10, 1906. He was seven years old when his family immigrated to the United States, and settled in Abingdon, Illinois. Although Abingdon was predominantly a Gentile community, Harry still attended the Jewish religious schools because his parents wanted him to have a religious education. Harry, on the other hand, sought out Gentile Christian friends because he did not want to associate with many of the Jews living in Abingdon.

Even though Harry's parents sent him to the Jewish religious schools, they allowed him to attend services at the First Methodist Church, pastored by the Rev. Dr. Bollinger. In fact, they not only allowed it, they *encouraged* it. His father went so far as to say, "…it would do me [Harry] good to watch the various insane beliefs that people had."[144]

The Bucalstein family moved to Brooklyn, New York in 1920. One day Harry's employer sent him out to collect some bills. He collected the money, but he did not return it to his employer. Instead, he kept the $17.80 for himself. Afraid to go home for fear of being caught and punished, He wandered the streets of New York, pondering the crime that he had committed. Several weeks passed, and one night in October 1921, as fifteen year old Harry walked the streets of Brooklyn, he heard a voice shouting above the noisy din of the city, "Repent, repent and believe the Gospel." He saw a crowd of people, and made his way toward the front of the crowd where the Rev. Charles Wiesenberg, a Jewish believer who was a minister and the superintendent of the Christian Witness to Israel, Inc., stood preaching.

As Harry listened, he recalled the times when he'd heard the message of salvation preached by Dr. Bollinger in the Methodist Church in Abingdon, Illinois. The Spirit of God touched his heart and he came under conviction—not only for stealing; he also recognized his need of a Savior.

After becoming a believer, Harry stayed at the Mission home of the Christian Witness to Israel with other believers. It wasn't long before the Holy Spirit brought further conviction upon his heart, and he confessed his theft of his former employer's money to Mr. Wiesenberg. Mr. Wiesenberg told Harry he needed to make restitution. Wiesenberg offered to go with Harry, so the two of them went to see Mr. LeGlaire, Harry's former employer.

When Harry confessed his crime to Mr. LeGlaire, and offered to make repayment, the kindly Jewish man told him it was not necessary. But Harry insisted because he wanted to have a clear conscience, so Mr. LeGlaire finally agreed that Harry could repay him at $1.00 a week until the debt was retired. He also agreed to rehire Harry so he could repay the debt!

With his sin confessed, and knowing that Yeshua was his personal Messiah and Saviour, Harry publicly professed his faith in Yeshua and was baptized on January 8, 1922.

When Harry's mother learned that he had been baptized, she was livid. She hadn't been upset over the fact that he'd stolen money and was wandering the streets of New York, but she was beside herself with rage over the fact that he'd confessed faith in Yeshua and had gone so far as to be baptized. She told him that Jews who become Christians should be killed. "…'Their hands and feet shall be broken.' Then she ran toward me with hatchet upraised. She did not bring the hatchet down. I stood perfectly still. Then I took my hat and went out. I rode the subway all night."[145]

Fearing further reaction from his mother, Harry did not return home. Instead, he went to his sister's home, but on January 16, 1922 he was arrested. The charge was "being a disorderly child." It had been brought by his mother under the statute of New York City which stated that "all children actually or apparently under the age of sixteen who desert their homes without good or sufficient cause shall be deemed disorderly children." Harry had deserted his mother's home to go to his sister's home—hence the arrest!

Harry spent four weeks in custody. He was about to be released when "The Jewish Big Brothers Association of Brooklyn" took up the case on behalf of his mother. They felt they would be able to keep Harry incarcerated by proving he was insane (At that time [and even in our day], incarceration was the practice of many Jewish families when their children accepted Yeshua as Messiah). But when the psychiatrists examined Harry, they declared him sane.

When Harry was released the Children's Court ruled that he would have to sleep at his mother's house. So every night he would return home. There he had to listen to his mother berate and curse him, with the ancient Jewish curses pronounced by Jews on those who have become apostate. She also forced him to accompany her to see various rabbis and other officials within the Jewish community as she attempted to have him "de-programmed."

In May 1922 the pressure on Harry was so great that he refused to go home; he broke his parole. Once again, he was arrested. This time he was on his way to prison!

As Christian friends and Jewish Christian friends (among them, Rabbi Leopold Cohn) heard of Harry's plight, they took up his cause. They knew he was simply being persecuted because of his faith, so they petitioned the court to appoint a legal guardian over Harry. During the trial, the following testimony was given by a Jewish man by the name of Mr. Teitch, an engraver by profession, who had no affiliation with any Christian group. He testified:

Mrs. Teitch told me that Mrs. Bucalstein is having some trouble with her boy. And I asked her just what the trouble was, and she told me that she is wishing that someone would aid her in some way or other to commit Harry Bucalstein to the Blackwell Island for becoming a Christian. She told me that he was a very good boy. 'And how is he now?' She told me that he was much better toward her than he was before, but she didn't want to have any Christian in her family.

Whereas I answered her, 'I would rather see the boy be a good Christian than a bad Jew.' And she further asked me if I would go to a rabbi of Brooklyn for the boy to bring him back to his first belief. And I told her I am not going to no rabbi before I see the boy myself. And the next day he came, with the consent of his mother.

Q. 'Came to your place of business, did he?' A. 'Yes, sir.' And I spoke to him about this matter and said to him 'Why did you change your belief?' and he answered me, 'I have not changed my belief at all but I have fulfilled the promise of God.' I asked him to show me how right he is, that he has fulfilled those words of God, and he has shown me many chapters of the Torah, has shown me in the Psalms of David, and he has convinced me through a firm belief that Christ Jesus is the suffering Messiah of the Israelites.[146]

In his testimony, Mr. Teitch also brought out that he had also tested Harry as to honesty and trustworthiness. He stated that he'd given Harry two hundred dollars and had sent him out to pay a bill. He said that Harry had paid the bill, and had returned with the signed receipt. He then sent him into the streets of New York City with over $1,000 worth of jewelry, and he stated that once again Harry had proved his trustworthiness by delivering the jewelry as promised. When questioned as to why he would want to test Harry in this way, Teitch testified:

I was told also when I was young that Christian people are not reliable, were murderers, and I have the same opinion all the time until I read a few passages of the Old and New Testament, and I have seen the action of Christian people, and I have found in my opinion that it is not so. Nor does it say in any part of the Old Testament whether Christian people ever existed at that time, but the Bible does say that there will come a day when there will be a new name of people as we have never heard of before, and I have been brought to this conclusion, that it is the Christian people, that they are the real people that God has said of this name.[147]

Finally Harry, himself, was allowed to testify. His argument at the trial (and throughout his lifetime) was that he was a descendant of the tribe of Levi (proven by his ancestry), not of the tribe of Judah. Therefore, he was not a Jew; he was a "Hebrew," even as Abraham was a Hebrew, not a Jew. He argued that even as a believer in Yeshua, he retained his Hebrew nationality. The four lawyers and the lawyer rabbi did not know how to respond to his argument, and throughout the rigors of their questioning they were unable to make Harry admit that he was no longer a Hebrew. He held fast to his position and to his faith. Eventually Harry was released; he became an emancipated minor after spending six months in prison for his faith.

From 1924 to 1927 Harry served as a clerk-typist in the U.S. Army. At the time of his discharge he had obtained the rank of sergeant. Knowing that God had called him to preach, he attended Moody Bible Institute, the University of Baltimore, Northern Baptist Seminary, and graduated from Minnesota Bible College in 1932. While pastoring his first church, the First Christian Church of Kenosha, Wisconsin, he met Lettie Smedley. They fell in love and were married in 1934.[148] For the next thirty years, Harry served as the pastor of a number of churches throughout the mid-western and western states.

In 1964 Harry resigned his pastorate in Culver City, California to give himself full-time to the ministry of reaching his own people with the Gospel. He and the author met during the Fall 1965 training sessions in Los Angeles. We continued to work together as co-pastors of the Mission's Messianic congregations as they were being established in Los Angeles and the western states, until Harry became one of the Mission's Field Evangelists. Harry was a popular speaker in the churches; as a Field Evangelist he traveled throughout the United States and Canada. God called Harry Bucalstein, a faithful servant and evangelist, into his presence on Monday, June 26, 1972.

OPPORTUNITY FOR MERGER IN CHICAGO

In New York, at the Directors' Spring 1965 meeting, Daniel Fuchs reported that he had received a letter from Dr. David Bronstein, director of the Aedus Center in Chicago, asking if the Mission was interested in taking over their ministry.[149] This was an answer to prayer, as the Mission's outreach in Chicago had almost completely deteriorated after the death of Joseph Cohn.

The Rev. David Bronstein and his wife, Sarah, opened their ministry in Chicago in 1933. Over the years, God had abundantly blessed their witness and many Jewish people had been reached with the Gospel. After the Lord called Rev. David Bronstein into His presence in 1961, the work was carried on by Sarah and by their son, Dr. David Bronstein. But David was also the American Secretary for the International Jewish Alliance, as well as being involved in a number of other ministries, so the primary responsibility for carrying on the work of Aedus Center in Chicago fell upon Mrs. Bronstein.

The Board of Aedus Center had decided to seek a merger between their ministry and the work of the Mission because they recognized that although Sarah Bronstein was remarkably active for her age (75 years), she would not be able to continue on forever. They also felt she was at an age where she was not able to recruit and train a competent new staff to assist her. Additionally, the neighborhood where their building was located had changed. It was no longer a Jewish neighborhood so the Board had sold the building and was looking for a new location.

After listening to Daniel's report, the Board of the Mission unanimously agreed to work toward a merge with the Aedus Center in Chicago. The Minutes of the next Board meeting state:

> Copies of the proposed agreement between Aedus Center and the American Board of Missions to the Jews, Inc. were studied at length and after discussion and changes, Mr. Leonard moved and Mr. Ivins seconded the motion that the Board go on record as being in agreement with the proposed agreement as amended between Aedus Center and the Board, with the understanding that copies of the revised agreement shall be mailed to all the Board members present and if there are any recommendations for changes to be made, they be made directly to Mr. Simmons, otherwise he shall be authorized to approve the agreement as amended. It was voted.
>
> Mr. Pretlove and Mr. Fuchs were in Chicago last week to look at property to purchase for the Aedus Community Center. Mr. Pretlove presented plans and pictures of a property on the North Side of Chicago, an excellent location for Jewish work. Mr. Fuchs moved and Mr. Melhorn seconded the motion and it was so voted, that the Executive Secretary be authorized to enter negotiations for the purchase of property in Chicago up to the amount $60,000.00.[150]

Once the agreement was approved, Mr. Harry Jacobson was transferred from the Minneapolis branch to Chicago.

HARRY JACOBSON—IN MINNEAPOLIS AND CHICAGO

Harry Jacobson was born of Jewish parents who immigrated from Russia to America in 1906. During his early boyhood years, his family lived in a rural farming area just outside of Buffalo, New York. He was one of seven children—five boys and two girls. There was very little formal religious training given to the children, nor did his parents maintain contact with other Jewish families. When they did socialize with other Jews, it was generally around Passover or Yom Kippur.

When Harry was nearing his teenage years, his father moved the family to the city of Buffalo. The neighborhood they settled in was openly anti-Semitic. Persecuted and hated by his Gentile classmates and neighbors, Harry often asked his father why the Jews are always hated if they are God's chosen people. His father would shrug his shoulders and a reply, "We are *The Chosen People* all right, chosen for persecution."[151] Harry recalled:

> After high school I turned completely away from God and became an atheist. It was not until after World War II, while attending the University of Washington, that I heard a minister make the amazing statement that Jesus Christ was a Jew. While I stood there speechless, I was informed also that the greatest Christian missionary who ever lived, the apostle Paul, was a Jew. I went home that night in a daze. I was 28 at the time and couldn't remember ever having talked with a Christian before about his faith.
>
> For two years I argued against the teachings of the New Testament, which I called 'the Gentile Bible,' before I settled down to read it in earnest. Then the more I read, the more I became aware that it was a book not of hate but of love.
>
> Several years later the Lord led me to Minneapolis to engage in administrative work with the electronic industries and it was in Minneapolis that I met the Christian girl who was later to become my wife. She attempted to tell me about her Saviour, the Lord Jesus Christ, but I always stopped her. Finally we decided to break up. On what was to be our last date, I told her, 'I'll never believe the way you do!' when suddenly the Holy Spirit came into my heart with such force that I dropped to my knees and wept. The next morning, Sunday, Donna called me, and asked me if I wanted to go to church with her. Although I felt weak and miserable, I told her I would.
>
> The church was the First Baptist in downtown Minneapolis, and it was Communion Sunday. At the close of the service, while the congregation was singing, 'Blessed Assurance, Jesus is Mine!' at that exact moment Jesus did become my Saviour and Redeemer.
>
> There were family heartbreak and trials at first. After my conversion, my heart turned to my own Jewish people and their need of the Gospel and the Lord led me into volunteer work for the American Board of Missions to the Jews. The doors definitely opened to me in November 1963 when I was accepted for full-time service with the Mission at the Minneapolis-St. Paul Branch.[152]

The worker for the ministry in Chicago was easier to secure than was a suitable building for the merged ministries.

The Mission's agreement with Aedus called for a building suitable for staff living quarters, as well as for enough space for meetings, counseling, etc. Both organizations were in agreement that the new facility should be located in a Jewish area such as the Rogers Park area on the North side of Chicago. It took eighteen months before such a building was located. Fuchs wrote:

> ...But no matter where we looked we were frustrated. The problem was one of parking space. We were looking for a two-family home—the upper apartment would be occupied by one of our workers, the lower apartment, the basement and the yard, would be for our various activities. There were many such buildings for sale but the zoning authorities would not permit such an arrangement unless we could provide off-street parking for those who attended the meetings. We even looked for empty lots and considered building on them but the cost was prohibitive. One day Mr. Jacobson called me. He had found a building which was just what we needed and there was an empty lot next to it. Investigation showed that the empty lot was also on the market. The location was excellent, the building was just what we needed and the vacant lot would not only provide parking but would permit future expansion.
>
> We praise God that we now have the building and the lot. Within a week after this issue of The Chosen People [June 1967] is mailed, Mr. Jacobson will, by God's grace, move into the upper apartment of the new building and work on the renovation and the parking lot will begin. Meetings will be held during the summer months but we are scheduling the dedication for Sunday, September 10th at 3 P.M. The building, which will be dedicated to the memory of the Rev. David Bronstein, will be called Aedus Community Center. The word Aedus in Hebrew means "witness" and we are already planning to add Henry Baar to our staff and maintain an effective aggressive witness for our Lord. We trust that many in the Chicago area will plan to attend the dedication service. The address will be:
>
> Aedus Community Center
> 6057 N. Kedzie Avenue
> Chicago, Illinois 60645.[153]

The building in Chicago was, indeed, dedicated on September 10, 1967 as projected. The Chicago branch of the Mission is still using the Aedus Community Center as its headquarters for reaching out to Jews of the Mid-western states with the Gospel. Interestingly, the Aedus Community Center has the rare distinction of being the only building within the United States, purchased by the Mission during the expansion years of 1964 to 1973, that the Mission still owns.

The transfer of Harry Jacobson from Minneapolis to Chicago left the ministry in Minneapolis in need of a worker, so Daniel Fuchs transferred David Woods from West Orange, New Jersey to Minneapolis. His route to Minneapolis included a "side trip" to Los Angeles where he went through Martin Rosen's training program.

David Woods— His Story

David Woods' history with the Mission went back to his childhood. His family lived in Brooklyn, near the Williamsburg branch of the Mission. They were one of the Jewish families that Miss Sussdorff visited. There were eleven children in the family—all of whom visited the Mission at one time or another. David sometimes attended meetings with his brother, Emanual. Both Emanual and David accepted the Lord and were baptized by Leopold Cohn. David was around eight or nine years of age at the time.

As the boys grew into manhood, Emanual felt the call of God on his life and surrendered for missionary service in Sao Paulo, Brazil. David, on the other hand, vacillated between attending meetings at the Mission and activities at the local synagogue. It was not until he was thirty-seven years of age that he surrendered his life to the Lord.

It was after he had joined the staff of the Mission, that David, who had been a member of Daniel Fuchs' woodworking class when he was a child, called Daniel to inquire whether he would speak at a meeting in Westbury, Long Island (a ministry begun by Max Doriani). Daniel wrote:

> Early in November [1959] I received a phone call from a young man named David Woods. David was one of the first boys who came to my classes in Brooklyn twenty-five years ago. For handiwork in that class I taught wood-working. Since the boys were very little, I was able, with my limited knowledge of woodworking at that time, to get away with it. In spite of the fact that I never could hit the nail with the hammer, I taught the class and David, unknown to me, learned to work with wood and grew up to become a craftsman in American colonial furniture. As a lad David accepted the Lord and was baptized by Leopold Cohn. His family moved to Long Island and for years it seemed as if the seed had perhaps fallen on stony ground. It looked as though it had not taken root and would wither away. But the Lord was faithful. He used even a synagogue service to show David the emptiness of the world. It was after he married and had a family that David, against the bitter opposition of both his and his wife's families, made a clean-cut profession of faith.

Shortly afterward the Mission began its ministries on Long Island. Mrs. Clara Rubin, the missionary at our Huntington Station Mission, remembered the Woods boys, sought David out, and he joined hands with us. Every time I saw him I found him growing in grace.

The telephone call I received from David was to tell me that he was taking the responsibility of arranging our meetings in Westbury, Long Island, and to invite me to speak at one of the meetings, which I promptly agreed to do.[154]

David Woods officially joined the staff in July 1960. His first duties were to assist in developing the work in Westbury, Long Island. Before he was transferred to Minnesota, he also established a ministry in West Orange, New Jersey. He also assisted Ruth Wardell, Eleanor Bullock, Burl Haynie and others with youth programs and the camping programs.

Terryl Delaney — Developing Denver

In the Spring of 1966, Daniel Fuchs transferred Terryl and Pauline Delaney from Los Angeles, California to Denver, Colorado. As has already been stated, Terryl's involvement with the Mission began when he joined one of Martin Rosen's evangelistic teams in 1961. At first his service with the Mission was a way of satisfying his Christian service assignment at BIOLA college, but he later realized that God had used that as a means of directing him into a ministry with Jewish missions.

After his graduation from BIOLA, Terryl applied for full-time service with the Mission and entered the training program. He was quick to learn Jewish history, customs, and traditions; he became an avid student of Rosen's abilities and tactics in witnessing to Jewish people. Many Jewish people expressed amazement at his knowledge and at his ability to communicate his knowledge in clever and unique ways. Martin, too, was aware of Terryl's unique God-given gifts and he was anxious to delegate areas of responsibility to this clever young man and his wife (Terryl married his college sweetheart, Pauline). Their first assignment as a missionary couple was as directors of religious education at the Los Angeles branch. Working together, the Delaneys soon had a large crowd of Jewish young people attending their special classes. During this period of time, Rosen, Delaney, Bucalstein, and the author became close friends and comrades as we labored for the Lord among the Jews of Los Angeles and its environs.

Rosen's long-range strategy called for Terryl Delaney to develop the "Rocky Mountain District." With the help of the Mission, the Delaneys purchased a home on Jasmine Avenue in Denver, Colorado and moved into that home during the Spring of 1966. Of the move and the challenges they were facing, Terryl wrote:

From my plane window I could see the lights of Denver, Colorado, glittering against the backdrop of the Rocky Mountains. Those lights reminded me of the 30,000 Jewish people who live in the Mountain States District (Colorado, New Mexico, Utah and Wyoming). I was once again challenged with the task which is ours—to reach these people with the message that the Deliverer has come, that He has brought the victory, and that He is soon returning.

True, the methods we use to accomplish this un-ordinary task are sometimes very unspectacular and common, but in the long-run they bear effective and long-lasting results.[155]

The methods used may have been unspectacular and common, but most of the workers of the Mission were spectacular "jewels" of the Lord. Two such jewels made Denver, Colorado their home—one was Hannah Wago (who led Martin and Ceil Rosen, and a host of others, to the Lord); the other was Mrs. Jewell A. Baer.

Jewell Baer was the widow of Max Baer, a famous prize-fighter. Max was Jewish; Jewell was a Gentile. When Jewell married Max, she was not a believer. It was not until after his death that the Lord spoke to her heart. She wrote:

As some of my friends know, my husband was Jewish and I loved him very much. But I am sorry to say that after his death I felt rather relieved that I would not have to feel embarrassed and pricked in my heart again listening to cruel jokes and painful jibes made about the Jews in his presence. Very often these were made by the kindliest of people, with no bad intentions, unaware that a Jew was present. But such thoughtless remarks distressed me, and I felt very sorry for him.[156]

In the mid-1950's, God touched Jewell's heart and she gave her life to the Messiah. Shortly afterward a prophetic Bible conference was held in her home church in Denver. For the first time in her life, Jewell heard about God's plan for the Jewish people and about His desire to see them come to faith in His Son. She wrote:

I attended many of the meetings and heard many wonderful things from God's Word that I had never heard before. But it was the tracts that first laid a heavy burden on my heart to witness to the Jewish people and to pray for their salvation.[157]

Of her marriage to Max, Jewell wrote:

> ...He led me to marry into the family of His covenant people,...He also put a special love in my heart for them and great burden to pray for them daily for their eternal salvation...[158]

Soon after attending the prophetic conference at her church, one of the church members told Jewell about Hannah Wago. When the two women met, an instant friendship was formed and the two women became inseparable. Of her friendship and admiration of Hannah, Jewell wrote:

> ...What a blessing this is to me to have her share her rich storehouse of Bible knowledge and practical experience of many years of service for the Lord with me.
>   Under her teaching and guidance the Bible has become a new book, and the people in it so very real, and I want to know more and more about God's wonderful Word. Mrs. Wago has also suggested to me ways to use our tracts and the information contained in them in witnessing to Jewish people.[159]

Jewell Baer was made an honorary missionary in Denver in 1961. During their years of ministry, both she and Hannah Wago were instrumental in introducing many Jewish people to the Gospel message.

The Delaney's settled into the house on Jasmine Avenue, and promptly joined Calvary Temple in Denver, where Pastor Blair was an innovative and creative communicator of the Gospel. Several members of his church were men whose professions were in the area of communications for large clothing firms, the automobile industry, etc. Pastor Blair had encouraged these men to use their expertise to communicate the message of Calvary Temple to the people in Denver. The result was that Calvary Temple was well-known to the citizens of Denver. Terryl was impressed, and he mused over what would happen within Jewish missions if the same marketing techniques were applied to presenting the message of the Gospel to Jewish people. He wondered if such marketing techniques could be used to reach the masses of Jewish people. He believed they could, and he wanted to try!

THE BEGINNING OF MEDIA EVANGELISM

One of the programs Martin Rosen had developed as a part of his training program was a dramatic presentation of Messiah in the Passover. From the time of Rabbi Leopold Cohn, workers of the Mission had been conducting demonstrations of "Messiah in the Passover" in churches throughout America. They were simple demonstrations, but effective. But Rosen, being a master at communications, had taken the demonstrations a step further. He'd added costumes and elaborate table settings, and had systematized the service so that the major points of the service and the table setting of the presentation could be duplicated by all of the Mission's workers. Oftentimes the demonstrations were expanded into full-blown Passover Seder Dinners, where each guest participated in the full story of Passover just as a Jewish family would celebrate the event.

These Passover demonstrations and dinners had become very popular. Calvary Temple, too, had scheduled such a banquet and it proved to be a great success. Afterwards Pastor Blair, Dick Maginot, and others approached Terryl with the idea of presenting a Passover demonstration on Television. The services at Calvary Temple were already being televised each week. Terryl was ecstatic! It was just the opportunity he had been praying about; it was a chance to see if Jewish people could be reached *en masse*, rather than just individually. Terryl immediately called Daniel Fuchs and told him of the great opportunity, and Daniel wasted no time in announcing the "first-ever" event in *The Chosen People* magazine. He wrote:

> As we are going to press we are excited by other news. On February 4th [c.1968] our Missionary in Charge of the Mountain States District, the Rev. R. Terry Delaney, will telecast the 'Christ in the Passover' service from Calvary Temple in Denver. The time of the telecast is 11 a.m.... Estimated ratings give this program a listing of 100,000 viewers. We have been advertising this telecast in the newspapers, and are using every known means to publicize this event. It is hoped that 5,000 Jews will see and hear the Gospel. Incidentally, when it snows in Denver, it is estimated that four times as many viewers generally use T.V. We are praying for snow.[160]

The May 1968 issue of *The Chosen People* magazine, included a glowing report of the telecast. Daniel wrote:

> On February 4th we were able to present the Gospel to more Jews and Gentiles than we have been able to reach at one time before this. Without any charge to the Mission, Terry Delaney, our indefatigable worker in Denver, gave an hour

long demonstration of the Gospel in his Passover presentation on six T.V. stations in Denver, Colorado Springs, Grand Junction, Montrose, Durango, Colorado, and Casper, Wyoming. It was made from Calvary Temple in Denver at no cost to the Mission.

Let me quote from one letter from an unsaved Jewish couple: 'We were at a resort for a convention. Before you came on my husband was upset because there was so much noise in the lobby we could not hear. Within 10 to 15 seconds after you began to present the passover, everyone stopped talking and began listening. The people in the cocktail lounge put down their drinks and came out to watch. It was very quiet; the silence made me feel like I was in a sanctuary. There were 15 to 20 people watching of whom four couples besides ourselves were Jewish. After you finished there was a great deal of discussion and many questions. Everyone thought the presentation was excellent.'[161]

In a report which Terryl Delaney submitted to Daniel Fuchs, he wrote:

Since the presentation of the passover, I have called on many Jewish families who have commented on their reactions. One orthodox man told me he felt it was beautifully presented, and was a fair interpretation. A reform family said they learned many things from watching the telecast, and were amazed to see how Christ was symbolized in their holiday.

The names of 170 Jewish families will be placed on our Shepherd of Israel mailing list as a result of the survey. Please pray that the Lord will do a work in many of their hearts as they rethink the truths they saw and heard. Pray that each month as they receive the Shepherd of Israel many may hear the voice of God speaking to their hearts about Jesus the Messiah.[162]

God used the Passover telecast done by Terryl Delaney as the catalyst to launch the Mission into using the media for evangelism. The question Terryl had asked was answered in the affirmative. Yes, Jewish people do respond en masse to the Gospel when it is presented within a Jewish context!

The Passover telecast also changed the direction of Terryl's career within the Mission. He went from serving as Missionary-in-Charge of the Rocky Mountain States District, to the position of Director of Communications for the Mission. As he worked to develop his position, and to promulgate the Mission and its outreach, he was affected by the increasing number of workers being hired by the Mission and by Martin Rosen's growing power base as it was developing within the Mission and among the many new workers.

Martin Rosen's power base within the Mission continued to grow as he developed the Missionary Training Program of the Mission—though the title of Director of Missionary Training had not as yet been conferred upon him. As the Missionary Director, all missionaries were to report directly to Daniel Fuchs (or to a Missionary-in-Charge who then reported to Daniel), but as Rosen's power base grew, many of the workers who had been recruited and trained by Martin felt a loyalty to him; oftentimes their reports to Daniel were first screened by him. By *de facto* leadership, but not by appointment, Martin Rosen was becoming Missionary Director of the Mission—a position he was never given.

CHANGES IN LEADERSHIP

At the June 1966 Board meeting, Martin Rosen was *officially* made Director of Missionary Training for the Mission. The Minutes state:

Mr. Fuchs moved that the Rev. Martin Rosen be appointed as Director of Missionary Training, his office to be located in New York and the move made as soon as feasible. Mr. Campbell seconded the motion and it was so voted.[163]

Only God knew the impact that this decision would ultimately have upon the Mission, the staff, and upon Martin Rosen, himself.

ENDNOTES

Chapter 10. The Vision Re-kindled

[1] *Minutes*, ABMJ, (October 8, 1953), p 102.

[2] *Minutes*, ABMJ, (April 29, 1953), p 100.

[3] *Minutes*, ABMJ, (October 8, 1953), p 103.

[4] *Minutes*, ABMJ, (January 28, 1953), p 97.

[5] *Minutes*, ABMJ, (October 28, 1953), p 106.

[6] *Minutes*, ABMJ, (December 14, 1953), p 109.

[7] *Minutes*, ABMJ, (October 24, 1956), p 150.

[8] *Minutes*, ABMJ, (October 28, 1923), p 106.

[9] *The Chosen People*, Vol. LIX, No. 6, (March, 1954), p 1.

[10] *Minutes*, ABMJ, (October 8, 1953), pp 102, 103.

[11] *The Chosen People*, Vol. LIX, No. 6, (March, 1954), pp 6, 7.

[12] See note above.

[13] See note above, p 8.

[14] *Minutes*, ABMJ, (October 28, 1953), p 106.

[15] *Minutes*, ABMJ, (January 26, 1955), p 127.

[16] See note above.

[17] *Minutes*, ABMJ, (April 27, 1955), p 132.

[18] *Minutes*, ABMJ, (December 14, 1953), p 108.

[19] *Minutes*, ABMJ, (April 28, 1954), p 117.

[20] *Minutes*, ABMJ, (March 1, 1955), p 130.

[21] *Minutes*, ABMJ, (October 26, 1955), p 137.

[22] *Minutes*, ABMJ, (January 25, 1956), p 140.

[23] *Minutes*, ABMJ, (January 16, 1957), p 156.

[24] *The Chosen People*, Vol. LIX, No. 1, (October, 1953), p 11.

[25] See Appendix E.

[26] *The Chosen People*, Vol. LIX, No. 1, (October, 1953), p 10.

[27] *The Chosen People*, Vol. LXV, No. 9, (May, 1960), pp 5, 6.

[28] *The Chosen People*, Vol. LXXXVII, No. 2, (February, 1981), p 12.

[29] *The Chosen People*, Vol. LIX, No. 4, (January, 1954), pp 7, 8.

[30] Moishe Rosen with William Proctor, *Jews For Jesus*, Old Tappan, New Jersey: Fleming H. Revell Co., 1974, p 24.

[31] *The Chosen People*, Vol. LIX, No. 4, (January, 1954), pp 7-10.

[32] M. Rosen with W. Proctor, *Jews For Jesus*, pp 26, 27.

[33] *The Chosen People*, Vol. LXXXVII, No. 2, (February 1981), p 13.

[34] M. Rosen with W. Proctor, *Jews For Jesus*, pp 26, 27.

[35] *Personal Interview*, Harold Sevener with Moishe (Martin) Rosen, (January 14, 1992), p 2.

[36] *The Chosen People*, Vol. LXIII, No. 4, (December, 1957), p 5.

[37] *Personal Interview*, H. Sevener with M. Rosen, p 3.

[38] *Personal Interview*, H. Sevener with M. Rosen, pp 3, 4.

[39] *Minutes*, ABMJ, (October 26, 1955), p 138.

[40] *Minutes*, ABMJ, (October 24, 1956), p 150.

[41] *Minutes*, ABMJ, (April 24, 1957), p 158.

[42] *The Chosen People*, Vol. LXIII, No. 4, (December, 1957), pp 5, 6.

[43] *Minutes*, ABMJ, (October 24, 1954), p 120.

[44] See Appendix F.

[45] *Minutes*, ABMJ, (January 26, 1955), p 126.

[46] *The Chosen People*, Vol. XXXV, No. 1, (October 1929), p 12.

[47] *Personal Interview*, Harold Sevener with Margaret Heydt, September 13, 1991.

[48] See note above.

[49] *Minutes*, ABMJ, (October 27, 1954), p 120.

[50] *Minutes*, ABMJ, (January 26, 1955), p 127.

[51] *Minutes*, ABMJ, (April 28, 1954), pp 118, 121.

[52] *The Chosen People*, Vol. LXI, No. 7, (March, 1956), p 4.

[53] *The Chosen People*, Vol. LXIII, No. 8, (April, 1958), p 9.

[54] *The Chosen People*, Vol. LXXVI, No. 10, (June, 1971), p 9.

[55] *The Chosen People*, Vol. LXXXIX, No. 9, (May, 1983), pp 13, 14.

[56] *Minutes*, ABMJ, (March 1, 1955), p 130.

[57] *Minutes*, ABMJ, (October 24, 1956), p 149.

[58] *The Chosen People*, Vol. LXII, No. 3, (November, 1956), p 5.

[59] *Minutes*, ABMJ, (January 16, 1957), p 156.

[60] *The Chosen People*, Vol. LXIV, No. 8, (April, 1959), p 8.

[61] *The Chosen People*, Vol. LXVI, No. 8, (April, 1961), p 6.

[62] *The Chosen People*, Vol. LXVII, No. 8, (April, 1962), p 7.

[63] *The Chosen People*, Vol. LXIX, No. 1, (September, 1963), p 6.

[64] *The Chosen People*, Vol. LXVIII, No. 1, (September, 1963), pp 14-16; *The Chosen People*, Vol. LXVIII, No. 2, (October, 1962), pp 15, 16.

[65] *The Chosen People*, Vol. LXX, No. 3, (November, 1964), pp 6, 7.

[66] *Minutes*, ABMJ, (October 19, 1984), p 1.

[67] *The Chosen People*, Vol. LXXXII, No. 4, (December, 1976), p 12.

[68] *The Chosen People*, Vol. LXIX, No. 9, (May, 1964), p 19.

[69] Zola Levitt, *Meshumed*, (Chicago: Moody Press, 1979), p 108.

[70] *The Chosen People*, Vol. LXXXII, No. 4, (December, 1976), p 12.

[71] Levitt, *Meshumed*, pp 108, 109.

[72] *The Chosen People*, Vol. LXXXII, No. 4, (December, 1976), pp 12, 13.

[73] See note above.

[74] *The Chosen People*, Vol. LXIX, No. 9, (May, 1964), pp 5, 6.

[75] Levitt, *Meshumed*, p 114, 115.

[76] *The Chosen People*, Vol. LXIII, No. 1, (September, 1957), p 9.

[77] *The Chosen People*, Vol. LXIII, No. 8, (April, 1958), p 8.

[78] *The Chosen People*, Vol. LXV, No. 6, (February, 1960), p 6.

[79] *The Chosen People*, Vol. LXIII, No. 1, (September, 1957), p 5.

[80] See note above, pp 6, 7.

[81] *Minutes*, ABMJ, (January 29, 1958), p 170.

[82] *The Chosen People*, Vol. LXIV, No. 4, (December, 1958), pp 7, 16.

[83] *The Chosen People*, Vol. LXVI, No. 8, (April, 1961), p 7.

[84] *The Chosen People*, Vol. LXVII, No. 2, (October, 1961), pp 5, 6.

[85] *The Chosen People*, Vol. LXIV, No. 5, (January, 1959), p 5.

[86] *The Chosen People*, Vol. LXIV, No. 8, (April, 1959), pp 7, 8.

[87] *The Chosen People*, Vol. LXVIII, No. 2, (October, 1962), p 7.

[88] *The Chosen People*, Vol. LXVIII, No. 10, (June, 1963), p 6.

[89] See note above.

[90] See note above.

[91] *The Chosen People*, Vol. LXIX, No. 3, (November, 1963), p 4.

[92] See note above.

[93] *The Chosen People*, Vol. LXXII, No. 10, (June, 1967), p 5.

[94] *The Chosen People*, Vol. LXXIII, No. 8, (April, 1968), p 4.

[95] *The Chosen People*, Vol. LXXIII, No. 2, (October, 1967), p 8.

[96] *The Chosen People*, Vol. LXIII, No. 1, (September, 1957), p 7.

[97] *Minutes*, ABMJ, (April 25, 1956), p 146.

[98] *The Chosen People*, Vol. LXII, No. 8, (April, 1957), pp 9, 16.

[99] *The Chosen People*, Vol. LXXV, No. 5, (January, 1970), p 8.

[100] *The Chosen People*, Vol. LXIX, No. 3, (November, 1963), p 6.

[101] See note above.

[102] See note above, p 6,7.

[103] *The Chosen People*, Vol. LXII, No. 9, (May, 1957), p 7.

[104] *Minutes*, ABMJ, (April 25, 1956), p 146.

[105] *The Chosen People*, Vol. LXII, No. 9, (May, 1957), p 7.

[106] See note above.

[107] *The Chosen People*, Vol. LXIV, No. 3, (November, 1958), p 8.

[108] See note above, p 9.

[109] *The Chosen People*, Vol. LXVI, No. 6, (February, 1961), p 7.

[110] See note above.

[111] *The Chosen People*, Vol. LXVIII, No. 6, (February, 1963), pp 8, 16.

[112] *The Chosen People*, Vol. LXIII, No. 1, (September, 1957), pp 8, 9.

[113] *The Chosen People*, Vol. LXIV, No. 6, (February, 1959), p 8.

[114] *Personal Interview*, Harold Sevener with Moishe Rosen, (January 14, 1992), p 8.

[115] *The Chosen People*, Vol. LXVII, No. 7, (March, 1962), pp 4, 5.

[116] See note above.

[117] *The Chosen People*, Vol. LXVIII, No. 9, (May, 1963), p 4.

[118] *The Chosen People*, Vol. LXIX, No. 7, (March, 1964), pp 5, 6.

[119] See note above.

[120] See note above.

[121] *The Chosen People*, Vol. LXXII, No. 1, (September, 1966), pp 12, 13.

[122] *The Chosen People*, Vol. LXXII, No. 3, (November, 1966), p 10.

[123] *The Chosen People*, Vol. LXII, No. 7, (March, 1967), p 9.

[124] Martin Waldman, *Personal Testimony/Application*, (May, 1978), p 1,2.

[125] *The Chosen People*, Vol. LXXXVII, No. 7, (July, 1981), pp 6, 7.

[126] See note above.

[127] *The Chosen People*, Vol. LXVIII, No. 7, (March, 1963), pp 3, 4.

[128] *Minutes*, ABMJ, (October 24, 1962), p 214.

[129] *Minutes*, ABMJ, (January 30, 1963), p 217.

[130] See note above, p 218.

[131] See note above.

[132] *Minutes*, ABMJ, (April 24, 1963), p 221.

[133] *Minutes*, ABMJ, (October 23, 1963), p 225.

[134] *Minutes*, ABMJ, (January 27, 1965), p 241.

[135] *Minutes*, ABMJ, (January 29, 1964), p 229.

[136] See note above.

[137] *The Chosen People*, Vol. LXIX, No. 8, (April, 1964), p 3.

[138] *The Chosen People*, Vol. LXX, No. 1, (September, 1964), p 2.

[139] See note above, p 3.

[140] *Minutes*, ABMJ, (December 8, 1964), p 236.

[141] *Reports: Salt Lake City Convention*, (November 14-15, 1966), p 1.

[142] See note above, Daniel Fuchs, *The District Method of Operation*, (November 14-15, 1966), p 2-4.

[143] *Minutes*, ABMJ, (November 17, 1965), p 252.

[144] *Jewish Boy Sent To Prison for His Religion*, Reprint from the Dearborn Independent, (November 3, 1923), p 1.

[145] See note above, p 2.

[146] See note above.

[147] See note above.

[148] *The Chosen People*, Vol. LXXVIII, No. 1. (September, 1972), p 5.

[149] *Minutes*, ABMJ, (May 5, 1965), p 244.

[150] *Minutes*, ABMJ, (September 15, 1965), p 251.

[151] *The Chosen People*, Vol. LXXI, No. 5, (January 1966), p 10.

[152] See note above.

[153] *The Chosen People*, Vol. LXXII, No. 10, (June, 1967), p 4.

[154] *The Chosen People*, Vol. LXV, No. 7, (March, 1960), pp 2, 3.

[155] *The Chosen People*, Vol. LXXII, No. 9, (May, 1967), p 5.

[156] *The Chosen People*, Vol. LXIX, No. 8, (April, 1964), p 6.

[157] See note above.

[158] See note above.

[159] See note above.

[160] *The Chosen People*, Vol. LXXIII, No. 6, (February, 1968), p 4.
[161] See note above.
[162] See note above.
[163] *Minutes*, ABMJ, (June 15, 1966), p 265.

I I

THE VISION IN KALEIDOSCOPE

"Woe to him who quarrels with his Maker,...Does the clay say to the potter, 'What are you making?'"[1]

Martin Rosen's appointment to the position of Director of Missionary Training of the Mission, coupled with the directive that the training program was to be relocated to New York, was something of a bitter-sweet experience for Martin. Neither the appointment, nor the possibility of relocating the training program, had come as a complete surprise to him; he and Daniel had spoken often about long-range plans for the Mission. But the timing of the appointment was not what Martin would have chosen for himself, nor was a move to the East Coast. Can the clay tell the potter how to shape it? Martin had made a commitment to serve the Lord in Jewish missions; more specifically, he had made a commitment to serve with The American Board of Missions to the Jews. He therefore accepted the directives of Daniel Fuchs and the Board as being God's directives.

When he was notified of his new appointment, Martin expressed feelings of ambivalence about the proposed move. He told the author that he felt he needed more "hands on" missionary experience before moving into a position of administration within the Mission. Further, he had hoped to be able to travel to England, Israel, and France to see about further developing ministry there before going to New York. He was also somewhat apprehensive about the "politics" of the Mission. On the West Coast, he'd had a free hand to develop the ministry as God directed him, but in operating the Missionary Training Program from the Headquarters in New York, he knew he'd be rubbing shoulders with the Mission's "troika" leadership—Harold Pretlove, Daniel Fuchs, and Emil Gruen—and he was not sure where he would fit in, since many of his plans and ideas for the Mission were controversial.

Three months prior to his appointment as Director of Missionary Training, Martin wrote to Rachmiel Frydland and mentioned his desire to go to England to do missionary work. Rachmiel, a Jewish believer and Talmudic scholar, was praying about joining the staff of the Mission when he received Rosen's letter of March 24, 1966. Rosen said:

> As you know I am extremely enthusiastic over the prospect of going to London. I feel that this might even be the apex of my career as a missionary to the Jews. I feel that by making such a trip that I could bring back an international viewpoint for our Mission, and if I am allowed to spend a month in Israel, I feel certain that I will be able to discover new ways and means to communicate the Gospel in this most difficult field.
>
> However, one such as myself is always in danger of confusing his will with God's will. The more I pray for the matter, the more enthusiastic I become that I ought to go and serve as a missionary.[2]

In his reply, Rachmiel did not encourage Martin in his desire to go to England. Instead, he wrote:

> I will join you in prayer that the Lord's will be done. Personally I can see your desire to go and be of benefit to the work in Israel, but England has little meaning. What you can get there in Jewish work, you can get in the USA and better. There was a time when we had to go England, in the time of Edersheim, John Wilkinson, David Baron, but today England's Jewish Mission live[s] only on the past greatness. The Jewish population is rich and almost unapproachable by Missions. I don't think that any of the Missions had three Jews come to Christ & be baptized for the last year. Maybe your presence can change it and maybe they need it, but what will become of LA and the work you are doing? Do you have anyone to take over the Training Center? the meetings? the organized Deputation Work that you have introduced? Will Jewish converts continue to come and co-work with the new person that you will appoint in your place? Of course if it is the Lord's will He will supply men and all that goes with it. But I can well see Daniel's point of view and his reluctance to let you go to England for a longer period. I am sure that he will well understand the desire to go for a month or two to Israel.[3]

Martin's response to Rachmiel's letter indicates the prayer and thought that he had given the matter. It was something that he really wanted to do. He wrote:

> Now let me take a moment and answer some of the things that you have said. You say that 'England has little meaning as far as Jewish Missions work is concerned.' This is perhaps one of the best reasons for me to go there. There are more than 300,000 Jews at London. You and I both know that the missions there are failing to meet the spiritual needs of the middle class Jews.
>
> If we have had any success at all it has been because we have met the needs of middle class Jews. If I volunteered to go to London to teach them how to do the work, I doubt if I would be received very well. However, if I go do the work, perhaps they will get some ideas.
>
> With regard to the present work that I am doing in Los Angeles. Let me say that I am not indispensable. Harry Bucalstein is prepared to take over the missionary operations when I leave. Harold Sevener has been trained as a teacher and has the classroom experience and can teach the training lectures. Emil Olsen has been trained in all phases of the deputation work, so Emil will be able to take over the deputation program. Believe me I know exactly what [I] am doing.
>
> So far as the Jewish converts are concerned, our aim has always been to get the converts into regularly established churches. Jewish people are constantly feeding in. I feel that the Hebrew-Christians who have known me will accept Harry Bucalstein's leadership. Of course I feel that I am a man set under authority and if Daniel orders me not to go, I will submit, and I believe that I can find a happy life in almost any situation.
>
> However, the one thing which no one seems to recognize is the fact that if I do go to New York and get involved in the work, and accept the burden of the labor there that I'll never have the opportunity again to go overseas.
>
> I do hope that things will continue to work out to enable you to work for the American Board. I believe that it is the best mission in the world for anyone who wants to win Jews to Christ.[4]

MOVING THE TRAINING PROGRAM TO NEW YORK

Daniel Fuchs was adamant in his position that Martin was not to go to England or to Israel—not even for a visit. He made it clear, even as the action of the Board indicates, that Martin would be transferred to New York, and to no other place. (One wonders what would have happened within the Mission, and to the whole cause of Jewish evangelism and missions, had Daniel allowed Martin to go to England!) An announcement about Martin's new title, and about the change in location of the Training Program was made by Daniel Fuchs in the September 1966 issue of *The Chosen People* magazine. The caption next to Martin's picture stated:

> At the last meeting of our Board of Directors, Mr. Rosen was appointed Director of Missionary Training. This program will be transferred from Los Angeles to New York as soon as feasible. Please pray for Mr. Rosen as he continues in this most important and strategic ministry.[5]

The author's two-year commitment to the Los Angeles ministry was drawing to a close when Martin was appointed Director of Missionary Training, and was asked to relocate to New York. As Rosen discussed his concerns and fears with me, and with Terryl Delaney, we both advised him against making the move to New York since he had such ambivalent feelings about the move. Then we agreed to pray with him about his decision.

As my immediate supervisor, Martin told me that Harry Bucalstein and myself would remain in Los Angeles and have a cooperative position as Missionaries-in-Charge. Harry Bucalstein was to share the responsibilities by being in charge of the deputation work, and by speaking at the Sunday afternoon meetings when he was in town. The author was to administrate and develop the missionary program.

Reluctantly, but believing it was God's will, Martin and his family made plans to once again make the long drive from one coast to the other. Before they made the move, however, Martin requested that he be allowed to renovate the Headquarters building in Manhattan so that it would have adequate office and classroom space.

The reader will recall that the Missionary Training Program of the Mission was originally established in New York under the name, "The Jewish Missionary Training Institute." This training program came under the direction of Dr. Henry Heydt in 1953—just months prior to the death of Joseph Hoffman Cohn. At the time of Martin Rosen's arrival in New York some classes were still being held. The infusion of Rosen's Training Program brought about a great deal of general confusion over who was conducting what—problems that were later resolved when Dr. Heydt graciously agreed to merge the Jewish Missionary Training Institute with the New York School of the Bible.

With the Headquarters building remodeled to house his Training Program, and most of the staff problems worked out, Martin and his family were ready to move to New York. But before they left Los Angeles Martin asked the author to promise that he (Martin) would be allowed to return to the Western District if things did not work out for him in New York. He suggested that the ministry in California could be divided between Southern and Northern California; he stated that he would develop the Northern part of the district, while the author could continue to develop the Southern district. We agreed to this "contingency plan," but we both prayed that it would never be needed.

RE-STAFFING LOS ANGELES

The Rosen family embarked upon their trip to New York in the late Spring of 1967. With them went the entire training program—equipment, files, mailing lists, etc.—as well as staff members (including Emil Olsen) who were involved with the program. The work in Los Angeles was left with a skeleton crew, and virtually devoid of equipment. The staff consisted of Harry Bucalstein, the author, and our faithful secretary/receptionist, "Mama Cohen" (Mrs. Faye Cohen—see Chapter Six). Martin did, however, leave behind a well-trained volunteer staff and a good "network" among the churches. Within the overall district, Rev. Kenneth Reeves was working in San Francisco; Miss Ruth Backus was working in Phoenix, Arizona; and Dr. Elias den Arend continued to serve as a Field Evangelist in the western states. Elias Zimmerman was retired, but he continued to take speaking engagements for the Mission.

THEODORE PAUL—HIS STORY

So it was that the work of re-staffing the Los Angeles branch began again. Rev. Theodore Paul was one of the first missionaries to be hired subsequent to the Rosens' move to New York.

Theodore (Ted) Paul was born of Ukrainian Jewish parents in 1920. Shortly after his father's death in 1926, Ted was placed in Girard School in Philadelphia—a school for orphan children, or for children whose fathers were no longer living and whose mothers were unable to support and care for their children. Girard School was run by Protestants. Ted was therefore brought up with very little Jewish religious training, but when he was with his mother he occasionally attended synagogue services.

Following his graduation from high school, Ted lived for awhile at the YMCA in downtown Philadelphia. There, he became acquainted with a young Jewish believer who began to witness to him, and who encouraged Ted to join him in attending services at a Jewish mission in Philadelphia. The mission was operated by The Christian Testimony to the Jew, under the direction of the Rev. A.M. Zegal. Ted didn't know what to expect when he went to the service for the first time, but he discovered that he liked what he heard so he continued attending the meetings. Soon the Lord convicted his heart. In April 1940 Ted prayed to receive Yeshua as his Messiah and Savior. He was baptized one month later at Wayland Memorial Baptist Church in West Philadelphia.

Ted served in the Army Air Force during World War II and during that time his interest in the things of Lord continued to grow. By the end of his tour of duty he felt that God was calling him into full-time ministry. Toward that end, he enrolled as a student at Syracuse University but he transferred to Wheaton College in 1947. At Wheaton his interest in Jewish missions and evangelism was aroused and he spent the summer of 1949 (following his graduation from Wheaton College) working for the Chicago Hebrew Mission.

Ted enrolled at Dallas Theological Seminary in the fall of 1949. In addition to his classroom work, he also worked with Rev. Kahle who had a small Jewish mission work in Dallas, called the Dallas Tenach Forum, and he did volunteer work for a Jewish ministry called Radio Revival. During his last year at Dallas, Ted spent the summer working in Detroit, Michigan as the youth director and as a missionary for Israel's Remnant, Inc.—a work begun by the late Dr. Fred Kendall.

After his graduation from Dallas Theological Seminary in 1953, Ted returned to Detroit to work full-time with Israel's Remnant. He became the assistant pastor of their congregation in Detroit. It was there that he met Miss Betty Evelyn Libby, whom he married in 1954.

Over the fifteen year span from 1953 until he was hired as a worker for the Mission, Ted's ministry with Israel's Remnant included doing visitation, leading Bible classes, and taking charge of a reading room, as well as working with that ministry's Hebrew Christian congregations in both Detroit, Michigan and in Brookline, Massachusetts. The Paul's also served on the staff of the Buffalo Hebrew Christian Mission. Ted opened a new ministry in Syracuse, New York for the Buffalo Hebrew Christian Mission. The new work was called the Syracuse Witness to Israel. God blessed the ministry and a number of Jewish people came to faith as a result of the Pauls' faithful witness there.

Ted was hired as a member of the Mission's Los Angeles staff on April 1, 1968. His primary responsibility was to carry on the visitation ministry in Los Angeles, North Hollywood, and San Fernando Valley but he also conducted Bible classes and spoke in numerous churches on behalf of the Mission. He was always (and still is) a persistent missionary to the Jewish people. Ted Paul faithfully served with the Mission until his retirement on December 31, 1982.

The ministry in Los Angeles continued to be blessed by God. New part-time workers and student workers were added to the staff, new meetings were opened throughout the district, and Jewish people were coming to faith in the

Messiah. But with the blessings of an expanding ministry came the need for additional office staff to assist in the administration of increased branch and staff activities and a growing mailing list. Our prayers for the "right person" were answered when God directed a Jewish believer, Mrs. Barbara Benedict, to the Mission.

BARBARA BENEDICT—HER STORY

Barbara had a position with the telephone company when God spoke to her heart and directed her to seek a position with the Mission. She has an excellent "telephone voice," and was fully qualified for the position of executive secretary. We later learned that she also has a beautiful singing voice, which she used in ministry by singing at various Mission functions. Barbara joined the Mission staff October 1, 1967.

Barbara became the author's "right hand man" during the years 1967 to 1972, and again from 1981-1991. Her capabilities and administrative skills enabled the author to feel confident that the office was running efficiently while he was traveling throughout the Western States District, opening new meetings, speaking at existing outreach ministries, conducting Bible conferences, and enlarging our base of ministry so more Jewish people could be reached with the Gospel. In fact, Barbara's efficiency and knowledge of the Mission and Mission affairs became so extensive that some of the workers lovingly referred to her as "Mrs. ABMJ."

No job was too small or too big for Barbara. When it was necessary, she remained at her desk long after others had gone home as she applied herself to getting a task done. Her faithfulness, loyalty, and ability was put to the test, and was further evidenced when she was asked to move to New York in 1979. Barbara loved California, and her husband, Ted, had a job that he loved—but they both set aside their personal desires and were willing to make the move to the East coast. Nine years later, when the Headquarters Office of the Mission was relocated to Charlotte, North Carolina, Barbara and Ted were once again willing to uproot their personal lives and make the move to a new community.

Over her twenty-five years of service with the Mission, Barbara held several titles while working with the author, including: secretary, Administrative Assistant, and Assistant to the President. Over the years she has also served as secretary to the Board. She and her husband, Ted, have been faithful and loyal workers for the Mission up to the time of the writing of this history. She is currently serving as Assistant to Rev. Sam Nadler, President of Chosen People Ministries, Inc., as well as secretary to the Board. Only eternity will be able to evaluate and reward Barbara and Ted for their dedication in the task of reaching Jewish people with the Gospel.

DEVELOPING SPECIAL SERVICES AND PROGRAMS

As the Los Angeles staff worked to penetrate the Jewish community with the Gospel, we began to develop more Messianic services and we introduced more "Jewish tradition and culture" into the various services of worship, holiday services, and Bible studies. We discovered that the Jewish people loved to come to the services because they included "yiddishkeit," Hebrew blessings, and other ceremonies and traditions that were familiar to them. The fact that the New Testament scriptures were read, and that Jesus was proclaimed to be the Messiah, did not offend them because they were included in the services in a Jewish context and Jewish culture. These services became the prototype for many of the Messianic congregations which sprang up in later years.

A MESSIANIC BAR MITZVAH

One unique service that was conducted was the "Messianic Bar-Mitzvah" service. The concept of such a service was new and unorthodox in the mid-1960's. When first introduced, the service was a source of controversy among missionaries to the Jews, within the Jewish community, and within Christian churches. Rabbi Leopold Cohn had introduced and conducted such services in his attempt to create a Messianic community of Jewish believers, but they had been discontinued because of the accusations of "Judaizing" and "legalism."

The first Bar Mitzvah service planned in the Los Angeles area was for a young Jewish boy whose family had come to faith in Yeshua through their contact with the Mission. The Charness family, including son, Michael, and daughter, Laurie, maintained a dynamic testimony for the Lord, and when Michael neared his thirteenth birthday they all felt the occasion could be used as a wonderful testimony to their Jewish friends and family members. At the time of Michael's Bar Mitzvah, the author wrote the following article for *The Chosen People* magazine:

Sunday, January 28th, [c.1968] was a great occasion for our mission in Los Angeles. It was even a greater occasion in the life of young Michael Charness, a Hebrew Christian. It was Michael's thirteenth birthday and according to Jewish tradition this is the age when a Jewish boy becomes a man. He is now responsible for his own sin, and, as a man, he takes on the responsibilities of Jewish life. He can now wear the Talith, the Tephillah or Phylacteries. He can participate in the Minyan and in the life of the Jewish community.

Michael's parents, Bob and Ruby Charness,...asked that we might have a Bar Mitzvah service for their son as a testimony to the rest of the family that accepting Jesus as Messiah and Saviour does not automatically cut one off from his Jewish heritage. After much thought and prayer, we agreed that this would be a unique and effective way to demonstrate what Christ can do in the lives of believers.

Our efforts were well rewarded. The Mission chapel was packed to capacity, with standing-room only for this special service. The family of Michael Charness was present, with all of the relatives and friends. For many this was the first experience and exposure to the person of Jesus our Messiah and Saviour. Michael recited the portions of the Torah and Haftorah, which he had learned in Hebrew, giving the appropriate prayers and blessings; and then gave his own personal testimony,...Needless to say, the family was impressed.

After the service we had the customary reception, at which time we were able to talk with the various members of the family and the friends who had come. I am convinced that we have not heard the last of this Bar Mitzvah service, for the seed of the Gospel which has been implanted in the lives and hearts of those present will come to fruition as the Lord blesses.[6]

Some criticism over the fact that we would conduct such a service was forthcoming, but we received far more favorable response than criticism. In fact, many other Jewish families subsequently wanted their sons and daughters to have "Bar Mitzvah" or "Bat Mitzvah" services so that they, too, could use the occasion as a means of testimony to family members and friends.

MESSIANIC HOLY DAY SERVICES

Jewish holidays, too, were occasions around which special services of worship were formed. One such Jewish holy day was *Yom Kippur*, the Day of Atonement. This most sacred of all Jewish holidays naturally lends itself to a witness of God's atoning work through the Messiah, but the branch ministries of the Mission had not capitalized on the opportunity to use it to share the Gospel message. Some of the Mission's branches had closed on Yom Kippur as a way of showing support for the Jewish community. Others had used the day as a special "day of prayer," with prayer meetings planned for, and attended by, believers. But none of the Mission's branches were holding Yom Kippur services as a means of preaching the Gospel.

The idea of using Yom Kippur as an opportunity for witness came to the author as he was reading the Los Angeles Times, and saw all of the ads for the High Holy Day Services. Each advertisement included a statement about the availability and cost of tickets needed for attendance at the High Holy Day services (Many Christians do not realize that synagogue membership is based upon dues and a fee schedule. These fees do not generally include the charges for High Holy Day tickets, which can get quite expensive!).

According to Jewish tradition, on Yom Kippur a Jew must hear and participate in the *Kol Nidre* service. Kol Nidre, meaning "all vows," is a Jewish prayer which gained sanctity to the Jewish community during the cruel and torturous treatment of the *Maranos* (Spanish Jews who were forced to convert to Christianity). The prayer, in effect, was to release them from any vow they had been forced to make (such as a vow to become a Christian). According to the rabbis, recital of the Kol Nidre does not absolve a worshipper from obligations made to his fellow man, it only absolves vows made between man and God. Such vows, according to Jewish tradition, can be absolved through prayer and repentance.

As the author read the ads, he mused over the numbers of Jews who would be clamoring to secure tickets for Yom Kippur services. He knew that for many, the Yom Kippur service is their annual trek to the synagogue; it is the only service they attend during the year. God brought to mind a question, "Why not conduct Messianic High Holiday Services, and advertise them in the newspapers, offering *free* seats?"

Our staff became excited about the special holiday services, and as we prayed and planned for the Fall "holy days," we included plans for a Rosh Hashanah (New Year) service, a Kol Nidre service on the eve of Yom Kippur, a Yom Kippur service, a Festival of Succoth (Feast of Booths) service, and a Simcha Torah (Rejoicing in the Law) service. Tickets were printed, ads were placed, and flyers were printed and mailed to Jewish homes throughout Los Angeles. With so many special services, the weeks of September and October were busy ones indeed!

In answer to our prayers for someone who could sing the Kol Nidre, God sent Joseph German, a young Jewish believer who had been trained as a cantor for the synagogue. Not only did he have a beautiful singing voice, he had memorized the various songs and liturgy of the Jewish ceremonies and services. Joseph also organized a choir and taught the choir members special songs and music for the holidays.

In sharing the results of one of the special services with readers of *The Chosen People* magazine, the author wrote:

For our recent Rosh Hashanah and Yom Kippur services we sent out over 200 tickets to interested Jewish people, completely filling our seating capacity. Mrs. Barbara Benedict, one of our missionary secretaries, writes:

'It is the Friday before Rosh Hashanah and 9:00 a.m. The staff has just met for prayer and committed the day to the Lord, asking especially that unsaved Jewish people will respond to the advertising and attend the holiday services. The telephone rings. It is a request for tickets to the services. "Why is it," the man asks, "that your ad states 'free tickets' when all the others charge?" We explain that our Center is not a temple, does not have a membership, nor do we charge for seats at any of our services; but we welcome anyone who wishes to attend. "You mean you have services all year long or just during the holidays?" is the next query. When told that we have regular services every Sunday afternoon as well as at Passover, Chanukah and other holidays he is amazed. When further explanation is made concerning the Jewish Christian aspects of our services he says, "Well, it is a place of worship isn't it? Send two tickets for my wife and myself." This is only one example of the dozens of calls. When we explain to those calling that we are Hebrew Christians who believe in Jesus as the Messiah and proclaim Him in our services, we can only give God the glory for the warm response from these Jewish people. We look forward with much anticipation to our holiday worship, trusting God to bring many into His family as a result of this ministry.'[7]

The response of the Jewish community of Los Angeles to the special Rosh Hashanah and Yom Kippur services was exhilarating. We saw the hand of God at work as our meeting rooms were packed to capacity. To accommodate the numbers of people who requested tickets, extra seating was arranged in several rooms of our Mission building. When the chapel was filled the over-flow crowd sat in adjoining rooms where the guests watched and heard the services on the closed circuit TV's we'd rented for the occasion. The windows and doors facing the large front porch of the building were also opened so that people who had gathered on the porch could catch a glimpse and hear some of what was happening. Many Jewish people came to faith in the Messiah as a result of the special services.

The service that was developed around the Festival of Succoth (Feast of Tabernacles) was another favorite with the Jewish community. Once again, the idea for the service originated from a newspaper ad. As the author read an October issue of the Jewish Press from Brooklyn, New York, he saw an ad for a pre-fabricated Succoth Booth. It seemed to be a wonderful prop for another holiday service, so the author spoke with Daniel Fuchs about placing an order, and he approved the expenditure.

During the Festival of Succoth, orthodox Jews build a booth in their yard, or a communal booth is built at the synagogue. According to Jewish custom and tradition (see Leviticus 23) the Jewish family is to "dwell" in the booth for eight days; it is a reminder of the Exodus and of God's provisions while the children of Israel wandered in the wilderness. Meals are taken in the booth, Scriptures are read, and prayers are offered. It is a holiday that beautifully lends itself to Messianic interpretation. It was at the Feast of Tabernacles that Yeshua declared Himself to be the Messiah; he spoke of the coming Holy Spirit at the time of "prayer for rain."

The staff enthusiastically endorsed the idea of the Succoth service, and of setting up a Succoth Booth. When the pre-fabricated booth arrived, it was set up in the parking lot of the Mission's building in Hollywood. Fruits and vegetables were hung from the ceiling of the booth; the walls were also decorated with the bounty of a harvest, and the roof was covered with palm branches. Tables and chairs were set up around the booth, while buffet tables were set up in the Mission's fellowship hall. The service, which was attended by hundreds of Jewish people each year, began outside with a short service of prayer and music. Then a procession was formed and the group paraded around the building with the *lulav* and *etrog*, finally entering the building to go through the buffet lines in the fellowship hall, and then returning to our seats outdoors. After the meal, the service included additional special music, prayer, and preaching about the Messiah, "Who tabernacled among us."

The special Passover services became so popular that it was impossible to accommodate the numbers of people in our Mission building. One year we rented space at the Civic Center. Another year, Douglas Pyle, one of our missionaries, negotiated with the Jewish Community in Culver City, California to use their facilities, but when the rabbi learned that the staff of the American Board of Missions to the Jews had leased his facilities for their Messianic Passover Banquet, he canceled the lease. He subsequently picketed our Passover Banquet which was held at the Santa Monica Civic Center.

As the special holy day services were planned and executed year by year, they synergistically opened more opportunities for witness; they drew people from the entire Los Angeles basin—from Santa Barbara to Desert Hot Springs and Palm Springs, and as far south as San Diego.

But the holy day services were not the only special meetings that were planned. As an outgrowth of the author's series of meetings at Bel Air Presbyterian Church, Jayne Meadows and Steve Allen offered to make their home available for meetings. Everyone in Hollywood and in Los Angeles knew of Jayne Meadows and Steve Allen. The staff was ecstatic over the opportunity of holding meetings in their home; we knew meetings there would attract many Jewish people.

The Allens graciously opened their home for a regular monthly Bible study class. They also allowed the Mission to host a special "kibbutznik night" (Israeli night) which was held in their back yard around their pool. The evening was a great success for the Gospel as several hundred people—most of whom were Jewish, and many of whom were from the motion picture and television industry—heard the message of the Messiah proclaimed and enjoyed the Israeli music and the delicious "falafel" and other Middle Eastern dishes that were prepared by an Israeli couple—owners of the Eilat restaurant in Los Angeles.

THE SUMMER INTERN PROGRAM

The number of meetings being held each week was increasing, and more workers were needed. To procure assistance, a "Summer Intern Program" (S. I. P.) was established during the summer of 1968. Through this program, which was geared to seminary students, individuals who had an interest in Jewish missions were trained to assist in the ministry on a part-time or on a volunteer basis. Flyers describing the S. I. P. program were sent to evangelical seminaries throughout the western states. The S.I.P program was the prototype for the S. T. E. P. (Summer Training and Evangelism Program) which has been offered since 1982. Morning hours were devoted to classes, while afternoon and evening hours were given to visitation, home Bible study meetings, street evangelism, etc.

LARRY JAFFREY JOINS THE STAFF

One of the seminary students who responded to the 1969 S.I.P. flyer was Larry Jaffrey, a student at the Conservative Baptist Theological Seminary in Denver, Colorado.

Larry was born October 27, 1943 into a Gentile family in the small rural town of Rush City, Minnesota. He, like Bill Ennis, was an individual whose background did not prepare him for Jewish missions and evangelism. That men like Larry Jaffrey enter the field of Jewish missions gives evidence to the fact that the calling and gifts needed to serve the Lord among the Jewish people are from God, not from man!

The home situation was difficult for Larry. His father died when he was only three years of age and although his mother did remarry, relationships within the family were strained. Further, there was little help forthcoming from the church the family attended; it did not preach the Gospel. At the age of fifteen, Larry left his mother's home to live with relatives in Wisconsin. They attended a small evangelical Baptist church. It was while attending services with them, that Larry first heard the Gospel.

When an accident claimed his brother's life, Larry began to question his own faith and beliefs. He began to realize that religious training did not make him a Christian, and after a Bible camp meeting in August 1959 Larry accepted Jesus as his Savior. Two years later he was baptized, and he joined the small Baptist church.

When Larry enrolled at the University of Minnesota in 1961 he had not given much thought to God's calling upon his life. His major was Dairy Husbandry; he was planning to enter some part of the dairy industry. But during his junior year in college (c.1964) he attended the tri-annual Urbana Missionary Conference sponsored by Intervarsity Christian Fellowship. At the conference he surrendered his life to the Lord; he told God he would be willing to serve Him any place and any time.

On June 25, 1966 Larry married Gail McCall, a young Christian girl from Anoka, Minnesota. In the Fall of that year he entered the Conservative Baptist Theological Seminary in Denver to study for the ministry. Terryl Delaney, the Missionary-in-Charge of the Denver Branch, was also taking courses at the seminary, and he had been asked to speak about the Mission in some of the chapel services. Larry had never before given thought to the need for sharing the Gospel with Jewish people and God used those chapel services to speak to his heart about devoting his life to a ministry in Jewish missions.

In the Fall of 1968, although he was still attending seminary, Larry was hired to assist Terryl Delaney on a part-time basis. At the end of the school year, he responded to the Mission's S. I. P. flyer. After attending this intense two-month period of learning and of witnessing, Larry returned to Denver all the more convinced that God was calling him into the field of Jewish missions. Following his graduation from seminary, Larry continued to assist Terryl in the Denver branch. In 1970 both men were transferred to work in the Mission's Philadelphia branch. Larry and Gail Jaffrey have been dedicated workers for the Mission since that time—a span of over twenty years.

RICHARD COHEN—HIS STORY

Richard Cohen, a young Jewish businessman, attended the S. I. P. program as well—and eventually joined the staff as a part-time worker, and then as a full-time worker.

Richard was born and raised in a traditional Jewish home in Los Angeles, California. Of his home life he said:

The earliest memory of my family life is of sitting on my grandfather's knee and having him feed me. I grew up in a

Jewish home where we were very close and where many of the Jewish traditions were practiced. Since I lived in Jewish neighborhoods most of my life, I never had much contact with Gentiles.[8]

While he was a student at Fairfax High School, which was a predominately Jewish high school at the time, Richard met Linda, a young Jewish girl whom he later married. After their marriage, Richard went into business with his father. The business prospered and the Cohens purchased a large home in San Fernando Valley. They had everything money could buy, and to the outward appearance they seemed happy as they pursued the life of a young successful Jewish couple. But Linda was lonely because of the long hours Richard devoted to his business career.

One day Jean Ambro, a Gentile Christian woman who did volunteer work for Dr. Fred Berger, knocked on the Cohens' door. Dr. Fred Berger was a missionary to the Jews serving with the American Baptist Home Mission Society. He had established an inter-faith Sunday School at the First Baptist Church of Van Nuys, California and Jean did visitation work for the Sunday School. It was a unique ministry; it reached out to the many families in the San Fernando Valley in which one spouse was Jewish and the other was Gentile—a dilemma that often left their children completely un-churched. (Before his death, Dr. Berger's ministry was merged with the work of the Mission, and Mrs. Ambro faithfully continued her witness to the Jewish people on a volunteer basis, and later as a staff member of the Mission, until her retirement on June 1, 1987.)

Just as Ceil Rosen had been open to the witness of Hannah Wago, Linda was open to the friendship and testimony of Jean Ambro. She not only loved the company, she found she was also curious and interested in the things Jean shared from the Scriptures about the Messiah of Israel. When Richard found out about Jean's visits, he was very upset and angry that Linda would allow a "missionary" in their home. He forbid Linda to allow Jean to visit again. But, like Ceil Rosen, Linda did not end the visits. One night when Richard came home from work he found that not only was Jean there, she had brought another Messianic Jewish believer with her. Despite his displeasure over having "missionaries" in his living room, Richard listened while they told him about the Messiah of Israel, and as they showed him from the Scriptures that Yeshua was the promised Messiah. Then and there he decided they were wrong, and he made the decision to study the Bible for himself just to prove them wrong. He later wrote:

After three months of study in my Old Testament I found out that what they had said about the Messiah was true and that I had been wrong. My wife was studying the Bible also and we accepted Jesus Christ as the Messiah of Israel and Lord and Savior of our lives. We found that the only real pleasure we had was to tell others about the Messiah and His saving grace.[9]

Richard and Linda were baptized, and they joined the Van Nuys Baptist Church. They were eager students of the Scriptures, and quickly grew in the faith. Richard had the distinction of being one of the youngest deacons to serve in Van Nuys Baptist Church. The Cohens also volunteered their time to a number of ministries within the church—from helping the blind, to starting a motorcycle club as a means of evangelizing cyclists. Richard also gave of his time to share his testimony and to witness to Jewish people at the Mission's Hollywood branch.

As they served the Lord through church involvement, both Richard and Linda began to feel God's call upon their lives to devote themselves to full-time ministry. Richard gave up his business and they sold their large home; he had decided to attend Prairie Bible Institute in Alberta, Canada. The mission helped them financially by giving him student aid. But their experience at Prairie Bible Institute was not a happy one. They were the only Jewish people for miles around, and they felt like fish out of water. But it wasn't just the lack of fellowship with other Jews that bothered them, it was the fact that at Prairie they were made to feel that they should renounce their Jewish heritage if they were going to serve the Lord. Richard knew he wanted to complete his studies for the ministry, but he also knew he and his family were Jewish; they could not give up their Jewish heritage. It became clear that they could not remain in Alberta.

Richard called the author and asked if there was any way that the Mission could help them. The author, in turn, called some friends at BIOLA College in La Mirada, California; they graciously agreed to see to it that Richard was accepted as a student there.

The Cohen's moved back to Los Angeles and Richard completed a few semesters at BIOLA. He then transferred to the Los Angeles Baptist College, in Newhall, California. During the years he spent studying for the ministry, Richard also continued working for the Mission on a part-time basis. He served with enthusiasm and soon developed a young adult ministry for the Hollywood branch, as well as a new ministry in North Hollywood.

DEVELOPING THE TRAINING PROGRAM IN NEW YORK

Utilizing the methodology taught by Martin Rosen, the author was developing the Western States District and

Terryl Delaney was developing the Rocky Mountain States District. As Director of Missionary Training, Martin Rosen was in New York developing his training program and laying plans to develop several new districts for the Mission. His vision for the Mission was to duplicate in the East, the Southeast, and the Atlantic states, the methods of outreach already being used in the Western District, in the Rocky Mountain District, and in the Southwestern District.

Martin Rosen's first six-month training program in New York had four candidates. A report of the program appeared in the March 1968 issue of *The Chosen People* magazine. Martin wrote:

> *The purpose of the training and orientation program …is to give incoming candidates both a theoretical and experiential knowledge of Jewish missions….*
>
> *…Each class of candidates should be four to six people, and they are in the program for approximately six months. This time is equally divided between classroom studies and practical work….*
>
> *Mogens R. Mogensen, a native of Denmark, has been in our work for six years and carried on a successful outreach in Pittsburgh, Pennsylvania. He is undergoing the training program as are other regular personnel transferred from one branch to another. Mr. Mogensen was an engineer and a ship's officer before he became a minister. He is an extremely creative individual and has played a significant role in designing our new sanctuary in New York City.*
>
> *Eliezer Urbach is a native of Poland. Not realizing that he was Jewish, the Russians had him jailed during the war for being a Nazi spy. He was released and served in the Russian army as a newspaper editor for a propaganda journal. Mr. and Mrs. Urbach are Hebrew Christians. He first heard the Gospel in Brazil and was later baptized in Israel. Besides the fluent, if slightly accented English, Mr. Urbach speaks a fluent Yiddish, Polish, Russian, Hebrew, Portuguese, and Spanish.*
>
> *Martin Klayman gave up a printing business to serve as a full time missionary with the A.B.M.J. He and his wife Pauline are Hebrew Christians and natives of New York. At the present time Mr. Klayman is president of the New York chapter of the Hebrew Christian Alliance. The Klaymans were baptized by Mr. Harry Bucalstein who serves as a missionary with the A.B.M.J.*
>
> *Arthur Katz, a Hebrew Christian, was a leftist and Communist sympathizer. For many years he taught American History at high schools in the Oakland, California system. He came to accept the Lord Jesus Christ as his Savior and Messiah in the city of Jerusalem, in 1964, through a series of life shaking circumstances. He went back to teaching in Oakland and diligently tried to relate his newly found faith in Christ to his students with the same zeal that he formerly proclaimed left-wing theories. Within a brief period, his testimony was known and felt in many areas of northern California. His wife Inger is a native of Denmark.[10]*

The stories of two of the candidates have since been published in book form. The story and testimony of Eliezer Urbach are given in a book entitled, *Out Of The Fury—the Incredible Odyssey of Eliezer Urbach.*[11] The story of how Arthur Katz came to faith in Yeshua is told in a book entitled *Apprehended By God—a Journal of a Jewish Atheist.*[12]

The second class of missionary candidates in Martin's training program in New York had an enrollment of seven. Of this group Martin wrote:

> *…The seven, who came from varying backgrounds, all have one thing in common. They are Gentiles. Nevertheless, through our training program they have become acculturated to the Jewish community and can move about with ease in Jewish circles. As part of their training, they received intensive instruction in the vocabulary of Jewish life. Regular synagogue attendance has accustomed them to Jewish worship. Classes were conducted to help them appreciate Jewish literature and folk music. They even learned to sing some of the folk songs of the Jewish people. The object of our training program was not to pass these people off as Jews, rather to help them think Jewish so that they might become, as Paul says, 'To the Jews, a Jew.' Frequently, the way to further conversation between Jew and Christian is opened up when the Jewish people see that a Gentile Christian has taken the time and trouble to become thoroughly acquainted with Jewish culture.*
>
> *Besides the training in culture, many of the lectures were given on technique; for example, lectures on 'How to Conduct an Outdoor Meeting.' 'How to Conduct a Bible Discussion Group,' and 'How to Carry Out Visits.' The candidates not only listened to the lectures, but they learned the methods of doing these things by being involved in all the various phases of the work carried on in New York City.*
>
> *This year's candidates who were trained in New York City are as follows:*
>
> *Paul Balthaser, a native of Hamburg, Pennsylvania, was graduated from Southwestern Baptist Theological Seminary in Fort Worth, Texas, just prior to entering our candidates' program. He was ordained in the Boulevard Baptist Church in Greenville, South Carolina. He is also a graduate of Bob Jones University in Greenville, South Carolina. While at Bob Jones University he met his wife, Jeanette, who is a Virginia girl. They have one son, David. Before*

attending seminary, Mr. Balthaser was employed as a schoolteacher, and his major was Religious Education. His knowledge and training in this field will be very valuable to us. The Balthaser's are presently residing in New York City awaiting assignment.

David Carlson, age 21, our youngest candidate, has a twin brother who is on the mission field in Mexico. Dave is a graduate of the Bethany Fellowship Missionary Training School in Minneapolis, Minnesota. His hobbies are electronics and photography. He is engaged and hopes to be married as soon as his fiancee graduates school.

Perrin Cook will bring some valuable experience to our field. For twenty years he has been a successful pastor of Baptist Churches in Alabama, Kentucky, and Mississippi. He left the pastorate of Handsboro Baptist Church in Gulfport, Mississippi, in response to a call to serve the Lord in bringing the Gospel to the Jewish people. Mr. Cook is a graduate of Baylor University in Waco, Texas, and Southern Baptist Theological Seminary in Louisville, Kentucky. He is married and has three sons and one daughter. He anticipates serving the Lord working among the Jews in the South. [Perrin eventually served the Mission in Atlanta, Georgia (c.1969) until that branch was closed in the early 1980's.]

Hannah Eurich is a native of Remscheid in West Germany. She is a graduate of Beatenberg Bible Seminary in Beatenberg, Switzerland. She is particularly interested in a ministry among young people and university students. She came to this country from Germany for the purpose of taking our candidates' course and serving in this field. She has acquired a remarkable use of the English language. She is presently anticipating service with the American Board of Missions to the Jews in Pittsburgh. Presently her hobby is singing and playing Yiddish and Hebrew folk songs.

Dan and Arlene Rigney are natives of Baltimore, Maryland. Mr. Rigney graduated from Moody Bible Institute in the Jewish Missions Course. Mrs. Rigney is also a graduate of Moody. Before entering our training program, they had spent their summers working in Jewish Missions, both in our Camp Sar Shalom and in a resort ministry with the Catskill Messianic Fellowship. They are presently assigned to work in New York City. [The Rigney's were eventually transferred to Baltimore where they worked with the Mission for several years before resigning to work with Jews for Jesus and Ariel Ministries.]

Mary Ann Sleichter graduated last June from Cedarville College in Cedarville, Ohio. Her home church is Chambersburg Bible Church in Chambersburg, Pennsylvania. She has a particular burden for working with children and young people and has demonstrated great skills. She has worked in our camping program and in Daily Vacation Bible School. Miss Sleichter hopes to be employed in a work among college students and young people. [The reader will recall that Mary Ann Sleichter went to Israel through the Mission's program. She worked with Martin Rosen and Jews For Jesus for awhile, and while working with Jews For Jesus she met the man she eventually married—Sam Nadler. Both Sam and Mary Ann (now Miriam) returned to work with the Mission.][13]

TENSION DEVELOPS OVER THE TRAINING PROGRAM

The relocation of the missionary training program from Los Angeles to New York entailed far more than just the physical transfer of the personnel and the setting up of new classroom facilities. There was a hurdle of suspicion and resentment which Martin Rosen had to cross. The veteran missionaries in the New York area were well familiar with the Jewish Missionary Training Institute that Joseph Cohn had established, and which had been under the direction of Dr. Henry Heydt for a number of years. Many had been trained there, and they were suspicious of Martin and of his new program; they resented the fact that they were being asked to go through "re-training." Additionally, most of the veteran missionaries were older than Martin; many remembered him from his student days at Northeastern Bible College, and it was difficult for them to accept him in an authoritative role.

The request that the veteran missionaries enter Martin's program for "re-training" would have been sufficient cause for the feelings of resentment—but the situation was aggravated further by the fact that when he moved to New York, Martin was not only given the title of Director of Missionary Training, he was appointed Missionary in Charge of the New York Headquarters *District*—an appointment that placed him over all the missionaries in the greater New York area. Prior to making the New York Headquarters a *district*, he'd had no authority over the other missionaries in charge within the New York environs; they all reported directly to Daniel Fuchs.

The veteran missionaries had been happy with their methods of reaching the Jews of New York with the Gospel. They felt their methods had proven to be effective, and they could see no reason for new methods and techniques. Further, they were not interested in changing their methods of doing ministry so that their programs would fit into the district program outlined by Martin.

NEW METHODOLOGY DEVELOPED

Martin, himself, soon discovered that not all of his new methods and techniques were effective in a bustling city such as New York. He wrote:

> In July of 1967 a new District was formed at our Headquarters which was designed to serve as a training center and to intensify the direct approach mission activity. It soon became apparent that methods and techniques which were effective elsewhere would not work as well in congested city living. A good example of this is to be seen in the canvassing ministry. In suburban areas, where most Jewish people live in family-type dwellings, we find more freedom to go from door to door, ring the bell, introduce ourselves, and offer some literature and a personal invitation to attend one of our Gospel meetings or Bible classes. However, in New York City, where most of the Jewish people live in apartments, we are unable to make personal contact because of doormen and double-locked entrances. Even if we had some way around the devices which people have set up to protect themselves from intrusions, it is doubtful that they would open their doors to such a canvass.[14]

Always the innovator, Martin attempted to solve this dilemma through telephone solicitation ministry. He and the staff composed a list of common Jewish names, then went through the Manhattan telephone directory, as well as the directories of the boroughs of New York, pinpointing Jewish names. Whenever a Jewish name was found, a telephone call was placed to that number. As a result of these calls, which were made at various times of day, several hundred Jewish people expressed interest in receiving information about the Mission, or in attending the Bible classes in their area.

Martin also set up an extensive visitation program, which he placed under the supervision of Eliezer Urbach. Eliezer maintained a detailed log of visitation records, and he set up the schedules for missionary candidates and new missionaries to go out, two by two, contacting Jewish people in their homes. Once a contact was established, the workers would seek to establish individual Bible study situations, and to encourage people to come to the Mission's meetings.

A department of Church Relations for the District was also established. This department was under the supervision of Mr. Emil Olsen. Emil furnished churches with literature, set up classes for Christians on "How to Witness to Jews," and arranged speaking dates for the missionaries and missionary candidates in churches throughout the district.

Some of the "old," established methods of ministry were used as well, such as the window display at the Headquarters building on 72nd St. This had always proved to be an excellent way to attract the attention of Jewish people passing by. Street meetings and other outdoors witness was utilized too. Martin wrote:

> While we use much of the newer methodology in communicating the Gospel, we have not abandoned the older tried and proven methods. We still carry on a ministry through the outdoor distribution of tracts and Gospel literature. Likewise, we regularly conduct Gospel meetings. Within twenty minutes after we set up our portable platform and the American flag [a requirement by law in the City of New York], we usually have a crowd of between 25 to 100 people listening to the message. Five or six of our staff members and candidates participate as a team. We continue this ministry usually from March to November, as long as weather permits, and a great many people are met and witnessed to.
>
> Though we haven't seen direct decisions made on street corners for Christ, we nevertheless continue to feel that this type of ministry is worthwhile because of the numbers of contacts we have gained. There are many Jewish people who come back regularly for the scheduled outdoor meetings. Some of these regulars come to outdoor meetings simply to enjoy the sport of heckling. However, there are a substantial number who attend because they are genuinely interested to hear what we have to say and who evidence some spiritual interest.[15]

Another phase of ministry that was duplicated was the establishment of an outreach on college campuses in New York. Martin had opened such ministries on the campuses of UCLA (University of California, Los Angeles) and USC (University of Southern California), but as he established college outreach in New York, he pursued it much more aggressively. He wrote:

> ...We make speakers available to different groups on the campus. Since what we have to say is somewhat unconventional and controversial, we get quite a number of invitations. Many of the campuses in the New York area have more than fifty per cent Jewish students, thus there is never any shortage of Jews to talk to at the campus level.[16]

Three of the veteran missionaries of the New York staff whom Martin involved in outreach were Jonas and Rachel Cohen, and Miss Lola Weir.

Lola Weir — A Veteran Missionary Joins the Staff
On a personal level, Lola Weir had been visiting Jewish people in the Bronx for some twenty-one years before she

learned of the American Board of Missions to the Jews.[17] Her affiliation with the Mission began in 1958, when she served as a volunteer on Long Island, visiting in hospitals and homes. Martin used her as a teacher for the "Golden Age Club," a class of retired women which met at the Headquarters building in Manhattan on Thursdays. Before her retirement, Miss Weir wrote about her ministry among the chronically ill:

> Of the fourteen Jewish contacts made over the years, only five are still living. Of those who have died only one refused to let me read the Bible, not even the Psalms, to her. Another woman would tell me on one visit that she loved Jesus and on the next visit would curse me. Still another would listen to me read and pray but never really committed herself to Him, as far as I could determine. Two were fearless witnesses to all around them. The others confessed Christ but not so openly. One had accepted Christ before coming to the hospital.[18]

Jonas Cohen—Last Baptized by Rabbi Cohn

Jonas and Rachel Cohen joined the staff of the Mission on September 1, 1957.

Jonas Cohen was born into an orthodox Jewish family on June 23, 1909. The Cohen family lived amidst the bustling Jewish community of New York's Lower East Side.

Jonas' first brush with Christianity came when he was just six years old—shortly after he started school. Some of his classmates taunted him by calling him a "Christ-killer." When Jonas asked them what that meant, they told him "the Jews killed Christ." Jonas was still confused. "Who is Christ?" he asked. "Christ was the Son of God, and the Jews killed Him," came their reply.

As young as he was, Jonas reasoned with himself that the events his friends were talking about had happened so long ago that neither he nor any Jew he knew could possibly be held responsible. It didn't make sense!

In his childish curiosity, Jonas continued to wonder about the person called "Jesus Christ." When he asked his mother, she promptly told him that Jesus was an imposter; she said some other uncomplimentary things too. Believing that his mother knew about such things, he let the matter drop.

Jonas' parents were concerned that their son be a "good" religious Jew. To ensure that their goals for him would be met, they not only insisted that Jonas attend Hebrew School, they also hired a rabbi to come to their home to tutor Jonas in the Hebrew prayers, the Old Testament, and the traditions of his people.

But Jonas had other plans for his life. As he grew older, he began to have doubts about God. He was uncertain about the inspiration and authority of the Scriptures. He was also uncertain about the traditions and teachings of the rabbis. Confused by it all, Jonas drifted from the Jewish religion and his orthodox way of life after his Bar Mitzvah. As he grew into manhood, he knew little about God and cared less.

Believing wealth was the key to success, Jonas pursued a career in the jewelry business. Soon he was working his way up the corporate ladder.

Stepping onto the elevator in the building where he worked, Jonas jokingly asked Eugene, the elevator operator, if he knew where Jonas could find some girls and some "good entertainment" in the city. Instead of the expected response, Eugene began to tell Jonas where he could find His Messiah. Recalling the incident, Jonas later stated:

> …This took place at the Passover season, and we stopped and talked about religion. I was amazed to hear that a Christian knew so much about the Jewish religion. He told me about the part that Jesus Christ plays in our Passover. Almost every evening we would meet and discuss 'religion.' By this time I had grown to be very cynical and looked with contempt upon all religion. The Bible, I told my new-found friend, is out-moded and should not be taken seriously in these times. 'After all,' I said, 'the Bible contains contradictions and cannot be trusted.' Then he proceeded to unfold the Bible to me in a remarkable way. He proved to me that the Bible, contrary to popular belief, contains no contradictions.[19]

Eugene continued to share God's Word with Jonas at every possible opportunity. Jonas recalled:

> …As he was speaking about the various parts of the law of Moses concerning the Passover and the various animal sacrifices, as well as the other Jewish holidays, and the importance that the Bible places on the 'lamb,' I was brought back to my childhood and I remembered studying about these things in Hebrew school.
>
> …in my earlier experiences with the name of Jesus I had heard that He was the Son of God, but when, at the age of twenty-six, I met this young man it was the first time I heard that Jesus was and is the Messiah of Israel.
>
> I had, of course, learned when I was a child that we Jews were expecting a Messiah. When I began to see that there was a possible relationship between the two I became frightened. (These discussions with my friend lasted for about a

year and a half.) I was frightened because I thought I would become a heretic if I allowed myself to believe in Jesus, and there seemed to be great 'danger' of that. So I drew back and avoided my friend.

At this time I was keeping company with a girl who later was to become my wife [Rachel], and when I visited her one evening I told her all that this young man told me only not as clearly, for I didn't understand too much about it. However, when I saw the look of alarm on her face, I immediately reassured her that I would never accept since, as I thought then, it would be the end of all our hopes and dreams. How little I knew the power of God!

When I could avoid him no longer, my friend and I again engaged in 'spiritual combat.' I was trying to destroy his faith and he was trying to give me faith. 'But faith in the Bible is impossible and impractical,' I said. 'The Bible is a collection of myths that no intelligent person can take seriously.'...

As I pondered on these things when I was alone, this thought occurred to me—perhaps it was too much like a fairy tale to be one; perhaps it appeared that way only because I did not understand it. So I began to investigate for myself. I then asked for and received a copy of the Old Testament that has been translated by the Hebrew Publishing Company, and I began to search the Scriptures. The first text that was shown to me was Isaiah 53, and I read it through carefully. It was then that I came, as it were, face to face with Jesus Christ. Even with my limited knowledge of the life of Christ, I was amazed to find a prophecy in the Old Testament that so clearly described Him.[20]

One day Eugene invited Jonas to attend a church service with him; Dr. Donald J. Barnhouse was speaking.

Jonas recalled that Dr. Barnhouse's message was from the Book of Revelation. He also recalled that the entire message went over his head. But something very significant happened after the service. Jonas met a Jewish believer whose name was William Samuels. Jonas had been certain that he was the only Jew in the service; he was surprised that another Jew had attended. As they shared, Samuels' loving words were all Jonas needed to confirm his need to study the Scriptures more diligently. He knew God was speaking to his heart. Later he stated:

By this time a little spark of faith was kindled in my heart. I had been married six months when I told my wife that I might accept the Lord Jesus, but that I must know and be sure that this was the truth.

Knowing that my wife knew more of Judaism than I did, I plied her with questions. One particular question I asked her was: 'We both know that according to the law of Moses we Jews had a lamb for a sacrifice as well as other animals. What do we have today, especially on the day of atonement (Yom Kippur)?' She answered, 'The chicken is our "Kapporah" today—that is, substitutionary sacrifice.'

It was then the revelation struck me as a bolt from heaven itself, and I cried out, 'That's it, Christ was our Kapporah!' My wife viewed me with alarm, but she said nothing.[21]

Fearing to go further with his thoughts, afraid of his wife's reaction, and generally confused about everything he believed, Jonas went to his rabbi hoping that he could supply some answers to his dilemma. He had to know if Jesus was really the Jewish Messiah. But it quickly became obvious to Jonas that his rabbi was not open to discussing such a topic. The rabbi's inability to answer Jonas' questions, and his deliberate dismissal of some questions, only served to convince Jonas that what he had been reading in the Bible was true; Jesus is the Messiah. He also realized that in order to have his sins forgiven, and be assured a place in heaven, he must have a sacrifice for his sins. He knew in his heart, that Jesus was that sacrifice for sins. He must accept him as his Savior and Messiah!

Jonas was twenty-six years old, sitting in a noisy commuter train headed for Manhattan, on the day when he quietly bowed his head and asked Jesus to forgive his sins and be his Savior and Lord. Neither he nor the other commuters saw flashing lights or heard bells or sirens as Jonas silently uttered his prayer to God that day, but the angels of heaven were rejoicing. A new child had come into the family of God. The searching jeweler had found the greatest Jewel of them all—Yeshua, the Messiah. Jonas said he simply felt a quiet assurance of God's presence in his heart. He knew without a doubt that God was real and that Jesus was his Messiah!

God's love radiated from Jonas! The joy of knowing Jesus permeated his entire life. Soon even Rachel's heart softened and she, too, received Jesus as her Messiah and Savior.

Friends told Jonas about Rabbi Leopold Cohn and the Mission, and Jonas and Rachel began attending the services. Rabbi Cohn became Jonas' mentor, discipling him in the Scriptures. Jonas Cohen has the distinction of being the last Jewish man Rabbi Leopold Cohn baptized before his death. One week after Jonas was baptized, Rachel Cohen was baptized by Joseph Hoffman Cohen.

Soon after his baptism, Jonas felt God's call to ministry among his own people. To prepare himself, he enrolled in the Mission's Jewish Missionary Training Institute in New York. He was ordained by the United Christian Church in February, 1957.

Both Jonas and Rachel served as missionaries in the greater New York area. Rachel served in the Ladies' Auxiliary, while Jonas was involved in visitation and in representing the Mission through church speaking engagements.

After Rachel entered her Lord's presence in 1972, Jonas carried on as a Field Evangelist with the Mission in the New York area until his retirement in 1975. A native New Yorker from beginning to end, Jonas Cohen proved a strong "voice in the wilderness" to God's chosen people.

As he attempted to develop his "district" methodology of missionary work, Martin Rosen did his best integrate new staff members with veteran workers, and new methodology with old methodology. His hope was that through the training program, and through his own involvement in the ministry in New York, his vision for the district method of operation would become a reality. His efforts were not just thwarted by the resistance of the veteran missionaries on staff; his program was often circumvented by Daniel Fuchs himself. This was not done deliberately by Daniel, but in his own zeal to reach Jews with the Gospel, Daniel would often make commitments to people and to programs. Some of these commitments later caused difficulty with existing staff and programs.

As the General Secretary/Missionary Director of the Mission, Daniel Fuchs was able to appoint new missionaries as he felt the Lord was directing him. He was also able to exempt veteran missionaries, or new missionaries, from the training program if he chose to. And this he did!

David Juroe—His Story

One worker who was appointed by Daniel Fuchs during this period of time was David Juroe.

David was the son of Herman and Esther Juroe. (The reader may recall that Herman Juroe was hired by Joseph Cohn in 1936, to serve as a Field Evangelist in the state of Iowa. Herman died of a heart attack on October 2, 1938. Joseph Cohn sent Emil Gruen to Des Moines to replace Herman Juroe as Field Evangelist. See Chapter Six.)

After her husband's death, Esther Juroe was both mother and father to her three boys—James, Theodore and David. She also continued to faithfully serve as a missionary in Des Moines, Iowa until the Fall of 1953, when she and the boys moved to Rochester, New York. Even in Rochester, Esther continued as a missionary for the Mission until her retirement.

As the boys reached college age, the Mission helped with their educations through the Student Aid ministry (a small scholarship fund which the Mission established, and which still exists today to help Jewish believers, and the children of staff members, with their educations. It was hoped that through this assistance children of missionary workers, and other Jewish believers, would join the staff of the Mission upon completion of their educations. Some, like Daniel Fuchs, Hilda Koser, Martin Rosen, David Juroe, Albert Runge, Richard Cohen, et al, did join the Mission's staff). David expressed the gratitude of many of the students when he wrote:

> I cannot fully express my appreciation to the American Board of Missions to the Jews for its Student Aid Program, which so generously helped my seminary education. Without it I would have found it almost impossible during those difficult days to carry a full load of studies, and at the same time support my family. With the help of the Mission I was able to give adequate time to my studies while I saw others with similar problems obliged to drop out of school because of financial worries. I shall always give thanks to the Lord that the Mission stood by me in those days, and any success He may be pleased to give me in my ministry is without doubt due in part to the support and encouragement of our dear friends in the Mission of which I shall always feel I am a part.[22]

While he was attending seminary, David served as one of the leaders for the Mission's summer camp—Camp Hananeel.[23] He applied to the Mission just before completing his seminary training at Eastern Baptist Seminary in May 1955,[24] but it was several years before he actually came on staff. Instead, he went into the pastorate after his graduation from seminary. In 1961, he expressed interest in working with the Mission as a Field Evangelist,[25] but once again, things did not work out. It was not until 1963 that David joined the Mission's staff. At that time, the health of Mr. Sam Kalmus, the Mission's worker in Washington D.C., would no longer permit him to carry on the ministry, so Daniel asked the Board to appoint David Juroe as Missionary-in-Charge of that branch. The Minutes state:

> As this move will leave a vacancy in our Washington Branch, Mr. Fuchs proposed that we employ Rev. David Juroe as our missionary in that area. As Mr. Juroe is an experienced pastor, has worked for the American Board in the past, during the last few years had taught in our Jewish Missionary Institute. Mr. Fuchs proposed that he be engaged as an experienced worker, rather than at the salary of a beginner in the work.[26]

Because David had been involved in the work of the Mission from time to time over the years, Daniel evidently did not feel it was necessary for him to go through the training program which, at that time, Martin was handling and developing in Los Angeles.

Under David's capable leadership, the ministry in Washington D.C. flourished, but he only remained there for a couple of years before Daniel transferred him to New York to take over the Manhattan ministry. The May 1967 *Chosen People* magazine gave the following detailed account of the ministry in Manhattan under David's direction:

> Our Manhattan Branch, with the Rev. David J. Juroe as missionary-in-charge, offers a warm welcome to all who may enter its doors. Free counseling service to aid with the problems of both the seeker and the believer, financial aid to the needy, spiritual instruction from the Word of God, and fellowship which is sincere and real make our ministry a far-reaching one. Many Jews over the years have become 'trophies of grace' in Christ because of such personal and consistent ministry.
>
> The regular meetings of the home mission station of Beth Sar Shalom are as follows:
>
> (1) 3:45 p.m. service every Sunday of the year. This service provides much group participation with a hymn sing and then followed by a plain but dignified worship service.... Occasionally, this service is a public baptism, which is a highlight as Jews and Gentiles join in praise and encouragement of those who have made recent professions of faith. The second Sunday of each month is set apart as the Communion service....
>
> (2) 7 p.m. Wednesday Bible Study Hour. This meeting's purpose is to study in depth the Word of God to nourish and help the Jewish believers grow in the faith. This meeting is followed by refreshments in the social hall.
>
> (3) 2 p.m. each Thursday—Ladies Bible Class. This class is under the capable instruction of Miss Lola Weir. She reports that the class has shown steady growth.... Much stress is given to bringing Jewish friends and soul winning....
>
> (4) The first Saturday of each month at 2-6 p.m. is the Ladies Auxiliary and Men's Fellowship meeting. Mrs. Rachel Cohen is in charge.... This group was formed in the fall of 1960 by Mrs. Sarah Braunstein.... As time went on Mrs. Sarah Braunstein felt that this group was incomplete without the men,...So a men's fellowship was formed. The women meet in the Chapel and men on the third floor in the headquarters building. Our missionary, Miss Lola Weir, teaches God's Word to the women, and Resident Pastor, Mr. Juroe, teaches the men....
>
> There are other various functions throughout the year for our Jewish people to promote fellowship and provide an evangelistic opportunity. An annual Passover Service has been a tremendous ministry. Last year all the branches in the greater New York area cooperated and several were saved.
>
> An annual boat ride in June up the beautiful Hudson River to Bear Mountain has become a blessed experience. A whole day is devoted to this outing, and our people truly enjoy the fresh air away from the city.
>
> Recently an annual weekend retreat has been included in our expanding work. The purpose in this ministry is to concentrate on the believer's daily walk and has been a means of encouraging Jewish people in spiritual matters.
>
> Street meeting work in New York presents a great challenge. An expanded ministry in this area is anticipated. We hope to have nursery care for young children soon to make it possible for young mothers to receive instruction and help.
>
> 'Are Jews being won?' is a question we are frequently asked. Only recently an elderly woman over sixty stood up in one of our Wednesday Bible hours and gave her first testimony. It was a great thrill to hear her speak of the grace of God in her life and hear her say what Jesus had come to mean to her.[25]

When Daniel transferred Martin Rosen from Los Angeles to New York, and made him Missionary-in-Charge of the New York Headquarters District, David Juroe was placed in the position of either having to work under Martin's authority, and go through the training program along with other veteran missionaries, or resign. David felt led of the Lord to resign, and the Lord led him to another field of ministry.

RAYMOND COHEN—HIS STORY

Another worker hired who was not required to go through Martin's training program was Mr. Raymond Cohen. Daniel hired Raymond in January 1969, to serve as a missionary in Miami Beach, Florida.

Raymond Cohn came to know the Lord through unique circumstances. Both he and his wife Lee were born into Orthodox Jewish homes and, for the first twenty or so years of their lives, lived in the East Bronx area of New York. They were married in 1943, shortly after Ray's induction into the Army.

Ray was discharged from the Army in 1946, and they were able to get an apartment in Fox Hills, Staten Island. Ray and Lee had two small boys by that time—one was twenty-two months of age, the other was just nine months old.

One evening they noticed that something very wrong with the older boy; he was obviously bleeding internally. They rushed him to Mt. Sinai hospital, and the doctors informed them he was suffering from acute leukemia. They were stunned by the diagnosis, and they cried out to God for help. That night, Raymond was awakened out of a sound sleep by an audible voice telling him that his son would be alright. For reasons unclear to himself, Raymond sensed that the voice was the voice of Jesus. He new nothing of Jesus, nor had he ever associated with those who did, and he didn't know what to do or what to say. In his testimony about this experience Raymond said:

> ...I just told Lee that God had answered our prayer. I couldn't tell her it was Jesus who answered us; nor was I sure why, when I prayed to God, He answered us.
>
> The hospital called the next day and told us that our son did not have leukemia and asked could we please leave him for further observation. During the next four years my son underwent six life-and-death operations. The doctors had given up all hope for his life, but each time he would somehow pull through. The one thought in my mind was the voice of Jesus saying, 'Your son will be alright.' During the ten intervening years, we had relocated to the Pelham Parkway section of the Bronx and then to Norwalk, Connecticut. In Norwalk my wife met a Gentile woman who went out of her way to be friendly. This woman questioned my wife about the Passover holiday and when Lee told her all she knew about the holiday, the woman went on to tell Lee much more than she ever knew. Amazed at her knowledge and interest in Jewish things, Lee asked her where she had obtained her information. She replied, 'From your Jewish book, the Bible.' She invited us to attend a Bible study class in her home, and when Lee asked if I would go, I jumped at the opportunity. You see I had now carried about with me the burning questions, 'Who is Jesus?' and, 'What do I as Jew have to do with him?' This was ten years after the original incident of His answering our prayers.
>
> At the very first class, the Gospel of John was being studied, and after I read the first fourteen verses in Chapter 1, I knew who Jesus was. Quietly in my own heart as I sat on the couch, I said, 'My Lord and my God.' I had no idea what being 'saved' was all about, but that day I received Him as my own.
>
> There is much to recount from that time, but let me condense it for you. I read the Old Testament constantly and incessantly and could see Jesus on almost every page. My wife became extremely angry with me. Our sons were studying for Bar Mitzvah at the Orthodox synagogue; and, as she put it, if I wanted to be a 'goy' I should change my name and leave her and the children alone. We studied with the rabbi as well as continuing with the Bible class in the home of our Gentile friends. At Lee's request, we discontinued studies with the rabbi for she said that he just did not have the answers to her questions.
>
> We were then introduced to other Jewish believers through the American Board of Missions to the Jews. After attending the meetings at Joe and Clara Rubin's house, my wife received Jesus as her own. We were both baptized in Norwalk, Connecticut by the Pastor who taught the original Bible class I mentioned previously.
>
> For the past eleven years we have been actively engaged in witnessing, in teaching, in preaching for Jesus. My son is now 25 years old and has a wonderful wife. Both are believers in Jesus. My other boy, now 24 years old and also a believer, has also found himself a young lady with whom he wants to share the rest of his life. She became a believer this past December.
>
> Last April, Lee and I decided we wanted to work for Jesus all the time, and so I left my position as planning manager with the Burndy Corporation and she her position as security secretary with the Perkin Elmer Corporation. Do we regret it? Not on your life! Jesus is the sweetest name we know. We now know why we are Jews. We now know how our heritage as Jews is completely fulfilled in Him. We have been completed. It is much better to be complete than incomplete, wouldn't you say so?[28]

Because Raymond was not required to go through Martin's training program (which was being carried on in New York at the time Raymond was hired), and because Daniel did not confer with Martin prior to hiring Raymond for the position in Miami Beach, Florida, the position for a missionary in Miami was duplicated. Martin had already trained Rev. Martin Klayman to develop the Mission's work in Miami. In fact, the Mission had purchased a new building, located at 16001 North East 18th Avenue, North Miami Beach, for the Klayman's ministry there. Mrs. Esther Bronstein, the widow of the founder of Aedus Center in Chicago (the ministry with which the Mission had merged—See Chapter 10) had given $9,000.00 toward the furnishings and equipment for the new Miami branch.[29]

Martin Klayman—His Story

Martin Klayman was born to an orthodox Jewish family in Brooklyn, New York. When he was growing up, if the children in the family even uttered the name of 'Jesus' they had their mouths washed out with soap.

> ...For Martin Klayman the word Jesus took on a new meaning when he was nineteen and wandered into an evangelistic tent meeting in the mistaken belief that he was going to a circus.
>
> Up to that hot August evening in 1935, he said that he felt a hollowness in traditional Judaism. 'There were many questions in my life and the rabbis couldn't give me answers. Where did I come from? Why was I here? Where am I

going? I was very conscious that I was a sinner. I had a feeling of guilt all the time. On the Day of Atonement, I'd fast, and then ask my father, "Are my sins forgiven?" All he said was, "Who knows?"...'

That evening in 1935 as he was riding his bicycle home from work, he stopped by what he thought was a circus tent. 'A man in a beautiful white suit greeted me at the entrance. He asked me if I was a Hebrew and I said I was. He almost shouted, "Praise the Lord, my Saviour was a Hebrew!" Then, in spite of his beautiful white suit, and although I was covered with perspiration, he threw his arms around me and hugged me. He told me he loved me, and this came as a big surprise. My parents had come from Poland, and there they had learned that Jews were hated by so-called Christians.'

The gentleman told Martin that the tent held a meeting, not a circus, and he invited the young man to come in. The music and hymns appealed to Martin and the message told the spiritual significance of the story of Abraham in the Bible.

At home, Martin Klayman did some soul-searching and some Bible searching. The next night he was back at the meeting and sat down in front. 'All my life I had believed there would be a personal Messiah,' Mr. Klayman said. 'I did not realize until August 1935, who the Messiah is, and that his name is Jesus. He came in fulfillment of all the Old Testament prophecies. It amazed me how the life of Jesus dovetailed with the prophecies of the Old Testament. When the second meeting was over, I indicated to the preacher that I wanted to commit my life to Jesus Christ.'[30]

It was Daniel's hope that the Klaymans and the Cohens could work together in building the ministry in Florida, but the Klaymans, who had gone through the Mission's "official" training program with Martin Rosen, thought they were in charge of the ministry, and the Cohens, who had been trained by Clara Rubin and hired by Daniel Fuchs, thought they were in charge. It soon became apparent that the two missionaries, trained to use different methodology, and reporting to two separate bosses, would not be able to work together. Daniel therefore left the Klaymans to develop the work in Miami, and he transferred the Cohens to Hollywood, Florida to begin a new ministry there. Raymond gave the following report to the readers of *The Chosen People* magazine:

On September 4, 1971 the Beth Sar Shalom Center of Hollywood, Florida opened for business—the Lord's business....

For some months my wife and I had been praying for the Lord to expand our ministry. Specifically we were praying that He would supply a meeting place for us, one that was strategically located in a Jewish community. Up to this point the Bible meetings were being held in our home; and although the attendance was good, we knew that unless we had a better outreach to our Jewish people, the work would not grow....

It wasn't too long when a new couple joined our Tuesday night Bible study. Mr. and Mrs. R. told us they had many Jewish friends and a home located in a predominantly Jewish area of Hollywood. After several weeks of attending our Bible study, they suggested that their home be used for meetings in the fall.[31]

During the months when the meetings were held in the home of Mr. and Mrs. R., members of the Bible study group looked for a building to lease, and they started a fund for the furnishings and equipment for a new facility once one was found. When a suitable building was located, they leased it immediately.

Raymond kept the ministry staffed through volunteer workers, and the new branch began to attract more and more Jewish people. Both the ministry of the Cohens in Hollywood, Florida and the ministry of the Klaymans in Miami were enjoying God's blessings. During the summer of 1972, however, Raymond Cohen felt led of the Lord to resign from the Mission. He subsequently established the branch in Hollywood as an independent missionary work to the Jewish people.

CHANGES ON THE HORIZON

Other workers, too, were exempted by Daniel Fuchs from participating in the Mission's training program in New York. Larry Jaffrey was excused on the basis that he had participated in the Summer Intern Program in Los Angeles before joining the Mission's staff. Terryl Delaney needed Larry Jaffrey to help him develop the ministry in Philadelphia. Robert (Bob) Gross attended the training program, but in his reports back to Terryl Delaney and to Daniel Fuchs, he stated that the program was not helping him so, over Martin's objections, he was excused from the training program and he, too, was hired to work with Terryl Delaney in the Philadelphia branch. The fact that Terryl did not send Larry Jaffrey through Martin's training program, and the fact that Robert Gross was feeding back mostly negative reports about the training program to Terryl, caused dissention between Terryl and Martin Rosen. Further, as Terryl shared information from Robert's reports with Daniel, Daniel's confidence in Martin's training program began to diminish.

Daniel Fuchs reasons for exempting some workers from the Missionary Training Program were not shared with the author, but it was known that he was a missionary at heart, and that he did not like personal confrontation between workers. If he saw potential in a prospective worker, and if he felt he might lose that individual by following established protocol, he was willing to by-pass some of the established channels to retain the prospective worker. Unfortunately, more often than not, by not following the established policy the worker was usually lost to the Mission anyway.

The hurdles of getting beyond the resentment of the veteran missionaries of New York, and of dealing with the over-lapping of Martin's ministry and Daniel Fuchs' involvement with missionary personnel were difficult and complex issues to overcome. But there was more. Rumor and innuendo began to sweep through the Mission about Martin's treatment of some of the Mission personnel in New York, and of the missionary candidates in particular.

Rosen had a vision for the Mission; he had a goal. With his appointment to the position of Director of Missionary Training, he believed he had a mandate from Daniel Fuchs, and from the Board, to fulfill that goal. But every time he tried to take steps toward meeting his goal, he ran into opposition. It came from every direction—from veteran missionaries, from new missionaries, from established policy (written and unwritten), and from his superiors in the Mission.

The biggest obstacles Martin faced was a lack of allocation of funds for his programs. As has already been discussed, after the death of Joseph Hoffman Cohn, the Board made a conscious decision to spend down the reserve fund of the Mission. By the time of Martin's move to New York this policy had been in force for fourteen years—years of rapid expansion without the benefit of programs and policies to ensure that the expenses of the new projects and personnel were adequately covered. During this same period of rapid expansion, several new Directors were added to the Board— most of whom knew nothing about Joseph Cohn or of his policies and vision for the Mission. They were men who knew Daniel Fuchs, or Harold Pretlove, or other members of the Board—fine Christian men who loved the Jewish people and desired them to come to faith in Yeshua.

Mr. Isaac James Leonard, a Christian businessman from Philadelphia was elected to the Board in March 1962. In 1964 Mr. Louis W. Ivins, a retired navy man, and Mr. John J. Kubach were elected to the Board. John was a close friend of Harold Pretlove. At the time of his election to the Board, John was Vice President of the Bankers Trust Company in New York City. In 1971 he retired from Bankers Trust and became Vice President and representative for the National Westminster Bank—the New York Branch of National Westminster Bank Ltd., London. Mr. Ivins retired from the Board in January 1981 and served as Director Emeritus until he went to be with the Lord. Mr. Kubach is now retired from his professional career, but he continues to serve on the Board of the Mission and on the Finance Committee of the Board.

During the summer of 1967, Mr. James W. Straub was elected to the Board. James is a graduate of New York University, and at the time of his election to the Board he was Vice President and director of the management consultant firm of Garnett, Stixrood, Straub, & Associates of New York. During his years of involvement with the Mission, Jim did consulting work for the Mission. In 1979 he became the Executive Vice President of the Mission—a position he filled until his retirement in May 1983. Mr. Straub remains an active member of the Board and he serves on the Finance Committee of the Board.

In April 1968, Harold B. Pretlove's declining health resulted in his resignation from his position as Executive Secretary of the Mission. He retired from active administration of the Mission, but he remained a member of the Board of Directors.[32] Many of the workers of the Mission presumed that Daniel Fuchs would step in to assume Pretlove's position and title, and that Martin Rosen would become the new Missionary Secretary, replacing Daniel Fuchs in that position. They further presumed that such a scenario would eventually place Martin in line for the position of President, or Executive Director, of the Mission. But instead, Daniel Fuchs took Pretlove's position and he took the title of General Secretary. He then surprised everyone by appointing Dr. Henry Heydt as Missionary Liaison Director—leaving Martin Rosen in his same position as Director of Missionary Training and Recruiting.

The move was like a slap in the face to Martin. By appointing Henry Heydt Missionary Liaison Director, Daniel was sending a clear signal to all of the workers on staff, and also to Martin, that he had no intention of making Martin his immediate successor in the work. To the veteran missionaries and Field Evangelists on staff who had been reporting directly to Daniel Fuchs, the message was an encouragement. But to workers who had been trained by Martin, and who reported to him (and even to a few of the veteran missionaries on staff), Daniel's message was a disappointment. Once again, division developed among staff members as they voiced their loyalties and their opinions as to who should run the Mission—Martin Rosen or Daniel Fuchs. But among the Directors there was no question about who should run the Mission. Daniel Fuchs was definitely in charge!

A major factor in Daniel's decision to create the new position of Missionary Liaison Director, and to give that position to Henry Heydt, was that in doing so the "troika" leadership was reduced to "dual" leadership. But of the two remaining leaders, he was the only man who was also a Board member, and thus his was the more powerful position. His decision placed him in a position where he would be able to set the vision for the Mission.

Focus of the Mission Program Changing

Daniel had first become enamored with the possibility of reaching masses of Jewish people when the Mission opened its booth at the New York World's Fair. Even before the era of television, he had been impressed with the reaction of Christians to the Passover demonstrations and to film strips like "I Found My Messiah," the story of a Jewish war veteran who came to faith in Yeshua. Daniel was a missionary at heart; he wanted Jewish people to hear the Gospel. If the use of film strips and media could enlarge the Mission's outreach, he was all for it. In April 1968, less than one year after transferring Martin Rosen to New York, Daniel proposed that funds be allocated to produce film strips which could be used to educate the Christian public. The Minutes state:

> For many years we have been using the film 'I Found My Messiah' for showing in the churches and adding to our ability to meet requests for presenting our work. This has helped stretch out the staff and make it possible to go to more churches. Mr. Fuchs presented a new idea which he has worked out for the use of film strips which tell of the Christian emphasis of the Passover which could be sold to the church for presentation in their evening services, Sunday schools, missionary societies, etc. This packet would consist of 54 film strips, a 12-1/2 inch record telling the story of the strips and a booklet which explains this story. It would cost about $4700 to produce 1000 of these packets. Mr. Fuchs moved and Mr. Kubach seconded the motion that $5000 be appropriated for preparation of film strips, records and books explaining the Passover Service. It was voted.[33]

The filmstrips were produced, but were never used as Daniel had envisioned because of the problem of finding and using filmstrip projectors. Eventually the filmstrips were sold.

Martin, too, was intrigued with the use of media. He, too, wanted Jewish people to hear the Gospel. But he was committed to communicating the Gospel *personally*, through direct witness, using missionary staff. Each man's vision of *how* the Gospel was going to be presented to the Jewish community was different. But Daniel's decision to eliminate the position of Missionary Director clearly placed him in a position to set the vision.

Terryl Delaney's opportunity to present the "Christ in the Passover" on television through Calvary Temple in Denver, Colorado once again intensified Daniel's desire to use the media as a means of sharing the Gospel with Jewish people. He therefore approached the Board with a new idea. The Minutes state:

> Two years ago Terry Delaney put on a television program of the Passover in Denver and it is believed that at least 10% of the Jewish people in Denver saw this program. The effect of the Passover presentation is tremendous. It is a good public relations vehicle and a good Gospel presentation. Mr. Fuchs said that he would like to have a professional television program made presenting the Passover and also a 16mm film to be shown by our field men on their projectors. At the Conference on Evangelism in Minneapolis, Mr. Fuchs talked with Paul Webb about the possibility of doing this and found that it would cost about $8600 to produce the film for television and if advertised in the Los Angeles area the cost would be $3500.
>
> After discussion, Mr. Ivins moved and Mr. Campbell seconded the motion that $12,000 be appropriated for the production of this television program and advertising it in the Los Angeles area. This is to be done in time for presentation during the Passover season in 1970. It was voted.[34]

MEDIA A PRIORITY

The focus of the Mission was slowly being turned away from the training of missionaries for the establishment of branch ministries to "media evangelism." As large amounts of money were being appropriated for the media projects, it became clear that funding was not available for the training program or for the future hiring of personnel, yet Martin was encouraged to look for larger quarters where he could train new missionary recruits. Martin could have developed a media program as a part of the overall training program, which could then have been integrated into the existing mission programs, but instead of involving him, Daniel turned to Terryl Delaney to develop a media program for the Mission.

While preparations were being made to make the Passover telecast, consideration was being given to moving the Missionary Training Program out of the Headquarters building in Manhattan to larger quarters. Property was located in Stony Point, New York, but the zoning board of Stony Point would not give the Mission a use permit.[35] Property was then located in Nyack, New York but once again the sale fell through.[36] By February, 1970 Daniel gave the following report of God's provision for the training program:

> During the past year our Board has considered the growing needs of the Mission. We have needed additional quarters, especially because of the training program. It is almost impossible to find suitable living quarters in the New York Metropolitan area without paying exorbitant rentals. We entered into a contract of sale for a building in Stony Point,

New York. However, no matter how we tried we couldn't please the officials. Since we didn't want to go to court, this door was closed. Then the fires in our Brooklyn buildings made it imperative that we get new space to provide storage for our growing literature ministry. We learned that a Carmelite Novitiate, which was already zoned for our purposes, was on the market in Nyack, New York. The asking price was $175,000. Several members of the Board of Directors, as busy as they are, gave up a week-end day and drove to Nyack where the premises were carefully examined and evaluated. Even though it was a good buy, it was a great deal of money, and the Board of Directors instructed me to see if some other place was available....

I spoke to our Rev. Daniel Rigney, ...and told him to be in touch with Mr. Rosen, our director of missionary training, to look further for a suitable place. I outlined an acceptable area to him 'as far south as Perth Amboy, New Jersey, and also Staten Island.'

The following Thursday afternoon Mr. John Camp, owner of radio station WPOW Inc.,...had for sometime wanted to see the Mission, [and] he took this opportunity to visit us.... Mr. Rigney took Mr. Camp through the building. As Mr. Rigney showed him the crowded quarters of our printing and mailing department, and the missionary training department, he told of our search for additional quarters. 'Why don't you use our building?' asked Mr. Camp. 'Station WPOW is located on 11 acres in Staten Island. On its facility there is a ten-bedroom house which we cannot sell or use.' When asked about rental, he replied, 'Just maintain the building and pay the taxes!'[37]

A Trip to Japan/A Change of Direction

Several months prior to this answer to prayer, during the Spring of 1969, while preparations were being made for the Passover telecast, and while the search for a suitable building for the training program was going on, Daniel made a trip to Japan. A group of Japanese believers who loved Israel and the Jewish people had written to him, inviting him to come to Japan to tell them about the Mission and its program. The trip impacted Daniel, and ultimately the Mission, in ways he never dreamed it would when he accepted the invitation.

When Daniel arrived in Japan he found the group of Japanese believers to be very unique. Some of them were thinking about immigrating to Israel; some were thinking about entering the Mission's training program. They called themselves a "tabernacle" movement. They informed Daniel that they did not believe in owning property because owning buildings and properties tied one down to a specific area and methodology and they believed the message of the Gospel was to "go!" As Daniel listened, he reflected on his own ministry. Since the death of Joseph Hoffman Cohn, he and Harold Pretlove had been responsible for purchasing over sixteen mission properties, and he had been contemplating purchasing more. Then and there he became convinced that his Japanese friends were right, and he decided to change the Mission's policy. The impact of Daniel's trip to Japan was spelled out at the November 1970 Board meeting, when he presented the following missionary policy:

Effective immediately we will change the directions of our ministry from being station-centered to people oriented. We will concentrate our ministry where the most people will be reached rather than the building up of centers. This will include ministries such as the Telecast, calendars, literature distribution, Israel radio, etc. In this way we will be able to do more work with less staff. We will also seek to use facilities which will be readily available to us, rather than the purchase of real estate for our own use. These facilities can be homes of Christians who will open their doors for Bible study, etc., various recreation halls, youth fellowship buildings, etc., the main difference is that we are to consider each mission station to be the means rather than the end to the means. Each mission station should be a 'beachhead' from which the Gospel will be proclaimed to the Jews throughout the area of the station. Formerly we have been preaching the gospel of 'come' but as far as our program is concerned, we have God's commission to 'go.'

Mr. Pretlove moved and Mr. Straub seconded the motion that the policy as outlined above be adopted. It was voted.[38]

When Daniel's new missionary policy was announced it hit the staff like a "bombshell." They couldn't believe what they were hearing. The Mission had *always* used a center approach; it had always provided an environment where Jewish people would feel welcome; it had developed programs where Jewish people could hear the Gospel and be stimulated in their spiritual growth. The Mission had *always* purchased property—out of necessity, because experience had taught that it was almost impossible to find suitable buildings owned by individuals who were willing to lease to a "Jewish Mission."

Daniel's new missionary policy further separated his vision for the ministry from Martin's vision, and from the Missionary Training Program he was developing—the program Daniel had so enthusiastically embraced a few years earlier. To many on staff, Daniel's new missionary policy seemed to be further evidence of the strained relationship that was developing between himself and Rosen.

THE PASSOVER TELECAST

Daniel's vision for using the media for "mass evangelism" was carried out by those of us who were involved in making the plans and preparation for the Passover telecast that was to be aired in the Los Angeles area. Terryl Delaney and the author met with writers, ad-men, artists, and executives of the Paul Webb agency in Los Angeles. The script was written and approved; the art work was completed. The Los Angeles staff compiled a list of over 50,000 Jewish families in the greater Los Angeles area, and 50,000 flyers advertising the Passover telecast were hand-addressed by volunteers from hundreds of churches in the area and then sent to Jewish people, encouraging them to watch the telecast. Additionally, a telephone calling team was organized, and over 30,000 telephone calls were made to Jewish homes, inviting the occupants to watch the special Passover telecast. Ads were placed in local newspapers, and space was reserved in the TV guide for the week of April 13th, 1970.

Many of the rabbis thought the Passover presentation was being put on by the Jewish community, and they encouraged members of their congregations to watch the telecast—and they did! A "trailer" was affixed to the end of the telecast with a special "write in offer." A special post office box number was rented so the Mission could determine the actual response to the telecast. And after the airing of the telecast a telephone survey was done to determine how large an audience the program had actually reached. Rita Klein, a Jewish believer and news correspondent, wrote for *The Chosen People* magazine:

> *...Last April, [April 13, 1970], enormous strides were made in the field of televised outreach to the Jews. The American Board of Missions to the Jews presented 'The Passover,' a television show which was seen by almost eighteen percent of the Jewish population in the city of Los Angeles alone, not to mention outlying areas which were reached by the station's broadcasting range. The response within the Jewish community has far surpassed the expectations of all concerned with presenting the program!*
>
> *Channel 5, KTLA in Los Angeles, aired the show during prime time television viewing time. KTLA broadcasts as far east as west Texas and throughout the states of Arizona and New Mexico.*
>
> *...'The Passover' was probably one of the most carefully organized, meticulously documented religious shows ever televised. More hours went into preparation for feedback on the show than on the actual production and presentation of the telecast itself.*
>
> *The show was unique in that, unlike many Christian evangelistic films and television programs, all the actors and staff who worked on the show were Christians, including the two children who took part in the televised Passover celebration. The members of the television 'family' who participated in the Passover service all attend Beth Sar Shalom in Los Angeles. It was an exciting venture which used Hebrew Christians to witness to their Jewish brethren.*
>
> *...It was truly an enormous step in the direction of mass evangelism for Christ. Letters poured in asking for the free booklet offered at the end of the program: 'Israel: A Modern Miracle.' Letters from Orthodox, Conservative, and Reform Jews praised the program and showed their enthusiasm for this new link between Judaism and Christianity. Many Christians wrote asking how they could help in future productions. Harold Sevener, missionary in charge of Beth Sar Shalom, stated, 'we were completely overwhelmed by the response to the television broadcast. The Lord blessed above and beyond all we could ask or think. We are still receiving requests from Jewish people for the booklet and tract materials [over 5,000 letters were received within the first week, after the broadcast]. Words of appreciation are now coming in from those who have received our literature. Requests for counseling, visits, and general interest in the claims of Christ are keeping our staff busy. We know and expect a great harvest of souls for our Lord. We have sown the Seed, and through the ministry of prayer it is being watered. Now we are thrusting reapers into the harvest.'* [39]

Daniel Fuchs was ecstatic about the results of the Passover telecast, and immediately began making plans for a nation-wide airing of the program in 1971. In his January 1971 salutation, he wrote:

...This year, by God's grace, our goal is to reach at least one million Jewish people as well as several million Gentiles with our Passover telecast. Last April we were astounded by the results of this telecast in Los Angeles. It was not just a 'shot in the arm' ministry; it resulted in crowds coming to our Los Angeles Branch for the Holy Days. We are still receiving mail about the literature we gave out and the calendars which were sent. Over 100,000 Jewish people viewed the telecast, and there were over 5,000 requests for literature. This year we are scheduling the telecast not only for Los Angeles but also for New York, Dallas, Denver, Miami, Minneapolis, Chicago, Philadelphia, Pittsburgh, and Washington D.C. These cities are where we have our own staff of missionaries for the necessary organization, preparation, mailing and follow-up. Already they are working on this tremendous task. There are several more cities in the United States where other Jewish missions may be able to take advantage of our offer for them to use this telecast. These include Boston, Detroit, and St. Louis. Besides this, the telecast will be shown in five of the largest cities in Australia under the auspices of The Jewish Evangelical Witness.[40]

STAFF CHANGES ADD TO TENSION

Even before the first airing of the Passover telecast in Los Angeles, as early as September 1969, Daniel was considering transferring Terryl Delaney from Denver, Colorado to Cherry Hill, New Jersey. The Minutes show the following:

Our missionary in Philadelphia, Mr. Harry Burgen, has grown old in service and is still carrying on a 'storefront ministry.' With the retirement of Mr. Walz in Camden it will be necessary to make plans for the development of our work in the Philadelphia-Camden area. Mr. Fuchs reported that he is seeking a younger man to be the area director and has contacted R. Terry Delaney of our Denver area regarding this. The work at 717 Walnut Street would be carried on as long as Mr. Burgen is able. It was the consensus that the reorganization of the Philadelphia area was within the powers given to the general secretary and no Board action was necessary.[41]

With the Board's approval to proceed, Daniel executed the transfer of Terryl to Cherry Hill, New Jersey. Terryl was made Area Director for the ministry in Philadelphia and New Jersey. Larry Jaffrey was transferred as well, to serve as Terryl's assistant. Daniel hired Mr. Elias (Eddy) Hildago for the Mission's work in Denver. The Mission also agreed to purchase the Delaney's home in Denver, for use as the Mission's branch.[42]

The transfer of Terryl Delaney to the Philadelphia area accomplished two purposes on Daniel's agenda: It allowed for the reorganization and expansion of the work in Philadelphia, and it brought Terryl closer to the New York area where he could be used to further develop the media work for the Mission. Terryl had taken classes in communications at the University of Colorado Graduate School of Communications. In Philadelphia he continued classroom work in communications at the Charles Morris Price School of Advertising and Journalism.

During this time, Daniel was grooming Terryl to become the Mission's Director of Communications, and he began turning over all of the Mission's magazine advertising to Terryl. Terryl also began to develop a new format for the radio ministry, using Dr. Charles Feinberg, *et al*, instead of just repeating the old tapes of Joseph Hoffman Cohn. The only communication vehicle in the Mission that Daniel did not turn over to Terryl was *The Chosen People* magazine and the direct mail contact with the donors of the Mission.

PLANS TO TRANSFER ROSEN

In the early 1970's, while Terryl and his family were settling into their new community of Cherry Hill, New Jersey, Daniel was making plans to move Rosen out of New York. The author and his staff in Los Angeles were "snowed under" in preparations for the April 1970 Passover telecast which was being aired in Los Angeles, when he began receiving telephone calls from Daniel Fuchs and Martin Rosen. Daniel felt he could no longer have Martin working in New York, and he wanted to fire him. Martin called, too, telling the author of the problems between himself and Daniel Fuchs. Martin also reminded the author of the promise we'd agreed to prior to his move to New York—the promise that if things became too difficult for him in New York, the author would let him return to Northern California to develop that area as a separate district.

As has been stated, Martin Rosen was an astute, imaginative, and very effective missionary. It was the author's conviction that it would be the Mission's loss if he were fired. In a telephone conversation with Daniel, the author shared his feelings with Daniel, and told him of my agreement with Martin before he embarked upon his move to New York. Daniel listened and finally said, "I'll agree to transfer Martin to San Francisco. However, I will not allow him to develop a separate region. He will have to work under your supervision. If you want him to stay in the Mission, that's the way it will have to be."

In sharing Daniel's response with Martin, a lengthy discussion ensued as to how things could be worked out. Both Martin and the author agreed that it would be best for him to remain with the Mission and move to San Francisco, rather than to leave the Mission. Daniel was informed of Martin's decision to remain with the Mission, and the necessary arrangements for Martin's transfer to San Francisco were made.

A CHANGE OF DIRECTION FOR ROSEN

Months earlier, as Daniel had focused on using the media approach of evangelism and had distanced himself from Martin and his training program, Martin had begun to question his move to New York, his position, and his ministry. Then his mother died. This prompted additional confusion in his mind. He later wrote:

One bombshell was my mother's death. She had never approved of my Christian commitment and rarely pulled any punches in conveying her disappointment. One day when we were riding past a Denver church in which I was scheduled to speak, I pointed out my name, posted in large letters on the bulletin board. She shook her head and said, 'It's like you stuck a knife through my heart.'

But despite our religious differences, we always loved each other and shared our common heritage with great relish. When she passed away, I felt that a part of me, a part of my own culture and history, had gone with her. I also realized I had been failing to develop my own personal identity as a Jew. I had been relying too much on memories of the past rather than continuing my family's vital Jewish traditions in my daily life.[43]

It was then that Martin began asking God to direct him—to help him find himself, and to show him what to do with his life. God answered those prayers in a most unexpected way. He was invited to speak at an Intervarsity Christian Fellowship meeting at Columbia University. He later wrote:

The hippie movement, antiwar protest, and general disenchantment of young people with the establishment were gaining momentum before I reached New York City. But, virtually oblivious to the social storm that was swirling about in the streets, I shut my office door and settled snugly into my new administrative role [at the Mission]....

My topic was 'Hippies, Radicals, and Revolutionaries,' and my approach was to make fun of them. As a rather narrow-minded organization man, I had little patience with anyone who rejected the old American work ethic and ran off into the hills to contemplate the flowers and the sky and strum a guitar all day long. I got a laugh at one point when I quoted Ronald Reagan's quip, 'A hippie is someone who dresses like Tarzan, walks like Jane, smells like Cheetah, says, "Make love, not war," but is incapable of doing either.'[44]

After the meeting, a friend of Martin's (and later a friend of the author), Bob Berk, told Martin how unhappy he was with his comments. Then he challenged Martin to get out of his ivory tower, and go into the streets and meet some of the hippies for himself. Bob Berk, a Jewish believer himself, was a social worker who lived and worked among the street people of New York. He also reminded Martin that a very large percentage of the "hippies" were Jewish.

Martin tried to forget Bob's reprimand, but he couldn't so he decided to take Bob's advice and go into the streets to meet and talk with street people. He soon learned they could not be approached by a person wearing a three-piece business suit, so he abandoned his "institutional" look. To his astonishment, he discovered that Bob Berk had been correct. Many of the hippies were Jewish and, surprisingly, many were looking for the truth about God, for answers to the mysteries of life, and for true peace!

REACHING OUT WITH BROADSIDES

Martin's heart was touched with the *need*, but he did not know how to reach this indigent segment of the population. The Mission's literature had always been written to appeal to the "scholarly" Jew, to the "Yiddish-speaking Jew" or to the "average" Jew, but never had its literature been targeted to the "Jewish hippie." Martin believed if he could reach Jewish hippies, and if enough of them accepted Yeshua, the whole field of Jewish missions and evangelism could be changed. In an effort to find ways to communicate with the street people, he called on his friend, Bob Berk. Recounting the event, Martin stated:

...I told Bob Berk about my problem one day, and he said, 'Don't be lazy, Moishe. You should write your own stuff. Tailor it to these people and the way they think. You can't be some kind of distant intellectual. That approach to Jewish hippies—any hippies, for that matter—is all wrong. You have to show them you really care.'

I scrawled out a simple homemade tract in my own hand on a single sheet of paper and experimented until I found an effective way to fold it. The tile was 'A Message From Squares,' and I drew a simple, obese figure of myself on the front. The hip jargon is dated now, but I found it got the message across:

Hey, you with the beard!

We think you are Beautiful.

God likes long hair and beards, too.

He didn't want the Israelites to trim their beards.

Can you just imagine Moses or Elijah with a crew cut?

You are brave to do your own thing.

Most of us don't have the heart to make the scene.

...We both want love but we settle for either sex or sermons. All want life. Most get a kind of living death called existence.

We try to be the saviours of the world, and we just end up sinning against those we want to save.

Maybe Jesus, the real Saviour, can save us, give us peace and help us come alive, to live and love…

> Then I quoted John 3:16.

> I signed my name and put my office address underneath. Although this little composition was not the greatest work of literature, I felt every word of it. I had no way of knowing this tract would be a forerunner of the later Jews-for-Jesus 'broadsides,' which we've distributed in the millions. I just wanted to communicate to these young people, and many of them sensed my genuine concern. I identified myself with the establishment, but I let them know I wanted to listen to them, too. Handing out a few of these around the Village helped start some conversations I'd never have dreamed possible a month before: 'Hey, man, this is way out!' I essentially have a middle-class outlook on life, but I've always believed in a revolutionary Christianity. And that belief was now motivating me to crack the stagnant mold I had constructed for myself. I began to keep my office door open, and I told our receptionist to send up any hippies who wandered in off the street.

> A major change was occurring in my approach to people: One year before, if a bearded kid wearing sandals had asked for me, he'd never have made it through the first layer of defenses I had set up to protect myself. Now, there was a steady stream of street people going in and out of my office. Some days, I'd end up with wall-to-wall hippies. They'd walk up to the receptionist and ask, 'Hey, man, does Moishe Rosen live here?' and she would send them up.[45]

The continuous entourage of "hippies" parading through the Headquarters building in Manhattan was disconcerting to some of the staff, as well as to some individuals who attended services there. Martin and "his hippies" became a source of controversy and conflict. Martin had found his "Message From Squares" tract to be very effective, and he wanted the Mission to print more of the "broadsides" for hippies and street-people. But the Editorial Committee felt the "broadside" tracts were incompatible with the other types of literature that the Mission was producing. They did allowed Martin to have broadsides printed "outside" the Mission, but they refused to print them as "official" literature of the Mission.

In one of the author's telephone conversations with Martin during the early months of 1970, as we discussed the possibility of his transfer to San Francisco, Martin spoke of his desire to reach that city's swelling population of street people and hippies. The author recalls saying to him, "Martin, you are almost forty years old. How can you expect to reach these Jewish street people with the Gospel? You have no experience in this area. Do you plan to become a forty-year-old hippie?" To which he responded that if given a chance, he could and *would* reach them. He stated that if the Mission would give him the chance, he would prove me wrong. And prove me wrong he did! There is nothing Martin Rosen likes better than a good challenge!

MOVING TO SAN FRANCISCO

After receiving approval to move to San Francisco, the Rosen family once again packed their belongings and headed to the West coast. Of that experience, and the thoughts he had about what was ahead for him, Martin later wrote:

> …So he [Daniel Fuchs] allowed me to resign my double role as missionary in charge [of the New York District] and as director of recruiting and gave me two of the mission's cars. In the summer of 1970, accompanied by eight females— my wife, two daughters, and five other girls who had either worked for the American Board or held other jobs in New York—I headed west. Even the family dog came along. I had a general idea that I wanted to continue to spread the gospel to Jews and also that I wanted to get involved with the youth culture. Beyond that, I didn't know what I was doing. I suspected that some of the evangelism techniques I had developed would be applicable to my new ministry, but I was also certain that I'd have a lot of learning to do.[46]

Martin and his family settled in Corte Madera, California (although *The Chosen People* magazine listed him as Missionary-in-Charge of San Francisco). For the next three years, he and his small band of helpers (including his wife and two daughters) worked among the street people of the San Francisco Bay area. He changed his name to "Moishe" Rosen, and he challenged the establishment, the Jewish community, the Christian community, and the Mission itself, as he learned to do "confrontational ministry" (for the Gospel's sake) on the streets of San Francisco. The author often witnessed his technique. He became an expert at setting up confrontation between others and his group—"Jews for Jesus" as they soon became known. Moishe always saw to it that the media was aware of "probable confrontation" and, more often than not, the evening news would pick up the story. Then the newspapers would print the story. As happens so often with media reports, the facts were frequently distorted. In the reports it often appeared that there were hundreds of Jews for Jesus involved, when in fact there was only a handful. Moishe had learned the secret of making the media work for him. In one report, he shared how the demonstrations began:

> The topless-bottomless craze featuring naked dancers began at North Beach in San Francisco.... Multitudes crowd the sidewalks as barkers try to entice people to come inside.
>
> San Francisco is filled with lonely people. Many of them gravitate toward North Beach, not so much because they welcome this kind of involvement, but rather because they want to be with a crowd. If the crowd does not give meaningful relationships, at least the clamor and sound and sights seem to insulate one from the realization of loneliness. The flashing bright neon lights seem to anesthetize the person against the throbbing loneliness of a life without Christ.
>
> It would have been difficult to conduct an ordinary type of outdoor meeting at North Beach. The hoarse voices of the barkers would interfere with the Gospel invitation, and the shoving crowd would make it difficult for anyone to stand in a place long enough to hear the Word of God proclaimed.
>
> Some of the Christians from the Christian World Liberation Front and the Jesus Mobilization Committee of Marin came up with a unique idea. They suggested that we conduct a demonstration, not merely to protest the sin of North Beach, but to attest the Lordship of Jesus Christ. There was immediate agreement. We felt that it was the leading of the Holy Spirit.
>
> Our group made up approximately fifty placards. On many of the placards we had a slogan, 'Jews for Jesus.' On the other side of the placards we used slogans such as: 'Sin is sickening, Jesus heals'; 'Jesus gives a more abundant life'; 'Smut is a rut, Jesus is our groove'; 'Jesus liberates women'; 'Love not lust'; etc.
>
> At the first demonstration two hundred young people appeared on the street, even though it was Saturday night and the busiest evening of the week. Their appearance was not lost in the crowds as they held their placards high, sang Gospel songs, chanted the slogans. At first the operators of the topless establishments mocked and ridiculed and made jokes. As the evening wore on and it was apparent that the demonstration was here to stay, their faces lost the sneers and smirks and they began to look worried and angry.
>
> There were many young people who were not carrying placards but were standing on the street corners with specially prepared Gospel tracts. They witnessed as to how the only real satisfaction in life could come through Jesus. That evening several young people chose to receive Christ as their Savior.
>
> Many of the usual patrons of these bars were shamed away and the owners agreed that what we were doing was bad for their business. We pointed out to many of the Jewish owners and managers the unfavorable light in which their activities place our Jewish people. One by one they presented themselves to us as legitimate businessmen who were just trying to make a living for their families. One owner of a particularly notorious bar came up to me and told me how he was a religious man himself. He had received his bar mitzvah. He said, 'I believe in God in my own way.' He admitted he had left most of the precepts and moral teachings of Judaism behind. Somehow, standing there with his vicuna coat and ostentatious jewelry, he was unconvincing as he pleaded poverty and legitimacy.
>
> We left about eleven o'clock, after picketing some three hours. During the week, I received an anonymous phone call, possibly because my name and address were on the Gospel tracts we handed out. The phone call said that we had better not come back or they would have a 'little surprise prepared for us.'...we spent an additional half-hour in prayer preparatory to the demonstration.
>
> This time when we went to North Beach, there were 300 of us; and with the enthusiastic singing and the brightly painted placards, we must have looked like 3,000 people. When we arrived, one establishment closed its doors and sent the bartenders and performers home. The general attitude of the owners and managers was there would not be much business on the street that night. Nevertheless, there was business—God's business. All of us who were engaged in the demonstration found people with hungry hearts. Almost every one of us had a chance to tell what Christ had done for us.
>
> However, at one establishment they were prepared to fight back. Hired thugs came out of the club and began shoving our young people off the sidewalk. Instead of responding in anger to the thugs, the only response was 'God bless you,' or 'Jesus loves you.' About ten of the dancers came out of the same establishment and began attacking our people. They seized the placards and ripped them into pieces; but the demonstrators picked up the pieces, held them high, and kept on marching. The manager came out with a water hose and began spraying water. We tried to call the police, but there was not a policeman to be found on the street. More than forty of our people were struck or beaten, but none so badly as to require hospitalization or treatment. With the placards it was another matter since three-fourths of them had been utterly destroyed.
>
> Finally the police did arrive and the owner who perpetrated the violence was taken in hand. Fearing prosecution, he made a concession to us. The following Saturday he would allow a group of us to come into his place to conduct a Gospel meeting!

The following Saturday we went to his establishment and found all of the dancers modestly attired. Paul Bryant led us in singing a few Gospel songs. Pat Matriciana, from the Christian World Liberation Front, stood up and gave testimony as to how God had transformed his life. Then Kent Philpott brought a brief Gospel message on the love of God. He did not rail against the people for their sin, but rather in a very positive manner showed what God wants from the life of each individual. He led in prayer, asking God's blessings on everyone that they might know the truth and be set free. We then left to conduct the demonstration elsewhere.

The threats continued. The San Francisco Police Department tried to remain neutral, but the owners and managers of these lewd businesses were putting tremendous pressures on them. The police asked us to cut down on the number of people demonstrating from 300 to 150. Even this proved to be an effective group during the next few weeks. The placards, the singing and chanting, the tracts being distributed have all had the effect of making people inquire, wanting to know more about Jesus Christ.[47]

While the demonstrations did provide opportunity for witnessing, they were really designed as "media events." Such media events fueled the fires of controversy that surrounded Moishe's ministry and gave Jews for Jesus the free publicity which gave the appearance that hundreds and thousands of Jewish hippies, or "street-people," were proclaiming Yeshua as Messiah. But Moishe did not limit his ministry to demonstrations. He established an excellent "networking" system for discipling the young people who came to faith in Yeshua. He reported to readers of *The Chosen People* magazine:

The biggest area of achievement for us during the past months was that of working with individuals. Through a series of circumstances that could have only been ordered by God, I found a group of hippies that were turning from dope and the hip life to the Lord. I wish I could say that I had been used to lead most of them to Christ, but that wasn't the case.

There is a man, named Mike Ward, at Coos Bay, Oregon, who has been dramatically used in the lives of these young people, most of whom are Jewish. Mike earns his living as an operator of a patrol boat, ...He and his wife Ann live on an isolated peninsula. Mike has been a merchant seaman and a science fiction writer and has a Masters in psychology. He has been given an unusual spiritual perception. He's been a Christian for six years. A couple of years back, God called on him to open up his house to love and feed anyone who came. He started picking up hitchhikers and taking them home to what he calls the Ranch.... The Ranch has several acres, and through foraging and gardening, he is able to feed the young people quite well.

The first of Mike Ward's young people that I met was Mitch G. [Glaser]. Mitch is nineteen and from New Jersey. He found one of our broadsides floating in on the tide in Sausalito and hitchhiked up to my home. Mitch was already on his way toward being saved but hadn't entered into the fullness of a commitment to Christ. Shortly after that, Marcia Black met ST, [Marcia was also on staff with the Mission and had been one of the missionary candidates in Moishe's last training program in New York. Marcia later married Baruch (Bruce) Goldstein; together they served as missionaries with Jews for Jesus], a friend of Mitch's, while she was distributing literature at the College of Marin. It was more than a coincidence. Even though S has not come to Christ yet, he was impressed that God was dealing with him.

Mitch went up to the Ranch in Coos Bay and made a commitment to Christ. This is how Mike Ward heard of us and our ministry. Without consciously thinking about it, we began working together. We sent several hippies up there and several have gotten saved.

But at any rate, Mitch was part of a large circle of hippie friends, most of whom come from New York. Two in this group were brothers from the Bronx. Two others were young men well known in the street scene of the Bay area where they have made their home for the last couple of years.

One Sunday I prayed with Jh'an [Moskowitz] one of the hippies, and he accepted Christ. Jim R. has also made a profession of faith; and one of their friends Alan M. came to Christ three weeks ago. I've been spending a lot of time working with these young people as individuals and they've been a great help to me in the street witnessing and the campus witnessing....

Now it seems that each one of these people had friends of their own and I began traveling in a wider circle of hippies. There have been several others beside this group to whom we have also had a ministry lately.

Again I mention Mike Ward because he has played a crucial role in the salvation of all these people. Because we don't operate a Christian house or commune, we've been sending our own contacts up to Coos Bay, which is about eight hours north of San Francisco. Up there, they have a wilderness experience and most of them come back committed to Christ. After a time at the Ranch, they come back down here and help us.

Most of my summer ministry has revolved around twelve to twenty individuals who were at the Ranch or some other Christian commune. What has developed is a good working fellowship which is mostly Jewish.

To give you some idea of our growth, last Thursday night we had thirty people out to our Bible study and not all of them were kids. Three were past fifty.

There have been some Gentile young people who have joined themselves to our group too, like Barbara Riddle, who first got a piece of our literature at the peace march on April 24 [c. 1971]. We corresponded for several months; then she came down to see me, stayed at Marcia's apartment for one night, and accepted Christ the next day. She's now attending Simpson College. Barry Ellegant is another Jewish young man who is attending Simpson through our influence. Barry is a former teacher from the Moline, Illinois school system. Bill Burdo, one of our regulars, met him and got him into Berachah House, a Christian commune, where Barry made a decision for Christ.

Certainly these months of witness, demonstrations, literature distribution and working with individuals has been fruitful for the cause of Christ in reaching Jewish young people.[48]

The influence, outreach, and effectiveness of this unusual branch of the Mission known as "Jews for Jesus" continued to grow rapidly. In reaching Jewish young people with the Gospel, it was far surpassing all other branch ministries. What Moishe could not accomplish in New York, he was accomplishing in San Francisco. Some of the missionaries who had been skeptical of Moishe's tactics and methodology were now visiting San Francisco, or inviting Moishe or his staff members to their areas, to learn techniques that would enable them to be more effective in their outreach to Jewish young people. In 1972, when the Mission participated in "Explo '72" in Dallas, Texas, one of the main attractions there was the Mission's "Jews for Jesus" booth.

PARTICIPATING IN EXPLO '72

The Mission's booth for "Explo '72" was designed by Bob Friedman, a former newspaper reporter and a creative writer who had a great sense of humor. Bob and his wife, Anita, were both Jewish believers. Anita accepted Yeshua (along with her sister Debbie, now Mrs. Louis Lapides) through the Los Angeles branch of the Mission. Bob came to faith in Yeshua after covering a story of Arthur Blessitt—a man who would chain himself to a cross on Sunset Strip in West Los Angeles. After accepting the Lord, Bob spent hours studying the Scriptures with the author. Both he and Anita had a desire to use their creative ability for the Lord, and they did. Bob wrote a number of books, and for a short time during the mid 1970's he served as Editor of *The Chosen People* magazine, and as the Mission's Communication's Director. In an article for *The Chosen People* magazine, Bob wrote:

Explo '72 never imagined that in the midst of all the grits and pone thousands of students would seek out a little cream cheese and lox for a special treat!

Explo '72—The International Congress on Student Evangelism recently held in Dallas, Texas, to train Christian youth how to share their faith, and, as an amazing, unplanned (by Explo) extra, to let them know that Jesus is Jewish.

Yes, the nightly meetings in the city's Cotton Bowl grabbed the headlines and Billy Graham was featured on the newscasts. Yet to one observant reporter from an Ohio newspaper the action was at the booth sponsored by The American Board of Missions to the Jews.

Hundreds of booths filled two giant buildings at Dallas' State Fair Grounds. Seminaries, foreign missions, colleges and a large variety of specialized mission work were represented in the booth areas. But, none were as crowded as the booth where the 'Jews for Jesus' were coming face-to-face with masses of curious Gentiles.[44]

Special over-sized buttons in blue and white were prepared for Jewish believers. They stated, "I'm a Jew for Jesus." Other over-sized buttons were prepared in yellow for Gentile believers. They read, "I'm for the Jews for Jesus." Thousands of these buttons were made, and in just a few days the entire supply was exhausted. They were seen on blouses, shirts, and sweaters all over the fair-grounds, the Cotton Bowl, and the city of Dallas. Friedman wrote:

Our booth was located in the best spot in the building, with our sign catching people's eyes as soon as they walked in. Across the back we had three 54 inch-high blowups. The first was an article appearing in Newsweek *about the 'Jews With a Smile'* New York Times *ad. The ad itself was blown up, as was a brilliant tract by Moishe Rosen in which he took an article rapping his 'Jews for Jesus' movement and used it to reach the curious. Mr. Rosen also contributed the most sought-after piece of literature. His pamphlet, originally entitled, 'How To Witness Simply and Effectively To The Jews,' was changed to read, 'How To Rap With Jews About Jesus.' This pamphlet was included with a few broadside tracts and other material about the ABMJ and Hebrew Christianity. These were inserted in an attractive kit along with the* Christian Life *article on Jewish believers.*[50]

Bob and Anita Friedman helped to man the booth, as did other Mission workers, part-time workers, students, and volunteers. Dr. Tom McCall, the Missionary in Charge of Dallas became a temporary dormitory leader, as workers and volunteers from New York descended on Explo, led by Miss Ruth Wardell, Baruch (Bruce) and Marcia Goldstein, and Martin Gruen (son of Dr. Emil Gruen).

In his report on Explo, Bob continued, saying:

> *Several delegates had dinner at the Mission following a seminar on Jewish evangelism which featured Rev. Harold Sevener of Los Angeles and Rev. Rosen. The seminar offered practical application of Scripture and taught common Jewish attitudes toward Judaism and Christianity.*
>
> *The results of ABMJ's work at Explo '72 may never be fully assessed, but thousands have been exposed to Jewish evangelism for the first time. We expect hundreds of Jews to suddenly discover that—Jesus was raised in a kosher home.[51]*

THE "JEWS FOR JESUS" BRANCH WINS APPROVAL

In many ways, the Mission's "Jews for Jesus" booth at Explo '72 put the "evangelical seal of approval" on Moishe's ministry in San Francisco. The presence of so many young Jewish believers at Explo '72, and the fact that so many evangelical Christians could see their zeal and commitment to Yeshua, and to the cause of Jewish evangelism, confirmed to them that Moishe's ministry could only be a work of the Lord (and it was!)—not some cultic phenomenon.

Moishe continued to draw around him greater numbers of creative and talented Jewish young people who now wanted to serve the Lord. Some were placed on staff in part-time positions, some were given student aid so they could attend Bible college, and others freely gave of their time and talents as volunteers. Some of the young people who identified themselves with Moishe, and with his ministry, were Steffi Geiser (now Steffi Rubin, wife of Barry Rubin, Director of the Lederer Foundation); Amy Rabinovitz; Alice Kress; Susan Perlman; Stuart Dauermann; Mary Ann Sleichter (now Miriam Nadler, wife of Sam Nadler); and Sam Nadler, President of the Mission (now called Chosen People Ministries, Inc.).

SAM NADLER—HIS STORY

Sam was born in Queens, New York on January 2, 1948. He considered his family to be "nominally orthodox" Jews. He attended synagogue services, kept some of the traditions, and observed the Jewish holy days. At age thirteen he was Bar Mitzvah. After high school, he enrolled at Queensborough Community College; he then transferred to Georgia State University. He was uncertain about what he wanted to do with his life, and was uncertain about the purpose and meaning of life as well so he went to his rabbi for answers. But the rabbi's answers made him feel that the rabbi was either hiding something, or that he did not know the answers to the questions himself. Sam's quest ultimately led him on a bizarre and treacherous path. The detailed account of how God worked in Sam's life to bring him to faith in Jesus is told in Moishe Rosen's book, *Jews for Jesus*. Moishe wrote:

> *Sam...came to Christ by another route that took him through a frightening and satanically-controlled realm of the counterculture. Sam was drafted into the army and was shipped off to Vietnam at the height of the war. He made it back in one piece and in his stateside duty station, he managed to establish a lucrative drug business. He decided he wanted to deal only in 'high class' drugs, so he became a 'clean dealer' who trafficked in marijuana, hashish, and psychedelics, not the hard stuff like heroin. While he was still in the army, Sam also set up a loan-sharking operation which netted him interest at the rate of about 600 percent annually.*
>
> *'Both the drug dealing and the lending operation were rotten things to do,' he said, 'but I didn't see anything wrong with them at the time; and I was doing very well financially. When I got out of the service, I believed that drugs were for everyone. After attending Georgia State University for a semester, I dropped out and started traveling across the country in a van, selling drugs when I needed the money. It was one continuous party. I'd sometimes have eighteen people in the van, with lots of girl friends, all that I wanted. It was the All-American dream.*
>
> *Sam stopped for a while in San Francisco, then moved to a small town in northern California to manage a saloon. He formed a band and played his harmonica and composed songs to his heart's content. Then things started to go wrong. He and his girl friend of the moment split up, his house burned down, and he lost his job.*
>
> *'Some friends of mine and I had staged an acid orgy with five Indian chicks we picked up, but when we got back to our place, it was nothing but ashes,' he explained. 'I decided the time had come to go back to San Francisco. It would be Jamaica for the winter. But again, I ran into trouble. I couldn't sell my van, and the novelty of the Jamaica idea soon wore off. I had started a nice drug business again, and so I decided to stay in the Bay area for a while.'*

'One day, in the fall of 1971, a girl I knew started telling me about some people she had met who called themselves Jews for Jesus. I said, "Okay, I guess everybody needs a label. But what will they think of next?" She kept pushing me to go to a Bible study with her, and finally I agreed. I met Moishe there, and frankly I was flabbergasted when he said he believed in a personal God. "You actually talk to Him, like you talk to me?" I asked. It was all so ridiculous.'

Sam said that he believed at the time that real spiritual truth lay in the occult, particularly in the I Ching and astrology. 'I was certain that there was a spiritual power that I could tap,' he said. 'Moishe had said that personal prayer worked for him, and because that seemed like part of the same bag I was into, I decided to try it. I still hadn't been able to get rid of my car, and so I said conversationally to God, "Can you help me get rid of it?" Soon afterwards, I sold the car, and I sensed somehow my prayer had been answered. I also found that the I Ching would give me the same reading over and over again, "You'll meet the great man." I got in the habit of walking up to people and asking, "Who's the great man?" With amazing frequency, they would answer, "Jesus Christ." But at that point, Jesus was still a lark with me.'

Unimpressed with these encounters with Christianity, Sam decided to throw himself heart and soul into the occult. 'I could actually find out what people were doing in an adjoining room just by getting a hexagram from coins. Then a heavy thing happened one night. I was sitting in the kitchen, rapping with some friends, and a strange presence or feeling filled the room. It grasped each of us to the point that we sat up straight, completely alert. We had a sense that something was about to happen. Although none of us were Christians, one guy started talking about Jesus. He talked for about ten or fifteen minutes, and the rest of us were transfixed. Then he got up and just as he left, another non-Christian friend came into the room and took up where the first guy had left off. Then the feeling seemed to dissipate, and we became aware of sounds outside the room. The first thing we heard was Billy Graham on the radio. He was saying, "Never before have so many young people been turning to Christ."'

This experience made Sam get serious. He went to his room and asked God to make Himself real, to reveal Himself if He were really there. But nothing happened immediately. A few days later, Sam started attending classes on how to use the occult to gain power over other people. One lecturer said, 'This is black magic I'm going to show you now. You can learn to control yourself and other people. You can communicate with the spirit world for whatever purposes you like, whether good or bad, moral or immoral.'

'A spade was finally being called a spade,' Sam said. 'That night I was shown that I was involved in something evil. I could now sense the difference between good and evil, between God and Satan. I knew I had been following Satan. I went home and began to sing every song I had ever written, and I thought, "These are all the good things I've ever done. I'm going to sing them to You, God." Then some of my neighbors started drifting in, heroin dealers and such, and it dawned on me the kind of social circle I was in. They filled the entire house that night. I knew Satan was present, and I became more and more frightened.'

Sam turned down the drugs that his friends offered him that evening, but he practically had to fight them off. 'It was a frightful night, trying to turn around, change my ways all at once. I can't tell you how sure I was that Satan was there, right there. You could feel the evil, the heaviness of it. I just knew I had to have Jesus in my life. I went to the stairs, fell to my knees, and asked Him into my life. As soon as I did it, as soon as I prayed, people started leaving. They had given no indication before that they were ready to go. It was God acting, no question in my mind. I was comforted, but I realized that I couldn't live in that house anymore. The people there were very much under Satan's control, into his trip.'

The next day, Sam sought out some Christians he knew and got in touch with me through them. Before the day was out, [c. January 10, 1972, Sam accepted the Lord] he had joined the tribe [Moishe's name for Jews for Jesus at the time]. Within a month, he was enrolled in Simpson Bible College.[52]

The author had the privilege of meeting Sam soon after he became a believer, when he flew to San Francisco for one of his regular planning and strategy meetings with Moishe. To avoid car rental expense, Moishe had arranged for Sam to meet me at the airport. He still looked like a young "hippie," with his long hair, sandals and jeans, but his love for the Lord was apparent and his desire to serve His Messiah quickly manifested itself. Sam had known the dark side of life—now he wanted to live in the light!

Sam soaked up the Word of God like the hot desert sand soaks up water. Among those discipling him, and helping him grow in faith, was Miriam Sleichter (When Mary Ann Sleichter moved to San Francisco to help Moishe Rosen, she changed her name to the Hebrew version, Miriam). Sam said he didn't like her much at first, but after several months he'd matured enough to appreciate such a godly woman so they met again—and ultimately fell in love. Sam and Miriam were married on June 9, 1973. They continued on staff with Jews for Jesus until rejoining the staff of the Mission in September 1979.

The Liberated Wailing Wall

Like Joseph Cohn, Moishe Rosen was always looking for new ways to share the Gospel. He soon discovered that among his group of young followers were some very talented musicians. Moishe and the author had often talked about using Jewish music in evangelism. We had witnessed many times Rabbi Sholmo Carlbach's charisma with the university crowds as he would speak to them through the use of music. Moishe, himself, had been enamored with the play, "Fiddler on the Roof." He knew many Christian people had been enamored by it too. He felt certain that the Christian public would react favorably to Messianic music, so he asked some of his young helpers to put together a music group. "The Liberated Wailing Wall" was the first group formed. In a report about the group, Steffi Geiser (now Steffi Rubin) wrote:

> ...A group of the kids here in Corte Madera have gotten together a Jews for Jesus presentation to perform at local churches. Calling themselves 'The Liberated Wailing Wall,' these Hebrew Christians present in song, drama and testimony, a little of what it means to be a Jew for Jesus. The music is Jewish in character and scriptural in content. The skits we perform deal with witnessing. In one colorful part of the service, Barry Ellegant dons a 'tallis' (prayer shawl) and chants in the manner of a true 'chazzen' (cantor) a prayer of thanksgiving for the Sabbath as it is sung in the synagogue. The program has been very well received, and the group, now led by Miriam Sleichter and joined by Shelley Korotkin, is opening up valuable opportunities of fellowship between the American Board of Missions to the Jews and the churches.[53]

The Liberated Wailing Wall soon toured the country on behalf of the Mission. They took meetings at any church that would allow them to share the Gospel and the message that Christians need to share the Gospel with Jews. The means they used were Messianic music, skits, and personal testimonies.

Within the space of less than three years, Moishe Rosen and his "tribe" of Jews for Jesus not only shook-up the city of San Francisco, they shook-up the Jewish community of the United States as they demonstrated that Jews could believe in Jesus and still be Jewish. What Moishe began in San Francisco changed forever the way Jewish missions and evangelism would conduct themselves and their programs. Steffi Geiser (Rubin) summed up this new style of ministry when she wrote for *The Chosen People* magazine:

> The Bay Area is spattered with colorful Jews for Jesus posters. The San Francisco residents are being bombarded with gospel literature. The airport and the Sausalito ferry dock have their comings and goings punctuated by a 'Shalom,' a smile and a fuzzy face or two greeting the passengers with the message of the Messiah. And local churches have become tuned into minor chords of Chassidic melodies to add to their worship services on Sunday mornings.
>
> New styles, new tunes and new faces have made what began as a handful of Jews for Jesus quite an issue in the San Francisco Bay Area. A different kind of zeal and a whole lot of 'chutzpah' (boldness) has made the placard a vital instrument in the sharing of the gospel, and has made ignoring Jesus excusable only to the blind and the deaf. There is no avoiding the live issue of Christ as a Jewish option.
>
> We are a small tribe-like group here on the coast. Our ministry is diverse and variety makes things interesting and gives many of us an opportunity to exercise our individual talents and energies as well as having the chance to work together on projects. What characterizes our ministry most is the emphasis on the need to get out into the streets.
>
> ...Bearing this in mind, the Hebrew Christians in the Bay Area have spent much of the past summer sunshine talking to the people on the streets of Sausalito, in the business district of San Francisco, amid the traffic of the airport. Passing out leaflets called 'broadsides,' wearing silkscreened T-shirts saying 'Jews for Jesus,' carrying colorful placards and sporting 'yarmulkes' (skullcaps), playing guitars and singing Hebrew Christian songs written by Stuart Dauermann, as many as seven Jews for Jesus would appear on busy Market Street presenting the gospel to the lunch-hour crowd. Organized demonstrations in front of the North Beach topless clubs or outside of the play 'Godspell' offered other chances to preach God's Word to the people, where they were.
>
> In keeping with the philosophy of approaching people in their own milieu, the literature that we have been using is aimed at being, above all things, relevant. It is run on a mimeograph machine in our office and written by the individuals in the group. Often an idea will go from hand to hand before a 'broadside' is completed. Last summer, when the American Medical Association held its convention in San Francisco, we were there to greet them with a tract called 'Dear Doctor'; and a broadside whose cover pictured a man being pounded on by a judge's gavel with the title 'Order!' greeted the American Bar Association when they convened at the Statler Hilton in the city. Now, with a total of over sixty different pieces of literature to run off, the mimeograph machine, manned by Sam Nadler and Mark Winter, is going almost constantly. And Baruch Goldstein, fastest tract passer in the West (or East) joined by other volunteers manages to unload as many as fifteen thousand gospel 'broadsides' on the streets each week.[54]

The diversity of Jewish backgrounds and the special gifts and talents of the young people Moishe incorporated as a part of his team helped to make Jews for Jesus the organization that it is today.

Moishe and his "tribe" had generated considerable publicity for the San Francisco branch—Jews for Jesus—and for the Mission, as its name was linked with Jews for Jesus. With all of the media exposure, and with the exposure given to the San Francisco ministry in *The Chosen People* magazine, Moishe was hoping and praying that the breach between himself and Daniel Fuchs would be bridged. He was hoping Daniel would see the potential in what he was doing and commit more funds and personnel to help him.

Daniel, however, had already committed the Mission to "Mass Media" evangelism, and the Board had committed themselves to move ahead with a nation-wide showing of the "Passover" telecast and to other mass media projects that were being considered. Daniel felt that while Moishe was accomplishing a very important ministry at the time, his approach through confrontational evangelism was limited to the "street-person" and to "hippie-type" young people. He believed, as did others on the Board, that the youth revolution would soon fade, while "media evangelism" would continue as a veritable means of reaching the whole of the Jewish community in the shortest period of time.

At the first Directors meeting following the transfer of Moishe Rosen to San Francisco, Daniel made his recommendations regarding revamping the missionary training program. The Minutes state:

> Due to the removal of Mr. Rosen from the New York area, it will be necessary to revamp the entire missionary training program. Mr. Fuchs gave each member of the Board a proposal for the Missionary Personnel Department and asked them to study it and report on it to him as soon as possible.
>
> With the removal of the training program to Staten Island, it will be necessary to have a missionary in charge of New York Headquarters District and a minister in charge of Beth Sar Shalom. Arthur Katz, now in the Plains States District has been asked to come to New York as missionary in charge and Rev. Daniel Rigney has been asked to continue as minister at Beth Sar Shalom.[55]

NEW DISTRICTS—NEW STAFF
ARTHUR KATZ

Arthur Katz had been one of the four candidates who attended Moishe Rosen's first Missionary Training Program in New York in 1968. When he completed the training program Arthur was sent to open a new district called the "Plains States District," and to serve as Missionary in Charge of a branch in Prairie Village, Kansas.

Art, an indefatigable worker and a gifted soul-winner, immersed himself in his new assignment. He wrote:

> ...We were fortunate that summer in having the assistance of Pauline Tieder, a Jewish believer on vacation from a Christian liberal arts college in Missouri. Together we worked out a telephone campaign in which Jewish families were called directly out of the telephone book and our new ministry introduced to them. By Summer's end, we had visited almost all the synagogues and reform temples in town, joined the Jewish Community Center, using its facilities and attending some of its functions, been interviewed on the local Christian radio station, driven about town with Beth Sar Shalom signs in our station wagon windows, had an Open House for the Christian and then Jewish communities, and by and large had made our presence and purpose known.
>
> One of our distinct purposes from the first was to establish the principle that a Jewish person who received Christ as his Messiah has in no way forfeited or rejected his Jewishness nor his prerogatives as a Jew in the Jewish community; on the contrary, he has but entered more completely into his heritage and has become a Jew in spirit and truth as well as by fact of birth. Unfortunately, we have not succeeded in this as much as we would have liked. One rabbi sent us a special delivery letter enjoining us from attending "his" temple—and this despite (or was it because of) the warm reception given us by several of the congregation who know our convictions and calling. His own secretary is one of our best contacts, challenged and disturbed within, though for the time being she has chosen expediency over truth....
>
> Still, souls are being saved—some seven in recent months including my own Aunt Sadie in London (en route to an evangelistic outreach in Jerusalem) and the doctor who delivered our last baby in New York (on the return trip from Israel on the way home to Kansas City). Locally, two college students received Christ—one at a state hospital where we visited him after he had suffered a nervous breakdown and the other at her campus in Tarkie, Missouri. One of my own former students now attending the University of Calif. at Berkeley was brought to the Lord through our correspondence; a dentist here in our first conversation; and the young teen-age daughter of a distraught woman to whom we had been ministering intensively. All of these are facing exceptional difficulties and impediments to spiritual growth and they need your prayers.
>
> While our weekly Bible study is at present only sparsely attended at best, the highlight of our months here was the

Chanukah party we gave which was attended by some thirty or more Jewish people, mostly unsaved. We had the good fortune to have Rev. Martin Rosen, Missionary-in-Charge of the Headquarters Branch in New York, as our speaker. The evening was a great success with many new contacts made.[56]

Arthur Katz continued to develop the Plains States District for the Mission until 1970, when Daniel Fuchs asked him to take over as Missionary in Charge of the Headquarters District in New York City. The Katz family moved to New York during the Fall of 1970, but their stay was shortlived. Art was, and is, a very charismatic speaker. He believes and was teaching that all gifts of the Spirit are for believers today—teaching that was in direct contradiction with the belief and teaching of many of the Mission's staff members, Board members, and supporters. Daniel soon began receiving telephone calls from staff members, pastors and supporters of the Mission, asking if the Mission had changed its doctrinal position.

Once again, Daniel was faced with a dilemma. The matter was resolved with the resignation of Art Katz from the Mission. Art went on to establish a ministry called "Ben Israel"—a ministry which is still actively reaching Jewish people around the world with the Gospel.

Following Arthur Katz' resignation from the position of Missionary in Charge of the Headquarters District in New York, the "New York District" was phased out of operation.

The transfer of Arthur Katz to New York left the Plains States District in need of a worker, so Daniel Fuchs hired Dr. Daniel Goldberg to take over the ministry there, and to serve as a Field Evangelist for that district. Dr. Goldberg was familiar with the ministry and with the district; he had worked for the Mission on a part-time basis since 1969, while finishing his doctorate (Th.D.) at Grace Theological Seminary in Winona Lake, Indiana. He joined the staff of the Mission as the Regional Director for the western states in 1979.

Daniel Goldberg

Daniel Goldberg was born of Jewish parents who had come to America from Europe. He was raised in the Boyle Heights section of Los Angeles. In his testimony, Daniel states that even as a young child he was required to fast on the Day of Atonement; he remembers well the long services of prayer and worship in the synagogue on Yom Kippur. He remembers, too, that the burden of sin troubled him at times, but he found no relief from it even after fasting and after the long synagogue services on Yom Kippur. Even the recitation at night of the Hebrew prayers his father taught him failed to give him peace or relief from the guilt of sin.

When Daniel was twelve years old, a Protestant minister spoke with him about his need to believe in Jesus. Daniel didn't know what he meant, but that night, as he prayed, he asked God to show him the truth about Jesus. Daniel said:

Then one day during my last year in Senior High a neighbor lady invited me to her house. She courteously asked me to sit in her living room and listen to a chapter in the Bible which she read from Isaiah, chapter 53. It was totally new to me and I found it difficult to believe that such a vivid description of Jesus was to be found in the Old Testament. I had never before read or been confronted with any Scripture, but this made an indellible [sic] impression upon my mind. Some time before this a school chum's mother gave me a copy of the New Testament which until then I had completely ignored. But the prophecy of Isaiah aroused my curiosity to know what was in the New Testament about this Jesus. Returning home that day I began reading the Gospel of John with absorbing interest and my soul was drawn toward this Son of God who was so loving and powerful. Right then and there, alone in my bedroom, I called on Jesus Christ to save me. At once I experienced a deep peace of heart and the burden of my sin was lifted. Two weeks later, when my Dad discovered the New Testament in my possession, he threatened and cursed me, demanding that either I leave home or give up the New Testament. I was then seventeen years of age, but Messiah Jesus had done so much for me, I knew that He would always come first. With real ache in my heart for my parents to know the salvation and peace of their Messiah, I packed my belongings and said good-bye. The promise found in Psalm 27:10, 'When my father and my mother forsake me, then the Lord will take me up,' sustained me.

I went to Chicago, Illinois, where Louis, my only brother, lived. About a year prior to this time Louis had found his Messiah through reading the Scriptures and observing the life of a true Christian fellow-employee who patiently witnessed to him. [Dr. Louis Goldberg served as Director of the Department of Jewish Studies at Moody Bible Institute for many years. The reader will recall that this is the Department which Dr. Solomon Birnbaum directed before coming with the Mission; it is the department that has trained many of the Mission's workers.] Actually the witness of Louis to me through letters and literature was a major factor in my coming to Christ. Louis and his wife shared their home with me and very soon I was led to study at the Moody Bible Institute where I was graduated in 1954. Since then I have received the B.A. and B.D. degrees from Goshen College and Northern Baptist Theological Seminary respectively.[57]

CHARLES EISENBERG

Although the "New York District" was phased out of operation after the resignation of Arthur Katz, the Headquarters branch ministry continued its ministry. In July 1971, Daniel appointed Charles Eisenberg as the Resident Missionary for the Manhattan branch.

Charles was, in some ways, another child of the Mission. He was raised in a Jewish home, and accepted Yeshua as his Messiah in October, 1954. By 1959 he recognized God's call on his life to preach the Gospel so he enrolled in BIOLA college in preparation for full-time Christian ministry. He graduated from BIOLA in June, 1963.

Like Arnold Fruchtenbaum and other young Jewish believers, Charles was involved in the Mission's summer camping programs. And, like Arnold Fruchtenbaum and others, it was at camp, while teaching and counselling, that he met Marilyn Hicks, one of the workers from the Mission's Pittsburgh branch. Charles and Marilyn were married in August, 1964.

Charles made application to the Mission for full-time service while he was completing his work at Talbot Theological Seminary. He and Marilyn wanted to work in the Pittsburgh ministry after Charles' graduation. However, the leadership of the Mission appointed Henry Johnson to the Pittsburgh branch.

Charles graduated from Talbot Seminary in June 1967, but at the time there were no openings in the Mission so he took the position of Minister of Outreach with Bethany Baptist Church in West Covina, California. In 1971 Daniel Fuchs called Charles and asked him if he would consider accepting the position of Resident Minister for the Manhattan branch—a position Charles happily agreed to accept.

INCOME VERSUS MEDIA

Daniel had done his best to fill the vacancies left by Moishe Rosen's transfer to San Francisco. In September 1970, four months after he had informed the Directors that the entire missionary training program would have to be revamped, Daniel asked the Board for a moratorium on the hiring of missionary personnel. The Minutes state:

> Mr. Fuchs reported to the Board that the costs of recruiting personnel have been spiralling and he would like to have a directive from the Board as to the matter of active recruitment of personnel. After discussion, the Board felt we should not actively recruit personnel for our training program at the present time but as applications are made and vacancies occur, the matter should be considered on an individual basis of our need.[58]

At the same Directors meeting, knowing that the salaries of the missionaries, as well as missionary projects and branch expenses, were being funded from a deficit budget, and knowing that media projects were expensive, Daniel forewarned the Board of upcoming expenses. The Minutes state:

> ...Beside the cost of the actual presentation there will be advertising expenses, printing of literature, postage, etc. Mr. Fuchs asked that the Board authorize an additional amount of $10,000 at the present time and when the arrangements are nearer completion, he will bring a request for funds to carry out the program. This may possibly run as high as $75,000 for the [Passover] Telecast outreach.
> Mr. Ivins moved and Mr. Straub seconded the motion that an additional amount of $10,000 be appropriated and put into the budget to be used for the TV Telecast in the spring of 1971. It was voted.[59]

The additional expenditures were authorized by the Board even though they knew it would increase the deficit spending for the year. Earlier in the meeting a new budget had been presented. The Minutes record:

> Mr. Pretlove moved and Mr. Straub seconded the motion that the financial report for the 11 month period ending August 31, 1970 showing receipts of $934,645 and disbursements of $1,365,583 be accepted as presented and placed on file and that the proposed budget for 1970-71 be adopted as presented. It was voted.[60]

Evidently, the Directors gave the matter of deficit spending some thought between meetings, because at their next meeting they took initial steps to set up a program whereby they could begin to replenish the investment fund of the Mission. The November, 1970 Minutes state:

> After discussion re: starting a deferred giving program, Mr. Kubach moved and Mr. Straub seconded the motion that the general secretary be authorized to include an article in the February issue of The Chosen People saying that with our expansion program our expenses are now far in excess of our income. Mention should be made if any of our friends would like our advice concerning either remembering us in their wills or through other plans of deferred giving we would

be happy to advise them. In counselling with our friends it would be most necessary that they be advised to consult with an attorney in their state as to the legal aspects of any gift. It was voted.[61]

Daniel wrote such an article for the February 1971 issue of *The Chosen People* magazine. In it he mentioned the Mission's need to develop a deferred giving program. (Under the leadership of Joseph Hoffman Cohn, the Mission had a very active deferred giving program which led, in part, to the large investment fund of the Mission, but the program was not advertized or developed further after his death.) Mr. Wesley J. A. Jones, one of the supporters of the Mission, read the article and offered his services to Daniel. After several meetings with Daniel, Wesley Jones became the Stewardship Director for the Mission—a position he held until his retirement in 1988.

The deficit in the operating fund of the Mission for the eleven months of 1970 was $430,938.00. The Board had authorized additional expenses on the Passover telecast projected to possibly run as high as $75,000.00. But, in fact, over $150,000 was spent on the 1971 telecast—a telecast that was subsequently canceled on most stations, resulting in a loss to the Mission of all monies spent on advertising (TV guide, newspapers, etc.). The Mission was, however, able to recoup most of the money for the canceled TV time.

Once again, the reader is reminded that from the time of Joseph Cohn's death, up to the period of time under discussion, the Board was operating according to the policy it had adopted, to use its reserve funds for missionary work. Reserve funds were sufficient to make up for the large deficits in income. However, the concern was that with each passing year the reserve funds were being depleted. The income of the Mission was not keeping up with the rate monies were being spent, nor with the rate of inflation. This was only seen as a moderate problem at the period of time under discussion, but it became a crucial problem within a few years.

OPPOSITION TO THE PASSOVER TELECAST

Through the remaining months of 1970, and the early months of 1971, Mission personnel were being prepared for the onslaught of telephone calls and letters that were expected in the aftermath of the nation-wide airing of the Passover telecast. But the pre-publicity which was sent out in advance of the telecast alerted the Jewish community to what was being planned. The Jewish community of Los Angeles had been caught unprepared, and were taken aback by the first showing of the Passover telecast in April, 1970. But this time they were prepared to stop the telecast, and they did it![62] Daniel Fuchs shared the news with *The Chosen People* family, saying:

> *Naturally, we were keenly disappointed and heartsick when so many of the TV stations on which we were scheduled panicked under the pressure of a very few people and canceled the Telecast showing. It is ominous that our freedom of speech and religion could be frustrated without, in most cases, our even knowing that we were accused. We would realize, however, that even the 'failure' is quite an accomplishment. Last year we were on one station in Los Angeles; this year we were in Los Angeles four times instead of once. We also had successful Telecast programs in Dallas and Amarillo, Texas, and Charleston, West Virginia. Besides, the Jewish Evangelistic Witness of Australia telecast The Passover in Australia's five largest cities, and HCJB in Quito, Ecuador, and five cable stations in Canada also carried the program. A conservative estimate would indicate possibly one million total viewers of which possibly 35,000 were Jewish. We reiterate, this is an educated guess. In Dallas we were able to run a survey which indicated that 15.5% of its 22,000 Jewish people did view the program....*
>
> *As we worked for the Telecast, the only real problem we faced was that we were all working so hard that the strain was showing. I never saw our workers, whom I have often described as the best in the world, so diligent; and all over the country faithful Bible-preaching churches helped us in many ways. They were as excited about the prospects as we were. An actual confrontation of the Jewish community with the Gospel was about to be made.*
>
> *This year the mailings went smoothly—no strikes nor complaints—and over one half million fliers were successfully mailed. It seemed as if we had only to wait for the responses from the Telecast.*
>
> *Early on March 25th, Terry Delaney called with the news of the threatened cancellation of our Passover Telecast on WOR-TV in New York. Terry is in charge of our North Atlantic District and has had special training in public relations. When our regular advertising agent could not get us on a station in New York, Terry personally went to bat. As far as WOR-TV is concerned, Terry did everything right. He told them who we are and our purpose, and showed them the Passover film. Even the Jewish staff members at WOR were impressed. The film was accepted; the date and the time were set. At the request of the station a 'tag' offering of our booklet of the telecast script was made rather than the booklet, 'Israel, A Modern Miracle,' as originally planned. We sent a check to our agent who sent his check to WOR-TV. That check was accepted and deposited. This briefly is the background of Terry's call.*
>
> *Terry said that our agent in Seattle had received a call from TV Guide in Seattle to the effect that WOR-TV had*

'put a stop' on the program. For weeks Terry had been dealing directly with the station's manager and now someone told someone in Seattle, three thousand miles away, that there was trouble. I asked Terry to get the facts directly from the management.

Then came another call that the Los Angeles station had canceled the Telecast. Would there be no end?

Following this a call came from Mr. Edward B. Fiske, religious news editor of The New York Times. He wanted to write an article on Missions to the Jews. This meant canceling a trip that had been planned, but it was one of the most important decisions I have ever made for without the publicity which was triggered by this article, which appeared on the front page of the April 2, 1971 edition of The New York Times, we would have been literally impotently buried.

When Mr. Fiske came for the interview on Missions to the Jews, he got the news of what was happening with our telecast. We gave him an 'exclusive' on the story.

All night long the phone rang with requests for interviews from other reporters. By God's grace, I determined on two policies: first, in every interview I would inject the Gospel so that everybody who read the interview report would have a clear-cut testimony; secondly, no matter how tired I was I would not lose my calm and never in any way say a word against our opponents or say anything that could be considered anti-Semitic. The policy evidently paid off. We received national coverage. The Jewish public was confronted with the Gospel as it never had been before in all history. Even the Jewish newspapers have printed the Gospel appeal from our Passover script, and frequently it was quoted without comment!

The response from our friends to the cancellation has been phenomenal? From all over the country pastors, teachers, ministerial associations, and lay-workers have written letters of protest. I firmly believe that this experience is one of preparation. When we do return to those stations which canceled our Telecast, the Lord willing, we will reach millions of Jewish people instead of hundreds of thousands. The fury of the opposition is the barometer of the effectiveness of this Passover Telecast.

Climaxing two weeks of tension, the April 12th [c. 1971] issue of Time magazine gave its religion page entirely to the Telecast in an article entitled, 'Is Passover Christian?'[63]

After the Board's action to take steps toward increasing income in the investment fund, Daniel also took some steps toward increasing income in the operating fund, and to cut some of the media expenses being paid out to varying agencies. At the June 1971 Board meeting, he made the following request:

Mr. Fuchs asked that Rev. R. T. Delaney be appointed in charge of public relations for the Mission, to be in charge of our radio work, magazine advertizing, etc. which we place in the United States. He would work closely with Dick Maginot in Seattle who handled much of the publicity for the telecast. Mr. Delaney would continue his work in the North Atlantic District. Mr. Fuchs moved and Mr. Straub seconded the motion that Mr. Delaney be appointed as head of the public relations department of the Mission. It was voted.[64]

With the cancellation of the nation-wide airing of the Passover telecast, Daniel and those working closely with him on the media projects learned that over-exposure of the Mission's plans could thwart further attempts to use the media for evangelism, so Daniel remained tight-lipped about the Mission's plans to air the Passover telecast during the Spring of 1972.

The "Smiling Faces" Ad

A new idea for mass evangelism was also being worked on by Daniel Fuchs, Terryl Delaney and the author. The idea had grown out of a conversation between Terryl and Mr. Dick Maginot, the vice-president of advertizing for a large, successful, department store chain. As Terryl revealed to Dick some of the problems we'd been having in trying to communicate the Gospel to Jewish people, Dick suggested that the Mission try newspaper advertizing. He then went on to say that the newest trend in ads was to present a group of "satisfied customers"—people endorsing and showing their satisfaction with a product. That suggestion was all Terryl needed to get his "creative juices" running. As he and Dick talked further, an ad began to take shape in Terryl's mind. The Mission's ad would involve a group of Jewish believers, looking up and smiling. The caption would read: "So many Jews are wearing 'That Smile' nowadays!"

When Terryl shared the concept of the "Smiling Faces" ad with Daniel and the author, we loved it! We saw it not only as another way to use the media for reaching Jewish people with the Gospel, but also as means of taking the focus of attack off the Passover telecast. With such a diversion, perhaps the Passover telecast could be quietly re-booked to air in 1972.

Terryl Delaney and Dick Maginot worked on the concept for the ad and on the copy. The author handled the matter of assembling a group of "credible" Jewish believers in Los Angeles who were not only willing to be photographed, but who were willing to have their picture appear in major newspapers across the United States. Additionally, each individual who appeared in the ad had to be willing to prepare a written testimony of how he came to faith in the Messiah so that a booklet presenting the testimonies of everyone in the group could be printed. The booklet was to be used as the "premium" for the write-in offer on the ad.

The inroads being made into the Jewish community by the Passover telecast, by Explo '72, and by Moishe Rosen's constant barrage of confrontational evangelism were significant. To counteract and invalidate the Gospel message, and the message that Jews who receive Yeshua remain Jews, many leaders of the Jewish community were saying that no "real Jew," or no "sane Jew," would ever accept Jesus as the Messiah. In an article in *The Chosen People* magazine, Terryl Delaney explained the Mission's use of media as a means of tearing down such misconceptions about Jesus and Jewish believers. He wrote:

> The first misconception that most Jews hold, is that any Jew who believes in Christ can no longer be Jewish. We felt that it was important to show the Jewish community that Jesus is Jewish, his disciples were Jewish, and the membership of the apostolic church was almost homogeneously Jewish during its first 25 years. Through the use of mass media, we were also able to show Jewish people many other Jews who believe in Christ today, thus, continuing the tradition of the early followers of Christ. After being exposed to our message, we wanted each viewer or reader to come away with the attitude that a Jew who accepts Christ today is not less Jewish than the early followers of Christ.
>
> The second misconception we wanted to attack was the impression that very few Jews accept Christ, and that the ones who do are weak and uneducated. We accomplished this by pointing out that 50,000 to 100,000 Jews follow Christ today, and the number is growing. On a percentage basis, there are as many Jews who believe in Christ as there are gentiles.
>
> By using large numbers of Jewish people in our projects, we are able to portray the fact that Jews not only remain Jewish when they accept Christ, but also there are a great many Jewish people who are following Him. We also give the Hebrew-Christians an opportunity to testify of their faith, and their testimony quickly dispels the fact that only weak and uneducated Jews accept Christ.[65]

In the early Fall of 1971, thirty-nine Jewish believers assembled in the parking lot of the Mission's building in Hollywood. A professional photographer was hired to take the group's picture. This he did from atop a tall ladder. The booklet containing an individual photograph and the testimony of how each person came to Yeshua (which was the reason for their smile) was compiled into a booklet entitled: "Here is The Story Behind All Those Smiling Faces." The group was a compilation of young and old, from all walks of life; there were doctors, lawyers, executive secretaries, businessmen, business women, ministers, homemakers, an aeronautical engineer, real estate brokers, students, etc. The photograph and the testimony booklet made it indisputable that Jewish believers in the Messiah were not a group of uneducated Jewish "kooks." They were real Jewish people—educated and of sound mind—saying openly to the world that they believe in Yeshua.

Daniel Fuchs gave the following report of the "Smiling Faces" ad:

> On December 10th [c. 1971] we 'redeemed the time' by purchasing a full page in The New York Times for this ad; and a new method of Jewish evangelism was born. Although the cost seemed high, this was actually one of the most inexpensive projects we ever made. Over a million copies were printed and delivered not only in New York but all over the United States for less than one cent a copy!
>
> The day of the ad there were 350 responses, not only from New York, but from New Jersey, Pennsylvania, Connecticut, Massachusetts, North Carolina, Florida, Illinois, California, District of Columbia, Oregon, Maine, Iowa, Ohio and Indiana....
>
> The results of the ad were more than gratifying. We had responses from the chief psychiatrist of a large Eastern hospital, a rabbi, several doctors, and numerous business men. One of them came from the president of the Hillel society of a famous Eastern College. He wrote:
>
> 'I saw your full-page advertisement in The New York Times of Friday, December 10, 1971 and was intrigued. I, in my official capacity as Hillel President, would be interested in knowing whether your organization sponsors speakers to discuss the concept of Jewish Christians. Please inform me in regard to the possibility as I feel certain that such a meeting would be informative and beneficial for all concerned.'
>
> 'Also send me a copy of your fascinating booklet.'
>
> Of course we received, as we were expecting, a full portion of four-lettered names. We confidently expect that

some of the writers who cursed us will some day sing the praises of the Lamb who was slain—the Lord Jesus Christ. Many of the letters, however, showed unusual spiritual concern.

'Please send me your booklet. I feel that "emptiness" you described in your Times advertisement of December 10, 1971. I want to stay Jewish—that is, continue to keep my cultural traditions, but perhaps for my emptiness I need Jesus Christ and His ideas. Perhaps not. But if you send me your material I can decide for myself.'

'Could you also send some to my friends. We've discussed it and I think they might want some. They are all Jewish.'[66]

Requests for the testimony booklets and reprints of the ad, as well as requests for information on the Mission, poured into Headquarters. Some people and organizations were requesting multiple copies. One missionary organization requested 50,000 booklets and 1,400 copies of the ad reprints. Daniel wrote:

We are sending 1400 copies of the ad, 1400 copies of the booklet, and 1400 copies of Martin Rosen's booklet, 'How to Witness Simply and Effectively to the Jewish People.' We will do everything in our power to help them get the 50,000 booklets. We rejoice in 1400 Gospel-preaching churches joining with us in bringing the Gospel to the Jews.[67]

Eventually over a half-million of the testimony booklets were printed and circulated among Jewish people around the world. Never before in the history of the Mission had such large numbers of requests for literature and Gospel materials been received. Nor had the Mission ever before had such media exposure. The Passover telecast, the Smiling Faces ad, Jews for Jesus demonstrations and witnessing campaigns, meetings booked by The Liberated Wailing Wall music group, the radio ministry—each outreach was generating interest in the Mission and in Jewish evangelism; they also generated a dire need for Mission personnel to help with follow-up work. Workers were needed to do visitation to new contacts, letters needed to be written and mailed, new literature needed to be prepared and printed—all in addition to the regular branch ministry of the Mission, both at home and abroad.

As the Los Angeles staff faithfully seized opportunities for witness, God continued to open doors for expanded ministry. Dr. John Feinberg, who is currently a member of the faculty of Trinity Theological Seminary, served as a part-time worker for the Mission's staff while he was attending Trinity seminary himself. He observed the growth of the L.A. ministry when he returned to assist us on his summer break. He wrote:

Another form of ministry that has blossomed since I was last in the Los Angeles area is the outreach on High School and University campuses. These outreaches were just beginning when I left, and it is a real joy to see how the Lord has been increasing them. At a time when we are constantly hearing about the availability of drugs on high school and college campuses, it is encouraging to know that a positive alternative, Jesus the Messiah, is also being presented to students. Douglas Pyle, who has been especially involved in this ministry, writes:

'At the University of California, Los Angeles, and at the University of California, Santa Barbara, where we have Beth Sar Shalom student groups registered on campus, hundreds of tracts and booklets have gone into the hands of Jewish students as they take literature from our tables. At UCLA we often have four or five Jewish students at one time crowding around the literature table, some asking pointed questions about the Messiah and others objecting to the answers.'

'Recently, Dr. J. Vera Schlamm, M.D., a survivor of two years in Bergen-Belsen Concentration Camp during World War II, shared her testimony with a crowd of over 100 students (the majority were Jewish) on the UCLA campus in a noon meeting. Several student members of the Chabad House (a Chasidic student movement) were present along with two Rabbis, a Jewish faculty member, and other Jewish students.'

'These incidents are typical of what is happening on our campuses. Further outreach is being planned and initiated on other campuses in the area.'

...there has also been an increasing ministry in the churches in the Southern California area. Pastors are becoming aware of the need for educating their people in Jewish evangelism ...As a result, there are more requests for meetings than there were a year ago....

It has been a great blessing to me to return to Los Angeles and see the ways in which the Lord is increasing the ministry here.[68]

God's abundant blessings on the ministry in Los Angeles were obvious, but for the staff the many new opportunities for witness were also difficult to keep up with!

New Training Program in Los Angeles

At the October 1971 Board meeting, the author was appointed to the position of Director of Recruiting and Training. The Minutes state:

> *Mr. Fuchs moved and Mr. Scharfman seconded the motion that Rev. Harold Sevener be appointed as director of Recruiting and Training. He will continue working in Los Angeles for the present. This was voted.*[69]

Having been a witness to the problems that developed when Moishe Rosen was appointed Director of Recruiting and Training, and was asked to move to New York, the author was understandably somewhat ambivalent about the appointment. However, at the time the appointment was made, there was no indication that the author and his family would be asked to relocate to New York. The moratorium on the recruitment and hiring of new missionary personnel was still in effect, and it seemed that the appointment would simply entail training a few workers to fill vacancies on staff as they occurred. Further, since the Mission's policy regarding the establishment of branches had been changed, with the emphasis now being on media evangelism and follow-up, rather than on the purchase of property for the establishment of branches, it appeared that the training program would be for a select few candidates, rather than upon training large groups of candidates. Hence, it appeared there would be no need for the program to operate from New York. The author therefore prayerfully accepted the position. Winnie Marriner (now the Mission's worker in Montreal, Quebec, Canada) and Irvin Rifkin (now the Mission's worker in San Diego) were among the first candidates trained by the author.

Changes in Policy Affect Branches

Many things converged to make 1970 and 1971 difficult years for Daniel Fuchs. The conflict between himself and Martin Rosen, the problem of finding workers to replace Martin after his transfer to San Francisco, the disappointment of the cancellation of the Passover telecast in the Spring of '71, and the strained financial position of the Mission all came at a time when he wanted to concentrate on the media projects. After the cancellation of the Passover telecast, he was determined that he was not going to divide his time between personnel problems and media projects and problems. Therefore, just three months after appointing the author to the position of Director of Recruiting and Training, Daniel went to the Board with a new proposal. The Minutes of January 26, 1972 state:

> *Our first venture into the field of mass media has proven that organizationally we are not geared to handle the results of this program. Mr. Fuchs has been studying the structure of our organization and feels that many changes will have to be made. As a first step he recommended that Rev. Harold Sevener, now missionary in charge of our Los Angeles work and Director of Student Training, immediately be appointed as Director of the Missionaries in Charge throughout the country. He will then handle many of the details and problems that arise in the missionary department and thus relieve Mr. Fuchs. As soon as it is practicable and possible, Mr. Sevener will come to New York to make this his headquarters. Mr. Kubach moved and Dr. Reifsnyder seconded the motion that Mr. Fuchs be empowered to make the necessary changes to put this first step of the reorganization into operation. It was voted.*[70]

Washington D.C.—Bob and Althea Miller

One of the first branches affected by the change in missionary policy, from being "station-centered" to a "people-centered" mission, as announced by Daniel Fuchs at the November 18, 1970 Board meeting, was the branch in Washington D.C. The reader will recall that Daniel hired David Juroe in 1963 to develop the Washington D.C. branch. When Juroe was later transferred to New York to serve as the Resident Minister (missionary) for the Manhattan headquarters branch of the Mission, Robert (Bob) E. A. Miller and his wife, Althea, were sent to take over the Washington D.C. ministry. They began their work there during the summer of 1966.

Bob and Althea were not strangers to the Mission. Bob's father, Rev. Paul Miller, had worked closely with Joseph Hoffman Cohn, developing the radio ministry for the Mission. Bob, himself, was introduced to the Mission as a small child, when he accompanied his father to the Mission's headquarter's in Brooklyn. Paul's love and concern for the Jewish people was transferred by example to his son, and Bob wrote:

> *Very early in life I learned the imperative of praying 'for the peace of Jerusalem.' I first heard my preacher-father pray for the salvation of Jewish people in our early morning family worship. I did not fully comprehend then the reason for such prayer. I only knew if my father prayed for them or for anybody's salvation, something happened. Little did I dream how those prayers would affect my later life.*
> *Father prayed four of six sons into the ministry. Although we all ministered to churches made up largely of Gentiles,*

we never forgot our responsibility to give the Gospel 'to the Jew first.' Dad set us a good example. If he felt it was important to devote the first Sunday of every year to the cause and challenge of Jewish evangelism in his pastorates, dare I do less? Reaching the Jew was always a live issue with me; it became a very personal responsibility and privilege. I had to do something about it.[71]

Bob did something about it? In all of his pastorates among the Grace Brethren churches, he demonstrated his love for the Jewish people and taught his congregations to love the Jews, and to support ministries to the Jews.

Bob was often invited to speak at the Mission's conferences. Joseph Hoffman Cohn mentioned Bob's participation in a Mid-Winter Bible Conference held at the New York headquarters building on January 13-20, 1952. He wrote:

Rev. and Mrs. Robert E. Miller came up from Roanoke, Virginia, and both of them delivered such welcome and inspiring messages, that the memory will remain with us for a long time to come. Some of our Jewish brethren had never thought possible that such a deep love for Israel could exist in the heart of a Gentile preacher. But they were delightfully disillusioned, and they found in Brother Miller a love that they had rarely seen even among the Jewish rabbis.[72]

Through the years, Bob and Althea's love for the Jewish people and for the Mission deepened. In 1964, they had the privilege of taking an extended study tour of Israel. It was a dream come true, and a trip which ultimately changed their lives and their ministry. Bob wrote:

After a heart-enlarging experience by way of an intensive Study Tour of Israel in 1964, I could not shake the thought that most Jewish people have not rejected Jesus Christ. You cannot reject someone you do not know. I was convinced that Jewish people don't know who Jesus Christ really is. With this conviction came another: I personally should do something about telling them who he is.

Hard upon the heels of these God-inspired stirrings in my heart, the hate-spreading Nazis came to our city of Glendale, California with the intention of setting up their western headquarters. In protest to them and all they stand for, I placed a 'mezuzah' on the doorpost of our church parsonage in similar fashion to what the Danes did in World War II to protest the Nazi hatred of the Jews in Denmark.

As I expected, these men did their best to discredit me, engage the sympathies of people, and organize their nefarious activities. But 'one with God is a majority,' and the Nazis were ejected from the city. The Jewish community of Southern California had evidently been watching this drama of opposition to anti-Semitism over TV and by the media of radio and press.

Doors of opportunity were opened in surprising numbers to give a witness to the grace of God in Christ. Literally thousands of Jews asked why I, a Gentile and a minister, defied Naziism and acted in behalf of Jewish people. All through this experience I sensed a deep hunger in the lives of most of these people. It is true, of course, that not all the Jewish folk to whom I spoke were interested in the spiritual implications of my stand in their behalf. Some were more curious about me than concerned about their own relationship to God. Nevertheless, these were wide open doors which I gladly entered.

God used all of these experiences to prepare me for His call to personally take the message of Messiah to the 'lost sheep of the House of Israel.' It was a thrilling realization for my wife and me to see how He prepared our hearts through our individual personality responses for the work of Jewish evangelism into which He has now thrust us.[73]

While God was preparing Bob's heart, He was also directing Althea toward ministry among the Jewish people. She stated:

Why am I a missionary to the Jewish people, ...No one event can be singled out as marking the actual moment of decision. I believe the capstone God used was an in-depth Study Tour of Israel in 1964. My eyes were opened to the enormous spiritual need of Jewish people the world over, even as I admired their initiative and dauntless courage. It was then that a long-standing love for this unique people was enlarged by a burden to share personally with them the message of salvation through Messiah-Christ. Somehow it was no longer enough for me to pray and give for someone else to do this work.

At the age of eight I came to know Jesus Christ as my own Saviour. I recall thinking how happy Jewish people must be that Jesus was a Jew according to the flesh. What a shock to discover that they had no joy in this fact, nor did they love Him. I wondered why.

A few years later the pastor of our church (who ultimately became my father-in-law [R. Paul Miller]) initiated the first conference on PROPHECY AND THE JEW ever to be held in Philadelphia. This was my introduction to the work of the

American Board of Missions to the Jews. I listened with rapt attention to the messages of Dr. Leopold Cohn, founder of this Mission, and his son, Dr. Joseph Hoffman Cohn. Even then I felt the first stirrings of concern for Jewish people envelop my heart. Over the years that concern never lessened; it increased until I was overwhelmed with God's call.

With no conscious effort on my part I have found myself thrown more and more frequently among Jewish people, making friends, learning to love them individually rather than as a people in general. Opportunities were many to tell them of their Messiah. Then one day God said to me as He once commanded Abram: 'Get thee out...unto a land that I will show thee' (Genesis 12:1). I said 'Yes,' to God, thus linking myself to this 'people of destiny.'

Now at my husband's side, we are giving the ageless Gospel message to Jewish people. Through the printed page in The Chosen People *my prayer is that fellow believers will be encouraged to love these special people with a godly love and to pray earnestly for the salvation of specific Jewish individuals.[74]*

After their 1964 Study Trip to Israel, Althea corresponded with Daniel Fuchs and he agreed to publish a report of their trip and experiences in Israel in *The Chosen People* magazine.[75] Althea is an accomplished free-lance writer, and her articles on Israel so impressed Daniel that when Charles Kalisky was no longer able to write the 'Jewish Notes' column in *The Chosen People* magazine, he asked Althea to write the column. This she did on a regular basis from March 1965 through 1974, in addition to the missionary work she and Bob were engaged in.

The Millers were excited about joining the staff of the Mission. They wrote:

Excitement of preparation, added to a keen anticipation of the unknown, reached fever pitch by the time the doorbell began to ring. Before it stopped ringing, 96 people had responded to our invitation to the fall season's first Family Night Fellowship and carry-in-dinner at Beth Sar Shalom, Washington, D.C. Center. And this in spite of pouring rain all day....

We were greatly honored to have with us the President of the Board of Directors of the American Board of Missions to the Jews, Mr. Francis Simmons, with his charming wife and family. Mr. Simmons spoke briefly, reminding the group of the deep passion of the Mission and its directors for the salvation of Israel.[76]

God blessed the ministry of Bob and Althea Miller while they served in Washington D.C., and the work grew. In sharing with readers of *The Chosen People* magazine they said, "God opens doors daily for witnessing to the hungry hearts among the 80,000 Jewish people in the greater Washington area."[77] Three years later they were reporting: "Nearly 200 people attended the 1969 Passover; 80 were Jews, saved and unsaved."[78]

In addition to the meetings they conducted, Bob Miller maintained an extensive prophetic Bible conference ministry, as well as a student training program. They also found time to write and edit a paper called 'Tehilah' (Praise), which was published from September through May, and mailed to Jewish truth-seekers, Hebrew Christians, and Gentile friends of Beth Sar Shalom. The paper served as a bulletin of the Mission's meetings; it also contained items of news, prayer requests, free literature offers, and it included a full page on 'Israel Today' by Althea Miller. The list of subscribers to their publication grew from less than three hundred readers to more than 1,000 readers each month.

Rev. Paul Balthaser, who completed the training program in New York, joined the Washington D.C. staff in March 1969. With his help, the Millers reported:

This additional help has resulted in stepped up visitation and many new contacts with local churches and pastors. Plans include an active youth program, Home Fellowship meetings in the greater Washington area, and a campus ministry at American University (70% Jewish students), University of Maryland, and possibly George Washington University.[79]

A summer campus ministry was begun in 1970. The Miller's reported that it involved:

...twelve weeks with two student trainees who worked particularly with young people. Donna Marovich, a recent university graduate, focused her attention on Jewish students on a local university campus. Martin Gruen's thrust was a program of discussions, outings and entertainment for teenagers, some of whom had been known and previously contacted. It was a pilot program with great potential. We have had a burden for reaching Jewish students on the university level, and the fields are so ripe.[80]

During the Fall of 1971, although the Millers had a deep burden for the Jews of Washington D.C., and although God was blessing and expanding their ministry there, they felt God was calling them to return to California. When they told Daniel Fuchs of their desire to relocate to the West coast, he took their request not only as the leading of the Lord for the Millers, but also as the leading of the Lord for the Mission. He was anxious to begin enacting his policy of eliminating Mission property. The new policy called for the Mission's workers to "go" into the community, using homes and rental space for ministry to the Jewish community. Washington D.C. was the first branch affected by this new policy.

DAN AND ARLENE RIGNEY

As a part of his new responsibilities as Director in Charge of the Missionaries,[81] the author was asked to explain the new policy and the consequences it would have on the Washington D.C. district to the Millers, as well as to Dan and Arlene Rigney who were being transferred to the Washington/Baltimore area. A report of that visit was submitted to Daniel in a letter dated May 26, 1972. It states:

> Just a brief report to let you know what I found regarding the branches I recently visited.
>
> First of all, in the Washington D.C. area I spoke at some length with the Millers and also with the Rigneys, separately and then together. Basically, I explained to them the shift of thinking regarding our reorganization: developing things on a local level, establishing administrative offices, with the work being carried out in the community over against establishing large branches with staffs, expecting the Jewish people to come to us. Both couples seemed to be in agreement with this.
>
> As for the Millers, I think under the circumstances it would be best to transfer them to the Long Beach area. Bob is quite willing to accept a position as being in charge of a branch in Long Beach as outlined, along with the oversight of the Orange County area and building of the deputation work in the Brethren churches, particularly in Orange County with the option for the State of California. The basic plan of operation would be for him to establish an office somewhere in the Jewish neighborhood of Long Beach and then for him and Althea to set up visitation programs, outreach meetings and training programs within the churches to carry out a Jewish mission work in the Orange County area and within the city of Long Beach. They would then coordinate their holiday meetings with the other missionaries in the district. I also pointed out that, as we have done with Martin, and will be doing in the other branches, for deputation they will be responsible for maintaining financially their own missionary program monthly, excluding salary. This is an idealistic goal which at least they should shoot towards fulfilling. The basic contacts with the churches can be done both on the local and district levels. Bob and Althea seemed agreeable to this and, in fact, rather enthusiastic about it.
>
> ...I asked Dan and Bill to scout around to find a suitable type office that we could rent in the Jewish area, where we could have window display advertising, etc., letting both the Jewish and Christian communities know of our presence in the area. Such an office should be found and set up prior to disposing of our present property, so that both the Jewish and Christian communities would know that we are simply relocating for a greater emphasis, rather than disbanding. I think it should also be timed for when the Miller's move, so that the property being disposed of and the Miller's move will accomplish essentially the same thing (e.g., rather than disbanding the ministry), simply a shifting to a re-emphasis of the ministry. The Rigneys would then carry out a coffee house ministry, a monthly program as presently constituted, renting a facility in one of the hotels or working through one of the local churches, training volunteer workers to help participate in the ministry and they will also assume responsibility of raising support to offset the expenditures for their local programs.
>
> If you and the Board are in agreement with this arrangement, please let me know and I'll notify Bob and Dan to begin the wheels rolling, getting appraisals, etc., and for the re-shifting of the operation on the moving of Bob Miller, etc. I trust that the above will meet with your approval.[82]

By motion, Daniel and the Board approved the transfer of the Millers to California, and they agreed to retain the Rigneys in the Baltimore/Washington D.C. area to develop a de-centralized type of ministry. They also voted to sell the Mission's building in Washington D.C.[83]

God continued to use Bob and Althea Miller as they developed meetings in the Long Beach, Orange County and the Palm Springs areas of Southern California. Throughout their ministry many Jewish people were touched with the Gospel and many came to faith in the Messiah. In August 1987 Bob and Althea retired from active missionary service with the Mission, but they remain active in their witness and in their commitment to reach Jewish people with the Gospel.

Dan and Arlene Rigney continued to develop the Baltimore/Washington area until they left the Mission to join the staff of Jews for Jesus. They served on staff with Jews for Jesus for a number of years, and then resigned to work with Ariel Ministries—a ministry begun by Arnold Fruchtenbaum shortly after he left the staff of the Mission. In 1992, in a special cooperative agreement with the Mission (now called Chosen People Ministries, Inc. [C.P.M.]), Ariel Ministries loaned the Rigneys to C.P.M. to help develop its new ministry in Kiev, in the Ukraine (the former Soviet Union).

Following the January 1972 Board meeting, and Daniel's announcement that the author had been appointed Director of Missionaries in Charge, and would be making New York his headquarters as soon as it was practical and possible, the author began taking steps to locate a successor for the Los Angeles ministry so that his move to New York could be executed during the Fall of '72.

PHILADELPHIA—TERRYL DELANEY

Terryl Delaney was also making plans to move. He planned to move to the state of Washington where he would be able to work more closely with Dick Maginot on the Mission's media projects. Daniel had also given Terryl permission to start his own ad agency. "Terryl Delaney & Associates" was established in Seattle, Washington. In addition to setting up his own agency, Terryl was asked to revive the missionary and deputation work that had been started in the Pacific Northwest years earlier by Dr. Walter Atkinson. Daniel's action in allowing Terryl to establish his own agency, while at the same time serving as Director of Communications for the Mission, was his attempt to prevent the Mission from having to pay the fees and commissions for the placement of ads and services done by an outside agency. It was hoped that by having Terryl in Seattle, the Mission could "kill two birds with one stone"—cut expenses, as well as to expand the missionary and deputation work.

During the author's years of ministry in the Los Angeles area, Dr. Emil Gruen used him extensively in Family Bible conferences that were held each summer at the First Conference Center, Washington; Mt. Hermon, California; Cedar Lake, Indiana; the Summers End Conference, New York, and others. There were also local church conferences, and the author worked closely with the Field Evangelists in mini-conferences. The conference schedule, plus the added responsibilities of helping with media events, and trying to recruit and direct the training of missionaries for the staff, in addition to the general supervision of the personnel within the district, had allowed little time to consider the eventuality that a trained successor may one day be needed.

With no trained successor "waiting in the wings" for the Los Angeles ministry, Moishe Rosen seemed to be the logical choice. He already had many friends in the area, he was doing a superb job developing the youth ministry for the Mission in San Francisco, and he had been well received the few times he had been a guest speaker at meetings in L.A. after his return to the West coast. But when the suggestion was presented to Daniel Fuchs, he felt it was out of the question.

God had abundantly blessed the work in Los Angeles; the ministry had grown to the point where two separate branches had been established—the main branch in Hollywood, and a second branch in North Hollywood. Additional meetings were also being held in homes throughout the Los Angeles county basin. It was a vibrant work; it needed a vibrant leader!

LOS ANGELES—RICHARD COHEN

Rev. Albert Stoltey, Rev. David Juroe, and other men who had assisted in the ministry were contacted, but each declined the opportunity to serve as Missionary in Charge of the Los Angeles branch. As the author continued to pray about the need, Richard Cohen's name began to be impressed upon him. Richard was already helping in a part-time capacity while he was finishing his training at the Baptist Seminary in Newhall, California. Through his fearless witness, many Jews and Gentiles had been led to the Lord and he had evidenced real potential for leadership. The more the author considered him as a possible candidate for the position, the more plausible the idea seemed.

Richard was still young in the faith. The strong anti-Jewish remarks and treatment he and his family had been subjected to at Prairie Bible Institute in Canada had created some negative feelings about Gentile Christians, but the author felt certain those feelings would dissipate with further training and spiritual growth. Daniel, too, felt that with continued on the job training, and with proper supervision, Richard Cohen was the right person for the position.

Dr. John Feinberg, too, was impressed with the accomplishment of Richard as a missionary. He wrote:

After finishing my year of study at Trinity [Trinity Theological Seminary], I decided to return to California and work with the Mission in Los Angeles for the summer. While in Chicago, I was involved in deputation for the Mission, so I was able to keep in contact with what was happening. I had heard that the projected programs of the previous summer had become realities. I was not fully aware, though, of the extent of the expansion of the work until I returned to Los Angeles. Certainly, part of the expansion was due to the overall increased ministry of the American Board of Missions to the Jews, but certain specific things were happening in Los Angeles, too....

...the Lord was expanding the old programs, but He was also opening up new areas of service. Before I left Chicago, Richard Cohen had been devoting much of his time and energy to reach the vast Jewish community in the sprawling San Fernando Valley. I can recall doing some visitation in that area and attending some of the meetings

Richard was conducting. The ministry was already well under way, but the projected plan was to open up a Valley Center and to have Richard devote all of his time to the work out there. This plan became a reality in November, 1971, when the Valley Center was opened. Has the work there been a success, or has it dwindled? You be the judge as Richard relates some of the various activities of the new branch:

'Our Tuesday evening Bible study has provided a place for elderly Jewish ladies and gentlemen to come and hear about their Messiah, and also to have a time of fellowship. With 60% unsaved out of a regular attendance of 20 to 30 people, we have had decisions for the Lord.'

'A new ministry which has appealed to various age groups is our Arts and Crafts Class which meets on Wednesday afternoons. It is a line into the community to introduce them to our work. Many Jewish people are afraid to come to any place where there is talk about the Messiah, yet through this class we are able to keep idle hands busy and to show the love of God.'

'Through an active street ministry and a reading room available to passers-by, we have distributed thousands of tracts so the Jews in our area might hear the Gospel....

'In our area of North Hollywood, there is a local Junior College with approximately 8,000 Jewish students. We have been making contacts on campus so that at the start of the next school year we will be having an extensive ministry amongst the students.'

'Through the last six months of our ministry here in North Hollywood we have had an average of two decisions per month. We plan in the months to come to expand our ministry to cover the entire San Fernando Valley where there are over 100,000 Jews who need to hear the about the Messiah.'[84]

Richard Cohen was a devoted missionary, and when the author spoke with him about the possibility of his becoming the Missionary in Charge of the Los Angeles ministry, he expressed a desire to accept the challenge, and a willingness to work on areas where his ministry skills and attitudes needed improvement.

There were other changes taking place within the structure of the Mission during 1972. In January 1972, the titles of Mission leaders were once again changed. The title of General Secretary, held by Daniel Fuchs, was changed to *Executive Director*; the title of Conference Secretary, held by Emil Gruen, was changed to *Conference Director*. Henry Heydt's title remained the same—Missionary-Liaison-Director.[85]

SAN FRANCISCO—MOISHE ROSEN

Moishe Rosen, too, was requesting changes for his ministry; he wanted to expand the work. The Minutes of the April 1972 Board meeting show the following entry:

When Martin Rosen was transferred to the San Francisco area nearly two years ago, he was given a very limited field of operation. He has done well out there and is an excellent missionary. He has now asked the he be allowed to enlarge his ministry—have a larger staff—open a coffee house ministry—do more work with the churches—publish more literature, etc. Mr. Fuchs was authorized by motion of Mr. Leonard to go into this matter very thoroughly with Martin, then take it up with the personnel committee and report back to the Board at the next meeting. The motion was seconded and carried.[86]

At the next Board of Directors' meeting, as agreed, Moishe's request to expand his ministry in San Francisco was discussed. The Minutes state:

After presenting Martin Rosen's request at the April meeting for an expanded work with the youth in the San Francisco area, Mr. Fuchs and Mr. Sevener met with him and they feel that he has done a very good work and that there is a need for a 'Christian House' in the area where Jewish Christians who have recently come to know the Lord may have a chance to grow in their Christian faith and life.

Mr. Rosen has asked that the Mission rent a large house in a convenient area where about a dozen young people can live on a temporary basis— where there will be room for printing of tracts and material—room for a coffee house that will accommodate about 50 people—room for Bible study that will accommodate between 50 and 75 people—an apartment for house parents—rooms and living quarters for from 10 to 12 young people and a place for transients who may stay two or three days. Bruce Goldstein and his wife, Marcia Black Goldstein, are mature enough to act as house parents.

After discussion, Mr. Straub moved that this project be approved with the understanding that it will be developed into a self-supporting program. It was further moved that the following rules of discipline as outlined by Mr. Rosen be *strictly adhered to. Mr. Leonard seconded the motion and it was voted.*

1. If it is forbidden in the Bible, it is forbidden in the house.

2. No use of narcotics or alcohol for purposes of intoxication allowed on the premises.

3. No pets except by prearrangement.

4. All teaching and conduct must be in accord with the evangelical Christian tradition as understood and taught by the Mission (no promotion of Pentecostal doctrine). [87]

The reference to "Pentecostal" doctrine was due to the growing "Charismatic" movement at the time—a movement which had caused a considerable amount of division within churches and ministries. The Board was trying to prevent such division among its staff and ministry.

The Board had invited the author to attend the June 1972 Directors' meeting; the reference to Martin's program being self-supporting was based upon his report as Director of Missionaries in Charge. The Minutes state:

Mr. Fuchs presented the Rev. Harold Sevener, director of the missionaries-in-charge. He gave a brief outline of the future plans for the mission work and presented an organizational chart for the American Board of Missions to the Jews. An explanation was given of the proposed plan for setting up programs in the cities in the midst to the Jewish population [100,000 or more] with a staff of not more than three—to enlist and train workers from the community itself—both from the Jewish and Christian community hopefully that within the course of at the most three years, this program would be both self-sustaining and self-supporting. A copy of the organizational chart is filed with the Board Minutes. [88]

Daniel Fuchs announced the plans to open a Halfway House in the city of San Francisco in the September 1972 issue of *The Chosen People* magazine. He wrote:

It is because of this moving of the Holy Spirit among Jewish youth that we are 'hoisting another sail.' By God's grace, we are opening a halfway house to minister to Jewish youths in the San Francisco-Berkeley area. It is to this area that countless Jewish youths are drifting. They are the alienated generation—alienated from their families, their synagogues and from society. These are the youths to whom Martin Rosen and his staff are ministering and we praise the Lord that many of them are accepting the Lord. But, whereas other young people in the streets can accept Christ and then return to their homes, this is not true of most Hebrew Christians. They need a great deal of acceptance, encouragement in Christian growth and Bible study.

To this ministry we have assigned Bruce (Baruch) and Marcia Goldstein. Bruce has been saved from a life of drug addiction. He has a warm heart of sympathetic understanding of the problems of those hooked on drugs. His wife, Marcia, is a graduate of Moody Bible Institute and has been a capable successful member of our staff for three years. Both Baruch and Marcia are young enough to become identified with the Jewish youth, and they are mature enough to give the house the stability that is necessary for discipline and Christian training. Please pray for them as we 'hoist another sail.' [89]

The Media Blitz Continued

As Moishe was moving ahead with his plans for a half-way house, and seeking to raise support to make it self-funded, Daniel's mind was occupied with the aftermath of the Smiling Faces ad, and with new evangelistic media ideas. In May 1972 he reported:

...The results of this ad [Smiling Faces] have been so gratifying that our Board of Directors authorized us to insert these ads in leading papers all over the country. In every city in the United States that has a Jewish population of 100,000 or more we will choose that newspaper that reaches most of the Jewish people. Here in New York City we will again use The New York Times but also add the New York Post, Newsday (Long Island), and the Long Island Press. In Los Angeles it will be The Los Angeles Times; in Washington, D.C., The Washington Post. We plan to give you the entire list in next month's issue. If we obtain a 50% penetration (this figure seems reasonable) we will reach 2 and one half million Jews, almost half of the Jewish population in the United States, in one day. We should realize that while our main purpose is to reach as many Jews as possible with the Gospel, we also desire to get into personal contact with those thousands of Jewish people who are hungry for this message. We know that there are throngs like this; but our problem has been, 'How can we reach them?' Until now, the doors have been closed. Now, as a result of the ad and the booklet of testimonies offered, we are still (three months later) receiving requests for visitation. Our Lord is opening doors. [90]

Daniel then gave examples of the many ways God was opening doors for the ministry, and concluded by saying:

There is a new climate in our ministry. A few years ago when our workers went out on the streets and college campuses, young people were chanting, 'God is dead;' 'Burn down the churches;' 'Kill the establishment.' Now some of these same young people are carrying Bibles, wearing 'Jews for Jesus' buttons and even testifying in the synagogues.[91]

If Daniel sounded enthused about the "media blitz" in the May '72 issue of *The Chosen People*, he was ecstatic when he wrote his Salutation for the June issue. He wrote:

'No weapon that is formed against thee shall prosper.' This promise, found in Isaiah 54:17, has always been a source of strength to us in our ministry. Last March our opponents forged a weapon against us. At first it seemed that their whetted sword would decapitate us. But the promise of God is sure, and 'the weapon' that was formed did not prosper. In fact, our Lord literally beat their swords in plowshares that have broken hard ground and made it a fertile field which, by His grace, is now being harvested. We will not know until eternity how greatly the cancellation of our Passover Telecast triggered the reception the Jewish youth are now giving the Gospel.

As I write this letter we are being buried with mail from our 'Smiling Faces' ad and also by the initial responses from our Passover Telecast. On March 12th [c. 1972], without any advance notice of what we were going to do, we placed the full-paged 'Smiling Faces' ad in newspapers in every city in the United States which has a population of over 100,000 Jewish people. The returns have been in the thousands.

The ad appeared in the following papers: The New York Times, The Los Angeles Times, The San Francisco Chronicle, the Chicago Tribune, The Boston Globe, The Long Island Press, The Philadelphia Inquirer, The Baltimore Sun, The Washington Post, and The Miami Herald.

The response has been gratifying. It indicates that many unbelieving Jews have a keen interest in the testimonies of Hebrew Christians....

Although, as we have stated, the replies have been in the thousands, these new contacts, in God's providence, have actually been part of the minor benefits. The ad has led to radio and television opportunities. The controversy it has generated in both the general and especially the Jewish press has reached as many Jews with the Gospel as did the original paid ad. I wish that it were possible for our Chosen People family to read all of the mail that we are getting. It would thrill your hearts. But, one of the greatest thrills to me is that we are finding out that hundreds of Jewish young people are accepting the Lord.

While all of the preparation for the 'ad' was taking place we were busy also with the Passover Telecast. Knowing that our opponents were actively undercutting us with the stations which had originally canceled the program, we tried to outflank them. The efficient, untiring vice-president and secretary of our Canadian ministry, Beth Sar Shalom Mission, is Mr. Tom Walker. While the pot was steaming here in the United States, Tom quietly negotiated with television stations all over Canada with the result that our Passover telecast was broadcast over 40 stations throughout the Dominion in the following cities: Vancouver, Victoria, Calgary, Lethbridge, Medicine Hat, Winnipeg, Barrie, Bancroft, Georgian Bay, Haliburton, Kitchener, Minden, Muskoka, Parry Sound, Peterborough, Toronto, Bon Accord, Moncton, Saint John, Antigonish, Caledonia, Canning, Halifax, Inverness, Sydney, Argentia, Bonavista, Cape Broyle, Central Nfld. Corner Brook, Deer Lade, Grandbank, Lawn, St. Alban's, St. John's, Signal Hill, Terranceville, Trepassey.

Here in the United States we offered the program to those stations that canceled and two, in Chicago and Pittsburgh, accepted. Besides this, the Miami station while not accepting the Passover has given us a wonderful opportunity to present our faith entirely free of charge....

Meanwhile, our field men in selected areas organized the evangelical clergy in various cities. These Bible-believing shepherds worked together, and, as local ministerial organizations, offered the telecast to stations in their own cities. In every case the Telecast was accepted, and in almost every case it was aired without charge on prime time as a public service!...

So, by God's grace, we are able to report on our new thrusts using mass media. Our report has necessarily been condensed. It is the story of the truth of the Scriptures, 'No weapon that is formed against thee shall prosper.' It is a story which will reach into eternity, therefore we can trust our Lord to close this salutation with a thankful TO BE CONTINUED![92]

The successes of the media projects were a "mountain peak" experience for Daniel, and for the entire Mission staff. But the mundane things of life kept our feet on the ground. The finances of the Mission continued to be a matter of concern.

Headquarters Moves Out of Manhattan

In New York, preparations were being made to sell the Headquarters building in Manhattan, and to separate the administrative work from the missionary outreach in New York. The Minutes of the June 1972 Board meeting record the reasons given for the sale of the Leopold Memorial Building on 72nd Street in Manhattan. They state:

> Mr. Fuchs reported that with the changing of our program and the fact that Rev. Harold Sevener will be coming to New York Headquarters, there is need for the room which is now being occupied by our printing and mailing departments.
>
> As of January 1, 1972 all tax exempt property was taken from the exempt rolls of the City of New York and new requests for tax exemption had to be filed. Our request for exemption of the property at 236 West 72nd Street, New York City was denied and we have been taxed $10,000 for one half year. This tax is being paid under protest and we will file again next year for exemption. One of the stumbling blocks to exemption may be that we have a printing department on the premises. Therefore Mr. Fuchs asked Rev. Burl Haynie to investigate the possibility of moving the printing and mailing department away from New York. A place was found in Zarephath, New Jersey where it was felt arrangements could be made with the Pillar of Fire School for a cooperative agreement for the printing and mailing of tracts. In order to do this effectively, it would be necessary to invest at least $65,000 in new equipment.
>
> This problem was discussed on two aspects:
>
> 1. The need of moving the mailing and printing department—there was general agreement about this need.
> 2. The purchase of additional equipment. It was felt that we should carefully investigate the wisdom of increasing investments in a 'captive plant' as well as problems relating to future management of such an operation.
>
> Later discussion revealed that this problem was not isolated—we must soon make major decisions about the possibility of moving from New York City and computerizing our system.
>
> Mr. Straub moved inasmuch as the printing department is only a part of the entire problem, that the directors work on the larger problem with as much speed as possible, and therefore resolve that no action be taken on individual parts at this meeting. Mr. Pretlove seconded the motion and it was voted.[93]

At the September 23, 1972 meeting of the Board the following Minutes were recorded:

> Mr. Fuchs reported that Rev. Burl Haynie had submitted his resignation [the reader will recall that Burl Haynie started with the Mission in Los Angeles. He later helped to man the Mission's booth at the New York World's Fair, as well as being in charge of the printing and mailing department of the Mission] and this would leave our printing department without a supervisor. In view of the discussion at the last meeting as to the wisdom of doing our own printing, Mr. Leonard moved and Mr. Straub seconded the motion that Mr. Fuchs be authorized to discontinue the printing department and to dispose of the printing equipment either by selling or leasing, whichever would be to the best advantage of the Mission. It was voted.[94]

Regarding the relocation of the administrative offices of the Mission, the Minutes of the same September 1972 meeting state:

> Mr. Fuchs reported, that as authorized by the Board at the last meeting, search has been made for a suitable location for moving our administrative offices. A place has been found at 460 Sylvan Avenue, Englewood Cliffs, New Jersey, which has 5000 square feet of space and would be sufficient for our needs. We have been offered a lease on this space at $5.75 a square foot for a five year lease with an option for five years more. The property would be renovated for our needs, janitor service would be provided, repairs would be taken care of, etc. Mr. Pretlove moved and Mr. Melhorn seconded the motion that the finance committee be authorized to negotiate a lease for the first floor in the property at 460 Sylvan Avenue, Englewood Cliffs, New Jersey for five years with option at $5.75 per square foot—or a better price if possible. It was unanimously voted.[95]

The Directors also voted to allow Daniel Fuchs to enter into a lease agreement with IBM for computer equipment "...on a rental basis at a cost of $2328.00 per month—not including one time costs for training personnel, etc."[96]

The Directors then authorized the sale of the Headquarters building in Manhattan (located at 236 W. 72nd Street). They also authorized the sale of the Mission building in Washington D.C. (located at 5917-16th Street NW).[97]

So it was that the Washington D.C. property and the Headquarters building in Manhattan (the Leopold Memorial Building) became the first two Mission properties to be sold—in accordance with Daniel Fuchs' change in missionary policy.

Director of Communications Appointed

At the January 1973 Board Meeting, Daniel introduced Terryl Delaney, Director of Communications for the Mission, to the Board. The Minutes state:

> He [Daniel] introduced Rev. Terry Delaney who gave a very comprehensive report of his work in mass-media—played tapes of some of the new approaches in the radio—his work in the line of TV and plans for getting a revised edition of Smiling Faces on campuses and in youth groups. When he finished Mr. Fuchs said, 'Terry, for myself and I think I speak for the Board, we want to tell you how much we appreciate your innovations, your originality and your drive for the work of the Board. I think you are one of the rising generation who has already changed the image of the American Board of Missions and its work for the Lord.'[98]

Not only was Terryl developing and placing the "Smiling Faces" ads in Newspapers nation-wide, he was also placing the Passover telecast on stations that agreed to air the broadcast. Additionally, he had begun a new radio broadcast for the Mission, called "The Promise of Tomorrow,"[99] and he was developing "spot" announcements for radio.

In February 1973, Daniel permitted Terryl to produce a special edition of *The Chosen People* magazine. Daniel thought the special edition might be used to further promote the Mission and thereby generate revenue which would help offset the rising costs of the media programs. Terryl hoped that by developing the special issue, Daniel would see the wisdom of bringing *The Chosen People* magazine under the umbrella of the Communications Department. However, this did not happen. Daniel gave Terryl a free hand to develop media, but *The Chosen People* magazine remained the exclusive domain of the Editorial Department under Daniel Fuchs.

The Mission's constituency was informed of the move of the Mission's administrative offices from New York City to Englewood Cliffs, New Jersey in the January 1973 issue of *The Chosen People* magazine. In that issue of the magazine, Daniel also made the first public mention of the financial strain the Mission was experiencing due to its rapid growth and expansion. He wrote:

> While we are grateful to our Lord for His many victories we must report that there are many grave problems which face us. One of these is financial.... In 1954 when I first edited a Report Issue [of The Chosen People magazine] our expenses for the year were $400,000. Last year our expenses reached $1,750,000. [What Daniel did not say was that the income was only $1,089,043 of which $203,420 was legacy income, and that $660,957 had been transferred from the investment fund to the operating fund in order to meet expenses.][100] We have built many new centers, quadrupled our missionary staff, and instituted daily radio programs beamed to Israel. Our ministry, by God's grace, has spiralled. In spite of all of this growth, we have firmly maintained our financial policy: we make our needs known but we never appeal for funds [this was never Leopold or Joseph Cohn's policy]. The Lord has honored this policy, and we do not plan to change it. However there were times last year when missionary payrolls were due, and the day before they were due we did not have the necessary funds in the bank. Your missionaries have been instructed to 'burn off the fat,' to cut expenses to the bone without weakening our ministry.
>
> In this economy drive we have had to take many long hard looks at our Mission's operational expenses. One of the hard looks we took was at our administrative offices in the heart of New York City. Our building at 236 West 72nd Street, cost $54,000 to purchase in 1942. Last year the maintenance cost alone for this building was over $65,000. And now New York City has assessed us $18,000 a year for real estate taxes. Besides this, the area has been deteriorating rapidly, and our people have a fear to come out after dark.
>
> We have some ethical questions we must answer. For instance, in the light of our faith in the imminent return of our Lord do we have the right to tie up the Lord's money in real estate? Should we continue to build centers or should we use the centers we now have as strategic areas from which we must move into other areas? There is a theology of missions in the Old Testament which can be distilled into one word, 'Come'....
>
> In the New Testament we have not merely a theology but a direct command from the Lord—'Go!' If we seek to maintain our ministry to the four walls of centers, we will fossilize.
>
> Thus, your Board of Directors has decided to move our administrative headquarters out of New York City into the suburbs.... This change alone will save us about $45,000 a year.[101]

Interestingly, Daniel said nothing about the expenses of the "media events" which had cost the Mission $250,000 to $300,000 a year over a period of two years, and the cost of those projects were on-going due to the fact that the Mission had to retain lawyers in an attempt to re-coup some of the funds lost when the many television stations had so abruptly canceled the Passover telecast without cause.

Daniel further told the readers of *The Chosen People*:

> We have been deeply grateful to the Lord for the marvelous reaction to our mass media ministry; and, although we had problems in follow-up, we believe our Lord has overruled. Last April our entire mailing system was short-circuited because of the tremendous response to our 'ad.' We simply were not equipped to handle the printing and mailing for this ad. It was almost three months before we finally completed the mailing of the booklets that were requested. It was weeks later before we were able to send the names and addresses to our workers and to the various churches for follow-up. Because of this, we have decided to computerize our mailing system. One operation will permanently file a name and address not only for mailing requested literature, but for all follow-up letters, invitations to special meetings, etc. We will be able to send daily recapitulation of names and addresses to workers and volunteers.[102]

THE AUTHOR AND HIS FAMILY MOVE TO NEW YORK

The actual move of the administrative offices of the Mission from New York City to Englewood Cliffs, New Jersey was scheduled for January 26, 1973. The author and his family had moved to New York in October 1972 and throughout the remainder of the year, and in the early weeks of January 1973, the author worked with Emil Olsen and Winnie Marriner (who was then serving as the author's secretary) in setting up the new offices in Englewood Cliffs. The three of us undertook the gargantuan task of assessing the situation and determining a plan to expedite the move. Over twenty-six years of accumulated files, equipment and literature had to be moved or disposed of, but Emil Olsen did a splendid job in organizing the task, and by January 26, 1973 the full administrative staff of the Mission occupied its new Headquarters office in Englewood Cliffs, New Jersey.

The Headquarters building in Manhattan was sold to the Metropolitan Baptist Association for $288,500. It was sold with the agreement that the Mission would have use of the entire sixth floor, and access to the meeting facilities for a five year period.[103] The Missionary Department and the Conference Department, under the direction of Dr. Emil Gruen who was planning to retire at the end of 1973, remained in New York. Dr. Henry Heydt also continued to maintain his office and his ministry in New York City. Dr. Heydt's title had remained unchanged; he remained the Missionary Liaison Director of the Mission. He was also the President of the Beth Sar Shalom Institute—the name given to the Missionary Institute program after it was merged with the New York School of the Bible. Henry also continued to write the "Question and Answer" column for *The Chosen People* magazine, and he carried on extensive correspondence. He continued to serve the Mission in this capacity even after his retirement and his move to Florida. Henry was an untiring servant of the Lord, carrying on the ministry from his home until a stroke incapacitated him.

Mr. Burl Haynie, who had resigned as the head of the Printing and Mailing Department of the Mission, continued doing work for the Mission. He secured rental space in Zarephath, New Jersey at the "Pillar of Fire" property. He then purchased the printing and mailing equipment from the Mission, and contracted with Daniel to do all of the printing and mailing for the Mission.

At the January 1973 Directors meeting, Daniel recommended that the author be present at Board meetings to present his report. The Minutes state: "Mr. Fuchs suggested in view of the fact that Mr. Sevener was taking over much of the work of Mr. Gruen, as well as many additional responsibilities, he should be present at Board meetings to give his report."[104]

At the April 1973 Board Meeting the author's title was changed to Missionary Director.[105] He then attended all of the Board meetings, and in many cases was invited to sit through the entire meeting, but he was not officially appointed as a member of the Board until the annual meeting on January 26, 1976.

In spite of the media campaigns, the extra efforts of the Field Evangelists to raise money, the sale of two Mission properties, and the relocation of the administrative offices out of New York City, the financial picture of the Mission continued to look grim. The computerization of the mailing list, which was expected to be of great assistance in processing literature requests and donor receipts, caused delays instead, and thereby affected the Mission's income. The Minutes of the June 1973 Board meeting state:

> The IBM conversion is progressing more slowly than had been hoped. Mr. Fuchs reported that he had authorized the delaying of the mailing of the calendars until the middle of August with the hope that conversion of the mailing list may be completed by that time. He will also delay the mailing of the September issue of The Chosen People until the second week in September.[106]

At the same Directors meeting, the Finance Committee presented a report that the Mission had outstanding bills in the amount of $50,000.00. It was their recommendation that the Mission should not sell any more of its securities, but that it should, instead, borrow money until the market turned around. Their recommendation was unprecedented! However, the Minutes state: "...After discussion, Mr. Scharfman moved and Mr. Fuchs seconded the motion that the finance committee be authorized to borrow against our securities up to $200,000, if needed. It was voted."[107]

The financial report, for the eight month period ending May 31, 1973, showed receipts of $942,684 and disbursements of $1,269,304—a deficit of $326,620! For the eleven month period ending August 31, 1973, the mission showed receipts of $1,236,692 and disbursements of $1,714,764—a deficit of $478,072![108]

Once again, the author would remind the reader that while these large deficits were a worry to the Directors of the Mission, they were astute businessmen and they knew that the Mission had sufficient assets to cover the liabilities. They were also men of faith, and they believed that God would supply the necessary funding to carry on the ministry.

Satan, on the other hand, was doing all he could to undermine and destroy the testimony and the growth of the Mission. He used one incident and the generosity of one supporter to rock the Mission and its programs.

A Gracious Gift Causes Problems

In December 1972, Daniel received a letter from a Mrs. Dessah Randall, a supporter of the Mission. Mrs. Randall had been a member of the church that Dr. Donald Grey Barnhouse had pastored in Philadelphia, Pennsylvania. She loved the Jewish people because of Dr. Barnhouse's teaching, and she wanted to make a $50,000.00 memorial gift in his memory. Daniel shared a portion of Mrs. Randall's letter in his Salutation in the March 1973 issue of *The Chosen People* magazine. It stated:

> 'Please advise me of any special needs that you have concerning your work. I expect to soon have $50,000 for Jewish work which you will get. This is in memory of Dr. Donald Grey Barnhouse who taught us the debt we owe to Israel. I like any donation to be used as soon as possible. Putting money in buildings or in funds to be used later does not interest me.'
> 'Reaching Jews for Christ NOW IS IMPORTANT.'[109]

Daniel went on to state: "Naturally, I replied and suggested our new thrust [media evangelism] and the donor agreed!"[110]

Daniel did not know his reply to Mrs. Randall would literally stir up a hornet's nest of controversy, but after it was made known who the donor was, Moishe Rosen notified Daniel that Mrs. Randall had contacted him and his staff about giving a gift to the Mission's work in San Francisco. Moishe felt that the original intent of the donor was to use the $50,000.00 gift to develop the halfway house which Daniel had announced in *The Chosen People*. Moishe was upset to think that Daniel had persuaded Mrs. Randall to give the gift for media evangelism instead.

Moishe's announcement that he, too, had been in contact with Dessah Randall and that he believed that Daniel had circumvented the gift for his own vision and programs, did not set well with Daniel. He was certain in his own heart and mind that Mrs. Randall wanted her gift used for media evangelism. The author, who'd had a number of telephone conversations with Mrs. Randall, also felt certain that her intent was that the gift was to be used for the Mission's media projects. In fact, the author was asked to personally meet with Mrs. Randall and to personally receive the check from her, and when she placed the check in my hand she stated that it was to be used for media evangelism. But through the misunderstanding between Daniel Fuchs and Moishe Rosen, the old feelings of mistrust once again rose to the surface!

Over a period of many years, the Mission's personnel had participated in summer family Bible conferences at the Firs Conference Ground in Bellingham, Washington. The summer of 1973 was no different. The author was one of the speakers, along with Dr. Charles Feinberg. Some of the members of the Los Angeles staff were also involved, including Richard Cohen, Doug and Paula Pyle, and missionary trainees, Mr. Bill Katin and Mr. Leslie Jacobs.

In making plans for the Los Angeles workers to participate in the conference at the Firs, it was decided that Bill Katin and Leslie Jacobs should spend a few weeks in San Francisco assisting and learning at the Jews for Jesus branch. But contrary to being the uplifting and helpful time we expected those weeks to be, Bill and Leslie arrived at the Firs with very disconcerting reports of the ministry in San Francisco. They reported activities that were contrary to the established policy by which Moishe was to work in his branch, and the time spent working with Moishe had been so upsetting to the men that they were ready to abandon their plans to work with the Mission.

The San Francisco Branch Closed

In a telephone conversation, the author reported the matter to Daniel Fuchs. He, in turn, caught the first plane out of New York to Seattle, and he made his way to the conference ground so that he could confer with Bill and Leslie and other members of the Los Angeles staff. The following day he flew to San Francisco. He telephoned the author later in the day to say that he had officially severed relationships with Moishe Rosen. It had been an extremely painful decision for Daniel; Moishe had been like a son to him.

The Minutes of the September 1973 meeting of the Board state: "After discussion of the San Francisco problems, Mr. Fuchs moved and Mr. Pretlove seconded the motion that the San Francisco Branch be closed as of September 30, 1973 and that the staff be terminated with salary until November 1, 1973. It was voted."[111]

At the same meeting it was moved by Mr. Kubach: "…that regular employees on the staff at San Francisco be given one month's severance pay for each year of service with the Mission. Mr. Straub seconded the motion and it was voted."[112]

In voting to close the San Francisco branch, the Board tried to be as generous as possible with the staff members. Not only did they extend to them salary and benefits, they allowed them to retain all of the equipment, furnishings, files and mailings lists because the Directors recognized the value in the ministry they were doing. But they also recognized that the direction and thrust of the two ministries were not compatible—no organization can have two heads and survive. The Board believed that by God's grace, both organizations—each with its own methodology—would continue to effectively reach Jewish people with the Gospel.

The Directors were right. It is God's desire that Jewish people have an opportunity to hear and respond to the Gospel. Jewish people, like Gentile people, are individuals—with individual ideas, needs and reactions. So it is that God's servants have differing ideas and individual gifts; He uses the kaleidoscope of talents and ideas to accomplish His purposes in bringing men and women to a knowledge of Himself. God uses people of faith and vision, and, in spite of their imperfections, and even in spite of their failures, He leads so that in all things His perfect will is accomplished for our good and for His glory!

Under the banner of His blessings, Jews for Jesus has grown into a world-wide organization which proclaims the Gospel to the Jewish people, and the Mission (the American Board of Missions to the Jews, Inc., now Chosen People Ministries, Inc.) has also continued its world-wide thrust of bringing the Gospel to all Jews everywhere.

Endnotes

Chapter 11. The Vision in Kaleidoscope

[1] Isaiah 45:9a

[2] *Personal Correspondence: Martin Rosen to Rachmiel Frydland,* (March 14, 1966), p 1.

[3] *Personal Correspondence: R. Frydland to M. Rosen,* (March 30, 1966), p 1.

[4] *Personal Correspondence: M. Rosen to R. Frydland,* (April 4, 1966), pp 1, 2.

[5] *The Chosen People,* Vol. LXXII, No. 1, (September, 1966), p 11.

[6] *The Chosen People,* Vol. LXXIII, No. 9, (May, 1968), pp 12, 13.

[7] *The Chosen People,* Vol. LXXVI, No. 4, (December, 1970), pp 10, 11.

[8] *The Chosen People,* Vol. LXXIV, No. 1, (September, 1968), p 13.

[9] See note above.

[10] *The Chosen People,* Vol. LXXIII, No. 7, (March, 1968), p 11.

[11] Eliezer Urbach as told to Edith S. Weigand, *Out of the Fury,* (Denver, Colorado: Zhera Publications, 1987).

[12] Arthur Katz, *Apprehended by God—a Journal of a Jewish Atheist,* (Laporte, MN: Ben Israel Publishers, 1993).

[13] *The Chosen People,* Vol. LXXIV, No. 7, (March, 1969), pp 10-12.

[14] *The Chosen People,* Vol. LXXIV, No. 5, (January, 1969), p 10.

[15] See note above, p 12.

[16] See note above, p 13.

[17] *The Chosen People,* Vol. LXXIII, No. 10, (June, 1968), p 8.

[18] *The Chosen People,* Vol. LXXIV, No. 4, (December, 1968), p 7.

[19] *The Shepherd of Israel,* Vol. 42, No. 1, (September, 1957), p 1.

[20] See note above, pp 1, 2.

[21] See note above, p 2.

[22] *The Chosen People,* Vol. LXVI, No. 9, (May, 1961), p 9.

[23] *The Chosen People,* Vol. LIX, No. 1, (October, 1953), p 16.

[24] *Minutes,* ABMJ, (March 1, 1955), p 130.

[25] *Minutes,* ABMJ, (February 14, 1961), p 198.

[26] *Minutes,* ABMJ, (April 24, 1963), p 222.

[27] *The Chosen People,* Vol. LXXII, No. 9, (May, 1967), pp 11, 12.

[28] *The Chosen People*, Vol. LXXVI, No. 3, (November, 1970), pp 8, 9.

[29] *The Chosen People*, Vol. LXXV, No. 3, (November, 1969), p 5.

[30] *The Chosen People*, Vol. LXXIX, No. 1, Reprinted in part from the North Dade Journal, N. Miami, Fla., (September, 1973), p 12.

[31] *The Chosen People*, Vol. LXXVII, No. 5, (January, 1972), p 8.

[32] *The Chosen People*, Vol. LXXIII, No. 10, (June, 1968), p 5.

[33] *Minutes*, ABMJ, (April 17, 1968), p 15.

[34] *Minutes*, ABMJ, (November 19, 1969), p 37.

[35] *Minutes*, ABMJ, (April 26, 1969), pp 27, 28; *Minutes*, ABMJ, (July 16, 1969), p 29.

[36] *Minutes*, ABMJ, (November 19, 1969), p 37.

[37] *The Chosen People*, Vol. LXXV, No. 6, (February, 1970), pp 2, 3.

[38] *Minutes*, ABMJ, (November 18, 1970), p 55.

[39] *The Chosen People*, Vol. LXXVI, No. 1, (September, 1970), pp 5-7.

[40] *The Chosen People*, Vol. LXXVI, No. 5, (January, 1971), p 3.

[41] *Minutes*, ABMJ, (September 17, 1969), p 35.

[42] *Minutes*, ABMJ, (January 28, 1970), p 41.

[43] Moishe Rosen with William Proctor, *Jews for Jesus*, (Old Tappan, New Jersey: Fleming H. Revell Co., 1974), p 58.

[44] See note above, pp 57, 58.

[45] See note above, pp 60, 61.

[46] See note above, p 63.

[47] *The Chosen People*, Vol. LXXVI, No. 4, (December, 1970), p 6,7.

[48] *The Chosen People*, Vol. LXXVII, No. 6, (February, 1972), p 8,9.

[49] *The Chosen People*, Vol. LXXVIII, No. 2, (October, 1972), p 10.

[50] See note above, p 11.

[51] See note above, p 12.

[52] M. Rosen, *Jews for Jesus*, p 82-85.

[53] *The Chosen People*, Vol. LXXVIII, No. 7, (March, 1973), p 11.

[54] See note above.

[55] *Minutes*, ABMJ, (April 22, 1970), p 44.

[56] *The Chosen People*, Vol. LXXIV, No. 10, (June, 1969), pp 11, 12.

[57] Daniel Goldberg, *A Personal Testimony*, (n.d.), p 1.

[58] *Minutes*, ABMJ, (September 16, 1970), p 52.

[59] See note above, p 51.

[60] See note above, p 50.

[61] *Minutes*, ABMJ, (November 18, 1970), p 53.

[62] See Appedix G.

[63] *The Chosen People*, Vol. LXXVI, No. 10, (June, 1971), pp 1-4.

[64] *Minutes*, ABMJ, (June 30, 1971), p 66.

[65] *The Chosen People*, Vol. LXXVIII, No. 6, (February, 1973), p 15.

[66] *The Chosen People*, Vol. LXXVII, No. 7, (March, 1972), pp 3, 4.

[67] See note above.

[68] *The Chosen People*, Vol. LXXVIII, No. 1, (September, 1972), pp 13, 14.

[69] *Minutes*, ABMJ, (October 20, 1971), p 69.

[70] *Minutes*, ABMJ, (January 26, 1972), p 76.

[71] *The Chosen People*, Vol. LXXII, No. 4, (December, 1966), p 11.

[72] *The Chosen People*, Vol. LVII, No. 6, (March, 1952), p 11.

[73] *The Chosen People*, Vol. LXXII, No. 4, (December, 1966), p 11.

[74] See note above, p 18.

[75] *The Chosen People*, Vol. LXIX, No. 10, (June, 1964), p 8; *The Chosen People*, Vol. LXX, No. 7, (March, 1965), p 15; *The Chosen People*, Vol. LXX, No. 10 (June, 1965), p 14.

[76] *The Chosen People*, Vol. LXXII, No. 4, (December, 1966), p 10.

[77] See note above.

[78] *The Chosen People*, Vol. LXXV, No. 3, (November, 1969), p 10.

[79] See note above, p 11.

[80] *The Chosen People*, Vol. LXXVI, No. 3, (November, 1970), p 10.

[81] *Minutes, ABMJ*, (April 19, 1972), p 76.

[82] *Personal Correspondence: Harold Sevener to Daniel Fuchs*, (May 26, 1972), p 1,2.

[83] *Minutes, ABMJ*, (June 21, 1972), p 81.

[84] *The Chosen People*, Vol. LXXVIII, No. 1, (September, 1972), pp 11, 12.

[85] *Minutes, ABMJ*, (January 26, 1972), p 74.

[86] *Minutes, ABMJ*, (April 19, 1972), p 77.

[87] *Minutes, ABMJ*, (June 21, 1972), pp 78, 79.

[88] See note above.

[89] *The Chosen People*, Vol. LXXVIII, No. 1, (September, 1972), p 3.

[90] *The Chosen People*, Vol. LXXVII, No. 9, (May, 1972), p 2.

[91] See note above.

[92] *The Chosen People*, Vol. LXXVII, No. 10, (June, 1972), pp 1-5.

[93] *Minutes, ABMJ*, (June 21, 1972), p 80.

[94] *Minutes, ABMJ*, (September 23, 1972), p 82.

[95] See note above, p 83.

[96] See note above.

[97] See note above.

[98] *Minutes, ABMJ*, (January 21, 1973), p 84.

[99] *The Chosen People*, Vol. LXXVII, No. 8, (April, 1972), p 4.

[100] See *Audited Financial Statement*, (year ended September 30, 1972), Appendix J.

[101] *The Chosen People*, Vol. LXXVIII, No. 5, (January, 1973), pp 2, 3.

[102] See note above.

[103] *Minutes, ABMJ*, (April 18, 1973), p 89.

[104] *Minutes, ABMJ*, (January 21, 1973), p 87.

[105] *Minutes, ABMJ*, (April 18, 1973), p 88.

[106] *Minutes, ABMJ*, (June 27, 1973), p 92.

[107] See note above, p 91.

[108] *Minutes, ABMJ*, (September 19, 1973), p 93.

[109] *The Chosen People*, Vol. LXXVIII, No. 7, (March, 1973), p 3.

[110] See note above.

[111] *Minutes, ABMJ*, (September 19, 1973), p 94.

[112] See note above.

12

THE VISION RE-FOCUSED

While Moishe Rosen led his small tribe of Jews for Jesus into the streets of San Francisco, to snatch Jewish young people from the city's "dens of iniquity," Daniel Fuchs continued to lead the American Board of Missions to the Jews into another stronghold of enemy territory—secular media.

Had the ultimate goal of the media blitz been to increase the size of the Mission's mailing list, or even to increase the Mission's support, Daniel and Terryl could simply have invested in Christian media, and advertised in Christian magazines and newspapers. But the goal of the media blitz was to reach Jewish people with the Gospel—and most Jews do not watch Christian television, nor do they subscribe to Christian magazines. The only means of reaching the Jews with the Gospel through media was to enter the stronghold of the enemy of the Gospel.

CONTROVERSY AND CONFRONTATION

Like angry bees attacking an intruder in their hive, the secular media pounced on the controversy created by the Mission's media events. Jews fighting among Jews, about Jesus? This was news!

As the publicity spread, leaders from both the Jewish community and from the Christian community began to take sides in the controversy. At issue were questions like, "Can Jews remain Jews and believe in Jesus?" "Do Christians have the right to 'convert' Jews?" "Is the American Board of Missions to the Jews using deceptive tactics in its attempt to convert Jews to Christianity?"

The heat of the controversy intensified as reporters interviewed Jewish and Christian theologians and missionaries who worked among the Jews, as they covered the "hot news story" of Jews who believe in Jesus. Daniel Fuchs wrote:

> We are living in exciting days. The entire Jewish world is being confronted with the Gospel. We have never dreamed that we would be able to see what is going on today. While the events of the day are, I believe, an act of the Holy Spirit Himself, I also believe that He has used the Mass Media ministry of our Mission as one of the tools in this present-day confrontation.
>
> Some of this excitement has not been very comfortable as the reaction of the Jewish community in many areas has been violent. There have been several bomb threats and demonstrations against us. On February 1st [c. 1973] our New York Branch was picketed and one of our workers attacked by the Jewish Defense League. We quote from a release from the Evangelical Press News Service:
>
> 'Some 12 picketing members of the Jewish Defense League gathered outside the mission headquarters on 72nd Street, New York City. The mission personnel had to call police when the demonstrators went inside the headquarters. They took a painting of an elderly Jewish man blowing the shofar and were outside again when the police arrived. Mogens Mogensen, a worker at the Mission who had painted the picture, went outside to continue witnessing to the demonstrators.'
>
> 'If you're such a good Christian,' one of the J.D.L. demonstrators challenged him, 'why don't you give me your coat? That's what Christ said to do.'
>
> The Rev. Mr. Mogensen immediately took off his coat and handed it to the man. Another picketer became so enraged by the act that he hit Mogensen with his fist, knocking him to the street and breaking his nose.
>
> A telephone bomb threat at 5:22 p.m. cleared the building and the loud voices of the young men and women dissenting against the meshumed ("traitors") were still by sundown. They left with Mogensen's painting and coat.'[1]

A few weeks later there was another demonstration at the tract table which the Mission maintained in the Port Authority Bus Terminal in New York City. Fortunately, the demonstration was stopped by Port Authority police because it was being staged on private property, but if it had not been squelched the Mission's workers would likely have been severely injured.

On Long Island, Bill and Jo Ennis began receiving threatening and abusive telephone calls at all hours of the day and night, and the Mission was forced to implement police protection for all Mission personnel and properties on Long Island.

In Israel, Victor Smadja, the printer whom the Mission was using to print the Jewish witnessing calendars, was attacked. The publicity about Jewish believers generated such intense hatred toward both Jewish believers and Christian missionaries that Chief Rabbi Goren called for the expulsion of all missionaries, and for "...legislation making it illegal to attempt to influence any person to change his religion."[2]

A friend of the Mission who lived in Israel wrote:

> *You will be interested to know that there has been a steady stream of reporting about Jews who believe in Jesus and the American 'Jews for Jesus' movement in the Israeli media in recent months. It seems that scarcely a day passes without some story or item about some aspect of it—in the Hebrew and/or foreign language press, on radio and T.V. The J.D.L. has been fanning the flames of zealotry, but one has the impression that they have little sympathy in most quarters. The believers active in literature and Bible distribution in Jerusalem seem to have been under the severest pressure.*[3]

Rabbi Dr. Maurice Eisendrath, president of the Union of American Hebrew Congregations, organized opposition to "evangelizing the Jews" in a campaign known as the "Key 73" campaign. Eisendrath's campaign, which began on December 25, 1972, not only involved mainline Jewish groups, it also involved mainline denominations, the Roman Catholic dioceses, and evangelical groups. The Associated Press carried an article announcing the "Key 73" campaign on December 3, 1972. The article stated that Rabbi Eisendrath "...has urged Christians to curb 'fundamentalist' evangelistic efforts aimed at converting young Jews to Christianity.... such efforts could damage the carefully cultivated roots of Christian-Jewish relations in our society and destroy the fabric of pluralism and religious freedom."[4]

Rabbi Eisendrath, whose organization represented seven hundred and ten Reform synagogues, with a combined membership of over one million Jewish members, stated that it was necessary to "...take every possible step to restrain the excessive zeal of the fundamentalist evangelical groups, particularly as these groups may subject young Jewish people and adults to repeated harassment and attempts at coercion."[5] Eisendrath then announced that his organization was planning to prepare materials and to launch programs which were designed to help Jewish youngsters challenge the statements of Christian evangelicals regarding the Jewishness of Jesus, His resurrection, and the Jewish ideas of the Messiah.

Rabbi Balfour Brickner, head of the Jewish organization's interfaith department, was also concerned about Christian fundamentalists who used Biblical proof texts to prove the Messiahship of Jesus, and he expressed the need for Jewish young people to learn how to respond to such tactics.

The strong reaction within the Jewish community began to spawn anti-missionary groups such as "Jews for Judaism," and Jewish missionizing groups such as "Hineni"—a group begun by Esther Jungreis, and sponsored by Rabbi Meir Kahane, which sought to bring Jewish young people back into Orthodox Judaism. In Israel, "Yad L'Chin" was formed by Shmu'el Golding. This organization is still active today. It publishes material against Jewish missionaries and teaches Jewish people how to "argue and defeat" the arguments of Jewish missionaries.

Anti-missionary articles began to appear in the Jewish press throughout the world. Rabbi Alan Maller, Rabbi Spivak, et al, took up the cause and began organizing anti-missionary groups among the Jews in America—focusing attention on major cities where the Mission's "Smiling Faces" ads had appeared and where numbers of Jewish young people were proclaiming Jesus as the Messiah, like Los Angeles, New York, Philadelphia, etc. In many of their articles they used scare tactics, or overstated the statistics of Jews who had accepted Jesus—thus adding fuel to the fires of controversy that were already raging.

If the Mission's media projects had accomplished nothing else, they had awakened the Jewish and Christian communities to the fact that there are Jews who believe in Jesus, and that those Jews still considered themselves to be Jewish!

As the controversy raged, many Jewish believers began to prefer the term, "Messianic believer," and in the '70's and '80's congregations of "Messianic believers" began to spring up throughout the country, and in Israel. Terms such as Hebrew-Christian and Jewish-Christian were set aside, as Jewish believers preferred to be identified, culturally, as Jews who believed in Jesus rather than as Jews who had converted to Christianity. Even organizations shed the connotation of being "Hebrew-Christian" and changed their names, as did the American branch of the International Hebrew-Christian Alliance which officially changed its name to the Messianic Jewish Alliance.

As Jewish believers and Jewish missions began to redefine terms and to rethink methodology, the leadership of the Mission sought to define the role of the Mission in the growing "Messianic Movement."

NEW MEDIA EVENTS

In the Spring of 1972, the Board authorized another "Smiling Faces" ad campaign which was to be directed toward Jewish youth on college campuses. In January 1973 the new edition of the ad was placed in college newspapers in the cities of San Francisco, Los Angeles, Denver, New York, Washington, D.C., Baltimore and Philadelphia. The caption read: "Not All Jews Are For Jesus."[6]

When the Passover telecast was canceled "across the board" in the Spring of 1972, some of the stations had agreed that they would air some other program produced by the Mission, and Terryl Delaney was asked to produce a new film that would be acceptable to the stations. WCIX-TV in Miami had suggested a live debate between representatives of the rabbinic community and representatives of the Mission, but no one from the rabbinic community wanted to debate on live TV. Terryl and the staff therefore developed a new concept for the presentation of our message, called "Les Crane Reports On Jews for Jesus!"

Les Crane was a twenty-nine year old secular news interviewer who had his own network show and was well known. Being youthful, he fit into the Jews for Jesus format that the Mission was trying to image. The title chosen was very forthright because one of the complaints lodged by the Jewish community against the Passover telecast was that they felt the title was deceptive.

The program was filmed on the campus of BIOLA college. Dr. Charles Lee Feinberg served as the most prominent guest being interviewed, although seventy-five other Messianic Jewish believers were assembled on campus. The purpose for having so many Jewish believers there was to show that being a Jewish believer in Jesus is not uncommon. But a few of the seventy-five were also interviewed. Among the testimonies featured in the special were those of Dr. Vera Schlamm, Stuart Dauermann, Mary Linderman, Bob Friedman, Richard Cohen, et. al.

The Les Crane special telecast was aired in Los Angeles, San Diego, Atlanta and Baltimore. Station WPIX-TV in New York City had also agreed to the format of the program, approved the concept, and had scheduled a time slot for it to be shown but, because of pressure from the Jewish community of New York, they canceled the telecast. The New York Daily News gave the following report:

> In another development this week, WPIX-TV suddenly canceled a scheduled special entitled, 'Jews for Jesus' because of what it said were objections by Jewish leaders. Richard N. Hughes, Vice-President of Community Affairs, for the station, declined to identify the protestors.
>
> 'Jews for Jesus' was produced by Beth Sar Shalom Hebrew Christian Fellowship [another name used for the work of the American Board of Missions to the Jews, now Chosen People Ministries, Inc.] in Los Angeles. The relatively new movement that seeks to convert Jews to Christianity has understandably aroused great controversy. But if WPIX-TV canceled 'Jews for Jesus' simply because someone opposed the thought of such a movement, then the question arises as to whether the station succumbed to censorship by outsiders.[7]

With this cancellation, Daniel announced to the readers of The Chosen People:

> ...we believe that we have a responsibility to the Lord's people in this matter. This is more than a conflict between the Jewish leaders and the American Board of Missions to the Jews. I believe this attack on us is also a thrust against the basis of evangelical Christianity. We are preparing litigation to enforce the contract we made with WPIX. We believe that it is the Lord's will to open TV for us in New York City.[8]

The Mission did press its litigation against WPIX-TV, but to no avail. The case went on for several years, a factor which increased the expense of the telecast considerably. It was finally settled out of court.

The door to the secular TV market was closed, as was the door to secular newspapers which also began to refuse further ads from the Mission. With rapidly decreasing investment funds and an over-stretched budget, the Mission's "media events," except for one last attempt in 1975, came to a sudden halt.

The last media event was announced in the June 1975 issue of The Chosen People magazine. In sharing the new plan for "radio spot evangelism," Daniel first informed readers of the magazine that the Mission's radio broadcast, "The Promise of Tomorrow," was being canceled. He then told readers:

> ...Our purpose is to reach all Jews everywhere with the Gospel, and so it was decided to drop the Promise of Tomorrow radio program and to concentrate on a radio ministry that would reach Jews everywhere.
>
> Our Mass Media Director, Terryl Delaney, was instructed to produce a series of spot announcements that would speak to the hearts of the Jewish people and to test-market them in Los Angeles, the same area where we first tested our

Passover telecast.

Mr. Delaney did his usual top-quality job for the Lord. He produced a series of four spot announcements that speak directly to the Jewish community right where it lives. The unique feature of these spots is that they don't talk just to the Jewish community, they reach to the core of spiritual questions that tear at the hearts and minds of all people. 'What happens to me after death?' 'I'm so lonely and no one cares!' 'How can I find reality in a life filled with empty promises?' These spots presented the Gospel so effectively that we budgeted $20,000 for pilot programs in Los Angeles, Chicago, and Philadelphia. We knew that God would provide.

Tests were started in these three areas and before they were completed the Lord gave us a greater area of ministry. Dan Rigney, Missionary-in-Charge of the Baltimore/Washington branch and our Camp Director, was asked to take part in a panel discussion at the National Religious Broadcaster's convention in Washington D.C. He took these spots with him and an unsaved Jewish radio executive heard them. He arranged for an audition of them for Dan with the President of Mutual Broadcasting System. Now for the 'miracle': When the President heard these tapes he was so impressed that he immediately offered to 'air' them on the Mutual network's 675 stations throughout the United States.

These stations were in population areas totaling 120,000,000 people. Any time a single spot was aired over the entire network, approximately two million people heard it. (It is estimated that a total of 18 million heard it.) What an opportunity! And the cost? Minimal! Each time a spot was aired over one station, it cost only $1.45 per spot per station. (It was at the same time over all the stations.) Add productions charges, mailing, etc., the cost was less than $2.10 per spot.[9]

Daniel then went on to say that time was of the essence, and that he had the approval of the Executive Committee of the Board to purchase six spots a day, Monday through Friday, for two weeks. He announced that the "radio spots" were to be aired from Monday, May 19, 1975 through Friday, May 30, 1975. He also pointed out to readers of the magazine that the expense of the project would be approximately $60,000 (He used the formula of 675 stations times $1.45 times 60 spots). He then related how the Mission's staff had contacted churches in areas where the spots were being aired, and that some of the churches had agreed to help with the cost. He wrote:

We also decided that it was imperative to share this ministry with the local churches. We couldn't even try to do this job ourselves and advertising our Mission was not our purpose. We immediately began working with local churches and the response was immediate and gratifying....

Many churches in cities where the spots were broadcast picked up 'the tab.' The tab for 60 spots was $125. We had time to make only minimal arrangements, but in the future we expect 100% coverage. In those areas where we were not able to assign a local church and phone number, we set up a national WATS line in our Dallas branch operating on a 5:30 a.m. to 10 p.m. schedule during the broadcasts.[10]

The June 1975 issue of *The Chosen People* magazine announcing the Mission's new "radio spot" evangelism program listed all 675 stations and the time of each broadcast. It also carried in it a special plastic "record" of the radio spots. In this way readers of the magazine had an opportunity to hear what the Mission was proposing.

The October 1975 issue of *The Chosen People* carried Daniel's report of the results of the "radio spot" evangelistic thrust. He told readers that there had been both positive and negative results. On the positive side was the fact that the spots had been aired and thus, potentially 18,000,000 people—many of them Jews—had been exposed to the Gospel. He also stated: "We are following up all of the contacts. Dr. Thomas McCall, Regional Director of our Southwest District, reports that 476 people called our WATS line in Dallas and more than 20 decisions were made for Christ."[11]

On the negative side was the fact that a number of hostile people had responded, spouting vituperative language. Many Christians who had volunteered to answer calls for their churches did not know what to say, and were offended by having to listen to such abusive language. (Gentile Christians who have not been exposed to Jewish street evangelism, or to door-to-door visitation, are often not prepared for the brutal, hostile, antagonistic remarks that missionaries to the Jews frequently deal with on a daily basis!)

Another negative factor had been the fact that the name of the Mission was announced at the end of each spot. This was a source of confusion to some listeners, and a source of irritation to others. (When the Mutual Broadcasting systems attorneys listened to the spots, they said the Mission would have to use the name American Board of Missions to the Jews, rather than Beth Sar Shalom, so it would not appear deceptive.) Also, the name of the Mission was so long that the names and telephone numbers of cooperating churches could only be mentioned once. Listeners did not have opportunity to write numbers down—a fact that limited the number of calls. Further, some disc jockeys had been antagonistic and had deliberately mispronounced the names of churches, or ridiculed the Mission and the message of the radio spots. Lastly, because the spots had been a new venture for both the Mission and for the Mutual Broadcasting Network, there had been problems in communication between Mutual in New York and their sister stations throughout the United States.

Daniel told readers of the magazine that the Mission would continue making the radio spots, but that the name of the Mission would no longer be used. Instead, the spots were to be given to local churches to sponsor. Thus, the "radio spots" ceased being a Mission-sponsored media event, and they became, instead, a vehicle for local churches to attempt reaching Jewish people in their communities.

Responses from the various media projects continued to pour into the Headquarters office. Christian names were added to The Chosen People mailing list, while Jewish surnames were added to The Shepherd of Israel mailing list. The names were then sent out to the various branches so the Mission's workers could follow up with personal visitation. In areas where there were no missionaries, volunteers were used, or the Field Evangelists were asked to make the visits.

Separating From the Name "Jews For Jesus"

The media events of the Mission and the popularization of the term "Jews for Jesus," as the press described the activities of Moishe Rosen and other highly visible areas of outreach being done by the Mission, made the names "Moishe Rosen," "Jews for Jesus," "American Board of Missions to the Jews," and "Beth Sar Shalom" nearly synonymous. This link caused widespread confusion—both within secular circles and within Christian circles—once the Mission severed its relationship with Moishe and his ministry. As Moishe Rosen and the Liberated Wailing Wall began booking meetings, many pastors and churches thought they were supporting an arm of the ABMJ.

Even after the separation of the two ministries, the secular press continued to use the phrase "Jews for Jesus" to describe everything being done to evangelize the Jews—a fact which Moishe, always the master strategist and communicator, used to his new organization's advantage. Although Moishe's ministry was originally begun under the name "Hineni Ministries," it was not long before his outreach became identified generically with the Jews for Jesus movement. Thus, in many newspaper articles of the day the name, "Jews for Jesus," was overshadowing the Mission's name. Oftentimes "the American Board of Missions to the Jews" was seen as a branch of "Jews for Jesus." This created even more confusion!

In an effort to stop further erosion of its name recognition within the media, the Mission attempted to trademark the name "Jews for Jesus" as a registered ministry name,[12] but the application was turned down and the staff was given a directive not to use the phrase "Jews for Jesus" on any materials, advertising, or program announcements of their local branches.[13] Since the phrase and name had been developed by staff workers of the American Board of Missions to the Jews, and was used by the Mission in its magazine, its publicity and its media events, this was a difficult step for the Mission to take. Severing its identity with the phrase "Jews for Jesus," the Mission lost much of the media exposure it had already gained. Sadly, when one examines the special "Eightieth Anniversary" edition of The Chosen People Magazine, printed December, 1974, there is no mention of Jews for Jesus and the impact which the formation of that unique Messianic youth movement had upon the Jewish community in the late sixties and early seventies when it was a significant outreach of the Mission.

Implementing New Mission Policy

Decentralizing the Mission's branches in accordance with the Mission's new policy of using its existing branch properties for administrative offices and training centers, rather than as a "branch" of the ministry where Jewish believers heard the Gospel and were discipled, proved to be a more difficult task than envisioned. The missionaries on staff had all been trained to establish branches—the historic way of reaching Jewish people with the Gospel—and most of them felt that through visitation, street ministry, and programs that penetrated the Jewish community, they did "go" to the Jews of their area.

In attempting to explain the Mission's new missionary strategy and methodology, the author wrote:

We have found that we are living in a highly mobile society. People are moving in and out of the urban areas at an increased rate, and the Jewish community is no exception. Years ago, Jewish people were either forced, or chose to live in ghetto areas in the large metropolitan areas. A missionary could be assigned to that area and plan to minister there for a number of years. The mission could purchase property for a large center in order to maintain a witness in that community. Today, this is rapidly changing. With the urban exodus and the emphasis on suburban living, we are finding that we have to change our programs in order to effectively reach the Jewish community. We have found that we can move into an area and rent a building in the heart of the Jewish community, advertise our meetings and our presence, and use that office as a hub for activities which are held in other parts of the community.

We called this new strategy a 'decentralized' mission program. The small center becomes a training center, and a beehive of activity, as our missionary workers are busily putting into practice a program of evangelism for the whole community. Reaching out from that center, they are establishing home fellowship meetings, campus works, reaching into hospitals, the homes for the aged, children's work, etc.

We combine these forms of outreach with television, radio, newspaper advertising, Jewish art calendars, and other forms of media. The combined effect of outreach produces an effect similar to that mentioned in the Book of Acts as our missionaries begin to turn the cities 'upside down.'

As the Lord tarries, and as we have funds available, we are continuing to expand our staff and train our workers in this exciting ministry of sharing the gospel with the Jewish people.[14]

As the Mission's workers began to implement the new decentralized/branch approach, workers in many areas of the country began to report exciting results.

THE MINISTRY IN MARYLAND

On October 16, 1972 *The Sun*, a Baltimore newspaper, ran an article telling of the exciting ministry of Dan and Arlene Rigney in the greater Washington/Baltimore area. The article mentioned Bill, Michael, and Robyn—Jewish young people who had become believers in the Messiah and who were among the twenty-plus Jewish young people who attended the Thursday night Bible study held in the Rigneys home on Sudvale Road in Pikesville, Maryland. It also mentioned Dr. and Mrs. Henry Einspruch, directors of the Lederer Foundation, who frequently joined the Rigneys when they were putting on a Passover demonstration, or passing out "broadsides" (tracts). Dan Rigney gave this report in *The Chosen People* magazine:

Mr. Stuart Dauermann, a well-accomplished musician and schoolteacher from Brooklyn, New York, assisted us in our ministry here in Baltimore from September until the end of December [c. 1972]. His versatile ministry was very valuable.... Lynda, a Jewish girl who called us and later wrote us, said she made a decision for the Messiah as a result of the broadside he gave her....

Robyn D. and Mike C. (mentioned in The Sun *article) are students at one of the universities here in the Baltimore area. They have arranged for us to have a "Jews for Jesus" Bible study on campus every week. Mike and Robyn have been a blessing and encouragement in our ministry. They are also members of our 'Broadside Brigade.'*

During the school year I taught Messianic prophecy at a campus to some Christian students to help in their witness to Jewish friends.... This is a ministry in that we are training volunteers to witness to the Jewish people.

Mr. Jim Morrow, a long-time friend of the ABMJ has been conducting Hebrew classes at the Wheaton Center on Saturdays.

The Lord has blessed us with many dedicated volunteers and helpers, and we cannot list them all. We are grateful for the ministry of Mr. Robert Wilson, presently a student at the Capitol Bible Seminary.... He is presently helping with young people in the Washington area....

Another part-time worker that the Lord has sent us is Mrs. Robert Scovner [Linda Scovner had served as one of Moishe Rosen's secretaries when he was in Los Angeles and in New York] who has recently moved to Baltimore. She is helping in the new office of the Baltimore ministry as receptionist and secretary. The Scovners have been a big help to us and have participated in our broadside distribution activities.

We have had Bible studies in our home since 1971. The work progressed and we had to find other facilities. The Lord opened a wonderful opportunity for us to have an office on the busiest street in Baltimore's Jewish community....

The Mission's Washington area Center was also relocated, and is presently in Wheaton, Maryland, a suburb of Washington. It is located across from a busy shopping center. At both Branches, we are seeing the Lord's blessing in a wonderful way....

At Christmas time, we gave out about 20,000 'Christmas is a Jewish Holiday,' and had a very good response from both Washington and Baltimore on it.

At about this time one of the local Rabbis spoke on 'Jews for Jesus, Then and Now,' and we decided to go to the synagogue. Much to our surprise, several of the people were reading "Christmas Is A Jewish Holiday" [one of the broadsides used at the time]. Eight Jews for Jesus were there. The Rabbi said that he felt Judaism had neglected the spiritual needs of the people, and that was the main reason the young people were going to Jews for Jesus and Beth Sar Shalom. He even mentioned the 'Smiling Faces' ad which was in the Baltimore paper. He said he did not think people would have to go to Beth Sar Shalom. Later in the reception line, I introduced myself as the Director of the local Beth Sar Shalom and the Rabbi was quite taken aback. Interestingly enough, at least two young people from his synagogue had come to know the Lord previously....

In September [c.1972], a very objective six-page article on Jews For Jesus was written by Mr. Turan of The Washington Post for the magazine section. We were able to witness for three hours during the interview and many things were cleared up for him. Strangely enough, he grew up in the same neighborhood that Stuart Dauerman did, and went to the same high school. This prompted further radio response in our area. Dr. Daniel Fuchs, Rev. Rachmiel Frydland, Dr. Henry Einspruch and myself were invited to be on WWDC, which is a network station in the Washington area, for a talk show. The time was free. The Lord is definitely using these means of mass media in our work here.

Another friend is Mr. Bob Hanna, director of THE WAY OUT, a Christian coffeehouse. We helped him get started in January 1972 and worked with him until June. We realized this would be a very profitable means of reaching Jewish youth and several Jewish young people did accept the Lord through this ministry....

An encouragement of our ministry has been seeing some who received the Lord in the fall of 1971-72 continue on to serve the Lord. One such Jewish youth is Sue. She came to our home in November of 1971 as a result of a broadside she had received at a street festival. She talked to us for about an hour at our home. We did not realize, but she told us later that it was at that time that she accepted the Lord as her Savior. She continued to fellowship with us and attend our Bible studies. Her parents thought it was just a fad and sent her to Israel for the summer to avoid having her see us. Now it is more than a year later and her parents realize that it is a serious thing. She praises the Lord and it is wonderful to see her and other Jewish believers going on with the Lord.[15]

THE MINISTRY IN LOS ANGELES

Exciting things were happening in the Los Angeles ministry too. Richard Cohen wrote:

Within a one-month period recently I had opportunity to visit four different synagogues in the Los Angeles area at their invitations. God seems to be opening many doors and we are grateful to Him for these times of witness.

First I visited a Conservative Synagogue. I had been invited to speak to their confirmation class, the graduating class of the Temple Religious School. They had asked me to explain the differences between fundamental Christianity and Judaism, and for an hour we told of the similarities and differences of our faiths....

The second visit was also to a Conservative Synagogue, one of the largest in the San Fernando Valley. The Rabbi had asked me to bring four young Hebrew Christians who would give their testimonies to the youth group. This would be followed by questions and answers and general discussion.... The Rabbi was very cooperative and friendly and assured me that we would be invited again. We gave literature and New Testaments to the young people. The Rabbi instructed the students to read the tracts and said that they would discuss them the following week. He also said that the New Testament would be required reading for the course and we agreed to supply the number needed....

For our third meeting we were invited by a group in Simi Valley. This is a small congregation presently meeting in different homes while trying to start their synagogue, and they have a student Rabbi.... Again, the Lord permitted us to give a good testimony and to provide an explanation of what a Hebrew Christian is. We offered literature as we left, and one of the ladies told us she had been receiving our publication, The Shepherd of Israel, for many years. She did not know how she came to be on the mailing list, but she read the paper every month then passed it on to her children. Praise God. This lady took one of the New Testaments and several tracts stating that there was a possibility she could be wrong in her opinions and wanted to look into it further....

Then we were invited to a Reform Synagogue in the San Fernando Valley area to speak to their Saturday and Sunday morning classes.... The Rabbi was also there, and gave several reasons why Jewish people should not believe in Jesus. Then it was my opportunity to tell why Jewish people should believe in Jesus. The Rabbi told me later that he had learned fundamental differences in our two beliefs and that we had destroyed several of the myths that he previously had believed about Christians....

It was our privilege earlier this year to conduct an evening service on a Jewish theme at the First Baptist Church of Van Nuys. This large church has always been interested in Jewish evangelism. (It was through this church that I came to know my Messiah.)

Nine believers wanted to be baptized, so the pastor, Dr. Harold Fickett, and myself arranged for a baptismal service before the regular service. The good attendance blessed our hearts and many were unsaved Jewish people.[16]

THE MINISTRY IN MIAMI BEACH

The Miami branch, under the direction of Martin and Pauline Klayman, experienced exciting growth too. They wrote:

Our Friday evening class grew to such proportions that we had to split it into six classes per week. Tuesday evening we have a class in south Hollywood in the home of a Jewish couple, the Newburgs. We have had several young people make decisions here. Barry Newburg and I share the ministry, and we have taught many Bible doctrines....

On Thursday mornings we meet in the Matassa's home in North Miami Beach. This small class has been growing and at our last session there were sixteen present. A Lebanese lady was saved and it is a joy to watch her beaming smile and radiant joy.

Thursday nights we meet in a Bible study at the home of Mr. and Mrs. Ravenna in North Hollywood. This couple dearly love the Jewish people.... One night a young girl was brought to the class and she was saved! . . .

For four years on Friday mornings we have had a Bible class in a Nursing Home in North Miami. This has been a blessed, fruitful ministry....

Our largest class of the week is on Friday evenings, with average attendance around 55. Many people have been saved at these meetings....

We believe the Lord is establishing a children's class this year. I thank God for the training we had with Miss Koser of the Coney Island Branch. Mrs. Klayman teaches the children and I am the helper....

Another method of operation for us is to become involved with people who live in hotels and people who are in hospitals. As we visit we always have opportunities to talk to new people, and hospital patients rarely refuse our prayers in their behalf.

Our facility has been used in many ways. We have had two weddings here; a number of times we've had groups of young people meet here; we had a surprise party for a fine Bible teacher, etc.

Recently we had a picnic and there were many good opportunities to speak with Jewish people. We have had small Passover services in our home ...We have also conducted the Passover for the past two years on a large scale in restaurants. We have found this to be a method with good results. During these Seders eight souls were saved....

In May, the ad, 'Not All Jews Are For Jesus' appeared in the University of Miami newspaper. As a result I was invited to take part in a campus forum. It was on the whole friendly and I felt that the students were sincere....

Now for a word about our faithful volunteers. Several men give of themselves unselfishly. Some drive their own cars bringing people back and forth to the classes. One man not only takes people home, but he continues the message where I ended and has led several people to the Lord.

One interested Pastor brings an airport limousine to our home on Fridays for use in transportation to and from the meetings—at no charge whatsoever.[17]

Reports From Other Branches
In the April 1974 "Report from the Missionary Director," the author included the enthusiastic reports of several of the workers:

...in Denver, Eliezer and Sarah Urbach reported that they had four recent decisions for the Lord,...

In San Diego, California, Irv Rifkin ...had just recently led two Jewish people to the Lord and has another two ready for baptism....

At Chicago, Harry Jacobson reports that two ladies there also accepted Christ in one month and ...a lady who has been ill...for 41 years believed in Jesus as her Savior.

In the New York area, Rev. Charles Eisenberg reports two recent decisions for the Lord and an opportunity to work together with several missions to use cable television in the New York area as a means of witness, using young Hebrew Christians as writers, directors, etc. They have put together a half-hour program which will be aired free on cable television reaching a potential audience of approximately 200,000. The only cost is the making of television tapes, which cost has already been subsidized by Christians interested in this project.

Eleanor Bullock reports decisions for the Lord, and Bill Ennis likewise. Clara Rubin, an indefatigable worker, reports that she and her husband Joe stayed up until 1:30 in the morning to lead to Christ a man to whom they had been witnessing for several years.[18]

Larry Jaffrey, too, reported that the Philadelphia ministry was experiencing increased attendance at meetings, and several decisions for the Lord. He wrote:

This past year was the beginning of four more regular Bible study groups in our area. The original Thursday evening study expanded to such an extent that we were able to divide the group into an adult study and a young people's study which is conducted by Mitch Triestman. A second study was started on Tuesday afternoon for those who could not come to the evening studies. Rev. Arthur Watson began a third study group in the Lower Bucks County area, reaching out to the Jewish population in that area. Finally, as a result of our prayers, a group is meeting in Wilmington,

Delaware for Bible Study....

As a result of our Bible studies and meetings in the Philadelphia area, we have made many new contacts with unsaved Jewish people. From these contacts several have come to receive Jesus as their Messiah, and some have even followed Him in baptism.[19]

But not all workers were able to adjust to the new de-centralized approach to ministry. At the time of the Mission's merge with Aedus Center in 1965 (See Chapter 10 of this history), Harry Jacobson was sent to develop the combined ministries. He did a fine job in Chicago, and when an opportunity came for him to enlarge upon a new work which was begun by volunteers in Houston, Texas, both the Mission and Harry thought he was the man for the job. Unlike Chicago, there was no centralized Jewish community in Houston; the Jewish population was scattered throughout the city. The work in Houston therefore called for a de-centralized approach, using rented office space, with meetings in hotels, churches, etc. Harry had believed that he could adapt to the new methodology even though his training had been in developing ministries around a branch/center approach.

As Harry labored in Houston, he established a good foundation for the ministry and he worked closely with a committee of concerned Christians and with several churches in the area. Several Jewish families came to faith in Yeshua as a result of his efforts, but eventually the differences in methodology created problems between Harry, members of the committee, and the Mission's staff in Dallas (where a branch ministry had been established). In December 1974, Harry felt led of the Lord to resign from the Mission's staff.[20]

When Harry resigned, the Mission transferred Bill and Jo Ennis from Long Island to take over the Houston work. As Bill and Jo continued to expand the ministry in Houston they reached many Jewish people for the Lord. They remained in Houston until their retirement from the staff of the Mission in December, 1985.

As Missionary Director of the Mission, it was the author's responsibility to be in touch with the missionaries on staff. The input from workers on the field made it abundantly clear that the combination of the Mission's "media events," the continuing impact of "Jews for Jesus," and the whole "Messianic Movement" was making the branch stations more necessary than ever. In an era when Messianic congregations were not yet an option as a place for worship and spiritual growth; a place where Jewish believers could meet and fellowship with one another; a place where they could strengthen their personal witness to their family members and friends, the Mission's branches were very much needed. The branch ministries gave an identity to Jewish believers; they also gave an identity to the Mission within cities where they were established. The Mission could not completely dissolve the "branch" ministry!

In an effort to utilize the best of the "branch" approach to evangelism, while at the same time maintaining the de-centralized approach to ministry, the author and some of the staff began to experiment with a "center" approach to doing ministry. The idea was that the evangelistic thrust of the work would be done using de-centralized methodology, but a "Mission Center" would also be maintained where congregational methodology could be developed. The long-range goal for the *centers* was that they would become financially independent of the Mission, and perhaps develop into congregations as the believers matured in the faith. We felt the *Center* approach to doing ministry was in keeping with the Mission's policy of de-centralization, while at the same time providing a vehicle where Jewish believers could worship together and grow in their faith. The Los Angeles ministry was used as one of the experimental areas for the *Center* approach to doing ministry.

CHANGES IN ADMINISTRATION

Not only was the Mission reorganizing on the field, it was reorganizing within its administration as well. In the October 1974 issue of *The Chosen People* magazine, Daniel Fuchs wrote:

The time has come in the administration of *The American Board of Missions to the Jews*, when it is necessary to follow Jethro's advice. You will observe that I have a new title: President. My job is the same. Under the Lord, I am still responsible to the Board of Directors for the operation of the Mission. But to work with me directing the various branches of the Mission, the Board has appointed 'able men.' We thank God for these men who have come up from the ranks. They have proven their capabilities for the chosen tasks and we believe they have the scriptural requisites....

My right-hand man in the reorganization is Harold Sevener, who is Vice-President and continues to be Missionary Director. He is in charge in my absence. He has faithfully handled these responsibilities with remarkable efficiency and effectiveness for the past two years.

The Rev. Terryl Delaney will carry on as Director of Mass Media. He has directed your Mission in undertaking the use of the media—TV, radio, and the press with astounding effect. We believe that the Media ministry will enable us to meet our goal 'to reach all Jews everywhere with the Gospel.'

I am happy to announce the appointment of the Rev. Arnold Fruchtenbaum as Editor of our publications. As a boy he found the Lord in our Brooklyn branch. He is a graduate of Cedarville College, Dallas Theological Seminary, and has studied at Hebrew University in Jerusalem. He is a capable editor.

Mr. Robert Hall, a graduate of Covenant Theological Seminary, is in charge of our computer operation. Mrs. Betty Schaffner, our office manager, works under Mr. Hall.

Mr. Richard C. Maund, our comptroller, is now also Assistant Treasurer.

Finally my wife Muriel, is now our Assistant Secretary. For years she has not only been my secretary, with all the responsibilities, but she has (without any public recognition) also been the managing editor of The Chosen People *and* The Promise of Tomorrow. *In the past I have been called the Editor, but actually she did the work.*[21]

Several things should be noted about this reorganization of the Mission's administration. First, the author's appointment to the position of Vice President (along with his duties as Missionary Director) was historic in that this was the first time a successor had been appointed to succeed the Director of the Mission in the event that the Director became incapacitated. Unlike his predecessor, Joseph Hoffman Cohn, Daniel was making plans for the future of the Mission.

Secondly, the appointment of Arnold Fruchtenbaum was historic in that up to then, the Director of the Mission had always been the editor of its publications. Daniel broke with tradition by appointing Arnold to this position. However, Daniel did not place Arnold Fruchtenbaum under Terryl Delaney, the Director of Communications for the Mission, which would have been the logical department for direct supervision. Instead, Arnold reported directly to Daniel and, in so doing, Daniel never really gave up the final right to edit *The Chosen People* magazine. Even after the author was appointed President, and Daniel Fuchs was made Chairman of the Board, he retained the right to the final editing of the Mission's magazine. The issue over who had the final say over what could, or could not, go into *The Chosen People* magazine was a constant source of irritation and conflict between the Communications Department and the Executive Department of the Mission.

As a further part of the administrative reorganization, although Daniel did not mention it in his Salutation, the Board approved the appointment of Mr. James Straub (a Board member) to be a consultant who was to help oversee the day-to-day operations of the Mission. The Minutes of the January 1974 meeting state:

After discussion of the problems and needs of the Mission to set up an effective and economical method of operation, Mr. Scharfman moved and Mr. Fuchs seconded the motion that Mr. Straub be appointed to spend one day a week at the Mission on a management consultant basis and later if less time is needed to make this survey, a day a month, …This was unanimously voted with one abstention and grateful thanks were given to Mr. Straub for his willingness to do this for the work of the Lord and the Mission.[22]

Jim Straub graciously agreed to cut his consultant fee in half so the Mission could afford his services. When the author was elected President of the Mission in January 1979, Jim Straub was elected to the full-time position of Executive Vice-President—a position he held until his retirement on April 30, 1983.[23]

The reorganization of the administration and assignment of new titles necessitated amendment of the by-laws to allow for the new positions and titles. Until this time (c. 1974), the title of "President" had been reserved for the presiding officer of the Board of Directors (although the title had been given to Dr. Rabbi Leopold Cohn, but he had refused it, preferring his old title of "superintendent"). The title given to the paid chief operating officer had always been "Executive Director," or "General Secretary." With the title "President" now assigned to the chief operating officer, Daniel Fuchs, the title of the "President" of the Board was changed to "Chairman" of the Board.[24]

In the late Spring of 1974, during a routine physical examination, Daniel Fuchs' doctor observed changes in a small birthmark just below his knee. The doctor suggested that a biopsy be performed, but Daniel was on his way to Israel so he told the doctor he would attend to it when he got back home. Daniel wrote of that occasion:

After my return [from Israel] I had it removed and the surgeon sent a sample to the lab for a biopsy. No problem, no pain, just a little discomfort. A few days later after a day at the office I took my usual four-mile stroll around Rockland Lake. I felt great.

On my return, my wife greeted me, 'The doctor wants to see you at once.' We knew it was something serious, as it was a Friday night when the doctor was usually away from his office. 'Your report is very serious. There are three kinds of skin cancer. Two of these present no great difficulty, but unfortunately the type you have is very invasive. We must act at once.' Within thirty minutes arrangements were made for admission to the hospital for numerous tests and several operations.[25]

The exploratory surgery was done on Friday, August 9, 1974. A report to the staff on August 12, 1974, said:

> We are glad to report that Dr. Fuchs has come through the first phase of the operation successfully. The cancer on his leg has been removed and skin was grafted over the incision.
>
> After a week of recuperation in the hospital, he will be home for two weeks before returning to the hospital for an operation on the lymph gland. Tests have shown no sign of cancer in that area, so we are hopeful that the lumps on the gland will prove to be benign.
>
> Thank you very much for continued prayer for Dr. Fuchs, for Mrs. Fuchs, who still spends half a day in the office, and for the rest of the Mission staff as the work is carried on.[26]

A final memo regarding Daniel's condition was sent to the staff on September 13, 1974. It stated:

> Dr. Fuchs has gone through the surgery and the doctors were able to remove all of the tissue as the cancer had not spread.
>
> He will be in the hospital for ten days or so, recuperating, and expects to be back on the job in a few weeks.[27]

God answered prayer on behalf of Daniel. There were no complications from his surgery, nor did he ever experience a recurrence of the cancer. During his absence from the office the daily work of the Mission continued to run smoothly and efficiently, and with the help of Jim Straub additional steps were taken to help reduce the expense of running the computer department of the Mission.

In "pre personal computer" days, everything was done on main-frame computers. To handle the volume of names and information needed in the Mission's data base, expensive equipment was required. So Jim Straub suggested the idea of forming a separate Not-for-Profit corporation that would not only handle the Mission's data processing, but would solicit data processing from other Christian organizations and thereby reduce the cost of each participating organization's data processing. The computer equipment was to be run twenty-four hours a day, thus making it more economical to own or to lease. The Minutes of the October 1974 Directors meeting state:

> Mr. Straub mailed to each member a copy of his report which is on file. He emphasized two things: one is, the marvelous co-operation of all the staff in Dr. Fuchs' absence. The organization worked very well.
>
> The other thing is the paragraph in his report on the Data Management Center. The center has been set up and contact with other mission organizations has been made. The New York Bible Society (now the International Bible Society) agreed to go on this center and possibly before the end of the year, another organization about the same size we are, will join which means that the center will be set up as an independent organization and it will cost the A.B.M.J. considerably less than it now costs us to use the new data center rather than doing it ourselves.
>
> John Burtis and Robert Hall have done a yeoman job on it. Dr. Fuchs helped in dealing with the proper individuals in other mission organizations. We have a viable data center going with good service.[28]

The Board was enthusiastic about the idea, and gave their approval. Thus, ECOMCO was born. The initials stood for: The Eastern Computer Organizations for Mission Corporations. ECOMCO remained in existence until June 30, 1985;[29] as an organization it saved the Mission substantial funding of its computer operations.

Jim Straub also was able to arrange for the Mission to join The Inter-Mission Annuity Fund. This allowed the Mission to pool its annuities with those of other Christian organizations—thus cutting costs while, at the same time, securing and protecting the Mission's annuities according to the laws of New Jersey.

MISSIONARIES AND SUPPORT

Because of the media exposure and the growing "Messianic movement" a resurgence of interest in Jewish ministry was born, and the Mission began receiving more applications than it could process. But the Mission's investment funds were insufficient to hire new workers, and the income was insufficient to support new workers. At the January, 1975 Board meeting, the author proposed a possible solution to ease the situation. The Minutes state:

> In his report Mr. Sevener noted we now have applicants waiting for appointment but funds are not available. Mr. Sevener suggested that we consider adopting the historic policy of faith missions throughout the world; namely, that after a missionary has been accepted he would become responsible to raise his support. Our Director of Church Relations would work closely with the new appointees.

The Board voted to send copies of Mr. Sevener's report to the members who were absent for their comments on this new proposal so that action would be taken at the next meeting. Mr. Sevener was instructed to immediately process all applicants and enlist them in the training program.[30]

The matter of missionaries raising their own support was not an issue easily resolved. Most of the Board members preferred the way the Mission had always operated—to hire missionaries and pay them from the General Fund; if the General Fund could not support their salaries and programs, money from the Mission's Investment Fund was used. Many of the members of the Board still felt that the purpose of the Investment Fund was to get missionaries into the field as quickly as possible, or to pay for programs to evangelize the Jewish people as quickly as possible—before the Lord returned!

As Missionary Director, the author recognized the need for the Mission to hire new missionaries, but he was also concerned about the drain on the Mission's investment funds should workers be hired without being required to raise their own support. And there was the concern for the senior missionaries on staff who had given years of their lives to the Mission. What would happen to them if the Mission could no longer afford to pay their salaries and expenses? They had made a commitment to the Mission, what responsibility did the administrator of the Mission have to that "life-time" commitment?

The Board had instituted a pension program, but the pension fund was tied into the Investment Fund of the Mission, and some of the Board members felt if the fund continued being spent down in direct evangelism nothing would be available to meet the pensions. As a part of the pension program, the Board took out life insurance policies on all of its workers; the policies were converted to an annuity for the worker at the time of his or her retirement. But as funding was needed to meet the ever-increasing costs of the Mission's expanding program, the Board voted to borrow against the policies (because of the lower interest rate), rather than to further deplete its investment account. The interest earned from the investment account was also used in the operating fund.

Once again, the author reminds the reader that the Board was acting in a responsible fiscal manner. Since the time of Joseph Cohn's death its philosophy had been to use all monies for direct evangelism rather than to build up large reserve funds. But the author, and many of the younger and newer members of the Board and staff, felt that a sufficient reserve fund was needed to guarantee the commitment made by the Mission when it placed new workers on staff. Not being a Board member at the time, the author could only submit proposals and prayerfully trust that God would give the Directors wisdom as they dealt with long-range planning and financing of the Mission's staff and programs.

At the June 1975 Board meeting the proposal concerning missionaries raising their support was again discussed, but the matter was tabled. The Minutes state:

There was considerable discussion on the proposal at the January Board meeting that missionary appointees raise their own support initially because of budget problems.

This matter was tabled until the next meeting. In the meantime, Richard Maund, Assistant Treasurer, was instructed to prepare an item in next year's budget for several missionary appointees' support in places where the Mission has need of workers and candidates are available. Also, Harold Sevener will report to the Board of Directors at the October meeting on the individual missionary appointees.[31]

The author made his report at the October 1975 Directors' meeting, and once again the issue of missionary support was discussed. The Minutes state:

Harold Sevener in his report has reviewed the missionary support policy so that both sides of the question have been satisfied. We are continuing our old policy of supporting the mission and not individual missionaries.[32]

Three main factors entered into the Board's decision to continue with the policy of not requiring missionaries to raise their support. First, it was the historic way the Mission had always done things. Second, there was great concern over the idea of giving the names of supporters of the Mission to individual missionaries. Historically, the names of all donors, or potential donors, were sent directly to headquarters; missionaries had no contact or correspondence with individual donors. Since missionaries had never had the names of donors, there was concern that this "confidential" information could be misused. Third, there was grave concern over what would happen to the names on an individual missionary's "donor file" when he or she left the Mission.

STAFF CHANGES CREATE NEW PROBLEMS

Both the positive and negative sides of the matter of missionaries accessing donor lists were addressed, and solutions for possible problems were proposed, but concern over individual missionaries having access to donor information and financial information turned to resolve against such a policy when Daniel Fuchs announced that Rev. Terryl Delaney, Director of Mass Media; Rev. Daniel Rigney, Missionary-in-Charge of the Baltimore/Washington Branch; and Rev. Arnold Fruchtenbaum, Editor of *The Chosen People* magazine had all resigned and would be leaving the staff of the Mission at the end of the year. Daniel then announced the appointment of Mr. Bob Friedman as Editor of *The Chosen People* magazine, and he announced that Bob's wife, Anita, had been appointed the new Mass-Media Director.[33]

The resignations of Emil Olsen, Director of Church Ministries; Henry Johnson, Missionary-in-Charge of the Pittsburgh branch; and Hannah Eurich, missionary on staff in Pittsburgh had been announced by Daniel at the previous Board meeting.[34] Emil had resigned to help Moishe Rosen with his work (he eventually formed his own organization). Dan Rigney also left to join the staff of Jews for Jesus. Henry Johnson and Hannah Eurich left because they felt torn in the competition that was developing between the two organizations.

The announcement of the resignations of these workers hit the Board members hard; the resignations hit at the heart of the Board's reorganization of the Mission's administration. Terryl had just been lavishly praised in *The Chosen People* magazine as the "author" of the Mission's mass-media evangelism. The Board was unaware that a "pot of frustration" had been boiling in Terryl for some time.

Following the nation-wide cancellation of the Passover Telecast in 1972, a number of factors converged as hindrances to the job Terryl wanted to do as Director of Mass Media. Television closed to the Mission as an avenue of communicating the Gospel to the Jews. Then newspapers refused to accept further ads from the Mission. There were problems with the Mutual Broadcasting Network in trying to air the Mission's radio spot announcements, and there was the high cost of media evangelism. Additionally, the missionaries began complaining that they were already swamped with names of Jewish people to visit, and some said their meetings were getting too crowded; the missionaries had grown weary of the extra work "media evangelism" added to their already-busy schedules. With media doors being shut, and the Mission's inability to fund further media events, the challenges of Terryl's involvement in media evangelism had come to a standstill by 1974.

Added to Terryl's growing frustration over not being able to produce more media projects for the Mission was the fact that he was not even able to coordinate all of the "media" of the Mission—the magazine, donor letters, tracts, etc.— because communication with the donors, and with the general public through the medium of the written page, remained under the control of the Editorial Department.

The "straw that broke the camel's back" came when Daniel Fuchs authorized Bob Friedman, who was not yet on staff, to produce an audio tape for the Mission entitled: "A Jewish Odyssey—From Abraham to You." As has already been mentioned, in his excitement to use media, and in his excitement to get the Gospel to the Jewish people, Daniel sometimes ran ahead of himself. It was not deliberate, but it still caused problems for others involved.

Bob Friedman was a Jewish believer who enjoyed a dual profession: He was a newspaper reporter; he was also a comedian. After coming to faith in Messiah, he used his writing skills for the Lord. His clever way of communicating, combined with his Jewish humor and wit, made his books and articles very popular among the Christian public. His autobiography entitled "What's a Nice Jewish Boy Like You Doing in The First Baptist Church?" was an immediate success.

The Jewish odyssey tape which he produced for the Mission was developed as a tape for both Jews and Gentiles. It was rich with Jewish humor. It told the history of Israel, while including humorous, but pointed, skits on Messianic prophecy. It was designed as a witnessing tape which Christians could either give to their Jewish friends, or share with Jewish friends in the friendly atmosphere of their own homes. It was well done—on a low budget—and Daniel was so impressed with it that he began advertizing it in the magazine. Terryl, who had not been consulted about this new "media" project, felt deeply hurt and betrayed.

But despite his feelings, Terryl's commitment to the Mission and to its workers compelled him to remain in his position as Director of Mass Media through 1975 so he could help lay the groundwork for the Mission's major Prophetic Bible Conference which was held in Philadelphia in July 1976, in honor of our country's Bi-Centennial Celebration.

Ironically, by hiring Bob and Anita Friedman as Editor and Director of Mass Media respectively (this had been Anita's professional field in the secular world), Daniel came close to bringing *The Chosen People* magazine and the media department under one umbrella.

Arnold Fruchtenbaum also resigned due to frustration. As Editor of the Missions publications, he was not able to effect change in his department, and he was limited in the development of the magazine. He was also frustrated over the placement of some personnel within the Mission. Arnold also wanted to teach, but the Mission had dropped its Christian radio ministry to use those funds for media evangelism, and the only teaching opportunity the Mission afforded was in Bible conference ministry and in church meetings.

Shortly after leaving the staff of the Mission, Arnold joined the staff of the Christian Jew Foundation where he became one of the teachers on their radio broadcast. A few years later, he resigned from the staff of C.J.F. and he established "Ariel Ministries." Over the years, a close working relationship has existed between Arnold and the workers on the staff of the Mission, and cooperative programs have been established between the two ministries. The most recent of these cooperative ventures was the loan of Dan and Arlene Rigney, workers on staff with Ariel Ministries, to work in the Mission's branch in Kiev (as mentioned in Chapter Eleven).

FIRST ANNUAL WORKERS' CONFERENCE

The month of October 1975 held two significant events. The first annual Workers' Conference was held at the Keswick Conference Grounds in Keswick, New Jersey. It was the first time the entire staff of U.S. and Canadian missionaries and the field evangelists had gathered together since the missionaries had been called to New York for a conference in 1953, just after the death of Joseph Hoffman Cohn. Jim Straub reported to the Board:

> ...that he attended the Workers' Conference at Keswick. He was impressed with the workers' willingness to try new methods of attaining their goals. The conference was an excellent balance of the spiritual and the practical and Harold Sevener is to be commended. Mr. Straub encouraged the Board of Directors to attend part of the conference next year. This would encourage and help the missionaries to meet the Board members.[35]

After hearing Mr. Straub's report, the Board voted and approved that "...the October 1976 Board meeting be scheduled at the time of the Workers' Conference at Keswick and that the conference be scheduled so that the Board members can spend a day there with the workers, and that the Board meeting be also scheduled for that date."[36]

A MESSIANIC STATEMENT CREATES CONTROVERSY

The second event which took place that October, and which greatly impacted the Mission, was the annual meeting of the Fellowship of Christian Testimonies to the Jews (FCTJ) which was also held at Keswick, New Jersey from October 16-19, 1975. At that time, the FCTJ had both individual and organizational membership. Individuals could approve the actions of the FCTJ, however any proposals or actions which would affect member organizations were to be approved by each organization's board before being released to the press, or made public. At this particular meeting, a resolution on Messianic synagogues was worked on and adopted. Among those who worked on the resolution were the author, Arnold Fruchtenbaum, Marvin Rosenthal, William Currie, et. al. The Resolution of the FCTJ stated:

> INASMUCH AS many within the modern movement of Messianic Judaism publicly declare themselves to be a fourth branch of Judaism, we of The Fellowship of Christian Testimonies to the Jews,...feel constrained to make the following statement:
>
> WHEREAS a segment of Messianic Judaism strives to be a denomination within Judaism alongside of orthodox, conservative, and reform Judaism, thus confusing law and grace, we of the FCTJ affirm that the New Testament teaches that the Christian faith is consistent with, but not a continuation of Biblical Judaism, and is distinct from rabbinical Judaism.
>
> WHEREAS a segment of Messianic Judaism claims to be a synagogue, and not a church, we of the FCTJ affirm that the New Testament clearly distinguishes between the synagogue and the church; therefore, Bible-believing Hebrew Christians should be aligned with the local church in fellowship with Gentile believers.
>
> WHEREAS a segment of Messianic Judaism encourages Gentile Christians to undergo a conversion to Judaism, we of the FCTJ affirm that this violates the tenor of the New Testament in general and the Books of Galatians and Hebrews in particular for it involves converting to a religion that clearly denies the messiahship of Jesus.
>
> WHEREAS a segment of Messianic Judaism adopts the practices of rabbinic Judaism (instituted by Jewish leadership who rejected the Person and work of Jesus Christ), e.g. kosher laws, wearing skull caps and prayer shawls, et al, we of the FCTJ affirm that any practice of culture, Jewish or non-Jewish, must be brought into conformity with the New Testament.
>
> WHEREAS a segment of Messianic Judaism isolates itself from the local church rebuilding the 'middle wall of partition,' thus establishing a pseudo-cultural pride, we of the FCTJ affirm the necessity of the Hebrew Christian expressing his culture and his spiritual gifts in the context of the local church thus edifying the Body of Christ as a whole, and not an isolated pseudo culture.
>
> WHEREAS a segment of Messianic Judaism opposes the usage of terms such as 'Jesus,' 'Christ,' 'Christian,' 'cross,' et al, and insists on using the Hebrew terms exclusively, we of the FCTJ affirm that though we endorse tactfulness in witness, we reject a presentation of the Gospel which is a subtle attempt to veil and camouflage the Person

and work of our Lord Jesus Christ.

WHEREAS segments of Messianic Judaism, by portraying themselves to be synagogues with rabbis for the purpose of attracting unsuspecting Jews, employ methods which are unethical, we of the FCTJ affirm that Jewish missions must be honest and Biblical in their message and approach, and reject the concept that 'the end justifies the means.'
BE IT RESOLVED, therefore, that we of the FCTJ stand apart from and in opposition to Messianic Judaism as it is evolving today.[37]

Evidently Marvin Rosenthal mistakenly thought that since each of the individuals who worked on the resolution was an officer within their mission organization, they would also have the approval of their Board to release such a resolution. However, this was not the case. The author specifically told the committee that while he was an officer of the Mission, he was not a Board member, and that such a resolution would need ratification by the Mission's board. But copies of the FCTJ resolution were released to the media and to churches and Christian leaders prematurely. And to make matters worse, the resolution was released over the endorsement of the organizational names of those individuals who had been involved in working on the resolution, rather than over the endorsement of the individuals themselves. Among the organizations listed were the American Board of Missions to the Jews, the American Messianic Fellowship, Bible Christian Union, Catskill Messianic Fellowship, Friends of Israel, Messianic Fellowship Center, Midwest Messianic Center, Message to Israel.

The Directors of the Mission may have been in agreement with many of things stated in the FCTJ Resolution, but they were upset that it was released using the endorsement of the Mission without giving them an opportunity to first ratify the resolution. The Directors had just cause for their indignation!

The purpose of the resolution was to address what were perceived as "excesses" within the Messianic Jewish movement. It is unfortunate that the resolution was released before the individual boards of the cooperating mission agencies had a chance to read the resolution and to correct and amend it as they saw fit. It is also unfortunate that the final statement of the resolution was a blanket condemnation of all Messianic Judaism, rather than specifically addressing the segment within Messianic Judaism which was carrying some things to excess. As a participant in the development of the resolution, the author shares the blame for not catching this oversight.

In the wake of the release of the FCTJ Resolution, a number of pastors and Christian leaders wrote to the Mission expressing their concerns as to where the Mission stood on the issues of "confrontational evangelism," the establishment of "messianic synagogues," the local church, and the Mission's methods of evangelism, and the Directors felt compelled to make a policy statement to clarify the Mission's position on these issues.

The controversial policy statement on Messianic Synagogues was adopted by the Board at their October 29, 1975 meeting. It stated:

A. *Doctrinal*
   The A.B.M.J. strongly affirms its doctrinal principles which are founded on the fact that both the Old Testament and the New Testament are ONE BOOK, the inspired Word of God.
B. *Missionary Principle*
   The A.B.M.J. believes that the Gospel must be preached to all people within the context of their own historic culture whenever those cultures do not conflict with the Scriptures. There is an essential Jewishness of the Gospel which is recognized by all and at the same time does not mitigate against the universality of the Gospel message. We must realize that the Gospel transcends all cultures. To form a Messianic Synagogue on the basis of cultural background is no more valid than a group of Muslims organizing an Arabian Mohammedan Christian Mosque.
C. *Ecclesiology*
   We recognize that the Lord Jesus Christ and His apostles established only one visible institution, the local congregation of believers. The Church of Jesus Christ is not a building, nor a Sunday School, nor an ecclesiastical organization. It is an organism, 'a living body of believers bound together in a shared life.' Believers do not just go to church. They are the church. The church consists of Jews and Gentiles who have been 'called-out' (Church—ECCLESIA—called out) and redeemed by the blood of Christ. Any attempt to rebuild the middle wall of partition between Jew and Gentile is wrong and sinful.
D. *Missionary Method*
   The purpose of the ABMJ is to reach all Jews everywhere with the Gospel and, by God's grace, we use all valid methods to attain our goal. We continue to use all of the new tools our Lord has given us to attain this end. However, we will continue to use these tools, wielding them in love. We do not approve of methods that seek to provoke a violent reaction from the Jewish community just for the purposes of publicity. Our various stations have been picketed but we

do not picket synagogues. Our workers have been physically attacked, our stations bombed and workers' homes set afire, but we will not retaliate. During the last decade we have become highly visible. We are thankful for this. We intend to use this visibility not to show off but to show Him, the Lord Jesus Christ who has 'shined in our hearts to give the light of the knowledge of the glory of God in the face of Jesus Christ.'[38]

This policy statement on Messianic Synagogues was then printed in the January 1976 issue of *The Chosen People* magazine, along with the following commentary written by Daniel Fuchs:

Once Dr. Joseph Hoffman Cohn told of Sadie's persistent calls to the hospital to see how her Ben was. The nurse faithfully checked the charts and accurately reported 'He's improving!'

Yet when Sadie continued to call every hour on the hour the nurse just said 'He's improving' without checking his chart. That night Ben had a relapse and died.

When a friend later asked Sadie the cause of Ben's death she said, 'He died from improvements.'

This really isn't funny. Some improvements could kill us.

In recent years the Lord has given us many new tools in Jewish evangelism, particularly in the area of mass media: radio spots, T.V. and newspaper ads. (And one our most effective efforts is the least expensive—the Jewish Art Calendar advertised in local newspapers.)

As a result of new methods of presenting the old Gospel we are amazed to learn of thousands of young Hebrew Christians. Most are talented, enthusiastic witnesses who love the Lord and their people. It's exciting!

In their desire to effectively witness to their friends and relatives some of these enthusiasts have come up with a 'new method,' the Messianic Synagogue.

The American Board of Missions to the Jews has spent decades teaching the Church of Jesus Christ her responsibility in witnessing effectively to the Jewish people in her community.

This ministry has succeeded and we can testify to the truth that now most Bible-believing, evangelical churches are vitally interested in Jewish evangelism. Now some of the Jewish believers who have been won to the Lord by churches and the Mission are being weaned from the churches into the Hebrew-Christian Synagogues.

We protest!

In all fairness we must reveal that this movement was not started by Hebrew Christians, but by a well-intentioned and successful Gentile missionary to the Jews who wrote a best-selling manual: Everything You Need to Grow a Messianic Synagogue.

This comes complete with synagogue number application, Sabbath services and a Messianic Synagogue stewardship program that is a whopper in three easy lessons: The Obvious Goniff, The Subtle Goniff, *and* The Unwitting Goniff.

Goniff is thief in Hebrew. A thief is a thief. Calling him a goniff won't help and a Gentile wearing a yarmulke will not make him Jewish.

We cannot understand how one can confuse a 'Messianic Synagogue' with the Body of Christ. We decry any movement no matter how well-intentioned that would erect the 'middle wall of partition between us' which our Lord destroyed....

The ABMJ rejoices with every organization which wins Jews to our wonderful Lord, but we vigorously protest any movement which ignores truths taught in the Scriptures concerning the Church of Christ.

Particularly those truths written in the Letters to the Romans, the Galatians, the Ephesians and in the Revelation.[39]

Daniel's commentary and the policy stirred up a hornet's nest, and shortly after it was published several representatives of the Messianic Synagogue Movement and other Messianic Jewish believers paid Daniel Fuchs and the author a visit. The main topic of discussion was the Mission's policy statement. Daniel agreed that he had not attended services or visited any of the Messianic synagogues, nor had he attended any of the annual Messianic Alliance conferences which were averaging more than seven hundred Messianic Jews in attendance. His commentary and the Mission's policy were written in reaction to the "excesses" evident within the Messianic movement, and in reaction to the many letters he had received from Christian leaders about the "excesses" among those in the Messianic movement. Daniel agreed that he should visit some of the Messianic centers and explore further what was happening among the growing numbers of Messianic Jews.

THE GROWING MESSIANIC MOVEMENT

In June 1976, Messianic Jewish leaders and Jewish mission leaders met together with the following men: Dr. Arthur

F. Glasser, Dean of Fuller Theological Seminary's School of World Missions; Dr. J. Herbert Kane, President of the American Society of Missiology; and Dr. Paul Feinberg, Professor of Philosophy of Religion and Theology, Trinity Evangelical Divinity School. The conference was called in order to confront attacks made on the Messianic Movement by pastors, Christian leaders, and Jewish mission agencies and to confront statements made by the Messianic Movement against Jewish missions. A lengthy and intensive discussion on the problems connected with Jewish evangelism and the Messianic Jewish movement ensued, and the following resolution was unanimously adopted:

> We, as leaders of Messianic Jewish outreach organizations, met in Chicago, June 21-23, 1976. Because of conflicts and misunderstandings we came together for the expressed purpose of seeking greater mutual recognition and trust.
>
> We sincerely regret the recriminations of the past, and pledge our cooperation with and support of one another in the days ahead. We call on those who differ to seek to communicate directly with one another before drawing conclusions or making public statements.
>
> We affirm our united commitment to the authority of the Old and New Testament scriptures and our belief in the unity of all believers in Jesus the Messiah.
>
> We recognize that different methods may be used to communicate the message of Jesus the Messiah to the Jewish people. We accept the validity of various congregational structures and modes of worship for Jewish believers. However we call upon our brethren to exercise caution in the use of traditional Jewish nomenclature when describing their distinctive characteristics.
>
> We express our gratitude to the evangelical churches for their long years of sympathy and support in the work of Jewish evangelism and for their abiding concern for the welfare of our Jewish people.
>
> We rejoice in any and all who are faithfully and courageously communicating the gospel of Jesus the Messiah to the Jewish community.[40]

In the very formative stages, the Messianic Movement involved many Jewish young people who were "Jews" in name only—many had grown up in completely non-religious homes. By becoming involved in the Messianic Movement these young people took a stand to prove the rabbinic community wrong in its accusations that Jews who believe in Jesus were converts to another religion and could not, therefore, still be Jewish. They wanted to show the "establishment" that this was not the case. There were also some Jewish believers who eagerly embraced the Messianic Movement because they'd felt that once they'd become members of churches their Jewish heritage had been lost to them—and certainly to their children. Messianic congregations provided an opportunity for them to regain their heritage, and to share it with their children. Retaining their Jewish culture, both in worship and in home life, opened new opportunities for Jewish believers to witness to family members and friends. It also provided a way for the children of Jewish believers to carry on their Messianic heritage!

Some members of the Mission's staff had very strong feelings about the need for Messianic congregations, and they wanted to use the Messianic congregation approach in reaching Jewish people with the Gospel. The Mission had come full circle. The vision of Rabbi Leopold Cohn had been to develop a Messianic congregation that would maintain a support ministry for Jewish believers, as well as to carry on evangelistic outreach to the Jewish community. His vision was being rekindled in Jewish believers who saw the Messianic Movement as a valid expression of their Jewish-Christian faith.

JEROME AND MILDRED FLEISCHER—IN SAN FRANCISCO

Two such workers were Jerome and Mildred Fleischer, the Mission's workers in San Francisco. They had left the staff of Friends of Israel Ministry, and had joined the staff of ABMJ because of the Mission's willingness to use "messianic congregations" and Jewish culture as methods of reaching Jewish people with the Gospel. Jerry was already involved in the leadership of the Messianic Jewish Alliance when he joined the staff of the Mission. He was an experienced missionary to the Jews, and he felt very strongly that more Jews could be reached through the Messianic Movement than through other approaches. He came to the Mission so he would be free to use this approach in reaching the Jewish community of San Francisco, California and the surrounding environs.

Jerome (Jerry) Fleischer had a unique background. He was born on the S.S. Rotterdam while his orthodox Jewish parents made their way from Europe to the United States. Like other Jewish immigrants, the Fleischer's settled in New York; Jerry was raised on the East Side of New York City where he attended the Jewish schools and studied Talmud and the commentaries of Rashi, etc., with the rabbis. He had a great love of learning, of Judaism, and of his Jewish people.

When World War II broke out, Jerry found himself overseas. His base was attacked by enemy bombs and the sight of men killing one another made him wonder if there was really a God who cared for mankind. His search for peace and for the answers to his questions led him to the Protestant chaplain on base, but when he asked about the differences between Judaism and Christianity the chaplain was evasive and was unable to answer Jerry's probing questions. Jerry's questions were still unanswered when he returned home; life seemed to have no sane pattern. Of that time in his life, Jerry said:

> …It was at this time that the Lord saw my need and sent one of His servants to me. This Christian service man expressed his love for Jewish people, and then witnessed to me concerning the promised One, the Messiah of Israel, also giving me a New Testament, (Old Testament Prophecy Edition)…. Then, as I read the Scriptures, God spoke to my heart. I realized my need and received Jesus as my Savior and Messiah. This beloved brother in Christ has been a close friend to us through the years, and I thank God for using him to bring me the love and peace which I had sought. It was at the Bible Class on our base (where this friend taught us), that I met my wife-to-be, Mildred, and after our marriage and subsequent discharge from the service, we studied at Bible School together (Moody Bible Institute and Emmaus Bible School), where we felt led of the Lord to take the message of salvation to my own brethren. We have ministered in this field since 1948; first in Charlotte, N.C. for six years, then in Dayton, Ohio, for nearly ten years, where I also served as the Radio Pastor for the Christian Radio station there—WFCJ-FM.
>
> In 1963, our family moved to the San Francisco area to take up the work of a retired Jewish missionary representing the Friends of Israel Missionary and Relief Society (now renamed The Friends of the Gospel ministry), whose headquarters is in West Collingswood [Bellmawr], N.J.
>
> In San Francisco, we find the challenge of a tremendous population and need of the Gospel. We conduct Hebrew Christian Felleowship and other Messianic Jewish Bible Meetings in our home and other homes, where we gather the people from all over the area to hear God's Word and to fellowship. I have the privilege of ministering in many churches, lecturing also in colleges, schools and seminaries, and over the Christian radio station in S.F., KEAR-FM. In the light of current happenings, both in Israel and other areas of the world, there are many unanswered questions which perplex people, and I seek to answer these both in the light of the Bible and of Judaeo-Christian history. I also minister weekly on college campuses, reaching many students who are searching for the answers to life.[41]

Jerome and Mildred Fleischer's daughter, Ruth Fleischer also joined the staff of the Mission. As a worker in the San Francisco area, Ruth developed Bible study programs apart from those being carried on by her parents. Since she was a young person herself, her thrust was mainly among the college-career aged group. Ruth then moved to the East coast, where she became a full-time worker in New Jersey as a member of the Communications Department of the Mission. Through the ministry of the three Fleischer's, many Jewish people came to accept Jesus as their Messiah and Savior. Jerome and Mildred remained faithful workers of the Mission until their retirement from active service in March 1986. During their years of ministry they established several Messianic congregations in the San Francisco Bay area.

RACHMIEL FRYDLAND

Another worker on staff who felt strongly about the need for Messianic congregations, and who resigned from his position on staff in order to be a part of the Messianic Movement, was Rachmiel Frydland, Missionary in Charge of Toronto, Ontario, Canada. (More of Rachmiel's story will be told in the chapter devoted to Canada in this history.) In a letter to the author, Rachmiel wrote:

> I want to stress again that I was most happy with ABMJ and happy with all the Mission did for me providing for me and my family so graciously and abundantly, but as I said to Leslie [Jacobs—another one of the Mission's workers in Toronto] to-day, 'My time of retirement and rest is fast drawing to an end and I was persuaded perhaps by human persuasion, but perhaps divine, to try something different, before I die or retire. Perhaps this is a better way to reach our people.' If it proves wrong then I have only lost materially, but if I did not try it, perhaps I would always think that I should have tried it.[42]

Rachmiel left the staff of the Mission to pastor a Messianic congregation in Cincinnati, Ohio.

NEW TITLES, NEW POSITIONS, NEW POLICIES

From the mid-1970's until the late 1980's, the Mission's staff and programs made use of both the de-centralized approach and the branch/center/Messianic congregation approach. From time to time, the media were used for specific projects or programs. The broad spectrum of methodology allowed the missionary staff of the Mission to use their particular God-given gifts and talents, as well as to experiment with and to develop a variety of programs and creative ways of proclaiming the Gospel message to the Jewish communities where they served. The author never forgot Daniel Fuchs' words to him at the time he was hired. Daniel had said, "You can use any means you want, as long as you preach the Gospel!" When the author was appointed Missionary Director, he wanted the other missionaries to have that same opportunity!

Historically and currently, the rugged individualism and creativity in getting the job done has distinguished the missionaries who have served on the staff of the Mission. This has been said to have been both the strength and the weakness of the organization. God calls leaders into the ministry and He gifts them accordingly. As an administrator of the Mission, it was the author's joy to seek to utilize the gifts and talents of each worker to produce a unified effort of reaching Jewish people with the Gospel.

At the January 28, 1976 meeting of the Board of Directors, the author was elected a member of the Board and his title was changed from Vice President to Executive Vice President.[43] With the new title came a new job description—not just to serve in Daniel's absence, but to begin working with Daniel in all areas of the Mission's administration.

With the election of the author to the Board, two "salaried" staff members were once again serving as Directors, in addition to Jim Straub who was serving as both a consultant to the Mission and as a Director.

James W. Straub was a New York businessman who had become a member of the Board of Directors during the summer of 1967. He was born in Brooklyn, but was reared in Hollis, in the Borough of Queens. His parents were Christians—members of the Bellerose Baptist Church. Jim came to know the Lord when, as a teen, he attended meetings at the Pinebrook Bible Conference in Stroudsburg, Pennsylvania—a time during which Pinebrook was under the leadership of Percy Crawford.

Jim's interest in the salvation of Jewish people, and in the Mission, came through his personal study of the Scriptures. When he joined the Board in 1967, he stated:

> Bible study is of particular interest to me. I am active in a local home Bible-study class which I helped to found over twenty-five years ago. My interest in the salvation of the Jews is based on my study of the Old Testament and the Israel-centered Gospels, followed by the harmony of the remainder of the New Testament. While God is dealing equally today with both Jew and Gentile, it is particularly thrilling to show a Jewish person the New Testament fulfillment of the Old Testament prophecies of God's promises to Israel. We, who are Christians and ambassadors for Christ, must diligently urge in every possible way the unsaved Jew and Gentile to be 'reconciled to God.' It is especially rewarding to point a Jewish person to the Reconciler, Jesus Christ.[44]

At the time of his Board appointment, Jim was serving as Vice-President and Director of the management consultant firm of Garnett, Stixrood, Straub, & Associates of New York. He had served in a similar capacity with other firms, including: Brennan Associates, Inc., New York; Rich Plan Corporation, Utica, New York; the Merchants Refrigerating Company, New York. His involvement in Christian ministries included serving as Vice President of the New York Bible Society (now The International Bible Society); Vice Chairman of the official board of Community Bible Church, Richmond Hill, New York; and member of the Cornell Club of New York.

As a consultant to the Mission, Jim gradually increased the number of hours he devoted to the Mission until, in January 1979, he was hired as a full-time employee of the Mission.

At the time of the author's election to the Board, the list of directors included: John E. Melhorn, Daniel Fuchs, James W. Straub, John J. Kubach, Harold B. Pretlove, George Savage, Louis W. Ivins, David Reifsnyder, Harvey Scharfman, Tom Walker, Isaac J. Leonard, and Harold A. Sevener. Except for Harold Pretlove and John Melhorn, all members of the Board had been elected after the death of Joseph Hoffman Cohn. (George Savage was elected to the Board at the June 18, 1975 meeting; also Tom Walker was appointed an ex-officio member of the Board. Both George Savage and Tom Walker were Board members of Beth Sar Shalom of Canada, CPM's affiliate work in Canada.)

In spite of having been witness to the conflict that developed between Harold Pretlove and Daniel Fuchs when both men held staff positions and Board positions, the Directors evidently thought such conflict would not develop between Daniel Fuchs, Jim Straub and the author. They evidently did not consider the fact that the appointment of the author began movement toward a "troika" leadership of the Mission once again.

By 1976, the financial needs of the Mission were the primary consideration of the Board: the salary and benefit programs of the employees; the financing of the missionary programs; the cost of media evangelism. Related problems which also impacted the Mission's finances were: the image of the Mission in view of the growing strength and recognition of Jews for Jesus as an organization; the development of literature for evangelism and support; the direction and thrust of the Mission's evangelism program in view of the Messianic movement, Messianic synagogues, and the growth of other Jewish Missions.

A Pension and Salary Program

The Personnel Committee of the Board was comprised of Daniel Fuchs, Jim Straub, and the author. In his capacity as a consultant, Jim Straub spent one to two days each week at the Headquarters office. Personnel Committee meetings were planned for a day when Jim was planning to be in the office. The committee's recommendations were then presented to the Board for approval, rejection, or further refinement. The committee worked on and submitted recommendations to the Board for a new Pension Program, a Salary Administration Program, and a plan for a Regional Division of Missionary Work.

Jim Straub presented the Personnel Committee's recommendations for a new Pension Program to the Board. It provided that all workers whose date of employment was subsequent to January 1, 1968 would have vested an amount established under the "gradual vesting" schedule (IRC #411). This meant that after five years of service, an employee of the Mission would have 25% vested, after 10 years 50%, and after 15 years 100% vested. It further provided that workers with a date of employment prior to January 1, 1968 were to receive credit for prior years of service at an additional 10% for each full year of service prior to using the "gradual vesting" schedule.[45] The program addressed all of the issues needed for a "qualified" pension plan according to the minimum government requirements of the Employee Retirement Income Security Act of 1974, and even included a Planned Security Program—a life insurance policy in the event an employee died prior to age 65; after age 65 it served as a paid up policy.

The Personnel Committee's recommendation for a "Salary Administration" program included a salary structure for the various positions in the Mission. Prior to this recommendation missionaries had, for the most part, been paid a salary amount which was negotiated at the time of hiring. There was no set dollar amount per position. The dollar figure arrived at was often based upon the employee's need at the time of hiring.

The Salary Administration program set up categories for each missionary position: Category I Missionary; Category II Missionary-In-Charge I; Category III Missionary-in-Charge II; Category IV District Director; Category V Regional Director. A minimum and maximum salary range was assigned to each position.

It was the recommendation of the committee that the proposed salary program go into effect only from increased income. Forty percent (40%) of any excess income over the budgeted income was to go into a Salary Increment Fund so that at the end of the fiscal year the forty percent could be divided among the missionary staff, using the proposed Salary Administration Plan as the guide. The increase was to be in excess of the regular cost of living adjustment given by the Board each year. The Board voted on and approved the Personnel Committee's recommendations.[46]

A Volunteer Missionary Program

Prior to the establishment of the Salary Administration Program, the author, in the capacity as Missionary Director, had presented to the Board several proposals for increasing the income of the Mission, while developing the missionary work. The proposal of a "missionary support" fund-raising category, discussed earlier, was considered but not adopted by the Board. Another proposal was the "volunteer program." The proposal was that each branch of the Mission would train and develop volunteers who would help them expand their outreach into communities where the Mission could not afford to place a worker. The author outlined the program in the December 1974 issue of *The Chosen People* magazine. He wrote:

> Perhaps you are an individual who has had a special burden to share the Gospel with the Jewish people. Maybe God has been speaking to you already; however, because of your age, work, family commitment, etc., you feel that you cannot be a full-time missionary to the Jews. Under this new program you may qualify to become a 'volunteer missionary.'
>
> For the past few years we have been experimenting with this program and now can say without hesitation that some [of] our most successful branches are being run by volunteers: in Phoenix, Mrs. Dorothy Mellow; in Santa Barbara, Mrs. Dorothy Wilkerson; in Portland, Oregon, Mrs. Bea Watson; in Palm Springs, Mr. Glenn Webb. These dedicated Christians have volunteered their time and effort for a most rewarding ministry.
>
> Simply put, our program works in this way:
> 1. You let us know if you would like to serve as a volunteer missionary with the ABMJ.
> 2. The missionary on staff with the ABMJ will train you in witnessing and visitation techniques. He will further assist you in setting up home Bible study classes and in the operation of a monthly home fellowship-type meeting in your area. The missionary-in-charge, under whom you are trained, will always be available for assistance, speaking, planning holiday services, etc.
> 3. The personnel, resources, and literature ministry of the ABMJ would be available to you in your designated area to assist you in reaching the Jewish people for Christ.
> 4. Volunteer missionaries would be listed in The Chosen People magazine with names and addresses so that individuals

wishing to contact these workers in order to have them visit Jewish friends will be able to have that information at hand.

It is our hope and prayer that as God blesses this program, we may be able to open up an additional thirty-four branches in the United States and Canada, staffed by trained volunteer workers.[47]

The response to the Volunteer Missionary Program was excellent. The Mission received over one hundred thirty applications for volunteer missionary service.[48] The Mission has continued the Volunteer Missionary Program, and during the years of 1975 through the mid-1980's there were as many as thirty volunteer stations operating at one time. In more recent years, because of changing times and different methodologies being employed in its outreach, the Mission has used fewer volunteer missionaries.

A Regional Missionary Program

Another time-consuming program which occupied both the Personnel Committee's and the Board's agenda, was the regional division of the missionary work in the United States (this was eventually extended to Canada as well) which was established by the author during the Spring of 1975. Under this program, the country was divided into five regions: the Northeast; the Southeast; the mid-West; the Southwest; and West. The missionary work, deputation work, and support staff within each geographical division was to function under the supervision of a Regional Director. The Regional Directors reported to the author.

The reason for establishing the regions was for the purpose of tracking responses to the Mission's media events, to more carefully monitor the Mission's sources of income, and to determine the effectiveness of the various programs and methodology being used by the Mission's workers. The installation of the computer at the Headquarters office made such tracking possible, and it was hoped that the information would lead to a stronger, more financially-sound ministry.

A chart of accounts was set up so that the expenses and the income raised by each missionary on staff could be tracked. The activity reports of workers were compared with computer generated reports to assess the effectiveness of programs being used in a given area. If the reports indicated that more decisions for the Lord were being made in a particular area of the country, an analysis of the workers, programs, etc. was done to determine whether the results were caused by a special working of the Holy Spirit in that area, or if they were the result of particular programs or projects that could be duplicated in the other regions with the same, or better results. It was hoped that such information would enable the Mission to build up support in areas where it was weak.

The "downside" of the regional system was that it was necessary to give each Regional Director the financial information for his region, the donor listing for his region, and the oversight of the personnel within his region. In initiating the regional division program, the author perceived the financial and donor information to be management tools that were necessary for the regional plan to function. Some Board members, however, felt that such information was to be kept confidential. This difference in perception eventually led to problems.

After attending one of the Regional staff meetings, held at Bear Mountain, New York in the Spring of 1975, Jim Straub reported to the Board:

...he attended the Conference of Regional Directors at Bear Mountain and feels that the right people are serving as Regional Directors. They are enthusiastic and capable. The work will be better organized under the regional directors. Mr. Straub reported that at this time he can see the Lord's blessing on the ABMJ, both in personnel and in the contributions.[49]

Mr. Straub's mention of the contributions was a reference to the Treasurer's report he had made earlier in the meeting. The Minutes state:

Mr. Straub referred to the Treasurer's Report. Budget income was $1,097,435 and the actual receipts were $1,103,341—$5,906 over the budget. The report indicated an increase of $119,542 in income over last year. Legacies were off 20.9%. This financial report is for the eight month period.[50]

The Regional Directors at that time were: Northeast: acting, Harold Sevener; Southeast: Rev. Larry Jaffrey; Midwest: Rev. Ben Alpert; Southwest: Dr. Thomas McCall; Western: Mr. Richard Cohen.

The Bi-Centennial Celebration

As has been mentioned, Terryl Delaney, Director of Mass Media, had submitted his resignation and his employment with the Mission was to terminate at the end of 1975. Bob and Anita Friedman were hired to fill the positions of Editor and Director of Communications respectively (although the masthead of the magazine lists Anita as associate Director). For the first time, the magazine was under the direction of the Communications Department (although Daniel still retained final editorship).

The Friedmans were eager to create an appealing publication that would communicate the Mission's message to it donors and to the Jewish and Christian public at large. They felt that *The Chosen People* magazine, which was produced in just under a 6 x 9 inch black and white format, was outdated; it lacked space for copy, photos, and illustrations. It also required special printing and binding, a more expensive process. A popular size and format for magazines was a little over 8x10 inches—as used by *Time, Newsweek*, etc.

The author worked closely with Bob and Anita in re-designing *The Chosen People* magazine. After many hours of prayer and planning, it was decided that the new format would be a little over 8x10 inches (the popular magazine format size), it would have sufficient "white-space," with modern and readable type, and it would include a careful selection of photographs that would image the ministry of the Mission. It was also decided that the magazine would be produced with some color, using offset printing to reduce the cost. The masthead was also changed to carry the names of the missionaries under the region in which they worked, along with a telephone number where they could be reached. It also listed the volunteer branches (then twenty-one), with names and telephone numbers for contact.

The first issue of the newly formatted Chosen People magazine appeared in December 1975. The magazine has undergone some cosmetic changes since then, but the essential format remained the same through July 1993. (Interestingly the new format of 8 x 10 was nearly the same size as the original magazine first produced by Rabbi Leopold Cohn in 1895. The magazine went to the smaller format in February 1913.) The response from the Mission's donors, both by way of letters and increased donations, made it abundantly clear that the change in format had been directed by the Lord in answer to prayer. During the Spring of 1993, the Board voted to discontinue publication of *The Chosen People* magazine, substituting in its place a monthly Chosen People newsletter.

THE CONGRESS ON PROPHECY IN PHILADELPHIA

Every indication was that the year 1976 was going to be an exciting year for U.S. citizenry. Plans were being made throughout the country to celebrate the 200th anniversary of our nation's birth. The Mission was looking forward to an exciting year as well, as plans were being made for the Bicentennial Congress on Prophecy and the many special projects and conferences spawned by this major event.

As plans for the Bicentennial year were made, "brainstorming" sessions were held. As an outgrowth of those sessions a Bicentennial logo was designed to update the image of the Mission and to promote the Mission's Bicentennial Prophecy Congress which was to be held in Philadelphia, Pennsylvania from June 27 through July 3, 1976. (After the Bicentennial Prophecy Congress Mr. George Samson made a few minor changes on the Bicentennial logo; it then became the official logo for the Mission and has been used to this present day without further change.) The brainstorming sessions also resulted in the selection of a Mission theme for the year. "Looking Back So That We Can Look Forward—'76" was the theme chosen.

Looking forward to the upcoming new year, the newly formatted December 1975 issue of *The Chosen People* magazine featured both the new Bicentennial logo and the Mission's theme for the new year. The coordination of the Editorial Department and the Communications Department can be seen in the opening "Letter from the President" which replaced the "Salutation" of the older magazine format. Daniel began his remarks by stating:

> *LOOKING BACK SO WE CAN LOOK FORWARD! We are excited as we introduce our Bicentennial motto and logo to our world-wide CHOSEN PEOPLE family.*
>
> *Beginning the first of this month every letter we send and every publication printed will remind you of our great Bicentennial Congress on Prophecy to be convened in Philadelphia June 27-July 3, 1976 as we celebrate the 200th anniversary of our nation's birth.*[51]

The idea for the Bicentennial Congress on Prophecy was developed by Terryl Delaney, and he did much of the preliminary planning before he resigned and left the staff of the Mission at the end of 1975. The Congress plans were then turned over to Bob and Anita Friedman, who continued to develop the project with the help of Dr. Thomas McCall, the Mission's Conference Director, and the Regional Directors.

Prior to 1974, the position of Conference Director was filled by Dr. Emil Gruen, and then by the author. In 1974 the author appointed Tom McCall to the position because he had developed good rapport with many Christian leaders and pastors across the United States. Joseph Cohn had built up his support and donor base by networking with the Christian leaders of his day; the prophetic Bible Conference ministry allowed us to continue this network and to expand on it.

In his position as Conference Director (a job he undertook in addition to his regular responsibilities as Regional Director for the Southwest), Tom's work load was greatly increased in 1976. He made all the arrangements for the speakers being featured at the Bicentennial Congress on Prophecy (Hal Lindsey; Dr. W. A. Criswell; Dr. Douglas MacCorkle; Dr. John Walvoord; Dr. Earl Radmacher; Dr. Charles Feinberg; Dr. Larry Ward). He also made the arrangements for the site, transportation, housing, and for the printing of messages presented at the Congress. Additionally, he set up fifteen smaller conferences on prophecy (family Bible conferences) which were held throughout the United States during 1976.

One new feature which the author added to the program of the Mission's family Bible conferences was a seminar conducted by Mr. Wesley Jones, the Mission's Stewardship Director. This was added to further develop deferred gifts for the Mission. It proved to be most successful. In his report, Daniel Fuchs told the Board:

> As far as Mr. Jones is concerned, he is working well. As Mr. Sevener told in his report Mr. Jones attended the conferences in the San Joaquin Valley and was very helpful in notifying people in that area of the meetings. He will attend the Dallas Conference early in February. Mr. Jones and I have kept in close touch.[52]

A Special Media Ad

The Bicentennial Congress was by far the largest conference the Mission had ever arranged. It was planned not only as a prophetic Congress which would bring together the leading prophetic Bible teachers of the day (including those on the Mission's staff), but also as a strategically-timed media campaign. Past experience had taught leaders of the Mission to keep media events a secret until the day of their release. On July 1, 1976 the Mission's dramatic full-page ad, "God's Timepiece" ran simultaneously in the New York Times, the Chicago Tribune, and the Los Angeles Times. The ad copy read:

> If you want to know where we are in history, look at the Jewish people.
> They are God's timepiece and people of prophecy. Part of an eternal clock ticking away as an everlasting reminder that although other peoples or nations may come or go, these people will remain forever.
> Because that's the way God wants it. Promised it. And planned it. Long ago.
> He made a covenant with Abraham, promising a large portion of the Middle East as an inheritance for him and his descendants.
> No mortgage. No lease. And no divine or human right of eminent domain to ever pop up later.
> The covenant was unconditional. Just like His love.
> And because of God's love He made another promise through Abraham. That through his seed all nations of the earth would be blessed.
> This is history past. For the seed which came through Abraham, Isaac and Jacob…Ruth, Jesse and David…came to fruition as the Messiah of Israel.
> We, as believers in the Messiah, know Him to fulfill ancient promises while bringing love, joy and peace to us now. This is history today.
> And as the Jewish people continue to return to their promised land by the thousands, they take part in fulfilling prophecy today. And history tomorrow. Bringing us one step closer to the most important event of all. The return of the Messiah.
> Because the Jewish people are the people of prophecy, they are the people of the land.
> And we, knowing Him who made the promise, totally support the people and land of Israel in their God-given, God-promised, God-ordained right to exist.
> Any person or group of nations opposed to this right isn't just fighting Israel. But God and time itself.[53]

At the bottom of the ad was the statement: "The following churches fully believe in God's promises to Israel and in His everlasting love for Her."[54] Listed below this statement were the church names and cities of one hundred and five of the leading evangelical churches in America. They represented a cross-section of evangelical Christian persuasion, crossing over denomination lines, all showing their love and support of Israel and the Jewish people.

The ad featured a sharp black background with a white "Mogen David" (The Star of David) suspended on a chain. The Mogen David was photographed in slow motion photography so that it looked like the "swinging pendulum" of a gigantic clock, ticking away the seconds of history. Below the ad copy, but above the names of the churches which endorsed the ad, was a coupon that gave the name and address of the Mission, as well as a book offer for a copy of "Israel, A Modern Miracle."

The ad was timed to hit the newspapers during the middle of the week when the Mission's Bicentennial Congress on Prophecy was being held—thus focusing more media attention on the Congress, and upon the concern of evangelical Christians for the Jewish people.

In sharing his excitement about the ad, the Congress on Prophecy, and the Saturday afternoon rally which was held on July 3, 1976 at the Centrum in Cherry Hill, New Jersey, Daniel wrote:

The parade of ships [Daniel was referring to a parade of beautiful tall-masted sailboats (Operation Sail '76) which made their way up the Hudson River in celebration of the Bicentennial] seemed a fitting climax to what was undoubtedly the greatest week in the history of the American Board of Missions to the Jews. It was our Bicentennial Congress on Prophecy in Philadelphia. It seemed as if the quintessence of our more than eighty years of ministry was distilled into that one week.

It began on Sunday, June 27th, with a week's series of meetings in five of the outstanding evangelical churches in the Philadelphia area:

Bethel Baptist Church, Wilmington, De.
Calvary Memorial Church, Philadelphia, Pa.
Church of the Saviour, Berwyn, Pa.
Cherry Hill Baptist Church, Cherry Hill, NJ.
Tenth Presbyterian Church, Philadelphia, Pa.

We were able to bring together the finest prophetic scholars in the United States including:

Dr. Charles L. Feinberg, Dean Emeritus, Talbot Seminary and Professor of Semitics and Old Testament;
Dr. W. A. Criswell, Pastor, First Baptist Church, Dallas, Tx;
Dr. Douglas MacCorkle, President, Philadelphia College of Bible;
Dr. John F. Walvoord, President, Dallas Theological Seminary.

Toward the middle of the week our staff (who knew what was ahead) could hardly keep their 'secret.' At the Thursday morning session of the Congress July 1st, I was able to announce that on that day we had exploded a three-fold media bombshell.

A beautiful ad, prepared by our media department was published simultaneously in three of the greatest newspapers in the United States . . .

In this one thrust we reached about one-fifth of all the Jews in the United States....

The effect was immediate and startling! Believe it or not, within the hour we received a telephone call from The Jerusalem Post with the result that the pastor of every one of the co-operating churches has received a letter from the North American Director of The Jerusalem Post which says:

'Dear Pastor,

In response to my request, the ABMJ office in Englewood, New Jersey, has given me your name and full address. The New York Times statement you endorsed this morning makes me feel goosebumps and I hasten to write directly and thank you personally. What a magnificent statement of solidarity! What profound concern!

As the North American Director of The Jerusalem Post newspaper, I have telexed a description and the full text of your statement to the Editor, Mr. Ari Rath, in Jerusalem. At the same moment in history when an Air France plane has been hijacked and the Israeli government is being forced to trade human lives, the visual imagery of the Jewish star as a pendulum and the force of your words warm my, and all our hearts. I, personally, thank you. One phrase I often use to describe The Jerusalem Post is: "a personal voice in an impersonal world." This morning, however, as a direct result of your statement, this phrase certainly seems invalid.'

At last many evangelical churches throughout the country are communicating the love of the Lord Jesus Christ to the Jewish community.[55]

PROCLAMATION ON ISRAEL, AND RALLY

As plans for the Congress on Prophecy were being made, a Proclamation on Israel and the Jewish people was prepared. It was hand written in beautiful calligraphy on a parchment scroll. At the bottom of the Proclamation there was a place for the signatures of the speakers of both the Congress and the Rally, as well as signatures of the pastors of participating churches. The Proclamation was addressed to: The Honorable Simcha Dinetz, Ambassador To The United States, Israeli Mission, Washington D.C. It read:

Dear Ambassador Dinetz:
I believe the Bible, including the Old and New Testaments, is the inspired Word of God...

That in the Bible God vigorously proclaims His love for the Nation of Israel and the Jewish people and...

Through the Nation of Israel came the promised Messiah and according to Scripture, the Messiah will return to Jerusalem to reign as King, and...

God has made a promise of love to Israel to insure her existence today, tomorrow and forever.

God has made a promise to Abraham, effective throughout history and to this present day, that any nation cursing Israel shall be cursed and any nation blessing Israel shall be blessed (Genesis 12:3)...

I, therefore, protest the recent action of the United Nations which equated Zionism with racism as being contrary to the Word of God and, as throughout history, self-condemning to any body or individual nation voting against Israel's right to exist.

Signed this 3rd day of July, 1976, at the Bicentennial Congress on Prophecy in Greater Philadelphia, Pennsylvania.[56]

Copies of the Resolution (as it appeared in the January 1976 issue of *The Chosen People* magazine) were printed and distributed to individuals who attended the Congress and the closing rally, and people were encouraged to sign their copy of the resolution and send it to the Mission. Tear-out copies of the resolution were also included in *The Chosen People* magazine so that individuals who could not attend the Congress were able to participate in taking a stand for Israel. They, too, were encouraged to sign the resolution and return it to the Mission. All told, over seven thousand additional signatures were collected.

A report telling about the signing of the Proclamation, and a brief account of the Rally, held on Saturday July 3, 1976 was given in September 1976 issue of *The Chosen People* magazine. It stated:

The giant rally held at the Centrum at Cherry Hill, NJ. marked the grand finale of the Bicentennial Congress on Prophecy.

One of the highlights, if not the main point of interest, was the signing of a beautiful proclamation which asserted our love and enthusiasm, as believers in the Messiah of Israel, for Israel and her people.

The featured rally speakers eagerly applied their names to the scroll: Hal Lindsey, author of The Late, Great Planet Earth; Dr. Larry Ward, president of Food For the Hungry; and Dr. Criswell.

Our speakers from the morning sessions as well as pastors from our participating churches also endorsed the document.

The rally came alive with the 200-voice choir from the First Baptist Church, Dallas. They mixed spiritual with patriotic songs for a well-balanced, highly enjoyable program.

Donna Jean Wood, a Hebrew-Christian singer from Beverly Hills, CA, was the featured soloist....

Calvin Marsh, formerly with the New York Metropolitan Opera, was also a featured soloist. He was accompanied by Duncan Holms on the piano for a perfect blend of instrument and voice.[57]

Throughout the Bicentennial Congress on Prophecy, the missionaries from the Mission's staff in Philadelphia, New York, and New Jersey, as well as selected staff from California, Texas, and other parts of the country, were on the streets of Philadelphia distributing literature to Jewish people. Some members of the Jews for Jesus staff and people from other Jewish missions organizations in the Philadelphia area also joined in the campaign and were present to distribute their special Bicentennial literature and "broadsides."

One particular event stands out in the author's mind. During the conference a special luncheon was arranged with a leading rabbi from the New York area. A group of the speakers, including Dr. W.A. Criswell and the author, joined the rabbi at lunch. It was a time of informal discussion about Israel, prophecy, the Congress, etc. When the conversation reached a lull, Dr. Criswell, in his own inimitable way, turned to the Rabbi and quietly said, "Rabbi, this last year I have been preaching through the book of Isaiah and on every page, in every chapter, in every line, I see a portrait of the Messiah. Rabbi what do you see? Does it ever occur to you that these prophecies might be a reference to the Messiah, Jesus?" The Rabbi was quiet, not knowing what to say. He looked down, thought, and chose his words very carefully. "Dr. Criswell," he said, "Where I went to seminary it was taught that this prophecy was fulfilled historically, and is a reference to the nation of Israel in its entirety. It never once enters my mind that the book of Isaiah contains any reference to the Messiah!" Nothing more was said, and the table talk continued.

As we were walking back to our hotel after the luncheon, I commented to Dr. Criswell that I had appreciated the way he'd been able to weave something about the Messiah into the conversation. I also mentioned how sad it was that modern-day rabbis had no concept of the Messiah as they read and studied the Scriptures. With a twinkle in his eye, Dr. Criswell responded, "And this rabbi will never again be able to read the Book of Isaiah without thinking about the Messiah!" We both laughed, and knew that the seed of God's Word had been planted in the mind and heart of the rabbi!

Perhaps, one day, God will use it to open his heart and mind to the Gospel of the Lord Jesus Christ.

The excitement of the Congress and the rally, the media ad, the Proclamation, and the involvement and encouragement of so many pastors, churches, and Christians for the work of Jewish evangelism buoyed the spirits of the missionaries and the staff, and they refocused their energies and dedication to the vision and task of reaching all Jews with the Gospel.

For Daniel Fuchs and the author, the Bicentennial Congress had a bittersweet ending. At the end of the week Bob Friedman informed us that he and Anita would be leaving the staff of the Mission and returning to California. The reasons for Bob's sudden decision were never spelled out. He simply indicated that he felt the Lord could better use his talent and witness for the Messiah in the secular world. Perhaps the Friedman's felt stymied after the June 1976 Board meeting when they set forth a media campaign to the Board. The Minutes of June 16, 1976 state:

> After a full discussion of Robert Friedman's report on the Proposal for New York-Los Angeles Media Campaign, it was agreed to use only ad #1 - "God's Timepiece" at the present time.
>
> Motion was made and voted that Mr. Friedman be authorized to place Ad #1 "God's Timepiece" in The New York Times and The Los Angeles Times for one day during the last week in June 1976.[58]

The sudden resignation of the Friedman's was a shock to the Mission personnel and to the Board, but Bob did not leave the Mission without a replacement for his position. In April 1976 he had hired Jonathan Singer, another Jewish believer, to be his associate Editor. When he was hired, Jonathan had only been a believer in the Lord for one year.

Jonathan Singer—His Story

Jonathan's story reveals the grace of God in a life. He was raised in an orthodox Jewish home, rich in tradition and Jewish heritage but his parents never told him about God, nor did they demonstrate that they personally had faith in God even though they kept Jewish traditions. By the time he reached his teen years, Jonathan was essentially an agnostic. In his late teens he began to experiment with drugs; they seemed to add a mystical dimension to his life. Like many teenagers, he was enamored with the teen-age rock stars and music stars. He admired them very much and he enjoyed expressing his feelings through journalism. He eventually found a position writing about the latest rock and roll stars. As he listened to them, and studied them, he became convinced that their music was inspired—it came from someplace, or from someone, outside themselves. He began to read the literature of the Hare Krishna's, Transcendental Meditation, and Scientologists, but he soon rejected them all. Nothing gave him the peace he was searching for.

In 1969 Jon married his college sweetheart, Nancy. However, even in marriage he did not find happiness or peace. In 1973 he and Nancy separated, and for one year they did not communicate with one another. Jon remained in New York City where he pursued his writing career at CBS, and did free-lance work for several popular music journals. Nancy moved to Ithaca, New York. There, she became involved in Teen Challenge of Greater Ithaca. When Nancy joined Teen Challenge, Jon thought perhaps she needed "religion" as some kind of buffer against the bad breaks she had suffered in her life.

During the summer of 1974, Jon was sent to New Orleans to cover a story about one of the most creative musicians in America. He was a reclusive, enigmatic personality—a musician no one had yet written about. The story was to be Jon's "exclusive"—the "big one" that would put him over the top career-wise. He hung around New Orleans for three weeks, hoping that his big break would come and he would have an opportunity for an interview. During those long hot days, he began to notice the differences between himself and those around him who said they believed in Jesus. He began to wonder, "Why do some people believe in Jesus and others do not?" His thoughts started to disturb him. He began to feel perverse somehow, and heinous because of his rejection of God. His agnostic beliefs seemed to be in contradiction with the "wholesome American custom" of believing in God, especially as expressed in the "Bible belt!"

A hurricane cut short Jon's stay in New Orleans. He was able to get a seat on the last airplane leaving the stormy New Orleans airport. As the plane took off, for the first time in his life, he began to pray. He didn't even know to whom! Or, Why! He just wanted to live and not become another statistic in a plane crash!

During this same time in his life, Jon began receiving letters from Nancy. In her letters Nancy witnessed to Jon, and at one point she even visited him and gave a copy of *Good News for Modern Man* (a translation of the Bible), but he ignored her pleas to accept Yeshua.

Determined to finish his "scoop" on the reclusive musician, Jon steeped himself in the man's music. Hoping to discover more about the man through the words of his music, he listened to the words intently and was shocked to discover that the man had faith in God. He realized that it would be impossible to write about the man without including the fact that he was a man of faith in God—and he didn't want to write about a God he didn't believe in!

Suffering from acute writer's block, Jon's life was on hold. He was living alone, with no income (as he couldn't write), and he was miserable. From time to time, in his loneliness and desperation he would pick up the Bible Nancy had given him and read from it.

When the spring of 1975 arrived Jon was three seasons late with his story, and to his dismay he discovered that another journalist had picked up on the story and had written it. He'd lost his once in a lifetime opportunity! Jon wrote:

> I had to face utter failure as a writer. I was left looking at myself not as a self-exalted journalist, but as a fear-filled shell of a man. Even that shell of a man was a front. I wanted to run, but I couldn't. Time had passed me by, there was nowhere to forget.[59]

When the reclusive musician from New Orleans was in New York City to perform a live concert, Jonathan attended. He later wrote:

> ...After the concert I walked alone into the night. My professional life was a complete washout. Moreover, a burning festering sore on my chest convinced me I was in fact dying. I wanted to live. I wanted to live right. On April 30 [c.1975] at 4 a.m. I called my wife long distance. I told her I was coming to live with her. I wanted to make peace with God. That wasn't enough, she said. She told me I had to have faith. I told her that was all I had. We prayed. I gave everything to Jesus. The next day I felt washed and free.[60]

After accepting Yeshua as his Messiah and Savior, Jon and Nancy reconciled and Jon continued to grow in his faith as he and Nancy studied the Scriptures together and had fellowship with other believers. He wrote:

> ...And I have been learning to trust Jesus as my Lord and Savior more and more. Learning that the trustworthiness of God's Word seals my salvation, not the way I feel when I wake up in the morning.
>
> One day in early January [c.1976], I asked God frankly for a job in an area of His ministry where I could utilize my talents and receive spiritual food. I xeroxed 20 copies of the first honest résumé of my life. I distributed them amongst the Ithaca area's advertising agencies. But I knew the Lord just didn't want me there. For several days in mid-Feb, a mysterious back ailment literally kept me on my back from distributing the rest of my résumés. One of these bedridden afternoons, I heard 2 ABMJ speakers on the radio. After the show, Roy Schwarcz and Dan Siegel dropped by my house for some much-needed fellowship. For some reason I felt particularly led to give Roy my résumé and some copies of my work—a "longshot." My wife and I love the country, but we know this move, 15 minutes from our "past" is of the Lord: "Go back to your town, and tell what wonderful things, God's done for you."[61]

Roy Schwarcz gave Jon's résumé to Bob Friedman, and Jonathan was hired as Bob's associate editor. Jon began his work for the Mission on April 1, 1976. Through the years, he faithfully and diligently used his God-given talents to develop *The Chosen People* magazine into an award-winning magazine. He eventually became the Creative Director for the Mission. In April 1992, after sixteen years of faithful service with the Mission, Jonathan and Nancy felt led of the Lord to use their gifts, talents and abilities in another area of God's vineyard.

GEORGE SAMSON JOINS THE STAFF

One individual whose ideas and contacts were of immeasurable help in the planning and execution of the Bicentennial Congress on Prophecy, was Mr. George Samson. The author first met George Samson when he introduced himself following a service at the Grace Conservative Baptist Church in Nanuet, New York. The author had been the guest speaker that morning, and God spoke to George's heart during the message. The whole concept of Jews coming to faith in the Messiah, and end-time events, fell into place for George and after the service he enthusiastically announced that he wanted to do something for Israel and the Jewish people.

George had been doing communications work for IBM; he had helped to develop their image, magazines, in-house communications, etc. In fact, some of the training films he'd produced for IBM were on exhibit at the Smithsonian Institute. Since he was planning to retire (although he continued working for IBM on a consultant basis), he stated that he would be available to help the Mission if we would be interested in using him.

The following day, the author told Daniel Fuchs and Bob Friedman about Mr. Samson's offer, and within a few days they met together. The Mission's staff was hard at work on preparations for the Bicentennial Congress on Prophecy and George Samson "jumped in with both feet," enthusiastically volunteering his time. With his assistance and expertise in media, public relations, and planning, the Mission was able to make the Congress on Prophecy into the media event that it was. It was through George and his contacts that the Mission was able to print the beautiful parchment scroll of the Bicentennial Proclamation on Israel and the Jewish people.

When Bob and Anita Friedman resigned their positions as Editor and Communications Director, Daniel and the author asked George Samson if he would take over the media and communications department of the Mission. Because he was also doing consultant work for IBM, George was not able to serve on a full-time basis. The Mission therefore contracted with him for his services as the Mission's Program Communications Consultant.

George Samson was not alone in his enthusiasm for Israel and the Jewish people. It was a time in history when a great number of evangelical and fundamental Christians had become enraptured by the role of the Jews in prophecy, and were vocal in their support of Israel. The Mission's media events had been instrumental in this "awakening of thought" within such Christians.

When the United Nations equated Zionism with racism, strong protests erupted from the evangelicals, while liberal Christians for the most part remained silent. Members of the Jewish community were impressed by this new block of support for the nation of Israel and for the Jewish people.

One very outspoken rabbi, Meir Kahane, welcomed this new support and wrote an article entitled, "Christians for Zion," which appeared in the January 24, 1975 issue of the Jewish Press in Brooklyn, New York. His article expressed the feelings of many Jewish leaders, as well as the feelings of evangelical Christians in support of Israel. Of the vast resource of evangelical support, Kahane wrote:

> The failure of the government of Israel to appreciate the enormous potential of this weapon is understandable only when one realizes that the leadership of the Jewish State is one that cannot bring itself to conceive of the kind of faith in the Bible that these people have and that, on the contrary, finds such thoughts in Jews, to be outlandish, medieval, dangerous and mystical. It is thus understandable that they have no affinity to the fundamentalist Christian groups who have such power and potential.
>
> It is the clear task of American Jews to work to persuade the fundamentalist Christian community to organize an active and politically militant 'Christians for Zion' committed to the unconditional opposition to Israeli retreat and American pressure against the Jewish State. It should be a group based strictly on Christians' self-interest which would give political muscle to its religious beliefs by making it clear to President Ford that his support in the Bible belt—without which he is a clear loser in 1976—will vanish unless he takes a firm stand on behalf of Israel and ceases American pressure. The fundamentalists believe that those who oppose Israel are doomed ('Blessed is he that blesseth thee and cursed is he that curseth thee,' Numbers 24:9). This belief must be imparted to Ford and the political threat made a clear and present one. That is the language that the President understands even more clearly than the Kissinger lectures on Realpolitik.
>
> Since neither the government of Israel nor the American Jewish Establishment is likely to have the imagination or the courage to work on this, it is important for local Jewish groups to begin. Bear in mind that these fundamentalist groups are zealous missionaries, but the Jewish head—if used—can overcome that.[62]

Articles such as this one by Rabbi Meir Kahane became the catalyst for the establishment of organizations such as Bridges For Peace, the Christian Embassy, etc. Realizing that there was value in such organizations, as long as evangelism was included, the leaders of the Mission began to think of ways to utilize the Jewish community's and Israel's willingness to be involved with evangelical Christians.

The closing rally of the Bicentennial Congress on Prophecy was not the end of the planned events. The Congress and the "God's Timepiece" ad had opened new opportunities for communication between evangelical Christians and Zionist leadership. Further, the signed Proclamation was to be presented to Ambassador Simcha Dinetz (along with the 7,000 resolutions signed by individuals) at a luncheon at the Madison Hotel in Washington D.C. on October 28, 1976.

When the Directors met for their regular meeting on October 25, 1976 there was an air of excitement as they discussed the Mission's involvement in further dialogue with the Jewish community. The Minutes state:

> Mr. George Samson, ABMJ Program Communications Consultant, presented a report on the involvement of the Mission as a liaison between the Evangelical Christian leadership and the Zionist leadership. He outlined the background beginning with the Resolution printed in the January 'Chosen People' followed by Herb Zwickel approaching Rabbi Siegel, Director of Inter-Religious Affairs for the Zionist Federation. While Rabbi Siegel did not wish to talk with a Hebrew Christian he would communicate with Mr. Samson. Many meetings with the leadership have resulted culminating in a meeting with Dr. Samuel Cohen, Executive Director of the American Zionist Federation and Rabbi Siegel.
>
> Projects were suggested—one of which is a national telecast which would be paid for by the Zionist group. Evangelical

Christians would direct and produce it.

The Proclamation which was signed at the Rally of the ABMJ Congress on Prophecy in Philadelphia by the Evangelical leaders was shown and read to the Board of Directors. This Proclamation, as well as over 7,000 signed resolutions by Christians in support of Israel, will be presented to the Honorable Simcha Dinetz, the Israel Ambassador to the United States, at a luncheon given by him on Oct. 28th in Washington, D. C. Mr. Samson outlined the program which will be preceded by a prayer breakfast led by Dr. Fuchs with the evangelical leaders.

Mr. Samson reported that a pamphlet by Dr. Criswell, 'Israel and America' will be mailed to 20,000 pastors with a letter telling them about the significant happenings and urging them to become more involved in Jewish evangelism.

This report was accepted with thanks and with a request that the program be undergirded with prayer.[63]

As the special luncheon with Ambassador Dinetz was being held, Daniel Fuchs and the author were asked to wait in an adjourning room. We were told that, as "missionaries to the Jews," our presence at the luncheon would have been a public embarrassment to the Ambassador and to the State of Israel. The Ambassador was willing to accept the Proclamation, the good will, and the love and support of evangelical Gentile Christians, but he did not want to publicly have any dealings with a "mission to the Jews" or with "Hebrew-Christians."

When the luncheon was over, Ambassador Dinetz met with Daniel and the author. He apologized for not being able to publicly recognize the work the Mission had done in preparing the Proclamation. In typical Israeli fashion, he hugged both of us, and thanked us for involving and encouraging so many evangelical Christians to love and support Israel.

As a result of the luncheon with Ambassador Dinetz, the presentation of the Proclamation and resolutions, and the involvement of so many churches, Mr. George Samson received an invitation (at government expense) to present the Proclamation (and the resolutions) to the curator of the Archives Building in Jerusalem, Israel, where it is kept on permanent display. George was selected for this honor because he was a "safe" representative of the Mission; he was a consultant to the Mission, but he was also a Gentile Christian.

Recognizing the value of what had been accomplished through the Congress, and with the Proclamation, but also recognizing that Jewish leadership in America and in Israel would never be willing to work directly with the Mission, the author and George Samson, with the approval of Daniel Fuchs, laid preliminary ground work for the formation of a sister organization called "Christians United for Zion." The author presented information about the new sister organization at the January 1977 Board meeting. The Minutes record:

Mr. Sevener presented his report and distributed copies to the Board members. In addition he presented a Preamble and Statement of Purpose of the new organization to be formed, 'Christians for Zion.'[64] *[The Board approved that] the preliminary legal work in the formation of the Christians For Zion organization will be undertaken by a lawyer and will be presented to the Board at its next meeting.*[65]

EVANGELICALS UNITED FOR ZION ESTABLISHED

Along with legal counsel, George Samson proceeded in setting up the new sister organization. The name was changed to "Evangelicals United for Zion" (EUZ). The Board of EUZ was inter-locked with the Board of ABMJ. The purpose of EUZ was to work directly with Jewish and evangelical leaders in combatting anti-Semitism, in increasing support for Israel on the part of evangelical Christians, and to demonstrate to Jewish leaders in America and in Israel that a continued anti-missionary stance on the part of Israel and the Jewish community would erode their support among evangelical Christians.

Unfortunately, this sister organization and its affiliation with the Mission was problematic. Since its membership was only open to Gentile Christians (because of the Jewish community's refusal to deal with Jewish believers), the Mission's own staff did not approve of the Mission's affiliation with, and support of, the EUZ. Staff members who were Jewish could not be involved, even if they wanted to be. This was difficult to accept. However, in spite of the objections of some of the staff, the Board approved the publication of an Evangelical Israel Newsletter. It was mailed out twice a month to the 20,000 plus evangelical churches who had taken part in the original signing of the Proclamation. The Board Minutes state:

Dr. Fuchs requested permission to proceed with the publication of an Evangelical Israel Newsletter. This will be published twice a month and offered at a subscription rate. It will involve a correspondent in Israel and the budget including printing, etc., will be $15,000 a year. This should become self-supporting after a year.[66]

It was hoped by Daniel, George, and the author that by keeping pastors and churches informed about Israel and the

Jewish people through the Evangelical Israel Newsletter, their concern and interest would be sustained. We also envisioned that some of the material from the newsletter could be used in a special "Israel" section in *The Chosen People* magazine, and we had hoped that through the newsletter and the magazine additional churches would be opened to the Mission's ministry, thus increasing the support base of the Mission. But the growing gap between actual income and actual expenses caused the cessation of the newsletter.

Struggling With Vision and Finances

Until his appointment to the Board in January 1976, the author had had only partial access to the Mission's financial information. But after becoming a Board member, he was given full access to the Mission's funding and financial records. As has been stressed, the philosophy of the Board was *not* to build up reserve funds. Most Board members felt strongly that God would provide for the needs of the Mission, and that if the General Fund was insufficient to provide for the programs and personnel of the Mission, they would make up the difference from the Investment Fund. However, each year more money was needed from the Investment Fund to make up for new programs launched and new personnel hired.

The years of the late 1970's through the mid 1980's were both painful and blessed—"bittersweet" is an apt description. They were years filled with changes for the organization, and personal changes. As the author began to see and understand the in-depth picture of the Mission's finances, his vision for the Mission was not always shared by Daniel Fuchs, and vice versa. Mistakes were made—some out of inexperience on the part of the author; some out of the reaction of the varying personalities involved to circumstances, some simply out of the shortcomings of being human beings. Looking back, the author is made aware again that the work of God, although done through men, is not of men, but of God. The Mission was, and will continue to be, an ongoing testimony to God's grace as He uses imperfect individuals to accomplish His perfect purpose in reaching the lost with the Gospel.

When the Directors approved the Salary Administration Program in January 1976, the author was a newly appointed Board member who had previously had limited access to the financial statements of the Mission. The financial statements which the author and Regional Directors had available to them indicated an item listed as "transfers from investments." It was assumed that this was normal practice since the Financial Statement showed that expenses were in line with the income. We did not realize that "transfers from investments" referred to the amount of funds needed to balance the income to the expenses. We therefore mistakenly believed that if we could just increase income, the salaries of the missionaries and other staff members would be increased as well. We had no idea that any increase in income would have to close the large gap between income and expenses before salary increases could become a reality.

As a Board member, the author began to examine the Financial Statements in light of the definition of "transfers from Investments," and what that meant. The fact that the transfers often totaled amounts in excess of $450,000.00 was a shocking revelation! Realizing that this directly impacted the Salary Administration Program, and the administration of the regional districts, the author shared the information with the Regional Directors. They, too, were shocked, and we realized that implementation of the salary increase program was a virtual impossibility. Unfortunately, the disappointment of this fact plus the author's sharing such specific financial information with the Regional Directors began a credibility gap between the members of the Board and the Regional Directors which took several years to correct.

Determined to increase the income of the Mission and decrease expenses, the author began to devote his time to projects and programs that would help accomplish that goal. One of the first steps taken toward increasing the income was a marketing study of *The Chosen People* mailing list. Jim Straub called upon the services of Dr. Francis Brown, an expert in the field. After analyzing the Mission's donor base, Dr. Brown suggested that the Mission begin developing additional programs which would be of interest to the Mission's existing constituents, as well as to stimulate greater interest in the ministry with new donors.

A step taken to decrease the expenses was to persuade Daniel Fuchs to drop a proposed program to bring Mr. Peter Eliastam from South Africa to tour the United States and Canada with his "Homage to Messiah" art exhibit. Daniel was convinced that through the use of "mass media" all Jews everywhere would hear the Gospel. Any program or project that would help accomplish this goal he was for 100%. He wanted Mr. Eliastam to display his exhibit on college campuses, shopping centers, etc., and the Board had already approved $5,000.00 for the project.[67] Jim Straub and the author estimated that if the Mission went ahead with the project, it would add an additional $100,000 to $200,000 of expenses to the budget—something the Mission could not afford!

This incident is mentioned because it was the first in a series of incidents which evidenced that the author's vision for the Mission and the vision of Daniel Fuchs for the Mission were not eye-to-eye. Daniel was fully convinced that it was the responsibility of each missionary to work himself out of a job. He felt that successful missionaries would eventually turn their work over to local churches, or to trained volunteers, thus eventually making the branches of the Mission unnecessary. The Mission could then carry out its vision through media evangelism, specialized staff, and volunteers. But having served on the staff of the Mission as a missionary, as Missionary Director, and as Executive Vice President still maintaining close contact with the Regional Directors, the author knew the staff did not see things this way. They saw the media only as a means to an end. At best, it provided exposure to the Gospel, but it could never replace person-to-person evangelism and the discipleship needed to bring Jewish people to the assurance of their faith in the Messiah. The branches were necessary. A staff was necessary. Messianic Congregations were necessary. Under certain circumstances Daniel agreed, but he was firm in his conviction that the Mission's priority for spending its resources should be in the area of "mass media evangelism."

SEEKING TO RELOCATE HEADQUARTERS

The matter of property ownership was another area where Daniel Fuchs' and the author's vision for the Mission differed. It was certainly true that in some areas it was preferable to lease property, but the author felt it was important to the stability of the organization, and to its image in the Jewish and Christian communities, that the Mission own its Headquarter's property.

Knowing that the five-year lease on the building being used for the Mission's Headquarters in Englewood Cliffs, New Jersey was only one year from termination, the Finance Committee brought three proposals to the Board at their June 1977 meeting: (1) Try to purchase the existing building in Englewood Cliffs; (2) Buy land and build a new building to meet our needs; (3) Renew the lease on the existing building for another five years. The committee's recommendation to the Board was that they accept proposal number two—that the Mission purchase land and build a building to suit its needs.[68]

Jim Straub and the author had already located land in Englewood Cliffs, as well as a developer who'd agreed to erect a building for the Mission for $495,000.[69] As individuals, some of the Board members shared Daniel's philosophy and were adamantly opposed to the idea of the Mission owning property and buildings. But when it came to a vote, the Directors approved the Finance Committee's recommendation to purchase land and build a suitable Headquarters office.

One of the Directors who approved of the Mission owning its Headquarters office was Mr. Albert Pasche, from Dallas Texas. Albert was elected to the Board at this crucial June 15, 1977 Board meeting.

Albert was a member of the First Baptist Church of Dallas, Texas; he was the Chairman of their Missions Committee. In his professional life, he was one of the executives with Mobil Oil Company.

As a couple, the Pasches were a great source of help and encouragement to the Mission's branch in Dallas. Their love for the Jewish people and their desire to see Jews come to faith in Yeshua was evident. They often opened their own home for meetings, and they quickly rallied to any cause to fight anti-Semitism or prejudice toward the Jewish people.

As the staff of the Mission got to know Albert, he became a champion to many because of his willingness to go witnessing with them. He would stand on the street corners and pass out tracts, or visit in the homes of unsaved Jewish people. He always showed practical and genuine concern for their well-being and he had a wonderful blend of spiritual and practical knowledge.

Albert felt very strongly that the Mission should own property in areas where it ministered, and his arguments proved most persuasive at the Board meetings. He remained active on the Board until the Lord called him home on December 6, 1985.

The vote of the Board on owning property was not unanimous, and the issue over whether to own or to rent property for the headquarters was never really resolved. While the motion passed for the Mission to build, the basic philosophic question still remained unanswered—owning versus renting.

When the zoning board turned down our variance request to build in Englewood Cliffs, New Jersey, the search for another piece of property on which to build began. Through Mr. Robert Clemensen, a Christian attorney in Rockland County, New York, we learned of a 3.68 acre parcel of land on Dutch Hill Road in Orangeburg, New York. When Jim Straub and other members of the Finance Committee looked at the property, they discovered that it was in an excellent location—right off the Palisades Parkway which provided a direct route into New York City. The property was ideally suited for the Mission's needs so the committee members moved ahead with the purchase, after which their action was approved by the Board. "RESOLVED that the action of the Finance Committee purchasing 3.68 acres in Orangeburg, New York, as a site for the construction of a headquarter's building is hereby approved."[70]

With the Board's approval and with all of the permits in place except for one—a sewer permit, which the seller and our attorneys assured us was not needed since we would be connecting onto existing sewer lines already in place on the property—we ordered a 10,000 square foot pre-fabricated steel "Butler" building which was to be erected on the property and finished to the Mission's specifications. (In checking into building costs, we learned that this was the least expensive way to build to get the space we required.)

With plans seemingly falling into place, a ground-breaking ceremony was planned. Members of the Mission's New York staff, ministers from the area, friends of the Mission, and the media were all present as Daniel, the author, and other members of the Board who were able to attend attempted to break the ground with the spade—but to no avail. We laughed and joked about not being able to build on the site because the ground was too hard. Little did we know that we would not be able to build on the site, but not because the ground was too hard.

Our ground-breaking ceremony had alerted members of the Jewish community to the fact that a "Jewish mission" was moving into their neighborhood and they began to put pressure on the public officials to stop our building program.

We were ready to build. All of the necessary permits had been issued—except for one, the sewer permit. The one permit which we had been assured was not needed, was the very thing the Jewish community used to create an insurmountable obstacle! Bowing to the pressure of the Orthodox Jews, town officials informed the Mission that the town would give a sewer permit only if the Mission would agree to put in a complete sewer system for the town, at the Mission's expense. The town would not permit us to connect up to the existing sewer system even though it went through our property and the neighboring shops were using it.

As in the case of Joseph, what had been meant for harm, God used for good, and within a matter of weeks Robert Clemensen, the attorney who had brought the Dutch Hill Road property to our attention, called and asked if we could meet him at property located at 100 Hunt Road (80 Blaisdell Road) in Orangeburg, New York—just two or three miles from the property on Dutch Hill Road. As we approached the designated property, we saw a building nearly identical in style and structure to the building we had planned to build. Not only did it have 10,000 square feet of office space already configured in a floor plan similar to the one we had designed, it also contained a warehouse with 20,000 square feet of space. There was a total of 30,000 square feet—and the asking price was $668,000.

The owner of the building was one of Mr. Clemensen's clients who wanted to relocate his offices to another town in Rockland County, New York. And miracle of miracles—he already had the property, all he needed was a building. When Bob told him about the Mission's situation, he said he would be willing to sell us his property and take our steel "Butler building" as the down-payment. The balance, of $600,000 could be handled with some cash and an assumable mortgage of $450,000.00. Recognizing the hand of God in the situation, the Board agreed, at their June 1978 meeting, to purchase the building at 100 Hunt Road, Orangeburg, New York.[71]

But the purchase transaction did not go as smoothly as expected. Although the seller had assured the Mission that the mortgage of $450,000.00 was assumable, the lenders did not want to let a "Jewish mission" assume the mortgage. In wrestling with the problem, the Finance Committee checked into the possibility of getting the needed money from outside lenders, but their interest rates were exorbitant. The committee therefore decided to put up the Mission's securities as collateral; they were then able to borrow at a more reasonable interest rate. They also discovered that one of the Mission's large contributors had agreed to allow funds which she had invested in a revocable trust to be substituted for a first mortgage on the property.[72] By pooling the first mortgage and the collateral loan, the Finance Committee was able to raise enough money to purchase the Orangeburg property. The transaction was therefore consummated, and the physical move was made. The Mission's new Headquarters Building was dedicated on Sunday, October 22, 1978. The first official Board meeting was held there on the previous day—October 21, 1978.

A NEW ORGANIZATIONAL CHART

During the months of negotiations on the Dutch Hill property and the months subsequent to the termination of that "deal," the Mission's workers continued to faithfully proclaim the Gospel message. But within the administration, thought was once again being given to reorganization, and a new organizational chart was being prepared. This new chart was presented to the Board at the June 21, 1978 meeting.

The new organizational chart called for changes in the by-laws of the Mission to allow for the Chairman of the Board (or the President of the Board) to receive a salary. The Vice-President, Treasurer, and Secretary of the Board would also be allowed to receive salaries if the member directors so desired.[73] The change in the by-laws also created the positions of Chairman Emeritus and Member Director Emeritus. The Board formally adopted the changes in the by-laws, and with it the new organizational chart, at their annual meeting on January 24, 1979. The Minutes state: "It was moved and voted unanimously that the changes in By-Laws voted on at the June 21, 1978 meeting of the Board of Directors be approved by the Member-Directors and the new organizational chart be implemented as of January 24, 1979."[74]

The new organizational chart placed Daniel Fuchs as Chairman of the Board (John Melhorn, the former Chairman, became Chairman Emeritus); Harold Sevener, President; James (Jim) Straub, Executive Vice-President. In his new position, Jim was hired as a full-time worker for the Mission. Once again the Mission had "Troika" leadership. Each position reported to the Board; each position was held by a Board member; each position was salaried (thus making the person holding the position an employee). The President was to work directly under the supervision of the Chairman of the Board, but was held accountable to the Board for all of his actions. The Executive Vice-President was to work under the supervision of the President, but also to report to the Board and to be held accountable to them. The Chairman of the Board reported to the Board as an employee, but at the same time he prepared the agenda for the Board, chaired the meetings, and generally had the oversight of the organization. In Daniel Fuchs' case, the Chairman of the Board was also the "behind the scenes" editor of *The Chosen People* magazine, the Shepherd of Israel, and other publications of the Mission.[75]

Daniel Fuchs, Jim Straub, and the author had worked closely as a team for a number of years. We had been working together in this fashion "unofficially" for several years, and making it "official" seemed the natural and logical step. However, when things become "official," responsibility and accountability take on a different perspective and meaning. When things go wrong, who is responsible? When things go right, who is responsible? As President, the author knew that while his work was supervised by Daniel, it was ultimately the Board that held him accountable for the effectiveness of the Mission's program, its financial growth, its expansion, its staff—or for its failures! The Scriptures are correct: "the little foxes spoil the vine."[76]

In many ways, the next several years were not only difficult years for the three employee-directors, the troika leadership made for an uncomfortable situation for the entire Board. As changes in vision, methodology, programs, and staff were presented to the Directors, their loyalties, friendships, and willingness to go beyond the "status quo" were often stretched to the limit. As Christian brothers, through prayer, discussion, and, yes, argument—all of the Directors were determined to work through problems, for the glory of God and for the well-being of the Mission. It was a time of growth for each Board member. A few members of the Board felt so strongly about certain issues that they prayerfully submitted their resignations; a few retired; and the Lord called some home. Of the original Board approving the organizational changes [c.1978-1979], only John Kubach, James Straub, and the author remain as active Board members.

NEW BOARD MEMBERS ELECTED

As new Board members were elected, they were the most affected by the "troika" leadership of the Mission. Three new Directors were elected to the Board during the years 1979 through 1982. Mr. C. Robert Clemensen, an attorney in Rockland County, New York, was elected June 20, 1979. He served through 1990. Mr. Roy Adams was elected on October 15, 1980. He is currently serving as Vice-Chairman of the Board. Roy served as Vice-President and Treasurer of the Mission's Canadian Board and was a Senior Internal Auditor with the DuPont Corporation in Canada. Dr. John L. Pretlove was elected October 22, 1982. He is an active Board member and is currently serving as Chairman of the Board. John was professor of New Testament/Greek at Criswell Bible Institute in Dallas, Texas. These men each played a vital role in the molding and shaping of the Mission as it re-focused on its vision to reach Jews with the Gospel.

REORGANIZATION OF STAFF

During the years that the author served as Vice President and as Executive Vice President of the Mission, he also continued as Missionary Director of the Mission. But in planning for the new reorganization, with the Board's approval, the author appointed a new Missionary Director to assume the responsibility for the National Missionary work. The Foreign branches remained under the supervision of the author during the years he served the Mission as Executive Vice-President, and then as President.

Mr. Richard Cohen, the Jewish believer who was appointed as Missionary in Charge of the Los Angeles ministry when the author moved to New York, had proven himself to be a capable, hard-working leader. When the Regional program was established, he became the Regional Director for the Western States. For a time he also served as interim Regional Director for the Mid-west region.

Richard was appointed Missionary Director of the Mission in the Fall of 1978. As a part of the administrative staff of the Mission, he moved his family to the East coast in the Spring of 1979; he occupied one of the offices in the new Headquarters building in Orangeburg, New York.

Restructured and reorganized, but still struggling with its "focus" and "vision", the Mission's programs moved ahead. As Executive Vice-President, Jim Straub was in charge of finances and administration. As Media Consultant, George Samson was in charge of communications. As Missionary Director, Richard Cohen was in charge of the missionary department. Each of these departments reported to the President and, together, we looked for ways to increase evangelism to the Jews, while at the same time developing the image of the Mission so that the support base of the ministry would be increased. We needed to increase income, cut expenses, and balance the budget!

A NEW LITERATURE PROGRAM

Our strategy, as an administrative team, included updating the Mission's literature to give it a fresh, contemporary look, re-establishing evangelistic radio ventures, using tours, conferences—and even an ark—to create an awareness of the Mission's existence and purpose among the Christian community. The missionaries continued the evangelistic thrust of the ministry.

CHANGES IN THE JEWISH CALENDAR

Since 1912, the Mission had produced a Jewish calendar each summer for the beginning of the Jewish year in the Fall of the year. Because *The Chosen People* magazine was not published during the summer months, a "Midsummer Letter" was sent out to supporters of the Mission, along with a copy of the free calendar. After a time, the calendar evolved into two separate calendars—one for Christians (each page included a photograph of one of the missionaries, a prayer request, and a suggested tract to send in for); the other calendar was produced for unsaved Jewish people (it contained Scripture verses and suggested tracts to send in for).

In seeking for ways to cut expenses, but at the same time to utilize the calendar for evangelism, it was decided to once again produce only one calendar. It was to be a calendar that could be used in Jewish evangelism—as a pre-evangelism piece; it was to be something that could be given or sent to a Jewish person (At the time, only Jewish mortuaries and funeral homes provided free Jewish calendars). The calendar was to look modern and attractive; it was to be something a Jewish person would want hanging on his wall, while still including all of the essential information such as Scripture readings, candle lighting information, Jewish dates, etc. It was also decided that instead of mailing the calendars to every name on the mailing list (not knowing if they were wanted or not), they were to be offered free upon request, with additional copies available at a small charge. In the 1979 Mid-Year Report, the author wrote:

> We are really excited about our calendar ministry this year. We have completely redesigned the Jewish art calendar. It is now a prophetic Jewish calendar. We have used full-color pictures of Israel; pictures taken by Dr. Daniel Fuchs, Dr. Frank Prewitt [the author's father-in-law] and myself, and with each month of the Jewish calendar we have listed a Biblical prophecy of Israel and its fulfillment in modern history. This calendar is unique, and we feel that it will be used of God to open many Jewish eyes to what God is doing in our world today. Not only does it list modern Biblical prophecies being fulfilled in the land of Israel, but it also has a section on Messianic prophecy pointing to the fact that indeed Jesus is our Messiah, our Lord, and our Savior. Picture these calendars hanging in thousands of Jewish homes. God's promise is that His Word will not 'return unto me void, but it shall accomplish that which I please, and it shall prosper in the thing whereto I sent it' (Isa. 55:11).[77]

The calendars were an immediate success. Christians everywhere wanted one. Copies were sent to Israel, to members of the Knesset—one even hung on the wall in the Prime Minister's office! Through the years the Mission has continued to refine the calendar, using different themes, and it continues to be one of the more effective tools in reaching Jewish people with the Gospel.

CHANGES IN THE MID-SUMMER LETTER

The format of the "Mid-Summer Letter" was changed as well. Where it had previously been a theological letter, or study of a passage of Scripture, it became the Mission's Mid-Year Report—a report to the supporters and friends of the Mission, telling them what their prayers and financial support was enabling the Mission to accomplish. In keeping with the Mission's long history, it was given a "corporate look"—as if it was a report to the stock-holders of a corporation. In a sense, each supporter was a "stock-holder" or a "stake-holder" in the Mission, and they had a right to know what their investment in the Mission was accomplishing.

Producing The Midyear Report was made possible in part because of the regional system of operation which required each Regional Director to submit a monthly reporting of monies spent and received, and of the activity within his region. A standardized form was developed for this statistical reporting. In the August 1979 Mid-Year Report, the author wrote:

> How we do praise God for what He has accomplished in these past six months through your missionaries. I could not help but shout 'Praise the Lord' when Rev. Richard Cohen, our Missionary Director, gave me the report of the ministry of the American Board of Missions to the Jews in the United States. Your missionaries were involved in 1,334 meetings where the Gospel was preached by them to 2,469 unsaved Jewish people. We were also able to visit in 1,790 Jewish homes where we were invited in to sit down and share the Gospel. During the last six months we produced and distributed 300,488 pieces of Gospel literature.
> In the last six months we have also had 55 Jewish people and 44 Gentiles make decisions for the Lord. A total of 99 decisions for our Lord.[78]

The Mid-Year Report has continued to be a vehicle though which the constituents of the Mission are kept informed about the Mission. Some issues have featured special emphasis on South America, Israel, and the Soviet Union—or a special event, worker, or branch. Without much change except for more color and updates in type style and graphics, it remains a major communication piece of the Mission.

Changes in the Jewish calendar and the Mid-year Report, and the addition of a July issue of *The Chosen People* magazine (making eleven issues a year), resulted in the summer income of the Mission increasing rather than decreasing.

RADIO MINISTRY

Radio was again looked at as a medium whereby the Mission could strengthen its image and its income, and the possibility of enacting a merge, or a cooperative program, with another Jewish mission organization was looked into. In 1977 Dr. Charles Halff, of the Christian Jew Foundation, had expressed interest in a possible cooperative program between his ministry and ABMJ, so Jim Straub and the author met with Dr. Halff on several different occasions to discuss such a venture.

It was finally agreed that a cooperative program would be entered into and that, if the cooperative effort worked, the two organizations would move toward formally enacting a merge between the two ministries.[79] The cooperative broadcast schedule, listing all of the stations where the Christian Jew Hour was broadcast was included in the March 1978 *Chosen People* magazine. The following announcement appeared with the radio-log listing:

> *Would you like to hear ABMJ missionaries on radio? Now you can. Through a special arrangement with the Christian Jew Foundation, Rev. Richard Cohen, our Missionary Liaison Director, will co-host with Dr. Charles Halff an outstanding Jewish Christian broadcast. Beginning this month [March, 1978] ABMJ and CJF's new radio format will include excellent Bible teaching and from time to time direct missionary reports from the field.*
>
> *We know that you will appreciate the ministry of Dr. Charles Halff and Rev. Richard Cohen, so check the schedule on this page for the time and station in your area. Drop us a line and let us know if you've enjoyed the program. Happy listening![80]*

The Board also allocated funds so that the Mission could begin its own radio program in the event that a final merger could not be worked out with The Christian Jew Foundation.[81]

As a part of the negotiations in setting up the cooperative radio program, with Richard Cohen as the speaker, the author involved the Mission's former Communications Director, Rev. Terryl Delaney. Terryl had closed his media agency in Seattle and had become the pastor of Grace Brethren Church in Los Angeles, California. Through the years the author and Terryl had stayed in touch, and when mention of the possibility of a merge with the Christian Jew Foundation was made, and of a cooperative radio ministry, Terryl was very interested. He knew the impact that a merge would have on both ministries and on Jewish evangelism as a whole. He immediately saw the potential and agreed to help. With his experience in communications, Terryl became the liaison person between the two organizations.

The cooperative program worked well for the first few months, but negotiations for the merge of the two missions reached an impasse as consideration was given to a new ministry name for the combined organizations, the logistics of integrating mailing lists and Boards, salary and benefits packages to be offered, etc. The leaders of each organization became convinced that each ministry should continue in its own specialized area of Jewish evangelism.

Terryl Delaney's involvement with Dr. Halff and the radio ministry, as he had served as the liaison person in the merger negotiations, had convinced him that God was calling him to help Dr. Halff develop the radio and media for his ministry. He therefore resigned from his church and moved his family to San Antonio, Texas, where he joined the staff of the Christian Jew Foundation. But within a matter of two or three months, the author received a call from Terryl saying that his heart was still with the Mission. He was calling to see if there was any possibility for him to join the staff of the Mission once again.

The Board had already approved the funding for a radio broadcast. Those funds had remained untouched during the negotiations with The Christian Jew Foundation. The development of a radio ministry had been a matter over which the author had spent much time in thought and prayer. Terryl's call seemed a direct answer to those prayers. The author spoke with the members of the Executive Committee and the Personnel Committee of the Board. Approval to once again hire Terryl Delaney to assist with the development of the Mission's new radio program was given at the October 1979 Directors meeting.[82]

The Delaneys quickly sold their home in San Antonio, Texas and moved to New York. In his usual competent manner, Terryl soon had a sound studio set up at the Mission's headquarters building and broadcast-quality equipment installed (prior to the installation of the equipment at the Headquarters building, Grace Conservative Baptist Church in Nanuet graciously allowed us to use their studio to make our radio tapes).

"The Chosen People News Hour" began on January 7, 1980. It was a fifteen-minutes daily program, Monday through Friday, which focused on prophecy, current events, and the work of the Mission. Terryl also produced a bi-monthly publication for the broadcast called "End Times." The author did the Bible teaching for the broadcast, Terryl did the production, editing, and the general oversight of the production. The purpose of the "End Times" publication was to get new names for the Mission's mailing lists. By building a separate mailing list for the radio work it was simpler to track names and donations so the Mission could evaluate more carefully if the radio was supporting itself, or if it was drawing income away from missionary programs.

The response to The Chosen People News Hour was excellent! The name helped supporters of the Mission to focus on two words—Chosen People. One result of the marketing survey done by Dr. Francis Brown was that it indicated that there was a great deal of confusion over the Mission's name. It was too long. People could not remember it; they often reversed the words. However, they did remember the name of the Mission's magazine, *The Chosen People*. A later survey showed that the Mission's constituents would not be averse to a name change, if handled properly. *The Chosen People* magazine, The Chosen People News Hour, Chosen People Ministries—they fit together to a produce a synergistic effect in communicating the Mission and its message to both Christians and Jews.

When the author moved to New York as Missionary Director in the Fall of 1972, he also assumed the leadership for the Northeast region. In subsequent years, Mr. Herb Zwickel became the acting Regional Director for the Northeast region, and later Rev. Richard Cohen assumed the responsibility along with his other duties. But it had been difficult to find a trained worker who had the ability to administrate the region, who wanted to live and work in New York City.

CHANGES IN THE MINISTRY IN NEW YORK

New York was home to the largest concentration of Jewish people in the world and God had blessed the Mission by providing a number of faithful, capable, dedicated missionaries who were living and working in New York and its boroughs. But one of our goals was to increase the staff in New York. The Board had adopted the author's recommendation that the Mission seek to place full-time missionaries where the Jewish population was the most dense—a minimum of one missionary per 100,000 Jews. Using that criterion, New York was an area where the largest staff of missionaries was needed. Yet without proper leadership we were stymied.

In the Fall of 1979, the author received a telephone call from Sam Nadler. He said he and his wife, Miriam, had just resigned from Jews for Jesus. Sam said he and Miriam both felt called to minister to the Jews of New York; he was calling to ask if the Mission could use him in New York. What a marvelous answer to prayer! Sam and Miriam were both trained missionaries and Sam was a capable leader. Under Jews for Jesus he had already established a strong ministry in New York City. Further, both Sam and Miriam had been on the staff of the Mission before the separation of the two organizations; they knew the Mission. The author told Richard Cohen, our Missionary Director, "get this nice Jewish boy back home!" On October 1, 1979 Sam and Miriam Nadler officially joined the staff of the Mission once again.

As the Mission approached the 1980's, Jewish people were being reached with the Gospel, missionary support was increasing, the General Fund was growing—but to keep the momentum going, several other projects were initiated.

RESPONSIBLE JEWISH EVANGELISM

A new public relations program called "Responsible Jewish Evangelism" was created under the direction of George Samson, Steve Schwartz, and Jonathan Singer. Ads were placed in *Christianity Today*, *Moody Monthly*, and *Christian Life* magazine which reflected the roots of ABMJ and encouraged Christians to join the Mission in doing Jewish evangelism. Press releases to all major publications were issued monthly to keep the Christian world informed of the Mission's activities. A portfolio was developed which included information on the various programs of the Mission, missionaries in need of support, etc. for individuals who responded to the ads and press releases, inquiring about the Mission's programs. The portfolio also included information on the Mission's stewardship program for deferred gifts.

A program of Major Donor Visitation was embarked upon by several members of the Board, and the portfolios were also made available to them for their visits. It was a way of thanking major donors for their support, while at the same time showing them visually what their prayers and support were accomplishing. It was also hoped that this personal contact would strengthen the relationship between the donors and the Mission, and that their support of the ministry would be confirmed and perhaps even increased. Several of the Board members became involved in this program, among them Albert Pasche and Jim and Tedie Straub. Jim and Tedie have faithfully participated in the major donor visitation program for over ten years (at the time of the writing of this history) and their dedicated efforts have won many friends for the Mission, and have substantially helped the income of the Mission to grow. Only eternity will reveal the total impact of their visitation ministry. The author believes they will have a special reward!

In October 1979, Jim Straub attended the strategy and planning sessions for the Evangelical Council for Financial Accountability (ECFA)—an organization being formed to monitor and approve the financial accountability of member Christian organizations. Jim reported to the Board on the importance of the Mission being involved with this historic organization and, following through on the theme of "Responsible Jewish Evangelism," the Board unanimously approved that the Mission should become a charter member of the ECFA.[83] In telling of this area of the Mission's responsible stewardship, Daniel Fuchs wrote in his salutation:

> ...We have a biblical yet legal organization where everyone has his own responsibilities and where everyone, including the Chairman of the Board, is responsible to higher authority. As Paul reported to the church in Jerusalem, everyone of your workers from the cleaning man to the President and Chairman of the Board is responsible to the Board of Directors, as well as to the Lord.
>
> 'Not slothful in business.' We scrupulously handle our mail so there is no way whereby we can be criticized for not safeguarding your gifts. Donors receive receipts which are recognized by the Internal Revenue Service as valid evidence for income tax deductions. We carefully check and cross check so that we can account for every penny received. Not only do we check and cross check our receipts, we do the same for our expenses. Our books are carefully audited by Certified Public Accountants. There is also a special Auditing Committee which meets with the accountants. Each member of our Board of Directors received a complete audit weeks before our annual meeting, and the administrative officers are examined by our Board of Directors. Each director takes his responsibility very seriously. One of the evidences of our responsible Jewish evangelism is our responsible Board of Directors.
>
> 'Not Slothful in business.' We do not send out frantic begging appeals. Our Lord has always honored this responsible policy.
>
> We believe that this is as it should be. We expect that we, together with other missionary agencies, are going to face examination by government agencies in the future. We accept this as a fact of life and can see some reason for this, although we resist all attempts for government control, with all of our strength.
>
> A few years ago a religious group which called itself a 'missionary' organization was investigated and the investigation revealed that only five cents of every dollar received was used for missionary efforts; the other 95 cents wound up in the pockets of fund-raisers and rip-off artists.
>
> Editorial writers and congressmen vied with each other calling for the government to regulate all charities and missionary organizations.
>
> Against this background, we, together with many other biblically-oriented mission societies, helped organize a new organization called the Evangelical Council For Financial Accountability.[84]

Ark II—Stanley Watin

Another project that was entered into, although it did not meet with the approval of everyone on staff, was a special project called "Ark II." This project was the brain-child of a Jewish believer whose name was Stanley Watin.

Stanley came to faith in Yeshua because of his Jewish friend, Mel. They had not seen one another for some time, but they bumped into one another in a grocery store. Both men had been taxi cab drivers in New York City. Of that God-appointed meeting, Stanley later said:

> One day I ran into an old friend ...'Hey, Mel,' I shouted, ...'you look great! What are you into lately?'
>
> He seemed to be weighing his words carefully. But finally the truth tumbled out, 'I've accepted the Lord Jesus Christ as my Lord and Savior.'
>
> 'But Mel,' I protested, giving him a look of disgust, 'you're Jewish!'
>
> 'Yes,' he said quietly, 'and so was Jesus.'
>
> I never knew that! I thought that Jesus, the man on the cross, was for the Catholics and the Protestants but not for us Jews.
>
> A few weeks later, after studying the Bible, I bowed my head, confessed my sins and asked Jesus to come into my life. In just three weeks my initial outrage with Mel turned into a deep love for the Jewish Messiah. I had been born again.
>
> Ironically, I am more Jewish now than ever before because now my beliefs coincide with the only lasting truth to be found anywhere on this planet—the truth of the Word of God.[85]

Using his training as a cab driver, Stanley soon took to the streets proclaiming his faith in the Messiah. He was an outspoken evangelist for his Lord. Soon Stanley enrolled at Nyack Missionary College, Nyack, New York, to prepare himself for the ministry—but not just any ministry. God had given him a vision of portraying the Gospel, live, on the stage of the world-famous Radio City Music Hall. He wanted to reach the millions of Jewish people living in the "Big Apple," or the "Big Bagel," as he called it.

Richard Cohen met Stanley when Richard was asked to speak to the students at Nyack Missionary College. An immediate friendship developed, and Stanley shared his vision of portraying the Gospel story live on the stage of Radio City Music Hall. Everyone he'd shared his vision with had told him he was crazy, but Richard listened quietly and then suggested that Stanley visit the Mission and discuss his plans with the author.

Stanley followed through on Richard's suggestion, and when Stanley told me what he wanted to do, I, too, was skeptical. I asked how he planned to finance such a project, and he responded by telling me about the Ark he was building. "An Ark?" I exclaimed. I'd heard correctly. Stanley went on to tell me he was building an Ark out of an old bus. He said he was planning to travel around the country, telling people about the Messiah, Jesus, and trying to interest them in supporting a live presentation of the Gospel story at Radio City Music Hall in order to reach Jewish people with the Gospel.

Stanley's plan was intriguing. The more I listened to him, the more I felt God would surely use such a bold witness in reaching Jewish people with the Gospel. I reasoned that even if Stanley never accomplished his goal of making a live presentation of the Gospel in Radio City Music Hall, many would hear the Gospel in the process of trying, so we set up a time for George Samson, Richard Cohen, and the author to see Stanley's Ark.

In seeing the Ark for myself—a converted school bus that had been transformed into a replica of a large boat, with a platform on which Stanley stood while proclaiming the Gospel, and equipped with living quarters built inside—the author was convinced that such a vehicle would command attention. It was a most unusual "soap box" from which to proclaim the Gospel. I therefore told Stanley, "If the Board approves, I'll recommend funding for your travel. Anything you raise above your expenses will go toward the Radio City Music Hall performance of the Gospel, if you can get them to agree to the performance."

The Board approved the project, and Ark II was launched. It was controversial, objectionable, conversational—but above all, it reached Jews and Gentiles with the Gospel. In sharing the story of Stanley Watin, readers of *The Chosen People* magazine were told:

> When Stanley Watin drives through town, people turn their heads and stare. But when he preaches the Gospel, people bow their heads and invite Jesus into their hearts.
>
> How many heads have been bowed? According to the last count, 53 individuals—nine of them Jewish—have placed their faith in the Lord Jesus Christ directly as a result of the Ark II ministry....
>
> When ABMJ sent Stanley and his traveling companion, Randy Jones, out to the harvest 15 months ago, we had no idea how abundantly God would bless the new mobile ministry....
>
> Stanley's message isn't new...but his manner of preaching is refreshingly different. His God-given sense of humor melts even the most hardened hearts of those who hear him speak. And his unique ark-on-top-of-a-bus gives him ample opportunity to preach wherever he goes. Truly, the world is Stanley's pulpit.
>
> Driving from New York to the west coast and back, Stanley and Randy have spoken in a number of prisons, bringing a message of hope and freedom to those without either. They have driven more than 35,000 miles to preach the Gospel in more than 144 churches.
>
> Because of the 'temperamental' nature of the ark-bus, many garage mechanics have heard the Word of God. On this, her maiden voyage, Ark II has needed two new engines, one transmission overhaul, three batteries, five alternators and three tires—and Stanley is not the type of person to sit quietly while the mechanics work.
>
> Stanley is the type of person who loves people too much to be silent about their eternal destiny. Stanley is the type of person who unashamedly tells people, 'You don't have a prayer if you don't know Jesus' and 'There are just two types of people in the world—believers and make-believers.'
>
> Stanley, it seems, was born to share the Gospel. In Chicago he visited the Sears Tower observation deck. When he stepped into the crowded elevator for the quarter-mile descent, he commented to the people, 'If the cable breaks, Jesus is your only hope!' But this time someone did Stanley better. A man in front responded, 'Even if the cable doesn't break, Jesus is still your only hope!' Wouldn't you know it—Stanley had unknowingly boarded the elevator with a missionary home on furlough from the Central African Empire.
>
> Wherever Stanley and Randy go, people take notice ...and the Ark II crew quickly point them to the true Ark of Safety—the Lord Jesus Christ....
>
> While he had hoped to raise enough money on the road to rent Radio City, the offerings and gifts weren't as bountiful as anticipated. In fact, they were barely enough to keep Ark II's thirsty gas tank satisfied.
>
> Nevertheless, Stanley is undaunted. He knows that ABMJ can't afford the tremendous expenses involved with staging a production in New York City. But he is praying for a miracle.
>
> So are we.[86]

Stanley was never able to raise enough money for the production of the Gospel on the stage of the Radio City Music Hall. But, while traveling, he did meet a lovely young woman who eventually became his wife. Stanley and his wife and family still live in New York where he continues a bold and active witness to Jews and Gentiles alike.

A UNIQUE TOUR DEVELOPED

During this time in the history of the Mission the "See Israel through Jewish Eyes" tours to Israel were being developed. Mention has already been made of Mr. Gary Selman's assistance in developing this program, and of the effectiveness of the tours in raising the Mission's profile in Israel.

THE CONFERENCE MINISTRY—TOM WALKER

In addition to the tours, the conference ministry was helping to raise the image and profile of the Mission throughout the world. The appointment of Mr. Tom Walker as the Mission's International Conference Director opened many doors for the Mission in Scotland, Ireland, and England, in addition to conferences and meetings he arranged within Canada and the United States.

Tom Walker had been associated with the Mission for over twenty-five years, and had assisted in the work of the Mission as a volunteer until December, 1979. He was a Board member in Canada, and a Board member ex-officio of the American Board. In the Fall of 1979, the author asked Tom to step down as a Board member of the American Board so that he could accept the position of International Conference Director—a full-time salaried position with the Mission.[87] Tom was born in Motherwell, Scotland. As a child, he attended Shields Road Gospel Hall (Plymouth Brethren) in Motherwell along with other members of his family. At the age of nine, Tom professed his faith in the Lord Jesus as his personal Savior. Not long after Tom's profession of faith, Rev. Mark Kagan, who was then representing the Mission in the United Kingdom, visited the Gospel Hall. For a period of eight years or so, Rev. Kagan returned to the church on an annual basis. As Tom listened to the messages of this Jewish believer, he was impressed with Rev. Kagan's sincerity and knowledge of Scripture.

When World War II erupted, Tom enlisted in the Navy. He said God used the memory of Mark Kagan's sermons, and the teaching he'd received at the Gospel Hall to keep him from submitting to the many temptations which faced him during those war-torn years.

Tom immigrated to Canada in 1948, after his service in the Navy. He lived in Toronto for a short time, and then moved to Hamilton, Ontario, where he was employed by Canada Packers, Inc.

After Tom's move to Hamilton, he met two people who became very important in his life. The first was his wife, Gloria. The second was Mr. William Jones, the honorary treasurer of the Mission in Canada. Tom was delighted to learn that this was the same Mission which Mark Kagan served with. Tom and Gloria were active Christians. They were involved with the Gideon's, their church, and a number of other evangelistic outreaches. Tom was also responsible for setting up meetings for the "Male Choir" of Canada—a choir that traveled all over the world.

After meeting William Jones, Tom and Gloria asked how they could become involved with the Mission. Gloria became involved in the office work, while Tom, a gifted soloist, began representing the Mission through a music ministry in churches. Tom's music ministry took him to Woodstock, where he met Dr. Alexander Marks and several other staff members of the Mission. Impressed with the messages and with the sincerity of Dr. Marks and the others, Tom once again asked if there was more he could do to help in the Mission's work.

Tom was a "doer"—a "go-getter." He had the energy and the drive to get things done. And, he could be very tenacious and convincing. These traits, plus his dedication to the work of the Mission, made him a "natural" for work in setting up the Mission's conferences—a position Tom was asked to take in 1960. His abilities opened doors for Mission representatives to have conferences or meetings in churches in Southern Ontario, the Maritime Provinces, and many churches between Rochester and Buffalo, New York.

When Tom took early retirement from Canada Packers, it was a natural transition for him to accept a full-time position with the Mission. By 1979 Tom McCall had resigned as the United States Conference Director, and it was decided that Tom Walker should develop the entire conference ministry—arranging for the Mission's conferences in Canada and the United States, as well as international conferences. He was therefore appointed International Conference Director. He took to the job like a duck takes to water!

Tom could schedule more conferences than the mission had speakers. With his friendships and contacts in the United Kingdom, he set up annual six-week Bible conference tours for the author and himself. The author did the speaking; Tom did the singing. The first such tour included meetings in Northern Ireland, Scotland, and England. Later tours included meetings in Europe. Funds raised in the meetings were used to further the Mission's ministry overseas.

As the years of the 1980's slipped by, the cost of travel increased to the point where it became apparent that the

Conference ministry of the Mission was costing more than it was producing. The Regional Directors of the Mission had begun to use the missionaries within their own regions to raise support within churches, and special speakers arranged through the Conference Department were no longer perceived to be as necessary for the task of opening churches to the work of the Mission as they had once been. Additionally, the Mission had begun to develop "Simcha" conferences—great "in-gatherings" of Jewish believers for fellowship and discipleship; these replaced the need of the conference ministry in some parts of the country.

By the late 1980's it was decided to place the conference ministry of the Mission under the Regional Directors—thus cutting back the need for a separate Conference Department. The Mission's work in Canada had also changed (see chapter on Canada). Tom Walker's position as International Conference Director was phased out by 1987 and Tom's wife, Gloria, subsequently resigned her support position in December 1987.

By 1980, with many new programs underway, the income up, and goodly numbers of Jewish people coming to faith in Yeshua, it seemed as if the Mission was poised for further expansion and even greater evangelism of the Jewish people.

But the enemy of the Gospel knows just when to strike. If anyone dares to believe that Satan does not do everything in his power to stop the Gospel message from reaching the Jewish people, they have not studied history or been involved first-hand in witnessing to Jewish people. Not only does Satan know when to strike, he also knows where to strike and his plan of attack always includes three D's—doubt, discouragement, division.

A FINANCIAL CRUNCH

As has been stated, the circumstances surrounding the purchase of the Mission's Headquarters building in Orangeburg, New York necessitated pledging the Mission's securities as collateral—leaving the Mission limited access to the securities. It further meant that the expenses of the Mission *had* to remain on target with budget, and that the market value of the securities had to remain high; any drop in their value would result in less money available for transfer into the operating fund of the Mission. The Finance Committee had established the amount needed to supplement the operating budget of the Mission and support for the Mission's programs.

The inevitable happened in 1980. The woman who had agreed to fund the first mortgage on the Headquarter's property, wrote and requested that at least half of the money be returned.[88] It seemed that the retirement village where she lived had a clause in their lease which prohibited the majority of residents' funds from being held in non-liquid assets (because of their long-term health care provisions), such as the Mission's first mortgage. She had been told that her lease would not be renewed if she did not have sufficient liquid assets on hand for health emergencies, so she requested that her money be returned within thirty days—by June 30, 1980.

Although the income for the previous eight months showed an increase of 5.54% ($73,525 over the budget), expenses had also increased (to $123,499 over the budget during the same eight-month period). The increase was due in part to Administrative expenses because of higher interest rates, equipment purchases for the sound and recording equipment for the radio broadcast, and some unusually high repair bills on Ark II.[89] The Mission's securities in the Investment Fund had been pledged as collateral on the property loan and could not be tapped to return the funds securing the first mortgage. For the first time in its recent history, the Mission was faced with a serious and immediate cash flow problem!

DIFFICULT DECISIONS AND MUCH PRAYER

Recognizing the severity of the situation, and realizing his responsibility as President of the organization, the author met in a number of informal sessions with members of the Executive Committee and Personnel Committee (from January 1979 until the mid-1980's the Executive Committee and the Personnel Committee were comprised of Daniel Fuchs, James Straub, and the author) to determine solutions to the financial crisis. Based on those meetings, and on discussions he had engaged in with other Board members, the author took steps toward rectifying the financial emergency.

After much prayer, and careful evaluation of the immediate and the long-range effects of the steps under consideration, the decision was made to make immediate and deep cuts from the top of the administration to the bottom level of the staff and programs. Implementing the cuts was the most difficult task the author has ever undertaken; they involved eliminating the positions of close personal friends—individuals who had been doing good work for the Mission!

The cuts from the administrative level involved the Communications Department and the Missionary department. George Samson's position in the Communications Department was terminated. George had become increasingly more involved in developing the new organization, Evangelicals United for Zion (EUZ). Terryl Delaney was handling the radio ministry for the Mission and George agreed that it was a good time to put the radio, publications, media, etc. all under one department. He therefore submitted his resignation so that he could continue to develop EUZ as a separate organization.

The cut from the Missionary Department was also difficult, but once again the timing seemed to be of the Lord. For a number of months the Mission had been receiving telephone calls and letters from pastors and concerned Christian friends about the increasing "anti-Gentile" and "anti-Church" messages given by our Missionary Director, Richard Cohen. In a meeting with Richard, the author expressed concern over the feedback he'd been getting from pastors and others. Mention was also made of the Mission's financial crisis, and Richard was informed that serious consideration was being given to phasing out the Missionary Director's position. Although he was told that the Mission would transfer him to another position within the organization, Richard responded that he, too, had been praying and thinking about his future and about his role in the ministry. He felt the time had come for him to return to the business world, to use his gifts and abilities there. In his letter of resignation, Richard expressed some of those feelings:

> For some time now I have felt God leading me out of the administrative capacity of the ministry. I feel that God is directing me toward a more personal one-to-one involvement with my Jewish people. I feel that I can better maintain this witness through secular employment and without the problems associated with being a 'professional missionary.'
>
> If, in the future, I feel that God should be leading me back into a full time missionary position with a Jewish mission organization, I would certainly like to re-apply to the ABMJ.[90]

The severance of Richard's position was reported to the Board at their June 1980 meeting. The Minutes state:

> Mr. Sevener reported on the acceptance of the severance of Rev. Richard Cohen, Missionary Director.
>
> Motion was made and adopted supporting Mr. Sevener's action in making the difficult decision concerning the severance of the Missionary Director.[91]

Richard returned to the secular business world and has become a very successful businessman. From time to time he and the author visit. I trust that God will one day lead Richard and Linda back into full-time active service for the Messiah.

In the field, the budget cuts involved the closing of several branches in areas where there were fewer than 100,000 Jewish people (the minimum set by the Board to warrant placement of a full-time missionary and a branch ministry). The cuts also involved the termination of some secretarial positions and part-time workers, as well as cutbacks on the printing of literature and materials.

In executing the cuts, the author discovered what every CEO eventually learns; it is very lonely at the top—even in Christian ministry. In spite of the fact that the staff and program cuts had been discussed and agreed upon by committee members of the Board, not all of the Directors were happy about the cuts. As feed-back from the staff began to filter back to the Directors, some began to feel that the author had sacrificed staff and programs of ministry for buildings and properties. Once again, the issue over whether the Mission should rent or own property surfaced and, while it was not voiced, some members of the Board felt that had the Mission not purchased the headquarters property in Orangeburg the financial crisis would never have happened. The three D's—doubt, discouragement, division—had taken a foothold.

The author's argument for the Mission owning its Headquarters building was based on tactics used by the military— establish a beach-head. Having fought for and won your beach-head, further attack can be launched against the enemy. The author saw the Mission's International Headquarters as its "beach-head" from which to launch our attack against the enemy of our souls. I believed that the headquarters property, owned and secured, was a testimony to both the Jewish and Christian communities that the American Board of Missions to the Jews, Inc. is an established organization involved in *responsible* Jewish evangelism. However no amount of rhetoric or argument could get around the fact that the Mission was facing a serious crisis for which solutions had to be found!

As a result of the dissatisfaction on the part of some Board members over the cuts made by the President of the Mission (the author), and in an effort to find a way of returning the monies that had been requested by the deadline of June 20, 1980, an Ad Hoc committee was formed. The Ad Hoc committee was comprised of Daniel Fuchs, John Kubach, George Savage, Harold Sevener, and James Straub. The committee met on May 29, 1980, and again on the morning of June 23, 1980. The committee then presented their recommendations to members of the Board at their meeting on June 23, 1980. They recommended that the Mission sell the Dutch Hill property (the original lot purchased for the Headquarters building), and the Orangeburg Headquarters property. They also recommended the sale of the Pittsburgh property and the Dallas property. They further recommended that the Mission's Pension Fund no longer be funded through insurance policies, but that it be funded through a Trust Fund established by a local accredited bank, without any right of the Mission to borrow against the Pension Fund or to use it as collateral. The Board unanimously approved all of the Ad Hoc committee's recommendations, including their recommendation to sell the Mission's Headquarters building.

The Minutes state: "Motion was made and unanimously voted to authorize the Executive Committee to negotiate the sale or the refinancing of 100 Hunt Road, Orangeburg, N.Y., property owned by ABMJ [the Headquarter's building].[92]

When the motion was made to "negotiate or refinance" the Headquarters building the author was startled by his own thought—"Why not tell our constituents about the problem the Mission is in. If they pray with us, and if enough of them feel the Mission should own its Headquarters property, let them tell us through a special offering. Perhaps God would so burden their hearts that the entire debt on the building would be retired!" The author made the thought a matter of prayer, and later shared it with Terryl Delaney, asking him to consider helping to write a letter that could go to the Mission's constituents informing them of our special need. Terryl, too, felt that such a letter could be used by God, and within a matter of a few days the letter was written.

An informal Board/committee meeting was arranged between Daniel Fuchs, Jim Straub, Terryl Delaney and the author to discuss using the letter as a special "appeal" mailing for the Headquarters building. Daniel had always opposed financial appeals; he often said, "the Mission never makes appeals for funds," which was true under his administration but it was not true under the administration of either Leopold or Joseph Cohn. During Daniel's administration there was no need for the Mission to make appeals because the Board had agreed to use the investment fund as the support arm of the Mission, for as long as it would last. Also, Daniel had changed the policy of the Mission from owning property to renting property.

After lengthy discussion on the issue of fund raising in general, Daniel agreed to allow for the mailing of such a letter, pending the approval of other Board members. With Daniel's tentative approval, the other Board members were approached and soon all agreed that we could send out the letter. But before the letter was ready for mailing, an emergency session of the Executive Committee was held to review the sale of all real estate pending. The date was August 9, 1980. The Minutes of that meeting state:

> The Executive Committee asked Jim Straub to assume full responsibility for the financial administration of the Mission. He is to submit a balanced financial plan to the Board of Directors for approval. It will be his responsibility to keep all spending within its limits. All mission expenditures must be reviewed and approved by him. This does not affect Harold Sevener's position as President of the Mission and his responsibility for all of the missionary and other outreaches. The Executive Committee recommends to the Board that Jim Straub be appointed to the additional office of Treasurer.[93]

God Answers Our Prayers

Once the expense of the appeal letter was approved, it was prepared for mailing and was delivered "on the wings of prayer." God marvelously answered those prayers! By the end of the year (c.1980), the Mission's supporters had contributed so generously that the Mission's Investment portfolio was freed. As we entered 1981, the gifts still coming in helped to substantially reduce all outstanding debts on the property. This was in addition to the regular income which was also substantially higher!

The Minutes of the January 28, 1981 Directors meeting state:

> Mr. Sevener also requested the Board to consider rescinding the motion passed by the Directors at its June 23, 1980 meeting to sell the Orangeburg property. This request was made because of the generous response of the donors to the appeal letter concerning debt reduction on the property.
> Motion was made and unanimously voted to rescind the motion on the sale of the Orangeburg property.
> However, if a good offer comes along, the Board will reconsider its sale.[94]

In seven months (God's perfect number), through the generous and sacrificial gifts of God's people, the debt on the Mission's Headquarters building was retired and the Mission's finances were once again able to support most of its programs. Only the problems of implementing the Salary Administration Program, fully funding the Pension Program with a trustee outside the Board, and removing legacy income from the General Fund still remained beyond the realm of achievement. It was a modern-day miracle, and the author saw it as a clear indication that God wanted the Mission's Headquarters right where it was—at least until He indicated otherwise!

A Support-Raised Program Adopted

With one of the cost-cutting measures being the temporary suspension of the position of Missionary Director, the author, as President, again assumed the responsibility for this position and began to work directly with the Regional Directors.

At the January 28, 1981 Board meeting, the members voted unanimously to adopt a fund-raising program for the Mission's five regions. The goal was to make each region self-supporting. The Minutes state:

Motion was made and unanimously adopted that the President is authorized to implement the following program immediately:

1. That the Board clarify to each worker of the ABMJ that he/she is an employee of the corporation and is hired to fulfill a specific responsibility, as defined by the Board.

2. That all full-time workers serving with the ABMJ be appointed by the Board to serve for a period of two years. Each employee will be evaluated every six months in three specific areas:

1) spiritual conduct
2) missionary service
3) support needs

The six-month evaluation will be done by the Personnel Committee of the Board, along with the Department Head of the worker being evaluated. A written report will be made, a copy given to the worker, as well as a copy placed in his/ her personnel file.

3. That the Board specify that each region be responsible for the entire support of their particular area. The support will include:

1) The Chosen People responses from the area.
2) church support from the area
3) individual support for each worker
4) church meetings of each worker
5) percentage of literature sold in the area, such percentage to be determined by the publication department.

The principle is that each region should become self-supporting, with income and expense goals set by the Board and determined by the program of evangelism for that particular area.[95]

Exactly six years earlier, at the January 1975 Board meeting, the author had presented a proposal that the regions, missionaries, and programs of the Mission become self-supporting but the matter had been tabled by the Board. Now, however, several Board members were in favor of the program. The overall consensus was that something had to be done to ease the financial pressure and this was one available option.

DEVELOPING A POLICY MANUAL

While the Board wrestled with financial concerns, the issue of missionaries raising support, the reduction of missionary staff and programs, on-going discussions regarding owning property versus renting, and matters of concern regarding the establishment of Messianic congregations, the Regional Directors set about to define policies which would help them govern and manage their regions. A policy manual was needed. Functioning as a management team, the R.D.'s developed job descriptions for each position in the Mission; they developed policies for hiring, evaluations, and the dismissal of workers; they set up ethical, moral, and doctrinal standards for missionaries and staff workers. In general, they developed a policy manual which fit the developing image of the Mission as it had been re-organized by the Board, and to fulfill the requirements of the adopted proposal to raise support.

The issue of raising support was not a problem as far as the Regional Directors were concerned. They accepted this responsibility. Their concern was that they wanted to have a voice in how funds raised within their regions were to be spent. They wanted to know the percentage that would be allocated for salaries, benefits, and evangelism programs for their regions versus the percentage that was to be spent on foreign ministries, literature, etc. They wanted assurances that the Board would not decide to use all of the monies raised within their regions for media campaigns or for other national missionary projects, rather than for the priorities established for the staff and evangelism within their regions.

The Board of Directors approved each section of the policy manual as it was developed. The Minutes of the June 1981 Board meeting state:

Mr. Sevener reported that the directors had received a copy of the Table of Contents of the Policy Manual, which included a Job Description for Regional Directors, Area Directors and Missionaries.

Mr. Sevener recommended that the office of Missionary Director be temporarily discontinued from the Organizational Chart and that the position of Assistant to the President be created. Evaluation of the Personnel to be made by the President and the Personnel Committee.

Motion was made and voted to accept the Index and sections of the Policy Manual submitted to date.[96]

The Minutes of the October 1981 state: "Mr. Sevener included the Organizational Chart in the Policy Manual given to the Directors. The office of Missionary Director has been held in abeyance and the office of International

Missionary Director has been added for future use. Mr. Sevener requested that the Directors study the Policy Manual as compiled to date and send Mr. Sevener any changes or suggestions by the end of November."[97]

Incorporating some minor changes and suggestions by the Board, the official Policy Manual of the Mission was adopted by the Board in 1982. The Minutes state: "The Directors urged that the Policy Manual be implemented and that Mr. Sevener personally present the policy manual to the staff."[98]

The adoption of an official "policy manual" forced the Board to face some of the philosophical issues that had been dividing its members, as well as members of the Mission's staff. Once again, the Board struggled with issues regarding the release of financial information and donor names to the Regional Directors. But the major issue dividing the staff and Board was the issue of Messianic congregations.

As mentioned earlier, Daniel Fuchs and some Board members were adamantly opposed to the establishment of a Hebrew-Christian Church or Messianic synagogues. Daniel's policy statement and editorial expressing the Mission's opposition to the establishment of Messianic synagogues was well known. Yet he did recognize the value and the ministry which a large segment of the Messianic movement was accomplishing. He even attended some of their meetings as he had promised to do.

THE CHICAGO MINISTRY DEVELOPS A PILOT PROGRAM

In the field, the ministry in Chicago—a work that had had a long and difficult history—was about to emerge as the new experimental laboratory for the Mission.

Shortly before Harry Jacobson was transferred from Chicago to Houston, Texas in 1974, the author interviewed Ben Alpert as a potential worker for the Mission. At the time, Ben was a student at the Baptist Bible College in Springfield, Missouri. He was planning to enter the field of Jewish missions following his graduation from Bible college.

BEN ALPERT

Ben was raised in a Reform Jewish home. Like many Jewish young people of his day, he did not know what he believed—but knew he couldn't believe in Jesus and still be Jewish. However, while he was working at the City Ambulance Company in Montgomery, Alabama he became acquainted with a young man who was a committed believer. This young man witnessed to Ben every day, telling him that he needed to accept the Lord. As the two men worked together side-by-side, helping people in life and death accident situations, Ben began to see the peace that his companion's faith in Jesus gave him in every situation. Finally, on August 30, 1970, after reading the New Testament for himself, Ben accepted Jesus as his personal Savior and Messiah. He joined the Perry Hill Road Baptist Church in Montgomery, Alabama and was baptized on September 13, 1970. Five days later, Ben surrendered his life to full-time Christian service. On the advice of his pastor, he enrolled in the Pastors' course at Baptist Bible College in Springfield. In May, 1971 he enrolled there as a full-time student.

In September of 1971, Sanford Mills, one of the Mission's Field Evangelists, was invited to be the guest speaker at a chapel service at the college. After his message, when Sanford offered to meet with any of the Jewish students enrolled at the college, Ben Alpert responded. Sanford suggested to Ben that if he felt called to minister among the Jews, he should contact the ABMJ. Sanford in turn gave Ben's name to Daniel Fuchs.

While attending Baptist Bible College, Ben met a fellow student, Bonnie Clave. Bonnie was raised in a Christian home, although several of her mother's relatives were Jewish. Bonnie had always been active in church, and she admitted that the only reason she went to Bible college was because some of her friends were going. Shortly after she enrolled, however, she attended a revival service and it was there that she realized she needed to accept Yeshua as her own personal Savior. Right then and there she accepted the Lord, and she knew God had His hand upon her life. Then God brought Ben into her life and, together, they knew He was calling them to minister to the Jewish people. Soon they married.

Ben had followed through on Dr. Mills advice to contact the Mission. Through that contact he was able to enroll in the Mission's Student Aid program. As Ben and Bonnie learned more about the Mission, and had more contact with Mission personnel, they became convinced that God was calling them to work with the Jewish people on staff with the Mission.

After Ben's graduation from Baptist Bible College in the Spring of 1974, he and Bonnie were sent to Chicago where they were to receive "on the job" training. They were also to receive formal training in the Mission's training program in Los Angeles. In telling about their arrival in Chicago and about their "on the job" training as missionaries among the Jews, Bonnie wrote:

> From all appearances, the sixty-hundred block of Chicago's North Kedzie Avenue is no different from any other residential street. The street itself is undergoing construction changes; but other than that, children ride bikes, play on the sidewalks, and parents go about their daily tasks. However the building that houses the Midwestern District

Headquarters of ABMJ hasn't been quite so normal during the last year.

Ben and I and our son Michael arrived in Chicago a year ago to begin our work in the Jewish community and after living in Missouri, moving to Chicago was a traumatic experience. We arrived not many hours after Ben's graduation from Baptist Bible College. We didn't know anyone in Chicago, or even how to get to the Mission; but, because we knew that God wanted us here, we were determined to make the necessary adjustments and face whatever was to come.

Our first encounter with the people of the Mission came by means of a Ladies Auxiliary meeting. The ladies greeted us with open arms and we shared a pot-luck dinner, ...We knew that we had a lot to accomplish in Chicago, but that these ladies were behind us with prayer and that our almighty Savior was directing our steps.

During our first month Ben was able to make a very valuable contact at the Israeli Embassy. Ben was allowed to see the Consulate General for five minutes. He was also able to talk with the Consulate's press secretary for over an hour, during which time he was able to share the plan of salvation. At the close of the meeting, our Mission was listed as a Messianic Jewish organization that was friendly to Israel, and we were put on the mailing list.

Not long after our arrival in Chicago, one of our Thursday night classes was interrupted by a telephone bomb threat. The caller said that the bomb was to go off in thirty minutes. While the police searched the building, we continued our meeting in the parking lot. I'm sure the bomb threat was meant to discourage us, but instead it turned out to be a victory for the Lord. The people who were in the parking lot attracted curious neighbors who otherwise would never attend a meeting.

At the end of our first summer, God sent us a young man who had been working in two other branches of the Mission. Michael Rydelnik, from Brooklyn, N.Y. has a testimony that really thrilled our hearts.... [Michael was a student at Moody Bible Institute. The continuing ministry of Michael Rydelnik will be enlarged upon at a later point in this history.]

Michael is doing an excellent job in fulfilling his calling. Along with classmates from Moody Bible Institute there have been over 10,000 tracts passed out to the people of Chicago. The first time they went out there were four professions of faith made as result of the tracts. Satan retaliated: the Mission was stoned causing minor damage, but we realized anew that Chicago was in desperate need of the Gospel. As a result of our tract ministry, since January, ten people have accepted Jesus Christ as Lord and Messiah....

The outreach of the ministry is ever-increasing, especially since the Volunteer Missionary Program was instituted. Five families in communities where there are sizeable Jewish populations have volunteered their homes for this outreach. The purpose is to teach Gentile Christians to effectively witness to and reach Jewish people for Christ. The volunteer missionaries are deeply dedicated and the Lord is blessing their lives. We have seen many souls won to the Lord throughout these outreaches....

According to our plans, July was to have been a month of vacation, but instead it turned into one of trial: Sunday, July 20th [c.1975], our building was fire-bombed.

I awoke about 4 a.m. and smelled smoke. I got up and walked about ten feet from our bedroom door and the smoke became so thick that I couldn't see. I ran back into our room, woke up Ben, (I never saw him get up so fast!) grabbed Michael, and headed down the back stairs. The smell of gas and smoke was almost unbearable by the time we reached the back door, but we knew that we had to get out. Ben called the fire department while I unlocked the back door and went outside. I never knew such fear in my life, not knowing where the fire was, or how bad it was; but yet I was able to praise God that we were still alive. As I reached the front of the house I was greeted by flames and a large can of flammable liquid. Ben was able to put out most of the fire with an extinguisher before the fire department arrived. The fireman told us that we were lucky to have gotten out of the house alive. They went on to explain that in most fires, where wooden doors such as ours are involved, the occupants of the buildings are usually overcome with smoke before the fire ever gets really bad.

After the fire trucks left and the arson squad finished their tests, we attempted to clean up and get things back to normal as much as possible. Because the front door was completely burned away, we have the front entrance boarded up....

That night we were visited again. This time red spray paint was used to spell out, 'Let my people alone,' across the front of our building and parking signs. Two days later our front office window was smashed and shortly after that, someone attempted to smash our living room window.

Numerous police and fire officials have been in and out of the Mission because so much has happened in the past weeks. They cannot understand why we are trying so hard to share Jesus with the Jewish community. We have had the opportunity to share the Gospel with a lot of people because it is impossible to explain what we are, or what we are trying to do without explaining the plan of salvation.

We have learned in the last year, not only about Jewish missions, but also what it means to be totally committed to the Lord Jesus Christ.[99]

The building in Chicago was not the only branch of the Mission threatened or fire-bombed during the mid-1970's. Because of the Mission's media exposure through its telecasts, newspaper ads, etc., branches in New York, Los Angeles, Toronto, Israel, Dallas, etc. had also been affected. And, as has already been discussed, the publicity surrounding Jews for Jesus activities and the Messianic Movement had also created general feelings of hostility among fringe groups within the Jewish community.

The controversy and continual harassment of Ben's ministry in Chicago began to affect people who attended the meetings and some, fearing retaliation or harm, stopped coming. But Ben was a tenacious worker. Like Joseph Cohn, he, too, was a "networker" and he spent much of his time making contacts. Those contacts paid off as pastors in the area began asking him to speak in their churches. Soon he was traveling throughout the region setting up meetings, training volunteers, and raising support for the Chicago ministry.

In 1975 Ben was asked to assume the leadership of the Midwest Region. Ben had established volunteer ministries for the Mission in Des Plains, Illinois; Detroit, Michigan; Indianapolis, Indiana; South Bend, Indiana; and Milwaukee, Wisconsin. To assist Ben with the supervision of his expanding ministry, a number of new workers were added to the Chicago staff in mid-1975 and early 1976. New workers included Myron Schweitzer, Barry and Dyann Budoff, Steve Besser, and Mr. and Mrs. Frank Gillis. But Ben was still in need of additional help. In the Spring of 1976, Mr. John Bell, a former class-mate and friend from Baptist Bible College in Springfield, Missouri, volunteered to help Ben with the work of the Mission.

John Bell

Chicago was John's home town. He was born into a Gentile-Christian home, and was saved at the age of eight. While he was in high school, he dedicated his life to the Lord and he knew God was calling him into ministry. As John prayed about where to go to college, God directed him to Baptist Bible College in Springfield, Missouri. It was there that a friendship developed between himself and Ben Alpert.

After John's graduation from Baptist Bible College in 1972, he married a fellow-student, Linda Rhode. He then took post-graduate courses at Southwest Missouri State University and taught physical hygiene and took a coaching position at Baptist Bible College. When he gave up his coaching position and returned to Chicago, he did so with the goal of beginning an independent Bible Baptist Church in the inner-city of Chicago. But when John heard about the trials Ben and Bonnie had been facing in their ministry among the Jews, he volunteered to help.

The more John visited with the Jewish people, the greater became his sensitivity toward them. He realized for the first time that Jewish people do not necessarily reject the Jesus of the Bible, they reject the Jesus of Christian culture. He discovered that many Jewish people know nothing about the Jesus of the Bible!

As John and Ben prayed together, and talked about the strategy for their ministry together, they became convinced that as a Jew and a Gentile they could work together to reach Jews and Gentiles. Their strategy would be to use the Mission's building to establish an independent congregation, called Messiah Baptist Church. John would pastor the church—a church that would reach both Jews and Gentiles with the Gospel—and the members of the congregation would help Ben in doing the missionary work. But their plans did not materialize. Instead, John became more and more involved in the Chicago ministry. He joined the staff of the Mission as a full-time worker and by the end of 1976 he was appointed Missionary in Charge of Chicago. John gave this report of his ministry:

This past year in Chicago [1976] has been one of provision and blessing of God. We have done some new things and some old ones in taking the Gospel to the Jewish people.

Some of the old things including calendar contacts, door-to-door visitation and tract distribution have proved successful and will continue to remain a vital part of this ministry.

Some new areas have opened up for us, however, and it is these I would like to share with you.

Northeastern University had been in sore need of a Hebrew Christian Club for purposes of evangelism and fellowship. Under the direction of Barry Budoff, one of our staff, and a faculty advisor, a Messianic Jewish club is now a reality.

God has provided volunteer workers to open up four new Jewish fellowships. These include Oak Lawn, Hoffman Estates, Des Plaines, and Rogers Park.

This past year, a new ministry, Shalom Pamphlets, appeared in Lincolnwood, a Jewish suburb. This was a series of six pamphlets with a view toward progressively explaining the message of Jesus the Messiah.

In September [c.1976], the pamphlets were followed up with a survey by volunteers from Moody Bible Institute going door-to-door to get reactions.

We have also had two nursing home ministries open up to us with sizeable Jewish populations. Here is another area where God is blessing and showing us His provision. By this time next year we want to be involved in three campus ministries. We want to present the Gospel to over one thousand new Jewish contacts.

We want to get involved in three more nursing home ministries, and finally we would like to begin a Jewish Evangelism Seminar this summer in Chicago.[100]

The evangelistic outreach of the Chicago ministry continued to thrive under John's leadership, while the Mission's exposure within the churches continued to thrive under Ben Alpert's ministry. Ben was an excellent Field Evangelist!

Toward the end of 1976 the Alpert's were transferred to the Northeast, and Ben was asked to use his talents to develop support for the missionary work of the Northeast region—an area with the largest concentration of Jewish people and, hence, an area which needed the largest staff of missionaries. The Northeast had traditionally been one of the most difficult areas in the country in which to raise support, but Ben proved equal to the challenge. He moved his family to Endicott, New York and began opening churches to the Mission's ministry.

Our Sovereign God, who knows when the fields are ready for harvest, brought three additional workers, almost simultaneously, to work with John Bell in Chicago. To each one, the Lord had given a vision of establishing an indigenous Messianic congregation—using the Mission's property, but keeping it independent of the Mission. The workers were Roy Schwarcz, Linda Block (now Mrs. Linda Herman), and Michael Schiffman.

ROY SCHWARCZ

Roy Schwarcz began his ministry with the Mission working in New York with Herb Zwickel, Eleanor Bullock, and others. In the spring of 1976 the Mission transferred Roy to Albany, New York to develop and expand a volunteer ministry he had begun there. In telling readers of *The Chosen People* how his ministry in Albany was established, Roy said:

As a new missionary, my first duty was to continue the work I had begun in Albany, N.Y. It was suggested that I start in earnest on the college campus and wait for the further leading of the Lord. I met weekly with other interested Christians at the State University of New York at Albany and had a book-and-question table in the Campus Center. Our group was called 'Jesus is a Jew.' We also began a similar ministry at Cornell University and Harper College in addition to personal work with young Jewish believers in Cortland, Ithaca, Binghamton, Utica and Albany.[101]

In relating the story of how he came to faith in Yeshua, Roy wrote:

'Hey Jew,' someone shouted. 'Did you know you and your family killed Jesus?'

I had never heard anything like that at home in Long Island, where being Jewish was nothing unusual. But my parents wanted me to have discipline, so at the age of fifteen I moved to Carolina Military Academy, which was to be my home and school for two years. The head of the school had told my family that it was one big, happy family, and it seemed like a good place to go.

What the headmaster had failed to tell us was that there were no other Jewish students in this happy family, and I was considered a 'New York Jew,' which wasn't exactly flattering. The other boys resented the fact that I was Jewish, and it didn't help matters when they heard that I was allowed to sleep in while they were required to attend church on Sunday mornings....

When I finally returned to New York to attend college, it's no wonder that I was cynical and on-guard. I didn't like the status quo of the world, and I saw a lot of injustice around me. I couldn't understand a world where there was hatred and distrust, a world where people seemed to enjoy a society full of wrongs.

It was the era of college unrest, and my roommate was an outspoken radical. Our late night discussions prompted me to think about the state of the world. He advocated violence, but I couldn't see how that would create anything but more problems. Instead, I wanted to see the world changed from within the system. I was convinced that the American legal system provided the answers to mankind's great problems.

It was inevitable that I would be disillusioned. As long as there are problems in the hearts of men, there will be problems in the legal system. I discovered that money means power and power means everything. I began to wonder if there was any real truth at all.

Through drugs and Eastern philosophies, I looked within myself, or at least that's what I thought I was doing. I studied the occult and a wide range of mystical teachings. I began to see that the spiritual realm was real, but I could tell that I wasn't seeing the truth in these ventures. As a matter of fact, I sensed evil.

I felt like my search was doomed. Perhaps the world could only offer me choices, relative decisions. I longed for something absolute, something of real substance.

I decided to get a taste of 'real life' and wandered across the country. In LaCrosse, Wisconsin, I encountered for the first time a group of real Christians. After some hesitation, I told them I was Jewish. Much to my surprise, one of the fellows shouted, 'Praise the Lord! Our Messiah was Jewish, and the Jews are God's Chosen People....'

...They told me more about Abraham and Moses and all my ancestors than I myself knew. They also told me that Christ had given His life voluntarily for the sins of all people....

They challenged me to ask God for myself, so as I prepared to move on from LaCrosse, I skeptically mumbled a prayer asking God to show me if Jesus was the Messiah.

By the time I returned to school two months later, I had forgotten my prayer. However, I hadn't forgotten the impression these people made on me. When we studied Milton's Paradise Lost in English class, I was once again confronted with the existence of an absolute in the world. In this poem I saw the god of this world, a god of absolute evil. But as I saw this, I realized that there must also be a God of the universe, a God of absolute good.

...God was still on my mind when a friend came to visit me in November. He agreed to travel with me back to LaCrosse during my winter vacation. I wanted to be with those people again.

On the way, we stopped at Niagara Falls. Seeing this awesome beauty I asked my friend, 'Do you believe there really was a flood?'

'If there is a God, He can do anything,' my friend replied....

At a friend's house later that night, I noticed a book on studying the Bible. While the others talked, I leafed through it and found myself reading how God had given the rainbow as a sign to mankind. At once, everything fell into place. I knew that God was speaking to me. I knew that God was real....

...Within a few days I had accepted the Lord and committed myself to doing whatever He wanted.[102]

On Roy's first trip across country, one of the people he met in La Crosse, Wisconsin made a profound impact on him—a girl named Joanne. In spite of the fact that he continued his trip and eventually returned to school in New York, Roy did not forget Joanne. He married her!

Roy and Joanne moved to Chicago in December 1977. The transfer allowed Roy to attend Moody Bible Institute, while at the same time doing missionary work in the Chicago area. As he did door-to-door visitation, Roy led many people to the Lord. But he discovered he had nowhere to take new Jewish people to church where they would feel comfortable. As he discussed the problem with his Regional Director, John Bell, the two men agreed that a solution was needed for this dilemma!

LINDA BLOCK

Linda Block was a brilliant pre-med student. She was raised in a traditional Jewish home, and like so many of the young people of her day she searched to know the meaning of life. When she found it in the Messiah, the Lord Jesus, she was rejected by her family, but she continued to lovingly witness to them and to pray for them.

God had gifted Linda in a very special way. She had the ability to strike up a conversation with anybody, anywhere and the conversation would always turn so that she could share her testimony, some Scripture, or something about the Messiah. Linda was a soul-winner! This was evidenced through her experiences while she was working for the Mission in New York City. She told readers of *The Chosen People* magazine:

A few weeks ago I boarded a bus to Manhattan. About a mile from my home, three Israelis got on. These women were conversing out loud and I said to another woman next to me, 'I've studied some Hebrew but I sure can't speak as well as they do.'

'I'm a Hebrew teacher,' she replied. We had quite a conversation about Israel, prophecy and how the Jewish people have strayed from the God of our forefathers.

During this time I noticed another woman was listening intently to our conversation. When the Hebrew teacher got off, the other woman came running over. 'I've been listening to you.'

I thought she was going to rebuke me. (I knew she was orthodox because she got on in the orthodox section of my neighborhood and she was wearing a wig as many of the religious women do. She happens to be the wife of an orthodox rabbi.)

Instead she said, 'You speak with such feeling.' She slipped her name and phone number into my hand and asked me for mine.

'I'd like to have you over to our synagogue to meet the young people.'

I told her that I was not orthodox but she told me that it didn't matter because 'I had something.' That something of course is the Spirit of the God of Israel!

I said goodby to her in Hebrew. Then, a Czechoslovakian Jewish woman began to talk to me.... Incidentally, all this happened in twenty-five minutes.

I spoke with Rabbi M three weeks ago. He's known me for about ten years. He kept bringing up the word 'tradition' while I emphasized the importance of having a relationship with the living God.

He said that the Bible is a closed book without the commentaries. I told him that Isaiah the prophet predicted that the literate of our people would say that (Isa 29:11).

If I read the Hertz Bible which has some commentaries, he will read the Gospel of Matthew in both Hebrew and English.

Last week I had a profitable appointment with a rabbi from a sizeable congregation. He's a very honest, friendly man who is sincerely attempting to be a good shepherd for his people.

He has been stirred recently with a desire to know the Lord better, for the Lord to be his friend and personal God. He can accept much of our theology except Jesus being the Messiah.

Older Jewish people too are very open to the claims of Jesus. Recently I had the privilege of dealing with an older Jewish woman in a nursing home. She prayed and asked the Lord Jesus to come into her heart. There was no theological problem. She wanted the Lord.

I've also seen two young Jewish men receive the Lord over the telephone, one, whom I've known two years and another who was a follower of Rev. Moon.

Yesterday I visited a Jewish family for the first time. They are very Jewish in outlook. The mother was reared in Orthodoxy. The daughter went to Yeshiva. I've contacted most of the Jewish people on their block and they are the only open ones....

I had a good, spirited, friendly exchange with a Lubavitcher (orthodox) young man last week.

He couldn't see why if Jesus was the Messiah there is still evil in the world.... I challenged him with Daniel 9:26 where it is stated that after Messiah is cut off in Jerusalem and the temple would be destroyed.

He said he couldn't trust my translation. (I forgot my Jewish Bible that day.) So I urged him to check his own....

Every week there are miracles like these. Miracles of timing, openness, blessing, and most of all, belief.[103]

Linda left New York to attend graduate school at Wheaton College. She wanted to further prepare herself for missionary work and cross-cultural communication. Since she had served on the staff of the Mission in New York, it was natural for her to gravitate to the Mission in Chicago, to meet John Bell and to renew fellowship with Roy Schwarcz whom she had met in New York.

MICHAEL SCHIFFMAN

Michael Schiffman joined the staff of the Mission in the Spring of 1977. Michael was born and raised in a traditional Jewish home in Phoenix, Arizona. After coming to faith in the Messiah, he began to witness to his own people. It wasn't long before his witnessing brought him in touch with the Mission's volunteer workers in Phoenix, Arizona and then with the missionaries of the Western Region, who recruited him as a campus worker. In relating some of his campus ministry experiences, Michael told readers of *The Chosen People*:

'Born again, but not a Christian!' That's what worker Michael Schiffman ...described himself as, one afternoon when another Jewish student took issue with him at Mike's book table on Arizona State U.'s campus.

'He told me he had seen the German concentration camps and this was the way "Christians" had treated the Jewish people,' related Mike. 'I told him that if his definition of a Christian is an anti-Semite, then not to think of me as a Christian, but as a believer in the Scriptures and a believer in Jesus the Messiah.' After the inquirer learned Mike was not ashamed of this Jewish heritage, the stumbling block was removed and a discussion ensued on the Messiahship of Jesus.

'The lesson I learned,' Schiffman concluded, 'is that before you can sow seeds you sometimes have to break up the hard ground.'[104]

Michael's desire to be fully prepared in his outreach to Jewish people led him to enroll in the Jewish Studies course at Moody Bible Institute, in Chicago. While he was there, the Mission employed him to work in the Chicago branch. Michael shared some of his first experiences as a missionary in Chicago:

As a new ABMJ missionary here in Chicago, I noticed one big difference between visitations here and in my home city of Phoenix. In Phoenix, most people live in one story dwellings, so when you ring a doorbell, you see the person you're talking with.

Not so in Chicago. Most people live in apartment buildings, with high security precautions. When I ring the buzzer, people will shout down to me three flights, and I have to shout up to them. I wind up not even seeing the faces of most people I contact. Couple this situation with my dislike for the weather here, and you have one very homesick, discouraged but nice Jewish believer.

About two weeks ago on visitation, a miracle happened. I was invited to come upstairs and talk. As I approached the third flight of stairs, I was greeted by a Jewish girl in her mid-twenties. We spoke outside her door for about fifteen minutes, and she invited me into her apartment.

She asked me to explain how a Jew could believe in Jesus, and still remain a Jew. In the course of the afternoon, we discussed prophecy, the existence of God, and tradition.

She indicated that her only objections to Jesus were that her parents wouldn't understand, and she didn't want to commit herself to 'my group' (Beth Sar Shalom). After informing her that her only commitment should be to the Lord, and that she didn't have to tell her parents until she felt the time was right, she prayed to accept her Messiah.

As I pondered these events, I realized that everything is just as it should be, that this is where the Lord wants me, warm weather or cold. I am here for his glory, not my comfort.[105]

Michael's willingness to suffer discomfort for the Gospel's sake was again tested when he went to the colleges and universities in the Chicago area where he set up book and literature tables, as he had done in Phoenix. He wrote:

The first time I had a literature table out at Bradley U.... I conversed with ten Jewish students. The next week, someone threw a brick through our storefront in response. The next few times I was on campus things were quiet. But the last time I was on campus I had a sign on the table saying 'We believe Jesus is the Messiah. Prove us wrong.'

Six students called campus security to have Michael thrown off campus. After they learned he had permission to be there they threatened violence. (They could have been the ones who also threw the brick.) 'I prayed,' recalled Mike. 'Then four Jewish students stopped by to inquire as to what we were all about. The Lord worked it for His own glory. No harm came to me and I was able to witness to the four students.'[106]

THE OLIVE TREE CONGREGATION

As John Bell, Linda Block, Roy Schwarcz, and Michael Schiffman compared notes about the different aspects of their ministries, and as they prayed together for God's direction for the ministry in Chicago, thoughts about the formation of a Messianic congregation began to germinate within each one of their hearts. The interest on the part of Gentile Christians in Jews who believed in Jesus, and the hostility on the part of Jews toward Jews who believed in Jesus convinced them of the need for a congregation of Messianic Jewish believers, where their "Jewishness" and belief in Jesus would not be questioned or doubted. Prayerfully, they began working on the by-laws and on a constitution for such a congregation. The idea was to create a Messianic congregation where Jewish customs and traditions could be utilized, but not legalized. They wanted the congregation to be free to celebrate cultural holidays that were important to Jews, and if those occasions had theological implications, they wanted to use them to show how they related to the Messiah and to Biblical Christianity. They envisioned that the congregation would be established as an indigenous church—self-supporting and self-propagating.

When John Bell approached the author with the concept and formative plans, I believed that God was directing them, and gave them the "green light" to proceed. It was an area of ministry I'd personally seen the need for since my student days in Israel in the early 1960's. I asked that the workers involved (John Bell, Roy Schwarcz, Linda Block and Michael Schiffman) document their "experiment" so the entire staff of the Mission and the Board could see this new methodology at work. I am happy that they did, as the issue over Messianic congregations nearly split the staff and the Board.

The first mention of the new "congregational approach" to ministry was made in "Insight"—an "in-house" paper initiated by the author in 1972 as a means of keeping the staff and the Board apprised of changes, staff appointments, new policies and procedures, etc. Through the years this publication has continued under different names, and is still published from time to time as a staff information piece. In the August 1978 issue of Insight, the following notice appeared:

NEW CONGREGATION STARTED IN CHICAGO

John Bell, Roy Schwarcz, Linda Block and Michael Schiffman have come up with a good idea. It is an alternative. Many areas do not have churches who accept Jewish believers readily, including the area around our Chicago branch, so the 'Olive Tree Congregation' was formed. It is a place where both Jewish and Gentile believers can worship together and feel comfortable. Good Work, Chicago!

If you want to know more about their new plan, let me know and I will send you their introductory pamphlet including their Covenant, Constitution and Articles of Faith.[107]

The next mention of the Mission's new methodology in establishing Messianic congregations appeared in a two-page spread in the January, 1979 issue of *The Chosen People* magazine. The article included pictures and a report of the first meeting of the congregation. One caption read: "The Olive Tree Congregation—'A Fellowship With a Vision.' Chicago's newly-formed congregation is growing by leaps and bounds, reports Roy Schwarcz. 'People are really getting committed.'"[108]

The February 1979 issue of *The Chosen People* magazine included an article telling about the merits of the "congregational approach" to doing ministry. The article, written by Michael Schiffman, stated:

As a new believer some five years ago, my family's reaction to my beliefs affected me so strongly that for a long time whenever I shared the Gospel, I was overcautious not to offend the individual. I didn't apologize for my faith, I was just careful not to seem too zealous.

In the past month here in Chicago, instead of maintaining a somewhat low-key witness, we've tried something new. We've gone door-to-door inviting Jewish people to our Olive Tree Congregation and then shared with them why they need to receive and accept Jesus as Messiah.

I have shared with Jewish people in the past, but never on such a scale. We made almost two hundred contacts. Even more startling was the response I observed. I saw over sixty people flatly reject the Gospel, but I saw five Jewish women accept the Lord and about seventy others were very open to coming to the meetings.

In the past, I would visit, share with that person, leave some literature and call again—a type of friendship evangelism. As I would re-visit the individual, I befriended them and attempted to lead them to the Lord.

What we have been doing recently is basically the same except my visits seem to have more of a definite purpose. I am inviting people to our congregation, the Olive Tree. The Olive Tree doesn't sound too foreign and it intrigues them. The second distinctive in our new visitation outreach is that we share with each person how they can receive the Lord on the first visit.

This was somewhat of a shock to my 'non-offensive' stance. But what if that person (God forbid!) died that night? I have an obligation to share with them how they can receive Him. What they do with the Gospel is between them and the Lord. I am very careful not to offend my Jewish friends with culturally offensive language or attitude, but beyond that, I will not withhold from them the Jesus of the Bible and of my life.

This is what the Lord has taught me from Olive Tree's outreach. If we can share the Gospel with a Jewish accent, we can have a local congregation with a Jewish flavor that is reaching out to Jews and Gentiles. By the grace of our great God, I will be an effective missionary to His Chosen People.

We believe this an alternative that God would have for us here in our outreach in Chicago—not the method but a workable, unoffensive outreach for Him to Jewish people.[109]

As the Olive Tree Congregation grew, more missionaries on staff began to experiment with the "congregational approach" in reaching Jews with the Gospel. But some of the Regional Directors remained adamantly opposed to this new approach. They felt Messianic congregations competed with local churches in their areas; they worried that such congregations would be confused with "Messianic synagogues"; they were concerned that Christians would see such congregations as re-building the middle wall of partition between Jews and Gentiles. Because of differing opinions on the issue, the Regional meetings became a debating forum where each side presented its views on this controversial issue. One thing could not be argued with however—the documented statistical evidence showing the ministry results of the Olive Tree Congregation.

In 1984, John Bell compiled the documented results of the Jewish-oriented church called the Olive Tree Congregation in a pamphlet entitled, "Why Plant Jewish Oriented Churches?" The documentation covered the founding of the congregation in 1978, when Roy Schwarcz was its first pastor, up to 1984, when another Mission worker, Barry Berger, was the pastor. John wrote:

...The following is a compilation of the result of this ministry through early 1984:
122 Jewish people have come to know the Lord.
132 Gentiles have come to know the Lord.

88 new believers have completed a regular 36-week program of discipleship.

5 have completed a 17 week course in evangelism.

5 men have been called into full time ministry.

3 men have been ordained.

5 Jewish missionary agencies have had members in this local church. This has helped break down barriers and promote unity of ministry.

5 young people participated in S.T.E.P, ABMJ/Chosen People Ministries' Summer Training and Evangelism Program. Financial support was raised for each person.

The Christian Broadcasting network, Pacific Garden Mission, and other area churches and ministries have established a policy of turning over all Jewish contacts to OTC [Olive Tree Congregation].

Members of OTC have travelled on Sunday evenings to other area churches and conducted entire services to help them discover the Jewishness of their faith.

Hundreds of people from around the country have come to Chicago just to see the Olive Tree Congregation; others have written for literature and information. As a result, we are constantly in fellowship with the larger body of Christ.

Moody Bible Institute chose Barry Berger, a worker with ABMJ/Chosen People Ministries and the pastor of OTC, as its "Pastor of the Week" and gave him the opportunity to preach three messages on its radio program.

OTC supports six missionaries at $100 a month, including Howard Silverman of ABMJ/Chosen People Ministries. In one 48-hour period, OTC sent fourteen trained members to Cleveland to evangelize with Howard Silverman. In this time, 3,000 tracts were distributed and 387 homes in a Jewish community were visited.

Thousands of homes have been visited locally.

80,000 pieces of literature have been distributed.

The two missionaries who started the work are free to perform other evangelistic duties while the local outreach continues with greater impact.

About 120 people now meet each week as an independent congregation for worship, fellowship, prayer, evangelism, and discipleship. This has made a dramatic impact in the Chicago area. Their dynamic testimony is much greater than their size. God used OTC to accomplish His purpose and ABMJ/Chosen People Ministries is viewed as a pioneer in this field, and I believe God has given the mission spiritual, financial, and ministry blessings because of this role.[110]

MESSIANIC CONGREGATIONS IN OTHER AREAS

As the Regional Directors of the Mission saw the results of the congregational approach being used in Chicago, they gradually became more supportive of the approach. Other workers of the Mission established Messianic congregations as well. The San Francisco branch, under the leadership of the Rev. Jerome Fleischer, developed into a congregation and Eliezer Urbach established a congregation in Denver, Colorado.

The Mission's outreach in Brighton Beach, under the leadership of Steve Schlissel (as discussed in Chapter Six of this history), developed a "cultural" approach to ministry before becoming an independent congregation. This approach was taken because at the time when the Mission purchased its property in Brighton Beach [c. 1979], this section of Brooklyn had a large influx of Russian Jewish immigrants. Miss Judi van Dyk, a young woman who spoke fluent Russian, was hired to work among the immigrants. In a report on the Brighton Beach ministry, readers of *The Chosen People* magazine were told:

Next the Lord provided a building in Brighton Beach....

Not only is the building situated in the heart of a Russian Jewish neighborhood, it also has an established place within the Jewish community since it was a former training facility for rabbis!...

The provision of this building comes at a crucial time. Russian Jewish immigrants now number in the thousands....

At the present time they face a totally new situation which has no meaningful link with their former life. This is where ABMJ missionaries serve a continuing role. The message of God's redeeming love which we shared with them has not changed....

Mission workers have seen the plight of the immigrants and are ministering to their basic needs. Clothing is being distributed. The center will be renovated so that housing can be made available. ABMJ missionaries are attempting not only to restore material security to these people but also a sense of their own human dignity.

We look in faith to the time when the Brighton Beach center will provide the essentials these immigrants require: housing, English instruction, finding employment and counselling. It is in faith, too, that we anticipate their greatest need of all being met as they place their trust in the Lord.[111]

Although the ministry done by Steve and Jeanne Schlissel developed into an independent congregation, the Brighton Beach area has remained an area comprised of a large population of Russian Jews and the Mission has continued its outreach among Russian Jewish immigrants and the Jewish community of Brighton Beach. As the author stated in Chapter Six of this history, the outreach in Brighton Beach is currently being done under the leadership of Rev. Israel Cohen and his wife, Judy. Assisting the Cohen's are Mr. and Mrs. Michael Wechsler. Mrs. Wechsler (Lydia) is a Russian Jewish believer who has been a great source of help in this outreach.

The Policy Struggles Continue

For the Board, and for some members of the Mission's staff, such a diversified program of reaching Jewish people with the Gospel was confusing and seemed contradictory to established Mission policy. Then, too, as the Mission entered its eighty-eighth year in 1982, many philosophical issues remained unsolved as Board members continued to wrestle with the on-going financial concerns, issues regarding support raising by missionaries and staff, the establishment of Messianic congregations, owning versus renting property, publication of literature, the regional system of operation, the funding of the Mission's pension program, the use of investment funds, radio, the wisdom of merging the Mission with another Jewish mission organizations, etc. (During 1982-1983 consideration was being given to the merger of the Mission with the American Association for Jewish Evangelism [AAJE], however there was reservation about such a merger by several of the Board members.)[112]

Although the members of the Board loved one another as Christian brothers, the twenty-four month period from June 1980 (the deadline for returning the funds securing the first mortgage on the Headquarters building in Orangeburg) to June 1982, was stressful and sometimes tense due to differences of opinion. One's perception of things is the culmination of many ingredients, and reports and findings are based on one's perception of the situation being studied.

As has already been stated, the author and Daniel Fuchs clearly had differences of opinion in several areas—among them was the matter of owning versus leasing the Mission's Headquarters building, whether or not the Mission should hold substantial investment funds, methodology of establishing Messianic congregations, releasing of financial information and donor names to the Regional Directors, fund raising, etc. These differences prompted the author to call upon the services of a Jewish believer from Los Angeles for counsel and advice.

Frustrated by the continual financial problems that had been created by "deficit" spending through the years, and unable to increase income sufficiently to maintain the Mission's current budget and expenses, the author asked Joseph (Gerald) Caplan, a man known for his ability in finances, management of personnel, and development of policy for major corporations to come to New York to do an "internal audit" of the Mission's finances and administration.

Joseph Caplan

Joseph (Gerald) Caplan was the only child of poor Jewish immigrants. He was born in the Salvation Army home in London, England. His father started a struggling "rag" business in London, and was determined that his son would have the best education money could buy. Joseph's parents scrimped and saved and sent him through Dulwich College, England (1943-1950), and then through the Honorable Society of Lincoln's Inn Law School, England where he received the Degree of Barrister at Law in 1954.

Joseph worked as a barrister (attorney-at-law) for a number of years, but when his father became seriously ill Joseph was forced to take over his business. Joseph said:

> ...It was a bitter blow. I was sure that I had tumbled from the top of the tree. Little did I realize that this was going to be my first step toward untold wealth.
>
> Within 13 years I had graduated from the rag business into money lending, real estate and commercial banking. I had even become an industrialist. I was soon chairman of 7 public companies in London, and I owned 86 other companies, employing between 10,000 and 14,000 people. The poor Jewish boy from London was now listed as the twenty-second richest entrepreneur in England. My holding company had assets of $300 million, and I was its largest shareholder.
>
> It seemed as though my wife [Valerie] and I had everything. We had homes in three countries, a beautiful 72-foot yacht in the South of France and a luxurious Rolls Royce Phantom. It was difficult to be humble in such circumstances.
>
> Beside all the material luxuries of life, I had a good education, culture and a socially proper amount of religion. Surely, Jesus was pointing His finger at me when He accused the Pharisees of going to the synagogue simply to be seen sitting in the best seats. I was filled with pride and all kinds of ungodly values. This didn't bother me, however, because I believed money could cover almost every sin.
>
> Then the day came when the economy in England almost collapsed [c.1973]. Our stock market plummeted from

450 to 150, which would be like the Dow Jones going from 1,000 to 500. Almost overnight, my empire crumbled. Everywhere I turned I was faced with financial and legal crises.

We moved to the South of France, where I fell into a deep depression. Then we moved to the United States. But everything I tried failed. Nothing in life had prepared me for such failure.[113]

After coming to America, Joseph had to face the ultimate crises. His heart was so bad that his doctor told him he was going to die. Joseph wrote:

A short time later, I lay motionless for over seven hours on an operating table in west Los Angeles. For no less than three of those seven hours my heart was detached from my body, as life-support systems labored to keep both me and my heart alive. Later my doctor told me I had fallen into 'the lowest ebb a human being can reach and still survive.'

You can imagine my wife's shock when the doctor called to tell her of my deteriorating condition. Neither my wife nor I had been deeply religious to this point in our lives; but she sensed that if I was going to survive, it would only be by God's grace. In the desperation of that moment, she cried out, 'God, I'm a Jewish girl, and I really don't know how to do it, but I will give You the rest of my life if You give my husband back to me.'

Miraculously, God answered her prayer, and I survived the operation.... I was optimistic that time would restore my health, but I wasn't nearly so confident about my impossible financial situation. It seemed that I had come back to life only to face the same disastrous circumstances that I had left behind when I entered the operating room....

When I came home, she [Valerie] told me how she had called out to God and how He had answered her. I wasn't sure what it all meant, but somehow I sensed that God could help me too. So we began to pray together.

A short time later, a little old lady and her husband approached me on the street. I had never met either one of them before. So I was astonished when the woman boldly walked up to me and declared, 'God has sent me to save you.' I knew she had to be crazy. But for a reason I have never been able to explain, I invited her to my home.

She and her husband patiently shared the Gospel with us. I saw something in them I had never seen in the rulers of industry, the politicians or my wealthy friends. They had a real relationship with God.

I tried to understand what they were telling me, but I couldn't. I had always thought Jesus was only a rebel who had gotten tied up in politics 2,000 years ago. It would have been so easy for them to have given up on me, but they didn't. Instead, they directed us to a Hebrew-Christian Bible study in West Los Angeles.

Both Valerie and I were overwhelmed by what we saw and heard at that Bible study. We had already learned by this time that we could never buy a relationship with God. Now we were ready for whatever God had for us.[114]

After the Bible study that evening, although neither knew the other was praying, both Joseph and Valerie knelt and prayed to receive Yeshua as Messiah and Savior. Not many months later their two children, Valerie's parents, and Joseph's parents also accepted the Lord.

Shortly after coming to faith in the Messiah, Joseph met Dr. Daniel Goldberg, the Western Regional Director for the Mission. As Daniel encouraged him in his faith, Joseph's desire to serve the Lord increased and it wasn't long before he had enrolled at Talbot Theological Seminary to prepare himself for full-time missionary service among the Jews.

It was while Joseph was a student at Talbot Seminary that the author first met him. After our initial meeting a friendship developed and Joseph became involved with the Mission—first as a volunteer, then as a consultant, and finally as an employee on an administrative level.

On a volunteer basis, Joseph put together an advisory council of outstanding Jewish-Christian leaders for the Los Angeles branch. This was part of an experimental program which the author had suggested to the Board as a means of involving more Jewish believers in the ministry and to develop contacts for potential Board members, while at the same time raising the profile of the Mission in areas where we had ministry. In his role on the Advisory Council, Joseph also worked to bring about healing of tensions and problems which had long existed between the various Jewish missions in the California area—a ministry which God blessed by restoring fellowship among brethren.

After Joseph joined the staff of the Mission, it was the author's intent for him to serve in the position of Assistant to the President (A position outlined in the newly adopted policy manual, tentatively replacing the position of Missionary Director). But that appointment was being held at bay until after his graduation from Talbot Seminary. In the meantime, the author was concerned about the Mission's finances and felt there was need of an internal audit from an impartial qualified business man. He therefore asked Joseph to produce such a report.

A very comprehensive report on all departments of the Mission was produced. In the report, Joseph included a number of suggestions—some of which were excellent and were quickly adopted. But some areas of his report touched upon departments of the Mission that were under the jurisdiction of Board committees—committees that were doing their own audits. Further, in the area of finances, Joseph's report was based upon his accounting knowledge in the "for profit" business world, not upon "not for profit" fund accounting.

Impressed with Joseph's report, and certain that it would help the over-all structure of the Mission, the author's zeal ran ahead of his wisdom. I asked Joseph to share his report with the full Board at their next meeting.

While several items in Joseph's report were appreciated by the Board, and were later adopted, there were items that directly contradicted the reports of the committees of the Board. As has been stated, the contradictory information was not in the failure of Joseph or the committees to present the proper facts and figures. The reports appeared contradictory because of the perspective from which they had been written.

The end result was that the author had to extend his apology to the members of the Board and to the committee members, as well as to Joseph Caplan. The author's error in judgement had brought about a situation which was humiliating for every one concerned. However, the damage was done. It could not be reversed.

The fiasco at the Board meeting made the appointment of Joseph to the position of Assistant to the President an impossibility. However he did continue to work with the Mission for a short time, assisting the author with the development of major donor programs and banquets, and in radio broadcasts.

Memo From a Board Member

The incident with Joseph Caplan and the pressures of many unresolved philosophical issues came to a head when Mr. C. Robert Clemensen, one of the Mission's newest Board members (elected to the Board June 20, 1979), sent a memorandum to Daniel Fuchs, Chairman of the Board. It stated:

Since I am probably the youngest member of the Board of Directors, I must apologize for any presumption implied or expressed in this memorandum. However, by virtue of my training and vocation, I have become increasingly aware of what seems to be a universal deficiency in Christian organizations. This deficiency can be expressed in terms of evolution away from the spiritual inspiration that gave rise to the original organization. Perhaps this is an oversimplification, for I certainly do not believe that ABMJ is 'evolving away' from its original purpose, but since such evolution is epidemic in Christian organizations, I believe the possibility exists that certain elements of the composition known as ABMJ may not presently be where God would want them to be. The process works something like this: An organization is formed by individuals inspired by God with a sense of mission. The organization grows and develops internal paths of activity, which paths of activity often develop over time in directions offering the least resistance. In the beginning such evolutions are generally harmless since the fundamental goal of the organization is so clearly defined in the minds of its constituents, that no decision would be made counter-positional to the goal. However, as the years go by, the organization grows in sophistication. Individual circumstances arise that when taken individually do not seem inconsistent with the goals of the organization, but taken in the aggregate are in reality counter-positional.

The American Board of Missions to the Jews Inc. is entering its 88th year and can look back upon a fine history of seeking God's will and implementing programs and policies with an avowed purpose of bringing glory to God. However, this is not to say that all is well. I believe that the role of the Board of Directors of the Mission is to assess the existing policy and its relation to procedures to determine whether we still maintain our original mission.

More specifically, I view the role of the Board of Directors as follows:

1. To prayerfully consider and subsequently define the philosophy and ideology of the involvements of ABMJ.

2. To formally establish through policy, the administrative functions to carry out the goals of the Mission.

3. To assess current involvements in all areas to determine that the Mission is indeed fulfilling its mission.

Realizing that over the past several years we as a Board have been confronted with a number of financial crises, I can understand that we have been more concerned about procedure than policy. However, now that it appears that our major financial difficulties have been solved, I believe it is time for the Board of Directors to once again address those policy matters for which they have been appointed. To that end I recommend that a special Board meeting be held wherein the agenda be directed to a prayerful consideration of the fundamental mission of ABMJ. From that consideration, the Board should entertain a critical self-evaluation of current mission involvements. This would include:

a. That alternative involvements be considered.

b. That current line and staff functions be re-assessed.

c. That current fiscal policy be re-assessed.

d. That current policies regarding compensation of employees be re-assessed.

e. That current policies regarding ownership consideration and/or control of real property be re-assessed.

f. That associations with other Christian organizations be re-assessed.

g. That policies regarding 'Beginning New Works' be re-assessed.

h. That involvements in foreign countries be re-assessed.

i. That media involvement be re-assessed.

j. That current solicitations for giving be re-assessed.

> *It may well be tht [sic] as a result of such a meeting very few if any changes will be made. However, I believe it is the duty of a Board committed to following the Will of God that it continually 'Try the spirits to see whether they be of God.'[115]*

Clemensen's memorandum touched a nerve in all of the Directors. Coming from the newest Board member and a "non-employee," his report was seen as objective—not as an attempt to take sides or to polarize the Board. It verbalized the unspoken concerns that many of the Directors had, and caused them to focus on the philosophical differences that were causing division among them and within the Mission.

THE BOARD RESPONDS

A special Board meeting to consider the "Clemensen Memorandum" was called for Saturday, April 17, 1982. Members present were: Daniel Fuchs, C. Robert Clemensen, Albert Pasche, Harold Pretlove, Harold Sevener and James Straub. Members absent were: Roy Adams, John Kubach and John Melhorn.

As the Directors shared both their positive and their negative thoughts about the Mission—its programs and its purpose—they realized that their differences were not as great as they had thought; the "philosophical issues" dividing them were distressing, but not beyond finding solutions. Each Director affirmed that his primary goal in serving on the Board was to see Jewish people come to faith in the Messiah.

The meeting resulted in several important developments. First, was the determination to set forth a "Statement of Purpose" for the Mission. The Minutes state:

> *It was agreed that each individual area of the ministry should be analyzed on the basis of what is being done toward fulfilling the goal of ABMJ. This will include the examination of time and money expended.*
>
> *Mr. Sevener expressed a three-fold purpose of ABMJ:*
>
> *(1) Propagation of the Gospel (evangelism)*
>
> *(2) Discipleship*
>
> *(3) Establishment of indigenous congregations such as those established in the Mid-West Region; or the referral of believers to local churches.*
>
> *Mr. Pasche emphasized the need for church involvement in Jewish evangelism and the support of ABMJ's ministry. Also, the need for education and involvement of educators and preachers in Jewish evangelism. This would help to counteract anti-Semitism. He also felt that the image of ABMJ (who we are and what we are doing) needed to be transmitted to the churches and educators. The methods of ABMJ in raising funds should be evaluated as well.[116]*

The second development that came from the meeting was the appointment of an Ad Hoc committee. The Minutes state:

> *The Board shall as a result of this meeting appoint Ad Hoc representatives to assess the involvements of the mission, which involvements shall be identified by the President, and these Ad Hoc representatives shall be sent to the appropriate center of activity (branch, personnel, headquarters, literature, radio, foreign, stewardship, fund-raising, mergers and acquisitions) and that the Ad Hoc representative would do an analysis of that particular involvement of the mission. The Board would then receive his written and oral report, together with a written and oral report from the President or appropriate administrator, together with a written and oral report of that individual charged with that element of the outreach. The Board would seriously and prayerfully consider what has been brought up and make decisions and implementations.*
>
> *The Directors appointed to undertake the evaluation on behalf of the Board of Directors are:*
>
> *(1) C. Robert Clemensen—Southwest, Midwest, and Western Regions.*
>
> *(2) Albert Pasche—Northeast and Southeast regions.*
>
> *(3) Roy Adams—administrative staff and functions at headquarters....*
>
> *Foreign ministries will not be included in the evaluation at this time.[117]*

The primary function of the Board of any corporation is to set policy for that organization in order for it to fulfill its stated purpose; to oversee the finances, making certain that they are properly used; and to evaluate the corporation's chief executive officer. As a general rule, it is not wise for Board members to become involved with staff, programs, procedures on a local level. However, most organizations do not have three of their top executives serving on the Board.

At the time, the Chairman of the Board was an employee of the corporation. Further, the President and Executive Vice President of the corporation were both Board members. The Personnel Committee was comprised of Board member/employees only, while the Executive Committee was comprised of a majority of Board member/employees. Although there were some members of the Board who'd had reservations about these arrangements, they said nothing. The report of the Ad Hoc committee began a move by the Board to put an end to "employee control" of the Mission, establishing the Mission as a "Board controlled" organization. The Ad Hoc Committee's recommendations, as presented at the June 12, 1982 Board meeting were as follows:

1. *That the President make a personal visit to each ABMJ missionary at least once every second year....*
2. *That on an annual basis, a representative from the Board, other than salaried Directors, visit each Region for a minimum of two days and spend time with both the Regional Director and the missionaries....*
3. *That until a new Missionary Director is appointed, the President convene a meeting of the Regional Directors each spring and fall. These meetings to be used for developing and analyzing plans and policies for all Regions....*
4. *That consideration be given to arranging an ABMJ annual conference for Directors and Regional Workers....*
5. *That prompt steps be taken to improve communications between Headquarters and all staff....*
6. *That an adequate policy of remuneration be developed and implemented no later than October 1, 1982....*
7. *That a Church Relations program, similar to that developed for the Northeast Region be set up on a national basis....*
8. *That goals of the Data Processing Manager be monitored closely to ensure that proper progress is made....*
9. *That the Radio ministry be terminated....(This was amended to a six month test for a new radio program).*
10. *That the first meeting of the Regional Directors referred to above, develop an appropriate literature policy for review by the Board at at [sic] early date. This meeting should also consider setting up a training/development program that will be sufficiently 'portable' to be used in all ABMJ regions. The seminar in 'Jewish' counselling techniques should also be treated as an urgent request....*
11. *That the Board appoint a Committee to review the goals, methods, costs and all other relevant data concerning 'The Chosen People.' The Committee to bring a recommendation to the next meeting of the Board....*
The Ad Hoc Evaluation Directors (Messrs. Adams, Clemensen and Pasche) will comprise this committee. It was agreed that none of the salaried Directors should serve on this Committee investigating The Chosen People magazine costs, but the salaried Directors will be consulted by the Committee for interaction....
12. *That consideration be given to appointing a non-salaried Director to the Personnel Committee....*
13. *That the Executive Vice-President be asked to develop a supplementary set of financial statements, tied into the audited statements, that present the Mission's Operating Fund on a cost-centered basis....*
14. *That the Executive Committee meet on a regular basis and not by telephone....*
15. *That the Board consider a mission policy on fund-raising and methods of increasing revenues.*[118]

Many of the recommendations of the Ad Hoc Committee went into place immediately, some had already been put into place as a result of the Committee's visits and the knowledge of their recommendations. Still others, were to be considered at a later time. Following the involvement of the Ad Hoc Committee, the Board of the Mission became, and still is, a very active working Board on behalf of the Mission and its staff. Meetings of the Directors now last two or more days, rather than just a few hours, and in between Board sessions the various committees of the Board work on issues that need resolution.

The Ad Hoc committee's recommendation to cancel the radio was amended by the Board and allowed to continue for an additional six months in order to give Joseph Caplan an opportunity to test the new radio format. However, increasing costs of the broadcast and decreasing revenue resulted in the cancellation of the radio broadcast on June 30, 1983—six months longer than the Ad Hoc committee had recommended because the Board wanted to give it every chance to succeed.

The first Major Donor Banquet was held on April 30, 1983 in Los Angeles. Dr. Daniel Goldberg and his staff, working with Joseph Caplan, made the arrangements for this pilot program. It had been decided that if such banquets were successful in Los Angeles, they would be planned for other regions of the country. The banquet was, from all appearances, a great success. But it was "bitter sweet." The Regional Directors and the Board members knew that it would be Joseph's last banquet with the Mission. Except for the radio ministry, scheduled to end in June, it was to be his last assignment with the Mission.

Joseph was well liked by most of the Regional Directors and many of the missionaries on staff, and when he resigned the Regional Directors and some members of the administrative staff asked to meet with the Board. The Board graciously agreed, and they arranged for a special meeting with the R.D.'s and select staff members. The meeting was held on June 17, 1983 at Nyack College in Nyack, New York in conjunction with the regular Board meeting and staff retreat.

In response to questions put forth by the Regional Directors, the Board assured them that each one of their concerns had been addressed carefully and prayerfully. The Board assured the R.D.'s that a long-range plan and program affecting all of their concerns (the pension plan, salary program, etc.) would be put into place. With regard to the pension plan, the Directors told the men that action had been taken. The Minutes of the June 1982 Board meeting reflect the following recommendation made by James Straub: "...since there was an increase of income over expenses, ...ABMJ set up a formal pension fund."[119] At that time, the Board had instructed Jim to proceed with an actuarial study as the first step toward establishing this formal pension plan. At the same meeting, the author had urged the Board to grant salary increases to the missionaries and Regional Directors, suggesting that monies saved from the cancellation of the radio program or from the cuts in the Communications departments, or that the cash reserves from increased income, be used. The Board deferred increasing salaries, but did extend to each worker a bonus check of $1,000, with the promise that a new salary administration program would be put in place as a part of Ad Hoc Committee's reports and evaluations.[120]

With regard to Joseph Caplan, the R.D.'s were assured that the Board felt their decisions had been in the best interests of the Mission. They encouraged the Regional Directors to continue to give their input regarding ideas for the ministry, and even suggested policies, but with the understanding that it was the Board, as directed by the Lord, that would ultimately decide the course and direction the ministry should take.[121]

This historic meeting between the Regional Directors and the Board did much to accomplish a growing confidence in the Board. The staff realized anew that members of the Board were committed to the ministry and to the staff's well being as workers of the Mission. They also began to realize, some for the first time, the amount of time and effort members of the Board give to the Mission. The Regional men had been impressed with the concern that the Ad Hoc Committee members demonstrated when they visited in their regions. While a number of issues about the vision and direction of the ministry still needed to be resolved, the work of the Ad Hoc Committee, and this meeting, was a giant step forward.

The Regional Directors who attended the historic meeting with the Board were John Bell, Rocky Freeman, Daniel Goldberg, Larry Jaffrey, Sam Nadler, and David Sedaca. Of these, only Larry Jaffrey was a part of the original team of Regional Directors.

THE WESTERN REGION UNDER DANIEL GOLDBERG

Dr. Daniel Goldberg was originally hired as a part-time field evangelist for the Mid-west. He worked for the Mission in this capacity for a number of years, but then returned to a full-time teaching position. In 1979, when Richard Cohen (one of the original team of R.D.'s) was transferred to New York, Daniel Goldberg was re-hired by the Mission as the Regional Director for the western states. As such, he had the oversight of a large staff of salaried and volunteer workers and the responsibility of raising support for the continuation and expansion of the missionary outreach in his region.

In developing his region, Daniel Goldberg spent much of his time speaking in churches, conferences, Bible colleges and seminaries. He is an excellent speaker and the contacts he made gained support for his region which, in turn, enabled the missionary work of the region to expand.

At the time of his appointment as Regional Director, the staff of the Western Region included: Irv and Cordelia Rifkin, missionaries in San Diego; Sid Stern in Phoenix, Arizona; Bill Katin, Fred Emery, Mr. & Mrs. Wilbur Freeman, Louis Lapides, Robert & Althea Miller, Ted Paul, and Ruth Wardell in Los Angeles; Donna Jean Wood, musical concert singer for the Mission in Beverly Hills; Jerome and Mildred Fleischer in San Francisco. Mr. Barry Wilson in Seattle, Washington; Eliezer and Sarah Urbach in Denver, Colorado. In addition, volunteer branches had been set up in a number of places including: Albuquerque, New Mexico under the leadership of Gilda Steinhouse; Palm Springs, California under Mr. M. Gale Beals; Portland, Oregon under Mrs. Bea Watson; Sacramento, California with Mr. S. J. Garst; San Gabriel Valley, California under Miss Sandra Wingate and Mrs. Sarah Garrison; and Santa Barbara, California under Mrs. Dorothy Wilkerson.

Daniel's wife, Madeline, was also a veteran missionary to the Jews; she had worked with several Jewish missions prior to joining the staff of the American Board of Missions to the Jews. Madeline Goldberg carried out an active outreach ministry in the San Fernando Valley until her retirement in 1990. Through her patient and loving witness many Jewish people came to faith in Jesus. Others were discipled and grew in their faith under her faithful teaching.

Eliezer and Sarah Urbach had been transferred to Denver, Colorado shortly after Terryl Delaney's move to the Philadelphia area.

Eliezer Urbach

Eliezer was born in 1921 in Skoczow, Poland. He was a teenager when the Nazis invaded his native land, and disrupted his once-peaceful religious Jewish home. Before being sent to Auschwitz, where they eventually perished, Eliezer's parents tearfully sent him away. Their hope was that at least one member of their family would survive to tell the world of the horrible atrocities that had befallen the Jews of Poland.

Forever etched in Eliezer's memory is the picture of his father, standing erect like an old soldier, fearing that he would break under the emotional strain of sending his eldest son away to an unknown fate.

His father's hand tightly gripped the hand of Eliezer's mother; her face and eyes were glistening with tears as she quietly wept for the son she knew she would never see again. Standing next to Eliezer's mother was Ernest, his younger brother—a boy who never knew the joys of manhood, for his young life was cruelly cut off by Hitler's "final solution."

The family recited the "Aaronic Benediction" together, and afterwards Eliezer left, knowing he would never again feel the warmth and love of his family. He was right. Each perished, as Hitler sought to rid Europe of the Jewish people.

Eliezer spent the next six years of his life running and hiding. It was only the grace of God that kept him as he sought to evade the military powers.

In 1940 Eliezer escaped into Russia, only to be caught and deported to a Siberian labor camp. When he was freed in 1941, he was gaunt from hunger and overrun with lice. Because he had no travel or work papers, he was unable to find work or a place to live. "Perhaps," he thought, "I can seek asylum in Afghanistan." But in his attempt to reach the border he was caught by a Russian patrol and sent back to prison.

Eliezer later recalled that many of the prisoners died of typhus, scurvy, dysentery, and diarrhea. Because the camp was devoid of effective medicines—there were no antibiotics, nor did they have any opiates to kill pain—and likewise had no fresh vegetables or fruits to prevent diet deficiency diseases, it was not uncommon for prisoners to lose all of their teeth, or to develop ulcers. Life was unbearable, and Eliezer knew that unless he was soon released, or unless he escaped, there would be no hope for his survival.

Because of his rapidly deteriorating condition, Eliezer was admitted to the infirmary for 10 days of rest—and regular meals. The infirmary would have been a welcome change had it not been for the fact that over-crowded conditions often required that two men share one bed.

One night a sickly old man was dropped into Eliezer's bed. The man was delirious, and in his delirium he threw himself on top of Eliezer. Throughout the night, Eliezer had to push the old man's body off of him. When morning came, to his horror, Eliezer found that the man had died during the night.

Prior to the War, Eliezer had never really taken his Orthodox Judaism seriously, but prison, the daily sights of his people being tortured, and the reality and finality of death caused him to recall some of the prayers and ceremonies which he and his family had known. In his desperation, he knew he needed God and for the first time in his life, Eliezer made a conscious decision to pray. He still remembers his prayer:

> *God of my father and my mother, forgive me if it was my fault that Ernest (Eliezer's brother) died. Maybe I did wrong to try to cross that border. If we hadn't tried to do that, maybe Ernest would not have died in prison. I feel responsible, but I don't know what to do about it now. If I am to die also, please, God, let me die a free man, and not in this filthy prison. There will be no one here even to close my eyes. Oh, God, I don't know what to do.*[122]

It was several years before Eliezer realized that God had answered his prayer.

Even when he was finally released from prison, Eliezer was still not free. He was haunted by memories, by the furtive lifestyle he had been forced to live as he sought to stay one step ahead of his captors.

Searching for peace, Eliezer's quest took him throughout Europe, and finally to Israel. In Israel, he met, and later married, Sarah Leiner. Sarah, too, was from a family of Polish Jewish immigrants. The two were wed on January 28, 1947.

Even in marriage peace was elusive to Eliezer. There was certainly no peace around him. Israel was engaged in the War of Independence, and Eliezer was called to arms. After the war peace continued to elude him. Without work, and with a family to support, he began to think about immigrating to Brazil where one of his uncles had offered him a job.

In 1954, Eliezer, Sarah and their two children said tearful farewells to Sarah's parents before they boarded the train to Haifa. From Haifa, a ship would take them to Brazil. They did not know that God would use this voyage to Brazil as the catalyst to bring faith and peace to their hearts.

Struggling to find work in Brazil, and to care for his family, Eliezer made friends with Laerte Modolo. It didn't take Eliezer long to recognize that Laerte had something in his life that brought him joy, peace and happiness. When Laerte invited Eliezer to attend a church service with him, Eliezer agreed to go.

Eliezer found the people at the Presbyterian church to be very friendly and open. They even provided him with a

Bible. Their love and genuine faith impressed Eliezer. They were so different from the "Gentiles" he had fled from in Russia and Poland. They talked and prayed as if they really knew God.

During the third meeting he attended, one of the church members asked Eliezer if he believed in God. "Yes," he answered. It was a truthful answer. From the time he had prayed in prison, Eliezer had been convinced that God was real—but he did not know Him. His friend then asked, "Do you believe in Jesus Christ?" Eliezer was not prepared for that question. He was Jewish. He knew the people in the congregation did not know that he was Jewish—nor would that have made any difference to them. Their only concern was that Eliezer be saved.

Sensing the man's genuine concern for him, Eliezer searched his heart. In that moment, he knew he did believe that Jesus is the Messiah. From that night until now, Eliezer Urbach has openly confessed his faith in Jesus. As he lovingly shared his faith with his wife, Sarah, she also began attending the church. Sarah, too, accepted Jesus.

Shortly after their confessions of faith, Eliezer and Sarah and their children returned to Israel. God was completing Eliezer's odyssey. In Haifa, Eliezer met Solomon Ostrovsky—a Brethren missionary. The Ostrovsky family took the Urbachs under their wings and discipled them. Solomon Ostrovsky baptized Eliezer in the Sea of Jaffa in 1957.

As Eliezer and Sarah grew in faith, they began to recognize God's call upon them to bring the gospel to the Jewish people. When an opportunity came for missionary service with Chosen People Ministries, Eliezer applied. His quest was over. He had found peace and joy. Eliezer and Sarah served with Chosen People Ministries until their retirement in 1991.

Two young Jewish believers who were hired during the late 1970's and early 1980's to do campus ministry in the Los Angeles area were Louis Lapides and Bill Katin.

LOUIS LAPIDES

Louis Lapides was born on March 27, 1947 in Newark, New Jersey. His was an "ultra-conservative" Jewish home. Like other young Jewish boys, Louis spent six years in Hebrew school in preparation for his Bar Mitzvah. Even as a youth, he questioned his relationship with God. He knew he daily failed to keep God's Laws; he also knew he could never find forgiveness according to the Levitical ordinances of sacrifices. He loved the Jewish customs and traditions, but he longed to know God in a personal way. In sharing his testimony, Louis wrote:

> ...Somehow I identified the rabbi with God, to such an extent, that I always desired to kiss him, so I could kiss God.
>
> Not only did I love God, but I had a tremendous sense of fear and an attitude of awe towards Him. I even felt compelled to hide my eyes when the Ark containing the Torah scrolls was opened, because God's glory and holiness seemed to be revealed.
>
> One time I wanted to practice my Bar Mitzvah speech in the main sanctuary of the temple. I was all alone when I noticed a button on the floor. Being a curious twelve year old, I stepped on it. Much to my surprise, the doors of the Ark began to open. I felt like Moses standing before the burning bush. I was afraid God would 'sizzle' me right there on the spot.
>
> On the day of my Bar Mitzvah the Rabbi asked me if I would like to continue my relationship with God and my training in Judaism. Since I was standing in front of my family and relatives on that memorable day, I knew I had to give the right answer. YES! But if I had been more honest, I would have told my rabbi I couldn't give my life to a God I didn't really know.
>
> I didn't think I could know a holy God personally as long as I couldn't meet His demands, described in the Bible. Who was I to change the Word of God? Yet my Jewish training taught me that the way to God was through prayer, charity and good deeds. This seemed inconsistent with what the Scriptures taught and, thus, led me to disbelieve the reality of God and the tenets of Judaism. I realized, no matter how many times I kissed my rabbi, I still could not get any closer to God.[123]

The years passed, during which time Louis spent two years in the United States Army. Of that time he stated:

> ...I was trained as a Marine engineer to work on Army amphibious craft and small boats. When I was ordered to go to Vietnam I wasn't too worried. I knew my job did not call for any combat duty.
>
> I took it very lightly that I was to spend one year in a war zone, until I landed in Saigon. While still on the plane I noticed flashes of light below me. Inquiring about it from one of the other men I was told it was only heat lightning. I thought to myself, 'Since when does lightning come from the ground?' The flashes were actually bombs going off. Suddenly I realized that God just might come in handy during the next year.
>
> To cope with the suffering and death all around me I started smoking pot. This was simply a way to escape the reality of war and the dreariness of army life.[124]

After his discharge from the Army, Louis decided to move to Southern California. He landed a job working as a camera man in a graphic arts studio; he also studied at the Los Angeles Art Center College of Design. He later wrote:

Southern California, with its melting-pot of religions and 'way-out' life style, provided fertile ground for a confused Jewish kid.... Los Angeles also exposed me to seance meetings, Satan worship, religious chanting and Scientology.

No matter how involved I became in these pagan religions I continued to be aware of the great differences between their gods and my Jewish God. Because of my Jewish roots and studies as a child I knew that something just wasn't kosher about these religions.

The more I searched for God, the more it seemed I could not find Him. Out of desperation and frustration I concluded, that if I could not find God outside of myself, I must be God. Taking hallucinogenic drugs made this very easy to believe.

Thinking I was God I believed I could perform miracles such as walking on water. After reading some mystical books about Jesus I was convinced that, as God, I should even be able to resurrect myself.

In my mind these were sound assumptions, until I was challenged to demonstrate my 'divine powers.' I was approached [c. August 1969] by Rev. Barry Wood, who at that time had a ministry on Sunset Strip. [Rev. Wood was also the pastor of the First Baptist Church of Beverly Hills.] As we were sharing ideas someone said, 'If you are God, create a rock.' I hallucinated a rock in my hand, but nobody else could see it. Then I was told, 'When God performs a miracle, everyone can verify it.' I realized I was a very small god. Besides, whoever heard of a god who took drugs?

My ideas of self-exaltation were completely shot down and this opened the door for Barry to share his faith with me. First, he asked me if I had ever read the Bible. I told him I had studied the five Books of Moses as a child. Then he proceeded to show some of the prophetic Scriptures to me. Initially, I was quite upset. 'What was this gentile doing with my Jewish Bible?'

He explained to me that he believed Jesus is the Jewish Messiah solely on the basis of the Jewish Scriptures. I was shocked!! This was the first time that I had encountered a true representation of the claims of Jesus. I stood waiting for the 42nd Street 'Hell-fire and brimstone' message, but it never came. Instead, his manner and conversation flowed with love and concern.

I was once again prompted to investigate my Jewish Scriptures, but I would not read that 'skinny gentile book' known as the New Testament. I only wanted to know what the God of Abraham, Isaac and Jacob had to say about Jesus.

During the following four months I read the Bible from Genesis to Malachi without any outside influence or guidance except that of God Himself.

The passage which was most striking to me was Deut. 18:15, where Moses says to the children of Israel, 'The Lord your God will raise up for you a prophet like me from among you from your countrymen; You shall listen to him.' Which prophet could have been greater than Moses? It seemed reasonable to me that only Jesus could be this one. The Holy Spirit continued to confirm in my heart, through Psalm 22 and Isaiah 52, that Jesus is my Messiah.

God taught me that the core of my problem is my own human nature and that righteousness could only be found in Him. I recognized that all the meditation, discipline, study and self-will could not make me right before God. But the work of the Messiah Jesus in His sacrificial death, broke the power of sin over my life and accomplished what I never could.

He alone met all the requirements of the Levitical Law which demanded a blood atonement for the forgiveness of sin. I knew all these things in my head, but I needed to have it in my heart.

God began speaking to me bringing me to the realization that He was a real, objective, living Person who was not a product of my imagination or of drugs. When I was at this point I literally saw my whole life pass before me. Everything that I had read about God or Jesus in the Bible came upon me at once. I could not do anything but think about God.

In the face of God's grace I said to God, 'I don't understand everything you want me to know, but whatever you want me to believe about Jesus, I do. You have shown me that Jesus is Your Son and the Messiah of Israel, and that's enough for me.'

After I prayed to God I wanted to ask Him one small favor. 'God, I will never ask you for anything again, but please answer this one prayer. You know that I have been...wishing for the girl of my dreams. Send me the girl with the rock.'

The significance of the rock was related to my search for God. Since one of those I had met on Sunset Strip had asked me to create a rock, the rock had become for me symbolic of God, His power, His miracles, and everything about Him. And the girl of my dreams would have the Rock.

Even before my search began the concept of God being the Rock was prominent in my thinking. I even went to a Buddhist chanting meeting, where they claimed they have the power to chant for anything, and asked them to chant for the Rock.

In the next few weeks after my prayer to God I noticed a definite change in my heart. I had no psychological need for drugs. My thoughts were different. I had a joy that had not been there before. I had a great desire to share my experience with God with my co-workers at the photographic studio.

One day on my lunch break I decided to eat at a nearby restaurant. I noticed a girl who looked quite familiar to me. She greeted me and reminded me that we had met at a party. She told me her name was Deborah. When I went back to work I couldn't get her out of my mind. So I wrote a letter to a friend asking what she knew about Deborah. She replied that Deborah was a Jew who believed in Jesus. That was enough for me!

Strangely enough, it worked out that Deborah and I were both invited to the same party soon after my discovery. Deborah needed a ride so naturally I volunteered. She knew nothing about me, nor about my experience with the Lord. After the party as I drove her home she pulled out a New Testament. She said that she wanted my opinion on some passages: she read from the 'love chapter,' 1 Corinthians 13.

After listening I asked her, 'How can you have this kind of love?' She casually answered, 'If you have the Rock you can have this kind of love.' As our friendship developed I discovered that Deborah had never referred to Jesus in that way before. It should be no surprise that we were married a year later![125]

Shortly after Louis' marriage to Deborah, the author received a telephone call from Louis' brother-in-law, Bob Friedman. Bob's wife, Anita, was Deborah's sister. (The story of Bob and Anita Friedman's involvement with the Mission was mentioned earlier in this chapter.) The author, who was serving as Western District Director and Missionary in Charge of the Los Angeles ministry at the time, knew Bob, Anita, and Deborah through their attendance at the Mission's meetings from time to time. As the telephone conversation progressed, Bob revealed that Louis felt God was calling him into full-time ministry; he wanted the author to meet with Louis to discuss the Mission's student aid program.

With the Mission's financial assistance, Louis attended Dallas Bible College. He also worked part-time for the Mission at the Dallas branch during that time. Following his graduation from Dallas Bible College, Louis and Deborah returned to Los Angeles and Louis enrolled as a student at Talbot Theological Seminary. He also continued to serve on the Mission's staff; for a short period of time he served as Missionary in Charge of the Los Angeles ministry. However, the ministry in Los Angeles began to take a different direction under Daniel Goldberg's leadership, and Louis wanted to pursue further education at Talbot. He therefore resigned from the Mission on July 31, 1980.

Louis remained in Jewish ministry. He served as a missionary on the staff of Ariel Ministries in Los Angeles and subsequently founded Beth Ariel Fellowship in West Los Angeles. Beth Ariel Fellowship is now an independent Messianic congregation and Louis continues to serve as its pastor.

BILL KATIN

The other worker hired for campus ministry was William (Bill) Katin. Bill was born in Chelsea, Massachusetts on January 29, 1952. His father had made his career in the United States Army; Bill's childhood was therefore spent shuttling between New England and Berlin, Germany. Although his father was Jewish (the family included several famous rabbis who were uncles and cousins), Bill did not grow up in a religious home. Instead, "education" and "knowledge" were touted as the supreme gift Judaism had to offer. At an early age he discovered that his scholastic interests were in the areas of music, math and science and he was determined to excel in those areas as a way of demonstrating his "Jewishness."

Bill first heard about Jesus from his classmates in school. At home he asked his mother if Jesus was Israel's Messiah; her response was brief and to the point—"No." This answer satisfied him until he reached his junior year of high school, when a Christian girl named Sharon struck up a conversation with him. Sharon was a "mere" sophomore, but she was attractive and Bill thought he'd like to get to know her better. Some time later he summoned up the courage to ask Sharon for a date; she responded by informing him that she only dated Christian boys. Bill was stunned! Since he'd had no religious training, he'd always thought that being moral made a person a "Christian"; by his definition, he *was* a Christian. But his definition did not satisfy Sharon. Bill therefore decided to look up the definition of "Christian" in the dictionary. To his dismay, he learned that a Christian was defined as "a follower of Jesus." Bill knew he wasn't a follower of Jesus. As a matter of fact, he'd developed a hatred of Jesus, based on what he'd read and heard about the hatred and persecution of the Jewish people—all done in the name of Jesus.

Bill knew he could not call himself a Christian, yet he knew his "Christian" friends were somehow different from the "followers of Jesus" whose persecution of the Jews had left such a wake of destruction and sorrow. He decided he should find out what his "Christian" friends really believed.

For the next year, during his lunch break, Bill met with Sharon and other Christian friends to study the Bible and to talk about Jesus. During that year he also learned (to his great surprise) that his physics teacher, whom he greatly admired, was a Christian.

The longer Bill studied with Sharon and his other Christian friends, the more convinced he was that the Scriptures were true. More than once tears stung his eyes as Sharon explained truths about the promised Messiah of Israel, and told him of the peace and forgiveness Yeshua offered to all who put their faith in Him. He knew Sharon was telling him the truth, but his pride would not let him admit it—until the Spring of 1968 when, one evening, the conviction of the Holy Spirit broke through his defenses and in desperation Bill called Sharon, asking her how to invite Jesus into his heart.

Bill's life changed after he accepted Jesus. The fears and worries that had plagued him before, disappeared. In their place, he discovered the peace that Sharon had told Him Yeshua would give.

After graduating from Yucaipa high school in 1969, with a California State Scholarship (a music scholarship), and a Bank of America achievement award in the field of fine arts, Bill enrolled at the University of California in Los Angeles (UCLA). He wanted to pursue a career in physics.

When he enrolled at UCLA, Bill didn't know that the student body was forty to sixty percent Jewish. He made that discovery after being on campus for a while, and after volunteering to work on campus with Campus Crusade For Christ. As he shared his testimony and the Scriptures with students on campus, Bill began to experience a growing burden for the Jewish students on campus. He made his concern a matter of prayer, and God answered his prayers by arranging circumstances so that he was brought into contact with Douglas and Paula Pyle, workers on staff with the Mission who had just established a Messianic ministry at UCLA.

Bill Katin and Doug Pyle became immediate friends. Through Doug, Bill became interested in the work of the Mission; he joined the Mission's staff as a part-time student worker in January 1972.

After Bill's graduation from UCLA in 1973, he enrolled in Talbot Theological Seminary; he graduated from Talbot with a Master of Divinity degree in 1976. He then enrolled in a Ph.d. program with specialization in the Dead Sea Scrolls at the Claremont Graduate School. Bill's continuing studies and scholastic achievements have served to open doors of witness to many Jewish students on the campuses where he has studied. He continued to work for the Mission in Los Angeles through the mid-1980's, when God led him to apply for a teaching and administration position with the Christian school system. His career has led him to schools in Europe and America. Wherever God leads him, Bill Katin's life and testimony proclaim Yeshua as Messiah and Lord.

One faithful campus worker, Mr. Curly Dalke, was not "officially" on staff; he maintained a "liaison-support" raised position with the Mission.

CURLY DALKE

Curly Dalke is a Gentile believer who has a great love for the Jewish people. He faithfully and fearlessly served as a "campus representative" for the Mission for a number of years. During the summer of 1985, Curly attended the Mission's S.T.E.P. program. At the time, he was twenty-six years of age. In a report that shared something about each participant in the S.T.E.P. program, the following information was included about Curly Dalke:

> According to the doctors, Curly is well beyond his life expectancy. Curly suffers from neurofibromatosis (the elephant Man's disease), and tumors riddle his body. This degenerative illness has already claimed the life of Curly's father. But Curly wanted to be a missionary to the Jewish people. Ask Curly (or anyone on the STEP team), and they will tell you that STEP has been the thrill of Curly's life. On the college campuses where he ministers as a volunteer for ABMJ/ Chosen People Ministries, Curly has 'won the right' to share the Gospel with many Jewish professors.[126]

Curly shared one incident when he was told he had no right to share his faith. He wrote:

> 'What gives you the right to be here? I don't think they should allow groups like yours to be on campus at all!' Before I could say a word, the angry young man who stood in front of my literature table at California State University at Fullerton turned on his heel and stomped away.
>
> I don't think I'll ever get used to that kind of anger, but I've learned that it presents a wonderful opportunity to pray. So that's just what I did for this disgruntled student. Even still, I realized it would take a miracle just to get him to stop and listen to me.
>
> A week later I'd all but forgotten him as I walked into the classroom of a Jewish professor to hear his evening lecture. The professor knew of my beliefs and was aware of my involvement with campus evangelism, but he still extended a friendly invitation to visit his class. On this particular evening, I decided to take him up on his invitation.
>
> During the break, I went up to say hello to the professor and was greeted warmly as he gave me a big hug and asked about my mother. We talked for a few minutes, and then he turned aside and introduced me to a student who was standing nearby, Avner. Avner was silent for a few seconds. 'We've met,' he finally said.

When the professor walked away, Avner turned to me and said, 'I'm really sorry for the way I acted at your table.' I couldn't believe it! It was the same angry student who wanted me kicked off campus. He seemed a little bit puzzled at his teacher's response to me and a little embarrassed over our past encounter.

After that night, Avner and I got together again. Since he made rings, he even offered to fix my broken ring. Little by little a friendship and a mutual respect began to grow between us. We have even been able to discuss spiritual matters and our views of life.

On one occasion I was invited to go on a field trip with Avner's class, and (as God would work it!) I drove to the site with Avner and the professor.

There is no doubt in my mind that God is working in both their lives. I'm asking our Chosen People family to join me in praying for their salvation. Yes, it would take a miracle for either of them to come to faith. But as I think of the angry young man who has become my friend, I remember that miracles can happen.[127]

Curly continued to serve on the Mission's staff through the mid-1990's, when he felt led of the Lord to continue his ministry on the campuses through the Bethel European Mission in Santa Barbara, California.

As the campus ministry was being developed in Los Angeles, a music and concert ministry was being developed by Donna Jean Wood. Donna Jean was never hired as a missionary, but she was employed by the Mission to present Messianic Jewish concerts in churches, Mission meetings, conferences, etc. throughout the United States and Canada.

DONNA JEAN WOOD

Donna Jean began her music ministry with the Mission during the mid-1970's. Her concerts opened opportunities for her to share her testimony and to encourage her audience to a deeper commitment to studying God's Word and living by its principles. In time she began to receive invitations to present a combined program of music and teaching seminars among women's groups. She faithfully carried on her concert/teaching ministry on behalf of the Mission and other Christian groups through the mid-1980's.

In sharing the story of Donna Jean's testimony and ministry, readers of *The Chosen People* magazine were told:

The life of Donna Jean Wood reads like the story of a Jewish Cinderella. She's attractive, she's talented, she has a lovely family, she lives in Beverly Hills, California, and she's married to the city's [Beverly Hills] handsome fire marshall [George Wood].

Now, that city of the rich and the famous has honored her by recently setting aside a day and calling it, 'The Donna Jean Wood Day' [January 28, 1980].[128]

But life wasn't always so beautiful for Donna Jean. She grew up in the midwest and moved to California at the age of seventeen when her parents were divorced.

It was especially painful for her to leave her father behind in Ohio even though she would be living closer to her mother's relatives. Her life was further complicated by the fact that both she and her mother had become believers in Jesus which was something her Jewish relatives could not understand or accept.

From all outward appearances, Donna Jean was destined to live a dull and dreary life in the shadow of her more affluent and influential relatives. But God had given her two gifts that she began to develop to His glory. First, He had put deep inside her spirit a bright and bubbly personality. And, He had also given her a strikingly beautiful voice.

By the time Donna Jean was twenty-four, she had been invited to sing on the Lawrence Welk Show and she had performed for the Los Angeles Civic Light Opera. As opportunities began to unfold, her concern turned to how she could use her talents for Jesus.

Donna sought the advice of a couple of well-known Christian performers about her developing career. They counselled her to take the secular road to success and fame. They urged her to begin accepting engagements at the nationally famous night clubs in Las Vegas. For weeks, Donna struggled with their suggestions. Deep down in her heart she knew, from a worldly point of view, their advice was probably right. Sadly, if she was to ever win the love and acclaim of the Christian community, she would probably have to first win the applause and approval of the world.

Fortunately, the young singer listened with her heart as well as with her ears. She heard the Holy Spirit reminding her that Satan sometimes uses godly people to give ungodly advice. Then He whispered to her, 'Follow Me, I have a better plan and purpose for your life....'

...Donna Jean soon learned the secret of our Lord's words in John 12:24, 'Except a grain of wheat fall into the ground and die, it abideth alone; but if it die, it bringeth forth much fruit.' She knew the spotlight had to be turned away from her and on to Jesus. So she set aside her own dreams and desires and began serving God.

Everywhere she goes people hear about Jesus. On a recent trip to New York, Donna Jean visited the United

Nations building with her daughter. As the tour ended, the guide turned to the mother and daughter and exclaimed, 'Thank you for showing me such love today.' Before they left the building, they were able to share the secret of their love with this young Jewish girl. She didn't accept the Prince of Peace that day ...But she confessed, as they departed, 'I really want what you have.' Donna Jean is still sharing the love of Christ with her through the mail....

Now, Donna Jean ministers to thousands of women across America, in conferences and retreats, as a popular speaker. Recently, over 1,000 people enjoyed her ministry at a statewide conference for women of Florida.

In the eyes of the natural man, it seemed for a time as though God had made Donna Jean one of the nobodies of this world, only to make her an ambassador from the courts of heaven.... He has shown the world through her life how He can use a yielded and ordinary vessel to attract people to His Son. And just as He said would happen, the world eventually honored that ordinary vessel.

...even in a sophisticated and affluent city like Beverly Hills.[129]

God used the gifts and abilities He'd given to Donna Jean Wood to open many doors of opportunity for the Mission, and to lead many Jewish and Gentile people to a saving knowledge of Himself. In retirement, Donna Jean and George Wood are still actively serving the Lord.

SIDNEY STERN

Mr. Sidney Stern was another worker who was serving on the Mission's staff as a full-time missionary at the time of Daniel Goldberg's appointment as Regional Director for the western states. As Daniel worked to expand the ministry in Los Angeles, a number of new missionary workers were added to his staff. He also transferred workers from other locations to Southern California to assist in opening outreach ministries in strategic locations throughout the Los Angeles basin. This was the case with Mr. Sidney Stern, who was transferred from Phoenix, Arizona to Los Angeles.

Prior to his retirement, "Sid" Stern held a position with the government; he was a photo engineer who helped to analyze high speed film tests for nuclear testing. When he retired, he moved to Phoenix, Arizona. It was in Phoenix that his affiliation with the Mission began.

In sharing the story of how God broke through his defenses and proved to him that Jesus, His Son, is the promised Messiah, Sid wrote:

There wasn't any need for religion in my nicely ordered life. After all, I had a beautiful home, a good career, a wonderful wife, two children of whom I was immensely proud, two cars and a great set of golf clubs.

And so, when my fourteen-year-old daughter, Sheryl, announced, 'Dad, Jesus is the Messiah, and you should believe in Him,' I just said, 'Forget it. Jews don't believe in Jesus.'

I know a lot of Jewish fathers might have been angry. But, after all, I was an engineer at Los Alamos, New Mexico, one of the chosen few selected to work on 'The Hill.' I was too intelligent to be angry over something as simple as God, and after all, I had long since left the Orthodox training of my family far behind.

I had raised my children to be independent, thoughtful and to learn by challenging their curiosity.

So naturally I just brushed off her news, until one day, after I made some crack about her activities, Sheryl asked, 'Can you prove Jesus isn't the Messiah?'

To an engineer, 'prove it' is a challenge that cannot be ignored!

Could I prove it? You bet I could! I marched to the bookshelves and resolutely removed a yellowed and stiff-paged Bible that had been a Bar Mitzvah gift thirty-seven years before.

I perched on a nearby chair, opened the book and full expected to turn right to a passage that said, 'Jews do not believe in the Gentile God,' or at least one that said, 'When the real Messiah comes there will be absolute peace on earth.' Then I could say with absolute certainty, 'See, I told you, Jesus isn't the Messiah.'

Funny, I was so sure it would be there, but it wasn't. Instead, as I read the Bible, I realized this was the Word of a Supreme Being. Every night for the next year I read that Bible. Despite my resolve to disprove Christianity, eventually I had to face the fact that God had something specific to say about the Messiah.

I came to the point where, if I didn't have a golf game and Sheryl pleaded hard enough, I attended church on Sunday mornings. When the pastor suggested I read the New Testament, I said, 'I might do that,' but I thought, 'I'll never do that.'

Then one night something changed. During my Bible reading I read the following: 'Behold, the days come, saith the Lord, that I will make a new covenant with the house of Israel, and with the house of Judah: Not according to the covenant that I made with their fathers in the day that I took them by the hand to bring them out of the land of Egypt; which covenant they broke, although I was a lord over them, saith the Lord: But this shall be the covenant that I will make with the house of Israel; After those days, saith the Lord, I will put my law in their inward parts, and write it in their hearts; and will be their God, and they shall be my people.' (Jeremiah 31:30-32)

'A new covenant,' I thought. 'I wonder what that means?' I went in and got Sheryl's Bible. It was a New Testament. That entire night I sat with 'that book' on my lap. Unopened.

I knew I was being irrational and foolish. Yet long-forgotten scenes flashed before me. I was eight years old again, and a stocky Gentile boy was pummeling me, screaming, 'Christ killer!' I thought of all 'they' had done to 'us.' And the New Testament remained unopened.

By the next night, I felt that I had to look at this book. After all, what could it hurt? It didn't take me very long to discover that the New Testament was a very Jewish book written by Jews to Jews about the Jewish Messiah.

I saw that it spoke of the Messiah, and I realized that Jesus was, indeed, an incredible Person. But was He God? To believe that was so, well, so Gentile.

While all this was going on at home, my career was going exceptionally well. I had been offered a terrific job, mine on the condition I pass a rigorous physical exam. Right before I had to go for the physical, I contracted a very painful case of hemorrhoids.

I found myself praying my first real prayer, 'God, if You are real, and if Jesus is the Messiah, and if You can remove this pain, then I will accept Jesus and live for Him.'

The day of the physical, I woke up without pain. Completely forgetting my prayer, I went to the doctor and passed the exam with flying colors. In taking my medical history after the exam, the doctor said a strange thing, 'I can see that you never had hemorrhoids and probably never will.'

On the way home, driving up the lonely mountain road to Los Alamos, I remembered my prayer. I pulled to the side and without a person or a car in sight, I prayed my second real prayer. 'Thank You, God, for showing me You are real.'

I knew, sure in my heart, that all I had read in the Bible and seen in my life was real.

'Thank You for loving me and sending Your Messiah to die for the sins that separated me from You. Please come into my life and give me Your life.'

The search was over. The proof was in. But for me, that was when things were just beginning.[130]

As Sid grew in his faith and understanding of the Scriptures, God burdened him to begin sharing the Gospel with his Jewish friends and neighbors. When he retired from his position with the government, he was able to give more of his time to Jewish evangelism. He eventually became a volunteer worker for the Mission. In 1979 he enrolled in the Mission's training program, and upon completion of the program he returned to Phoenix where he served as a full-time missionary until he was transferred to Southern California to open a new outreach in the Los Angeles area. Sid retired from active missionary service in December 1990, but he remains active in his witness and testimony for His Savior and Lord, Yeshua.

WILBUR AND EDITH FREEMAN

Wilbur and Edith Freeman joined the Los Angeles staff in July 1977. Edith was raised in a Jewish home; Wilbur (Bill) was raised in a Gentile home.

In sharing her testimony with readers of *The Chosen People* magazine, Edith wrote:

I was brought up in an Orthodox home in Brooklyn, New York. My mother and grandmother taught me Hebrew prayers, to light candles, to speak Yiddish and to keep a kosher home; but I never knew God loved me nor had I heard about the Messiah. At age twenty I left Brooklyn and moved to Los Angeles and got away from my religious upbringing. I read an ad about the Sunday School for interfaith families and began attending.

It was there my Scriptures began to have meaning to me and give me pride in being Jewish. I was invited to a monthly Hebrew Christian meeting held at First Baptist Church of Van Nuys and met Jewish believers for the first time. The speaker said, 'I was born a Jew. I will die a Jew but more than that, I am a completed Jew.' He gave his testimony and this was the first time I had ever heard anything like this.

I continued attending the Sunday School weekly and God began to show me that I was a sinner in need of an atonement. I became angry and tried to justify my life but more and more became convicted of my sins. After nine months of searching I accepted the prophecies of the coming of the Messiah as fulfilled in Jesus and asked Him to forgive my sins and take over my life. That was seventeen years ago [c. 1960] and I love Jesus more and more and have a deep love and concern for my people Israel.[131]

Bill shared his testimony with readers of the magazine too. He wrote:

I am the gentile in our marriage but praise God, His only begotten Son Jesus included me when He died for lost sinners. I never remember hearing the gospel message in church where I grew up in Kansas. From 1940 when I graduated from high school and moved to California, to 1957 I wasn't in any church more than a handful of times. In November 1957 a Christian lady I was interested in witnessed to me. As a banking officer I tried to convince myself I was a good respectable person.

In a way I led two lives. I worked during the week and on weekends was a tennis bum and out on the town. Often I would hear myself thinking 'there must be a better life than this.' I attended my friend's church just to please her. As the months rolled by the powerful Word of God began to penetrate my mind and heart and on April 6, 1958 I surrendered my life to Jesus.[132]

Because of their consistent and loving witness, Bill and Edith were used of the Lord to lead many Jewish people to the Lord. They remained active members of the Mission's staff until December 1987 when they retired from full-time missionary service.

New workers, Fred and Linda Emery, Mrs. Trudy (nee: Simons) Sherbourne, Barry and Joyce Wilson (Seattle area) and Karl Thames, were recruited and hired to assist with the expansion of the western region, but they only remained on staff for a short time.

ARTIS CLOTFELTER

New "volunteer workers" were also recruited; among them was Mrs. Artis Clotfelter, who joined the Mission's staff as a "volunteer missionary" in the early 1980's. Through her dynamic witness to Jewish people, and her persistent encouragement to Christians and pastors to witness to the Jewish people of their community (Sacramento, California), a growing branch of the Mission was established. Artis enrolled in the Sacramento Bible Institute, and the Mission subsequently hired her as a part-time missionary. In sharing her testimony with readers of *The Chosen People* magazine, Artis wrote:

I always felt different from the other kids.

An ugly duckling, I was too tall, always awkward and no matter what mother did with my thick black hair it stuck straight out. Even during those Depression years most kids had mothers who stayed at home and cooked. My mom was divorced and worked to support her invalid parents and me.

I always suspected the divorce was my fault. If only I'd been prettier, not quite so odd, my parents would have stayed together.

I felt different in other ways too. We lived in a predominantly Catholic neighborhood so my two best friends were Catholics. One time, stepping into their European style cathedral, I was reminded how different it was to be Jewish.

Just inside the door stood a mammoth statue of Jesus on the cross. It must have been 10 or 15 feet high. Worshippers would climb a ladder-like stairway in front of the statue and kiss the nail-scarred hands and feet.

I climbed the ladder and kissing that cold, imposing body a terrifying voice suddenly stabbed my heart: 'Thou shall have no graven images before thee.' Shaking, I climbed down.

As if it wasn't enough being different from my friends, mother never quite let me forget I was also very different from her.

She was a people-person. Strong and charismatic, she never seemed to feel inadequate. She loved pretty dresses and parties. I wanted to be a Northwest Mounted Policeman. More often than not you could find me alone somewhere, in my room, eyes drooping as I stayed awake to read the latest Jack London book.

Our house overflowed with Bohemian immigrants, people who loved laughter and music. I stayed outside the crowd, watching and listening, alone....

In school, I was well ahead of my class but frequently bored.

Always asking questions, I was considered too outspoken, another trait my mother didn't approve of.

One time during confirmation studies I remember questioning the rabbi about Isaiah 1:18.

'Look,' I showed him. 'It says my sins are like scarlet but they can be white as snow. Why are they scarlet? How can they be white?'

'Don't ask such questions,' he said, 'and don't argue. If you would live a good life, do mitzvot (good deeds) and be a good person, instead of being a troublemaker, you would understand these things.'

Naturally mother was exasperated. 'Why can't you just sit there and keep quiet?' she pleaded....

Mother remarried when I was about ten. When I was 14, my stepfather, an engineer, moved us to Monterrey, Mexico where he had a very good job offer. Though I was 5'10" and loomed over everyone, at last it seemed that the ugly duckling was going to turn into a swan.

I was accepted by an older, faster crowd and went to gala balls. We were very involved in the Jewish community and there were constant parties and activities.

The fun ended when mom got worried about the company I kept. It was, she feared, too loose and fast for a young teen. Before I knew what had happened, I was whisked off to live with a complete stranger: my father.

Dad and his wife Lillie led a quiet, refined life in Washington, D.C. Lillie's father was a Civil War veteran and she had always lived in a somewhat genteel, antebellum atmosphere. Neither Lillie nor I was prepared for the culture shock of a rebellious, Jewish American Princess moving into her home.

Doubt and insecurity hit me harder than ever. I was attending a high school where most of the kids were from families of ambassadors and high level government officials. For once I wasn't the brightest in my class. Washington turned the swan from Mexico back into an ugly duckling.

Gloria Steinem, one of the early founders of Women's Lib., was in my high school class and just recently I heard her confess she felt like an awkward outsider in school. If so, it didn't seem that way to me. She and her friends seemed like the 1952 version of the 'beautiful people.'

After high school, I snared a job at the Pentagon and began to date Len Clotfelter, a handsome airman. Len had come to Christ when he was 12, but was never grounded in the Word of God.

Our relationship bloomed and we married. When Len got out of the Air Force we moved to southern California, and began attending First Baptist Church of Lakewood with his sister.

For several months, Len grew as a Christian and I was willing enough to go to services with him. Everyone was praying for me, but I was completely oblivious to the idea that there was some decision I had to make.

Oh, I was curious. One time after an altar call I wanted to see this 'prayer room' they invited people to. After the service I quietly opened the door. All I saw were choir members taking off their robes.

It was after seeing Oil Town U.S.A., a Billy Graham film, that I ended up in that prayer room. The counselor asked, 'Do you believe the New Testament is the Word of God?'

'Yes,' replied a prim and proper woman next to me.

'No!' I said, incredulous at the question.

The counselor called for Bob Ellif, Chairman of the Deacon Board. Bob had a special sensitivity to me, and after talking, said, "What you're saying is you'd like to find out more, right?'

'Yes,' I agreed, relieved.

Pastor Harold Carlson came over and went through much of the same information Bob Ellif had. He explained that all of us were sinners, separated from God, and in need of a Savior. He showed me that Jesus said He was that Savior.

It's all a little hazy to me, but before I knew what had happened, Pastor Carlson and a bunch of others were congratulating me. I didn't feel any different, except I knew I had invited Jesus to come into my life and accepted that He died in my place on the cross. What good would that do, I thought. I could work all my life and still not be good enough to please God.

It wasn't until a few weeks later that I realized what had happened. The Scripture—'It is by grace you have been saved, through faith, and this is not from yourselves, it is the gift of God, not by works, so that no one can boast' (Eph. 2:8, 9)—suddenly came alive.

God had given me eternal life! I had never felt quite good enough, pretty enough, popular enough, or bright enough. No wonder I felt I could never be good enough for God.

But God had already done it all! He wasn't disappointed that I was different; He had made me that way!

I went wonderfully wild. Accepted by God? Assured of eternal life with His glory? It was the best discovery that I had ever made. When I told my mother, I was so excited that I hardly noticed the frost in her voice when she said. 'Are you trying to tell me your grandmother is in hell? . . .'

The cold war that began that day lasted almost 30 years, until a month before Mother died, and she accepted His salvation. For one month, mother and I shared His praises, no longer separated by our differences....

When the joy of God first impressed me, I took out my childhood Bible, the one I had used growing up in the synagogue and turned to the section marked 'Birth.' The words I wrote there still make me want to sing:

'The most important in all of eternity for me, April 1954, born again to be a child of God through the precious blood of the Lamb of God of Isaiah 53.'[133]

Artis was never too busy for the people God sent her way. She was always willing to adjust her personal schedule of activities in deference to opportunities to share the Gospel. This is evidenced by her report of a Jewish man named Larry. She wrote:

Larry was on a journey to find himself. It was partly geography, and partly whim, that landed him in Sacramento, but once here, he seemed to be on a direct path to God. What happened is this: he was having some work done on his car and went into the auto dealer's office to make a call. While there he flipped through the Yellow Pages. Casually he was looking at the churches, and one seemed to stand out.

So while he was at the phone...he thought he'd call the church.

A friend of his back home in Vancouver had been witnessing to him for years. 'But you're not Jewish,' he kept telling her, 'and Jews don't believe in Jesus.'

Then she introduced him to a Jewish believer. But that still didn't help. Larry just couldn't believe in Jesus. Until that day in Sacramento, when his eyes sought out a church listing and he called and asked them if they knew any Jewish believers.

They didn't. But they referred him to someone, who referred him to someone else, and eventually, I got a call from a friend. 'Artis, there's a Jewish fellow in town who would like to meet a Jewish believer. Would you give him a call?'

'Oh, Lord, help!' I prayed. It was already late morning. I had a class that afternoon. Church that night. I was leaving town the next day. In my spare time I had volunteered to sew costumes for our church Christmas pageant. Yet when I called to talk to him, and I asked him if he had time to stop by our house, he said yes.

That afternoon we sat and talked for three hours and discussed how to recognize the Messiah. I brought out my Bible and, beginning at Genesis 3:15, went through an overview of Messiah. He recognized the Bible we were using as a Jewish version, so when we got to Isaiah 53, I handed it to him to read. A few verses along, he said, 'This is Jesus!'

'Larry,' I pointed out, 'this is the Jewish Bible.'

'I know, but this is Jesus.'

'Well, read on,' I replied.

A few verses further he stopped again. 'This has got to be Jesus.'

'Well, the rabbis say it is Israel.'

'But it can't be Israel.'

It was time for me to leave for church, and he had other plans, so (with a great deal to think about) we parted ways. 'If you'd like to come back here tonight when we get back from church, my husband and I would be happy to have you as our guest for the night.'

He accepted my invitation, and when I returned from church he came back. As I sewed costumes, we resumed our discussion of earlier that day.

Finally, about 11:30, I turned and looked at him. 'Larry, are you convinced Jesus is the Messiah?'

'Yes,' he replied.

'Would you like to receive Him as your atonement?'

'Yes.'

We got down on our knees and prayed together. We rejoiced together as I explained what God had brought into his life through this new birth. And next morning, as I left for my trip I praised God and prayed for this man who set out to search for himself and ended up finding God.[137]

Artis and her husband, Len, have remained in the Sacramento area and Artis continues to serve the Lord on the staff of the Mission. Through the years, God has used her to lead many Jewish people to the Lord.

CHRISTOPHER MELISKO

Chris and Marsha Melisko were hired as missionaries and congregation planters for Los Angeles in January 1987. In December 1990, Chris was promoted to the position of Area Director for Los Angeles and the Western Region.

Christopher Melisko was born on November 14, 1958 in Endicott, New York. His family background was Roman Catholic. Shortly after his sister, Stephanie, was born the family moved to the Elmira-Corning area of New York, where Chris grew up.

There seems to be little in Chris's early background to indicate that he would one day be drawn to the field of Jewish missions. In relating his testimony, he shared:

Before I was saved, I put my faith in drugs, alcohol, and rock and roll. By the time I graduated high school, I was drinking heavily and partying steadily. But there was something in me that kept saying, 'This is getting out of control.' One night, dead drunk, I got in my car and drove to the police station at 2:00 a.m. and said, 'I give up. I'm a drunk. I need help....'

By the time Chris was 20, he was introverted, unhappy, and often depressed. He didn't like his life but was powerless to control it. One day on his way to work (he was working the second shift at a nearby factory), he stopped by a bookstore. He spotted the book The Late Great Planet Earth by Hal Lindsey. The cover appealed to him, maybe because it seemed to promise answers.

He started reading the book after work, about midnight, and read straight through to 6 a.m. 'When I put it down I thought Jesus was coming back at 7:00 a.m. And I was scared.'

A few days later, he bought a Bible.

For eight months his life was a living contradiction. 'Every day I read the Bible convinced that it was true. But at night, I was powerless to stay away from bars. I'd get home late at night and toss and turn, tormented by an inward pull, yet convinced I didn't have the strength to give up my life and my friends. It wasn't much, but it was all I knew.'

He started attending a small church on Sunday mornings. He was drawn to the people and to God's Word. He made more trips to the bookstore looking for books on prophecy.

Because the Jewish people played such an important role in prophecy, he also perused books on Jewish evangelism. He bought one called Our Jewish Friends by Dr. Louis Goldberg. It was his introduction to Jewish people as people, as a culture in America, and as people who were blind to God's plan of salvation, yet whom God loves with a special heart.

'Night after night I considered God,' Christopher remembers. In a sense, he was like the Jewish people about whom he was reading. He was faced with an opportunity to be one with God, but unable to spiritually commit himself. He knew God's Spirit was drawing him. Then he'd go and get drunk and forget the spiritual pain inside.

'Then one night a friend and I were leaving a bar, totally smashed. I put him in the passenger seat and wobbled around to the driver's side. Just as I was getting in, a car drove by and smashed into the open door.'

It wasn't so much the brush with death that affected Christopher, but the isolation while his car was in the shop. 'I was out of commission. Forced to stay home, I faced God soberly. The first week I had wheels, I went to a nearby church. I went back the second Sunday, and when they gave an altar call, there was no doubt in my mind. I accepted the Lord.'

The layman who prayed with Christopher that day was Ed Sabol. Ed and his wife Marcia, had just returned from their second trip to Israel, and Marcia was soon to begin a dissertation on the Holocaust. As spiritual parents, their love of the Jewish people was infectious. However, Marcia remembers that 'from the very first time we talked to Chris, we noticed he had an intensity about Jewish people that we had never seen before.' The second time Christopher was at the Sabols' home, Marcia recognized a uniquely God-given sensitivity to Jewish people. 'You have a Jewish heart,' she told him.

'What's that?' Chris asked.

'That's when God places a special love and concern for the Jewish people in your heart, and you sense a need to see the Jewish people know Messiah; it's a Jewish heart.'

Christopher agreed, but wasn't certain what to do about it. 'Scripture says the Lord created all things for Himself, and I kept thinking, "What am I created for?"'

While waiting for the Lord to answer, Chris kept busy, spending evenings in the homes of church members, sitting and listening, asking questions about his faith. The Sabols were surprised when they heard of Christopher's previous activities. 'God seemed to gift him with a maturity that never flagged. He never looked back. He didn't just learn, he soaked up learning. He was gentle and compassionate. Upbeat and positive. It was impossible to think of him as someone who was confused and depressed.'

A few months later Christopher went to a Jewish Evangelism seminar. After listening to speaker Manny Brotman, Christopher knew his calling. 'I walked out that day and said, "I'm called to the Jewish people. I really think I am."' [135]

In 1983 Chris entered the pastoral studies program at Moody Bible Institute. He believed his call would be fulfilled through ministering to Jewish people in a church. When he arrived at Moody, he discovered his roommate was Chosen People worker Jeff Seif. Living with a Jewish person and seeing first hand what it meant for a Jew to accept Jesus, strengthened his heart's leaning.

The next semester, he roomed with another Chosen People worker, Jerry Gross. "Being part of Jeff's and Jerry's lives showed me the victories and struggles that Jewish people undergo, especially with their families. The next year, I went into Jewish studies."[136]

Two other life-changing events came into Christopher's life during his first two years at Moody. He met Dr. Daniel Goldberg, the West Coast Regional Director for Chosen People Ministries, and learned that the ministry was committed to planting congregations that would be sensitive to Jewish evangelism. He also met a farm girl from Kansas—Marsha Mindedahl—who would later become his wife. She recalled, "From the first time I met Christopher at Jays (a hamburger stand near Moody), I knew he was intense and single-minded about the Jewish people. He and I were friends, but I never thought I'd be a teacher, a pastor's wife, or a missionary. It was obvious his wife would be all three."[137]

Two years later, Christopher was committed to entering Jewish missions. By that time Marsha felt her calling was to Christopher, to do whatever she could to make his ministry successful even though she still didn't know many Jewish people, and was still unfamiliar with Jewish culture.

A teacher recommended Marsha for a job at the YMCA, teaching an aerobics class. All but one of her students were Jewish. Every job she had after that put her in predominantly Jewish settings, and she met Jewish people of every age and every socio-economic group. She discovered that she too loved these people and desired for them to know her Lord.

In May 1986 Christopher and Marsha were married, and in January 1987 they joined the staff of Chosen People Ministries. They moved to Southern California, where they worked with Howard and Janet Silverman in helping the Shepherd of Israel Congregation get started.

Christopher works on campuses most days, talking to Jewish students about the Lord. He is the person others call at midnight when they've got problems, because he is always there for people.

Marsha's love of art led her to pursue training in graphic arts. She enrolled in a two-year college course to become a designer-artist, with the hope of combining the skills she learned with her desire to create Jewish-oriented curricula for churches and Messianic congregations. She said, "I want to see the Gospel presented through the arts, using interesting and attractive posters and publicity for our outreaches that speak to Jewish people."[138] Marsha's art teacher and several classmates were Jewish, and she found that they were intrigued with the art samples she brought to class. Over the years, she has had an active ministry with women and children—an important part of The Chosen People work in Los Angeles.

In addition to his responsibilities as Area Director for the ministry in Los Angeles, Chris also serves as the pastor of the Shepherd of Israel Congregation (established by the Mission). In sharing the congregation's unique approaches for evangelism, he reported:

> Our congregation has a variety of approaches to minister to the diverse L.A. Jewish community. Beside our high-profile ministries—a book table at a local campus (where recently ten Israelis stopped by in one day) and our ads in the L.A. Times (which reach 250,000 people with the headline 'We Have Found the Messiah')—we are involved in more 'sensitive' outreaches. For instance, we have a ministry to unsaved spouses, traditionally more defensive than the rank-and-file unbeliever. Our special holiday services allow the Spirit of God to work in the hearts of these beloved marriage partners of our congregants.[139]

God has blessed the evangelistic program of the Shepherd of Israel congregation. Mr. Rich Goldstein is just one of the many Jewish people who have come to faith in Jesus as a result of their effective outreach. The April 1992 Chosen People magazine included the testimony of Rich Goldstein. It stated:

> As a boy, Rich Goldstein was always full of questions. But whenever he had deep questions about the Jewish faith or he asked his parents why he was to believe the things Jewish people believed about God, he was always given the same answer: 'Because you're Jewish!'
>
> 'That just wasn't good enough for me,' Rich, 33, states emphatically, recalling his Jewish childhood in California's San Fernando Valley. For Rich, now in the construction industry, growing up in a Jewish home meant going to synagogue during the High Holy Days, attending Hebrew school and being bar mitzvahed [sic] ('against my will').
>
> While at college, he accompanied Gentile friends to several different church services. 'I always had an open mind,' he recalls. 'I was also looking for answers to questions I had about Judaism.'
>
> Eventually, Rich's wife, a Gentile believer, accompanied him to Chosen People Ministries' Shepherd of Israel Congregation in Canoga Park, CA. Slowly, things began to fall into place for Rich as Chris Melisko and others from Chosen People Ministries explained the faith from a Jewish perspective.
>
> Still, confronting the traditions and teachings he learned growing up in a Jewish home—in light of what he was now learning—was no picnic.
>
> 'Being Jewish you're brought up with a lot of guilt even saying the name Jesus,' he remembers with some pain.
>
> Then last year, his wife took him to Shepherd of Israel's Messianic Passover seder. Rich admits he didn't know what to expect. But the tables were set much the way he remembers his own family's seders.
>
> Rich found the service answered questions about the atonement he hadn't even framed in his own mind yet. At the end of the seder, when a woman at his table asked him if he was a believer, Rich just blurted out 'yes.'
>
> Growing by leaps and bounds in his faith since then, Rich and family continue to attend the Shepherd of Israel Congregation. With obvious excitement he recounts a milestone in his new life that occurred recently. 'I had my first hour long conversation with my mother about what I believe,' he says excitedly.
>
> 'In one breath she said she believed in reincarnation, and in the next breath she said you return to the earth.' But

her main argument, Rich recalled, was that she believed what she believed because 'that's the way it's always been.'

And 'that's the way it's always been' was never good enough for Rich. But now, he has found real answers and is able to follow God completely.[140]

STEVEN SINAR

As the missionary workers of the Western Region faithfully carried on an evangelistic outreach to the Jewish people, support staff was needed to assist in scheduling church meetings and to handle the myriad of other administrative tasks which are a part of the work. Mr. Steven Sinar entered the Mission's S.T.E.P. program in June 1990. He was hired in the fall of 1990 as the Regional Church Ministries Coordinator for the western states. Steve is representative of the fine support staff God supplied for the on-going work of the Mission. The responsibility of the Mission's "church ministries coordinators" is to contact churches and organizations, with the goal of arranging meetings at which the missionaries of the region can share the work of the Mission.

Readers of *The Chosen People* magazine were given a glimpse of Steven Sinar's life and testimony:

The pleasant voice on the telephone now greeting churches in Southern California for Chosen People Ministries belongs to Steve Sinar,...a friendly, likeable person with a ready smile. It's difficult to believe that this cheerful voice once carried a scared, frantic tone—the urgency of a man getting deeper in debt with each passing day.

In a sense, Steve Sinar was a product of his environment. He was the first-born son of a nice, middle-class Jewish family living in a suburban Jewish neighborhood and belonging to the country club.... In short, he had the conventional 'Bar Mitzvah and bagels' Jewish upbringing.

'When I was growing up in Pikesville, Maryland,' Steve reflects, 'my environment seemed to be so full of superficial things. It was as if the only things people thought were important were the trappings of success. Where people went, what they did, and what they drove were more important than who they were.'

'My first look at something different came when I counseled at a youth camp during summer vacations. Working with teenagers, learning to share their hurts and fears, and having the opportunity to add a little something to each child's life, gave me a new look at people.'

It was my first real opportunity to notice that there were all types of people in the world...and all types of needs other than those in the world I had seen around me in Pikesville.'

Then, social science degree in hand, Steve entered the 'real world.'

'I worked as a youth counselor and was really caught up in my job. Here was my opportunity to affect people's lives.'

'I thought everything was perfect until I ran into major disappointment: I came up short on a state qualification test to continue youth counseling as a full-time position.'

'Hurt and disappointed, I started bouncing from job to job, always looking for that same satisfaction I received from counseling. I wanted to help and care for my fellow man. It's almost as if I believed that the job and the title could also make me a different person.'

Eventually Steve ended up in Baltimore, selling insurance and making big commissions.

'In no time at all, I racked up more bills than I could possibly handle. If something made me feel good, I bought it. It didn't make any difference whether I needed it or could afford it.'

'Did I have a new girl friend? Then I needed a new wardrobe. Was there a new disco? Then I had to be there.'

'My whole identity seemed to be linked to what I was on the outside rather than who I was on the inside. On the outside I was smiling, as if everything was wonderful. On the inside I was hurting, and I knew it.'

'My bills—and my life—were out of control....'

'During my time selling insurance, sometimes I'd go into homes where I noticed the people were religious. In many of these homes I noticed a difference. These people—the ones who seemed to truly believe in Jesus—were always interested in me....'

Into this directionless life came a phone call from Don Goldvarg. Don was recruiting Steve to enter a multilevel marketing plan. Needing more money, and being attracted to the evident enthusiasm in Don's voice, Steve agreed to meet with him.

'From the time I met Don and his wife, Leslie, I knew something was different. They had joy, especially Leslie. She just bubbled over with joy. I enjoyed going over to their house for the sheer pleasure of being with them. I recognized the quality they had as love. Once they shared with me that their love came from the Lord.

It didn't even dawn on me to ask any questions about their faith, that's how consumed I was with my own way of living. It never occurred to me there could be a better way for me.

Noticing that Steve did not have plans to attend Yom Kippur services, the Goldvargs invited him to their congregation, which, by the way, is a Messianic Jewish congregation of believers in Yeshua, the Messiah. The Goldvargs mentioned that their twelve-year-old son was taking Bar Mitzvah lessons there.

'I agreed to go because I knew I wouldn't have gone to any other services. (I wasn't a member of any of the neighborhood synagogues.) Also, I admit that, by this point, I was a little curious....'

'When we arrived, I noticed right away that the building was packed and that the people all appeared to be Jewish. I noticed that there was life and joy in the congregation, that there was something wonderful there. Sometime during the service, I understood that the difference was the Lord God of Israel, and I allowed His Spirit to penetrate my heart.'

'Right away, I felt a change. I knew that Yeshua was my Messiah. What a great day to come to know Messiah— on the Day of Atonement. What a joy I felt to understand the true atonement of God.'

'Perhaps most people want to hear about the one-step, two-step, three-step way I prayed to receive the Lord. But all I know is that at some point, my spirit opened itself up and turned to God. I came out changed.'

Steve was never the same after that Yom Kippur service. He met with the pastor of the congregation and became grounded in his faith, studying Scripture to understand that Messiah had given him a new life.

'Actually, during this time it was really hard. I knew I was a new person, but I was living with my girlfriend, and I didn't want to give up that relationship. Eventually, I couldn't get rid of the feeling that it was either her or the Lord. I couldn't live for both and she wouldn't live for Him. I moved from the bedroom into the den.'

'After six months I decided to move out. At the last minute I couldn't leave. I called the movers to tell them not to come. But they had already left the warehouse and were soon at my door, ready to move me.'

'The congregation became like a family to me, a place to grow in the Lord, and always very supportive. Yet, I remember being scared at first to enter the building. I was afraid that someone would recognize me.'

'The biggest change that happened in my life, though, took place right after I came to faith. One day I sat down with my pastor and said, "I know God doesn't want me to live this way. He wants me to be responsible to Him, and it's clear what He expects of me."'

'We got out every one of my bills and labeled several envelopes by category. Three months of overdue car payments went into one envelope. Electric bills, telephone bills, car insurance, and other notes went into another envelope. Miscellaneous expenses went into another. Then he helped me work out a payment plan to catch up on every bill.'

'I quit my commission job, got a salaried position, and went on a budget. We staged a garage sale and sold almost everything I owned. Slowly but surely each debt was conquered.'

Over the next several years, other changes occurred in Steve's life. He began to witness. Instead of seeing people as dollar signs who were going to give him fat commission checks, he began to care about them as people.

'When I'd make a sale or win an award, I'd praise the Lord in the office, always giving God the glory. This testimony to my unbelieving colleagues started to evoke feelings that I hadn't had since I was counseling teenagers! I saw that God could use me to make a difference in people's lives.'

After three years, Steve began to think about serving the Lord in full-time ministry.

'Here was my opportunity to help people again, as I had once hoped to. I wanted to share God's love, especially to my own Jewish people, who are so in need of answers. I saw hope and answers and healing in Yeshua, and I just couldn't keep quiet about it.'

'I knew I would have to do some explaining to my parents and sister, because we were really close. I knew I was bucking the system, and I was concerned about how they'd feel in front of their friends.'

'But as I looked around me and listened to the believers I respected, I knew that my duty was to be a full-time committed believer. If that meant being in the ministry, then I had to do it. Each one had worked through similar situations when God called them to service....'

'When I look back on how I was before I knew Messiah, I can only see the big difference the Lord has made in me. Scripture reminds us that "if anyone is in Messiah, he is a new creation, the old has gone, the new has come" (2 Cor. 5:17). Praise God! I can see how true it is!'[141]

THE SOUTHEAST REGION UNDER LARRY JAFFREY

While Daniel Goldberg was developing the Western Region, Larry Jaffrey was developing the Southeast and Atlantic States regions of the Mission. As has been mentioned, Larry Jaffrey was transferred from Denver, Colorado to the Philadelphia, Pennsylvania area in 1970, along with Terryl Delaney. After Terryl's appointment as Director of Mass Media for the Mission, Larry Jaffrey was appointed as Missionary in Charge of Philadelphia; Larry was later appointed Regional Director of the Southeast Region (c.1975). The Southeast Regional Office was established in Silver Spring, Maryland in December 1975.

ARTHUR WATSON

One of the first workers hired by Terryl and Larry for the work in Philadelphia was Mr. Arthur Watson. Arthur, who was fifty-five years of age when he was hired on October 15, 1971, was replacing Mr. Harry Burgen who had retired. Arthur Watson remained on staff in the Philadelphia area until he retired on October 15, 1979.

Arthur Watson was a Gentile who came to faith in Jesus on December 10, 1965. After becoming a believer, even though he worked full-time as Project Engineer for the Arcos Corporation in Philadelphia, Arthur took evening classes at the Philadelphia College of the Bible for four years. He received his diploma in 1970. He had a deep love for the Jewish people, and concern for their salvation. This love and concern prompted him to become involved with the Hebrew Christian Alliance in Philadelphia; for over three years he also served as the Bible teacher for the First Hebrew Congregation, then located at 1907 Chestnut St., Philadelphia. After joining the staff of the Mission, Arthur wrote:

> Looking back over the past year, I want to praise the Lord for the opportunities He has given me to serve Him through my association with the American Board of Missions to the Jews. Two areas of service immediately come to mind. The first opportunity is in the area of visitation. I praise the Lord for using me to direct two Jewish brothers (5 years and 9 years old) to a local Daily Vacation Bible school. At the school one boy accepted his Messiah and now both brothers are attending Sunday School regularly.
>
> Several months ago the Lord gave me the opportunity to lead a 14-year old Jewish boy to his Messiah. Since that time, he has seen that God is a prayer-answering God as his mother, sister and brother have accepted their Messiah and have joined a fundamental church. Now, in answer to prayer, his father has attended two Christian Business Men's meetings with me and is becoming open to the Gospel. This after twenty-four years of refusing to hear about his wife's Messiah! Praise God for answered prayer.
>
> I think of another family where the two girls (6 and 10 years of age) and their Gentile mother accepted Christ as their Savior. Even now the Jewish stepfather is telling people that he is nearly a Hebrew Christian. May the Holy Spirit continue to convict Him.
>
> God has used me to provide both spiritual and physical comfort to an 83-year-old gentleman who has had two strokes. He lives alone and has just returned home after undergoing a rather serious operation. God gave him a Christian roommate and he was able to see the difference between a Gentile and a Christian by this man's actions and brotherly concern. I believe he has accepted his Messiah, but only God knows for sure. It was in answer to his request for a 'Smiling Faces' booklet of testimonies that I first visited him.[142]

For many years the Mission leased a building at 717 Walnut Street in downtown Philadelphia. This was the building in which Rev. Harry Burgen faithfully proclaimed the Gospel to Jews or Gentiles who paused to observe his window display, or who ventured inside the building. The building and Harry's ministry had become a landmark known by both the Jews and Christians in Philadelphia.

As he ministered from the building at 717 Walnut Street, Arthur Watson wrote:

> Working in our Walnut Street Branch, I can see the limitless opportunities that exist here. Many people pass by our display which features a large print copy of the poem 'The Jew.' Some stop in for copies of the poem and other literature, while others come in out of curiosity. It is a joy to see how the Lord is using this window ministry to bring many Jewish people in to hear about their Messiah.
>
> Last week, two students from the Jefferson Medical College came into the Center. One young man, who was Jewish, did not appear to be interested in the Messiah, but he listened attentively to the discussion I was having with his friend. Upon leaving, both accepted the literature that was given to them. [This booklet was produced by the Mission and sent to Jewish people responding to the Mission's media ads][142]

As plans for the Mission's Bi-centennial Congress on Prophecy were under way, it was decided that the building on Walnut Street was in need of remodeling. Arthur told readers of *The Chosen People* magazine:

> This last November we progressed to the point in remodeling here at Walnut Street that we were able to have our first monthly meeting. We had forty-three people in attendance, of which at least four were unsaved Jewish people. In December we had a Chanukah meeting at which time Dr. Gary Cohen of the Biblical School of Theology spoke on the history of Chanukah, and how Messiah relates to Chanukah. Again we had a number of unsaved Jews at the meeting.
>
> We have just started a Bible study for the Jewish people who have attended our monthly meetings. While the

number in attendance has not been large, I'm sure that the Lord will send in those He wants here.[144]

During the time that Arthur Watson was seeking to re-vitalize the Walnut Street ministry in downtown Philadelphia, Larry Jaffrey was attempting to develop a Jewish outreach in the southeast region of Philadelphia. He wrote:

> *Our goal is to present the message of Christ to over 400,000 Jewish people in Philadelphia and surrounding areas. It is impossible for our staff of three full-time missionaries [Larry Jaffrey, Arthur Watson, and Mitch Triestman] to accomplish this goal. With this in mind, our secondary goal is to train local churches and individuals in Jewish evangelism, so they can also minister to the Jewish community. Our aim is to have a trained witness in every community where there are 2500 or more Jewish people.*
>
> *At present, we have such ministries in Wilmington, Delaware [directed by volunteer missionary Albert Rosevich] and Harrisburg, Pennsylvania [directed by volunteer missionary Milt Maimon]. In these communities, we have individuals and churches co-operating in reaching God's Chosen People with the Gospel message. They supply the manpower, and we help them in formulating a program of outreach. For example, we go to these areas once a month with a special meeting to which Jewish people can be invited to hear God's truth in a manner not offensive to them. The local believers then bring their unsaved Jewish friends to the meeting. This acts as a catalyst for further witnessing opportunities.*
>
> *Our other areas of outreach include two centers in the city of Philadelphia, plus an outreach to college students at Temple University [conducted by Mitch Triestman].*
>
> *Our center on Castor Avenue [Philadelphia] serves as a focal point for our entire outreach in the area. Out of this office come the various mailings each month, such as announcements for meetings and prayer letters.*
>
> *This center is also a point for many Jewish people in this section of Philadelphia. Every week there are two Bible studies conducted for Jewish people. Over the past year, the attendance at these Bible studies has greatly increased. Once a month there is a special meeting which focuses on a Jewish holiday or some other topic geared to bring in unsaved Jewish people.*
>
> *All the meetings and Bible studies provide an opportunity where Jewish believers can meet other believers of the same background, thus strengthening their faith. These times of fellowship also give unsaved Jewish people a chance to meet Hebrew Christians.*
>
> *As a result of these meetings, many doors are opened for visitation. There have been entire families reached because one member of the family came to a meeting.*
>
> *One lady, who responded to our recent Jewish Art Calendar ad, decided to come out to our Bible studies. Each time she came, she invited someone new to come with her. She enticed them to come by saying, 'You're going to have to come and see the love they have at Beth Sar Shalom.' After coming out with her friends for about two months, this Jewish woman accepted Christ as her personal Savior. Now she has that love she saw in others. Stories like this can be repeated as we reach out for the Messiah from Castor Avenue.[145]*

The ministry at Castor Avenue continued to see growth, but the ministry at Walnut Street was diminishing. The Walnut Street neighborhood had changed, and the emphasis of the ministry in Philadelphia had shifted to the suburbs. By the time Arthur Watson retired in 1979, the work at Walnut Street had been phased out. The closing of the Walnut Street storefront ministry brought the Mission's ministry in downtown Philadelphia to an end—an outreach that had begun over fifty years earlier.

The building on Castor Avenue in Philadelphia was owned by St. Luke's Lutheran Church, but the pastor, the Rev. Mr. Bruce Lieske, had a great love for the Jewish people and a desire for their salvation. He had been a long-time supporter of the Mission, and he was delighted to allow the Mission to lease the facility. The Mission carried on a Gospel outreach from Castor Avenue until the mid-1980's when, once again, a new location and new methods were needed to reach the shifting Jewish population of Philadelphia. (Interestingly, Rev. Bruce Lieske went on to direct the Lutheran Institute for Jewish Evangelism, which trains congregations of Lutheran churches to establish Messianic congregations, and gives instruction to members of Lutheran churches regarding their responsibility to share the Gospel with the Jewish people.)

As mentioned by Larry in his report in the April 1975 Chosen People magazine, the missionary work in the Philadelphia area was, at that time, being carried on by three full-time workers—himself, Arthur Watson, and Mitch Triestman, but in the summer of 1975 Mr. David Bowers was hired to be a youth and campus worker.

MITCHELL TRIESTMAN

Mitchell Triestman was born into a conservative Jewish family in Brooklyn, New York in the year 1947. Twenty-two years later, in 1969, he came to faith in Jesus as his Messiah and Lord. In sharing the story of how he came to faith in Yeshua, Mitch told readers of *The Chosen People* magazine:

Most people would never think of a nice young Jewish boy as being a crook. But that's what I was. By the time I had graduated from high school, my life was filled with gambling and stealing. Then I graduated to writing bad checks and using drugs. Somehow I had become a slave to sin.

How did it happen? I had all the advantages of a middle-class environment. My parents loved me. Being brought up in a Conservative Jewish home, I was taught high ethical and moral principles. How had I become a slave to sin? And more importantly, how did I gain my freedom?

Although Jesus was the One who eventually became my deliverer, I learned only contempt for His name while I was a child. God sent many Christians across my path during my 'growing up' years, but my religious training at home nullified the testimony of these born-again believers. I was taught that gentiles believe one way and Jews another—no matter how 'right' their faith appeared, Jesus simply was not for me.

At the age of 13 I became Bar Mitzvah and continued to attend religious services for a short while. But soon I became disillusioned with the Jewish rituals. There didn't seem to be much in them for me, and the emotional experiences I received weren't worth the bother. While I was still proud of my Jewish heritage, I decided I'd only observe the most important holidays.

As I drifted away from the Jewish religion, I also lost respect for authority. Up to this point, the only thing that kept me from misbehaving was the fear of punishment. But as I broke one religious rule after another without being punished by God, I began to feel I could do anything I wanted without fear …just as long as I didn't get caught. And what I wanted to do was gamble.

All my life I was intrigued by gambling, and by my early high school years I was hooked. I wouldn't do anything without having money on it. Everything from exams at school to athletic events had some money riding on them. When I was winning, I had lots of money, friends and girls around, and we frequently celebrated my good fortune by getting drunk.

But when I was losing I felt alone and depressed. Soon I started stealing to get enough money to get into card games. At first, I only took small change from my brother's closet. I figured I would put the money back after winning, but somehow I always forgot to replace the money.

Once I started stealing, I progressed to bigger and more serious forms of crime. I broke into parked cars to steal items locked inside. I broke into homes and eventually I stole cars. I even robbed the charity collection cans in restaurants! I had certainly fallen very low…but I was nowhere near the bottom yet.

In college I graduated to cashing bad checks. Then in the spring of 1966 my life of crime caught up with me. Four of my friends and I were caught cashing checks, and we were told we'd have to repay all bad checks traced to us in order to escape prosecution. Somehow we managed to come up with the money, but I was still unchanged inside.

At the end of the semester I left Southern Illinois University and entered Loop Junior College in Chicago. I lied about the circumstances surrounding my leaving SIU, but when the truth was discovered, I was told to pick up my books and get out.

With nowhere else to turn but God, I turned in the opposite direction and joined the army, where I knew I could continue my life of gambling and hustling to make a quick buck. But in the army, something new was added to my life—drugs. In-between card games I experimented with marijuana and LSD.

Then I met a most unusual man. He was a Jew …but he was also a Christian. I'd never met anyone like him before and was intrigued by his life and his words. He shared his faith with me in a way that I just couldn't ignore. But I still didn't feel that Christ was for me.

After an early discharge from the service (because of my tour of duty in Vietnam), I started working at a department store. While there, a Christian girl was hired to work in my department, so I had plenty of opportunity to observe how a Christian acts in many different circumstances. For the first time in my life I became aware of the 'abundant life' and witnessed someone who was living it.

This Christian girl started bringing me to a coffeehouse where I met several other Christians. As it turned out, it was through these Christian young people that the Spirit of God chose to work with me. After three weeks of hearing their testimonies—and hearing the inner voice of the Holy Spirit—I realized my need for salvation …and God saw fit to save me.

Because of my compulsive gambling, my stealing and use of drugs, I'd probably be behind bars today if it weren't for Jesus. Instead, Jesus freed me from the slavery of sin and commissioned me to bring the Gospel of freedom to my Jewish brothers.

Several years ago a popular book and song told about the joy of being 'born free.' But I know that we're not born free. We are free only when we are born again.[146]

After becoming a believer, Mitch knew God was calling him into full-time missionary service so he enrolled in the Philadelphia College of the Bible. He began his affiliation with the Mission as a student worker on the campus of Temple University. He joined the staff of the Mission in 1973. Of those early days on the campus of Temple University, Mitch wrote:

Temple University, once a Baptist school, has become one of the most difficult campuses to reach with the Gospel. Temple has a large Jewish student enrollment and is predominantly a commuter campus. Students are constantly bombarded with communist propaganda, ultra liberal politics, and a rapidly changing morality. These three combine for an extremely anti-Christian atmosphere. It was to this campus, where the Gospel had for so long been unable to gain a foothold, that the Lord led us to minister for the past three years.

Most productive has been the privilege of setting up a publicity table in the Student Activities Center. At the table we placed a sign proclaiming 'Jews for Jesus,' and on the table we displayed assorted Gospel literature for Jewish students. Hundreds of students pass the table daily. Many take literature, and others stop for discussions.

The other main area of outreach has been contacting students on a one-to-one basis. Through both ministries we have much for which to praise the Lord. Perhaps the greatest single blessing from God is that we are no longer alone on campus. There are now three other Christian organizations working along with us at Temple. As a result, thousands of students have been reached with literature; hundreds have been contacted personally; dozens have come to a saving knowledge of the Messiah; and many committed Christian students are participating in Bible studies and learning how to effectively share their faith with their fellow students.[147]

Not only did Mitch have good rapport with students, God had gifted him in the area of personal evangelism. It seemed that no matter where he went, Mitch could turn any occasion into an opportunity to present the Gospel. From the time that he joined the Mission's staff in 1973 until the time that he left the staff of the Mission in 1990, almost every issue of *The Chosen People* magazine contains a story about a Jewish student, young person, businessman, family, etc., who had come to faith in Jesus because of the bold witness of Mitch Triestman. One typical story was shared in the January 1983 issue of *The Chosen People* magazine. It stated:

'Hey, why don't you let us louse up your day?' I [Mitch Triestman] shouted. 'You don't want to play alone.' I was getting ready to play golf with my friend Bill, when we spotted a young fellow approaching the first hole with his clubs.

He heard me calling and immediately came over. We introduced ourselves, and as we moved along the golf course, I learned more and more about Larry Gaines.

By the time we reached the eighteenth hole, I knew more than just the fact that he hits the ball long and putts left-handed. I knew something far more important—I had been granted a glimpse into his life.

Larry was brought up in a Conservative Jewish home much like my own, where the High Holy Days and Passover were observed. He was Bar Mitzvah (made a son of the Law), but once that was accomplished, he felt there was no reason to attend synagogue any longer. He confessed to me that by the time he grew up, he felt direction-less. He had been looking into Transcendental Meditation because drugs, gambling and girls hadn't done much for him.

I felt this was good opportunity to direct our conversation toward spiritual things. So I told Larry that man always feels a need to have a relationship with something in his world. He keeps choosing different things until he finds something to fill this need in his life. Larry quietly listened as I went on to tell him that God had designed a way for man to come to Him,...only it's not just another man-made way.

Larry understood this, but he was more interested by now in finding out a little about me. So he asked, 'What do you do for a living?'

I told him that I was a minister and he looked surprised. 'That's funny,' he said, 'I thought you were Jewish.'

'That's right,' I replied, 'I am Jewish.'

With a sudden look of confusion on his face, he asked, 'Oh, then you mean you're a rabbi?'

Without knowing it, he had given me the perfect chance to share my testimony with him. I began by telling him that I was brought up in a Jewish home and later came to know that Jesus was the Messiah promised to the Jews and to all people. I told him that I believe in the Scriptures, follow the Christian faith and am still Jewish.

Larry tried, but he couldn't fully understand what I was telling him, so we stood and talked at the eighteenth hole for a while. He wondered how I could be so happy with my life. He knew there must be something stronger at work here than human will—it must be a difference only God could make. He wanted the same for himself, but he couldn't see how believing in the Messiah could be the answer.

Finally, as we were about to part that day, I gave him a piece of ABMJ literature called 21 Reasons. On it, I wrote my name, address and phone number and told him, 'Now, if you have any questions or if you want some more information, just give me a buzz.'

As it turned out, Larry read the pamphlet I gave him, but then he misplaced it. He didn't misplace it intentionally, however. He truly wanted to contact me and know more about how he could have the same peace in his life, but he couldn't even remember my name. How would he ever find me?

He visited church after church with a description, as far as he could relate, of what I believed in. Eventually, a minister in a liberal church sent him to a Baptist church, commenting, 'That sounds like their thing.'

Larry didn't find me at the Baptist Church either. But, he found Jesus, his Savior!

Four years later, when I was interviewing a band called 'Foundation' to play at our Beth Sar Shalom fellowship, the Lord had a pleasant surprise for me.

Two young well-dressed Hebrew-Christian men came in with their instruments. Before I heard them play, I wanted to know a little about how they met their Messiah.

One began to tell his story. It sounded familiar. It was the story of a direction-less young man who met someone on a golf course who told him about Christ. Suddenly, he saw the pamphlet, 21 Reasons, in my pocket.

'That's it? That's the same pamphlet he gave me.' Suddenly he paused. We knowingly smiled at each other simultaneously, rejoicing as we realized that I was the man who witnessed to him on the golf course. What a blessing to hear that I was the one who had planted that first seed four years earlier. I thanked the Lord. For Larry, once a lonely young man on a golf course, had now found his purpose in life—loving and serving the Lord.

Ever since that day when Larry and I found each other again, he and his musical partner, Larry Frieberg, also a Jewish believer, have become a vital part of our fellowship. In addition to his musical talents, Larry Gaines offered the use of his apartment for Bible studies, and soon our gatherings grew into an exciting new fellowship we now call Beth Simcha. Through Beth Simcha, God has enabled us to spread His Word outside of our fellowship.[148]

David Bowers

David Bowers, who joined the Mission's staff during the summer of 1975, was raised in a Gentile Christian home. He had attended Philadelphia College of the Bible. By nature, he was a quiet man—a man who was sensitive to the leading of the Lord as he sought to share the Gospel on campus; but as the Lord directed him, he was bold in his witness. Speaking of his ministry, David wrote:

In my two years with the ABMJ [c. May 1978] I have found that one can't always judge the effectiveness of one's witness just by the number of decisions for salvation. It may take many months just to build a friendship, and years until a person comes to know the Lord as personal Savior. And then again, after years of prayer, friendship and witnessing, a person may choose not to accept Jesus.

God, in His grace, has done everything that's needed to be done for salvation and left the final decision up to the individual. (Whosoever believeth in Him shall not perish but have everlasting life, John 3:16.)

As a missionary, my job is simply to make the Gospel of salvation by grace very clear to the person and to encourage this person to respond positively to that which he has just heard.

At Temple University in Philadelphia, I have done much in the way of seed planting seemingly without much tangible evidence of 'growth.'

The steward's job is to keep on being faithful, no [sic] what the results; and it is the Lord's job to convict, draw, and regenerate people. There is no reason to feel discouraged if I am doing my job, because God is certainly doing His.

It does help, however, to get some kind of feedback.

A few weeks ago I had the blessing of receiving just such feedback from a girl named Tracy, whom I had led to the Lord over a year ago at a meeting on the Temple University campus. She wrote a brief letter thanking me for taking the time to speak to her about Christ. In her letter she said that it has made all the difference in her life and that she thanks God every night for all of us who had a part in her salvation.

I thank God for this encouraging feedback from Tracy, and I thank Him for using me even though 'results' may not be readily evident.[149]

As David continued his witness on the campus of Temple University, God blessed him with other evidences of His grace. He reported to readers of *The Chosen People* magazine:

Scott casually leafed through our stacks of literature. Like many other campus organizations, we were making our beliefs known to the students at Temple University. I had seen Scott walking through the various literature tables, stopping to talk at some, bypassing others. I particularly noticed that he spent several minutes at a nearby table set up by an anti-missionary group—so I was curious when he came up to our table. Would there be fireworks, as I had seen so many times that day when angry, hostile students rejected the message of the Lord?

No, there were no loud words, no arguments, just a mild curiosity. We bantered back and forth as he asked questions about scientific research which supported the authenticity of the Bible.

Each time I was on campus, Scott would come by, listen as I explained Scripture, and ask questions. He was always polite, always friendly, but never showed any deep spiritual interest.

Then Scott stopped coming by our table. From time to time I'd pray for him, but I pretty much decided my ministry had been to sow the seed. I would have to wait for eternity to find out the results.

One night, almost a year after I had last seen Scott, he called me at home. My first thought was that he had deep spiritual questions. But no, he just said he was looking for a place to live and remembered I knew a lot of people. On an off chance, I invited him to our Friday night worship service. I was surprised when he accepted the invitation and was even more surprised when he showed up.

Throughout the service, Scott seemed to be the same, quiet Scott. He listened politely, seemed agreeable, but also seemed unreachable. After the service he talked to several of the believers. It was during this time I realized Scott was very open and very interested in the Gospel.

'I've never seen anything like this,' I overheard him saying.

As we began to talk, I realized he was absorbing every word. When we talked about man's sinfulness, he said, 'That's true. I know I can't live up to God's standard.'

As I explained how God has bridged the gap that separates us from Him, I could see that God was closing the gap in Scott's life.

'Scott,' I finally said, 'knowing all this isn't enough. God wants us to accept it personally. Would you like to?'

Then this quiet young man made a very bold announcement. 'Yes,' he said, 'I'd like to do that very much.' Together we prayed as Scott invited Jesus into his life.

Sometimes I pray more for those students who outwardly seem to be in the midst of a deep spiritual quest. Scott is a reminder that one really never knows what is happening in another's heart. Even now as a Christian, Scott's still a little quiet and retiring. But as I watch him grow in the Lord, I'm grateful that God sees beyond a man's behavior and knows his heart.[150]

David Bowers continued to serve as a member of the Mission's staff through 1987, when God directed him to another field of service. During his years of campus ministry, God used David to reach many Jewish students on the campus of Temple University.

Two additional workers were added to the staff in Philadelphia—Mr. Tom Huckel and Mr. Larry Caruvana.

Tom Huckel

Tom Huckel was raised in the Roman Catholic church. He came to faith in Jesus as a result of being invited to become a member of a church basketball team. After a year of involvement with the team, the youth director prayed with Tom as he received Jesus as his Savior and Lord; Tom was nineteen years old. Through his church involvement, Tom met and ultimately married a Jewish believer, Sharon. God has blessed Sharon with a beautiful singing voice, and she was often asked to sing and to share her testimony at the Mission's meetings in Philadelphia.

After his marriage, Tom began a career as a businessman, but with each passing year he had a greater desire to be in Christian ministry. Toward that end, he enrolled in the Philadelphia College of the Bible. With a family to support, it was a financial struggle and a time of stress for both Tom and Sharon, but he graduated from the college with a degree in Bible Ministries.

Because of Sharon's involvement with the Mission, both Tom and Sharon had come to know the staff in Philadelphia and they felt certain that God wanted them in Jewish missions as well. Tom therefore applied to the Mission; he first served as a part-time staff member. In March 1986, he was hired as a full-time missionary.

Tom and his co-worker, Mitch Triestman, became close friends. In sharing a report about their joint witness to a Jewish man, Mitch and Tom told readers of *The Chosen People* magazine:

Dolf Bergman lost his entire family in Poland in the Holocaust. He was embittered and alone. After wandering aimlessly for a number of years, he met Hank and Janet Clugston. They loved Jesus. But, more important to him, they had a special love for Jewish people too. They took him in and treated him like one of the family. Dolf accepted their love, but rejected their Savior.

Seven years ago the Clugstons introduced me [Mitch Triestman] to Dolf. He came to a few of our meetings. But, it was obvious that he had no interest in spiritual things. He was so bitter about the Holocaust that he would hear nothing about God.

After a few months, we lost contact with Dolf. We told the Clugston family that although he had no interest, they should continue to help him and continue to pray for him. They did for the next seven years.

...after all those years, my wife, Jackie, received a phone call from Janet. She was calling from the hospital, where he had spent the last three days.... 'I'm sure you don't remember me, but your husband once witnessed to a Jewish friend of our family.' Jackie could sense the desperation in her voice as she said, 'Mrs. Triestman, this is an emergency. Our friend is dying. He's been in a coma and was expected to die last night. But, today he has suddenly come out of the coma.... He's lucid and talking, but his time is short. Could your husband please come right away and talk to him?' At that moment, however, I was fifty miles away teaching a Bible study in New Jersey.

Jackie knew I wouldn't be able to make it, but she assured Janet that we would send somebody....

...I was fifty miles away, and he might not be alive by the time I reached the hospital. The situation seemed impossible. Then I remembered that Tom Huckel, one of our missionaries, lived only a few minutes from the hospital. I told Jackie to send Tom.

It wasn't until after I got off the telephone that I remembered that Tom isn't Jewish. The people at the Bible study questioned the wisdom of sending him. Sure, he was close to the hospital but he was a Gentile Christian. If the Gentile Christians who had befriended him for almost 30 years could not bring him to the Lord, what could another Gentile Christian do...and a stranger at that!

God laid on my heart, then, three things to share with the people at the Bible study. First, oftentimes just hearing from another person about the Gospel confirms the truth that they've previously heard. Second, Tom is trained in Jewish evangelism and experienced in dealing with older Jewish people. And third, I told them we're going to pray! We're going to send Tom into a battlefield that has been prepared by the Spirit of God. So, as we began to pray, Jackie called Tom on the telephone....

I [Tom Huckel] hadn't been home more than fifteen minutes when Jackie called and relayed the message from Mitch. I immediately headed for the hospital to present the Gospel to the dying Jewish man. The situation seemed hopeless and futile from a human standpoint, but I took comfort in the fact that I had come armed with God's Word and the Holy Spirit. As I sped toward the hospital, I asked the Lord to prepare the man's heart and to grant me clarity of thought.

When I arrived, Hank and Janet Clugston were anxiously waiting in the lobby. The moment I saw Dolf I could clearly see that he was losing the battle against the cancer that was slowly destroying his body. Dolf was lying in bed, obviously in pain, and was having difficulty breathing. The oxygen mask over his face limited his ability to speak more than a word or two at best. His eyes kept shutting as he winced in pain, so it was impossible for him to look at the Scriptures. But he could still hear. How I took comfort as I recalled, 'Faith comes by hearing, and hearing by the Word of God.' So I shared some Scriptures, and when I asked if he understood, he nodded, 'yes.' I don't remember everything I said, but I do remember a small illustration I used that seemed to touch his heart. I told him that even without looking into the Scripture, one could see God's plan of salvation in nature (Rom. 1:20). God deemed it necessary that in order for our physical lives to continue, some form of life must give itself for us whenever we eat. The same principle is true in our spiritual lives. God bridges the gap between Himself and man in Jesus Christ. I explained to Dolf that when Jesus gave His life as a sacrifice for our sins, it was an eternal act designed by God to give us eternal life.

I asked Dolf if he would trust Jesus for the forgiveness of his sins and for eternal life. He nodded, 'yes.' We prayed with Dolf—that Jesus would come into his heart.

Janet couldn't believe it! She asked him if he understood everything I had said, and again he nodded 'yes.' Janet began crying tears of joy as the angels in heaven were rejoicing. The faith of everyone involved was strengthened by Dolf's salvation.

The following morning Janet Clugston called and told me that Dolf went home to be with the Lord just 90 minutes after I left the hospital.[151]

Over the next few years God used Tom and Sharon Huckel to lead a number of Jewish people to the Lord. The Mission also produced a musical cassette recording of Sharon singing hymns and Messianic songs. The cassette was well received by both Jewish and Christian people. In 1991 Tom Huckel resigned from the Mission's staff to take a position with The Evangelization Society of Philadelphia, Inc., known as Hananeel House. He and Sharon are still actively witnessing to the Jewish people in the Philadelphia area.

LARRY CARUVANA

Larry Caruvana was also recruited for the Philadelphia ministry. Larry was a "child of the Mission"; he found the Lord through the Coney Island ministry, under the leadership of Miss Hilda Koser. He had worked as a student worker in the Coney Island branch before being sent to Los Angeles for training.

In 1973, after completing the training program, Larry was sent to Peoria, Illinois to direct the ministry there following a merger between the Mission and the Peoria Messianic Testimony. Four years later, during the summer of 1977, Larry was transferred to Philadelphia to help develop the young people's ministry and to assist in developing the Mission's camping programs.

In sharing his testimony with *The Chosen People* family, Larry wrote:

> *My mother's background was Jewish and my father's was Italian, and neither was very religious, so I was not raised either way. As a 'mixed' Jew, I'm thankful I found the Messiah of Israel as my Saviour.*
>
> *When I was 13, I first came in contact with the American Board of Missions to the Jews and attended meetings at the Coney Island Branch. My mother was the first one in my family to be saved, and then she let my brother and me attend meetings at the Mission where she was saved.*
>
> *My acceptance of the Lord Jesus Christ did not come as a great climatic decision. I simply realized I was a sinner and needed to accept Christ as my Saviour, and I did. Soon after, my brother was saved, and several years after that, at a New Year's Eve candlelight service at the Coney Island Mission, my father acknowledged that he too had accepted Christ as his Saviour.*
>
> *During high school, when able to do so, I taught Sunday school and helped Miss Koser at Coney Island. She challenged me to go to Bible school and asked me to pray about it. When I graduated from high school, my main desire was to get a job and make some money. After working for a year, however, I realized I was getting nowhere and needed further education. I applied to Staten Island Community College and was accepted, although I was still praying about going to Bible school.*
>
> *In June 1960 I went to Miss Koser and told her that I felt the Lord was leading me to Bible school. We prayed about it, and a month later I applied to Northeastern Bible Institute, and was accepted. The Lord was leading me all right,...in the second semester of my junior year I realized He was leading toward the field of Jewish missions....*
>
> *I graduated from Northeastern's 3-year course in 1963, and spent 1964 studying at the Nyack Missionary College. However, Northeastern this year inaugurated a 4-year course with a degree, so I am returning to Northeastern and will graduate this coming June with a B.R.E. degree in missions. At that time I hope to go into full-time ministry among the Jews, for which I covet your prayers.*[152]

After his transfer to the Philadelphia area, Larry found that his real love was in working with the Mission's camping program. As the Mission's Camp Director and also serving on the staff in Philadelphia, Larry reported:

> *Once again we praise the Lord for His blessing on our camping program July 30—Aug. 18 [c.1979], in Honeybrook, Pa. Camp Sar Shalom continues to be a place of harvest for children and teenagers (84 kids this year!) who hear the Word at our various Mission stations throughout the year. This year the Lord again gave us a great staff. They were Daniel Siegel (Assistant Director), Cynthia Rydelnik, Paula Fischer, Sandy Morse, Stefanie Saldana, Barry Budoff, Angelo Giammona, Scott Dellana, Ronald Elkins and Guy Perrodin....*
>
> *...When camp began we felt there were two young people, a brother and sister, who were not believers.... Our staff meeting always closed with earnest prayer for unsaved campers.*
>
> *About midway through our first week of camp, we received a phone call from Jim Bates one of our missionaries. He wanted to know if he could bring Karen, an unsaved nineteen-year-old Jewish girl to camp. Of course we said, 'yes.' Karen's mother was a believer but Karen wasn't. She arrived at camp with her whole weekend already planned out. Friday she would participate in camp activities; Saturday she would sightsee off the camp grounds; Sunday she would leave for home. But the Lord had different plans for Karen.*
>
> *Friday she joined in camp activities and...sat in on the meetings that Friday night, but she still seemed bored with things. Even the emotional Hebrew songs didn't seem to interest her. Yet, I sensed God at work. When she woke up Saturday she had already changed her plans. Instead of sightseeing off camp grounds, she decided to stay for the activities.*
>
> *That evening 'Ammi' the ABMJ singing group from our Coney Island group presented a program led by Steve Schlissel. The music was inspiring and the testimonies spoke clearly to hearts of Messiah's love.... At the close of the program I gave an invitation to which there was no response. I looked at Karen and noticed no apparent interest.*

I learned later she was very much interested and absorbed in the program. After the program, Karen posed the question, 'What is this being born again all about?' Stefani Saldana, one of our counsellors, took her aside and spent the rest of that evening opening the Scriptures and dealing with Karen's questions. We were all praying. About midnight, Stefanie came in with a big smile on her face. Karen had just accepted Jesus as her Messiah and Savior!

The next morning even Karen's face showed a change had taken place. After breakfast she called her mother to tell her the good news. Of course Karen did not leave after lunch that day as she had planned. Instead she stayed until the close of teenage camp! ...At the end of our teen camp, I asked her if she would like to stay for junior camp as a helper. 'Could I really?' she asked, obviously very happy.

The first night of our junior camp, she gave her first public testimony.... she told the group,...she had received Him just a week ago, proving that it's never too late to know Him.

Another camp highlight was the skit the counsellors presented based on the parable of the Seed and the Sower. It was humorous and yet had a pointed spiritual message for each camper. After the last scene, we closed with an invitation. Two teenage girls responded. Lisa was one of the teens we had been praying for since camp began....

The next morning I learned that still another decision was made by a camper that night. In the quiet of his cabin, Scott opened the Scriptures, realized who Jesus really was, and accepted Him as his Savior, all on his own. Scott was the brother of Lisa who had also made a decision the same night.

God had answered our prayers regarding the salvation of these two teenagers (remember the sister and brother we prayed for at the beginning of camp?)...

Many other commitments were made by both the teens and juniors at camp. We only trust that these decisions would bring forth fruit in their lives. As the Parable of the Seed and the Sower stated, we hope to see some bring forth thirty, sixty and even one hundred fold as they seek to live for their Messiah.[153]

During his years of ministry in Philadelphia, God used Larry Caruvana to reach many Jewish young people with the Gospel. In December 1985, Larry submitted his resignation to the Mission because of personal problems he was working through. Coincidentally, his resignation came about the same time that the workers in Philadelphia decided to close the Castor Avenue office and de-centralize the Philadelphia ministry.

The reader will recall that at the Salt Lake City Convention in 1966, Daniel Fuchs had announced his "Expansion Program" of the Mission, using Martin (Moishe) Rosen's idea of "District" development of the Mission (see Chapter Ten of this history). Under this expansion program, missionary staff of each district reported to the "Missionary in Charge," but each Missionary in Charge and all other personnel within districts were to report to Daniel Fuchs. In 1970, after Daniel's trip to Japan, this policy was abruptly changed when he announced to the staff that the Mission would no longer be developing "branch" ministries.

In seeking to follow the directives of Daniel Fuchs, and still find a "workable" solution for effectively reaching Jewish people with the Gospel, the author developed the "regional structure." Under the regional structure, each "region" was under the supervision of the "Regional Director." Within the regions, the methodology of evangelistic outreach was dictated by the needs of the community where ministry was being done.

As Southeast Regional Director, Larry Jaffrey's region included areas as far north as southern New Jersey, as far south as Florida, and as far west as the Mississippi. His was the first region to feel the effects of the "decentralization" of the branch ministries (as mentioned in Chapter Eleven of this history, when the Mission's Washington D.C. branch was closed and the building was later sold).

In the spring of 1977, in attempting to expand the outreach of the Southeast Region, the Mission transferred Barry and Dyann Budoff to work at the Pittsburgh branch—a branch that had been without workers since the resignation of Henry Johnson in 1975.

BARRY AND DYANN BUDOFF

Barry and Dyann Budoff were both Jewish believers. Each felt called of the Lord to serve in the field of Jewish missions and evangelism. In preparing themselves for ministry, each had enrolled in the Jewish studies program at Moody Bible Institute. Barry and Dyann joined the Mission's staff during the late spring of 1976, as part-time workers for the Chicago branch. Following their graduation from Moody, they were transferred to Pittsburgh.

Barry Budoff was born on August 3, 1950. Both of his parents were Russian Jewish immigrants. His conservative Jewish home, Barry said, provided him with a fairly good Jewish education.

Following his Bar Mitzvah, Barry left all religious training far behind him as he sought to experience life on his own. After high school graduation he entered Hunter College in New York City, but his first experience with college was not successful. After one year at Hunter, he was expelled for academic reasons. He then enrolled in Bernard Baruch School of Business, but once again he was expelled after one semester—this time for selling drugs.

Determined to get an education, and to get his life in order, Barry enrolled in the Lake City Florida Forest Ranger School. He kept his promise to himself and earned a certificate in Forestry. He was also inducted into the National Honor Society, Phi Theta Kappa; he became the editor of the campus magazine, The Phoenix; he was a member of the Associate Collegiate Players Association; and he was the captain of the debate team.

While he was still a student at the school of forestry, Barry decided that he wanted to become a veterinarian. Toward that end, he enrolled in the University of Georgia, College of Veterinary Medicine after his graduation from forest ranger school. He kept himself afloat financially by taking a job as a Veterinary Nurse/Assistant. It was while he was working in this position that God touched his heart, and changed his life and his life's direction. Of that time in his life, Barry wrote:

> I wanted to sell one of my dogs,…and in asking around concerning buyers, I was introduced to Randy Somers, a minister at Rehoboth Baptist Church in Tucker, Georgia. At first, talking to Randy was a joke; but as things progressed [over a period of several months], I began to see the seriousness of the Messianic claims of Yeshua. Finally, one Saturday night while lying in bed, I prayed to G-d for forgiveness through the Messiah. All I can say is that it worked. There weren't any angels flying over my bed (or at least I didn't see any) and no flaming fingers writing on the wall; but it was real, and it worked. I was baptized the next night and became a member of Rehoboth, where I received my grounding in the faith.
>
> After a few months as a believer, I began to wonder what G-d wanted me to do. I sought prayer from the elders of my church and undertook a period of prayer and fasting. G-d eventually answered my prayers through His word. Isaiah 58 begins with these words: 'Cry loudly, do not hold back; Raise your voice like a trumpet and declare to My people their transgressions, and to the house of Jacob their sins.' All I can say is that G-d called me to do exactly that, to cry loudly to His people.[154]

Shortly after receiving God's call to minister among the Jewish people, Barry began applying to Jewish mission agencies for missionary service. He first applied to the American Messianic Fellowship in Chicago and was accepted, working with Mr. John Fischer during the summer of 1974. In January 1975 he was accepted for missionary service with the Peniel Center in Chicago (a Jewish ministry founded Dr. David Bronstein Sr.). It was while he was working at Peniel Center that Barry met, and later married, Dyann Silver. As students at Moody Bible Institute, Barry and Dyann came in contact with workers from the Mission, and felt led of the Lord to apply to ABMJ for full-time missionary service.

Dyann was born on August 4, 1949. She was raised in a reform Jewish home in New York. In sharing her testimony, Dyann wrote:

> …I was raised in New York in a Jewish home, although being Jewish was only important to get out of school on holidays. The only time I ever heard the name Jesus was when it was used as a swear word. I was told that, as a Jew, I was not to believe in Him or to talk about Him. I went through a lot of persecution because I was Jewish, and I became very ashamed of my heritage.
>
> At 13 I was involved in witchcraft. I talked with spirits and hated the Jews. The psychiatrists thought I was mentally ill. I spent years in and out of hospitals because of the power of Satan.
>
> I always wanted to be a social worker and work with minorities. During the 1960's I was very involved with civil projects. I wanted so much to give something to the lower class people, but soon got very frustrated because I realized I had nothing to offer. I knew there was a lacking in my life. That's when drugs started to enter my life. I was about 16 when I entered the world of drugs. It started with pot, pills, ups and downs, LSD, and soon I was addicted to heroin. I did anything necessary to pay for my habit, and I was convinced that there was no God.
>
> At 21 I was traveling around the country with my 2 month old baby—hungry, lonely, and with no home. I had reached my dead end, when a Christian lady picked me up while I was hitch-hiking. As a favor to this gracious lady, I went to her church; and I have been going ever since. I accepted Jesus into my life shortly afterward…. I was immediately delivered from drugs.
>
> The lady who did pick me up was Carolyn Roper, wife of David Roper, who is one of the pastors of Peninsula Bible Church in Palo Alto, California (Pastor Ray Stedman). After six years of living in a nightmare and now seeing the love and reality of the lives of the people who were 'born again,' I knew right away that this was what I had been looking for all my life. I knew I had found the answer to life.[155]

After accepting the Lord, Dyann became involved with the Friends of Israel ministry in San Jose. She wrote:

He [Rev. Paul Yates] asked me if I would be interested in helping him contact Jewish people. I laughed and turned down the offer. The second time I said, 'Never! I'm going to Israel' and turned down the offer again. Then a married couple was hired as full-time workers in San Jose. I volunteered to help them get settled …by letting them live at my apartment, introducing them to all the Jewish people in town, and getting them started in the ministry. (Since I was doing volunteer work for Paul Yates, I knew pretty much his routine.) I began to have doubts as to whether or not the Lord wanted me to go to Israel, as I had been planning for a year.

Penny and David, the missionary couple,…then felt they were not called to Jewish missions and wanted to leave. At the same time, my volunteer ministry was being blessed.

When Penny and David resigned from the mission, I felt personally hurt. If they did not go to my people, who would? I felt it was my job and right to take on what they would not. I felt it was my responsibility…. I called up Paul and asked him to write to the mission and find out if I could take over the work that Penny and David came to do.

I was immediately accepted and loved every minute of it…. To me, mission work is like breathing…it is part of my life.[156]

With a desire to improve her education and training for her ministry in Jewish evangelism, Dyann enrolled in Central California Bible Institute, a night accredited school from the Multnomah School of the Bible in Portland, Oregon. She later moved to Chicago, where she enrolled in evening classes at Moody Bible Institute in Chicago.

As the Budoffs' worked to develop the ministry in Pittsburgh, Barry reported to *The Chosen People* magazine:

About two years ago I visited an older Jewish woman named Mrs. A. for the first time. Our first meeting was not highly successful as you can tell from this reconstruction:

'Hi, my name is Barry Budoff. I'm from Beth Sar Shalom Hebrew-Christian Fellowship, and if you have a few moments I'd like to speak with you.'

'Are you the ones who try to convert Jews into Christians?'

'No, we can't convert anybody, but we do believe that Jesus is the promised Messiah.'

'I'm not interested! Go away and don't bother me again! I'm a Jew and I want to remain a Jew!' (Slam!)

Under ordinary circumstances I probably would have left her alone, but for some odd reason I just couldn't.

Two-and-a-half months later I was back at her door. While she was still far from open, she wasn't quite as abrupt. So I decided to visit her once a month, and this continued for about a year-and-a-half.

Finally, on one particular occasion Mrs. A. just 'happened' to have a friend visiting with her. After introducing the two of us, her friend hit me with a barrage of questions, all of which were pertinent to Mrs. A. as well. After more than an hour of answering these questions I had to leave, but not before noticing that a striking change had come over Mrs. A. For the first time she said to me, 'I want to talk to you about why the Messiah had to die.'

I visited her home four more times since then, and we discussed the need for a blood atonement and Messiah's death. One blessed day Mrs. A. said to me, 'I want to accept Jesus' sacrifice for my own. What do I do?' I explained the plan of salvation to her, and when I was done she asked me to pray with her, which I most joyfully did. Her comment afterwards: 'I wish I had known sooner!'

Please pray for Mrs. A. as she continues to grow in her new faith in Messiah. She has begun to attend a local church, and at age 68 has finally begun to enjoy the abundant life.[157]

Barry also included hospitals in his visitation program. *The Chosen People* magazine reported:

When ABMJ's Barry Budoff first arrived in Pittsburgh he led a gentile lady to the Lord while he was on a hospital call. She began growing in the Lord and started sharing her faith with others in the hospital. One day she met a Jewish patient and began witnessing to him. He was moved by her testimony, but he wanted to meet a Jewish believer. She called Barry who went to visit the man. During Barry's visit the man accepted Christ as his Savior. Four days later he went home to be with his Master. God's timing was perfect.[158]

Barry and Dyann and several other workers of the Mission also became involved in attempting to save the life of a Russian Jewish baby girl named Jessica Katz. Barry, along with Arthur Watson and Larry Caruvana (workers of the Philadelphia branch) gathered over 4,000 signatures on a petition, which Barry then presented to Senator Schweiker (R. PA) urging the Soviet Union to accept U.S. help for little Jessica, who was suffering from mal-absorption syndrome. Barry told readers of *The Chosen People* magazine:

At a recent fair here, [Pittsburgh] Beth Sar Shalom had a booth where we distributed almost 900 pieces of literature. At the same time we were circulating a petition to help a Russian Jewish baby dying of a rare disease. The U.S. has developed a cure but the U.S.S.R. will not allow it to be shipped in.

The response was quite interesting. There was some name calling and yelling at us, but the vast majority of the people who came by our booth showed at least minor interest in what we were all about. Pray that our presence at the fair and at other similar activities will open doors in the Jewish community. Also, pray that the petitions which were signed will be of some effect in aiding Jessica.

Interestingly enough a local newspaper was sufficiently interested in our involvement with Jessica that they ran a story about us on the front page.

Continue to pray for our fellowship. I have begun training eight volunteers in Jewish evangelism, and beginning in August [c. 1978], we will be 'hitting' the streets to share our faith. Pray that God would give these eight people confidence both in learning the lessons that are being taught and in sharing their faith.[159]

Barry and Dyann were able to train, recruit and disciple many Jewish and Gentile believers for the work in Pittsburgh. From those discipled and trained, the beginnings of a Messianic congregation were formed; this nucleus of believers eventually established themselves as an independent congregation. They resigned from the staff of the Mission in late 1980, feeling that God was calling them to establish Messianic congregations. Through the years God has used them to build several such congregations. Barry is presently serving as the spiritual leader and "Messianic rabbi" of Congregation Adat Hatikvah in Chicago, Illinois.

As mentioned earlier, the Pittsburgh branch was one of the earliest branches established outside New York City, but following the resignation of the Budoffs the Pittsburgh branch of the Mission was closed. The building was leased to the Messianic congregation formed under the leadership of the Budoffs; the congregation later purchased the building. Although the Mission no longer has an outreach ministry in Pittsburgh, the congregation continues to bring the Gospel to the Jewish people and Gentile people of that area.

In May 1981, after the retirement of Perrin Cook, the Mission also closed the Atlanta, Georgia branch.

PERRIN COOK

Perrin Cook had participated as one of the "missionary trainees" in Martin Rosen's first training session in New York in 1968. After completing the training program, he remained in New York as the Resident Minister of the Manhattan branch. He was transferred to Atlanta, Georgia in 1969 (a time when the "District" method of operation was still being developed).

Perrin Cook was born into a Gentile Christian home in Phoenix, Arizona on February 22, 1922. In 1924 his family moved to Crystal Springs, Mississippi, where Perrin lived until after his graduation from high school in 1940. He was ten years of age when he openly professed his faith in Jesus at the First Baptist Church of Crystal Springs. Later, with the conviction that God was calling him to preach the Gospel, Perrin surrendered his life to God for full-time service. In preparation for the ministry, he attended Baylor University in Waco, Texas. After graduating from Baylor in 1950, he attended the Southern Baptist Theological Seminary in Louisville, Kentucky. He graduated from seminary in 1954.

In 1946, Perrin married a Christian girl whose name was Mildred Sanders. Mildred and Perrin had three sons and one daughter. Before applying to the Mission, Perrin spent over twenty years as a successful pastor of Baptist churches in Alabama, Kentucky, and Mississippi. He left the pastorate of Handsboro Baptist Church in Gulfport, Mississippi in response to a call to serve the Lord in bringing the Gospel to the Jewish people. Interestingly, Perrin had had no previous experience in Jewish evangelism. God had used his study of the Word and his contact with Mission personnel to burden his heart for the salvation of the Jewish people.

In sharing the story of how his ministry began in Atlanta, Perrin wrote:

The ABMJ opened the South Central Atlantic District in Atlanta in the Fall of 1969. Prior to that time some of our field men had ministered in churches of the area, but now through many contacts, God has opened the door for our personal ministry.

Mrs. H, a Hebrew Christian, saw our name in The Chosen People *and called, telling us that prayers had been answered. She, along with many others, had been praying to have a full-time ministry for the Jewish people, such as our Board has in Dallas, where her daughter lives. She had a reception for us in her home, where we had the privilege of meeting others who had been working with Jewish people. Out of this meeting, two couples played an important part in the beginning of our ministry. One couple, Mr. and Mrs. F, invited me to teach a Bible class in their home. They had been having a Home Fellowship Bible Class for more than six years where Jewish people were invited to come. Mrs. F.*

and other women had done door-to-door visiting and invited Jewish people to the class. Through this ministry, several had been led to faith in the Lord Jesus Christ. Another couple, Mr. and Mrs. L., had a ministry with Jewish people, and he interviewed me on his radio program. He has been a valuable helper in contacting Jewish people. Through this couple we were invited to a supper meeting in the home of Mr. and Mrs. S., Hebrew Christians, in Gainsville, Ga. She was teaching a morning Bible Class and asked me to come and supply several times for her. This gave opportunity of meeting other Christian friends who were interested in reaching Jewish people with the Gospel. She came to Atlanta and we met at the Jewish Home for the Aged where she sang and visited. We are thankful for these many doors of witness and ministry....

Our first public meetings were held in a community room of the Atlanta Federal and Savings building. From our first meeting with two people present, it has grown to as many as forty-two in attendance—and still growing! The public meetings have been strengthened from time to time by speakers from Mission Headquarters, Dr. Fuchs, Dr. Gruen and Dr. Heydt, as they were in the area.

When a Christian couple, Mr. and Mrs. P. in another city, learned of our desire to reach the college age group, they volunteered to help finance the enclosing of our double carport. Now, thanks to the prayers of so many, we are approaching the finishing stages of the room and plan on holding our fellowships in it in the coming weeks. All of the new recruits in our college group are anxious to bring their friends and to get started in a real relationship of understanding with their own people.

We have made two visits to our neighboring high schools. Both visits were for the purpose of bringing an understanding with the students about their Jewish friends and their traditions. The classes responded well for they seemed eager to know more about the Jewish heritage and their contribution to world history.

Our work includes several unique ministries, one of them being home 'personal' care. We have had the privilege of helping Hebrew Christians help themselves through recovering from hospital surgery. We have had the joy of bringing young Hebrew Christians to our home from the hospital. They felt relaxed and comfortable being in a family situation.[160]

The major thrust of Perrin's ministry in Atlanta was personal visitation and follow-up ministry to Jewish people from all walks of life. Once contacted or visited, invitations were extended to attend the various meetings held in the Atlanta area. Perrin faithfully visited all the Jewish people who were referred to him. Telling of Perrin's visits and loving concern for him, one individual, named Howard, sent a letter to the Mission's headquarters. He wrote:

I am writing to thank you and tell you how much your man, Rev. Perrin Cook, has done for me. I contacted him while I was serving time in jail and he came to see me.

In three to four weeks I will be released [c. 1977]. I could never have done these six months without Rev. Cook's help. He opened my eyes to the Lord Jesus Christ and now I have accepted Him as my Messiah.

Ever since I accepted Him things started to happen to speed up my release. My parents have also gotten closer to me.

All the time I was in jail, Rev. Cook was the only one to come to see me. He would come over and sit 20 or 30 minutes and we would talk and pray together. I don't know if you understand what this means to someone sitting in jail. It was like God knew I was there alone and sent Rev. Cook so I would be saved.

I am twenty-eight years old and Jewish. I was Bar Mitzvahed [sic] and did not attend temple much after that. After reading about Jesus Christ in the books Rev. Cook brought me I decided to ask Christ into my heart.

On February 3, 1977 I was reborn. Since that day I feel like a new man and I know I can go out and conquer anything I try. I only hope I can serve the Lord the way He wants to be served.

I am in deepest gratitude to your organization for being there when I need you and for having people that think of others as much as themselves—like Rev. Perrin Cook.

I pray many people find out how wonderful it is to be wanted by people like you and God.[161]

The Lord used Perrin Cook to reach many of the Jewish people of Atlanta with the Gospel. He also used him to teach many Christians the need for Jewish missions and evangelism.

During the early 1980's, as Larry Jaffrey worked to build the ministry in the Southeast Region, his wife, Gail, became very ill. She saw doctor after doctor, but the cause of her illness remained a mystery to them. No one seemed to be able to diagnose her problem. She almost lost her life before it was discovered that she was suffering from acute allergic reaction to a number of things, including air pollution and food allergies.

Once Gail's illness was diagnosed, it became clear to the Jaffreys that they would have to move from the congested Silver Spring, Maryland area to an area where there was less air pollution. In 1984 the Southeast Regional Office was therefore moved to its current location of Marshall, Virginia.

Although the move and Gail's road back to health were difficult, the new location did open a new area of witness for the ministry. The regional office was established in the Jaffreys' home, and when Gail was able to assist Larry, she was hired as his secretary. Additionally, like most missionaries' wives, she also helped with the Bible study and training classes that were held in the home.

Living in the rural suburbs of Washington D.C. did not limit the Jaffreys' concern for the Jewish people who lived and worked in large cities such as the Washington D.C./Baltimore, Maryland area. The Mission had long sought to maintain a branch ministry in the Nation's capitol, but it had always been a difficult city to reach with the Gospel.

When Larry first became the Regional Director for the Southeast region, Dan and Arlene Rigney were serving as missionaries in the Baltimore/Washington area. After the Rigneys resigned to work with Jews for Jesus, the Mission hired Dean Freeman and Delbert Holloway to work in that area but they eventually left the staff of the Mission to seek different careers.

Following the resignations of Freeman and Holloway, the Jaffreys faithfully conducted Bible study classes and other outreach ministries in the Washington D.C./Baltimore area. At times, Larry was able to arrange for special meetings at the Pentagon; other meetings were held in churches in the area, or in homes. Through the years, they managed to maintain a nucleus of Jewish and Gentile believers who were vitally interested in Jewish evangelism. This faithful core group, along with other Mission personnel, made the need for an outreach in the Washington D.C. area an important matter of prayer. God wonderfully answered those prayers in 1988 when Scott Brown, a young Jewish believer, was hired as a full-time worker for the Washington D.C./Baltimore, Maryland area.

Scott Brown

Scott Brown was born in Washington D.C. on June 9, 1954. He described his home as a typical modern, but traditional Jewish home. The story of how Scott came to faith in Jesus, was given by him in the following graphic and moving words:

I am yet another member of the east coast Ashkenazim; 2nd generation America-born and of Polish/Russian stock. The orthodoxy of my European forebears dwindled significantly by the time it reached me, which may account for my casual outlook on Jews and Judaism during the early post-Bar Mitzvah years. 'Identity' was something akin to achievement; it had to be accomplished.... Anyway, everyone was Jewish, as far as I could tell ...and commonness, to this teenager, was something to be scorned. So up on the shelf went my heritage and all the accouterments. I sought idols instead.

That's really what it means to seek out a purpose, to look for meaning in anything other than God: Idolatry. Not that I forsook Him; I just didn't pursue Him, but chose, rather, to pursue 'ways which seemeth right unto a man' (Prov. 14:12). But each 'way' had its corresponding idol: Ecology/Ralph Nader; college/professors; motorcycles and girls/ ...And on goes the list which, if I were to itemize it here, would suggest something like 'secular dispensationalism'; distinguishable ages in the outworking of Scott's plan, characterized by repeated unfulfillment.

I was working on college level idolatry [Beloit College, Beloit, Wisconsin; c. 9/1972-6/1974] when a fellow student mentioned in passing that he would like to buy some land one day. This was in the days when masses were streaming 'back to the land'; when Christmas sales claimed more Foxfire books than poinsettias. [The Foxfire books were popular in the early 1970's. Edited by Eliot Wigginton, they focused on teaching youth through a return to their cultural heritage.] *The craze had infected me, too, but before my friend's expressed daydream it had never occurred to me that just anyone could go out and buy land.... People inherited land, I thought, or otherwise found themselves on a parcel which no one had noticed before, ...It wasn't just another thing to own or study, it was something to become a part of; bigger than you. And the accessory images were so luscious! Shovels and hoes, tractor, garden, root cellar, cabin, family, fireplace.... This was a heritage I could buy to replace the one I had shelved. It was something new to worship.*

I bought forty wilderness acres and an axe. My zeal more than compensated for the fact that I had never before strayed more than nine yards from central air conditioning. Despite my mother's impassioned reminders that Jewish boys don't do this sort of thing, I built a tiny cabin and lived in it for nearly three years. This was in the wooded outskirts of a little no-light town called Cornell, Wisconsin. When my mother's friends asked her where I was and what I was doing, she would say, 'He's studying hard at Cornell' and quickly change the subject.

I learned much in that time of 'studying.' I learned that, indeed, all men are without excuse; God's qualities are clearly seen in His creation (Rom. 1:19,20). I also learned that I'm not such a bigshot after all....

I spent about one year working with a small crew of carpenters. Two of these fellows were particularly peculiar. Peculiar, ...in a positive sense. It was not just that their behavior was different, though it surely was (at work on time, no swearing, no complaining, no back-stabbing, etc.). It was a difference in quality; a quiet confidence which seemd [sic] to lay bare my own lack thereof. One of them, Jim, cared about me in a way which was neither contrived nor calculated, and I grew to appreciate him. One day at quitting time, Jim tossed me a little brown book. As I caught it I heard him say, 'Read this; there's life in it.' I thanked him, but I knew what the book was: It was that Gentile Bible, that primer for antiSemitism, the source of so much pain and suffering for the whole of Jewry. I took it home and stuffed it in the back of a drawer, where I intended it to remain. I would have thrown it away immediately were it not for the fact that Jim had given it to me. Jim cared about me, so I kept his gift.

Months passed, and I changed jobs. I was searching for something in my cabin one evening when I came across the little testament. Something (some One?) grabbed me by the impulse and I was overcome with curiosity. What were its contents? Was it mysticism? Mythology? I convinced myself that I was obligated to justify my distaste for the book. After all, I had never really seen one....

By the dim light of a kerosene lamp I began reading what appeared to be the most Jewish book I had ever read. I was totally bewildered. Jewish genealogies, Jewish history, Israel...what did the Gentiles see in this? I soaked it in. But whenever the words 'Jesus Christ' appeared on the page, they tore into me, so thick was the rind of misbeliefs enshrouding my understanding. But why was the name so deeply offensive? I had never considered the question until now.

In the ensuing weeks, my disposition toward the book changed dramatically.... It commanded respect without having to qualify its authority. The words of this Jesus wrenched secrets from my heart and mind of which even I was unaware. The book challenged me, and I became its disciple.

In 1977 I proposed to my high school sweetheart. She followed with two proclamations: 1) 'Yes.' 2) 'I'm not into the Bible like you are, so don't presume it upon me.' Four years later, she was into the Bible like I was, and together we had become quite knowledgeable in the Scripture...and remained quite dead in our sins. In the summer of 1981, a local church in town posted notices that they were going to show a series of films depicting events which the Bible says will occur at the end of this age. It was Jim the carpenter's church. The films were free and we love movies, so we went.

How does one describe the internal ministry of the Holy Spirit on the unregenerate soul? We knew enough Bible to trust the film's depiction of Revelation. The people on the screen were identifiable types; we were much like them. But they were being forced to make decisions that would shape their destinies, decisions based solely on their relationship to Jesus Christ. They were either His or they weren't. If they weren't they were condemned. Their death was obviously imminent, given the times. Was our death, though less obvious, any less imminent? Where did we stand with Him?

I was too distracted by my own suffocating conviction to notice that Margie was experiencing the same. With white-knuckled determination we resisted the altar call, after which we silently left the church, silently drove home, silently sat on the furniture in the living room. At least one eternity passed before I choked out the obvious: 'We have to pray.' In our four years of marriage, we had never prayed. My wife sat beside me on the couch, we held hands and I stumbled through a prayer of brokenness that took 27 years to compose. We were born again that night.

...I won't attempt to describe the subsequent transformation in our lives. But...I must mention the glorious fact that God not only resurrected my spirit, He has quickened what I thought to be forever dead: My sense of relevancy as a Jew. That useless heritage I shelved...was like a puzzle with a missing piece; full of potential, beautiful in places, almost fulfilling...but in the end, totally useless. Jesus is the missing piece. The puzzle has come down and it all makes perfect sense....

...Upon arriving at the Alaska Bible Institute to begin a two-and-one-half year course of study, one of my first private prayers was this: 'Lord, I'm yours. Build me and use me. Show me your will for my life and I'll follow it. Send me anywhere,...except to the Jews.' I could write volumes...about the means God has used to answer that prayer. Suffice it to say, He has turned my heart completely around, back in the direction of my people.[162]

Some of the first Jewish people God sent Scott to as a "missionary" were the members of his own family. He began by sharing the Gospel with his father, Dick Brown. At first, Dick just thought his son was going through another one of his passing "fads." He said:

He was young, and I figured it was just another one of his passing phases. Then, the more he talked, the more I put my guard up. To be perfectly honest, it was so foreign to hear that a Jew—especially my son—could believe in Jesus. I just couldn't accept it....

I was the next thing to an agnostic. I was raised partially by Orthodox aunts who made observing Judaism seem like paying penance. I ended up pushing it away. But when Scott started talking about God, I (falling back on my training) said that Jews don't believe in Jesus. I think I was just looking for something to say. I thought that if I could ignore this phase, he would grow out of it....

Over the months I could tell Scott was changing. Before, he had always sounded like he was looking for something. He had always had a searching look in his eyes. Now I could see the changes. He looked peaceful. He talked like he had a purpose....

I was a mortgage banker, a successful salesman, and I knew when I was being sold; it was obvious Scott was sincere. I remember thinking how much I wished something like that would happen to me.[163]

Scott stayed in close contact with his parents when he went off to attend Bible school in Alaska. It was while he was away at Bible school that Scott learned about the Bible study that Larry Jaffrey held in the Washington D.C. area; it was near his parents' home. Scott suggested to his parents that they attend the Bible study—just to see more about what he believed. His father stated:

Normally I'd have made an excuse to avoid going to a Bible study. I wasn't interested. But something compelled me to go. When I met the people there, something happened to me. It was inbred in me to look for the worst in people, to be cynical, to be suspicious of their motives. But I was just plain jealous of these people. They seemed to get so much out of something so simple. There was harmony inside them—blissful sounds corny—but it was something. And it was obvious they really loved me. They were strangers who were not strangers.

I kept looking for the gimmick in all this, telling myself that it couldn't be real, that he [Scott] had to be into some scam. So I went up to him for myself.[164]

When Dick Brown arrived in Alaska and went to visit the Bible School that Scott attended, he was amazed. Scott wrote:

My dad was overwhelmed by the love of the people at Bible school. One night he came to see me, almost furtively, and said, 'It's ironic—I own, or have owned, almost everything I ever wanted. But I wish I had the peace you have.'[165]

Dick returned to Washington D.C., and when his wife asked him if he was going to continue attending Larry Jaffrey's Bible study classes, he replied, 'Yes.' When she asked if he was doing it because of Scott, he responded, "No," he was doing it for himself. As he began to grasp an understanding of God's Word, Dick sent a letter to Scott in which he said:

Did you know there were about 400 years between the Old and New Testaments? Did you know that the first mention of the Messiah was in Genesis 3 and that Daniel foretold the coming of the Messiah in Daniel 9? Mom and I were fascinated by our first real exposure to Messianic Jews. Here were people who had Jewish names, sounded Jewish, looked Jewish, and yet believed that Jesus is the Messiah. Now, I understand what you were trying tell me, Scott.... As for me, well, I am ready to go further by attending future get-togethers at Larry's house.[166]

Although Scott was thrilled that God was working in his parents' lives, his own days were still filled with turmoil. He knew God was calling him into full-time ministry in Jewish Missions and evangelism, and he know God was calling him to work with ABMJ/Chosen People Ministries. But he also knew that his parents wanted him to prosper in the secular business world, and while they were open to the Gospel, he was not sure how they would receive the news that he wanted to be a "missionary to the Jews." Remembering that time in his life, Scott later stated:

There were still hard times ahead. For instance, when I knew I was going to quit my job and apply to Chosen People Ministries. It had taken me years to come to this point, and I prayed, rehearsed, practiced, and prayed some more before I told my parents. When I finally told them, my parents were very still, clinging to every word. My mother began to cry and left the room. Only later did I learn that this reaction was from conviction in her heart and that the very event I feared might harden her to the Gospel would be a catalyst for her coming to faith.[167]

Scott's father recalled the events of those days, when he wrote:

I wondered how Scott would raise his family. I had always made a lot of money and thought my children would too. Scott had such a promising future. I couldn't believe he'd give it all up. Then I looked at my own life. I had plenty of everything money could buy, and it was obvious that it hadn't been enough.[168]

Then came a day when Dick Brown's world came crashing down around him—the day he was told he would have to undergo emergency triple bypass surgery. Faced with his own mortality, he called his son, Scott. Dick later said:

> I called Scott to pray with Him. There was something about having triple bypass surgery that made me start to ask, 'I wonder exactly where I stand, right now and for all eternity?' I had never had time in my life to listen to my children. I was glad God had changed me enough so that I was listening to them now.
>
> I can see the changes God has made, and I trust Him. It's a miracle. That's really all I can say about it. It's truly a miracle.[169]

Scott, too, remembers that ominous day. It's a day he will never forget. He said:

> ...I'll never forget the day my dad called. He was going in for triple bypass surgery. He told me he knew he was a sinner and was separated from God. He wanted to pray with me to be reconciled with God. There I was, praying over the phone at work, crying my eyes out as he accepted the Messiahship of Jesus and acknowledged Him as his sin-bearer.
>
> The Lord has fulfilled the promise of Ezekiel 11:19 in our family: 'And I shall give them one heart, and shall put a new spirit within them. And I shall take the heart of stone out of their flesh and give them a heart of flesh.' My father, who was always generous, now has a tender heart. It's the greatest thing God has done.[170]

Scott completed his studies at the Alaska Bible Institute in Homer, Alaska and in 1985 he attended the Mission's S.T.E.P. program. In 1986 the Mission sent him on a mini-tour of Alaska. The tour's purpose was to open the churches of Alaska to the ministry of the Mission by giving them an opportunity to hear the testimony of a Jewish believer, and by giving Scott an opportunity to share with Christians of Alaska their need to reach Jewish people with the Gospel. When Scott and his wife, Marjorie, returned to the Washington D.C. area, Scott volunteered his time and abilities to Larry and the Mission. In June 1988 Scott joined the Mission's staff as a full-time worker for the Washington D.C./Baltimore area.

Soon after he joined the Mission's staff, Scott felt led to establish a new Messianic congregation. The Son of David congregation was therefore established, with Scott Brown as its pastor. Not only did Scott's parents come to faith in Jesus, his brother, Jeffrey, also accepted Jesus. Jeffrey now works together with Scott in the Son of David congregation. God's blessings on the ministry of the Browns' and the ministry of the Son of David congregation can be seen in the following report which appeared in *The Chosen People* magazine:

> Chosen People Ministries' Son of David Congregation sign (Silver Spring, MD) apparently draws its share of curiosity seekers. Several months ago, two Jewish women—independent of each other—saw the sign and called Scott Brown and Winn Crenshaw (CPM Greater Washington Area). Both women have since accepted Messiah.
>
> Debbie called after seeing the sign and receiving a brochure about the congregation. Scott met with her for five weeks of Bible study, tracing the principle of redemption in the first four chapters of Genesis.
>
> After she came to faith, her testimony at the time of her immersion (baptism) was 'one of the most powerful "Jewish" testimonies' Scott said he ever heard.
>
> 'In effect she said that her Jewishness was not contrary to this faith, but rather her Jewishness was fulfilled by it,' said Scott.
>
> The Son of David Congregation sign also prompted Marsha to call. New in the area, Marsha thought Son of David was a typical Jewish synagogue.
>
> Winn Crenshaw explained that Son of David congregants believed Jesus to be the promised Jewish Messiah.
>
> 'Well, I've heard that,' Marsha said, agreeing to attend the next service.
>
> After meeting with Winn, she prayed to receive the Lord. Marsha was also immersed with Debbie during October [c. 1991].[171]

The Chosen People magazine also reported the following story of a young Jewish man who came to faith in Jesus because of the witness of Scott Brown:

> When Steve Twain first met Chosen People missionary Scott Brown two years ago [c. 1990], he was quite surprised and intrigued. While visiting church with his wife, a believer, Steve heard Scott speak; Steve had a friendly discussion with Scott after the service.
>
> Steve came away with many questions. Here was Scott, a Jewish man, who believed in Yeshua (Jesus) as his Savior, while still maintaining a vibrant Jewish identity and lifestyle. The whole idea didn't seem possible to Steve—who

is also a Jew—yet here was living proof of it.

So in meeting Scott, one of Steve's long-held beliefs was shattered, but Steve wasn't willing to explore it any further. After all, he thought, I'm young, successful, and quite satisfied with the course my life is taking.

He continued to attend church from time to time with his wife, but that was enough for him. Scott offered to talk more with Steve, but they could never seem to get together.

Two years later, in April of this year [c.1991], Steve once again sat listening to Scott. This time, Scott was sharing on the Messiah in Passover. The presentation was both enlightening and compelling, and Steve was moved. He sought Scott out after the service with an enthusiastic greeting: 'Remember me?'

Scott did indeed remember Steve, but was surprised at the change in him. Gone was the confident, self-assured businessman he had met two years ago. In his place stood a man of uncertainty with an emptiness inside; a 'poverty of spirit.' He ventured a question: 'Where are you, Steve, regarding Jesus?'

Steve shrugged his shoulders and answered, 'Somewhere in no-man's land. I'm feeling really frustrated.'

Steve began to voice some of his fears regarding Jesus; he felt he could never measure up to God's standards. 'Steve,' Scott asked, 'do you know what it is that saves a man?' Although a bit taken aback by the direct question, Steve paused for only a moment before responding, 'Well…would you tell me?'

This was all the catalyst Scott needed. He quickly reminded Steve of the life-for-life principles of atonement he had just explained during the Passover demonstration: that the One who did 'measure up' was and is willing to exchange His life for Steve's, if only he would receive it.

Steve was excited and wanted to do something about it. 'You can do something about it right now,' Scott shared. 'This is a very personal issue, between you and God alone, but I would be happy to help you finalize your decision through prayer.'

So Steve, his very thankful wife, the pastor and Scott all knelt to pray. Steve's heart was both tender and broken as he received his Messiah and Lord. He wept tears of release and repentance, of surrender and security.

It was a moment profound in its impact. Long after the service had ended, in the quietness and serenity of the sanctuary, those four individuals demonstrated something so often forgotten. The only time we can measure up is when we are down on our knees.[172]

Through Scott Brown and the Son of David congregation, the witness of the Gospel continues to be effectively proclaimed to the Jewish people in the greater Washington D.C. area.

As previously mentioned, Larry Jaffrey was a member of the original team of "Regional Directors." Daniel Goldberg replaced Richard Cohen as Regional Director for the western states. The original team also included Rev. Ben Alpert as Regional Director of the Mid-West and Dr. Thomas McCall as Regional Director for the South West.

John Bell replaced Ben Alpert in Chicago, so Ben could do field work for the Mission. In the Spring of 1979 Ben resigned from the Mission's staff to work for The Friends of Israel Ministry. Ben re-applied to the Mission in June 1984; he was hired as a Field Evangelist for the Southeast Region (new title: National Ministries Representative)—a position he continues to hold with the Mission.

The Southwest Region Under Irwin (Rocky) Freeman

Dr. Irwin (Rocky) Freeman replaced Dr. Thomas McCall as Regional Director for the Southwest Region. (Tom resigned from the Mission's staff effective September 30, 1982.) Rocky was hired on July 15, 1982. He was sent to New York for specialized training, after which he returned to Dallas. His ministry there began on October 1, 1982.

"Rocky" was no stranger to the Mission. For many years he had been supplying the Mission with the names of interested and concerned Christians so that they, in turn, could receive The Chosen People magazine. As an independent evangelist, Rocky was well-known throughout the Southwest and Southeast. He regularly recommended the use of the Mission's materials and missionaries when pastors or individual Christians asked him for help in reaching Jewish people with the Gospel. Because of his interaction with the Mission through the years, Rocky and the author had become good friends by way of telephone visits and personal correspondence.

Rocky was raised in an orthodox Jewish home in Nashville, Tennessee. Even though he didn't live in a heavily populated Jewish community, he was raised in orthodox tradition. At the age of four he was enrolled in the local Hebrew school and was speaking Hebrew by the age of five and beginning to memorize the Torah (first five books of Moses). His intensive education and training continued until he was made Bar Mitzvah at the age of thirteen.

Rocky said it wasn't easy growing up in an orthodox Jewish home in Nashville. He was frequently mocked and cursed. As he grew older, he became impressed with material things, and he had a difficult time accepting the fact that he lived in a lower-middle class home. He also had difficulty accepting the reality that there were a lot of ungodly

Gentiles who seemed to enjoy endless prosperity. He struggled with the age-old question, "Why do the godly find life such a struggle, while the ungodly have life so easy?"—or so it seemed! Eventually he came to the conclusion that God may have worked in the lives of the Jewish people in ages past, but He certainly wasn't working in their lives in this day and age. Of that time in his life, Rocky wrote:

…Once I arrived at that decision, I was left on my own to forge a godless life that was soon to become an embarrassment to my family.

By this time, I had already made two important decisions. First, I had had enough persecution for being Jewish …Second, I decided that I was going to make more money and have more material possessions than any other person I knew.

Since the crowd I hung around with was in the habit of drinking, I decided to drink too. In the two years between my thirteenth and fifteenth birthdays, I had graduated from beer to moonshine. I soon found that I could drink half a pint of moonshine and still walk a straight line. It wasn't long before drinking became a daily ritual for my friends and I even while we were in school.

Naturally, it wasn't long before we earned a bad reputation. Even though we never became a formal gang, wherever 18 to 20 of us could be found, trouble was never far behind.

I was scheduled to graduate from high school at 16 because I had been advanced two years between the first and third grades. Two weeks before final exams I announced to my mother that I was going to quit school and join the Army.

She was shocked. After a long argument, it was decided that I couldn't join the Army or the Navy. My mother agreed to let me quit school only with the hope that I would return to school the next day. But, that night I ran away to join a carnival.

For three to four months I worked with the carnival. I was impressed by the fact that my co-workers were a strange breed of people, and it wasn't long before I learned that they had very few morals. It also wasn't long before my own moral standards plummeted even below theirs.

When the excitement of the midway began to wear off, I decided to return home. My mother told me I could stay on one condition—I had to finish school. As hard as it is to believe, when I reached two weeks before my final exams, I once again decided to quit.

So, at 17, I finally found myself in the Navy. It was almost like a dream come true. I could buy a bottle of beer for a dime and champagne for a dollar. In six months, I consumed $750 worth of booze.

I came back from overseas strapped to a bed on the aircraft carrier. The doctor on the carrier told me if I continued drinking the way I had been, a time would come when I wouldn't be able to quit.

This warning really scared me. My mind immediately flashed back to a time when I was a child and my mother called me to the window of our home. She pointed to a drunk man who was staggering down the street and said, 'You see him?' I said, 'Yes, Mama.' She warned, 'He's a Christian, and if you're not careful, you'll grow up to be just like him.'

So, when the ship's doctor told me I would be a drunk for the rest of my life, I was scared. I equated this warning with being a Christian, and I thought, 'Man, I don't want to be a Christian.'

Although my drinking habits did change once I got back to Nashville, my living habits didn't….

Then something happened to change the direction of my life. A young man named Paul was working for us….

…He told me his life had been changed by Christ. Then Paul invited me to his church so I could find out for myself what he was talking about….

One day, I went to a church softball game with Paul. As we watched the game, a honey blond, blue-eyed dream came walking by. Instantly, I knew I had to get to know her better. It wasn't easy, but I finally got her telephone number and called.

To my dismay, she wasn't the least bit interested in going out with me. I called her every day for six months, and the answer was always the same—'no!' Finally, she agreed to go out with me, but only if we went to church for a Wednesday prayer meeting.

I began attending church regularly on Wednesdays, but it didn't have any effect on me. I didn't know what was going on, and I didn't care.

As time passed, however, I couldn't help noticing the sincerity of these Christians. They persisted in telling me about Jesus, and I just as persistently ignored them. I was convinced that religion didn't work….

No matter how hard I tried to discourage these people they weren't about to give up. Every Wednesday night, and eventually on Sunday too, I would take this young lady to church. First, I'd hear about Jesus, and then I would take her home with my heart full of hope that she would respond affectionately toward me. But, it was always the same. She would read a couple of chapters out of the Bible, pray for me, and she would see me to the door. As I left, she would invariably say, 'It's been a wonderful evening. I hope we can do it again soon....'

Many of my friends were now either in prison or on their way. Two had been put to death in the electric chair. What hope was there for me?

One day as I sat in church wrestling with these thoughts, God spoke to me through a Scripture verse. Its promise rang out in my mind, 'He that cometh to me, I will in no wise cast out.' As the choir sang, I began to cry. I was both surprised and embarrassed by my sudden uncontrollable demonstration of emotions. 'What will people think?' I ask myself. As I looked around the sanctuary, however, I saw that no one was watching me.

Then another verse of Scripture came to me, 'And ye shall seek me, and find me, when ye shall search for me with all your heart.' At that very moment I felt an arm around my shoulder. I almost panicked as I thought to myself, 'That preacher has come back to get me!' But, as I glanced back I was even more startled. Nobody was there.

When I looked up at the pulpit, my amazement was complete. The preacher was gone and in his place there stood a man dressed in a brilliant white robe. I couldn't distinguish any features because his countenance shone with the most brilliant and blinding light that I had ever seen.

I don't remember walking up the aisle that day and falling on my knees in front of 1,100 people. All I know is the next thing I became aware of was the pastor asking me what I wanted.

I cried out, 'Man, I don't know what I want.' He said, 'What are you doing here, then?' And once again I cried out, 'Man, I don't know.'

The pastor called the chairman of the deacons to his side, saying, 'Brother Ward, this man is lost. Will you pray with him and ask God what He wants Rocky to do?'

I prayed with Brother Ward that day, pleading, 'Lord, if you'll let me know right now that Jesus Christ is Your Son and if You let me know that He can do for me what these people are saying, I will accept Him.'

At that very moment, the guilt and the burdens of my life were lifted. They were gone and now I had total peace. It was all true. Even a person like me—even I could be forgiven! As I knelt before God, I told Him with a heart full of gratitude that I would accept the gift I finally believed could be mine.[173]

God soon called Rocky into the ministry. Pat, the girl who had so diligently shared the Scriptures with Rocky, and prayed for him, also became his wife.

Rocky served as the Mission's Southwest Regional Director until September 1989, when he resigned to return to the ministry he and Pat had founded—the Rocky Freeman Evangelistic Association.

Another Regional Director who attended the historic meeting with the Board was Sam Nadler. As has been stated, Sam and Miriam Nadler re-joined the Mission's staff in September 1979. They had a burden to work with the Jewish community in New York City. When Sam came on staff, Richard Cohen was still the Missionary Director, and acting Regional Director for the Northeast. The author later appointed Sam to the position of Northeast Regional Director—a position he held until March 1, 1989 when the Board appointed him the Executive Director of the Mission.

David Sedaca was also at the historic meeting. David was the Regional Director for Canada. Insight into David's ministry in Canada and South America is related in other chapters of this history. Suffice it to say here, the missionary work and staff of Canada (during this period of time, up to the present) was treated as if it was another region of the Mission. This was done to systematize policies and procedures of the ministry being done in Canada and the ministry being done in the United States.

National Church Ministries Director Appointed

In addition to the Regional Directors, some members of the administrative staff were also invited to be present at this historic meeting with the Board. Rev. Terryl Delaney, Director of Communications for the Mission (he also carried the title of Editor in *The Chosen People* magazine) was invited to attend. Barry Rubin, hired in October 1982 as the Mission's National Church Ministries Director, was also invited. Barry's position had been created in conjunction with the Ad Hoc committee's recommendation to standardize the Church Ministries departments throughout the regions.

Before coming on the Mission's staff, Barry had served as the Executive Director of the Messiah Has Come Ministries, a work with headquarters in Chattanooga, Tennessee (formerly, the Southern Hebrew Mission to the Jews). Barry and his wife, Steffi, lived in Baltimore, Maryland. When Barry was hired by the Mission it was agreed that the Rubins could continue to live in Baltimore while they set up a pilot program under the supervision of Larry Jaffrey, the Southeast Regional Director. If the program proved successful, Barry was then to be transferred to New York to set up a similar program for the Northeast Region, and for the rest of the country.[174]

Both Barry and Steffi are highly creative individuals; they were also trained and experienced missionaries to the Jews. They had a wide range of administrative and media experience. Both had been former staff members of Jews for Jesus, and Steffi Rubin (nee: Geiser) had worked closely with Moishe Rosen and was one of the founding team members of the San Francisco "tribe" when it was still a part of the Mission.

Barry Rubin—His Story

Barry was raised in a traditional Jewish home. Like many Jewish young people, he could not find the practical relationship between "tradition" and faith in God. He wrote:

> I remember the day before my Bar Mitzvah. I was a Jewish boy of 13 and, according to Jewish tradition, responsible for obeying the laws of Torah. But I didn't see it that way. Although I intuitively held the books of Moses in reverence as any 'good' Jew would, I couldn't seem to apply their principles to my life. I had to be honest about my feelings, so I told my father I wasn't going through with the ceremony.
>
> 'Dad,' I exclaimed, 'I don't believe in God; neither do you; and neither do most of the people in the synagogue.' Deep thinking for a 13-year old? Well, I was also just plain scared to stand up and read Hebrew before all those people. But my Dad convinced me to get it over with. That was the last time I would set foot in a synagogue for many years. Still, something inside me yearned to know the meaning of life, even if I wasn't interested in the meaning of Jewish tradition.[175]

After Barry's graduation from college in the late 60's, he once again began to question the meaning of life and the existence of God. People were talking about "peace" and "love," yet those around him had very little of either. Believing that Jews could not even consider the claims of Christianity if they wanted to remain "Jewish," his search led him to consider the Eastern mystical religions. He soon became involved in the practices of Transcendental Meditation. Of his involvement, Barry wrote:

> …'TM,' marketed as 'a simple relaxation technique to relieve stress and help people fulfill their human potential,' is actually a form of Hinduism. The religious aspect is cleverly hidden behind the mask of 'self-awareness.' It sounded good to me, and soon I had become involved in an ancient mystical religion without knowing it.
>
> Morning and evening I would practice the ritual of TM. Over and over again I would vainly repeat my 'mantra.' It was merely a sound on which I was instructed to meditate. 'It will allow you to relax and find inner peace,' I had been told. But what was actually happening was that I was sliding deeper into sin and further away from God. Yet, at that time, I didn't know that, and I didn't really care about God.
>
> Funny thing about being Jewish—like many other Jews, I had no desire to know God and yet I still felt a strong tie with my Jewish background. So I wasn't too frightened of TM until I experienced a strange sensation once while in deep meditation. I felt as if my soul were leaving my body. I was shaken and needed something to take my mind off what had just happened. So I looked around the hotel room where I had been staying on a TM retreat for something to read. My eyes focused on a Gideon Bible placed by my bedside. Picking it up, I turned to the New Testament for the first time in my life.
>
> At first I was afraid to read it and then I found that I had nothing to worry about. I discovered that it was all about Jews—Matthew, John, Peter, Paul. I had always thought it was a book about Gentiles. Even the teachings of Jesus were compatible with the basic tenets of Judaism and the Old Testament. I was surprised to find that I actually felt drawn to this man called Jesus.[176]

Not long after that experience, Barry saw an ad in the local newspaper advertising an ABMJ (Chosen People Ministries) Hebrew Christian Rosh Hashanah service. Barry was intrigued by the ad. He had no idea what a Hebrew-Christian was. He thought perhaps it meant intermarried couples—like Jews and Christians. The more he thought about the service, the more appealing it sounded, so he went. He had no idea how that service and the Mission's missionaries, Dan and Arlene Rigney, would impact his life!

In relating the story, Barry wrote:

> …There I met Jews who believed that Jesus is our Messiah, just like the Jews I had read about in the New Testament. Unlike my ancestors, it seemed they had a good experience with Jesus and had no trouble saying His name. They even prayed in His name. 'This is interesting,' I thought, 'but not for real Jews like me.' I continued to go, however, because the people were so warm and friendly, and the atmosphere was welcoming. During this time, I became preoccupied with the Bible and began to read it daily. Its messages were becoming vivid parts of my memory by now.[177]

Even though he was regularly reading the Scriptures, hearing the testimonies of other Jewish people who had accepted the Messiah, and enjoying the fellowship of other believers in the Lord, Barry stubbornly refused to trust in Yeshua for his salvation. Then came April 15, 1972—a day when Barry joined a sailing cruise on the Chesapeake Bay. Of that fateful cruise, he recalled:

> We were moving along beneath the Bay Bridge. I looked up to watch some of the construction, marveling at the new span being added to the old bridge. Suddenly the serenity was shattered as a piece of steel tumbled from the bridge, crashing down onto our boat. It landed with an ear-splitting crack, so close to me that it broke my watch crystal. Fortunately, it did not break through the bottom of the boat.
>
> The others I was with raced over to where I stood, their voices high-pitched, full of panic and disbelief. Yet only one thought reached through to my numbed consciousness: Would God bring about something like this to make His point? Scripture teaches that Jews seek for a sign. But this? Or was Satan trying to kill me before I applied what I had heard about salvation in the Messiah?
>
> I found that I was strangely calm about the fact that I had almost been crushed by the piece of falling steel. What made me shake, though, was the enormity of the spiritual decision that lay before me. Although I had studied Isaiah 53, although I had calculated the time of the coming of the Messiah in Daniel 9, although I had understood how a Jew could believe in Yeshua, I was still reluctant to yield my life to the Lord.
>
> That night I attended a Passover Seder, the service that recounts the freeing of the Jewish people from slavery in Egypt thousands of years ago. It was a Messianic service led by Dan Rigney [CPM missionary]. It was held in Baltimore at a place called The Lederer Foundation.... I listened as the elements of Passover were described with their full Messianic meaning. I knew I now believed.
>
> That night, in the quietness of my home, I prayed to the God of Abraham, Isaac, and Jacob that Yeshua, His Messiah, would be my Savior.
>
> It was later that I discovered how many people had been praying for me in Baltimore, Washington, and all across the country. From time to time I still meet people who were praying for me back in 1972. One of those people who was praying was a nice Jewish girl originally from the Bronx named Steffi. She and I met a few months after I received Yeshua. We were married two years later and God has blessed us with two lovely daughters, Rebecca and Shira.[178]

STEFFI (GEISER) RUBIN—HER STORY

Steffi Rubin (Geiser), first came into contact with Moishe Rosen in January 1971—during the early days of the Mission's outreach in the San Francisco Bay Area. Moishe had been teaching a Bible study in cooperation with the Christian World Liberation Front on the campus of the University of California. At the time, Moishe had only been in the San Francisco area for about six months, having recently been transferred from New York.

Steffi had been attending the University of Buffalo in New York. She'd gone to California on her winter break. While living in New York, Steffi had worked as a designer and illustrator, and despite the fact that she was into the "drug scene" (as many were in those days), she gained knowledge and experience in the whole area of the graphic arts. While she was in California, one of her girlfriends talked Steffi into attending Moishe's campus Bible study. Steffi later wrote:

> When I first saw Moishe,...he looked very hokey to me,...I thought that whole Bible-study thing was very absurd. One girl came over to me and just stared. Her eyes were crossed and she was wearing an old lady's hat and fur coat. The entire experience was bizarre. But I needed a place to stay, and some of the kids in the Bible study invited me to their house. I didn't know it at the time, but Moishe bought food for me and other people who needed it. When I got to the house where these Christian kids were staying, I began to read one of the Bibles they left lying around, partly because they had been nice to me and partly because I was really curious.
>
> Two days later, on Sunday, I accepted the Lord,...Everybody in the house was really ecstatic about my decision and congratulated me over and over again. I called Moishe and said, 'Mr. Rosen, I accepted Jesus.' He said, 'Are you sure?' I said, 'Uh, yeah.' Then he replied, 'That's nice, but we have some people here for dinner. I'll call you on Tuesday.' Frankly, I was expecting him to jump up and down and appear immediately, but he was pretty cool about it. I know now that's his style, and I think it's probably wise because some young people jump into a commitment without thinking through all the implications.[179]

After accepting the Lord, Steffi began to hang around the Jews for Jesus office, enjoying the fellowship of the other believers and growing in the Lord. Moishe kept asking her to work on "broadsides" for him. But she kept putting him off—she wanted no responsibility. Moishe was persistent however, and soon Steffi gave in. She did one, then another, then another. By June 1971 she was spending her days and nights writing, illustrating, and doing art work for Moishe and for the Jews for Jesus branch of the Mission. In the Fall she enrolled at Simpson Bible College and began working part-time for the Mission. A sample of her creative writing appeared in *The Chosen People* magazine in her report entitled "A Day In The Life Of A Hebrew Christian":

> When I visited New York City in December I got up all my nerve and took my father's car into the Sunday night midtown traffic. I was on my way to a concert at Carnegie Hall given by a Hebrew Christian named Paul Stookey and more commonly known simply as Paul when surrounded by 'Peter' and 'Mary.'
>
> I had successfully parked the car and was on my way toward Carnegie Hall with an armload of broadsides I'd written called, 'Organic Health Foods.' (A broadside, incidentally is a handmade-type-looking do-it-yourself tract.) Having had extensive experience handing these out on the streets of Sausalito and the campus at Berkeley I was ready take on 57th Street. So there I was, walking down the street handing out literature in the cold between 6th and 7th Avenues; and I saw a crowd of people gathered around a movie theater like Otto Preminger is about to drive up or something. Well, what could please a nice tract-passing Jewish girl more, I ask you? As I walked around through the crowd passing out the literature, this policeman gives me a pushy nudge and tells me I'm not allowed to be doing this sort of thing. Well, I know otherwise. And, following in the footsteps of a certain minister I know who has a moustache and shall remain nameless (he is a staff member of ABMJ), I, in a somewhat louder-than-normal voice, reply, 'I have a perfect right to be handing this out because it's religious literature.' The policeman looks at the cover of the pamphlet and snarls, 'This is about health foods.' I tell him I know what it's about because I wrote it, and it's definitely about Jesus. He takes me firmly by the arm, (the crowd is very interested) and I declare in my best Hamlet-soliloquy voice, 'This police officer is violating my right to pass out religious literature and won't even examine it to find out if he's wrong!'
>
> Well, here I am with the sympathy of the crowd and one furious, embarrassed cop. I was shaking in the general area of my knees, and praying in the general area of the back of my mind, and speaking undauntedly and loudly in the general area of my mouth. I proceeded to hand out about 50 pieces of literature to the anxious crowd who wanted to know what this controversial scribble had to say.[180]

Writing tracts and other materials, distributing tracts, composing music and traveling with the music team—the Liberated Wailing Wall—Steffi used her gifts and talents for the Lord. In June 1973 she graduated summa cum laude from Simpson Bible College. Her talents were utilized in every area of the early formation and founding of Jews for Jesus.

Barry organized a pilot program for the Church Ministries Department which was very successful and which was adopted and adapted for all regions of the Mission. A modified version of the program is still being used.

S.T.E.P. Program Developed

Barry also designed and implemented the Summer Training and Evangelism Program (S.T.E.P.). He prepared a proposal for STEP which the author presented to the Board at the August 27, 1982 meeting. They were delighted with the proposal and unanimously adopted it.[181]

The STEP program provided the Mission with a unique recruiting and training program, expanding opportunities for witnessing not only in the city where the training was being held, but in cities across the United States and Canada where the STEP teams travel. The program also provided for increased income to the Mission. It was designed to have two phases. Phase One provided for classroom instruction and for opportunity to apply the lessons through doing evangelism and missionary work in the city where the program was being held. Phase Two was an itinerant program with the STEP candidates being divided into teams. The teams then ministered in different areas of the country for several weeks. Each team had an established itinerary, arranged through the Church Ministries Department and coordinated with the Regional Directors and staff in the areas where they were to minister. As the teams traveled and spoke in churches they raised support for the Mission; they raised awareness of the need for prayer support for the Mission; they raised awareness for the need for Christians to witness to their Jewish friends; and they recruited new STEP candidates for subsequent programs. Each candidate attending STEP was required to raise the "tuition" fees for attending the program.

The author shared his excitement about the STEP program in the August 1983, Midyear Report. He said:

> We are really excited about our expanded summer ministry in the New York area this year under the leadership of Barry Rubin. We are confident that God will use this Summer Training and Evangelism Program (S.T.E.P.) to touch thousands of Jews and Gentiles with the Gospel of Christ. We are thrilled to see the large numbers of dedicated young people God has raised up to participate in this program. First, they received classroom training from our veteran missionaries and regional directors. Secondly, they had practical, on-the-spot training by ministering in the New York

area. With their training completed, six teams are being sent throughout the United States and Canada. They are going into the highways and byways proclaiming the message of Jesus to Jew and Gentile alike.[182]

The success of the STEP program was immediately apparent. Jewish people were reached with the Gospel. There were decisions for the Lord. New workers were recruited for the Mission. New churches were opened as missionary and prayer support for the Mission increased. The September issue of *The Chosen People* magazine carried some of the reports of those who attended the first STEP program in New York City. Among those attending were Jerry Gross, (who later became a full-time missionary with the Mission); Melissa Honig (who became a part-time worker with the Mission); Pat Meese (a missionary with the Harrisburg Messianic Hebrew Christian Fellowship, in Harrisburg, Pennsylvania); Lena Gibson; Mark Kion; Patrica Freeman, (wife of Rocky Freeman, Regional Director of the Southwest region).[183] Each wrote of their experiences, telling how God used them to lead Jewish people to the Lord as they witnessed on the streets of New York.

Since its inception, God has continued to use the S.T.E.P. program as an effective summer training and evangelism program. With some modifications, it remains a part of the missionary program of the Mission.

POLICY ISSUES AND PROGRAMS

Prior to the June 1983 Board meeting, the author sent six written proposals to the members of the Board which he wanted them to consider in a special "think-tank" session. The proposal included the following points for consideration and discussion: (1) A Working Board versus an Influential Board. (2) A Fund Raising Policy. (3) Property Ownership and/or Leasing. (4) Regional Representation at Board Meetings. (5) ABMJ 5 Year Program. (6) Enforcement of the Policy Manual.

As the Board sessions got underway on June 18, 1983, the members decided to consider the issue of Fund Raising first. They proposed that each Director prepare a written statement indicating the goals and priorities he perceived for the Mission over the upcoming five year period. A working document on each issue was to be prepared from the written statements of the Directors. A deadline of July 15, 1983 was given, and a date for the special Board "think-tank" meeting was set for August 7, 1983.

At the same Board meeting (June 18, 1983) several other important items of business were approved by the Board. One was the authorization for Sam Nadler "...to look for property on Long Island, either for rent or purchase."[184] This was important as it directly addressed one of the issues—renting versus leasing—that was to be discussed at the special Board meeting in August.

The Board also unanimously passed resolutions, expressing their appreciation to Dr. Daniel Fuchs, Mrs. Muriel Fuchs, and Mr. James Straub—all three of whom had presented their requests to the Executive Committee at the January 24, 1983 meeting to retire from full-time active ministry with the Mission, effective April 30, 1983.[185]

At the time of his retirement from active service with the Mission, Daniel Fuchs, then age 71, had served for over forty-six years. Muriel Fuchs had served for thirty-three years. Jim Straub, then age 65, had served as a volunteer Board member since 1967, as a paid consultant since the mid-70's, and as Executive Vice-President in a full-time salaried position for five years.

With the retirement of Daniel Fuchs and James Straub as employees of the corporation, the author remained the only employee who was also a Board member. It was the first time since the days of Joseph Hoffman Cohn (except for the first few years after Cohn's death when Harold Pretlove served as the Executive Director) that only one employee was responsible for the organization and accountable to the Board. However, while Daniel Fuchs and James Straub retired from active service as "employees" of the corporation, they continued to serve on the Board of Directors—Daniel as Chairman of the Board, and James Straub as a member of the Executive Committee, the Finance Committee, and the Personnel Committee. With Harold Pretlove still serving on the Board, the ten-member Board had three retired staff members and one actively employed staff member among its membership. The major committees of the Board were still controlled by employees, either active or retired!

Part of the tension felt within the Board was the pull between the members who were employees and/or retired members who were volunteers. This tension affected many of the issues confronting the Board, especially with many of the new changes in policy and personnel. It was this very aspect of the Board which had prompted the author to include the topic of a "Working Board Versus an Influential Board" on his points for consideration and discussion at the "think tank" session of the Board. The author was convinced that for the future of the Mission, for its growth and continued development, a strong working volunteer Board of committed believers was essential.

Not only did Daniel and Muriel Fuchs and James Straub retire, Terryl Delaney also submitted his resignation during the summer of 1983. The changes brought about by the Ad Hoc Committee and their recommendations, the resignation of Joseph Caplan, and the re-organization of staff and administration to handle the retirement of Daniel, Muriel, and Jim Straub had created a great strain and burden on the Communications Department of the Mission. Though understaffed, the department was handling the monthly publication of *The Chosen People* magazine, printing and publishing tracts and materials for Jewish evangelism, and producing and coordinating materials for the regions and the Church Ministries Department. Terryl was also producing the radio broadcast, "*The Chosen People* News Hour," for which the author, Joseph Caplan and Terryl were speakers. On top of this, the department was handling the fund raising activities (such as they were), the publicity, and the public relations pieces for the Mission.

At about the time of the formation of the Ad Hoc Committee, Terryl submitted a proposal to the Board for additional staff and funding for his department, but the Board felt it could not act on his proposal until after the Ad Hoc Committee had had an opportunity to complete an in-depth study of the entire communications program of the Mission. When the committee completed its report, they recommended that a number of steps be taken to reduce the expense of the Communications Department.

When Terryl was told that his department was not going to be increased in size, either with personnel or additional funding, but that it would be decreased instead, he was deeply hurt. He asked to be removed as the Director of Communications and retained as the Editor of *The Chosen People* magazine. However, the Board felt that this would not be the right thing to do. Terryl subsequently submitted his resignation in August, 1983.

A year or two prior to his resignation from the Mission, Terryl had begun a Bible study in his home. Following the program of establishing congregations, the group soon organized itself into a local church and when Terryl resigned from the Mission the congregation voted to affiliate with the Conservative Baptist Home Mission Society with a view to establishing themselves as a Conservative Baptist Church in Monroe, New York. Terryl was asked to serve as the pastor of the church. With God's blessings, the church has grown and is being used to reach both Jews and Gentiles with the Gospel.

The special "think tank" session of the Board was held, as planned, on August 7, 1983. All members were present except for John Kubach, John Melhorn, and Harold Pretlove. Present by invitation were Jim Rees and Tom Walker. Jim Rees had taken over the responsibility of the finances and administration of the headquarters office after Jim Straub retired. He was not a Board member. Tom Walker was also present since he was still acting President of the Canadian Board, a member of the Mission's Canadian Board, and was International Conference Director for the Mission. He was no longer a member of the American Board of Directors.

The papers presented by the various Board members made it evident that the issue over the Mission's planting of indigenous congregations was still not resolved in the minds of some of the Directors. In an effort to glean additional insight into this area of ministry, it was decided that John Bell and Roy Schwarcz would be invited to the next Board meeting, to present the church planting ministry of the Mission.

The Board members continued to wrestle with questions such as, "What happens when Mission congregations become independent and want to associate with fellowships or denominational groups not in accord with the Mission's doctrinal position?" "How much control should the Mission exercise over the congregations?" "Does the Mission establish a fellowship or a denomination for the congregations it establishes?" These were new questions for the members of the Board, but they were questions which the Regional Directors had already discussed and argued through. Already on the author's drawing board was a plan for a fellowship of Messianic congregations—a fellowship for congregations that were in agreement with the doctrine and vision of the Mission. This had been discussed at the Regional meetings, and workers who were involved in congregational planting were already laying the groundwork to establish an independent organization called the Fellowship of Messianic Congregations. (This organization was established and is now a fellowship comprised of many Messianic congregations—some of which were established by the Mission, others through independent Messianic believers or other organizations, but united in faith, fellowship and doctrine for the common purpose of reaching more Jewish people with the Gospel through established Messianic congregations.)

The Board also wrestled with the issue of the "mission of the Mission." The Minutes record the following discussion:

> *Mr. Sevener presented the thought that, if a goal is to be a goal, it must be measurable and obtainable. Should 'to reach all Jews everywhere with the Gospel' be changed to 'reaching Jews with the Gospel,' leaving out all and everywhere. These words seem to imply that we need to be doing something wherever in the world there are Jewish people, regardless of numbers.*
>
> *Also to be considered is the definition of what 'the Gospel' is. Is it not only proclamation but also discipleship? These two areas could be:*
> 1) *Direct Evangelism, where we would bring the Gospel directly to the Jewish community.*
> 2) *Indirect Evangelism, where we are ministering to Christians, not only to witness, but to gain prayerful and*

financial support for the ongoing work of our ministry.

The mission cannot exist as an entity unto itself. It must be an extension of the local church within the community. Our goal is to be a handmaid to the churches to fulfill the Great Commission to the Jews.

Perhaps, rather than a goal for ABMJ, it is the purpose of the Church to 'reach all Jews everywhere with the Gospel.' This would mean that ABMJ is the 'arm' of the local church in reaching the Jews in their area with the Gospel. We must help the local church to understand that we are helping them to accomplish their work. Rather than viewing the ABMJ as a competitive ministry, we must educate the churches to realize that, if they were doing their task, we would have no reason to exist....

Mr. Sevener pointed out the statistics concerning the changing Jewish communities and the need to look toward the areas where the people are going, as we formulate programs and goals for the future. We must evaluate the areas as well as the ministry. We must be ready to move from a particular area if things are not working to accomplish the set goal(s) of the mission. The best way to make a missionary dispensable in an area is the establishing of a local congregation. In this way, when the mission moves its people and outreach, the witness continues in the community.[186]

Discussion also centered around fund-raising, the question regarding the use of the mailing list—its access and availability to staff and others. Also discussed was the whole question of vision versus budget—does the Board set the priorities for the ministry by the budget, or in faith, should the vision and course of the organization be determined, with the budget drawn up around that vision? These questions were not easily answered or resolved, but the fact that they were being raised and discussed was helping to expand the thinking and vision of all Board members as they looked to the Mission's future. One thing that was agreed upon by all of the Directors was the fact that fund raising was necessary if the vision of the Mission was to continue.

A further area of discussion centered around the regional approach to ministry, and the issue of Mission property—purchase versus renting or leasing. As for the regional method of operations the Minutes state:

Mr. Sevener presented what might be considered a basic rationale for staffing a region:
1) Regional Director—involved in missionary and field work.
2) Secretary—general office and correspondence.
3) Church Ministries Secretary.
4) Field Evangelist.
5) Missionaries—total dictated by the number of Jewish people to be reached, considering the three areas of center ministry, church planting and home/hotel Bible studies.
The above would provide for five missionaries for a population of 500,000, plus two secretaries. It was stated that we whould [sic] not be rigid in formula, but should look to the potential of an area and the needs within a particular region, keeping in mind the sensitivities and backgrounds of the people.[187]

With regard to the issue of property, at the time the Mission was faced with an immediate need for property on Long Island and in Van Nuys, California. With the issue over the regional structure resolved, it was not a difficult matter for the Board to resolve the issue over property. The type of ministry needed in a particular area would determine the type of building; it would also determine whether the Mission should purchase or rent/lease property. The Minutes state:

Mr. Sevener pointed out that the situation on Long Island is immediate. We need to vacate the church property. In the New York area we have established a congregation in White Plains [Light of Israel—Sam Nadler, pastor] and it is evident that we need a center ministry on Long Island.

In California, however, the situation is somewhat different. The Van Nuys office must be vacated, but the North Hollywood branch is not in jeopardy, even though the landlord does not make improvements. If we determine that we should not have a center-type ministry there, but instead go the direction of church planting, we might be able to rent smaller office space for the regional facilities and missionaries.[188]

The discussion then turned to the Communications Department of the Mission, and the need of hiring a new Communications Director. Since the issues of the image and vision of the organization were still being debated by the Board, and the struggle over the control and editorship of the magazine, literature, direct mail appeals, etc., had not yet been resolved, the author suggested that the hiring of a new Communications Director be postponed.[189] He did so based on his belief that until clear direction was given in these areas, the hiring of a new Communications Director would only increase problems because his or her new ideas, suggested changes, etc., would not be able to be implemented.

The depth and scope of the Directors' discussions regarding the magazine and literature produced are reflected in the Minutes. They state:

Dr. Fuchs suggested that we again form an Editorial Committee to deal with the needs of literature and publications.

Concerning The Chosen People magazine, it was agreed that the Board must decide which direction to take with the publication. It was suggested that we consider changing format, paper, size, etc. It was also suggested that we seek advice from someone with expertise in this area. Do we want a magazine? Do we want a house organ that could be produced less expensively? It was agreed that we do not want a magazine for a magazine's sake. We do want a publication that will bring to the Christian public the need for Jewish missions, through Bible studies and prophecy, and information as to what the Holy Spirit, through the ABMJ, is doing. It must be clearly identified with the ABMJ all the way through.

Could we work toward two separate publications? One which would be the house organ of the ABMJ, simply produced, reflecting our ministry, free of charge, etc. At the same time, we could approach perhaps Christianity Today to begin to work toward a publication such as a Hebrew Christian Journal, etc....

Jim Straub pointed out that we are dealing with two types of people: those who are already interested in the mission and would read any piece of literature, and those who are new and who we want to attract to becoming involved with ABMJ. Perhaps what we need are two pieces, one plain and the other more sophisticated.

Dr. Fuchs suggested that a possibility might be to publish 10 months of The Chosen People in a smaller, less expensive style and use the eleventh month to publish a more sophisticated (perhaps even four color) issue. This special issue could be printed in enough numbers to use for presentation to large donors and to introduce people to the mission.

Mr. Sevener will try to secure appointments with some men who have expertise in this field,...to discuss our issues, goals and needs and bring a recommendation to the Board at their next meeting.

Immediate steps will be taken to increase the use of the ABMJ name and logo within the magazine and all other materials published by the mission....

Concerning the content of the magazine, it was suggested that perhaps we consider other areas of Bible study in addition to prophecy. Also, to include helps on 'how to' witness to Jewish people for the greater Gentile readership.

The Board did agree that The Chosen People magazine should be the official organ of the ABMJ and that, although it will carry a subscription rate, it will be offered free.

Mr. Sevener stated that he had been talking with Amy Rabinovitz and that she expressed an interest in reworking The Shepherd of Israel, making it into something more contemporary. Our workers are presently not using it to its full potential, because it does not reach the Jewish person of today. There has been some discussion about possibly changing the name as part of the revision.

[Amy Rabinovitz came to faith in the Messiah through the witness of her friend, who took her to the Denver branch of the Mission where Eliezer and Sarah Urbach were working. On that particular night, the author was the guest speaker and he met Amy, who was still searching for truth. Eliezer and the author spoke to Amy about her need to accept Yeshua. Shortly after that encounter Amy accepted the Lord.

As Amy grew in her faith, she wanted to serve the Lord so she involved herself in doing volunteer projects for the Mission. Her home was in Texas, and when the Mission participated in "Explo '72," Amy was there to help. About that time, Moishe Rosen needed a worker with secretarial and writing skills, as well as administrative skills. Knowing that Amy was a very creative writer who possessed good administrative skills, the author suggested that we interview her for the job. Amy was hired to work with Moishe. When Jews for Jesus was separated from the Mission, Amy stayed with the newly formed organization—thus becoming one of its founding members. Several years later, she left the Jews for Jesus organization to do free-lance writing. The Mission once again utilized Amy's writing skills as she was asked to write for *The Chosen People* magazine and other publications. She continued to write for the Mission until 1992, when the Communications Department decided to bring all of its writing "in-house."]

It was agreed that the broadsides, as is presently being done, would continue to be printed in the various regions as they see the need and develop them. Headquarters reserves the editorial rights on all printed materials, however.

Such broadsides and some tracts printed by headquarters can be defined as pre-evangelism materials. We need to develop a secondary line of tracts, by updating many of those previously published and developing new ones, which would be teaching material. A third line would be thesis type booklets, prepared for both Jews and Christians. This would enable ABMJ to provide material that is peculiar to the ministry of reaching Jews with the Gospel.

Along with this, we need to develop a cassette ministry, including all of the men on our staff who currently are involved in speaking and teaching ministries. For a minimal investment, the mission could realize a new source of income, while at the same time helping these men to become better known publicly, thus increasing the opportunities for speaking dates.

It was noted that we should monitor very carefully the use of special projects, for which funds are designated and set aside, so that this does not jeopardize the General Fund.

Dr. Pretlove [John] mentioned that he had experience with other Christian organizations who had received legacies and spread them over a five year period, wondering if the ABMJ had ever considered this. It was agreed that it is imperative that these funds be segregated from the General Fund for use on special projects. These are part of the endowment that must be built for the future ministry.[190]

The matter of segregating legacy income from General Fund income was one issue which the author and some of the other Board members felt strongly about. We believed if the Mission was going to grow, these funds needed to be segregated so they could be used for special projects, or for non-recurring expenses. Using legacies for salaries, benefits, programs, etc., as was the practice after the death of Joseph Cohn, caused the General Fund to be inflated which resulted in financial difficulties such as those the Mission had been facing. Unfortunately, the issue over the purpose and use of the Investment Fund, legacies, etc. was not resolved until several years after this meeting of the Board.

The days, weeks, and months after that fateful day in May 1980, when the Mission received notification that the funds securing the first mortgage on the Mission's Headquarters building had to be returned, had been both stressful and joyful. The missionary work continued to grow and flourish. As missionary reports heralded the news that Jewish people were opening their hearts to Yeshua around the world, the news was passed on to the members of the "Chosen People family" (donors and friends of the Mission). Each issue of *The Chosen People* magazine carried the testimonies of new Jewish believers and reports of the growing impact of our missionaries. In South America, Israel, France, Canada, and the United States it seemed that a "field white unto harvest" was being reaped by the workers of the Mission. By the time of the special "think tank" session of the Board, it seemed that the Mission, the Board, and the staff were finally beginning to share a common vision and program. We thrilled at God's faithfulness, and knew He could be trusted in the present, and for the future!

But the days were stressful, too. By mid-1983 the author began to experience some health problems. These problems culminated in September 1983 when the author found himself in a hospital bed, facing triple bypass surgery. Among the lessons learned during this abrupt interruption in his activities, was the fact that no one is "indispensable" in the Lord's work. Serving in a leadership role in the Lord's work is a privilege, not an "inalienable right." Over a four-month period, the author appreciated anew the wonderful staff of workers God had given to the Mission, the faithful and dedicated members of the Board, and the wonderful "Chosen People family" of prayer and financial supporters.

With the position of Executive Vice President still unfilled (following the retirement of James Straub April 30, 1983), and with the position of Missionary Director still unfilled (the author assumed those duties after the resignation of Richard Cohen in 1980), the author's sudden and serious health condition focused the Board's attention on the fact that there was no one to "fill in the gap." Daniel Fuchs, in his position as Chairman of the Board and as the past President of the Mission, therefore once again assumed the duties of President during the author's illness and recuperation.

During those weeks "back in the harness," Daniel met with members of the staff and he joined the Regional Directors at one of their meetings. As he listened to the reports of the R.D.'s—their vision for the ministry, their grievances, etc.—he realized that some of the unresolved issues of the Board were affecting the Regional Directors and, ultimately, the staff of the Mission. He also realized, perhaps for the first time, that the scope, direction and vision of the ministry which the Regional Directors were pursuing greatly impacted on many of those issues. This realization served as a catalyst to once again focus on the many "unresolved issues." These issues therefore once again become the topics of much discussion at the Board meetings held subsequent to Daniel's meeting with the R.D.'s.

The October 29, 1983 meeting of the Board was held at the home of the author, who was still recuperating from surgery. The meeting was historic in that at this meeting the issue of the Mission establishing Messianic congregations was finally resolved.

John Bell was invited to address the Board on the topic of Messianic congregations. He presented a paper which included three areas of discussion: 1) Why Church Planting is necessary for today. 2) What has happened as a result of Church Planting. 3) What is the future of Church Planting.

With regard to John's presentation, the Minutes state:

...Dr. Fuchs stated that he felt many of the questions had been answered. It was agreed that the Church Planting program will continue as one aspect of the overall ministry of the ABMJ. For future congregations consideration will be given to location (primarily in Jewish communities where new believers would not have access to an evangelical

congregation), need of the people in that location for a congregation, capable personnel to pastor the flock, etc. Congregations will not be started merely for the sake of starting congregations, but only as the Lord leads in order to meet the needs of those to whom the ABMJ is ministering.

John Bell was commended for the paper he presented and it was suggested that the ABMJ copyright the material and, with proper editing, publish it, perhaps in booklet or some other form.[191]

The Mission did edit and publish John's paper in booklet form, and it became the official policy for the church planting ministry of the Mission. Later, a policy manual and an operations manual was developed as the Mission continued to expand its church planting ministry.

Barry Rubin was also invited to the October 1983 Board meeting, to present a report on the Mission's Church Ministries Department. His report and the new policies for the Church Ministries Department of the Mission were unanimously accepted. The Minutes state:

Dr. Fuchs summarized the priority of Mr. Rubin's report as recommending the employment of a Church Relations Director in each region who would contact churches for meetings for the missionary staff, thereby tapping a potential of hundreds of churches which do not now support us. Mr. Rubin amplified this by stating that he believed this to be the 'bread and butter' of ABMJ. By reaching these churches the ABMJ would also be reaching those individuals, led of the Lord, who would become involved in the ministry through prayer and giving.

Upon motion and second, it was unanimously carried to officially change the name of the Church Relations Department to the Church Ministries Department, since our relationship with the churches is not merely to raise funds, but to minister to them and assist them in Jewish evangelism.[192]

The Church Ministries Department, as outlined by Barry Rubin to the Board, had the full support of the Regional Directors. It has been a very effective program for the Mission, and it continues with some modifications to the present day.

By January 1984, the author was back "on the job" following his surgery. As the Directors met together at the end of January, three major considerations dominated the discussions. One was the re-establishment of the Field Evangelist position—a position which had been phased out as the regional program became operative. The Regional Directors felt it was time to re-institute this position, and their proposal that this be done had been presented to the Board at their previous meeting. The Minutes of the January 27, 1984 meeting state:

Mr. Sevener presented a proposal from Rocky Freeman that had first been presented to the directors for consideration last October for the establishment of a position of Field Evangelist. This would be a regional position, with the person reporting directly to the regional director. While the missionaries would be seeking their individual support, the Field Evangelist would be seeking support for the overall ministry of the region. As he traveled from place to place to speak in churches, he would also be responsible for evangelizing amongst the Jewish people in those communities. The salary for this position would fall in the Missionary II category of the salary schedule. It was moved and voted to approve the establishment of the position of Field Evangelist as outlined in the proposal with the appointment of such subject to budgetary limitations.[193]

The use of Field Evangelists was soon implemented; it continues today with minor adaptations and changes—one of which was the change of title from Field Evangelist to National Ministries Representative.

Another major consideration at the January 1984 Board meeting was the author's proposal to the Board that they consider the possibility of changing the name of the Mission to "Chosen People Ministries, Inc."[194] As a result of the discussions on this subject, it was agreed that the possibility of a name change would be discussed with individuals in marketing and communications to determine the impact of such a change upon the Mission.

The author also presented a proposal that all prospective Board applicants complete an application and a doctrinal questionnaire—something that had never been done before. The Board had been concerned about recruiting new Board members, but the author believed that before new members were recruited, guidelines needed to be established as to the type of board member needed, background, etc. Further, the Board needed to establish standards for membership so the vision and work of the Mission would continue. With some modifications in the application and procedure, the Board adopted the Board Member Application and recruitment procedure proposal at their May, 18, 1984 meeting.[195]

A recommendation was also made to once again secure the services of Dr. F. E. Brown to do an in-depth study of the Mission's ministry objectives and image among its staff, Board members, and constituents. The Minutes state:

It was the recommendation of the Budget Committee appointed by the Board that the Executive Committee retain the services of Dr. F.E. Brown and Dr. John Walvoord to examine the philosophy of the mission particularly in the area of fund raising. Reports will be forth-coming from both gentlemen in a few weeks.[196]

The results of Dr. Brown's survey were presented at the May 1984 Board meeting. The meeting was held at Schroon Lake, New York, in conjunction with the Mission's annual staff retreat. Present at the meeting, by invitation, for the discussions on the survey were the Regional Directors—Rocky Freeman, Daniel Goldberg, Larry Jaffrey, Sam Nadler, Tom Walker.

The survey indicated that the Mission, when compared to other organizations surveyed, rated above average on every area and issue—with the exception of one, the area of control.[197] Dr. Brown's report indicated that the Mission's greatest strength was also its greatest weakness—the rugged individualism of its leadership. He pointed out that this indicated that the Mission was composed of strong individuals who possessed vision and direction (as leaders often do), and that the goal of the Mission should be to effectively harness that leadership ability so that it would function to fulfill a common goal. (It is difficult for people of vision and individual drive to work together, yet within the Mission's structure it was happening! This had been true of the Mission since the days of the Cohns.)

Following the presentation of Dr. Brown's report, the Board voted to hold a special meeting in July for further discussion and analysis of the report, and for the development of the Mission's objectives and the Board's recommendations in light of the findings of the report. The special Directors meeting was scheduled to begin at noon on July 20, 1984 and to extend through Sunday, July 22, 1984. The Regional Directors were asked to submit their thoughts and input to the President in written form. He, in turn, was asked to forward the responses from the R.D.'s to the other Board members by mail.

Policy Statement Formulated

The July 20-22, 1984 Board of Directors meeting was historic. It took place at the Bear Mountain Inn, Bear Mountain State Park, New York. Board members present included: Daniel Fuchs, presiding; Roy Adams, Albert Pasche, Harold Pretlove, John Pretlove, Harold Sevener, and James Straub. Absent were: C. Robert Clemensen, John Kubach, and John Melhorn. Present by invitation, but not a Board member was Jim Rees, the Controller for the Mission.

The meetings were the most comprehensive discussions the Board had held to date. Many of the statements and policies from the meetings set the direction and vision for the future of the Mission, and are still in effect within the Mission's structure today.

After a detailed consideration and discussion of the survey tabulated by Dr. Brown, the Board discussed and took action on a number of issues. They once again affirmed the guideline of a minimum of 100,000 Jews per area in determining cities to which full-time missionaries were to be assigned. The Directors recognized that this figure was a "rule of thumb," and that exceptions were to be allowed in instances where merit was found for deviation. Cities where the Jewish population was not large enough to merit a full-time missionary in residence, were to be included within the itineraries of the Field Evangelists or the S.T.E.P. teams.

It was also moved and adopted that each S.T.E.P team would have a veteran missionary accompany them as they traveled. This was to eliminate any problems encountered because of the inexperience of newly trained S.T.E.P. workers, as well as to give opportunity to further evaluate the ability of the team members to work together as a missionary team.

The Directors unanimously agreed and voted to discontinue the publication of The Shepherd of Israel—a publication that had been produced since 1920. A careful evaluation of the publication had revealed that it was no longer an effective means of communication. The changes made by Amy Rabinovitz had not improved its effectiveness. It was therefore agreed that it had outlived its usefulness.

The financial statements and liquidity reports of the Mission were also reviewed, and comparative statements from previous years shown. It was clear that the new communications programs, developed in conjunction with an outside agency, were helping to increase the Mission's donor base and income. The decision was made to retain the services of outside agencies to assist in the fund raising of the Mission.

The Directors also discussed the fact that there was a growing atmosphere of mutual trust between themselves and the Regional Directors. Recognizing the need for the R.D.'s to have access to financial information of the Mission which affected their ability to properly administer their respective areas, the Board took the following action:

...As the Board establishes objectives for all regions, it must be with the understanding that they are guidelines and may not work in every region. However, it is important that the Regional Directors have this direction from the Board, in order to use the talents and gifts of all of their staff.

It was moved, seconded and unanimously adopted that the Regional Directors be made privy to financial information of the Mission at the discretion of Harold Sevener. It was agreed that the previous arrangement of sharing printed material only at a specific meeting was preferable.[198]

Another area of discussion was the setting of goals for the Investment Fund of the Mission. This matter was referred to the Finance Committee of the Board, and they were asked to come back to the Board with specific recommendations for its use.

The Board also approved the policy of a Workers Conference, to be held every two years, as an opportunity for the staff and Board to fellowship together, and for the Mission's leaders and Board members to discuss Mission policy and its implications. This policy has been continued to the present, and has proven to be a benefit for the entire Mission.

But the greatest achievement coming out of the special meeting of the Board in July 1984 was a unified Statement of Purpose for the organization. The Minutes state:

It was moved, seconded and unanimously carried that the following be adopted as the Statement of Purpose of the American Board of Missions to the Jews, Inc.

'To serve as an arm of the local churches of the Lord Jesus Christ in fulfilling the Great Commission, with specific emphasis on the Jews.'[199]

A list of specific objectives and goals was then unanimously adopted by the Directors.

SPECIFIC OBJECTIVES
A. *In relation to the Jews*
　1. *Present the Gospel to Jews.*
　2. *To lead Jews to trust in Jesus Christ as their Lord, Saviour and Messiah.*
　3. *To disciple those who trust in Christ.*
　4. *To integrate those who trust in Christ into local churches, existing or new.*
B. *In relation to local churches*
　1. *Teach the Scriptures concerning God's plan for the Jews.*
　2. *Teach their responsibility for Jewish evangelism.*
　3. *Teach Christian responsibility in support of Jewish evangelism in prayer and in giving.*
　4. *To teach Christians methods of personal evangelism which have been found useful in winning Jews.*
SPECIFIC GOALS
A. *For the Mission*
　1. *In relation to Jews.*
　2. *In relation to local churches.*
B. *For each missionary*
　1. *In relation to Jews.*
　2. *In relation to local churches.*
METHODOLOGY
A. *Evangelism*
The methods will vary and change. The fundamental criterion: any method must be designed to present the claims of Jesus Christ as the crucified Messiah, in the power of the Holy Spirit, in such a way that an individual is invited to trust Jesus Christ alone for his salvation and begin to follow Him as Lord.[200]

With some slight variation in wording this Statement of Purpose, as adopted by the Board at this historic meeting, still remains the operative statement of the Mission's purpose in fulfilling its ministry.[201]

In keeping with the Directors' desire to increase the number of Jewish believers on the Board, and with the new Board application and doctrinal questionnaire policy in effect, Rev. Albert Runge was interviewed for Board membership at the May Directors' meeting.[202] His nomination was unanimously approved and carried at the October 1984 Board meeting.[203] (Albert Runge's testimony was given in Chapter Ten of this history.)

New Staff for the Northeast

The missionary staff, too, was being increased. Michael Rydelnik, who had worked for the Mission on a part-time basis while he was a student at Moody Bible Institute, was hired in 1984 as a full-time missionary.

MICHAEL AND EVA RYDELNIK

Michael was another "child of the Mission." His mother had become a believer while she was living in Germany prior to World War II. After she accepted the Lord, she began studies as a novice in the Lutheran Sisterhood. When the war broke out, and Hitler began his program of rounding up the Jews of Germany for the "final Jewish solution," Michael's mother was among the Jews who were rounded up and placed in a concentration camp. She miraculously survived those years, and was liberated by the allies.

Before immigrating to the United States, Michael's mother married a Jewish man who did not believe in Yeshua as Messiah. When the family settled in Brooklyn, Mr. Rydelnik forbade his wife from attending church or from having fellowship with other Christians. He also forbade her from telling their children about her belief in the Messiah.

The four Rydelnik children were raised in orthodox Jewish tradition. They attended synagogue regularly and were given a solid Jewish education. Michael, like the other orthodox Jewish boys, was made Bar Mitzvah at age thirteen. Jewish tradition and Zionism became his religion.

Mrs. Rydelnik kept her promise to her husband, and did not reveal her belief in Yeshua to her children, but through the leading of God, Michael's brother also came to faith in Yeshua. He made the mistake of wearing a cross around his neck, and when Mr. Rydelnik saw it he immediately accused his wife of breaking her promise. He threatened to leave her unless she renounced her faith. This was more than she could take! Keeping silent had been one thing; to renounce her faith was another! She refused, and she told her husband he could never make her stop believing in Yeshua. Furious with her for her defiance, Mr. Rydelnik left the family and obtained a divorce.

After her husband left, Mrs Rydelnik began to attend the meetings at the Coney Island branch of the Mission; she began to talk openly to her children about her faith and about Yeshua. Her friends from the Mission began showing up at their house and they, too, spoke about Yeshua. They showed Michael the prophecies from the Bible, and told him that he, too, needed to accept Yeshua as his Messiah and Savior, but their words made Michael angry. Following the example set by his father, he steeled himself against their testimony. He had been raised as a traditional Jew. Jesus was for the Christians—Jesus was not for the Jews, or so he thought!

One evening when Michael went to the Mission to pick up his mother, he met Hilda Koser, the Missionary-in-Charge of the Coney Island branch. Hilda, who was a masterful missionary, had learned that Michael was looking for a summer job so she asked if he would work for her, straightening out the books in her library. For Hilda, it was a perfect witnessing situation. She planned to be nearby as Michael arranged the books in her library—just in case he had any questions. During the lunch hour she shared Messianic prophecies with Michael, and demonstrated that Jews can believe in Jesus and still be Jewish. In recalling those noontime meetings and subsequent events, Michael later wrote:

> At noontime, I was very confident. But late at night, I'd lie in bed and wonder about her interpretation of Scripture. 'Could she be right?'
>
> As it became increasingly apparent that there was validity to these Messianic prophecies, I began to pray that God would show me if Jesus was truly the Messiah.
>
> Then one day, Miss Koser pointed out that the Law required a blood sacrifice for sin. This Judaic practice had ceased two millennia ago, she maintained, because Jesus was that final sacrifice for sin.
>
> For the first time, I recognized my need. Maybe I wasn't a druggie, but I was a sinner.
>
> Repentance would not be enough. I needed an atoning sacrifice. It seemed logical that the Messiah would die in exchange for my life.
>
> Still, I was hesitant. I was convinced that if I believed that Jesus was both the Lord and Messiah, I would have to forfeit my Jewish identity. That fear kept me from making any decision.
>
> Even though I had refused to attend any meetings at the center, I was invited there to see a film about Israel. As a Zionist, I felt this would be OK, so I went.
>
> While watching 'His Land,' I saw how the restoration of Israel had been foretold by Hebrew prophets. I realized then that the same prophets had also spoken of a Messiah to be born in Bethlehem (Mc. 5:1, 2), One who would die for the sins of Israel.
>
> It had to be Jesus. 'If the Jewish Scriptures spoke of Him, then—to be the best Jew I could be—I had to believe in Him.
>
> Though some people had persecuted Jews in Jesus' name, I knew He wept over every drop of spilled blood. And that day, after a lifetime of hostility, I said, 'Yes, Jesus is the Messiah. I'm receiving Him as my Savior and putting my life in His hands.'
>
> Now my life has real purpose and stability, because I'm anchored to the Rock of Israel. My sins have been forgiven, and I have a personal relationship with God.[204]

Two years later, in 1974, Michael enrolled in the Jewish Studies program at Moody Bible Institute to prepare himself for full-time missionary service among the Jewish people.

While attending Moody, Michael met a young woman who was also a student in the department of Jewish Studies. Her name was Eva McCollum. With their common interest in the Jewish people, and desire to see Jews saved, Michael and Eva soon fell in love. They were married in May 1976.

Eva was raised in a Gentile Christian home, in the Chicago suburb of Calumet Region, Indiana. At the early age of four, Eva remembers her mother telling her that Jesus was a Jew. The early recognition that Jesus was Jewish never left Eva. Later, at the age of thirteen when Eva openly professed Jesus as her Lord and Savior, she also thought about the Jewish people's need to accept Him as their Messiah and Savior. Eva was in high school when she visited Maxwell street—the old Jewish neighborhood in Chicago. As she left, she felt saddened and burdened for Jewish people who lived without hope or knowledge of the true Messiah.

After graduating from high school, Eva decided to take a trip to Israel. While she was there, she went through Yad VaShem (the Holocaust Memorial to the six million Jews slaughtered in the death camps of Europe). It was an experience that made her weep. After her return home, she began reading everything she could on the Jewish people. It was then that she began to realize God's call upon her to work among the Jews.

Eva enrolled in the Jewish Studies Department of Moody Bible Institute in the Fall of 1973. She also became the personal secretary to Dr. Louis Goldberg, the Director of the Jewish Studies Program. As she worked closely with Dr, Goldberg, her knowledge of Jewish people, customs, and traditions increased. She wrote:

> An exceptional part of the training at Moody, was the required field education/summer intern experience. I spent two summers working with Chosen People Ministries—one in the Coney Island branch, one with a traveling evangelistic team and children's camp program. This valuable field training, a forerunner of Chosen People Ministries' Summer Training Evangelism Program (STEP) gave me a wealth of experience in all phases of Jewish ministry.
>
> The first summer I worked with Chosen People Ministries, 1974, I met a Jewish-believer who was working part-time with Chosen People Ministries and entering Moody in the fall. We shared many common interests, especially our commitment to sharing the Good News with the Jewish people. Although I planned to reach out to Jewish people as a single woman, God was beautifully orchestrating another plan for my life, and in May 1976, Michael Rydelnik and I were married.[205]

After completing their work at Moody, Michael and Eva took additional graduate work. Eva received her BA in Biblical literature from Azusa Pacific College; she also earned a Master of Arts degree in Counseling at Wheaton College. The Rydelniks then moved to Dallas, Texas where Michael completed his work on a Masters of Theology degree at Dallas Theological Seminary.

During the years that Michael and Eva were completing their educations, they either worked with the Mission or with other Jewish missions (Jews for Jesus and Ariel Ministries). Michael also pastored a Messianic congregation in Columbus, Ohio.

In 1984 Michael and Eva Rydelnik returned to New York to serve as full-time missionaries with the Mission. The Messianic Bible study which they inaugurated in their home on Long Island grew into a fully functioning congregation, called Olive Tree Congregation. It is located in the Mission's building in Plainview, Long Island—in the heart of the Jewish community. This congregation has developed a Messianic children's program, called "Kibbutz Ha Or" (Community of Light). They have also developed Bible studies and discipleship groups.

When Sam Nadler was appointed Executive Director of the Mission in 1989, Michael Rydelnik was appointed Regional Director for the Northeast—a position he held until December, 1993.

STEVE AND LISA CAGAN

Another missionary couple added to the staff in 1984 was Steve and Lisa Cagan. In telling the "Chosen People family" about this new missionary couple, it was reported:

> Steve and his wife, Lisa, are two of ABMJ's newest missionaries. Steve is a musician with a degree in music education from the University of Bridgeport. He came to Christ while he was traveling with the ever-popular 'Up with People' musical troupe. From the time he was saved, he knew he wanted to be a missionary, but it wasn't until he was studying at Multnomah School of the Bible that he realized God was calling him to Jewish missions.
>
> 'I was always a little frightened of Jewish missions,' Steve explains. 'I remembered how hostile I had been when I heard the Gospel, at once being both attracted to the message and repelled by the implications of accepting the Lord.

However, while I was studying for a graduate certificate in Bible at Multnomah, it slowly began to dawn on me that I could be an especially effective witness to my own people. Precisely because I understood their resistance and hostility, I knew that I could help break through these barriers. It wasn't until I attended a missions conference at school, however, that I told God I was willing to go wherever He wanted me. At the end of the conference, we had a challenge to stand up if we would go wherever God sends us. When I stood, it was to present myself to God. By that time, I knew He was sending me to the Jewish people. Heartbreaks and heartaches included, I was going to my own stiff-necked people, and for the first time I had a real joy about that decision.'[206]

Steve Cagan was born in New York City, New York in November 1955. He was raised in Yonkers. His parents were Reform Jews—very liberal in their commitment to both God and to the synagogue. By the time Steve made Bar Mitzvah, although he had respect for the faith of his ancestors, the traditions and observances held little meaning to him. In telling a little bit about how he came to faith in Yeshua, Steve said:

To my 12-year-old mind, the synagogue was a holy, awesome place,...One day as I finished my lessons in preparation for my Bar Mitzvah, I walked into the sanctuary. With the eternal light glowing at one end, it seemed to be the 'gate to God.' I walked through the rows of scarlet-covered seats. Although they were empty, they would soon hold my family and friends, who would be there to listen to my reading of the Torah. On that day I would be proud but nervous. But there in that synagogue alone, I wanted to talk to God just for a moment....

I don't remember exactly what I said, but even now, 16 years later, I still remember that I wanted to know God.

Years later when I first heard the Gospel, I wrote to the rabbi of that synagogue: 'Tell me, what should I make of all that I've heard about Jesus? Can He possibly be the Messiah?' When I got the rabbi's reply, I realized that the answer to knowing God would not be found in the synagogue. The rabbi seemed to be discussing doctrines that were abstract and impersonal. The Christians who told me of Jesus spoke of a living and real God. I began reading the New Testament, and by the time I got to Matthew 8, I realized I had found God at last. Jesus was the Jewish Messiah, the only way any person, Jew or Gentile, could know God.[207]

Lisa grew up in a Christian home, and she remembered her family as always having an interest in missions. Her father was a minister of music, so she knew the pressures of being in full-time Christian ministry. In her testimony, Lisa stated:

...Still, I wanted to go wherever God wanted me. In high school, I became aware of Jewish missions when I met a number of Jewish youngsters. I could see that they had a different culture than I did. They reacted to the Gospel differently from others I had known. There was a sort of hostility and unwillingness and at the same time a special receptivity. A friend lived with us for a while whose father was Jewish, and I realized from knowing her that Jewish people weren't likely to come to faith one, two, three. However, when she did accept Christ, I felt a special excitement and thrill that made me realize how much I loved this field of ministry.[184]

When Steve and Lisa were planning to be married, they agreed that they both felt God's call upon their lives to go into full-time ministry in Jewish missions. Readers of *The Chosen People* were told:

...Lisa had also attended Multnomah, where she graduated with an associate of arts degree in biblical studies. While at school, she was very active in the Jewish prayer group. Like Steve, Lisa is very musical. She plays the piano and guitar and has written a number of songs.

Both Steve and Lisa were excited about becoming full-time missionaries and applied for staff positions on the American Board of Missions to the Jews shortly after being married in December 1982. They were told, however, that they would have to go through the special Summer Training and Evangelism Program (S.T.E.P.) the next summer before their applications could be accepted.

'Frankly,' Lisa admits, 'I was a little put off. Both Steve and I had a lot of Bible education, and we both had experience in witnessing to Jewish people. We planned to spend the summer of 1983 in Israel, and the thought of canceling our trip just to go on a witnessing and training program was frustrating.'

S.T.E.P. was a surprise to both of the Cagans. Despite Steve's background, he discovered there was a lot about his own Jewishness that he didn't understand. Lisa felt that her Christian upbringing taught her many of the things she learned in the S.T.E.P. classroom sessions, but the experience she gained on the streets was eye-opening.

Steve says, 'Living like a missionary every day showed me a lot about what being a full-time missionary is like.

Meeting so many people who come from such a wide range of interests was also a lesson. I was always challenged and constantly needed to turn to God. If I hadn't been committed to full-time ministry before S.T.E.P., I would have been by the end of the program.'

Lisa adds, 'I saw the special problems and blessing involved for a Gentile in Jewish missions. One man I witnessed to in Birmingham, Alabama, was a special blessing. He was Jewish and not at all hostile to hearing the Gospel. At the same time, he wasn't ready to believe and accept. At one point in our conversation, he asked, "Are you trying to get me to convert?"'

I was able to say, 'No, you don't need to convert. As a matter of fact, I as a Gentile had to be converted to the God of Israel. Now I'm bringing His message back to His chosen people. You only need to return to the God of our fathers.' He was so moved when he heard that, it was like a light that he hadn't seen before. I realized that being a Gentile in Jewish missions didn't have to be a disadvantage.

Steve and Lisa successfully completed the S.T.E.P. program. They are now explaining their work in various churches before they go to their permanent assignment in New York.[209]

Steve and Lisa Cagan worked in the New York area for several years before being transferred to Boston, to work with Gary and Mary Lou Derechinsky in the Mission's branch there. Steve and Lisa also used their musical talent in writing, composing, and recording Messianic music for the Mission. In 1991 the Cagans were transferred to Los Angeles where they continued in their ministry for the Lord through June 1993.

JERRY GROSS

Another missionary added to the staff of the Northeast in 1984 was Jerry Gross. Jerry told *The Chosen People* magazine family:

I grew up in a Jewish home in the Bronx where Jesus was not exactly a household word. As a matter of fact, His name wasn't any sort of a word at all, except when used occasionally as a curse.

Then my older brother, Richie, came home and said he had received the Lord. My family was upset and outraged. At 17 years of age, I was old enough to sympathize with my parents completely.

Richie tried to share his faith with me, but I was very angry that he'd even attempt such a thing.... I felt Richie was intruding on me by pulling this Jesus thing.

It wasn't that I felt Judaism had the answer—just the opposite. I had been Bar Mitzvah in an orthodox synagogue, yet even at age 13, I sensed I could never find God in the trappings and formality of the synagogue....

...By the next summer,...I had a job in the Catskills (the Jewish Alps) and was having the time of my life.

A friend warned me not to burn the candle at both ends, but I just laughed and said, 'I can do whatever I want. I can burn the candle at both ends, in between and on the sides. Just watch.'

God has a way of humbling us. Or at least He did me. I came home with mononucleosis. For four months I was in bed, depressed, inactive. My friends were all out doing other things.

Needless to say, there was plenty of time to think. I thought about my real purpose for living and the reality of a world that seemed to ignore the weak and helpless....

The long hours passed slowly and silently, while inside my mind I kept hearing questions about God and life.

'What is life all about anyway?' I wondered. 'Is there something more out there that I'm not letting myself see?'

A few months after my recovery, I was watching television one day and saw Orson Welles advertising a movie called The Late Great Planet Earth. *I liked Orson Welles, so I figured the movie might be interesting. Was I surprised!*

The movie was about Bible prophecy and the second coming of Messiah. I was amazed that it pointed out that Jesus is the Messiah promised throughout the Bible. I was equally surprised how relevant the Bible seems to be to today's world.

The movie made me think about my life. 'What will I do when He returns?' I wondered. 'Where will this leave me?'...

Since Jesus was the question at hand, I got a copy of the New Testament and began to read. Not wanting to hurt my parents (after all, I was the good son who wouldn't betray them like my brother had), I did my reading at night underneath the blankets.

It was a strange way to study the Bible, but no stranger than what I found there—teachings and miracles of a Man who was obviously more than a human being.

Even though part of me kept saying, 'You're Jewish. You should not be reading this,' the words and life of Jesus were a magnet. I could not stop reading the New Testament.

As I accepted this truth about Jesus I acknowledged in my heart that He alone is worthy of my trust and that He is the God of Israel.

When I finally told my parents, their reaction was even worse than I had feared. Their hurt, concern and confusion caused them to do whatever they could to convince me I was wrong.

My girl friend's parents gave me a clear choice: Give up their daughter or give up this Jesus. I wavered in my faith for some months before knowing that there was really no choice. God was calling me.

Hesitantly, I recommitted my life to God and began to understand the implications of Jesus' words in John 14:6, 'I am the way and the truth and the life. No one comes to the Father except through me.' I knew I really wanted to serve Him and live the way He wants.

Actually, this deeper commitment came about in a strange way. Through a number of seeming coincidences, I met a fellow at a train station who said he was a Jewish believer in Jesus. He urged me to commit myself to God.

I visited his church one day and felt very uncomfortable....While I was there, though, I picked up some tracts.

One day, for no apparent reason other than that it was a nice day and I felt a strange stirring inside me, I decided to stand out on a street corner and hand out the tracts I got from that church.

While I was handing out the tracts, I met a fellow believer who encouraged me to become more involved with the Lord. He recommended a fellowship in Queens and gave me the address.

I decided to go to the fellowship and got hopelessly lost while looking for the street....

After looking around for some time, I crossed the street and stopped the first passer-by I saw to get directions. He was a well-dressed man with a long beard. He looked at the address and shook his head. 'It doesn't exist,' he said....

Then he introduced himself as Vince Morgan and told me that he was a fellow believer called by the Lord to minister to the Jewish people. Starting that day, Vince discipled me and helped me grow in my faith. [Vince Morgan had attended the Mission's training program and worked with the Mission as a student. He then went to New York to work the Christian Missionary Alliance in their Jewish work in New York City. Later he worked with Conservative Baptist Home Mission Society, seeking to establish Jewish congregations in New York.]

As I grew, I longed to serve God. I decided to attend a Bible camp for Jewish believers. My parents told me that they had had enough. 'If you go there, don't return,' they warned.

We had been leading to this break for some time, as my parents had become progressively more hostile to my beliefs. As I prayed about going to camp, I knew God wanted me to stand for Him.

At the Bible camp I met the Miaman family; they invited me to move in with them....

I stayed with the Miamans for a year then knew God was calling me to enter the ministry. I went to Moody Bible Institute. Then, in June 1984, I joined the staff of Chosen People Ministries.[210]

On December 20, 1987 Jerry Gross married another missionary who was serving with the Mission in New York. Her name was Martha Aller.

MARTHA ALLER

Martha Aller was born into the home of a missionary couple who were serving in South America. She came to know the Lord at a young age. Because of her concern for the Jewish people, she applied to the Mission's S.T.E.P. program. In October 1986, after completing the S.T.E.P. program, she joined the Mission's staff as a part-time worker. In January 1987, she became a full-time worker assigned to the Westchester County area of New York, where she worked under the supervision of Sam Nadler.

Readers of *The Chosen People* magazine were given a glimpse of Jerry and Martha's wedding (which served as a witness to Jerry's Jewish family and friends) through an article written by the author. It stated:

It was a traditional Jewish marriage ceremony which had been modified to give witness to their family members and their friends of their love for one another and of their love for the Messiah, the Lord Jesus.

Our New York and New Jersey workers, Sam Nadler and Larry Feldman officiated. Other staff members and friends provided the Messianic music which was interwoven throughout the ceremony.

All eyes were fixed on the radiant bride and groom as they walked arm-in-arm down the aisle and took their places under the large white chupah [the marriage canopy]. They were surrounded by their parents and the wedding party.[211]

Shortly after their marriage, Jerry and Martha resigned their positions with the Mission so Jerry could attend Talbot Theological Seminary.

Highlights of the Ministry—1985

By January 1985, there was much for which to praise the Lord. There was a surplus of income over expenses (the financial report given by Jim Rees showed that the audited report from Fox and Company for the period ending September 30, 1984, indicated revenue exceeding expenses by $155,890.00[212]) and God's hand of blessing upon the world-wide ministry was evident. At the Directors meeting, held January 25, 1985, the President (the author) highlighted some of the exciting events happening in the ministry:

> SOUTH AMERICA—*In December 1984 Mr. Sevener visited the Buenos Aires branch and was greatly blessed and encouraged by the ministry as it is being conducted by Rev. Roberto Passo. Mr. Passo has organized the 'Friends of ABMJ,' a group of volunteers ministering in Argentina, Brazil, Chile and other South American countries. Six members of this group met together with Mr. Sevener in September.*
>
> *Mr. Sevener shared several testimonies of the ministry which is reaching out through Bible classes, evangelistic meetings, radio broadcasts, holiday services, visitation, literature, etc. Mr. Passo is also very actively ministering to churches, challenging them to become involved in Jewish evangelism and with the ABMJ. Mr. Jose Abadi, chairman of the South American Board, often shares church meetings by presenting slides of Israel which he has taken on his trips to that country. The numbers of Jewish people being reached is increasing, but the needs of the ministry are also increasing....*
>
> SOUTHWEST REGION—*Mr. Sevener cited the growing outreach under the leadership of Dr. Irwin (Rocky) Freeman. He shared some of their statistics: 101 church meetings, 134 Bible studies, 7,121 tracts distributed, 21 salvation decisions (19 Jewish, 2 Gentile), and ten Jewish people baptized. Income from church meetings has also been increasing.*
>
> SOUTHEAST REGION—*Under the leadership of Rev. Larry Jaffrey, this area is also experiencing growth in ministry and outreach. Out of a total of 1100 meaningful contacts and conversations, 500 were with unsaved Jewish people. They conducted 300 Bible studies. There were fifty-nine salvation decisions (25 Jewish, 34 Gentile).*
>
> WEST REGION—*Dr. Daniel Goldberg had reported 401 church meetings in his region, 4,515 pieces of literature distributed (plus 100,000 pieces during the Olympics), 457 scheduled meetings and Bible studies and 13 salvation decisions.*
>
> *Concerning the planting of new congregations, one has been started in London, Ontario, Canada, under John Bell's direction. Two groups presently meeting in New Jersey and on Long Island will be monitored as possibilities for future congregations.*
>
> CONFERENCE MINISTRY—*Tom Walker had arranged a total of 21 Bible conferences in the United States, ministered in and through churches. There were also five weekend conferences: Camp of the Woods, Lucerne Conference Center, Mt. Hermon Conference Center, The Firs Conference Center and Word of Life. The projection is to repeat these weekends, with the exception of Lucerne, and introduce a new one in Oregon as well as in the Midwest....*
>
> LITERATURE—*A camera-ready copy of the church planting booklet was shown to the Directors. Finished copies should be available in a few weeks. Also being worked on is a book dealing with the Jewish holy days, written by Dr. Fuchs.* [This book was finished and published by Loizeaux Brothers Publishing Company, and is still available through the Mission] *Anticipated completion date is April 1985. As finances allow, the goal is to update (textually and graphically) one tract per month from those previously printed by the mission. Dr. Louis Goldberg has edited the texts and Barry and Steffi Rubin will handle the graphics and arrangements for printing.[213]*

The President also reported to the Board that since the Mission had filed to trademark the phrase "See Israel Through Jewish Eyes," the Mission's tour slogan, three Jewish agencies had filed opposition to the trademark being issued to the Mission. The Board authorized the author, as President, to proceed with legal action to obtain the Trademark.[214] Eventually, however, it was decided to withdraw the legal action because the expense involved was escalating and it was felt that the money would be better spent on the missionary program of the Mission. The Mission continues to use the phrase "See Israel Through Jewish Eyes" without the trademark to this present day.

Continued Financial Concerns

While the January 1985 meeting of the Board ended on a high note, with a surplus of income over expenses, the June meeting, held at Schroon Lake in conjunction with the Workers' Conference, was not as bright. Income was holding, but expenses were increasing. It was clear that if they continued, the Mission would show a deficit for the fiscal year.

The Investment Fund of the Mission was once again the subject of discussion. Opinions over the use of these funds were still divided. Some members of the Board felt the Investment Fund was a holding fund to be used for current income needs of the Mission. Other members (including the President) felt that only the *interest income* from the Investment Fund should be used for funding projects or helping the Operating Fund when needed.

In their report to the Board, the Finance Committee stated: "...we do not want to build up a big portfolio. We should use the money received from our people for His glory, so His Word can get out."[215] When it came to a vote, the Board voted to accept the recommendation of the Finance Committee, with some modifications, and the following motion was approved at their evening meeting: "Concerning our portfolio of securities, it is agreed that the principal purpose of our investments in securities is to provide income for current use by ABMJ, not appreciation in value."[216] The wording of the motion was an attempt at compromise between the two positions. It did not spell out which position the Finance Committee should take. Instead, the wording was open for interpretation by the Finance Committee, the administration, and the Board. This was not resolved until 1991, when the Mission established *The Chosen People Ministries Foundation* to provide long-term funding for the Mission, its staff and programs.

To bring about better control of expenses, and to utilize available capital for the missionary programs of the Mission, the Finance Committee was asked to involve itself in three other areas of the Mission's holdings and activities. First, the Committee was directed to sit in on the preparation of the annual budget. Second, the Committee was asked to specifically approve, before any commitment was made, any capital expenditure in excess of $10,000 which had not been previously approved by the Board when it adopted the annual budget. Third, the Committee was directed to analyze all of the Mission's real estate holdings, both domestic and foreign, to determine if each was serving its purpose and providing for the optimum use of resources.[217]

The latter point was an important change and addition. The question of owning versus leasing/renting had already been resolved and the administration, in conjunction with the Finance Committee, had developed some ratios of expense in owning versus leasing property. Based on those studies, it had been determined that if the Mission could recoup its investment over a ten to fifteen year period, it was preferable for the Mission to purchase property. While this was not an established policy, it served as a guide when trying to determine which direction to go in a given area, and for a specific ministry.

The new directive to analyze *all* of the Mission's real estate holdings included the Mission's Headquarters building in Orangeburg, New York. It had become increasingly apparent to the members of the Board that the cost of maintaining the Headquarters building, and the staff working there, was escalating at a rapid rate. Because of the high cost of living in the suburban areas surrounding New York City, it was difficult to find competent office workers who were willing to accept the salary levels offered by the Mission. The pool of prospective workers was limited further by the fact that the Mission would only hire believers. The problems of finding competent help, and the cost of maintaining that staff, plus cost of maintaining the building and property, was an increasing concern.

These problems and concerns had prompted the author, James Straub, and C. Robert Clemensen to do some investigation of the value of real estate in the Orangeburg area. Mr. Clemensen reported on the findings at the June 1985 Directors meeting. The Minutes state:

> ...His [Clemensen's] *research shows an approximate capitalized value for this property of $1.43 million.* [The original purchase price in June 1978 was $668,000. As it turned out, Clemensen's estimate was low. The Mission sold the Headquarters property in 1987 for $1,850,000.] *He believes that this may be a realistic sales price in Orangetown and feels that the market conditions at present are positive.*
>
> *It was his view that the mission should not consider renting other facilities, since 1) it is often difficult to secure leases because ABMJ is a mission to the Jewish people, and 2) by renting the mission would not have the benefit of tax exemption. The question posed was: 'What would happen if ABMJ would find a relatively inexpensive piece of property to purchase?'*[218]

In his usual adroit manner and clear logical presentation, Clemensen's report struck a responsive chord from all of the members of the Board. Obviously, if a suitable Headquarters property could be found for less money than the Orangeburg property sold for, this would be good stewardship of the Lord's money.

Clemensen already had another property in mind, as well as a builder who was willing to build a new, low maintenance, high efficiency building, built to the Mission's specifications for approximately $800,000. If the figures held true, the net savings to the Mission would be $630,000—capital that would go a long way toward fully funding the Mission's Pension Program and further developing the ministry of reaching Jewish people with the Gospel. The Minutes state: "The Board concurred that Mr. Clemensen should proceed with investigation of possible buyers for the Orangeburg property."[219]

ROY ADAMS JOINS THE STAFF

At this same Board meeting (June 11, 1985), Daniel Fuchs recommended that Mr. Roy Adams be appointed to serve as Administrative Vice President of the American Board of Missions to the Jews, Inc., with the understanding that he would be serving in the same position with Beth Sar Shalom Mission in Canada. The appointment was approved by the Directors.[220]

Roy was the Senior Internal Auditor for the Dupont Corporation of Canada—an active Christian layman who had served on the boards of other Christian missions in Canada, in addition to his involvement in his local church. He had been a member of the Mission's Board of Directors in Canada since 1976, filling the positions of Treasurer, Vice President, President, and Chairman of the Board. The Directors of the American Board had elected him as a member at their October 15, 1980 meeting. Roy thus possessed an extensive working knowledge of the Mission, as well as expertise in the secular world of finance and administration.

The recommendation of Roy Adams for Administrative Vice President came as a complete surprise to the President! Although the position of Executive Vice President had been vacant since June 30, 1983 when James Straub retired, the author had been considering several other non-Board members for the position.

Daniel apparently felt the position should be filled by another Board member since that is what had been done in the past. However, it was the author's position that while the President should be a member of the Board, all other offices of the corporation should be non-Board member positions—employees who would be responsible to the President for their activities. Having been a witness to the fact that some of the problems of the past had been exacerbated because the Board was comprised of too many employees, the author felt the Board should hold the President of the corporation accountable for the affairs of the Mission, and for the actions of the staff.

As Chairman of the Board, Daniel had proceeded on his own to secure the approval of the other Board members for the appointment of Roy Adams for the work in Canada, and for the position as Administrative Vice President of the United States as well. The one Board member Daniel had not discussed the appointment with prior to the June 1985 Board meeting was the President (the author).

Even Christians err. The history of the Mission (and any other Christian church or organization if truthfully analyzed) gives evidence to the fact that in spite of human failures, God patiently works through His children to ultimately bring glory to His Name and blessing to those who seek to serve and glorify Him. The author was admittedly upset, but as he told Roy and other members of the Board, it was not the appointment of Roy that upset him—it was the *way* in which the appointment was made. Once again, the Mission was moving back toward dual, or "troika" leadership.

As early as May 1985, the author had received a telephone call from Roy Adams during which time Roy mentioned that he had an opportunity to take an early retirement from Dupont. Roy wanted to know if there was some way that he could be used in the Mission in Canada (Roy and his wife, Ella, were Canadian citizens). The author's response to Roy was that he felt certain that the Board (both the U.S. Board and the Canadian Board) would be happy to use him in an administrative capacity in Canada. The author made mention of this telephone conversation with Roy at the May 29, 1985 Personnel Committee meeting. The Minutes state:

> Mr. Sevener mentioned that Mr. Roy Adams is considering an early retirement from his position with Dupont in Canada. He has offered his services to the Beth Sar Shalom Mission. Since he needs to make a decision by the end of June 1985, this will be discussed with him during the Workers' Retreat.[221]

The author's intention was to present a recommendation to the Board at the June 11, 1985 Board meeting that Roy be used full-time in Canada. This, however, became a moot issue.

As the author reflected upon the action that had been taken, he reminded himself of the fact that when God's people prayerfully seek to do His will, even though you may disagree with them, you must wait upon the Lord. A number of the Directors gave words of encouragement, and after a season of prayer and thoughtful reflection, Roy Adams and the author met together. Roy Adams is a man who has a deep love for the Mission and its work, and as we spoke and compared notes we found that we had a similar vision for ministry; we felt we would be able to work together in harmony.

Following the meetings, there was the matter of working through the logistics of how Roy Adams, who lived in Canada, could divide his time to allow him to supervise the staff and handle the administrative duties of the Canadian outreach, as well as the staff and the administrative duties of the overall ministry from the Headquarters office in New York. It was decided that he would spend two weeks of each month at the Hamilton, Ontario office, and two weeks at the Headquarters office in Orangeburg, New York—an arrangement that was difficult for his wife and family, and expensive to the Mission, as it entailed travel and lodging when he was States-side. After several months, it became apparent that the problem of trying to find suitable lodging for Roy, at a reasonable rate, was becoming an arduous and time-consuming job. The Mission therefore purchased a condominium for use by Roy and his wife, or other staff as needed.

The next few years were difficult ones for Roy and Ella. Their ministry involvement was divided between two countries and two Missions—the Mission in America and the Mission in Canada. Yet, as true servants of the Lord, they persevered and God blessed their efforts and their ministry. In accepting the challenge of the financial and administrative responsibility of the Mission, Roy soon discovered there was a vast difference between managing the financial department of a large corporation and the tasks which had become his at the Mission. At Dupont, he'd had financial resources, personnel, and even the personnel of other departments at his disposal, while at the Mission the financial resources and personnel were limited. As a result, Roy worked long and grueling hours to help establish sound administrative and financial policies, insurance programs, salary administrative programs, and a funded pension program.

A New Missionary Director—John Bell

The Ad Hoc Committee of the Board had recommended that the President appoint a Missionary Director and a Communications Director as soon as possible. But at the time of their recommendation the Board was still struggling through the problems of the regional system of operations, congregation planting, and the image and vision of the Mission. To appoint individuals to these positions seemed counter-productive. By 1986 the Board had resolved enough of these issues to move ahead with the appointments.

The author had spoken with Barry Rubin about filling the position of Communications Director. As National Church Ministries Director, Barry, with the help of Steffi, had already been developing many of the communications pieces used by the Mission. But after praying about the matter, Barry decided that he did not want to move his family to New York. The position was therefore left open and the author and Jonathan Singer, the Editor and Creative Director of the Mission, ran the Communications Department. As a cost-cutting measure, all direct mail programs were brought back to the Communications Department, and the use of outside agencies to handle fund-raising was terminated.

The position of Missionary Director was easier to fill. The author, in conjunction with the Personnel Committee, recommended Rev. John Bell for the position.

As has been mentioned, John served as Regional Director of the Mid-west; he had been a leader in the establishment of the Mission's first Messianic congregation—the Olive Tree congregation in Chicago; he had documented and established the Church Planting program of the Mission. The author believed that appointing John to the position of Missionary Director would guarantee, at least for the foreseeable future, that the Mission would continue its policy of establishing Messianic congregations. John also had the respect of the missionaries on staff and of the other Regional Directors.

An invitation was extended to John to attend the January 1986 Board meeting. After a lengthy interview and discussions with the Board members, he was given the position. The Minutes state: "…it was agreed that John Bell be appointed Missionary Director, effective August 1, 1986."[222] Following his appointment to the position, John moved his family to New York. They later moved to Charlotte, North Carolina.

As a Regional Director, John had done a good job assembling his staff into a working missionary team for the Midwest region. He had recruited workers from the Jewish Studies Program at Moody, as well as from some of the Messianic congregations being established in the Chicago area. As these workers became active on staff they, in turn, recruited others. Because of the active Messianic congregations in the Chicago area, the opportunities for ministries, the team spirit of John's staff, and the availability of facilities for training, it was decided to transfer the S.T.E.P. program of the Mission from New York to Chicago. All new workers of the Mission (and some veteran workers) were required to go through the S.T.E.P. program. Having the program in his region gave John further opportunity, as Missionary Director, to evaluate them and work with the other Regional Directors in placing them.

New Workers for the Midwest

John had recruited two new workers for the Mission during 1982—Barry Berger, the pastor of the Olive Tree Congregation in Chicago and his brother-in-law, Rev. Galen Banashak.

Galen Banashak

Galen was born in Chicago. He was raised in a Polish-Roman Catholic home. His father, a war hero, died in the war when he was two years old. Although he had no memory of his father, he enjoyed a happy childhood. When he reached his teenage years, however, he began searching for some meaning and purpose in life. It was during his first semester at the University of Illinois, Chicago Circle, that he first heard the message of salvation.

A friend from work invited Galen to attend the Messiah Baptist Church, then located in Broadview, Illinois. Galen went because he had been impressed with the kind of life his friend lived and he wanted that same peace, joy and love in his life. As the minister preached the Word of God, the Holy Spirit brought conviction to Galen's heart. He knew he was a sinner in need of eternal salvation. For the first time he realized that this "gift" from God could only come through faith in Jesus.

The following Sunday, Galen accepted the Lord Jesus as his Lord and Savior. Knowing that God had forgiven him and cleansed him from sin, Galen's life changed. He joined a discipleship class, was baptized, and became very involved in his new church home.

During the summer, the youth group of Messiah Baptist Church went on a mission trip to Mexico; Galen was one of the members of that group. It was while he worked with the other young people among the people of Mexico that God burdened his heart for full-time ministry and missionary work. He was so thankful for what God had done in his life, that he wanted to share the message with others. He knew that faith in Jesus was the only hope for mankind, and he wanted to share the message with as many people as possible.

In preparation for the ministry, Galen attended the Baptist Bible College in Springfield, Missouri. After his graduation in 1976, he and his wife, Carol, left for Guadalajara, Mexico to start a church. They completed a one-year course in Spanish at Queretaro Spanish Language School in Queretaro, Mexico and spent the next two and one-half years laboring to establish a church in Guadalajara. Galen's goal was to spend one term in Guadalajara before moving to a different area to begin another new church. But God had other plans for the Banashaks.

Before Galen and Carol left for Mexico, John Bell spoke to them about the necessity of missionary work among the Jews. The seed was planted in Galen's heart. As they labored in Mexico, they also thought and prayed for their family members. Galen's wife, Carol, and John Bell's wife, Linda, were sisters—so every time the Banashaks prayed for John and Linda, they remembered their missionary field among the Jewish people in Chicago.

Galen did not feel God's call upon him to work among the Jews until April 1982. That year he made a trip to New York and Boston with a Jewish believer. As they travelled, visited, and shared the Gospel, Galen could see the burden that his Jewish friend had for his family and friends. He recognized the desperate need to communicate the Gospel to the Jewish people in the language and culture they would understand. Galen shared the fact of his increasing burden to reach Jews with John Bell, and John suggested that he begin to pray specifically about serving with the Mission. Galen followed through on John's advice, and as he did, God began to open the doors. Upon their return from Mexico, the Banashaks were accepted for missionary service in the Chicago area. It was an answer to prayer for Galen. He was back in his home town, yet he was still in "foreign" missions.

Roy Schwarcz took Galen under his wing, and soon the two men were inseparable—wherever Galen was, Roy was. The Mission staff jokingly named them "Frick" and "Frack." Together, Roy and Galen expanded the Olive Tree congregational ministry into a second Messianic congregation, which was named the Vineyard congregation. Later, as additional help was needed in Canada, Roy and Galen divided their time between Chicago, Toronto, and Montreal in an effort to establish congregations and supervise the missionary activity in Canada. Galen became so burdened for the Jewish people of Canada that he and his family were seriously praying about moving there, but once again, God had other plans for them.

After John Bell's appointment as Missionary Director, Roy Schwarcz was named Mid-west Regional Director. Galen Banashak continued as the Area Director for the Chicago ministries; he was also asked to become the Director for the S.T.E.P. activities in Chicago, and to become the Regional Director for Canada.

In September 1991, as the Mission was once again undergoing organizational changes, Galen resigned from the Mission, feeling that God could better use his gifts and abilities in another area of service.

Barry Berger

Barry Berger was also recruited by John Bell in 1982. His testimony was shared with the readers in the April 1987 issue of *The Chosen People*. Barry said:

Speaking at a missions conference a few years ago, I was taken totally by surprise when another of the guest speakers, whom I did not know, began pointing at me from the pulpit saying, 'That man was the most vindictive, volatile person I'd ever met.'

A very quiet moment passed before he smiled and said, 'If God could save him, God can save anyone.'

Then I remembered. This man was the pastor who had once come to my house with my friend John Reid. They had come to tell me about Jesus.

At first, sitting at my kitchen table, we were all very polite. But when the talk switched to Jesus, I got a little testy, and when they told me that I wasn't really happy and that I needed Jesus, I demanded they leave.

My friend John was probably used to my kicking him out of the house. I had done it almost every week for a year and half. John would come to my house to pick up his products (I was his Amway distributor), and without fail he would speak to me about Jesus. And without fail, I would tell John to leave.

The last thing I needed was Jesus. It wasn't that I was so religious. Even though I had been raised as an Orthodox

Jew, I hadn't been to synagogue since I was fourteen. It was just that I already had everything I wanted.

I really meant that too. I had a great job in graphic arts. A beautiful apartment. Sharp clothes. Expensive vacations. A new car every year. And good times whenever I wanted them. Now I can look back and say I was without real purpose, but it was everything I wanted back then....

It was during this time that John told his mother about me.

This guy Barry Berger has everything he wants: money, clothes, cars ...he's so happy. Happy without knowing the Lord Jesus.

His mother told him that I wouldn't always be so happy and to start to pray for my salvation....

The Reid family is black. John, his parents (Rev. and Mrs. Reid), and family attended a black Baptist church on the south side of Chicago. Every Sunday John would place my name on their church's prayer list for my salvation.

For the next year and a half, the people of Grove Heights Baptist Church prayed faithfully for the salvation of Barry Berger, John's Jewish friend. It was about that time that my world began to fall apart.

I lost my job and was blackballed from my trade. I had lost my source of income, but continued to live the life style that I was accustomed to. I just went on partying, drinking, gambling, and running around. My bills mounted up into thousands of dollars. I knew my life was deteriorating fast and all the things I loved were disappearing.

I had never known what it meant to feel unsatisfied and frustrated. I'd never really thought about the quality of my life. But when my good times went bad and the things that I loved began to lose their glitter and importance, I realized there had to be something more substantial to life. With almost angry frenzy, I began to study astrology and eastern religions, searching to find peace and purpose in my life.

All the time, John's church was praying for me, and every Wednesday night before John would go to prayer meeting at his church, he'd come over and tell me about Jesus. When John tried to tell me about how Jesus was the long-awaited Messiah of the Jewish people, I'd get so mad I'd see stars. My life was falling apart, but no matter how desperate I got, I would never believe in Jesus.

'Don't you try and tell me about Jesus,' I'd yell. 'I know what you Christians really think about the Jews and how you treat us.'

I had already had my nose broken six times because I wasn't the kind to ignore a fight when some 'Christian' hollered 'dirty Jew' or 'Christ-killer' at me.

I knew all about Christians and about what Jesus stood for. The Crusades. The Spanish Inquisition. The Russian pogroms. The Holocaust. I might be desperate but I would not betray my ancestors.

Then one Saturday morning after I had been out late the night before, I struggled awake to watch a basketball game at 11:30. The next thing I knew, it was 7:30 in the evening and I could not account for the hours in between. I had lost a whole day.

I had no idea what had happened, except for a vague recollection of spending eight hours pacing up and down my living room in total depression, smoking cigarette after cigarette, trying to make sense of my life.

When I realized it was night and that I had lost a day, I realized I had seen a picture of what it was like to lose my whole life. Crying, confused, and miserable, I walked into my bedroom and shouted, 'God, why are You doing this to me? Help me!'

My eyes were drawn to an orange book on my night stand. It was a Bible John had left with me. I picked up that Bible as if it were a Ouija board, opened it and poked my finger down onto a verse. 'You will not be cleansed by me until I have put all my wrath upon you.'

Since I've never found that passage again, I'm not sure if I read it right or not. But that terrifying night in a southside Chicago apartment, I knew that I had been warned by God.

I picked up the phone and called John.

'Please come over, John. I need you.'

In fifteen minutes he was standing at my door, puzzled to see me in this state. Me, the carefree person who had refused to talk about God for almost a year and a half.

I tried to tell him what had happened. I pointed to the piles of astrology, occult, and metaphysical books around my room.

'I don't know what's right,' I cried. 'I don't know what to believe.'

John, in his quiet, confident sort of way said, 'Why don't you pray and ask God what you should believe?'

'God, I don't even know how to pray,' I began, because it suddenly seemed that I had no idea what to say or how to address God. 'I just need for You to show me what to believe.'

I was at the end of my rope. It was survival or nothing. Anything would be acceptable as long as it gave me peace from the awful, and awe-filled, confrontation I had been having. For the next five days everything I heard, saw, or read *was Bible, Bible, Bible. I went to the store and heard two women talking abut the Bible. I turned on the radio and heard people talking about the Bible. I opened a magazine to an article about the Bible.*

Now I'm occasionally stupid, but I'm not dumb. By the following Wednesday, January 27, 1976, I knew God was answering my prayer and telling me to believe the Bible.

It all culminated when I turned on the Mike Douglas show at 3:30 in the afternoon. Basketball star Jerry Lucas was promoting his new book.

Since I had been a big fan of his, I was naturally awed as my hero showed his photographic memory by having the hundreds of people in the audience stand and give their name. Then, at random, Mike Douglas would point to someone, mid-row, mid-audience, and Lucas would call off his name. He also showed his speed-reading skills. I was awed that he could read, comprehend, and remember with such skill and speed.

I didn't move during the commercial break. When they returned, Lucas was talking about his personal life.

'I had everything,' he said, 'more money than I'd ever want, fame, a great career, the whole thing. But wasn't happy; I wasn't at peace.'

When his wife was born again, Jerry Lucas read through the Bible three times in one night. The message of the Bible, he had discovered, was that the only way to have real peace was Jesus.

When he said Jesus had given him the only peace he had ever had, I knew I had to have that too.

I called up John. 'What are you doing tonight?'

> *'Going to church.'*

> *'Can I come along?'*

I don't remember very much about that night, only that when the pastor issued an invitation for those who wanted to receive Jesus, I knew he meant me. There wasn't anything I wanted more than to give my life to the Jewish Messiah …Jesus.

And when I did, there were no bells, no whistles, no lump in my throat. Just a quiet assurance of peace. And the knowledge that at last, everything was going to be all right.[223]

Barry continued to grow in the Lord, and when the Olive Tree Congregation was established he became involved. Soon afterward he began to recognize the call of God upon his life for full-time ministry. In preparation for ministry, he enrolled in the Jewish Studies program at Moody Bible Institute. In December 1980, the Olive Tree congregation called Barry Berger as their pastor.

When Barry joined the staff of the Mission in 1982, he was hired to work as the Field-Evangelist (National Church Ministries Representative) for the Mid-west—a position he held until 1992, when he felt led of the Lord to resign to join the Christian Jew Foundation.

HOWARD SILVERMAN

Another worker who was recruited as a worker for the Midwest region was Howard Silverman. Howard came to faith in Yeshua through the witness of Roy Schwarcz. In his testimony to *The Chosen People* family, he said:

I grew up in a Conservative, observant Jewish home. I revered God. I loved and honored my parents. I thought being Jewish was great. I didn't rebel against keeping kosher or going to synagogue. I tutored boys preparing for their Bar Mitzvah and read Torah regularly during Sabbath service. I never ever conceived of believing anything apart from what my rabbi and parents taught.

The closest I came to questioning what I was taught was that I often wondered if I could ever know God. Sure, I believed in God. I thought about God. But I knew I didn't know God.

One time when I was about sixteen, I was driving down the street, and I remember asking out loud, though no one was with me, 'Can I ever really know God personally?' It didn't become an issue with me, but it didn't go away either.

It was three years later that my thoughts about God were rudely challenged. Home from college for summer break, I began to date a nice Jewish girl named Marsha.

Marsha had become a believer a few weeks before we started to date. One night she sat me down and said, 'I have something to tell you.'

I couldn't imagine what to expect, but when she told me she believed in Jesus, I was dumbfounded. I was disgusted. It was a travesty! It was horrifying. I couldn't believe that she didn't understand such a thing was impossible! Obviously she hadn't had much of a Jewish upbringing and, quite probably, she had serious emotional problems.

But for all the things she wasn't…she was nice. And I did like to be with her. So after reminding myself how liberal and open-minded I was, I decided, 'Oh well, who am I to try and rule her?'

The next time we were together I told her if it made her happy she could believe in it and that if she wanted to talk about it I wouldn't get mad.

So all summer she'd tell me about 'her Messiah' and give me tracts. One time I patiently explained that you can't be Jewish and Christian at the same time, because if you believe in Jesus, you're not Jewish anymore.

'But Jesus is the Messiah of Israel.' she said, 'and Jewish people should believe in Him. It's not only Gentiles who are Christians.'

I thought this girl needed a psychiatrist and I needed out of the relationship, but then I reminded myself that there was no need to argue over religion, and I continued seeing her.

Every so often Marsha would mention a Jewish believer named Roy Schwarcz. 'He could really answer a lot of your objections,' she'd say.

I kept putting her off. I thought there must be something wrong with him too. What could he possible have to say? After all, who ever heard of a Jew named Roy anyway?

Finally, one day we went to Roy's Bible study. There was a fair share of what I considered weirdos there, like the man who told me that God had healed his tape recorder. 'Just what I figured,' I thought, 'This is the kind of Jew who believes in Jesus.'

The one thing (besides the occasional strange folks) that struck me about the group, however, was the mix of people who were there.

I thought it would be all college students, but there were people of all ages, a lot of housewives and professionals. It lent it a little bit of credibility.

I talked with Roy that day and read several of the tracts he had. As I got to know him better, I don't remember much about what he said or what I read, but I was incredibly impressed with Roy Schwarcz.

'Here,' I thought, 'is a Jewish man who lives like a Jew and has something real. When he talks about the Bible, it's like listening to someone talk about the newspaper.'

What really surprised me was the New Testament he gave me. At first the New Testament posed an awkward situation. I was home for the summer, living with my parents and working for my father.

The only time I could read the New Testament was at night. So I'd tell my parents I was going for a drive, and would go out to the middle of nowhere and read the New Testament.

I'd sit there in my car thinking, 'I can't believe I'm doing this. I can't believe I'm reading this book. I can't believe I'm sneaking around my parents and locking this book in my glove compartment and actually reading it at night.'

Roy told me to read Romans 9,10, and 11. That posed my second problem with this strange book. I had always been sure that the New Testament said one of two things about the Jews: nothing or only negative things.

Yet this book I was reading portrayed Jewish people in a very positive way. I was flabbergasted. I went back to Matthew and started reading straight through.

The more I read, the more I saw this belief might have some validity. I still couldn't see what Jesus had to do with the Messiah I had always expected to come, or why His coming should matter to me, but I did see you didn't have to be a lunatic to believe.

Roy explained that the Messiah was to be a suffering servant as well as a reigning king. I was impressed with Isaiah 53, but Isaiah 59:2 stunned me: 'Your iniquities have separated you from you God; your sins have hidden his face from you, so that he will not hear.' With a sickening feeling, I saw that just being Jewish might not be enough to satisfy God.

One night I went with Roy to a church where he was speaking. Sometime during that service I realized I was thinking that the whole thing made an awful lot of sense. I had to force myself to remember that Jews don't believe in Jesus.

The next few weeks were hard. Admitting I believed this would break my parents' hearts. I kept looking in the mirror and saying, 'Who is this person who is ready to see his parents die of shame?' I, who had never rebelled before, was considering this atrocity. Even worse, I wasn't convinced in my own mind that I would still be Jewish if I finally did acknowledge Jesus.

It was a huge help when I heard music recorded by Lamb, a Messianic music group. They sounded so Jewish and presented the Gospel in such a Jewish way that I wanted what Roy and Marsha had. I wanted it so much I got scared that I might decide to accept Jesus as Messiah and nothing would happen.

I wasn't sure how to pray because all my prayers before had been memorized for services and synagogue. One night I sat on the edge of my bed and started talking, 'God? My name is Howard.'

At first I felt stupid, but finally I got around to asking Him to show me if Jesus was the Messiah.

Over the next few days I knew inside of me that it was true, but I still couldn't admit it. I wanted to believe. I also wanted it all to go away.

During one of my talks with God, alone in my room, I made a decision: it was to be yes or no, but not this in-between.

With false bravado but a serious desire to settle the matter, I prayed, 'God, if Jesus is the Messiah, I want to believe. If not, I want to forget it.'

Suddenly I knew. I was elated. I felt so good I wanted to laugh. I felt like I had just been born. I knew, without doubt. I didn't want to deny it anymore. Jesus was the promised Messiah, the Lord God of Israel, the one way I could have a personal relationship with the God of my fathers.

The next morning I called Marsha and Roy. Marsha was elated. Roy was at a retreat, so I left my number. He called me back a few hours later; then I went up to the retreat with him and we prayed together. It was all so new and exciting that I felt consumed by it.

I went back to college that fall without telling my parents. It wasn't until I was home for the High Holidays that I found myself explaining to them that something the rabbi said during his Rosh Hashanah sermon was wrong.

'You know, the way the rabbi was talking about Christians and Jews, well, did you know that a Gentile is not automatically a Christian?' I said.

My mother looked at me with a what-are-you-talking-about stare. Without realizing it, I began to explain to her about Jesus being the Messiah.

With fear and trepidation, her eyebrows raised, she half whispered, 'Do you believe that?'

I nodded my head.

My parents were overwhelmed, but since I had to get back to school, there wasn't any time to talk. My mother hugged me as I left, half sobbing, 'Don't forget to come home again.' In their mind, I was about to be lost for good.

It was years before my parents became reconciled to my beliefs, years of struggles and misunderstandings, but lots of love. When I graduated from college I decided to go to Moody's Advanced Studies Program, and after that I joined the ABMJ/Chosen People Ministries.

My mom recently told me that my parents had considered me sort of a miracle baby, coming ten years after they were married. Right after I was born, she prayed that God would use me. She admits that what turned out wasn't exactly what she had in mind when she prayed. But, after all, what else could happen when a nice Jewish boy finds God?[224]

Howard joined the staff of the Mission as a Field Evangelist for the state of Ohio. In 1981 he married Janet, a Christian girl he met at the Messianic congregation he was attending. In the fall of 1986, after doing missionary work in Cleveland, Ohio, Howard and Janet Silverman were transferred to Los Angeles to work with the Mission there, and to help establish a Messianic congregation in the San Fernando Valley. Howard served as the Area Director for Los Angeles, but by 1990 he felt God was calling him to return to Ohio to pastor a Messianic Congregation there. He resigned from the Mission, effective November 30, 1990.

The decision of the Board at their June 1985 meeting, to allow Mr. Clemensen to proceed with an investigation of possible buyers for the Orangeburg property opened the idea of the feasibility of moving the Headquarters office of the Mission out of the state of New York. The argument was raised that if the Headquarters was being moved to reduce expenses, why not move to an area where the cost of maintaining administrative and personnel staff could also be reduced. Although, historically, the missionary work and the administration of the Mission had always been combined in one building (as it was in Brooklyn and Manhattan), when the administration of the Mission was relocated to Englewood Cliffs, New Jersey in 1972, the missionary work and the administration were separated. From that time on, the missionary work in New York was maintained under the regional structure of the Mission, while the Headquarters office became an administrative function. Changing methodology, the regional structure of the Mission, and a world-wide ministry and outreach had dictated that maintaining missionary work and administrative work under one roof was no longer necessary.

At the January 1986 meeting of the Board, the author presented a report on the progress of an offer on the Orangeburg headquarters building. The offer was still not confirmed. As a part of the author's recommendations, he asked that the administration be allowed to consider out-of-state property in its search for a new location for the Mission's headquarters building. The Board approved the recommendation.[225]

With this recommendation approved, a Building Site Committee was formed to look at prospective building sites in areas outside of New York state. The Committee was comprised of the author, as President; Roy Adams, Administrative Vice-President; and John Bell, Missionary Director—the management team of the Mission. A twenty-page questionnaire was drawn up, detailing the specific requirements which the administration of the Mission felt were necessary in the location and a building. Of primary concern was the cost of the building and the cost of upkeep on a building, as well as the cost of living within each area investigated. The committee visited a number of cities including Dallas, Texas; Kansas City, Missouri; and Raleigh/Durham and Charlotte, North Carolina.

The Directors recognized the need to add Jewish believers to their membership, and with this in mind the names of two Jewish believers were submitted for consideration at the January 1986 Board meeting—Ms. Goldie Rotenberg, and Mr. Jose Abadi.

Mr. Jose Abadi is a Jewish Christian businessman in South America. He is the President of his own company in Argentina, called Fabril Encuardernadora, Inc. He is also President of the Mission's South American Board. It was the author's hope that having Mr. Abadi on the Board would further consolidate the working relationship between the South American ministry and the American Board. Submission of Mr. Abadi's name was also an attempt to make the Board of the Mission more global in their thinking. The American Board was already comprised of Canadians and U.S. citizens and it seemed a good time to include members from other countries where the Mission had established works. However, because Mr. Abadi did not have a working command of the English language, and because of the expense in bringing him to meetings, it was felt that he should be made an Honorary Board member (with no vote); he would be welcome to attend the Directors meetings at his own expense.[226]

Goldie Rotenberg—Her Story

Ms. Goldie Rotenberg is a Jewish believer who is a practicing real estate attorney in New York. At the time of her appointment, Goldie was a member of the Light of Israel congregation—a Messianic congregation established and pastored by Sam Nadler. The question of having a woman on the Board was raised, but was quickly resolved when the Board was reminded that a number of women had served on the Board in years past. It was decided that the Directors would have an opportunity to review Goldie's completed application and doctrinal questionnaire, after which she would meet with several members of the Board in an informal setting. If she met with their approval, a recommendation to approve her as a Board member would be made to the entire Board.

Goldie Rotenberg was unanimously approved to serve on the Board at the June 20, 1986 Directors meeting. She was, at the time, the only woman on the Board and she had the distinction of being the youngest member of the Board as well, replacing C. Robert Clemensen. The Board membership was comprised of: Dr. Daniel Fuchs, Chairman; Roy Adams, C. Robert Clemensen, John Kubach, John Melhorn, Harold Pretlove, Dr. John Pretlove, Albert Runge, Harold Sevener, and James Straub. John Kubach, John Melhorn, and Harold Pretlove were no longer actively attending Board meetings, although John Kubach remained an active member of the Finance Committee, and met regularly with the other members in person or via telephone conversations. By 1986, Daniel Fuchs was the only "active" Director who had known the Cohns. A new generation of staff and Board members were taking the reigns to perpetuate the work of the Mission in reaching Jewish people with the Gospel.

God's timing is always perfect. Goldie came on the Board at a most expedient time. Her expertise in real estate law, contracts, etc., proved invaluable as the Mission prepared to sell its Headquarters property in New York and move to Charlotte, North Carolina. Her knowledge of the law, and her contacts with other attorneys proved to be of enormous help in establishing new personnel policies, revising existing policy and generally moving the Mission from antiquated by-laws and policies to modern, efficient methods of conducting its ministry world-wide. Goldie continues to be a valuable member of the Board of Directors, and she chairs some of its committees. Her testimony was shared with the readers of *The Chosen People* magazine and is included here. She wrote:

> I was a nice Jewish kid from the Bronx, one of two daughters of immigrant parents who were survivors of Nazi death camps.
>
> We were raised with a lot of Jewish culture and spoke Yiddish at home. During my teens, after school or on weekends, I went to a Workmen's Circle School (a school where Jewish culture was taught). Yet despite all my Jewishness, what little sense of God I had disappeared while I was still in junior high school.
>
> Perhaps more than anything in my childhood, though, I was influenced by my parents' special background. Like many children of immigrant parents, there was almost a role reversal in our home. My sister and I quickly learned to cope with the alien culture and wanted to take care of our parents. Plus, because of what they had been through during the war, I wanted to protect them from being hurt.
>
> Even in college, when my friends were rebelling against authority, I was very aware of my need to watch out for my parents. One time, on hearing that I was going on a peace march to Washington, my mother became frantic. She knew, firsthand, that you didn't have to do something illegal to go to prison. I gave up my seat on the bus and stayed in New York, working on posters.
>
> Between my staunch Jewish pride and my strongly developed sense of logic, I wasn't interested in hearing about

Jesus. To top it off, I was quite hostile toward 'Christians,' a term I considered synonymous with Gentiles and some of whom had been among the Nazis. Without Margaret Reitz, I probably would have continued to accept that idea as fact.

Margaret Reitz was a quiet, gentle country mother and wife, not quite old enough to be my mother but somehow very mature, established, and peaceful. I was a fast-talking, fast-thinking, city kid.

We were so different that it is amazing we became such dear and abiding friends. Yet from the first time I met her, I knew she had two qualities no one else I had ever known had: a very special calm and an extra-ordinary sense of love.

I met Margaret in 1971, the summer after I was graduated from Harpur College. I had planned to help a girl friend move to Albuquerque where she had a new job, but the night before we left, her new job was canceled. Since we had already rented a car and packed our bags, we decided to take a short vacation in Lancaster, Pennsylvania. Through a series of word-of-mouth referrals, we ended up staying at a tourist home run by the Reitz family.

For those first few days I stayed at the Reitz home, my conversations with Margaret reflected the friendly differences I sensed. Seeing the 'Chai' necklace I wore, she remarked on my being Jewish.

'If I weren't born a White Anglo-Saxon Protestant, I would have liked to be a Jew,' she said. 'The Jews are God's chosen people.'

'Chosen for what?' I responded. 'Slaughter?'

Another time she asked what I would do when I got to the end of my rope and couldn't depend on myself.

'I'd probably invent God, just like everyone else does,' I told her, completely confident that I would never come to such an end. 'Then, when the crisis was over, I'd come to my senses and realize I had made the same mistake everyone else who believes in God makes.'

Yet despite all differences, our friendship grew. After I left, we frequently exchanged letters and visits. My letters to Margaret over the next few years reflected much of what I was thinking about God:

'Dear Margaret: There's a certain logic (of the 'soul' if not the pure mathematical logic of the mind) to at least some of what you say. If you keep it up, you may yet convince me of something, though I'm not altogether sure of what.... I was, however, genuinely tickled pink by your letter, and I promise if you make no progress with me, I will someday give you a chance with my children. I don't know if you will have much influence with them either in terms of religion (you know what they say about the mother's influence), but it wouldn't take them long to learn love from you.'

Dear Margaret:...Let me (for a change) disagree with another of your theories. Evil in the world proceeds not from man's refusal to bow his will, intellect, and body to anybody greater than himself, but rather from some men's desire to subjugate others to their will. I don't believe I have argued that man is basically good. In fact, my tendency is to believe he is not. His failure is not so much in not bowing to greater powers than himself but rather in not recognizing the value of other human beings to be as great as his own.'

'Dear Margaret:...You should, I think, understand it is precisely [my successes and accomplishments] that makes me so closed to philosophies that are outside the realm of what I already believe. I just have a constitutional aversion to changing. I've had more than my share of successes, [and] every incident is just a reinforcement that ...I must be doing something right.'

Despite (or perhaps underneath) my glib and frequent barbs to Margaret about her faith, I was quite aware of some things that I found very difficult to express. One was a genuine envy of the surety Margaret had in her faith. The second was a deep desire that this dear friend be completely justified in her trust of a loving God who cared for the fate of individuals.

Dear Margaret:...I've been putting off for about a page now trying to tell you something that I'm not sure I've got straight enough in my mind to express adequately. And even if I do, I'm sure you'll never hear me admit it in a face-to-face meeting. Even though I can't get past the intellectual block and therefore can't really approach it with anything bearing a vague resemblance to an open mind, I would like to be able to believe in God and have been in that position for almost as long as I haven't believed.

I suppose the reason now of wanting to be convinced is the worst one I've come up with in a long time. But it's true nonetheless. I would like to believe now because I would like to know that you are right. Both because it is so important to you as an individual and because I find you so special a person.'

Thus it went until 1975. I even went so far as to read parts of the Bible. Though I was impressed by Romans 9, 10, and 11, it was with a cool intellectual appraisal, acknowledging that the barrier between Jews, Gentiles, and Christians might not be as firm as I had considered it. I continued to be unmoved and untouched spiritually and if at times there did emerge an honest quest for God, I completely suppressed it.

In 1975, having completed law school, I went to spend a few days with the Reitz's. One Sunday evening we went to a slide show on Israel.

The accompanying narrative traced the biblical prophetic record along-side Israel's history. That night, for the first time, I faced a crisis of faith.

I had looked at God as man's invention and the Bible as folklore. Yet someone had taken the Bible and compared it with history. Confronted with the facts, I knew that I would finally have to admit that perhaps, even probably, God was real. Given the amount of energy I had spent denying God, this was a crushing blow.

Four years of my words and wise-cracks suddenly dried up. As Margaret and I sat to the wee hours of the morning, we barely spoke. Instead I sat silently as much of what I'd heard for the past years about a loving God fell into place, a God who cares, a personal God, the God of Israel who was and is and always will be. He is a God of fact as well as faith; He is a God who is real not only for gentle, soft Margeret [sic] Reitz, but also for a fast thinking, overachieving Jewish lawyer from New York.

Margaret gave me a choice, perhaps the only one I was capable of making just then. 'Are you willing to give God a chance to show you?'

For several hours I was unable to answer that question. I knew what it meant, what I would be acknowledging. I was afraid God would show me that Jesus was real. I sat quietly at times, crying at times, tormented by my need to avoid causing my parents any pain.

I had placed logic on a pedestal, and now I realized logic had taken me as far as it could. The only 'logical' conclusion was to take a leap of faith. I saw in one flash that the Bible was valid. It had something to say to me.

Finally I was able to break through and I answered 'yes.'[227]

Following her appointment to the Board, Goldie recommended that the author interview another Jewish believer, Mr. Jeffrey Branman, as a potential Board member.

Jeffrey Branman—His Story

Jeff was born in Chicago, Illinois but during his childhood the family moved to Southern California. Like other young Jewish boys, he attended Hebrew School and Temple. But his parents were not practicing Jews. In fact, after his Bar Mitzvah, Jeff's parents told him quite frankly that the only reason they had sent him to Hebrew School was to appease his grandfather, who would have been upset had they allowed Jeff to break with tradition and not be made Bar Mitzvah.

Jeff's recollection of the first time he heard the name of Jesus Christ is vivid! The words of his little playmate, "You dirty Jew, you killed Jesus Christ and you're going to burn in hell" had left him confused and perplexed. In Hebrew School he had been taught that God loved the Jewish people; he had been taught that the Jews were special because they had a special relationship with God. But no one had mentioned Jesus Christ. Who was he? With his playmate's words still ringing in his ears, Jeff marched straight home to ask his parents about her accusation.

Mr. and Mrs. Branman had already braced themselves for the day when their son would ask about such an allegation. They knew the day would come, and they had their explanation ready. "Jesus," they said, "was a Jewish man who was killed by the Romans, and after his death Gentile Christians made him their God. The Christians believe that the Jews killed Jesus, and that's why they hate the Jews." Continuing, they told Jeff, "Christians made up the story about hell to scare people into obeying their orders, but Hell doesn't really exist!"

Calmed by his parents reassurance that he had not killed anyone, and that he was not going to burn in hell, Jeff tried to put his playmate's ugly words out of his mind. He liked the things he learned about God in Hebrew School. It was good to know that God loved the Jewish people when there were all those Christians out there who hated Jews.

One day when Jeff was talking to his mother about the lessons he was learning about God, she announced, "We don't really believe in God. If God were real He wouldn't have allowed six million Jews to die in Nazi Germany"—a response which, for the second time in his young life, left Jeff completely confused and perplexed. If his own parents didn't believe in God how could he, a young Jewish boy, believe in Him? The lessons of Hebrew School had taken root in his heart and he wanted to believe God was real, but his mother's words shook the foundation of his faith and greatly impacted his image of God.

Following his Bar Mitzvah, both Jeff and his parents stopped attending services at the Temple. Jeff found new interests and new friends, and he made the amazing discovery that there are many people in the world who do not hate Jews. He was shocked, but delighted, to find that in the areas of the arts, history, theater and drama his Jewishness was actually an advantage to him!

Jeff loved the excitement of the theater. By the time he was in Junior High School he was chosen for many of the leading roles in school plays—a status he continued to enjoy throughout his High School years as well. His leading roles in school plays made him a part of the "in" clique of the Drama Department. Puffed up with own self importance, he used his "limelight" platform to criticize other students for their lack of dedication to the "art form." Not surprisingly, he found he had few friends outside the Drama Department.

During Jeff's junior year in High School things began to change. "Jesus Freaks" began to appear on campus; they seemed to infiltrate every classroom and every school activity—including the Drama Department. They made him nervous. Their words brought back the ugly memory of his childhood playmate—especially when they would corner him and say, "turn or burn Jeff!" Within months several of his closest friends confided that Jesus had changed their lives, and they told him, "Jesus loves you Jeff Branman." But Jeff's response was always the same: "Too bad—I don't love Him," or "That's alright for you, but not for me. I'm Jewish!"

The thought of having to endure a conversation with one of the "Jesus freaks" was more than Jeff could bear, and he began to avoid Christians like the plague. He wanted nothing to do with them or the "Jesus-God" they worshipped. He set about to conduct his own search for peace of heart and mind, and he threw himself with gusto into the theater, parties, marijuana—anything he could find that would put distance between himself and those "Jesus Freaks."

In spite of his determination to steer clear of Christians, Jeff surprised himself one day as he heard his own voice agreeing to go to church with one of his young friends. After agreeing to go, he justified his response to himself by musing that it would be interesting to watch the "freaks" in action; he was curious about what they actually did in their church.

Looking at the sea of faces surrounding him inside the church, Jeff was amazed to see that the audience was mainly comprised of young people. The songs were unfamiliar to him, and the atmosphere was foreign, yet he found that he was enjoying the service. His enjoyment ended when the pastor began to teach from Isaiah 42:1, and identified the "servant" as Jesus. Since he did not have a Jewish Bible with him, Jeff could not disprove what the pastor was saying but he knew that Jesus was not in his Jewish Bible!

Jeff could hardly wait to get home! As soon as he reached the house he made his way to his father's room. There, hidden away under the stacks of books and papers, he found his father's unused copy of the Jewish Scriptures. He fumbled through the pages until he found Isaiah 42:1. It was just as he had suspected! The Christians had changed the Bible! His Jewish version of the Isaiah 42:1 stated, "Behold my servant *Israel*...." It did not say Jesus. From that moment on, convinced that the teachings of the Christians could not be trusted, Jeff militantly turned a deaf ear to the comments of anyone who tried to tell him about the claims of Jesus.

By the time he entered the University of Redlands, in Redlands, California, three things became the center of Jeff's life—girls, marijuana, and the theater. Although he no longer concerned himself with the message proclaimed by the "Jesus Freaks," and although his busy social calendar left little time for reflection, he was vaguely aware of an emptiness in his life. He began to realize that most of his friends were just like himself—people who were going through life pretending; they were people with no depth, no reality. With that realization, he decided he wanted to be a true artist— not just another pretentious creep!

Leaving his University of Redlands friends, Jeff began making friendships with the Johnston College people. Throughout the 1972 school year, he lived in their dorms and ate in their commons. At last he felt he had found some true "artists." His new friends were idealistic, free-thinking, and morally lax. Some were spiritually attuned—but not to God!

One such "spiritually attuned" individual was a young man whose name was Pat. Jeff and Pat became immediate friends; they seemed to be able to communicate supernaturally, linking up with one another mentally and emotionally whenever necessary. They began to believe that the "spiritual power" they had was God, and that they were special because they knew about it and no one else did.

Jeff returned to the Redlands campus during the Fall of 1973, but he continued to maintain contact with his friends at the Johnston campus. The Johnston commons was a favorite lunch-time hangout. It was there that Jeff and his friends would sit and plan their futures. As he walked towards the commons in October 1973, he was unaware of a group of young people who were performing in the commons that day—a group whose songs and skits would make him see red!

The performing young people were from the organization known by the name, "Jews For Jesus." The group's name was the Liberated Wailing Wall. They had come to the Johnston campus to share the Gospel message through songs and gospel skits. But Jeff saw them as impostors—Christians dressed up like Jews, trying to make the *real* Jews look bad. He was furious, and he stood up and yelled, "I want to eat my lunch in peace!" Taking their cue from Jeff, other Jewish students began yelling, cat calling, and making noises with their plates. Standing on a chair, Jeff led the rally cry to throw the "pretenders" off campus. But despite his efforts and antics the concert continued. Livid with anger, Jeff spotted the director of student life standing in the crowd. He jumped off his chair, ran over to him, and shouted in his most angry theatrical voice, "Get these...creeps out of here." Frightened by Jeff's demeanor and overwhelming anger, the director of student life ordered that the plug to the electrical sound equipment be pulled. Without amplification the songs of the Liberated Wailing Wall were no match for the shouting of the angry mob; the group was escorted off the platform and the concert ended. Jeff was pleased with what he had accomplished, but for days afterward his anger would not subside and he continued to curse out "those Jews who believe in Jesus."

Jeff's encounter with the Liberated Wailing Wall shook him to the very marrow of his bones; it awakened him to an awareness of his deep-rooted hatred of Jews who dared to believe in Jesus. At the same time, he began to realize that his special friendship with Pat was breaking down. It was time for a change, so Jeff decided to call the whole "school thing" quits for awhile. Some friends he knew had invited him to go with them to Mexico, where the marijuana was better. Jeff had been smoking marijuana heavily, and the thought of getting some real "good stuff" was appealing. He knew that his companions were not going to Mexico just for the marijuana; they wanted to buy cocaine. But he didn't care what they bought; he just wanted to be with different people in a different place.

As they made their way toward Mexico, Jeff sat in the back of the pick-up truck, watching the yellow line disappear over the horizon as the highway rose and dipped. He looked out across the expanse of the desert, observed the strange shapes of the cactus plants as they drove, and became aware of the intense heat of the desert sun. Everything seemed to rush by with tremendous speed and he thought, "I'm going further and further into hell!" In his mind's eye he saw a mountain with a road leading to its base. At the base of the mountain the road forked; one road went to the right, the other to the left. In his vision, Jeff had turned to go down the left fork of the road when he felt an angel lift him above the top of the mountain. From that vantage point he could see where the two roads ultimately led. He could see that one led toward God and life, while the road he had chosen led only to darkness and to death. In his vision, he recognized that the friends he was with were agents of the Devil; they had brought him along to lead him to his death. He saw them trying to pass a semi-truck on the road, and crashing into an oncoming car. He saw himself thrown out of the truck, killed as he was crushed in the twisted wreckage. He also saw that his two companions survived the wreck, and were given honors from Satan for a job well done.

Just as Jeff's vision ended, he became aware that the driver of the pick-up truck was starting to pass a huge truck. He could hear the whine of the engine as the driver pushed down on the accelerator. Then he heard the voice of God— words Jeff later said he will never forget: "Obey Me. Leave these two companions and choose life, or choose to die." In a split second, though not one audible word was spoken, Jeff spoke to God saying, "Lord I want life." "I want to live."

As the words faded from his mind, and with his heart still pounding as if it would leap out of his chest, Jeff realized they had safely passed the big semi-truck. He knew God had saved him from certain death and he decided that he would part company with his traveling companions the moment they reached the small town of Nuleje. Jeff could hardly wait to jump out of the truck, knowing that somehow he had chosen life over death.

Trusting God to direct him, Jeff made his way back to the Redlands campus. He was not sure what had happened to him on the road to Mexico; what he did know was that for the first time in his life he was experiencing a kind of peace he'd never before known.

At the close of the semester Jeff decided to return to the area where he grew up. He transferred his credits to the University of Southern California and set about to resume his acting career. One of his childhood friends, Jack McCullough, lived close to his parents home. Jeff had known Jack since junior high school. What Jeff did not know about Jack was that Jack had become a born again believer. The two young men decided to car-pool. They also had the same acting classes. Whenever they were together Jack would bring up the subject of Jesus. He was persistent in his witness to Jeff, but sensitive to his moods, and because Jack was a Gentile his faith in Jesus did not anger Jeff. Whenever Jeff was down, Jack would remind him that Jesus was the answer to this quest for personal peace.

One day Jeff and Jack agreed to give a ride to a new classmate, Monica MacClean. To Jeff's dismay, Monica was also an outspoken born again believer. Like Jack, Monica talked a lot about Jesus and when Jeff asked her why she seemed so happy she replied, "Because Jesus loves me!" "How trite," Jeff thought, yet he longed for that peace and happiness in his own life.

Before their evening class that day, Jack and Jeff stopped for a cup of coffee. As they talked, Jack once again reminded Jeff that Jesus loved him. But Jeff didn't want to talk about Jesus. To close the subject he said, "I can't believe in that, I'm Jewish." But Jack quickly responded, "Jesus came as the Messiah for the Jewish people." Jeff was at a loss for words. He knew nothing about a Jewish Messiah. Embarrassed, he bluffed and said, "I don't believe that stuff." Not deterred, Jack continued to talk to Jeff about the Jewish Messiah and the promises about Him in the Bible. He told Jeff why the Messiah was supposed to come, and what the Bible meant about sin. He told Jeff that God loves us; He doesn't want us to die because of our sin—that's why the Messiah came. "But I'm Jewish," blurted out Jeff, knowing full well that his excuse no longer held any weight in their discussion. Jack sat back, paused a moment, and then said, "Jesus said that He came so that 'we might have *life* and have it more abundantly' and that's more than you need Jeff."

Jeff was floored. He head tingled, his heart pounded. He turned the words over and over again in his mind. Life. Life abundantly. Jeff remembered his vision in the back of the pick-up truck; he remembered his decision to choose life. Once again, he was being given the choice. He felt the presence of God speaking to him, "This is the life that I have given to you. This is your chance of have life." As God spoke to his heart, Jeff hardly heard Jack telling him to "think about it."

Class went on as usual for everyone else, but for Jeff it was an hour of warfare—spiritual warfare. At times the struggle was so intense he felt he wanted to die. When the class was over, Jeff told Jack about his struggle with life and death and his thoughts of suicide to end the raging inner battle. Quietly Jack said, "Jeff, Jeff, you are so close to knowing Jesus that Satan will do anything to keep you from accepting Jesus as your Messiah and Savior." As they drove home, Jeff told Jack he wanted to accept Jesus—but not while they were driving. It was when they stopped the car to let Monica out that Jeff knelt down to accept Jesus as his personal Savior and Lord. Jeff later stated that as he prayed, confessing his sin and asking forgiveness, no big spiritual bliss fell upon him, but he knew that God had heard his prayer and he knew that at that moment he became a child of God. Jeff prayed to receive Jesus on August 9, 1974 at 11:30 P.M. He was baptized at Corona Del Mar, California on August 30, 1974 by one of the pastors at Calvary Chapel of Costa Mesa.[228]

Today Jeff is a successful businessman in Southern California. He currently serves on the Board of Directors of Chosen People Ministries, Inc.

In addition to the Board's unanimous approval to make Goldie Rotenberg a Director, the agenda of the Board's June 1986 meeting included several additional items which are noteworthy.

John Bell, as Missionary Director, was invited to make a report to the Board. He shared the listing of the Messianic congregations which had joined The Fellowship of Messianic Congregations—the new Messianic organization that the Mission had helped establish. John pointed out that six of the member congregations had been established by the Mission.[229]

The Mission's Name is Changed

The author reported to the Directors that the name, "Chosen People Ministries," was in the process of being trademarked.[230] Later, at the October 1986 Board meeting the Directors unanimously passed a resolution authorizing that the name "The American Board of Missions to the Jews, Inc.," be changed to "Chosen People Ministries, Inc.," effective immediately.[231]

The Williamsburg Mission to the Jews, established in 1894, which had become The American Board of Missions to the Jews, Inc., was now Chosen People Ministries, Inc. But unlike the name change from The Williamsburg Mission to the Jews to The American Board of Missions to the Jews, a new corporation was not established. In changing the name of the ministry to Chosen People Ministries, Inc., only the name was changed.

The proposal to change the Mission's name was first submitted for the Board's consideration at the January 1984 Directors meeting. Knowing that such a change would need to be handled through a gradual process so as not to confuse the Mission's constituents, the change was initiated by dropping the use of the full ministry name for an abbreviation of the name, using the initials ABMJ. The initials were highlighted to alliterate the purpose of the Mission—"Always Bringing Messiah to the Jews." In the November 1984 issue of *The Chosen People* magazine, emphasizing the world-wide scope of the Mission's ministry, the author used his "From the President" column to write:

> I am amazed at how many people think that the American Board of Missions to the Jews is a ministry reaching only the American Jew. Perhaps it is because of our name, the American Board.
>
> In reality, however, the ABMJ is an international ministry reaching around the world. We have workers in Canada, in Paris, France; Jerusalem, Israel; Athens, Greece; and Buenos Aires, Argentina....
>
> Yes, ABMJ is more than a mission simply to the American Jews. It is the ABMJ—Always Bringing Messiah to the Jews. It is a world-wide ministry with a vision to see the lost sheep of the house of Israel come to a saving knowledge of Jesus as their Messiah, their Lord, and their Savior.[232]

The next step was to use the initials "ABMJ," along with the name, "Chosen People Ministries"—using the two names together: ABMJ/Chosen People Ministries. This was done so that the name could be legally trademarked; at the same time the Mission's constituents were being familiarized with the new name. By the end of 1986, and during the early months of 1987, all of the Mission's publications and communications carried the name Chosen People Ministries along with the Mission's "logo"—the logo that had been developed for the Bicentennial Congress on Prophecy in 1976.

Report of the Ministry — 1986

By June 1986, the Directors also authorized Sam Nadler, as Northeast Regional Director, to begin looking for a home that could serve as a dwelling for himself and his family, as well as to serve as the regional headquarters office for the Northeast. The Northeast Region had grown considerably under Sam's leadership, and the need for a facility from which to operate the region was acute. The Board empowered the Executive Committee to spend up to the sum of $225,000 for such property.[233]

Some years prior, Mr. Wesley Jones, who was serving as the Stewardship Director for the Mission, had set up a Trust for a faithful supporter of the Mission. When the supporter died, it was the desire of the trustees that the monies be made immediately available to the Mission to be used as a "Missionary Housing Fund." Working with their attorneys, the Board set up what was called a "contract to deed," whereby missionaries of the Mission were to receive credit for monthly payments which they made to the Mission toward the future purchase of houses originally purchased by the Mission.[234] As the missionary was able to purchase the home from the Mission, it would then free funds to provide housing for other workers. The program was a way of providing affordable housing for missionaries who were forced to live in some of the most expensive cities in the United States in their endeavor to reach Jewish people with the Gospel. This fund was able to provide housing for workers in New York and California. The property being sought for the Nadlers was to have been a part of this program.

The Directors also adopted an Agreement of Alliance between ABMJ and Beth Sar Shalom Mission of Canada (ABMJ's affiliate organization) at their June 1986 meeting. The agreement was drawn up with the help of legal counsel so that there would be no misunderstanding as to the control and ownership of the Mission and its properties and programs in Canada. After adopting the agreement the Board further approved that such agreements should be effected with ABMJ's branches in South America and France.[235]

In an effort to further strengthen the agreement between the U.S. Board and the Canadian Board, Mr. Gary Smith (who was already a member of the Canadian Board) was elected to the U.S. Board at the Directors January 1987 meeting.[236] At the same meeting, the name of Mr. David Weland, another Canadian Board member, was submitted for consideration as a U.S. Board member. However, he declined. David was subsequently elected to the American Board at the June 1987 Board meeting. Gary Smith is a Christian businessman and David Weland is charter accountant.

In the 1986 Mid-Year Report, the author reported that in the first six months of the year the workers of the Mission had led 135 Jewish people to the Lord. Over 157,000 tracts were given out to Jewish people. More than 1,485 Bible studies were conducted in homes. Hundreds of services, special events, and Bible studies were held in churches, centers, and meeting rooms. Throughout the United States, Canada, South America, Europe and Israel, small groups were regularly meeting to evangelize, disciple and train Jewish and Gentile believers.[237]

Board members, John Melhorn and Harold Pretlove, were made Members Emeritus of the Board in January 1987, as both suffered from health problems which prevented them from attending meetings. Harold Pretlove had served on the Board for forty years; John Melhorn had given over thirty years as a Director.

Five-Year Plan Adopted

The January 1987 Board meeting was also noteworthy because at that meeting the Board adopted a Five-Year Plan for the Mission. The program was developed by Roy Adams, John Bell and the author in response to the suggestion of the Ad Hoc Committee that the Mission needed a plan of projected goals whereby the Board could measure the health and vitality of the ministry in light of the Mission's Statement of Purpose.

The Five-Year Program was a comprehensive program utilizing the unifying policy and programs which the Board had already agreed to. It involved building up an extensive ministry in Israel, continuing development of the ministry in Europe and expanding the ministry into the United Kingdom, Australia and South Africa. It called for expansion of the ministry in South America, and for the establishment of a radio broadcast to the Soviet Union. Within the United States, the plan called for reducing the regional districts from five to four by adding to the Southeast region and the Northeast region. It called for an increase in the number of Field evangelists (National Church Ministries representatives), and for the establishment of additional Messianic congregations throughout the United States and Canada. Evangelistic "media campaigns" were planned in strategic cities in North America, culminating in a centennial celebration of the Mission in New York City. It envisioned missionary internship programs in local churches and Messianic congregations, conferences, and the establishment of a Chosen People Ministries Bible Institute which was to offer daytime, evening, and correspondence classes. It also envisioned training and re-training for present workers in specialized areas.

The goals for the Five-Year program were stated clearly and precisely; responsibility for each item was assigned, and a time-schedule was given. Since the program was comprehensive and inter-dependent, it required that each program become self-supporting. Thus, before any new project could be funded, the plan required that all existing projects and programs be fully funded. This apparently was not understood by all members of the Board.

At the time that the Five-Year plan was approved and adopted, the Mission was considering the purchase of property outside of the state of New York for its Headquarters and administrative offices. It was also proposing the purchase of a regional headquarters building (and home for the Nadlers) in the Northeast. It was seeking to fully fund its Pension Program, and it was faced with the need to increase and adjust the salaries of current workers. Additionally, it was in the throes of a name change.

After the Five-Year Program was adopted the finances did increase, but they had not increased sufficiently to completely meet the needs of the existing programs and personnel, let alone the additional programs and personnel proposed in the Five-Year Plan. One year later, at the January 1988 Board meeting, with the pending relocation of the Mission's Headquarters office and changes within the Mission's administrative and missionary staff, and to prevent the Mission from going into additional deficit spending, the author requested that the Board put the Five-Year Program on a "temporary hold" for re-evaluation.[238]

HEADQUARTERS MOVED SOUTH

At the June 1987 Board meeting, the Directors unanimously approved a resolution authorizing the President and the Administrative Vice President to purchase property for the relocation of the Mission's Headquarters office to Charlotte, North Carolina. The property was located in the Coffee Creek development of Charlotte. At the same meeting, Mr. John Gotberg, an engineer who worked with the Missionary Tech Team, presented to the Directors his findings on the proposed building site and his plans for the new building. The plans had been carefully prepared subsequent to Mr. Gotberg's visit to the Orangeburg office, at which time he queried each department head and assessed the space needs of each department and for the building as a whole. The Board approved the plans.[239]

The author shared the news of the relocation, and some of the Board's reasoning for the selection of the Charlotte site, in the August 1987 Mid-Year Report. He stated:

After much prayer and searching, we believe that God led us to the Charlotte, North Carolina area. Charlotte, North Carolina fits all of the criteria that we had established, plus offers us some bonuses [among the criteria established were an international airport, Eastern Standard Time, a strong economic base, a strong Christian community to draw upon for administrative staff, access to major businesses and industries for equipment, service, repair, etc.]. Last year the Sudan Interior Mission (SIM) relocated their international headquarters to Charlotte, North Carolina; we would have Christian neighbors.

The American Chamber of Commerce, in establishing a Cost of Living Index for the major cities across the United States, rated New York at 141.2%, the national average being 100%. Charlotte, North Carolina is rated at 98.7%, which is a 42.5% difference between the averages. In other words, by relocating our receipt, mail, publication and communication services to Charlotte, North Carolina, potentially we could reduce our administrative costs by 30%.

This is an answer to prayer and is exciting! It is a way for us to be wise stewards of the Lord's resources.

As we explored the city of Charlotte, God directed us to a brand new business park called Coffey Creek. It is located right off the Billy Graham Parkway, near the new International Airport and the new Coliseum, parks and recreational facilities that are being developed. It is a perfect location.

We were able to purchase a 2.8 acre parcel of land, which will more than adequately meet our needs, and as soon as our building is sold in New York we will begin to build a 15,000 sq. foot office building on this property.

We are praying that by next July we'll be able to move into a new building in Charlotte, North Carolina. Amazingly, the total cost for the land and the building is approximately $750,000. In New York, we couldn't even begin to purchase the land for that price.[240]

Without even having to list the Orangeburg building with a realtor, the Mission's headquarters building was sold, and the purchaser agreed to allow the Mission to remain in the building until the new building in Charlotte was complete or until the end of 1988, whichever came first. Staff members not being transferred were given generous severance allowances and the Mission paid for job placement service for those who needed it. Through the effective leadership of John Gotberg and Roy Adams, the new headquarters building was built within budget ($750,000), and on time. The move was accomplished "decently and in order"; the Headquarters staff of the Mission occupied the building the first week in August, 1988. Without Roy Adams' help and meticulous care for details, and the high level of confidence that the Board had in his abilities, the Mission could never have enjoyed such a smooth transition.

An Open House was held for friends of the Mission and for visitors during the afternoon hours on both Saturday, October 1, 1988 and Sunday, October 2, 1988 and a Dedication Service for the building, featuring Dr. John Walvoord as the main speaker, was held at 7:30 P.M. on Saturday evening.

But the relocation of the Mission's Headquarters office was not the only change within the Mission during 1988. The year 1988 proved to be a historic year for the Mission. There were many changes.

During the first six months of 1988, Chosen People Ministries missionaries led thirty-five Jewish people to the Lord (United States and Canada); they distributed 55,000 pieces of Gospel literature; they made 3130 visits, of which 905 were to unsaved Jewish people; they held 247 Bible studies, with 5577 people in attendance. Seventy-five Gentiles were led to the Lord and sixteen people were baptized. The Mission also hired new workers for Israel—Avner and Rachel Boskey (See Chapter Seven of this history).

But by far, the most unexpected and startling change was the swift and sudden death of Dr. Daniel Fuchs, on May 24, 1988. Daniel was the last link on the Board to have known the Cohn family personally. His death, in many ways, signaled the end of an era. By the time of his death the Mission was no longer known as The Williamsburg Mission to the Jews, or as The American Board of Missions to the Jews, or even as Beth Sar Shalom; it was now known as Chosen People Ministries, Inc. The missionary work and the administrative work of the Mission no longer shared a facility, due to many factors, including the frequent bomb threats and violent actions of anti-missionary groups. The Mission's Headquarters building was no longer in Brooklyn, or Manhattan—one of the largest Jewish population centers in the world; it was being relocated to Charlotte, North Carolina—one of the smallest Jewish population centers in the world. The Mission's publications were no longer in Yiddish and illustrated in stylized Hebrew or "Jewish" letters; its materials and publications were done in modern up-to-date graphics. The Mission was no longer a "family run" organization; it was now directed by an efficient and competent group of outside Directors. Over the years the Mission had changed dramatically from what it had been, but its message and vision remained true to the vision of its founders—to reach Jewish people with the Gospel.

Plans For the Future

In December 1987, knowing that the Headquarters of the Mission was being relocated to Charlotte, North Carolina in a matter of seven to eight months, Daniel Fuchs asked the author if he could stop by the office for a visit. As Chairman of the Board, he had often made such requests for visits with the author, to discuss Mission affairs.

On this occasion Daniel began to talk about the history of the Mission. He spoke of the many changes that had taken place, and mentioned some of the disagreements we'd had over the vision and direction for the ministry in more recent years. Each of us had been trying to serve the Lord as we believed He was directing. Although we realized we would not always agree, we both wanted what was best for the Mission.

Finally, Daniel broached the subject he'd come to address—the future of the ministry. He stated that he believed the time had come for both of us to step aside; he believed it was time for the development of a new leader to take over the reigns of the ministry. He stated that his biggest fear was that if he stepped aside, "Harvard businessmen" would step in and run the Mission, rather than missionaries. He stated that the Mission's name change, the relocation of the Headquarters office, and the many new programs of the Mission all indicated to him that perhaps the time was right for a change in leadership as well.

As we spoke, the author agreed that if changes were to be made, it seemed like a good time to bring strong Jewish-Christian leadership into the executive positions of the Mission—especially with the congregation-planting ministry and the increasing visibility of the Messianic movement. The author agreed to pray with Daniel for God's leading and direction in the matter. However, the author also made it clear that if such a course of action were to be pursued, he (the author) would want a Search Committee of the Board formed and responsible to interview candidates, who would then be presented to the Board for further interviews and selection. The author also stated that he felt prospective candidates should be selected from outside the Board, and that if the Board wanted to make that individual a Director after his selection, it would be their decision.

The Mission had come a long way in its nearly one hundred year history. By 1988 the Board of Directors was comprised of Christian volunteers—both Jewish and Gentile—who gave themselves unselfishly as they labored on behalf of the Mission. The Board was strong in their convictions, competent in their judgments, wise in their decisions, and they sought the Lord in all of their deliberations.

At the close of our meeting together, Daniel and the author prayed together and embraced.

At the January 1988 annual meeting of the Board, the author made the President's Report on the ministry. The report included the accomplishments of the ministry during 1987. It also included a number of recommendations for study and action by the Board in the new year. The Minutes state: "Harold Sevener also made recommendations ... that a Search Committee be appointed by the Board to find, within the organization, successors for the offices of President and Executive Vice-President."[241]

New Leadership Positions Outlined

Included with the recommendation for the formation of a Search Committee was the recommendation that the Board draw up job specifications for the positions they wanted to fill; it was a recommendation that they give consideration to the type of President they wanted leading the organization. Did they want a figure-head President? Did they want a Gentile or a Jewish believer? Did they want to combine C.E.O. [Chief Executive Officer] and C.F.O. [Chief

Financial Officer] duties? Did they want the President of the Mission to be a scholar, writer, preacher, etc.[242]

In making these recommendations the author knew he was in essence laying his position on the line, and he had prayerfully considered the consequences. He also knew the organization would never grow, unify and move toward the fulfillment of a common vision without the commitment of the entire Board of Directors.

The Board discussed the recommendation at length and decided to defer the matter until the next meeting to give the individual Directors more time for thought and prayer on the matter.[243] The next meeting was scheduled for May 5-7, 1988.

Before the May meeting could be held, a special meeting of the Board was called for April 4 & 5, 1988 in Toronto, Canada. The meeting was called by the Chairman to focus on what the Board desired in a President, but it was also held to evaluate the author in light of those expectations.[244] Since the meeting was an evaluation of the author, as President, and a definition of the role which the Board wanted the author to fulfill, the author was not invited to attend the first part of the meeting. However, after the Board had defined what it wanted in the role of President, the author was invited to join the discussions of how the Directors viewed the position of President for the Mission, and any strengths the author could bring to the office as they had structured it.

In effect, the Board had structured the office of President around what they perceived the author's strengths to be—preaching, writing, managing and editing of *The Chosen People* magazine, the writing of letters to the ministries constituency, visiting with the Mission's major donors, writing papers and books, and conducting tours to Israel. In general, all of the responsibilities that they defined for the President were in the areas of public relations and communications. In essence, they defined the position of President as being a "figure-head" who was also to be closely involved with the communications of the Mission.

The author was then informed that the Board was planning to create a new position which they planned to call the Executive Director. The Executive Director of the Mission would be responsible for day-to-day affairs of the Mission, thus allowing the President to concentrate on the areas they had outlined and specified.[245]

It was further stated that the Executive Director, and the President would both report directly to the Board. The Board had asked Roy Adams to assume the responsibility of Executive Director until such time as another candidate was appointed to the position. The Board then unanimously passed the following resolution:

THAT THE BOARD INFORM THE PRESIDENT:
(1) that we thank God for him, for his gifts, and for the fact that the Lord allows him to serve as President of Chosen People Ministries;
(2) that we recognize that his gifts are, in general, gifts that are related towards our constituency, rather than gifts in acting towards our organization as a Chief Executive Officer;
(3) that we propose to work with him to redefine his job specifications to reflect those gifts and to maximize his usefulness;
(4) that we propose to seek for a person to whom the functions of a C.E.O. can be given.[246]

Needless to say this was not an easy meeting. It was not easy for the Board to make their evaluations and recommendations, nor was it easy for the author to accept their evaluation. Yet, this was what I had asked the Board to do in making the recommendation that a "Search Committee" be formed. Knowing that the members of the Board were men and women of God who had diligently prayed about the matter, and sought the Lord's direction and wisdom for the future leadership of the ministry, the author accepted the position of President as defined and outlined by the Board. My major reservation in accepting the position was the fact that, once again, the Mission was to be under the leadership of two leaders—both of whom were to report directly to the Board. I felt that the Mission would once again have difficulty in defining its vision and policies. The Board was concerned about this as well, and they tried their best to write a job description for the position of Executive Director that would address some of these concerns.

The May 6, 1988 Board Minutes state:

Daniel Fuchs appointed a Search Committee to look for a new Executive Director. This Committee will consist of John Pretlove, Goldie Rotenberg and Gary Smith. The first task of this Committee will be to draw up job specifications and requirements for this position. Daniel Fuchs will work on requirements and specifications with this Committee. The Committee will then report back to the Board for approval of their work and then proceed with the search.[247]

As Daniel Fuchs and the author had discussed at their meeting together in December 1987, the Search Committee was comprised of one Director who had served on the Board for several years and two Directors who were recent members of the Board; all were volunteers; none were employees, nor had they ever been employees of the Mission. The author believed that this was important if the Mission was going to develop and expand its ministry under new leadership.

The job description for the position of Executive Director which the Search Committee presented, and which the Board approved at their November 18, 1988 meeting, was carefully worded to balance the areas of responsibility and communication between the President and the Executive Director. It stated:

1. *The Executive Director is a Senior Officer of the Mission.*
2. *The Executive Director is a Member of and reports to the Board of Directors.*
3. *The Executive Director will be responsible for the formulation of policy and the preparation of long and short range plans, all to be submitted to the Board of Directors for approval. He/she will be responsible for the execution of these plans, working with the President and the Executive Vice President when appropriate, all within the policy and budgetary constraints established by the Board. He/she will report to the Board on progress and problems and make any recommendations for change.*
4. *Either directly, or through a person to be named, the Executive Director will supervise all missionary activities, domestic and foreign. Within this area of activity, he/she will delegate responsibilities and be responsible for monitoring performance of subordinates. He/she will work with the Personnel Committee of the Board in the administration of personnel policy, including recommendation of position and salary changes.*
5. *The Executive Vice President will report to the Executive Director to whom he will be responsible for the administrative and financial areas of the ministry.*
6. *The current President will report directly to the Board. It is realized that the communications and donor relations functions managed by the President and the administrative and financial areas managed by the Executive Vice President, and the planning and missionary activities managed by the Executive Director, are inter-related and a high degree of cooperation among these areas is required to carry out the objectives of the Mission effectively. There shall be a regular exchange of information and full access to all functions among these three divisions.*
7. *The President will serve as the Editor of* The Chosen People *magazine, which shall be available to the Executive Director to be used as the vehicle for sharing the vision and activities of the Mission. The President and the Executive Director will work together in the planning of each issue of the magazine.*[248]

As indicated, this was not an easy job description to write but the Search Committee did its best to define a working relationship between the President and the Executive Director. Ironically, Daniel Fuchs, who was to help in drawing up this job description, was called home to be with the Lord. His death was sudden and unexpected. It came as a shock to everyone!

THE DEATH OF DANIEL FUCHS

Daniel had been having circulatory problems in his leg; he also suffered from diabetes. The discomfort in his leg was discouraging to him; he loved to walk, but the pain made it difficult for him. By the spring of 1988, his doctors discovered that a blood clot had formed in his leg. They were fearful that it might cause a heart attack, or a stroke, so they hospitalized him. After a few days, when it became apparent that nothing was helping the circulation in the leg, Daniel's doctors informed him they would have to amputate his leg below the knee.

The author visited Daniel in the hospital within hours after he was admitted. He was confident that the Lord would heal his leg, yet he was prepared if God chose not to. When the doctors told him that his leg would be amputated, Daniel said, "if that is what the Lord wants for me I'll use crutches and learn to walk with an artificial leg." As his friends and members of the Board visited with him, each one found him confident in God's sovereignty over his life.

During the week of Daniel's hospitalization, the Northeast region was holding its annual "Simcha" (Joy) Conference at the Word of Life Conference grounds in Schroon Lake, New York. Because the author was one of the scheduled speakers at the conference (as were others from the New York staff), we were unable to be at the hospital the day Daniel's leg was amputated, but Muriel Fuchs (Daniel's wife) kept us informed.

On his return from the conference, the author stopped at the hospital to visit with Daniel. He was sitting in a chair, reading material about the care and use of an artificial leg. His spirits were excellent. He could hardly wait to start practicing walking again. He was determined to resume his regular schedule of activities, including walking several miles around a near-by lake. He was delighted to hear the good report of the "Simcha" conference, and of the many decisions for the Lord which the Mission's workers had reported in recent weeks. We read Scripture together, prayed, and the author left to return home and to resume his responsibilities at the Mission.

During the very early morning hours, on May 24, 1988, Daniel Fuchs' heart failed. God called his faithful servant into His presence. Daniel was 76 years old; he had served with the Mission for over 50 years. He was well loved by the

Mission's staff and by the members of the Board.

The July 1988 issue of *The Chosen People* magazine was dedicated to the memory and to the work of Dr. Daniel Fuchs. It was a special memorial edition which included notes from various Christian leaders such as Dr. Douglas McCorkle, former President, Philadelphia College of the Bible; Dr. Charles Halff, President, Christian Jew Foundation; Dr. Leslie Flynn, Pastor, Grace Conservative Baptist Church; Dr. W.A. Criswell, Pastor, First Baptist Church, Dallas, Texas; Dr. Maxwell Coder, Dean of Education Emeritus, Moody Bible Institute; Dr. John Walvoord, Chancellor, Dallas Theological Seminary; Dr. Richard Halverson, Chaplain, U.S. Senate, Washington D.C.; Dr. Moishe Rosen, Executive Director of Jews for Jesus; Dr. Louis Goldberg, Chairman, Jewish Studies Department, Moody Bible Institute; Dr. Jack Wyrtzen, Founder/Director, Word of Life Fellowship Inc.; Dr. Charles Lee Feinberg, Dean Emeritus and Professor of Old Testament, Talbot Theological Seminary. The memorial issue also included notes written by various staff members.

A Daniel Fuchs Memorial Fund was established to further Jewish missionary work in New York City. A resolution was also passed by the Board of Directors on June 17, 1988, in recognition of the faithful service of Daniel Fuchs. It stated:

> WHEREAS, Dr. Daniel Fuchs has been an honored member of the Board of Directors of Chosen People Ministries, Inc. (American Board of Missions to the Jews, Inc.) since January 1957, and
> WHEREAS, Dr. Fuchs has served as Chairman of the Board since 1977, and . . .
> WHEREAS, Dr. Fuchs served Chosen People Ministries for over 50 years, . . .
> WHEREAS, Dr. Fuchs had a genuine love for his Jewish people, and a desire to see them accept Jesus as their Messiah and Saviour, and
> WHEREAS, on Tuesday, May 24, 1988, the Lord called Dr. Daniel Fuchs home to be with Himself and to reward him for his faithful service as a missionary and minister of the Gospel,
> THEREFORE, BE IT RESOLVED, that we, the Board of Directors of Chosen People Ministries, Inc., express our deep gratitude to our Lord for Dr. Daniel Fuchs and for his years of effective ministry with us, and
> BE IT FURTHER RESOLVED, that May 24th be set aside annually as a special Day of Prayer in all the branches and congregations of Chosen People Ministries, Inc., praying especially for the salvation of Jewish people, the needs of Jewish believers and the peace of Jerusalem,...[249]

One of the vignettes quoted in the special memorial edition of *The Chosen People*, written by Dr. Jack Wyrtzen, typifies Daniel's spontaneity in seizing every moment as an opportunity to present the Gospel. Jack wrote:

> The first time I ever met Dan, he took me to Coney Island, back in the 30's when I was a Christian businessman in downtown N.Y. There were six of us in the car. Dan said, 'Let's pray before we go down the boardwalk for our street meeting.'
> So we rolled up the windows and prayed. We were so intent on our prayer that we did not even notice that there was a crowd gathering around. They thought we had died, suffocated or something, in the car and they called a policeman.
> The policeman knocked on the window. Dan looked up and the policeman said, 'What are you doing?' Dan said, 'We're praying.' The policeman looked and said, 'I can't believe it.' We finished our prayer. We didn't bother going to the boardwalk; we got outside and we had a ready-made street meeting. That was the story of Dan's life.[250]

And so it was! Daniel, a missionary at heart, loved the spontaneous idea—the creative moment that could be turned into a tract, a media event, a program for reaching all Jews everywhere with the Gospel! He had labored long and hard to serve his Lord and Messiah.

With the death of Daniel Fuchs, the Mission entered a new era of ministry!

ENDNOTES
Chapter 12. The Vision Re-Focused
1 *The Chosen People*, Vol. LXXVIII, No. 10, (June, 1973), p 1.
2 See note above, p 2.
3 See note above.
4 *The Chosen People*, Vol. LXXVIII, No. 7, (March, 1973), p 3.
5 See note above.

[6] See note above, p 2.

[7] *The Chosen People*, Vol. LXXVIII, No. 10, (June, 1973), p 3.

[8] See note above, p 4.

[9] *The Chosen People*, Vol. LXXX, No. 10, (June, 1975), pp 3, 4.

[10] See note above, pp 4, 5.

[11] *The Chosen People*, Vol. LXXXI, No. 2, (October, 1975), p 2.

[12] *See Correspondence: Dorothy Chesley*, January 23, 1973; March 7, 1973.

[13] *Insight*, ABMJ, 1973.

[14] *The Chosen People*, Vol. LXXVIII, No. 6, (February, 1973), p 20.

[15] *The Chosen People*, Vol. LXXVIII, No. 9, (May, 1973), pp 11-14.

[16] *The Chosen People*, Vol. LXXIX, No. 2, (October, 1973), p 11.

[17] *The Chosen People*, Vol. LXXIX, No. 1, (September, 1973), p 12.

[18] *The Chosen People*, Vol. LXXIX, No. 8, (April, 1974), pp 4, 5.

[19] *The Chosen People*, Vol. LXXIX, No. 9, (May, 1974), p 10.

[20] *Minutes*, ABMJ, (October 23, 1974), p 112.

[21] *The Chosen People*, Vol. LXXX, No. 2, (October, 1974), pp 2, 3.

[22] *Minutes*, ABMJ, (January 23, 1974), p 104.

[23] *Minutes*, ABMJ, (January 28, 1983), p 7.

[24] *Minutes*, ABMJ, (June 26, 1974), pp 105, 106.

[25] *The Chosen People*, Vol. LXXX, No. 4, (December, 1974), p 6.

[26] *Memo to Staff from Harold Sevener*, (August 12, 1974), p 1.

[27] See note above, September 13, 1974.

[28] *Minutes*, ABMJ, (October 23, 1974), p 110.

[29] *Minutes*, ABMJ, (June 11, 1985), p 4.

[30] *Minutes*, ABMJ, (January 25, 1975), p 115.

[31] *Minutes*, ABMJ, (June 18, 1975), p 120.

[32] *Minutes*, ABMJ, (October 29, 1975), p 123.

[33] See note above.

[34] *Minutes*, ABMJ, (June 18, 1975), p 121.

[35] *Minutes*, ABMJ, (October 29, 1975), p 122.

[36] See note above.

[37] Reprint of FCTJ *Resolution*, (October 16-19, 1975).

[38] *Minutes*, ABMJ, (October 29, 1975), p 124.

[39] *The Chosen People*, Vol. LXXXI, No. 5, (January, 1976), p 14.

[40] *Insight*, Reprint of Proclamation, (June, 1976), p 3.

[41] *Fact Sheet: Jerome Fleischer*, n.d.

[42] *Personal Correspondence: Rachmiel Frydland to Harold Sevener*, (April 20, 1975), p 2.

[43] *Minutes*, ABMJ, (January 28, 1976), p 1.

[44] *The Chosen People*, Vol. LXXIV, No. 2, (October, 1968), p 5.

[45] See note above, p 4.

[46] See note above, p 6.

[47] *The Chosen People*, Vol. LXXX, No. 4, (December, 1974), pp 14, 15.

[48] *The Chosen People*, Vol. LXXX, No. 10, (June, 1975), p 5.

[49] *Minutes*, ABMJ, (June 18, 1975), p 119.

[50] See note above.

[51] *The Chosen People*, Vol. LXXXI, No. 5, (January, 1976), p 4.

[52] *Minutes*, ABMJ, (January 23, 1974), p 102.

[53] *The Chosen People*, Vol. LXXXII, No. 1, (September, 1976), p 6.

[54] See note above.

[55] See note above, pp 4, 5.

[56] See note above, p 7.

[57] See note above, p 10.

[58] *Minutes*, ABMJ, (June 16, 1976), p 4.

[59] *Personal Testimony of Jonathan Singer*, p 5.

[60] See note above.

[61] See note above.

[62] Meir Kahane, *Christians For Zion*, (Brooklyn, NY: The Jewish Press Inc., January 24, 1975), p 16.

[63] *Minutes*, ABMJ, (October 25, 1976), pp 1, 2.

[64] *Minutes*, ABMJ, (January 26, 1977), p 2.

[65] See note above, p 5.

[66] *Minutes*, ABMJ, (October 19, 1977), p 4.

[67] *Minutes*, ABMJ, (October 25, 1976), p 3; *Minutes*, ABMJ, (January 25, 1977), p 4; *Minutes*, ABMJ, (October 19, 1977), p 4.

[68] *Minutes*, ABMJ, (June 15, 1977), p 2.

[69] See note above, p 3.

[70] *Minutes*, ABMJ, (June 21, 1978), p 6.

[71] See note above.

[72] *Minutes*, ABMJ, (January 24, 1979), p 5.

[73] See note above, pp 3, 4.

[74] See note above, p 1.

[75] See Appendix J. Job Descriptions as adopted by the Board, January 24, 1979.

[76] Song of Solomon 2:15.

[77] *A Mid-Year Report*, ABMJ, (August, 1979).

[78] See note above.

[79] *Minutes*, ABMJ, (October 21, 1978), p 3.

[80] *The Chosen People*, Vol. LXXXIII, No. 7, (March, 1978), p 14.

[81] *Minutes*, ABMJ, (October 21, 1978), p 4.

[82] *Minutes*, ABMJ, (October 20, 1979), p 2.

[83] See note above, p 3.

[84] *The Chosen People*, Vol. LXXXV, No. 10, (June, 1980), pp 2, 3.

[85] *The Chosen People*, Vol. LXXXVI, No. 4, (December, 1980), p 5.

[86] See note above, pp 4, 5.

[87] *Minutes*, ABMJ, (January 23, 1980), p 1.

[88] *Minutes*, ABMJ, (June 23, 1980), p 4.

[89] See note above, p 2.

[90] *Personal Correspondence: Richard Cohen to Harold Sevener*, (May 8, 1980), p 1.

[91] *Minutes*, ABMJ, (June 23, 1980), p 2.

[92] See note above, pp 4, 5.

[93] *Minutes of Executive Committee*, ABMJ, (August 9, 1980), p 2.

[94] *Minutes*, ABMJ, (January 28, 1981), p 2.

[95] See note above.

[96] *Minutes*, ABMJ, (June 17, 1981), p 4.

[97] *Minutes*, ABMJ, (October 21, 1981), p 5.

[98] *Minutes*, ABMJ, (June 11/12, 1982), p 6.

[99] *The Chosen People*, Vol. LXXXI, No. 3, (November, 1975), pp 8-12.

[100] *The Chosen People*, Vol. LXXXII, No. 5, (January, 1977), p 7.

[101] *The Chosen People*, Vol. LXXXIII, No. 2, (October, 1977), p 9.

[102] *The Chosen People*, Vol. XCI, No. 8, (March, 1985), pp 9, 14.

[103] *The Chosen People*, Vol. LXXXII, No. 11, (July, 1977), pp 4, 5.

[104] *The Chosen People*, Vol. LXXXIII, No. 2, (October, 1977), p 10.

[105] *The Chosen People*, Vol. LXXXIII, No. 5, (January, 1978), p 6.

[106] *The Chosen People*, Vol. LXXXIV, No. 2, (October, 1978), p 7.

[107] *Insight*, ABMJ, (August, 1978), p 2.

[108] *The Chosen People*, Vol. LXXXIV, No. 5, (January, 1979), pp 8, 9.

[109] *The Chosen People*, Vol. LXXXIV, No. 6, (February, 1979), p 4.

[110] John Bell, *Why Plant Jewish Oriented Churches?*, (Orangeburg, New York: ABMJ/Chosen People Ministries, 1984), p 15-17.

[111] *The Chosen People*, Vol. LXXXV, No. 1, (September, 1979), pp 6, 7.

[112] *Minutes*, ABMJ, (April 17, 1982), p 4.

[113] *The Chosen People*, Vol. LXXXIX, No. 3, (November, 1982), pp 8, 9.

[114] See note above.

[115] *Memorandum from C. Robert Clemensen to Dr. Daniel Fuchs*, copy Minutes, ABMJ, (April 17, 1982), p 5.

[116] *Minutes*, ABMJ, (April 17, 1982), pp 2, 3.

[117] See note above, pp 3, 4.

[118] *Minutes*, ABMJ, (June 11/12, 1982), pp 6-9.

[119] See note above, p 5.

[120] See note above.

[121] *Minutes*, ABMJ, (June 17, 1983), p 3.

[122] *The Chosen People*, Vol. XCX, No. 5, (January, 1989), pp 11, 12.

[123] *The Shepherd of Israel*, Vol. 63, No. 3, (Spring, 1979), pp 1, 2.

[124] See note above.

[125] See note above, pp 2-4.

[126] *The Chosen People*, Vol. XCII, No. 2, (October, 1985), p 6.

[127] *The Chosen People*, Vol. XCI, No. 2, (September, 1984), p 11.

[128] *The Chosen People*, Vol. LXXXV, No. 8, (April, 1980), p 4.

[129] *The Chosen People*, Vol. LXXXVIII, No. 3, (November, 1981), pp 6-8.

[130] *The Chosen People*, Special Issue, (October, 1987), pp 8, 9.

[131] *The Chosen People*, Vol. LXXXIII, No. 1, (September, 1977), p 11.

[132] See note above.

[133] *The Chosen People*, Vol. XCIII, No. 3, (November, 1986), pp 3-6.

[134] *The Chosen People*, Vol. XCVI, No. 7, (March, 1990), pp 8, 9.

[135] *The Chosen People*, Vol. XCVI, No. 4, (January, 1990), pp 3-5.

[136] See note above.

[137] See note above.

[138] See note above.

[139] *The Chosen People*, Vol. XCVII, No. 9, (May, 1991), p 10.

[140] *The Chosen People*, Vol. XCVIII, No. 8, (April, 1992), p 6.

[141] *The Chosen People*, Vol. XCVII, No. 8, (April, 1991), pp 3-5.

[142] *The Chosen People*, Vol. LXXVIII, No. 8, (April, 1973), p 11.

[143] *The Chosen People*, Vol. LXXIX, No. 9, (May, 1974), p 13.

[144] *The Chosen People*, Vol. LXXX, No. 8, (April, 1975), p 12.

[145] See note above, pp 10, 11.

[146] *The Chosen People*, Vol. LXXXVI, No. 4, (December, 1980), pp 6, 7.

[147] *The Chosen People*, Vol. LXXVIII, No. 8, (April, 1973), p 12.

[148] *The Chosen People*, Vol. LXXXIX, No. 5, (January, 1983), pp 3, 4.

[149] *The Chosen People*, Vol. LXXXIII, No. 9, (May, 1978), pp 8, 9.

[150] *The Chosen People*, Vol. XCI, No. 2, (September, 1984), p 10.

[151] *The Chosen People*, Vol. LXXXVIII, No. 1, (September, 1981), pp 5-7.

[152] *The Chosen People*, Vol. LXXI, No. 1, (September, 1965), p 12.

[153] *The Chosen People*, Vol. LXXXV, No. 3, (November, 1979), pp 10, 11.

[154] Barry Budoff, *Personal Testimony*, p 1.

[155] Dyann Budoff, *Personal Testimony*, pp 1, 2.

[156] See note above.

[157] *The Chosen People*, Vol. LXXXV, No. 4, (December, 1979), pp 7, 8.

[158] *The Chosen People*, Vol. LXXXIII, No. 1, (September, 1977), p 11.

[159] *The Chosen People*, Vol. LXXXIV, No. 2, (October, 1978), p 6.

[160] *The Chosen People*, Vol. LXXVII, No. 8, (April, 1972), pp 10, 11.

[161] *The Chosen People*, Vol. LXXXII, No. 9, (May, 1977), p 12.

[162] Scott Brown, *Personal Testimony/Application*, ABMJ, (August, 1987), pp 1-4.

[163] *The Chosen People*, Vol. XCVII, No. 10, (June, 1991), p 10.

[164] See note above, p 11.

[165] See note above.

[166] See note above.

[167] See note above, p 11.

[168] See note above.

[169] See note above.

[170] See note above.

[171] *The Chosen People*, Vol. XCVIII, No. 5, (January, 1992), p 15.

[172] *The Chosen People*, Vol. XCVIII, No. 9, (June, 1992), p 3.

[173] *The Chosen People*, Vol. LXXXIX, No. 5, (January, 1983), pp 8-11.

[174] *Minutes: Personnel Committee*, ABMJ, (May 28, 1982), p 1.

[175] *The Chosen People*, Vol. LXXXIX, No. 7, (March, 1983), p 4.

[176] See note above.

[177] See note above, p 5.

[178] Barry Rubin, *You Bring the Bagels, I'll Bring the Gospel*, (Old Tappan, New Jersey: Fleming Revell Co., 1989), p 195-196.

[179] Moishe Rosen with William Proctor, *Jews for Jesus*, (Old Tappan, New Jersey: Fleming H. Revell Co., 1974), p 78.

[180] *The Chosen People*, Vol. LXXVII, No. 9, (May, 1972), pp 5, 6.

[181] *Minutes*, ABMJ, (August 27, 1982), p 1.

[182] *Midyear Report*, ABMJ, (August, 1983), p 2.

[183] *The Chosen People*, Vol. XC, No. 1, (September, 1983), pp 6-9.

[184] *Minutes*, ABMJ, (June 18, 1983), p 6.

[185] *Minutes of Executive Committee*, ABMJ, (January 24, 1983), p 1.

[186] *Minutes*, ABMJ, (August 7, 1983), pp 1, 2.

[187] See note above, p 4.

[188] See note above, p 6.

[189] See note above, p 7.

[190] See note above, p 8.

[191] *Minutes*, ABMJ, (October 29, 1983), p 286.

[192] See note above, p 1.

[193] *Minutes*, ABMJ, (January 27, 1984), p 5.

[194] See note above, p 7.

[195] *Minutes*, ABMJ, (May 18, 1984), p 7.

[196] *Minutes*, ABMJ, (January 27, 1984), p 6.

[197] *Minutes*, ABMJ, (May 18, 1984), p 1.

[198] *Minutes*, ABMJ, (July 20, 21, 1984), p 4.

[199] See note above, p 2.

[200] See note above, pp 4, 5.

[201] *Minutes*, ABMJ, (October 19, 1984), p 9.

[202] *Minutes*, ABMJ, (May 18, 1984), p 7.

[203] *Minutes, revised*, ABMJ, (October 19, 1984), p 1.

[204] *The Chosen People*, Vol. XCI, No. 6, (January, 1985, reprinted courtesy of Moody Monthly), p 7.

[205] *The Chosen People*, Vol. XCVIII, No. 9, (May, 1992), p 11.

[206] *The Chosen People*, Vol. XCI, No. 1, (August, 1984), pp 10-12.

[207] See note above, p 10.

[208] See note above, p 11.

[209] See note above, pp 11, 12.

[210] *The Chosen People*, Vol. XCIV, No. 8, (April, 1988), pp 4-7.

[211] *The Chosen People*, Vol. XCIV, No. 6, (February, 1988), p 9.

[212] *Minutes*, ABMJ, (January 25, 1985), p 3.

[213] See note above, pp 2, 3.

[214] See note above, p 11.

[215] *Minutes*, ABMJ, (June 10, 1985), p 1.

[216] *Minutes*, ABMJ, (June 11, 1985), p 5.

[217] See note above, p 5.

[218] See note above, p 10.

[219] See note above.

[220] See note above, p 6.

[221] *Minutes: Personnel Committee*, ABMJ, (May 29, 1985), p 2.

[222] *Minutes*, ABMJ, (January 24-25, 1986), p 7.

[223] *The Chosen People*, Vol. XCIII, No. 8, (April, 1987), pp 12-14.

[224] *The Chosen People*, Vol. XCII, No. 11, (July, 1986), pp 7-9.

[225] *Minutes*, ABMJ, (January 24,25 1986), p 3.

[226] See note above, p 7.

[227] *The Chosen People*, Special Issue , (October, 1987), pp 15, 16.

[228] Jeffrey M. Branman, *Personal Testimony*, pp 1-8.

[229] *Minutes*, ABMJ, (June 20, 1986), p 1.

[230] See note above, p 2.

[231] *Minutes*, ABMJ/Chosen People Ministries, (October 17, 1986), p 4.

[232] *The Chosen People*, Vol. XCI, No. 4, (November, 1984), p 2.

[233] *Minutes*, ABMJ, (June 20, 1986), p 4.

[234] *Minutes*, ABMJ/Chosen People Ministries, (October 17, 1986), p 2.

[235] *Minutes*, ABMJ, (June 20, 1986), pp 3, 4.

[236] *Minutes*, ABMJ/Chosen People Ministries, (January 30-31, 1987), p 1.

[237] *Mid-Year Report*, ABMJ, (August, 1986), p 2.

[238] *Minutes*, ABMJ/CPM, (January 29,30, 1988), p 5.

[239] *Minutes*, ABMJ/CPM, (June 4, 1987), p 1.

[240] *Mid-Year Report*, ABMJ, (August, 1987), p 3.

[241] *Minutes*, President's Report, ABMJ/Chosen People Ministries, (January 29, 1988), p 5.

[242] See note above, p 6.

[243] See note above, p 5.

[244] *Minutes*, Special Meeting ABMJ/Chosen People Ministries, (April 4-5, 1988), p 1.

[245] See note above, p 2.

[246] See note above.

[247] *Minutes*, ABMJ/Chosen People Ministries, (May 6, 1988), p 4.

[248] *Minutes*, CPM Job Description for Executive Director, (November 18, 1988), p 1.

[249] *The Chosen People*, Vol. XCIV, No. 11, (July, 1988), p 15.

[250] See note above, p 9.

13

THE VISION: ONE HUNDRED YEARS AND BEYOND

So many changes! Some of the Mission's workers must have felt that Rabbi Leopold Cohn and his son, Joseph Hoffman Cohn were, to use a common phrase, "turning over in their graves!" By mid-August, 1988, the Mission's International Headquarters Office had a new address—1300 Cross Beam Drive, Charlotte, North Carolina—and a new name, Chosen People Ministries, Inc.

ADJUSTING TO CHANGE

Many of the workers on staff had greater difficulty adjusting to these changes than did the Mission's constituency— especially workers in the Northeast and the Midwest, who felt the Mission's administration had deserted them by relocating the Headquarters office across the Mason-Dixon line. Workers in the South and the West were not as deeply affected by the relocation of the administrative offices, but the name change, the reorganization, the personnel changes, and the break with some of the traditions of the past affected the entire staff during the years 1988 to the present (c. 1993).

As has been stated, the meticulous planning and attention to every detail by Roy Adams resulted in a transition which was executed smoothly and without incident. Prior to the actual relocation, he had interviewed prospective support staff for the office in Charlotte. Individuals who were hired were already being trained for their various tasks by the time the moving vans arrived in Charlotte.

Missionary Director, Rev. John Bell, moved his family to Charlotte as soon as the Board approved the relocation and the Charlotte building site. He served as an "advance man," contacting churches and Christian leaders in and around Charlotte, letting them know of the Mission's impending move to the area.

Following the sudden death of Daniel Fuchs, the Board nominated Mr. James Straub to serve as Chairman of the Board on an interim basis. The Board ratified this nomination at their September 29,30, 1988 meeting.[1] They also elected Mr. Jeff Branman, a Jewish believer, to the Board. Jeff had served on the staff of Jews for Jesus before becoming a successful businessman with expertise in marketing and sales. He currently serves as Chairman of the Personnel Committee of the Board.

The Mission, like many other Christian organizations, had been organized with a self-perpetuating Board; the members succeeded themselves year after year. Generally speaking, self-perpetuating Boards do not require that the officers rotate. Hence, the Chairman or other officers can serve for as many terms as they are re-elected. In the case of the Mission, the Board was established as a self-perpetuating body because of the problems of finding dedicated Christian business people—people who were genuinely concerned about reaching Jewish people with the Gospel—who were willing to give of their time. For many years such Christians were few and far between, but by the 1980's this was changing.

By the time of Daniel Fuchs' death, there were many more Christians, both Jews and Gentiles, who were willing to serve on the Mission's board. Realizing this, and having established definitions of the role of a Board member, the Nominating Committee proposed that the time had come to limit the number of terms the Chairman could serve. This proposal prompted discussion about the number of terms other Board members could serve as well. The Board was not yet willing to move to a Board-rotation policy, but the decision to elect James Straub on an interim basis gave the Board time for two major considerations: (1) to define a job description for its Chairman (2) to determine if a limit should be set on how long a Chairman could serve.

The sale of the Mission's Headquarters building in New York provided the Mission, at last, with sufficient reserves to secure the Pension Fund for the workers. The fund was placed in the hands of an outside trustee and, for the first time, a formal pension program, based on the guidelines for qualified pension programs as outlined by the Federal Government, was established.

Throughout the summer and into the fall of 1988, the members of the Search Committee worked on the job description for the Executive Director's position; it received the approval of the Board at their November 1988 meeting.

As the committee narrowed their search, two candidates, both of whom were already on the Mission's staff, emerged—John Bell, the Missionary Director, and Sam Nadler, Regional Director for the Northeast Region.

When John learned that he was being considered as a candidate for the Executive Director's position, he was both flattered and apprehensive. He spoke to the author about his ambivalence. On the one hand, he wanted the position because he believed he had a lot to give to the Mission, and because he felt a certain loyalty to fellow workers who were encouraging him to interview for the position. On the other hand, he believed that the Mission needed a Jewish believer in the Executive Director's position. In personal conversation with some of the Directors, he confided that he felt the position should be held by Sam Nadler. Further, he was not sure that he wanted to be responsible for the myriad details and problems that go hand-in-hand with administrating a world-wide ministry, and working with a Board and committees.

John talked about his desire to return to the pastorate and about his love of ministering directly with people, rather than through the delegated authority of a large staff. He was still a young man, and he was fearful that he might not have an opportunity to go back to into a pastorate if he became the Executive Director of the Mission. On the other hand, he knew he would likely never have another opportunity to be in charge of the Mission if Sam was selected as the Executive Director.

As John shared his concerns with the author, we agreed to continue in prayer about his situation, letting God guide and direct in the decisions of the Search Committee.

Sam Nadler had concerns as well—some of which he shared with the author. He was concerned about the fact that he had never worked in the Mission's administration on a national level, nor did he have any experience in working with a Board. He knew God had gifted him as a soul winner; he was an evangelist, and he wasn't sure he wanted to be involved in administration at the expense of evangelism. The author's evaluation of Sam was that he possessed both gifts—evangelism and administration.

THE NORTHEAST REGION, UNDER SAM NADLER

When Sam re-applied for missionary service with the Mission during the fall of 1979, the Northeast Region was still rebounding from changes initiated in 1972 when the administrative Headquarters was moved away from Manhattan to Englewood Cliffs, New Jersey. That historic transition ended seventy-eight years of tradition; for the first time, the administrative work of the Mission and the missionary work were separated.

From its very inception, the administrative work and missionary work of the Mission had functioned under one roof. The local ministry was viewed as an outgrowth of the administration. Over the years, the branches in the Northeast (particularly those in New York) felt an affinity and closeness to the administration of the Mission—something that was not shared by other branches of the Mission because of the distances involved. The local missionaries were able to stop to visit with the staff and the leadership of the Mission, or to pick up materials. By virtue of their proximity to the Headquarters office, the missionaries felt somewhat involved in every new project undertaken. But when the administration was relocated, the branches of the entire Northeast were placed under the supervision of a Regional Director and they were treated like all other regions of the Mission.

In many ways, the situation and attitudes of the missionaries in Manhattan and the boroughs of New York could be likened to those of an eldest child in a family. They had enjoyed their somewhat "favored" position, and they found it difficult to accept the new leadership and the many changes imposed upon them when the administration of the Mission was moved out of Manhattan.

After the relocation of the Headquarters office to Englewood Cliffs, the New York branches began to experience a gradual change of character. In 1973, Ruth Wardell was transferred to Los Angeles, affecting a great part of the children's ministry being done on Long Island. The outreach on Long Island was further affected when Bill and Jo Ennis were transferred to Houston, Texas in 1975, and Herb Zwickel became the Missionary in Charge of the Hollis branch. The Coney Island branch changed too. Miss Koser retired in 1978. She moved to Florida, while the Coney Island ministry moved to Brighton Beach—a forced relocation brought about when the city of New York took over the Mission's property in Coney Island. The ministry in Manhattan underwent change as well, when Rev. Charles Eisenberg resigned as pastor/missionary, and when the lease on the West 72nd Street building was due to expire. Clara and Joe Rubin continued their ministry in Huntington Station, Long Island, but they felt isolated and alienated as their fellow workers were transferred, left the staff of the Mission, or retired.

As new missionary staff was hired for the New York ministries, the innovative ideas and different approaches of the new workers for reaching the modern, secular Jew caused further feelings of alienation and isolation among the "senior" staff; additional tension and even suspicion entered the picture when Sam Nadler was hired to join the New York staff during the fall of 1979.

Sam was known to the Mission's workers in New York. As workers on staff with Jews for Jesus, Sam and Miriam had been sent to New York City to begin a branch for Jews for Jesus. The workers of the Mission saw this endeavor by Jews for Jesus as a threat to their own ministries, and as an affront to the Mission. After all, New York was the birthplace of the Mission. Although other Jewish ministries had been established in New York, the American Board of Missions to the Jews was the most well-known and was considered by its staff and by others to be the most effective.

As Jews for Jesus grew and developed as an organization, competition between the two organizations began to develop both on the field (as each ministry sought to reach more Jewish people with the Gospel) and in church relations as each ministry sought support for its outreach. It is the latter area that unfortunately produced a somewhat unhealthy type of competition.

A strange phenomenon exists among churches with regard to missionary dollars. While most churches regularly support a host of mission agencies and individual missionaries to the Gentiles in varying foreign countries, relatively few churches include even one Jewish mission or missionary in their budgets. Fewer still consider undertaking the support of more than one Jewish mission within their missionary budgets. As the number of Jewish missionary agencies has grown, this phenomenon has resulted in unhealthy competition between Jewish mission agencies and individual missionaries as they vie for support.

Many workers of the Mission were incensed that Moishe Rosen would open a branch of Jews for Jesus in the Mission's own backyard. It appeared that he was deliberately throwing down the "gauntlet"—deliberately trying to build his ministry in the areas where the Mission was already established, rather than to open works in other parts of the country or the world. When Jews for Jesus began doing ministry in New York there was an attempt toward cooperative programs and evangelism campaigns, but that ended as rumor and innuendo about the tactics of their competitor spread among the staff of the Mission, and as it became clear that the two organizations were in direct competition with one another.

Missionaries are human. Like other Christians, they are "sinners saved by grace." The attacks of Satan, the flesh and the world are as real to a missionary or to a pastor as they are to any other child of God—perhaps more so because they are on the cutting edge of repelling evil and accomplishing God's presence and power in this world by proclaiming the Gospel.

As Sam Nadler developed his ministry for Jews for Jesus in New York City, and as he gained support in the churches and the Christian community, the battle lines for "missionary territory" were being drawn. In some cases feelings went so deep that friendships were severed. Thus, when Sam and Miriam decided that the Lord was directing them to leave Jews for Jesus and to serve, once again, with The American Board of Missions to the Jews, the news hit the Mission's staff like a bomb-shell! Some believed the maneuver was a plot by Jews for Jesus to take over the Mission; others suspected internal problems in Jews for Jesus if the Nadlers were leaving. The rumor mills cranked out their stories and scenarios—none of which were right. In some of the rumors there was just enough truth to keep everyone unsettled—a ploy of Satan in his attempt to divide and conquer!

The truth is, that the Nadlers left Jews for Jesus over the issue of autonomy and direction. They believed that God had called them to minister in New York City. Moishe, however, wanted to transfer them back to San Francisco. Further, Moishe had asked them to conduct two separate Jews for Jesus music and drama teams which were being scheduled to travel across the United States—Sam was to head one team, while Miriam was to head the other. The teams were scheduled to take different routes, thus separating them from one another and from their child for several months. It was an arrangement which was unacceptable to them; they did not want to be separated from one another and from their child, nor did not want to leave New York City for San Francisco. As they sought God's will in the matter, they felt led to remain in New York. The situation finally reached an impasse and they had no choice but to resign from the staff of Jews for Jesus.

As the situation between the Nadlers and the directives of Moishe Rosen grew more tense, Moishe telephoned the author and informed him that Sam and Miriam would likely be leaving his staff. He inquired whether or not there would be a place for them on the staff of the Mission. The author assured him that the Mission would prayerfully consider hiring the Nadlers if they felt led of the Lord to rejoin the Mission's staff. Assurances were also given that the Mission would make a smooth transition, so as not to cause support or image problems for either organization. The assurances given were evidently conveyed to the Nadlers, for within a few days the author received a telephone call from Sam, inquiring about a staff position that would allow them to continue their ministry in New York City.

Once they had rejoined the staff of the Mission, Sam and Miriam were caught in the cross fire between individuals and the two organizations; they felt totally isolated. The staff members of the Mission were skittish, uncertain as to how they should react to the presence of the Nadlers in their ranks. On the other hand, the Nadlers were totally ostracized by the Jews for Jesus staff. Their closest friends from the staff of Jews for Jesus would no longer speak to them because they felt Sam and Miriam had betrayed them by going over to the other side. (Sam and Miriam Nadler were not the only former Jews for Jesus staff members who experienced this type of "shunning." Barry and Steffi [Geiser] Rubin told the author that they experienced the same thing when they left Jews for Jesus and joined the staff of the Southern Hebrew

Mission [Messiah Has Come Ministries] and that the shunning had intensified when they joined the staff of the Mission. Others who have left the Jews for Jesus organization have had similar experiences.)

Once again, much of the unhealthy competition and the resulting rumors and innuendo goes back to the issue of support. When workers, such as the Nadlers, leave a Jewish mission agency they generally take a large percentage of their support with them, thus closing the donations of those supporting churches to the mission agency being left.

The issue over the support of Sam and Miriam Nadler came to a head when the author received a telephone call from Moishe Rosen in early December, 1979. The author's response by letter is quoted to emphasize the problems that erupt when missionaries to the Jews transfer from one mission agency to another. Jewish missions are, in reality, foreign missions working at home. But where matters of support are concerned, the missionaries do not have the same advantages or opportunities. In his letter dated December 5, 1979 to Moishe Rosen, the author wrote:

> Dear Martin:
>
> I am deeply concerned about your telephone call on Monday, December third regarding Sam Nadler....
>
> ...you state that you are upset because Sam has been contacting churches who have previously supported his ministry while serving with 'Jews for Jesus' and informing them that he is now serving with the ABMJ. As I told you on the phone, it was your responsibility to write to Sam's supporting churches and/or individuals, and let them know that Sam and Miriam Nadler are no longer serving with 'Jews for Jesus' as of October 1, 1979. This should have been done immediately, and I would think, should be standard operating procedure for you as a Mission. It is a policy that we adhere to, as do other mission organizations.
>
> We have instructed Sam to contact churches in the New York area and churches who are presently supporting the ABMJ, or who have supported our ministry in the past. Again, this is standard operating procedure for the ABMJ. Some of these churches will likewise have been supporting 'Jews for Jesus,' and perhaps even Sam and Miriam Nadler. This is why I told you it was imperative for you to contact churches and individuals who may have been supporting their ministry, and to let them know immediately that they are no longer serving with 'Jews for Jesus.' If you do not, I am sure that you will receive letters from pastors and individuals questioning the operating procedure of 'Jews for Jesus.'
>
> As you mentioned to me on the telephone, this is already December and so far you have not notified any supporting churches. I do not see how you can hold Sam or the ABMJ responsible for an oversight on your part. You mentioned to me on the phone, as an implied threat, that if Sam contacted any more churches you would mail out a copy of the contract that he had signed when working with 'Jews for Jesus.' As you well know, such a contract has no binding effect upon Sam or upon any employee once an employee resigns. In fact, I don't know of any other Christian organization apart from Bible colleges and seminaries that issue a contract to its individual workers. This is certainly not standard missionary practice.
>
> Nevertheless, to send such a contract out in an attempt to make it appear that Sam has violated some agreement with 'Jews for Jesus' is not in the best interest of Jewish missions, Christian fellowship or brotherly love.
>
> Sam and Miriam felt led of the Lord to remain and work in New York City, and God's evident blessing upon their ministry has confirmed to them and to us that this was God's direction and leading in their life.
>
> Martin [Moishe], as you well know, when any missionary resigns from an organization, there will be questions from their supporting churches, from friends and from other staff members. As these questions are raised Sam and Miriam have been answering them truthfully, and never once to my knowledge have they or any other staff member of the ABMJ spoken negatively about 'Jews for Jesus.' Nor do we intend to. We have enough to do trying to fulfill our commitment of reaching all Jews everywhere with the Gospel without having disputation or problems with other organizations.
>
> I would request that you prayerfully consider sending out a letter to those who have supported the Nadlers as quickly as possible and refrain from any action that would reflect negatively upon them, upon 'Jews for Jesus,' upon the ABMJ, or upon the cause of Jewish missions and evangelism.[2]

The author's letter both helped and hindered the Nadlers' cause. It helped to clarify the confusion over the Nadlers' supporting churches, but on a personal level it hindered the Nadlers because they were declared "persona non grata" as far the Jews for Jesus staff was concerned. Sadly, it also deepened the rift between the two organizations. Moishe responded by sending out a letter stating "We have been hurt!"—implying that the support of the ministry of Jews for Jesus had been hurt by the tactics of its former staff members, the Nadlers.

Once again, the author would remind the reader that during this time Jews for Jesus, as a newly formed organization, was struggling to gain financial support and to develop a consciousness of its message and image within the Christian community. Moishe wanted his organization seen as a distinct organization—apart from ABMJ/CPM—which was worthy of support in its own right. The Mission, too, was struggling with its own image and the need for support. As a part of this, the Mission was distancing itself from the high profile of street and confrontational evangelism which characterized Jews for Jesus.

To the Mission, Sam and Miriam were an answer to prayer. At the time that they rejoined the staff, the ministry in New York had undergone sweeping changes as workers had resigned, retired, or been transferred to other branches within the ministry. New York, with one of the largest Jewish populations in the world, has always been one of the most difficult areas in which to place and to keep workers. The Mission desperately needed missionaries who had a definite calling from God to work among the Jews in New York—Sam and Miriam had that calling!

In spite of the difficulties he faced, Sam soon rallied the staff in New York and enlisted the help of a group of volunteers; together, they began to blitz the city with Gospel literature. In his first article in *The Chosen People* magazine, Sam wrote an "apologetic" on his "broadside" ministry. He wrote:

> *For many believers in Jesus, there is some confusion as to the uses of Gospel tracts and literature. And with the confusion comes non-use. This is unfortunate and unnecessary, since Gospel tracts can be instrumental in communicating the Good News of Jesus.*
>
> *Generally there are two varieties of Gospel pamphlets: (1) those that answer questions, and (2) those that raise questions. We can all appreciate the need to answer questions. And we generally prepare ourselves to have many answers to the myriad of questions that the world may possibly throw at us. So we feel the need to explain the existence of God, the Trinity, and the mystery of the incarnation.*
>
> *We, of course, expect our literature to bolster our answers with scholarly content and thus meet the objections of all who doubt or verbally assault. Hopefully also, the sincere inquirer will receive the information that will lead to faith and salvation.*
>
> *The second use of Gospel tracts has been the most neglected. Actually, some believers don't fully understand its importance. Some would think that raising questions sounds close to 'starting an argument' or 'picking a fight.' Of course, this not at all what we are talking about.*
>
> *Let us understand that the world in general, and my Jewish people in particular, cannot be characterized as the Philippian jailer who asked, 'What must I do to be saved?' (Acts 16:30). They are not asking questions about God. Indeed, for the most part, the world is not interested. You see, the world and my people have 'written off' Jesus and faith in Him as an irrelevant and unimportant issue.*
>
> *All they may know about 'Christianity' is Santa Claus and Easter bunnies. They may never have heard and understood the real Gospel, only the 'traditions of men' that they think constitute faith in Christ.*
>
> *There is a need to have people think about the real issues of Scripture, so they may ask valid questions concerning their relation to God. Most, however, just do not care. Therefore, I have found the need to distribute literature that will communicate to the Biblically ignorant and the spiritually insensitive. This can result in: (1) they may question their own unbelief and the 'religious' stereotypes they had continually taken for granted and then (2) they may question me regarding the 'hope that lies within me.'*
>
> *Right now they are unconcerned. The Messiahship of Jesus is not dinner conversation in most Jewish homes. But Christ in us loves them too much to leave them there. So we (the New York City staff and several volunteers) have been distributing tens of thousands of pieces of Gospel literature with catchy titles.*
>
> *As we hand out the literature to the busy multitudes of New York City, we just depend on God to get it into the hands of those with 'ears to hear' and responsive hearts. And the way that He does it is really all His doing.*
>
> *Take, for instance, a man named Carl. When visiting his sister in Mexico, this Jewish young man was attracted to a Gospel pamphlet on her living-room coffee table.*
>
> *It seemed she had received it a year before when she was visiting her family in New York City. One of us had handed it to her as she hurriedly passed by. She didn't know why she kept it so long.*
>
> *As Carl recalls it, he found himself intrigued with Jesus. When he came back to New York City, he came to my office there and inquired further. Now he had real questions to ask. Praise God for the answers!*
>
> *As we looked over Isaiah 9:6 and other Old Testament portions which point to Messiah's first coming, he realized the truth about Jesus. After explaining the Gospel and how to receive Christ, he prayed with me to Jesus to forgive his sins and asked for eternal life in the Messiah.*
>
> *There are many Carls who have a hunger but don't know where to look. They have need but have written off 'Christ' of Christendom and have never considered the real Jesus of the Scriptures who can eternally meet their needs. We need to go forth with lives and literature that will whet their thirst and then lead them to the fountain of living water that will quench and satisfy, and indeed they 'shall never thirst' again.[3]*

Not only did Sam excel at getting tracts into the hands of Jewish people, he is a gifted soul-winner. This, too, quickly became apparent. Speaking of some of the opportunities which God had opened up, he told *The Chosen People* family:

> Rosh Hashanah—or the Jewish New Year—is also a good time to share the Messiah. Actually, this holiday is the Biblical Feast of Trumpets (Leviticus 23:24-25). Each year I use the Biblical truth of "trumpets" to speak of the urgent hour in which we live when at any moment the last trump may sound.
>
> During a Bible study in our apartment at this time of year, a young Jewish woman named Robin accepted the Lord. While she had been pondering the question of Jesus for quite some time, God spoke in a fresh way to her heart. The Feast of Trumpets showed her the need for an immediate response to Jesus, for 'no man knows the hour' and 'now is the day of salvation.'
>
> This past Passover offered a wonderful opportunity to share the Lamb of God. A local church invited me to share 'Christ in the Passover'—a demonstration ABMJ missionaries conduct all over the country during the Passover season.
>
> Only one unsaved Jewish person showed up—a woman named Rose—but I was glad to see 150 others who had come to hear. The pastor estimated that only one-fifth of those present were born-again believers. What a great opportunity to present the Hope of Israel...and the world!
>
> After I explained how the Passover Seder (order of service) pointed to Jesus and His work of redemption, I asked if anyone would like to receive Christ for the first time and know the forgiveness of sins. So many hands went up that I lost count![4]

When Sam and Miriam rejoined the Mission's staff in October 1979, the New York staff consisted of Rev. Richard Cohen, the Regional Director; Mr. Martin Gruen, in church relations; Mr. Ray Gordet, missionary in Bergen County; Mr. Steve Schlissel, Miss Linda Schwarcz, and Miss Judith van Dyk, missionaries in Brooklyn; Miss Eleanor Bullock, Rev. David Hodges, Mrs. Cynthia Rydelnik missionaries in Hollis, Long Island; Mrs. Clara Rubin, missionary in Huntington Station, Long Island; Mr. Jim Bates and Mr. Daniel Siegel, missionaries in New York City; Miss Molly Hurley, missionary in Rockland County.

As Sam carried on his ministry he demonstrated administrative leadership. He soon became the Missionary-in-Charge of Manhattan—with Jim Bates, Daniel Siegel and Elaine Fenchel reporting to him. The author appointed Sam as Northeast Regional Director in the Fall of 1980, following the resignation of Richard Cohen. At first, Sam was reluctant to assume this position as he did not want anything to take him away from doing direct missionary work and evangelism. Additionally, having been severely hurt over the way things had developed in Jews for Jesus, he was reluctant to become too closely aligned with any organization. He was happy doing missionary work—leading people to the Lord—and he wanted nothing to do with the politics, policies, or the personalities that come into play within leadership positions of organizations. However, he prayed about the position and as we discussed the areas of responsibilities involved in the position, and what might be accomplished if he took the position, Sam began to feel more peace about accepting the job.

Not all of the New York staff shared his sense of peace however. Sam had a reputation as a fair, but hard, taskmaster. He is a workaholic who expects and requires much from himself; he also requires equal dedication from those under him. The "rumor mill" had already cranked out several versions of a story that Sam was a plant by Moishe Rosen to take over the Mission, to make it another Jews for Jesus. It wasn't long, therefore, before a number of the newer workers in the New York area began to submit letters of resignation, or requests for a transfer to other branches within the Mission. Fortunately, the senior missionaries had learned that the "rumor mill" was untrustworthy. They had learned to accept the decisions of the Board and the President, or Missionary Director, realizing that God would overrule if those decisions were not within His will. Until that time, they purposed within their hearts to carry on their ministries as God directed.

Sam was directing a region where, historically, the branches had operated almost totally independently of one another. It was his task, as Regional Director, to unify and solidify the branches within the region so that they functioned as a team, under a unified policy. As he attempted to accomplish this goal, and as one by one workers left the New York region, Sam came to the author on a number of occasions to discuss whether or not he should be replaced as the Regional Director. The author reminded Sam that in churches, business and in government, it is not uncommon for the staff of previous leadership to be dismissed so that the new leadership has a free hand to develop new programs. After prayer together and words of encouragement to buoy him up, Sam would leave our meetings with determination to build a Class A team of missionaries for the Northeast. Within a few years he was able to accomplish this goal and much more!

As has been mentioned, when Sam was made Missionary-in-Charge of Manhattan, three workers reported directly to him—Daniel Siegel, James Bates, and Elaine Fenchel.

DANIEL SIEGEL

Daniel Siegel joined the staff of the Mission as a full-time worker for the Manhattan ministry in July 1974. He served under the leadership of Rev. Charles Eisenberg. "Danny," like Sam Nadler, is a soul winner; he has the gift of evangelism and he excelled at doing personal, one-on-one evangelism on university campuses, etc. In relating his story to the readers of *The Chosen People* magazine, Danny said:

> From my dungaree jacket littered with 'Stop the War' and 'McGovern' buttons right down to my bellbottom pants, I was a true sixties radical. Even if someone had bothered to tell me about Jesus Christ, I would have laughed. After all, everyone knew that Christianity was just like Karl Marx said it was—the opiate of the masses, an elaborate system of mind control that kept the poor in their poverty and the pope in his palace.
>
> I'm not sure why I was so harsh on Christianity. Maybe because I grew up in New York City and had never met a true Christian. Maybe because I viewed reality as being only those things I could touch and hold. Whatever the case, my freshman year at Butler University in Indianapolis opened my eyes to a lot of things.
>
> First of all, I saw that true Christians were concerned, involved people. I made this observation while sitting in the Louisville jail where I had been placed under arrest for being in an open housing sit-in at Churchill Downs Racetrack. As I looked around me, I saw a lot of people like me, members of Students for a Democratic Society. We seemed to have a lot of questions but no answers. I also saw some Christians who were there because they were trying to show their faith in action, trying to make the world a place that matched their beliefs. They seemed to be honestly concerned with others and were doing what they thought God wanted of them. The concept of a God who expects something from man was a new idea for me.
>
> It was also during my freshman year that I first read the Bible. When I was growing up, I had years of religious instruction, Orthodox Jewish training, that taught me how to read Hebrew, say prayers, and keep kosher. But I had never studied the Bible. It wasn't until a friend who was majoring in religion lent me his Bible that I saw the reality in Scripture. Too soon, my friend had to study for finals and wanted his Bible back. Since I had no idea where to buy a Bible, my Bible reading seemed to come to an end.
>
> The summer of 1967, an unsettling one for our nation, was even more so for me. Israel won the Six Day War, and I realized that a miracle had occurred. But for me to say it was a miracle meant I believed in a God who performed miracles. Did such a God exist? I wondered.
>
> Then I took a good look at my friends and fellow radicals. They were unhappy people searching for answers and equipped only with questions. One high school friend committed suicide while on an LSD trip. Another, a leader in our class, flunked out of college. What was happening around me? Was the world headed for a living hell?
>
> I went to hear a leading Communist spokesman. It was obvious he didn't have the answers. He wouldn't even let us ask questions that challenged his beliefs.
>
> Unfortunately, I wasn't in much better shape than anyone else. I had lots of questions, nowhere to go for answers, dreams of a better society, but no place where I could see it working. I realized I loved mankind but didn't know how to love my neighbor. It was confusing and disheartening.
>
> One day I helped a friend get ready to move. In return he gave me several books of Green Stamps. As I looked at them, I remembered when I was a kid I had seen Bibles in the stamp catalogues. I went to the redemption center and got my first Bible: a large, black, Nelson edition of the Revised Standard Version.
>
> Then I met another Christian who gave me food for thought. I had returned to Indiana to organize Fort Wayne for an antiwar effort called Vietnam Summer. Going door-to-door, I met a Strategic Air Command pilot. I was ready for him to be very hostile to my efforts but much to my surprise, we got involved in a long, reflective conversation. I soon found myself telling him about my confusion and disillusion.
>
> This all-American looking man told me that once he had been an unhappy and confused drunk. Jesus, he told me, changed his life. As the evening wore on, he offered to drive me back to my boarding house so I wouldn't have to make the ten-mile walk. It may seem like a small thing but I didn't know many people who would go out of their way to help a stranger. I recognized it as a special kind of love. A love that I lacked and one that I wanted.
>
> That night I prayed for the first time in my life. 'God, I don't even know if You are there. If You are, show me what this man said is true.'
>
> When school started again, I switched my major to religion. I was determined to understand God. Unfortunately, most of my professors were not Christians, and they only confused me. I tried to behave like the Bible described. This confused me even more, because it was obviously impossible to live like God wanted.
>
> One Sunday morning I met a fellow in the dorm who was dressed in a suit. He was going to church. It never dawned on me that people actually went to church on Sundays. I asked if I could go with him. There, to make matters

worse, I found that even though I wanted to respond to the altar calls given each week, something held me back. I felt like I would be embracing the enemies of my people. It seemed anti-Jewish.

The harder I tried to live like God wanted, the more I became aware of my inability to do so. It became a depressing series of efforts and failures.

Finally I realized that I had to make a choice. Either everything was real—the Bible, Jesus, the need of salvation—or the whole thing was a lie. I read Romans 10:9,10, 'That if thou shalt confess with thy mouth the Lord Jesus, and shalt believe in thine heart that God hath raised Him from the dead, thou shalt be saved. For with the heart man believeth unto righteousness, and with the mouth confession is made unto salvation.'

There was only one way I would know if it was real. I turned to God. 'Show me, God. Show me if it is real.' Then I thought about the verse, and I knew if my prayer was to mean anything, I needed to come to God through Jesus. So I closed my prayer in His name.

I felt a release, a new beginning, a cleansing that come from God. It was wonderful to believe I had experienced new birth. But during the next few weeks I still sinned. Every time I did, I felt worse than before.

One night when I was walking around the dorm, I saw a fellow I knew lounging by an open door. I went over and discovered an end-of-the-year Pizza party sponsored by InterVarsity Christian Fellowship.

Throughout the summer I attended the InterVarsity Bible studies. One night we were sharing our testimonies, and I guess something I said raised some doubts. Actually, what I said expressed the doubts I still had. One of the people took me aside and explained salvation and assurance. Though I had prayed before, it was then that I committed my life to Christ, realizing I wasn't saved by my up-and-down feelings, but by faith alone.

Later in the summer I attended a Navigator's summer conference and was challenged to reach my campus for Christ. I was also challenged to believe that prayer really works. I praise God for these two campus organizations that were so influential in my life.

It was several years later that God showed me He wanted me to reach out to my own Jewish people, and I became a missionary with the ABMJ. It's been exciting to minister to others who, like I once was, are skeptical but searching for the God of Israel. When I meet a cynical student, I remember how much I wanted to change the world. And I thank God again that He alone gives changed lives and new hearts, the most world-changing elements any revolution can claim.[5]

Danny Siegel led many Jewish people to the Lord as he ministered on the campuses and on the streets of New York. On September 16, 1979 Daniel Siegel married Miss Helen Schaefer. Helen was also a Jewish believer, and the couple used their wedding ceremony as way of witnessing to their family members and friends. They later shared some incidents of their honeymoon with members of *The Chosen People* family. Daniel wrote:

...I must say that the Lord opened up numerous opportunities to share our Messiah with people wherever we went. Some were very open, divine contacts. We also met believers wherever we traveled.

Perhaps the most unusual contact came as we ate dinner one night at a restaurant requiring reservations. The establishment misplaced our reservation, so they asked my wife and me if we'd mind eating with another couple. We said fine and so did they. It turned out that they too were on their honeymoon and that they too were Jewish. As we enjoyed each other's company during the meal, the conversation turned to our occupation. I said I was with Beth Sar Shalom [one of the ministry names used by the Mission for its branch and center ministries] ...an answer which surprised him greatly. He said his mother and he received our Prophetic Jewish Calendar. And as the evening came to a close, I offered him a New Testament which he enthusiastically and thankfully received.

Contacts like this just don't happen by chance. Pray for this couple—that they might soon let the Messiah enter into their marriage relationship.[6]

When Sam Nadler established the "Light of Israel" Messianic congregation in White Plains under the Mission's Church Planting department in January 1983, Daniel and Helen Siegel were there to help. God used Daniel's involvement in the growing congregation to speak to his heart about furthering his training so that he would be prepared to pastor a Messianic congregation.

In August 1984, Daniel became a full-time student at the Conservative Baptist Theological Seminary in Denver, Colorado. Throughout his years as a student at the seminary, he continued serving on the staff of the Mission as a part-time missionary worker for the Denver branch. He assisted Eliezer Urbach, visited in Jewish homes, worked on college campuses, and assisted in the Messianic congregation established there.

After Daniel's graduation from seminary, he and Helen returned to New York to again work with the Mission.

However, the Lord closed the door. The condominium home which God had provided for them while they were in seminary did not sell and they were forced to return to Denver; God evidently wanted them to remain in Denver awhile longer. When they were able to return to New York again, Daniel became involved in helping to establish a Messianic congregation among the Russian Jewish immigrants in the Brooklyn area of New York. The March 1991 issue of *The Chosen People* magazine included the following report:

'While I was at seminary,' Danny [Daniel Siegel] reflects, 'I regained a strong sense of justice. When I was first saved, I distrusted anything that had been part of the natural me.' This time, as Danny sensed a need to work with people, and on their behalf, he realized that this desire had been refined by the Lord.

When he returned to New York, he found himself drawn to Brighton Beach, always one of his favorite areas. 'I don't know why,' he says. 'I think way back my family was Russian, but I just like Brighton Beach with its colorful community. The signs are in Russian, the menus are in Russian, the area is a little Russian community. Best of all are the people themselves. They are sweet, gentle people.'

Once back in Brighton Beach, Danny recognized his burden to reach these people for the Gospel as well as to minister to their needs.

'These people don't know how to fend for themselves in a strange land,' Siegel explains. 'They don't know how to shop in American stores or how to cook American foods. They never leave the Brighton Beach area, because it's the only place where things are familiar.'

'They don't know how to get things done in our country. I've met doctors and engineers who are at a loss when it comes to getting through the system and practicing their professions. Everything is new to them,' he emphasizes.

This very newness, however, is one reason why the Russian Jews are open to the Gospel. 'All their lives, they've lived under tight authority,' he says. 'Now, for the first time, they have complete freedom. They're willing to discuss and debate new ideas. I'll hand out tracts along the street, then walk back through after people have had a chance to read them. Groups of people will stop me. If there are six or seven people, each one will have a opinion,' he smiles. 'They want to discover for themselves and make decisions for themselves. They don't want to accept any authority that tells them what to believe. Interestingly, it's just the opposite for American Jews: Heeding authority is what often keeps them from hearing the Gospel—that sense of 'it's not the Jewish thing to do....'

Through a translator, Danny talks to the Soviet Jews he meets. He tells them about American life and customs, where to find the best bargains, and about the Messiah. Some of his Soviet Jewish friends stay in America; others, whose visas expire, return to the Soviet Union— with Danny's address and phone number tucked in their pockets.

Danny's dream is to see a Messianic congregation spring up in his area, a center where believers can meet and have classes in American culture: cooking, shopping, even something as simple as picking up packages from the post office. ('You wouldn't believe,' he says, 'how much we take for granted about the way we get around in our country!')

The Soviets are a warm people and enjoy hospitality and stopping by for tea and talk, so he hopes the center can become a social hall of sorts. Or, more appropriately, a fellowship hall in the truest sense of the word.

It seems, as always, that Danny Siegel, ever the maven, has once again found the right place to be at the right time. 'I think God is allowing the Jews to leave Russia for the Gospel's sake,' he concludes. 'In post-World War II Japan, as Emperor worship was dying, there were real spiritual opportunities. I think we've got that same type of opportunity right now among Soviet Jews. And I want to be there.'[7]

The congregation became a reality and the work among the Russian Jews in Brooklyn has continued to grow as other staff members have joined in this effort. The July 1991 issue of *The Chosen People* magazine included a report of Daniel Siegel's involvement in the Mission's new Russian-Jewish Messianic congregation in Brighton Beach. It stated:

We meet every Sunday afternoon in a joint service with the Conservative Baptists. It's amazing to see how some people are just waiting to receive the Lord! The service, which is in Russian and English, has been attracting a number of recent Soviet immigrants as well as visitors from the Soviet Union.

As much as possible, Lydia Onbreit (a Soviet Jewish believer) and I try to meet with the people afterward. [Lydia is now one of the Mission's staff members. She married Mr. Michael Wechsler, a part-time worker with the Mission.]

One man, Kirill, who attended, was so comfortable with matters of faith that only later did I realize he was not a believer. Although he is Jewish, he reminded me of the Gentile Cornelius, who was waiting to be told about Jesus, who was ready to have a personal relationship with Him. As soon as we shared the Gospel with him (Lydia was translating) and asked if he wanted to receive the Lord, he began to pray!

Since then, we've been helping Kirill complete stacks of paperwork and have discovered that he is seeking political *asylum. He looks like a boxer whose nose has been broken repeatedly. We discovered that our assumption was only half true: His nose had indeed been broken but not because he is a boxer.*

Actually, he was frequently harassed and arrested as an active Zionist in the Soviet Union. He was often beaten by one of the anti-Semitic groups which are increasingly active in the Soviet Union.

The vigor that Kirill once applied to Zionism is now being used by the Lord. The Sunday after he came to Yeshua, he gave a public profession of faith. He's been witnessing with us since, and he is growing steadily in a discipleship program.

Not long after Kirill received the Lord, Lydia and I [Danny Siegel] were witnessing in Brighton Beach, and we ran into Lena, a woman who was coming to our Sunday meetings.

Lena was visiting the United States and was coming to the meetings with a friend. As Lydia and Lena exchanged pleasantries, their conversation turned to the Gospel.

Soon Lydia found it was very natural to ask Lena if she wanted to receive the Lord.

'Oh yes,' she replied, and immediately wanted to pray with us.

She's back home now, hopefully being followed up by Jewish believers in contact with our mission. But what a great remembrance of her trip to America she has taken back with her![8]

Daniel Siegel remained on the Mission's staff until August 1992, at which time he resigned. He was not able to raise sufficient funding to continue his support and ministry in Brighton Beach.

The other full-time missionary who reported to Sam Nadler when he was Missionary in Charge of the Manhattan branch, was Jim Bates. Jim joined the staff of the Mission in 1978. He was hired to work on campuses, along with Linda Block and Daniel Siegel.

JIM BATES

Jim Bates was a most unlikely candidate for Jewish missionary work. He was a Gentile Christian—a giant of a man, big and muscular. Before becoming a believer he was a "bouncer" at one of New York City's more notable nightspots. Readers of *The Chosen People* magazine were told:

Most people wouldn't think that being a bouncer is very good preparation for being a missionary, but Jim thinks otherwise (and, frankly, I wouldn't want to disagree with him). He notes that his previous occupation has made him very observant—quick to notice a way to share the Gospel and quick to observe a person's sensitivities. In addition, he has spent a lot of time with young people and is able to relate to them well even though he has attained the advanced age of 36 [c. 1981].[9]

Jim entered the Mission's training program in 1979. The program, which was held at the Headquarters building in Orangeburg, New York offered classes in Jewish theology, Jewish history, tradition and the Hebrew language. Jim was a good student, with a burning desire to put the things he was learning into practice. Since he was already working in New York City, it seemed a forgone conclusion that his ministry would remain there, but even prior to joining the staff of the Mission Jim told the Missionary Director, Richard Cohen, that he felt God was calling him to work among Jewish students on the many campuses in and around Boston, Massachusetts.

Interestingly, while Jim was still in the training program, several Christian businessmen from The Society For Promoting Christianity Among the Jews, an old established Jewish Mission in Boston, contacted the Mission. They explained that they had not been able to locate a capable worker to replace their missionary who had left. They wanted to know if the Mission was interested in placing a missionary in Boston. They went on to say that if the Mission wished to place a worker in Boston, they would use the remaining resources from their ministry to support such a worker. This was a wonderful answer to prayer. Not only did the Mission have an interest in opening a branch in Boston, we had a trained worker who had already indicated that he'd felt the call of the Lord to go to Boston. Further, through the generosity of the businessmen from The Society for Promoting Christianity Among the Jews, the Mission had the funding to send a missionary there.

Jim Bates was elated when he was told he was being transferred to Boston. Even though he was not Jewish, and not among the "educationally elite," his abundance of love for the Jewish people made him an excellent worker among the Jewish students of Boston. It wasn't long before he was given an opportunity to speak on the campus of Harvard University—one of the oldest and most respected universities in the country. Liane Rozzell of the Dunster Christian Issues Table invited him to speak at Dunster House (a dormitory facility serving sophomores, juniors and seniors) on Election Day, 1980. Jim accepted the invitation immediately. A report of that incident appeared in the February 1981 issue of *The Chosen People* magazine:

Some Jewish students, however, objected when they found out that a representative of a Hebrew-Christian group was scheduled to speak on campus, but Jim showed up right on time. So did they.

The students seemed to gravitate toward those with an identical faith—the Christians on one side of the room and the Jewish students on the other. And there at the front—right in the middle—was Jim Bates.

'I voted today,' he began, 'for a man I believe would support Israel and their right to exist. I think that America today has been blessed by God and will continue to be blessed by God only if we support Israel.'

Noting that God gave the land of Israel to Abraham and his descendants through Isaac and Jacob, Jim stated that 'one of the ways that I, as a Biblical Christian, can best show my support for the Jewish people is by calling myself a Zionist.'

Although most of the 90 minutes was used in presenting the case for the right of Israel to exist, Jim couldn't resist sharing the Gospel. After all, he is a missionary.

'My Jewish friends might not like what I'm about to say, but I have to defend what I believe is the truth. The Apostle Paul, writing to the church at Rome, said: "I say then, have they (the Jewish people) stumbled that they should fall? God forbid! but rather through their fall salvation is come unto the Gentiles, for to provoke them to jealousy."'

'How do I, as a gentile Christian, provoke someone to jealousy?' he asked. 'By loving them and letting my light so shine before men that they might see my good works and glorify my Father Who is in heaven.'

'It's a lifestyle,' he stressed. 'I must be obedient to God's Word and that's why I share the Good News of Jesus being the Messiah with anybody who is willing to listen.'

Just before the question-and-answer time, Jim told about the work of Beth Sar Shalom—of the soup kitchens we started during the war, of the services we provide to Russian Jewish immigrants in the Brooklyn area. 'That's what it means for me to be a Christian—to help my neighbor, and that's what we're all about at Beth Sar Shalom.'

After the meeting the Jewish students immediately got up and walked to the front of the conference room. There they met Jim with smiles, handshakes and friendly words. It seems his great love for the Jewish people had gotten through to them.

One final note—the Jewish student who was most opposed to Jim's appearance made a luncheon date with Liane, the Christian who had invited Jim on campus. They are now friends and meet once a week to discuss the Scriptures.

ABMJ's first experience at Harvard turned out to be a good one—a fact for which we praise the Lord.[10]

The third member of the staff reporting to Sam Nadler was Elaine Fenchel—a Jewish believer who joined the staff of the Mission in 1970 as a missionary-receptionist at the Mission's Headquarters building in Manhattan, and faithfully served in that capacity until her retirement in January 1990.

ELAINE FENCHEL

Elaine grew up in a Jewish family in the Bronx. There were six children in the family. Her mother and father were "from the old country"; they spoke Yiddish and English. Even as a child, Elaine was interested in Jewish culture and history. When she became a believer in the Messiah, her interest in her own Jewishness and in her own family members intensified. She told readers of *The Chosen People* magazine:

My grandmother died in Russia during World War II. I never met her, and I automatically assumed she had never heard of the Lord. My mother came to this country when she was a young woman, and though she told me many stories about my grandmother and growing up in Russia, there was one story I didn't hear until after I accepted the Lord.

When I became a believer and started working for the ABMJ [Chosen People Ministries] at our former office on 72nd Street in Manhattan, my mother came to visit me. She brought me lunch and, though she didn't say it, she probably wanted to see what this Jewish mission her daughter was working for was all about. She was startled, as she put it, to see 'it's so Jewish!?' It was shortly afterward that she told me the following story about my grandmother.

One day in the early 1900's, my grandmother had to visit a dentist in the big city of Kishinev. She was gone several days, and when she returned home she told everyone that in Kishinev she saw a building with a large window that displayed a Torah, a Jewish candelabra, and other Jewish artifacts.

In czarist Russia, well-known for its anti-Semitism, these items were rarely displayed. But what was really strange was the open book that was also on display. It was a New Testament! My grandmother had apparently stumbled upon a place where Jews who believe in Jesus as Messiah came to study and pray.

I couldn't contain my curiosity. 'Was Grandma angry when she saw this?' 'No,' my mother replied nonchalantly. 'She thought it was interesting.'

Did my grandmother really happen upon what could have been perhaps the only Jewish Christian congregation in all of Russia? Maybe she was confused and simply returned home with nothing more than a bubbeh miceh (pronounced 'bub-eh mice-eh;' in Yiddish, 'a grandmother's story, a fanciful tale.')

Sometime after this, I began to think about grandmothers (and grandfathers) dying without the Lord, when I came across a book called Famous Hebrew Christians. *One particular chapter was about a Jewish man from Kishinev (the city my grandmother visited) named Joseph Rabinowitz, who visited the Holy Land in the late 1800s.*

While climbing the hill near Golgotha, the words of Isaiah 53 came to him, and he knew in that instant that Jesus was the One spoken of who was wounded for our transgressions. Rabinowitz returned to Kishinev and established a congregation of Jewish believers in Jesus. This was during the time my grandmother lived near and visited Kishinev [The reader may want to re-read the testimony of Joseph Rabinowitz in Chapter Seven of this history].

I'm not saying that my grandmother was a believer, that she was member of Rabinowitz's congregation, or that she had even met Rabinowitz. What I do find interesting are the 'odds,' if you will, of a Jewish woman in czarist Russia stumbling across a Jewish Christian congregation.

What a coincidence that after my mind was gripped by the question of grandparents dying without the Lord, I should find a book confirming the existence of such a congregation—the tiniest shred of evidence that maybe my grandmother did know the Lord. I've seen enough 'coincidences' in my life to know when the Lord is working. Then maybe again He wasn't. The story does prove, though, that we don't always know the details of another's life.

When I found the Lord, my children were away at summer camp. If I had died before they returned, they would never have known of my new birth. My grandson, Joshua, would wonder if I were in heaven just the way I wonder about my grandmother.

The ways of God are far above our human understanding. Perhaps the view to take is one I posed to a young woman who was worried about her dead grandmother. 'How would you like to end in hell,' I asked her, 'only to find out that your grandmother is in heaven? First make sure you are going to be with the Lord. Then trust the Lord for your grandmother. After all, "Shall not the Judge of all the earth do right [Gen.18:25]?"'[11]

Elaine has long been convinced that there are no coincidences in life, only divine appointments. Her first big job after graduating from New York's City College was with the publishing giant, Simon and Schuster. As she met some of the authors who came into the building, or had opportunity to read the writings of many of them (Elaine is an avid reader), she developed a deep burden for their salvation, and she began to pray for ways to witness to them (those who know Elaine, know that she is not only a woman of prayer, she is fearless in her testimony). As she prayed, Elaine became particularly burdened for the salvation of Nobel laureate, Isaac Bashevis Singer. She later wrote:

'I got this tremendous desire to pray for him,' she recalls, 'after reading his A Little Boy in Search of God. *Then next week guess who I saw on the streets?'*

'He had won the Nobel Prize, but he still went unrecognized on the street. I wasn't sure it was him, so I walked up and said, "Isaac?"'

'He just looked at me and nodded, so I asked if I could talk with him. He said okay, if I'd walk with him where he was headed. I told him I'd read A Little Boy in Search of God. *and that I was a little girl who searched for God but that I'd found Him, and He was Yeshua, Jesus.'*

'He's a short man, his eyes were level with mine, and he looked at me eye to eye and said, "You must write and tell me more" so I left a New Testament and some literature with his doorman, but I never heard back.'

'I met him two other times, and one time I handed him a copy of A Little Boy...*to autograph, and said just sign it "To a little girl who found God" and he looked at me and said, "You can't find God."'*

'The third time I was on a street corner and saw him and I said hello. It just so happened that on my way out of the house that day I had picked up David Cooper's The God of Israel *[a scholarly treatment of the Messiahship of Jesus] and so I asked if he'd take it, which he did.'*

'Did he read it?' she says, exasperated. 'I just know God gives him lots of opportunities to hear about Messiah.'[12]

Elaine also has witnessed to, or left tracts for, other "famous" people such as Philip Roth, Marvin Hamlisch, Lauren Bacall, Tony Randall, and Joseph Heller. She stated:

...'other believers could and should avail themselves of these "everyday" miracles.'

'People could pray for things like this to happen to them,' she says excitedly....

'...one of my favorite Scriptures is "Call upon me and I will answer you and show you great and mighty things..." (Jer. 33:3). 'I think it's a great and mighty thing for me to pray and meet and witness to an Isaac Singer....'

The world of books and famous authors is a glamorous, heady orbit. But nowadays the best-sellers on Elaine's shelf are either gathering dust or are being displaced by titles of spiritual import. For, no matter how these best-sellers tickle the ears, they're 'junk,' as Elaine puts it, if they're not leading a man to consider the God who lives.

'Only one life—will soon be past,' she concludes. 'Only what's done for Jesus will last.'[13]

Elaine continued to keep her "divine appointments" with the Jewish people of New York, and even in retirement she maintains a vibrant witness and testimony for the Lord. As a result of her faithfulness, heaven will be filled with Jewish people whose lives were touched by the loving and faithful testimony of Elaine Fenchel.

As Jim Bates continued to develop the ministry in Boston, it became clear that he needed assistance. The Mission complied by sending Mrs. Marjorie Mogensen and Gary and Mary Lou Derechinsky. (The faithful work of Marge Mogensen and her husband, Mogen, is mentioned in Chapter Ten of this history.) Marge and Mogens served as missionaries at the Mission's Pittsburgh branch before they moved to New York. When the Boston work opened, Marge requested a transfer.

GARY AND MARY LOU DERECHINSKY

Gary and Mary Lou Derechinsky first joined the staff of the Mission during the spring of 1975. At that time, they served as missionaries for Bergen County, New Jersey and Rockland County, New York. In sharing his testimony with readers of *The Chosen People* magazine, Gary said:

I was raised in an Orthodox Jewish home. From five years old to age thirteen I went to Hebrew school four days a week.

I wanted to play baseball with the rest of the guys but, coming from an Orthodox Jewish home, I was supposed to learn about my God and the Scriptures.

At thirteen, when I was bar mitzvahed [sic], my father said 'You are a man now. You are a son of the Law. You are now responsible for your own sin according to Rabbinical Law.'

My father was responsible for my every act until I became a man. Now I was responsible. 'If you want to continue your studies in Judaism that is fine,' he said. 'If not, you don't have to.'

I chose not to.

When I was in school my best friend used to say to me 'The way I get to God is through Jesus,…'

…In Hebrew school I always asked my rabbi 'What is this with Jesus? Who is He?'

I must have gotten on his nerves. One day he said, 'Joseph (that was my name in Hebrew), get out of the class.'

He put me out because I kept asking about Jesus….

A few years passed by before I heard something very startling:

Charley Rizzo, a guy I went to high school with—and used to take drugs with—was studying to be a pastor in a church!

This was too much to believe so I went to see him.

'Charley, what's going on? What's this all about?'

'It's real, Gary.'

'I can't accept it. I'm a Jew. This isn't for Jews.'

What was there in Christianity? I already had Abraham, Isaac, Jacob and the Old Testament. I didn't need anything else. I thought gentiles were supposed to believe in Jesus and Jews weren't.

'Rather than argue with you, Gary,' Charley said, 'I'll tell you what. If you're willing to read it I'll give you a Bible.'

'Okay, fine.'

He went upstairs in the church and took a Bible from a pew. I didn't realize Bibles were given away by churches because in synagogues they don't do that. I thought he was stealing the thing.

…I began to read and it said 'Jesus Christ, the son of David, the son of Abraham.'

Immediately I wondered what these Jewish guys were doing in this gentile part of the book!

It just didn't click with me. But that got me to reading on.

And then I found Jesus to be totally different from what anybody had told me about Him.

Christians might have said some things that were true, but I had to find out for myself. When I saw what Jesus had to say about Himself I knew it was credible and I could believe it….

About seven months after I had given up taking drugs I was invited to a rock concert.

We camped out in Washington, D.C. and for two days there was no problem. The third day I decided to take anything that came my way.

Pills, drugs and alcohol—I just dumped them all down. When I got up the next morning it was terrible…

When I arrived home and walked in the house something hit me smack in the face. It was the fact that before I had left for the concert I was praying to Jesus—one of the things I did when I was reading the Bible. Charley told me I couldn't understand it unless I prayed. Every time I'd open the Bible I would pray to Jesus 'If You're real then show me. Amen,' and would then start reading.

Before I went to the concert I prayed and said 'Jesus, I haven't taken drugs for about seven months and I'm going to this concert where there will be drugs. I'm not going to give in to that temptation.'

'But if I do (and I knew I would) you've got my life. It's yours.'

I walked into the house and remembered I had prayed and I thought if I started in on drugs I was to give Him my life and the Lord was saying to me 'Now—or not at all.'

It was my decision.

I went into the bathroom because we didn't have locks on other doors. If my parents walked into my bedroom while I was praying they would have thought I was crazy.

I didn't have to kneel, but I did—using the hamper like an altar—and I prayed. 'Jesus, You've got my life. Come into my life' and (with the same breath) 'make me a witness to my Jewish people.' That was my concern.

When I walked out of that bathroom I had to tell someone about Jesus! I walked into the kitchen were my mother was doing the dishes.

'Hey, Mom, I found the Messiah of Israel. It's Jesus.'

'Did you hear what your son just said?' I heard a paper rustling and my father came in and…'What are you talking about Jesus?' Yelling. Screaming. Dishes flying….

Wouldn't you know it, but that prayer I said when I accepted the Lord made me a witness to the Jewish people—exactly to the day.

I was born again May 1st and four years later to the day—May 1st [c.1974]—the ABMJ gave me a call and told me I was on staff starting that day as a missionary to the Jewish people.[14]

Gary was enthusiastic in his witness; he soon organized a small army of volunteer workers to help him and his wife, Mary Lou, as they handed out tracts at shopping centers, downtown business areas, airports, etc. As they developed their technique, they discovered that it was easy to strike up conversations in the airports if they stood in areas where people were waiting for arriving flights. These conversations often led to decisions actually being made for the Lord. At other times they were able to extend an invitation to attend their Bible study or church services. In reporting on the Derechinskys' ministry, an article in *The Chosen People* magazine stated:

'We met another fellow at the airport,' Gary recalls, 'who had tried to commit suicide. It had been necessary for him to commit himself to a mental hospital in order to receive help.'

'After leaving the hospital he still needed help—he was still searching.'

'He met one of our girls who was handing out tracts on a street corner. About a week or two later he came to our church and—gave his life to the Lord.'

A young Jewish man had been attending Gary's Bible studies while considering Jesus as his Messiah. One week, two weeks—finally a month went by.

One night he left, still full of questions, but returned the next day and accepted his Lord and Messiah into his heart. He is now praying for God to bring peace to his family.

Along with the blessings comes the tsuris, the trouble, but all for a purpose. Gary's wife, Mary Lou, is a beautiful petite believer whose natural shyness has to flee when she's thrown into a heated situation while witnessing.

Once an older Jewish woman began yelling and shaking her fist at Mary Lou, telling her she had no right to proselytize Jewish people. Gary says his wife was scared but held her ground as the woman became more and more agitated.

'How could Jews believe in Jesus?' she asked Mary Lou.

She explained that she, herself, was not Jewish but nevertheless loved the Jewish people and fully supported the State of Israel. She then explained from Scripture and several related testimonies how a Jewish person, such as her husband, could believe in Jesus as the Messiah.

The woman quieted down—listened intently—took a tract and patted Mary Lou on the head.

'I don't know whether I should say "The Lord bless you" or what,' the woman said, half astonished, 'but keep up the good work.'

Praise God that Gary, his wife, and their army of enthusiastic believers are doing just that.[15]

Because of their bold witness, the local newspapers andmedia of Bergen County began to make frequent references to Gary's ministry. One day, a leading rabbi of Bergen County invited Gary to his synagogue for a dialogue on the credibility of Hebrew Christianity. The incident was reported in *The Chosen People* magazine:

> By the time the usual Friday night Sabbath service was completed at 7:30, two hundred people had jammed the small building completely blocking and overflowing the center aisle, front entrance and outlying sidewalk and street.
>
> The debate began with an opening statement by the rabbi—the atmosphere emotion-charged as he upheld his position. After his remarks several Hebrew Christian testimonies were delivered then Derechinsky took the floor.
>
> 'We made some strong comments in defense of Hebrew Christianity—many revolving around Isaiah 53 and Isaiah 7:14,' Gary recalled. 'Many Jewish people were greatly touched by the Scripture references and by our consistent and sincere faith.'
>
> A lively question-and-answer session followed the speaker's formal remarks, often interrupted by emotional outbursts from the mixed gathering.
>
> 'Before we went to the debate our group was praying that at least one Jewish soul would give his life to the Lord,' said Gary. 'A Hebrew-Christian who attends our church brought his mother to the debate and she was deeply touched by what was said. The next Sunday evening he brought his Mom to church and she gave her heart to the Lord. So God did answer our prayers.'[16]

Gary and Mary Lou's ministry in Bergen County soon developed into an informal congregation. Gary wrote:

> As the ministry developed, we were confronted with the need to disciple those Jews who had made a personal decision to accept Jesus as their Messiah in addition to our goal of bringing the Gospel to unbelieving Jewish people.
>
> Particularly important in discipling these Jewish believers was the need to encourage them in their Jewish heritage so that they might preserve their Jewish identity. Quite often it was suggested to us that we begin a worship service so that these believing Jews could worship the Lord in a Jewish cultural setting.
>
> Through the efforts of both Jewish and Gentile believers who have committed themselves to the ministry of the American Board of Missions to the Jews in our area, the service became a reality.
>
> Currently, our services are held at the Elmwood Park Bible Church every Friday evening. It was interesting to see how God guided us as we were considering the right place for these services. Looking back on that initial period, I could see that God was not only burdening our hearts for this type of ministry, but also the hearts of those who attended the Elmwood Park Bible Church.
>
> The thought of using the facilities of this church occurred to me after having shared with the congregation the work of the American Board of Missions to the Jews.
>
> Two primary reasons for choosing this building were, first of all, its size. It wasn't too big and rather had a homey atmosphere. Secondly, its location. It was very close to one of the largest Jewish communities in Bergen County which has approximately 20,000 Jewish families, and yet it was not right in the middle of that community so as to be threatening to them.
>
> It was close to three major highways in Bergen County making it rather accessible for many. I later found out that the church had been praying for the past few years that they might be directly involved in a Jewish work in their community. This was also seen as an answer to their prayers. So, it was God who was working both with us and with the church.
>
> Our services have a distinct Jewish flavor to them. The order of service includes singing, prayers and reading from the Law, the Writings, the Prophets and the New Testament in both Hebrew and English. These services have not only served to bring the Gospel to unbelieving Jews and to disciple Jewish believers, but to help the church better understand the culture and traditions of their Jewish friends and neighbors.[17]

Not long after Gary accepted the Lord, his friend and pastor, Charley Rizzo, brought him to the Mission to visit with the author. Gary felt certain that God wanted him to be a missionary to his own people. He mentioned that he was already enrolled in the pastors' course for the Nazarene church, and he wanted to know if any additional education was needed. Gary heeded the author's advice to get more education and he enrolled in Northeastern Bible College. He did so well scholastically that soon after his graduation from Northeastern, he was accepted into Dallas Theological Seminary.

Both Gary Derechinsky and Larry Feldman (mentioned in Chapter Six of this history) enrolled in Dallas Theological Seminary in the Fall of 1979. Larry, who had been the Missionary in Charge of the Coney Island branch, continued his ministry with the Mission on a part-time basis by assisting Rev. Tom McCall at the Dallas branch. After his graduation from seminary, Larry and Fran Feldman returned to the Northeast to work with Sam Nadler.

Gary, too, helped in the Dallas ministry while studying at Dallas Theological Seminary. Toward the end of Gary's program at Dallas, Mary Lou became ill—the diagnosis was multiple sclerosis. Their research into the illness and into innovative physicians and medical centers for the treatment of the illness revealed that Boston, Massachusetts provided the best programs. Gary therefore asked that the Mission consider transferring them to the Boston branch. The Mission agreed, and the Derechinsky's moved to Boston to work with Jim Bates and Marge Mogensen in 1981.

Subsequent to their move to the Boston area, Gary enrolled in Gordon-Conwell Seminary where he finished his seminary training. While attending seminary, he also studied at Harvard's Department of the History of Religion: Judaism. This training served him well! When Dr. Henry Heydt was no longer able to handle the Question and Answer Column for *The Chosen People* magazine, the author asked Gary to write the column and to answer the questions. Gary wrote that column for three years—from March 1984 through April 1987.

With three workers in Boston, one of whom was a Jewish believer, the work soon on new life! *The Chosen People* family was told:

> *The Boston branch of ABMJ is now or soon will be involved in:*
> *Sharing the Gospel with the 7,000 Jewish students on the campus of Boston University.*
> *Vigorous on-the-street witnessing and distribution of Gospel literature.*
> *Two Bible studies already in progress and three more 'in the works.'*
> *A nursing home ministry.*
> *Numerous speaking engagements throughout the greater Boston area, presenting the Gospel to unbelievers and the work of ABMJ to Christians.*
> *Recruiting volunteers to help spread the Gospel without drawing on the limited funds available.*
> *Working with other campus groups. We've helped such groups as The Navigators, Inter-Varsity Christian Fellowship and Campus Crusade understand more about Jewish evangelism.*[18]

After Gary's graduation from Gordon-Conwell Seminary in June 1982, he was made Missionary in Charge of the Boston ministry.[19] Jim Bates was transferred to Florida, where he was to re-activate the ministry there.

Long before God directed the Derechinskys to the Boston area, He had spoken to the heart of another believer in that area. Her name was Marguerite Eckhart. In the early 1950's God burdened Marguerite's heart to share the Gospel with the Jews. She responded by beginning a Bible Club in her home in Sharon, Massachusetts. To her disappointment, more Catholic children than Jewish children attended, but she never lost her vision or her faithfulness in praying for her Jewish neighbors.

Marguerite enlisted the help of several other women. Among them was a friend whose name was Ruth Baker. When Marguerite went home to be with the Lord, Ruth carried on her efforts to reach the Jewish people of her neighborhood with the Gospel.

By the time the Derechinskys made their move to the Boston area, the little "bedroom community" of Sharon had a population of approximately 16,000; it was about 70% Jewish. The Derechinskys thought Sharon would be a good place for a Jewish outreach ministry, but rents were high. Like other young couples, Gary and Mary Lou hoped that one day they could own a home. As they prayed about finding a home to purchase, and as word of their ministry spread among the Christians in the Sharon area, God answered prayer by arranging circumstances so that they were put in touch with Ruth Baker. A report in *The Chosen People* magazine continues the story:

> *Just about that time the Bakers were thinking about selling their home. When they heard about the Jewish ministry, and saw the fruits of Gary's Bible study, they believed it was God's will to sell their home to Gary and Mary Lou at a far-below-the-market value.*
> *Ruth correctly described this charming home as 'smack in the middle of the harvest field.'*
> *She also added that what made it even better was seeing that it was God's will, and knowing 'that I was part of God's answer to dear Marguerite's prayer.'*[20]

Gary fit right into the "intellectual" stream of Boston. With God's blessings, the Bible study group which they established in their home prospered. After a few years, Gary and Mary Lou and other members of the Bible study class began praying about establishing a Messianic congregation, as Gary had done in Bergen County, New Jersey. As they prayed, God directed, and in 1987 the Beth El Shaddai congregation was established. The Mission sent Steve and Lisa Cagan to Boston to help the Derechinskys with their new congregation.

When the Beth El Shaddai congregation was established the Jewish community of Sharon was outraged! Once again, Gary found himself in the center of controversy as articles pro and con Jewish believers in the Messiah, Yeshua, began appearing in the local newspapers. Reacting against the congregation and against Gary's ministry, the Jewish community sponsored anti-missionary statements, anti-missionary seminars, anti-missionary literature and anti-missionary lectures. Members of the Jewish community also formed a consortium of local and national groups and funded *Mogan Avraham*, a joint effort to respond to the local Boston branch of missionaries led by Gary Derechinsky.

Readers of *The Chosen People* magazine were given updates on the Boston ministry from time to time. In the November 1988 issue they were told:

> ...Then last year [c. 1987], several Jewish believers asked Gary to work with them in planting a Messianic congregation from which they could reach out to the community.
>
> Gary agreed that to reach Jewish families in a structured environment, a congregation seemed the best, most stable, environment.
>
> After prayer and consideration, such a congregation was started: Congregation Beth El-Shaddai (House of the Almighty God). Yet, from the first week that the congregation put a small notice in the weekly church listings, Sharon's rabbis were upset.
>
> When the congregation offered Jewish art calendars with prophecies explaining the Messiah, the furor broke.
>
> Full page ads warned Jews to stay away from Beth El-Shaddai. Reporters called Gary. Lecture series, ads and a whole slew of anti-missionary propaganda warned Jewish people about this 'deceitful group.'
>
> The congregation, less than two dozen people, many of them new believers in the process of being discipled, was at first bewildered. What had they done? Only taken out an ad inviting Jewish people to come hear about the Messiah and offering them a calendar with Scripture.
>
> What should they do? 'We really didn't have many choices,' Gary explains. 'As a ministry, we continued our campus outreach, Bible studies and discipleship. As a congregation, we invited people to our services, learned about God and worshipped together.'
>
> As reporters called, at first the attention was all on Gary. 'I was either a pure saint or a wicked sinner. But soon it became obvious to everyone, the press included, that our congregation posed no possible threat and was very open in our statement.'
>
> 'Then we learned how to turn the attention to Yeshua, so that people could see He was the real issue. Who did Yeshua say He was? Should Jewish people have the choice of accepting or rejecting His statements?'
>
> Gary is quite frank in admitting he's not a media super-star looking for attention. 'I don't like the controversy. I'm basically a person who likes people, who likes books, who likes quiet. But I've seen how this creates a climate of inquiry and an opportunity to challenge the community with the claims of Messiah.' For the congregation, it became a matter of being faithful to the opportunity God had given them.
>
> The hope is that all of this will bring people to Messiah and lay a solid foundation for the congregation.
>
> 'We're certainly learning what it means to be weak,' Gary confesses, 'because there is no way in the natural world that we have the resources to take this on as a fight. We don't have a mega-staff; we don't have mega-bucks; we don't even have a permanent facility to meet in.'
>
> 'I'd like to say the controversy is not a waste of time, even if no one comes to faith as a result of it, because I know these circumstances were ordained by an all-powerful God. But even more, I want to believe it will result in people coming to faith.'
>
> 'What I'd like to see is a congregation of Jewish punims (faces), praising the Lord, growing in the Lord, experiencing the joy of salvation in Jesus, free from controversy so that others would join us.'
>
> 'Because, despite the ruckus out there, I think that there are many, many people around us in Sharon who feel the emptiness of not having a relationship with God. For now, they lack the opportunity and courage to join us. But perhaps in the future things will quiet down and these people will know where to find us ...and they will.'[21]

God continued to bless Gary's ministry and the Beth El Shaddai congregation, as that group of believers proclaimed the Gospel to the Jewish people. Mary Lou's health continued to deteriorate however, and both she and Gary came to the realization that Gary's ministry schedule was posing a hardship for them. Oftentimes when Mary Lou needed Gary the most, he was away from home doing ministry for the Mission. After giving the matter much prayer, the Derechinskys resigned from the Mission's staff May 1992. Gary is now the pastor of New Hope Chapel in Arnold, Maryland.

With the resignation of the Derechinskys, the transfer of Steve and Lisa Cagan to the Western Region, and the retirement of Marge Mogensen, the Mission's branch in Boston was closed. However, the witness for the Gospel continues through the Beth El Shaddai congregation and the group of volunteers whom Gary and Mary Lou trained.

As has been mentioned, a number of the workers in the Northeast submitted resignations, or requested transfers to other branches of the Mission after Sam Nadler's appointment to the position of Northeast Regional Director in 1980. But as the Lord provided capable workers and funds, new workers were hired to replace those who had left. Among those hired were Israel and Judy Cohen.

ISRAEL AND JUDY COHEN

Israel Cohen was born in Philadelphia, Pennsylvania on March 18, 1942. His parents were Conservative Jews; they were not very religious. During his boyhood—from age eight until age thirteen—Israel was taught stories from the Jewish Bible, as well as the traditions of the Jewish people in preparation for Bar Mitzvah. Occasionally he and his father also attended synagogue—particularly during the High Holy Days in the Fall.

After his Bar Mitzvah, Israel's Jewish education came to a end. His father wanted him to become an electronics engineer, but Israel admits he was not a very good student; he wound up in the lowest quarter of his high school graduating class. He knew that his grade point average would prevent him from getting into college. He also knew he was eligible for the draft and he did not want to serve in the Army, so in May 1960, Israel joined the Navy.

Away from his parents and his home for the first time, Israel found the temptations of the world alluring. He had not been allowed to drink at home, so he began to indulge in this vice at every opportunity—and in the Navy he found plenty of opportunity!

After eight weeks in boot camp and eight months in communications school, the Navy issued Israel's orders. He was being sent to Arabic Morocco—a Moslem country where Jews were not accepted. Little did he know that in that Moslem country, he would be introduced to the Jewish Messiah. Such are the wonders of our Sovereign God!

Sitting alone in his barracks during the afternoon of May 16, 1961, Israel was wishing for a drink to ease his loneliness when a young Gentile sailor by the name of Art Hammers approached him. The sailor asked Israel if he wanted to talk and when Israel said, "Yes," the sailor responded by asking Israel if he was Jewish. When Israel again responded in the affirmative, the sailor shocked him by asking if he had a Jewish Bible. Israel said that he did and, again, the Gentile sailor amazed him by asking if Israel would teach him about being Jewish from his Jewish Bible. Recalling that moment, Israel later wrote:

> I got my Jewish Bible out but didn't know where to turn. We seldom read it in Hebrew School. So he asked me to turn to Isaiah. When he saw I was having trouble finding it, he found it for me and turned to Isaiah 53rd chapter.
>
> 'Read this aloud,' he said, and I did. At first I thought I had the wrong Bible. It sounded so much like what my Gentile friends used to say about Jesus.[22]

As their discussion continued, Art took a New Testament out of his own pocket. He asked Israel to read the third chapter of John. Israel went on to say:

> Art Hammers explained that Jesus was Jewish, the New Testament was written by Jews and tells all about the Jewish Messiah. I had never heard such things before. There I was—an 18-year-old Jewish boy in a Moslem country talking to a Gentile Christian about the Jewish Messiah. Never in my life had I been so confused!
>
> But after three hours of talking and reading from both of our Bibles, my confusion started to disappear. I now understood that I was a sinner and in need of the salvation offered by Jesus, the Jewish Messiah.
>
> I couldn't sleep that night, nor could I keep myself from crying as I tried to fall asleep. The knowledge of my great sinfulness so overwhelmed me that I knew I needed Jesus—but I also knew I was Jewish and couldn't accept Jesus as my Messiah.
>
> I pulled my blanket over my head so the others couldn't hear my weeping. And then I turned on a flashlight so I could read the New Testament my Christian friend had given me.
>
> As my tears fell upon the pages in the Book of Romans, I could no longer resist doing what I knew I had to do— I prayed to accept Jesus into my life asking His forgiveness for my sins. A few moments later I went peacefully to sleep.
>
> But the following morning at 6 a.m. the barracks wasn't peaceful any longer. A sailor could be heard from one end of the barracks to the other running around shouting, 'I'm saved! I'm saved!'
>
> That sailor was me [Israel Cohen].[23]

Israel's exuberance continued for a time. He wrote:

> While I was in the Navy, I was in a state of born-again bliss as I memorized Scripture, studied God's Word, and walked with the Lord. But when I got back home, though I didn't plan on backsliding, I soon decided that I had been overly ambitious in my plans to attend Bible college. Gradually I quit attending church and spent less time reading the Bible.
>
> Before long I had become quite ill. When I told my doctor that I was sick because I was running away from God, he said I needed a psychiatrist. Well, I wasn't ready for that, but when my boss gave me the phone number of a 'nice Jewish girl,' I thought he might have the answer.
>
> By my third date with Judy, I realized I was getting serious and we needed to have a heart-to-heart talk.
>
> 'Listen, you've got to know something,' I explained. 'I believe in Jesus and I can't marry you if you if you don't believe in the same thing.'
>
> Before I could continue, she was screaming at me and insisting I take her home. The next morning she telephoned me and gave me an ultimatum in no uncertain terms: 'You've got to give up this Jesus stuff. You're Jewish and that's all there is to it.'
>
> By that time I had suffocated the voice of the Lord so often that I went along with her. After a few more months, I proposed.
>
> 'Will you marry me if I say OK?' I asked.
>
> 'Yes,' she agreed.
>
> So we set our wedding date. A month before our wedding, we held our little 'funeral service' with the garbage men for all the remaining memories of my relationship with God.
>
> The trunk, filled with Bibles, study books, and notes from dozens of Bible studies I had attended, was so heavy it took both of us to haul it out to the trash. As I watched the garbage men heave it onto the truck and mash it between two steel plates, my heart was so heavy I could hardly stand there. But one look at my fiancee reminded me that now we could get married. Now that I had fulfilled my promise to 'bury this Jesus nonsense.'
>
> For five years things went from bad to worse. Business was thriving, but though I had buried my Bibles, I couldn't bury the living Word that had been planted in my heart. Our marriage was a farce; we barely got along. Socially we were very involved in a Jewish lodge, and though I liked our friends, I couldn't stand their mores and values, which had no basis in God. Torment is a very strong word, but even that can't describe the unhappiness I was suffering underneath my carefree salesman's banter.
>
> One day I was driving home and suddenly everything broke. I began crying uncontrollably. Because I couldn't see through my tears, I had to pull off to the side of the road. I couldn't live this way any longer. Two Scripture verses came to mind—Matthew 6:33 and Psalm 119:9-11. I knew I had to begin seeking God's righteousness and I had to begin studying the Bible. Still out of control, I cried out, 'If You are real, God, and if Jesus is the Messiah, bring me a Bible now.'
>
> With my prayer, a fog that had been inside of me for years suddenly cleared. I looked up and, much to my amazement, saw that I had stopped my car right in front of a Christian book store. I marched in and said, 'I want a Bible.'
>
> I realized I wasn't exactly free from all fear when the woman began showing me a large selection of Bibles.
>
> 'No, no,' I explained frantically, 'my wife isn't a believer and I need something small.' I bought a pocket-sized King James Version, and when I got back into my car, I took out a red marking pen and wrote inside the cover, 'Back with Jesus this day, 9/20/70.'
>
> I was back on the track. Sort of.
>
> For two years I secretly read that Bible, careful not to make Judy suspicious. I never told anyone what I was doing. One day I knew this couldn't continue. I called Judy into the living room.
>
> 'Sit down, you're not going to like this,' I said. 'I'm going to go to church. I'm quitting the lodge.'
>
> Hysterical isn't even the word to describe what happened next. Within minutes she was on the phone with her mother, the two of them frantically deciding what to do. They finally agreed that the best plan was to call a minister and have him talk me out of this betrayal. Judy got the name of a nearby church and called.
>
> 'It's my husband,' she began rationally enough. 'He's Jewish and he—he believes in Jesus!' Then Judy broke down. 'He wants to quit the lodge. Won't you talk him out of it? Won't you tell him he can't do this and...!' She probably would have continued for some time if the pastor hadn't interrupted her and asked to speak with me.
>
> Pastor Goodheart (Judy could hardly believe that was his real name) spoke with me briefly, offering to come right over. I was more appreciative for his love than I could express, but we decided the next night was soon enough.
>
> When Pastor Goodheart came and listened to our tale, I don't think Solomon could have been more tactful or wise. He had us agree that I would continue going to the lodge and Judy would begin coming to church with me. Well, it was

wise, but it didn't work. After two trips to church, Judy refused to continue.

We put in an emergency call to Pastor Goodheart. Judy agreed to try again. This continued for several months. Screaming refusals to continue going to church, threats of leaving me, and my insistence that Jesus was Messiah and that I wasn't going to deny Him.

Finally we came to an uneasy truce by living separate lives. I was involved in my activities; she went out with her friends. Her name remained at the top of the list in the prayer group I attended, but there seemed no hope on the horizon.

Then one Sunday night when I got home from church, I knew something had happened. Judy was already home, even though she made it a practice to purposely stay out late when I was at church.

'Sit down,' she said solemnly.

That night when she went roller-skating with a group, one of the people said he had to go to church to lead the singing. Judy asked if she could go with him. During the service, God spoke to her and she came under conviction. Afterward she told her friend, 'I think my husband is right. What can I do to be saved?'

So when we sat down for our talk, it was to tell me she had received Christ and to ask my forgiveness for what had happened during the past years. Two weeks later she was baptized.

Not long after all this, Ruth Wardell, an ABMJ missionary, spoke at our church and put Judy and I in touch with a group of other Jewish believers. As we took part in the fellowship, I knew God was calling me into full-time service.

When I look back on the years I was away from God, I am amazed at His faithful loving-kindness. How glorious that though I took it upon myself to 'bury Jesus,' no force could keep Him from the resurrection victory and the surety of His living in my life.[24]

After being united in faith and in their love for the Lord, Israel enrolled at Northeastern Bible College. While he was a student there, he was involved with the Mission and with Jews for Jesus. He and Judy were members of the Beth Yeshua congregation in Philadelphia, where Marty Chernoff was the pastor.

Ten years after writing the words, "Back with Jesus this day, 9/20/70," after graduating from Northeastern Bible College, Israel Cohen joined the staff of the Mission. He was hired as full-time worker on June 1, 1980. He later served as an assistant to Larry Feldman with the Beth Messiah congregation he was establishing.

Israel Cohen's exuberance and enthusiasm in sharing the Gospel is contagious! He has been a valuable and loved worker on the Mission's staff. He has currently been studying the Russian language so he will be a more effective missionary to the Russian Jews in his Brooklyn neighborhood. Riding the subway from Brooklyn to Grand Central Station, where he and other missionaries on staff go to witness and to distribute tracts, many Russian Jews eye him with interest as he studies his Russian language books. He told readers of *The Chosen People* magazine:

'They look over my shoulder,' Israel laughs, 'and ask me why I'm studying Russian. I tell them "because I want to share the Messiah with Russian Jews," and bingo! I'm already sharing my faith.'[25]

At the time of this writing, Israel and Judy Cohen continue to be faithful and dynamic members of the Mission's staff as they seek to reach the Jewish people of New York with the Gospel.

Another worker appointed to the New York staff to assist Sam Nadler in the ministry there, was Frank Potter. Frank joined the staff of the Mission in October 1982.

FRANK POTTER

Frank Potter was born into a Jewish family in 1934. He was raised by his father's eldest sister in an essentially non-traditional, quasi-agnostic Jewish home. From the time he was a small child, Frank was introspective. He believed in God, and would speak to Him, but no matter how hard he searched or studied, he couldn't seem to figure out how to know Him personally.

While he was in college Frank decided to explore more about his Jewish heritage. For a few years he attended synagogue faithfully and studied Jewish history, customs, and traditions but he discovered that there was an emptiness in his life that traditional Judaism could not fill.

After college Frank attempted to bury his "emptiness" in business and in the things of the world—but to no avail; he knew there was more to life. He knew there had to be some way to have a personal relationship with God!

Several years passed before Frank met a lovely young woman named Rosanne. Rosanne was a Christian, but she never forced her faith on Frank. Instead, she lovingly invited him to attend church with her. Of that time in his life, Frank wrote:

...Fifteen years later at the behest of a young woman whom I ultimately married, I attended a church service. She had not witnessed to me, nor do I recall hearing an evangelistic message, but I was touched by the Holy Spirit. A week later in my bedroom at 11 p.m. on a Sunday night, the Lord appeared to me in a sort of vision and I asked Him into my heart. I felt a warm surge throughout my body and began praising God. It was at that moment that I was saved and reconciled back to God.

From the time I was saved, I attended the New City [a town in the suburbs of New York] Gospel Fellowship with my wife and felt a sense of calling to the ministry.[26]

In 1982 Frank made application to the Mission. He was accepted and he became the Mission's representative in Rockland County, New York and in the surrounding environs. He soon developed a ministry among the many convalescent hospitals and homes in the New York area. God has gifted Frank with a loving heart and the willingness to listen to others—gifts which enabled him to be greatly used as he ministered to the many abandoned and disenfranchised residents who occupy the homes for the aged. In giving a report of this special ministry, Frank wrote:

Their names come to me as easily as those of my own children: Anna, Sam, Mimi, and Victor, just to name a few.

Who are these people, and why are their names important to me—and to you? These dear souls are a very small, but significant cross section of the elderly Jewish residents—some sick and dying—of the nursing and adult homes in the Rockland County area of New York.

As you might guess, people like Anna and Victor are here primarily because their families can no longer care for them. All too often, however, that means total abandonment, because they have become a burden and an imposition on the families they raised and nurtured and for whom they sacrificed so much in their productive years.

I have commiserated much with these beautiful mothers and fathers as part of my ministry to the elderly in nursing homes and homes for the elderly. Although my heart has often been heavy as I ministered to them, there has also been much fruit and moments of ecstatic joy.

I think of the blessing that will always be mine for having known Louis, who was a diabetic and an amputee. Louis had also been crippled by a severe stroke. His speech was slurred, and when I first began to visit and share the Gospel with him, I could hardly understand his replies.

Then as I tuned in more carefully each week, I began to decipher his utterances and communicate with him in a more meaningful way. Louis placed his faith in Messiah Jesus, and I continued to minister to him from the Word of God until he went to be with the Lord.

Then there was Jack, a wonderfully warm and beautiful man. A grandfather many times over, he was terminally ill with a severe kidney disease. What wonderful conversations we had and times of sharing together in the Psalms, which he so dearly loved. Jack too gave his heart to Messiah Jesus and several months later joined Louis in the presence of his Lord.

But the joy of introducing these men to their Messiah was tempered by the heartbreak of my uncertainty about Nathan. For six months or so I had witnessed to him and shared with him from the Scriptures. Then one day Nathan was rushed to the coronary care unit of a local hospital. I remember standing over him while he struggled to survive with the aid of a respirator. He was in a semicomatose state.

I'll never forget Nathan's eyes as I told him one final time of Messiah's love for him and his need to be cleansed, forgiven, and saved. I watched the life force slowly and systematically slip away as Nathan entered an eternity from which there would be no return, no second chance.

I prayed the sinner's prayer with Nathan, and hoped that he had prayed it with me and had meant it in his heart. As I left the hospital to continue my rounds, all I could think of was the story of the rich man and Lazarus in Luke 16:19-31. I sat in my car and wept and hoped that Nathan had not met that same fate.

Yes, there is joy and sorrow in reaching out to the aged 'lost sheep of the house of Israel.' The rewards are indescribable and they are also available to you! These precious souls are all around you—in your neighborhood, your local hospital and nursing home, your city or town.[27]

Not only does Frank have a gift for ministering among the aged and sick Jewish people, he also has the gift of "helps." He willingly filled in where he was needed the most. One year he was asked to join one of the Mission's evangelistic teams. Frank gave the following report of the unique way God blessed:

Can you imagine sharing the Word one-to-one on the streets of Moscow? The thick Russian accents of passers-by enveloped me and a stiff wind made me turn my collar up. But I wasn't behind the Iron Curtain or even in Europe.

We were in Rochester, New York outside an apartment complex of mostly Russian and Rumanian Jewish families.

Myself, Israel Cohen (ABMJ missionary, New Jersey) and several ABMJ missionary trainees were winding up a Northeast evangelistic tour. The host church where we had just finished a Jewish Evangelism Seminar suggested we drive over to the complex.

Finding a well-lit courtyard area in the complex we began singing some Hebrew/Jewish songs. Strollers began to drift over joining in on the ones they had known in Russia. Then we began to share.

'Come over here, listen to what these people are saying,' shouted Mikael, a young Russian Jew who beckoned more of his countrymen over to us.

'They're talking about God, the Messiah.'

Mikael confided in Israel Cohen that he had been to a Gentile believer's Bible study.

'I know why you are here. You've come to tell us that Jesus is the Messiah and we need to believe in Him in order to get to heaven.'

Pulling Israel away from the crowd, he put his thumb and index finger together and whispered, 'You know Israel, I think I even believe a little bit. But I need to hear and learn more.'

As I looked around the considerable throng of people that had gathered I saw Stephanie Rivera and Jacob Cohen, two missionary trainees talking with Rachel an attractive middle-aged Russian Jew.

Rachel shared that both she and her husband were unemployed. Jacob and Stephanie promised to pray for their situation. As Jacob shared the Word in Hebrew, Rachel suddenly excused herself and ran upstairs.

She returned moments later clutching a Russian Bible she had received at a stopover point in Italy. Her husband had tried to get her to leave it behind because he thought their baggage would be overweight for their trip to America. She had stood her ground though and now proudly displayed it. (Incidently through prayer and some legwork by Stephanie and Jacob, Rachel and her husband were able to find work. But best of all Rachel accepted the Lord!)

While animated conversations were happening all around me I found myself surrounded by eight men and women. As I shared with a woman who was a Russian schoolteacher, Manny, who didn't speak any English heard me through an interpreter in Hebrew!

'In Russia, they told us there is no God,' Manny exclaimed in Russian.

As I continued to share biblical passages on sin, salvation, and forgiveness through the Messiah, one woman snapped that what I was saying, was the talk of a 'meshumed' (traitor).

But as she listened more intently she wound up agreeing that I made sense!

The hour was growing late and as people began to drift back to their apartments we shook hands warmly and parted.

Some days later I learned through word from the Rochester host church that much fruit resulted from our visit. A Russian Jewish man dying of cancer accepted the Lord and so did many other Jewish people.[28]

When John Bell was appointed Missionary Director in August 1986, he and his family moved to New York and John maintained an office at the Mission's Headquarters building in Orangeburg, New York. It did not take him long to recognize Frank's unique gifts of helps, administration, and witnessing and he asked that Frank be transferred to his department to become his assistant. When the administrative operation of the Mission was relocated to Charlotte, North Carolina in August 1988, Frank and his family made the move along with others of the Mission's administrative staff.

In Charlotte, North Carolina Frank not only assisted in the Missionary Department, he also served as a National Church Ministries Representative for North and South Carolina. At the time of this writing (c.1993) Frank Potter and his family are preparing to return to the Philadelphia area to assist in a Messianic congregation being established by the Mission in that area.

LARRY FELDMAN REJOINS THE STAFF

After graduating from Dallas Theological Seminary in June 1983, Larry Feldman participated in the Mission's S.T.E.P. program. He led the evangelistic tour which traveled throughout the Southeast for the summer, after which he and his family returned to the Northeast.

As mentioned in an earlier chapter, Larry first joined the staff of the Mission in June 1974, when he was hired as the assistant to Miss Hilda Koser in Coney Island. He became the Missionary in Charge of the Coney Island branch when Miss Koser took her sabbatical in Florida and subsequently decided to retire. (See Chapter Six for details.) Both Larry and Fran have a love for music and young people, and during their years of ministry in Coney Island they organized a Messianic music group called "Ammi" (meaning "My people," taken from Hosea 2:1). Even prior to their years of missionary service in Coney Island, Larry and Fran had been involved with Messianic music from groups like Lamb, Kol Simcha, and the Liberated Wailing Wall.

Larry rejoined the staff of the Mission as a full-time missionary working under Sam Nadler in the New York/New Jersey areas in August 1983. They established Beth Messiah (the House of the Messiah), a Messianic congregation in the town of Livingston, New Jersey—a "bedroom community" of New York City comprised of 100,000 Jewish people. One of the first things Larry and Fran did after establishing the congregation was to start a new "Ammi" Messianic music group.

Beth Messiah congregation reflects the community in which it is located. There are many singles in their late twenties and early thirties, as well as young families. Typically, fifty to sixty people attend the Friday night services, and seventy to one hundred attend special events. "Over and over again newcomers tell Larry, 'My family will never listen to the Gospel.' Eventually, though, most do. They come to weddings, baby dedications, High Holiday services, and Passover Seders."[29] Howard Rothbard, one of the members of Beth Messiah said:

> I've had some of my best opportunities to share Messiah because I attend a Messianic congregation. I can take my friends there and know they'll be comfortable. When my daughter was born, 19 of my unsaved family members came out to the dedication and saw that our beliefs and commitment were to the God of Israel. I know that when they come to Beth Messiah, they'll be comfortable and they'll hear the Gospel.[30]

Robert Kaplan, another member wrote:

> I didn't want my faith to be a hindrance to my family and friends, and Beth Messiah gave me a place that bridged the gap. I could grow in the Lord, worship Him, and be a witness to unbelievers. For instance, originally my mother was alienated from my faith, but I took her to Beth Messiah and she really enjoyed it. I think she could identify with God in that setting.[31]

As Messianic congregations were established in the Northeast, and throughout the country, the need for a children's camping program resurfaced. The Mission's summer camping program had been suspended in 1980 due to the fact that after the Mission cut back on its branch and center type outreach, there was no longer a nucleus of children from Messianic Jewish families to draw from. Secondly, the emphasis had turned to college campus ministry, and to ministry among older youth who were coming to faith in the Messiah. But the Messianic congregations were comprised of many young Jewish families and a summer camping program was needed to further evangelize the children. The camping program was seen as a valuable way to train and disciple the next generation of Messianic Jewish believers. The younger workers of the Mission also felt that the camping program was important for their own children; it is a way the "MK's" (missionary kids) can meet one another and be strengthened in their faith in the Lord, while identifying with other children whose parents are involved in Jewish missions.

Larry Feldman was asked to assume the responsibility as Camp Director of the children's camping program, "Camp Simchat Yeladim" (Joy of Children), which was re-established in August 1988.[32] Larry and Fran Feldman were the perfect couple for this very important ministry and Camp Simchat Yeladim continues to be an essential part of the ministry of the Mission to the present day.

In sharing the importance of instilling within their children an understanding of their Jewish culture and heritage, along with a strong belief in Jesus as the Messiah, Larry and Fran Feldman told readers of *The Chosen People* magazine:

> We want our children to know that we are Jewish believers in Yeshua. We don't see this as two separate parts of their lives, but rather as one identity.
>
> I know this means that they'll have to sort out some things. For instance, last year Rachel [Larry and Fran's oldest daughter] was shocked when she found out that all Jews aren't believers in Messiah. My mother says Rachel will be confused when she's older, but just the opposite is happening. She is growing strong and confident in the Lord and in her sense of being Jewish.
>
> This confidence is one of the most important things this generation of Messianic Jewish parents can give their children. Right now, a lot of Jewish believers, especially those in their twenties and thirties, are awkward about being Jewish believers. They try very hard not to offend their Gentile Christian brothers and sisters, so hard that sometimes they unnecessarily offend their Jewish families. Other times they try so hard not to offend their Jewish families, they aren't completely forthright in their testimony of Messiah's salvation.
>
> There is a better way, and I think raising our children with a right sense of what it means to be Jewish and what it means to be a believer will change this awkwardness.
>
> Why is it important to me that my children understand they're Jewish? Because as I trace Genesis 12:3; 15:1-6;17; and Jeremiah 31:35-37, I see that God raised up the Jewish people to be a testimony to His faithfulness. Acts 15

explains that Gentile believers do not have to become Jews in order to follow the Jewish Messiah, implying that Jewish believers do not have to 'become' Gentiles. All of this tells me that we shouldn't cast aside our Jewishness.

The emphasis obviously must come in the home. Deuteronomy 6 says that the home is the best place to teach our children about God. In our home we do this through creating our own 'customs.' For instance, Friday night dinner with chalah (braided bread) and the candles has been a custom in Jewish homes for thousands of years. In our home, we have dinner, we light the candles, and we have the chalah . But as we light the candles we give thanks that Messiah, the Light of the World, has come; as we break the bread we give thanks to Yeshua, the Bread of life.[33]

Fran Feldman added:

Jewishness has a beautiful, rich history and culture, and we want our girls to appreciate this. So as Rachel (and Rebekah, when she is old enough to understand) learns about her heritage, she will not only see the connection between the Bible and the people of the Bible, but she will gain something to pass on to her children.

I can't imagine denying them this tie with their past. My parents went through the Holocaust, and I want my children to understand their history. Sometimes we'll all sit around, and my dad will tell us stories of Europe—what it was like to live in a ghetto or how he almost escaped from a labor camp once. Rachel, like the rest of us, will cry and laugh at his stories. How can I ignore teaching her what it means to be part of this people.

Of course, I know that some Christians fear that we'll pull our children from the Church. But just the opposite is happening! Our Jewish testimony is drawing others to the Lord. My parents are now believers—my whole family is— and they've got strong testimonies even though—or actually because—they maintain their Jewish identity.[34]

The Feldman's Messianic lifestyle and consistent witness for their Lord is producing "fruit" in the lives of their own children. In 1991, eleven year old Rachel Feldman wrote a letter to the Mission telling of her experience with the Lord. The letter was published in *The Chosen People* magazine. She said:

From the age of two, my parents taught me about Yeshua. At four and a half years old, I asked Yeshua to come into my heart. Since then I have known that I am saved, and desire to know more about Him.

For the last three years at Simcha [the annual Messianic conference sponsored by the Mission], I have seriously thought of immersion, but have not worked up the courage to do it.

At Simcha on June 8th 1991, there was an afternoon class on immersion. I was glad to be at the class. That night I was immersed. It was one of the greatest times of my life.

Afterwards, I felt good and cleansed. From then on I have felt stronger about living for God. I also want to win souls for Him like it says in Scripture, Proverbs 11:30, 'He who is wise wins souls.'[35]

Still another worker who joined the staff to help Sam Nadler in the Northeast was Stewart Weinisch. As a student at Moody Bible Institute, Stewart served as a part-time worker in the Mission's Chicago branch. He was hired as a full-time missionary for the New York City area in January 1984.

Stewart and Shoshannah Weinisch

Stewart was born in the Bronx, New York on February 21, 1958. His was a Conservative Jewish family. He recalled that while he was still a teenager, a good friend of his showed him Isaiah 53 and implied that it was a reference to Jesus. Stewart became so angry that he threw his friend out of his house and did not speak to him again for several years.[36] However, the seed was planted. In January 1979, Stewart opened his heart to receive Yeshua (Jesus) as his Messiah and Savior. His testimony was shared with readers of *The Chosen People* magazine in the February 1992 issue. It stated:

'Someday...' I promised God at my Bar Mitzvah, 'Someday I'll take the time to know more about You.' Stewart Weinisch was thirteen when he made that promise. Thirteen years old, ready to experiment with the temptations of being a teenager, but, for the moment, awed as he stared at the open ark (where the Torah scrolls are kept in the synagogue).

'For that minute I really meant it. I wanted to know God ...But not now. Not today.'

Stewart grew up in the Bronx, one of three children. 'My dad was active in the synagogue, a macher (important person). On high holidays, when the children met in a different building for their own services, Dad would often be the one honored to carry the Torah from the big synagogue to our service.'

'I can still picture him walking down the street, hugging the Torah, wrapping it protectively with his tallis, guarding

it with his life. I knew there was something very valuable in the Law, something worth living for....'

'As I was going through high school, I became friends with a divorced lady in my neighborhood, and became sort of a big brother to her two sons. Then the mother and I grew from friends into really good friends. At 18 years old I was all ready to marry her.'

'Then she got saved, and said she couldn't marry someone who didn't share her faith.'

Frustrated over her beliefs, which Stewart assumed were 'strictly Gentile,' he was still emotionally involved with her and her children.

'Over the next nine months, we started a whole new relationship. We spent a lot of time reading the Bible. It went from one to two hours at a time, to four or five hours at a time. Pretty soon, whenever we were together, we were reading the Bible.'

'Now this whole time we were only reading the Old Testament, because of course I told her that Jews don't believe the New Testament, and that it was written for the Gentiles....'

'Eventually,' Stewart concedes, 'I began to get the idea that all this reading I was doing in the Bible was about Jesus, but that only made it more plain that it didn't have anything to do with me. I was Jewish....'

Stewart came to the conclusion that things would look different if they were not reading from the 'Gentile Old Testament,' so he went out and bought a Jewish Bible from the Hebrew Publication Society and compared the texts word by word.

'What I found was that they were the same ...almost. Certain key passages that talked about Messiah were different. For instance, in the Hebrew Publication Society Bible, Isaiah 9:6 read like this: "Pele Yoetz, El Shaddai [sic. El Gibbor], Avi Ad, Sar Shalom.'

'It was transliterated Hebrew.'

'In tiny, tiny type off to the side was the actual translation: "His name will be called Wonderful Counselor, Mighty God, Eternal Father and Prince of Peace."'

...Everything else was a regular English translation of the Hebrew Scriptures. Stewart was puzzled, thoughtful and more than a little apprehensive about what he was learning.

...On Christmas Eve, Stewart and his girlfriend went to a midnight service at an evangelical church in Brooklyn. Expecting to hear about Jesus and the manger, or 'more about what Christians really thought,' Stewart was stunned when the pastor preached about Abraham's faith. It was so Jewish.

'That night, I walked out of church feeling so high I couldn't believe it. It was a wonderful, pure, clean feeling and I knew I had found God. Faith wasn't a Jewish/Gentile thing any more.'

But as soon as they got in the car, a feeling of dread and distrust gripped him. 'I had a sense that this was the devil, drawing me away from Judaism, doing what Hitler and all other anti-Semites hadn't been able to do, shake Jewish people at their roots and destroy them. I convinced myself that the high I felt was an emotional experience.'

For two weeks Stewart convinced himself that no self-respecting Jew would believe in Jesus.

'I ignored the whole thing as much as I could. Then, one day I took the D train home (like I always did) and expected to meditate (like I always did) and expected to come out of my meditation at the stop nearest my home (like I always did).'

'Instead, I came out of my meditation and found myself in Brooklyn, not the Bronx. I had taken the D train all right, but in the wrong direction.' To his surprise, Stewart found himself only a block or two from the church he had attended on Christmas.

'It was a Tuesday night, but the church was open for a Bible study. No one was there yet. Well, one person was—a deacon who had met me on Christmas. He saw me standing there and came over. "Hey brother," he asked, "When did you get saved?"'

'Uh, I'm Jewish,' I replied.

Minutes later Stewart was talking to the deacon, and to a friend of his who was, not coincidentally, a Jewish believer.

'For the first time I heard the Gospel from a Jewish perspective. It was astounding. We read Jeremiah 31 and I realized this was a new covenant...a new testament.'

In one fell swoop, everything Stewart had heard and read made sense. He remembered that three years before a friend had tried to tell him about Jesus. 'I remembered I threatened to kill him if he ever talked to me again,' and he also remembered that his friend had left a New Testament . . .

'I went home and dug that Bible out; the Bible that made me so mad when he gave it to me. And I started reading. I read from the first page in Matthew where it says, "The genealogy of Jesus Christ (I knew that Christ meant Messiah), Son of David, Son of Abraham." At that moment it all came together. Jesus was the Jewish Messiah and trusting in*

Him was the most Jewish thing a Jewish person could do.'

The next week, Stewart went to a Bible study with his girlfriend. The sermon was about belief, and the difference between believing in the heart and believing in the head.

'Right after the message, I made a commitment to God. I knew I had already made up my mind, but now I made a commitment in my heart also.'

A week after his commitment to Messiah, Stewart was walking with his girlfriend when she mentioned a Jewish neighbor.

'I wish there was some way I could tell this woman about her Messiah,' she said.

In a flash of understanding, Stewart realized '...that one day I'd be witnessing to Jewish people ...that this is what I wanted to do ...what God wanted me to do.'

Not long after, an 'old drinking buddy' introduced his aunt to Stewart. His aunt, also a Jewish believer, introduced Stewart to Sam Nadler.

'Sam discipled me and encouraged me to go to Moody Bible Institute where I completed the Jewish Studies Program.'

It's been over twenty years since Stewart made that 'someday' promise to God. And he's traveled a lot of miles since he took the train going in the 'wrong' direction. Yet somehow God used it all for His grace as Stewart took the D train to God.[37]

The relationship between Stewart and the girlfriend who had been so instrumental in bringing him to faith in the Messiah, ended soon after Stewart became a believer. God had brought her into his life for a purpose, however she was not to be the helpmate God wanted for Stewart in the ministry.

After completing his studies at Moody Bible Institute, Stewart returned to New York where he joined the staff of the Mission as a full-time missionary. As a part of his ministry, he helped Sam Nadler with the Light of Israel congregation and with Bible study classes in New York City. Through his ministry in the congregation, he met a beautiful young Jewish believer—Shoshannah Tilleman. Shoshannah and Stewart were married on August 2, 1986.

Shoshannah (Tilleman) Weinisch's testimony appeared in October 1989 special "Jewish" issue of *The Chosen People* magazine. The article stated:

'A story like mine wouldn't speak to a lot of people,' says Shoshannah Weinisch, 'people who have it "all together," who don't think they're miserable. A lot of people can go through this life without the Lord and be happy, because they don't think about the consequences of what comes after death. But a person who has really hurt and struggled, someone who knows what it is to be hurt, broken and miserable, these are people I can speak to from my experience. These are the people who know they don't have life like it was meant to be.'

It's difficult to see her today and think of her as being miserable. All her life, she wanted to be married and she is ...to a man devoted to her. All her life she wanted children ...she has two (two year old Melissa and six month old Jonathan). She has always enjoyed art ...last year her hand-designed wearable art, 'Originals by Shoshannah,' was featured in a promotion at Nordstroms, a fashionable department store.

To all outward appearances, her life has always been pleasant. She was the daughter of a middle-class Jewish family. After high school she moved to California where she worked while attending college. She held a high profile job for a computer related firm, where she was very successful.

For many people, including Shoshannah, the pleasant life is a myth. She was a lonely child in a family where her parents constantly fought. 'My parents never told me they loved me,' she remembers, 'Neither one ever told me they did. My great grandfather's house became a haven for me. I used to spend every summer at his house. His whole life revolved around synagogue and God. He'd get up in the morning and walk to shul, and then he'd come home and daven for hours—chanting and rocking. Then he'd eat and then pray some more.'

'At home, my parents fought all the time, and my mother eventually left my father with four kids. I took on the role of mom, but none of us were close. But at my great grandfather's, it was full of love. He couldn't even speak to me ...he spoke no English, and I spoke no Yiddish, but I knew he loved me and I knew God was in his home. I knew what was missing from my family.'

After high school, Shoshannah went West to find herself. Like many teenagers in the early 1970's, she tried a combination of spirituality, knowledge, and philosophy. The spirituality was mostly eastern; time spent in an ashram. The knowledge was from college classes; majors in dance, art, music. The philosophy was primarily that of Mexican writer Carlos Castanada; he preached that life was a void which one must jump into.

'Life never seemed to make sense, never seemed to come together. I was always an outsider. All the life philosophies, all the mystics, sounded great on paper, but I couldn't make it right for me. I just couldn't get there. And I got unhappier

and unhappier. My life revolved around relationships that I'd try desperately to make work. It wasn't that I disliked myself. After all, I knew I was pushy at work, but that was okay, because I was also successful. I could justify my hurt in relationships because I was a nurturing person.'

'What I couldn't get over was that I was always very, very lonely. I felt this big empty hole in my inner being that nothing could fill. I kept trying to fill it with relationships but it was an emptiness that only God could fill. These relationships hurt me so badly that one time, I laid on the floor of my apartment for two days. I couldn't answer the phone or eat, I was so depressed, internally destroyed because of the pain of my relationships.'

'Eventually I tried everything I knew. Dancing, business, choreography. Looking at it now, I feel like I was being swallowed alive. You know, on the outside, people who saw me thought I had it all together. I looked busy and happy and successful. But I knew better. I knew I was dying.'

'In a class I was taking we had to discuss the meaning of life. I pondered the whole weekend, and on Monday, I was the only one who came up with the answer the teacher was looking for: there is no purpose in life.'

About that time, in a series of subtle ways, a different spirituality entered Shoshannah's life when she picked up a Bible someone had left in her apartment and began to flip through it.

'For the first time out of any of the things I had been studying, something made sense. It was totally different reading the Bible than anything else. And as I read, it began to permeate my life. I started to try to do what it talked about, about turning the other cheek or submitting and humbling myself in a situation instead of trying to beat people over the head. And it worked! I couldn't believe it.'

'When I did things the way that God says to do them it worked out for my benefit. It was real. It was working. Not only that, but it was bringing peace into my life.'

'From reading the Bible, I sensed that I was in the same situation as Jesus had been when he confronted the Jewish leaders: they owed their disbelief to a power and political struggle—the establishment versus the truth—rather than a spiritual truth. I realized my unwillingness to make any deeper commitment to Jesus was the same struggle: what I had been taught was right vs. what was the truth.'

'So one night I got on my knees in my bedroom and said, "God, if this is true—if Jesus is really the Messiah—You've got to prove it supernaturally. It goes against everything I've been taught and I can't do it on my own.'

Within 24 hours, Shoshannah's prayer was answered. She went to pay her rent, and her landlady invited her in for coffee, something she had never done, and even more astounding, the landlady initiated a conversation about the gospel. When Shoshannah left, twelve hours later, she was unable to sleep, so she went to a neighbor's. The neighbor had never talked about spiritual matters, until this day, when she felt compelled to share her beliefs that Jesus was Messiah. That same night, Shoshannah went to her waitressing job and overheard some of her customers talking about Jesus.

'When they noticed me eaves-dropping,' Shoshannah remembers, *'they asked me if I was a Christian. I said no, I was Jewish. They said it was possible to be both and asked if they could have a Jewish believer in Jesus call me.'*

On her second visit with Martha Jacobs, the Jewish believer her customers had contacted, she knew what God wanted. 'Martha asked me if I wanted a personal relationship with Yeshua and I knew I did want to. I wanted to please God. To belong to Him. To have a relationship with Him.'

Since that time, Shoshannah Weinisch has never looked back. 'God is always there, under your feet. If you can just remember what you're standing on, you don't fall. I know He's always there. I am very conscious that there's no one in the world who seemed further from God than me, but that God forgave me, loved me, saved me. God has filled the longings of my heart, He's given me a family and life filled with Himself, filled with love. For me, faith is a life-long dream I'm living every day.'[38]

In his position as a missionary in the "jungle" of New York City, Stewart distributed thousands of tracts and witnessed to countless Jewish people as they paused to accept the hand-outs. Both he and Shoshannah actively participated in the Light of Israel Congregation, giving themselves to teaching, visiting, etc. They also served as camp counselors in the Mission's summer camping program. Later, God opened the door for them to begin monthly Bible study classes in Ansonia, Connecticut and, as the Weinischs followed God's leading, the study grew into the Joy of Israel Messianic Congregation.

In 1991 the Mission promoted Stewart to the position of Area Director. With that appointment the Weinischs moved back to New York City where they are currently working among the Jewish people in Queens, Brooklyn, Manhattan and the other boroughs of New York.

Michael Rydelnik (whose testimony and background was given in Chapter Twelve of this history), joined the staff of the Mission as a full-time missionary in the Queens/Long Island area on October 1, 1984. As mentioned earlier, his ministry of evangelism, discipleship, and Bible study resulted in the establishment of the Olive Tree congregation.

The Olive Tree congregation occupies a remodeled church building which the Mission purchased—a facility located on the edge of the Jewish community in Plainview, New York. Because of its strategic location, the congregation has been the subject of controversy, hatred, and persecution as some leaders within the Jewish community have attempted to shut it down. But Michael and the members of the congregation have used the wrath of the Jewish community as a further testimony for the Gospel. As a result, the Olive Tree congregation has been used of God to reach many Jewish people with the Gospel. But not only are Jewish people coming to faith through the congregation's ministry, Muslims, too, are being reached. Michael told readers of *The Chosen People* magazine:

> *I never dreamed I would see a Muslim come to know the Lord, but Jewish ministry is full of surprises! This is what happened. Several months ago, Alan, a Jewish believer, began attending Olive Tree Congregation with his Iranian Muslim wife, Sheila [not her real name]. This bright, lovely, and attractive woman was in no way hostile to her husband's faith. In fact, it was she who nudged him to find a place to worship.*
>
> *But her Islamic upbringing kept her from seeing Jesus as anyone more than a prophet. 'There is no God but Allah,' she said, 'so Jesus can not be God.' Remarkably, approaching a Muslim is not very different from sharing the Gospel with a Jew.*
>
> *Sheila attended consistently, while I and others shared with her regularly. She and her husband joined a home fellowship which was especially helpful in establishing friendships and demonstrating the Gospel. The Lord also brought a new woman to the congregation who is an Iranian believer. She was able to explain the Good News in Farsi (the Iranian language).*
>
> *At our Passover Seder, I asked Sheila what was keeping her from becoming a believer. She said, 'It's harder for me, I have to become Jewish first!' I explained that wasn't necessary and showed her Acts 15.*
>
> *The following Sunday, Resurrection Day, I preached on John 20, where Thomas was transformed from disbelief to faith in Messiah's deity. Immediately after the service ended, Sheila came to me and said with tears in her eyes, 'I'm ready!'*
>
> *Sheila is growing in her faith. Pray for her as she shares with her parents who now are also attending the congregation.[39]*

On March 1, 1989, Michael Rydelnik was promoted to Regional Director for the Northeast Region of the Mission, replacing Sam Nadler who was appointed Executive Director of the Mission. Shortly after he became the Regional Director for the Northeast, Michael gave the following report of the Region's activities:

> *One minute I'm in Central Park*
> *Then I'm down on Delancey Street,*
> *Up on the Bowery to St. Marks,*
> *There's a syncopated beat.*
> *I'm street wise, I can improvise.*
> *I'm street smart, I've got New York City heart!*

> *Recently I took my sons to see Disney's Oliver & Co., an animated update of Dickens' Oliver Twist. The Artful Dodger character, with the voice of Billy Joel, sang the above lyrics. As I listened, I couldn't help but think of our New York City staff.*
>
> *The missionaries we recruit for Chosen People Ministries staff must all have a passion for godliness, a courageous spirit, and a deep burden for Jewish people. But for the New York City staff we look for one more quality—we look for people who are 'street wise' and 'street smart!' Men and women who can communicate the good news in the rough and tumble city of New York, the greatest Jewish city in the world.*
>
> *As a native New Yorker, it's easy for me to spot someone who has New York City heart. It would have to be someone like Israel Cohen, who affably talks to dozens of Jewish people at the Kings Plaza Shopping Mall in Brooklyn while his wife, Judy, shops.*
>
> *Last Fall, after Yom Kippur, Israel would ask Jewish people if they had attended synagogue for the High Holy Days. When they said 'yes,' he asked if they were certain their sins were forgiven. 'We can only hope so!' was the common reply, to which Israel responded by showing from Scripture how everyone can know so. New York City is the only place where there are so many Jews that even Israel won't run out of enough people to talk to.*
>
> *Or Irving Salzman, whose quiet demeanor may cause people to miss his holy chuzpah (boldness). Once, while Irv and some others distributed literature at a Brooklyn subway station, an anti-missionary sought to discourage passers-by*

from taking the pamphlets by shouting 'These are missionaries—don't read this!' By and large he was succeeding, until Irving, in an equally strong voice, spoke up: 'Think for yourselves, this man doesn't trust you to think for yourself.?' The subway riders began to ignore the anti-missionary and take Irving's tracts.

You'd spot Stew Weinisch as a native New Yorker even though he is currently a congregation planter in the Connecticut suburbs of New York. Besides being famous for his biking and paddle ball skills, Stew is equally noted for his arrest on Christmas Eve for giving out tracts in front of Bloomingdale's. Stew thought it was his constitutional right to be there, and by the way, so did the judge.

Whether it's Rob Styler, who can match one-liners with any New York street comic, or Larry Feldman who can direct you to the best kosher delis in Brooklyn or Manhattan, or Elaine Fenchel who carries Bibles, tracts, and her lunch in her New York luggage (i.e. a shopping bag), these are all people with New York City heart. What is more, they are all people who have a heart for New York City.

Congregation Planting—We start Bible-believing, Messiah-centered congregations that reflect the Jewish culture around them. In the last several years, four such congregations have been planted in the suburban areas of Westchester, North Jersey, Southern Connecticut, and Long Island.

Bible Studies—We have several evangelistic Bible studies around New York City. Please pray as we seek to develop one in Brooklyn.

Tract Distribution—Thousands upon thousands of Gospel leaflets are distributed weekly around New York City. In 1988 alone, our missionaries distributed 223,280 pieces of Gospel literature. Whether in shopping areas, at train stations, or ball parks, the good news is faithfully proclaimed.

Questionnaires—In malls and neighborhoods our staff and volunteers reach out with religious questionnaires, sharing Messiah Yeshua with those who respond.

Advertising—Our ads appear regularly in local papers and even on the radio. We announce special services as well as the Good News itself.

Special Services—High Holy Day services, Chanukah and Purim parties, and Passover Seders are used to proclaim Jesus as Messiah and Savior. For example, four Jewish people trusted in the Lord at the Long Island Passover Seder in New York last April [c.1989].

Book Tables—At the World Trade Center, Grand Central Station, Pennsylvania Station, and on the streets of Midtown Manhattan, …book tables allow inquiring Jewish people to take literature and speak with our staff and volunteers and Yeshua the Messiah.

Follow-up—Our Chosen People magazine family, local churches, and other believers give us names of interested Jewish people. Our staff diligently meets and shares with all these contacts to help them understand and receive the Gospel.[40]

Two additional workers came on staff to assist Sam Nadler with the task of sharing the Gospel with the Jewish community of the Northeast—Irving Salzman, and Rob Styler (the reader will learn more about Rob Styler in the chapter on Canada).

IRVING SALZMAN

Irving Salzman was born in Montreal, Canada in September 1959. He joined the staff of the Mission as a part-time worker for the Brooklyn branch while he was attending the Philadelphia College of the Bible. In 1987, after he completed his theological training, he became a full-time missionary. In sharing his testimony with the readers of *The Chosen People* magazine, Irving said:

My father was born in Poland in an observant home. His father, a devout, pious man who was a Torah reader in the synagogue, died when my father was months old.

Some of my ancestors were rabbis, and perhaps if World War II had not broken out, things would have been different in my father's life and in mine. But my father's religious training was interrupted by the war when he was fourteen years old, and for five years he was on the run throughout Europe, hiding from the Nazis.

Eventually he emigrated from Europe to Israel, where he fought in the War of Independence. He then came to Canada, where he met my mother, an English Jewess.

Both my parents were committed to raising my brother and me in a home where Judaism was evident. But because my father's religious upbringing was interrupted, we didn't have the heavy religious obligations that were traditionally 'old world.'

So it was that we lit the Sabbath candle and observed the holidays and my brother and I went to Hebrew school from the time we were small.

Although it makes sense now to say that my father's Holocaust experiences should have greatly colored my childhood, he exhibited great love by sheltering us from the bitterness of the tragedy.

Instead, I was greatly influenced by my parents' love of Jewishness and Judaism. From a very young age, I understood that being Jewish meant something special.

I believed in God and His Messiah when I was very young. My first remembrance of this was when I was about five. I had gone to bed as usual, reciting the Sh'ma as my evening prayer. I had hardly fallen asleep when I woke up from a bad dream which I knew had to do with death.

Frightened, wanting to be comforted, I crawled out of my bed and went off to find my parents.

My father gently reassured me, 'Don't worry. One day Messiah will come and raise people from the dead,' he promised.

As young as I was, there was great comfort in hearing about this wonderful Messiah. It was a promise I always held dear to me.

During the next few years, my knowledge of God came from the synagogue and the Hebrew classes I took after my regular school. About the time I was beginning to prepare for my Bar Mitzvah, my father decided he wanted me to go into a yeshiva for my high school studies.

The yeshiva was run under the auspices of the Lubbavichers (an ultraorthodox, evangelistic community). While there, I fell in love with this ordered, disciplined Judaism I was being taught.

There was something very peaceful and beautiful to me in the rules we observed, and it was a joy to learn about my heritage. Studying God and observing His Law gave me a sense of purpose.

Before long, I adopted the religious observances I saw around me and took to wearing a yarmulke (skull cap) and tsisis (ritual fringes) at all times.

Because the dietary laws were important to me, my parents began to observe kashrut (kosher laws) in our home. Religious observances had now become part of my life style rather than just part of my studies.

Along with my deep interest in Judaism, I made another discovery during this time: I was gifted with a very good memory and had the other skills necessary to be a Torah reader in the synagogue.

A Torah reader is a skilled individual held in great esteem in the Jewish community. Most synagogues read the five books of Moses in a cycle each year. The books are divided into fifty-two sections, one to be read each week, and the Torah reader is the person who reads them in the synagogue.

Being a Torah reader is a difficult task, requiring as many as six hours of preparation a week, because the section must be read from the scroll, which does not include the dots and dashes that make up the vowels in Hebrew. The weekly portion must also be chanted in a prescribed method, according to specified musical notes.

From the time I was in high school, and almost every week until only a few months ago, my Saturdays were spent in various synagogues, reading these lengthy Hebrew portions for the congregations.

Unfortunately, I had very little time to become involved in the meaning of the words I was memorizing, since the mechanics were so difficult and the preparation so intense. Even though I deeply enjoyed the readings, being a Torah reader was more of a challenge than an inspiration.

After I graduated from high school, I went to college, a year in Canada and a year in Israel. After Israel, I went to school in New York and then moved back to Montreal.

Through all this, I had lost some of the rigidity of the Jewishness I knew, and although I still had a deep sense of identity, I found myself drifting through life with no great purpose at hand.

Sometimes, to kill time, I would call special phone lines where you called in and met someone over the phone, usually hoping to meet someone of the opposite sex with whom you might form a relationship.

One day I called the phone lines and was connected to a sixteen-year-old named Peter. At first I thought I would just talk for a moment and then hang up, but Peter turned out to be so opinionated and interesting that we talked for hours.

He mentioned to me that he was born again and that he called the phone lines to talk to people about what he believed.

I was fascinated. It was the first time anyone had said that there was anything worth sharing in Christianity. Though I wasn't searching for anything spiritual, I was curious.

Until that time, I had always assumed that Christianity was mostly symbols: vast churches with crosses, nuns, priests, images that made me a little frightened to think about because they all represented a forbidden 'unwelcome' sign to the Jews.

Peter and I began to talk frequently, and at one point we made a pact: If he could show me that what he believed was true, I would believe it also. Likewise, if I could convince him that what I believed was true, he would believe that.

In fact, both of us were thoroughly convinced that there was no possible way the other was right.

Nevertheless, over the next two years, I watched my beliefs slowly fade away, which was traumatic. Everything I had built my life on was being shattered.

It wasn't any one thing he said, but rather bits of things that made me realize my faith was not as solid as Peter's. His was based on something of which he was so certain, and mine ...it was based more on tradition and heritage.

More and more, I found myself thinking that an intelligent, educated Jew could well consider Jesus (Yeshua) to be the Messiah.

'Except,' I often told myself, 'if it is so right, the rabbis would have believed it long ago.'

I found myself listening for other confirmations of what he was telling me. Weekly I was calling a taped Bible message (a ministry of Chosen People worker Winnie Marriner) and started to listen to those around me for other evidences from the Scripture. I wanted to hear more evidence that this was true.

Then one night, something different happened. I was stretched out comfortably on my bed half-listening, half-thinking as Peter and I spoke. Peter asked if he could read me something, as he often did during our conversations. This time, the words he read entranced me.

'Blessed are the poor in spirit, for theirs is the kingdom of heaven. Blessed are those who mourn, for they will be comforted. Blessed are the meek, for they will inherit the earth. Blessed are those who hunger and thirst for righteousness, for they will be filled.'

Peter read me the Sermon on the Mount, and at the end of it, I knew the speaker was no mere rabbi, no man like all others. The beauty, wisdom and depth of those words called out to me across the reserve that had been in my heart.

I told Peter how beautiful I found those words, but even more, I began to notice that something was different. I knew I could never look at Yeshua the same way again.

Shortly after that, Peter moved and we lost touch for a while.

Gradually, with no great revelation, I realized that within myself I had accepted that Yeshua was the Jewish Messiah.

I continued to work at the synagogue as a Torah reader, and I appeared very much the same person on the outside. Yet in my heart, I recognized that something momentous had occurred.

Then, almost a year after my last conversation with Peter, he called again. As we spoke, he recognized that the tenor of our discussion was different.

'You believe, don't you?' he asked me.

To this stranger, whom I had known so long but had never met, I admitted the truth.

'Yes, but I'm afraid to say I believe. I don't know if I can be truly sincere, if I truly want Him to have control of my life.'

'You can only do what you know best at any given time,' Peter wisely counseled. 'God will give you the power you need to believe more. Would you like to receive Jesus now? Personally? We can pray together on the phone.'

'No, I don't think I want to pray on the phone,' I answered, feeling somewhat embarrassed and awkward.

'Let me call you back.'

The phone went dead, and for just a moment I hesitated. What would this mean in my life? Do I really want this? Can I live up to such a commitment? Could I offer myself to Him and mean it?

I knew that to have salvation, atonement and eternal life, I needed to receive the Messiah. Silently I prayed.

Minutes later I called Peter back and told him what I had done. I did not feel any different or see any great flashes of light. But I knew in my heart, and Peter assured me, that God was faithful to my prayers.

Shortly after turning my life over to the Messiah, I contacted Winnie Marriner and attended a fellowship meeting at her house, where I met many of The Chosen People workers who serve in the Northeast.

About three years later, they encouraged me to attend Bible college, which is what I'm doing now, as I prepare to enter the ministry.[41]

Because of his unique background, Irving has a special burden to reach his orthodox Jewish brethren with the Gospel; his ministry with the Mission has been among the orthodox Jews in Brooklyn. A report of his ministry among the "ultra-orthodox" Jews appeared in the April 1992 issue of *The Chosen People*. It stated:

...Irving has continued to seek opportunities to witness to these men (and women) who, with their austere black dress, flowing beards, and side curls, seem forever stranded in medieval Europe.

> 'One of the things we've done in the New York City ministry,' Irving says, 'is to set aside time each week to pray for the Orthodox.'
>
> Since the New York staff began praying, Irving has noted a marked increase of interest in the Gospel by these latter day descendants of the Pharisees.
>
> Ministry to those steeped in Talmud and ultra-Orthodox Jewish tradition is a slow-going, long-term affair. Even the mention of the name Jesus is enough to evoke hostility and/or violence.
>
> One Orthodox young man came up to Irving Salzman and Israel Cohen's literature table in Grand Central Station.
>
> 'We spoke in Yiddish for half an hour,' says Irving. 'He had a pretty good knowledge of the Old Testament ...a lot of the Orthodox don't.'
>
> Irving guided the man to Isaiah 53. Reading out of the Hebrew, Irving showed him the passage that dealt with the Suffering Servant's death on behalf of Israel.
>
> The young man protested saying the passage said only that the Servant was 'pierced through,' not killed.
>
> 'His translational skills impressed me,' says Irving. 'I had to be sharp to talk with this guy.'
>
> After Irving pointed out the verse about the Servant being 'cut off out of the land of the living' (Isaiah 53:8), the young Orthodox man took a few minutes to read it in Hebrew.
>
> 'You're right,' he finally exclaimed. 'The Servant does die.'
>
> Noting the man's curiosity and lack of hostility, Irving further shared Leviticus 17:11 ('...the life of the flesh is in the blood . . .'), talking about atonement for several minutes.
>
> One recent sunny Saturday afternoon, Irving Salzman and Israel Cohen were doing some ministry among the Russian Jews in Brighton Beach, Brooklyn, when two young Orthodox students stopped to talk.
>
> 'I like going back to my Yeshiva (Hebrew school) personality,' admits Irving with obvious satisfaction. 'I like sharing with them on their own level—using their terms and expression, like calling God the way they call Him, Ha Shem [the name].
>
> 'It's like they're seeing a mirror-image of themselves,' says Irving. 'They see I have the Yiddish background, I've studied in an Orthodox Yeshiva, I talk like them, yet I've arrived at a different belief.'
>
> As the discussion wore on, these Torah students had to admit they didn't have the Old Testament knowledge that Irving had.
>
> 'They couldn't answer me,' says Irving. 'And they couldn't say I didn't have a good Jewish education.'[42]

While many Orthodox Jews have approached Irving Salzman and Israel Cohen with questions, others have violently protested against their witness. In another report in *The Chosen People* magazine, readers were given insight into God's protection over these courageous missionaries:

> On a cool, spring Saturday afternoon, Israel Cohen and Irving Salzman from our New York outreach, found out how 'hot' it could get while passing out tracts on Avenue M in Brooklyn.
>
> As they were handing out the literature, a Hasidic Jew approached Irving to talk. Another came up to Israel and started to push him. The pushing continued up the steps of the building until Israel was being pushed against a wall.
>
> The whole scene was observed by a N.Y Transit Authority policeman who stopped the situation and asked what was going on. Israel told him that he was being stopped from passing out tracts and that his Constitutional rights were being infringed upon. The officer asked Israel if he wanted to press charges, but Israel replied that all he wanted to do was pass out his tracts.
>
> The original transit officer was joined by several others who guarded Israel and Irving while they handed out tracts. Outside of this protective circle several Hasidic Jews began demonstrating.
>
> With all the commotion and the police, almost all the people passing by wanted the materials that were being handed out. Israel and Irving are praising God for His protection and the increase in people reached.[43]

Irving Salzman continues to faithfully share the Gospel message with the Orthodox Jews of New York City.

Thus, during the nearly nine years that Sam Nadler served as the Northeast Regional Director, both the missionary staff and the missionary outreach of the region were expanded. Under Sam's leadership, the missionary staff was reaching the Jewish community with the Gospel as well as challenging Christians of the Northeast to witness to their Jewish friends and neighbors.

After the Search Committee of the Mission had narrowed the search for an Executive Director down to two candidates—John Bell and Sam Nadler—the Board proceeded by embarking upon a series of personal interviews with the candidates, as well as by asking that the candidates complete a battery of psychological tests and evaluations by Christian psychologists and psychiatrists.

Choosing between the two men was a difficult task. Each man had his own unique gifts and strengths, as well as weaknesses. The Directors were cognizant of the fact that the choice could not be made without one candidate experiencing disappointment; it was possible that the choice might even result in the resignation of the man not chosen. Yet the process of selection was important to the Mission and to the Board; it was a historic departure from what had been done in the past. By their action, the Board was setting new policy and direction for the selection of future leaders for the Mission. They were desirous that their selection be the person God wanted to use to lead the organization to even greater victories for the Lord.

A NEW EXECUTIVE DIRECTOR APPOINTED

The Search Committee proposed that Sam Nadler be interviewed by the full Board at their November 18, 1988 meeting. This proposal was acted upon. After a lengthy interview by the Directors, Sam was unanimously elected to the position of Executive Director.[44] His position was to become effective March 1, 1989. On that same date, Sam was to be appointed to the Board of Directors of the Mission.[45]

When John Bell learned of the Board's decision to appoint Sam Nadler to the Executive Director's position, he requested a transfer back to Chicago. He felt he could not continue in his position as Missionary Director. The Board granted John's request, and agreed to assist him with the relocation costs.[46] However, John never assumed a position for the Mission once he had returned to Chicago. Instead, effective May 29, 1989, he submitted his resignation as Missionary Director of Chosen People Ministries. He took a pastorate in the suburbs of Chicago, where he continues to serve at the time of this writing.[47]

NEW BOARD MEMBERS ELECTED

During 1988 consideration was also being given to adding to the membership of the Board, and the author, along with other members of the Board, began interviewing prospective candidates who could help the directors fill the long range goals, plans, and statement of purpose of the Mission as contributing members of a working Board.

One candidate interviewed was Mrs. Jean Wheeler. Jean is a trained and licensed psychotherapist. At the time, she maintained an established and thriving counseling service. She also served on the faculty of King's College, in Briarcliff Manor, New York. She was a member of the Christian Association for Psychological Studies, Northern Westchester Mental Health; the American Association for Counseling and Development; the Association for Religious and Value Issues in Counseling.

Jean was invited to the January 27, 1989 meeting of the Board. She was unanimously elected to Board membership at the June 1, 1989 meeting of the Board. Jean has become an invaluable help on the Personnel Committee and Appraisal Committee of the Board.

Another candidate interviewed and elected to the Board was Mr. Darrell Winrich. Darrell was invited to meet with members of the Board at their January 26, 1990 meeting. He was unanimously elected to the Board at the June 8, 1990 meeting.

Darrell is an investment counselor. He founded Winrich Capital Management in 1976, and from 1968-1985 he served as a well-known financial and economic commentator for KABC Radio in Los Angeles. He came to know the Lord in the spring of 1950, through the witness of a fellow student at the College of the Pacific. That student—Carolee—later became his wife.

Throughout his adult life, Darrell has been actively involved in a variety of Christian ministries and he has served on boards of a number of Christian organizations, including Southern California Foundation, California Lutheran Homes, and the International Bible Society to name a few.

As a contributing member of the Board of Chosen People Ministries, Darrell has served on the Finance Committee, the Pension Committee, and the Audit Committee. His expertise in the area of finances has been of tremendous help in building a strong financial base for the Mission's current programs and personnel.

With the appointment of Sam Nadler as Executive Director of the Mission, and with his appointment to the Board of Directors, the author began to devote a great amount of thought and prayer to his own role as President of the Mission. Having served for nearly twelve years as President of the Mission, in a situation in which his fellow Board members served as employees of the Mission but were accountable to the Board, but not to him, he understood all too well the difficulties which both he and Sam would be facing. Dual leadership of the Mission was a situation the author had worked hard to change, but was faced with once again. This time the role was reversed. The author, not Daniel Fuchs, had control of the "communications" of the Mission (the magazine, fund raising, etc.)—the vehicles through which the vision and the image of the organization were communicated to the Christian and Jewish public. It was a department that directly impacted the support and income of the Mission. Sam Nadler, on the other hand, had been given responsibility for the expenses of the Mission, and the task of administrating Mission personnel and programs. The author was *well familiar* with the fact that if the support did not come in for the Mission's programs and personnel, Sam would be held accountable.

Through prayer and continued examination of the job descriptions which the Board had so carefully and prayerfully drawn up, the author became convinced that in spite of each man's best efforts, eventually a time would come when conflict would arise. Years of previous experience had taught the author the truth of the words: "it is the little foxes that spoil the vine!"[48] No organization, or family, can have two heads. With this conviction, the author believed that the Board and the staff needed to rally to the support of one leader who could set the vision for the Mission—that man would be Sam Nadler.

The need for just one leader was made very apparent on a trip to South America which the author and Sam Nadler made together in December 1989, not many months after Sam's appointment as Executive Director. It was Sam's first trip to South America. The author, on the other hand, had been there on numerous occasions during his years, as he had participated in Bible conference ministry throughout South America and as he had attempted to help Rev. Roberto Passo develop the work in South America. Although the author took care to introduce Sam as the new Executive Director of the Mission—the man who was now in charge of the foreign branches of the Mission, including South America—Sam was perceived as the author's "assistant." The author's title as "President" conveyed that idea of authority, while the title "Executive Director" conveyed the idea of limited authority. It became clear that Sam did not have authority over one of the most important areas of the ministry—the area of communications.

Reflecting upon the South American trip and upon the Mission—its history and its future—God began to bring about a conviction within the author's heart to speak to the members of the Appraisal Committee of the Board about placing Sam Nadler in charge of the entire Mission operations, and about conferring upon him the title President in addition to being the Chief Executive Officer. It was the author's conviction that this was the only way the Mission would continue to grow and develop; it was the only way the Board could exercise proper management over its President and Chief Executive Officer.

The author shared his convictions and ideas with members of the Appraisal Committee, and after a time of discussion and prayer they, too, agreed. At the January 26, 1990 Board Meeting it was agreed that an ad hoc committee would be formed to work out a transition in leadership and in transferring the title of President from the author to Sam Nadler.[49] The ad hoc committee, with the assistance and input of Sam and the author, drew up a proposal for the transition which was to become effective January 1, 1991.

There were changes being made in other departments of the Mission as well. Roy Adams submitted his resignation as Executive Vice-President, effective November 15, 1990. Following his resignation, Roy returned to his native Canada. He and his wife, Ella, later moved from Canada to Charleston, South Carolina. Roy remains an active member of the Board of Directors of the Mission.

A New Administrative Director—Bill Caldwell

On November 15, 1990 Paul W. (Bill) Caldwell was hired as the Administrative Director of the Mission.

Bill Caldwell was born on April 14, 1949 in Alpharetta, Georgia—the oldest of three children. When Bill was five years old his parents divorced. His mother remarried within a year. Although his stepfather was the only real father he knew, and many of the values Bill holds today were instilled in him by his stepfather, it was Bill's grandparents and step-grandparents who had the greatest spiritual influence upon his life. They were all Christians; each held strong convictions about Christ and about the Christian faith.

Bill began attending a strict Southern Baptist church at the age of six. One month prior to his eighth birthday, after a particularly stirring message, the Lord convicted Bill of his need of a Savior. He claimed John 14:6 as a promise made to him, and accepted the Lord Jesus as his personal Savior. For the next few years Bill was very active in the youth activities of his church and it was during this period of his life that he received the basic foundations of his faith as godly men and women influenced him.

When Bill was thirteen years of age, his mother was again divorced and the family returned to Atlanta, Georgia. For the next five years, confused by the disruption in his family and about life in general, Bill began to rebel against his mother and against her authority over him.

In high school, Bill became more interested in sports than he was in his studies. However, even in this, God's hand was upon him; his coach was a Christian, a real one. He took Bill under his wing and helped him get a scholarship to the Presbyterian College in Clinton, South Carolina. God also brought Catherine into his life—the girl he later married.

In College Bill once again came under the influence of Christian coaches who willingly spent time counseling him and helping him. In loving and practical ways, they demonstrated their Christian faith to him. Yet despite their witness Bill was determined to live life his way. He graduated college [c.1971] with a B.A. in English, and in December 1971 he enlisted in the army; he was commissioned as a 2nd Lieutenant.

Although thoughts of God and of following His truths was the furthest thing from Bill's mind during his military career, God had His eye upon His child! In September 1976, having achieved the rank of captain in under five years in the armed forces, Bill resigned his commission and moved his family to Racine, Wisconsin where his wife, Cathy, had family. Both he and Cathy knew they needed something, although they weren't sure just what that "something" was.

Through the testimony of the many Christian members of Cathy's family, and through the influence of the Bible-believing pastor and church they began to attend, Bill and Cathy began to realize that the "something" they had been searching for was a relationship with God, and they rededicated themselves to Him as Lord. Although Bill was employed by SC Johnson Wax Company, and was on the fast track of their executive management team and vice-presidency within the company, in the months following his rededication to following Jesus as his Lord, he found time to serve as a Sunday School teacher, High School Youth Coordinator, an Elder, a Deacon, and chairman of various committees in the church.

Both Bill and Cathy felt happy and fulfilled—until the day when Bill's doctors told him that he had cancer. During the next several months their faith was tested. Their prayers were answered in an amazing way when God granted Bill a complete healing. Knowing what God had done in his life, and with his trust in God strengthened and deepened, Bill wanted to express his thanks to God by sharing His Truth and His love with those who were still in darkness. Cathy shared his desire to enter some type of full-time Christian ministry. The question was, where and how?

God answered the Caldwells' prayers when they attended a conference where Sam Nadler was speaking. Sam and Bill became immediate friends, and Bill began to share Sam's burden for reaching Jewish people with the Gospel. When the Mission reorganized, and Sam was appointed Executive Director, and then President, there was a need for an Administrative Director for the Mission. It was then that God laid Bill Caldwell's name on Sam's heart. Bill had all of the qualifications and more!

When Sam shared the Mission's need with Bill, he promised that he and his family would pray about the matter. To Bill's surprise, even his children encouraged him to take the position with the Mission if he believed that was where God wanted him to serve. Bill Caldwell joined the staff of Chosen People Ministries and moved his family to Charlotte during the Fall of 1990. Since then, God has used Bill to oversee the administration of the Mission, worldwide, as well as in personal ministry as he speaks in churches and Bible studies for the Mission, and witnesses to Jews and Gentiles alike about the marvelous grace of God.

The President's Baton is Passed

The transition of Sam Nadler to the position of President of the Mission was to take effect on January 1, 1991. In preparing his statement for the donors and friends of the Mission, the author wrote the following article for the January 1991 issue of *The Chosen People* magazine:

'There is a time for everything, and a season for every activity under heaven.' So wrote the preacher in Ecclesiastes 3:1. The emphasis of this verse is on the positive. There is a right time for everything. This is as true in nature as it is for each of us individually. It is true in the life of an organization, as well as in the life of a nation. Things done in their proper time produce good results.

Too often within the life of churches and religious or mission organizations there is resistance to change. Individuals who occupy leadership positions cling to their positions long after the time and need for change. As a result, churches split, organizations falter, and God is not glorified.

Each of us in ministry, and especially those who are in leadership positions, should have able and competent younger spiritual leaders in training, individuals to whom we can turn over our leadership responsibilities at a proper time. None of us should make ourselves indispensable. Paul gave Timothy good advice when he said, 'Commit this to faithful men who will be able to teach others also' (2 Tim. 2:2). Younger leadership groomed and developed within the work of any organization is the future of that organization.

Since 1979 I have had the privilege of serving as the President of Chosen People Ministries. In September of last year, Grace and I completed our twenty-fifth year of service with this mission. It seems like just yesterday when the late Dr. Daniel Fuchs, then Missionary Director of Chosen People Ministries (formerly called The American Board of Missions to the Jews), interviewed us and asked that we work in the Los Angeles branch. Excited and enthusiastic and knowing that God was leading and directing our lives, we became missionaries in Southern California. Little did we realize then, that thirteen years later I would be asked to serve as President of the ministry. God's timing is always perfect, and, if we are willing to be led by Him, He always prepares in advance a place of ministry for His servants.

During our years of service with Chosen People Ministries, we have experienced, and I know that many of you have seen, God's hand of blessing upon this mission. Through the years there have been many changes, as we have sought to keep abreast of the changing needs of the Jewish community and to be wise stewards of God's resources. But our message and our purpose have always remained the same: To bring the Gospel to the Jew first, and also to the Gentile.

Over the years we have seen increasing numbers of Jewish people coming to faith in their Messiah, and we praise God! It is an evidence of God's blessing upon our methodology in witnessing and upon our missionaries' faithful proclamation of the Gospel.

But one of the greatest blessings to me, personally, has been working with the younger men whom God has directed to our work. Many of them are Jewish believers, Bible college and/or seminary trained. They are evangelists, church planters, able expositors of the Word of God; men who are able to teach and to train others. These younger men are the future of Chosen People Ministries into the decade of the 1990's and beyond—until our Lord returns.

With such wonderful, spiritual, creative leadership in place, and after much prayer, I felt the time was right for me to ask our Board of Directors to allow me to step aside as the President of the ministry. I asked the members of our Board to prayerfully consider the appointment of our present Executive Director, Sam Nadler, as President, effective January 1, 1991. I then asked the Board to consider reassigning my present duties and responsibilities so that I would have more time to write, speak, teach, and use my years of experience in Jewish evangelism to help train others. Such a reassignment would also allow me the opportunity to visit with some of you (our Chosen People family), to answer your questions about the ministry and to share ways in which you can become more personally involved with us in the great task of reaching Jewish people with the Gospel. Through the years, Grace and I have had many requests for visits, but our ministry responsibilities did not permit us time to do so. Now, by God's grace, we will.

After several months of prayer, evaluation, and thoughtful planning for the future, our Board of Directors unanimously accepted my endorsement of Sam Nadler as the new President of Chosen People Ministries. They also unanimously agreed to the reassignment of my duties and responsibilities and asked that I continue to serve as President Emeritus.

I am not retiring. I will remain active on the Board of Directors, and I will remain active in the work of Chosen People Ministries. With the reassignment of my duties, I will continue writing for the Chosen People magazine. . . , and I will continue to answer your questions on the Bible and on related Jewish subjects. Additionally, I will be speaking, doing more writing, paying those visits I mentioned, and so forth.

I believe the time is right for change and that this is a wonderful answer to prayer. Too often Christian leaders tend to view their organizations or churches as their own work (rather than God's work) and, therefore, become unwilling to relinquish the authority and leadership to the younger men.

This is not my work—it is God's work. Chosen People Ministries is a mission that was raised up by God and has been led by godly men and women seeking to do God's will in God's way, so that the Gospel is shared with the Jewish people.[50]

While the transition in the leadership of the Mission went smoothly, change always brings more change. There have been many adjustments within the Mission since the appointment of Sam Nadler as Executive Director of Chosen People Ministries in January 1989.

Not only was there a change in the leadership of the Mission, there was a change in the leadership of the Board of Directors. James Straub, who had been serving as the acting Chairman of the Board since the death of Daniel Fuchs in May 1988, felt that he could no longer serve in that capacity. Several Directors, including the author, were considered for the position. However, after the retirement of Daniel Fuchs on May 1, 1983 it was decided that the position of Chairman of the Board would no longer be a salaried position. In electing the author to the position, the position would have reverted once again to a salaried employee of the Corporation (Mission). Some members of the Board saw no problem with this. Others, including the author, did.

The author was flattered and honored in being considered for the position as Chairman of the Board. However, in giving consideration and prayer to the long-range ramifications of holding the position, the author realized that in accepting the position he would be vulnerable to many of the mistakes of the past. If the Mission was to continue to expand into the next century, it was essential that the mistakes of the past not be repeated; it was clear that the Mission needed to be controlled by a volunteer Board of Directors rather than by an employee controlled Board.

With this in mind, the Board revised its By-laws to state that the position of Chairman of the Board cannot be held by a salaried employee of the corporation.[51] Additionally, to correct problems created by "self-perpetuating" board membership, the Board changed its by-laws to read: "…The chairman shall hold office for three (3) years and shall not be eligible to serve more than two (2) consecutive terms."[52]

More recently [c. 1993] the Board established an ad hoc committee to study and to submit to the full Board a recommendation to change the membership of the Board from a "self-perpetuating board" to a "term membership board," allowing for a rotation policy to rotate members off the Board after a fixed number of terms. Such a policy allows for the development of new board members and the infusion of "new blood" and "spiritual insight" from a greater cross-section of the Jewish and Gentile Christian community.

Board and Staff Changes

Thus, in a historic departure from the past, the Board of Directors, desiring to have a volunteer Director serving as Chairman of the Board, unanimously elected Dr. John Pretlove as Chairman at the January 1991 Board meeting. As Chairman, John Pretlove has been a capable, dedicated, progressive leader of the Board—both in areas of spiritual guidance and in practical policy decisions. His guidance has already helped to stabilize the Mission and position it for ministry in the next century—or until our Lord returns.

Soon after assuming his role as Executive Director of the Mission, Sam Nadler began to experience *déjà vu* of his experience when he had been appointed Regional Director for the Northeast. Once again, he received the resignations of several staff members.

As already mentioned, John Bell, Missionary Director, had already resigned in May 1989. Dr. Rocky Freeman, Regional Director for the Southwest, resigned.[53] Shortly thereafter, Howard Silverman, who was to be transferred to Pennsylvania, resigned. Avner Boskey, Missionary in Charge in Israel, resigned. Roy Schwarcz and Galen Banashak from the Chicago ministry submitted their resignations, as did Mitch Triestman in Philadelphia and Tom Huckel in Philadelphia. Barry Berger, National Ministries representative for the Midwest region, also resigned. When a new Director of Communications was hired, John Singer, Editor and Art Director, resigned. In Canada, Ben Volman, the missionary in Toronto, resigned. In Denver, Eliezer and Sarah Urbach, retired. Sid Stern, missionary in California, also retired.

The Board fully supported Sam in the decisions made, and the policies and recommendations put forth, and although they did their best to assure the remaining workers on staff that the changes they were hearing about were a natural part of re-structuring when new leadership is put into place, many of the workers had uncertainty and doubts about their own futures with the Mission.

The staff retreat (which also included Board members and their spouses) held in December 1991 helped to alleviate the fears and confusion felt by some of the staff members. But for others, the retreat was a reminder to them of the many friends and co-workers not present; it therefore further polarized their feelings and attitudes toward the Mission and toward the Board. This led to additional resignations in 1992. But the staff that remained were committed to serving with the Mission and to diligently doing all *they* could to see the ministry expand further in its efforts to reach Jewish people with the Gospel, and God was preparing new workers to step in and carry on the vision and the message of the Gospel to His chosen people.

Not all of the resignations were directly related to Sam's appointment to the leadership of the Mission. In a case or two there was an indirect relationship, in that Sam's appointment as President and Chief Executive Officer indicated to them that any opportunity for them to be selected for the position in the future appeared out of the question. (Even missionaries and Christian workers have dreams of future leadership possibilities!) For others, the changes within the Mission brought about uncertainty and apprehension, and they began to look for other areas of ministry in God's vineyard. There were others who, although they were in total agreement with the policies and the direction and vision of the Mission, were simply ready to move on, and thus they submitted their resignations.

In answer to prayer, God directed new workers to the Mission. Mr. David Henschen was hired in September 1991 as the Mission's Stewardship Director, replacing Mr. Wes Jones who retired and Jack Anderson, who resigned.

David Henschen Joins the Staff

David Henschen was born on March 25, 1960 in Davenport, Iowa. His grandparents, who lived next door, attended a Lutheran church and they faithfully encouraged David to attend with them. In sharing his testimony with readers of *The Chosen People* magazine, David spoke about the influence of his grandparents in his life. He stated:

'They were my spiritual parents,…' 'Through their influence I came to faith at 14 and was a leader in the youth group throughout high school.'

Soon after David's spiritual birth, he participated in a course on lay ministry for evangelism where he was taught the essentials of evangelism. Going door to door and sharing the Gospel, David made an impact for the Lord among his fellow students.

Summing up this period of his life before college, David recalls, 'I experienced real growth at an early age.'

College, he admits, was not a time of spiritual growth. At the University of Iowa he began to drift away from the Lord and to follow a 'me-first' philosophy. 'God allowed me to experience the "fruits" of this philosophy for several years.'

During this time David met and married his wife, Nadine, who also was a Christian but who lacked a firm grounding in the Word. After three years of marriage their problems seemed insurmountable.

'I fell to my knees one day and cried out to God for help,' David admits. 'Remarkably, He removed the scales from my eyes.'

David mourned the years he and Nadine had lost, but not for long.

'As God's lordship was reinstated in our lives, He began healing our wounds and afflictions,' recalls David. 'Since then we have grown to the point of leading and discipling other couples in Messiah.'

While the stitches of their relationship were being knit together, their first child was born prematurely. Weighing under one pound, the infant died. It was a time of immense struggle. Miraculously, their delicate relationship with each other and the Lord deepened.

Through all of this, David was progressing in his career, building a solid reputation in a field that has seen the lightning rise and fall of many—the world of finance. By 1987 he was vice president and assistant branch manager of Shearson Lehman Brothers in Austin, Texas, specializing in wills and estate and tax planning for individuals and foundations. Previously he had served as a vice president at Paine Webber and as a financial consultant at Merrill Lynch.

Then several years ago David and Nadine sensed God's leading them into full-time Christian service.

'After nine years' experience as a financial consultant on Wall Street, I felt God asking me to put my skills to work for Him,' David says.

'I want to go wherever God wants us to go,' he remembers Nadine telling him one night.

After two years of prayer, the Henschens knew God was directing them to Chosen People Ministries.[54]

The Mission's Investment Fund—how it was to be used, as well as the long range plans for the fund—had been the subject of discussion and debate by the Board for many years. But in December 1990, just eight months prior to the hiring of David Henschen as the Mission's Stewardship Director, *The Chosen People* Ministries Foundation was established. The purpose of the CPM Foundation was to provide a funding arm for Chosen People Ministries; it was to be the organization holding the investment funds of the Mission. The interest generated by the funds are designated for the ministry and programs of the Mission. After David Henschen joined the staff, he was appointed as the Administrative Director of the Foundation. The Foundation is governed by the same Board of Directors as Chosen People Ministries and it continues to be a vital part of the financial funding for Chosen People Ministries.

In the Spring of 1993, David Henschen was appointed to the position of Director of Development for the Mission, bringing both the Stewardship Department and Communications Department of the Mission under his direct supervision.

With the funding arm of the Mission in place, Sam and the Board began the work of rebuilding the staff of the Mission and expanding the evangelistic outreach of the ministry.

Mr. Ken Alpren was hired as the Area Director for Philadelphia on June 1, 1992.

Ken Alpren—In Philadelphia

Ken was born in Philadelphia, Pennsylvania on March 17, 1955. His mother was raised Catholic, but she converted to Reform Judaism—the "denomination" of Judaism the family continued to follow, although the family was not very religious. His father was Professor of Education at Temple University, and his mother was a teacher; she later became the Assistant Superintendent of Council Rock School District. The family lived in a Jewish neighborhood in the suburbs of Philadelphia, where they sporadically attended synagogue and where Ken attended Hebrew school. But after his Bar Mitzvah, Ken gave up all involvement in religion.

The atmosphere within the home was strained and often filled with conflict as Ken's parents struggled to hold their marriage together. His home life was not conducive to reading, thoughtful reflection, or to concentration on studies at hand, so Ken turned his attention to other things he enjoyed—music composition and performance and competitive sports. In his early teens he played in a rock band and performed regularly at the overnight camp he attended. Of this period in his life, Ken later said:

As I progressed in my adolescent years, I began to long more and more for a discovery for meaning and purpose in existence. Henry David Thoreau opened up my imagination and search for answers in nature. I sought peace in the quiet of the woods—in vain. The Beatles and 1960's subculture drew me into the world of drugs (minor) and anti-government protests. At about this time, I met a fellow classmate who began showing me prophecies in the Bible. She was a Christian, and though very different culturally, persisted to befriend me and ignite my curiosity by the passages shown. I enjoyed the challenge, took my liberty to disagree, and kept coming back for more. It wasn't long before a very close friend of mine surprised me with some news: he'd become a born again Christian! He would no longer be engaged in any drugs or party-going. His entire life was different now!…it wasn't long before I accompanied him to a film being shown in the basement of a church by Mr. Harry Bristow.

After the film I went up to Mr. Bristow and tried to engage him in an argument. My questions were the same ones that had been irritating me constantly for the past few weeks, for which I still had no answers. How do we know there is God? A devil? A heaven or hell? Can you prove that these entities exist? The particular film I'd just viewed was right up my alley—a film on prophecy based on one of Hal Lindsay's books. I saw the return of the Jewish people to their land: the reality that what God said most certainly comes to pass (Ezek. 12:25, Prov. 22:21). Mr. Bristow took me through the Scriptures and showed me my need to receive Messiah. Though I did not understand it all, I prayed with him that night in April, 1972, to receive the Lord. That night I truly sensed a supernatural peace in my heart returning home. I knew something was different. The emptiness was gone, the 'ache' in my heart. God was real, and I knew Him. Two things immediately resulted: I experienced a conviction to get rid of my marijuana—I stopped at once and two weeks later flushed it all away; I had a new appetite for God's Word. I began to devour it, a little at a time but with great love and meditation.

The ensuing year of high school I was able to lead many others to the Lord. We held weekly Bible Study meetings in my parents home (with their reluctant tolerance) and saw quite a work of God which included a majority of Jewish salvations. Following the counsel of a Christian teacher I applied and was accepted at Gordon College which I found a bit disappointing [c.1974]. Preferring the 'unsaved' environment of a university, I went on to Temple University [c.1975], still seeking to find and follow God's career call. Through a clear direction the Lord called me to attend a Bible college in the East, where I grew in His Word [Maryland Bible College and Seminary c.1977; ordained July, 1977]. During my education I was asked to lead a Bible study which thereafter developed into what became my first pastorate.

At the time of my enrollment in Bible School, I expressed my convictions that I was called to the Jewish ministry. The pastor had affirmed that, and even gave me a special spot once a week on his radio program directed to the Jewish people. I visited the distanced [sic] synagogues and witnessed initially, but because we were not in a Jewish area, and the overall ministry had no vision of the Jewish people, I had no real outlet to pursue. During Bible School, every so often the 'call' would burden me, but I wasn't sure how to pursue it. Later, I kept busy pastoring and initiated occasional holiday services in the Bible college area, and then Shabbat services.

Throughout my two pastorates, while thankful to be pioneering and teaching God's Word, I felt a reccurring frustration at not being involved in Jewish missions.…

My discontentment grew in my second pastorate, and I clearly heard the voice of God speak (within) to me through the music of Lamb [Messianic music group] at a Messiah Conference [Messianic Jewish Alliance]. I was to plant a Messianic congregation.… I did not know where, but I knew I must,…I considered Montreal, Canada, and Nashville, Tennessee.…

I then asked a Jewish friend and graduate of the Bible college to pray about working with me. He had just returned from six months in Israel. He consented to visit Nashville with me, in response to the request of a few Jewish believers there. We visited, held meetings, and decided shortly thereafter to 'give it a go.'…The Lord provided a wonderful pastor to replace me in my church, and I moved on.[55]

In Nashville, Ken and his friend established a self-supporting congregation called "Beth Chaim" (House of Life). He was also able to inaugurate and maintain a daily radio program that was heard widely throughout the city of Nashville.

In 1991, desiring to do more to reach his Jewish people with the Gospel, Ken applied to the Mission and was accepted for the position of Area Director for the Philadelphia area—the city of his birth, where he continues to faithfully reach out to his Jewish people with the message of the Messiah.

James Fox—in the Northeast

Another worker who joined the staff of the Mission as of June 1, 1992 was James Fox. He was hired as a full-time missionary for the Long Island, New York outreach.

James (Jimmy) Fox, in every sense, is a product of the Coney Island ministry of the Mission. He was born on October 25, 1960 into a Catholic/Protestant home in the Coney Island section of Brooklyn, New York. His mother,

Evelyn Marie Kramer, was a Roman Catholic who was born and raised on Coney Island. His father, John Richard Fox, was originally a farm boy from Watertown, New York. Mr. Fox was raised as a Methodist, but he considered himself an agnostic. John Fox and Evelyn Kramer met when John, who was in the Navy, took shore leave on Coney Island—the "world's playground" as it was known then. The two were married shortly thereafter. By the time Jimmy was born, Coney Island was in a period of rapid decline. The streets that had once been filled with Jewish immigrants, tourists, and people looking for a good time, were fast becoming a battle-ground for street gangs.

Jimmy was only four years old when his mother began sending him and his cousins to the Coney Island branch of the Mission. Of that time in his life, Jimmy later wrote:

> ...My mother said it would keep me off the streets, and though I doubted very much that as a 4 year old a [sic] would spend much time on the streets I didn't complain because every Friday afternoon we had fun at Miss Koser's place [Miss Hilda Koser was the Missionary-in-Charge of the Coney Island branch]. None of us could ever doubt Miss Koser's love and concern for us. We would enjoy games and crafts as well as the manditory [sic] Bible story with an occasional [sic] Bible quiz thrown in.
>
> At seven years of age I was allowed to go to ABMJ's summer camp, and it was there that I first remember putting my trust, with the limited understanding of a seven year old, in my Messiah and Saviour Jesus. It wasn't until I was about 13 years old that I gave my decision any serious thought. I had continued coming to the meetings at Miss Koser's place and had helped with the various chores and working with the younger kids. I had also been going, when prompted by my mother, to Catholic Church. I made my first 'communion' there and at this time I was being tutored by a priest to make my confirmation. Seeing the vast differences in what I was bing [sic] taught in the Catholic Church and at the Mission, I decided that after my confirmation my association with the Catholic Church would come to an end.
>
> It was also at this time of my life that Larry Feldman came to Coney Island, fresh from Moody Bible Institute [Larry followed Hilda Koser as the Missionary-in-Charge of Coney Island]. Being one of the few teenage boys going to the Mission, and a minority in a community of Black and Hispanics (some of whom had developed a distinct dislike for Whites), I latched onto Larry as a mentor and friend. Larry broadened my scriptural understanding and urged me on to spiritual growth. It was from him that I learned more of Messianic terminology and it's importance in reaching Jewish people. It was also from him that I learned a bit of what being a pastor was about and the need for more Messianic pastors, because the Mission had now evolved into a congregation. The desire began to grow to became a pastor.[56]

By the time Jimmy was approaching high school graduation there were many changes on the horizon—for Jimmy, for the Coney Island ministry, and for Coney Island as an area. Jimmy Fox enrolled at Polytechnic University, where he majored in chemistry. Larry Feldman resigned from his position as Missionary in Charge of Coney Island to enroll in Dallas Theological Seminary. Steve Schlissel became the Missionary in Charge of the work, which was in the throes of change because the government took over the Mission's building, and under his leadership the ministry was moved to Brighton Beach, Brooklyn where it eventually became an independent Messianic congregation affiliated with the Christian Reform movement. (See Chapter Six for the story of Larry Feldman and Steve Schlissel in Coney Island.)

In spite of the many changes, Jimmy Fox continued to attend and he remained actively involved. He was even given opportunity to preach to the congregation on a number of occasions. But as the congregation changed, he was a witness to some of the problems that came up within the congregation as a result of its young pastor having no formal theological training. God used this insight to burden Jimmy with a desire to enroll in a program of formal Bible training so that he could become a pastor.

Jimmy graduated with a B.S. degree in chemistry, and was ready to embark upon a "career change" and enroll in Bible training when his parents—his mother in particular—reminded him they had paid for his schooling, and they expected him to do something with the degree he'd earned. In their thinking, ministry and chemistry didn't mix! As a way of appeasing his parents, and to give himself more time to consider his decision, Jimmy joined the Navy; he entered Officer Candidate School. His decision pleased his parents, especially his father who was a "Navy-man" himself. Jimmy's unspoken motive for enlisting was that he felt he would gain valuable leadership and management skills as a Naval officer—skills he could later use in the ministry, or in the field of service where God placed him.

Shortly before leaving for the Navy, Jimmy was introduced to Rebecca Grundstrom, who soon afterwards became his wife. Of the subsequent period, he wrote:

> ...My first year I was stationed in Philadelphia, Pa., so I made frequent trips back home. During my time in Philadelphia I assisted the ABMJ workers there in their teen outreach, usually by playing guitar and leading the singing for their

meetings and helping with the activities. After our marriage on Feb. 12, 1983, I was transfered [sic] to an ammunition ship stationed in NJ, and it was there in Monmouth County that we made our home....

Toward the end of my time in the Navy we had learned that Larry Feldman was starting a congregation fifty miles north of us in New Jersey. We started attending Beth Messiah [Larry's Messianic congregation] once a week and upon my release from active duty we moved to West Orange to be closer to our congregation. Originally, I wanted to go to Seminary straight from the Navy, but at that time Rebecca was pregnant with our second child....

Having become reunited with my mentor I started learning anew from the information and experiences he had accumulated at Dallas Seminary. I also learned more about the needs of the others in the congregation and tried to assist Larry as much as possible. We also went with Larry occassionally [sic] as he spoke at Churches for Chosen People as well as participating in the congregation's singing group "Kol Ammi." I provided for my family during our time in West Orange by working for a gym equipment company in New York.[57]

Jimmy spent two years assisting Larry Feldman at Beth Messiah congregation, during which time the Lord was impressing upon him the need to pursue his seminary training. Rebecca had always known of his desire to go into the ministry, but that did not make the move away from people she loved any easier. On August 1, 1988 Jimmy and Rebecca and their children bade farewell to their friends and family members. Jimmy had been accepted into Dallas Theological Seminary; they were moving to Dallas, Texas.

RICH AND JULIA FREEMAN—IN THE NORTHEAST

In Dallas, the Fox's were met by Rich and Julia Freeman. Rich, too, was a Jewish believer who was attending Dallas Theological Seminary. In sharing his testimony of how he came to faith in Yeshua, Rich wrote:

Life seemed so normal, so sane. I worked hard and loved my family. If someone had bothered to tell me about Jesus, I would have had all the answers: First of all, I was Jewish and everyone knew Jews didn't believe in Jesus. Not Jews like me, anyway, who were proud of their heritage and had a good Jewish upbringing.

What's more, I didn't want to be a Christian. I thought Christianity was Roman Catholicism, statues, mysterious conversion ceremonies, and anti-Semitism. Of course, my wife wasn't anti-Semitic and she was Catholic, but that was different. She respected my beliefs and I respected hers.

But most of all, there was no reason to be a Christian. I was more like Christ than a lot of Christians I knew. No one could tell me I was a sinner.

So that was where I stood. I believed in God, lived a good life, did the best I could, and probably would have continued like that if God hadn't interrupted my serenity with a real Southern gentleman—Mr. B.R. Walton.

There's been an age-old conflict between those above and below the Mason-Dixon line, and to tell you the truth, I was a little anxious about meeting my new boss.

We hit it off immediately, however. To top it off, he had something in his life that made me jealous—peace, calm, and joy.

One day I asked him about this peacefulness. Imagine my surprise when he pulled out a Bible! 'I read this every day, Richard. My wife and I pray and read the Bible together, and what you see comes from this time we spend with God.' I'm not quite sure what else he said because once I realized he was talking about Jesus, I ruled myself out. Shortly after this conversation, B.R. was transferred out of New York.

About this same time, my wife Julia started attending a Bible study [Julia, an Italian/Catholic became a born-again believer in 1982, and began praying for Rich's salvation]. We had always had an easy-to-live-with understanding about our religious differences, and I was willing to listen to her, but when the subject got too personal, I'd change the topic.

One night when Julia got home from her Bible study, I said hello, then turned back to the TV program I was watching. Everything seemed normal until Julia started crying like her world was coming to an end. I'm an accountant, cool, calm, and collected. So, I let her cry for a few minutes, then asked what was wrong.

'I'm so unhappy,' she blurted out. 'You're not going to heaven with me.'

My calm disappeared. 'What do you mean? Do you know anyone who is a better person than I am? Don't you ever, ever tell me that again!'

A quiet truce fell over our home, and it seemed like things were back to normal, when our five and one-half year old son Brian fell off a slide and broke his arm. X-rays showed a cyst the size of an orange wrapped around the bone. The doctor was very solemn. Cortisone treatments, surgery, bone graft, all of these words tumbled around inside of me.

During the months Brian's break was healing, we could no nothing but wait; I felt like I was falling apart. Meanwhile, my normally emotional wife was calm and assured. She reminded me that people were praying for Brian. She had a foundation and surety that was missing in my life. I found myself praying when I was alone. At first I prayed that if God was real, He would show me. Soon I found myself praying to Jesus. 'If you really are God, show me.'

The day came when more X-rays were to be taken. I sat at work anxiously waiting. When Julia finally called and I heard her crying, my heart sunk. I knew the worst had happened, Brian had to be rushed into emergency surgery.

My own hope at a low, I almost missed what she was saying: The x-rays revealed that the cyst was shrinking. It was going away. I knew God had worked a miracle and inside of myself I felt a change. But I didn't really understand what to do next.

God did not leave me hanging. Julia met Jeanne Rees, whose ministry of music and evangelism had greatly encouraged her. Jeanne suggested that we attend a nearby Messianic congregation, and when Julia hesitantly brought it up to me, I said 'Sure.' Julia was surprised at my willingness, since I really hadn't let her know what was going on inside of me.

The week we planned to visit the congregation there was a snowstorm. We stayed home. The second week we woke up to find the roads covered with ice. 'Julia, I'm not risking life and limb just to go to a religious meeting.' Within an hour a light rain started, and the streets, though messy, were passable. Off we went to the Light of Israel congregation.

The only service I had ever been to outside of the synagogue was a Roman Catholic mass, and I half expected this service to be similar. Instead I found people who looked pretty much like me. There were no hushed tones, just people sitting around in chairs, singing songs and praying in English. There were no crosses, no statues.

Why, then, if everything was so ordinary, did I have the strangest feeling? Why did I feel hot and cold at the same time? Why, at the end of the service when Sam Nadler gave an invitation, was I paralyzed? I wanted to raise my arm but I couldn't. As soon as the service was over, we left.

The following Thursday night I began to thumb through a copy of The Chosen People Julia had brought home. In it was a testimony by Rocky Freeman. 'Imagine that,' I thought, 'someone whose last name is the same as mine.' And what a testimony he had! God had certainly performed a miracle in this man's life.

I knew God wanted to do a miracle in my life too. But I just couldn't let go. I thought about this as I turned the page. Staring up at me was an article about ABMJ's summer STEP program. The headline was 'Take the BIG STEP,' and there was a picture of a wing-tip shoe exactly like a pair I wore all the time [see January 1983 issue of The Chosen People magazine]. Even the creases were the same? 'Julia' I said, 'what do I have to do to get saved?'

The next night we returned to the Messianic congregation, and this time there was no paralysis when I wanted to raise my hand. This time there was joy. I asked the Messiah to come into my heart as Lord and Savior of my life.

It's been almost two years since I personally accepted the Lord [c. 1982]. Shortly after I came to faith, a specific Scripture was very meaningful—Ephesians 2:8, 9: 'For by grace are ye saved through faith; and that not of yourselves: it is a gift of God: Not of works, lest any man should boast.' This Scripture still speaks to me of total dedication and trust, two things which I praise God He had for me long before I had Him.[58]

For six years Rich and Julia Freeman and their children enjoyed the teaching ministry of Sam Nadler, and the fellowship of the other believers at the Light Of Israel congregation, but as the years went by Rich began to recognize the call of God upon his life. He later said:

Picture this: You're an accountant with a Fortune 500 Company. Good future. Great house in a good suburb of New York. Active in a nice congregation. A wife and three beautiful children, one of them a newborn. The kids are in a good school. You build up some equity in the house and kick back for the long haul, right?

Maybe, but not yet. That still, small voice seems to be calling you into full-time ministry, calling you to give up that secure job, nice home, supportive congregational life, and enroll in seminary.

So you hand in your resignation; and you sell the great house, and you schlep your wife and three children 1,600 miles to foreign soil (Dallas, Texas).[59]

It was there—in Dallas, Texas—that Rich and Julia Freeman welcomed and befriended James and Rebecca Fox. To support his family while he was attending seminary, Rich took a computer accounting job. He also served as a part-time worker for the Mission, assisting the work of the Dallas branch. Jimmy Fox immediately volunteered to help the Freemans by helping with the music ministry and by teaching at the Friday night Bible study.

The appointment of Sam Nadler to the position of Executive Director for the Mission brought about major changes for Rich and Julia Freeman. Sam's appointment meant that he had to resign from his position as pastor of the Light of Israel congregation in New York and relocate his family to Charlotte, North Carolina. When the Freeman's heard that the congregation was in need of a pastor they were understandably concerned. Richard later wrote:

> 'The pace in Dallas was very, very difficult, ...But when we prayed about returning to New York to take the pastorate, the answer seemed to be no.' Still, the matter seemed unsettled in his mind. 'I didn't really have peace that I could put the position behind me. I remember asking the Lord, "If it is not Your will for us to stay in Dallas, please clearly show us."'
>
> Events began to shape an answer to Rich's prayer.
>
> In May 1989 Rich was told his computer job was going to relocate to Kansas City. At the same time, Rich's father, who had courageously battled brain cancer for nearly three years, took a serious turn for the worse and lapsed into a coma.
>
> 'Julia and I felt that the Lord was leading us back to New York. We wanted to be near my mother, and the Lord's timing seemed to be at hand.'
>
> When the Freemans were in New York to visit Rich's father, Rich and Julia interviewed with the congregation's pastoral search committee. In early July [c.1989], Rich candidated at Light of Israel, and on July 15, the congregation voted to call Rich as pastor.
>
> The congregation, without a full-time pastor since March [c.1989], was eager for the Freemans to move. As of November, however, their home in Dallas still had not sold, and until they were financially free of the house, the Freemans couldn't leave Dallas. Finally, the family made the hard decision that Julia and the children would stay in Dallas until the house sold. Rich would go to New York.
>
> 'Every time someone comes through the house, I tell myself, "Don't get excited, they might not buy it. Don't get your hopes up. Trust the Lord,"' Julia admits. 'After all, if there is anything being in Dallas has taught me, it's the real day-to-day presence of the Lord in every detail of our lives.'[60]

On December 22, 1989, just three days before Rich's installation service as pastor of the Light of Israel congregation, God sent a buyer for the Freeman's home in Dallas. Rich continues to serve as pastor of the Light of Israel congregation.

When the Freemans returned to New York, Jimmy Fox volunteered to take over the areas of responsibility which Rich had handled in the Dallas branch of the Mission. Jimmy graduated from Dallas Theological Seminary in May 1992 and on June 1, 1992 he joined the staff of the Mission as a full-time missionary working among the Jewish people on Long Island.

Following the resignation of Missionary Director, John Bell, who had once served as the Missionary-in-Charge of the Chicago branch, and then as Regional Director for the mid-West, the Chicago branch of the Mission lost nearly all of its missionary staff. Roy Schwarcz, Galen Banashak, and Barry Berger all submitted their resignations. But Michael Campo faithfully continued on with the Gospel outreach to the Jewish community of the Chicago area, and on June 15, 1992 Kirk Gliebe was appointed to the Chicago staff.

KIRK GLIEBE — IN THE MIDWEST

Kirk was born in Santa Rosa, California on April 11, 1966. His parents were both Jewish but neither one had practiced any sort of Judaism. His paternal grandfather was a noted psychologist who held to typical Freudian views, and thus did not bother with religious training for his children. His father therefore received no religious education. His mother had no knowledge of her Jewish heritage until she was old enough to piece together something of her family history through her cousins and a grandfather. Her father was of Swedish background. Her mother's family, though Jewish, had become Christians in Russia and they had become absorbed into the mainstream of Christianity in Russia, Europe, and the United States.

By the time of Kirk's birth, both of his parents had become believers in the Messiah, but neither was living a consistent Christian life and their marriage was a very unhappy one. Although they took their children to church, the example of their personal lives made the Christian "words" seem a farce and Kirk became very critical of "Christians." He wrote of his experiences:

> As I grew into my teen years my critical attitude kept boiling and I started to consider myself an agnostic. However, I really was very interested in finding God and peace from the trouble at home. So I considered Judaism, but my only religious Jewish friend was reformed [sic] and he seemed worse off than me. At this time I was very fortunate to have some very godly friends from the Church youth group who were willing to discuss things with me. They figured that I must be a believer since I had been going there all my life, but they probably were confused when I asked them, 'How can a person find peace?' 'Who is Jesus really anyway?' Due to their witness and the fact that I could see in their lives

that they really did have a peace and faith that I didn't, I prayed to believe in Jesus as my Messiah on July 30, 1981.

> *From that day on I knew that God wanted me to go into ministry full time. I started doing evangelism and became a leader in my Youth Group. I figured that I would study to become the next Billy Graham so I decided on Moody Bible Institute because they offered a degree in Evangelism. When my Mother heard about Moody she actually tried to interest me in the Jewish Studies Program but I was totally not interested. I left for Moody in 1984 and was involved in a variety of outreaches and helped start a couple of Evangelism events which continue to this day. During my first semester Dr. Goldberg spoke in one of my classes to discuss Jewish Evangelism. He reminded me so much of my Grandfather I became extremely angry. It was the strangest feeling. Up to this point I was like my Father in that I didn't have much interest in Jewishness besides history and politics. But now I felt like my Father and Grandparents had denied me such a wealth of information and heritage. I decided to find out more so I got to know the other Jewish students on campus and started associating with them.*[61]

By the time Kirk was nearing his fourth semester at Moody Bible Institute, he was identifying himself as a Messianic Jewish believer but his pastor at his home church in Santa Rosa told him he was a "Christian" and that was it! He criticized Kirk for "rebuilding the middle wall of partition" between Gentile and Jewish believers in the Messiah, and counselled Kirk that he didn't need to pursue anything "Messianic." Kirk began to feel he would either have to abandon his "Jewishness" or abandon his church and many of his "Gentile" Christian friends. Thanks to the encouragement of friends at Moody Bible Institute who challenged him not to abandon his "Jewishness" despite the pressure of his pastor and friends, Kirk remained at Moody. He not only completed his diploma in the Evangelism Department, he went on to complete a BA in the Jewish Studies Department.

By the fall of 1991, with a secure job, a wife (Kirk married Carla in the Spring of 1988) and new home, it looked as if the Gliebes were pursuing the "American Dream," but God began speaking to their hearts about being in full-time ministry. Kirk wrote:

> *...My job was going very well but we were longing to find a ministry that we could effectively serve with. I had interacted with Chosen People Ministries for years, first with Roy Schwarcz and then Michael Rydelnik. When the Chicago Branch began to plan a new local Bible study I became involved as a volunteer with Michael Campo and Leon Engman. On March 6, 1992...I prayed to the Lord on my way to work for a very definite sign to show us if he wanted us to go into full time ministry. That day, at 3:00, I was summoned to the Owner's office to be told that due to their miscalculations in sales and a very bad cash flow problem that they admitted was due to their causing they laid me off. Needless to say I was shocked but Carla and I both knew that the Lord had given us the sign that we had asked for.*[62]

Kirk immediately contacted Michael Rydelnik, the Area Director for the Northeast, who encouraged him to submit an application for missionary service with the Mission. Today, the Gliebes serve in the Chicago branch of Mission, along with Michael and Sandra Campo.

MICHAEL CAMPO—IN THE MIDWEST

Michael Campo was hired as a full-time missionary for the Chicago ministry on February 1987, but prior to joining the Mission's staff Michael and his wife, Sandy, served as volunteers in the work of the Mission for a number of years. In 1985 Michael joined the staff in a "support raised" category (meaning that the Mission paid him a salary based upon the funds he was able to raise as he spoke in churches and in doing deputation for the Mission).

Michael was born on October 25, 1940. His parents were Gentile people who made their home in Chicago, Illinois. He came to faith in Jesus at the age of thirty-three (July 1974) as a result of the faithful witness of several Gentile Christian women who frequented a beauty salon business he owned.

During the summer of 1974, Michael went on a camping trip in Colorado. While he was there, the peacefulness and the beauty of his surroundings caused him to reflect on the things the women had told him about God, and about his need of a Savior. He wanted to believe in God; he wanted a personal relationship with Him; he just wasn't sure it was possible. In the stillness of the evening hours, amidst the hush of the forest, Michael bowed his head and asked God to reveal Himself to him. God heard his prayer, and in a most humbling and personal way, His answer confirmed to Michael that everything the women had shared with him was true.

One of the first things Michael did after returning home, was to locate the Mount Prospect Bible Church—the home church of the customers who had witnessed to him for over three years. In the weeks that followed, as he attended services at the church, and as the Word of God was quickened to his heart, Michael prayed to receive Jesus as his Savior and Lord.

As his faith grew, and his knowledge of the Scriptures increased, Michael began to sense a burden to share the Gospel with Jewish people. His love for the Jewish people and faithful testimony to his Jewish customers soon brought Michael to the attention of the Mission's staff in Chicago.

Michael and Sandra soon became involved in helping the Mission's staff with the establishment of the Vineyard Congregation in Buffalo Grove, Illinois—a suburb of Chicago. For a time, Michael served as the Associate Pastor of the congregation, and Sandra was in charge of the Sunday School Department.

After he became a full-time worker on the Mission's staff, Michael's responsibilities included leading three of the Mission's STEP teams on missionary tours through the West and Midwest. He and Sandra also assisted in the establishment of a Messianic congregation in Columbus, Ohio—the Olive Branch Congregation, where Michael serves as congregational leader.

In 1992 Michael was asked to assume the responsibility of the Chicago area ministry. He is currently in charge of the Chicago branch of the Mission. He is also starting new works in Milwaukee, Wisconsin and in the northern suburbs of Chicago. Through Michael's personal and public ministry, many Jewish people in the Midwest have come to faith in the Messiah, Jesus.

Winn Crenshaw—in the South

After the resignation of Jim Bates, the Florida ministry was also in need of staff. Mr. Winn P. Crenshaw, who was hired November 1, 1990, was transferred to vivify the Florida ministry.

Winn was born in Sherman, Texas on February 22, 1947. He was the only child of a Gentile family of the "Baptist" tradition. His parents attended church occasionally, but they never mentioned God, the Bible, Jesus, or prayer in their home—God was not a part of their everyday lives. Although they considered themselves to be Christians, they lived their lives as practical atheists, and for the most part could be considered non-believers. In telling of his decision to accept Jesus and to follow Him, Winn wrote:

> I received Christ as my Saviour at age 13 when an elderly, Baptist couple [Walter & Vera Steadman] came and shared His death, burial, and resurrection with me. I was baptized a few days later. Attending Sunday School was as close as I got to discipleship. As a child I didn't know what to do next, so after a few months, I lost interest and dropped out of church. However, because of the faithfulness of God, I believe that I was saved at that time, I just never grew.
>
> During my senior year of high school, I began attending church again and reading the Bible on my own for the first time. This was my first real growth experience. That summer I worked at a Baptist camp and by the end of the summer felt that God had called me 'to preach.' While in college, I became very involved in Baptist Student Union, Campus Crusade, and Inter-varsity. After graduation from college [Stephen F. Austin State University, Nacogdoches, Texas; B.A., c.1970], I went to Southwestern Baptist Theological Seminary for part of a semester, but was not prepared for the Wellhausen theory and other 'higher criticism' teachings dominant at the school. I left SWBTS and transferred to Dallas in 1972 [Dallas Theological Seminary]. I didn't graduate, but while there I learned Bible study methods and have loved the Bible ever since.[63]

Continuing his testimony, Winn told readers of *The Chosen People* magazine:

> Seminary unearthed my feelings of inadequacy; I realized that I was not ready to make a commitment to the ministry. The words of one of my professors, Dr. Howard Hendricks, rang in my ears: 'If you can do anything besides the ministry, do it. The world needs dedicated Christian laymen.'
>
> I left seminary and became a Dallas police officer. I wanted to make a difference in the world, to be a bridge of understanding, to be a light to society.
>
> Instead of making a difference in the world, the world began to make a difference in me. A black cloud began to fill my life. All I was seeing was the seamy side of life day in and day out. Like so many police officers, I became hard. The hardness affected my emotions and extended to the very depths of my spirit.
>
> 'The world is too trashed out to believe You are seriously involved,' I often told God.
>
> In an attempt to put God away from me, I threw out all my Bibles. With this attitude, it is no surprise that bitterness and hopelessness, skepticism and cynicism steadily grew in my heart.
>
> As time passed, though, I saw what kind of person I was becoming; I knew I needed a change. So I left the police department and became a program director for the YMCA [c.1978]. There I was able to work with people and interact with them more positively.
>
> The difference in my outlook was immediate, but the spiritual deadness remained. I was unable to reconnect with

God because of my bitterness, yet His Spirit continued to woo me. I'd lay in bed at night, knowing He was calling me. Finally I went out and bought a Bible, but I only read it once in a while, as if a part of me was ashamed of my distance from Him.

Then, one day, between matches at a racquetball tournament, for no reason I could explain, I wanted (really wanted!) to read the Bible [c.1981]. I went to my car and drove around to the back of the building where I could be alone.

The Bible seemed to open itself to Psalm 51. I was confronted with myself in an entirely new way. I had been looking at the problems in the world. Now I realized that the problems weren't confined to 'everyone else.' The problems were in me as well.

I saw my arrogance, my separation from God, my own sins. For the first time, I saw God's deep love and, even more, His abiding commitment to me. I began to confess my bitterness and all that had grown from it. My sin, my separateness from God, became crystal clear. I needed to renew my relationship with God. I realized I needed forgiveness for the hardness I'd allowed to enter my life. I read the psalm over and over and found myself crying and saying it aloud as a prayer to God.

From that day on, my life was completely turned around. Daily I read, I devoured, the Bible. God and my relationship with Him were real. He became an active presence in my life. The hurt and bitterness that had dominated me were gradually being replaced by joy and light.

I felt like a new man. The vague feeling that I had always lived with—always thinking I had to prove myself and had to battle the world—disappeared.

Then I met sweet Dana, a lovely woman who had been a committed Christian since she was very young. Everything seemed complete. Dana and I were married [c. February, 1983], and we moved to Columbus, Indiana. There with a promotion to executive director, my ascent in the YMCA 'career mainstream' began. For the first time in my life, I was both satisfied and settled. We thought this was what we'd do forever. It probably would have been too, if I hadn't met a group of Jewish believers. [In 1985, Winn attended a concert presented by the Liberated Wailing Wall from Jews for Jesus. Impressed with what he heard, Winn purchased Moishe Rosen's book: *Share The New Life With A Jew*. After reading through the book, Winn began to pray that God would lead him to some Jewish people. He didn't know any, but now wanted to share Messiah with them.]

Meeting Jewish people who believed in Messiah made me realize how far we had come from the roots of our faith. I started thinking how much the Church was missing by not understanding its Jewish roots. Even more, I realized that true New Testament Christianity had to be 'to the Jew first.'

I didn't know much about the Jews (only that when I was in junior high school, the Jewish kids had more holidays than we did). Yet I began to pray for Jewish missions and then for Jewish people. Soon, I was praying that God would let me meet Jewish people with whom I could share my faith.

Bigger, better career opportunities opened up in the Muskogee, Oklahoma, YMCA, and off we went. Among our first friends there were a Jewish couple. That spring they invited us to attend a Seder with them. Even though it was a Reform ceremony, I got chills when I heard the many references to the Messiah and saw how clearly this ceremony pointed to my Lord. More than ever, I appreciated the deeper aspects of my faith that were part of understanding the Jewish roots of Christianity. More than ever, I longed for Jewish people to know their Messiah.

My career aspirations glowed, and our life looked better than ever. But I wanted to do more for the Lord. I was dissatisfied, not with life, but with the way I was using the time God had given me. [Desiring to witness to Jewish people, Winn applied and was eventually accepted as a volunteer co-laborer on the staff of Jews of Jesus. He spent part of his 1988 vacation in Boston, handing out broadsides with the Boston staff of Jews for Jesus.]

As executive director for the YMCA [Anniston, Alabama], I was often a spokesman and a seller of ideas. However, the more I worked with Jewish missions, the more I realized that if I was going to be speaking—or selling an idea—I wanted it to be the idea that Jews and Gentiles can only find life through the Jewish Messiah.

Fifteen years after leaving seminary, I was once again faced with Dr. Hendricks' words. This time I realized that I could no longer be a layman. I felt that I had no choice but to be in the ministry.

But I was 43 years old with a family to support. It didn't seem logical to take a new position at half the money and with none of the security of my present one. Yet I had an inescapable feeling that I was not going to be at peace until I was actively reaching Jewish people for Messiah.

During this time as my love for God's people deepened, so did my love for God and the impact of the Bible in my life.

It wasn't only me either. As a family, we wanted to create family traditions and incorporated several Biblical Jewish celebrations into our home. The object lessons of these celebrations made our family grow together spiritually *and gave us opportunities to share our faith as a family.*

As I read and studied Romans, Paul's words burned into me. In chapter 11, he addresses the Gentiles, reminding them that their faith was supported by Jewish roots and that their salvation is part of making the Jewish people yearn for salvation. The chapter then talks of God's mercy, an unsearchable, unknowable mercy. This mercy had been extended to me.

'Therefore,' Romans 12 begins. Because of the great mercy of God. Because of His great love. Because of His gift to me. Because of all this, He was asking me to present myself as a living sacrifice to Him. Not only myself, but my family. My Career. My future. My life.

During the summer of 1990 I took part in Chosen People Ministries' Summer Training and Evangelism Program (STEP) as preparation for full-time missionary service.[64]

After Winn completed the STEP program, the Mission sent him and his family to the Baltimore/Washington D.C. area for further training under Larry Jaffrey, Missionary in Charge of the Washington D.C. area, and Scott Brown, pastor of the Son of David congregation in Rockville, Maryland.

In the fall of 1992, Winn and Dana Crenshaw were transferred to Florida. They purchased a home in Coral Springs, Florida—a city of 80,000 where the average age is thirty-four, and approximately 35% of the population is Jewish. Since their move to Florida, Winn has carried on an aggressive campaign of evangelism which has caught the attention of the Jewish community. At the writing of this history, God continues to bless the efforts of Winn and Dana as they proclaim His truth to the Jewish community in Florida.

The Russian Ministry Re-opens

World events during 1989, and the threatened May 5, 1990 pogrom of the Jews in Russia, brought the plight of the Jews in the Soviet Union and in east European countries to the foreground. The Mission's outreach in the east European countries had been closed since 1930, when its property in Ekaterinaslav, Russia was seized by the government, and its worker, Mr. Guberman, was never heard from again. But when the Berlin Wall fell, and when God moved in history to bring about an opening of doors whereby individuals from the Western countries were permitted to enter the Soviet Union, and to openly distribute Bibles, plans were made for Sam Nadler and for Albert Davis [Israeli] (Albert is a Russian Jew who had came to faith after his family immigrated to Canada—See Chapter Seven) to visit Russia. Reporting on how God opened the door for their visit to the Soviet Union, and sharing the results of that visit, Sam told readers:

Last year the Lord began stirring my heart as I saw all the changes taking place in Eastern Europe. I was moved to share my burden for Soviet Jewry with our Board of Directors. They agreed that the Lord might be leading.

So we spent the spring [1990] preparing to go. In May, Albert Davis [Israeli] (our Russian Jewish missionary from Toronto, Ontario), and I prayerfully planned an itinerary and formulated goals for our visit.

We prayed that the Lord would give us seeing eyes, hearing ears and understanding hearts. We wanted to do everything He wanted us to do.

Almost as soon as we landed in Moscow, we found open doors of witness—on street corners, in restaurants and even in synagogues!

We found great opportunities for mass evangelism as we handed out hundreds of Gospel tracts in front of department stores on Red Square. Always it was the same reaction—crowds would form to ask us more about our faith.

One Jewish musician spent a great deal of time trying to explain to us the way things are there—how the Soviet system has crushed the spirit of the people and left them without any hope.

I was able to sense this man's despair and was able to share with him that many times despair is the starting point of God's work in our lives. Many times God brings us to an end of ourselves ...that we might look to Him.

As the curtain of despair began to be drawn back by these words of hope, the musician's heart became tender to the Lord.

But it was in Kiev that we received our greatest blessing. Kiev, a city of three million, with a Jewish community of 150,000 to 300,000, is the capital of the Ukraine.

When we got there on Wednesday, we had only a few contacts. Our plan was to stay only a few days and return to Moscow on Saturday.

But God changed our plans.

When we arrived, we met with the pastor of the local congregation in Kiev. He invited us to speak to the church the following evening, which was a special day in Russian Orthodox tradition, Ascension Thursday.

Our message was that the ascended Lord would have us go 'to the Jew first.' To the natural eye, we explained, going 'to the Jew first' might not seem to be the most expedient way to evangelize. But we taught that only as we set our minds and hearts upon things that are above (Colossians 3:1-4) are we able to appreciate God's perspective and priorities.

We were pleased that night when one Gentile person came to faith. We were further encouraged by the pastor, who told the congregation that though he had never before heard the message "To the Jew First," before, [sic] he recognized it as being biblical. The pastor concluded that they must, therefore, share Messiah with their Jewish friends and neighbors.

From the pulpit, the pastor invited us back to speak at the Sunday service and exhorted the congregation to bring Jewish neighbors to hear the Gospel.

Sensing God's hand in our affairs, we decided to stay in Kiev and canceled our trip to Moscow.

During the next several days we witnessed one-on-one to many individual Jewish people. But on Sunday morning as we looked out from the church pulpit, we saw a great sea of hungry souls.

The church building had about 400 seats, but there were over 1,000 people jamming the aisles. The congregation had heeded their pastor's instruction: Over 200 Jewish people had accepted their invitation to come and hear the message of Messiah!

Even more touching, Christians were getting up from their seats and giving them to visiting Jewish people. Then these wonderful Christian brethren slipped quietly into the aisles to stand for the rest of the service—a service that would last for two and one-half hours!

With Albert Davis translating, we were able to share not only our testimony, but the very love of God from Jeremiah 31:3. The first words that we proclaimed were, 'Am Yisrael Chai!—The People of Israel Live!' because the God of Israel lives and loves His people and will not forsake them.

As we spoke we could see many faces visibly soften as the Spirit of God was ministering in their midst. Some of the people in the congregation started to cry during our presentation.

At the end of the service, an invitation was given to Jewish people to respond to the message. Those that wanted to receive Messiah into their hearts were asked to come forward and trust Him as their Savior and Lord.

We didn't know what to expect—but we were thrilled as we saw Jewish people get up from their seats and come forward...then more Jewish people...and more filling up the front! Finally, there was no more room—and people were still wanting to come forward!

At the end of the service we took them all off to a side room where we prayed with them, taught them from the Scriptures, gave them all New Testaments and exhorted them in the faith.

The pastor thought there were over 100 Jewish people that morning who gave their hearts to the Lord. We have the names of over 70 that made solid decisions for Messiah.

We spent a great deal of time after the service instructing the Jewish believers in the Scriptures and encouraging their hearts. Then we gave an interview on Radio Kiev proclaiming the Gospel throughout the city.

That evening, another 75 to 100 Jewish people came back to hear more about Messiah. We taught on Jeremiah 31:31-34, the New Covenant, explaining that the New Covenant is like a wedding contract and that the kind of relationship God wants to have with us can be understood in the picture of a marriage relationship.

At the end we invited them to come forward and receive Messiah and to enter into that eternal, intimate relationship with the Living God.

Another 20 or so Jewish people came forward and gave their hearts to the Lord that night. We gave them each a New Testament, prayed with them and wrote down their names for follow-up.

At the end of the evening, I noticed one gentleman in the back of the church who had been waiting patiently all night just to speak with us.

'I just wanted to praise the Lord with you,' he said with tears in his eyes. 'I brought four Jewish families, and three of them accepted the Lord tonight.'

We embraced and praised the Lord for His goodness. I, too, found myself weeping.

The Christians of Kiev are begging us to return, and we are more than willing to do so. We are planning to return this summer and want to bring thousands of Bibles for the Jewish people there. We know that Bible are being sent over, but they are not reaching Jewish hands. We want to put Bibles into Jewish hands.

Please join us in praying for the follow-up and for the ministry to the Jews in Russia. Pray that many more will come to faith in Yeshua, the Messiah of Israel.[65]

Before Sam and Albert left the Soviet Union to return home, they made arrangements for the new Jewish believers to be discipled in a weekly Bible study. The work in Kiev has grown rapidly!

Upon their arrival home, Sam told the Board there were two priorities: to obtain Bibles to be sent for distribution among the Jews of Russia, the Ukraine, and in East European countries; to begin working toward obtaining legal standing as a Mission in the Soviet Union. With God's blessings, both objectives were accomplished! Thousands of Bibles were obtained and distributed without cost to Jewish people, and by August 1991 (just fourteen months after their initial trip to the Soviet Union) the Mission was established as a legal mission organization in the former Soviet Union. It was the first Jewish Mission to be so established since before the Communist Revolution!

In the August 1991 *Mid Year Report*, Sam Nadler gave the following report:

> *Of late, the Jewish community in the Soviet Union has been doing all that it can to try to hinder our ministry there. But the Lord has overruled their efforts, and our staff has been seeing many people come to faith. The Soviet Jewish believers we've discipled are bold and courageous and are effectively being used for the Gospel.*
>
> *One incident that occurred several months ago particularly stands out in my mind. It was during a Holocaust remembrance at Babi Yar (the scene of a tragic mass execution of Jewish people during World War II) outside Kiev. Jewish people from all over Eastern Europe came, and our staff was there walking through the crowds sharing the Gospel. Normally the Holocaust is one of those subjects where Christians fear to tread with the Gospel, wanting to be sensitive to Jewish feelings. Yet as a result of our workers' witness, more than a hundred Jewish people came to our meetings in Kiev to hear how the Messiah can change their lives!*
>
> *We are blessed to have the work in the Soviet Union supervised by Albert Davis [Israeli], who makes regular trips there. His trips no longer originate from Canada, because this past spring we moved him and his family to Israel. Why Israel? So Albert, who is fluent in Hebrew and Russian, could be an effective witness to both newly arriving Soviet Jews and to the Israelis. Albert and Gretta Davis, as you may know, are Soviet Jewish believers who both have Israeli citizenship.*[55]

VLADIMIR WINER—IN KIEV

Although Albert Israeli continued to make regular trips to Kiev, a facility in which to hold meetings and a full-time worker were much needed! After several months, the Mission hired Vladimir Winer. In December 1990, Vladimir held a special Chanukah service for new Jewish believers and for their non-believing family members and friends. Their service was interrupted by a group of ultra-Orthodox Chassidic Jewish people who demonstrated their contempt for the Jewish believers by disrupting the service. The incident was reported in *The Chosen People* magazine and readers were encouraged to pray for the Kiev ministry and for the new Jewish believers. The report stated:

> *'Come downstairs and join some real Jews,' shouted one of the Chassidic men to the group of 75 Jewish believers and nonbelievers meeting in a Kiev community hall.*
>
> *When none of the believers followed the Chassidim downstairs where they were holding their Chanukah party, the latter directed their threats toward Vladimir Winer, who was presiding over the believers' Chanukah service.*
>
> *'If you don't leave,' the Chassidim warned, 'we're going to come back with ten men to beat you up.'*
>
> *Still no one left the room.*
>
> *'Now we see what you're like,' said one of the Jewish nonbelievers addressing the Chassidim, 'and we're not coming to your synagogue. We're staying here. We want to hear what these people have to say.'*
>
> *The Russian Jewish believers prevented the Chassidim from physically harming Vladimir, but not before a riot broke out.*
>
> *When the building's manager witnessed the riot, he expelled the Chassidim and allowed the believers to continue their service.*[67]

DAN AND ARLENE RIGNEY—IN KIEV

The Mission later purchased an apartment in Kiev which was used for meetings, as well as for living quarters for Vladimir. But as the ministry in Kiev continued to grow, Satan launched his attack by using issues over doctrine, methodology, and finances to cause friction and division among the growing numbers of believers. In 1992 Vladimir Winer resigned from the Mission to work for another mission organization. To maintain the momentum already gained in the outreach, Sam Nadler contacted Arnold Fruchtenbaum, founder of Ariel Ministries, and arranged to send their workers, Dan and Arlene Rigney (former staff members with the Mission, and veteran missionaries) to Kiev as missionary "house parents" to the new believers. The Rigneys were able, through translators and through the help of Albert Israeli and others, to develop the fledgling believers into a small, but growing, congregation.

During the summer of 1993, six of the Russian Jewish believers were brought to the United States for participation in the Summer Training and Evangelism Program (S.T.E.P.). It is hoped that this intensive training and discipleship program will result in new workers readied for leadership positions within the ministry in Kiev.

Lydia (Onbreit) Wechsler — Her Story

The ministry among the Russian and East European Jews has not been limited to the geographical area formerly known as the Soviet Union. Russian and East European Jews have flooded into the United States, Israel, and Canada as the doors for them to immigrate have opened. To meet the challenge of reaching the Soviet Jews in New York, the Mission hired another Russian Jewish believer. Miss Lydia Onbreit joined the staff of the mission as a "student missionary" in February 1992, but for several months prior to that, Lydia served as a volunteer with the Mission. Her story and testimony appears in the November 1991 issue of *The Chosen People* magazine. In it she states:

Two things in my mother's heart greatly influenced my life when I was young. The first was her desire to know God. The second was fear, fear she and my father felt if they were to attend synagogue.

I was born in 1967 in a Jewish family in Leningrad, Russia, at a time when Leonid Brezhnev ruled. The State was 'supreme,' and 'religion' was for 'illiterate fools who were unworthy of the great opportunities the State could make available.'

My parents knew, as did everyone else, that they would be considered disloyal to their country if they went to synagogue. It was every Jew's fear during worship to see the edges of a flash, knowing that the KGB was recording their presence on film.

You have to live under this kind of system to know what it means, to understand how effectively and powerfully it can threaten your life and job.

However, no system can shut out God.

My mother had a great desire to be close to God and to see that I loved Him too. For this reason she took me to the Russian Orthodox church when I was about eight years old. There we were both baptized. After all, there was only one synagogue for the authorities to watch, but there were many Russian Orthodox churches.

I still remember that day. The awe-inspiring richness of the church with its silver and gold trimmings and beautiful icons led me to feel a deep peace and reverence for God.

And so, although I did not understand what I did that day, in all my life I was never to forget it. From that day on, I began to tell everyone that I believed in God. You must realize that the Soviet Union is primarily an atheistic country, so that what I was saying was considered to be very out of step.

I seemed to be more out of step as I grew older.

My parents worked very hard to have me accepted at a high school that specialized in English. There, in addition to our other school work, we memorized articles and political texts about our leaders so we'd be ready to explain our policy and peaceful intentions to foreigners.

It was fully understood that we were expected to become Communists when we graduated from high school.

But from the American and British political essays I read, I knew that there was much wrong with the Communist system. Deep in my heart I knew there was something very wrong with what I was being taught, with more than just the political system.

We were told that rich people had made up the idea of God to exploit the poor. This I just could not believe!

I knew there was a God. I felt He had great love. Still, I had no knowledge of how to follow Him, and so I continued along the path that our 'system' set out for me.

After high school, because I had been good at mathematics and foreign languages, I went to the Railway Engineering Institute to study civil engineering. This was a time when I should have been entirely devoted to logic, to my future …to becoming a productive Soviet citizen. Strangely, what began to grow most in me was a curiosity about my Jewishness.

Suddenly I wanted to know more about what it meant to be Jewish, to understand the culture, the holidays, the history. I began to attend synagogue on the holidays, hoping to discover more about what it meant to be a Jew. Yet the synagogue was very crowded on the holidays (perhaps people felt less intimidated because of the crowds) and since the service was in Hebrew, I didn't really understand anything that was going on.

Throughout my years at the institute, my longing to know more about my Jewishness grew. I didn't seem to be able to do much about this longing except to ask questions of my grandparents. Occasionally I'd pray, trusting in the rote prayers I had learned in the Russian Orthodox church.

Then I was invited to an international ball at the Palace of Youth. This hall housed the social and political activities of the Komsomol (Communist Union of Youth). Affiliation with the Komsomol was prelude to becoming a Communist Party member.

At this dance, I met a girl from Finland. Always trying to practice my English, I began to talk with her. We agreed to exchange letters after she left the Soviet Union.

In her first letter she told me she believed in God.

As we corresponded, she challenged me to think about God and what He meant in my life. She also mentioned that she would be praying for me and my family.

God answered her prayers in two ways.

First, a friend (who knew I wanted to practice my English) invited me to see the movie Jesus of Nazareth. This was the first time I had seen or heard that Jesus was Jewish. The final scene, when Jesus told His disciples that He would be with them always, left me with the feeling that I could truly believe and trust Him.

The second event happened after I graduated from the institute. I was working as an engineer. Again while trying to practice my English, I met American students who invited me to the Baptist church.

Go to a Baptist church? At first I was afraid. I had heard the Baptist church was a cult, a sect, full of fanatics and illiterates.

Still, something inside prodded me to form my own opinion, so I went. There I met some people who had a house church, and (again listening to that inner curiosity, that prodding) I began to attend their Wednesday night Bible studies.

The Bible studies were in a little two-room apartment, where a pastor, his wife, and seven children lived. Often the services were as long as two hours, and because 30 or more people would sometimes come, there would be standing room only.

Still, what I noticed wasn't the small apartment or the long stand. It was the excitement I felt in hearing people talk about God and the Bible.

It was the first time I learned about the Bible in a way I could understand it, and I continued to go to the study. At home I was praying very often, and at work I was telling people about God. I had stopped caring about being an engineer and a Communist, as if I had ever really cared to begin with. I was eager to be completely God's.

On Easter Sunday, I felt that I wanted to make my beliefs public, but my mother was at the service with me, and the words just wouldn't come out. However, a few weeks later during service, I felt God calling me [May 7, 1989].

The pastor asked if anyone wanted to receive the Lord. All at once everything I had always felt for God seemed to well up inside me. I was full of peace and cleansing, full of the beauty and awe of the God of Israel.

I started to pray to receive the Lord, but could hardly finish because I was crying so much. Then came an overwhelming feeling of newness and satisfaction—a part of me had found something I had always been looking for.

Within weeks the Lord was using me to witness and hand out Gospel literature on the streets of Leningrad. By August 1990 (three months later), God had opened a door for me to visit New York.

At Calvary Baptist Church in Manhattan, I met Israel Cohen and, through him, Danny Siegel (both Chosen People Ministries workers in New York). Like me, Danny had recently arrived in New York and also had a desire to reach Russian Jews with the message of salvation. [note: Danny Siegel had returned to New York from Denver, Colorado after completing his theological studies at Denver Seminary.] *He had only one problem: He could neither speak nor understand Russian. We began to work as a team.*

I have learned a lot about my Jewish identity during the last six months as a volunteer with Chosen People Ministries. This summer [c.1991], I was part of STEP, learning how to serve Him as a missionary. As I look at all God has done in my life, I know that 2 Corinthians 5:17 is true: 'If anyone is in Messiah, he is a new creation; the old has gone, the new has come!'[68]

In December 1992, Lydia married Michael Wechsler, a part-time staff member. Lydia and Israel Cohen continue their work with the large Russian Jewish community of Brighton Beach, Brooklyn—a ministry that includes sharing the love and truth of God in word and in deed.

FULL CIRCLE

In many ways, God has brought the Mission full circle in its one hundred years of ministry to the Jewish people. In 1894 Rabbi Leopold Cohn's mission (the Williamsburg Mission to the Jews) began ministering in Brooklyn, New York. His ministry was to the immigrant Jews from Russia, Hungary, Poland, and other East European countries. Then, as now, as the Gospel was boldly proclaimed to the Jewish people, it often provoked great hostility! The Cohns' experienced throughout their years of ministry, and the staff in New York continues to experience such hostility—as evidenced by a report in the July 1993 *Chosen People* magazine which stated:

Any time Chosen People Ministries runs an advertisement for an upcoming Seder dinner, they always hope the turnout will be good. The crowd that gathered outside Kings Highway Church in Brooklyn, NY for the Russian Seder wasn't just good—it was phenomenal! However, this crowd didn't come to join in the fellowship and worship of the evening service. Their intent was to be disruptive and hostile.

It was a simple ad that ran in a Russian newspaper in New York City inviting those interested to attend a Russian Seder dinner hosted by Chosen People Ministries at Kings Highway Church on April the tenth. Lydia Wechsler, A Russian speaking staff member of CPM, had been taking reservations for the upcoming Seder. She told missionary Stewart Weinisch to plan for about 65 people, but Lydia had reason to believe that the count would not be accurate.

Some of the reservations that were called in seemed suspicious. One such call came a few days before the Seder from a Mr. Weismann. Because Lydia detected his Yiddish accent, she asked the man if he spoke Russian. He ignored the question at first asking for the address of the church and making a reservation.

So Lydia asked again, 'Do you speak Russian?' He then admitted he spoke Yiddish.

'How did you find out about the Seder, then?' she questioned.

'My wife knows Lydia and Michael Wechsler,' he replied.

'Well, I'm Lydia . . .?' The man seemed to want to ignore this also.

On the night of the Seder in the basement of the Kings Highway Church, the tables had been set, the caterers had delivered the kosher meal, big bright yellow signs had been posted directing the guests to the church, and Chosen People staff members Israel Cohen and Michael Wechsler were about the town picking up those guests who needed transportation. Nothing seemed out of the ordinary—except the four or five Hasidic Jews wandering around the church grounds. The Chosen People staff had expected the newspaper advertisement to draw some opposition, but these few men didn't seem like much to worry about.

The staff had intended to start the service at 6:00 P.M. but decided to wait in hopes that the no-show reservations were just late rather than pranks by Orthodox opposers. Almost an hour later, the service started with 45 guests. No one seemed concerned with the clock and the guests appeared to enjoy the time of fellowship with one another.

While Michael and Lydia Wechsler were filling the basement with worshipful music, the street in front of Kings Highway was filling up with Orthodox protesters. The group of five Hasidic men had grown to 50. A member of the church staff had called the police.

By the time the church volunteers had served the Seder meal, the group of 50 had swelled to 200 or more!

Although the chanting of the crowd could not be heard in the church basement, The Chosen People staff were aware of the commotion outside....

The Orthodox Jewish people made accusations, saying that ignorant Russian Jews were being held against their will and Russian children had been kidnapped. The police inspected the church building but found no evidence of criminal activity. They reported this to the accusers, but the Orthodox were not satisfied.

So police then came down to the Seder requesting permission to admit two of the men from outside the church. Stewart gave his approval with the condition that the men could not be disruptive.

A rabbi and a young Hasidic man were escorted to the basement. They began inspecting the food to see if it was kosher. Both were verbally harassing the Russian people. The rabbi told them, 'You will be protected and cared for, if only you will leave this place and come with us.'

The police intervened, removing the men from the Seder, and Stewart felt he had some explaining to do. He told the Russian Jews, 'The Religious [the Orthodox Jews] thought we were holding you against your will. If you would like to leave now, we will not keep you here.'

Stewart was pleased; no one deserted. Then he asked, 'Would you like to finish celebrating the Passover?' The group responded with cheering and clapping. The Chosen People staff was elated.

The Seder continued—but not without interruptions. At one point, six men pushed in the door. One young man strew anti-missionary literature all through the church building; another confronted Lydia. He asked her in Russian, 'Why have you invited these people?'

'To teach them about the Passover and the sacrifice the Messiah, Jesus, gave,' she answered.

He was angry, screaming at her telling her she was Satan.

At the end of the service, Stewart asked the people if anyone desired to receive forgiveness through Jesus, the Passover Lamb. Twelve people raised their hands, and Stewart led them through a prayer to receive salvation.

Thirty policemen were there to control the scene. By their estimations, the mob outside the church was now 400 strong.

With police protection, the Russian Jewish guests braved the crowd and left the building to go to their cars. Some of the Orthodox were asking children to sit in front of the vehicles so that no one could leave the parking lot....

Israel Cohen and Michael Wechsler were the first of the CPM staff to leave the building. They both had Russian guests that needed to be driven home....

Israel had three people to take home: two elderly Jewish ladies and a seven-year-old girl.... It took six officers and 15 minutes of negotiation to get the people who were standing in front of the car to back away.

After Michael Wechsler managed to get out of the parking lot and drop off his passengers, he went back to King's Highway because his wife, Lydia, was still there. He parked the car two blocks away and walked to the church....

When Michael reached the gate, the police would not let him enter. They told him everyone would be brought out in just a few minutes....

An Orthodox man then began to address the crowd. He told them that the Christians were brainwashing Russian Jews. That it must be prevented.... Michael debated with himself as to the wisdom in speaking to this man. Finally, he could stand it no more and responded. 'If you care so much, why are you out here harassing us?...

Quickly a circle of men surrounded him and the Orthodox man to whom he spoke.

'How are we harassing you?' he asked....

The spokesman...asked Michael, 'Why don't you talk to these people about what it means to be Jewish—about their heritage?'

'Being Jewish is more than a heritage,' Michael replied, 'Being Jewish is believing in God's Word and accepting His atonement that He's provided for us through the Messiah.'

'Atonement!' the man spat the word as if it was distasteful. 'Obeying the Torah, doing mitzvoth [good deeds], these are what God wants!'

'This is what the rabbis say; not what God says,' Michael refuted. 'When did God abrogate His requirement for atonement? In Leviticus 17:11 it says 'by blood on the altar.'

'Leviticus?' the man's face was reddening with anger. 'Every morning I repeat, "Shema, Yisrael, AdoShem Elokheynu, AdoShem echad"—the Lord is one, and He doesn't change!'

Michael answered him: 'I know; the Lord is one and He doesn't change. Neither does His requirement for sin.'

At this point, Michael was surprised the mob had not touched him. The Orthodox man was now yelling that Michael spoke garbage. Michael decided further conversation would be useless, so he turned to make his way back to the gate. A policeman there recognized him and told the other officer to let Michael in.

The police were ready to move. They formed a lane with their bodies that extended from the church to a van parked close by. The Chosen People staff walked through the lane as the mob struggled violently to grab them.

Everyone reached the police van, and except for some scratches they were all fine.[69]

Rabbi Leopold Cohn, an immigrant "Hasid" from Hungry, looking very much like those who even today demonstrate against the Mission's workers, wandered the same streets of Brooklyn in his search for the Messiah of Israel. His search ended when he was given a small Yiddish New Testament and he read the words, "A record of the genealogy of Yeshua Messiah the son of David, the son of Abraham:"[70] With those words, God touched the heart of Rabbi Leopold Cohn and opened the eyes of his understanding to recognize His Son, Yeshua—the Messiah of Israel and of the whole world. The truth of the words sealed themselves to Rabbi Cohn's heart, and in spite of great persecution he faithfully proclaimed that truth throughout the remainder of his life.

One hundred years later, the ministry founded by Rabbi Leopold Cohn continues to proclaim the Gospel message that Yeshua, God's Son, is the promised Messiah of Israel. The staff and missionaries of the Mission continue to proclaim the very same message that Rabbi Leopold Cohn and his son, Joseph Hoffman Cohn proclaimed to the immigrant Jews in America and to the Jews scattered around the world—the message that through Yeshua's atonement, all mankind—Jew and Gentile alike—can find forgiveness of sin and can accept His gift of eternal life.

During the period from October 1992 through May 1993, Chosen People Ministries world-wide led 593 people to the Lord, of whom 184 were Jewish people and 409 were Gentile people.[71]

In the United States during the same period of time, CPM missionaries led forty-seven Jewish people to the Lord and forty-seven Gentiles, for a total of ninety-four decisions. The 1993 STEP program included seven Russian Jewish believers, three Canadian believers, and one worker from the Arbetisgemeinschaft fur das Messianische Zeugnis an Israel (AmZi) in Basil, Switzerland.

In Canada, for the same period there were nineteen decisions for the Lord—seven Jewish people and twelve Gentiles. The Messianic congregations in Toronto and Montreal are growing and Jewish people are coming to faith in Jesus.

In Israel there were nine decisions for the Lord—in spite of continued anti-Semitism and anti-missionary activity. During the last week of May 1993, Albert Israeli participated in a three-day evangelistic campaign in Haifa and had hundreds of conversations with Russian Jews. In July 1993, Albert worked with Operation Mobilization in distributing more than 500,000 tracts in northern Israel, near Haifa.

In Kiev, (the Ukraine) there were 124 decisions for the Lord, fifty-nine were Jewish people and sixty-five were Gentiles. Eighteen people were baptized. The staff now includes Dmitri Riznik (full-time), Samuel Lichtman (part-time), Alexander (Sasha) Duchno (part-time), and Ludmilla (Luda) Riznik (part-time).[72] A system of delivering humanitarian aid to the Jewish believers in Kiev has also been set up.

In South America, there were 347 decisions for the Lord. Sixty-three were Jewish people and 284 were Gentiles. The staff in South America includes Rev. Roberto Passo, Elias Habif, Telma Passo, Alejandra Passo, Betsabe Leon and Stephen Riviore. A new building has recently been purchased to house the growing congregation of Jewish believers who now attend the meetings. Three new groups of "the Friends of Chosen People Ministries" have been established: one in Bahia Blanca (Buenos Aires, Argentina); one in Embalse (Cordobe, Argentina); and one in Trujillo (Trujillo, Peru). The total number of "volunteer branches" in South America is now thirty-one (twenty-four in Argentina, and seven outside Argentina—in Mexico, Chile, Peru, Paraguay, and Uruguay).

Additionally, the radio program "Oye Israel" is being broadcast on over forty stations in South America. The Spanish edition of *The Chosen People* magazine, El Pueblo Elegido, is also being distributed throughout South America. Further, the new Bible Messianic Institute (I.B.M.) began its first year on March 12, 1993 with twenty students.

Thus the vision and message of Rabbi Leopold Cohn goes on. The Mission's name has changed three times. The personnel have changed. The methodology has changed. But the truth of the message is changeless: "The Gospel of the Lord Jesus Christ is the power of God unto salvation to all who believe, to the Jew FIRST, and also to the Gentile."[73]

The Rabbi's Vision will continue on into the next century—or until the Messiah returns!

ENDNOTES

Chapter 13. The Vision: One Hundred Years and Beyond

[1] *Minutes, ABMJ/Chosen People Ministries,* (September 29, 30, 1988), p 1.
[2] *Personal Correspondence: Harold Sevener to Martin (Moishe) Rosen,* (December 5, 1979), pp 1, 2.
[3] *The Chosen People,* Vol. LXXXV, No. 8, (April, 1980), pp 9, 10.
[4] *The Chosen People,* Vol. LXXXVI, No. 1, (September, 1980), p 7.
[5] *The Chosen People,* Vol. XCI, No. 2, (September, 1984), pp 6-8.
[6] *The Chosen People,* Vol. LXXXVI, No. 1, (September, 1980), p 11.
[7] *The Chosen People,* Vol. XCVII, No. 7, (March, 1991), pp 7, 8.
[8] *The Chosen People,* Vol. XCVII, No. 11, (July, 1991), pp 6, 7.
[9] *The Chosen People,* Vol. LXXXVII, No. 2, (February, 1981), p 5.
[10] See note above, pp 5, 6.
[11] *The Chosen People,* Vol. XCI, No. 1, (August, 1984), pp 6, 7.
[12] *The Chosen People,* Vol. XCX, No. 10, (June, 1989), pp 13, 14.
[13] See note above.
[14] *The Chosen People,* Vol. LXXXI, No. 9, (May, 1976), pp 9, 10.
[15] See note above, p 8.
[16] *The Chosen People,* Vol. LXXXIII, No. 1, (September, 1977), p 9.
[17] *The Chosen People,* Vol. LXXXIV, No. 6, (February, 1979), pp 6, 7.
[18] *The Chosen People,* Vol. LXXXVII, No. 2, (February, 1981), p 5.
[19] *Minutes of Personnel Committee, ABMJ,* (March 17, 1982), p 1.
[20] *The Chosen People,* Vol. XCX, No. 3, (November, 1988), p 5.
[21] See note above, pp 5, 6.
[22] *The Chosen People,* Vol. LXXXVII, No. 4, (April, 1981), p 14.
[23] See note above.
[24] *The Chosen People,* Vol. XCI, No. 12, (July, 1985), pp 8-10.
[25] *The Chosen People,* Vol. XCVII, No. 7, (March, 1991), p 9.
[26] Frank Potter, *Personal Testimony/Application ABMJ,* (April 5, 1982), p 3.
[27] *The Chosen People,* Vol. XCI, No. 1, (August, 1984), p 9.
[28] *The Chosen People,* Vol. XC, No. 5, (January, 1984), pp 12, 13.
[29] *The Chosen People,* Vol. XCVII, No. 7, (March, 1991), p 4.
[30] See note above, p 5.

31 See note above, p 4.

32 *The Chosen People*, Vol. XCIV, No. 6, (February, 1988), pp 10, 11.

33 *The Chosen People*, Vol. XCIII, No. 1, (September, 1986), p 5.

34 See note above.

35 *The Chosen People*, Vol. XCVIII, No. 1, (September, 1991), p 15.

36 Stewart Weinisch, *Personal Testimony/Application*, (June, 1983), p 3.

37 *The Chosen People*, Vol. XCVIII, No. 6, (February, 1992), pp 3-5.

38 *The Chosen People*, Vol. XCVI, No. 2, (October, 1989), pp 7, 8.

39 *The Chosen People*, Vol. XCVII, No. 3, (November, 1990), p 6.

40 *The Chosen People*, Vol. XCX, No. 10, (June, 1989), pp 4, 5.

41 *The Chosen People*, Vol. XCIV, No. 4, (December, 1987), pp 8-11.

42 *The Chosen People*, Vol. XCVIII, No. 8, (April, 1992), p 9.

43 *The Chosen People*, Vol. XCVIII, No. 9, (May, 1992), p 9.

44 *Minutes*, Chosen People Ministries, (November 18, 1988), pp 2, 3.

45 *Minutes*, Chosen People Ministries, (January 27, 1989), p 1, 2.

46 See note above, p 2.

47 *Minutes*, Chosen People Ministries, (June 1, 1989), p 1.

48 Song of Solomon 2:15.

49 *Minutes*, Chosen People Ministries, (January 26, 1990), p 4.

50 *The Chosen People*, Vol. XCVII, No. 4, (January, 1991), pp 2, 3.

51 *Chosen People Ministries Bylaws*; revised: 9/25/92; 4:15; p 8; 5.5; p 13.

52 See note above, 5.2: p 12.

53 *Minutes*, Chosen People Ministries, (June 1, 1989), p 1.

54 *The Chosen People*, Vol. XCVIII, No. 3, (November, 1991), p 14.

55 Ken Alpren, *Personal Testimony/Application*, (December 19, 1991), pp 4, 5.

56 James Fox, *Personal Testimony/Application*, (June 1, 1992), p 3.

57 See note above, p 4.

58 *The Chosen People*, Vol. XCI, No. 3, (October, 1984), pp 6-8.

59 *The Chosen People*, Vol. XCVI, No. 6, (February, 1990), p 9, 10.

60 See note above.

61 Kirk Gliebe, *Personal Testimony/Application*, (March, 1992), p 2.

62 See note above, p 3.

63 Winfred P. Crenshaw, *Personal Testimony/Application*, (January 18, 1990), p 5.

64 *The Chosen People*, Vol. XCVII, No. 6, (February, 1991), pp 3-5.

65 *The Chosen People*, Special Issue, (August, 1990), pp 6-11.

66 *Mid-Year Report*, CPM, (August, 1991), pp 2, 3.

67 *The Chosen People*, Vol. XCVII, No. 6, (February, 1991), p 13.

68 *The Chosen People*, Vol. XCVIII, No. 3, (November, 1991), p 7, 8.

69 *The Chosen People*, Vol. XCIX, No. 11, (July, 1993), pp 4-6.

70 Matthew 1:1.

71 *President's Report*, CPM Board Meeting, (June 18-19, 1993), p 2.

72 *See note above, p 4.*

73 Romans 1:16.

14

THE VISION IN THE DOMINION OF CANADA

During the late 1930's the outreach of the Mission just naturally spilled over the Canadian border, as churches and conference grounds in Vancouver, Winnipeg, Toronto, Hamilton and throughout the Dominion of Canada invited Joseph Hoffman Cohn, the Field Evangelists, or missionaries to present the work of the Mission.

CANADIAN HEADQUARTERS IN HAMILTON, ONTARIO

In Hamilton, Ontario, the Rev. Donald J. Mackay, pastor of Philpott Tabernacle, expressed his interest in the work of the Mission and his concern for the salvation of the Jews in the city of Hamilton. His interest and concern prompted Mr. A.B. Machlin, the Missionary in Charge of the Mission's Buffalo branch, to establish an extensive visitation program in the city of Hamilton, Ontario, Canada—a program which ultimately led to the establishment of the Mission's first "official" outreach in Canada. From the outset, however, it was clear that contributions given to the Mission in Canada would, of necessity, have to remain for use in that country. The July 1940 Minutes record Joseph's explanation to the Directors regarding this matter. He stated:

> Conditions surrounding the present exchange rate as between Canadian and American funds are such as to be adverse to the interests of our Canadian contributors. We have now established a small Jewish work in Hamilton, Ont., Canada,…and hereafter all Canadian contributions will be used in Canada. 750 copies of The Shepherd of Israel go from this office each month and are mailed to the Jews of Hamilton. Mr. Machlin visits Hamilton regularly and does visitation among the Jews of that city.[1]

The Board authorized a resolution establishing Rev. Donald J. Mackay as the Canadian Treasurer for the American Board of Missions to the Jews for the Domain of Canada; the work became an outreach of Philpott Tabernacle. By 1941 Pastor MacKay was appointed the Director of the Hamilton branch of the Mission. The Headquarters for the Canadian ministry was housed in the Bible House of Hamilton.

In reporting on the new ministry in Canada, Joseph Cohn told readers of The Chosen People magazine:

> Spontaneous and enthusiastic has been the response from our Canadian friends ever since we announced a few months ago that the Lord had been definitely leading us to undertake a testimony to the Jews in our neighboring country, Canada. With generosity and wholeheartedness our beloved brother Rev. Donald J. MacKay, Pastor of the Philpott Tabernacle in Hamilton, came forward to give his services freely as Honorary Treasurer of the American Board of Missions to the Jews, in Canada. And quickly our Canadian friends responded, so that from all over the Canadian Provinces, came letters and gifts to Pastor MacKay for the Canadian work. We now are seeking to branch out a little farther into the Jewish field there, in addition to what we are now doing in the city of Hamilton itself. In Hamilton, aside from the treasurer's office in the study of the Philpott Tabernacle, we have a center at 39 King William Street. These are the quarters occupied by the Bible House of Hamilton with Mr. W. Jones in charge. We are sharing the rent with him now, so that one-half of the store is ours, and thus we have half of the window display. In the window we are continually exhibiting various tracts both for Jews and for Christians and these exhibits are being frequently changed and they are attracting attention continually.
>
> We are also sending into Hamilton some 700 copies of the 'Shepherd of Israel' each month, addressed to 700 Jewish families in that City.
>
> To reach out into other parts of Canada, we have taken as a first step a little service in one of the Detention Camps, where there are a great many refugee Jews who have been sent there from Great Britain. In this particular Camp there is Mr. Alexander George Lichtenstein, son of our own missionary, Pastor Emanuel Lichtenstein of Vienna, Austria [see chapter seven of this history]. This young man was studying in London for the ministry, and quite suddenly

in the fifth column scare which spread over England, many Jews were taken and shipped away to Detention Camps, some even as far as Australia. Among these aliens thus taken, was this young man. To him we have been sending Gospel literature because he wrote us that there is a fine opportunity there to reach many with good Christian reading matter.[2]

In 1943, as World War II engulfed Europe, Mr. William O. Jones, Director of the Bible House, took on the added responsibility of directing the Mission's activities in Hamilton when Pastor Donald J. MacKay was called into active military service as a chaplain.[3]

Joseph Cohn's policy had always been to help as many Jewish believers as possible with their educations. He did so with the hope that upon graduation at least *some* of the men and women would be led to join the staff of the Mission, but when they did not, he expressed confidence that they would be used in other ways to help reach Jewish people with the Gospel.

One young Jewish student who received financial assistance for his education from the Canadian ministry, but did not feel led to join the Mission's staff, was Martin Chernoff.[4]

The Ministry in Montreal

Karl Goldberg also received financial assistance through the Canadian office; he, on the other hand, joined the Mission's staff. Karl was a refugee boy who immigrated to Canada from Vienna.[5] He came to faith in Yeshua through the ministry of Rev. Emanuel Lichtenstein in Vienna. Even before he graduated from Toronto Bible College, Joseph had decided to use Karl to open a second branch of the Mission in Canada. The Montreal branch was opened during the summer of 1942. The Dedication Service was held October 15, 1942.

Karl Goldberg

In reporting to the Board on the opening of the Montreal branch, Joseph stated that the Mission had secured a small building on the outskirts of Montreal, the rent being $70.00 a month. He further reported that Mr. Karl Goldberg had been hired as the missionary of this new branch.[6]

Following his standard procedure, Joseph established a central committee to oversee the work in Montreal. The committee was under the leadership of Rev. Stanley Stock, pastor of the Madison Baptist Church. Rev. Stock, a graduate of Dallas Theological Seminary, had a great love for Israel and the Jewish people and he was delighted to be involved with the Mission in Canada.[7]

Stanley Stock first became acquainted with the Mission when, as a young man, he heard Rabbi Leopold Cohn speak at the Erieside Bible Conference in Cleveland, Ohio. That message implanted within him a burden for the Jewish people which never left him, and ultimately resulted in the Montreal branch of the Mission being established.[8]

In sharing the story of the opening of the Montreal branch Joseph Cohn told readers of *The Chosen People* magazine:

...Even the choosing of this hall seemed ordered of God; for every other building with whose owner we were negotiating, was deliberately refused to us. In one case, while the owner was willing to rent, the Outremont City Council refused to give us permission to open a hall for the preaching of the Gospel of the Lord Jesus Christ to the Jews. As is well known, Montreal is a strongly Roman Catholic city.

At last came the day of opening and dedication, and at this point I think it may be best to have our beloved brother, Rev. Stanley Stock, the pastor of the Madison Baptist Church, and the chairman of our Montreal Committee, give the story. So, here it is, from his own pen:

'On the evening of October 15th, 1942, there was assembled a very happy company in the City of Montreal, Que., Canada. About seventy friends of Israel had gathered in a spacious store at 357 Laurier Avenue W., to celebrate the opening of a new branch of our Canadian work. This marked the culmination of the hopes and prayers of a number of faithful believers that something might be done toward the evangelization of the upwards of 80,000 Jews of this great metropolis. Now, at last, we were to witness the official opening of the work by Rev. J. Hoffman Cohn, our beloved General Secretary....'

'At the suggestion of Mr. Cohn the Committee through its chairman approached our dear brother Mr. Karl Goldberg, who was then about to complete his work at Toronto Bible College. We found in him a young man of charming personality as well as a devout and consecrated Christian. Again we were impressed that "This thing was of God." After prayer, arrangements were made for Mr. Goldberg to come to Montreal in April after his graduation.'

'A thorough survey of the city by our missionary was undertaken to determine the most suitable place in which to locate. Again the guidance of God was very manifest. Our present mission premises impressed us all as ideal, but

permission was refused by the Bank which owns the building. Slightly crestfallen, but assured that God would over-rule, we continued in prayer.... Then, as so often happens in answer to prayer, a sudden change of attitude was shown by the Bank and a remark made to Mr. Goldberg by the manager led us to believe that they might reconsider their decision. The Chairman of the Committee presented our case to him, and after several days the Bank consented to lease the premises to us.'

'By the Grace of God we have secured a large well-equipped, heated store at the heart of the middle class Jewish section of the city. We are in the City of Montreal and but two blocks removed from the border of Outremont, a suburb with 6,000 Hebrew inhabitants. Since we are but two doors removed from an important crosstown intersection, the advertising value of our store front is excellent. All this we have secured at a very reasonable rental, less than many middle class people are paying for rent of their homes in Montreal.'

'As we looked around us on the happy evening, we remembered with thanksgiving that God had supplied Christian friends for our brother Karl, who in glad co-operation with him had performed the necessary alterations at a cost to us of material only. We have been able, then, to subdivide the large store so that we have a good sized office and prayer room and adjoining that a very necessary kitchen which together occupy the rear ten feet of the store. Directly in front of these is our meeting room proper for public services, curtained off from the front of the store at about fifteen feet leaving that amount of space for a reading room which is screened from the curious eyes of the passer-by by Venetian Blinds. The windows are attractively furnished with signs of invitation, a Hebrew, a Yiddish and a German Bible are open at impressive passages, and tracts with titles calculated to arrest the attention of those who pass, are carefully laid out so they can be read by the one looking in.'

'Hundreds of Jewish homes have been visited by Mr. Goldberg, and tracts have been left. We are now beginning to reap spiritual results from the faithful sowing. One refined Hebrew lady was attracted by the prospect of learning to read and write English which she already speaks well. A Christian lady, a school teacher in a city school has undertaken this work and this receptive Jewess is learning the 53rd chapter of Isaiah by heart that she may accept and love the Lord Jesus, Who is so beautifully depicted therein. A Jewish man, in great trouble came into the store and after long conversation was presented with a New Testament. He told Mr. Goldberg that he reads it constantly, even on the street car, to his great comfort of heart. A young man of nineteen was much impressed by a visit of our missionary and desired Mr. Goldberg to visit his young men's club at the Synagogue and lead in a friendly debate afterward. These are but drops which are beginning to fall, of the blessings which we believe will in the future come in showers.'[9]

Karl Goldberg was tireless in his efforts to evangelize the Jewish community of Montreal and its environs. He often distributed upwards of four to five hundred copies of the Shepherd of Israel in a month, as well as a number of New Testaments and tracts. He told readers of The Chosen People magazine:

Last Saturday we started a children's campaign and the result was that we had nine children attend our children's meeting. Every child was from a Jewish home. There would have been more coming but one of the bigger boys prevented them from entering the Mission. He told the children that we were teaching them about Christ and how to eat unclean things. Some of the little ones of course were afraid to enter the Mission. That is one of the things we have to put up with, trusting the Lord will bring the children in, in spite of these handicaps and hardships. The children who came enjoyed the meeting very much and promised to come back next Saturday....

...throughout this month we made new contacts through visitation and them visiting us. Also many of our old contacts are being followed up carefully and they are being revisited from time to time.... But one new contact was rather remarkable. A middle aged man visited the Mission one morning. He asked for some tracts which are exhibited in the windows. After he received them from my hands he turned to me and said the following: 'You know I believe that we Jews are coming daily closer to your faith. After all, the great multitudes the New Testament talks about, who followed Christ in the beginning were all Jews, and I believe soon this multitude of Jews is going to follow Him again.' This inquirer was not a Gentile (for he spoke Yiddish) neither a Hebrew Christian for he told me he is from an orthodox home. He accepted one English New Testament (he preferred an English edition). We trust and pray that while reading it the Lord will speak to him as an individual, that he may become one of the multitude which we trust soon will follow their true Messiah.[10]

HELEN CARRELL

The work in Montreal prospered under Karl Goldberg's leadership and it became a training ground for new missionary workers. One individual who was sent to Montreal for "expanded missionary training" was Miss Helen Carrell. Helen, a member of the Brethren Churches of America, had begun her training in Los Angeles, California; she was being trained to become an assistant missionary to Rev. Elias Zimmerman.

When Helen arrived in Montreal for missionary training, she did not expect to fall in love. But fall in love she did! Cupid's arrows pierced the hearts of both Karl Goldberg and Helen Carrell the moment they were introduced to one another. It was "love at first sight"—but each one was too shy to tell the other.

Many years later, Daniel Fuchs told this writer how he and his wife, Muriel, had gone to Canada to speak on behalf of the Mission, and to try to open new doors of support for the missionary program. While they were there, Karl told Daniel how much he loved Helen, but was to shy to tell her his feelings. Helen likewise told Muriel Fuchs of her love for Karl. Daniel knew Helen's missionary training period was about to conclude, after which she would be returning to Los Angeles, so he wasted no words. He said, "Karl, what you do, do quickly!" Evidently Karl followed Daniel's advice, for on September 28, 1944 Helen and Karl were married. Joseph Cohn told readers of *The Chosen People* magazine: "And so instead of being the assistant to Mr. Zimmerman, she has become a very permanent assistant to Karl Goldberg!"[11]

As the head of the committee overseeing the Mission's work in Montreal, Rev. Stanley Stock wrote to Joseph and jokingly complained that since Miss Carrell had become Mrs. Goldberg, he had lost a worker (actually he had gained one, but it was a good ploy anyway); he therefore asked Joseph for another worker to replace Miss Carrell.

MARTHA SINGER

Joseph responded to Rev. Stock's plea for another worker by sending Miss Martha Singer, daughter of Mr. Herbert Singer, the Mission's worker in charge of the refugee work in New York. Martha was a graduate of the Bible Institute of Pennsylvania, and a capable worker who had trained under Miss Sussdorff, Miss Rose, and Hilda Koser in Coney Island.[12]

Martha Singer gave the following report of the first seven months of her ministry in Montreal:

> As I look back over the seven months of service with our Mission here in Montreal, I can truly praise the Lord for His wonderful guidance and blessings that He has poured upon His work. Although there is much opposition from all sides, we are able to have two children's classes, two English classes and one Mother's class every week. On Monday and Friday of each week, Jewish girls from the age of seven up to fourteen years of age come to the Mission to sew and hear the Gospel taught to them....
>
> Our reading room is open from morning to night and many Jewish people stop in to read and discuss our tracts. Here we find marvelous opportunities in talking to men and women and many of them have left the Mission with a new Testament and tracts, promising to read them.
>
> One day, returning from an errand, I noticed a Jewish man standing in front of the Mission. I asked whether I could help him and he hesitatingly asked me to type a business letter for him. I at once saw another opportunity of witnessing for the Lord and so I invited him in and typed the needed letter for him. While doing this, Mr. S. was looking around the room, reading several of the tracts. Upon finishing his letter, Mr. S. was greatly touched when I refused to accept money for the work. The Lord then gave me a wonderful chance to talk to him, and when he left, after a two-hour discussion, he carried with him a New Testament and several tracts which he promised to read. The following week, both his girls came to my classes and have come ever since!
>
> There are many wonderful experiences, but the greatest joy came when I had the privilege of leading a Jewish soul to the acceptance of the Lord Jesus Christ....
>
> These are just a few of the high lights in the work that the Lord has given us. It is my sincere desire to be greatly used of the Lord among 'the lost sheep of the house of Israel.'[13]

As with other branches of the Mission, retaining staff in Montreal, an area hostile to the Gospel, was not an easy task. The missionaries there were not only rebuffed by the Jewish community, they were also surrounded by the large Roman Catholic community which saw the Mission and its workers as a threat to their own church and missionary programs. Eventually, Karl and Helen Goldberg were transferred to Buffalo, New York to work in the Mission's branch there. They later left the staff of the Mission to further develop the Buffalo Hebrew Christian Mission independently of the American Board of Missions to the Jews. Miss Martha Singer was also transferred, and later resigned from the Mission.

NEW STAFF IN MONTREAL

When the Goldberg's and Martha Singer were transferred to other areas of the ministry, the Mission hired Miss Gladys Midgley to take over the mothers' and children's ministry in Montreal; Rev. G. Vanderlip was hired to handle the teaching ministry. Both were hired in 1946. The February, 1947 Chosen People magazine included their respective reports. Gladys Midgley wrote:

Although I have not been with the Mission for the complete year, I praise God that He has called me to work among His chosen people. The experiences of the missionary are varied in every home. Our task is to enter the home, win their confidence and tell them of their Messiah. The Mothers' class, held once a week, has proved to be a time when they learn more of the One who saves, and of the way of the Christian life…. We rejoice to have the children step in occasionally and tell us the things of their interest. This affords an opportunity to have personal chats with them, beside weekly classes. The women who come for help with the English language, often discuss with us the things of God. The New Testament is used for reading lessons. We are surrounded by Jews who are very friendly. One from a neighboring store, asks for literature, both to read and to send to his parents. We trust that the Lord will use our humble efforts and bless His Word to the salvation of many from Israel's race.[14]

Rev. Vanderlip reported:

Israel was like a beautiful ornament upon which the Artist had put His name in many different ways…. That marvelous piece of pottery is broken and its fragments are scattered over the earth, and only the hand of the Master can bring these beautiful pieces of broken pottery together. God has placed in Montreal a few pieces of that broken pottery…and we are trying to collect these fragments, to lay them down at the feet of the Master, so that He again can make it another vessel as seemeth good in His sight. There is a great variety of broken pottery. Here comes the Jewish man who loves to chant the Psalms of David, followed up by an intelligent Jewish lady, sharing the evening meal with us; there is that high school student, Zionist and communist, and also the boys and girls in their teens coming to our Mission. We do our best to introduce them all to the One who has said, 'Come unto me all ye that labor, and I will give you rest.'[15]

A MONTREAL REPORT — 1949

The May 1949 issue of *The Chosen People* magazine included a comprehensive report of the Mission's outreach in Montreal. The report was given by Arnold Seidler, who visited the branch prior to accepting a position as Missionary in Charge of the Pittsburgh branch after John Solomon's retirement (see Chapter Nine of this history). He wrote:

…The Mission is pleasantly situated; and a large sign, reaching well out into the street, proclaims the message preached in the Hall: 'Jesus Christ, Israel's Messiah,' in English and Hebrew. These words arrest the curiosity and interest of every passing Jew. Jews who have passed the Mission in a streetcar have been known to return on foot in order to find out the meaning of this sign. The windows are attractively arranged and well stocked with open Bibles and tracts showing clearly the purpose of the work of the American Board. Here is the same spirit in which the work in Manhattan and Brooklyn is carried on….

Sitting indoors one has a perfect view of everyone who stops at the window to read the prophecies concerning the first coming of our Lord Jesus Christ. These, by the way, are written on a large roll of paper and displayed by an ingenious device like a telegram or ticker-tape, being operated by a small motor. This is the work of Mr. Vanderlip, who has completed several rolls on different topics and displays them alternately.

On one occasion a Jew stayed for well over twenty minutes following the Scriptures attentively. Another, after reading with apparent interest the Scriptures for a similar period, came in and asked for literature, which was gladly given. That same day a brilliant pianist and architect (a newcomer to Canada) entered and enquired about English lessons which are given free of charge and advertised in the window. It was a delight to witness to him of the saving power of our Saviour. Although one felt that the Truth had made upon him a deep impression, one could notice too the inner fear of what would happen to him and his family if he accepted the Truth. He has not found employment yet and it seems that it is difficult for Jews to find any.

A young Jew converted two years ago is still without any work; no Jew or Christian will have him. Another Jew, convinced of the Truth, said to Mr. Vanderlip, 'I dare not acknowledge Him as my Saviour; they will crucify me when they hear of it.' It makes it difficult for the missionary to pursue his aim, knowing that every convert has to face such a future….

A young Jewish woman read with interest the Scriptures in the window and it was interesting to watch her features as she did so. After some time she entered the Reading Room and requested to be allowed to look at some of the reading matter put on the tables for the use of visitors. After reading quietly for a period she entered into conversation with Miss Midgley, our lady missionary. They had a heart-to-heart talk at the end of which she said: 'I wish I could believe as you do; for I see you have real happiness.' She left with the promise to come again. To our surprise and joy she returned the same evening with the express purpose of seeing Miss Midgley again….

During the afternoon two Jewish gentlemen entered the room. While the younger approached Mr. Vanderlip, the elder selected a number of tracts and copies of The Shepherd of Israel, *and stuffed his pockets with them. They were father and son, attached to the leading liberal synagogue of Montreal; and they asked questions concerning the purpose and aim of our missionary efforts. They were told that we preached Christ Jesus as the only way of salvation for Jew and Gentile, for He came in fulfillment of Old Testament prophecies. He then asked if we hated the Jews; to which he received the reply, 'We do not, and we dare not. The Jews are the people of God's choice and no real Christian can hate the brethren of our Lord according to the flesh.' He then made known the real purpose of his visit. He was the organizing secretary of the Young People's Society of the Shaare Sion Synagogue and wished that a worker of the American Board of Missions to the Jews would take part in a public symposium held for the young people at the synagogue a few weeks hence. The subject will be, 'Anti-Semitism, its Solution.' Mr. Vanderlip happily agreed to be the speaker for the Mission....*

That night the English classes were held. Nineteen Jews and Jewesses were present, newcomers to Canada. I cannot help but think that Canada is a very privileged country. The cream of the Jewish intellectuals were gathered in our hall. Six different classes were in operation. When it came to conversation, it centered around the land, the people, the Messiah. When it was time to read, all classes united; and sitting around a long table, we read the first two chapters of Genesis. After that, Mr. Vanderlip asked me to say a few words and I spoke to them in Yiddish and German....

...After the English lesson it was 9:35 p.m.; there was a knock at the door. Two young Jewish students, who had been reading the Word of God in our window, desired a talk. At first they seemed on their guard, but they were disarmed immediately when they heard that we were friends of Israel, friends of the Jewish people, and trying to alleviate their sufferings both spiritual and physical. The conversation continued until 11:50 p.m. and faithful witness was given, not without making some impact upon them. We met one of them since then, while traveling in a streetcar, and he came across and spoke to us, not afraid to be seen with those who love the Saviour....

We are often asked: Is Jewish work worthwhile? Are all the expenses justified? In one day at our Montreal Branch nearly ten Jews and Jewesses who never before had heard of the Saviour were told of Him, and nearly thirty unconverted Jews heard the Gospel. Another Jewess who accepted Christ as her Saviour is waiting to be baptized; ...

Is it worthwhile? ...Of course it is worthwhile. 'Inasmuch as ye have done it to the least of these my (Jewish) brethren, ye have done it unto me!'[16]

As God poured out His blessings on the missionary outreach in Canada, He also blessed the work financially. The Minutes of the January 1950 annual meeting of the Board state: "Mr. Jones presented the financial report of the Canadian work for the year 1949. This showed receipts of $22,707.44, and disbursements of $20,496.96. Mr. Pretlove moved that the report be received and placed on file with appreciation from the Board. The motion was seconded and unanimously carried."[17] For the fiscal year 1950, the Board was able to add an additional $4,632.40 to their cash surplus for further expansion of the ministry in Canada.[18]

The work in Montreal remained under the close supervision of Rev. Stanley Stock and despite the difficulty of maintaining a staff, the work was thriving. Mr. Vanderlip resigned during the Fall of 1951 and the work continued without the benefit of a Missionary in Charge until the Spring of 1952, when Joseph Cohn transferred Mr. Paul Wilson to the Montreal branch.[19] Paul Wilson had been serving in Cuba, but it was no longer safe for him to minister there (See Chapter Nine of this history).

When he arrived in Montreal, Paul was impressed to find that the Mission was still holding twice-weekly English language classes for refugee Jews; the weekly attendance ran from thirty-five to forty adults. In addition, there were twice-weekly English language classes for children conducted by Miss Gladys Midgley and Miss Ruth Belding. The classes in English were used as Bible classes, to give each student an understanding of the Gospel. When they were not teaching classes, the staff members did personal visitation in homes and distributed gospel literature to the Jewish people of Montreal. The first Friday of each month was devoted to a special prayer meeting for the friends of the Mission.[20]

Despite Paul Wilson's enthusiasm for the ministry in Montreal, his commitment was to ministry among Spanish speaking Jews (Sephardic), rather than among the French speaking and East European Jews who were immigrating into Montreal. By the end of 1952 Paul resigned from the Mission. He returned to Florida to work among the Jewish people there.[21]

ASHTON HOLDEN AND MARGARET SEIDLER

In 1953, hoping to expand the work in Montreal, Joseph transferred Rev. Ashton Holden from the Los Angeles branch to the Montreal branch. Ashton had been serving as an assistant to Rev. Elias Zimmerman.

Six years later (c.1959) the Montreal branch was relocated to a facility in the heart of the city's orthodox Jewish section—a move which was met with such opposition on the part of the orthodox neighbors that for the first few months they would cross to the other side of the street whenever they passed the Mission's building. Gradually, however, they became more tolerant of the Mission's presence in their midst. Some even stopped to look at, and to read, the materials displayed in the window. Ashton Holden wrote:

> There has been a steady growth in attendance at our meetings. A year ago, on account of increased numbers, we split our Young Peoples' Meeting into two, and now find it necessary to hold four meetings a week for the same reason. These meetings are a great help in establishing contact with parents, some of whom on several occasions (having ostensibly called to see if their children were at the Mission) stayed through the gospel meeting....
>
> While street meetings are not permitted in the Province of Quebec, we are able to distribute gospel leaflets and Scripture portions in different languages.[22]

In 1960, shortly after the death of her husband (c.1959), Mrs. Margaret Seidler was transferred to the Montreal branch. Margaret Seidler was Ashton Holden's sister. The Seidlers (as mentioned in Chapter Nine of this history) had served for more than ten years as missionaries on the staff of the Hebrew Christian Testimony to Israel in London, England prior to joining the staff of the Mission. Ashton, too, had served as a missionary to the Jews in London. He was hired to work in the Los Angeles branch about the same time Arnold Seidler was hired to serve as Missionary in Charge of the Pittsburgh branch.

It appears that Joseph Cohn hired a number of workers from England about the same time he was considering hiring Mr. Herman Newmark to be his associate in the work (c.1947-1950). All were former staff members of the Hebrew Christian Testimony to Israel, and while nothing is explicitly stated in the Minutes to indicate that Joseph Cohn was seeking to merge the two ministries, and thereby to strengthen his foreign work and his work in Canada, the implications from the Minutes, from correspondence, and from personal interviews which the author has undertaken with workers from that period of time suggest the possibility. If such a merger was in Joseph Cohn's thoughts, it was never culminated. Instead, several workers from the Hebrew Christian Testimony to Israel were hired by Cohn. Others decided against serving with the Mission and chose to remain with the Hebrew Christian Testimony to Israel.

One of the reasons that Daniel Fuchs transferred Margaret Seidler to Montreal was that the ministry was waning. Many of the programs that had been established to reach immigrant Jews no longer served a purpose, and had therefore been discontinued. Other programs were discontinued through attrition; some had become obsolete through failure to keep up with the changing Jewish community in Montreal. As a missionary "team," Ashton Holden and Margaret Seidler emphasized the mothers' and children's ministry. Margaret wrote:

> The Young People's classes for boys and girls recently went through a period of dwindling attendance. However, after much prayer and increased personal contacts through visitation, we now have a number of new members. We have proven that having a library for the young people to use has been a means of reaching out into the neighborhood. The youngsters come to the Center in order to join the library and take out books, but many stay to hear the Bible stories. There is a steady demand for Bibles and Biblical books.
>
> Both the girls and boys enjoy being together at handwork, playing games, or even studying their homework before the 'Clubs' begin. The emphasis is on personal interest and individual attention. This is a time when we may hear of a problem at school or at home or may get involved in discussing a Bible story from a previous meeting. Here are vital points of contact!
>
> Our reading room has also given us opportunities for some very personal talks with Jewish people. The majority of the New Testaments asked for are in Yiddish, but also some in Hebrew, English and French are given out.
>
> We seek further contacts with all age groups and are glad of the facilities offered by the apartment over the Mission. We often invite people to a meal on Sundays and take them to a local church afterwards. Also, as weather permits, we take groups of children or young people on short sight-seeing trips.
>
> One of the most important aspects of the work in Montreal is the time we spend in visitation. The Women's meetings have also been a great joy to both Rev. Holden and me and we are thankful for the growth of this group.[23]

Rev. Stanley S. Stock continued to serve as Honorary Director of the Montreal branch—a position he'd held from the inception of that branch in 1941—but when he retired from his position as pastor of Madison Baptist Church of Montreal in May 1965, he was able to devote his time to doing field work for the Mission.[24] When the Mission's work in Canada was incorporated as Beth Sar Shalom Mission in 1967, Rev. Stanley Stock was elected to serve as the Canadian Mission's first President.[25]

In reporting to the Directors of the Beth Sar Shalom Mission in November 1971, Stanley Stock read from letters he'd received from the Montreal workers—Margaret Seidler and Ashton Holden. The letters spoke of the personal contacts they'd made, but they included no statistical information regarding how many meetings had been held each week, how many attended, etc.—information which the Directors felt was necessary in order to ascertain what direction they should take to help the work. The Board therefore unanimously passed that the following statistical information be included in the Annual Missionary Reports in Canada:

1. the number of meetings per week including the average attendance.
2. the ages of those attending
3. the average number of visits per month
4. the number of those who have accepted the Lord.
5. the number of crafts [sic-tracts] that have been given out, also which particular craft [sic] is most important.[26]

The information requested was already being included in the missionary reports in the United States, and would simply have brought the Canadian missionary reports into conformity with reports being submitted in the United States, but Ashton Holden objected vigorously to giving statistical information in his reports to the Board. A full year passed without cooperation from Rev. Holden, and the Minutes of the Annual Board Meeting of the Beth Sar Shalom Mission of November 1972 record the following discussion:

> ...In corresponding with Rev. Holden, Rev. Stock mentioned the suggestion by the Board of Directors of the five points as formulated at the last board meeting. In reply, Rev. Holden objected to the holding of statistics and the reporting of same. This correspondence was forwarded to Dr. Fuchs who in turn, wrote to Rev. Holden and mentioned that the purpose in asking about details was not for advertising that we hold so many meetings and number of people attending and the number of souls saved because the issue of statistics is questionable.... However, the problem is not one of statistics but a matter of stewardship and as Members of the Board we are required to give an account of our stewardship and I feel that the questions that were asked were valid and that he should not hesitate in answering them. Rev. Holden was urgently requested to consider his decision to withhold these facts from us. On March 20th., Rev. Holden replied to say that he had a conviction and therefore could not comply with the request as he did not feel that statistics were necessary in missionary work. It was decided that this matter should be brought up later in the meeting under New Business.[27]

Under New Business, the Beth Sar Shalom Mission Directors agreed that Daniel Fuchs should discuss with Ashton Holden and Margaret Seidler the possibility of their joint retirement. This was accomplished, and their retirement became effective July 1, 1975. However, because Rev. Holden was not yet sixty-five (the effective age of the Mission's pension program), the two remained in Montreal. Shortly after their retirement, both Ashton Holden and Margaret Seidler returned to their native England.

The national headquarters of the Canadian outreach had remained in Hamilton, Ontario where the Mission continued to utilize part of the space at the Bible House. Canadian gifts were received and receipted from this office. Joseph Cohn was always careful to explain to the readership of *The Chosen People* magazine that funds raised in Canada were used for the ministry in Canada and in other parts of the world. He wrote:

> ...This work has been growing and has already experienced rich blessings at the Lord's hands. Here also has been established the business office for our Canadian friends, so that Canadian gifts can be sent to Hamilton and money used either for work in Canada, or for work in Great Britain, or sometimes to help our work in Palestine. In this way Canadian gifts suffer no shrinkage on account of adverse exchange rates.[28]

In 1945 the Board passed a motion to further clarify the separation of funds. The motion stated that the Canadian Treasurer for the Mission in Canada, "...accepts the duty of receiving such funds as may be contributed to our Mission in Canada, and disbursing the same according to directions which may be given to him from time to time by the General Secretary of the Board of Directors."[29]

The Mission Incorporated in Canada

It was not the intention of the Board to create two separate missions—one in Canada and one in the United States. The desire was to have one mission, controlled and operated by the Board of Directors in the USA. Cohn preferred to operate Canada's mission as he had the other "foreign" branches—through the oversight of a committee established in each country—and the Mission in Canada was operated in this way for many years. However, in November 1967, twenty-two years after the inception of the Mission's outreach in Canada, Harold Pretlove announced to the Directors of the American Board of Missions to the Jews that the Beth Sar Shalom (House of the Prince of Peace) Mission of Canada had legally incorporated and was registered in Canada.[30]

The first organizational meeting of the Beth Sar Shalom Mission of Canada was held November 13, 1967. The organizing Board was comprised of: "Mrs. H. Wilson, Hamilton, Rev. Stanley Stock, Montreal, Rev. Daniel Fuchs, Rev. Harold Pretlove, New York City and Mr. Tom Walker, Hamilton."[31]

As has been mentioned, Rev. Stanley Stock was elected president; Mr. Tom Walker, vice-president and secretary; Irene Wilson, treasurer; Harold Pretlove and Daniel Fuchs, directors. The Beth Sar Shalom Mission adopted an identical Doctrinal Statement to the statement held by the American Board of Missions to the Jews in the United States, and the two missions functioned with an inter-locking Board of Directors. This was apparent when Canadian members of the Beth Sar Shalom Mission were asked to sit on meetings of the American Board and vice versa.

In selecting a name for the Canadian ministry, anything with the word, "American," was avoided because of the strong national feelings in Canada against such organizational names. Beth Sar Shalom Mission was chosen, because it was a name under which many of the Mission's foreign branches had been established.

The Minutes record the following action taken as the Canadian Directors discussed the future of the Beth Sar Shalom Mission at their initial Directors meeting in November 1967:

> *With the re-organization of the Canadian work, the possibility of locating in Vancouver, B.C., Winnipeg, Manitoba and the enlarging of the work in Toronto, Ontario was suggested. This would require workers in the West, Mid-West, Central and Eastern Provinces and that there should be no boundary line between the United States and Canada. With a dividing line running north and south, a worker in a given area could extend his field of labour north into Canada or south into the United States. Offerings received in either country should be forwarded to their respective Head offices. e.g. Canadian funds to the Mission office in Hamilton and in the United States to the Mission office in New York.*[32]

The American Board authorized the transfer of all assets it was holding for the Canadian ministry to be transferred to the new Canadian Mission.[33]

The formation of a new corporation, allowing for the administration of its funds by a separate board, was a historic step for the Mission. For the first time a board, other than the American board, had the authority to determine how funds in their country would be used. This move toward decentralization of the American board's power and authority was far removed from the controlling hand Joseph Hoffman Cohn employed and wanted.

The Canadian board voted to continue the support of Victor Sedaca in Buenos Aires, of Peter Gutkind in Haifa, Israel (Canadian funds of the Mission had been used to purchase the apartment for Gutkind's use in Haifa), and also of Mrs. Wilkowsky in London, England. They also voted to continue, at least for a while, the policy set by the American Board with regard to the use of Canadian funds—that they be used in the foreign work of the Mission until such time as sufficient staff and branches could be developed in Canada to use all of the Canadian funds there.

TORONTO, UNDER FRED BREGMAN

One of the major concerns of the Canadian board was the need for a branch of the Mission in Toronto—a city with the largest and the fastest growing Jewish community in Canada. The Mission had workers in Montreal and volunteer workers in Hamilton, Ontario, but no outreach ministry had been established in Toronto. To meet the need of a Gospel testimony to the Jews in Toronto, the Canadian board hired Mr. Fred Bregman as a part-time missionary. The Glencairn Baptist Church of Toronto rented space to the Mission so Mr. Bregman would have a place to establish the Toronto branch of the ministry.[34]

Fred Bregman was the son of Rabbi Henry Bregman, a well known rabbi in England and Canada who had accepted the Messiah, Yeshua while he was still employed as a rabbi in Exeter, England. Mr. and Mrs. Sawkins, a Gentile Christian couple had asked Rabbi Bregman to teach them Hebrew, and during the hours, weeks, and months they spent together the love that Mr. and Mrs. Sawkins displayed for the Jewish people broke down the rabbi's barriers of fear and distrust. Because of their consistent and loving testimony, Rabbi Bregman began reading a Hebrew New Testament that had been given to him by Rev. C.T. Lipshytz of the Barbizon Mission in London.

After reading through the New Testament, Rabbi Bregman could no longer participate in Jewish tradition, liturgy, or prayers without thinking of Yeshua, Israel's promised Redeemer. He knew he should publicly profess Yeshua as his Messiah and Savior and yet, for "fear of the Jews," for fear of losing his position, for fear of becoming a hated "Christian," he could not bring himself to do it.

One day the conviction of the Holy Spirit to accept Yeshua weighed so heavily upon his heart that he left his home and wandered all day, searching for peace. At last he sat down by the river Exe and tried to sort out his life, his feelings, his faith. He later wrote:

> I wish I had a free pen to describe that day and the night which followed in order to give the reader a full conception of one of the darkest days in my life. The stillness that prevailed, and the darkness that filled the whole place, added to my battle with Satan. I walked in great despair till two o'clock in the morning when I saw a vision beyond my power of description, and heard a voice saying as from out of heaven, 'Man do not be foolish. Go home and rest, and to-morrow I will teach you the right way.'
>
> A new light was kindled in me, and sparks from heaven, filled with life, illumined my face. I walked home triumphantly, singing all the way, praising the Lord for His loving kindness and mercy. When I arrived home and found the door unbolted, I walked in, opened the Bible, and the passage, 'Come unto me, all ye that labour and are heavy laden, and I will give you rest,' appeared!
>
> I told the Lord Jesus of all my troubles, and went to bed quite happy, 'safe in the arms of Jesus.' In the morning I woke up happy in the Lord and was waiting for His guidance. As soon as I saw my landlady I revealed to her what had happened, and added I should now write to the president [of his synagogue], and tell him of the good news, that I had found Jesus as my Saviour.[35]

But instead of immediately writing the letter to the president of the synagogue, Rabbi Bregman told several members of his congregation about the spiritual unrest which had culminated in his acceptance of Yeshua as his Messiah and Lord. Appalled by his story, they tried to dissuade him from his beliefs and from writing the letter. They offered him more money, counseling, time to think things over—anything to keep him from openly professing this faith in Yeshua. Bregman wrote:

> …I then told them it was not money that would make me happy, only He who was waiting to receive me could make me happy and set me free from sin. I left them and went home and wrote to the president and told him I had found the Messiah, and it would not be right for me to remain in the synagogue under false pretenses. He called a special meeting the very morning he received my letter. They sent it on to the late Doctor Adler, the then Chief Rabbi of Great Britain, and he sent them another rabbi. Jews passed me in the street without looking at me. I was the topic of the day. Christian friends congratulated me and wished me all success in life in winning souls, especially amongst His ancient people.[36]

Shortly after Rabbi Bregman came to faith in Yeshua, he married Miss Clara Rowland of Trew Weir Paper Mills, Exeter. Persecution and the efforts of some of his Jewish neighbors to scandalize him and to destroy his marriage resulted in the Bregmans leaving Exeter. They went to London, where they stayed with Rev. C.T. Lipshytz; it was there, in the providence of God, that they met Rev. Louis Meyer who was visiting from Canada. Rev. Meyer opened the door for the Bregmans to immigrate to Toronto, Canada.

Once in Toronto, the Bregmans immediately joined the Knox church. Rabbi Bregman was baptized in Knox church by Rev. A.B. Winchester on December 7, 1906. The church record states: "Five infants and two adults received the seal of baptism. One of the latter was Rabbi Henry Bregman, one of God's ancient people after the flesh, and now re-created after the image of Jesus Christ unto good works."[37]

Rabbi Bregman's burden for the salvation of his own Jewish people prompted him to enroll as a student at Toronto Bible College. Later, when the Presbyterian Church in Canada opened their mission to the Jews in Toronto, he joined their staff. He served with them until 1916, when the Peterson Hebrew Mission contacted him and asked if he would take over their work among the Jews in Patterson and Passaic, New Jersey. Bregman and his wife moved to the United States, and under the auspices of the Peterson Hebrew Mission, he operated a reading room, Saturday and Sunday evening services, Sunday afternoon Bible classes, open air services, sewing classes for girls, visitation, a medical department and an extensive visitation program.

Three years later, on April 18, 1919 Bregman accepted a missionary position on the staff of the New York Jewish Evangelization Society. He had served with them for two and one half years when he received a call from the Board of Home Missions of the Presbyterian Church in Canada; they asked him to take over their work in Montreal, Quebec.

Henry and his wife returned to Canada, and had only been in Montreal for a year and a half before the Lord led him to return to Toronto. The year was 1923, and the Bregmans were back in Toronto. In seven years they had gone full circle!

In Toronto Rabbi Bregman met Rev. Oswald J. Smith, pastor of the Alliance Tabernacle. Smith helped him set up a committee through the church to reach the Jews of Toronto with the Gospel. The ministry was named Beth Dor'she' Emeth (the House of Seekers of Truth); it was incorporated in 1927, and became an interdenominational faith mission.

It was from this rich heritage and experience in Jewish ministry that Fred Bregman, Rabbi Henry Bregman's son, came to minister with the Beth Sar Shalom Mission of Canada.

The news of the Mission's new branch in Toronto was heralded in an article by Rev. Stanley Stock which appeared in the December 1966 issue of *The Chosen People* magazine. Rev. Stock wrote:

In our work it is especially true that 'the fields are ripe unto harvest, but the laborers are few.' A God-given love for Israel, a Scriptural background for the work, a call to the field, are essential to the equipment of any who labor in their field. Such an one we believe God has indicated for the work in Toronto. Fred S. Bregman is the son of ex-Rabbi Bregman who was well known as a Jewish missionary a quarter of a century ago in Toronto. Intimate acquaintance with the work of his father was followed by a period of association with him in the work, and succession to him for a short time. His steps were led away from the work by a combination of circumstances but his heart was always with his first love. Now he rejoices to return to the field in which his call was received, and he will soon, we hope, be at liberty to devote all his time to the challenging task. Ex-Rabbi Bregman was well known and beloved by us 34 years ago in Toronto. We are assured in our hearts that Fred has the spirit and zeal of his illustrious father. Again we see the marks of the guidance and blessing of God.[38]

But the work in Toronto did not progress as quickly as the board had hoped. Two years later, in spite of Fred Bregman's part-time visitation program among the Jews in the Glencairn area of Toronto, the Directors Minutes report:

...The work is progressing slowly, much prayer is needed and capable leadership is required. During the conference in May, Tom Walker will schedule three staff workers, namely: Mr. Fred Bregman, Toronto, Rev. Harry Jacobson, Missionary in charge, Chicago Branch, and Rev. H. Johnson, Missionary in charge, Pittsburgh Branch to call on homes in the Glencairn area, thereby, seeking contacts and to distribute literature, including an invite to attend a church service at Glencairn Baptist church. The speaker will be Rev. Martin (Moishe) Rosen of New York City.[39]

The Bible Conference Ministry

From the early years of the Mission's formation in Canada until the mid-1980's, Mr. Tom Walker very ably made the arrangements for the Mission's Bible conferences throughout Canada and in bordering cities of the United States. These conferences were the basis on which support for the missionary program was built.

In his report to the Board at their January 1969 meeting, Tom shared:

That the conference which commenced on Sunday, May 22 to June 4, 1968, a total of forty (40) meetings were scheduled in the following areas.
U.S.A.—Batavia, Rochester and Buffalo, New York.
Canada—Toronto, Hamilton, Burlington, St. Catherines, Niagara Falls, Fort Erie, Waterford, Ontario.
Guest speakers included: Dr. D. Fuchs, Dr. H. Heydt, Dr. T. Lawrence, Mr. A. Katz, Rev. Martin Rosen, Mr. Isaac Leonard, Rev. H. Johnson.[40]

Not only did Tom Walker set up the Bible conferences for the Mission in Canada, he also set up the itinerary for Field Evangelist, Dr. Alexander Marks (See Chapter Nine of this history) who, although he was blind, traveled extensively in Eastern Canada where he held church meetings. In the fall of 1971, Tom arranged for Dr. Marks to speak in a number of churches in Newfoundland. Never before had the Mission sent a representative to the island. In fact, according to reports of many the pastors on the island, Alexander Marks was the first Jewish believer ever to have spoken in the churches of Newfoundland.[41]

The conference ministry was successful in its efforts to raise funds for the Canadian outreach, but the problems of finding and retaining qualified staff members continued.

The work in Toronto continued to "limp along," evidencing no vitality under the leadership of Fred Bregman. Finally, the Board decided to close the work there, and to dismiss Fred Bregman effective April 30, 1970. Sadly, the work in Montreal, which had once prospered under the leadership of Karl Goldberg, had also essentially come to a stand-still. The Hamilton office remained active as the administrative office for the Mission in Canada, but no missionary work was being done in Hamilton. Further, in 1970, Mrs. Wallace, the woman who had been hired to handle the correspondence and the receipting of donors at the Hamilton office, was seriously injured and could not continue her responsibilities. On September 1, 1970, Mrs. Gloria Walker volunteered to take over Mrs. Wallace's duties.[42] This position became a full-time salaried position for which Mrs. Walker was hired on January 1, 1971—a position she competently and faithfully gave herself to until she resigned from the Mission in 1987.

Using the Media in Ministry

It was a difficult time for members of the Board in Canada. They had a deep concern for the Gospel to penetrate the Jewish communities of their country, and as reports of the Mission's activities in the United States were given it was only natural that the reports created an even greater longing in the hearts of the Canadian Directors to see similar activities and results in Canada. This was especially true when Daniel Fuchs reported the results of the Passover Telecast and its impact on the Jewish community of Los Angeles. In an effort to duplicate outreach and results, the Canadian Directors discussed the methodology and logistics of using the TV film on the Passover in Canada. The Minutes of the October 1970 Board meeting state:

> The following is suggested: That Rev. S. Stock and Tom Walker lay the ground work, to contact interested Pastors, invite them to a prayer breakfast meeting and the showing of the TV film on the Passover....
>
> The local Pastors should set up a committee in their churches that would forward a piece of advertising at the churches expense, to Jewish people in their neighborhood. This would announce the date of the TV showing. Prior to the actual date of showing, committee members should telephone the homes and invite the occupants to watch the TV film on the Passover.
>
> Rev. S. Stock and T. Walker accepted the responsibility.[43]

One year later, as the Canadian Directors met together for their November 1971 meeting, Daniel Fuchs spoke to them about the new methodology which had been adopted in the United States for doing missionary work. [At the November 1970 meeting of the American Board, Daniel had presented his new missionary policy of changing from a "station-centered to a people-oriented" ministry.] He told the Canadian Directors:

> ...To reach the Jewish person for the Lord we must go outside the Mission property to the campuses, the street corners, this is the only direction that is successful.
>
> At the workers meetings held in New York the following instructions were given:
>
> 1. Every district must open up a new college campus with a regular witness on this campus.
> 2. To have a new local church in the area that was vitally involved. That we teach the church members how to reach the Jew with the gospel and in turn, they go out and do the work. As a Mission, we cannot do the work alone.
> 3. In every area there are large homes in Jewish neighborhoods so let them invite their Jewish neighbors in and commence meeting there. In so doing, the work is then increased with half the normal staff.
> The plan of outreach will involve the mass media, radio and television, which will require expert advice. New methods of communicating and a new approach is needed today.[44]

The Canadian Directors had followed through on the plans to air the Passover Telecast in Canada, and Tom Walker gave a report to the Board at their November 1971 meeting. He stated:

> ...The presentation of the Passover film has created a challenge to us. We thank God for opening the way whereby 12 major stations have contracted to telecast the program and two others, namely, Ottawa and Toronto stations, have auditioned the film but will not commit themselves as to the acceptance of same until late January, 1972. Also most of the stations contracted have additional satellite stations for smaller areas. This gives us an additional coverage at no extra charge. This totals to 29 satellite and 12 major stations with two still pending. In addition, there is the possibility of securing a station in Vancouver for the telecast.
>
> The Island of Newfoundland which is a new field of endeavor for the Mission, will telecast the Passover on ten stations. Our initial outlay will be the cost of only one station.[45]

Just as the experiment of using the media had at first proven successful in the United States, the first ventures of using the media in Canada were exhilarating! Tom Walker gave the following report to the Directors at their November 1972 meeting:

> From coast to coast forty-two stations participated with a total expenditure of $3,830.00. The Kitchener station broadcast the Passover program at no charge to the Mission. A tremendous response was recorded across Canada with

the heaviest mailings coming from Vancouver and Winnipeg. In the Winnipeg area the Management of the T.V. station received over 500 calls on account of the broadcast. Many were opposed to the telecast but the majority were greatly in favour. It was unfortunate that the Toronto station refused to telecast the Passover but nevertheless, the surrounding areas telecast the program and part of the signal reached into the Toronto area. Mrs. Walker, secretary in the Hamilton Office, has compiled a complete list as per each province including the names and addresses of those who responded to the telecast. This was then forwarded to Dr. Fuchs in New York City and many will be placed on The Chosen People mailing list. The Lord willing, as the work progresses in Canada many of these names will serve as means of contact.[46]

Eventually, however, the expense of using the media and the continued pressure by the Jewish community in Canada forced the Mission to stop showing the Passover telecast on a regular basis. But on the occasions when stations would air the program, the response from Jewish people who watched was usually positive.

Meanwhile, the missionary work in Canada was at a standstill—a matter of grave concern to the Board in Canada, and a matter to which much prayer was devoted. The Directors were willing for the Mission in Canada to help support the foreign missionary work of the Mission, but they felt if funds were being raised in Canada, there should be an active missionary outreach to the Jews of Canada.

The answer to their prayers came in June 1972, when two Jewish believers submitted applications for full-time work. Both men were hired for the Mission's outreach in Toronto.

RACHMIEL FRYDLAND—HIS STORY

Rachmiel Frydland was a Jewish believer who joined the staff of the Mission as a part-time worker in 1964. He was one of the part-time staff members who assisted at the Mission's booth at the New York World's Fair in 1964 and 1965.

Rachmiel was a gifted Hebrew and Talmudic scholar. He was fluent in Hebrew, Yiddish, Polish, German and several other languages. He was a graduate of the University of London holding a B.A. degree, a B.D. degree and an M.A. degree, and he took graduate work at New York University, where he earned an M.A. in Hebrew Education and Culture. He also studied Bible at All Nations Bible College from 1947 to 1949. Through the years Rachmiel had not only been a capable missionary (on a part-time basis), he had edited and written articles for The Shepherd of Israel (the English/Yiddish missionary paper of the Mission), as well as some of the Mission's tracts. His willingness to serve on the staff of the Mission as a full-time worker was viewed as a wonderful answer to prayer for the work in Canada!

Rachmiel was born on March 15, 1919 into a very religious Jewish home in Poland. In telling how God brought him to faith in Yeshua, he wrote:

...As far back as I can remember, my father always wore a religious garb, with beard and peyoths (side curls) and all the other customary marks of Jewish orthodoxy.

The Jewish community where I spent my boyhood was small and poverty stricken. It was not in a position to maintain a Cheder (a Jewish religious school). But my father being a devout Jew felt it his duty to instruct his own five children himself, my four sisters and his only son, in the faith of his fathers. And when he no longer was able to devote the needed time and strength to that task he, out of his own meager resources, engaged a Belfer (a primary religious teacher) to continue our instruction.

It was the Belfer who started the Chumesh with me, but he did not stay long. For various reasons, chiefly financial, my father had to let him go. It was decided that I should be sent to a Cheder in a neighboring town to continue my religious training.

Accordingly, after Pesach (the Jewish Passover) having reached the ripe age of seven, my father took me by the hand and brought me to the Cheder about four miles away from our village.

I began to study the Talmud at the age of nine. A year later the Rebbe advised my father that he had advanced me in my studies as far as he was able, and that if he desired me to continue my Talmudical studies he should transfer me to a higher school of learning. My father joyfully took his advice, and soon after I was enrolled as a student in a Yeshivah.

Such was my life until I reached my 13th year of age, that is, until I became Bar Mitzvah (a son of the Law).

A year later found me in the capital city of Poland, Warsaw, continuing my Talmudical studies in one of the famous Rabbinical seminaries, at the end of which course of studies I expected to obtain my Rabbinical diploma. But this meant again a period of struggle and privation. This time it was not the food which was the problem, but the lodging. The food was provided by the seminary, but for lodging, I, like other needy students, had to find some Jewish store where I would act as night watchman, for which service I would receive shelter and sometimes a few pennies.

The teaching in the Rabbinical Schools was all 'spoon-fed'—that is, we had to learn by heart or memorize what we read in the books or what we heard from the lips of the Rabbi. Independent reasoning and questions were utterly discouraged. Those who inadvertently expressed a doubt or an opinion of their own not found in the books, were cruelly punished for their temerity. As a result, I carried around my problems and doubts, not daring to confide them to anyone.

At that time it became clear to me that however I tried, I would not go to heaven anyway. I felt I could not measure up to the requirements of the Torah. A Talmudical story about a famous Rabbi troubled me exceedingly. According to it, when his end was approaching, he was so terrified that he wept bitter tears. He did not know, he lamented, where he was going, to Heaven or to Gehenna. 'If such a Rabbi,' I said to myself, 'so famous for his devotion and sanctity, did not know whether he was good enough to go to Heaven, what chance had I to go there.'

At this point an incident occurred which completely changed the whole course of my life. I had a friend who was suspected of not being sufficiently orthodox according to the rigid conception of the Yeshivah I was attending. He belonged to a religious Zionist group, called the Mizrachi which was not tolerated by that Yeshivah. Though having nothing to do with this group, my association with this friend of mine nevertheless drew suspicion on me also.

Also at that time I became dissatisfied with the whole system of Rabbinical education. All of it was nothing except what the Rabbis long ago said or wrote. I desired to read and to study things which were outside the Talmudical curriculum. I craved to learn things other than which were taught in the Yeshivah.

That opportunity soon came. Walking in the streets of Warsaw, I met a friend, also a Talmudical student, standing in the street and selling things. I asked him why he was doing it. He said, 'I am fed up with the tyranny and fanaticism of the Rabbis. I am now earning my own living. I am no longer dependent upon the Yeshivah. Now I can think for myself and read what I like.'

A short time later, I too was standing in the street, selling things.

Then the storekeeper, who was giving me lodging on his premises, saw me thus in the street with my basket of goods. 'Aha,' he said, 'you are no longer in the Yeshivah? My store is only for Yeshiva Bocherim (students). You therefore can no longer sleep in my place.'

The only thing then for me to do was to find another lodging. This I succeeded in doing quickly in the home of a kindly motherly woman.

But this woman was attending meetings at a mission!

'What do they do at the mission?' I asked her. 'Come and see!' she replied. My curiosity was aroused, and so one day I accompanied her to the meeting.

The missionaries were not altogether unknown to me. I had heard of them before, and abhorred them. I had also seen some of their literature, but as soon as I looked into it, I tore it up. It seemed to propound the idea that Jews should believe in three gods and exchange the holy Torah for the teaching of the 'Hanged One,' whose name it was a sin for a Jew to take even upon his lips, because 'that One' was the cause of all the sorrows that had befallen Israel since His day nearly two thousand years ago.

Moreover, what I saw at the Mission that day filled me with ridicule. The missionary began the meeting by offering prayer in Yiddish! I could not help bursting out in laughter. With us, in the synagogue, only ignorant women prayed in Yiddish. The language of prayer for men was Hebrew, from the Siddur! [The Jewish prayer-book].

A little reflection, however, made me ashamed of my behavior. After all, I said to myself, God understood all the languages, even Yiddish. Then thinking back to Abraham, Isaac and Jacob and the prophets—they had no Siddur to pray from, and yet their prayers were accepted of God.

Then at the close of the meeting I heard the speaker make the following announcement:

'If any of you want a sign from the Tenach (Old Testament) that Jesus is the Messiah, let him remain until after the meeting, and I will prove to him with more than one sign that this is so.'

Hearing this I decided to stay. I was sure that he was wrong. I knew there were no signs in the Tenach by which he could prove his point. I knew also that I could demolish all his arguments, and show him that he was in error. I was therefore eager to hear what he had to say.

The missionary made a long speech, quoting many verses from the Tenach in his support. But I had an answer ready for every one of those verses. Some of them, I explained, may not apply to the Messiah, and of those that did, I showed him that it was not Jesus to whom they referred.

The only passage, however, for which I had no answer was Daniel 9:24-26.

I simply had to confess that I did not understand this passage at all. But I promised the speaker that I would study it and come back with the answer. What puzzled me was: Why was Messiah to be cut off?

As I continued to attend the meetings I learned to respect the people for their patience and humility. Further reflection and study made me feel that all my ready answers to the missionary's 'signs' were based, not upon the *unprejudiced study of the Bible, but upon what the Rabbis told me. I had to admit that the promises fulfilled in Jesus were too numerous to be explained away. There was an accumulation of evidence which could in no manner be set aside.*

But I wanted to get at the bottom of the whole matter. I therefore obtained a copy of the New Testament in Hebrew to learn first hand who Jesus was, and what He came to do and to teach. I read it through carefully, comparing the many references in it to the Old Testament.

Slowly it dawned upon me that Jesus must be the Messiah!

Looking back upon my life, I realized that step by step the hand of God was upon me, leading me. All the circumstances of its course seemed to combine to bring me to that decision. It was the hand of God which I could not and would not resist and it was the Spirit of God, who still broods over the chaos of this world and over men's souls, darkened through sin, crying: 'Let there be light!'

It was a lonely decision to take. I could not consult my parents or friends. They would not have understood. They would have been bitterly opposed to it. Nevertheless I knew that my next step was to make an open and public confession of my faith in the Messiah. But I lacked the courage to come out boldly.

Then came the winter of the year of 1937. There was a meeting at the mission, and on that occasion, it was composed wholly of Jewish believers. The speaker was a Gentile woman, who talked about the Temple of Jerusalem, explaining how all things in it—its construction and its furniture—all pointed to the fact that all men were sinners, and that the Lord Jesus was the sacrifice for the sins of all.

'How is it,' I asked myself 'that a Gentile woman knew more about the Bible and about the significance of these things than I, a student of the Yeshivah? Does this not prove that it is because we as a nation have rejected our Messiah?'

When the speaker was done, we were invited to kneel and to pray. Then the unexpected happened. In spite of my Jewish reluctance to kneel, I immediately sank upon my knees before all, and prayed that God might open my eyes to the Truth, and forgive me my sins for not acknowledging openly before men that Jesus was my Messiah.

God answered my prayer. A new assurance filled my soul. I was no longer afraid to confess Him before men. I was no longer afraid of the consequences.[47]

Rachmiel's decision to accept Yeshua as his Messiah coincided with the Nazi invasion of Warsaw, Poland toward the end of September 1939. As Warsaw shook under the thunderous bombing and shelling by the Nazis, Rachmiel and several other Jewish believers rallied to the cause of the resistance in trying to defend the besieged city. Because he believed bearing arms was contrary to his faith, he was given physical work to do. As the Nazis surrounded the city, all supplies were cut off and soon the city was without food and other necessities of life. Within a month the city of Warsaw was crushed and the triumphant Germans marched in.

One day as Rachmiel and some of his friends (also Jewish believers) stood in line to receive their meager rationing of food, one the young men was recognized by a Nazi guard. He was quickly pulled out of line, beaten and sent away hungry. The guards made it clear that the soup was for Polish citizenry, not for any "Jew." Knowing that he, too, would be recognized, Rachmiel decided to leave Warsaw and go to the village of Plock about seventy-five miles away. Before he left the city, his pastor gave him a certificate showing that he had been baptized, and was now a Christian. Since Jews were not allowed to use any of the public conveyances, he set out on foot but when he reached the outskirts of the city he was stopped by a Nazi soldier. In recalling the incident, Rachmiel later wrote:

'Are you a Jew?' he demanded. Without a word, I handed him my certificate. He looked at it and then spat out? 'Yes, but you are still a Jew!' He seized a shovel and slammed it into my back, knocking me into a ditch. There I was ordered to join fellow Jews who were digging graves for dead horses. It was my first taste of Nazi brutality, but actually mild in comparison with what awaited so many others.[48]

That evening the soldiers took Rachmiel and the other Jews to a work camp for the night. At the camp Rachmiel shared his faith with some of the other Jews. Later, when it was dark, he left the camp in full sight of the guards and the other captured Jews, but no one raised a hand to stop him. Three days later he arrived in Plock, and was received with open arms by the believers there.

As Nazi brutality intensified, and as more restrictions were placed upon the Jews of Europe, Rachmiel decided to return to Warsaw to see if he could help the Jewish people, and members of his family, now trapped in the infamous "Warsaw Ghetto." He realized that he was placing his life on the line by returning, but he felt he had to do something to help. When he reached Warsaw he learned that one of his sisters had died from typhus. He realized there was very little he could do, so he continued walking toward his native village—one hundred fifty miles southeast—to see about his parents and other family members. He later wrote:

My parents could hardly believe I was still alive when I arrived in mid-December. One of my sisters also returned home, and we settled down, hoping to wait out the war. We knew, however, that our blue-and-white armbands, marking us as Jews, were a constant hazard to our lives. I was forced to work with slave laborers, building a road, but managed to escape when starvation swept the camp. Home again, my mother told me that I must stop telling my Jewish friends about the Messiah. But the spreading pall of suffering and death caused people to reach out for some hope or answer for the dreaded future. [During this time, Rachmiel often risked his own life to travel to the nearby villages in an effort to obtain the necessities of life for his family and for the other Jewish people in their village. And while the Jews of the village did not approve of his belief in Yeshua, they began to respect his faith because of his living testimony. God used his testimony of words and deeds to produce faith in other members of his family.]

One day my sister came to me. 'I read your Bible,' she said, 'and I heard your discussions. I believe, and if God gives us peaceful days, I want to be baptized.' My mother came to me and said, 'I have watched you and you are a different person. I was reading your New Testament and I don't see anything wrong in this Jesus. Why are our rabbis so much against Him?' My father never admitted anything to me. However, he stopped hiding my Bible and rebuking me for speaking about Jesus. He began secretly to read the Bible.

The blossoming faith of my family was a great blessing to me as death drew nearer in 1942. We saw trucks and trains loaded with Jewish people rolling toward the extermination camp at Sobibor. One by one and village by village they disappeared. My father, my mother, my sisters, my newly wedded wife, and all other relatives except a brother-in-law perished.[49]

Rachmiel knew that he, too, was on the list to be sent to the gas chambers and crematoria located about twelve miles from his village. He wrote:

On August 30th, 1942, I received the order to go to the gas chambers. I did not go; but stayed at home and awaited the mercy of the Lord. On September 24th the village mayor came and told me, while I was at work, (helping one of the peasants in the cutting of wood) that he had received orders to hand me over to the Gestapo.... The man who led me had pity on me and hinted that I should escape. I did so and fled to the woods....

...We hid ourselves in the high grass that grew in the woods. They discovered and took away all our food, but our lives were spared. That night heavy snow fell some three feet deep. We had to go and get some food. Alas! when we reached the road leading to the village, the police were there, What were we to do? There were shouts of 'Stop! stop!' and shots. For quite a time I did not know what I was doing and where I was running, nor what was happening. I did not think; I just ran and ran as shots whistled over my head and round my ears.

At last there was silence; no one was pursuing me any longer.

I flopped onto a tree-trunk; I could neither speak nor pray. My sweat chilled me. I gathered some sticks, made a fire and gradually became able to think. No one was near to comfort me; only the flame of my little fire broke the darkness around....

But there still remained the Lord, the same yesterday and to-day. He began to speak to me with His soft voice. 'You have enough of My grace. Had not Job enough; had not Paul enough?' I became silent to hear what the Lord had to say to me, and He said much.[50]

Once again Rachmiel tried to get to the Warsaw Ghetto to help the Jews there. He wrote:

...I got to Chelm safely; here brethren helped me to get a railway ticket for Warsaw. I arrived there on December 20th, 1942. I returned to Chelm for Christmas, but was caught again on Christmas Day as I was going from our village to Chelm. Approaching the town, I stopped and told my captor that I was not going to move until I prayed. His protests and threats had no effect on me as I knew that only a few hundred yards further were the Gestapo quarters. I knelt and prayed, yielding my life to God. When I arose my captor began to talk to me softly and finally let me go free. I returned to Warsaw, where I stayed awaiting the Grace of God.

From time to time I went around the walls of the ghetto thinking of the possibility of getting inside. One of the places where I was permitted to spend a night or two in hiding was in the shop of a Christian undertaker. With another Jewish Christian boy we put chips in one of the unfinished coffins and thus spent the night. (Alas, this boy, too, was later caught and killed). Here in the spring of 1943 I became acquainted with Jews who worked outside the Ghetto for a German firm adjacent to this Christian undertaker. As they had a special permit for ten to leave and enter the Ghetto, one Friday they took me in with them instead of the tenth who did not leave the Ghetto on that day. Thus a week before the liquidation of the Ghetto I was able to get inside for the week-end. I met some of our precious Jewish believers. They *told me their miraculous stories. Some had already died of starvation or were imprisoned and tortured to death. S. Eizenberg, a young man who accepted his Messiah immediately before the war, had received special permission for a Polish Pastor, Mr. Krakiewicz, to enter the Ghetto and baptize him there. He was later imprisoned for being late to work and as he was awaiting death, he wrote a verse of his favorite hymn on the wall. It so happened that the German officer came in on that day and asked his Polish interpreter to translate all the inscriptions of the victims. When they came to his hymn and heard the words (it was a Polish hymn translated from the German) he stopped and did not go further, but demanded that the one who wrote it should confess, otherwise all would be guilty. Stasiek confessed. The officer went away, but in a few hours Stasiek Eizenberg was released. As they were now awaiting definite extermination, I tried to comfort them as best as I could. They insisted that I leave the Ghetto, for God who preserved me until now would keep me to the end of the war, and then I would be able to tell the Christians of those woes. I left the Ghetto and was probably one of the last to leave before the liquidation began. Time dragged on slowly. I had to learn to trust the Lord for each minute. Whether spending the night with a Christian family who risked their lives to take in a Jew for the night, or in a coffin in the shop of a Christian undertaker, or in some barn, there was the same assurance that the Lord wanted me to live and as long as He wanted it, I was ready.*

Finally the hour came, and no more was I hunted and condemned to die just because I was a Jew. However my heart longed for freedom and fellowship with others who believe, likewise, that Jesus is their own personal Messiah and Saviour. God granted me the desire of my heart and helped me to leave Poland and get to England. Later God opened for me the way into the U.S.A. and afterwards I went to Israel and spent there four years among my own brethren. There I married a Jewish believer in the Messiah. She also suffered under the Nazi occupation in France. We have four children, two girls and 2 boys, whom we try to bring up in the faith of God and the Messiah.[51]

Rachmiel joined the staff of the Mission as a full-time worker in the fall of 1972 but, due to difficulties in obtaining entry papers into Canada, his ministry in Toronto did not get underway until the spring of 1973.

Rachmiel Frydland's presence in Toronto triggered a flurry of debates and discussions within the Jewish community of Toronto. His experiences, his rabbinic and theological training, could not be disputed by the orthodox Jewish leaders of Canada. In his report to the Board, he stated:

...The Jewish population of Toronto is between 125, and 140,000 people. It is a well organized Jewry and they have been brought closer together by the "threat" they think lurks from such missionary organizations as the A.B.M.J. Thus, though in times past the Conservative, Reformed [sic], and Orthodox Jews were mutually despising one another and were hardly on speaking terms, now they want to show a united front. On one occasion Rev. Frydland reported before a Conservative Synagogue which had invited another Hebrew Christian and himself to present their views so that they may know what makes them 'tick' and to ask questions. They were later denounced by Orthodox and 'Lubavitcher' leader—Rabbi Schochet for permitting them to come into a Jewish conservative synagogue to present their views. All of this has a certain advantage for it makes people curious to know what the Mission is all about and gives the opportunity to present our case. The opportunity has also presented itself to start a small Bible Study Group in the home of some 'hippie' students who live in a large apartment house and share the cost of the rent and food. Some of these students are of Jewish birth. Some have professed faith in Christ and have approached Rev. Frydland, who in turn, spoke to a Pastor of a local Christian & Missionary Alliance Church, and asked permission to baptise [sic] them and to extend the right hand of fellowship. Permission has been granted and upon return to Toronto after the Christmas recess the baptismal service will take place.[52]

Although the ministry in Toronto continued to grow under his leadership, Rachmiel became increasingly drawn to the growing Messianic movement. As mentioned in Chapter Eleven of this history, he wanted to establish a Messianic congregation. At the time, the Mission had not formulated a policy on the planting of Messianic congregations; this was especially true in Canada, where the Board members were opposed to the establishment of Messianic congregations.

In the spring of 1975, Rachmiel Frydland received a call to become the Messianic teacher of the Beth Messiah congregation in Cincinnati, Ohio. After prayerful consideration, he submitted his resignation to the Mission. His resignation was regretfully accepted, effective June 15, 1975.

LESLIE JACOBS—IN TORONTO

The second worker hired during the Fall of 1972 for the Toronto ministry was Mr. Leslie Jacobs. Leslie was born in Canada. His father was a Jewish believer, but he was separated from Leslie's mother. Leslie and his sister, Sandi, were raised by their father. In sharing his testimony of how he came to faith in Jesus, Leslie wrote:

...It was a beautiful spring day of April 1960 in Newmarket, Ontario, at a Bible club meeting that my sister and I said yes to Jesus. We both stayed after the meeting knowing exactly what we wanted and that was to invite the Lord Jesus into our hearts. This is exactly what Sandi and I did, and we have been growing every day with the Lord since that day.

Much of my earlier history had a great influence on my decision of inviting Jesus into my heart. My father was much involved in Jewish work in Toronto and in Winnipeg. I saw how God was blessing the work and how the work had so few workers yet the need was so great. I also had alot [sic] of fellowship with the Hebrew Christian Alliance branch of Toronto. My father was proud of being a Jew and he wanted his children to also be proud of their heritage....

Coming from a broken home I had alot [sic] of things to learn, but I had a father that really loved me and wanted the best for me. Finishing public school I applied to a private christian high scool [sic].... After high school the Lord led me to Bible school at the Briercrest Bible Institute.... This year [1972] I will be graduating after three years of study...

Through the years the Lord has been molding my life. Since the summer of '66, each summer I've been getting involved in camp work with the Japanese of Toronto, YMCA, and the Canadian Sunday School Mission. Through this avenue of service the Lord has impressed on me the need for dedicated workers.[53]

After joining the staff of the Mission Leslie was sent to Los Angeles to complete the six month training program. He began his ministry in Toronto in the Fall of 1973—just months after Rachmiel Frydland arrived in Toronto. Leslie rented office space near York University, and he quickly proceeded to gather around him a group of volunteers to assist him in developing a campus ministry, Bible studies, and a ministry of distributing tracts and broadsides. In a report of his initial work in Toronto, he wrote:

Upon arrival in my home town I realized the going was going to be tough,...I started from scratch,...My task was to develop a continual work on York University which has 6,000 Jewish students. There is a strong Jewish Student Federation which is financially secure and has alot [sic] of good programs along with a free Jewish University, ...To date we have a regular book table ministry run by Christian students, we have had training sessions for witnessing and still have a continuous Bible study ministry on campus. What has been the result? There have been many good discussions, debates, counselling sessions and much literature distribution...The whole school has at one time or the other discussed the work that is being done on the campus.

...I have developed a...core group that has worked as a team. The team has spent many hours together praying, sharing, studying the Bible and distributing the folling [sic] amounts of literature. Tracts—185,000 Posters—11,000.

Besides this ministry and office work we have witnessed together at Jewish rallies such as the Canadian Jewish Congress, Synagogue meetings and as of late a short debate with Rebitzen Esther Jungreis along with several hundred Jewish people. The group has also participated in street work, church deputation and one on one witnessing. Many of us have been accosted by the JDL and TETAR which are active in the Toronto area....

Special Programs and Events. There have been many special programs that we have been able to use for the furtherance of the Gospel. The following are some of the programs that we developed that were very effective for the ministry.

    1. Passover Banquet
    2. Sabbath meals
    3. Sukkot, Chanukkah, Rosh Hashanah-Yom Kippur festival celebrations.
    4. Messianic Music Concert at the Universities
    5. Simchat Torah Rally/Soviet Jewry Walk[54]

The ministry of Leslie Jacobs was out-going, confrontational and flamboyant, while the ministry of Rachmiel Frydland was steady, non-confrontational (unless necessary) and more in keeping with the work being done by the Mission's branches in the United States and Europe. Leslie was enamored with the "Jews for Jesus" movement; he wanted to use their techniques and tactics in his ministry in Toronto. Because of the vast differences in the two approaches to ministry, it was possible for the two missionaries to work within the same city (Toronto) without conflict between the ministries. In many ways the two ministries complemented one another; each approach drew into its circle of influence individuals who would never have been won by the opposite approach. In his report to the Board, Rachmiel Frydland wrote:

Leslie Jacobs has carried on a more aggressive ministry and last month he invited a partly Hebrew Christian Musical group from Cincinnati called "LAMB." They gave a Hebrew Christian concert on York Campus and I was invited to be the speaker and to answer questions. A number of rabbis also came to challenge us including David Schochet, brother of Immanuel Schochet. The discussion and conversations lasted for several hours and we had at least one good response from a female student who wanted my booklet "Joy Cometh..." and other literature.... At the downtown campus there is also at least one good prospect and also another who we hope will come to a full knowledge of the Gospel and thus also bring our labors to success and fruition.

Leslie Jacobs felt that he should take the young people to a lecture of the "rebbetzin" Esther Youngreiss [sic], a lady who has put it as her task to bring back to Judaism those Jewish young people who according to her have strayed away to Christianity. This led to it that one of our young man [sic] was brought in the home of Immanuel Shochet [sic] the rabbi who is on the mailing list of every Jewish Mission and Missionary to receive our literature in order to 'refute' it. The rabbi began to work hard on the heart and mind of this young man and his faith was shaken for a while, but Leslie brought him to our home and I was able to show the unfair arguments and misinterprations [sic] taking advantage of this young man Nathan because he did not know the original Hebrew and Aramaic. This brought back Nathan in renewed faith and confidence, but now he wants me to go and renew the witness to the student and to this rabbi. Although these encounters do not give me much joy as the opposing party uses all the bad manners and bad words against Christ and Christianity and against Jewsih [sic] believers and myself, I feel that there is no way out and we must also give witness before the rabbis and the sanhedrin and trust the Lord for giving us the strength and knowledge to resist and to answer. It also makes us better known in the Jewish community. But we may also face the fiery attacks of the JDL [Jewish Defense League] and other active opposers of Jewish Missions.[55]

Through his campus ministry and other ministry contacts, as well as through the classes he was taking at the University, Leslie Jacobs developed many friendships among the Orthodox and Hassidic students. As he became more involved with the university scene, however, and more closely drawn to his Orthodox friends, a subtle change began to take place in Leslie's theological perspective. This led to an inner conflict between theology and Jewish evangelism and methodology which began to affect his ministry.

Leslie shared some of his thinking with the author, who was serving as the Missionary Director for the Mission at the time. He spoke of his concern that perhaps some Orthodox Jews or Hassidic Jews who really tried to be righteous according to Jewish law, may indeed be saved—a position which the Mission has never accepted. The Mission was founded on the principle that without faith in Jesus, and belief in His death, burial and resurrection, both Jews and Gentiles are lost. The author suggested to Leslie that he take a leave of absence to re-study his position. He also suggested that Leslie consider enrolling in a theologically sound seminary where he could study and re-think this most important issue. It was suggested that once the matter was resolved he could re-apply to the Mission for active missionary service if he felt led of the Lord to do so.

On April 15, 1976 Leslie requested an extended leave of absence from the Mission in Canada. He did not attend seminary or re-apply to the Mission, but he has continued in fellowship with some of the Messianic believers in Canada.

NEW BOARD MEMBERS ELECTED

Once the Toronto ministry was staffed, the Canadian Board began to consider the need to add new Directors to the Board. Mr. Robert Slessor was elected to the Board in the mid-1970's. He had an automobile dealership in Ontario, and he had graciously been supplying automobiles to the workers of the Mission, and for speakers at the Mission's Bible conferences.

Two additional members were appointed to the Canadian Board at the November 30, 1973 Directors meeting—Mr. George Savage, and the author.

George Savage was the President of the Guarantee Company of North America, with headquarters in Montreal, Quebec. His acquaintance with the Mission covered a span of over thirty years; he had been an active supporter of the ministry throughout those years.

The author became a member of the Canadian Board by virtue of the fact that he was appointed to the position of Missionary Director of Canada—the same position, with the same authority (as it affected the Missionary program of Canada) which he held in the United States.[56]

Following the appointment of the two new Board members the Canadian Board was comprised of the following members: Dr. Daniel Fuchs, Rev. Harold B. Pretlove, Mr. George Savage, Rev. Harold A. Sevener, Mr. Tom Walker, Mrs. Irene Wilson and Mrs. Gloria Walker as Secretary to the Board. Tom Walker was elected Vice-President of the Board; he was later elected President.

Two years later, at the January 1975 meeting, Mr. James Straub was elected to the Canadian Board. He replaced Rev. Harold B. Pretlove who had resigned from the Board. Later that year, at the annual meeting in November 1975, Mr. George Savage was elected Chairman of the Canadian Board.

Following the November 1972 Board meeting, Daniel Fuchs carried out the directive of the Board to talk to Ashton Holden and Margaret Seidler about their joint retirement. But, as has been mentioned, Mr. Holden was not yet sixty-five. They therefore remained in Montreal until their retirement in July 1975. The author, in his position as Missionary Director of Canada, was asked to carry out the change of staff in Montreal.

On May 15, 1975 Mrs. Winnie Marriner was hired as a "temporary" replacement for Ashton Holden and Margaret Seidler in Montreal. That temporary assignment has become a eighteen year commitment, during which time Winnie Marriner has faithfully proclaimed the Gospel to the Jewish community of Montreal!

Winnie Marriner—Her Story

Winnie first made application to the Mission on November 30, 1971. She was accepted into the Mission's six month training program in Los Angeles in the spring of 1972. She was an unlikely candidate for missionary service among the Jewish people. She was born into a Gentile home in Montreal, Quebec, Canada; it was a home that was fractured by discontent, and when she was less than one month old her parents separated. Her mother left town, leaving Winnie in the care of her paternal grandparents in Montreal. They were Irish Catholics who were strict in the traditions of the Catholic church.

As Winnie grew up, she knew she had the love of her grandparents, but something still seemed to be missing. As hard as she tried to find peace and happiness, it seemed to elude her. She thought perhaps if she could just get to know her parents the emptiness she always felt would dissipate, but it didn't happen. When Winnie was twenty-six years old her Mother returned to Montreal. They were strangers to one another, but Winnie was anxious to have a relationship with her Mother so she invited her to be her roommate. Unfortunately, when Winnie's father learned that the mother was living with her, he disowned Winnie and would not speak to her up to the day that he died.

Seeking happiness and security, Winnie married. She and her husband had two daughters. At last she had security, love, and all that money could buy—but the emptiness persisted. Soon her marriage began to crumble. In despair, she sought the Lord by going to Mass at the Catholic church. After Mass she would hurry home to watch Billy Graham or Oral Roberts on television. Oftentimes she would kneel on the kitchen floor, pleading with God to save her and to come into her life. But nothing changed.

One day Winnie's sister-in-law, who was a believer, invited Winnie to attend a church service with her. Of that eventful and life-changing day, Winnie later wrote:

> …While the people were singing…I began to shake and cry. The minister stopped the service and asked if anyone would like to give their heart to Jesus. Before I knew what I was doing, I ran down to the fron [sic], fell down on my knees, and cried for over two hours. When I got up, I knew I was different….
>
> …How wonderful that God saves us at exactly the right moment! I…had everything a woman would want or need (including luxuries) but nothing satisfied. An unhappy marriage was more than I could cope with, and then, just as Satan almost won …Christ came and loved me with an overwhelming love![57]

For the first time in her life, at the age of thirty-three, Winnie knew God's peace which passes all understanding. As the Pastor dealt with her, and showed her the way of salvation, she experienced the assurance of God's presence in her heart!

The pastor and his wife continued to disciple Winnie, and during their hours together the love that they had for the Jewish people was very evident. They often invited Winnie to join them as they visited in Jewish homes. God used these times to instill a love for the Jewish people in Winnie's heart; having been brought up in a strict Catholic community, she knew how religion and tradition could be used by Satan to blind one's understanding to their need of God's grace.

As Winnie resolved to follow the Lord, her own family rejected her. Her husband filed for a legal separation. When Winnie was awarded custody of their daughters, her husband claimed that she was a "religious fanatic," and he tried to have the courts revoke their decision. Winnie wrote:

> …I prayed for over a year about a solution to this problem and one day I very definitely felt the Lord tell me to let my husband take the responsibility of the children. I felt in prayer that when my husband saw that he could not manage, he would turn to me for help in raising the girls. This is exactly what happened! God kept His word, and my husband contacts me all the time when he has any problems or does not know what kind of privileges or curfew to administer.
>
> The four of us are closer now than we have ever been in our lives, and I have only The Lord to thank for this.[58]

Shortly after becoming a believer, Winnie took a position as executive secretary for a Protestant minister. This position, added to her beliefs, only served to further alienate her from her Catholic family. But she continued to faithfully witness to them—especially to her mother who was still living with her. Winnie wrote:

I have tried to win my mother to Jesus Christ ...however, the relationship is a very unusual one and my mother will not accept Christ in case the family rejects her. When I became a Christian the family was very much against me ...however, with the passing of time, The Lord has healed the breach considerably, and I am now welcome in the homes of my relatives....

...I had the privilege of witnessing to my grandmother just before she died, and the person she was with when she died told me that she called upon Jesus as she was expiring![59]

As Winnie earnestly prayed for the salvation of her own family members, she found that her heart was increasingly concerned for the salvation of Jewish people as well. In fact, God placed such a heavy burden upon her heart for the Jewish people that she often used her after-work hours to meet with Jewish friends and acquaintances so she could share the Messiah with them. Then she heard about the work of the Mission, and she immediately began corresponding with Daniel Fuchs about missionary opportunities; he, in turn, shared Winnie's name with the author.

When I began corresponding with Winnie, I told her that because of her background it might be difficult for her to become a missionary on the Mission's staff. I suggested, however, that perhaps her skills could be used in the administrative branch of the Mission. In her response, Winnie wrote:

I would not be opposed to doing office work if it would afford opportunities to deal with people. However, I cannot see myself doing nothing more than shorthand and typing, bookkeeping, etc. with never a chance to deal with flesh and blood.[60]

Winnie made application to the Mission's training program, and was accepted. She proved to be a real soul winner, and she was greatly loved by all of the Jewish people she met. She excelled at "acculturation" and cross cultural communication. In addition to the Mission's training, she took classes being offered at synagogues, temples, and Jewish universities. One of the first courses she took was a Hebrew language course (she already spoke fluent French).

When Winnie finished the training program she remained in Los Angeles, doing ministry among the women as well as on college and university campuses. She also helped the author with her very capable secretarial skills. When the author was transferred to New York in the Fall of 1972, Winnie was willing to move to the east coast to fill the secretarial position for the author until such time as he could find someone else. She made it clear, however, that she was making the move on the condition that she would still have opportunity to witness to Jewish people. She was a missionary first, and a secretary second!

In New York, Winnie not only served as the author's secretary, she served as the receptionist for the Mission's Headquarters Office in Manhattan—a position she used to exercise her gifts as a missionary. She shared the Gospel with every salesman and with every person who called or who came into the building, and she led many of them to the Lord!

In January 1973, as preparations were being made to separate the administrative work of the Mission from the missionary outreach in New York, Winnie's assistance was invaluable as she helped in the gargantuan task of relocating the Mission's headquarters office from Manhattan to Englewood Cliffs, New Jersey.

After the relocation of the Mission's Headquarters, Winnie continued to give of her secretarial skills, but she also served as a missionary for Bergen County, New Jersey and Rockland County, New York. She was happy and content in her place of service; she did not know God had another place of service for her.

Winnie had made application for United States citizenship, but it was turned down. To her dismay, she was told that her visa would not be renewed and that she would have to return to Canada. The news was a shock at first, but as Winnie and others of us gave it further consideration, we could see God's hand at work. The year was 1975—Ashton Holden and Margaret Seidler were due to retire in July 1975, and a bi-lingual, trained missionary who was a real soul winner was needed in Montreal. Montreal was Winnie's home. It seemed clear that God was opening the door for Winnie to return to Montreal to re-establish her ministry there. The Canadian Board agreed.[61]

Winnie returned to Montreal in the Fall of 1975. In her usual manner, she bathed her plans in prayer and then set out to share the Gospel. She was bold in her witness, courageous, and persistent in her missionary effort. She left no stone un-turned in the city of Montreal. In sharing the work with readers of *The Chosen People* magazine, she wrote:

In spite of our efforts to secure an ideal location for our mission station in Montreal, God continually closed the doors. Not only did we walk the streets for months, but even had three real estate agents at our disposal.

We walked and talked, phoned and moaned, but all to no avail.

God knew the location He had chosen for us was right next to a synagogue, that at His appointed time the former tenant would move out and the building agent would place an ad in the Montreal Star! The rent is one-half that of the other locations we had considered and we have a two-year lease.

About fifteen or twenty years ago the gentleman said we had been very kind to his wife and daughter when they went into our mission on Laurier Avenue.

They had gone in to ask questions and the man said we had 'even given them a free Bible.'

Truly there is no god like the wonderful God of Israel!

The Lord has just opened the door for a literature table at Concordia University, Sir George Williams Campus—with two other campuses as definite possibilities.

Young people are so exciting to work with and I am looking forward to God's challenge.

Two ladies who have supported the mission for years have begun a 'mailing ministry' with a difference.

The difference being that fervent prayer will be made on behalf of all persons who ask us to remove their names from our mailing list—since they will have already cast their ballots against the Lord!

Our prayer is for God to spare them and, through His mercy and long suffering, continue to deal with them in love.

We have also taken literature to radio and television stations, banks, newspapers, shopping centers, the Jewish mayor of my municipality, synagogues, B'nai B'rith lodges, Jewish service organizations, Chabad House and the office of the Israeli Ambassador to Canada.

We have taken literature to a Roman Catholic priest, co-chairman of Montreal's Jewish-Catholic Relations, because of the Vatican's 'apparent' refusal to acknowledge Israel as an independent nation.

God has permitted me to boldly declare at Jewish-Catholic meetings that regardless of what human councils decree, God's Word makes it clear you cannot separate the Book from the Land—or the Land from the People—or the People from the book.

The three are interwoven.

God has allowed me to publicly discuss the issue of 'deicide' with both priest and rabbi, and to declare the truth of what Jesus said in the tenth chapter of the Gospel of John.

We have also discussed at length the difference between a Gentile and a Christian—all to the praise and glory of God.

God is so anxious for the truth to be told to His people! Someone once said that 'Evangelism is simply one beggar telling another beggar where to find food.' We need to shout it from the rooftops that Messiah is the Bread of life![62]

As Winnie continued to develop the ministry in Montreal she, the members of the Board, and others prayed that God would direct young Jewish believers, young men, to eventually take over the ministry. She understood her limitations as a woman in Jewish ministry—especially in the growing Messianic movement. However, God's answers to her prayers were not forthcoming. In the meantime, Winnie continued to use her special and unique God-given gifts in reaching the Jewish people of Montreal with the Gospel.

In addition to her missionary endeavors, Winnie continued her Jewish education and "acculturation" at Concordia University, and through the years she has developed enough credits for a graduate degree in Jewish studies. But it was not the degree she sought. Winnie knew that the university campuses served as a means of a continuing witness to her fellow-students and to professors alike. An illustration of this was her encounter with an Orthodox rabbi. She wrote:

The nameplate on the front door told me a rabbi lived here. When he opened the door, I spoke to him in English. The rabbi apologized for not being able to speak English or French very well.

'That's no great problem,' I said in Hebrew, 'I speak your language!' His grey eyes twinkled as he put his hand to his long, grey beard and pulled his talit (prayer shawl) a little tighter.

'Come in,' he said. 'Come in.'

As Richard Lavallee, my French brother in Christ [Richard Lavallee served as a volunteer worker who assisted Winnie], and I stepped into the rabbi's study, my eyes darted across the four walls, going from floor to ceiling. Books! Nothing but books! Books also covered the large dining room table that the rabbi used as his desk.

He welcomed us and sat down after Richard and I had made ourselves comfortable.

'So, you speak Hebrew,' he said. 'You're Jewish.'

'No,' I replied, 'but when I came to believe in Jesus as my Messiah, God gave me a Jewish heart!'

Once again his hand quickly stroked his beard as he shifted slightly in his chair.

'What is it exactly that you wish to discuss with me?' he asked in broken English.

'I would like to ask you about the Tenach (Old Testament) and the B'rith Hadashah (New Testament),' I said. 'Do you as a rabbi read the Tenach daily, and do you believe it is the Word of God sent down to mankind?'

'Of course I read it, all the time,' he said, pointing to the commentaries on the table.

'Yes, I see the commentaries,' I said, 'but my question is this: Do you spend more time reading the Tenach itself or

the commentaries on the Tenach? To which do you devote most of your study time?'

'Well,' he said, 'you can see right here in the middle of the page, this is the Tenach.'

'Yes, I understand,' I said, 'but the little portion of Tenach is completely surrounded on all four sides by the commentaries of men. Which is the more important to you personally?'

'Well,' he said, 'I am the rabbi of all the people in this district, and I must know what the sages have said and taught.'

'Oh,' I said, 'then may I ask, which school do you follow, that of Shammai or that of Hillel?'

'How do you know such things?' he asked. 'Do you study with someone?'

'No, not exactly,' I said. 'But I read my Tenach regularly, and when I discover some Jewish tradition that is contrary to the Tenach, I go to the Jewish library and look for some answers. However, I must add that I meet with many discrepancies and differences of opinion among the sages.'

'But,' he said, 'you are on the outside looking in. You must come right in and study on the "inside."'

'By "inside" do you mean Judaism?' I asked.

'Yes,' he replied. 'You are so close—but you must come right in, and then you will learn and understand everything.'

'But, Rabbi, if I do come right in, does that mean I must leave Jesus "outside"?'

The rabbi hesitated. Finally, in a very gentle way, he said, 'Of course.'

'But why?' I asked. 'Wasn't Jesus Jewish?'

'Again I repeat,' he said, 'you must come in.... you are so close!'

I asked if I might ask him some very personal questions, and he nodded his head. 'When do you think Mashiach (Messiah) will come, Rabbi? And how will the Jewish people first recognize Him?'

'Who knows?' he replied. 'This is why we must study the commentaries all the time. We have our answers right here.'

'The prophet Zechariah told us that Mashiach would come on an ass, and yet Daniel insists that Mashiach will come on the clouds of heaven. Who has the truth?? I asked.

The rabbi shook his head, almost in unbelief. 'Whoosh!' he said. 'You are so close! How is it that you know of such things?'

I replied, 'I truly meant it when I told you that I read my Tenach regularly, praying that God will interpret the truth of His Word for me. Surely God's prophets do not contradict one another. I believe with all my heart that Mashiach came the first time riding on an ass, not because all of Israel was unworthy, as the sages have taught, but because the whole world needed to experience His redemption.'

'He came as God's Servant and poured out His soul unto death for our sin. Rabbi, I also believe with a perfect faith that Mashiach will come again on the clouds of heaven and that He will receive an everlasting kingdom. I'm happy that the Bible tells me I will someday see Mashiach vindicated when the inhabitants of the earth finally discover the truth. Then everything will be clear.'

'People will know then and believe that Mashiach was born of the virgin as a miraculous sign to the whole house of David, pointing them to the truth that Mashiach was more than just a man!'

The rabbi lowered his head and with a voice full of kindness, he said, 'You know of such things also?'

'Yes,' I replied, as I quoted Isaiah 7:14 and part of Zechariah 12:10, 'You see, Rabbi, the Jewish Mashiach is my personal sinbearer and Savior. I love Him with all my heart, and I love His people too. It's very personal,' I said. 'The Jewish Mashiach was pierced through for my sins, and I accept Him as my atonement.'

'Rabbi,' I said, taking a deep breath, 'I could never leave my Jewish Sinbearer outside.... He must be with me everywhere I go, for He is my Kapparah (covering, atonement) for now and for all eternity. Someday I will go to be with Him and thank Him personally for dying for me, a lost Gentile sinner. Mashiach did for me that which I could never do for myself. He made me acceptable to God and gave me His peace.'

Sensing our visit had drawn to a close, I stood up to leave.

'Thank you for opening our home to us today, Rabbi,' I said as Richard and I prepared to leave.[63]

Winnie's years of faithful witness have brought many Jewish people and Gentile people to faith in Jesus, but she was never able to establish a "branch" or a "center" type ministry in Montreal, nor was she able to get a Messianic congregation started. Part of the difficulty she faced, and which workers in Toronto faced as well, was the involvement of some of the Board members into the day-to-day activities of the ministry.

As mentioned earlier, the ministry in Canada was begun with the oversight of a Committee. The Board's continued involvement was a natural evolution; its members continued to function as the Committee had. Although the Canadian Board had appointed the Missionary Director from the United States to serve as the Missionary Director for the Canadian ministry, and had extended to that Missionary Director the same authority he had in the United States, some members of the Board in Canada still wanted the Canadian staff to report to them. This involvement sometimes generated problems as staff members felt free to approach Board members to "lobby" for programs, etc., and when Directors felt free to evaluate the work of the missionaries.

In the spring of 1976 Roy Adams was elected to the Canadian Board. At the time, both he and George Savage were living in Montreal and both men helped with the supervision and oversight of Winnie's ministry. But when Roy moved to Ontario, and George Savage resigned from the Board, Winnie was, for the most part, on her own again.

STAFF PROBLEMS AND REORGANIZATION

The moratorium on the hiring of new missionary personnel requested by Daniel Fuchs in September 1970, and the organizational changes within the American Board during the late 1970's and early 1980's, greatly impacted the work in Canada and attempts to place new workers there. However, at the November 1981 meeting of the Canadian Board, the author presented the name of David Sedaca as a possible worker for Toronto. David had already completed the missionary training program and he and his family had been looking forward to doing ministry in Canada. The sudden death of David's father, Victor Sedaca, had interrupted those plans and dreams, and David had returned to South America after the training program, to become Missionary in charge of the Mission's branch in Argentina (See Chapter Seven of this history).

After some discussion, the Canadian Board agreed to extend a call to David. Their intention was to bring him to Canada as Missionary in Charge of Toronto, but their long-range goal was to appoint him as Regional Director for Canada—an appointment which would give him supervision of the ministry in Montreal. Ultimately, they wanted to consider him for the position of Missionary Director of Canada.[64]

David and his family arrived in Toronto during the summer of 1982—six years after Leslie Jacobs left the staff of the Mission. One year later, David gave a report of his first year's activities. He wrote:

> Beth Sar Shalom Toronto began with a home Bible study. Only a few weeks later we were so crowded that we were forced to find a larger meeting place, one that was closer to the Jewish community. From there, we realized we would soon require our own center to accommodate our well-attended activities. Now, only one year after it all began, here we are at 343 Eglinton Avenue East. [This was a building the Canadian Board leased as an office and meeting place for the Toronto ministry. It was planned that eventually the Canadian Mission's administrative office would be moved from Hamilton to Toronto].
>
> Our work here is very important as Toronto is one of the fastest growing Jewish communities in North America. It has a large Orthodox and Hasidic contingency, heavily influenced by their brethren in New York. Toronto has recently replaced Montreal as Canada's largest and most dynamic Jewish community. Due to the large number of immigrants (from such places as Russia, Israel and Montreal), Toronto's Jewish population has almost doubled from approximately 80,000 ten years ago to close to 150,000 today.
>
> Not a single day goes by that I don't receive a phone call from an unsaved Jewish person asking questions or interested in or upset by our work. But the important thing is that we are sowing seeds. Already we have shared the Gospel through our Passover (Seder) banquet, weekly worship services and Bible studies.
>
> Pray with us as we plan to start a ladies' study and youth outreach. Truly the fields of Toronto are now white unto harvest.[65]

Under David's leadership, the ministry in Toronto flourished and at the Canadian Directors March 1983 meeting, Daniel Fuchs (who was still serving as President of the Canadian ministry) gave the following report:

> I have just had one of the most heart-warming experiences of my career. Knowing David Sedaca, I expected to have a very good report of progress in organizing our Toronto ministry. I am happy to say that what I have experienced has far exceeded my highest expectations. In all of my forty-six years of missionary work I have never seen a mission station operating in such a short period of time. Wednesday night I enjoyed teaching a group of about 30 believers, I think that all were Jewish except one. Before the meeting I spend [sic] several hours with David, I probed deeply into his theology, missionary philosophy and methods, his experience, plans for growth and expansion. I am happy to report that at last we have a trained, competent, highly motivated Hebrew Christian who, I believe, will be used of our Lord to build our evangelistic ministry. As members of the Board of Directors of BSSM [Beth Sar Shalom Mission], we must provide him with the essential tools which he needs. I believe that if our Lord tarries, we at last will begin to fulfill the task which our Lord has assigned to us. We are now opening the door of opportunity.
>
> For many years our staff in Canada has splendidly 'stood by the stuff' so that David will be able to build on a good

foundation. We are deeply grateful to the memory of William Jones, first honorary treasurer for Canada of ABMJ, to his daughter Mrs. Irene Wilson, and to Gloria Walker, who has so admirably and efficiently organized our administrative department. Also Tom Walker who has splendidly organized and developed the world-wide conference ministry of which he is the Director. We thank God for all of them.

I believe that we are at a climactic point in our history. We are now going to have to make crucial decisions which will decide whether our new ministry in Ontario, together with our one worker in Montreal [Winnie Marriner] will be all that we want it to be. I believe that in our Lord's will we must implement a plan of growth which will bring the Gospel to the Jews in all the Dominion of Canada. God help us to be faithful to Him.

I respectfully suggest that we adopt a step by step program, with defined goals which will enable us to fulfill God's purpose for Beth Sar Shalom.

A. We should define the purpose of Beth Sar Shalom Mission, Inc. as 'to reach all Jews in the Dominion of Canada with the Gospel.' This will mean that all activities of the Mission will be supportive and subjective to our one ultimate purpose.

B. In order to attain our purpose, we must realize that Beth Sar Shalom, Inc. and ABMJ are a unit operating in complete synchronism.

C. As far as is legally and practically possible, we must erase the boundary line that now exists.

D. We must adopt the same policy manual as ABMJ. (There may be legal and geographic differences which will have to be defined.)

E. At the next annual meeting the President of ABMJ should also be the President of BSSM.

F. We must provide the tools for our growth. Last Wednesday's meeting was a blessing in spite of the fact that it was in a church setting which is very uncomfortable to unsaved Jewish people. We must rent an adequate meeting place, some office space. We must relieve our missionary from details of janitorial and office routine. A competent secretary can frequently quadruple the effective ministry of a missionary. I suggest a goal of providing meeting and office space in Toronto and at least a part time Secretary by January 1, 1984.

G. Since continued growth will be dependent on increased receipts, I suggest that we recruit a church relations minister or a field evangelist by January 1, 1985.

H. We must undergird our work in Montreal. This is a bi-lingual ministry and recruiting will be very difficult. Goal—a missionary couple in Montreal by January 1, 1986.

I. Goal: A ministry in the Maritimes by January 1, 1987.

J. Another Goal: A ministry in Western Canada by January 1, 1988.

It is my sincere conviction that unless we answer God's challenge NOW we will become the 'Ichabod Mission to the Jews.'

Also, I would like us to consider sometime in the immediate future, the question, 'Is Hamilton the best location for our headquarters?' If not, we should schedule a change perhaps within three years or at least by the time our present lease expires.[66]

The Board enthusiastically endorsed and adopted Daniel's proposals and recommendations.

A building was leased in Toronto for David's ministry, and new staff members were hired. Miss Diana Holditch, who had participated in S.T.E.P. (The Mission's Summer Training and Evangelism Program) was hired effective September 1, 1983, to serve as a missionary in Toronto. And a part-time worker was hired to help Winnie Marriner in Montreal. At last, the missionary outreach in Canada was moving ahead!

As mentioned in Chapter Twelve of this history, the author underwent triple bypass surgery in September 1983. Upon his arrival home from the hospital, he received word that David Sedaca had been relieved of his missionary responsibilities in Canada (Because David's ministry had been so successful, the Canadian Board was following through with their initial plans for David; by the Fall of 1983, he was serving as Regional Director of Canada). It seems that culturally, and administratively problems had developed between David and some of the Board members, as well as between David and some members of his own staff. Recognizing that there was fault on both sides, the Canadian Board asked that a Committee be set up to deal with the problem, and to recommend to the American Board that David be transferred back to Buenos Aires, Argentina or to another Latin America country.[67]

When the Sedaca family returned to Argentina, David decided not to work with the Mission in Latin America. Ultimately, the Lord led him to take a position with another Jewish mission work.

In many ways the problem with David Sedaca was unavoidable. There were simply too many supervisors and too many Board members involved with the workers. The Directors in Canada recognized the problem, and at the February 1984 Board meeting they agreed on the following recommendation:

In order to avoid problems in the future regarding the supervision of missionaries on staff, it was agreed that it would be wise if major directives to staff missionaries could be issued from Orangeburg.[68] [The Mission's Headquarters Office in New York.]

Following the dismissal of David Sedaca, Sam Nadler, who was then serving as Eastern Regional Director in the United States, as well as pastor of the Light of Israel Messianic congregation, was asked to make a trip to Canada to evaluate the work in both Toronto and Montreal. His report was given to the Board at their February 1984 meeting. His findings were, for the most part, negative. He felt closer supervision was needed, as well as more training of the current workers. He recommended that Diana Holditch be sent to New York for three to four months of additional training.

A REGIONAL STRUCTURE FOR CANADA

The Board then asked the author to develop a program whereby the staff in Canada would be supervised directly by the Regional Directors of the United States.[69]

At their May 1984 meeting, the Canadian Directors acted on the author's recommendation to bring the missionary work in Canada under the supervision of the U.S. Regional Directors. The following men were appointed as Regional Directors for the Canadian Region:

Sam Nadler: Eastern Canada (Quebec, New Brunswick, Nova Scotia, Newfoundland and P.E.I. [Prince Edward Island].
John Bell: Central Canada (Ontario, Manitoba)
Dan Goldberg: Western Canada (Saskatchewan, Alberta, British Columbia and N.W.T. [Northwest Territory]).[70]

It was also recommended that John Bell release Miss Diana Holditch from active missionary service.[71]

With a regional structure in place for Canada and supervision of Canadian personnel under the direction of Regional Directors, the ministry in Canada once again began to develop. The Regional men requested that the Canadian Directors determine a set budget for each region; they requested the immediate employment of missionaries for the Toronto area; they requested that the ministry in Montreal be expanded through monthly and weekly Bible studies and through the celebration of the Jewish holidays. Daniel Goldberg began to develop church relations in Western Canada as a means of raising support; the monies were to be designated for hiring missionaries. Dan recognized that once the requirements for missionaries for Toronto and Montreal had been met, missionaries could be hired for other areas of the country. The missionary quota targeted for the ministry in Canada was identical to the quota set in the United States—one missionary per one hundred thousand Jews.

MORE NEW BOARD MEMBERS APPOINTED

At their September 1984 meeting, the Canadian Board appointed two Directors to the membership—Mr. David Weland, and Mr. Gary Smith. And four months later, at the January 1985 Board meeting, Rev. Albert Runge was elected to the Board (Albert Runge's story and testimony appear in Chapter Ten of this history).

David Weland is a Charter Accountant. His firm had been handling the auditing of the Mission's books—a contact through which David developed an interest in the Mission and a love for the Jewish people. He gave freely of his time to handle the Mission's books. Eventually he was elected Treasurer for the Mission in Canada.

Gary Smith was serving as vice-president of marketing and sales for a national paper company in Canada at the time he joined the Board. His dedication to the Mission and his leadership abilities have made him a valued member of the Board. He currently serves as Chairman of the Canadian Board, in addition to serving on a number of committees.

With the appointment of the U.S. Regional Directors as supervisors of the Canadian missionary work, one of the "defined goals" mentioned by Daniel Fuchs at the March 1983 Board meeting was essentially met—that of erasing the boundary line between the two countries.

NEW WORKERS AND PROGRAMS IN PLACE

By June 1984 a new work in Canada had begun. The following report from John Bell, Roy Schwarcz, Galen Banashak and Sam Nadler was presented to the Board at their January 1986 meeting:

The goal set before the workers in Toronto was to build credibility in Jewish Missions especially Beth Sar Shalom Mission in Toronto; build a work that would be responsible for itself; obtain folks who would take over the work and leadership. It is felt this was partially accomplished.

A Hanukkah service was held along with a special Yom Kippur Service.

The Congregation was started on January 13, 1985 on a bi-weekly basis at the Holiday Inn, Toronto Yorkdale. On July 1, 1985, weekly meetings began. Over half of the congregation is Jewish.

During the month of December the Lord sent a Russian family, Jewish Believers, whose grandfather is a rabbi in Israel.

The Sunday school has been divided. There is a class for teenagers and during the worship service a class for the younger children. A young Jewish boy named Jeremiah accepted the Messiah recently.

LONDON AREA:

A Bible Study is arranged once a month on the first Thursday evening. There are not many Jewish people attending and very few Jewish believers in the area. The attendance is...30-50 and there is a real zeal among those attending.

PASSOVER:

well attended with 145 maximum attending at the Park Lane Hotel. Others turned away.

RECOMMENDATIONS: Rob Styler has visited the area on two occasions. Once with Galen Banashak and another longer weekend with his wife and family. Rob has worked as a volunteer in the Chicago area while attending school. He has a great desire to work in Jewish Mission outreach. He is an aggressive young man, 30 years of age, very sharp and a good teacher. He has agreed, if the Board approves, to move his family to Toronto in September, 1986.

Also...Ben Volman, who has worked in Jewish Missions for some time and has pastoral qualities, is attending the congregation in Toronto and working with the group. John Bell recommended him as a good co-worker with Rob Styler and Ben would be considered some time in December. Ben Volman will attend S.T.E.P. this summer [c.1986].

UNION OF MESSIANIC CONGREGATIONS:

In November [c. 1985] a meeting was held at Orangeburg and an agreement on articles of faith and a constitution has been established. [This was for a new independent organization call The Fellowship of Messianic Congregations]. There will also be some guidelines with regards to Bible Teachers and Sunday School material geared to Hebrew Christian congregations. The new guidelines will reach out to disciple Jewish Believers and hope to bring congregations together for instruction, fellowship, etc.

SAM NADLER, Eastern Region

Israel Cohen is visiting the Montreal Area on a monthly basis. Israel has the heart of an evangelist so is concentrating on door to door and street ministry. The meetings have increased and approximately 50 people are attending regularly.

Names were submitted of those who have accepted the Messiah and new people who are attending the services.

GOALS:

Book tables—on the Campus of 3 Universities. Concordia University will be considered first with the hope of establishing 'Shalom Club' to reach those interested.

Discipleship of the new converts—Sam wants to see them growing, settle in the faith and to that end, meetings are being held with the individuals on a weekly basis.

Tract distribution—in order to have a visibility in Montreal, street ministry will take place twice a week for approximately two hours at a time, handing out gospel literature. The point of this outreach is that we will be able to be found.

Door to door ministry will take place twice a week when the weather breaks. Israel's trips to Montreal will be increased to twice a month, if this is feasible.

SPECIAL EVENTS:

Passover Banquet, Holiday Inn, April 19, 1986.

Conference, Word of Life, hoping that some of the believers from Canada will attend. Various Holidays, e.g. High Holy Days, a program will be arranged.

CHURCH MEETINGS: approximately 60 church meetings were arranged. Plans are underway for further contacts with the churches in Quebec and Eastern Ontario.

SUMMARIZING: 382 Visits were made. 129 were with unsaved Jewish people. This will continue. 19 Bible Studies with 16 unsaved people attending.[72]

At the May 22, 1986 meeting of the Board, it was reported that John Bell had been appointed Missionary Director for the United States. The appointment was to be effective August 1, 1986. After discussion, the Canadian Board approved the appointment of John Bell as Missionary Director for Canada as well, effective August 1, 1986.[73]

At their May meeting the Board also interviewed Rob and Sharon Styler as prospective missionaries for Toronto (The Stylers had already been interviewed and approved for missionary service by the Regional Directors). After the interview, they unanimously approved the Stylers appointment for missionary service in Toronto.

ROB STYLER — IN TORONTO

Rob Styler was born April 2, 1953 in Elizabeth, New Jersey. His parents were devout Roman Catholic people who attended church every Sunday; Rob went with them. His parents insisted that he attend Sunday School classes so he would be prepared for his first communion and confirmation. But, like Jewish boys who are Bar Mitzvah, Rob stopped attending church once he was confirmed. He had no desire to attend church; in fact, he had no curiosity about God.

By the time Rob entered high school he and his friends started to experiment with drugs. He developed the attitude that school was like church—optional. He didn't like school, he didn't want to go, and he didn't do well in school. He decided that he wanted to become a hairdresser, so he enrolled in a local vocational school. After graduating from the vocational school, he found a job as a hairdresser and continued his lifestyle of work and drugs.

Two years after graduating from vocational school, Rob met and fell in love with a girl named Sharon, but even after they were married his lifestyle did not change.

Four years passed, and Rob went from job to job, never feeling satisfied with anything in life. One day a friend called to tell him that he was opening a new salon; he wanted Rob to work for him. Rob felt it would be a good opportunity, so he gladly accepted. It was at the new salon that Rob was introduced to a fellow worker whose name was John.

As Rob worked with John, he realized that his life was different. He was a good worker. He could be counted on. One day John brought some tracts to work. Rob had never seen a tract before. That night, before he left the shop, he picked up one of the tracts and put it in his pocket so he could read it at home. Reading the tract, Rob couldn't believe its claims! Since he'd never read the Bible, he didn't know if what was written was true or not. But it certainly made him curious!

Rob began to take more tracts—each night he took a different one home. Then he began to ask John questions about the claims made in the tracts. John responded by asking Rob if he had a Bible. When Rob said he didn't, John went out and bought him one. After that, Rob began to read the Bible to see if the claims written in the tracts were true. Recalling that time in his life, Rob wrote:

A few weeks later I was sitting home alone and I realized I was going to hell. I remember thinking about it, I was going to hell and I hadn't even been concerned. I got out one of the tracts and read the prayer in the back. Then I did it again to make sure it was right. Even though I didn't know exactly what happened, I knew that Jesus had paid for my sins, and now thru Him, I was right with God. I felt relieved![74]

Sharon wasn't interested in the tracts Rob had been bringing home, but she did notice the difference in Rob after he started reading them and the Bible. By the time Rob accepted the Lord, Sharon knew that she, too, needed the peace and joy which Rob was beginning to experience in his life. After reading a book that Rob's co-worker had sent home, Sharon, too, knelt before God, repented of her sins, and received Jesus as her Lord and Savior (c. 1977).

The Stylers began attending a small Baptist church. But strangely, Rob also found himself drawn to the nearby Hasidic community of Jewish people. He started buying books so he could read about the Jewish people, and as he frequented their stores he began to develop casual relationships with the Jewish owners of bookstores. He thought surely he was the only Christian alive who was concerned about the Jewish people.

One Sunday a woman in their church gave Rob a copy of *The Chosen People* magazine. As he read through the pages a whole new world opened to him. He was amazed to learn that there were others who shared his burden for Jewish people. Rob learned, too, that the Vineyard congregation in Chicago (a Messianic congregation established by Chosen People Ministries) was not too far from them. After making this discovery, Rob and Sharon began regularly attending the services at the Vineyard, and were discipled in Messianic teaching.

Through a friend, Rob learned of the Jewish Studies program at Moody Bible Institute. He enrolled and was accepted. After his graduation from Moody, the Stylers entered the S.T.E.P. program of the Mission; they were then sent to Toronto.

BEN VOLMAN — IN TORONTO

About the same time that Rob and Sharon Styler were hired for the Toronto ministry, Ben Volman was also hired. In sharing his testimony with readers of *The Chosen People* magazine, Ben wrote:

The sunlight of early spring poured into the professor's office. As we sat around her desk discussing the meaning of philosophy, I grew more dissatisfied with her every answer.

'How did I make this mistake?' I thought. 'What made me think that philosophy would lead to understanding or give my life meaning?'

The face of my teacher was lined with her own troubles. I tried to explain my dilemma.

'I always thought that studying philosophy would lead to truth, to wisdom for life.'

'No, Ben,' she began. 'Those things are not the purpose of our study. We are examining the history of ideas....'

Outside in the reviving March air, I felt the freedom that comes from giving up false illusions. It was mixed with disappointment. What would I do now? As I started walking, trying to sort things out, some nagging questions spoke up. Does God have anything to do with this? Who is Jesus really? ...

From my route I could see the emerging skyline of the city center. My parents had come to Toronto from Israel in the early 1950's, and I was born while they still lived in the teeming Kensington Market when it was full of postwar Jewish immigrants. Soon afterwards they moved uptown, but not to one of the usual Jewish areas.

I was always very conscious of my Jewishness. Not that my parents were very religious. We celebrated all the holidays, but our identity did not revolve around Passover or Yom Kippur.

We were stirred instead by my mother's stories of growing up in Israel in the 1930's and 1940's. My mother's family had fled to Israel from Germany in 1933. My father was a Holocaust survivor and had been in the War of Independence. Hebrew was the second language in my home. Then, as now, I called myself a Zionist.

When I was a boy I thought that being Jewish meant being smart, and being bothered by the other kids. In the schoolyard I felt the bitter sting of anti-Semitism, but I did well in class. I had goals of excellence.

Despite all kinds of personal success in school, I was always aware of a deep-rooted bitterness. I could trace that, too, back to my Jewish heritage. It seemed as though we were almost reliving a part of the Holocaust in the daily talk around the kitchen table or at family gatherings. Whenever the stories were told of aunts, uncles, grandparents, or young cousins, they all ended in tragedy. They died in the camps, in the streets, or in a way too horrible for my parents to talk about,

The thought of those who died was like a weight, and the memory of those crimes against the innocent burned inside me like unresolved anger. I blamed it for my occasional mean streak and sometimes for my bleak sense of humor.

If there was a God, the Holocaust proved that He didn't matter.

I remember during the last hectic year of high school, while I was yearbook editor, that an acquaintance told me he went to church. I thought it was a joke. 'Nobody,' I said to myself, 'believes in God today.'

In the fall of 1974 I entered the University of Toronto. My college, Innis, was the smallest and most 'radical' of the undergraduate colleges in Canada. In spite of the time frittered away playing pinball or having a good time, I was planning on a career as a writer by taking courses in English and philosophy.

My first philosophy class was particularly disarming. Imagine my surprise when the distinguished lecturer closed his class this way? 'Ladies and gentlemen, I hope you will study many philosophers in the years ahead, but I hope that you will also discover that the greatest philosopher who ever lived is Jesus Christ.'

Despite that unexpected beginning, philosophy did attract me. (The Philosophy Department at the university was one of the largest in North America.) Strangely enough for me, the philosophers were always taking about God. In fact, their reasons for believing that there was a God seemed, well, almost convincing. Descartes, Spinoza, Kant, even the modern philosophers continued the discussion. Some of them even believed.

I had always assumed that no one educated after the Dark Ages believed in God.

Later I became fascinated by the book Pensees, a collection of thoughts by Blaise Pascal, the seventeenth-century French mathematical and scientific genius. Pascal actually recounted a moment of meeting Jesus personally.

He was the author of a brilliant little essay called 'The Wager.' He offered two alternatives? 'Either God is or God is not...and you must wager.' I had never seen it put that way before.

'Let us weigh up the gain and the loss involved in calling heads that God exists...if you win you win everything; if you lose you lose nothing.'

Pascal points out that there is an eternity of hope in having this faith, and otherwise there is none. It is foolish not to wager on God, and though being faithless gains you nothing, it may also lose you everything. I had to laugh and concede that he had won his point.

Slowly I was being drawn into a God consciousness of some kind. It weaved through readings in the occult and mysticism. How was I going to put it all together?

One weekend my elder brother brought home a Bible he was reading. My interest was aroused. I went to one of the campus bookstores and rummaged through every Bible in stock. Finally, I found one of the most cumbersome paperback editions I have ever seen. I bought it, and I read it.

The Bible was the most powerful literature I had ever encountered. In a life devoted to great literature, I was overwhelmed by its poetry, beauty, eloquence, and vividness.

The writing was wonderful. I even asked myself if I might ever live by Jesus' teaching. I decided I might want to, but I never would. I'm not saint material.

Then one summer day I stumbled onto a reference to John 14:6. Jesus says there, 'I am the way and the truth and the life. No one comes to the Father except through me.' I studied the passage for long minutes. ' Yes,' I concluded, 'Jesus is actually saying here that He is God.'

'I'm Jewish,' I thought. 'I can't believe this.'

I closed the Bible and put it away. And that, I assumed, closed the book on Jesus.

I entered my second year at the university. As months went by I found that I could not shake the conviction that God exists. This time, though, I was not looking at Him, but at myself. Life seemed rather shallow from this end. Beside the wonderful promise of hope spoken of by Pascal, my life seemed like an empty routine without joy or reason.

One night I lay in bed, painfully aware of the void inside. 'Dear God,' I began. I really did want to pray, but then stopped. My heart was not in it. Tears came. My heart had lapsed into a long and bitter winter. For the first time I knew how deep the gulf was between God and man.

The study of philosophy began to disappoint me as well. The closer I looked at the teachers (with the one exception of that first professor), the less I found to emulate or admire. The ones I knew all seemed to take for granted a life of spoiled ideals.

It was for this very reason—one last attempt at finding truth and meaning—that I had gone to my professor's office, only to have her say, 'No, Ben, those things are not the purpose of our study.'

As I walked through the wintry streets from the professor's office, I looked forward to lunch with my friends. I was only steps away from the college when a yellow poster caught my eye. In bold red letters it announced: Arthur Katz. For some reason I stopped to look. Underneath was a biography. I began to read about his spiritual journey from Marxism to that which led him to 'expound on the Person of Jesus Christ.'

I looked again at the name. With a name like that, he must be Jewish....

The meeting started at 1 o'clock. It was now 1:15. The auditorium was on the other side of the campus. I would have to skip lunch.

'What the heck,' I thought. 'I want some spiritual food.'

I arrived quietly and slipped into a back seat of the hall. As I sat there, I heard the speaker's dramatic and intelligent voice repeat things that had been going through my mind for over a year....

Katz spoke of living moment by moment with the Lord, and I knew that this was how I wanted to live.

After the stirring address, I went forward to talk to him in person. So did some others from the audience. I hadn't noticed before that a little group of my Jewish friends from Innis had been sitting near the front. We stood around talking, waiting to meet Arthur Katz.

I asked the one question that held me back. 'What about the Holocaust?' To be honest, I don't remember his answer....

I realize now that the only answer to the Holocaust, to evil in any and every form, is to end the will to evil that lives in our own hearts. To receive inner healing we must receive the Prince of Peace. We can't change history, but we can change, with God's help.

Art looked at me closely. 'You're ready to come, aren't you?' 'Yes,' I said.

He took me aside, and there in front of my Jewish friends I let God have His way in my life. I felt like a brick had fallen off my chest. A few minutes later I felt flooded with the joy of peace beyond understanding.

I had received the God of Israel as my God, and Jesus as my personal Messiah. And I felt inside that They had received me.[75]

Under the leadership of John Bell, Roy Schwarcz, and Galen Banashak an Olive Tree congregation had been established in Toronto. Ben was hired to co-pastor the congregation with Rob Styler. Unfortunately, it wasn't long until tension developed between the two men over leadership roles in the congregation, and over the missionary work in Toronto. In July 1987, John Bell reported to the Board that he would be transferring Rob Styler to Long Island, New

York where he was to work under Michael Rydelnik in the region supervised by Sam Nadler.[76] Ben was to remain in Toronto in charge of the missionary activity and as pastor of the Olive Tree congregation.

The news of Rob Styler's transfer back to the United States was a disappointment to Canadian Directors, but they were willing to abide by John Bell's decision in the matter. Some of the disappointment was abated when John went on to announce that Albert & Gretta Davis [Israeli] had been hired by the American Board, effective June 1, 1987. They were to work among the Russian Jews in Toronto. (For the full story of Albert and Gretta Davis [Israeli], see Chapter Seven of this history.) Not only was Canada getting a new missionary, they were getting a missionary whose salary and expenses were being paid by the American Board, thus freeing up an already tight budget in Canada.

The three men—John Bell, Missionary Director of the Mission, Roy Schwarcz, Regional Director for the Midwest and Canada, and Galen Banashak, Area Director for Toronto—assumed more and more control of the missionary work and the administrative work in Canada. After Tom Walker's position as International Conference Director was phased out in the late 1980's, the conference work in Canada was shifted to them as well. They chose to follow the methodology that was set up in the United States; all conferences and church meetings were arranged for through the Church Ministries Department of the Mission—each region hired Church Ministries Coordinators to carry out the department's goals. Miss Janice Buerling was hired as the Canadian Church Ministries Coordinator in January 1988.

As Missionary Director, John Bell recognized the hardship imposed on the Regional Directors as each man tried to juggle his missionary activities, oversight of his particular region (West, Midwest, Northeast), maintain his relationships at home, and travel to Canada to carry out his ministry oversight there. At the January 1988 meeting of the Board, John's Missionary Report included the suggestion that since Canada was being treated as region, perhaps it should have its own Regional Director. The Minutes state: "Galen Banashak has been asked to consider the position on a permanent basis. Galen has indicated that he would be willing to be "acting" regional director for a period of two years. At the end of that two years a decision would have to be made and would involve Galen moving to Canada."[77] The Board agreed to the proposal, and thereafter Galen was considered the "acting Regional Director" of Canada.[78]

John continued his report to the Board by presenting Galen Banashak's Missionary Report to the Directors. The report stated:

MONTREAL: Galen has visited Winnie [Marriner] in Montreal…She leads Bible studies on Tuesday and Wednesday nights and has now moved her Bible study to the Holiday Inn in Point Claire with 20 to 25 in attendance….
TORONTO: Albert Davis [Israeli] is holding a Bible study on Wednesday evenings with about 20 in attendance, 6 of which are unsaved Russian Jews.
Albert is very busy with a tract ministry and spends 2 days per week working on his radio ministry….
OLIVE TREE: There is a good spirit and unity present in the congregation…. The last meeting of the congregation had about 50 in attendance. This is up from approximately 30 or 35, 60% are Jewish.
Ben has 15 signed up for a discipleship program and has just completed 3 baptisms with 3 more to follow shortly.
HAMILTON: Janice Berling [sic] is working …as Church Ministries Coordinator…. Janice will also be working on a Messianic curriculum in conjunction with the Olive Tree Congregation.
Ben Volman has completed a tour of the Maritimes visiting 12 churches.[79]

God continued to bless, and the workers of the Mission rejoiced together as the Olive tree congregation saw several more Jewish people baptized. Albert Davis' [Israeli] Bible classes also continued to grow, and eventually developed into a Russian Jewish congregation.

It had been three years since the Board had taken on any new members, and the Directors began to consider the names of prospective candidates. Mr. John MacKinnon was elected to the Canadian Board at their October 1, 1988 meeting. John is a member of the Canadian Royal Mounted Police; his election to the Board was an effort to include more Canadian citizens on the Board and to thereby to keep the work indigenous.

The report of the missionary activity in Canada given to the Board at their October 1988 meeting was, once again, one of encouragement. Galen Banashak reported that in the five-month period since his last report to the Board, there had been 223 meaningful conversions; 47 Bible Studies for evangelism; 39 Bible Studies for discipleship; 4 Jewish decisions and 2 Gentile decisions. He further informed the Board that 646 churches had been contacted, 60 had been booked for the Fall season (c. 1988).[80]

STAFF CHANGES AND REORGANIZATION

But clouds hovered on the horizon. The changes taking place within the Mission in the United States were about to move across the border into Canada as well. On March 1, 1989 Sam Nadler was appointed Executive Director of Chosen

People Ministries in the United States; he was also elected to the U.S. Board of Directors. Subsequently, the Canadian Board, at their October 1989 meeting, elected Sam as President of Chosen People Ministries of Canada, and appointed him to the Canadian Board.

As indicated in Chapter Thirteen of this history, Sam's appointment as Executive Director of Chosen People Ministries in the United States (and his subsequent appointment as President of *The Chosen People* Ministries in Canada) triggered a number of resignations—among them, the supervisory staff, and missionary staff, of the Canadian ministry. John Bell, Galen Banashak, Roy Schwarcz and Ben Volman all resigned from the staff of the Mission. Additionally, although they did not resign from the Mission's staff, Albert & Gretta Davis (Israeli) left Canada; they were transferred to Israel to take over the ministry there. (In Israel, the Israelis' have continued their work among Russian Jewish immigrants who have poured into Israel, and Albert has continued to effectively direct the Mission's ministry in Kiev and its environs.)

Once again, the ministry in Canada was devoid of missionary staff. The entire staff (except for Winnie Marriner who faithfully continued her ministry in Montreal) and outreach had to be rebuilt. But this time the work would be rebuilt under a new ministry name.

As stated in Chapter Twelve of this history, the Mission's Directors in the United States had unanimously passed a resolution, in October 1986, authorizing that the name of the Mission be changed to "Chosen People Ministries, Inc." The name change became "official" during the Spring of 1988. Shortly after the American Board voted to change the Mission's name, the Canadian Board voted to change the name of the Canadian work from "Beth Sar Shalom Mission of Canada" to "Chosen People Ministries (Canada)." The first official Directors meeting of Chosen People Ministries (Canada) was held October 27, 1989 at the Marriott Residence Inn, Charlotte, North Carolina.

With the strong conviction that it was God's will that the Jews of Canada have an opportunity to hear the Gospel message (although it seemed evident that Satan was opposing the work on every front!), the Canadian Board set about to re-staff. On April 1, 1991 they approved the hiring of Larry Rich as Area Director for Canada. His appointment was a wonderful answer to prayer! Larry is a Jewish believer who is not only a veteran missionary to the Jews, he was raised in one of the early Messianic congregations in the city of Chicago.

LARRY RICH—AREA DIRECTOR/CANADA

Larry Rich was born into a Russian-Jewish family on October 1, 1941. His parents had immigrated to the United States while they were in their teens; they met one another in Chicago, and later married. Although both had been raised in Orthodox homes, they chose to live a fairly secular lifestyle. In telling about his background, Larry wrote:

> *...approximately four years before I was born my mother (who was not in good health) had a housekeeper who 'happened' to leave some literature laying on a table in our home. After my mother had read quite a bit she said to the housekeeper, 'I was interested in what I was reading here until I came to the name of "Jesus." You know, we Jews don't believe in Jesus.' The housekeeper (who was not Jewish herself) replied, 'Well, I'll take you to some who do!'*
>
> *My mother came to a women's Bible class and met, among others, Esther and David Bronstein—pioneer leaders in interpreting the Gospel of the Jewish Messiah in the Chicago area. After several weeks of attending the classes my mother confessed Jesus (Yeshua) as her Messiah and Savior.*
>
> *For my father the process was a good deal longer. He studied the Bible with Mr. Bronstein and others, came to the camp in Michigan run by the Bronsteins and engaged in the daily Bible studies there, and then eventually—about a year after my mother's experience with Yeshua—came to faith himself. He became quite active in the congregation led by Mr. Bronstein (then know [sic] as the First Hebrew Christian Church of Chicago), serving as an elder for some twenty years until his death in 1959.*
>
> *After I was born, I was raised in the fellowship of the First Hebrew Christian Church. As a young boy I made a specific commitment to Yeshua as Messiah and Savior, although it had been something that had seemed to be a part of me from my earliest memory. I looked up to Mr. Bronstein and others and considered 'the ministry' as a calling from the Lord (although there were still the dreams of one day playing for the Chicago Cubs). In my high school days I got actively involved in youth groups and Bible clubs, and later went to college—during which time I experienced a very specific and somewhat dramatic calling from the Lord to go into full time ministry.*
>
> *After seminary and graduate school [Taylor University, Upland, Indiana. B.A.1963; McCormick, Chicago, Ill. 1966. M.Div.; Wheaton Graduate School; 1966; M.A.] I was called to serve as director of Peniel Center and pastor of the First Hebrew Christian Church—formerly under the leadership of Mr. Bronstein and then later his brother-in-law, Morris Kaminsky. In later years I taught Bible at Trinity College in Deerfield, Illinois, and then served five years as General Secretary of the Messianic Jewish Alliance of America.*

As might be expected, my understanding of myself and my faith has grown and been modified over the course of these many years. Very significant has been my evolving identity as a Jew. Even as believers in Yeshua, my parents still placed a limited emphasis on Jewish practice and so I was raised knowing that I was a Jew and feeling okay about it, but with limited knowledge of Jewishness. While serving at Peniel Center I became more and more aware of the Messianic Jewish movement that was surfacing in several places in the country, and through contacts with such people as the Martin Chernoff family—then in Cincinnati, began to give serious thought to the relationship between Jewish identity and practice—and believing in Messiah Yeshua. For some years now it has been a major topic of personal study and a part of a still developing life orientation.

Remarkably, in 1980, I returned to serve—for the second time—as the spiritual leader of the congregation in which I was raised. We are known as Adat haTikvah now (Congregation of the Hope), and are one of the many Messianic congregations that can be found today in the large Jewish population areas throughout the United States. Throughout the eighties there has been congregational growth and many blessings from the Lord. An important milestone was a year ago when the Congregation became independent after fifty-five years of affiliation with the Presbyterian Church.[81]

After being appointed Area Director for Canada, Larry Rich and his family moved to Toronto where they have labored to once again develop the ministry there. Welcoming Larry Rich to the staff of the Mission was like welcoming one of the "Mission's boys" because, as mentioned in Chapter Ten of this history, the Bronsteins' ministry (Aedus Community Center) was merged with the Mission in 1965.

As steps have been taken to re-staff the Toronto and Montreal ministries, God has once again supplied His choice servants for the task. In August 1991 Rob Styler and his family returned to Toronto to take over the ministry there. God has blessed by supplying a new worker for Montreal as well. Mr. Percy Johnson was hired on July 1, 1992. He will eventually assume the leadership of the work in Montreal.

Percy Johnson—in Montreal

Percy Johnson was born May 18, 1950 in Lima, Peru. His father came from a Sephardic Jewish background. His mother was a Roman Catholic. Percy wrote:

I come from a family, that without being religious, we learned high moral standards. My father has always been a moral person and I would say a religious person in his own way. My mother's side is Catholic, and I would add nominal Christians. Their moral standards were not as high as my father's were and are.... When I was 15 years old I began college at the Catholic University of Lima, Peru. I was studying Civil Engineering and I needed to take four semesters of Catholic Doctrine. I took the course and memorized it. In that way I had a good grade, but I did not believe in what it taught. The priest, who was the professor, had a very licentious life and he boasted about it. As a college freshman I visited my friend's ranch. Here I saw another priest preach to the poor people, who were workers from the ranch, telling them that God made them poor in order to inherit the heavens. Later on the same day while eating with the ranch owner, the priest mocked what he said in the morning. These two experiences with the institutional religion made [me] become a complete agnostic and later on an atheist.

At the same time in the Catholic University were some professional students who were paid by the communist party to try to entice young people into their ranks. They used the religious people's hypocresy [sic] and their institutions and blamed the government for everything that was wrong. Because I was completely disoriented in my beliefs, I began listening to these people. Many things that they said made a lot of sense to me. It was easy for me then to come to the conclusion that religion was an invention of man in order to exploit his own kind and we needed to take away that sperstition [sic] from man. This pilgrimage would help me later in my own search for the truth. During this time I arrived home one day from working late in the university on a special research, when I saw some people crying. The first thing I thought was something happened to my mother. I ran and asked what was going on and they told me that my oldest brother Jimmy had been in an accident and was very critical at the hospital. I rushed to the hospital and I saw my brother. The doctors told me they could not do anything for him. Two days later he died. I did not know why I could not cry or feel anything. I made all the funeral arrangements because my father was completely destroyed by this tragedy. After the funeral my father told me that he lost all his hopes for the future because his first born died. I told him that he still had other children and I was ready to take my brother's responsibilities. But he said that he had only one first born and nobody could replace my brother. I knew [it] was impossible to replace my brother, but I wanted to help so bad. During this time a missionary couple, the Ditmores, were supporting my family. My youngest brother had had a genuine conversion and he invited these missionaries to my home the day of the funeral. Later we met another couple from the Wycliff Bible Translators, the Lyons, who were also Southern Baptist. We became good friends with these two couples and my parents would invite them sometimes to have supper with us. The Lyons invited me to spend time with them at their home in the Wycliff Bible Translators base. I did and met their children. Christmas we invited Nathan (the Lyons' son) to spend time with us. I became like a big brother to him. December 23rd, 1972 he took the plane back home, but never got to its destination. Nathan died and my memories were still fresh from my brother Jimmy. As a result of the Lyons' example, I saw God's love and peace that I had never seen before. They gave me a New Testament which I started reading. The Lord changed my heart through the reading of His Word and the silent, but the loud example of Christian hope and love in the lives of the Ditmores and Lyons. I dedicated my life to the Lord, surrendering everything from me to Him.

Since that day I have been serving Him. Missionary Steve Ditmore was an excellent help for my discipleship and he led me to love the Lord Jesus and to know more about Him. I went to South Western Baptist Theological Seminary in Fort Worth to prepare myself so that I could preach the Word of God. I left my profession as professor of thermodynamics in the University in Peru. To this day I do not have any regrets. I believe that all my experiences and training I have had were used to prepare me to serve my Lord better in the call of missions which He has given me. I learned with so much love that Jesus was a Jew and now I feel proud to be one and tell other Jews that Yeshua Ha Mashiach; Jesus is the Messiah.[82]

Percy Johnson and his family moved to Montreal in July 1992; they are actively developing and expanding the ministry there.

The most recent change in the Canadian ministry took place during the Spring of 1993 when the administrative office of the Mission in Canada was relocated from the city of Hamilton to Toronto—a move that had long been discussed by the Canadian Board.

In Canada, as in the United States and around the world, there is still much to be done! The "fields are white unto harvest, but the laborers are few."[83] The constant prayer of the Directors of the Canadian Board, as well as of the Directors of the American Board, is that the Lord of the harvest will supply more workers for the field.

As the Mission in the United States prepares to celebrate its Centennial, the Mission in Canada will celebrate fifty-four years of testimony to the Jewish community of Canada. It is our prayer that, should our Messiah tarry, the Mission in Canada will continue under the banner of His blessings, and that one day it, too, will celebrate a "Centennial of faithful ministry."

ENDNOTES
Chapter 14. The Vision in the Dominion of Canada

1 *Minutes*, ABMJ, (July 29, 1940), p 5.
2 *The Chosen People*, Vol. XLVI, No. 4, (January, 1941), pp 11, 12.
3 *The Chosen People*, Vol. XLVIII, No. 5, (February, 1943), p 6.
4 *The Chosen People*, Vol. XLVII, No. 8, (May, 1942), p 12.
5 *The Chosen People*, Vol. XLVII, No. 1, (October, 1941), p 12.
6 *Minutes*, ABMJ, (October 21, 1942), p 5.
7 *The Chosen People*, Vol. XLVIII, No. 6, (March, 1943), pp 8-10.
8 *The Chosen People*, Vol. LXXI, No. 6, (February, 1966), p 12.
9 *The Chosen People*, Vol. XLVIII, No. 6, (March, 1943), pp 9, 10.
10 *The Chosen People*, Vol. XLVIV, No. 3, (December, 1943), p 11.
11 *The Chosen People*, Vol. L, No. 5, (February, 1945), p 14.
12 See note above.
13 *The Chosen People*, Vol. LI, No. 2, (November, 1945), p 13,14.
14 *The Chosen People*, Vol. LII, No. 5, (February, 1947), p 9.
15 See note above.
16 *The Chosen People*, Vol. LIV, No. 8, (May, 1949), p 12-14.
17 *Minutes*, ABMJ, (January 25, 1950), p 64.
18 *Minutes*, ABMJ, (January 25, 1951), p 80.
19 *The Chosen People*, Vol. LVII, No. 5, (February, 1952), p 17.
20 *The Chosen People*, Vol. LVII, No. 7, (April, 1952), p 12.
21 *Minutes*, ABMJ, (January 26, 1955), p 127.

[22] *The Chosen People*, Vol. LXIX, No. 1, (September, 1963), p 8.

[23] *The Chosen People*, Vol. LXXIV, No. 5, (January, 1969), p 4.

[24] *The Chosen People*, Vol. LXXI, No. 6, (February, 1966), p 12.

[25] *Minutes*, Beth Sar Shalom Mission, (November 13, 1967), p 1.

[26] *Minutes*, Beth Sar Shalom Mission, (November 19, 1971), p 1.

[27] *Minutes*, Beth Sar Shalom Mission, (November 3, 1972), p 1.

[28] *The Chosen People*, Vol. XLVIII, No. 5, (February, 1943), p 6.

[29] *The Chosen People*, Vol. L, No. 5, (February, 1945) p 5.

[30] *Minutes*, ABMJ, (November 15, 1967), p 7.

[31] *Minutes*, Beth Sar Shalom Mission, (November 13, 1967), p 1.

[32] See note above, p 2.

[33] *Minutes*, ABMJ, (November 15, 1967), p 7.

[34] *Minutes*, Beth Sar Shalom Mission, (March 27, 1970), p 2.

[35] Henry Bregman, *The Conversion of a Rabbi, or My Life Story*, (Toronto: Beth Dor'she Emeth, n.d.), p 44,45.

[36] See note above, pp 46, 47.

[37] See note above, p 49.

[38] *The Chosen People*, Vol. LXXII, No. 4, (December, 1966), p 5.

[39] *Minutes*, Beth Sar Shalom Mission, (March 22, 1968), p 2.

[40] *Minutes*, Beth Sar Shalom Mission, (January 31, 1969), p 2.

[41] *Minutes*, Beth Sar Shalom Mission, (November 19, 1971), p 3.

[42] *Minutes*, Beth Sar Shalom Mission, (October 19, 1970), p 1.

[43] See note above, p 3.

[44] *Minutes*, Beth Sar Shalom Mission, (November 19, 1971), p 3.

[45] See note above, p 4.

[46] *Minutes*, Beth Sar Shalom Mission, (November 3, 1972), p 4.

[47] Rachmiel Frydland, *Why I Believe*, (Englewood Cliffs, New Jersey: Sar Shalom Publications, n.d.).

[48] Rachmiel Frydland, *Why I Believe*, (Chattanooga, TN: Messianic Fellowship, n.d.), p 3.

[49] See note above, p 4.

[50] Rachmiel Frydland, *I Escaped From the Nazis*, (Willowdale, Ontario: Rachmiel Frydland, n.d.), p 1.

[51] See note above, p 2.

[52] *Minutes*, Beth Sar Shalom Mission, (November 3, 1972), p 5.

[53] Leslie Jacobs, *The Discovery That Made Me Complete*, Personal Testimony/Application, (n.d.), p 1,2.

[54] Leslie Jacobs, *Board Report—Toronto, Ontario, Canada*, (October, 1974), p 1,2.

[55] Rachmiel Frydland, *Report to the Board*, (December, 1974), p 2.

[56] *Minutes*, Beth Sar Shalom Mission, (November 30, 1973), p 1,2.; *Minutes*, Beth Sar Shalom Mission, (Special Meeting, June 18, 1974), p 1.

[57] Winnie Marriner, *Personal Testimony/Application*, (November 30, 1971), p 2,3.

[58] See note above.

[59] See note above.

[60] See note above.

[61] *Minutes*, Beth Sar Shalom Mission, (January 10, 1975), p 10.

[62] *The Chosen People*, Vol. LXXXI, No. 6, (February, 1976), p 10.

[63] *The Chosen People*, Vol. XCII, No. 1, (September, 1985), pp 6-8.

[64] *Minutes*, Beth Sar Shalom Mission, (November 17, 1981), p 2.

[65] *The Chosen People*, Vol. XC, No. 4, (December, 1983), p 9.

[66] Daniel Fuchs, *Report*, Beth Sar Shalom Mission, (March 25, 1983), pp 1, 2.

[67] *Minutes*, Beth Sar Shalom Mission, (December 2, 1983), p 2.

[68] *Minutes*, Beth Sar Shalom Mission, (February 9, 1984), p 1.

[69] See note above, p 2.

[70] *Minutes*, Beth Sar Shalom Mission, (May 17, 1984), p 1,2.

[71] See note above.

[72] *Minutes*, Beth Sar Shalom Mission, (January 10, 1986), pp 3, 4.

[73] *Minutes*, Beth Sar Shalom Mission, (May 22, 1986), pp 1, 2.

[74] Robert Styler, *Personal Testimony/Application*, (January, 1985), p 3.

[75] *The Chosen People*, Vol. XCIV, No. 1, (September, 1987), pp 4-8.
[76] *Minutes*, Beth Sar Shalom Mission, (June 13, 1987), p 1.
[77] *Minutes*, Beth Sar Shalom Mission, (January 30, 1988), p 2.
[78] See note above, pp 2, 3.
[79] See note above, p 3.
[80] *Minutes*, Beth Sar Shalom Mission, (October 1, 1988), p 2.
[81] Larry Rich, *Personal Testimony/Application*, (April, 1991), pp 1, 2.
[82] Percy Johnson, *Personal Testimony/Application*, (May, 1989), pp 11-13.
[83] Matthew 9:37.

Epilogue

Chosen People Ministries, Inc. continues to fulfill the vision of its founder, Rabbi Leopold Cohn. It is the first mission in the twentieth century to have established a missionary policy of establishing indigenous Messianic congregations.

Today, both the Board of Directors and the Mission's staff are united in their stand behind the Mission's policy which states that the sole purpose of the Mission is to reach Jewish people with the Gospel, to disciple new Jewish believers, and to encourage Jewish believers to affiliate with Scripturally sound Messianic congregations or local churches where their cultural and spiritual heritage as Jews can find true expression within the Body of Messiah.

The Board of Directors of Chosen People Ministries is currently comprised of the following members: Roy Adams, Vice-Chairman of the Board; Jeffrey M. Branman; John J. Kubach; Sam Nadler, President/CEO; Dr. John L. Pretlove, Chairman of Board; Goldie Rotenberg, Assistant Treasurer; Harold A. Sevener, President-Emeritus; Gary W. Smith, Chairman, Canadian Board; James W. Straub; David C. Weland; Jean C. Wheeler; Darrell J. Winrich. Additionally, in accordance with its by-laws, the Board has elected two officers who are not board-members, and thus have no vote. These individuals may attend board meetings to give reports, etc., but they do not sit through the entire meeting. These two officers are: Barbara Benedict, Secretary; C. James Rees, Treasurer.

Board committees include several standing committees as well as appointed committees. Each board member is assigned to a committee, and members may serve on more than one committee. Committee assignments are made by the Nominating Committee, or an assignment may be made by an appointment of the Chairman. In making committee assignments, consideration is given to areas of "expertise" of the individual Board members, and assignments are made accordingly.

The committees of the Board are: The Appraisal Committee, consisting of: Jean Wheeler, Chairman; Roy Adams, Jeffrey Branman, Gary Smith, James Straub, and David Weland. The Audit Committee, consisting of: Roy Adams, James Rees (without vote), David Weland, Darrell Winrich. The Executive Committee, consisting of: John Pretlove, Chairman; Roy Adams, Jeffrey Branman, Sam Nadler, Goldie Rotenberg, Harold A. Sevener, and Darrell Winrich. The Finance Committee, consisting of: John Kubach, David Henschen (without vote), James Rees (without vote), James Straub, and Darrell Winrich. The Foreign Committee, consisting of: Sam Nadler, John Pretlove, Goldie Rotenberg, Gary Smith, and Darrell Winrich. The Nominating Committee, consisting of: Jeffrey Branman, Goldie Rotenberg, Gary Smith, James Straub, Jean Wheeler. The Pension Committee, consisting of: Roy Adams, James Rees (without vote), James Straub, David Weland, and Darrell Winrich. Personnel Committee, consisting of: Jeffrey Branman, Chairman; Roy Adams, Sam Nadler, Goldie Rotenberg, Harold A. Sevener, Gary Smith and Jean Wheeler.

The Canadian Board of Directors consists of the following members: Roy Adams, Vice-Chairman; John MacKinnon, Secretary; Sam Nadler, President/CEO; Dr. John L. Pretlove, Chairman American Board; Harold A. Sevener, President-Emeritus; Gary W. Smith, Chairman; David C. Weland, Treasurer.

The overall work and staff of Chosen People Ministries is divided into four main categories—National Ministries, U.S. Ministries, Development, and Administration. This structure allows for proper supervision and evaluation of each department as it carries out its functions and duties. The current staff is comprised of the following workers:

NATIONAL MINISTRIES:
Sam Nadler, President & CEO; Barbara Benedict, Assistant to the President.
Harold A. Sevener, President Emeritus; Grace Sevener, Secretary to the President Emeritus.

U.S. MINISTRIES:
Larry Jaffrey, U.S. Ministries Director; Miriam Nadler, National Church Ministries Coordinator; Michelle Barnett, Church Ministries Coordinator; Dot Pringle, Regional Church Ministries Coordinator; Teri Gee, Church Ministries Coordinator.

DEVELOPMENT DEPARTMENT (Stewardship & Communication):
David Henschen, Development Director; Judy Weiser, Secretary; Zahea Nappa, Major Donor Coordinator; Shelvie Hostetler, Media Coordinator; Constance Steinberg, Resource Coordinator; David Gage, Donor Relations Representative, Bryan Hinkle, Donor Caller.

ADMINSTRATION:
Bill Caldwell, Administrative Director.

FINANCE:
James Rees, Treasurer; Priscilla George, Administrative Assistant; Susan Turner, Senior Data Preparation Clerk.

DATA PROCESSING:
Bruce Altemose, Data Process Manager; Sandra Avery, Data Entry Operator; Duncan Hurst, Analyst/Programmer; Nancy Lopez, Assistant to the Data Process Manager; Janice Northrop, Programmer/Operator; Betty Roble, Data Entry Operator.

BUILDING SERVICES:
Andrew Barnett, Building & Office Services Manager; Robert Cachine, Sr., General Mail/Inserter Operator; Lewis Turner, General Mail/Inserter Operator.

GENERAL OFFICE:
Marilyn Gravitt, Office Manager; Ruth Clewis, Church Report Clerk; Linda Human, Data Preparation Clerk; Ann Jackson, Data Preparation Clerk; Eileen Miller, Secretary/Receptionist; Peggy Tucker, Church Report Clerk; Mennie Wright, Literature Clerk. Connie Behn, Susan Ferrell, and Judith McCord serve as volunteer workers.

 While the "Regions" of the Mission are no longer clearly defined for the supervision of the missionary personnel and the support staff of the Mission, they are still maintained as boundaries for determining areas of support and for specific mission activities. The supervision of Mission personnel within the various regions may therefore become the responsibility of Larry Jaffrey, the U.S. Ministries Director, of Michael Rydelnik as Regional Director, or of Miriam Nadler, as National Church Ministries Coordinator.

 The "Northeast Region" is comprised of ministry being carried on in the New York Metropolitan area, Long Island, and Northern New Jersey. (At the present time, there are no Mission workers stationed in Boston, Massachusetts.)

 The main office for the Northeast Region is located at 88 Southern Parkway, Plainview, New York (Long Island). Michael Rydelnik is the Regional Director for the Northeast Region. His area of supervision also currently includes the Midwest. The Long Island staff includes Joseph Dorais, support staff (full-time); Stacy Dorais, support staff (full-time); Susan Kurtzer, Regional Church Ministries Coordinator (part-time); Eva Rydelnik, Missionary (part-time); Teri Gee, Regional Church Ministries Coordinator (working out of the Charlotte Headquarters office).

 Within the Northeast Region, the ministry in the Northern New Jersey area is under the leadership of Larry Feldman, Area Director. His staff includes Irving Salzman, Missionary (full-time); and Lisa Spadafino, support staff (part-time).

 The ministry in the New York Metropolitan area is under the leadership of Stewart Weinisch, Area Director. His staff includes Shoshannah Weinisch, support staff (part-time); Israel Cohen, Missionary (full-time); James Fox, Missionary (full-time); Lydia Wechsler, Student Missionary; Michael Wechsler, Missionary Aide (part-time).

 The main office of the "Midwest Region" is located at 6057 N. Kedzie Ave, Chicago, Illinois. At the current time there is no Midwest Regional Director and, as stated, supervision of the region has been designated to Michael Rydelnik. Michael Campo and Kirk Gliebe serve as full-time missionaries for the Midwest Region. Leon Engman serves as a missionary in a Support-Raised catagory; he is trying to raise his support so he can join the staff as a full-time missionary. The Midwest staff also includes: Patricia Fletcher, Support Staff (full-time); Sherry Gotbaum, Regional Church Ministries Coordinator. Yvonne Becker, Harold Cohen, Wayne Kaipainen, and Wilma Koch serve as volunteer workers in the Midwest.

 The "Southern Region" is comprised of two regions formerly called the Southeast Region and the Southwest Region. As with the Midwest Region, there is no Regional Director. Supervision of the Southern Region is under Larry Jaffrey, whose title has been broadened from Southeast Regional Director to U.S. Ministries' Director. The main office for the Southern Region is located at 819 Woodward Rd., Marshall, Virginia. Gail Jaffrey serves as support staff (full-time) for the region; Mark Wachtel is a volunteer worker. The Church Ministries office for the region is located in Dothan, Alabama. Sheila Stephens serves as the Southern Regional Church Ministries Coordinator (part-time).

Within the Southern Region, the ministry in the greater Philadelphia area is being done by Ken Alpren, who serves as the Area Director and Frank Potter, who assists as a Missionary (full-time). Ministry in the Washington DC area is being carried on by Scott Brown, Missionary (full-time); Marjorie Brown, assists Scott as his secretary (part-time); Mr. Charles Burrall serves as a volunteer worker. In South Florida, Winn Crenshaw has established a work in the Coral Springs area. Winn serves as a Missionary (full-time). Steve Cohen has been hired as a Missionary (part-time) for ministry in Dallas, Texas.

Also stationed in the Southern Region is Ben Alpert, who serves as a National Ministries Representative for the Mission. Bonnie Alpert serves as Support Staff (part-time).

The main office for the "Western Region" is located at 7041 Owensmouth Ave., Suite 102, Canoga Park, California. Like the Midwest Region and the Southern Region, the Western Region does not have a Regional Director. Supervision of the Western Region is the responsibility of Larry Jaffrey, as the U.S. Ministries' Director.

The ministry in the Los Angeles area is being carried on by Christopher Melisko, Area Director; Phyllis Adams, Support Staff (full-time); Steven Sinar, Regional Church Ministries Coordinator; and Dr. Daniel Goldberg, the International Ministries Representative. In Sacramento, Artis Clotfelter serves as a Missionary (part-time). In San Diego, Irvin Rifkin serves as a Missionary (full-time). Irv's wife, Cordelia, serves as a Missionary (part-time).

Foreign branches of Chosen People Ministries are currently located in Argentina, Canada, Israel, and the Ukraine.

The main office for the ministry in Argentina, is located at Billinghurst #417, 1174 Buenos Aires. Workers in Argentina include Roberto Passo, Director for the South American ministry; Elias Habif, Missionary (full-time); Stephan Rivoire, Missionary (full-time); Alejandra Giampaolo, Support Staff (full-time); Betsabe Leon, Support Staff (full-time); Thelma Passo, Support Staff (part-time). The work in South America is known by the name, Junta Americana De Misiones A Israel (JAMI).

The main office for the work in Canada is now located at 291 Sheppard Ave W., North York, Ontario. In the greater Toronto area, Larry Rich is the Area Director. The Canadian staff also includes: Janice Beurling, Regional Church Ministries Coordinator; Rob Styler, Missionary (full-time); Lorraine St. Onge, Support Staff (full-time); Margaret Lee Wo, Support Staff (part-time). In Montreal, Quebec Percy Johnson serves as a Missionary (full-time).

The main office for the ministry in Israel is located in the village of Kfar Saba. Albert Israeli is the Missionary (full-time); Ora Braithwaite, Support Staff (full-time).

In the Ukraine the ministry is currently being carried on by Dimitri Riznik, Support Staff (full-time); Luda Riznik, Support Staff (part-time); Alexander Duchno, Support Staff (part-time); Samuel Lichtman, Support Staff (part-time).

Messianic congregations which the Mission has established, and which continue to be pastored by Mission personnel, include: the Shepherd of Israel congregation, Woodland Hills, California, Christopher Melisko, leader; Son of David congregation, Rockville, Maryland, Scott Brown, leader; Beth Messiah congregation, Livingston, New Jersey, Larry Feldman, leader; Olive Tree congregation, Plainview, New York, Michael Rydelnik, leader; Hope of Israel congregation, Philadelphia/Cherry Hill, New Jersey, Ken Alpren, leader; Beth Sar Shalom, Toronto, Canada, Rob Styler, leader.

The publications printed by the Mission have been cut back in recent years. As of September 1993, *The Chosen People* magazine, which was established and was continuously published since 1895, was discontinued. In its place, the Mission began publishing *The Chosen People* Newsletter—an eight page newsletter designed to promote the ministry in an updated format.

Many tracts and booklets previously produced by the Mission have been discontinued. In some cases, the materials have been reworked into more modern vehicles of communication such as audio or video cassettes. Tracts and booklets which continue to be produced by the Mission include:

BOOKS:
How To Be Like the Messiah - John Bell.
How To Introduce Jewish People To the Messiah.
I Have Loved Jacob - Joseph Cohn.
Passover Haggadah - Harold A. Sevener, Editor.

The Mission stocks and sells many other books—some written by staff members but printed and distributed by other publishers.

TRACTS:
Debt of Love; Importance of Passover; Twenty-One Reasons; L'Chaim; What is a Christian/Who is a Jew?; How Would You Know The Messiah?; Twenty-Seven Prophecies; Isaiah 53; Dear Rabbi; The Broken Matzo; Why Did Messiah Die;

Jewishness & Hebrew Christianity; Ministry of Beth Sar Shalom; Did God Reject His People?; An Astonishing Yom Kippur Prayer (Yiddish); The Dead in Christ.

Other tracts are also printed and distributed by the staff of the Mission. These are called "broadsides," and are printed through the individual regions for distribution in special missionary activities.

AUDIO CASSETTES:
History of ABMJ - including interviews with Dr. Daniel Fuchs, Chairman of the Board of Directors (now deceased)
    and Rev. Harold A. Sevener, President of ABMJ (now President-Emeritus).
The Temple in Prophecy - Harold A. Sevener.
The Middle East in Prophecy - Harold A. Sevener.
Why Witness to Jewish People - Larry Feldman.
How to Witness to Jewish People - Larry Feldman.
Passover Music/Prayers.
God's Love For Israel - Sam Nadler.
Simcha '92, 6 Messages on Simcha/Joy—Phillipians.

VIDEO CASSETTES:
Armageddon.
The Temple At Jerusalem.
The Messiah.
Messiah In The Passover.
Messiah In The Day Of Atonement.
Messiah In The Day Of Pentecost.

The Mission also produces a special *Jewish Art Calendar* each year. These are made available prior to the Jewish New Year in September/October.

A Messiah in the Passover kit has also been produced. It is a "do-it-yourself" kit which includes: a step-by-step Haggadah (guide for the service), a Leader's Manual with Christological insights into the Passover service, full-color posters for advertising, a cassette of traditional and Messianic music, a how-to-prepare booklet with menus and recipes, and a Passover song book.

Through its "Book Room," the Mission offers special greeting cards from Israel, as well as numerous other items to assist Christians who want to reach Jewish people with the Gospel.

One Hundred years ago Rabbi Leopold Cohn had a vision—a vision of a Messianic community where Yeshua (Jesus) would be celebrated as Messiah, Savior, and Lord by his Jewish brethren. In our day that vision has become a reality. By God's grace, the Messianic Jewish community is growing. It is the prayer of the Board and the staff of Chosen People Ministries that the Messianic Jewish community will continue to grow, and that Chosen People Ministries will continue to be used of God to evanglize and disciple Jewish people until our Messiah returns.

A Chronology Of Important Events

1850	Beginning of "The Golden Age of Jewish Missions." Jewish people accepting the Lord, immigrating to the United States in great numbers.
1858	The oath "on the true faith of a Christian" is abolished in England; Jewish disabilities removed.
1860	The Alliance Israelite Universelle founded.
1881	Many Jews begin to leave Russia in the wake of terrifying pogroms.
1892	March 2, 1892. Rabbi Leopold immigrates to the United States from Hungary looking for the Messiah. He accepts Jesus as his Messiah and Savior.
1894	Rabbi Leopold Cohn begins an independent Jewish mission work among the Jews in the Brownsville section of Brooklyn, New York. His work becomes known as the Brownsville Mission to the Jews.
1894	The Dreyfus Affair—the arrest and imprisonment of Captain Alfred Dreyfus and charges of espionage.
1895	Rabbi Leopold Cohn begins publishing *The Chosen People* magazine, seeking to gain supporters for his ministry.
1895	Theodor Herzl's *Judenstaat* is published.
1896	Rabbi Leopold Cohn opens a new mission station in addition to the Brownsville Mission, it is called the Williamsburg Mission to the Jews. The new mission station is located in the Williamsburg section of Brooklyn, New York.
1896	Rabbi Leopold Cohn begins receiving support from the American Baptist Home Mission Board and the Brooklyn Long Island Church Extension Society.
1897	The Mission establishes its headquarters on Throop Avenue in Brooklyn. The Mission now becomes known as the Williamsburg Mission to the Jews.
1897	The First Zionist Congress is held in Basil.
1898	B.M. Gordon, the first missionary assistant to Leopold Cohn, is appointed.
1898	The Mission opens its first outreach for Jewish women and children.
1901	President McKinley is assassinated.
1907	Mr. Philip Englander joins the staff as an assistant missionary to the Cohns.
1908	The mission receives a large donation from Miss Francis Huntley. The gift is designated for the purchase of the first building for the Mission.
1909	Tel Aviv, first new all Jewish city is founded in Israel. *Degania*, the first Kibbutz (collective village) founded in the Galilee.
1911	Joseph Hoffman Cohn, son of Rabbi Leopold Cohn joins his father in the work.
1911	September 30, 1911. The Mission is legally incorporated as the Williamsburg Mission to the Jews.
1912	Miss Augusta Sussdorff and Miss Grace Bigelow join the staff—the first women missionaries on staff outside of the Cohn family members.
1914	World War I begins, the War to end all wars.
1916	The Gospel Mail Department of the Mission is established, initiating the beginning of the world-wide ministry.
1916	The Mission establishes *Machpelah*—the first cemetery for Jewish believers in the United States.
1917	The Mission holds its first Congress on Prophecy in New York, called "The Jew in Prophecy."
1917	The Russian Revolution takes place.
1917	The Balfour Declaration is signed. The Cornerstone of the Hebrew University on Mount Scopus is laid.
1917	The British army, with Jewish contingents, begins liberation of the Holy Land from the Turks.
1919	The Plaza branch of the Mission is opened in New York.
1920	The first issue of *The Shepherd of Israel* is published in Yiddish/English and sent to over 10,000 Jewish names.
1921	The Mission purchases a missionary home on Hewes Avenue in Brooklyn.
1922	The British Mandate over Palestine is confirmed by the League of Nations.
1924	The American Board of Missions to the Jews is founded as the world-wide ministry arm of the Williamsburg Mission to the Jews. Mission is now called the American Board of Mission to the Jews.
1925	The Hebrew University opens on Mount Scopus.
1925	The Peel Commission proposes partition of Palestine, one part as a Jewish state.

1925   Hitler publishes first volume of *Mein Kampf*.

1926   On December 21, 1926 the Mission establishes its first branch outside of New York; it is established in Philadelphia, Pennsylvania. The branch was under the direction of Mr. Harry Burgen who had worked with the Mission since 1916.

1926   The first foreign branch of the Mission is established by Simon Aszur in Lithuania.

1928   The Mission opens a second branch outside New York; it is established in Atlantic City, New Jersey.

1929   Stock market crashes. Beginning of the Great Depression.

1929   The second foreign branch of the Mission is established in Riga, Latvia; on June 6, 1929. Gregory Guberman established a work in Dnjesperprotowsk, Ukraine.

1929   An Arab attack is carried out upon the Jews in Palestine in dispute over the Western Wall.

1929   A third branch outside New York is opened. It is established in Pittsburgh, Pennsylvania by Mr. John Solomon.

1929   The Mission establishes a branch ministry in Chicago. Mr. Solomon Birnbaum is appointed to supervise the Chicago ministry.

1930   Charles Lee Feinberg, a young rabbinical student is led to the Lord by John Solomon in the Pittsburgh branch of the Mission.

1930   The Mission begins to minister to the Jewish people of Canada by sending evangelists into Jewish areas.

1930   Wheaton College confers a Doctor of Divinity degree upon Rabbi Leopold Cohn.

1931   The Mission begins taking out full page ads in *Moody Monthly* and *The Sunday School Times* to promote its ministry among the Jews.

1932   Franklin D. Roosevelt is elected President of the United States.

1933   April 19, 1933 the Mission begins supporting Mr. Frank Boothby and the Gospel Gate Room ministry in Palestine (Jerusalem, Israel).

1933   Hitler becomes Chancellor of Germany and his Nazi party begins the "Nazi Holocaust."

1933   The Mission establishes a partnership ministry with Keith L. Brooks who published the "Prophecy Newsletter." This liaison placed the Mission in the forefront of prophetic teaching.

1934   The Mission opens a branch ministry in Warsaw, Poland. Mr. & Mrs. Moses Gitlin were the appointed missionaries.

1935   The Nuremberg laws place the Jews beyond the pale of citizenship. Poland, Lithuania, Latvia, Rumania and Hungary adopt anti-Jewish measures.

1935   June 15, 1935 the Mission dedicates the new headquarters building built in Brooklyn, New York, called "Marston Memorial Hall."

1935   The Mission opens the Paris branch ministry under the supervision of Pastor Henri Vincent. Mr. Andre Frankl is appointed as missionary.

1935   The Mission places Elias Zimmerman as a Field Worker for California.

1935   The Mission opens a new ministry in Los Angeles; Elias Zimmerman is appointed Missionary-in-Charge.

1936   The Mission opens a branch in Des Moines, Iowa with Mr. and Mrs. Herman Juroe serving as missionaries.

1936   The Mission opens a branch ministry in Vienna, Austria. Emanuel Lichtenstein is the appointed missionary.

1937   Herbert Singer is appointed as the Director of Relief to help the refugee Jews in Europe. Soup kitchens are opened throughout Europe to feed starving and refugee Jews.

1937   The Mission places Mr. and Mrs. Oscar Wago as Itinerant Missionaries for Ohio.

1937   The "Dalton" family is the first Jewish refugee family resettled by the Mission in Montevideo, Uruguay. This begins the Mission's attempt to re-settle refugee Jewish believers in South America.

1937   The Buffalo, New York branch of the Mission is opened by Mr. Abraham B. Machlin.

1937   The Los Angeles Baptist Seminary (BIOLA) confers a Doctor of Divinity degree upon Joseph Hoffman Cohn.

1937   December 11, Rabbi Leopold Cohn, founder of Chosen People Ministries dies.

1937   Joseph Hoffman Cohn, son of the founder, is appointed the General Secretary of the Mission.

1938   The Mission hires Mr. & Mrs. Leon Awerbach to help distribute relief funds to the Jewish believers in Kischineff (Russia) and Bessarabia.

1938   Austria adopts the entire body of anti-Jewish legislation.

1938   Jews are attacked in the *Kristallnacht* (Broken Glass) pogrom in Germany.

1938   The Mission establishes a refugee ministry to care for the needs of Jewish people being persecuted in Europe and Russia.

1938   The Mission takes over the mission work among German speaking Jews begun by the father of Emil Gruen.

The Mission hires Emil Gruen as a Field Evangelist.

1938   The Coney Island branch of the Mission is opened by Miss Dorothy Rose and Miss Augusta Sussdorff.

1938   The Mission takes on the support of workers in Romania to help distribute relief funds to persecuted Jewish people.

1939   The Seattle branch of the Mission is opened by Herbert Amster.

1939   Goering given orders to devise an over-all plan for the "final solution" of the Jewish question.

1939   The Mission, through its worker Otto Samuel, establishes a "Soup Kitchen" in Brussels, Belgium to feed and assist refugee Jews.

1939   The British "White Paper" limits Jewish immigration and land purchase in Palestine.

1940   Miss Hilda Koser is transferred from the Pittsburgh branch to the Coney Island branch to assist in the ministry.

1940   The Mission works out a cooperative effort with Dr. Henry Einspruch, Director of Lederer Foundation, to publish a Yiddish translation of the New Testament.

1940   The Summer Camp for children is established by the Mission.

1940   The Mission extends a call to Victor Buksbazen to join the staff. The Buksbazen family is re-located from London to New York to work in the Brooklyn ministry and the Buffalo ministry. (January 27, 1943 Victor Buksbazen leaves the staff and later founds the Friends of Israel Gospel & Relief Society, Inc., now called The Friends of Israel.)

1940   The Mission opens a branch ministry in Washington D.C. Sanford Mills is the appointed missionary.

1940   The Mission officially incorporates in Canada. Headquarter offices are established in Hamilton, Ontario. Rev. Donald MacKay, Pastor of the Philpott Memorial Church is named honorary treasurer.

1941   Pearl Harbor is bombed by the Japanese. The United States enters World War II.

1941   Hitler breaks his pact with Stalin and marched into Russia. Jewish population of the invaded territories is systematically exterminated by the "Einstazgruppen" a special S.S. unit.

1941   The Mission establishes refugee work in London, England under the supervision and direction of Mr. and Mrs. Awerbach. Mrs. Awerbach is appointed to carry on the ministry after her husband's death in 1942.

1941   The Mission organizes and sponsors the American Fellowship of Jews to help re-settle refugee Jews.

1941   The Zionist movement calls for a Jewish State.

1942   Deportation to the "death camps" begins.

1942   The Jews of Kiev are massacred and buried at Babi Yar on the eve of Yom Kippur.

1942   Emanuel Lichtenstein escapes from the Nazis. The Mission relocates the Lichtensteins to Buenos Aires, Argentina. In Argentina, Emanuel opens a Mission branch to minister to the refugee Jews fleeing Europe. The Buenos Aires branch of the Mission is started.

1942   Sanford Mills is sent to Columbus, Ohio to open branch ministry and field work for the Mission.

1942   The Mission hires Dr. Harry Marko to be the Field Representative in Texas.

1942   The Erie, Pennsylvania branch of the Mission is opened by Mrs. Thelma Blair.

1942   The Mission opens a branch ministry in Montreal, Quebec. Karl Goldberg is the appointed missionary.

1943   The Warsaw Ghetto uprising takes place on the eve of Passover.

1943   The Miami, Florida branch of the Mission is opened by Mrs. Lindsey and Mr. Leslie Batchelder.

1943   The Indianapolis, Indiana branch is opened by Esther Hoyt and Lulu Sommers.

1944   A split within in the Board of Directors over the leadership of Joseph Cohn causes a split in the missionary work. As a result, the American Association for Jewish Evangelism (AAJE) is formed. A number of missionaries leave the Mission's staff to serve with this new organization.

1945   The Auschwitz death camp is captured and liberated.

1945   World War II ends. Six million Jews have died in the "death camps." Three out of four Jews in Europe—dead. Two out of five Jews in all the world—dead.

1945   The Mission begins a nation-wide radio broadcast called "The Chosen People Broadcast." Joseph Cohn is the radio speaker; Mr. Paul Miller is the program director and producer.

1945   The Mission appoints Miss Anne Rayner to be a missionary in London, England.

1945   The Mission dedicates its new headquarters building in Manhattan on West 72nd. St. called the "Leopold Cohn Memorial Building."

1945   The Mission opens a branch ministry in Havana, Cuba. Mr. Paul Wilson is the appointed missionary. The Mission also begins a radio ministry in Spanish and English to Cuba.

1946   The first "Summer's End" (Prophecy) Conference is held at the new headquarters building in New York City.

1946   The Mission organizes and sponsors the World Fellowship of Jews in Paris, France in order to help re-settle refugee Jews after World War II.

1946   Anglo-American Committee favors admission of 100,000 displaced persons to Palestine.

1947   November 29—United Nations General Assembly adopts partition plan providing for the establishment of the Jewish State.

1948   The State of Israel is proclaimed: On May, 14. May 15, the British withdraw. Arab armies invade the new Jewish state.

1950   On October 6, 1950, Dr. Harry Ironside sends a letter of apology to Joseph Cohn and reconciles with the Mission.

1949   The War of Independence ends in Israel. Armistice agreements are signed with Arab neighbors.

1949   Election of first Knesset in Israel takes place. Dr. Chaim Weizman is elected the first President.

1950   The Law of the Return is enacted to confirm the right of every Jew to dwell in Israel.

1950   The Korean War begins.

1950   The Jews of Yemen are airlifted to Israel.

1950   The Jews of Iraq are airlifted to Israel.

1951   The Mission officially incorporates in London, England and is called the American Board of Mission to the Jews, Limited. Mark Kagan is appointed honorary Director.

1951   The State of Israel declares the 27th of Nissan as *Yom HaSho'ah* (Holocaust Remembrance Day), in memory of the six million Jews killed by the Nazis.

1953   Harold B. Pretlove, a member of the Board of Directors of the Mission is elected by the Board to be the new Executive Secretary of the Mission.

1953   October 5, 1953 Joseph Hoffman Cohn is called home to be with the Lord, ending the Cohn Era.

1953   The Mission appoints Ruth Backus to open a branch of the Mission in Portland, Oregon.

1953   The Mission holds the first staff meeting of all the missionaries (54) in New York. The Mission's film "I Found My Messiah" is released for use in ministry.

1953   The Mission hires Henry Heydt as the new president for its Jewish Missionary Training Institute.

1954   The Mission appoints Harold Bruce Pretlove to the position of Executive Secretary.

1954   The Mission opens a new branch ministry in Minneapolis, Minnesota. Joseph Herschkowitz is appointed as missionary.

1955   Daniel Fuchs begins writing the "Salutations" in *The Chosen People* magazine and is named as Editor of the Editorial Committee of the Mission's publications.

1955   The Mission sends Elias and Margaret den Arend to San Jose, California to begin missionary and field work.

1955   The Mission administration is re-organized into a "troika" leadership. Emil Gruen is appointed Conference Director; Daniel Fuchs is appointed Director of Missionary Activity; Harold Pretlove's title is changed to Executive Secretary.

1955   The Mission opens the Levittown branch under the supervision of Miss Ruth Wardell.

1955   The Mission opens a new Mission branch in Flushing, New York in the home of Mr. and Mrs. Gilbert Maggi.

1955   The Mission opens the East New York branch in January, 1955. This was the old Brownsville section of Brooklyn where the Mission first started.

1956   The Sinai Campaign begins.

1956   The Mission opens a new Mission branch in Huntington Station, Long Island in the home of Clara and Joe Rubin.

1956   The Mission opens the Rockaways and Five Towns branch. Max Doriani is appointed missionary.

1957   The Mission opens the Westbury Long Island branch.

1957   The Mission hires Martin Meyer Rosen (Moishe) to be the new Missionary-in-Charge of Los Angeles.

1958   The Mission opens the San Diego branch; Kenneth Reeves is sent as missionary.

1959   The Mission opens a new branch in Dallas, Texas. Bill & Jo Ennis are appointed missionaries.

1959   The Mission opens a new branch ministry in Phoenix. Ruth Backus is transferred from Portland, Oregon to begin this ministry.

1960   Adolph Eichmann is arrested and stands trial in Israel.

1962   Adolph Eichmann is executed in Israel.

1962   The Mission opens a branch ministry in Haifa, Israel. Peter Gutkind is the missionary.

1963   President John F. Kennedy is assassinated in Dallas.

1963   The Mission begins a new Recruiting and Training Program under Martin Rosen (Moishe) in Los Angeles.

1963   The Mission purchases and dedicates a new building for the Los Angeles ministry. The building became the

Regional Headquarters for the Western ministry.

1964   The Mission opens an Evangelism Booth at the New York World's Fair, beginning its use of media to reach Jews with the gospel.

1964   The Mission begins a "District Method" of operation—an organized attempt to reach major Jewish population centers with the gospel.

1966   Martin Rosen (Moishe) is appointed Director of Missionary Training.

1966   The Mission purchases and dedicates on September 11, 1966 a building for the Dallas ministry. The building became the Regional Headquarters for the Southwest ministry.

1966   The Mission opens a branch ministry in Toronto. Mr. Fred Bregman is the appointed missionary.

1967   The Six Day War takes place in Israel. Jerusalem is re-united as the capital of the Jewish state.

1967   Harold Sevener is appointed Missionary-in-Charge for the Western District.

1967   Martin Rosen (Moishe) and the Training Program are transferred to New York City.

1967   The Mission opens a new Chicago branch called "Aedus Center."

1968   Harold B. Pretlove resigns as Executive Secretary of the Mission. Daniel Fuchs is appointed General Secretary. Henry Heydt is appointed Missionary Liaison Director.

1968   The Mission begins a radio ministry to Israel and the Middle East over HCJB and TWR.

1968   The Mission dedicates a new building for the Long Island ministry in Hollis, New York.

1968   The Mission begins a Summer Intern Program (SIP) for the training of seminary students interested in Jewish evangelism.

1969   The Mission appoints Joseph Alkahe to be their missionary in Tel Aviv, Israel.

1969   Golda Meir is installed as Israel's fourth Prime Minister.

1969   The first man lands on the moon.

1969   The Mission purchases a building and property in Buenos Aires for its ministry. The building serves as the headquarters for the South American ministry.

1969   The Mission hires Demetrius Papanikolaou to open a branch in Athens, Greece.

1969   The Mission hires Jacob and Leah Goren to be missionaries in Jerusalem, Israel.

1969   The Mission opens a new branch in Prairie Village, Kansas and creates a new Plains States District under Arthur Katz.

1969   The Mission opens a new branch ministry in Atlanta, Georgia. Perrin Cook is the appointed missionary.

1969   The Mission sends Martin and Pauline Klayman to Miami, Florida to open a new branch ministry.

1970   Martin Rosen (Moishe) begins ministry among the Jewish "street people" and "hippies" of New York. Rosen creates the Mission's first "broadside" tracts.

1970   The Mission transfers Terryl Delaney and Larry Jaffrey from Denver to Philadelphia to expand the ministry in the Atlantic District.

1970   The Mission produces its TV production, *The Passover*. It aired for the first time in Los Angeles. Thousands of Jewish people responded to the telecast.

1970   The Mission begins to use the term "Jews for Jesus" to describe their ministry among the Jewish young people and street people.

1970   The Mission transfers the Recruiting and Training program back to Los Angeles under the direction of Harold Sevener.

1970   The Mission transfers Martin Rosen (Moishe) to San Francisco to open a new branch ministering to Jewish young people and street people—the Jews for Jesus branch.

1970   President Nassar of Egypt dies. Anwar Sadat is nominated as President by the Central Committee of the Arab Socialist Union.

1971   The Mission appoints Raymond Cohen to open a branch in Hollywood, Florida.

1971   The Mission's Passover Telecast scheduled to be on nation-wide television is canceled. The cancellation creates media stir that propels the Mission and its ministry to national recognition.

1971   The Mission creates and places full page ads in the major newspapers across the United States. The headline reads: "Why Are So Many Jews Wearing That Smile Nowadays!" The response once again provokes national publicity and thousands of responses from Jewish people requesting information about Jesus.

1971   The Mission is able to air the Passover telecast in Australia and Canada. Once again national publicity is received and Jewish people respond.

1971   The Mission produces a testimony booklet of the thirty-nine Jewish people who appeared in the full-page ads. Over 500,000 booklets sent out.

1971   *Time* magazine, *The New York Times*, and major newspapers and periodicals carry stories about the Mission's ministry of reaching Jewish people with the gospel.

1972   Harold Sevener is transferred to New York as the Missionary Director/Conference Director for the Mission.

1972   The Mission participates in the Campus Crusade rally "Explo '72". Its Jews for Jesus booth began to popularize the movement.

1972   The Mission creates, through its Jews for Jesus branch, the singing group "The Liberated Wailing Wall."

1972   The Mission moves its administrative headquarters to Englewood Cliffs, New Jersey, separating its International Administrative Offices from its New York Missionary work for the first time since it began in 1894.

1972   The Mission airs *The Passover* telecast across Canada. Response creates publicity and requests for gospel literature.

1973   The Yom Kippur war erupts in Israel.

1973   The Mission begins a de-centralized approach to reaching Jewish people with the gospel using the "media" as its main thrust.

1973   The Mission takes over the Peoria Messianic Testimony in Peoria, Illinois. Larry Caruvana is appointed missionary.

1973   The Mission closes its San Francisco branch on November 1, 1973, allowing Jews for Jesus (Hineni Ministries) to become a separate organization.

1974   President Richard Nixon resigns in the wake of Watergate.

1974   The Palestine National Council meets in Cairo to draft political principles to be followed in the PLO's political offensive.

1974   Dr. Daniel Fuchs is appointed President of the Mission. Harold Sevener is appointed Vice-President.

1974   The Mission opens a new branch in Houston, Texas. Harry Jacobson is transferred from Chicago to begin the ministry in Houston.

1975   The Vietnam war ends.

1975   The Suez Canal reopens after eight years.

1975   The U.N. General Assembly approves a resolution equating Zionism with racism.

1975   A new San Francisco branch is opened by the Mission with Jerome & Mildred Fleischer serving as missionaries.

1975   The Mission holds its first staff conference at Keswick Conference grounds in New Jersey since 1953. It inaugurates Bi-Annual staff conferences for training and fellowship.

1975   The Mission produces and airs "Gospel Radio Spot Announcements" directed to the Jewish people over the Mutual Broadcasting Networks 675 stations nation-wide.

1975   The Mission creates a new format for *The Chosen People* magazine increasing its readership and interest among Christians and Jews.

1975   To supervise its growing staff and to maintain visitation and contact with Jewish people responding to the media campaigns, the Mission establishes a Regional system for ministry in the United States—having a Northeast Region, a Southeast Region, a Midwest Region, Southwest Region and a Western Region. Missionaries and staff workers now reported to their Regional Director.

1976   The Mission holds a major Congress on Prophecy in Philadelphia, Pennsylvania to celebrate the nation's Bi-Centennial.

1976   The one hundred Jews are held hostage at Entebbe airport near Kampala, Uganda were rescued by an Israeli commando raid.

1976   The United States celebrates its Bi-Centennial birthday.

1976   The Mission creates a sister organization "Evangelicals United for Zion" to deal directly with the leaders in Israel and the Jewish communities of the world.

1976   The Mission launches a new media campaign entitled "God's Timepiece." Full-page ads were place in major newspapers supporting Israel and giving a gospel witness.

1976   The Mission produces a "Proclamation on Israel" signed by major Christian leaders across America and presented to the Ambassador from Israel in a special luncheon meeting in Washington D.C.

1978   Mission purchases and dedicates a new headquarters building in Orangeburg, New York on October 22, 1978.

1978   The Mission establishes its first independent Messianic Congregation in Chicago, called the Olive Tree Congregation.

1979   The Board of Directors elects Harold A. Sevener to be the President of Chosen People Ministries.

1979	Egypt's president, Anwar Sadat, visits Jerusalem and a peace treaty is signed whereby Israel withdraws from the Sinai.
1979	The Mission opens a new branch of ministry in Boston. Jim Bates is appointed to develop this ministry.
1979	The Mission re-organizes its administrative officers. Daniel Fuchs is appointed Chairman of the Board. Harold Sevener is appointed President of the Mission. James Straub is appointed Executive Vice-President.
1980	The Mission launches "Ark II" a mobile van that looked like Noah's ark from which Stanley Watin could preach the gospel to Jews and Gentiles. Stanley and his "Ark" travelled throughout the United States.
1981	A nuclear reactor near Baghdad, Iraq is destroyed by Israeli commando units.
1982	Israeli Defense Forces invade Lebanon to stop PLO terrorist attacks.
1982	The Mission launches a new evangelism program called STEP (Summer Training and Evangelism Program). The program is developed by Barry Rubin.
1983	The Mission establishes a new Messianic Congregation in East Hanover, New Jersey (later moved to Livingston, New Jersey), called Beth Messiah by Larry Feldman.
1983	STEP in New York—teams are sent across the United States and Canada.
1984	Training and evangelistic extension programs begin in cities throughout South America under the direction of Roberto Passo.
1984	Jerusalem becomes the largest city in Israel.
1984	December training and evangelistic program begins in Buenos Aires, Argentina.
1984	STEP in New York—teams are sent across the United States and Canada.
1985	The Mission establishes a new Messianic Congregation in White Plains, New York, later moved to Yonkers, New York by Sam Nadler. The congregation is called "The Light of Israel."
1985	STEP in New York—teams are sent across the United States and Canada.
1985	Annual "Simcha" (Joy) Conferences at Word of Life, Schroon Lake, New York for Messianic believers and their families are begun.
1985	Israel withdraws troops from Lebanon.
1986	The Mission opens new branch in Plainfield, New York (Long Island), with Michael Rydelnik serving as missionary. A Messianic congregation called the "Olive Tree Congregation" was established.
1986	STEP in New York—teams sent across the United States and Canada.
1986	Harold Sevener, the President of Chosen People Ministries presents thousands of signed proclamations supporting Israel and the Jewish people to the Prime Minister at a special meeting in the Knesset in Israel.
1987	STEP in Chicago—teams are sent across the United States and Canada.
1987	The Mission begins a special October Evangelistic Edition of *The Chosen People* magazine to be given to Jewish people. It is utilized in evangelism world-wide.
1987	December 7, marks the beginning of the "Intifada" (literally, "shaking off"), the Palestinian uprising against the military rule of the Israeli in the "occupied territories.
1987	The Mission begins a radio broadcast to the Soviet Union with Albert Davis [Israel] as the radio voice. The broadcast helps pave the way for future ministry in the former Soviet Union.
1988	The uprising of the Palestinian "Intifada" against the Israeli armies is carried out in the "occupied territories."
1988	Dr. Daniel Fuchs is called home to be with the Lord on May 24, 1988. James Straub is appointed Chairman of the Board on September 29, 1988.
1988	STEP in Chicago—teams are sent across the United States and Canada.
1988	The Mission appoints Avner and Rachel Boskey to be missionaries in Tel Aviv, Israel.
1988	The Mission establishes a Messianic Congregation called "Olive Tree" in Toronto, Canada.
1988	The Mission establishes a ministry to the Russian Jews through Albert & Greta Davis [Israeli].
1988	The Mission officially changes its name to Chosen People Ministries to reflect its world-wide ministry.
1988	The Mission moves its administrative offices to Charlotte, North Carolina to reduce administrative expenses and increase missionary outreach.
1988	Mikhail Sergeevich Gorbachev continues to introduce changes into the Soviet Union through "glasnost" (openness) or "Peristroika" (restructuring).
1989	STEP in Chicago—teams are sent across the United States and Canada.
1989	The Mission appoints Sam Nadler as their Executive Director.
1989	November 9, the Berlin Wall that had divided eastern and western Germany comes crashing down.
1989	The eastern bloc of Communist nations overthrows their leadership and begins to turn to democracy.
1989	The Soviet Union begins to open its doors to the West.

1990   John Demjanjuk (identified as "Ivan the Terrible") is sentenced to death for war crimes against the Jews. His sentenced is appealed.

1990   The Mission sends Sam Nadler and Albert Davis [Israeli] to Russia and the Ukraine for evangelism and to open a new branch ministry there.

1990   STEP in Chicago—teams are sent across the United States and Canada.

1990   The Mission establishes a Messianic Congregation to minister to the Russian Jewish believers.

1990   August 2, Saddam Hussein and the armies of Iraq invade Kuwait.

1991   Crisis in the Persian Gulf due to Saddam Hussein's invasion of Kuwait. United States forms an alliance with Arab and Western nations, without Israel, and attacks Iraq.

1991   January 18, eight modified Scud-B missiles, dubbed by the Iraqis "El Hussein", fall on Tel Aviv. January 19 another four missiles fall on Tel Aviv.

1991   The break of the Soviet Union into 15 different republics is called the Commonwealth of Independent States. The fall of Communism in the Soviet Union is accomplished.

1991   The Mission develops Jewish Holiday video tapes for TV and evangelism, *Messiah In The Passover; Messiah In the Day Of Atonement, Messiah In the Day of Pentecost.*

1991   STEP in Chicago—teams are sent across the United States and Canada.

1991   The Mission appoints Albert & Greta Davis [Israeli] to be their missionaries in Kfar Saba (Tel Aviv suburb), Israel.

1991   The Mission establishes a branch ministry in the Ukraine to minister to the Jewish people.

1991   The Mission appoints Sam Nadler as President. Harold Sevener becomes President Emeritus of the organization.

1991   Dr. John Pretlove is elected Chairman of the Board of Directors for Chosen People Ministries.

1991   Middle East Peace Conference takes place in Madrid, Spain.

1992   The Mission takes out full-page evangelistic ads in the New York newspapers.

1992   Summer Evangelistic Program is conducted on the beaches and cities in Israel in cooperation with the Messianic believers and missions in Israel.

1992   STEP in Chicago—teams are sent across the United States and Canada.

1993   Yassar Arafat and Itzsak Rabin shake hands at the White House after signing a preliminary peace accord. Israel and the PLO officially recognize one another.

1993   Summer evangelistic tract distribution program is conducted on the beaches and cities in Northern Israel in cooperation with the Messianic believers, missions in Israel, and Operation Mobilization.

1993   STEP in New York. First international training program with representatives from the Ukraine and Europe. Teams ministered in New York City.

1993   The Mission moves its administrative office from Hamilton, Ontario to Toronto to cut overhead costs and expand the ministry in Toronto.

1993   Chosen People Ministries begins publishing *The Chosen People Newsletter* and launches *Shalom 2000*, a worldwide evangelistic outreach.

APPENDIX A: JOURNAL ENTRIES

Brooklyn Baptist Church Extension Society. Ninth Annual Report, 1896.

An interesting addition to the Society's work has been its assistance of an evangelical effort among the Hebrews at 'Brownsville.' This work has been pursued with encouraging results for some time past, but without connection with any organized body. It is in the midst of a colony of from twelve to fifteen thousand Jews, and is superintended by one of their own race, an earnest, Christian man of sagacious qualities of leadership and of cultured mind. Upwards of twenty men have, through his teaching, declared their faith in Jesus Christ. Their place of meeting is without necessary accommodations and very uninviting, but the work is prospering, and it seems to demand of us a much more liberal support than we have been able to give. For a Hebrew to make a confession of faith in the Christ is to invite ostracism and discharge from employment. The sacrifice called for in such a profession is in itself a safeguard against imposture and should ensure our practical sympathy and support.

Tenth Annual Report. 1897

During the present year this work [Brownsville] has greatly increased in proportions and interest and has been extended to another Jewish settlement in the Eastern District where a similar effort has been met with most gratifying results. In the 'Brownsville' district there are some six thousand Jewish families, and the way was providentially opened to one of that race, Rev. Leopold Cohn, and [sic] educated and devout Christian, to labor among his own people. His effort to overcome the prejudices of Judaism met with great difficulty. The lack of means and sympathetic assistance was a serious impediment. But when his work was made known to this Society and its importance was recognized means were provided whereby it was more effectively organized and cared for. This Soc. shares with the American Baptist Home Mission Society the expense of labor on these two fields. More than 50 Jews are reported to have professed faith, 150 mean [men] and women attending meetings. [A] Night school has been opened for secular instruction.... Racial religious prejudice is strong....

1898: "Jewish mission in 'Brownsville' reports a continued interest in the means used to bring the Gospel.... there are 50,000 Jews in the two districts affected by this work.... 5 meetings are held weekly, attended by about 150 adults and 200 children.... Rev. Leopold Cohn, Superintendent estimates number of believers at 50. Six, baptized."

1899: "Now two fields of labor in the city; One Brownsville, and other in eastern District.... Racial prejudice is very bitter.... School for girls established, teaching plain sewing and truths of the Gospel are worked in with the play of needle and thread.... Help is needed...especially teachers. $605.00 reported in treasurers report as given to Hebrew mission."

1900: "...Mission has been assisted to the extent of $600. yearly ...racial opposition strong . . ."

1901: "...work sustained in connection with the A.B.H.M.S. by payment of $600."

1902: "Contributions made to Hebrew mission in Brownsville and Williamsburgh, in cooperation with A.H.M.S."

1903: "...work continued in Brownsville and Williamsburgh among the Jews.... Joint committee of Brooklyn Bapt. Ch. Extension Soc. Long Island Association and American Home Mission Society report ...The American Baptist Home Mission Society at present aids in the support of the Jewish Mission in Williamsburgh and Brownsville. A union of forces and resources to some extent it deemed desirable for the more vigorous and systematic cultivation of these fields, which have a population of over one and one-half million people. The entire time and energies of a valuable man are needed...make suty [study] of new fields, etc., etc. It was agreed to employ a Superintendent of Missions, whose salary, expenses and time be apportioned among these Societies.... Edwin P. Farnham selected."

1904:   "Rev Leopold Cohn, assisted by 2 women supported by the Woman's Home Mission Society of Chicago working among almost 100,000 Jews."

1905:   "Work continuing."

1906:   "A committee of five—three from this Society and two from the A.B.H.M.S. has been created to work with Rev. Cohn in ministering to the Jews ...Christian people of many denominations have contributed to the work...."

1907:   "Committee of Five work in close relation with Rev. Cohn. No final report to make."

1908:   "The Hebrew-Mission under the leadership of Rev. Leopole [sic] Cohn is conducted independently of our denomination and is no longer supervised by us nor receiving aid from either our Home Mission or Church Extension Societies."

Long Island Baptist Association report for 1907:

"Mr. Joseph Cohn, a son of the Rev. Leopold Cohn, spoke for the Hebrews in a very bright address."

APPENDIX B

The Sworn Affidavits of Max Kahan and David Kahan, of Detroit, Michigan,
who stated that they were nephews of Mr. Leopold Cohn.
Quoted from the official documents
"In the Matter of the Investigation of Charges Preferred against LEOPOLD COHN."

"Max Kahan of the City of Detroit in the County of Wayne and the State of Michigan being first duly sworn on oath deposes and says that he was born in Visoorszi, Marmoros Mejgi about 21 years ago, that he continued to live and reside in the same place until August 9, 1911 when he left said place coming to the City of New York in the United States of America where he arrived on August 30, 1911. Deponent further says that his father's name was Joseph Kahan, which name, to the best of deponent's information and belief, his father always bore. Further deponent saith that his father, Joseph Kahan, is a nephew of Isaac Leopold Kahan (or Leopold Cohen which is the name of the same person) of 27 Throop Ave. Brooklyn, New York City, and that when deponent left Visoorszi to come to New York, his father gave to him a letter of introduction to said Leopold Kahan or Cohen and that deponent frequently called on and visited said Leopold Kahan in New York City. Deponent further says that his father, Joseph Kahan has often and frequently talked with him about and told him of said Leopold Kahan, whom he always spoke of as Isaac Leopold Kahan, and that his father during said conversations often told the deponent that he, Joseph, and said Leopold studied together for several years in Marmoros, Sziget, and that said Leopold was always known as and went by the name of Isaac Leopold Kahan, according to the information given this deponent by his father. Further deponent says that his father told him of numerous occasions that said Isaac Leopold Kahan was a rabbi before he came to the United States and that he officiated as such and followed the vocation of rabbi until he left for the United States of America, and that he never ran or conducted a saloon or public drinking house or inn in the old country."

"Deponent further on oath says that his father's father and said Isaac Leopold Kahan were brothers and the deponent's grandfather's family name and the name by which he was known during his life time was Kahan and that he personally knew his grandfather by the name of Kahan."

"Further deponent says that his uncle, Getzel Kahan, is well known to deponent, said Getzel Kahan having been employed by Joseph Kahan, the father of deponent, within the past six years and that he always knew his uncle by the name of Kahan. Further deponent on oath says that he frequently talked with his uncle, said Getzel Kahan, regarding said Isaac Leopold Kahan and that said Getzel Kahan told deponent that said Isaac Leopold Kahan was a rabbi and that he, Getzel, and Isaac Leopold were about the same ages."

"Deponent further on oath says that said Isaac Leopold Kahan, deponent's great uncle, was well known in Visoorszi and that he has frequently heard other persons not members of his family say that said Isaac Leopold Kahan was a rabbi and that he officiated as such up to the time he left the old country for New York."

"Deponent further on oath says that after coming to New York and during his frequent visits with said Isaac Leopold Kahan, said Isaac Leopold told deponent that he, Isaac and deponent's father, Joseph, studied together at Marmoros, Sziget, for several years and said Isaac Leopold frequently talked to this deponent of other relatives in the old country, calling them by the names by which this deponent knew such relatives so that this deponent knows that said Isaac Leopold Kahan of 27 Throop Avenue, Brooklyn, New York City is the same person who studied with deponent's father as aforesaid and was known by the same name both while pursuing his studies and while officiating as rabbi in the old country...."

"David Kahan of Detroit, Michigan, being first duly sworn on oath deposes and says that he is about 22 years of age, that he was born in Visoorszi, Marmoros, Mejgi, that his father's name is Joseph Kahan and that this deponent is a brother of Max Kahan who made, subscribed and swore to the annexed affidavit."

"This deponent further says that he came to America with his brother, Max, arriving in New York City on August 30, 1911. Further deponent says that he is personally acquainted with said Isaac Leopold Kahan (or Leopold Cohn) which is the name of the same person of 27 Throop Avenue, Brooklyn, New York City."

"Further deponent on oath says that he has read the foregoing and attached affidavit by Max Kahan, his brother, and that the statements therein contained and the information therein conveyed are known to this deponent and that all of the statements therein contained are true to the best of this deponent's information and belief and that his information has been acquired from his father, Joseph Kahan, his uncle Getzel Kahan, and from other persons residing in and about Marmoros, Mejgi."

"This deponent further says on oath that he has from various sources learned that said Isaac Leopold Kahan was a rabbi and officiated as such before emigrating to the United States of America and that in Marmoros, Mejgi he was known by the name of Isaac Leopold Kahan and deponent never heard of him going by or being known by any other name."

APPENDIX C

Employment Contract. Mr. John Solomon.
Quoted from Minutes; the Executive Committee of the American Board of Missions to the Jews, Inc.,
June 4, 1929, pages 94,95.

1. We are to engage Mr. Solomon as our missionary for the Pittsburgh district. Salary to be up to $200.00 per month, but we are not responsible for any amount, nor do we guarantee any salary. The salary is only payable as funds specified for Pittsburgh work shall warrant.

2. Mr. Solomon agrees to present the work before the churches and individuals for the purpose of securing contributions. All moneys received by him, either from individuals or from collections or through any other source whatsoever, for Jewish work, shall be forwarded by him promptly to us, with a report as to the sources of such contributions, and all such funds shall be handled through our treasury and through our office.

3. Aside from the maximum salary of $200.00 contingently provided for above, there is also to be allowed for the expenses of the Pittsburgh work a sum not to exceed $2600.00 a year. This is also contingent, as is the salary above mentioned, upon Mr. Solomon's raising the money, and pending funds coming in to our treasury, specified for Pittsburgh.

4. For the present requirements of the situation, no more than a maximum of $5,000.00 shall be spent for the Pittsburgh work in any one year, including the salary of Mr. Solomon and the expenses of the work. If it should so happen that the funds received by us for the Pittsburgh work in any one year should exceed $5000.00, we shall not be obligated to pay out this surplus, but it shall be carried over as a balance in the Pittsburgh work for the following year.

5. All moneys that shall be received by Mr. Solomon and reported by him, either in cash or in pledges, shall be credited by us to the Pittsburgh account, whether so specified or not.

6. Pledges will only be credited as they are paid.

7. Mr. Solomon is to be our missionary and under our full direction in every way; he is to be responsible to us for the conducting of the work in Pittsburgh and outlying territory. He is to have freedom as to general plans and methods, as the Lord may lead him, but in any decision of importance he is to yield to our judgment.

8. It is within the meaning of missionary work if Mr. Solomon should for the first four or five months of his connection with us deem it wise not to open a Mission hall in Pittsburgh, but to do itinerant missionary work among the Jews in the towns where he goes to present the work to the churches.

9. Mr. Solomon shall give us at least one full monthly report [this was subsequently changed to two] of his activities, particularly stressing any reports of interviews with Jews, and any conversions.

10. We are to co-operate with Mr. Solomon in any conference he may arrange which may be acceptable to us. Our Field Secretary will speak at such conferences and his expenses only will be charged to the conference. The balance of the money raised is to be charged to the Pittsburgh account.

11. Effective date of these arrangements is as of June 1st, 1929.

12. We are to underwrite $100.00 a month for 6 months.

APPENDIX D

LIST OF SPEAKERS FOR THE 1ST NATIONAL CONGRESS/PROPHECY

Rev. William Ward Ayer, D.D.
Pastor, Calvary Baptist Church
New York, New York

Rev. Louis Bauman, D.D.
Pastor, First Brethren Church
Long Beach, California

Rev. R.S. Beale, D.D.
Pastor, First Baptist Church
Tucson, Arizona

Rev. Dean Bedford
Pastor, Brighton Community Church
Rochester, New York

Rev. John W. Bradbury, D.D.
Editor, *Watchman Examiner*
New York, New York

Rev. Keith L. Brooks
Editor, *Prophecy*
Los Angeles, California

Rev. C. Gordon Brownville, D.D.
Tremont Temple
Oakland, California

Rev. Henry E. Burke, D.D.
Pastor, Melrose Baptist Church
Oakland, California

Rev. H.B. Centz
Philadelphia, Pennsylvania

Rev. Lewis Sperry Chafer, D.D.
President, Dallas Theological Seminary
Dallas, Texas

Rev. Joseph Hoffman Cohn, D.D.
Brooklyn, New York

Rev. V. Ray Erickson, D.D.
Pastor, University Presbyterian Church
Seattle, Washington

Rev. Charles Lee Feinberg, Th.D.
Dallas Theological Seminary
Dallas, Texas

Rev. David Otis Fuller, D.D.
Pastor, Wealthy Street Baptist Church
Grand Rapids, Michigan

Rev. Harris H. Gregg, D.D.
Lookout Mountain, Tennessee

Rev. Joseph W. Hakes
Pastor, Twentieth Street Baptist Church
Huntington, West Virginia

Rev. Adam J. Hunter
Pastor, Independent Bible Church
Tacoma, Washington

Rev. Harry A. Ironside, D.D.
Pastor, Moody Memorial Church
Chicago, Illinois

Rev. Albert Johnson, D.D.
Pastor, Hinson Memorial Baptist Church
Portland, Oregon

Rev. Albert Lindsey, Jr.
Immanuel Presbyterian Church
Detroit, Michigan

Dr. Herbert Lockyer
Preacher and Author
Editor, *Christian Digest*

Rev. Donald MacKay
Pastor, Philpott Tabernacle
Hamilton, Ontario, Canada

Rev. J. Palmer Muntz, D.D.
Pastor, Cazenovia Baptist Church
Buffalo, New York

Rev. Harold Ockenga, D.D.
Pastor, Park Street Church
Boston, Massachusetts

Rev. W.E. Pietsch, D.D.
Des Moines, Iowa

Rev. R.L. Powell, D.D.
Pastor, Temple Baptist Church
Tacoma, Washington

Rev. W.H. Rogers, D.D.
Author and Bible Teacher
New York, New York

Rev. L. Sale-Harrison, D.D.
Chancellor Hall
Philadelphia, Pennsylvania

Rev. Charles H. Stevens
Pastor, Salem Baptist Church
Winston-Salem, North Carolina

Rev. B.B. Sutcliffe, D.D.
President, Multnomah School of the Bible
Portland, Oregon

Rev. Louis Talbot, D.D.
President, Bible Institute of Los Angeles
[BIOLA]
Los Angeles, California

Rev. John F. Walvoord, Th.D.
Dallas Theological Seminary
Dallas, Texas

Rev. I L. Yearby, D.D.
Pastor, First Baptist Church
El Paso, Texas

Appendix E

Ratification of Directors' motion for a Pension Plan for Mission employees.
Quoted from official Minutes, the American Board of Missions to the Jews,
April 27, 1955, page 133.

"Employees will be eligible for coverage after two years employment, except for female clerical employees, for which five years of employment will be necessary. They must be at least 25 years of age to qualify."

"The formula is at the rate of 1 1/3% per year but not in excess of 25 years of continuous service, and this percentage will be computed on the average annual basic earnings during the last five years of employment. This will provide for a maximum of 33 1/3% of the average annual earnings during the last five years of service. Employees must be at least 65 years of age to retire."

"The Mission shall have the privilege of either funding the plan themselves or carrying specific insurance on any employee who meets the requirements. No individual insured plan shall be started for anyone who is over 55 years of age."

"Employees shall have no rights or incidents of ownership in the fund or the insured policy until the time of retirement. For insured coverage the Mission shall retain all rights, privileges, benefits, options, and elections granted to or covered upon the insured by the policy. It being intended that the insured shall have no legal incidents of ownership in any insured policy."

APPENDIX F

Explanation by Joseph Hoffman Cohn regarding Rabbi Asher Tzakik Levi's credentials as a rabbi
(See The Chosen People, Vol. LIX, No. 1, October, 1953, page 10).

Rabbi Leopold Cohn's failure to retrieve his Haturah (ordination paper and rabbinic references) after he came to faith in Yeshua resulted in making it virtually impossible to prove his claim—hence the "Investigation of Charges Preferred Against Leopold Cohn."

Joseph Cohn was well aware of the problems created in not being able to verify one's claims of being a rabbi without documentation. He (Joseph Cohn) therefore made certain that Rabbi Asher Tzakik Levi's credentials were kept on file. These papers included letters of service from Synagogue BEVIS MARKS, London, the oldest Sephardic Synagogue in England, and letters from other synagogues where Rabbi Levi had served, including synagogues in Los Angeles, Brooklyn, Constantinople, Brussels, and New York.

Appendix G

Articles from: *The New York Times* Company, Friday, April 2, 1971;
Time, The Weekly Newsmagazine, April 12, 1971.
Reprinted by permission in *The Chosen People* magazine, Vol. LXXVI, No. 10, June, 1971, pages 3 and 4.

The New York Times, by Edward B. Fiske:

"Station WOR-TV disclosed yesterday that it had canceled plans to broadcast a controversial and widely advertised television program depicting the Jewish Passover as a forerunner of Holy Communion and other Christian practices."

"The sponsored program, entitled 'The Passover,' was produced by the American Board of Missions to the Jews, a Manhattan-based Protestant organization dedicated to converting Jews to Christianity."

"Michael McCormick, general manager of the station, said the half-hour program—which had been scheduled for Monday at 7:30 P.M.—was being withdrawn because the management had decided 'it would be offensive to a great number of people.'"

"The Rev. Dr. Daniel Fuchs, general secretary of the missions board, said his organization was 'tremendously disappointed' by the decision and that he was seeking legal advice on what further steps might be possible."

"Dr. Fuchs, whose parents were converted from Judaism, said the program would be shown during the next week in 11 major cities, mostly in prime evening time. He estimated the cost of the time and promotion at $100,000. including $5,000 for the time on WOR-TV."

"Mr. McCormick said: 'We did not think that airing the program would serve the best interests of the New York television audience.'"

"He confirmed that as a result of widespread publicity the station had received many protests from individual Jews as well as from the New York Board of Rabbis, the Synagogue Council of America and the Anti-Defamation League of B'nai B'rith."

"Mr. McCormick added, however, that the decision to cancel the broadcast was not made because of the protests. 'The calls and mail simply made us take another and closer look,' he declared."

"The program is one of the most ambitious projects to be undertaken by the American Board of Missions to the Jews, which was founded in 1894 by Leopold Cohn, a Brooklyn rabbi who became converted."

"The organization has an annual budget of $1.5-million and a staff of 100, including 65 missionaries to Jews in the United States, Israel and four other countries. It also supports relief work among converted Jews and educational activity among Jewish youths."

"The television program reflects the fundamental conviction of the American Board that Christianity is the fulfillment of Judaism and that a convert is not repudiating his heritage by 'accepting Christ as Lord and Savior.'"

"'We feel that we are still good Jews,' Dr. Fuchs said."

"The program begins with an announcer describing the historical background of the Passover and the Exodus. While actors depict the religious feast at a table set with the appropriate religious articles, the announcer describes what they are doing and interprets its significance."

"There is no indication at the beginning that the film is Christian in orientation rather than a straight documentary, but gradually Christian references begin to appear. The announcer suggests, for instance, that the three pieces of matzoh 'represent Father, Son and Holy Spirit.'"

"The program concludes: 'Year after year now, for some 35 centuries, the Jewish people have been repeating the story of redemption in the Passover. But as we have seen it is also a clear prophecy of a greater story. The story of redemption through Christ the Messiah, the Lamb of God, Who lived and died and rose again for the redemption of all who will believe.'"

"Rabbi Harold Gordon, executive vice president of the New York Board of Rabbis, said yesterday that he accepted the right of the Protestant group to proselytize, but he said of the television program: 'It was full of inaccuracies and given under false pretences [sic]. Everything was calculated to give the impression that it was Jewish, and we don't think this was fair.'"

REPRINTED BY PERMISSION FROM TIME:

"Jewish Easter. The Rev. Daniel Fuchs, general secretary of the American Board of Missions to the Jews (and himself the son of converts from Judaism), was puzzled by the uproar. When the show was broadcast last season in Los Angeles, Fuchs says, the board received 5,400 requests for literature, more than half of them from 'Jewish names.' At least six of the inquirers, he says, were converted to Christianity, and only about 20 letters were critical."

"It would be difficult to deny the program's proselytizing intent. In its hard-sell conclusion, the film argues that Passover is 'a clear prophecy of a greater story, the story of redemption through Christ the Messiah, the Lamb of God, who lived and died and rose again for the redemption of all who believe.' That reading is based on a long tradition of Christian exegeses of the Hebrew Scripture, which sees prefigurings of Jesus' mission in many Old Testament passages and practices. Jewish criticism, accordingly, was not so much aimed at the fact of proselytizing as at the method. Some Jews assailed the program for using their own festival in an attempt to evangelize them; others were resentful because the Christian message was slyly introduced into what first appeared to be a documentary."

"Christians, of course, will now miss the show, too—and its other message, which was to inform them of their own heritage in the Jewish feast. Ironically, in a spot radio broadcast for Easter and Passover on New York's WINS this week, Ecumenicist Rabbi Marc H. Tanenbaum is reminding Christians of that religious link. The events of Holy Week, he pointed out, 'cannot be understood, as Jesus and his early followers understood them, apart from their profound rootedness in First Century Judaism.' There is, of course, the obvious fact that the Gospels record the Last Supper as a Passover meal. But Tanenbaum goes further: 'The pilgrimage to Jerusalem with palms was a traditional practice of the country Jews of Palestine, who inaugurated the Passover festival by such rites...The retreat to the Mount of Olives was based on the practice of King David, who made a pilgrimage there to wrestle in a cave for seven days with the spirit of death, only to emerge victorious.'"

"Tanenbaum speaks from considerable historical evidence. Which suggests another question and perhaps another documentary: How Jewish is Easter?"

WORKS CITED

BOOKS

Bernstein, A. *Some Jewish Witnesses For Christ*. London:
Operative Jewish Converts' Institution, Palestine House, 1909.

Bregman, Henry. *The Conversion of a Rabbi, or My Life Story*. Toronto. Beth Dor'she Emeth, n.d.

Charlotte, Elizabeth. *Israel's Ordinances: A Few Thoughts on Their Perpetuity*. New York. I.P. Labagh, 1844.

Cohn, Joseph H. *I Have Fought a Good Fight*. New York: American Board of Missions to the Jews, 1953.

Cohn, Leopold. *A Modern Missionary to an Ancient People*. Brooklyn. American Board of Missions to the Jews, 1908.

Colby, Philip. *The Conversion and Restoration of the Jews*. Boston. Perkins and Marvin, 1836.

Down on Throop Avenue. Brooklyn: The American Board of Missions to the Jews, Inc., n.d.

Graetz, Heinrich. *History of the Jews*. Vol. III, Ch. VII. Philadelphia: The Jewish Publication Society of America, 1967.

Karp, Abraham J. *Golden Door to America: the Jewish Immigration Experience*. New York. Viking Press, 1976.

Katz, Arthur. *Apprehended by God—a Journal of a Jewish Atheist*. Laporte, Mn. Ben Israel Publishers, 1993.

Koser, Hilda. *Come & Get It*. Orlando. Golden Rule Book Press, Inc., 1987.

Kushner, Harold. *When Bad Things Happen to Good People*. New York. Schocken Books, 1981.

Levison, Frederick. *Christian and Jew—Leon Levison—1881-1936*. East Lothian, Scotland. The Pentland Press, 1989.

Levitt, Zola. *Meshumed*. Chicago. Moody Press, 1979.

Mead, Frank S., ed. *The Encyclopedia of Religious Quotations*. New Jersey. Fleming H. Revell Co., 1965.

Pragai, Michael J. *Faith and Fulfillment*. London, England: Valentine, Mitchell and Company, Ltd., 1985.

Rosen, Moishe; Proctor, William. *Jews For Jesus*. New Jersey. Fleming H. Revell Co., 1974.

Rubin, Barry. *You Bring the Bagels, I'll Bring the Gospel*. New Jersey. Fleming Revell Co., 1989.

Singer, Isidore. ed. *The Jewish Encyclopedia*. New York: Ktav Publishing House, Inc., n.d.

Thompson, A. E. *A Century of Jewish Missions*. Chicago. Fleming H. Revell Co., 1902.

Urbach, Eliezer; Weigand, Edith S. *Out of the Fury*. Denver. Zhera Publications, 1987.

PERIODICALS

Angel, Bernhard. *The Hebrew Christian*. "The Story of the Conversion of Rev. Bernhard Angel, B.D," March 1894.

—. *The Hebrew Christian*. "Mistakes," July 1896.

"Announcement." *The Hebrew Christian*. December 1894.

Brooks, Keith L. *Prophecy magazine*. January 1951.

Kahane, Meir. *The Jewish Press, Inc.* "Christians For Zion". Brooklyn. 24 January 1975.

The Chosen People. Vol. 1, No. 5, February 1896.

The Chosen People. Vol. 2, No. 1, October 1896.

The Chosen People. Vol. 2, No. 2, November 1896.

The Chosen People. Vol. 2, No. 3, December 1896.

The Chosen People. Vol. 2, No. 6, April 1897.

The Chosen People. Vol. 3, No. 4, January 1898.

The Chosen People. Vol. 4, No. 1, November 1898.

The Chosen People. Vol. 4, No. 2, December 1898.

The Chosen People. Vol. 4, No. 4, January 1899.

The Chosen People. Vol. 4, No. 5, February 1899.

The Chosen People. Vol. 4, No. 7, April 1899.

The Chosen People. Vol. 5, No. 8, December 1899.

The Chosen People. Vol. 7, No. 4, January 1902.

The Chosen People. Vol. 8, No. 8, May 1903.

The Chosen People. Vol. 9, No. 5, February 1904.

The Chosen People. Vol. 10, No. 2, November 1904.

The Chosen People. Vol. 10, No. 4, January 1905.

The Chosen People. Vol. 12, No. 2, November 1906.

The Chosen People. Vol. 12, No. 5, October 1907.

The Chosen People. Vol. 13, No. 2, November 1907.

The Chosen People. Vol. 13, No. 3, December 1907.
The Chosen People. Vol. 13, No. 6, March 1908.
The Chosen People. Vol. 13, No. 8, May 1908.
The Chosen People. Vol. 14, No. 2, November 1908.
The Chosen People. Vol. 14, No. 3, December 1908.
The Chosen People. Vol. 14, No. 4, January 1909.
The Chosen People. Vol. 15, No. 1, October 1909.
The Chosen People. Vol. 15, No. 5, February 1910.
The Chosen People. Vol. 16, No. 3, January, 1911.
The Chosen People. Vol. 17, No. 1, October 1911.
The Chosen People. Vol. 17, No. 2, November 1911.
The Chosen People. Vol. 18, No. 2, November 1912.
The Chosen People. Vol. 18, No. 3, December 1912.
The Chosen People. Vol. 18, No. 4, January 1913.
The Chosen People. Vol. 18, No. 8, May 1913.
The Chosen People. Vol. 22, No. 2, November 1916.
The Chosen People. Vol. 22, No. 3, December 1916.
The Chosen People. Vol. 22, No. 5, February 1917.
The Chosen People. Vol. 22, No. 6, March 1917.
The Chosen People. Vol. 23, No. 1, October 1917.
The Chosen People. Vol. 24, No. 5, February 1919.
The Chosen People. Vol. 24, No. 8, May 1919.
The Chosen People. Vol. 25, No. 3, December 1919.
The Chosen People. Vol. 26, No. 1, October 1920.
The Chosen People. Vol. 28, No. 8, May 1923.
The Chosen People. Vol. 29, No. 1, October 1923.
The Chosen People. Vol. 29, No. 3, December 1923.
The Chosen People. Vol. 30, No. 1, October 1924.
The Chosen People. Vol. 31, No. 2, November 1925.
The Chosen People. Vol. 32, No. 4, January 1927.
The Chosen People. Vol. 32, No. 7, April 1927.
The Chosen People. Vol. 34, No. 3, December 1928.
The Chosen People. Vol. 34, No. 7, April 1929.
The Chosen People. Vol. 34, No. 8, May 1929.
The Chosen People. Vol. 35, No. 1, October 1929.
The Chosen People. Vol. 35, No. 6, March 1930.
The Chosen People. Vol. 35, No. 8, May 1930.
The Chosen People. Vol. 36, No. 1, October 1930.
The Chosen People. Vol. 36, No. 3, December 1930.
The Chosen People. Vol. 36, No. 6, March 1931.
The Chosen People. Vol. 37, No. 3, December 1931.
The Chosen People. Vol. 37, No. 5, February 1932.
The Chosen People. Vol. 37, No. 8, May 1932.
The Chosen People. Vol. 38, No. 2, November 1932.
The Chosen People. Vol. 38, No. 8, May 1933.
The Chosen People. Vol. 39, No. 2, November 1933.
The Chosen People. Vol. 39, No. 5, February 1934.
The Chosen People. Vol. 40, No. 2, November 1934.
The Chosen People. Vol. 40, No. 6, March 1935.
The Chosen People. Vol. 41, No. 1, October 1935.
The Chosen People. Vol. 41, No. 2, November 1935.
The Chosen People. Vol. 41, No. 3, December 1935.
The Chosen People. Vol. 41, No. 4, January 1936.
The Chosen People. Vol. 41, No. 6, March 1936.

The Chosen People. Vol. 41, No. 7, April 1936.
The Chosen People. Vol. 41, No. 8, May 1936.
The Chosen People. Vol. 42, No. 1, October 1936.
The Chosen People. Vol. 42, No. 2, November 1936.
The Chosen People. Vol. 42, No. 3, December 1936.
The Chosen People. Vol. 42, No. 4, January 1937.
The Chosen People. Vol. 42, No. 5, February 1937.
The Chosen People. Vol. 43, No. 2, November 1937.
The Chosen People. Vol. 43, No. 3, December 1937.
The Chosen People. Vol. 43, No. 4, January 1938.
The Chosen People. Vol. 43, No. 5, February 1938.
The Chosen People. Vol. 43, No. 6, March 1938.
The Chosen People. Vol. 43, No. 7, April 1938.
The Chosen People. Vol. 44, No. 2, November 1938.
The Chosen People. Vol. 44, No. 3, December 1938.
The Chosen People. Vol. 44, No. 4, January 1939.
The Chosen People. Vol. 44, No. 5, February 1939.
The Chosen People. Vol. 44, No. 6, March 1939.
The Chosen People. Vol. 45, No. 1, October 1939.
The Chosen People. Vol. 45, No. 2, November 1939.
The Chosen People. Vol. 45, No. 3, December 1939.
The Chosen People. Vol. 45, No. 4, January 1940.
The Chosen People. Vol. 45, No. 5, February 1940.
The Chosen People. Vol. 45, No. 6, March 1940.
The Chosen People. Vol. 45, No. 7, April 1940.
The Chosen People. Vol. 45, No. 8, May 1940.
The Chosen People. Vol. 46, No. 1, October 1940.
The Chosen People. Vol. 46, No. 2, November 1940.
The Chosen People. Vol. 46, No. 4, January 1941.
The Chosen People. Vol. 46, No. 5, February 1941.
The Chosen People. Vol. 46, No. 6, March 1941.
The Chosen People. Vol. 46, No. 7, April 1941.
The Chosen People. Vol. 46, No. 8, May 1941.
The Chosen People. Vol. 47, No. 1, October 1941.
The Chosen People. Vol. 47, No. 3, December 1941.
The Chosen People. Vol. 47, No. 4, January 1942.
The Chosen People. Vol. 47, No. 5, February 1942.
The Chosen People. Vol. 47, No. 7, April 1942.
The Chosen People. Vol. 47, No. 8, May 1942.
The Chosen People. Vol. 48, No. 1, October 1942.
The Chosen People. Vol. 48, No. 2, November 1942.
The Chosen People. Vol. 48, No. 5, February 1943.
The Chosen People. Vol. 48, No. 6, March 1943.
The Chosen People. Vol. 49, No. 2, November 1943.
The Chosen People. Vol. 49, No. 3, December 1943.
The Chosen People. Vol. 49, No. 5, February 1944.
The Chosen People. Vol. 49, No. 7, April 1944.
The Chosen People. Vol. 50, No. 1, October 1944.
The Chosen People. Vol. 50, No. 2, November 1944.
The Chosen People. Vol. 50, No. 3, December 1944.
The Chosen People. Vol. 50, No. 5, February 1945.
The Chosen People. Vol. 50, No. 8, May 1945.
The Chosen People. Vol. 51, No. 2, November 1945.
The Chosen People. Vol. 51, No. 3, December 1945.

The Chosen People. Vol. 51, No. 5, February 1946.
The Chosen People. Vol. 51, No. 6, March 1946.
The Chosen People. Vol. 51, No. 7, April 1946.
The Chosen People. Vol. 52, No. 1, October 1946.
The Chosen People. Vol. 52, No. 2, November 1946.
The Chosen People. Vol. 52, No. 3, December 1946.
The Chosen People. Vol. 52, No. 4, January 1947.
The Chosen People. Vol. 52, No. 5, February 1947.
The Chosen People. Vol. 52, No. 7, April 1947.
The Chosen People. Vol. 52, No. 8, May 1947.
The Chosen People. Vol. 53, No. 1, October 1947.
The Chosen People. Vol. 53, No. 3, December 1947.
The Chosen People. Vol. 53, No. 4, January 1948.
The Chosen People. Vol. 53, No. 7, April 1948.
The Chosen People. Vol. 54, No. 2, November 1948.
The Chosen People. Vol. 54, No. 7, April 1949.
The Chosen People. Vol. 54, No. 8, May 1949.
The Chosen People. Vol. 55, No. 1, October 1949.
The Chosen People. Vol. 55, No. 2, November 1949.
The Chosen People. Vol. 55, No. 7, April 1950.
The Chosen People. Vol. 56, No. 1, October 1950.
The Chosen People. Vol. 56, No. 3, December 1950.
The Chosen People. Vol. 56, No. 6, March 1951.
The Chosen People. Vol. 56, No. 7, April 1951.
The Chosen People. Vol. 56, No. 8, May 1951.
The Chosen People. Vol. 57, No. 5, February 1952.
The Chosen People. Vol. 57, No. 6, March 1952.
The Chosen People. Vol. 57, No. 7, April 1952.
The Chosen People. Vol. 58, No. 1, October 1952.
The Chosen People. Vol. 58, No. 3, December 1952.
The Chosen People. Vol. 58, No. 4, January 1953.
The Chosen People. Vol. 58, No. 7, April 1953.
The Chosen People. Vol. 59, No. 1, October 1953.
The Chosen People. Vol. 59, No. 3, December 1953.
The Chosen People. Vol. 59, No. 4, January 1954.
The Chosen People. Joseph Hoffman Cohn
   Memorial Edition, January 1954.
The Chosen People. Vol. 59, No. 5, February 1954.
The Chosen People. Vol. 59, No. 6, March 1954.
The Chosen People. Vol. 59, No. 8, May 1954.
The Chosen People. Vol. 60, No. 3, December 1954.
The Chosen People. Vol. 60, No. 6, March 1955.
The Chosen People. Vol. 60, No. 7, April 1955.
The Chosen People. Vol. 61, No. 7, March 1956.
The Chosen People. Vol. 61, No. 8, April 1956.
The Chosen People. Vol. 61, No. 9, May 1956.
The Chosen People. Vol. 62, No. 3, November 1956.
The Chosen People. Vol. 62, No. 8, April 1957.
The Chosen People. Vol. 62, No. 9, May 1957.
The Chosen People. Vol. 63, No. 1, September 1957.
The Chosen People. Vol. 63, No. 4, December 1957.
The Chosen People. Vol. 63, No. 6, February 1958.
The Chosen People. Vol. 63, No. 7, March 1958.
The Chosen People. Vol. 63, No. 8, April 1958.

The Chosen People. Vol. 63, No. 10, June 1958.
The Chosen People. Vol. 64, No. 3, November 1958.
The Chosen People. Vol. 64, No. 4, December 1958.
The Chosen People. Vol. 64, No. 5, January 1959.
The Chosen People. Vol. 64, No. 6, February 1959.
The Chosen People. Vol. 64, No. 8, April 1959.
The Chosen People. Vol. 65, No. 6, February 1960.
The Chosen People. Vol. 65, No. 7, March 1960.
The Chosen People. Vol. 65, No. 8, April 1960.
The Chosen People. Vol. 65, No. 9, May 1960.
The Chosen People. Vol. 66, No. 6, February 1961.
The Chosen People. Vol. 66, No. 7, March 1961.
The Chosen People. Vol. 66, No. 8, April 1961.
The Chosen People. Vol. 66, No. 9, May 1961.
The Chosen People. Vol. 67, No. 2, October 1961.
The Chosen People. Vol. 67, No. 7, March 1962.
The Chosen People. Vol. 67, No. 8, April 1962.
The Chosen People. Vol. 68, No. 2, October 1962.
The Chosen People. Vol. 68, No. 1, September 1962.
The Chosen People. Vol. 68, No. 6, February 1963.
The Chosen People. Vol. 68, No. 7, March 1963.
The Chosen People. Vol. 68, No. 9, May 1963.
The Chosen People. Vol. 68, No. 10, June 1963.
The Chosen People. Vol. 69, No. 1, September 1963.
The Chosen People. Vol. 69, No. 3, November 1963.
The Chosen People. Vol. 69, No. 4, December 1963.
The Chosen People. Vol. 69, No. 5, January 1964.
The Chosen People. Vol. 69, No. 7, March 1964.
The Chosen People. Vol. 69, No. 8, April 1964.
The Chosen People. Vol. 69, No. 9, May 1964.
The Chosen People. Vol. 69, No. 10, June 1964.
The Chosen People. Vol. 70, No. 1, September 1964.
The Chosen People. Vol. 70, No. 3, November 1964.
The Chosen People. Vol. 70, No. 7, March 1965.
The Chosen People. Vol. 70, No. 9, May 1965.
The Chosen People. Vol. 70, No. 10, June 1965.
The Chosen People. Vol. 71, No. 1, September 1965.
The Chosen People. Vol. 71, No. 5, January 1966.
The Chosen People. Vol. 71, No. 6, February 1966.
The Chosen People. Vol. 72, No. 1, September 1966.
The Chosen People. Vol. 72, No. 3, November 1966.
The Chosen People. Vol. 72, No. 4, December 1966.
The Chosen People. Vol. 72, No. 6, February 1967.
The Chosen People. Vol. 72, No. 7, March 1967.
The Chosen People. Vol. 72, No. 9, May 1967.
The Chosen People. Vol. 72, No. 10, June 1967.
The Chosen People. Vol. 73, No. 2, October 1967.
The Chosen People. Vol. 73, No. 6, February 1968.
The Chosen People. Vol. 73, No. 7, March 1968.
The Chosen People. Vol. 73, No. 8, April 1968.
The Chosen People. Vol. 73, No. 9, May 1968.
The Chosen People. Vol. 73, No. 10, June 1968.
The Chosen People. Vol. 74, No. 1, September 1968.
The Chosen People. Vol. 74, No. 4, December 1968.

The Chosen People. Vol. 74, No. 5, January 1969.
The Chosen People. Vol. 74, No. 7, March 1969.
The Chosen People. Vol. 74, No. 10, June 1969.
The Chosen People. Vol. 75, No. 3, November 1969.
The Chosen People. Vol. 75, No. 5, January 1970.
The Chosen People. Vol. 75, No. 6, February 1970.
The Chosen People. Vol. 76, No. 1, September 1970.
The Chosen People. Vol. 76, No. 3, November 1970.
The Chosen People. Vol. 76, No. 4, December 1970.
The Chosen People. Vol. 76, No. 5, January 1971.
The Chosen People. Vol. 76, No. 6, February 1971.
The Chosen People. Vol. 76, No. 10, June 1971.
The Chosen People. Vol. 77, No. 1, September 1971.
The Chosen People. Vol. 77, No. 4, December 1971.
The Chosen People. Vol. 77, No. 5, January 1972.
The Chosen People. Vol. 77, No. 6, February 1972.
The Chosen People. Vol. 77, No. 7, March 1972.
The Chosen People. Vol. 77, No. 8, April 1972.
The Chosen People. Vol. 77, No. 9, May 1972.
The Chosen People. Vol. 77, No. 10, June 1972.
The Chosen People. Vol. 78, No. 1, September 1972.
The Chosen People. Vol. 78, No. 2, October 1972.
The Chosen People. Vol. 78, No. 5, January 1973.
The Chosen People. Vol. 78, No. 6, February 1973.
The Chosen People. Vol. 78, No. 7, March 1973.
The Chosen People. Vol. 78, No. 8, April 1973.
The Chosen People. Vol. 78, No. 9, May 1973.
The Chosen People. Vol. 78, No. 10, June 1973.
The Chosen People. Vol. 79, No. 1, September 1973.
The Chosen People. Vol. 79, No. 2, October 1973.
The Chosen People. Vol. 79, No. 6, February 1974.
The Chosen People. Vol. 79, No. 8, April 1974.
The Chosen People. Vol. 79, No. 9, May 1974.
The Chosen People. Vol. 80, No. 2, October 1974.
The Chosen People. Vol. 80, No. 4, December 1974.
The Chosen People. Vol. 80, No. 6, February 1975.
The Chosen People. Vol. 80, No. 8, April 1975.
The Chosen People. Vol. 80, No. 10, June 1975.
The Chosen People. Vol. 81, No. 2, October 1975.
The Chosen People. Vol. 81, No. 3, November 1975.
The Chosen People. Vol. 81, No. 5, January 1976.
The Chosen People. Vol. 81, No. 6, February 1976.
The Chosen People. Vol. 81, No. 9, May 1976.
The Chosen People. Vol. 82, No. 1, September 1976.
The Chosen People. Vol. 82, No. 4, December 1976.
The Chosen People. Vol. 82, No. 5, January 1977.
The Chosen People. Vol. 82, No. 9, May 1977.
The Chosen People. Vol. 82, No. 11, July 1977.
The Chosen People. Vol. 83, No. 1, September 1977.
The Chosen People. Vol. 83, No. 2, October 1977.
The Chosen People. Vol. 83, No. 5, January 1978.
The Chosen People. Vol. 83, No. 7, March 1978.
The Chosen People. Vol. 83, No. 9, May 1978.
The Chosen People. Vol. 84, No. 2, October 1978.

The Chosen People. Vol. 84, No. 5, January 1979.
The Chosen People. Vol. 84, No. 6, February 1979.
The Chosen People. Vol. 85, No. 1, September 1979.
The Chosen People. Vol. 85, No. 2, October 1979.
The Chosen People. Vol. 85, No. 3, November 1979.
The Chosen People. Vol. 85, No. 4, December 1979.
The Chosen People. Vol. 85, No. 6, February 1980.
The Chosen People. Vol. 85, No. 7, March 1980.
The Chosen People. Vol. 85, No. 8, April 1980.
The Chosen People. Vol. 85, No. 10, June 1980.
The Chosen People. Vol. 86, No. 1, September 1980.
The Chosen People. Vol. 86, No. 4, December 1980.
The Chosen People. Vol. 87, No. 2, February 1981.
The Chosen People. Vol. 87, No. 4, April 1981.
The Chosen People. Vol. 87, No. 5, May 1981.
The Chosen People. Vol. 87, No. 7, July 1981.
The Chosen People. Vol. 88, No. 1, September 1981.
The Chosen People. Vol. 88, No. 3, November 1981.
The Chosen People. Vol. 89, No. 3, November 1982.
The Chosen People. Vol. 89, No. 5, January 1983.
The Chosen People. Vol. 89, No. 7, March 1983.
The Chosen People. Vol. 89, No. 9, May 1983.
The Chosen People. Vol. 90, No. 1, September 1983.
The Chosen People. Vol. 90, No. 4, December 1983.
The Chosen People. Vol. 90, No. 5, January 1984.
The Chosen People. Vol. 91, No. 1, August 1984.
The Chosen People. Vol. 91, No. 2, September 1984.
The Chosen People. Vol. 91, No. 3, October 1984.
The Chosen People. Vol. 91, No. 4, November 1984.
The Chosen People. Vol. 91, No. 6, January 1985.
The Chosen People. Vol. 91, No. 8, March 1985.
The Chosen People. Vol. 91, No. 12, July 1985.
The Chosen People. Vol. 92, No. 1, September 1985.
The Chosen People. Vol. 92, No. 2, October 1985.
The Chosen People. Vol. 92, No. 8, April 1986.
The Chosen People. Vol. 92, No. 11, July 1986.
The Chosen People. Vol. 93, No. 1, September 1986.
The Chosen People. Vol. 93, No. 3, November 1986.
The Chosen People. Vol. 93, No. 8, April 1987.
The Chosen People. Vol. 93, No. 9, May 1987.
The Chosen People. Vol. 94, No. 1, September 1987.
The Chosen People. Special Issue, October 1987.
The Chosen People. Vol. 94, No. 4, December 1987.
The Chosen People. Vol. 94, No. 6, February 1988.
The Chosen People. Vol. 94, No. 8, April 1988.
The Chosen People. Vol. 94, No. 11, July 1988.
The Chosen People. Vol. 95, No. 3, November 1988.
The Chosen People. Vol. 95, No. 7, March 1989.
The Chosen People. Vol. 95, No. 9, May 1989.
The Chosen People. Vol. 95, No. 10, June 1989.
The Chosen People. Vol. 96, No. 2, October 1989.
The Chosen People. Vol. 96, No. 4, January 1990.
The Chosen People. Vol. 96, No. 6, February 1990.
The Chosen People. Vol. 96, No. 7, March 1990.

The Chosen People. Special Issue, August 1990.

The Chosen People. Vol. 97, No. 3, November 1990.

The Chosen People. Vol. 97, No. 4, January 1991.

The Chosen People. Vol. 97, No. 6, February 1991.

The Chosen People. Vol. 97, No. 7, March 1991.

The Chosen People. Vol. 97, No. 8, April 1991.

The Chosen People. Vol. 97, No. 9, May 1991.

The Chosen People. Vol. 97, No. 10, June 1991.

The Chosen People. Vol. 97, No. 11, July 1991.

The Chosen People. Vol. 98, No. 1, September 1991.

The Chosen People. Vol. 98, No. 3, November 1991.

The Chosen People. Vol. 98, No. 5, January 1992.

The Chosen People. Vol. 98, No. 6, February 1992.

The Chosen People. Vol. 98, No. 8, April 1992.

The Chosen People. Vol. 98, No. 9, May 1992.

The Chosen People. Vol. 98, No. 9, June 1992.

The Chosen People. Vol. 99, No. 11, July 1993.

The Missionary Review of the World. "General Missionary Intelligence,. May 1893.

The Missionary Review of the World. "General Missionary Intelligence,. November 1899.

The Missionary Review of the World. "General Missionary Intelligence,. August 1901.

The Shepherd of Israel. Vol. 20, No. 11-12, July/August 1938.

The Shepherd of Israel. Vol. 28, No. 7, March 1946.

The Shepherd of Israel. Vol. 30, No. 6, February 1948.

The Shepherd of Israel. Vol. 34, No. 5, January 1951.

The Shepherd of Israel. Vol. 36, No. 11, July/August 1953.

The Shepherd of Israel. Vol. 63, No. 3, Spring 1979.

OTHER SOURCES CITED

Alpren, Ken. *Personal Testimony*. C.P.M. Employment Application, December 1991.

Bell, John. *Why Plant Jewish Oriented Churches?* Orangeburg, New York. ABMJ/Chosen People Ministries, 1984.

Brown, Scott. *Personal Testimony*. ABMJ Employment Application, August 1987.

Budoff, Barry. *Personal Testimony*. ABMJ Employment Application, n.d.

Budoff, Dyann. *Personal Testimony*. ABMJ Employment Application, n.d.

Chesley, Dorothy. *Letter to author*, 23 January 1973.

Clemensen, C. Robert. *Memorandum to Daniel Fuchs*, 17 April 1982.

Cohn, Joseph. *Letter to Henry Ironside*, 7 March 1945.

—. *Letter to J. R. Miller*, 13 July 1945.

—. *Letter to Jean Tanguy*, 11 November 1939.

—. *Letter to Henri Vincent*, 21 November 1938.

—. *Letter to Henri Vincent*, 13 December 1938.

—. *Personal notes*. Morton Hotel, Grand Rapids, MI: n.d.

—. *Work Sheets*, 25 April 1944.

Cohen, Richard. *Letter to author*, 8 May 1980.

Crenshaw, Winfred P. *Personal Testimony*. C.P.M. Application, January 1990.

Evearitt. Daniel Joseph. *Jewish-Christian Missions to Jews. 1820-1935*. Ann Arbor. MI.
    University Microfilms International Dissertation Information Service, 1989.

Fleischer, Jerome. *Fact Sheet*. ABMJ Employment Application, n.d.

Fleming, R. *Letter to Joseph Cohn*, 27 March 1944.

Fox, James. *Personal Testimony*. C.P.M. Employment Application, June 1992.

Frydland, Rachmiel. *Letter to Martin Rosen*, 30 March 1966.

—. *Letter to author*, 20 April 1975.

—. *Why I Believe*. Englewood Cliffs, New Jersey. Sar Shalom Publications, n.d.

—. *Why I Believe*. Chattanooga, TN. Messianic Fellowship, n.d.

—. *I Escaped From the Nazis*. Willowdale, Ontario. Rachmiel Frydland, n.d.

—. *Report to the Board*, December 1974.

Fuchs, Daniel. *The District Method of Operation*. Salt Lake City Convention, 14-15 November 1966.

—. *Report: Beth Sar Shalom Mission*, 25 March 1983.

Fuller, Otis; Powell, R. *Telegram to Joseph Cohn*, 12-15 May 1944.

Fuller, Otis. *Letter to R. L. Powell*, 14 June 1944.

Gliebe, Kirk. *Personal Testimony*. C.P.M. Employment Application, March 1992.

Gitlin, Moses. *Letter to Joseph Cohn*, 24 April 1944.

Goodrow, Elizabeth. *Letter to Grace Bredehoft*, 3 May 1944.

Hall, Douglas. *Letter to Joseph Cohn*, 23 June 1945.

Houghton, W. H. *Letter to Keith L. Brooks*, 6 September 1944.

Insight. ABMJ, New York, 1973.

Insight. Reprint of "Proclamation." ABMJ, New York, June 1976.

Insight. ABMJ, New York, August 1978.

Ironside, H. A. *Letter to Keith L. Brooks*, 14 February 1945.

—. *Letter to Joseph Cohn*, 6 October 1950.

—. *Letter to Joseph Cohn*, 24 November 1950.

Jackson, P. R. *Letter to Emil D. Gruen*, 31 October 1944.

Jacobs, Leslie. *Personal Testimony*. ABMJ Employment Application, n.d.

—. *Board Report: Toronto, Ontario, Canada*, October 1974.

Johnson, Percy. *Personal Testimony*. C.P.M. Employment Application, May 1989.

Machlin, A. B. *Letter to Joseph Cohn*, 15 April 1944.

—. *Letter to Irwin H. Linton*, 29 May 1944.

Marriner, Winnie. *Personal Testimony*. ABMJ Employment Application, November 1971.

Mc Leod. Alexander. *Address to the Christian Public by a Committee of the Board*. New York: American Society for Meliorating the Condition of the Jews, 1822.

Memorandum and Articles of Association of the American Board of Missions to the Jews Limited, 12 September 1951.

Mid-Year Report. ABMJ, New York, August 1979.

Mid-Year Report. ABMJ, New York, August 1983.

Mid-Year Report. ABMJ, New York, August 1986.

Mid-Year Report. ABMJ, New York, August 1987.

Mid-Year Report. ABMJ, Charlotte, August 1991.

Minutes. ABMJ Board of Directors, 28 October 1923.

Minutes. ABMJ Board of Directors, 25 January 1928.

Minutes. ABMJ Board of Directors, 17 October 1929.

Minutes. ABMJ Board of Directors, 22 January 1930.

Minutes. ABMJ Board of Directors, 15 April 1931.

Minutes. ABMJ Board of Directors, 17 January 1932.

Minutes. ABMJ Board of Directors, 19 October 1932.

Minutes. ABMJ Board of Directors, 19 April 1933.

Minutes. ABMJ Board of Directors, 25 October 1933.

Minutes. ABMJ Board of Directors, 17 October 1934.

Minutes. ABMJ Board of Directors, 16 October 1935.

Minutes. ABMJ Board of Directors, 10 December 1935.

Minutes. ABMJ Board of Directors, 12 April 1936.

Minutes. ABMJ Board of Directors, 15 April 1936.

Minutes. ABMJ Board of Directors, 28 October 1936.

Minutes. ABMJ Board of Directors, 27 January 1937.

Minutes. ABMJ Board of Directors, 21 April 1937.

Minutes. ABMJ Board of Directors, 20 October 1937.

Minutes. ABMJ Board of Directors, 20 April 1938.

Minutes. ABMJ Board of Directors, 17 October 1938.

Minutes. ABMJ Board of Directors, 19 October 1938.

Minutes. ABMJ Board of Directors, 19 April 1939.

Minutes. ABMJ Board of Directors, 19 October 1939.

Minutes. ABMJ Board of Directors, 24 January 1940.

Minutes. ABMJ Board of Directors, 15 May 1940.

Minutes. ABMJ Board of Directors, 29 July 1940.

Minutes. ABMJ Board of Directors, 30 October 1940.

Minutes. ABMJ Board of Directors, 22 January 1941.

Minutes. ABMJ Board of Directors, 16 April 1941.

Minutes. ABMJ Board of Directors, 15 October 1941.

Minutes. ABMJ Board of Directors, 16 October 1941.

Minutes. ABMJ Board of Directors, 30 December 1941.

Minutes. ABMJ Board of Directors, 28 January 1942.

Minutes. ABMJ Board of Directors, 13 May 1942.

Minutes. ABMJ Board of Directors, 21 October 1942.

Minutes. ABMJ Board of Directors, 27 October 1943.

Minutes. ABMJ Board of Directors, 27 January 1943.

Minutes. ABMJ Board of Directors, 27 April 1943.

Minutes. ABMJ Board of Directors, 27 January 1944.

Minutes. ABMJ Board of Directors, 25 April 1944.

Minutes. ABMJ Board of Directors, 24 May 1944.

Minutes. ABMJ Board of Directors, 10 June 1944.

Minutes. ABMJ Board of Directors, 21 June 1944.

Minutes. ABMJ Board of Directors, 19 July 1944.

Minutes. ABMJ Board of Directors, 1 August 1944.

Minutes (notes). ABMJ Board of Directors. 24 October 1944.

Minutes. ABMJ Board of Directors, 23 January 1945.

Minutes. ABMJ Board of Directors, 27 January 1945.

Minutes. ABMJ Board of Directors, 24 April 1945.

Minutes. ABMJ Board of Directors, 23 April 1946.

Minutes. ABMJ Board of Directors, 22 October 1946.

Minutes. ABMJ Board of Directors, 28 January 1947.

Minutes. ABMJ Board of Directors, 22 April 1947.

Minutes. ABMJ Board of Directors, 28 October 1947.

Minutes. ABMJ Board of Directors, 27 January 1948.

Minutes. ABMJ Board of Directors, 31 August 1948.

Minutes. ABMJ Board of Directors, 26 October 1948.

Minutes. ABMJ Board of Directors, 26 January 1949.

Minutes. ABMJ Board of Directors, 27 April 1949.

Minutes. ABMJ Board of Directors, 30 August 1949.

Minutes. ABMJ Board of Directors, 26 October 1949.

Minutes. ABMJ Board of Directors, 25 January 1950.

Minutes. ABMJ Board of Directors, 26 April 1950.

Minutes. ABMJ Board of Directors, 30 August 1950.

Minutes. ABMJ Board of Directors, 25 October 1950.

Minutes. ABMJ Board of Directors, 24 January 1951.

Minutes. ABMJ Board of Directors, 25 January 1951.

Minutes. ABMJ Board of Directors, 25 April 1951.

Minutes. ABMJ Board of Directors, 23 April 1952.

Minutes. ABMJ Board of Directors, 28 January 1953.

Minutes. ABMJ Board of Directors, 29 April 1953.

Minutes. ABMJ Board of Directors, 8 October 1953.

Minutes. ABMJ Board of Directors, 28 October 1953.

Minutes. ABMJ Board of Directors, 14 December 1953.

Minutes. ABMJ Board of Directors, 28 April 1954.

Minutes. ABMJ Board of Directors, 24 October 1954.

Minutes. ABMJ Board of Directors, 27 October 1954.

Minutes. ABMJ Board of Directors, 26 January 1955.

Minutes. ABMJ Board of Directors, 1 March 1955.

Minutes. ABMJ Board of Directors, 27 April 1955.

Minutes. ABMJ Board of Directors, 26 October 1955.

Minutes. ABMJ Board of Directors, 25 January 1956.

Minutes. ABMJ Board of Directors, 25 April 1956.

Minutes. ABMJ Board of Directors, 24 October 1956.

Minutes. ABMJ Board of Directors, 16 January 1957.

Minutes. ABMJ Board of Directors, 24 April 1957.

Minutes. ABMJ Board of Directors, 29 January 1958.

Minutes. ABMJ Board of Directors, 14 February 1961.

Minutes. ABMJ Board of Directors, 23 May 1962.

Minutes. ABMJ Board of Directors, 24 October 1962.

Minutes. ABMJ Board of Directors, 30 January 1963.

Minutes. ABMJ Board of Directors, 24 April 1963.

Minutes. ABMJ Board of Directors, 23 October 1963.

Minutes. ABMJ Board of Directors, 29 January 1964.

Minutes. ABMJ Board of Directors, 8 December 1964.

Minutes. ABMJ Board of Directors, 27 January 1965.

Minutes. ABMJ Board of Directors, 5 May 1965.

Minutes. ABMJ Board of Directors, 23 June 1965.

Minutes. ABMJ Board of Directors, 15 September 1965.

Minutes. ABMJ Board of Directors, 17 November 1965.

Minutes. ABMJ Board of Directors, 15 June 1966.

Minutes. ABMJ Board of Directors, 19 April 1967.

Minutes. ABMJ Board of Directors, 15 November 1967.

Minutes. ABMJ Board of Directors, 17 April 1968.

Minutes. ABMJ Board of Directors, December 1968.

Minutes. ABMJ Board of Directors, 26 April 1969.

Minutes. ABMJ Board of Directors, 16 July 1969.

Minutes. ABMJ Board of Directors, 17 September 1969.

Minutes. ABMJ Board of Directors, 19 November 1969.

Minutes. ABMJ Board of Directors, 22 January 1969.

Minutes. ABMJ Board of Directors, 28 January 1970.

Minutes. ABMJ Board of Directors, 22 April 1970.

Minutes. ABMJ Board of Directors, 16 September 1970.

Minutes. ABMJ Board of Directors, 18 November 1970.

Minutes. ABMJ Board of Directors, 30 June 1971.

Minutes. ABMJ Board of Directors, 20 October 1971.

Minutes. ABMJ Board of Directors, 26 January 1972.

Minutes. ABMJ Board of Directors, 19 April 1972.

Minutes. ABMJ Board of Directors, 21 June 1972.

Minutes. ABMJ Board of Directors, 17 August 1972.

Minutes. ABMJ Board of Directors, 23 September 1972.

Minutes. ABMJ Board of Directors, 21 January 1973.

Minutes. ABMJ Board of Directors, 18 April 1973.

Minutes. ABMJ Board of Directors, 27 June 1973.

Minutes. ABMJ Board of Directors, 19 September 1973.

Minutes. ABMJ Board of Directors, 23 January 1974.

Minutes. ABMJ Board of Directors, 26 June 1974.

Minutes. ABMJ Board of Directors, 23 October 1974.

Minutes. ABMJ Board of Directors, 25 January 1975.

Minutes. ABMJ Board of Directors, 18 June 1975.

Minutes. ABMJ Board of Directors, 29 October 1975.

Minutes. ABMJ Board of Directors, 28 January 1976.
Minutes. ABMJ Board of Directors, 16 June 1976.
Minutes. ABMJ Board of Directors, 25 October 1976.
Minutes. ABMJ Board of Directors, 25 January 1977.
Minutes. ABMJ Board of Directors, 26 January 1977.
Minutes. ABMJ Board of Directors, 15 June 1977.
Minutes. ABMJ Board of Directors, 19 October 1977.
Minutes. ABMJ Board of Directors, 21 June 1978.
Minutes. ABMJ Board of Directors, 21 October 1978.
Minutes. ABMJ Board of Directors, 24 January 1979.
Minutes. ABMJ Board of Directors, 20 October 1979.
Minutes. ABMJ Board of Directors, 23 January 1980.
Minutes. ABMJ Board of Directors, 23 June 1980.
Minutes. ABMJ Board of Directors, 28 January 1981.
Minutes. ABMJ Board of Directors, 17 June 1981.
Minutes. ABMJ Board of Directors, 21 October 1981.
Minutes. ABMJ Board of Directors, 17 April 1982.
Minutes. ABMJ Board of Directors, 11 June 1982.
Minutes. ABMJ Board of Directors, 28 January 1983.
Minutes. ABMJ Board of Directors, 17 June 1983.
Minutes. ABMJ Board of Directors, 18 June 1983.
Minutes. ABMJ Board of Directors, 7 August 1983.
Minutes. ABMJ Board of Directors, 29 October 1983.
Minutes. ABMJ Board of Directors, 27 January 1984.
Minutes. ABMJ Board of Directors, 18 May 1984.
Minutes. ABMJ Board of Directors, 20 July 1984.
Minutes. ABMJ Board of Directors, 19 October 1984.
Minutes. ABMJ Board of Directors, 25 January 1985.
Minutes. ABMJ Board of Directors, 10 June 1985.
Minutes. ABMJ Board of Directors, 11 June 1985.
Minutes. ABMJ Board of Directors, 24 January 1986.
Minutes. ABMJ Board of Directors, 20 June 1986.
Minutes. ABMJ/CPM Board of Directors, 17 October 1986.
Minutes. ABMJ/CPM Board of Directors, 30 January 1987.
Minutes. ABMJ/CPM Board of Directors, 4 June 1987.
Minutes. ABMJ/CPM Board of Directors, 29 January 1988.
Minutes. ABMJ/CPM. Special Meeting. 4/5 April 1988.
Minutes. ABMJ/CPM Board of Directors, 6 May 1988.
Minutes. CPM Board of Directors, 29 September 1988.
Minutes. CPM Board of Directors, 18 November 1988.
Minutes. CPM Board of Directors, 27 January 1989.
Minutes. CPM Board of Directors, 1 June 1989.
Minutes. CPM Board of Directors, 26 January 1990.
Minutes. Beth Sar Shalom Canada, 13 November 1967.
Minutes. Beth Sar Shalom Canada, 22 March 1968.
Minutes. Beth Sar Shalom Canada, 31 January 1969.
Minutes. Beth Sar Shalom Canada, 27 March 1970.
Minutes. Beth Sar Shalom Canada, 19 October 1970.
Minutes. Beth Sar Shalom Canada, 19 November 1971.
Minutes. Beth Sar Shalom Canada, 3 November 1972.
Minutes. Beth Sar Shalom Canada, 30 November 1973.
Minutes. Beth Sar Shalom Canada, 18 June 1974.
Minutes. Beth Sar Shalom Canada, 10 January 1975.
Minutes. Beth Sar Shalom Canada, 17 November 1981.

Minutes. Beth Sar Shalom Canada, 2 December 1983.
Minutes. Beth Sar Shalom Canada, 9 February 1984.
Minutes. Beth Sar Shalom Canada, 17 May 1984.
Minutes. Beth Sar Shalom Canada, 10 January 1986.
Minutes. Beth Sar Shalom Canada, 22 May 1986.
Minutes. Beth Sar Shalom Canada, 13 June 1987.
Minutes. Beth Sar Shalom Canada, 30 January 1988.
Minutes. Beth Sar Shalom Canada, 1 October 1988.
Minutes. Executive Committee ABMJ, 10 March 1920.
Minutes. Executive Committee ABMJ, 24 March 1920.
Minutes. Executive Committee ABMJ, 20 December 1921.
Minutes. Executive Committee ABMJ, 25 April 1922.
Minutes. Executive Committee ABMJ, 16 October 1922.
Minutes. Executive Committee ABMJ, 21 November 1922.
Minutes. Executive Committee ABMJ, 13 March 1923.
Minutes. Executive Committee ABMJ, 14 May 1923.
Minutes. Executive Committee ABMJ, 7 November 1923.
Minutes. Executive Committee ABMJ, 16 July 1924.
Minutes. Executive Committee ABMJ, 21 December 1926.
Minutes. Executive Committee ABMJ, 21 June 1927.
Minutes. Executive Committee ABMJ, 3 October 1927.
Minutes. Executive Committee ABMJ, 19 March 1928.
Minutes. Executive Committee ABMJ, 5 March 1929.
Minutes. Executive Committee ABMJ, 8 October 1929.
Minutes. Executive Committee ABMJ, 24 May 1934.
Minutes. Executive Committee ABMJ, 2 October 1934.
Minutes. Executive Committee ABMJ, 5 June 1935.
Minutes. Executive Committee ABMJ, 10 December 1935.
Minutes. Executive Committee ABMJ, 18 June 1936.
Minutes. Executive Committee ABMJ, 8 December 1936.
Minutes. Executive Committee ABMJ, 30 March 1937.
Minutes. Executive Committee ABMJ, 4 June 1937.
Memo to Executive Committee. 18 August 1937.
Minutes. Executive Committee ABMJ, 27 September 1938.
Minutes. Executive Committee ABMJ, 12 June 1939.
Minutes. Executive Committee ABMJ, 11 September 1940.
Minutes. Executive Committee ABMJ, 24 June 1941.
Minutes. Executive Committee ABMJ, 9 December 1942.
Minutes. Executive Committee ABMJ, 8 May 1944.
Minutes. Executive Committee ABMJ, 18 February 1946.
Minutes. Executive Committee ABMJ, 14 March 1946.
Minutes. Executive Committee ABMJ, 9 April 1947.
Minutes. Executive Committee ABMJ, 8 October 1947.
Minutes. Executive Committee ABMJ, 9 August 1980.
Minutes. Executive Committee ABMJ, 24 January 1983.
Minutes. Investigation of Charges Against Leopold Cohn, 1916.
Minutes. Personnel Committee ABMJ, 17 March 1982.
Minutes. Personnel Committee ABMJ, 28 May 1982.
Minutes. Personnel Committee ABMJ, 29 May 1985.
Minutes. President's Report. January 29, 1988.
Minutes. Williamsburg Mission to the Jews, 30 September 1911.
Minutes. Williamsburg Mission to the Jews, 4 June 1912.
Minutes. Williamsburg Mission to the Jews, 15 January 1913.
Minutes. Williamsburg Mission to the Jews, 11 June 1913.

Minutes. Williamsburg Mission to the Jews, 21 January 1915.

Minutes. Williamsburg Mission to the Jews, 19 January 1916.

Minutes. Williamsburg Mission to the Jews, 27 June 1916.

Minutes. Williamsburg Mission to the Jews, 8 November 1916.

Minutes. Williamsburg Mission to the Jews, 17 January 1917.

Minutes. Williamsburg Mission to the Jews, 17 April 1917.

Minutes. Williamsburg Mission to the Jews, 20 November 1917.

Minutes. Williamsburg Mission to the Jews, 16 January 1918.

Minutes. Williamsburg Mission to the Jews, 13 June 1918.

Minutes. Williamsburg Mission to the Jews, 4 November 1918.

Minutes. Williamsburg Mission to the Jews, 5 December 1918.

Minutes. Williamsburg Mission to the Jews, 7 January 1920.

Minutes. Williamsburg Mission to the Jews, 28 January 1920.

Minutes. Williamsburg Mission to the Jews, 3 March 1920.

Minutes. Williamsburg Mission to the Jews, 2 June 1920.

Minutes. Williamsburg Mission to the Jews, 25 January 1922.

Minutes. Williamsburg Mission to the Jews, 15 September 1924.

Minutes. Williamsburg Mission to the Jews, 24 January 1934.

Muntz, J. P. *Mass mailing to his constituency and others,* 1 June 1944.

—. *Circular letter to supporting mailing lists,* 1944/45.

Passo, Roberto. *Personal Testimony.* ABMJ Employment Application, May 1982.

Potter, Frank. *Personal Testimony.* ABMJ Employment Application, April 1982.

Reports. *Salt Lake City Convention.* 14-15 November 1966.

Reprint. *Annual Banquet and Business Meeting.* Buffalo Hebrew Christian Mission, 2 December 1927.

Reprint. *Buffalo Evening News,* 20 January 1921.

Reprint. *The Dearborn Independent.* "Jewish Boy Sent to Prison for His Religion," 3 November 1923.

Reprint. *Resolution.* FCTJ, 16-19 October 1975.

Rich, Larry. *Personal Testimony.* C.P.M. Employment Application, April 1991.

Riley, W. B. *Letter to Irwin H. Linton,* 14 April 1945.

Rogers, W. H. *Letter to A. L. Griswold,* 20 February 1945.

Rosen, Martin. *Letter to Rachmiel Frydland,* 14 March 1966.

—. *Letter to Rachmiel Frydland,* 4 April 1966.

Sedaca, Victor. *Letter to author,* 30 January 1976.

Sevener, Harold A. *Letter to Daniel Fuchs,* 26 May 1972.

—. *Letter to David Sedaca,* 25 May 1977.

—. *Letter to Moishe Rosen,* 5 December 1979.

—. *Memo to Staff,* 12 August 1974.

—. *Memo to Staff,* 13 September 1974.

—. *Personal Interview with Henri Vincent,* 19 April 1990.

—. *Personal Interview with Margaret Heydt,* 13 September 1991.

—. *Personal Interview with Moishe Rosen,* 14 January 1992.

Singer, Jonathan. *Personal Testimony.* ABMJ Employment Application, n.d.

Styler, Robert. *Personal Testimony.* ABMJ Employment Application, January 1985.

Talbot, L. *Letter to Keith Brooks,* 21 November 1944.

Vincent, Henri. *Letter to Joseph Cohn,* 14 February 1939.

—. *Letter to Joseph Cohn,* 18 April 1939.

—. *Letter to Joseph Cohn,* 20 June 1939.

—. *Letter to Joseph Cohn,* 10 September 1939.

—. *Letter to Joseph Cohn,* 18 November 1944.

—. *Letter to Joseph Cohn,* 10 March 1945.

—. *Letter to Joseph Cohn,* 12 June 1945.

—. *Letter to Joseph Cohn,* 7 July 1945.

—. *Letter to Joseph Cohn,* 8 August 1945.

Waldman, Martin. *Personal Testimony.* ABMJ Employment Application, May 1978.

Weinisch, Stewart. *Personal Testimony.* ABMJ Employment Application, June 1983.

Why We Resign From the American Board of Missions to the Jews, Inc.. Winona Lake. The American Association for Jewish Evangelism, Inc., 1944.

Sources Referenced But Not Cited

A Handbook of Foreign Missions. London. Religious Tract Society, 1888.

American Board of Commissioners for Foreign Missions. *Missions to the Jews.* Boston: ABCFM, 1851.

American Society for Meliorating the Condition of the Jews.

The Report of the American Society for Meliorating the Condition of the Jews. New York: Gray and Bunce, 1823.

Baron, David. *The Jewish Problem.* New York: Fleming H. Revell Co., 1891.

Berger, David and Michael Wyschogrod. *Jews and "Jewish Christianity".* Philadelphia: KTAV Publishing House, 1976.

Black, James. ed. *The Christian Approach to the Jews.* London. Edinburgh House Press, 1927.

Brandes, Joseph. *Immigrants To Freedom- Jewish Communities in Rural New Jersey Since 1882.* Philadelphia. University of Pennsylvania Press, 1971.

Buksbazen, Lydia. *They Looked For a City.* Philadelphia. The Friends of Israel, 1955.

Cohn, Joseph. *The Chosen People Question Box.* Brooklyn, NY: American Board of Missions to the Jews, Inc., 1945.

—. *Beginning At Jerusalem.* New York. American Board of Missions to the Jews, Inc., 1948.

Davis, Alan T. *Anti-Semitism And the Christian Mind—The Crisis of Conscience After Auschwitz.* New York. Herder and Herder, 1969.

Dunlop, John. *Memories of Gospel Triumphs Amongst the Jews During the Victorian Era.* London. S.W. Patridge & Co., 1894.

Einspruch, Henry. *When Jews Face Christ.* Brooklyn, NY. American Board of Missions to the Jews, 1932.

Eichhorn, David Max. *Evangelizing the American Jew.* Middle Village, NY. Jonathan David Publishers, 1978.

Ellegant, Barry. *Jews for Jesus.* Plainfield. Logos International, 1973.

Fisher, Eugene J.; Rudin, James A., Tanenbaum Marc H., eds. *Twenty Years of Jewish-Catholic Relations.* New York. Paulist Press, n.d.

Frank, Arnold. *What About the Jews?* Belfast. Graham & Hislop, 1944.

—. *Witnesses from Israel.* Edinburgh. Oliphant, Anderson & Ferrier, 1903.

Freedman, Theodore, ed. *Anti-Semitism in the Soviet Union. Its Roots and Consequences.*

New York. Freedom Library Press of the Anti-Defamation League of B'nai B'rith, 1984.

Freshman, Jacob. "Baptism." in *Second Annual Report for the Year 1883: Hebrew Christian Work, New York City.* New York. Wm. Knowles, 1883.

Frey, Joseph S.C.F. *Narrative of the Rev. J.S.C.F. Frey.* New York. W.B. Gilley, 1817.

—. *The Object of the American Society for Meliorating the Condition of the Jews.* New York. Daniel Fanshaw, 1827.

Fruchtenbaum, Arnold G. *Hebrew Christianity: Its Theology, History and Philosophy.* Washington D.C.: Canon Press, 1974.

Gartenhaus, Jacob. *Famous Hebrew Christians.* Chattanooga. International Board of Jewish Missions, Inc., 1979.

Gidney, William Thomas. *At Home and Abroad.* London. Operative Jewish Converts Institution, 1900.

—. *The History of the London Society for the Propagation of Christianity Amongst the Jews.* London. London Society for the Propagation of Christianity Amongst the Jews, 1908.

—. *The Jews and Their Evangelism.* London. Volunteer Missionary Union, 1899.

—. *Missions to Jews.* London. Operative Jewish Converts Institution, 1897.

—. *Sites and Scenes.* 2 Vols. London. Operative Jewish Converts Institution, 1897-99.

Goble, Phillip E. *Everything You Need to Grow a Messianic Synagogue.* South Pasadena. William Carey Library, 1974.

Goldberg, Louis. *Our Jewish Friends.* Chicago: Moody Press, 1977.

Grinstein, Hyman B. *The Rise of the Jewish Community of New York 1654 - 1860.* Philadelphia. The Jewish Publication Society of America, 1945.

Grose, Peter. *Israel In The Mind Of America.* New York. Alfred A. Knopf, 1983.

Gutwirth, Jacques. *Les Judeo-Chretiens d'aujourd'hui.* Paris, France. bd Latour-Maubourg, 1987.

Halff, Charles. *Forty Wonderful Years.* San Antonio. The Christian Jew Foundation, n.d.

Harris, Lis. *Holy Days-The World of a Hasidic Family.* New York. Summit Books, 1985.

Hect; Shea; Clorfene, Chaim. *Confessions of a Jewish Cultbuster.* Brooklyn, NY. Empire Press, 1985.

Hefley, James C. *The New Jews.* Wheaton. Tyndale House Publishers, 1971.

Hertzberg, Arthur. *The Jews in America—Four Centuries of an Uneasy Encounter: A History.* New York. Simon and Schuster, 1989.

Historical Sketch of the Chicago Hebrew Mission. Chicago. Chicago Hebrew Mission, 1912.

Karp, Abraham J. *Golden Door to America. The Jewish Immigrant Experience.* New York: Viking Press, 1976.

Kiell, Norman, ed. *The Psychodynamics of American Jewish Life. An Anthology.* New York. Twayne Publishers, Inc., 1967.

Levine, Samuel. *You Take Jesus, I'll Take God. How to Refute Christian Missionaries.* Los Angeles: Hamorah Press, 1976.

Lew, Leslie K., comp. *From Hitler's Hell To God's Peace-The Life Story of Dr. Ben David Lew.* Oak Park. Israel's Evangelistic Mission, n.d.

Littell, John S. *Some Great Christian Jews.* Keene, NH. The Author, 1913.

Meyer; Lewis; Rausch, David A., eds. *Eminent Hebrew Christians of the Nineteenth Century.* New York. Edwin Mellen Press, 1983.

Narrative Of A Mission Of Inquiry To The Jews From The Church Of Scotland In 1839. Philadelphia. Presbyterian Board of Publication, 1845.

Norris, H.H. *The Origin, Progress, and Existing Circumstances of the London Society for Promoting Christianity Amongst the Jews. An Historical Inquiry.* London. J. Mawman, 1825.

Ornish, Natalie. *Pioneer Jewish Texans—Their Impact On Texas And American History For Four Hundred Years 1590 - 1990.* Dallas. Texas Heritage Press, 1989.

Poll, Solomon. *The Hasidic Community of Williamsburg.* New York. The Free Press of Glencoe, Inc., n.d.

Pressler, Robert L.; Currie, William; Maas, Arlene & Eliezer; Tabor, Wesley, eds. & comps. *One Hundred Years of Blessing: The Centennial History of the American Messianic Fellowhip 1887-1987.* Lansing. American Messianic Fellowship, 1987.

Pruter, Karl. *Jewish Christians In The United States.* New York. Garland Publishing, Inc., 1987.

Rausch, David A. *Messianic Judaism. Its History, Theology, and Polity.* New York. Edwin Mellen Press, 1982.

Rischin, Moses, ed. *The Jews Of North America.* Detroit. Wayne State University Press, 1987.

Rivkin, Ellis. *The Shaping of Jewish History-A Radical New Interpretation.* New York. Charles Scribner's Sons, 1971.

Rubenstein, Richard L. *After Auschwitz—Radical Theology and Contemporary Judaism.* New York. The Bobbs-Merrill Company, Inc, 1966.

Sandmel, Samuel. *Judaism and Christian Beginnings.* New York. Oxford University Press, 1978.

Seay, W.M. *A Tale of Two Peoples: Gentiles and Jews.* Atlanta: Home Mission Board of the Southern Baptist Convention, 1927.

Schonfield, Hugh J. *The History of Jewish Christianity. From the First to the Twentieth Century.* London. Duckworth, 1936.

Shenker, Israel. *Coat Of Many Colors.* New York. Doubleday & Company, Inc., 1985.

Sherman, Shlomoh. *Escape from Jesus—One Man's Search For A Meaningful Judaism.* Mount Vernon. Decalogue Books, 1983.

Silberman, Charles E. *A Certain People—American Jews And Their Lives Today.* New York. Summit Books, 1985.

Sobel, B.Z. *Hebrew Christianity. The Thirteenth Tribe.* New York. John Wiley & Sons, 1974.

Stern, David H. *Messianic Jewish Manifesto.* Jerusalem, Israel. Jewish New Testament Publications, 1988.

Stevens, George H. *Jewish Christian Leaders.* London. Oliophants, 1966.

Stuart, Moses. *The Conversion of the Jews.* Andover, Mass.. Flagg and Gould, 1831.

Sutcliffe, B.B. *The Responsibility of the Church in Relation to Israel.* Chicago. Chicago Hebrew Mission, n.d.

Tatford, Fred. A. *That The World May Know—The Restless Middle East.* Vol. 1. Bath, Avon, England. Echoes Of Service, 1982.

—. *That The World May Know—Dawn Over Latin America.* Vol. 2. Bath, Avon, England. Echoes Of Service, 1983.

The Cruise of the Eight Hundred To and Through Palestine. New York City. The Christian Herald Press, 1905.

Wheatley, Joseph. *The Life and Letters of Phoebe Palmer.* 2 Vols. New York. W.C. Palmer, Publisher, 1876.

Wilkinson, Samuel Hinds. *The Evangelization of the Jews in Russia.* London. Mildmay Mission to the Jews, 1899.

—. *The Great Pogrom.* London. Mildmay Mission to the Jews, 1906.

—. *In The Land of the North.* London. Marshall Bros., 1905.

—. *The Life of John Wilkinson, the Jewish Missionary.* London. Morgan & Scott, 1908.

Wyman, David S. *The Abandonment Of The Jews—America And The Holocaust 1941 - 1945.* New York. Pantheon Books, 1984.